GENERAL MOTORS | CHEVY
1964-88 REPAIR MANUAL

CHILTON'S

Covers all U.S. and Canadian models of
Chevrolet Chevelle, El Camino, Laguna S-3,
Malibu and Monte Carlo; including SS models
and diesel engines

by Kevin M. G. Maher, A.S.E.

CHILTON *Automotive Books*

PUBLISHED BY **HAYNES NORTH AMERICA**. Inc.

AUTOMOTIVE
PARTS &
ACCESSORIES
ASSOCIATION MEMBER

Manufactured in USA
© 1994 Haynes North America, Inc.
ISBN 0-8019-8594-3
Library of Congress Catalog Card No. 93-074299
9012345678 9876543210

Haynes Publishing Group
Sparkford Nr Yeovil
Somerset BA22 7JJ England

Haynes North America, Inc
861 Lawrence Drive
Newbury Park
California 91320 USA

ABCDE
FGH

Contents

Contents

SAFETY NOTICE

Proper service and repair procedures are vital to the safe, reliable operation of all motor vehicles, as well as the personal safety of those performing repairs. This manual outlines procedures for servicing and repairing vehicles using safe, effective methods. The procedures contain many NOTES, CAUTIONS and WARNINGS which should be followed, along with standard procedures to eliminate the possibility of personal injury or improper service which could damage the vehicle or compromise its safety.

It is important to note that repair procedures and techniques, tools and parts for servicing motor vehicles, as well as the skill and experience of the individual performing the work vary widely. It is not possible to anticipate all of the conceivable ways or conditions under which vehicles may be serviced, or to provide cautions as to all possible hazards that may result. Standard and accepted safety precautions and equipment should be used when handling toxic or flammable fluids, and safety goggles or other protection should be used during cutting, grinding, chiseling, prying, or any other process that can cause material removal or projectiles.

Some procedures require the use of tools specially designed for a specific purpose. Before substituting another tool or procedure, you must be completely satisfied that neither your personal safety, nor the performance of the vehicle will be endangered.

Although information in this manual is based on industry sources and is complete as possible at the time of publication, the possibility exists that some car manufacturers made later changes which could not be included here. While striving for total accuracy, the authors or publishers cannot assume responsibility for any errors, changes or omissions that may occur in the compilation of this data.

PART NUMBERS

Part numbers listed in this reference are not recommendations by Haynes North America, Inc. for any product brand name. They are references that can be used with interchange manuals and aftermarket supplier catalogs to locate each brand supplier's discrete part number.

SPECIAL TOOLS

Special tools are recommended by the vehicle manufacturer to perform their specific job. Use has been kept to a minimum, but where absolutely necessary, they are referred to in the text by the part number of the tool manufacturer. These tools can be purchased, under the appropriate part number, from your local dealer or regional distributor, or an equivalent tool can be purchased locally from a tool supplier or parts outlet. Before substituting any tool for the one recommended, read the SAFETY NOTICE at the top of this page.

ACKNOWLEDGMENTS

Portions of materials contained herein have been reprinted with the permission of General Motors Corporation, Service Technology Group.

1

GENERAL INFORMATION AND MAINTENANCE

HOW TO USE THIS BOOK

Chilton's Repair Manual for Chevrolet Mid-Size cars is intended to help you learn more about the inner workings of your vehicle and save you money on its upkeep and operation.

The first two sections will be the most used, since they contain maintenance and tune-up information and procedures. Studies have shown that a properly tuned and maintained car can get at least 10% better gas mileage than an out-of-tune car. The other sections deal with the more complex systems of your car. Operating systems from engine through brakes are covered to the extent that the average do-it-yourselfer becomes mechanically involved. This book will not explain such things as rebuilding the differential for the simple reason that the expertise required and the investment in special tools make this task uneconomical. It will, however, give you detailed instructions to help you change your own brake pads and shoes, replace spark plugs, and do many more jobs that will save you money, give you personal satisfaction, and help you avoid expensive problems.

A secondary purpose of this book is a reference for owners who want to understand their car and/or their mechanics better. In this case, no tools at all are required.

Before removing any bolts, read through the entire procedure. This will give you the overall view of what tools and supplies will be required. There is nothing more frustrating than having to walk to the bus stop on Monday morning because you were short one bolt on Sunday afternoon. So read ahead and plan ahead. Each operation should be approached logically and all procedures thoroughly understood before attempting any work.

All sections contain adjustments, maintenance, removal and installation procedures, and repair or overhaul procedures. When repair is not considered practical, we tell you how to remove the part and then how to install the new or rebuilt replacement. In this way, you at least save the labor costs. Backyard repair of such components as the alternator is just not practical.

Two basic mechanic's rules should be mentioned here. One, whenever the left side of the car or engine is referred to, it is meant to specify the driver's side of the car. Conversely, the right side of the car means the passenger's side. Secondly, most screws and bolts are removed by turning counterclockwise, and tightened by turning clockwise.

Safety is always the most important rule. Constantly be aware of the dangers involved in working on an automobile and take the proper precautions. See the procedure in this section Servicing Your Vehicle Safely and the SAFETY NOTICE on the acknowledgment page.

Pay attention to the instructions provided. There are 3 common mistakes in mechanical work:

1. Incorrect order of assembly, disassembly or adjustment. When taking something apart or putting it together, doing things in the wrong order usually just costs you extra time; however, it CAN break something. Read the entire procedure before beginning disassembly. Do everything in the order in which the instructions say you should do it, even if you can't immediately see a reason for it. When you're taking apart something that is very intricate (for example, a carburetor), you might want to draw a picture of how it looks when assembled at one point in order to make sure you get everything back in its proper position. (We will supply exploded views whenever possible). When making adjustments, especially tune-up adjustments, do them in order; often, one adjustment affects another, and you cannot expect even satisfactory results unless each adjustment is made only when it cannot be changed by any other.

2. Overtorquing (or undertorquing). While it is more common for over-torquing to cause damage, undertorquing can cause a fastener to vibrate loose causing serious damage. Especially when dealing with aluminum parts, pay attention to torque specifications and utilize a torque wrench in assembly. If a torque figure is not available, remember that if you are using the right tool to do the job, you will probably not have to strain yourself to get a fastener tight enough. The pitch of most threads is so slight that the tension you put on the wrench will be multiplied many, many times in actual force on what you are tightening. A good example of how critical torque is can be seen in the case of spark plug installation, especially where you are putting the plug into an aluminum cylinder head. Too little torque can fail to crush the gasket, causing leakage of combustion gases and consequent overheating of the plug and engine parts. Too much torque can damage the threads, or distort the plug which changes the spark gap.

There are many commercial products available for ensuring that fasteners won't come loose, even if they are not torqued just right (a very common brand is Loctite®). If you're worried about getting something together tight enough to hold, but loose enough to avoid mechanical damage during assembly, one of these products might offer substantial insurance. Read the label on the package and make sure the product is compatible with the materials, fluids, etc. involved before choosing one.

3. Crossthreading. This occurs when a part such as a bolt is screwed into a nut or casting at the wrong angle and forced. Cross threading is more likely to occur if access is difficult. It helps to clean and lubricate fasteners, and to start threading with the part to be installed going straight in. Then, start the bolt, spark plug, etc. with your fingers. If you encounter resistance, unscrew the part and start over again at a different angle until it can be inserted and turned several turns without much effort. Keep in mind that many parts, especially spark plugs, used tapered threads so that gentle turning will automatically bring the part you're threading to the proper angle if you don't force it or resist a change in angle. Don't put a wrench on the part until it's been turned a couple of turns by hand. If you suddenly encounter resistance, and the part has not seated fully, don't force it. Pull it back out and make sure it's clean and threading properly.

Always take your time and be patient; once you have some experience, working on your car will become an enjoyable hobby.

TOOLS AND EQUIPMENT

▶ **See Figures 1 and 2**

Naturally, without the proper tools and equipment it is impossible to properly service your vehicle. It would be impossible to catalog each tool that you would need to perform each or any operation in this book. It would also be unwise for the amateur to rush out and buy an expensive set of tools on the theory that he may need one or more of them at sometime.

The best approach is to proceed slowly gathering together a good quality set of those tools that are used most frequently. Don't be misled by the low cost of bargain tools. It is far better to spend a little more for better quality. Forged wrenches, 6 or 12-point sockets and fine tooth ratchets are by far preferable to their less expensive counterparts. As any good mechanic can tell you, there are few worse experiences than trying to work on a vehicle with bad tools. Your monetary savings will be far outweighed by frustration and mangled knuckles.

Begin accumulating those tools that are used most frequently; those associated with routine maintenance and tune-up.

In addition to the normal assortment of screwdrivers and pliers you should have the following tools for routine maintenance jobs:

1. SAE (or Metric) or SAE/Metric wrenches-sockets and combination open end/box end wrenches in sizes from 1/8 in. (3mm) to 3/4 in. (19 mm) and a spark plug socket 13/16 in. or 5/8 in. (depending on plug type).

If possible, buy various length socket drive extensions. One break in this department is that the metric sockets available in the U.S. will all fit the ratchet handles and extensions you may already have (1/4 inch, 3/8 inch, and 1/2 inch drives).

2. Jackstands for support.
3. Oil filter wrench.
4. Oil filler spout for pouring oil.
5. Grease gun for chassis lubrication.
6. Hydrometer for checking the battery.
7. A container for draining oil.
8. Many rags for wiping up the inevitable mess.

In addition to the above items there are several others that are not absolutely necessary, but handy to have around. These include oil dry, a transmission funnel and the usual supply of lubricants, antifreeze and fluids, although these can be purchased as needed. This is a basic list for routine maintenance, but only your personal needs and desire can accurately determine your list of tools.

The second list of tools is for tune-ups. While the tools involved here are slightly more sophisticated, they need not be outrageously expensive. There are several inexpensive tach/dwell meters on the market that are every bit as good for the average mechanic as a professional model. Just be sure that it goes to a least 1,200-1,500 rpm on the tach scale and that it works on 4, 6, and 8 cylinder engines. (A special tach is needed for diesel engines). A basic list of tune-up equipment could include:

9. Tach/dwell meter.
10. Spark plug wrench.
11. Timing light (a DC light that works from the vehicle's battery is best, although an AC light that plugs into 110V house current will suffice at some sacrifice in brightness).
12. Wire spark plug gauge/adjusting tools.
13. Set of feeler blades.

Here again, be guided by your own needs. A feeler blade will set the points as easily as a dwell meter will read dwell, but slightly less accurately. And since you will need a tachometer anyway. . . well, make your own decision.

14. In addition to these basic tools, there are several other tools and gauges you may find useful. These include:
- Compression gauge. The screw-in type is slower to use, but eliminates the possibility of a faulty reading due to escaping pressure.
- Manifold vacuum gauge.
- 12v test light.
- Induction meter. This is used for determining whether or not there is current in a wire. These are handy for use if a wire is broken somewhere in a wiring harness.

As a final note, you will probably find a torque wrench necessary for all but the most basic work. The beam type models are perfectly adequate, although the newer click types are more precise.

Special Tools

Normally, the use of special factory tools is avoided for repair procedures, since these are not readily available for the do-it-yourself mechanic. When it is possible to preform the job with more commonly available tools, it will be pointed out, but occasionally, a special tool was designed to perform a specific function and should be used. Before substituting another tool, you should be convinced that neither your safety nor the performance of the vehicle will be compromised.

Some special tools are available commercially from major tool manufacturers, while others are available from the dealership. The tool manufacturer can also be contacted directly at: Service Tool Division Kent-Moore 29784 Little Mack Roseville, MI 48066-2298.

SERVICING YOUR CAR SAFELY

It is virtually impossible to anticipate all of the hazards involved with automotive maintenance and service, but care and common sense will prevent most accidents.

The rules of safety for mechanics range from "don't smoke around gasoline," to "use the proper tool for the job." The trick to avoiding injuries is to develop safe work habits and take every possible precaution.

Dos

• Do keep a fire extinguisher and first aid kit within easy reach.

• Do wear safety glasses or goggles when cutting, drilling, grinding or prying, even if you have 20-20 vision. If you wear glasses for the sake of vision, they should be made of hardened glass that can serve also as safety glasses, or wear safety goggles over your regular glasses.

• Do shield your eyes whenever you work around the battery. Batteries contain sulfuric acid. In case of contact with the

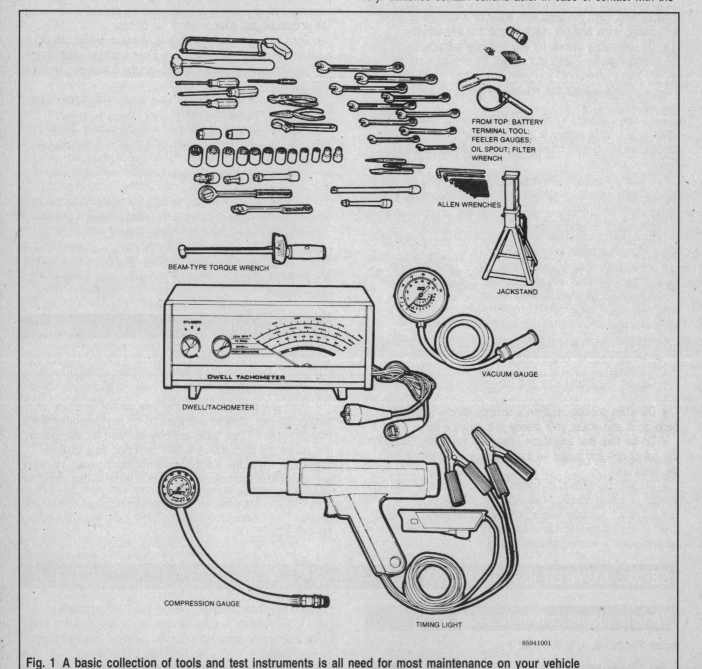

BEAM-TYPE TORQUE WRENCH

DWELL/TACHOMETER

COMPRESSION GAUGE

FROM TOP: BATTERY TERMINAL TOOL; FEELER GAUGES; OIL SPOUT; FILTER WRENCH

ALLEN WRENCHES

JACKSTAND

VACUUM GAUGE

TIMING LIGHT

85941001

Fig. 1 A basic collection of tools and test instruments is all need for most maintenance on your vehicle

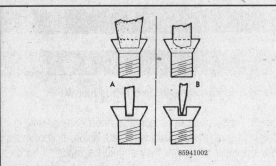

Fig. 2 Keep screwdrivers in good shape. They should fit the slot as shown in "A". If they look like those in "B", they need grinding or replacing

eyes or skin, flush the area with water or a mixture of water and baking soda and get medical attention immediately.

• Do use safety stands for any undercar service. Jacks are for raising vehicles; safety stands are for making sure the vehicle stays raised until you want it to come down. Whenever the car is raised, block the wheels remaining on the ground and set the parking brake.

• Do use adequate ventilation when working with any chemicals or hazardous materials. Like carbon monoxide, the asbestos dust resulting from brake lining wear can be poisonous in sufficient quantities.

• Do disconnect the negative battery cable when working on the electrical system. The secondary ignition system can contain up to 40,000 volts.

• Do follow manufacturer's directions whenever working with potentially hazardous materials. Both brake fluid and antifreeze are poisonous if taken internally.

• Do properly maintain your tools. Loose hammerheads, mushroomed punches and chisels, frayed or poorly grounded electrical cords, excessively worn screwdrivers, spread wrenches (open end), cracked sockets, slipping ratchets, or faulty droplight sockets can cause accidents.

• Likewise, keep your tools clean; a greasy wrench can slip off a bolt head, ruining the bolt and often ruining your knuckles in the process.

• Do use the proper size and type of tool for the job being done.

• Do when possible, pull on a wrench handle rather than push on it, and adjust your stance to prevent a fall.

• Do be sure that adjustable wrenches are tightly closed on the nut or bolt and pulled so that the face is on the side of the fixed jaw.

• Do select a wrench or socket that fits the nut or bolt. The wrench or socket should sit straight, not cocked.

• Do strike squarely with a hammer; avoid glancing blows.

• Do set the parking brake and block the drive wheels if the work requires a running engine.

Don'ts

• Don't run the engine in a garage or anywhere else without proper ventilation-EVER! Carbon monoxide is poisonous; it takes a long time to leave the human body and you can build up a deadly supply of it in your system by simply breathing in a little every day. You may not realize you are slowly poisoning yourself. Always use power vents, windows, fans or open the garage door.

• Don't work around moving parts while wearing a necktie or other loose clothing. Short sleeves are much safer than long, loose sleeves; hard-toed shoes with neoprene soles protect your toes and give a better grip on slippery surfaces. Jewelry such as watches, fancy belt buckles, beads or body adornment of any kind is not safe working around a car. Long hair should be tied back under a hat or cap.

• Don't use pockets for toolboxes. A fall or bump can drive a screwdriver deep into your body. Even a wiping cloth hanging from the back pocket can wrap around a spinning shaft or fan.

• Don't smoke when working around gasoline, cleaning solvent or other flammable material.

• Don't smoke when working around the battery. When the battery is being charged, it gives off explosive hydrogen gas.

• Don't use gasoline to wash your hands; there are excellent soaps available. Gasoline may contain lead, and lead can enter the body through a cut, accumulating in the body until you are very ill. Gasoline also removes all the natural oils from the skin so that bone dry hands will suck up oil and grease.

• Don't service the air conditioning system unless you are equipped with the necessary tools and training. The refrigerant, R-12, is extremely cold when compressed, and when released into the air will instantly freeze any surface it contacts, including your eyes. Although the refrigerant is normally non-toxic, R-12 becomes a deadly poisonous gas in the presence of an open flame. One good whiff of the vapors from burning refrigerant can be fatal.

• Don't use screwdrivers for anything other than driving screws! A screwdriver used as an prying tool can snap when you least expect it, causing injuries. At the very least, you'll ruin a good screwdriver.

• Don't use a bumper jack (that little ratchet, scissors, or pantograph jack supplied with the car) for anything other than changing a flat! These jacks are only intended for emergency use out on the road; they are NOT designed as a maintenance tool. If you are serious about maintaining your car yourself, invest in a hydraulic floor jack of a least 1½ ton capacity, and at least two sturdy jackstands.

SERIAL NUMBER IDENTIFICATION

Vehicle Identification Number (VIN)

▶ **See Figures 3, 4, 5, 6, 7 and 8**

The 1964-67 vehicle serial number is stamped on a vehicle identification plate, attached to the left front door hinge pillar.

On 1968 and later cars, the Vehicle Identification Number (VIN) is stamped on a plate located on the top left hand side of the instrument panel, so it can be seen by looking through the windshield.

The VIN is a thirteen digit (1968-80) or seventeen digit (1981 and later) sequence of numbers and letters important for ordering parts and for servicing. The VIN is also part of the Federal Vehicle Theft Prevention Standard and cannot be removed or altered in anyway.

➡Model years appear in the VIN as the last digit of each particular year (6 is 1976, 8 is 1978, etc.) until 1980 (which is A). This is the final year under the thirteen digit code. The seventeen digit VIN begins with 1981 (B) and continues 1982 (C), 1983 (D), etc. Once the vehicle year lettering system began, any letter that might be mistaken for a number was skipped, therefore 1988 was J not I, because I might be mistaken for the number 1.

Fig. 4 The VIN plate on most vehicles is visible through the lower corner of the windshield

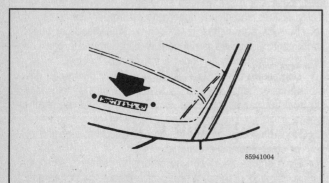

Fig. 3 For 1968 and later vehicles, the VIN plate is located on the driver's side of the dash

Fig. 5 Most vehicles covered in this manual are equipped with a body identification plate, located on top of the cowl

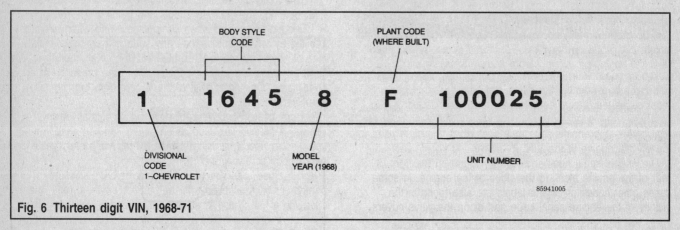

Fig. 6 Thirteen digit VIN, 1968-71

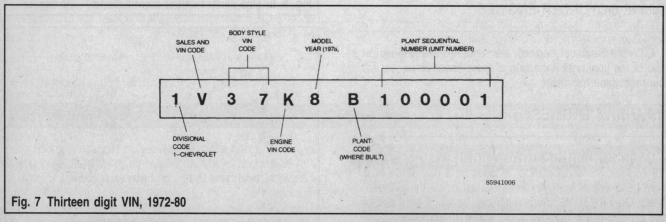

Fig. 7 Thirteen digit VIN, 1972-80

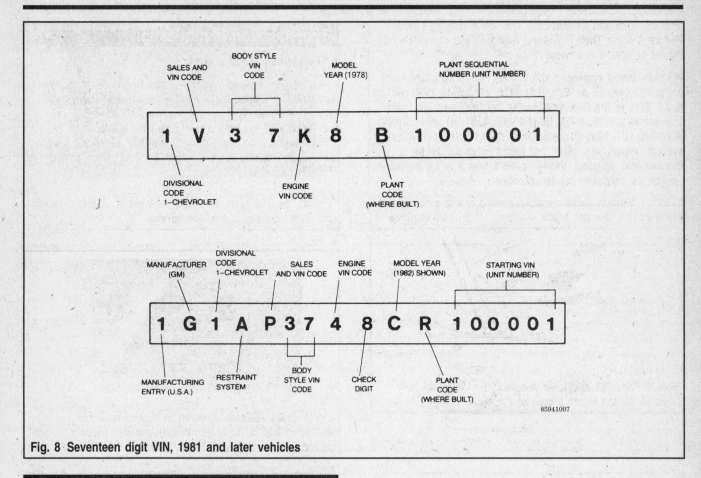

Fig. 8 Seventeen digit VIN, 1981 and later vehicles

Engine Identification

▶ See Figures 9, 10 and 11

The engine serial number is stamped on an engine block pad in order to identify the place and time of manufacture. In most cases the engine serial number will also contain a 1-3 digit code that identifies the engine type. In the case of single digit codes, this engine code may conform to the code used to identify the engine in the VIN.

The engine serial number is usually found on the front or rear of the engine block to the sides of the engine. In some cases other codes or engine labels are also found in the vicinity of the engine serial code pad or on the valve covers.

INLINE 6-CYLINDER ENGINES

On inline 6-cylinder engines, the serial number is found on a pad at the front right hand side of the cylinder block, just to the rear of the distributor.

V8 AND V6 ENGINES

On the 229 V6 (1967-84), 265 V6 (1985 and later) and most V8 engines, the serial number is found on a pad at the front right hand side of the cylinder block, just below the cylinder head. On the 231 V6, the number can be found on a pad on the left side of the cylinder block, where it meets the transmission.

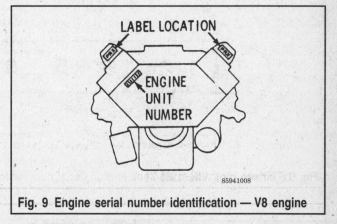

Fig. 9 Engine serial number identification — V8 engine

Fig. 10 Engine label locations — 231 V6 engine

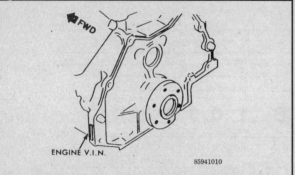

Fig. 11 Engine serial number located at the extreme left rear of the cylinder block — some V6 and V8 engines

Transmission Identification

▶ **See Figures 12, 13 and 14**

A transmission serial number is stamped on each transmission. Like the engine serial number, the transmission serial number is intended to identify the time and place of manufacture along with the particular transmission model identifier.

Placement of the serial number will vary depending on the transmission model, but it is normally found on the side or rear of the transmission housing.

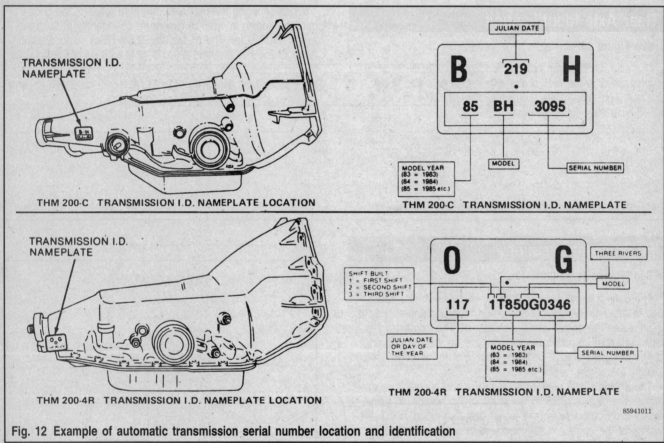

Fig. 12 Example of automatic transmission serial number location and identification

Manual Transmissions

	Year																							
	64	65	66	67	68	69	70	71	72	73	74	75	76	77	78	79	80	81	82	83	84	85	86	87	88
Muncie 3-speed	✓	✓																							
Muncie 3-speed, Fully Synchronized					✓	✓	✓	✓	✓	✓	✓														
Saginaw 3-speed, Fully Synchronized			✓	✓	✓	✓	✓	✓	✓	✓	✓	✓	✓	✓	✓	✓	✓								
Muncie 4-Speed	✓	✓	✓	✓	✓	✓	✓	✓	✓	✓	✓														
Saginaw 4-speed			✓	✓	✓	✓	✓	✓	✓	✓	✓	✓	✓	✓	✓	✓	✓								
Warner T-16, 3-Speed				✓	✓																				
Warner 4-Speed															✓	✓	✓	✓							
Saginaw 4-Speed, Overdrive											✓	✓	✓	✓	✓	✓	✓	✓	✓	✓					

Fig. 13 Manual transmission application guide

Automatic Transmissions

	Year																								
	64	65	66	67	68	69	70	71	72	73	74	75	76	77	78	79	80	81	82	83	84	85	86	87	88
Power Glide	√	√	√	√	√	√	√	√	√	√	√	√	√	√	√	√	√								
Turbo Hydramatic 350						√	√	√	√	√	√	√	√	√	√	√	√	√							
Turbo Hydramatic 400			√	√	√	√	√	√																	
Turbo Hydramatic 200															√	√	√	√							
Turbo Hydramatic 250											√	√	√	√	√	√									
Turbo Hydramatic 200C																			√	√	√	√	√	√	
Turbo Hydramatic 250C																			√	√	√				
Turbo Hydramatic 350C 4-speed																			√	√	√				
Turbo Hydramatic 200-4R overdrive 4-speed																		√	√	√	√	√	√	√	√
Turbo Hydramatic 350C 3-speed																			√	√					

85941c08

Fig. 14 Automatic transmission application guide

Rear Axle Identification

▶ **See Figure 15**

The axle identification number is located either on a metal tag (attached to the rear of the differential) or stamped onto the front right side of the axle tube, about three inches outboard from the differential cover.

When servicing the rear axle, the third letter of the code must be known in order to determine the identity of the rear axle manufacturer. The codes are: B for Buick, C for Buffalo, G for Chevrolet-Gear and Axle, K or M for GM of Canada, O for Oldsmobile, P for Pontiac and W for Warren.

On late model vehicles, the axle ratios are designed to meet emission standards for areas of operation.

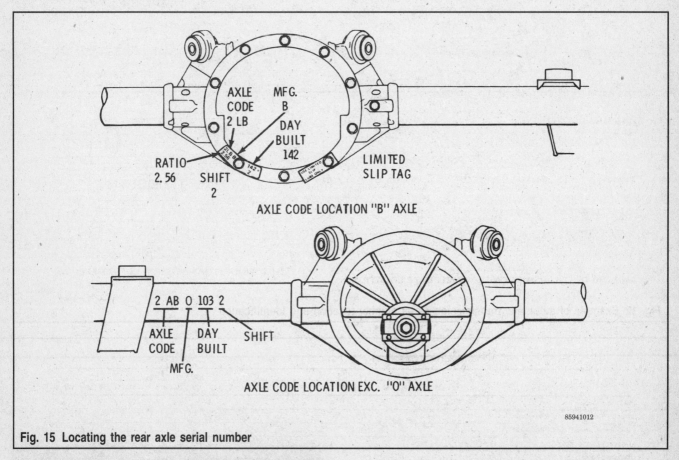

AXLE CODE
2 LB

MFG.
B

DAY
BUILT
142

RATIO
2. 56

SHIFT
2

LIMITED
SLIP TAG

AXLE CODE LOCATION "B" AXLE

2 AB O 103 2

AXLE
CODE

MFG.

DAY
BUILT

SHIFT

AXLE CODE LOCATION EXC. "O" AXLE

85941012

Fig. 15 Locating the rear axle serial number

Vehicle Emission Control Information Label

▶ **See Figure 16**

The Vehicle Emission Control Information Label is located in the engine compartment (fan shroud, radiator support, hood underside, etc) of every vehicle produced by General Motors. The label contains important emission specifications and setting procedures, as well as a vacuum hose schematic with various emissions components identified.

The Vehicle Emission Control Information Label will often reflect changes in specification made during a given manufacturing year that are applicable to that particular vehicle. This label should always be checked for up-to-date information pertaining specifically to your car.

➡**Always follow the timing procedures on this label when adjusting ignition timing.**

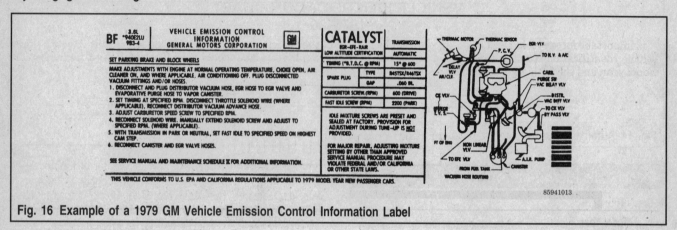

Fig. 16 Example of a 1979 GM Vehicle Emission Control Information Label

VEHICLE IDENTIFICATION CHART
1976-80

It is important for servicing and ordering parts to be certain of the vehicle and engine identification. The thirteenth digit Vehicle Identification Number can be used to determine engine application and model year. The sixth digit indicates the model year, and the fifth digit identifies the factory installed engine. It can be interpreted as follows:

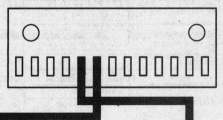

Model Year Code		Engine Code					
			Displacement				
Code	Year	Code	Cu. In.	Liters	Cyl.	Carb.	Eng. Mfg.
6	'76	D	250	4.1	6	1	Chev.
		G	262	4.3	6	2	Chev.
		Q	305	5.0	8	2	Chev.
		V	350	5.7	8	2	Chev.
		L	350	5.7	8	4	Chev.
		U	400	6.6	8	4	Chev.
		S	454	7.4	8	4	Chev.
7	'77	D	250	4.1	6	1	Chev.
		U	305	5.0	8	2	Chev.
		L	350	5.7	8	4	Chev.
8	'78	M	200	3.3	6	2	Chev.
		A	231	3.8	6	2	Buick
		D	250	4.1	6	1	Chev.
		U	305	5.0	8	2	Chev.
		L	350	5.7	8	4	Chev.
9	'79	M	200	3.3	6	2	Chev.
		A	231	3.8	6	2	Buick
		D	250	4.1	6	1	Chev.
		J	267	4.4	8	2	Chev.
		G	305	5.0	8	2	Chev.
		H	305	5.0	8	4	Chev.
		L	350	5.7	8	4	Chev.
A	'80	K	229	3.8	6	2	Chev.
		A	231	3.8	6	2	Buick
		3	231	3.8	6	Turbo	Buick
		J	267	4.4	8	2	Chev.
		H	305	5.0	8	4	Chev.
		N	350	5.7	8	Diesel	Olds.

85941C01

VEHICLE IDENTIFICATION CHART
1981–88

It is important for servicing and ordering parts to be certain of the vehicle and engine identification. The VIN (vehicle identification number) is a 17 digit number visible through the windshield on the driver's side of the dash and contains the vehicle and engine identification codes. The tenth digit indicates model year and the eighth digit indicates engine code. It can be interpreted as follows:

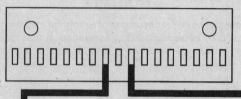

Engine Code						Model Year	
Code	Liters	Cu. In. (cc)	Cyl.	Carb.	Eng. Mfg.	Code	Year
K	3.8	229	6	2	Chev.	B	1981
9	3.8	229	6	2	Chev.	C	1982
A	3.8	231	6	2	Buick	D	1983
3	3.8	231	6	Turbo	Buick	E	1984
Z	4.3	262	6	TBI	Chev.	F	1985
V	4.3	263	6	Diesel	Olds.	G	1986
J	4.4	267	8	2	Chev.	H	1987
G	5.0	305	8	4	Chev.	J	1988
H	5.0	305	8	4	Chev.		
7	5.0	305	8	4	Chev.		
6	5.7	350	8	4	Chev.		
N	5.7	350	8	Diesel	Chev.		

85941C02

ENGINE IDENTIFICATION CHART
1964–70

Engine identification code letter follows immediately after engine serial number.

No. Cyls.	Cu. In. Displ.	Type	Year and Code						
			1964	1965	1966	1967	1968	1969	1970
6	194	M.T.	GF, G	AA	AA				
6	194	HDC	GG, GB	AC	AC				
6	194	AC	GM, GK	AG	AG				
6	194	HDC, AC	GN, GL	AH	AH				
6	194	Taxi	GH, GK	AK					
6	194	PG	K, KB	AL	AL				
6	194	PG, Taxi	KC, KD	AN					
6	194	PG, AC	KJ, KH	AR	AR				
6	194	w/ex. EM			AS				
6	194	w/ex. EM, AC			AT				
6	194	PG, w/ex. EM			AX				
6	194	PG, w/ex. EM, AC			AY				
6	230	HDC				BC	BC	BC	
6	230	HDC, AC				BB	BB	BB	
6	230	PG	BE				BF	BF	
6	230	PG, w/ex. EM	BN		BL			AN	
6	230	Hyd., AC						AR	
6	230	PG, w/ex. EM, AC			BM				
6	230	Hyd.						AD	
6	230	w/ex. EM			BN				
6	230	w/ex. EM, AC			BO				
6	230	PG, PCV, AC	BP						
6	230	M.T.		CA	CA	CA	BA	AM	
6	230	M.T.	LM	CB	CB				
6	230	3 Spd. AC	LN, LL			CB		AP	
6	230	PG		CC	CC	CC			
6	230	PG, AC	BM	CD	CD	CD	BH	AQ	
6	250	3 Spd. or OD				CM	CM	BE	CCL
6	250	3 Spd. AC				CN	CN	BF	
6	250	3 Spd. or OD w/ex. EM				CO			
6	250	3 Spd. AC w/ex. EM				CP			
6	250	PG				CQ	CQ	BB	CCM
6	250	PG, AC			CR	CR	BC		
6	250	Hyd.						BD	CCK
6	250	PG, w/ex. EM				CS			
6	250	Hyd., AC						BH	
6	250	PG, AC w/ex. EM				CT			
8	283	3 Spd.	J	DA	DA	DA			
8	283	4 Spd.	JA	DB	DB	DB			
8	283	PG	JD	DE	DF	DE			
8	283	3 Spd., 4 Bbl.	JH	DG	DG				
8	283	PG, 4 Bbl.	JG	DH	DH				
8	283	w/ex. EM			DI	DI			
8	283	PG, w/ex. EM			DJ	DJ			
8	283	4 Spd., w/ex. EM		DK	DK				
8	283	4 Bbl., w/ex. EM			DL				
8	283	PG, 4 Bbl., w/ex. EM			DM				
8	283	HDC				DN			
8	307	Hyd.						DD	CNF

85941C03

ENGINE IDENTIFICATION CHART
1964–70

Engine identification code letter follows immediately after engine serial number.

No. Cyls.	Cu. In. Displ.	Type	Year and Code						
			1964	1965	1966	1967	1968	1969	1970
8	307	Hyd.						DD	CNF
8	307	M.T.					DA	DA	CNC
8	307	4 Spd.					DE	DE	CND
8	307	PG					DB	DC	CNE
8	307	HDC					DN		
8	327	M.T.	JQ	EA	EA	EA	EA		
8	327	HP	JR	EB					
8	327	w/ex. EM			EB	EB			
8	327	SHP	JS	EC			ES		
8	327	PG, w/ex. EM			EC	EC			
8	327	w/T. Ign.	JT	ED					
8	327	3 or 4 Spd. (325 H.P.)				EP			

85941c3a

ENGINE IDENTIFICATION CHART
1964–70 (cont.)

Engine identification code letter follows immediately after engine serial number.

No. Cyls.	Cu. In. Displ.	Type	Year and Code						
			1964	1965	1966	1967	1968	1969	1970
8	327	HDC, 3 or 4 Spd. w/ex. EM (325 H.P.)				ER			
8	327	HDC (325 H.P.)				ES	ES		
8	327	HDC (275 H.P.)				ED	ED		
8	327	PG	SR	EE	EE	EE	EE		
8	327	PG, HP	SS	EF					
8	350	M.T.						HA	
8	350	Hyd.						HB	
8	350	2-BBL.						HC	
8	350	2-BBL., Hyd.						HD	
8	350	PG						HE	CNM (250)
8	350	PG, 2-BBL.						HF	
8	350	M.T.						HP	CNI (250)
8	350	M.T.						HR	CNJ (300)
8	350	PG						HR	CNK (300)
8	350	Hyd.						HS	CRE (300)
8	396	HDC			ED	ED	ED	ED	
8	396	HP			EF	EF	EF	JC	
8	396	SHP					EG	JD	
8	396	w/ex. EM			EH	EH			
8	396	HP, w/ex. EM			EJ	EJ			
8	396	PG			EK	EK	EK	EK	
8	396	PG, HP			EL	EL	EL	EL	
8	396	PG, w/ex. EM			EM	EM			
8	396	PG, HP, w/ex. EM			EN	EN			
8	396	Hyd. (325 H.P.)				ET	ET	ET	
8	396	Hyd. (350 H.P.)				EU	EU	EU	
8	396	w/ex. EM (325 H.P.)				EV			
8	396	w/ex. EM (325 H.P.)				EW			
8	396	M.T.						JA	CZX (265), CTX (350), CKT (375), CKO (375)
8	396	HP, 3-sp. Hyd. 400						JE	
8	396	Hyd. 400						JK	CTW (350)
8	396	SHP, Hyd. 400. (#-CKP only)						KF	CTY (375), CKP (375), CKU (375)
8	396	M.T.						KG	
8	396	Hyd. 400						KH	CKN (325)
8	396	M.T., HP						KB	
8	396	M.T.						JV	
8	396	SHP, M.T.						KD	
8	396	M.T.						KI	
8	396	M.T., HDC							CTZ (350), CKQ (375)

85941C04

ENGINE IDENTIFICATION CHART
1964-70 (cont.)

Engine identification code letter follows immediately after engine serial number.

No. Cyls.	Cu. In. Displ.	Type	Year and Code						
			1964	1965	1966	1967	1968	1969	1970
8	400	M.T. (330 H.P.)							CKR
8	400	M.T., HDC (330 H.P.)							CKS
8	454	M.T. (390 H.P.)							CRN, CRT
8	454	Hyd. 400 (390 H.P.)							CRQ
8	454	Hyd. 400 (450 H.P.)							CRR
8	454	Hyd. 400 #(450 H.P.)							CRS
8	454	M.T. (450 H.P.)							CRV

AC—Air conditioned
HDC—Heavy duty clutch
HP—High performance
SHP—Special high performance
M.T.—Manual transmission
OD—Overdrive
PG—Powerglide transmission
PCV—Positive crankcase ventilation
w/ex. EM—with exhaust emission
w/T. Ign.—with transistor ignition
4 Bbl/—Four barrel carburetor
Hyd.—Hydramatic
#—Aluminum heads

85941c4a

ENGINE IDENTIFICATION CHART
1971–80

No. Cyls.	Cu. In. Displ.	Type	Year and Code									
			1971	1972	1973	1974	1975	1976	1977	1978	1979	1980
6	200	All								M	M	
6	229	All										K
6	231	All								A	A	A
6	250	All	CAA	D	D	D	D	D	D			
8	267	2bbl										J
8	305	2bbl						Q	U	U		
8	305	4bbl									H	H
8	307	All	CCA	F	F							
8	350	MT 2bbl	CGA	CKA	CKA							
8	350	MT 4bbl	CGK	CKK	CKB							
8	350	MT 2bbl w/EEC		CDA	CKC							
8	350	MT 4bbl w/EEC		CDG	CKH							
8	350	PG	CGB	CKB								
8	350	PG w/EEC		CDB								
8	350	TH350 2bbl		CTL	CKL							
8	350	TH350 4bbl	CGL CGD	CKD	CKJ							
8	350	TH350 2bbl w/EEC		CMD	CKK							
8	350	TH350 4bbl w/EEC		CDD	CKD							
8	350	Police		CSH								
8	350	Police/EEC		CAR								
8	350	2bbl				H	H	V				
8	350	4bbl				J	J	L	L	L	L	
8	350	4bbl DE				T	T					
8	400	MT	CLL CLS	CLA CLS								
8	400	MT w/AIR		CTA								
8	400	MT w/HD 3sp.		CTH								
8	400	AT 2bbl		CLB								
8	400	AT 4bbl	CLB			R	U	U				
8	400	AT 2bbl w/AIR		CTA								
8	400	AT 4bbl w/AIR		CTB								
8	454	MT 365 hp	CPG CPA	CPA	CWA							
8	454	AT	CPO CPP	CPD	CWB	Y	Y					
8	454	AT w/AIR		CRW								
8	454	AT w/EEC			CWD	Z						
8	454	MT w/AIR		CRX	CWC							

85941C05

ENGINE IDENTIFICATION

Year	Engine Displacement cu. in. (liters)	Engine Series Identification (VIN)	No. of Cylinders	Engine Type
1981	229 (3.8)	K	6	OHV
	231 (3.8)	A	6	OHV
	267 (4.4)	J	8	OHV
	305 (5.0)	H	8	OHV
1982	229 (3.8)	K	6	OHV
	231 (3.8)	A	6	OHV
	263 (4.3)	V	6	OHV
	267 (4.4)	J	8	OHV
	305 (5.0)	H	8	OHV
1983	229 (3.8)	9	6	OHV
	231 (3.8)	A	6	OHV
	263 (4.3)	V	6	OHV
	305 (5.0)	H	8	OHV
	350 (5.7)	N	8	OHV
1984	229 (3.8)	9	6	OHV
	231 (3.8)	A	6	OHV
	263 (4.3)	V	6	OHV
	305 (5.0)	H	8	OHV
	350 (5.7)	N	8	OHV
1985	231 (3.8)	A	6	OHV
	262 (4.3)	Z	6	OHV
	305 (5.0)	G	8	OHV
	305 (5.0)	H	8	OHV
1986	262 (4.3)	Z	6	OHV
	305 (5.0)	G	8	OHV
	305 (5.0)	H	8	OHV
1987	262 (4.3)	Z	6	OHV
	305 (5.0)	G	8	OHV
	305 (5.0)	H	8	OHV
1988	262 (4.3)	Z	6	OHV
	305 (5.0)	G	8	OHV
	305 (5.0)	H	8	OHV
	307 (5.0)	Y	8	OHV

85941C06

REAR AXLE IDENTIFICATION AND RATIO

Codes	64	65	66	67	68	69	70	71	72	73	74	75	76	77	78	79	80	81	82	83	84	85	86	87	88
AA																2.56				2.56					
AB															2.56	2.73	2.73	2.73	2.73	2.73	2.73	2.73	2.73	2.73	2.73
AC										2.73	2.73	2.73	2.73	2.73		3.08	3.08	3.08				3.08	3.08	3.08	3.08
AD										3.08	3.08	3.08	3.08			3.23	3.23								
AE																				3.42					
AF														3.08											
AG															2.93	2.93		2.93							
AH												2.56	2.56				2.29	2.29	2.29	2.29	2.29	2.29	2.29	2.29	
AJ										3.42	3.42	3.42				2.41	2.41	2.41	2.41	2.41	2.41	2.41	2.41	2.41	2.41
AL																2.73									
AS																					3.42				
AT																	2.29	2.29	2.29	2.29					
AU																									
AV																	3.08	3.08	3.08		3.08	3.08	3.08	3.08	3.08
AW																	2.93								
AX															2.73	2.73	2.73	2.73	2.73	2.73	2.73	2.73	2.73	2.73	
AY																2.56	2.56	2.56	2.56			2.56	2.56	2.56	
AZ															2.41	2.41	2.41	2.41	2.41	2.41	2.41	2.41	2.41	2.41	
BA															2.56	2.56									
BB															2.73	2.73	2.73	2.73	2.73	2.73	2.73	2.73	2.73	2.73	
BC																3.08		3.08				3.08	3.08	3.08	3.08
BD																3.23									
BG															2.93	2.93		2.93							
BH															2.29	2.29	2.29	2.29	2.29	2.29	2.29	2.29	2.29	2.29	
BJ																2.41	2.41	2.41	2.41	2.41	2.41	2.41	2.41	2.41	2.41
BL																2.73									
BS																					3.42				
BT																	2.29	2.29	2.29	2.29					
BU																		3.23							
BV																3.08					3.08	3.08	3.08	3.08	3.08
BW																	2.93								
BX															2.73	2.73	2.73	2.73	2.73	2.73	2.73	2.73	2.73	2.73	
BY																2.56	2.56	2.56	2.56			2.56	2.56	2.56	
BZ															2.41	2.41	2.41	2.41	2.41	2.41	2.41	2.41	2.41	2.41	
CA	3.08	3.08	3.08	3.08	3.08	3.08																			
CB	3.36	3.36	3.36	3.36	3.36	3.36								2.56											
CC	3.73	3.73	3.73	3.73	3.73	3.73				2.73	2.73	2.73	2.73	2.73											
CD	3.07	3.07	3.07	3.07	3.07	3.07				3.08	3.08	3.08	3.08												
CE	3.08	3.08	3.08	3.08	3.08	3.08																			
CF	3.31	3.31	3.31	3.31	3.31	3.31	3.31	3.31	3.31					3.08											
CG	3.36	3.36	3.36	3.36	3.36	3.36																			

85941C09

REAR AXLE IDENTIFICATION AND RATIO

Codes	64	65	66	67	68	69	70	71	72	73	74	75	76	77	78	79	80	81	82	83	84	85	86	87	88
CQ	3.36	3.36	3.36			2.56																			
CR	3.70	3.70	3.70	3.70	3.70																				
CS	3.70	3.70	3.70			2.56																			
CT	3.73	3.73	3.73	3.73		2.73																			
CU	3.73	3.73	3.73	3.73	3.73																				
CV	3.70	3.70	3.70	3.70	3.70																				
CW	3.31	3.31	3.31	3.31	3.31	3.31	3.31	3.31	3.31																
CX	3.07	3.07	3.07	3.07	3.07	3.07																			
CY					3.07																				
CZ					2.73																				
CCA						3.08																			
CCD						3.07																			
CCE						3.08																			
CCF						3.31																			
CCH						2.73																			
CCN						2.56																			
CCO						2.56																			
CCP						2.73																			
CCW						3.31																			
CCX						3.07																			
CGA						2.56																			
CGB						2.56																			
CGC						2.73																			
CGD						2.73																			
CGG						3.36																			
CGI						3.36																			
CKC						2.73																			
CKD						2.73																			
CKF						3.55																			
CKJ						3.55																			
CKK						4.10																			
CRJ						2.56																			
CRK						2.56																			
CRU						3.31																			
CRV						3.31																			
CRW						4.10																			
FH					2.73	2.73																			
FI					2.73	2.73																			
FJ					3.08	3.08																			
FK					3.08	3.08																			
FL					3.36	3.36																			
FM					3.36	3.36																			
FN					3.55	3.55																			
FO					3.55	3.55																			
FP					3.70																				

85941C11

REAR AXLE IDENTIFICATION AND RATIO (continued)

Codes	64	65	66	67	68	69	70	71	72	73	74	75	76	77	78	79	80	81	82	83	84	85	86	87	88
FU					3.70																				
GA								2.56																	
GB	2.73	2.73						2.56																	
GC	2.73	2.73						2.73																	
GD	2.73	2.73						2.73																	
GE	2.73	2.73																							
GF								3.08	3.08																
GG								3.36	3.36																
GH								2.73	2.73																
GI								3.36	3.36																
GN								3.08	3.08																
KA					3.55	3.55																			
KB					3.55	3.55																			
KC					2.73	2.73																			
KD					2.73	2.73	2.73	2.73																	
KE						2.73																			
KF			3.55	3.55	3.55	3.55																			
KG			3.55	3.55		3.08																			
KH			3.55	3.55		3.08																			
KI			2.73			3.36																			
KJ			3.55	3.55	3.55	3.55																			
KK			4.10	4.10	4.10	4.10																			
KL			4.10	4.10		3.36																			
KM			4.56	4.56	4.56	4.56																			
KN			4.56	4.56		3.55																			
KO			4.88	4.88	4.88	4.88																			
KP			4.88	4.88		3.55																			
KW					2.73																				
KX					3.07	3.07																			
KY					3.31																				
KZ					3.31																				
K2					3.55																				
K3					3.55																				
K4					3.73																				
K5					3.73																				
K6					4.10																				
K7					4.56																				
K8					4.88																				
PC																2.41									
RA															2.29	2.29	2.29								

85941C12

REAR AXLE IDENTIFICATION AND RATIO (continued)

Codes	64	65	66	67	68	69	70	71	72	73	74	75	76	77	78	79	80	81	82	83	84	85	86	87	88
RB																	2.41								
RC															2.56	2.56									
RD															2.73	2.73	2.73								
RF																3.08									
RU								3.31	3.31																
RV								3.31	3.31																
RW								4.10	4.10																
RX															2.73	2.73		2.73							
SC																2.29									
SC																2.41									
SC																3.08									
TF																								3.73	3.73
TH																								3.73	3.73
WA												2.73	2.73												
WB										2.73	2.73														
WC										3.08	3.08	3.08	3.08												
WE										3.42	3.42	3.42													
XA										2.73	2.73	2.73	2.73												
XB										2.73	2.73														
XC										3.08	3.08	3.08	3.08												
XE										3.42	3.42	3.42													
ZE														2.73											
ZJ														3.08											
ZW														2.73											
ZY														3.08											

85941C13

REAR AXLE IDENTIFICATION AND RATIO

Codes	64	65	66	67	68	69	70	71	72	73	74	75	76	77	78	79	80	81	82	83	84	85	86	87	88
CH	3.70	3.70	3.70	2.73	2.73	2.73	2.73					2.56	2.56												
CI	3.73	3.73	3.73	3.73	3.73	3.73																			
CJ	3.07	3.07	3.07	3.07		2.56				3.42	3.42	3.42													
CK	3.07	3.07	3.07	3.07		2.56																			
CL	3.08	3.08	3.08			2.56																			
CM	3.08	3.08	3.08			2.56																			
CN	3.31	3.31	3.31	3.31		2.56																			
CO	3.31	3.31	3.31	3.31		2.56																			
CP	3.36	3.36	3.36		2.73	2.73																			

85941C10

ROUTINE MAINTENANCE

Air Cleaner

The air cleaner has a dual purpose. It not only filters the air going to the carburetor, but also acts as a flame arrester if the engine should backfire through the carburetor. The engine should never be run without the air cleaner installed unless an engine maintenance procedure specifically requires the temporary removal of the air cleaner. Operating a car without its air cleaner results in some throaty sounds from the carburetor giving the impression of increased power, but this will only cause trouble. Unfiltered air to the carburetor will eventually result in a dirty, inefficient carburetor and engine. A dirty carburetor increases the chances of carburetor backfire and, without the protection of an air cleaner, an underhood fire becomes a very real danger. The air cleaner assembly consists of the air cleaner itself (the large metal container or housing that fits over the carburetor), the element (paper or polyurethane) contained within the housing, and the flame arrester located in the base of the air cleaner. If your car is equipped with the paper element, it should be inspected at its first 12,000 miles, rechecked every 6,000 miles thereafter, and replaced after 24,000 miles for 1974 and earlier vehicles. For 1975 and later vehicles, air cleaners should be replaced at 30,000 mile intervals if the paper type (V6 and V8), and 15,000 miles if the oil wetted type (inline six). Inspections and replacements should be more frequent if the car is operated in a dirty, dusty environment. When inspecting the element, look for dust leaks, holes or an overly dirty appearance. If the element is excessively dirty, it may cause a reduction in clean air intake. If air has trouble getting through a dirty element, the carburetor fuel mixture will become richer (more gas, less air), the idle will be rougher, and the exhaust smoke will be noticeably black. To check the effectiveness of your paper element, carefully remove the air cleaner assembly and, if the idle increases, then the element is restricting air flow and should be replaced. If a polyurethane element is installed, clean or replace it every 12,000 miles. If you choose to clean it, do so with kerosene or another suitable solvent. Squeeze out all of the solvent, soak in engine oil, and then squeeze out the oil using a clean, dry cloth to remove the excess. The flame arrester, located at the base of the carburetor, should be cleaned in solvent (kerosene) once every 12,000 miles.

REMOVAL & INSTALLATION

▶ **See Figure 17**

For most vehicles, the filter element is easily accessible by removing the cover from the air cleaner assembly.

1. Loosen the wing nut(s) at the center of the air cleaner cover, and if applicable, the clamp fasteners along the cover's edge.

2. Remove the cover from the air cleaner assembly, then remove the air cleaner element from the housing.

Fig. 17 Loosen the wing nut in order to remove the air cleaner cover and access the filter element

3. If necessary, disconnect the air intake hose and, if applicable, the heat stove and/or vacuum line(s), from the air cleaner housing and remove the housing from the vehicle.

To install:

4. If removed, position the air cleaner housing on top of the carburetor or throttle body, then connect the air intake hose. If applicable, connect the heat stove and/or vacuum lines.

5. Install the air cleaner element to the housing, then position the cover onto the assembly.

6. Secure the cover using the clamp fasteners and/or wing nut(s).

Gasoline Fuel Filter

There are three types of fuel filters that may be found on these vehicles, internal (in the carburetor fitting), in-line (in the fuel line) and in-tank (the sock on the fuel pickup tube).

✳✳CAUTION

Before removing any fuel system component, always relieve pressure from the system.

FUEL PRESSURE RELEASE

Carbureted

To release the fuel pressure on the carbureted system, remove the fuel filler cap from the fuel tank in order to allow the expanded vapor to escape, then reinstall the cap. A rag should be placed around a fuel fitting before it is disconnected in order to catch any fuel which may escape.

Throttle Body Injection (TBI)

When servicing TBI vehicles, the fuel tank filler cap should be removed, in order to relieve tank pressure, then reinstalled. The TBI unit used on the 4.3L V6 engine contains a constant bleed feature in the pressure regulator that relieves pressure any time the engine is turned off. Therefore, no special relief procedure is required, however, a small amount of fuel may be released when the fuel line is disconnected.

✳✳CAUTION

To reduce the chance of personal injury, cover the fuel line with cloth to collect escaping fuel and then place the cloth in an approved container.

REMOVAL & INSTALLATION

Internal Filter

▶ See Figures 18, 19, 20, 21 and 22

The carburetor inlet fuel filter should be replaced every 12,000 miles for 1964-74 vehicles, every 15,000 miles for 1975 and later models or more often if necessary.

1. Disconnect the fuel line connection at the fuel inlet filter nut on the carburetor. A backup wrench should be used to prevent the fuel filter nut from loosening while trying to remove the line.
2. Carefully loosen and remove the fuel inlet filter nut from the carburetor.
3. Remove the filter and spring.

To install:

➡If a check valve is not present with the filter, one must be installed when the filter is replaced. The check valve is necessary in order to meet Motor Vehicle Safety Standards (MVSS) for roll-over.

Fig. 18 Whenever loosening fuel line connections, use a backup wrench to prevent overtorquing and damage to the lines

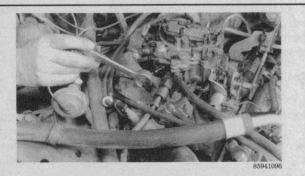

Fig. 19 If possible, use a line wrench to loosen the carburetor fuel inlet filter nut

4. Install the spring, filter and check valve making sure the valve end of the filter is facing the fuel line. Ribs on the fuel filter will prevent it from being installed incorrectly, unless it is forced into position.
5. Connect the fuel line to the filter inlet nut.
6. Start the engine and check for leaks.

Inline Filter

▶ See Figure 23

To locate the inline filter, follow the fuel line back from the carburetor or throttle body. Inline filters are often mounted to the frame rail underneath the vehicle. It may be necessary to raise and safely support the vehicle using jackstands in order to access the filter.

1. Disconnect the negative battery cable to prevent fuel spillage if the ignition is accidentally turned **ON**.
2. Using a backup wrench to prevent overtorquing the lines or fittings, loosen and disconnect the fuel lines from the filter. Be sure to position a rag in order to catch any remaining fuel which may escape when the fittings are loosened.
3. Loosen the retaining bolt, then remove the retaining bracket and/or fuel filter from the vehicle.

To install:

4. Position the filter and retaining bracket with the directional arrow facing away from the fuel tank, towards to carburetor or throttle body.

➡The filter has an arrow (fuel flow direction) on the side of the case, be sure to install it correctly in the system, the with arrow facing away from the fuel tank.

5. Install and tighten the filter/bracket retainer.
6. Connect the fuel lines to the filter and tighten using a backup wrench to prevent damage.
7. Connect the negative battery cable, then start the engine and check for leaks.

In-Tank Filter

To service the in-tank fuel filter, refer to the electric fuel pump removal and Installation procedure in Section 5 of this manual.

Diesel Fuel Filter

▶ See Figures 24 and 25

The diesel fuel filter is mounted on the rear of the intake manifold, and is larger than that on a gasoline engine because diesel fuel generally is dirtier containing more suspended particles than gasoline.

The diesel fuel filter should be changed every 30,000 miles or two years.

REMOVAL & INSTALLATION

1. Disconnect the negative battery cable.
2. With the engine cool, place absorbent rags underneath the fuel line fittings at the filter.
3. Disconnect the fuel lines from the filter. If possible, use a backup wrench to prevent overtorquing and damaging the fuel lines.

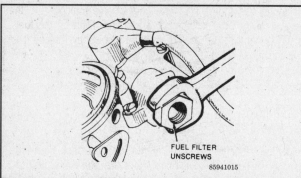

Fig. 20 Remove the large fuel line inlet nut and the fuel filter should pop out under spring pressure

Fig. 21 Remove the filter and spring from the inlet nut

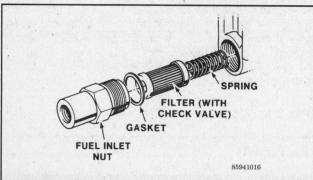

Fig. 22 Exploded view of a carburetor internal fuel filter assembly

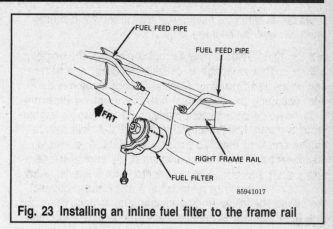

Fig. 23 Installing an inline fuel filter to the frame rail

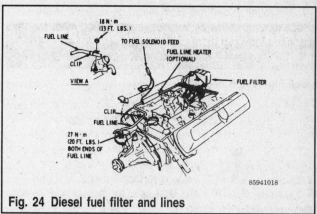

Fig. 24 Diesel fuel filter and lines

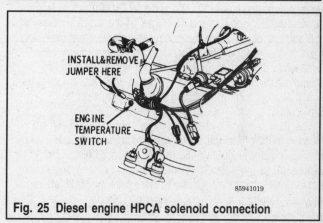

Fig. 25 Diesel engine HPCA solenoid connection

4. Loosen the fasteners and remove the filter from its bracket.

To install:

5. Position a new filter to the bracket and secure.

6. Connect the fuel lines to the fittings being careful nut to overtorque or damage the lines.

7. Connect the negative battery cable, then start the engine and check for leaks. Run the engine for about two minutes, then shut the engine off for the same amount of time to allow any trapped air in the injection system to bleed off.

GM diesel cars also have a fuel filter inside the fuel tank which is maintenance-free.

➡If the filter element ever becomes clogged, the engine will stop. This stoppage is usually preceded by a hesitation or sluggish running. General Motors recommends that after changing the diesel fuel filter, the Housing Pressure Cold Advance be activated manually, if the engine temperature is about 125°F. Activating the H.P.C.A. will reduce engine cranking time. To activate the H.P.C.A. solenoid, disconnect the two lead connector at the engine temperature switch and bridge the connector with a jumper. After the engine is running, remove the jumper and reconnect the connector to the engine temperature switch. When the new filter element is installed, start the engine and check for leaks.

Positive Crankcase Ventilation (PCV) Valve

◆ See Figures 26 and 27

Most gasoline engines covered in this manual are equipped with a Positive Crankcase Ventilation (PCV) system which must operate properly in order to allow evaporation of fuel vapors and water from the crankcase. This system should be checked at every oil change and serviced after one year or 12,000 miles. The PCV valve is replaced after 2 years or 24,000 miles. For 1975 and later cars, the service interval has been upgraded to one year or 15,000 miles, with PCV valve replacement scheduled for two years or 30,000 miles. Normal service entails cleaning the passages of the system hoses with solvent, inspecting them for cracks and breaks, and replacing them as necessary. The PCV valve contains a check valve and, when working properly, this valve will make a rattling sound when the outside case is tapped. If it fails to rattle, then it is probably stuck in a closed position and needs to be replaced.

The PCV system is designed to prevent the emission of gases from the crankcase into the atmosphere. It does this by connecting a crankcase outlet (valve cover, oil filler tube, back of engine) to the intake manifold with a hose. The crankcase gases travel through the hose to the intake manifold where they are returned to the combustion chamber and burned. If

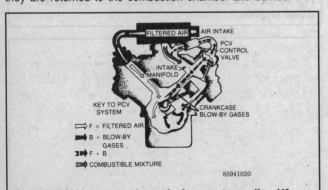

Fig. 26 PCV system schematic for most gasoline V6 and V8 engines

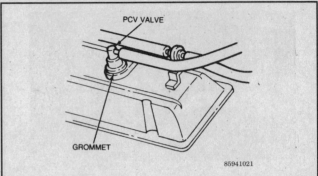

Fig. 27 The PCV is often grommet mounted in the valve cover on these vehicles

maintained properly, this system reduces condensation in the crankcase and the resultant formation of harmful acids and oil dilution. A clogged PCV valve will often cause a slow or rough idle due to a richer fuel mixture. A car equipped with a PCV system has air going through a hose to the intake manifold from an outlet at the valve cover, oil filler tube, or rear of the engine. To compensate for this extra air going to the manifold, carburetor specifications require a richer mixture (more gas) at the carburetor. If the PCV valve or hose is clogged, the additional air doesn't go to the intake manifold and the fuel mixture is too rich. A rough, slow idle results. The valve should be checked before making any carburetor adjustments. Disconnect the valve from the engine or merely clamp the hose shut. If the engine speed decreases less than 50 rpm, the valve is clogged and should be replaced. If the engine speed decreases much more than 50 rpm, then the valve is good. The PCV valve is an inexpensive item and is easily replaced during routine maintenance. If the new valve doesn't noticeably ©improve engine idle, the problem might be a restriction in the PCV hose. For further details on PCV valve operation see Section 4 of this manual.

REMOVAL & INSTALLATION

◆ See Figure 28

Almost all of the gasoline engines covered in this manual are equipped with a PCV valve which is mounted in a rubber grommet on one of the valve covers. Some of the earlier engines covered here may utilize a valve that is threaded into the rear of the carburetor base. Check the valve covers first, and if a valve cannot be found, look for a rubber hose that runs from the base of the carburetor to a valve cover or to the back of the manifold. If one is present, it should be a PCV valve. The valves which are threaded into the base of the carburetor are not difficult to find, but are often missed and neglected during maintenance. If your vehicle utilizes this alternate PCV valve mounting, it is even more important to check this valve's condition during maintenance as it was likely overlooked by past owners.

1. For vehicles equipped with a valve cover mounted PCV valve, grasp the valve and withdraw it from the valve cover. Holding the valve in one hand and the hose in the other,

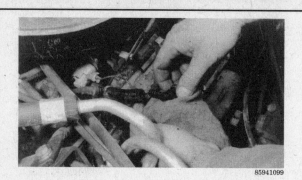

Fig. 28 Separate the PCV valve from the hose, then remove the valve from the vehicle

carefully pull the valve from the hose and remove from the vehicle.

➡ Some PCV valve hoses will be retained to the valve using a clamp. If so, use a pair of pliers to slide the clamp back on the hose until it is clear of the bulged area on the end of PCV valve nipple. With the clamp in this position, the hose should be free to slip from the valve.

2. For vehicles equipped with a carburetor mounted PCV valve, first disconnect the hose from the rear of the valve. Then carefully unthread the valve and remove it from the vehicle.

To install:

3. Check the PCV valve for deposits and clogging. The valve should rattle when shaken. If the valve does not rattle, clean the valve with solvent until the plunger is free or replace the valve.

4. Install the PCV hose to the grommet in the valve cover or to the back of the carburetor.

5. Connect the PCV hose to the valve assembly.

Crankcase Depression Regulator and Flow Control Valve

▶ See Figures 29, 30 and 31

Whereas gasoline engines utilize a PCV valve to control crankcase pressure and emission, diesel engines are equipped with a Crankcase Depression Regulator (CDR) or flow control valve. The CDR is found on 1981-84 diesels, while the flow control valve is used from 1978-80. These systems are designed to scavenge crankcase vapors in basically the same manner as the PCV valve on gasoline engines. The valves are located either on the left rear corner of the intake manifold (CDR), or on the rear of the intake crossover pipe (flow control valve). On each system there are two ventilation filters, one per valve cover.

The filter assemblies should be cleaned every 15,000 miles by simply prying them carefully from the valve covers (be aware of the grommets underneath), and washing them out in solvent. The ventilation pipes and tubes should also be cleaned. Both the CDR and flow control valves should also be cleaned every 30,000 miles (the cover can be removed from the CDR; the flow control valve can simply be flushed with

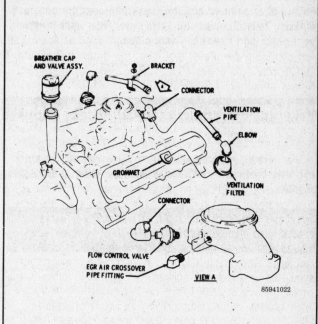

Fig. 29 Crankcase ventilation system found on 1978-80 diesel engines

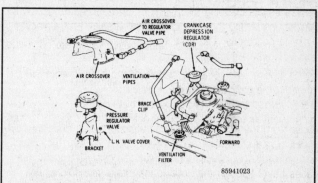

Fig. 30 CDR ventilation system found on 1981-84 V8 diesel engines

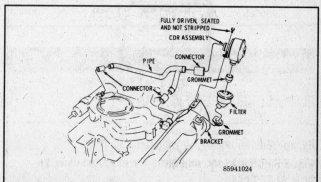

Fig. 31 CDR ventilation system found on 1981-84 V6 diesel engines

solvent). Dry each valve, filter, and hose with compressed air before installation.

➡ **Do not attempt to test the crankcase controls on these diesels. Instead, clean the valve cover filter assembly and vent pipes and check the vent pipes.**

Replace the breather cap assembly every 30,000 miles. Replace all rubber fittings as required every 15,000 miles.

Evaporative Emissions Control System

▶ **See Figure 32**

This system, standard since 1970, eliminates the release of unburned fuel vapors into the atmosphere. The only periodic maintenance required is an occasional check of the connecting lines of the system for kinks or other damage and deterioration. Lines should only be replaced with quality fuel line or special hose marked **evap**. On the 1970-71 vehicles, every 12,000 miles or 12 months, the filter in the bottom of the carbon canister which is located in the engine compartment should be removed and replaced. On 1972-1976 vehicles, this service interval is 24,000 miles or 24 months. For 1977 and later vehicles, the mileage interval has been increased to 30,000 miles, while the time interval remains the same. Not all canisters contain a replaceable filter. During the mid-1980's, the use a canisters which are replaceable as a whole assembly began. For further details on the Evaporative Control System please refer to Section 4 of this manual.

FILTER REPLACEMENT

1. Tag and disconnect all vapor hoses which are connected to the charcoal canister.
2. Loosen the retaining clamps or mounting bracket and then lift the canister from the vehicle.
3. Grasp the filter in the bottom of the canister with your fingers, then squeeze and pull it out from under the lip surface or from under the retainer bar.

To install:

4. Install a new filter to the bottom of the canister by squeezing and carefully inserting the filter into the canister. Make sure the edges are tucked under the canister lip.
5. Position the canister assembly in the vehicle and secure using the retainers.
6. Connect all vapor hoses to the canister as noted during removal.

Battery

FLUID LEVEL/SPECIFIC GRAVITY

Except Maintenance-Free Batteries

▶ **See Figures 33, 34 and 35**

Check the battery fluid level on all serviceable batteries at least once a month, more often in hot weather or during ex-

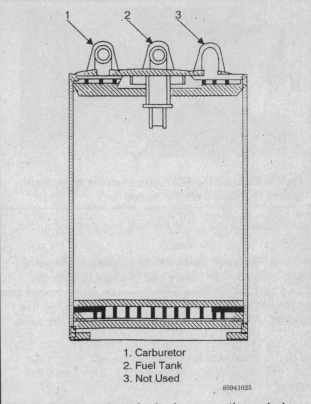

1. Carburetor
2. Fuel Tank
3. Not Used

85941025

Fig. 32 Cut-away view of a basic evaporative emission charcoal vapor canister

tended periods of travel. The electrolyte level should be up to the bottom of the split ring in each cell. Most batteries are equipped with an eye in the cap of one cell. If the eye glows or has an amber color to it, this means that the level is low and only distilled water should be added. Do not add anything else to the battery. If the eye has a dark appearance the battery electrolyte level is high enough. It is also wise to check each cell individually.

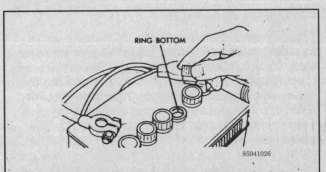

RING BOTTOM

85941026

Fig. 33 Each battery cell should be filled to the bottom of the split ring using distilled water — serviceable batteries

Fig. 34 On all serviceable batteries, a simple float type hydrometer may be used to check specific gravity

At least once a year, check the specific gravity of the battery. It should be between 1.20-1.26 in. Clean and tighten the clamps and apply a thin coat of petroleum jelly to the terminals. This will help to retard corrosion. The terminals can be cleaned with a stiff wire brush or with an inexpensive terminal cleaner designed for this purpose.

Specific Gravity Reading	Charged Condition
1.260–1.280	Fully Charged
1.230–1.250	¾ Charged
1.200–1.220	½ Charged
1.170–1.190	¼ Charged
1.140–1.160	Almost no Charge
1.110–1.130	No Charge

85941028

Fig. 35 Battery state of charge at room temperature

If distilled water is added during freezing weather, the car should be driven several miles to allow the electrolyte and water to mix. Otherwise the battery could freeze.

If the battery becomes corroded, a solution of baking soda and water will neutralize the corrosion, then the solution should be rinsed from the battery using cold water. Before applying the solution, make sure that the fluid caps are securely in place in order to prevent contaminating the electrolyte.

Some batteries were equipped with a felt terminal washer. This should be saturated with engine oil approximately every 6,000 miles. This will help to retard corrosion.

If a fast charger is used while the battery is in the car, disconnect the battery before connecting the charger.

➡ **Keep flame or sparks away from the battery; it gives off explosive hydrogen gas.**

Maintenance-Free Batteries
▶ **See Figures 36, 37, 38, 39 and 40**

All later model cars are equipped with sealed maintenance-free batteries, which do not require normal attention as far as fluid level checks are concerned. However, the terminals require periodic cleaning, which should be performed at least once a year.

The sealed top battery cannot be checked for charge by checking the specific gravity using a hand-held hydrometer, since there is no provision for access to the electrolyte. Instead, the built-in hydrometer must be used in order to determine the current state of charge:

1. If the indicator eye on top of the battery is dark, the battery contains sufficient fluid. If the eye is light, the electrolyte fluid is too low and the battery must be replaced.

2. If a green dot appears in the middle of the dark eye, the battery is sufficiently charged. Proceed to Step 4. If no green dot is visible, charge the battery as in Step 3.

✳✳CAUTION

Do not charge the battery for more than 50 amp/hours. If the green dot appears, or if electrolyte squirts out of the vent hole, stop the charge and proceed to Step 4.

3. Charge the battery referring to the charging rate amp/time chart for the necessary time span and rate of charge.

➡ **It may be necessary to tip the battery from side to side to get the green dot to appear after charging.**

4. Connect a battery load tester and a voltmeter across the battery terminals (the battery cables should be disconnected from the battery). Apply a 300 amp load to the battery for 15 seconds to remove the surface charge. Remove the load.

5. Wait 15 seconds to allow the battery to recover. Apply the appropriate test load, as specified in the chart or on the

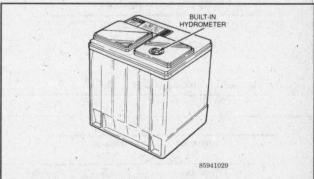

Fig. 36 Location of the built-in hydrometer on maintenance free batteries

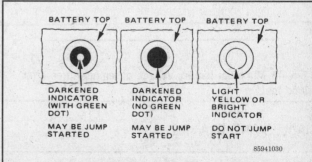

Fig. 37 The built-in hydrometer may be used to determine the current level battery charge — maintenance free batteries

battery label, for 15 seconds while reading the voltage. Disconnect the load.

6. Check the results against the minimum voltage chart. If the battery voltage is at or above the specified voltage for the temperature listed, the battery is good. If the voltage falls below what's listed, the battery should be replaced.

Charging Rate Amps	Time
75	40 min
50	1 hr
25	2 hr
10	5 hr

85941031

Fig. 38 Charging rate amp/time

Battery	Test Load
Y85-4	130 amps
R85-5	170 amps
R87-5	210 amps
R89-5	230 amps

85941032

Fig. 39 Standard batteries and test loads

Temperature (°F)	Minimum Voltage
70 or above	9.6
60	9.5
50	9.4
40	9.3
30	9.1
20	8.9
10	8.7
0	8.5

85941033

Fig. 40 Minimum battery voltage at temperatures after load test

CABLES AND CLAMPS

▶ **See Figures 41, 42, 43, 44 and 45**

➡ **In order to avoid the possibility of accidentally grounding the car's electrical system always remove the negative battery cable first. Failure to do so could allow a spark to occur exploding battery gasses and cause personal injury.**

Once a year, the battery terminals and the cable clamps should be cleaned. Loosen the clamps and remove the cables, negative cable first. On batteries with posts on top, the use of a puller specially made for the purpose is recommended. These are inexpensive, and available in auto parts stores. Side terminal battery cables are secured with a bolt.

Clean the cable clamps and the battery terminals with a wire brush, until all corrosion, grease, etc. is removed and the metal is shiny. It is especially important to clean the inside of the clamp thoroughly, since a small deposit of foreign material or oxidation will prevent a sound electrical connection and could inhibit both starting or charging. Special tools are available for cleaning these parts, one type for conventional batteries and another type for side terminal batteries.

Before installing the cables, loosen the battery hold-down clamp or strap, remove the battery and check the battery tray. Clear it of any debris, and check it for soundness. Rust should be wire brushed away, and the metal given a coat of anti-rust paint. Reposition the battery and tighten the hold-down clamp or strap securely, but be careful not to overtighten the retainer and crack the battery case.

After the clamps and terminals are clean, reinstall the cables, negative cable last. Never hammer on the clamps to install. Tighten the clamps securely, but do not distort them. Give the clamps and terminals a thin external coat of grease after installation, to retard corrosion.

Check the cables at the same time that the terminals are cleaned. If the cable insulation is cracked or broken, or if the

85941100

Fig. 41 DO NOT remove the positive battery cable before disconnecting the negative cable

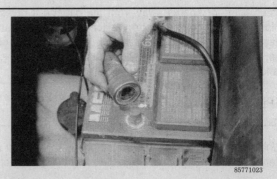

85771023

Fig. 42 A terminal cleaner or a wire brush may be used to clean battery post terminals

Fig. 43 Most terminal cleaner tools will also be equipped with a wire brush to clean the inside of the battery terminal clamps

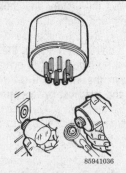

Fig. 44 Special tools are also available to clean the battery terminals and clamps on side terminal batteries

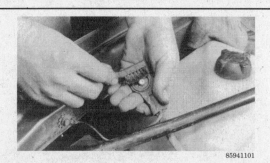

Fig. 45 If a terminal cleaner tool is not available, a wire brush may be used to clean most cable side mount clamps

ends are frayed, the cable should be replaced using a new part of the same length and gauge.

➡**Keep flame or sparks away from the battery; it gives off explosive hydrogen gas. Battery electrolyte contains sulfuric acid. If you should splash any on your skin or in your eyes, flush the affected area with plenty of clear water; if it lands in your eyes, get medical help immediately.**

REPLACEMENT

When it battery replacement becomes necessary, select a battery with a rating equal to or greater than the one which was originally installed. Deterioration and aging of the battery cables, starter motor, and associated wires makes the battery's job harder in successive years. The slow increase in electrical resistance over time makes it prudent to install a new battery with a greater capacity then the old. Details on the role the battery plays in the vehicle's electrical systems are covered in Section 3 of this manual.

1. Carefully disconnect the negative battery cable from the battery terminal.

✳✳CAUTION

Always use caution when working on or near the battery. Never allow a tool to bridge the gap between the negative and positive battery terminals. Also, be careful not to allow a tool to provide a ground between the positive cable and any metal component on the vehicle. Either of these conditions will cause a short leading to sparks and possibly, personal injury.

2. With the negative battery cable disconnected and out of the way, carefully disconnect the positive cable from the battery terminal.
3. Loosen the nut and/or bolt retaining the battery retainer strap or clamp. Remove or reposition the battery retainer.
4. Wearing an old pair of work gloves or using a battery lifting tool to protect from any remaining battery acid, carefully lift the battery out of the vehicle and place it in a safe location. Be sure to keep the battery away from open flame and to protect surrounding areas from acid.

To install:
5. Inspect the battery tray and cables for damage or corrosion. As necessary, clean or repair the tray and cables.
6. Carefully lower the battery into position in the tray, making sure not to allow the terminals to short on any bare metal during installation.
7. Position and secure the battery retainer strap or clamp.
8. Connect the positive battery cable to the battery terminal.
9. Connect the negative battery cable to the battery terminal.

Manifold Heat Control Valve (Heat Riser) 1964-74

This valve is located in the exhaust manifold under the carburetor on inline engines, and in either the right or left side exhaust manifold on V engines. It can be identified by looking for an external thermostatic spring and weight, along with hinge pins that run through the walls of the manifold. Check the valve for free operation every 6,000 miles and, if it binds or is frozen, free it up with a solvent.

➡**Certain early engines have a heat riser built into the manifold, which can only be repaired by replacing the entire manifold.**

Early Fuel Evaporation (EFE) System 1975 and Later

▶ **See Figure 46**

This is a more effective form of heat riser which is vacuum actuated. It is used on all carbureted engines built in 1975 and later. It heats the incoming air/fuel mixture during the engine warm-up process, utilizing a ribbed heat exchanger of thin metal that is located in the intake manifold. This pre-heating allows the choke to open more rapidly, thus reducing emissions and improving cold driveability. Problems with this system might be indicated by poor engine operation during warm-up.

This valve should be checked initially at 6 months/7,500 miles, and thereafter, at 18 month/22,500 mile intervals.

To check, move the valve through its full stroke by hand, making sure that the linkage does not bind and is properly connected. If the valve sticks, free it with a solvent. Also check that all vacuum hoses are properly connected and free of cracks or breaks. Replace damaged hoses or broken/bent linkage parts as necessary.

Belts

▶ **See Figures 47, 48, 49, 50, 51, 52, 53, 54, 55, 56, 57, 58 and 59**

TENSION CHECKING AND ADJUSTMENT

Check the drive belts every 7,500 miles or six months for evidence of wear such as cracking, fraying and incorrect tension. Determine belt tension at a point halfway between the pulleys by pressing on the belt with moderate thumb pressure. The belt should deflect about ½ in. at the halfway point if the distance between the pulleys (measured from the center of each pulley) is 13-16 in. The belt should deflect ¼ in. if the distance is between the pulley centers is 7-10 in. If it is noted that deflection is too much or too little, loosen the mounting bolts and pivot the component in order to properly adjust the belt.

➡ **The replacement of the inner belt on multi-belted engines may require the removal of the outer belts.**

Before you attempt to adjust any of your engine's belts, you should take an old rag soaked in solvent and clean the mounting bolts of any road grime which has accumulated on and around the bolt heads. On some of the harder-to-reach belts, especially on late model V8's with air conditioning and power steering, it would be especially helpful to have a variety of

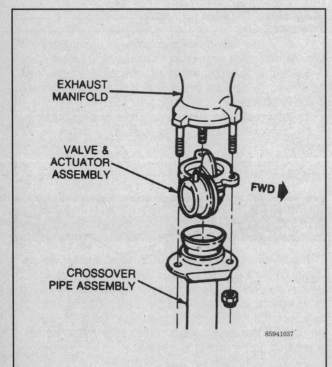

Fig. 46 The Early Fuel Evaporation (EFE) valve is mounted inline between the exhaust manifold and front exhaust pipe

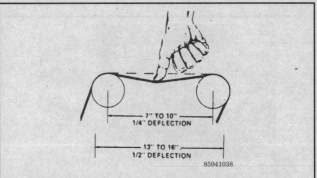

Fig. 47 A gauge is recommended, but you can check the belt tension using thumb pressure

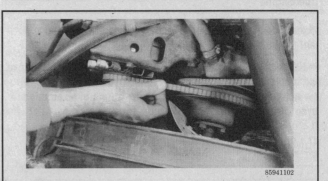

Fig. 48 The belt tension may be checked using thumb pressure

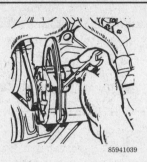

Fig. 49 To adjust the belt tension or to replace worn belts, first slightly loosen the component's mounting and adjusting bolts

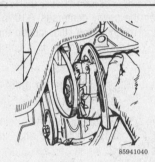

Fig. 50 If removing the belt, push the component toward the engine in order to loosen the belt, then slip the belt from the pulleys

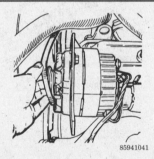

Fig. 51 When replacing a belt, slip the new belt over the pulley while the component is tilted inward toward the engine

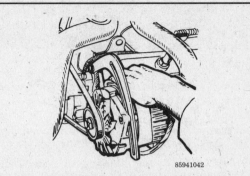

Fig. 52 Pivot the component away from the engine to tighten the belt

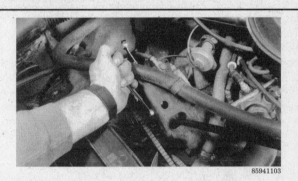

Fig. 53 Adjust the belt tension by pivoting the component outward

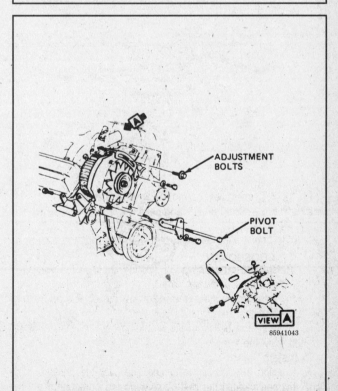

Fig. 54 Alternator mounting and drive belt adjustment — 1980-88 V8 engines

socket extensions and universals in order to access those hard-to-reach bolts.

➡When adjusting the air pump belt, if you are using a pry bar, make sure that you pry against the cast iron end cover and not against the aluminum housing. Excessive force on the housing itself will damage it.

REMOVAL & INSTALLATION

1. If you are working on or near the battery, disconnect the negative battery cable. This is also advisable in order to prevent personal injury should someone attempt to start the en-

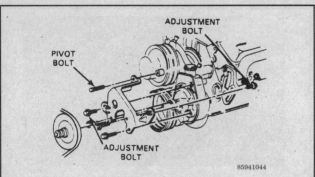

Fig. 55 Power steering pump mounting and drive belt adjustment — all except 1985-88 with A/C

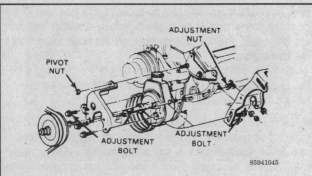

Fig. 56 Power steering pump mounting and drive belt adjustment — 1985-88 with A/C

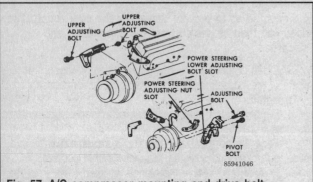

Fig. 57 A/C compressor mounting and drive belt adjustment — 1980-84 V8 engines

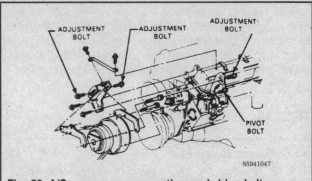

Fig. 58 A/C compressor mounting and drive belt adjustment — 1985-88 V8 engines

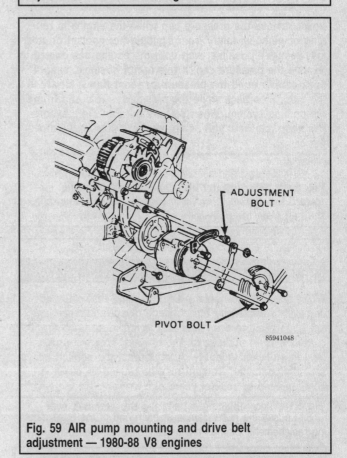

Fig. 59 AIR pump mounting and drive belt adjustment — 1980-88 V8 engines

gine while your hands and face are near the radiator cooling fan.

2. Loosen the mounting and adjusting bolts on the component whose belt is being removed.

3. Pivot the component inward toward the engine and slip the belt off of the component's pulley.

4. Remove the belt from the crankshaft pulley, then remove the belt from the vehicle.

To install:

5. Position the belt to the engine and over the pulleys.

6. Properly adjust the belt by pivoting the component outward until the proper tension is achieved, then tighten the component mounting and adjusting bolts.

7. If necessary, reconnect the negative battery cable.

Hoses

INSPECTION

Upper and lower radiator hoses along with the heater hoses should be checked for deterioration, leaks and loose hose clamps at least every 15,000 miles. It is also wise to check the hoses periodically in early spring and at the beginning of the fall or winter when you are performing other maintenance. A quick visual inspection could discover a weakened hose which would have left you stranded if it had remained unrepaired.

Whenever you are checking the hoses, make sure the engine and cooling system is cold. Visually inspect for cracking, rotting or collapsed hoses, replace as necessary. Run your hand along the length of the hose. If a weak or swollen spot is noted when squeezing the hose wall, the hose should be replaced.

REMOVAL & INSTALLATION

▶ **See Figures 60 and 61**

1. Remove the radiator pressure cap.

❊❊CAUTION

Never remove the pressure cap while the engine is running or personal injury from scalding hot coolant or steam may result. If possible, wait until the engine has cooled to remove the pressure cap. If this is not possible, wrap a thick cloth around the pressure cap and turn it slowly to the stop. Step back while the pressure is released from the cooling system. When you are sure all the pressure has been released, still using the cloth, turn and remove the cap.

2. Position a clean container under the radiator and/or engine drain cock or plug, then open the drain and allow the cooling system to drain to an appropriate level. For some upper hoses only a little coolant must be drained, to remove hoses positioned lower on the engine, such as the lower radiator hose, the entire cooling system must be drained.

❊❊CAUTION

When draining the coolant, keep in mind that cats and dogs are attracted by the ethylene glycol antifreeze, and are quite likely to drink any that is left in an uncovered container or in puddles on the ground. This will prove fatal in sufficient quantity. Always drain the coolant into a sealable container. Coolant may be reused unless it is contaminated or several years old.

3. Loosen the hose clamps at each end of the hose requiring replacement. Clamps are usually either of the spring ten-

Fig. 60 This screw tension clamp may be loosened using a screwdriver

Fig. 61 A hex socket driver may also be used on this type of clamp

sion type (which require pliers to squeeze the tabs and loosen) or of the screw tension type (which require screw or hex drivers to loosen). Pull the clamps back on the hose away from the connection.

4. Twist, pull and slide the hose off the fitting taking care not to damage the neck of the component from which the hose is being removed.

➡ **If the hose is stuck at the connection, do not try to insert a screwdriver or other sharp tool under the hose end in an effort to free it, as the connection and/or hose may become damaged. Heater connections especially may be easily damaged by such a procedure. If the hose is to be replaced, use a single-edged razor blade to make a slice along the portion of the hose which is stuck on the connection, perpendicular to the end of the hose. Do not cut deep so as to prevent damaging the connection. The hose can then be peeled from the connection and discarded.**

5. Clean both hose mounting connections. Inspect the condition of the hose clamps and replace them, if necessary.

To install:

6. Dip the ends of the new hose into clean engine coolant to ease installation.

7. Slide the hose clamps over the replacement hose and slide the hose ends over the connections into position.

8. Position and secure the clamps at least ¼ in. from the ends of the hose. Make sure they are located inside the raised bead of the connector.

9. If available, install a pressure tester and check for leaks.

10. Close the radiator or engine drains and properly refill the cooling system with the clean drained engine coolant or a suitable 50/50 mixture of ethylene glycol coolant and water.

11. Leave the radiator cap off, then start and run the engine to normal operating temperature. When the engine is at operating temperature and the thermostat has opened, continue to fill the radiator until the level stabilizes just below the filler neck.

12. Install the radiator pressure cap and check the clamped hose ends for leaks.

13. Shut the engine **OFF** and allow the engine to cool. Once the engine has cooled, check for proper coolant level and add, as necessary.

Air Conditioning

▶ See Figure 62

SAFETY PRECAUTIONS

Because of the inherent dangers involved with working on air conditioning systems and R-12 refrigerant, the following safety precautions must be strictly adhered to in order to service the system safely.

1. Avoid contact with a charged refrigeration system, even when working on another part of the air conditioning system or vehicle. If a heavy tool comes into contact with a section of tubing or a heat exchanger, it can easily cause the relatively soft material to rupture.

2. When it is necessary to apply force to a fitting which contains refrigerant, as when checking that all system couplings are securely tightened, use a wrench on both parts of the fitting involved, if possible. This will avoid putting torque on refrigerant tubing. (It is advisable, when possible, to use tube or line wrenches when tightening these flare nut fittings.)

➡ R-12 refrigerant is a chlorofluorocarbon which, when released into the atmosphere, can contribute to the depletion of the ozone layer in the upper atmosphere. Ozone filters out harmful radiation from the sun.

3. Do not attempt to discharge the system by merely loosening a fitting, or removing the service valve caps and cracking these valves. Precise control is possible only when using the service gauges and a proper A/C refrigerant recovery station. Wear protective gloves when connecting or disconnecting service gauge hoses.

➡ Be sure to consult the laws in your area before servicing the air conditioning system. In some states, it is illegal to perform repairs involving refrigerant unless the work is done by a certified technician.

4. Discharge the system only in a well ventilated area, as high concentrations of the gas which might accidentally escape can exclude oxygen and act as an anesthetic. When leak testing or soldering, this is particularly important, as toxic gas is formed when R-12 contacts any flame.

5. Never start a system without first verifying that both service valves are properly installed, and that all fittings throughout the system are snugly connected.

6. Avoid applying heat to any refrigerant line or storage vessel. Charging may be aided by using water heated to less than 125°F (50°C) to warm the refrigerant container. Never allow a refrigerant storage container to sit out in the sun, or near any other source of heat, such as a radiator.

7. Always wear goggles to protect your eyes when working on a system. If refrigerant contacts the eyes, it is advisable in all cases to see a physician as soon as possible.

8. Frostbite from liquid refrigerant should be treated by first gradually warming the area with cool water, and then gently applying petroleum jelly. A physician should be consulted.

9. Always keep refrigerant drum fittings capped when not in use. If the container is equipped with a safety cap to protect the valve, make sure the cap is in place when the can is not being used. Avoid sudden shock to the drum, which might occur from dropping it, or from banging a heavy tool against it. Never carry a drum in the passenger compartment of a car.

10. Always completely discharge the system into a suitable recovery unit before painting the vehicle (if the paint is to be baked on), or before welding anywhere near refrigerant lines.

11. When servicing the system, minimize the time that any refrigerant line or fitting is open to the air in order to prevent moisture or dirt from entering the system. Contaminants such as moisture or dirt can damage internal system components. Always replace O-rings on lines or fittings which are disconnected. Prior to installation coat, but do not soak, replacement O-rings with suitable compressor oil.

GENERAL SERVICING PROCEDURES

The most important aspect of air conditioning service is the maintenance of a pure and adequate charge of refrigerant in the system. A refrigeration system cannot function properly if a significant percentage of the charge is lost. Leaks are common because the severe vibration encountered underhood in an automobile can easily cause a sufficient cracking or loosening of the air conditioning fittings; allowing, the extreme operating pressures of the system to force refrigerant out.

The problem can be understood by considering what happens to the system as it is operated with a continuous leak. Because the expansion valve regulates the flow of refrigerant to the evaporator, the level of refrigerant there is fairly constant. The receiver/drier stores any excess of refrigerant, and so a loss will first appear there as a reduction in the level of liquid. As this level nears the bottom of the vessel, some refrigerant vapor bubbles will begin to appear in the stream of liquid supplied to the expansion valve. This vapor decreases the capacity of the expansion valve very little as the valve opens to compensate for its presence. As the quantity of liquid in the condenser decreases, the operating pressure will drop there and throughout the high side of the system. As the R-12 continues to be expelled, the pressure available to force the liquid through the expansion valve will continue to decrease, and, eventually, the valve's orifice will prove to be too much of a restriction for adequate flow even with the needle fully withdrawn.

At this point, low side pressure will start to drop, and severe reduction in cooling capacity, marked by freeze-up of the evaporator coil, will result. Eventually, the operating pressure of the evaporator will be lower than the pressure of the atmosphere surrounding it, and air will be drawn into the system wherever there are leaks in the low side.

Because all atmospheric air contains at least some moisture, water will enter the system and mix with the R-12 and the oil. Trace amounts of moisture will cause sludging of the oil, and corrosion of the system. Saturation and clogging of the filter/drier, and freezing of the expansion valve orifice will eventually result. As air fills the system to a greater and greater extent, it will interfere more and more with the normal flows of refrigerant and heat.

From this description, it should be obvious that much of the repairman's time will be spent detecting leaks, repairing them, and then restoring the purity and quantity of the refrigerant charge. A list of general rules should be followed in addition to all safety precautions:

1. Keep all tools as clean and dry as possible.

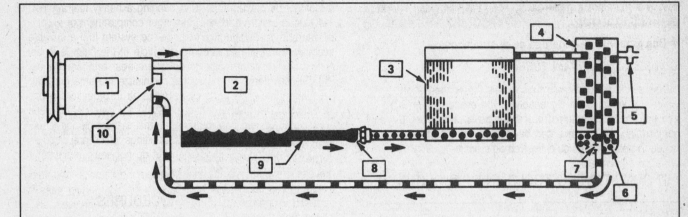

1—COMPRESSOR
2—CONDENSER
3—EVAPORATOR
4—ACCUMULATOR

5—PRESSURE CYCLING SWITCH
6—DESSICANT BAG
7—OIL BLEED HOLE

8—EXPANSION TUBE (ORIFICE)
9—LIQUID LINE
10—PRESSURE RELIEF VALVE

●●● LOW PRESSURE LIQUID
■■■ LOW PRESSURE VAPOR

▬▬ HIGH PRESSURE LIQUID
▭▭ HIGH PRESSURE VAPOR

85941049

Fig. 62 Example of the refrigerant path of travel in an A/C system

2. Thoroughly purge the service gauges and hoses of air and moisture before connecting them to the system. Keep them capped when not in use.

3. Thoroughly clean any refrigerant fitting before disconnecting it, in order to minimize the entrance of dirt into the system.

4. Plan any operation that requires opening the system beforehand, in order to minimize the length of time it will be exposed to open air. Cap or seal the open ends to minimize the entrance of foreign material.

5. When adding oil, pour it through an extremely clean and dry tube or funnel. Keep the oil capped whenever possible. Do not use oil that has not been kept tightly sealed.

6. Use only R-12 refrigerant. Purchase refrigerant intended for use only in automatic air conditioning systems. Avoid the use of R-12 that may be packaged for other purposes, such as cleaning, or powering a horn, as it is impure.

7. Completely evacuate any system that has been opened to replace a component, or that has leaked sufficiently to draw in moisture and air. This requires evacuating air and moisture with a good vacuum pump for at least one hour. If a system has been open for a considerable length of time it may be advisable to evacuate the system for up to 12 hours (overnight).

8. Use a wrench on both halves of a fitting that is to be disconnected, so as to avoid placing torque on any of the refrigerant lines.

9. When overhauling a compressor, pour some of the oil into a clean glass and inspect it. If there is evidence of dirt or metal particles, or both, flush all refrigerant components with

clean refrigerant before evacuating and recharging the system. In addition, if metal particles are present, the compressor should be replaced.

10. Schrader valves may leak only when under full operating pressure. Therefore, if leakage is suspected but cannot be located, operate the system with a full charge of refrigerant and look for leaks from all Schrader valves. Replace any faulty valves.

Additional Preventive Maintenance Checks

ANTIFREEZE

In order to prevent heater core freeze-up during A/C operation, it is necessary to maintain permanent type antifreeze protection of +15°F, or lower. A reading of -15°F is ideal since this protection also supplies sufficient corrosion inhibitors for the protection of the engine cooling system.

➡The same antifreeze should not be used longer than the manufacturer specifies.

RADIATOR CAP

For efficient operation of an air conditioned car's cooling system, the radiator cap should have a holding pressure which meets manufacturer's specifications. A cap which fails to hold these pressures should be replaced.

CONDENSER

Any obstruction of or damage to the condenser configuration will restrict the air flow which is essential to its efficient operation. It is therefore a good rule to keep this unit clean and in proper physical shape.

➡Bug screens are regarded as obstructions.

CONDENSATION DRAIN TUBE

This single molded drain tube expels the condensation, which accumulates on the bottom of the evaporator housing, into the engine compartment. If this tube is obstructed, the air conditioning performance can be restricted and condensation buildup can spill over onto the vehicle's floor.

AIR CONDITIONING TOOLS AND GAUGES

♦ See Figure 63

Test Gauges

Most of the service work performed in air conditioning requires the use of a set of two gauges, one for the high (head) pressure side of the system, the other for the low (suction) side.

The low side gauge records both pressure and vacuum. Vacuum readings are calibrated from 0 to 30 inches and the pressure graduations read from 0 to no less than 60 psi (414kPa).

The high side gauge measures pressure from 0 to at least 600 psi (4140kPa).

Both gauges are threaded into a manifold that contains two hand shut-off valves. Proper manipulation of these valves and the use of the attached test hoses allow the user to perform the following services:

1. Test high and low side pressures.
2. Remove air, moisture, and contaminated refrigerant.
3. Purge the system (of refrigerant).
4. Charge the system (with refrigerant).

The manifold valves are designed so they have no direct effect on gauge readings, but serve only to provide for the flow or cut-off of refrigerant through the manifold. During all testing and hook-up operations, the valves are kept in a closed position to avoid disturbing the refrigeration system. The valves are opened only to purge the system of refrigerant or to charge it.

When purging the system, the center hose is attached to a recovery station at the lower end, and both valves are cracked open slightly. This allows refrigerant pressure to force the entire contents of the system out through the center hose and into a suitable recovery station. During charging, the valve on the high side of the manifold is closed, and the valve on the low side is cracked open. Under these conditions, the low pressure in the evaporator will draw refrigerant from the relatively warm refrigerant storage container into the system.

Service Valves

For the user to diagnose an air conditioning system, he or she must gain "entrance" to the system in order to observe the pressures. There are two types of terminals for this purpose, the hand shut off type and the familiar Schrader valve.

The Schrader valve is similar to a tire valve stem and the process of connecting the test hoses is the same as threading a hand pump outlet hose to a bicycle tire. As the test hose is threaded to the service port the valve core is depressed, allowing the refrigerant to enter the test hose outlet. Removal of the test hose automatically closes the system.

Extreme caution must be observed when removing test hoses from the Schrader valves as some refrigerant will normally escape, usually under high pressure. (Observe safety precautions.)

Some systems have hand shut-off valves (the stem can be rotated with a special ratcheting box wrench) that can be positioned in the following three ways:

1. FRONT SEATED — Rotated to full clockwise position.
   a. Refrigerant will not flow to compressor, but will reach test gauge port. COMPRESSOR WILL BE DAMAGED IF SYSTEM IS TURNED ON IN THIS POSITION.
   b. The compressor is now isolated and ready for service. However, care must be exercised when removing service valves from the compressor as a residue of refrigerant may still be present within the compressor. Therefore, remove service valves slowly observing all safety precautions.
2. BACK SEATED — Rotated to full counterclockwise position. Normal position for system while in operation. Refrigerant flows to compressor but not to test gauge.
3. MID-POSITION (CRACKED) — Refrigerant flows to entire system. Gauge port (with hose connected) open for testing.

Using The Manifold Gauges

The following are step-by-step procedures to guide the user to correct gauge usage.

1. WEAR GOGGLES OR FACE SHIELD DURING ALL TESTING OPERATIONS. BACKSEAT THE HAND SHUT-OFF TYPE SERVICE VALVES.
2. Remove caps from high and low side service ports. Make sure both gauge valves are closed.

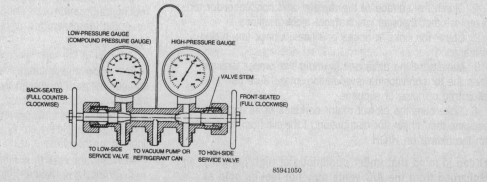

85941050

Fig. 63 A manifold gauge set is necessary for A/C system service

3. Connect low side test hose to service valve that leads to the evaporator (located between the evaporator outlet and the compressor).

4. Attach high side test hose to service valve that leads to the condenser.

5. Mid-position hand shutoff type service valves.

6. Start engine and allow for warm-up. All testing and charging of the system should be done after engine and system have reached normal operation temperatures (unless the recovery/charging station's manufacturer instructs otherwise).

7. Adjust air conditioner controls to maximum cold.

8. Observe gauge readings. When the gauges are not being used it is a good idea to:

a. Keep both hand valves in the closed position.

b. Attach both ends of the high and low service hoses to the manifold, if extra outlets are present on the manifold, or plug them if not. Also, keep the center charging hose attached to an empty refrigerant can. This extra precaution will reduce the possibility of moisture entering the gauges. If air and moisture have gotten into the gauges, purge the hoses by supplying refrigerant under pressure to the center hose with both gauge valves open and all openings unplugged.

SYSTEM INSPECTION

→R-12 refrigerant is a chlorofluorocarbon which, when released into the atmosphere, can contribute to the depletion of the ozone layer in the upper atmosphere. Ozone filters out harmful radiation from the sun.

The easiest and often most important check for the air conditioning system consists of a visual inspection of the system components. Visually inspect the air conditioning system for refrigerant leaks, damaged compressor clutch, compressor drive belt tension and condition, plugged evaporator drain tube, blocked condenser fins, disconnected or broken wires, blown fuses, corroded connections and poor insulation.

A refrigerant leak will usually appear as an oily residue at the leakage point in the system. The oily residue soon picks up dust or dirt particles from the surrounding air and appears greasy. Through time, this will build up and appear to be a heavy dirt impregnated grease. Most leaks are caused by damaged or missing O-ring seals at the component connections, damaged charging valve cores or missing service gauge port caps.

For a thorough visual and operational inspection, check the following:

1. Check the surface of the radiator and condenser for dirt, leaves or other material which might block air flow.

2. Check for kinks in hoses and lines. Check the system for leaks.

3. Make sure the drive belt is under the proper tension. When the air conditioning is operating, make sure the drive belt is free of noise or slippage.

4. Make sure the blower motor operates at all appropriate positions, then check for distribution of the air from all outlets with the blower on **HIGH**.

→Keep in mind that under conditions of high humidity, air discharged from the A/C vents may not feel as cold as expected, even if the system is working properly. This is because the vaporized moisture in humid air retains heat more effectively than does dry air, making the humid air more difficult to cool.

5. Make sure the air passage selection lever is operating correctly. Start the engine and warm it to normal operating temperature, then make sure the hot/cold selection lever is operating correctly

REFRIGERANT LEVEL CHECKS

▶ See Figures 64 and 65

✳✳CAUTION

Do not attempt to charge or discharge the refrigerant system unless you have access to a recovery station and are thoroughly familiar with the system's operation and the hazards involved. The compressed refrigerant used in the air conditioning system expands and evaporates (boils) into the atmosphere at a temperature of -21.7°F (-29.8°C) or less. This will freeze any surface that it comes in contact with, including your eyes. In addition, the refrigerant decomposes into a poisonous gas in the presence of flame.

1964-76 cars with factory installed air conditioners have a sight glass for checking the refrigerant charge. The sight glass is on top of the VIR (valves-in-receiver) which is located in the front of the engine compartment, usually on the left side of the radiator.

1977 and later models utilize Cycling Clutch Orifice Tube (C.C.O.T.) system which does not include a sight glass. The C.C.O.T refrigeration system is designed to cycle the compressor on and off to maintain desired cooling and to prevent evaporator freeze.

→If your car is equipped with an aftermarket air conditioner, the following system checks may not apply. Contact the A/C system manufacturer for instructions on system checks.

1964-76

This test works best if the outside air temperature is warm (above 70°F).

1. Place the automatic transmission in **Park** or the manual in **Neutral**, then set the parking brake.

2. With the help of the friend, run the engine at a fast idle (about 1500 rpm).

3. Set the control for maximum cold with the blower on high.

4. Look at the sight glass on top of the VIR. If a steady stream of bubbles is present in the sight glass, the system is low on charge. It is very likely that there is a leak in the system.

5. If no bubbles are present, the system is either fully charged or completely empty. Feel the high and low pressure lines at the compressor, if no appreciable temperature difference is felt, the system is empty or nearly so.

6. If one hose is warm (high pressure) and the other is cold (low pressure), the system may be OK. However, you are

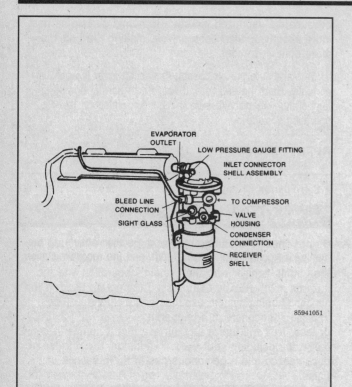

Fig. 64 Air conditioning VIR assembly showing sight glass and connections

Fig. 66 The service ports are usually found on or near the accumulator

Fig. 67 The high pressure port is on thinner A/C line as compared to the low side line

Check item \ Amount of refrigerant	Almost no refrigerant	Insufficient	Suitable	Too much refrigerant
Temperature of high pressure and low pressure lines.	Almost no difference between high pressure and low pressure side temperature.	High pressure side is warm and low pressure side is fairly cold.	High pressure side is hot and low pressure side is cold.	High pressure side is abnormally hot.
State in sight glass.	Bubbles flow continuously. Bubbles will disappear and something like mist will flow when refrigerant is nearly gone.	The bubbles are seen at intervals of 1 - 2 seconds.	Almost transparent. Bubbles may appear when engine speed is raised and lowered. No clear difference exists between these two conditions.	No bubbles can be seen.
Pressure of system.	High pressure side is abnormally low.	Both pressure on high and low pressure sides are slightly low.	Both pressures on high and low pressure sides are normal.	Both pressures on high and low pressure sides are abnormally high.
Repair.	Stop compressor immediately and conduct an overall check.	Check for gas leakage, repair as required, replenish and charge system.		Discharge refrigerant from service valve of low pressure side.

Fig. 65 Using a sight glass to determine the relative refrigerant charge

probably making these tests because there is something wrong with the air conditioner, so proceed to the next step.

7. Either carefully disconnect the compressor clutch wire or have a friend in the car turn the fan control on and off to operate the compressor clutch. Watch the sight glass.

8. If bubbles appear when the clutch is disengaged and disappear when it is engaged, the system is properly charged.

9. If the refrigerant takes more than 45 seconds to bubble when the clutch is disengaged, the system is more than likely overcharged. This condition will usually result in poor cooling at low speeds.

➡**If it is determined that the system has a leak, it should be repaired as soon as possible. Leaks may allow moisture to enter the system, causing an expensive problem with corrosion.**

1977 and Later

The air conditioning system on these cars has no sight glass.

1. Run the engine until it reaches normal operating temperature.

2. Open the hood and all doors.

3. Turn the air conditioning **ON**, move the temperature selector to the first detent to the right of COLD (outside air) and then turn the blower on HI.

4. Idle the engine at 1,000 rpm.

5. Feel the temperature of the evaporator inlet and the accumulator outlet with the compressor clutch engaged.

6. Both lines should be cold. If the inlet pipe is colder than the outlet pipe, the system is low on charge. Do not attempt to charge the system yourself unless you have access to the proper equipment.

DISCHARGING THE SYSTEM

▸ **See Figures 66, 67 and 68**

➡**R-12 refrigerant is a chlorofluorocarbon which, when released into the atmosphere, can contribute to the depletion of the ozone layer in the upper atmosphere. Ozone filters out harmful radiation from the sun.**

Consult the laws in your area before servicing the air conditioning system. In some states it is illegal to perform repairs involving refrigerant unless the work is done by a certified technician.

The use of refrigerant recovery systems and recycling stations makes possible the recovery and reuse of refrigerant after contaminants and moisture have been removed. If a recovery system or recycling station is available, the following general procedures should be observed, in addition to the operating instructions provided by the equipment manufacturer.

1. Check the system for pressure using the manifold gauge set. Take note, if a recovery system is used to draw refrigerant from a system that is already ruptured and open to the atmosphere, only air may be pulled into the tank.

Fig. 68 The lower pressure service port

2. Connect the refrigerant recycling station hose(s) to the vehicle air conditioning service ports and the recovery station inlet fitting.

➡**Hoses should have shut off devices or check valves within 12 in. (305mm) of the hose end to minimize the introduction of air into the recycling station and to minimize the amount of refrigerant released when the hose(s) is disconnected.**

3. Turn the power to the recycling station **ON** to start the recovery process. Allow the recycling station to pump the refrigerant from the system until the station pressure goes into a vacuum. On some stations the pump will be shut off automatically by a low pressure switch in the electrical system. On other units it may be necessary to manually turn off the pump.

4. Once the recycling station has evacuated the vehicle air conditioning system, close the station inlet valve, if equipped. Then switch **OFF** the electrical power.

5. Allow the vehicle air conditioning system to remain closed for about 2 minutes. Observe the system vacuum level as shown on the gauge. If the pressure does not rise, disconnect the recycling station hose(s).

6. If the system pressure rises, repeat Steps 3, 4 and 5 until the vacuum level remains stable for 2 minutes.

7. If A/C oil is expelled during the discharge procedure, before discarding the oil, measure the amount discharged in order to determine the proper quantity which must be added to the system during charging.

EVACUATING/CHARGING THE SYSTEM

Evacuating and charging the air conditioning system is a combined procedure in which the lines are purged, then refrigerant is added to the system in proper quantity. Charging is always conducted through the low pressure fitting. NEVER attempt to charge the air conditioning through the high pressure side of the system.

Once again, evacuation and charging should not be attempted unless the proper equipment, such as a charging station and a vacuum pump is available in order to properly service the system. If a charging station and pump is available, the following general procedures should be observed, in addition to the operating instructions provided by the equipment manufacturer.

1. The proper amount of fresh compressor oil must be added to the system after discharging, but BEFORE evacuation and charging. The total amount of oil which was lost from the system during discharge and from any repaired or replaced components must be added to the system. This can be accomplished by disconnecting the refrigeration suction hose at the accumulator outlet pipe connection and by pouring the fresh oil into the hose or pipe and then reconnecting the fitting.

2. Properly connect a manifold gauge set to the vehicle, then connect the manifold to a vacuum pump.

3. Turn the vacuum pump ON and slowly open the high and low side valves to the pump. Allow the system to evacuate for 20-30 minutes, then note the gauge reading. If the system is unable to reach 28-29 in. of vacuum, the system and vacuum pump must be checked for leaks and repaired before proceeding further.

4. After the system has been evacuated for a minimum of 20 minutes, close the gauge high and low side valves, then shut the pump OFF.

5. Watch the low side gauge for vacuum loss. If vacuum loss is in excess of 1 in. Hg (3.38 kPa), then leak test the system, repair the leaks and return to Step 1. Before leak testing, remember to disconnect the gauge high side connector from the service port.

6. If after 1-3 minutes, the loss is less than 1 in. Hg (3.38 kPa), then proceed with the system charging.

7. Disconnect the gauge high side connection from the service port and the gauge manifold from the vacuum pump.

8. Engage the center manifold connection to an R-12 source. If you are using a refrigerant drum instead of a charging station, place the drum on a scale to determine the amount of refrigerant being used.

9. Open the source and low side gauge valve, then monitor the weight of the drum or the rate at which the charging system is introducing R-12 into the system.

10. When 1 lb. of R-12 has been added to the system, start the engine and turn the air conditioning system ON. Set the temperature lever to full cold, the blower speed on high and the selector lever to the upper outlets. Under this condition, slowly draw in the remainder of the R-12 charge. The total charge should range between 3-3¾ lbs. depending on the model.

11. When the system is charged, turn the source valve OFF and continue to run the engine for 30 seconds in order to clear the gauges and lines.

12. With the engine still running, carefully remove the gauge low side hose from the suction pipe service fitting. Unscrew the connection rapidly to avoid excess refrigerant loss.

✳✳CAUTION

If the hoses of the manifold gauge set may be disconnected from the gauge, NEVER remove a hose from the gauge while the other end of the hose is still connected to an air conditioning system service fitting. Because the service fitting check valve is depressed by the hose connec- tion, this would cause a complete and uncontrolled discharge of the system. Serious personal injury could be caused by the escaping R-12

13. Install the protective service fitting caps and hand-tighten.

14. Turn the engine and air conditioning OFF.

15. If an electronic or open flame leak tester is available, test the system for leaks.

16. If there are no leaks, perform the refrigerant level test to verify proper system charging.

FREON CAPACITIES:

- 1964-72: 3 lbs.
- 1973-80: 3¾ lbs.
- 1981-88: 3¼ lbs.

LEAK TESTING THE SYSTEM

▶ See Figure 69

Whenever a refrigerant leak is suspected, begin by checking for leaks at the fittings and valves. There are several methods of detecting leaks in an air conditioning system; among them, the two most popular are (1) halide leak-detection or the "open flame method," and (2) electronic leak-detection. Use of an electronic leak detector, if available is preferable for ease and safety of operation.

The halide leak detector is a torch like device which produces a yellow-green color when refrigerant is introduced into the flame at the burner. A purple or violet color indicates the presence of large amounts of refrigerant at the burner.

An electronic leak detector is a small portable electronic device with an extended probe. With the unit activated the probe is passed along those components of the system which contain refrigerant. If a leak is detected, the unit will sound an alarm signal or activate a display signal depending on the manufacturer's design. Follow the manufacturer's instructions carefully. Move the detector probe at approximately 1 in. per second in the suspected leak area. When escaping refrigerant gas is located, the ticking/beeping signal from the detector will

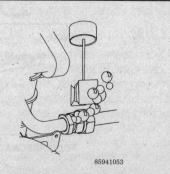

85941053

Fig. 69 A soap solution applied to a suspected area or fitting can be helpful in pinpointing a refrigerant leak

increase in ticks/beeps per second. If the gas is relatively concentrated, the signal will be increasingly shrill.

❈❈CAUTION

Care should be taken to operate either type of detector in well ventilated areas, so as to reduce the chance of personal injury, which may result from coming in contact with poisonous gases produced when R-12 is exposed to flame or electric spark.

If a tester is not available, perform a visual inspection and apply a soap solution to the questionable fitting or area. Bubbles will form to indicate a leak. Make sure to rinse the solution from the fitting before attempting repairs.

Windshield Wipers

▶ See Figure 70

For maximum effectiveness and longest element life, the windshield and wiper blades should be kept clean. Dirt, tree sap, road tar and so on will cause streaking, smearing and blade deterioration if left on the glass. It is advisable to wash the windshield carefully with a commercial glass cleaner at least once a month. Wipe off the rubber blades with the wet rag afterwards. Do not attempt to move the wipers by hand; damage to the motor and drive mechanism will result.

To inspect and/or replace the wiper blades, place the wiper switch in the **LOW** speed position and the ignition switch in the **ACC** position. When the wiper blades are approximately vertical on the windshield, turn the ignition switch to **OFF**.

Examine the wiper blades. If they are found to be cracked, broken or torn, they should be replaced immediately. Replacement intervals will vary with usage, although ozone deterioration usually limits blade life to about one year. If the wiper pattern is smeared or streaked, or if the blade chatters across the glass, the elements should be replaced. It is easiest and most sensible to replace the elements in pairs.

Most original wiper blades found on Chevrolet vehicles are easily replaceable. The wiper blade slides from the arm assembly once the catch is released. If your vehicle is equipped with aftermarket blades, there are several different types of refills and your vehicle might have any kind. Aftermarket blades and arms rarely use the exact same type blade or refill as the original equipment. Here are some common aftermarket blades, not all may be available for your car.

The Anco® type uses a release button that is pushed down to allow the refill to slide out of the yoke jaws. The new refill slides back into the frame and locks in place.

Some Trico® refills are removed by locating where the metal backing strip or the refill is wider. Insert a small screwdriver blade between the frame and metal backing strip. Press down to release the refill from the retaining tab.

Other types of Trico® refills have two metal tabs which are unlocked by squeezing them together. The rubber filler can then be withdrawn from the frame jaws. A new refill is installed by inserting the refill into the front frame jaws and sliding it rearward to engage the remaining frame jaws. There are usually four jaws; be certain when installing, that the refill is engaged in all of them. At the end of its travel, the tabs will lock into place on the front jaws of the wiper blade frame.

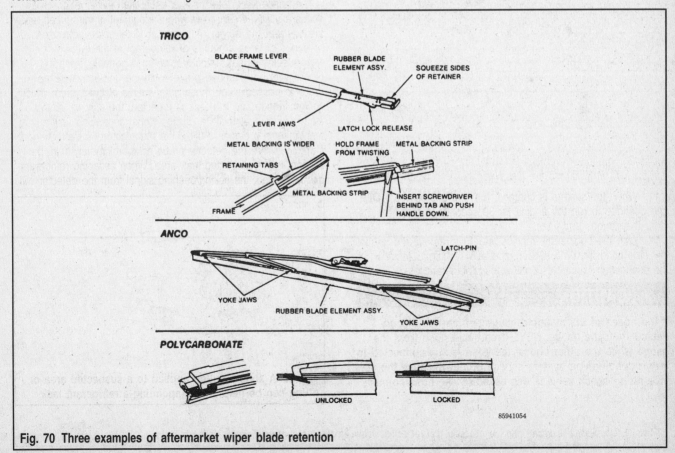

85941054

Fig. 70 Three examples of aftermarket wiper blade retention

Another type of refill is made from polycarbonate. The refill has a simple locking device at one end which flexes downward out of the groove into which the jaws of the holder fit, allowing easy release. By sliding the new refill through all the jaws and pushing through the slight resistance when it reaches the end of its travel, the refill will lock into position.

To replace the Tridon® refill, it is necessary to remove the wiper arm or blade. This refill has a plastic backing strip with a notch about 1 in. (25mm) from the end. Hold the blade (frame) on a hard surface so the frame is tightly bowed. Grip the tip of the backing strip and pull up while twisting counterclockwise. The backing strip will snap out of the retaining tab. Do this for the remaining tabs until the refill is free of the arm. The length of these refills is molded into the end and they should be replaced with identical types.

Regardless of the type of refill used, make sure that all of the frame jaws are engaged as the refill is pushed into place and locked. If the metal blade holder and frame are allowed to touch the glass during wiper operation, the glass will be scratched.

Tires and Wheels

▶ **See Figures 71, 72, 73 and 74**

Inspect your tires often for signs of improper inflation and uneven wear, which may indicate a need for balancing, rotation, or wheel alignment. Check the tires frequently for cuts, stone bruises, abrasions, blisters and for objects that may have become embedded in the tread. More frequent inspections are recommended when rapid or extreme temperature changes occur or where road surfaces are rough or occasionally littered with debris. Check the condition of the wheels and replace any that are bent, cracked, severely dented or have excessive run-out.

The tires on your car have built-in wear indicators molded into the bottom of the tread grooves. The indicators will begin to appear as the tire approaches replacement tread depth. Once the indicators are visible across 2 or more adjacent grooves and at 3 or more locations, the tires should be replaced.

Wear that occurs only on certain portions of the tire may indicate a particular problem, which when corrected or avoided, may significantly extend tire life. Wear that occurs only in the center of the tire indicates either overinflation or heavy acceleration on a drive wheel. Wear occurring at the outer edges of the tire and not at the center may indicate underinflation, ex-

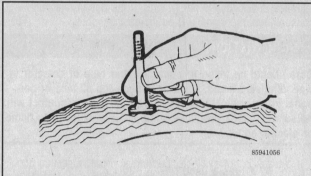

Fig. 72 Tread depth can be checked using an inexpensive gauge

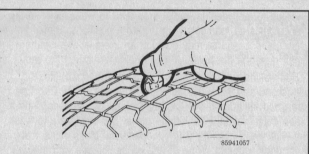

Fig. 73 If a gauge is not available, a penny may be used to check for tire tread depth; when the top of Lincoln's head is visible, it is probably time for a new tire

cessively hard cornering or a lack of rotation. If wear occurs at only the outer edge of the tire, there may be a problem with the wheel alignment or the tire, when constructed, contained a non-uniformity defect.

TIRE ROTATION

▶ **See Figure 75**

Tire rotation is recommended every 6,000 miles or so, to obtain maximum tire wear. The pattern you use depends on whether or not your car has a full-sized usable spare or a undersized "donut" spare. Because the compact or donut spare tire is designed for limited emergency use, it should not be included in normal tire rotation.

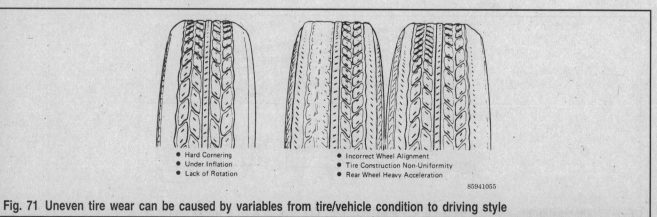

- Hard Cornering
- Under Inflation
- Lack of Rotation

- Incorrect Wheel Alignment
- Tire Construction Non-Uniformity
- Rear Wheel Heavy Acceleration

Fig. 71 Uneven tire wear can be caused by variables from tire/vehicle condition to driving style

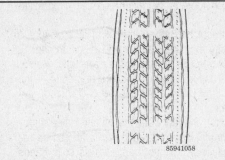

Fig. 74 If tires a used beyond the point of tread life, built-in wear indicators will begin to appear as lines perpendicular to the tread

Due to their design, radial tires tend to wear faster in the shoulder area, particularly in the front positions. Radial tires in non-drive locations, may develop an irregular wear pattern that can generate tire noise. It was originally thought the radial tires should not be cross-switched (from one side of the car to the other); because of their wear patterns and that they would last longer if their direction of rotation is not changed. The manufacturer's recommendations for tire rotation allows and even suggest cross-switching radial tires to allow for more uniform tire wear.

➡**Some specialty aftermarket tires may be directional, meaning they may only be mounted to rotate in one direction. Some snow tires and special performance tires/wheels will fall into this category and will be marked with directional rotation arrows on the tire sidewalls. NEVER switch the direction of rotation on tires so marked or poor performance/tire damage could occur. This should be taken into consideration in choosing a rotation pattern for directional tires.**

TIRE DESIGN

▶ **See Figure 76**

When buying new tires, give some thought to the following points, especially if you are considering a switch to larger tires or a different profile series:

1. All four tires must be of the same construction type. This rule cannot be violated, radial, bias, and bias-belted tires must not be mixed or vehicle handling and safety may be seriously jeopardized.

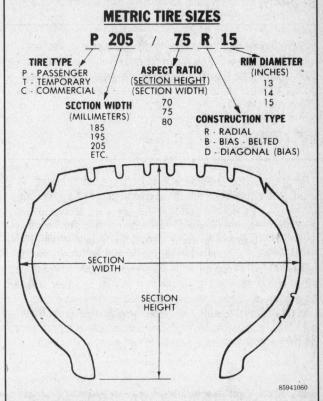

Fig. 76 Interpreting the metric tire size codes found on most late-model vehicles

2. The wheels should be the correct width for the tire. Tire dealers have charts of tire and rim compatibility. A miss-match will cause sloppy handling and rapid tire wear. The tread width should match the rim width (inside bead to inside bead) within an inch. For radial tires, the rim should be 80% or less of the tire (not tread) width.

3. The height (mounted diameter) of the new tires can change speedometer accuracy, engine speed at a given road speed, fuel mileage, acceleration, and ground clearance. Tire manufacturers furnish full measurement specifications.

4. The spare tire should be usable, at least for short distance and low speed operation, with the new tires.

5. There shouldn't be any vehicle body interference when loaded, on bumps, or in turns. If the tire hits the wheel-well under load, wear and the possibility of a blow-out will be significantly increased.

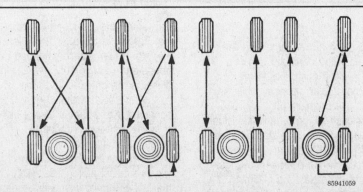

Fig. 75 Acceptable tire rotation patterns for radial and bias ply tires in 4 or 5 wheel rotations

STORAGE

Store the tires at the proper inflation pressure if they are mounted on wheels. Keep them in a cool dry place, laid on their sides. If the tires are stored in the garage or basement, do not let them stand on a concrete floor; set them on strips of wood.

INFLATION

Tires should be checked weekly for proper air pressure. A chart, located either in the glove compartment and/or on one of the vehicle's doors or door jambs, gives the recommended inflation pressures. Maximum fuel economy and tire life will result if the pressure is maintained at the highest figure given on the chart. Pressures should be checked with the tires cold before driving 1 mile or more since pressure can increase as much as six pounds per square inch (psi) due to heat buildup as the tire is warmed. It is a good idea to have your own accurate pressure gauge, because many gauges on service station air pumps cannot be trusted. When checking pressures, do not neglect the spare tire. Note that some spare tires require pressures considerably higher than those used in the other tires.

While you are about the task of checking air pressure, inspect the tire treads for cuts, bruises and other damage. Check the air valves to be sure that they are tight. Replace any missing valve caps. Dirt and moisture gathering in the valve stem could lead to an early demise of the stem and a subsequent flat tire.

Check the tires for uneven wear that might indicate the need for front end alignment or tire rotation. Tires should be replaced when tread wear indicators appears as solid bands across the tread.

CARE OF ALUMINUM WHEELS

If your car is equipped with aluminum wheels from an aftermarket application, they are normally coated to preserve their appearance. To clean the aluminum wheels, use a mild soap and water solution and rinse thoroughly with clean water. If you want to use one of the commercially available wheel cleaners, make sure the label indicates that the cleaner is safe for coated wheels. Never use steel wool or any cleaner that contains an abrasive, or use strong detergents that contain high alkaline or caustic agents, as they will damage your wheels.

FLUIDS AND LUBRICANTS

Fluid Disposal

Used fluids such as engine oil, transmission fluid, antifreeze and brake fluid are hazardous wastes and must be disposed of properly. Before draining any fluids, consult with the local authorities; in many areas, waste oil, etc. is being accepted as a part of recycling programs. A number of service stations and auto parts stores are also accepting waste fluids for recycling.

Be sure of the recycling center's policies before draining any fluids, as many will not accept different fluids that have been mixed together, such as oil and antifreeze.

Fuel and Engine Oil Recommendations

FUEL

Gasoline

All 1964-74 models are designed to run on either regular or premium grade fuel depending upon the particular engine's compression ratio. All engines having a compression ratio of 9.0:1 or less can run efficiently on regular gasoline, while any engines with a higher ratio must use premium fuel. All 1975 and later models have been designed to run on unleaded fuel. The use of a leaded fuel in a car requiring unleaded fuel will plug the catalytic converter and render it inoperative. It will also increase exhaust backpressure to the point where engine output will be severely reduced. In all cases, the minimum octane rating of the unleaded fuel being used must be at least 87, which usually means regular unleaded.

The use of a fuel too low in octane (a measurement of anti-knock quality) will result in spark knock. Since many factors such as altitude, terrain, air temperature and humidity affect operating efficiency, knocking may result even though the recommended fuel is being used. If persistent knocking occurs, it may be necessary to switch to a higher grade of fuel. Continuous or heavy knocking may result in engine damage.

➡**Your engine's fuel requirement can change with time, mainly due to carbon buildup, which will in turn change the compression ratio. If your engine pings, knocks, or diesels (runs with the ignition off) switch to a higher grade of fuel. Sometimes just changing brands will cure the problem. If it becomes necessary to retard the timing from the specifications, don't change it more than a few degrees. Retarded timing will reduce power output and fuel mileage, in addition to making the engine run hotter.**

Diesel Fuel

Fuel makers produce two grades of diesel fuel, No. 1 and No. 2, for use in automotive diesel engines. Generally speaking, No. 2 fuel is recommended over No. 1 for driving in temperature above 20°F (-7°C). In fact, in many areas, No. 2 diesel is the only fuel available. By comparison, No. 2 diesel fuel is less volatile than No. 1 fuel, and gives better fuel economy. No. 2 fuel is also a better injection pump lubricant.

Two important characteristics of diesel fuel are its cetane number and it viscosity.

The cetane number of a diesel fuel refers to the ease with which a diesel fuel ignites. High cetane numbers mean that the fuel will ignite with relative ease or that it ignites well at low temperatures. Naturally, the lower the cetane number, the higher the temperature must be to ignite the fuel. Most commercial fuels have cetane numbers that range from 35 to 65. No. 1 diesel fuel generally has a higher cetane rating than No. 2 fuel.

Viscosity is the ability of a liquid, in this case diesel fuel, to flow. Using straight No. 2 diesel fuel below 20°F (-7°C) can cause problems, because this fuel tends to become cloudy, meaning wax crystals begin forming in the fuel (20°F is often call the cloud point for No. 2 fuel). In extreme cold weather, No. 2 fuel can stop flowing altogether. In either case, fuel flow is restricted, which can result in a no start condition or poor engine performance. Fuel manufacturers often winterize No. 2 diesel fuel by using various fuel additives and blends (No. 1 diesel fuel, kerosene, etc.) to lower its winter time viscosity. Generally speaking, though, No. 1 diesel fuel is more satisfactory in extremely cold weather.

➡No. 1 and No. 2 diesel fuels will mix and burn with no ill effects, although the engine manufacturers will undoubtedly recommend one or the other. Consult the owner's manual for information.

Depending on local climate, most fuel manufacturers make winterized No. 2 fuel available seasonally.

Many automobile manufacturers publish pamphlets giving the locations of diesel fuel stations nationwide. Contact the local dealer for information.

➡Do not substitute home heating oil for automotive diesel fuel.

While in some cases, home heating oil refinement levels equal those of diesel fuel, many times they are far below diesel engine requirements. The result of using dirty home heating oil will be a clogged fuel system, in which case the entire system may have to be dismantled and cleaned.

One more word on diesel fuels. Don't thin diesel fuel with gasoline in cold weather. The lighter gasoline, which is more explosive, will cause rough running at the very least, and may cause extensive damage if enough is used.

OIL

▶ See Figures 77 and 78

The SAE (Society of Automotive Engineers) grade number indicates the viscosity of the engine oil and thus its ability to lubricate at a given temperature. The lower the SAE grade number, the lighter the oil; the lower the viscosity, the easier it is to crank the engine in cold weather.

Oil viscosities should be chosen from those oils recommended for the lowest anticipated temperatures during the oil change interval.

Multi-viscosity oils (10W-30, 20W-50 etc.) offer the important advantage of being adaptable to temperature extremes. They allow easy starting at low temperatures, yet they give good protection at high speeds and engine temperatures. This is a decided advantage in changeable climates or in long distance touring.

The API (American Petroleum Institute) designation indicates the classification of engine oil used under certain given operating conditions. Only oils designated for use Service SG should be used. Oils of the SG type perform a variety of functions inside the engine in addition to their basic function as a lubricant. Through a balanced system of metallic detergents and polymeric dispersants, the oil prevents the formation of high and low temperature deposits and also keeps sludge and particles of dirt in suspension. Acids, particularly sulfuric acid, as well as other byproducts of combustion, are neutralized. Both the SAE grade number and the API designation can be found on side of the oil bottle.

Synthetic Oil

There are excellent synthetic and fuel-efficient oils available that, under the right circumstances, can help provide better fuel mileage and better engine protection. However, these advantages come at a price, which can be three or four times the price per quart of conventional motor oils.

Before pouring any synthetic oils into your car's engine, you should consider the condition of the engine and the type of driving you do. It is also wise to check the vehicle manufacturer's position on synthetic oils.

Generally, it is best to avoid the use of synthetic oil in both brand new and older, high mileage engines. New engines require a proper break-in, and the synthetics are so slippery that they can impede this; most manufacturers recommend that you wait at least 5,000 miles before switching to a synthetic oil. Conversely, older engines are looser and tend to use more oil; synthetics will slip past worn parts more readily than regular oil, and will be used up faster. If your car already leaks and/or uses oil (due to worn parts or bad seals or gaskets), it may leak and use more with a synthetic inside.

Consider your type of driving. If most of your accumulated mileage is on the highway at higher, steadier speed, a synthetic oil will reduce friction and probably help deliver better fuel mileage. Under such ideal highway conditions, the oil change interval can be extended, as long as the oil filter will operate effectively for the extended life of the oil. If the filter can't do its job for this extended period, dirt and sludge will build up in your engine's crankcase, sump, oil pump and lines, no matter what type of oil is used. If using synthetic oil in this manner, you should continue to change the oil filter at the recommended intervals.

Cars used under harder, stop-and-go, short hop circumstances should always be serviced more frequently, and for these cars synthetic oil may not be a wise investment. Because of the necessary shorter change interval needed for this type of driving, you cannot take advantage of the long recommended change interval of most synthetic oils.

Finally, most synthetic oils are not compatible with conventional oils and cannot be added to them. This means you should always carry a couple of quarts of synthetic oil with you while on a long trip, as not all service stations carry this oil.

Engine

OIL LEVEL CHECK

▶ See Figures 79, 80 and 81

Every time you stop for fuel, check the engine oil making sure the engine has fully warmed and the vehicle is parked on a level surface. Because it takes a few minutes for all the oil

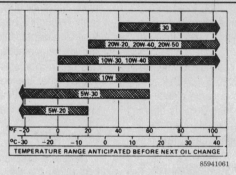

Fig. 77 Recommended SAE engine oil viscosity grades for gasoline engines. NOTE: do not use SAE 5W-30 for continuous high speed driving

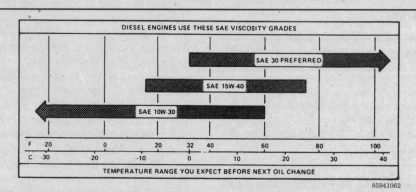

Fig. 78 SAE engine oil viscosity recommendations — Diesel engines

to drain back to the oil pan, you should wait a few minutes before checking your oil. If you are doing this at a fuel stop, first fill the fuel tank, then open the hood and check the oil, but don't get so carried away as to forget to pay for the fuel. Most station attendants won't believe that you forgot.

1. Make sure the car is parked on level ground.

2. When checking the oil level it is best for the engine to be a normal operating temperature, although checking the oil immediately after stopping will lead to a false reading. Wait a few minutes after turning off the engine to allow the oil to drain back into the crankcase.

3. Open the hood and locate the dipstick which will be in a guide tube mounted in the upper engine block just below the cylinder head mating surface. The dipstick may be located on the right or left side of the vehicle depending upon your partic-

Fig. 80 For an accurate reading wipe the dipstick clean with a rag, then re-insert it into the guide tube

ular engine. Pull the dipstick from its tube, wipe it clean and then reinsert it.

4. Pull the dipstick out again and, holding it horizontally, read the oil level. The oil should be between the FULL and ADD marks on the dipstick. If the oil is below the ADD mark, add oil of the proper viscosity through the capped opening in the top of the cylinder head cover (or oil fill tube on most Oldsmobile engines). See the oil and fuel recommendations listed earlier in this section for the proper viscosity and rating of oil to use.

5. Replace the dipstick and check the oil level again after adding any oil. Approximately one quart of oil will raise the level from the ADD mark to the FULL mark. Be sure not to overfill the crankcase and waste the oil. Excess oil will generally be consumed at an accelerated rate.

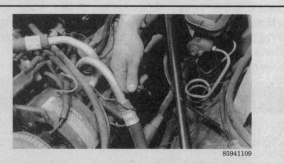

Fig. 79 The engine oil level is checked using the dipstick located on the side of the block, near an exhaust manifold

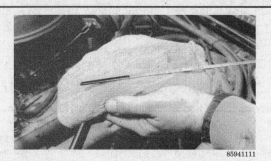

Fig. 81 To maintain a proper oil level, make sure it reads between the ADD and FULL marks on the dipstick

OIL AND FILTER CHANGE

▶ **See Figures 82, 83, 84, 85, 86 and 87**

If the vehicle is operated on a daily or semi-daily basis and most trips are for several miles (allowing the engine to properly warm-up), the oil should be changed every four months or 6,000 miles on all 1964-74 models. On 1975-78 models, the interval is six months or 7,500 miles. 1979 and later models increased the time interval to 12 months while keeping the mileage (7,500) the same (Diesel interval is 5,000 miles). Make sure that you change the oil based on whichever interval comes first.

If however, the vehicle is used to tow a trailer, is made to idle for extended periods of time such as in heavy daily traffic or if used as a service vehicle (police, taxi, delivery) or the vehicle is used for only short trips in below freezing temperature, the oil change interval should be shortened. Likewise, if your vehicle is used under dusty, polluted or off-road conditions, the oil should be changed more frequently. Under these circumstances oil has a greater chance of building up sludge and contaminants which could damage your engine. If your vehicle use fits into these circumstance, as most do, it is suggested that the oil and filter be changed every 3,000 miles or 3 months, whichever comes first.

The oil drain plug is located on the bottom of the oil pan (bottom of the engine, underneath the car). The oil filter is located on the right side of the inline 6-cylinder engine and on the left side of most other engines. Although most vehicles

Fig. 82 A wrench or a ratchet will be necessary to initially loosen the drain plug

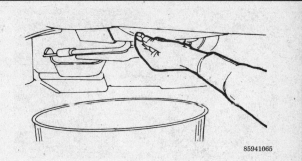

Fig. 83 By keeping inward pressure on the drain plug as you unscrew it, oil won't escape past the threads

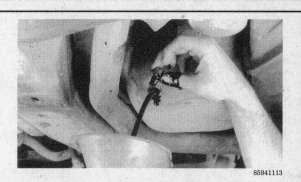

Fig. 84 Once the plug is fully unthreaded, withdraw it and quickly pull your hand out of the way

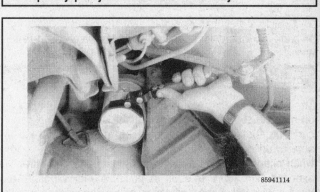

Fig. 85 A strap-type or equivalent filter wrench is usually necessary to loosen the oil filter

covered in this manual utilize a spin-on oil filter, some 1968 and earlier vehicles were originally equipped with a canister and cartridge type filter. On these earlier vehicles, the canister must be removed in order to access the cartridge.

Always drain the engine oil after the engine has been running long enough to bring it up to normal operating temperature. Hot oil will flow easier and more contaminants will be removed along with the oil than if it were drained cold. To change the oil and filter:

1. Run the engine until it reaches normal operating temperature.
2. Raise the front of the vehicle and support it safely using a suitable pair of jackstands.

Fig. 86 The new oil filter gasket should be coated using clean engine oil

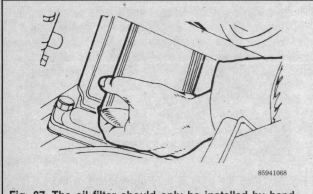

Fig. 87 The oil filter should only be installed by hand

3. Slide a drain pan of a least 6 quarts capacity under the oil pan. Wipe the drain plug and surrounding area clean using an old rag.

✻✻CAUTION

The EPA warns that prolonged contact with used engine oil may cause a number of skin disorders, including cancer! You should make every effort to minimize your exposure to used engine oil. Protective gloves should be worn when changing the oil. Wash your hands and any other exposed skin areas as soon as possible after exposure to used engine oil. Soap and water, or waterless hand cleaner should be used.

4. Loosen the drain plug using a ratchet, short extension and socket or a box-wrench. Turn the plug out by hand, using a rag to shield your fingers from the hot oil. By keeping an inward pressure on the plug as you unscrew it, oil won't escape past the threads and you can remove it without being burned by hot oil.

5. Quickly withdraw the plug and move your hands out of the way. Allow the oil to drain completely in the pan, then install and carefully tighten the drain plug. Be careful not to overtighten the drain plug, otherwise you'll be buying a new pan or a trick replacement plug for stripped threads.

➡**Although some manufacturers have at times recommended changing the oil filter every other oil change, we recommend the filter be changed each time you change your oil. The added benefit of clean oil is quickly lost if** the old filter is clogged and the added protection to the heart of your engine far outweighs the few dollars saved by using a old filter.

6. Move the drain pan under the oil filter. Unless your vehicle is equipped with a canister type filter, use a strap-type or cap-type filter wrench to loosen and remove the oil filter from the engine block. Keep in mind that it's holding about one quart of dirty, hot oil.

7. If equipped with a canister filter, remove the through-bolt retaining the canister to the engine, then carefully lower the canister for access to the cartridge. Make sure the old cartridge gasket was lowered with the canister and is not left on the engine. On these vehicles, it is not uncommon to find 2 or more gaskets which were left in place by a less experienced or attentive person who changed the filter before you.

8. Empty the old filter into the drain pan and dispose of the filter or the cartridge.

9. Using a clean rag, wipe off the filter adapter on the engine block. Be sure that the rag doesn't leave any lint which could clog an oil passage.

➡**Replacement cartridges for canister type filters may be difficult to find. If you cannot locate a replacement cartridge, most automotive supply stores will be able to supply you with an adapter kit which will allow you to use a standard spin-on filter.**

10. Coat the rubber gasket on the filter or cartridge with fresh oil. If equipped with a standard filter, spin it onto the engine by hand; when the gasket touches the adapter surface, give it another $1/2$-$1/3$ turn. No more, or you'll squash the gasket and it will leak.

11. If equipped with a canister filter, install the new cartridge into the canister. Make sure the gasket is in place, then install the canister and tighten the through-bolt.

12. Refill the engine with the correct amount of fresh oil. See the refer to the Capacities chart at the end of this section.

13. Check the oil level on the dipstick. It is normal for the level to be a bit above the full mark. Start the engine and allow it to idle for a few minutes.

✻✻CAUTION

Do not run the engine above idle speed until it has built up oil pressure, as indicated when the oil light goes out.

14. Shut off the engine and allow the oil to flow back to the crankcase for a minute, then recheck the oil level. Check around the filter and drain plug for any leaks, and correct as necessary.

Manual Transmission

FLUID RECOMMENDATIONS AND LEVEL CHECK

The oil in the manual transmission should be checked at least every 6,000 miles for 1964-74 models or every 7,500 miles for all 1975-81 models.

1. With the car parked on a level surface, remove the level/filler plug from the side of the transmission housing. If the

plug cannot be accessed with the car parked, it may be raised and supported by 4 jackstands so that the vehicle is level. DO NOT support the vehicle using cinder blocks, as they may crumble without notice and drop the vehicle suddenly.

2. If the lubricant begins to trickle out of the hole, there is enough and you need not go any further. Otherwise, carefully insert your finger (watch out for sharp threads) and check to see if the oil is up the edge of the hole.

3. If not, add oil through the hole until the level is at the edge of the hole. Most gear lubricants come in a plastic squeeze bottle with a nozzle; making additions simple. Some lubricant manufacturers will supply a small hose and hand-pump with their oil to further ease this process. If necessary, you can also use a common kitchen baster to introduce the oil into the transmission housing. Use only standard GL-5 hypoid-type gear oil - SAE 80W or SAE 80W/90.

4. Replace the filler plug and, if applicable, lower the vehicle to the ground.

5. Block the drive wheels and set the parking brake, then run the engine and check for leaks.

DRAIN AND REFILL

There is no recommended interval for the manual transmission but it is always a good idea to change the fluid if you have purchased the car used or if it has been driven in water high enough to reach the axles.

1. The oil must be hot before it is drained. Drive the car at highway speeds for 10-15 minutes or until the engine and transmission reach their normal operating temperatures.

2. If necessary for access, raise the front of the vehicle and support it safely using jackstands.

3. Clean the area surrounding the level/filler and drain plugs using a old rag. Remove the level/filler plug to provide a vent.

4. Place a large container underneath the transmission and then remove the drain plug. Remember to use a rag to protect your hands and to apply slight pressure to the plug as it is unthreaded in order to keep the oil from flowing freely until the plug is fully withdrawn.

5. Allow the oil to drain completely into the pan. Clean off the drain plug and replace it; carefully tighten it until it is just snug.

6. Fill the transmission with the proper lubricant through the level/filler plug bore as detailed earlier in this section. Refer to the Capacities chart for the correct amount of lubricant.

7. When the oil level is up to the edge of the filler hole, replace the filler plug.

8. If raised, remove the jackstands and carefully lower the vehicle.

9. Drive the car for a few minutes, stop, and check for any leaks.

Automatic Transmission

FLUID RECOMMENDATIONS AND LEVEL CHECK

▶ See Figures 88, 89, 90, 91 and 92

Check the automatic transmission fluid level at least every 6,000 miles for 1964-74 vehicles or every 7,500 miles for 1975 and later models. The dipstick can be found in the rear of the engine compartment. The fluid level should be checked only when the transmission is hot (normal operating temperature). The transmission is considered hot after about 20 miles of highway driving.

1. Park the car on a level surface with the engine idling. Shift the transmission into **Neutral** and set the parking brake.

2. Remove the dipstick, wipe it clean and then reinsert it firmly. Be sure that it has been pushed all the way in. Remove the dipstick again and check the fluid level while holding it horizontally. With the engine running, the fluid level should be between the upper notch and the FULL HOT line. If the fluid must be checked when it is cool, the level should be between the lower 2 notches.

3. If the fluid level is low add DEXRON®II automatic transmission fluid. The fluid must be added through the transmission dipstick tube, which is easily accomplished using a funnel. Add fluid gradually, checking the level often as you are filling the transmission. Be extremely careful not to overfill the transmission, as this will cause slippage, seal damage and overheating. Approximately one pint of ATF will raise the fluid level from one notch/line to the other.

➡Always use DEXRON®II ATF. The use of ATF Type F or any other fluid will cause severe damage to the transmission.

The fluid on the dipstick should always be a bright red color. If it is discolored (brown or black), or smells burnt, serious transmission troubles, probably due to overheating, should be suspected. The transmission should be inspected by a qualified technician to locate the cause of the burnt fluid.

85941116

Fig. 88 Like engine oil, the automatic transmission fluid level is checked using a dipstick

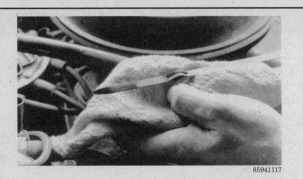

Fig. 89 Check the level on the dipstick after it has been wiped, re-inserted and withdrawn

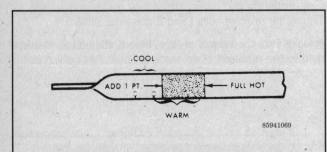

Fig. 90 Automatic transmission dipstick marks; the proper level for a hot transmission is within the shaded area

Fig. 91 Automatic transmission fluid is added through the dipstick guide tube

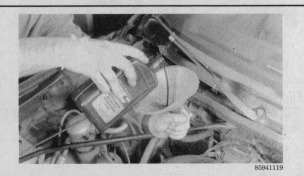

Fig. 92 If a standard funnel is hard to fit in the tube, try a funnel with a flexible neck

TRANSMISSION DRAIN AND REFILL/PAN AND FILTER SERVICE

The service procedures for automatic transmission fluid drain and refill, filter change and band adjustment are all detailed in Section 7 of this manual.

Rear Axle

FLUID RECOMMENDATIONS AND LEVEL CHECK

▶ **See Figures 93, 94, 95 and 96**

The oil in the differential should be checked at least every 6,000 miles on 1964-74 vehicles or every 7,500 miles for 1975 and later models.

1. With the car parked on a level surface and with the parking brake set or with the vehicle raised and supported safely by 4 jackstands so the vehicle is level, remove the filler plug from the front side of the differential.

2. If oil begins to trickle out of the hole, there is enough. Otherwise, carefully insert your finger into the hole (watch out for sharp threads) and check that the oil is up the bottom edge of the filler hole.

3. If not, add oil through the hole until the level is at the edge of the hole. Most gear oils come in a plastic squeeze bottle with a nozzle; making additions is simple. Some gear oil manufacturers will provide a small hand-pump and length of tubing which can be used to pump gear oil into the housing. You can even use a common kitchen baster. Use only standard GL-5 hypoid-type gear oil - SAE 80W or SAE 80W/90.

➡️**On all models equipped with the positraction/limited slip rear axle, GM recommends that you use only the special lubricant which is available at your local Chevrolet parts department.**

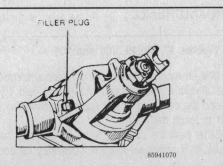

Fig. 93 The filler plug located on the side of the rear axle housing is used to check the fluid level and to fill the housing

Fig. 94 Clean the area surrounding the drain plug to prevent contamination the gear oil

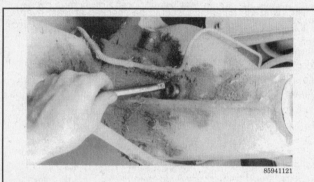

Fig. 95 Use a ratchet with an extension to loosen the square filler plug

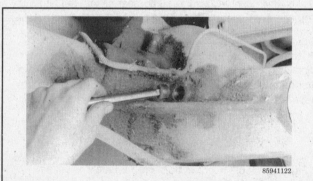

Fig. 96 Remove the filler plug from the bore in the rear axle housing

DRAIN AND REFILL

▶ See Figures 97, 98, 99, 100 and 101

There is no recommended change interval for the rear axle but it is always a good idea to change the fluid if you have purchased the car used or if it has been driven in water high enough to reach the axle.

1. Either park the car on a level surface and set the parking brake, or if additional room is necessary for access to the

housing, raise and support the rear of the vehicle using jackstands.

2. Remove the filler plug.

3. Place a large container underneath the rear axle. Clean the area surrounding the rear cover to help prevent dirt from entering the rear axle housing.

4. Unscrew the retaining bolts and remove the rear cover. When removing the cover, a small prytool may be used at the base of the cover to gently pry it back from the axle housing, breaking the gasket seal and allowing the lubricant to drain out into the container. Be careful not to use excessive force and damage the cover or housing.

To install:

5. Carefully clean the gasket mating surfaces of the cover and axle housing of any remaining gasket or sealer.

6. Install the rear cover using a new gasket and sealant. Tighten the retaining bolts using a crosswise pattern.

➡**Make sure the vehicle is level before attempting to add fluid to the rear axle or an incorrect fluid level will result.**

7. Refill the rear axle housing using the proper grade and quantity of lubricant as detailed earlier in this section. Install the filler plug, operate the vehicle and check for any leaks.

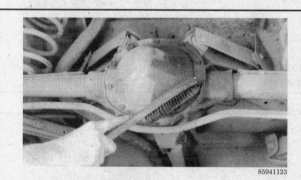

Fig. 97 Clean the area surrounding the rear axle cover to prevent contamination of the differential

Fig. 98 Remove the cover retaining bolts

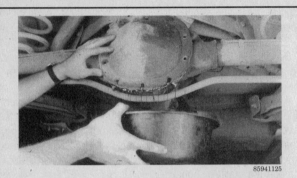

Fig. 99 Carefully lift or pry outward at the bottom of the cover, allowing the fluid to run into the drain pan

Fig. 100 Once most of the fluid has drained, remove the rear cover from the housing

Fig. 101 Carefully clean the gasket mating surfaces of all gasket and sealer traces

Cooling System

▶ See Figures 102 and 103

✳✳CAUTION

Never remove the radiator cap under any conditions while the engine is hot! Failure to follow these instructions could result in damage to the cooling system, engine and/or personal injury. To avoid having scalding hot coolant or steam blow out of the radiator, use extreme care whenever you are removing the radiator cap. Wait until the engine has cooled, then wrap a thick cloth around the radiator cap and turn it slowly to the first stop. Step back while the pressure is released from the cooling system. When you are sure the pressure has been released, press down on the radiator cap (still have the cloth in position) turn and remove the radiator cap.

Dealing with the cooling system can be dangerous matter unless the proper precautions are observed. It is best to check the coolant level in the radiator when the engine is cold. On early models this is accomplished by carefully removing the radiator cap and checking that the coolant is within 2 in. of the bottom of the filler neck. On later models, the cooling system has, as one of its components, a coolant recovery tank. If the coolant level is at or near the ADD/FULL COLD line (engine cold) or the FULL HOT line (engine hot), the level is satisfactory. Always be certain that the filler caps on both the radiator and the recovery tank are closed tightly.

In the event that the coolant level must be checked when the engine is hot on vehicles not equipped with a coolant recovery tank, place a thick rag over the radiator cap and slowly turn the cap counterclockwise until it reaches the first detent. Allow all hot steam to escape. This will allow the pressure in the system to drop gradually, preventing an explosion of hot coolant. When the hissing noise stops, carefully remove the cap the rest of the way.

If the coolant level is found to be low, add a 50/50 mixture of ethylene glycol-based antifreeze and clean water. On older models, coolant must be added through the radiator filler neck. On newer models with the recovery tank, coolant may be ad-

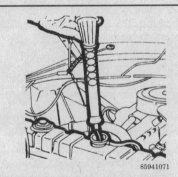

Fig. 102 Coolant protection can be easily checked using a float-type hydrometer tester

Fig. 103 If possible, a hand-held pressure tester should be used at least once a year to check system integrity

ded either through the filler neck on the radiator or directly into the recovery tank.

❋❋CAUTION

Never add coolant to a hot engine unless it is running. If it is not running you run the risk of cracking the engine block.

It is wise to pressure check the cooling system at least once per year. If the coolant level is chronically low or rusty, the system should be thoroughly checked for leaks.

At least once every 2 years, the engine cooling system should be inspected, flushed, and refilled with fresh coolant. If the coolant is left in the system too long, it loses its ability to prevent rust and corrosion. If the coolant has too much water, it won't protect against freezing.

The pressure cap should be examined for signs of age or deterioration. Fan belt and other drive belts should be inspected and adjusted to the proper tension. (See checking belt tension).

Hose clamps should be tightened, and soft or cracked hoses replaced. Damp spots, or accumulations of rust or dye near hoses, water pump or other areas, indicate possible leakage, which must be corrected before filling the system with fresh coolant.

FLUID RECOMMENDATION

When adding or changing the fluid in the system, create a 50/50 mixture of high quality ethylene glycol antifreeze and water.

LEVEL CHECK

▶ See Figure 104

On most late model vehicles, the fluid level may be checked by observing the fluid level marks of the recovery tank. The level should be near the ADD or FULL COLD mark, as applicable, when the system is cold. At normal operating temperatures, the level should be above the ADD/FULL COLD mark or, if applicable, between the ADD/FULL COLD and the FULL HOT marks. Only add coolant to the recovery tank as necessary to bring the system up to a proper level.

❋❋CAUTION

Should it be necessary to remove the radiator cap, make sure that the system has had time to cool, reducing the internal pressure.

On earlier vehicles and any vehicle that is not equipped with a coolant recovery or overflow tank, the level must be checked by removing the radiator cap. This should only be done when the cooling system has had time to sufficiently cool after the engine has been run. The coolant level should be within 2 in. of the base of the radiator filler neck. If necessary, coolant can then be added directly to the radiator.

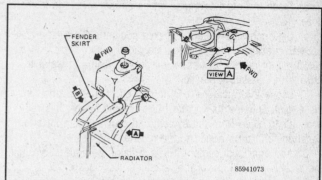

Fig. 104 If equipped, the coolant recovery/overflow tank is usually mounted to the right fender skirt

COOLING SYSTEM INSPECTION

Checking the Radiator Cap Seal

While you are checking the coolant level, check the radiator cap for a worn or cracked gasket. It the cap doesn't seal properly, fluid will be lost and the engine will overheat.

Worn caps should be replaced with a new one.

Checking the Radiator for Debris

Periodically clean any debris — leaves, paper, insects, etc. — from the radiator fins. Pick the large pieces off by hand. The smaller pieces can be washed away with water pressure from a hose.

Carefully straighten any bent radiator fins with a pair of needle nose pliers. Be careful — the fins are very soft. Don't wiggle the fins back and forth too much. Straighten them once and try not to move them again.

DRAINING AND REFILLING THE SYSTEM

▶ See Figures 105, 106, 107, 108, 109 and 110

1. Make sure the engine is cool and the vehicle is parked on a level surface, then remove the radiator neck cap and, if equipped, the recovery tank cap in order to relieve system pressure.

2. Position a large drain pan under the vehicle, then drain the existing antifreeze and coolant by opening the radiator petcock and/or engine drains. It is also possible to drain the system by disconnecting the lower radiator hose, from the bottom radiator outlet.

❋❋CAUTION

When draining the coolant, keep in mind that cats and dogs are attracted by the ethylene glycol antifreeze, and are quite likely to drink any that is left in an uncovered container or in puddles on the ground. This will prove fatal in sufficient quantity. Always drain the coolant into a sealable container. Coolant should be reused unless it is contaminated or several years old at which point it should be returned to a coolant recycling or hazardous waste disposal sight. Check your local laws for proper disposal methods.

3. Close the radiator/engine drains or reconnect the lower hose.

4. Determine the capacity of your coolant system (see capacities specifications). Through the radiator filler neck, add a 50/50 mix of quality antifreeze (ethylene glycol) and water to provide the desired protection.

5. Leave the radiator pressure cap off, then start and run the engine until the thermostat heats up and opens, this will allow air to bleed from the system and provide room for additional coolant to be added to the radiator.

6. Add additional coolant to the radiator, as necessary, until the level is within 2 in. of the radiator's filler neck base.

7. Stop the engine and check the coolant level.

8. Check the level of protection with an antifreeze tester, then install the radiator pressure cap.

9. If equipped with a coolant recovery/overflow tank, add coolant to the tank, as necessary to achieve the proper level.

10. Start and run the engine to normal operating temperature, then check the system for leaks.

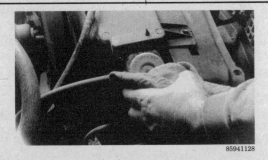

Fig. 105 When removing cap from a warm radiator, cover the cap with a rag and carefully turn to the first stop. Allow the pressure to release.

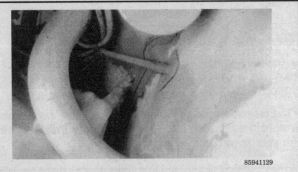

Fig. 106 The engine block drain plug should be removed if you are fully draining the cooling system

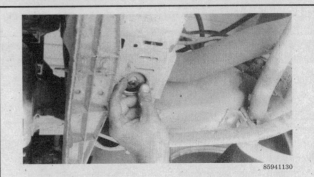

Fig. 107 Open the radiator drain cock in order to fully or partially empty the radiator of coolant

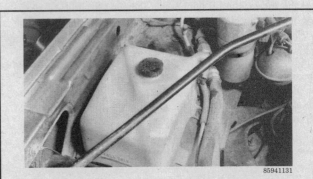

Fig. 108 Most vehicles covered in this book are equipped with a coolant recovery tank

Fig. 109 On a cold engine, the coolant level should be at the FULL COLD line

Fig. 110 If equipped, small amounts of coolant should be added through the coolant recovery tank

FLUSHING AND CLEANING THE SYSTEM

The cooling system should be drained, thoroughly flushed and refilled at least every 30,000 miles or 24 months. These operations should be done with the engine cold, especially if a backpressure flushing kit is being used. Completely draining, flushing and refilling the cooling system at least every two years will remove accumulated rust, scale and other deposits. Coolant in late model vehicles is a 50/50 mixture of ethylene glycol and water for year round use. Use a good quality antifreeze with water pump lubricants, rust inhibitors and other corrosion inhibitors along with acid neutralizers.

There are many products available for cooling system flushing. If a backpressure flushing kit is used, it is recommended that the thermostat be temporarily removed in order to allow free flow to the system with cold water. Always follow the kit or cleaner manufacturer's instructions and make sure the product is compatible with your vehicle.

1. Make sure the engine is cool and the vehicle is parked on a level surface, then remove the radiator neck cap and, if equipped, the recovery tank cap in order to relieve system pressure.

2. Position a large drain pan under the vehicle, then drain the existing antifreeze and coolant by opening the radiator petcock and/or engine drains. It is also possible to drain the system by disconnecting the lower radiator hose, from the bottom radiator outlet.

✳✳CAUTION

When draining the coolant, keep in mind that cats and dogs are attracted by the ethylene glycol antifreeze, and are quite likely to drink any that is left in an uncovered container or in puddles on the ground. This will prove fatal in sufficient quantity. Always drain the coolant into a sealable container. Coolant should be reused unless it is contaminated or several years old at which point it should be returned to a coolant recycling or hazardous waste disposal sight. Check your local laws for proper disposal methods.

3. Close the radiator/engine drains or reconnect the lower hose, as applicable and fill the system with water.

4. Add a can of quality radiator flush.

5. Idle the engine until the upper radiator hose gets hot and the thermostat has opened. This will allow the solution to fully circulate through the system.

6. Drain the system again.

7. Repeat this process until the drained water is clear and free of scale.

8. Close all drains and connect all the hoses.

9. If equipped with a coolant recovery system, flush the reservoir with water and leave empty.

10. Determine the capacity of your coolant system (see capacities specifications). Through the radiator filler neck, add a 50/50 mix of quality antifreeze (ethylene glycol) and water to provide the desired protection.

11. Leave the radiator pressure cap off, then start and run the engine until the thermostat heats up and opens, this will allow air to bleed from the system and provide room for additional coolant to be added to the radiator.

12. Add additional coolant to the radiator, as necessary, until the level is within 2 in. of the radiator's filler neck base.

13. Stop the engine and check the coolant level.

14. Check the level of protection with an antifreeze tester, then install the radiator pressure cap.

15. If equipped with a coolant recovery/overflow tank, add coolant to the tank, as necessary to achieve the proper level.

16. Start and run the engine to normal operating temperature, then check the system for leaks.

Brake Master Cylinder

FLUID RECOMMENDATIONS AND LEVEL CHECK

▶ **See Figures 111, 112, 113, 114, 115 and 116**

The brake master cylinder is located under the hood, in the left rear section of the engine compartment. It is divided into two sections (reservoirs) and the fluid must be kept within 1/4 in. of the top edge of both reservoirs. Some reservoirs will have minimum or maximum fluid level marks on an outer side wall in order to help determine if the fluid is at a proper level. The level should be checked at least every 6,000 miles for 1964-74 vehicles or every 7,500 miles for 1975 and later models.

➡ **Any sudden decrease in the level of fluid indicates a possible leak in the system and should be checked immediately.**

To check the fluid level, simply pry off the retaining bar and then lift off the top cover of the master cylinder, taking care not to allow any fluid to drip on painted surfaces. When making additions of brake fluid, use only fresh, uncontaminated brake fluid which meets or exceeds DOT-3 standards. Be careful not to spill any brake fluid on painted surfaces, as it will quickly eat the paint. Do not allow the brake fluid container or the master cylinder reservoir to remain open any longer than necessary; brake fluid absorbs moisture from the air, reducing its effectiveness and causing corrosion in the lines.

➡ **The reservoir cover on some 1978 and later models may be without a retaining ball. If so, simply pry the cover off with your fingers.**

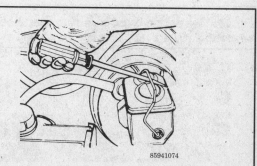

85941074

Fig. 111 If equipped with a metal cap, carefully pry the retaining bar from the top of the master cylinder reservoir cap

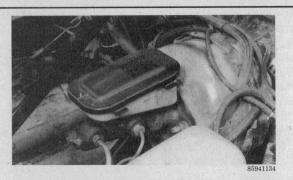

Fig. 112 Some master cylinder reservoirs are equipped with a plastic cap

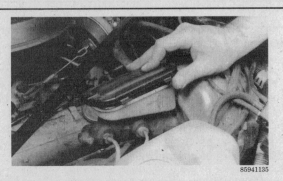

Fig. 113 For plastic retaining caps, carefully unsnap the cap from the reservoir using the tabs

Fig. 114 If equipped, remove the rubber diaphragm located under the cap

Fig. 115 If necessary, add only FRESH, clean DOT-3 brake fluid to the master cylinder reservoir

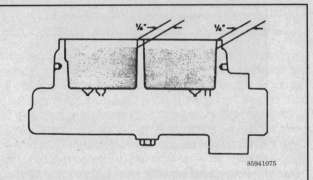

Fig. 116 Brake fluid level should be within ¼ in. of the reservoir's top edge

Power Steering Pump

FLUID RECOMMENDATIONS AND LEVEL CHECK

▶ See Figures 117, 118 and 119

Power steering fluid level should be checked at least once every 6,000 miles for 1964-74 vehicles or every 7,500 miles for 1975 and later models. Low fluid level usually produces a moaning sound as the wheels are turned (especially when standing still or parking) and increases steering wheel effort.

To prevent possible overfilling, check the fluid level only when the fluid has warmed to operating temperatures and the wheels are turned straight ahead (unloading the pump). If the level is low, fill the pump reservoir with suitable fluid until the fluid level measures full on the reservoir dipstick. For 1976 and earlier vehicles use DEXRON® Automatic Transmission Fluid, but 1977 and later cars require GM power steering fluid.

Windshield Washer Pump

FLUID RECOMMENDATIONS AND LEVEL CHECK

▶ See Figures 120 and 121

The windshield washer pump fluid reservoir is a plastic container usually found on the left side of the engine compartment, near the wiper motor. The reservoir should be filled to the top of the container using a wiper fluid solution which can

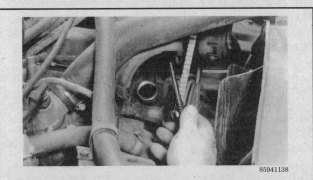

Fig. 117 Turn the power steering pump cap to unlock it, then remove it from the top of the pump

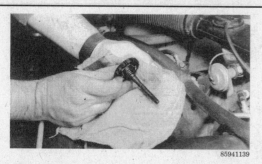

Fig. 118 Power steering fluid level can be checked using the dipstick attached to the pump reservoir filler cap

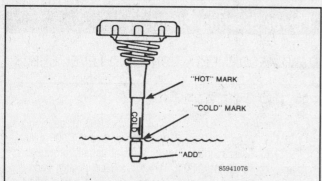

Fig. 119 Make sure fluid is at the appropriate level for the pump operating condition

"HOT" MARK
"COLD" MARK
"ADD"

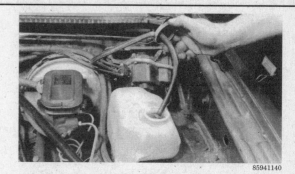

Fig. 120 The washer pump reservoir filler cap is usually attached to the pump feed tube

Fig. 121 When filling the washer reservoir, a funnel will help prevent waste

be found at most automotive stores. Do not further dilute the solution (unless it is sold in concentrate, then follow the manufacturer's instructions), as this will adversely affect its ability to keep from freezing at low temperatures. Also, never place another fluid, such as ethylene glycol antifreeze in the reservoir as other fluids could damage pump seals.

Chassis Greasing

▶ See Figures 122, 123, 124 and 125

Chassis greasing can be performed with a pressurized grease gun or it can be performed at home by using a hand-operated grease gun. Wipe the grease fittings clean before greasing in order to prevent the possibility of forcing any dirt into the component.

On most applications, the grease gun nozzle should be held onto or attached to the grease fitting, then the pump is operated to force fresh grease into the component. Some of the old, contaminated grease will usually be forced from the seams of a seal.

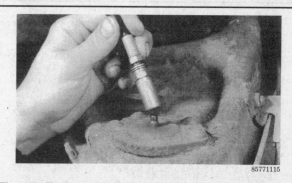

Fig. 122 There are various grease fittings located on the suspension, such as the control arm ball joints

Fig. 123 The steering linkage will also contain grease fittings

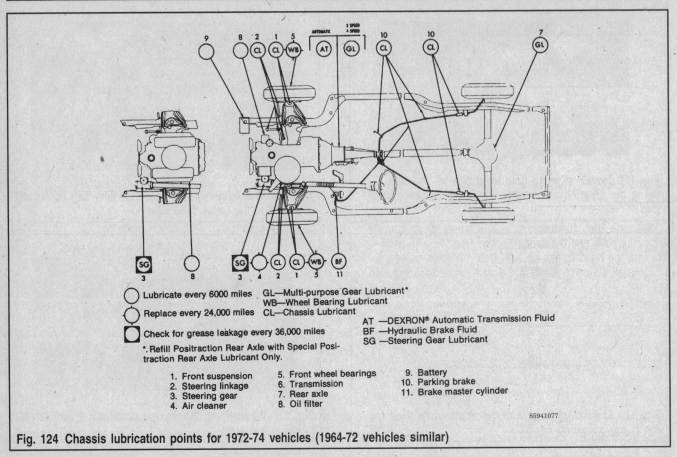

Lubricate every 6000 miles

Replace every 24,000 miles

Check for grease leakage every 36,000 miles

*. Refill Positraction Rear Axle with Special Positraction Rear Axle Lubricant Only.

GL—Multi-purpose Gear Lubricant*
WB—Wheel Bearing Lubricant
CL—Chassis Lubricant

AT —DEXRON® Automatic Transmission Fluid
BF —Hydraulic Brake Fluid
SG —Steering Gear Lubricant

1. Front suspension
2. Steering linkage
3. Steering gear
4. Air cleaner
5. Front wheel bearings
6. Transmission
7. Rear axle
8. Oil filter
9. Battery
10. Parking brake
11. Brake master cylinder

85941077

Fig. 124 Chassis lubrication points for 1972-74 vehicles (1964-72 vehicles similar)

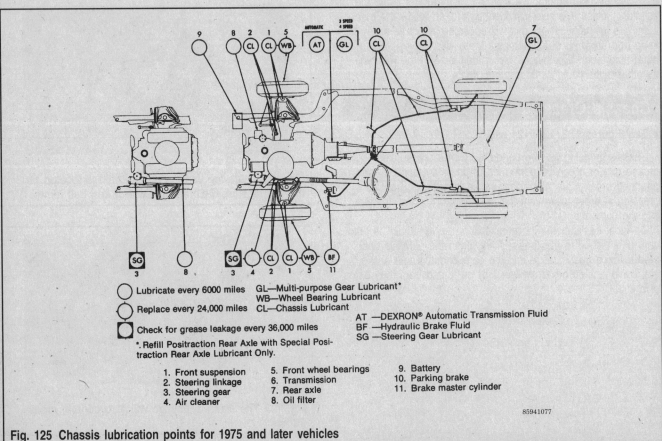

Lubricate every 6000 miles

Replace every 24,000 miles

Check for grease leakage every 36,000 miles

*. Refill Positraction Rear Axle with Special Positraction Rear Axle Lubricant Only.

GL—Multi-purpose Gear Lubricant*
WB—Wheel Bearing Lubricant
CL—Chassis Lubricant

AT —DEXRON® Automatic Transmission Fluid
BF —Hydraulic Brake Fluid
SG —Steering Gear Lubricant

1. Front suspension
2. Steering linkage
3. Steering gear
4. Air cleaner
5. Front wheel bearings
6. Transmission
7. Rear axle
8. Oil filter
9. Battery
10. Parking brake
11. Brake master cylinder

85941077

Fig. 125 Chassis lubrication points for 1975 and later vehicles

Body Lubrication

TRANSMISSION SHIFT LINKAGE

Lubricate the manual transmission shift linkage contact points with the EP grease used for chassis greasing, which should meet GM specification 6031M. The automatic transmission linkage should be lubricated with clean engine oil.

HOOD LATCH AND HINGES

Clean the latch surfaces and apply clean engine oil to the latch pilot bolts and the spring anchor. Use the engine oil to lubricate the hood hinges as well. Use a chassis grease to lubricate all the pivot points in the latch release mechanism.

DOOR HINGES

The gas tank filler door, car door, and rear hatch or trunk lid hinges should be wiped clean and lubricated with clean engine oil. Silicone spray also works well on these parts, but must be applied more often. Use engine oil to lubricate the trunk or hatch lock mechanism and the lock bolt and striker. The door lock cylinders can be lubricated easily with a shot of silicone spray or one of the may dry penetrating lubricants commercially available.

PARKING BRAKE LINKAGE

Use chassis grease on the parking brake cable where it contacts the guides, links, levers, and pulleys. The grease should be water resistant for durability under the car.

ACCELERATOR LINKAGE

Lubricate the carburetor stud, carburetor lever, and the accelerator pedal lever at the support inside the car with clean engine oil.

FRONT WHEEL BEARINGS

Once every 12 months or 12,000 miles, clean and repack wheel bearings with a wheel bearing grease. Use only enough grease to completely coat the rollers. Remove any excess grease from the exposed surface of the hub and seal.

It is important that wheel bearings be properly adjusted after installation. Improperly adjusted wheel bearings can cause steering instability, front-end shimmy and wander, and increased tire wear. For complete removal, lubrication installation and adjustment procedures, see the Wheel Bearing procedures in Section 8 of this manual.

RECOMMENDED LUBRICANTS

Item	Lubricant
Engine Oil (Gasoline)	API "SF/CC" or "SF/CD"
Engine Oil (Diesel)	API "SF/CC", "SF/CD"
Manual Transmission	SAE 80W GL-5 or SAE 80W/90 GL-5
Automatic Transmission	DEXRON® II ATF
Rear Axle–Standard	SAE 80W GL-5 or SAE 80W/90 GL-5
Positraction/Limited Slip	GM Part #1052271 or 1052272
Power Steering Reservoir	DEXRON® ATF—1964–76 Power Steering Fluid—1977 and later
Brake Fluid	DOT 3
Antifreeze	Ethylene Glycol
Front Wheel Bearings	GM Wheel Bearing Grease
Clutch Linkage	Engine Oil
Hood and Door Hinges	Engine Oil
Chassis Lubrication	NLGI #1 or NLGI #2
Lock Cylinders	WD-40 or Powdered Graphite

85941079

TRAILER TOWING

General Recommendations

Your car was primarily designed to carry passengers and cargo. It is important to remember that towing a trailer will place additional loads on your vehicle's engine, drive train, steering, braking and other systems. However, if you find it necessary to tow a trailer, using the proper equipment is a must.

Local laws may require specific equipment such as trailer brakes or fender mounted mirrors. Check your local laws.

Trailer Weight

The weight of the trailer is the most important factor. A good weight-to-horsepower ratio is about 35:1, 35 lbs. of GCW (Gross Combined Weight) for every horsepower your engine develops. Multiply the engine's rated horsepower by 35 and subtract the weight of the car passengers and luggage. The result is the approximate ideal maximum weight you should tow, although a a numerically higher axle ratio can help compensate for heavier weight.

Hitch Weight

Figure the hitch weight to select a proper hitch. Hitch weight is usually 9-11% of the trailer gross weight and should be measured with the trailer loaded. Hitches fall into various categories: those that mount on the frame and rear bumper, the bolt-on or weld-on distribution type used for larger trailers. Axle mounted or clamp-on bumper hitches should never be used.

Check the gross weight rating of your trailer. Tongue weight is usually figured as 10% of gross trailer weight. Therefore, a trailer with a maximum gross weight of 2,000 lbs. will have a maximum tongue weight of 200 lbs. Class I trailers fall into this category. Class II trailers are those with a gross weight rating of 2,000-3,500 lbs., while Class III trailers fall into the 3,500-6,000 lbs. category. Class IV trailers are those over 6,000 lbs. and are for use with fifth wheel trucks, only.

When you've determined the hitch that you'll need, follow the manufacturer's installation instructions, exactly, especially when it comes to fastener torques. The hitch will subjected to a lot of stress and good hitches come with hardened bolts. Never substitute an inferior bolt for a hardened bolt.

Cooling

ENGINE

One of the most common, if not THE most common, problems associated with trailer towing is engine overheating. If you have a standard cooling system, without an expansion tank, you'll definitely need to get an aftermarket expansion tank kit, preferably one with at least a 2 quart capacity. These kits are easily installed on the radiator's overflow hose, and come with a pressure cap designed for expansion tanks.

Another helpful accessory is a Flex Fan. These fans are large diameter units are designed to provide more airflow at low speeds, with blades that have deeply cupped surfaces. The blades then flex, or flatten out, at high speed, when less cooling air is needed. These fans are far lighter in weight than stock fans, requiring less horsepower to drive them. Also, they are far quieter than stock fans. If you do decide to replace your stock fan with a flex fan, note that if your car has a fan clutch, a spacer will be needed between the flex fan and water pump hub.

Aftermarket engine oil coolers are helpful for prolonging engine oil life and reducing overall engine temperatures. Both of these factors increase engine life. While not absolutely necessary in towing Class I and some Class II trailers, they are recommended for heavier Class II and all Class III towing. Engine oil cooler systems consists of an adapter, screwed on in place of the oil filter, a remote filter mounting and a multi-tube, finned heat exchanger, which is mounted in front of the radiator or air conditioning condenser.

TRANSMISSION

An automatic transmission is usually recommended for trailer towing. Modern automatics have proven reliable and, of course, easy to operate, in trailer towing. The increased load of a trailer, however, causes an increase in the temperature of the automatic transmission fluid. Heat is the worst enemy of an automatic transmission. As the temperature of the fluid increases, the life of the fluid decreases.

It is essential, therefore, that you install an automatic transmission cooler. The cooler, which consists of a multi-tube, finned heat exchanger, is usually installed in front of the radiator or air conditioning compressor, and hooked in-line with the transmission cooler tank inlet line. Follow the cooler manufacturer's installation instructions.

Select a cooler of at least adequate capacity, based upon the combined gross weights of the car and trailer.

Cooler manufacturers recommend that you use an aftermarket cooler in addition to, and not instead of, the present cooling tank in your radiator. If you do want to use it in place of the radiator cooling tank, get a cooler at least two sizes larger than normally necessary.

➡**A transmission cooler can, sometimes, cause slow or harsh shifting in the transmission during cold weather, until the fluid has a chance to come up to normal operating temperature. Some coolers can be purchased with or retrofitted with a temperature bypass valve which will allow fluid flow through the cooler only when the fluid has reached above a certain operating temperature.**

Handling A Trailer

Towing a trailer with ease and safety requires a certain amount of experience. It's a good idea to learn the feel of a trailer by practicing turning, stopping and backing in an open area such as an empty parking lot.

PUSHING AND TOWING

Push Starting

This is the least recommended method of starting a car and should be used only in an extreme case. Chances of body damage are high, so be sure that the pushcar's bumper does not override your bumper. If your Chevrolet has an automatic transmission it cannot be push started. In an emergency, you can start a manual transmission car by pushing. With the bumpers evenly matched, get in your car, switch on the ignition, and place the gearshift in Second or Third gear. Do not engage the clutch. Start off slowly. When the speed of the car reaches about 15-20 mph, release the clutch.

When using a pushcar to get your vehicle rolling, it is also advisable to have the driver of the pushcar brake and let your car roll away from the push vehicle before you release the clutch. This will prevent the pushcar from rear-ending you should your car buck, not start or should you hit the brake for any reason.

Towing

The car can be towed safely from the front ONLY if the transmission is in **Neutral** and if speeds are restricted to 35 mph or less. The car must either be towed with the rear wheels off the ground or the driveshaft disconnected if: towing speeds are to exceed 35 mph, towing distance is over 50 miles, or transmission/rear axle problems exist.

When towing the car on its front wheels, the steering wheel must be secured in a straight-ahead position and the steering column unlocked. Tire-to-ground clearance should not exceed 6 in. during towing.

JUMP STARTING A DEAD BATTERY

▶ **See Figure 126**

Whenever a vehicle must be jump started, precautions must be followed in order to prevent the possibility of personal injury. Remember that batteries contain a small amount of explosive hydrogen gas which is a byproduct of battery charging. Sparks should always be avoided when working around batteries, especially when attaching jumper cables. To minimize the possibility of accidental sparks, follow the procedure carefully.

❋❋CAUTION

NEVER hook the batteries up in a series circuit or the entire electrical system will go up in smoke, especially the starter!

Cars equipped with a diesel engine utilize two 12 volt batteries, one on either side of the engine compartment. The batteries are connected in a parallel circuit (positive terminal to positive terminal, negative terminal to negative terminal). Hooking the batteries up in parallel circuit increases battery cranking power without increasing total battery voltage output. Output remains at 12 volts. On the other hand, hooking two 12 volt batteries up in a series circuit (positive terminal to negative terminal, positive terminal to negative terminal) increases total battery output to 24 volts (12 volts plus 12 volts).

Jump Starting Precautions

1. Be sure that both batteries are of the same voltage. Most vehicles covered by this manual and most vehicles on the road today utilize a 12 volt charging system.
2. Be sure that both batteries are of the same polarity (have the same terminal, in most cases NEGATIVE grounded).
3. Be sure that the vehicles are not touching or a short could occur.
4. On serviceable batteries, be sure the vent cap holes are not obstructed.
5. Do not smoke or allow sparks anywhere near the batteries.
6. In cold weather, make sure the battery electrolyte is not frozen. This can occur more readily in a battery that has been in a state of discharge.
7. Do not allow electrolyte to contact your skin or clothing.

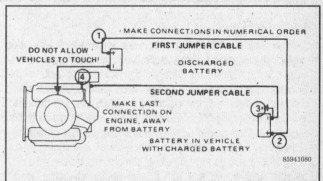

Fig. 126 Connect the jumper cables to the batteries and engine in the order shown

Jump Starting Procedure

1. Make sure that the voltages of the 2 batteries are the same. Most batteries and charging systems are of the 12 volt variety.
2. Pull the jumping vehicle (with the good battery) into a position so the jumper cables can reach the dead battery and that vehicle's engine. Make sure that the vehicles do NOT touch.
3. Place the transmissions of both vehicles in **NEUTRAL** or **PARK**, as applicable, then firmly set their parking brakes.

➡**If necessary for safety reasons, both vehicle's hazard lights may be operated throughout the entire procedure without significantly increasing the difficulty of jumping the dead battery.**

4. Turn all lights and accessories off on both vehicles. Make sure the ignition switches on both vehicles are turned to the **OFF** position.

5. Cover the battery cell caps with a rag, but do not cover the terminals.

6. Make sure the terminals on both batteries are clean and free of corrosion or proper electrical connection will be impeded. If necessary, clean the battery terminals before proceeding.

7. Identify the positive (+) and negative (-) terminals on both battery posts.

8. Connect the first jumper cable to the positive (+) terminal of the dead battery, then connect the other end of that cable to the positive (+) terminal of the booster (good) battery.

9. Connect one end of the other jumper cable to the negative (-) terminal of the booster battery and the other cable clamp to an engine bolt head, alternator bracket or other solid, metallic point on the dead batteries engine. Try to pick a ground on the engine that is positioned away from the battery in order to minimize the possibility of the 2 clamps touching should one loosen during the procedure. DO NOT connect this clamp to the negative (-) terminal of the bad battery.

❈❈CAUTION

Be very careful to keep the jumper cables away from moving parts (cooling fan, belts, etc.) on both engines.

JACKING

▶ **See Figures 127, 128, 129, 130, 131 and 132**

There are 2 different types of jacks which may be found in these vehicles. Most of the earlier vehicles were equipped with a bumper jack from the factory. This jack utilized slots in the bumper to raise the car. Later vehicles were equipped with a scissor jack that used a locating pin which was inserted into the vehicle's frame rails and the vehicle was lifted using the frame rail. The jack is used on the frame rail just behind or in front of the wheel well, whichever direction is just slightly toward the center of the car when compared with the wheel wells. The jack supplied with the car should never be used for any service operation other than tire changing. Never get under the car while it is supported by only a jack. Always block the wheels when changing tires.

❈❈WARNING

Never get underneath a car that is supported only by a jack or by cinder blocks. A jack may become released or could be knocked over and drop the vehicle rapidly. Likewise, cinderblocks could crumble with little or no warning. In either case, the vehicle could be dropped suddenly and violently causing severe personal injury or death to anyone underneath it.

Service operations in this book often require that one end or both ends of the car be raised and safely supported. The ideal

10. Check to make sure that the cables are routed away from any moving parts, then start the donor vehicle's engine. Run the engine at moderate speed for several minutes to allow the dead battery a chance to receive some initial charge.

11. With the donor vehicle's engine still running slightly above idle, try to start the vehicle with the dead battery. Crank the engine for no more than 10 seconds at a time and let the starter cool for at least 20 seconds between tries. If the vehicle does not start in 3 tries, it is likely that something else is also wrong or that the battery needs additional time to charge.

12. Once the vehicle is started, allow it to run at idle for a few seconds to make sure that it is properly operating.

13. Turn on the headlights, heater blower and, if equipped, the rear defroster of both vehicles in order to reduce the severity of voltage spikes and subsequent risk of damage to the vehicles' electrical systems when the cables are disconnected.

14. Carefully disconnect the cables in the reverse order of connection. Start with the negative cable that is attached to the engine ground, then the negative cable on the donor battery. Disconnect the positive cable from the donor battery and finally, disconnect the positive cable from the formerly dead battery. Be careful when disconnecting the cables from the positive terminals not to allow the alligator clips to touch any metal on either vehicle or a short and sparks will occur.

method, of course, would be a to use a hydraulic hoist. Since this is beyond both the resource and requirement of the do-it-yourselfer, a small hydraulic, screw or scissors jack or floor jack will raise the vehicle sufficiently for almost all procedures in this guide. But the vehicle must still be supported by two sturdy jackstands if you intend to work under the car at any time. An alternate method of raising the car would be drive-on ramps. These are available commercially or can be fabricated from heavy boards or steel. Be sure to block the wheels when using ramps. Never use concrete blocks to support the car. They may break if the load is not evenly distributed.

Regardless of the method of jacking or hoisting the car, there are only certain areas of the undercarriage and suspension you can safely use to support it. The front and rear crossmembers and the side frame rails and generally safe areas by which to support these vehicles. But be careful not to contact and damage other components such as stabilizer bars or the exhaust system. Also, it is advisable to protect the vehicle's undercarriage from scratches that will promote corrosion. To help prevent unnecessary scratches a block of wood should always be positioned between the jack or jackstand and the vehicle. Refer to the accompanying illustrations and make sure that only the noted areas are used to lift the car. In addition, be especially careful on vehicles built after 1974 that you do not damage the catalytic converter. Remember that various cross braces and supports on a lift can sometimes contact low hanging parts of the car.

Fig. 127 The vehicle's bumper jack should never be used for anything more than an emergency tire change

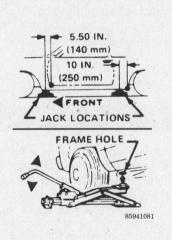

Fig. 128 Later model vehicles are equipped with a compact jack that utilizes a pin which fits into frame holes

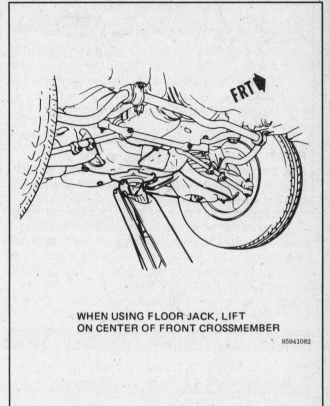

WHEN USING FLOOR JACK, LIFT
ON CENTER OF FRONT CROSSMEMBER

Fig. 129 A floor jack can be used at the center of the front crossmember

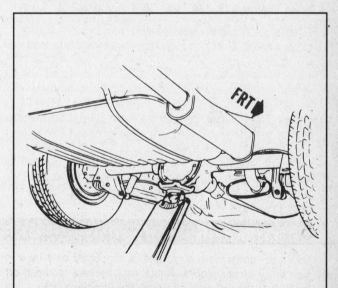

WHEN USING FLOOR JACK, LIFT
AT CENTER OF DIFFERENTIAL HOUSING—
NOT ON STABILIZER BAR (IF PRESENT)

Fig. 130 A floor jack can also be used at the center of the rear axle housing. If equipped with a rear stabilizer bar, make sure the jack does not contact and subsequently damage the stabilizer bar

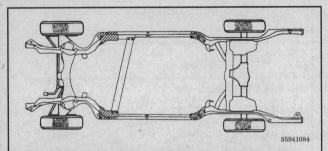

Fig. 131 Additional vehicle jacking and lifting points. Note that floor jacks may be used on the lined areas, but it is advisable to protect the vehicle's frame using a block of wood

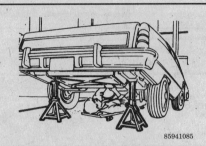

Fig. 132 Always use a pair of sturdy jackstands to support the vehicle. Never use cinder blocks or tire changing jacks to support the vehicle while you are working under it.

MAINTENANCE INTERVALS CHART FOR 1964-76 GASOLINE VEHICLES

Interval At Which Services Are To Be Performed	Service
LUBRICATION AND GENERAL MAINTENANCE	
Every 6 months or 7,500 miles	*CHASSIS-Lubricate ●*FLUID LEVELS-Check *ENGINE OIL-Change
At first oil change-then every 2nd	*ENGINE OIL FILTER-Replace (V-6 Replace each oil change)
See Explanation of Maintenance Schedule	TIRES-Rotate DIFFERENTIAL
Every 12 months	AIR CONDITIONING SYSTEM-Check charge & hose condition. TEMPMATIC AIR FILTER-Replace every other year.
Every 12 months or 15,000 miles	*COOLING SYSTEM-See Explanation of Maintenance Schedule
Every 30,000 miles	WHEEL BEARINGS-Clean and repack *AUTOMATIC TRANS.-Change fluid and service filter MANUAL STEERING GEAR-Check seals CLUTCH CROSS SHAFT-Lubricate
SAFETY MAINTENANCE	
Every 6 months or 7,500 miles	TIRES AND WHEELS-Check condition *EXHAUST SYSTEM-Check condition of system *DRIVE BELTS-Ck. cond. & adjustment. Replace every 30,000 miles FRONT AND REAR SUSPENSION & STEERING SYSTEM-Ck. cond. BRAKES AND POWER STEERING-Check all lines and hoses
Every 12 months or 15,000 miles	DRUM BRAKES AND PARKING BRAKE-Check condition of linings; adjust parking brake THROTTLE LINKAGE-Check operation and condition UNDERBODY-Flush and check condition BUMPERS-Check condition
EMISSION CONTROL MAINTENANCE	
At 1st 6 months or 7,500 miles-then at 18 month/22,500 mile Intervals Thereafter	THERMOSTATICALLY CONTROLLED AIR CLEANER-Check operation CARBURETOR CHOKE-Check operation ENGINE IDLE SPEED ADJUSTMENT EFE VALVE-Check operation CARBURETOR-Torque attaching bolts or nuts to manifold
Every 12 months or 15,000 miles	CARBURETOR FUEL INLET FILTER-Replace VACUUM ADVANCE SYSTEM AND HOSES-Check oper. PCV SYSTEMS-See Explanation of Maintenance Schedule
Every 18 months or 22,500 miles	IDLE STOP SOLENOID OR DASHPOT-Check operation SPARK PLUG AND IGNITION COIL WIRES-Inspect and clean
Every 22,500 miles	SPARK PLUGS-Replace ENGINE TIMING ADJUSTMENT & DISTRIBUTOR CHECK
Every 24 months or 30,000 miles	ECS SYSTEM-See Explanation of Maintenance Schedule FUEL CAP, TANK AND LINES-Check condition
Every 30,000 miles	AIR CLEANER ELEMENT-Replace

* Also Required Emission Control Maintenance
● Also a Safety Service

85941086

MAINTENANCE INTERVALS CHART FOR 1977 AND LATER GASOLINE VEHICLES

When to Perform Services (Months or Miles, Whichever Occurs First)	Services
LUBRICATION AND GENERAL MAINTENANCE	
Every 12 months or 7,500 miles (12 000 km)	● CHASSIS-Lubricate ● FLUID LEVELS-Check CLUTCH PEDAL FREE TRAVEL-Check/Adjust
See Explanation of Maintenance Schedule	*ENGINE OIL-Change *ENGINE OIL FILTER-Replace TIRES-Rotation (Radial Tires) REAR AXLE OR FINAL DRIVE-Check lube
Every 12 months or 15,000 miles (24 000 km)	*COOLING SYSTEM-See Explanation of Maintenance Schedule
Every 30,000 miles (48 000 km)	WHEEL BEARINGS-Repack CLUTCH CROSS SHAFT-Lubricate
See Explanation	AUTOMATIC TRANSMISSION-Change fluid and service filter
SAFETY MAINTENANCE	
Every 12 months or 7,500 miles (12 000 km)	TIRES, WHEELS AND DISC BRAKES-Check condition *EXHAUST SYSTEM-Check condition SUSPENSION & STEERING SYSTEM-Check condition BRAKES AND POWER STEERING-Check all lines and hoses
Every 12 months or 15,000 miles (24 000 km)	*DRIVE BELTS-Check condition and adjustment (1) DRUM BRAKES AND PARKING BRAKE-Check condition of linings; adjust parking brake THROTTLE LINKAGE-Check operation and condition BUMPERS-Check condition *FUEL CAP, TANK AND LINES-Check
EMISSION CONTROL MAINTENANCE	
At first 6 MOnths or 7,500 Miles (12 000 km)–Then at 24-Month/ 30,000 Mile (48 000 km) Intervals as Indicated in Log, Except Choke Which Requires Service at 45,000 Miles (72 000 km)	CARBURETOR CHOKE & HOSES-Check (2) ENGINE IDLE SPEED-Check adjustment (2) EFE SYSTEM-Check operation (If so equipped) CARBURETOR-Torque attaching bolts or nuts to manifold (2)
Every 30,000 miles (48 000 km)	THERMOSTATICALLY CONTROLLED AIR CLEANER-Check operation VACUUM ADVANCE SYSTEM AND HOSES-Check (3) SPARK PLUG WIRES-Check IDLE STOP SOLENOID AND/OR DASH POT OR ISC-Check operation SPARK PLUGS-Replace (2) ENGINE TIMING ADJUSTMENT AND DISTRIBUTOR-Check AIR CLEANER AND PCV FILTER ELEMENT-Replace (2) PCV VALVE-Replace EGR VALVE-Service

● Also a Safety Service
* Also an Emission Control Service
(1) In California, a separately driven air pump belt check is recommended but not required at 15,000 miles (24 000 km) and 45,000 miles (72 000 km).
(2) Only these emission control maintenance items are considered to be required maintenance as defined by the California Air Resources Board (ARB) regulation and are, according to such regulation, the minimum maintenance an owner in California must perform to fulfill the minimum requirements of the emission warranty. All other emission maintenance items are recommended maintenance as defined by such regulation. General Motors urges that all emission control maintenance items be performed.
(3) Not applicable on vehicles equipped with electronic spark timing (EST).

85941087

MAINTENANCE INTERVALS CHART FOR DIESEL VEHICLES

When to Perform Services (Months or Miles, Whichever Occurs First)	Services
LUBRICATION AND GENERAL MAINTENANCE	
Every 5,000 Miles (8 000 km)	*ENGINE OIL-Change *OIL FILTER-Change ●CHASSIS-Lubricate ●FLUID LEVELS-Check
See Explanation	TIRES-Rotation REAR AXLE OR FINAL DRIVE-Check lube
Every 12 months or 15,000 miles (24 000 km) Every 30,000 miles (48 000 km)	*COOLING SYSTEM-Check *CRANKCASE VENTILATION-Service WHEEL BEARINGS-Repack
See Explanation	AUTOMATIC TRANSMISSION-Change fluid and filter
SAFETY MAINTENANCE	
At first 5,000 miles (8 000 km) Then at 15,000/30,000/45,000 miles	*EXHAUST SYSTEM-Check condition
Every 12 months or 10,000 miles (16 000 km)	TIRES, WHEEL AND DISC BRAKE-Check SUSPENSION AND STEERING-Check BRAKES AND POWER STEERING-Check
Every 5,000 Miles (8 000 km)	*DRIVE BELTS-Check condition and adjustment
Every 12 months or 15,000 miles (24 000 km)	DRUM BRAKES AND PARKING BRAKE-Check THROTTLE LINKAGE-Check operation BUMPERS-Check condition
EMISSION CONTROL MAINTENANCE	
At first 5,000 miles (8 000 km) Then at 15,000/30,000/45,000 miles	EXHAUST PRESSURE REGULATOR VALVE
At first 5,000 miles (8 000 km) Then at 30,000 miles (48 000 km)	ENGINE IDLE SPEED-Adjust
Every 30,000 miles (48 000 km)	AIR CLEANER-Replace FUEL FILTER-Replace

●Also a Safety Service
*Also on Emission Control Service

85941088

CAPACITIES

Year	Engine No. Cyl. Displacement (cu. in.)	Engine Crankcase Add 1 qt. for New Filter	Transmission Pts. to Refill After Draining Manual 3-Speed	4-Speed	Automatic•	Drive Axle (pts.)	Gasoline Tank (gals.)	Cooling System (qts.) With Heater	With A/C
1964	6-194 6-230	4	2	—	15.2①	3.5	20	11.5	12
	8-283	4	2	2.5	15.2①	3.5	20	17	18
	8-327	4	2	2.5	15.2①	3.5	20	16②	18②
1965	6-194 6-230	4	2	—	15.2①	4	20	12	12
	8-283	4	2	2.5	15.2①	4	20	17	18
	8-327	4	2	2.5	15.2①	4	20	16②	18②
1966	6-194	4	2	—	6③	3.5	20	12	12
	6-230	4	2	2.5	6③	3.5	20	12	12
	8-283	4	2	2.5	6③	3.5	20	16	18
	8-327	4	3④	3	6.5	3.5⑤	20	15	17⑥
	8-396	4	3④	3	6.5③	3.5⑤	20	23	23
1967	6-230	4	3④	3④	6③	3.5	20	14	14
	6-250	4	3④	3④	6③	3.5	20	13	14
	8-283	4	3④	3④	6③	3.5	20	16	17
	8-327	4	3④	3④	6③	3.5	20	15	18
	8-396	4	3④	3④	6③	3.5	20	23	23
1968	6-230	4	3④	3④	6③	3.5	20	12	12
	6-250	4	3④	3④	6③	3.5	20	12	12
	8-307	4	3④	3④	6③	3.5	20	17	17
	8-327	4	2.5	3④	6③	3.5	20	16	16
	8-350	4	2.5	3④	6③	3.5	20	16	16
	8-396	4	2.5	3④	6⑦③	3.5	20	23	23
1969	6-230	4	3④	—	6⑧③	3.5⑤	20	13	13
	6-250	4	3④	—	6⑧③	3.5⑤	20	13	13
	8-307	4	3④	3④	6⑧③	3.5⑤	20	17	18
	8-350	4	3④	3④	6⑧③	3.5⑤	20	16	17
	8-396	4	3④	3④	8③	3.5⑤	20	23	24
1970	6-230	4	3	—	6⑧③	3.75⑨	20⑩	12	13
	6-250	4	3	—	6⑧③	3.75⑨	20⑩	12	13
	8-307	4	3	—	6⑧③	3.75⑨	20⑩	12	13
	8-350	4	3	3	6⑧⑪③	3.75⑨	20⑩	16	16
	8-400	4	3	3	8③	3.75⑨	20⑩	16	16
	8-396	4	3	3	8③	3.75⑨	20⑩	23	24
	8-402	4	3	3	8③	3.75⑨	20⑩	23	24
	8-454	4	3	3	8③	3.75⑨	20⑩	22	23
1971	6-250	4	3	—	6③	3.75	19⑩	12	—
	8-307	4	3	—	6⑧③	3.75	19⑩	15	16
	8-350	4	3	3	6⑧③	3.75	19⑩	16	16
	8-402	4	3	3	8③	3.75	19⑩	23	23
	8-454	4	—	3	8③	3.75	19⑩	22	23

85941089

CAPACITIES (continued)

Year	Engine No. Cyl. Displacement (cu. in.)	Engine Crankcase Add 1 qt. for New Filter	Transmission Pts. to Refill After Draining			Drive Axle (pts.)	Gasoline Tank (gals.)	Cooling System (qts.)	
			Manual					With Heater	With A/C
			3-Speed	4-Speed	Automatic•				
1972	6-250	4	3	—	6⑧③	4.25	19⑩	12	—
	8-307	4	3	—	6⑧③	4.25	19⑩	15	16
	8-350	4	3	3	6⑧③	4.25⑫	19⑩	16	16
	8-402	4	—	3	8③	4.25⑫	19⑩	24	24
	8-454	4	—	3	8③	4.25⑫	19⑩	23	24
1973	6-250	4	3	—	6⑧③	4.25	22	12.5	—
	8-307	4	3	—	5③	4.25	22	16	17
	8-350	4	3	3	5③	4.25	22	16	17
	8-454	4	—	3	8③	4.25⑫	22	23	24
1974	6-250	4	3	—	8③	4.25	22	12.5	—
	8-350	4	3	3	8③	4.25	22	16	17
	8-400	4	—	—	8③	4.25⑫	22	16	17
	8-454	4	—	3	9③	4.9	22	23	24
1975	6-250	4	3	—	8③	4.25	22	14	16
	8-350	4	3	3	8③	4.25	22	17	18
	8-400	4	—	—	8③	4.25⑫	22	17③	18
	8-454	4	—	3	9③	4.9	22	23	23
1976–77	6-250	4	3	—	8③	4.25	22	15	17
	8-305	4	3	—	8③	4.25	22	17	18
	8-350	4	—	3	8③	4.25	22	17	18
	8-400	4	—	—	8③	4.25	22	17	18
1978	V6-200	4	3	—	6③	3.5	⑯	16.8	18.8
	V6-231	4⑮	3	3	6③	3.5	⑯	14.7	14.7
	6-250	4	3	—	6③	3.5	⑯	14.6	14.6
	8-305	4	—	3	6③	3.5⑭	⑯	19.2	19.2
	8-350	4	—	3	6③	3.5⑭	⑯	19.2	19.2
1979	V6-200	4	3	—	8③	3.25	18	18.5	18.5
	V6-231	4⑮	3	—	8③	3.25	18	15.5	15.5
	8-267	4	—	3.4	8③	3.25	18	19.2	19.2
	8-305	4	—	3.4	8③	3.5⑭	18	19.2	19.2
	8-350	4	—	3.4	8③	3.5⑭	18	19.2	19.2
1980–81	V6-229	4⑮	3	—	8③⑰	3.25	18	18.5	18.5
	V6-231	4⑮	3	—	8③⑰	3.25	18	15.5	15.5
	8-267	4	—	—	8③⑱	3.25	18	21	21
	8-305	4	—	3.4	8③⑱	3.5⑭	18	19	19

85941090

CAPACITIES (continued)

Year	Engine No. Cyl. Displacement (cu. in.)	Engine Crankcase Add 1 qt. for New Filter	Transmission Pts. to Refill After Draining			Drive Axle (pts.)	Gasoline Tank (gals.)	Cooling System (qts.)	
			Manual					With Heater	With A/C
			3-Speed	4-Speed	Automatic•				
1982–84	V6-229	4 ⑮	—	—	7 ⑲	3.5 ⑭	⑬ ⑳	12 ㉑	13 ㉑
	V6-231	4 ⑮	—	—	7 ⑲	3.5 ⑭	⑬ ⑳	12 ㉑	13 ㉑
	8-267	4	—	—	7 ⑲	3.5 ⑭	⑬ ⑳	16.75	16.75 ㉒
	8-305	4	—	—	7 ⑲	3.5 ⑭	⑬ ⑳	15.5	15.5 ㉒
	8-350	4	—	—	7 ⑲	3.5 ⑭	⑬ ⑳	19.2	19.2
	V6-263 Diesel	6	—	—	7 ⑲	3.5 ⑭	⑳	13.4	14.4
	V8-350 Diesel	6	—	—	7 ⑲	3.5 ⑭	⑳	18.3	19.3
1985–88	V6-262	4 ⑮	—	—	7 ㉓	3.5 ⑭	17.6	13.1	13.1
	V8-305	4	—	—	7 ㉓	3.5 ⑭	18.1	16.7	16.7

•Specifications do not include torque converter
① Figure given is for dry refill
② 18 qts.—300 hp eng.; 19 qts.—350 hp eng.
③ Figure given is for drain and refill
④ 3.5 pts. with heavy duty trans.
⑤ 4 pts. with 8.875 in. ring gear
⑥ 16 qts.—350 hp eng.
⑦ 8 pts.—THM 400
⑧ 5 pts.—THM 350
⑨ 4.25 pts. with 8.875 in. ring gear
⑩ 18 gals.—station wagon
⑪ 8 pts.—360 hp eng.
⑫ 4.9 pts. with 8.875 in. ring gear
⑬ 18 gals.—Monte Carlo
⑭ 4.25 pts.—8.5 in. ring gear; 5.4 pts. with 8.75 in. ring gear
⑮ Figure is the same with or without a filter change
⑯ 18.1—Malibu, El Camino
    18.2—Malibu station wagon
    17.5—Monte Carlo
⑰ 7.0 pts.—1981
⑱ 6.0 pts.—1981
⑲ 6.0 pts.—THM 350
⑳ 25 gals.—Malibu
    22 gals.—Malibu station wagon
    27 gals.—Diesel coupe
    22 gals.—Diesel station wagon
㉑ Chevrolet-built V6; 15 qts. (heater) and 16 qts. (A/C) with Buick V6
㉒ Monte Carlo 21 qts., 267 V8; 19 qts. 305 V8
㉓ 10.0 pts.—THM 700-4R

85941091

2

ENGINE PERFORMANCE AND TUNE-UP

TUNE-UP PROCEDURES

In order to extract the full measure of performance and economy from your engine it is essential that it is properly tuned at regular intervals. A regular tune-up will keep your car's engine running smoothly and will prevent the annoying breakdowns and poor performance associated with an untuned engine.

➡ **All 1964-74 models use a conventional breaker point ignition system. In 1975, Chevrolet switched to a full electronic ignition system known as HEI.**

A complete tune-up should be performed at least every 15,000 miles (12,000 miles for early models) or twelve months, whichever comes first.

➡ **Because of improved materials and engineering, 1981 and later models have an increased tune-up interval of 30,000 miles.**

This appropriate interval should be halved if the car is operated under severe conditions such as trailer towing, prolonged idling, start-and-stop driving, or if a driveability problem such as hard starting or poor running is noticed. It is assumed that the routine maintenance described in Section 1 has been kept up, as this will have a decided effect on the results of a tune-up. All of the applicable steps of a tune-up should be followed in order, as the result is a cumulative one. Any adjustment made to the engine is normally performed only when it will not be affected by other adjustments that are yet to be made during the tune-up.

If the specifications on the underhood tune-up sticker in the engine compartment of your car disagree with the Tune-Up Specifications chart in this Section, the figures on the sticker must be used. The sticker often reflects changes made during the production run or revised information that apply to the particular systems in that vehicle.

Spark Plugs

▶ See Figures 1, 2 and 3

A typical spark plug consists of a metal shell surrounding a ceramic insulator. A metal electrode extends downward through the center of the insulator and protrudes a small distance. Located at the end of the plug and attached to the side of the outer metal shell is the side electrode. The side electrode bends in at a 90° angle so that its tip is just past and parallel to the tip of the center electrode. The distance between these two electrodes (measured in thousandths of an inch or hundredths of a millimeter) is called the spark plug gap. The spark plug does not produce a spark but instead provides a gap across which the current can arc. The coil produces anywhere from 20,000-25,000 volts (the HEI transistorized ignition produces considerably more voltage than the standard type, approximately 50,000 volts) which travels through the wires to the spark plugs. The current passes along the center electrode and jumps the gap to the side electrode, and in doing so, ignites the fuel/air mixture in the combustion chamber. All plugs used since 1969 have a resistor built into the center electrode to reduce interference to any nearby radio and television receivers. The resistor also cuts down on

erosion of plug electrodes caused by excessively long sparking. Resistor spark plug wiring is original equipment on all models.

Spark plug life and efficiency depend upon condition of the engine and the temperatures to which the plug is exposed. Combustion chamber temperatures are affected by many factors such as compression ratio of the engine, fuel/air mixtures, exhaust emission equipment, and the type of driving you do. Spark plugs are designed and classified by number according to the heat range at which they will operate most efficiently. The amount of heat that the plug absorbs is determined by the length of the lower insulator. The longer the insulator (it extends farther into the engine), the hotter the plug will operate; the shorter it is, the cooler it will operate. A plug that has a short path for heat transfer and remains too cool will quickly accumulate deposits of oil and carbon since it is not hot enough to burn them off. This leads to plug fouling and consequently to misfiring. A plug that has a long path of heat transfer will have no deposits but, due to the excessive heat, the electrodes will burn away quickly and, in some instances, pre-ignition may result. Pre-ignition takes place when plug tips get so hot that they glow sufficiently to ignite the fuel/air mixture before the spark does. This early ignition will usually cause a pinging (sounding much like castanets) during low speeds and heavy loads. In severe cases, the heat may become enough to start the fuel/air mixture burning throughout the combustion chamber rather than just to the front of the plug as in normal operation. At this time, the piston is rising in the cylinder mak-

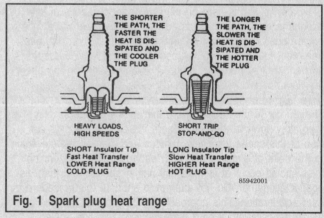

Fig. 1 Spark plug heat range

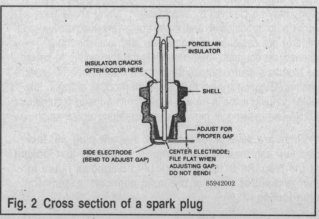

Fig. 2 Cross section of a spark plug

ing its compression stroke. The burning mass is compressed and an explosion results producing tremendous pressure. Something has to give, and it does; pistons are often damaged. Obviously, this detonation (explosion) is a destructive condition that can be avoided by installing a spark plug designed and specified for your particular engine.

A set of spark plugs usually requires replacement after 10,000-12,000 miles depending on the type of driving (this interval has been increased to 22,500 miles for all 1975-79 models and 30,000 miles for all 1980 and later models). The electrode on a new spark plug has a sharp edge but, with use, this edge becomes rounded by erosion causing the plug gap to increase. In normal operation, plug gap increases about 0.001 in. (0.0254mm) for every 1,000-2,000 miles. As the gap increases, the plug's voltage requirement also increases. It requires a greater voltage to jump the wider gap and about 2-4 times as much voltage to fire a plug at high speed and acceleration than at idle.

The higher voltage produced by the HEI ignition coil is one of the primary reasons for the prolonged replacement interval for spark plugs in 1975 and later cars. A consistently hotter spark prevents the fouling of plugs for much longer than could normally be expected; this spark is also able to jump across a larger gap more efficiently than a spark from a conventional system. However, even plugs used with the HEI system wear after time in the engine.

Worn plugs become obvious during acceleration. Voltage requirement is greatest during acceleration and a plug with an enlarged gap may require more voltage than the coil is able to produce. As a result, the engine misses and sputters until acceleration is reduced. Reducing acceleration reduces the plug's voltage requirement and the engine runs smoother. Slow, city driving is hard on plugs. The long periods of idle experienced in traffic creates an overly rich gas mixture. The engine does not run fast enough to completely burn the gas and, consequently, the plugs become fouled with gas deposits and engine idle becomes rough. In many cases, driving under the right conditions can effectively clean these fouled plugs.

To help clean fouled plugs in a running engine, first accelerate you car to the speed where the engine begins to miss and then slow down to the point where the engine smooths out. Run at this speed for a few minutes and then accelerate again to the point of engine miss. With each repetition this engine miss should occur at increasingly higher speeds and then disappear altogether. Do not attempt to shortcut this procedure by hard acceleration. This approach will compound problems by fusing deposits into a hard permanent glaze. Dirty, fouled plugs may be cleaned by sandblasting. Many shops have a spark plug sandblaster and there are a few inexpensive models that are designed for home use and available from aftermarket sources. After sandblasting, the electrode should be filed to a sharp, square shape and then gapped to specifications. Gapping a plug too close will produce a rough idle while gapping it too wide will increase its voltage requirement and cause missing at high speed and during acceleration.

➡️**There are several reasons why a spark plug will foul and you can usually learn what is at fault by just looking at the plug. Refer to the spark plug diagnosis figure in this section for some of the most common reasons for plug fouling.**

The type of driving you do may require a change in spark plug heat range. If the majority of your driving is done in the city and rarely at high speeds, plug fouling may necessitate changing to a plug with a heat range one number higher than that specified by the car manufacturer. For example, a 1970 Chevelle with a 350 cu. in. (300 hp) engine requires an R44 plug. Frequent city driving may foul these plugs making engine operation rough. An R45 is the next hottest plug in the AC heat range (the higher the AC number, the hotter the plug) and its insulator is longer than the R44 so that it can absorb and retain more heat than the shorter R44. This hotter R45 burns off deposits even at low city speeds but would be too hot for prolonged turnpike driving. Using this plug at high speed would create dangerous pre-ignition. On the other hand, if the aforementioned Chevelle were used almost exclusively for long distance high speed driving, the specified R44 might be too hot resulting in rapid electrode wear and dangerous pre-ignition. In this case, it might be wise to change to a colder R43. If the car is used for abnormal driving (as in the examples above), or the engine has been modified for higher performance, then a change to a plug with a different heat range may be necessary. For a modified car it is always wise to go to a colder plug as a protection against pre-ignition. It will require more frequent plug cleaning, but destructive detonation during acceleration will be avoided.

REMOVAL

◆ **See Figures 4, 5, 6, 7 and 8**

When you're removing spark plugs, you should work on one at a time. Don't start by removing the plug wires all at once because unless you number them, or they're going to get mixed up. On some models though, it will be more convenient for you to remove all the wires before you start to work on the plugs. If this is necessary, take a minute before you begin and number the wires with tape before you take them off. The time you spend doing this will pay off later when it comes time to reconnect the wires to the plugs.

1. Disconnect the negative battery cable from the negative battery terminal.

2. Twist the spark plug boot slightly in either direction to break loose the seal, then remove the boot from the plug. You may also use a plug wire removal tool designed especially for this purpose. Do not pull on the wire itself or you may separate the plug connector from the end of the wire. When the wire has been removed, take a wire brush and clean the area around the plug. An evaporative spray cleaner such as those designed for brake applications will also work well. Make sure that all the foreign material is removed so that none will enter the cylinder after the plug has been removed.

➡️**If you have access to a compressor, use the air hose to blow all material away from the spark plug bores before loosening the plug. Always protect your eyes with safety glasses when using compressed air.**

3. Remove the plug using the proper size socket, extensions, and universals as necessary. Be careful to hold the socket or the extension close to the plug with your free hand as this will help lessen the possibility of applying a shear force which might snap the spark plug in half. If the cylinder heads

Tracking Arc
High voltage arcs between a fouling deposit on the insulator tip and spark plug shell. This ignites the fuel/air mixture at some point along the insulator tip, retarding the ignition timing which causes a power and fuel loss.

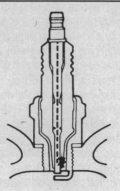

Wide Gap
Spark plug electrodes are worn so that the high voltage charge cannot arc across the electrodes. Improper gapping of electrodes on new or "cleaned" spark plugs could cause a similar condition. Fuel remains unburned and a power loss results.

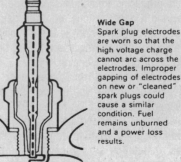

Flashover
A damaged spark plug boot, along with dirt and moisture, could permit the high voltage charge to short over the insulator to the spark plug shell or the engine. AC's buttress insulator design helps prevent high voltage flashover.

Fouled Spark Plug
Deposits that have formed on the insulator tip may become conductive and provide a "shunt" path to the shell. This prevents the high voltage from arcing between the electrodes. A power and fuel loss is the result.

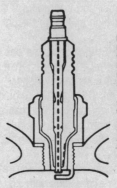

Bridged Electrodes
Fouling deposits between the electrodes "ground out" the high voltage needed to fire the spark plug. The arc between the electrodes does not occur and the fuel air mixture is not ignited. This causes a power loss and exhausting of raw fuel.

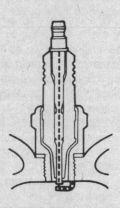

Cracked Insulator
A crack in the spark plug insulator could cause the high voltage charge to "ground out." Here, the spark does not jump the electrode gap and the fuel air mixture is not ignited. This causes a power loss and raw fuel is exhausted.

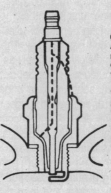

85942003

Fig. 3 Spark plug diagnosis

on the engine are original, then for all 1964-69 engines, and all V8s 1964-71, use a $\frac{13}{16}$ in. spark plug socket. 6-cylinder engines for 1970 and V8s from 1972 and later are equipped with tapered seat plugs which require a $\frac{5}{8}$ in. socket.

4. If removing the plug is difficult, drip some penetrating oil on the plug threads, allow it to work, then remove the plug. Also, be sure that the socket is straight on the plug, especially on those hard to reach plugs. Again, if the socket is cocked to 1 side a shear force may be applied to the plug and could snap the plug in half.

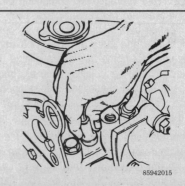

85942015

Fig. 4 Twist and pull on the rubber boot to disconnect the spark plug wires; never pull on the wire itself

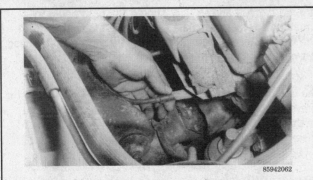

Fig. 5 Grasp the wire boot, twist it, and pull it from the spark plug

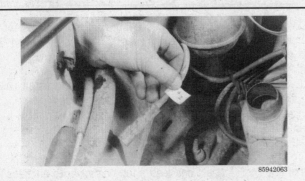

Fig. 6 Label the spark plug wires to assure proper installation

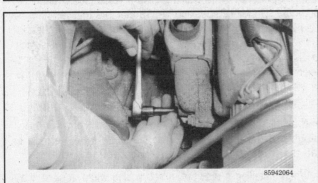

Fig. 7 Remove the spark plug using a suitable socket and driver

INSPECTION

▶ See Figures 9, 10 and 11

Check the plugs for deposits and wear. If they are not going to be replaced, clean the plugs thoroughly. Remember that any kind of deposit will decrease the efficiency of the plug. Plugs can be cleaned on a spark plug cleaning machine, which can sometimes be found in service stations, or you can do an acceptable job of cleaning with a stiff brush. If the plugs are cleaned, the electrodes must be filed flat. Use an ignition points file, not an emery board or the like, which will leave deposits. The electrodes must be filed perfectly flat with sharp edges; rounded edges reduce the spark plug voltage by as much as 50%.

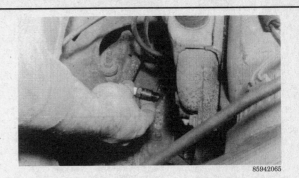

Fig. 8 Once the plug is loosened, finish unthreading it by hand and remove it from the cylinder head

Check and adjust the spark plug gap immediately before installation. The ground electrode (the L-shaped one connected to the body of the plug) must be parallel to the center electrode and the specified size gauge (see Tune-Up Specifications) should pass through the gap with a slight drag. Always check the gap on new plugs, too; since they are not always set correctly at the factory.

Do not use a flat feeler gauge when measuring the gap on used plugs, because the reading may be inaccurate. The ground electrode on a used plug is often rounded on the face closest to the center electrode. A flat gauge will not be able to accurately measure this distance as well as a wire gauge. Most gapping tools usually have a bending tool attached. This tool may be used to adjust the side electrode until the proper distance is obtained. Never attempt to move or bend the center electrode or spark plug damage will likely occur. Also,

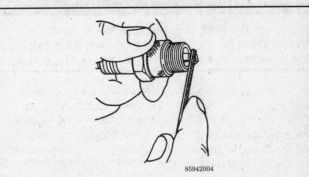

Fig. 9 Spark plugs that are in good condition can be filed and re-used

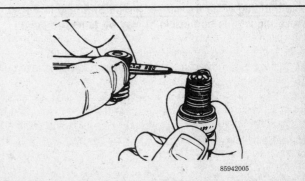

Fig. 10 Always use a wire gauge to check the electrode gap on used plugs

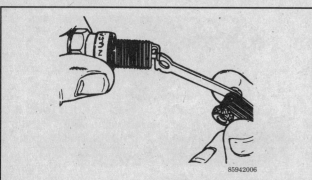

Fig. 11 Adjust the gap by bending the side electrode very slightly towards or away from the center electrode

be careful not to bend the side electrode too far or too often; if it is overstressed it may weaken and break off within the engine, requiring removal of the cylinder head to retrieve it.

INSTALLATION

1. Inspect the spark plugs and clean or replace, as necessary. Inspect the spark plug boot for tears or damage. If a damaged boot is found, the spark plug wire must be replaced.

2. Using a feeler gauge, check and adjust the spark plug gap to specification. When using a gauge, the proper size should pass between the electrodes with a slight drag. The next larger size should not be able to pass while the next smaller size should pass freely.

✳✳CAUTION

Do not use the spark plug socket to thread the plugs. Always thread the plug by hand to prevent the possibility of cross-threading and damaging the cylinder head bore.

3. Lubricate the spark plug threads with a drop of clean engine oil, then carefully start the spark plugs by hand and tighten a few turns until a socket is needed to continue tightening the spark plug. Do not apply the same amount of force you would use for a bolt; just snug them in. If a torque wrench is available, tighten the plugs to 11-15 ft. lbs. (15-20 Nm).

➡**A spark plug threading tool may be made using the end of an old spark plug wire. Cut the wire a few inches from the top of the spark plug boot. The boot may be used to hold the plug while the wire is turned to thread it. Because the wire is so flexible, it may be turned to bend** around difficult angles and, should the plug begin to crossthread, the resistance should be sufficient to bend the wire instead of forcing the plug into the cylinder head, preventing serious thread damage.

4. Apply a small amount of silicone dielectric compound to the end of the spark plug lead or inside the spark plug boot to prevent sticking, then install the boot to the spark plug and push until it clicks into place. The click may be felt or heard, then gently pull back on the boot to assure proper contact.

5. Connect the negative battery cable.

CHECKING AND REPLACING SPARK PLUG WIRES

Every 15,000 miles, visually inspect the spark plug wires for burns, cuts, or breaks in the insulation. Check the boots and the distributor cap tower connectors. Replace any damaged wiring.

Every 45,000 miles or so, the resistance of the wires should be checked using an ohmmeter. Wires with excessive resistance will cause misfiring and may make the engine difficult to start in damp weather. Generally, the useful life of the cables is 45,000-60,000 miles.

To check resistance, remove the distributor cap, leaving the wires in place. Connect one lead of an ohmmeter to an electrode within the cap; connect the other lead to the corresponding spark plug terminal (remove it from the spark plug for this test). Replace any wire which shows a resistance over $30,000\Omega$. Generally speaking, it is preferable that resistance be below $25,000\Omega$, but $30,000\Omega$ must be considered the outer limit of acceptability. It should be remembered that resistance is also a function of length; the longer the wire, the greater the resistance. Thus, if the wires on your car are longer than the factory originals, resistance will be higher, quite possibly outside these limits.

➡**If all of the wires must be disconnected from the spark plugs or from the distributor at the same time, be sure to tag the wires to assure proper reconnection.**

When installing a new set of spark plug wires, replace the wires one at a time so there will be no mix-up. Start by replacing the longest cable first. Install the boot firmly over the spark plug. Route the wire exactly the same as the original. Connect the wire tower connector to the distributor. Repeat the process for each wire. Be sure to apply silicone dielectric compound to the spark plug wire boots and tower connectors prior to installation.

GASOLINE ENGINE TUNE-UP SPECIFICATIONS

When analyzing the compression test results, look for uniformity among cylinders rather than specific pressures.

Year	Engine No. Cyl. Displacement (cu. in.)	hp	Spark Plugs Type	Gap (in.)	Distributor Point Dwell (deg.)	Point Gap (in.)	Ignition Timing ▲(deg.)●● Man. Trans.	Auto. Trans.	●Valves■ Intake Opens (deg.)	Fuel Pump Pressure (psi)	●Idle Speed▲ Man. Trans.	Auto. Trans.
1964	6-194	120	46N	0.035	31–34	0.019	8B	8B	62	4½–6	500②	500②
	6-230	155	46N	0.035	31–34	0.019	4B	4B	62	4½–6	500②	500②
	8-283	195, 220	45	0.035	28–32	0.019	4B	4B	32½	5¼–6½	500②	500②
	8-327	250, 300	44	0.035	28–32	0.019	8B	8B	32½	5¼–6½	500②	500②
1965	6-194	120	46N	0.035	31–34	0.019	8B	8B	62	4½–6	500②	500②
	6-230	140	46N	0.035	31–34	0.019	4B	4B	62	4½–6	500②	500②
	8-283	195, 280	45	0.035	28–32	0.019	4B	4B	32½	5¼–6½	500②	500②
	8-327	250, 300	44	0.035	28–32	0.019	8B	8B	32½	5¼–6½	500②	500②
	8-327	350	44	0.035	28–32	0.019	10B	—	54	5–6½	750②	750②
1966	6-194	120	46N	0.035	31–45	0.019	8B	8B	62	4½–6	500②	500②
	6-194①	120	46N	0.035	31–34	0.019	3B	8B	62	4½–6	700②	600②
	6-230	140	46N	0.035	31–34	0.019	4B	4B	62	4½–6	500②	500②
	6-230①	140	46N	0.035	31–34	0.019	4B	4B	62	4½–6	700②	600②
	8-283	195	45	0.035	28–32	0.019	4B	4B	32½	5¼–6½	500②	500②
	8-283①	220	45	0.035	28–32	0.019	4B	4B	32½	5¼–6½	700②	600②
	8-327	275	44	0.035	28–32	0.019	8B	8B	32½	5¼–6½	500②	500②
	8-327①	275	44	0.035	28–32	0.019	8B	2A	32½	5–6½	700②	600②
	8-327	350	44	0.035	28–32	0.019	10B	—	54	5–6½	750②	—
	8-396	325	43N	0.035	28–32	0.019	4B	4B	40	5–6½	500②	500②
	8-396	360	43N	0.035	28–32	0.019	4B	4B	56	5–6½	550②	550②
	8-396	375	R-43N	0.035	28–32	0.019	4B	—	44	5–8½	750	—
1967	6-230	140	46N	0.035	31–34	0.019	4B	4B	62	3½–4½	500②	500②
	6-230①	140	46N	0.035	31–34	0.019	4B	4B	62	3½–4½	700	500
	6-250	155	46N	0.035	31–34	0.019	4B	4B	62	3½–4½	500②	500②
	6-250①	155	46N	0.035	31–34	0.019	4B	4B	62	3½–4½	700	500
	8-283	195	45	0.035	28–32	0.019	4B	4B	38	5–6½	500②	500②
	8-283①	195	45	0.035	28–32	0.019	TDC	4B	38	5–6½	700	600
	8-327	275	44	0.035	28–32	0.019	8B	8B	38	5¼–6½	500②	500②
	8-327①	275	44	0.035	28–32	0.019	6B	6B	38	5¼–6½	700	600
	8-327	325	44	0.035	28–32	0.019	10B	—	54	5–6½	700②	—
	8-327①	275	44	0.035	28–32	0.019	10B	—	54	5–6½	750②	—
	8-396	325	43N	0.035	28–32	0.019	4B	4B	40	5–6½	500②	500②
	8-396①	325	43N	0.035	28–32	0.019	4B	4B	40	5–6½	700②	500②
	396	350	43N	0.035	28–32	0.019	4B	—	56	7¼–8½	550②	550②
	396①	350	43N	0.035	28–32	0.019	4B	4B	56	7¼–8½	700②	500②
	8-396	375	R-43N	0.035	28–32	0.019	4B	—	44	5–8½	750	—

GASOLINE ENGINE TUNE-UP SPECIFICATIONS

When analyzing the compression test results, look for uniformity among cylinders rather than specific pressures.

Year	Engine No. Cyl. Displacement (cu. in.)	hp	Spark Plugs Type	Gap (in.)	Distributor Point Dwell (deg.)	Point Gap (in.)	Ignition Timing ▲(deg.)■• Man. Trans.	Auto. Trans.	•Valves■ Intake Opens (deg.)	Fuel Pump Pressure (psi)	•Idle Speed▲ Man. Trans.	Auto. Trans.
1968	6-230	140	46N	0.035	31–34	0.019	TDC	4B	16	3½–4½	700	500② / 400
	6-250	155	46N	0.035	31–34	0.019	TDC	4B	16	3½–4½	700	500② / 400
	8-307	200	45S	0.035	28–32	0.019	2B	2B	28	5–6½	700	600
	8-327	275	44	0.035	28–32	0.019	TDC	4B	28	5–6½	700	600
	8-327	325	44	0.035	28–32	0.019	4B	—	40	5–6½	750②	—
	8-396	325	43N	0.035	28–32	0.019	4B	4B	28	5–6½	700②	600②
	8-396	350	43N	0.035	28–32	0.019	TDC	4B	40	7¼–8½	700	600
	8-396	375	R-43N	0.035	28–32	0.019	4B	—	44	5–8½	750	—
1969	6-230	140	R-46N	0.035	31–34	0.019	TDC	4B	16	3–4½	700	550/400
	6-250	155	R-46N	0.035	31–34	0.019	TDC	4B	16	3–4½	700	550/400②
	8-307	200	R-45S	0.035	28–32	0.019	2B	2B	28	5–6½	700	600
	8-350	250	R-44	0.035	28–32	0.019	TDC	4B	28	5–6½	700	600
	8-350	300	R-44	0.035	28–32	0.019	TDC	4B	28	5–6½	700	600
	8-396	325	R-44N	0.035	28–32	0.019	4B	4B	28	5–8½	800	600
	8-396	350	R-43N	0.035	28–32	0.019	TDC	4B	56	5–8½	800	600
	8-396	375	R-43N	0.035	28–32	0.019	4B	4B	44	5–8½	750	750/400
1970	6-250	155	R-46T	0.035	31–34	0.019	TDC	4B	16	3–4½	750	600/400
	8-307	200	R-43	0.035	28–32	0.019	2B	2B	28	5–6½	700	600/450
	8-350	250	R-44	0.035	28–32	0.019	TDC	4B	28	5–6½	750	600/450
	8-350	300	R-44	0.035	28–32	0.019	TDC	4B	28	5–6½	700	600
	8-396	350	R-44T	0.035	28–32	0.019	TDC	4B	56	5–8½	700	600
	8-396	375	R-43T	0.035	28–32	0.019	4B	4B	NA	5–8½	750	700
	8-400	265	R-44	0.035	28–32	0.019	4B	8B	28	5–8½	700	600/450
	8-402	330	R-44T	0.035	28–32	0.019	4B	4B	28	5–8½	700	600
	8-454	360	R-43T	0.035	28–32	0.019	6B	6B	56	5–8½	700	600
	8-454	390	R-43T	0.035	28–32	0.019	6B	6B	NA	5–8½	700	600
	8-454	450	R-43T	0.035	28–32	0.019	4B	4B	NA	5–8½	700	600
1971	6-250	145	R-46TS	0.035	31–34	0.019	4B	4B	16	3½–4½	550	500
	8-307	200	R-45TS	0.035	29–31	0.019	4B	8B	28	5–6½	600	550
	8-350	245	R-45TS	0.035	29–31	0.019	2B	6B	28	7–8½	600	550

85942008

GASOLINE ENGINE TUNE-UP SPECIFICATIONS

When analyzing the compression test results, look for uniformity among cylinders rather than specific pressures.

Year	Engine No. Cyl. Displacement (cu. in.)	hp	Spark Plugs Type	Gap (in.)	Distributor Point Dwell (deg.)	Point Gap (in.)	Ignition Timing ▲ (deg.)•• Man. Trans.	Auto. Trans.	•Valves• Intake Opens (deg.)	Fuel Pump Pressure (psi)	•Idle Speed▲ Man. Trans.	Auto. Trans.
1971	8-350	270	R-44TS	0.035	29–31	0.019	4B	8B	28	7–8½	600	550
	8-400	255	R-44TS	0.035	29–31	0.019	4B	8B	28	7–8½	600	550
	8-402	300	R-44TS	0.035	29–31	0.019	8B	8B	28	7–8½	600	600
	8-454	365	R-42TS	0.035	29–31	0.019	8B	8B	56	7–8½	600	600
	8-454	425	R-42TS	0.035	29–31	0.019	8B	12B	44	7–8½	700	700
1972	6-250	110	R-46TS	0.035	31–34	0.019	4B	4B	16	3½–4½	700	600
	8-307	130	R-44T	0.035	29–31	0.019	4B	8B	28	5–6½	900	600
	8-350	165	R-44T	0.035	29–31	0.019	6B	6B	28	7–8½	900	600
	8-350	175	R-44T	0.035	29–31	0.019	4B	8B	28	7–8½	800	600
	8-402	240	R-44T	0.035	29–31	0.019	8B	8B	30	7–8½	750	600
	8-454	270	R-44T	0.035	29–31	0.019	8B	8B	56	7–8½	750	600
1973	6-250	100	R-46T	0.035	31–34	0.019	6B	6B	16	3½–4½	700/450	600/450
	8-307	115	R-44T	0.035	29–31	0.019	4B	8B	28	5–6½	900/450	600/450
	8-350	145	R-44T	0.035	29–31	0.019	8B	8B	28	7–8½	900/450	600/450
	8-350	175	R-44T	0.035	29–31	0.019	8B	12B	28	7–8½	900/450	600/450
	8-454	245	R-44T	0.035	29–31	0.019	10B	10B	55	7–8½	900/450	600/450
1974	6-250	100	R-46T	0.035	31–34	0.019	6B	6B	16	4–5	800/450	600/450
	8-350	145	R-44T	0.035	29–31	0.019	4B	8B	28	7½–9	900/450	600/450
	8-350	160	R-44T	0.035	29–31	0.019	4B	8B	44	7½–9	900/450	600/450
	8-400	150	R-44T	0.035	29–31	0.019	—	8B	28	7½–9	—	600/450
	8-400	180	R-44T	0.035	29–31	0.019	—	8B	44	7½–9	—	600/450
	8-454	235	R-44T	0.035	29–31	0.019	10B	10B	55	7½–9	800/450	600/450
1975	6-250	105	R-46TX	0.060	Electronic		10B	10B	16	4–5	850/425	550/425 (600/425)
	8-350	145	R-44TX	0.060	Electronic		6B	6B	28	7½–9	800	600
	8-350	155	R-44TX	0.060	Electronic		—	6B	28	7½–9	—	600
	8-400	175	R-44TX	0.060	Electronic		—	8B	28	7½–9	—	600
	8-454	215	R-44TX	0.060	Electronic		—	16B	55	7½–9	—	600/500

85942009

GASOLINE ENGINE TUNE-UP SPECIFICATIONS

When analyzing the compression test results, look for uniformity among cylinders rather than specific pressures.

Year	Engine No. Cyl. Displacement (cu. in.)	hp	Spark Plugs Type	Gap (in.)	Distributor Point Dwell (deg.)	Point Gap (in.)	Ignition Timing ▲(deg.)■● Man. Trans.	Auto. Trans.	●Valves■ Intake Opens (deg.)	Fuel Pump Pressure (psi)	●Idle Speed▲ Man. Trans.	Auto. Trans.
1976	6-250	105	R-46TS	0.035	Electronic		6B	6B	16	3½–4½	850	550 (600)
	8-305	140	R-45TS	0.045	Electronic		—	8B (TDC)	28	7–8½	—	600
	8-350	145	R-45TS	0.045	Electronic		—	6B	28	7–8½	—	600
	8-350	165	R-45TS	0.045	Electronic		—	8B (TDC)	28	7–8½	—	600
	8-400	175	R-45TS	0.045	Electronic		—	8B	28	7–8½	—	600
1977	6-250	110	R-46TS	0.035	Electronic		6B @ 850	8B @ 600	16	4–5	750	550
	8-305	145	R-45TS	0.045	Electronic		—	8B @ 500	28	7½–9	—	500
	8-350	170	R-45TS	0.045	Electronic		—	8B @ 500	28	7½–9	—	500
1978	6-200	95	R-45TS	0.045	Electronic		8B	8B	28	7½–9	700	600
	6-231	105	R-46TSX	0.060	Electronic		15B	15B	17	6–7	600	500
	8-305	145	R-45TS	0.045	Electronic		4B	④	28	7½–9	600	500
	8-350	170	R-45TS	0.045	Electronic		—	8B	28	7½–9	—	500
1979	6-200	all	R-45TS	0.045	Electronic		8B	14B	34	4½–6	700	600
	6-231	all	R-46TSX	0.060	Electronic		15B	15B	16	4.2–5.7	600	500
	8-267	all	R-45TS	0.045	Electronic		4B	10B	28	7½–9	600	500
	8-305	all	R-43TS	0.045	Electronic		4B	4B	28	7½–9	600	500
	8-350	all	R-43TS	0.045	Electronic		—	8B	28	7½–9	—	500
1980	6-229	115	R-45TSX ⑤	0.045	Electronic		8B	12B	42	4½–6	700	600
	6-231	110	R-45TSX	0.060	Electronic		—	15B	16	4¼–5¾	—	560 (600)
	6-231 Turbo	170	R-45TSX	0.060	Electronic		—	15B	16	4¼–5¾	—	550 (600)
	8-267	120	R-45TS	0.045	Electronic		—	4B	28	7½–9	—	500
	8-305	155	R-43TS	0.045	Electronic		4B	4B	28	7½–9	700	500 (550)
1981	6-229	110	R-45TS	0.045	Electronic		6B	6B	42	4¼–6	⑥	⑥
	6-231	110	R-45TS8	0.080	Electronic		—	15B	16	4¼–5¾	—	⑥
	6-231 Turbo	170	R-45TS	0.040	Electronic		—	15B	16	4¼–5¾	—	⑥
	8-267	115	R-45TS	0.045	Electronic		—	6B	28	7½–9	—	500
	8-305	150	R-45TS	0.045	Electronic		6B	6B	28	7½–9	700	500

85942010

ENGINE PERFORMANCE AND TUNE-UP   2-11

GASOLINE ENGINE TUNE-UP SPECIFICATIONS

When analyzing the compression test results, look for uniformity among cylinders rather than specific pressures.

Year	Engine No. Cyl. Displacement (cu. in.)	hp	Spark Plugs Type	Gap (in.)	Distributor Point Dwell (deg.)	Point Gap (in.)	Ignition Timing (deg.) Man. Trans.	Auto. Trans.	Valves Intake Opens (deg.)	Fuel Pump Pressure (psi)	Idle Speed Man. Trans.	Auto. Trans.
1982–84	6-229	110	R-45TS	0.045	Electronic		—	6B ⑥	42	4½-6	—	⑥
	6-231	110	R-45TS	0.045	Electronic		—	15B ⑥	16	4½-6	—	⑥
	8-267	115	R-45TS	0.045	Electronic		—	6B ⑥	44	7½-9	—	⑥
	8-305	145 ⑦	R-45TS	0.045	Electronic		—	6B ⑥	44	7½-9	—	⑥
1985	6-262	130	R-43CTS	0.035	Electronic		—	⑥	44	9-13	—	⑥
	8-305	150 ⑧	R-45TS	0.045	Electronic		—	⑥	44	5½-6½	—	⑥
1986	6-262	140	R-43TS	0.035	Electronic		—	⑥	44	9-13	—	⑥
	8-305	150 ⑧	R-45TS	0.045	Electronic		—	⑥	44	5½-6½	—	⑥
1987–88	6-262	145	R-45TS	0.035	Electronic		—	⑥	44	9-13	—	⑥
	8-305	150 ⑧	R-45TS	0.035	Electronic		—	⑥	44	5½-6½	—	500 ⑨

NOTE: The underhood specifications sticker often reflects tune-up specification changes in production. Sticker figures must be used if they disagree with those in this chart.

▲ See text for procedure
● Figures in parentheses indicate California
■ All figures Before Top Dead Center
*When two idle speed figures are separated by a slash. the lower figure is with the idle speed solenoid disconnected
NA—Not available
① Equipped with the Air Injection Reactor System
② A/C on
③ Lower figure is with idle solenoid disconnected
④ 49 states—4B
  Calif.—6B
  High alt.—8B
⑤ With A/T—R-45TS
⑥ See underhood specifications sticker
⑦ 150 hp. 1983–84
⑧ 180 hp—SS Model
⑨ 600 rpm—SS Model

85942011

DIESEL ENGINE TUNE-UP SPECIFICATIONS

Year	Eng. V.I.N. Code	Engine No. Cyl. Displacement (cu. in.)	Eng. Mfg.	Fuel Pump Pressure (psi)	Compression (lbs.) ▲	Ignition Timing (deg.) Auto. Trans.	Intake Valve Opens (deg.)	Idle Speed• (rpm)
1980	N	8-350	Olds.	5.5–6.5	275 min.	5B ②	16	750/600
1981–84	N	8-350	Olds.	5.5–6.5	275 min.	①	16	①
1982–84	V	V6-263	Olds.	5.5–6.5	275 min.	①	16	①

NOTE: The underhood specifications sticker often reflects tune-up specification changes in production. Sticker figures must be used if they disagree with those in this chart.
▲ The lowest cylinder reading should not be less than 70% of the highest cylinder reading
• Where two idle speed figures appear separated by a slash. the first is idle speed with solenoid energized; the second is with solenoid disconnected
① See underhood specifications sticker
② Static

85942014

FIRING ORDERS

➡ To avoid confusion, remove and tag the wires one at a time, for replacement.

♦ See Figures 12, 13, 14, 15 and 16

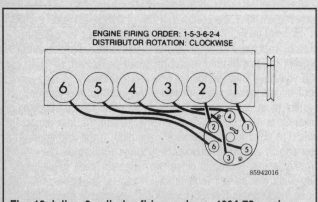

ENGINE FIRING ORDER: 1-5-3-6-2-4
DISTRIBUTOR ROTATION: CLOCKWISE

85942016

Fig. 12 Inline 6-cylinder firing order — 1964-79 engines

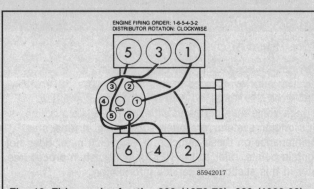

ENGINE FIRING ORDER: 1-6-5-4-3-2
DISTRIBUTOR ROTATION: CLOCKWISE

85942017

Fig. 13 Firing order for the 200 (1978-79), 229 (1980-83) and the 262 (1984 and later) V6 engines

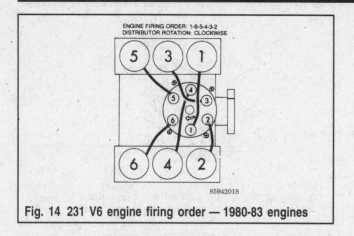

Fig. 14 231 V6 engine firing order — 1980-83 engines

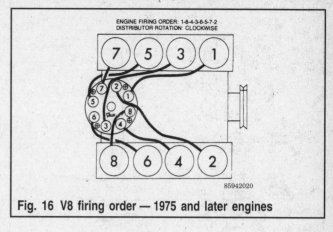

Fig. 16 V8 firing order — 1975 and later engines

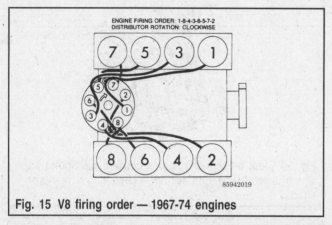

Fig. 15 V8 firing order — 1967-74 engines

POINT TYPE IGNITION

Breaker Points and Condenser

▶ See Figures 17 and 18

➡A point type ignition was originally installed on all 1964-73 vehicles covered in this manual. Most 1974 vehicles were also equipped with a point type distributor, though some may be found with the HEI system option. HEI ignition systems are often substituted in repairs or maintenance on these vehicles. If your distributor does not contain points, refer to the HEI ignition system procedures later in this section for service information.

The points function as a circuit breaker for the primary circuit of the ignition system. The ignition coil must boost the 12 volts supplied by the vehicle's charging system to as much as 25,000 volts in order to fire the plugs. To accomplish, the coil depends on the points and the condenser to make a clean break in the primary circuit.

The coil has both primary and secondary circuits. When the ignition is turned on, the battery supplies voltage through the coil and to the points. The points are connected to ground, completing the primary circuit. As the current passes through the coil, a magnetic field is created in the iron center core of the coil. When the cam on the distributor shaft turns, the points open, breaking the primary circuit. The magnetic field in the primary circuit of the coil then collapses and cuts through the secondary circuit windings around the iron core. Because

of the physical principle called electromagnetic induction, the voltage is increased to a level sufficient to fire the spark plugs.

When the points open, the electrical charge in the primary circuit tries to jump the gap created between the two open contacts of the points. If this electrical charge were not transferred elsewhere, the metal contacts of the points would start to charge rapidly. The function of the condenser is to absorb excessive voltage from the points when they open and thus prevent the points from becoming pitted or burned.

If you have ever wondered why it is necessary to tune-up your engine occasionally, consider the fact that the ignition system must complete the above cycle each time a spark plug fires. On a 4-cylinder, 4-cycle engine, two of the four plugs must fire once for every engine revolution. If the idle speed of you engine is 800 revolutions per minute (800 rpm), the breaker points open and close two times for each revolution. For every minute your engine idles, your points open and close 1,600 times (2 x 800 = 1,600). And that is just at idle. Just think at the work your points are performing at 60 mph and you will begin to realize why periodic engine tuning is so important.

There breaker point gap may be checked in either of 2 ways: with a feeler gauge or with a dwell meter. In both cases setting the points means that you are adjusting the amount of time (in degrees of distributor rotation) that the points will remain open. If you adjust the points with a feeler gauge, you are setting the maximum amount that points will open when the point rubbing block is on a high point of the distributor

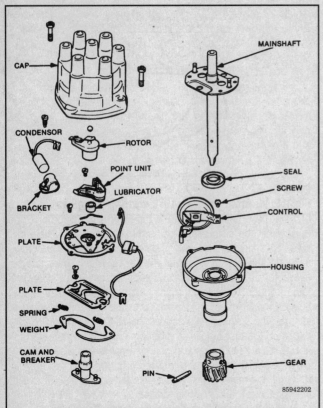

Fig. 17 Exploded view of a common 6-cylinder point type distributor

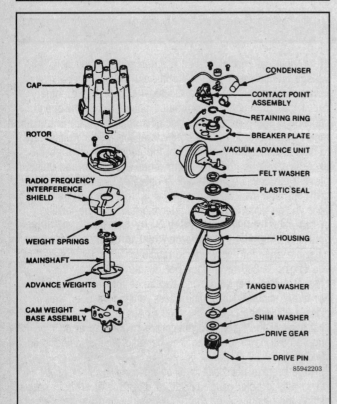

Fig. 18 Exploded view of a common 8-cylinder point type distributor

Fig. 19 The distributor cap on most 6-cylinder engines is held in place using 2 captive screws

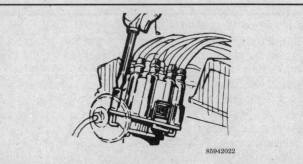

Fig. 20 Most 8-cylinder engines utilize a distributor cap which is retained using spring latches with screw-type heads

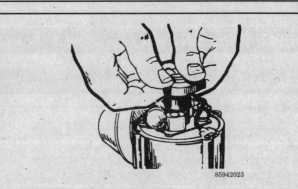

Fig. 21 For 6-cylinder engines, the rotor is removed by pulling straight upward

cam. When you adjust the points with a dwell meter, you are measuring the number of degrees (of distributor cam rotation) that the points will remain closed before they start to open as a high point of the distributor cam approaches the rubbing block of the points.

If you would like a demonstration of how the points function mechanically, take a friend, go outside, and remove the distributor cap from your engine. Make sure the parking brake is set and that the transmission is not in gear, then have your friend operate the starter for a few seconds as you look at the exposed parts of the distributor. Be sure to keep yourself and your clothing away from any moving engine parts for safety reasons. You should see the points open and close as the distributor rotates.

There are two rules that should always be followed when adjusting or replacing points. The points and condenser are normally replaced as a set; when replacing the points, the condenser should also be replaced. If you change the point gap or dwell of the engine, you will affect the ignition timing. Therefore, if you adjust the points, you must also adjust the timing.

REMOVAL & INSTALLATION

1964-74

▶ See Figures 19, 20, 21, 22, 23, 24, 25, 26, 27, 28, 29 and 30

The usual procedure is to replace the condenser each time the point set is replaced. Although this is not always necessary, it is easy to do at this time and the cost is negligible. Every time you adjust or replace the breaker points, the ignition timing must be checked and, if necessary, adjusted. No special equipment other than a feeler gauge is required for point replacement or adjustment, but a dwell meter is strongly advised. A magnetic screwdriver is handy to prevent the small points and condenser screws from falling down into the distributor.

Point sets using the push-in type wiring terminal should be used on those distributors equipped with an R.F.I. (Radio Frequency Interference) shield (1970-74). Points using a lock-screw-type terminal may short out when installed in these distributors due to contact between the shield and the screw.

1. Disconnect the negative battery cable. Loosen the distributor cap by either unscrewing the captive retaining screws or by pushing downward and turning on the spring loaded latch screws, as applicable. Remove the distributor cap from the assembly and position aside. You might have to unclip or detach some or all of the plug wires to remove the cap. If so, tag the wires and the cap before disconnecting the wires in order to ease installation.

2. Clean the distributor cap inside and out using a clean rag. Check for cracks and carbon paths. A carbon path shows up as a dark line, usually from one of the cap sockets or inside terminals to a ground. Check the condition of the contact button inside the center of the cap and the inside terminals. If wear, cracks or carbon paths are present, cap replacement is required.

3. Either, pull the 6-cylinder rotor up and off the shaft or remove the two screws and lift the round V8 rotor from the

distributor assembly. There is less danger of losing the screws if you just back them out all the way and lift them off using the rotor. Clean off the metal outer tip if it is burned or corroded, but DO NOT file it. Replace the rotor if it is necessary or if one was supplied with your tune-up kit.

4. Remove the radio frequency interference shield if your distributor has one. Watch out for those little screws! The factory says that the points don't need to be replaced if they are only slightly rough or pitted. However, sad experience shows that it is more economical and reliable in the long run to replace the point set while the distributor is open, than to be forced to do this at a later (and possibly more inconvenient) time.

5. Pull one of the two wire terminals from the point assembly. One wire comes from the condenser and the other comes from within the distributor. The terminals are usually held in place by spring tension only. There might be a clamp screw securing the terminals on some older versions. There is also available a one-piece point/condenser assembly for V8s. The radio frequency interference shield isn't needed with this set. Loosen the point set hold-down screw(s). Be very careful not to drop any of these little screws inside the distributor. If this happens, the distributor will probably have to be removed to get at the screw. If the hold-down screw is lost elsewhere, it must be replaced with one that is no longer than the original to avoid interference with the distributor workings. Remove the point set, even if it is to be reused.

6. If the points are to be reused, clean them with a few strokes of a special point file. This is done with the points removed to prevent tiny metal filings from getting into and damaging the distributor. Don't use sandpaper or emery cloth

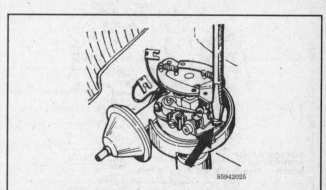

Fig. 23 The points are retained by screws. If possible, use a magnetic screwdriver when removing the screws

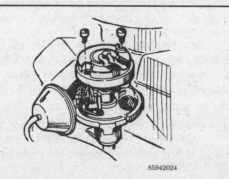

Fig. 22 To remove the rotor on most 8-cylinder engines the 2 rotor retaining screws must first be removed

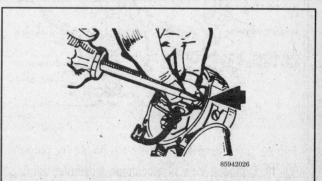

Fig. 24 The condenser is usually held in place with a screw and a clamp

as they are not fine enough and will usually cause rapid point burning.

7. Loosen the condenser hold-down screw and slide the condenser free of the clamp. This will save you a struggle with the clamp, condenser, and the tiny screw when you install the new one. If you have the type of clamp that is permanently fastened to the condenser, remove the screw and the condenser. Again, be careful not to lose the screw.

To install:

8. The distributor cam lubricator should either be switched or replaced at each tune-up. If your distributor is equipped with the round kind, turn it around on its shaft at the first tune-up and replace it at the second. If you have the long kind, switch ends at the first tune-up and replace it at the second.

➡Don't oil or grease the lubricator. The component's foam is impregnated with a special lubricant.

If your tune-up kit did not supply a lubricator, your distributor is not equipped with one, or it looks like someone removed the lubricator, don't worry. Under these circumstances, just rub a match head size dab of grease on the cam lobes.

9. Install the new condenser. If you left the clamp in place, just slide the new condenser into the clamp.

10. Replace the point set and tighten the screw on all V8 engines that are equipped with a hex adjuster bolt. Leave the screw slightly loose on 6-cylinder engines or any distributor that does not contain an adjustment bolt. Connect the two wire terminals, making sure that the wires don't interfere with any moving components within the distributor assembly. Some V8

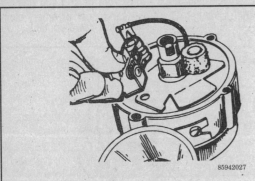

Fig. 25 Position the point set on the breaker plate, then attach the wiring

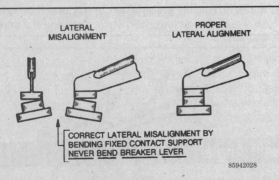

Fig. 26 After installation, check the points for proper alignment

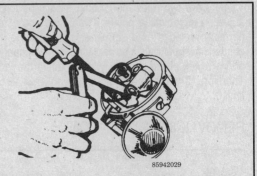

Fig. 27 A screwdriver may be used to lever the points closer together or farther apart on 6-cylinder engines

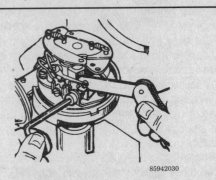

Fig. 28 You will need a hex wrench to adjust the point gap on most 8-cylinder engines

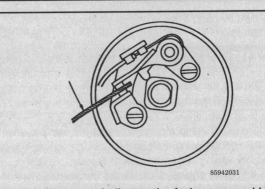

Fig. 29 The arrow indicates the feeler gauge which is used to check the point gap

distributors have a ground wire that must go under one of the screws.

11. Check that the contacts meet squarely. If they don't, bend the tab supporting the fixed contact.

➡If you are installing preset points on a V8, go ahead to Step 16. If they are preset, it will say so on the package. It would be a good idea to make a quick check on point gap, anyway. Sometimes those preset points aren't.

12. Turn the engine until a high point on the cam which opens the points just contacts the rubbing block on the point arm. You can turn the engine by hand if you can get a wrench on the crankshaft pulley nut, or you can grasp the fan belt and

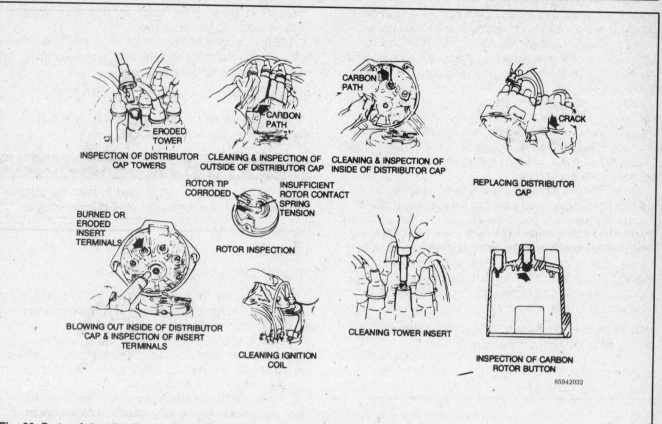

Fig. 30 Parts of the distributor assembly which should be inspected during a tune-up

turn the engine by hand if the spark plugs are removed to relieve compression.

✳✳CAUTION

If you try turning the engine by hand, be very careful not to get your fingers pinched in the pulleys.

An alternative is to bump the starter switch or use a remote starter switch. Though using the starter is not a very accurate method and will usually require multiple attempts.

13. On a 6-cylinder engine, there should be a screwdriver slot near the contacts. Insert a screwdriver and lever the points open or closed until they appear to be at or near the gap specified in the Tune-Up Specifications. On a V8, simply insert a 1/8 in. hex wrench into the adjustment screw and turn. The wrench is sometimes supplied with a tune-up kit.

14. Insert the correct size feeler gauge and adjust the gap until you can push the gauge in and out between the contacts with a slight drag, but without disturbing the point arm. This operation takes a bit of experience to obtain the correct feel. Check by trying the gauges 0.001-0.002 in. larger and smaller than the setting size. The larger one should disturb the point arm, while the smaller one should not drag at all. Tighten the 6-cylinder point set hold-down screw, then recheck the gap, because it often changes when the screw is tightened.

15. After all the point adjustments are complete, pull a white index card through (between) the contacts to remove any traces of oil. Oil left on the points will cause rapid contact burning.

➡You can adjust 6-cylinder dwell at this point, if you wish.

16. Replace the radio frequency interference shield, if equipped. You don't need it if you are installing the one-piece point/condenser set. Push the rotor firmly down into place, taking care to make sure it is firmly seated. The rotor will only install one way, but if it is not installed properly it will probably break when the starter is operated. Tighten the V8 rotor screws.

17. Install the distributor cap and connect the negative battery cable.

18. If a dwell meter is available, check the dwell.

1975 and Later

These engines use the breakerless High Energy Ignition (HEI) system. Since there is no mechanical contact, there is no wear or need for periodic service. There is an item in the distributor that resembles a condenser; it is a radio interference suppression capacitor which requires no service.

Dwell Angle

Dwell angle is the amount of time (measured in degrees of distributor cam rotation) that the contact points remain closed. Initial point gap determines dwell angle. If the points are set too wide they open gradually and dwell angle (the time they remain closed) is small. This wide gap causes excessive arcing at the points and as a result, point burning. A small dwell doesn't give the coil sufficient time to build up maximum energy and so coil output will also suffer. If the points are set too close, the dwell is increased but the points may bounce at higher speed, the idle becomes rough and starting is made harder.

Remember when adjusting the dwell angle that the wider the point opening, the smaller the dwell and the smaller the gap, the larger the dwell. Adjusting the dwell by making the initial point gap setting with a feeler gauge is usually sufficient to get the car started and running, but a finer adjustment should then be made using a dwell meter.

Connect the red lead (positive) wire of the meter to the distributor primary wire connection on the Positive (+) side of the coil, and the black ground (negative) wire of the meter to a good ground on the engine. The dwell angle may be checked either with the engine cranking or running, although the reading will be more accurate if the engine is running. With the engine cranking, the reading will fluctuate between 0° dwell and the maximum figure of that angle. While cranking, the maximum figure is the correct one.

➡Dwell angle is set electronically on HEI distributors, requiring no adjustment or checking.

ADJUSTMENT

1964-74

Dwell can be checked with the engine running or cranking. Decrease dwell by increasing the point gap; increase dwell by decreasing the gap. Dwell angle is simply the number of degrees of distributor shaft rotation during which the points stay closed. Theoretically, if the point gap is correct, the dwell should also be correct, or at least very close. Adjustment with a dwell meter produces more exact and consistent results since it is a dynamic adjustment. If dwell varies more than 3° from idle speed to 1,750 engine rpm, the distributor is worn.

1. To adjust dwell on a 6-cylinder engine, trial and error point adjustments are required. On a V8 engine, simply open the metal window on the distributor and insert a ⅛ in. hex wrench. Turn the adjustment screw until the dwell meter shows the correct reading. Be sure to snap the window closed when the adjustment is finished.

2. An approximate dwell adjustment can be made without a meter on a V8 engine. Turn the adjusting screw clockwise until the engine begins to misfire, then turn the screw outward ½ of a turn.

3. If the engine won't start, check:
   a. That all the spark plug wires are in place.
   b. That the rotor has been installed.
   c. That the two (or three) wires inside the distributor are connected.
   d. That the points open and close when the engine turns.
   e. That the gap is correct and the hold-down screw, if applicable, is tight.

4. After the first 200 miles or so on a new set of points, the point gap often closes up due to initial rubbing block wear. For best performance, recheck the dwell (or gap) at this time.

This quick initial wear is the reason the factory recommends 0.003 in. more gap on new points.

5. Since changing the gap affects the ignition timing, the timing should be checked and adjusted as necessary after each point replacement or adjustment.

1975 and Later

The dwell angle on models equipped with the HEI ignition is electronically set and is not adjustable.

Ignition Coil

TESTING

1964-74

PRIMARY CIRCUIT WITH VOLTMETER

A quick, tentative check of the 12 volt ignition primary circuit (including ballast resistor) can be made with a simple voltmeter, as follows:

1. With engine at normal operating temperature, but stopped, and the distributor side of the ignition coil grounded using a jumper wire, hook up a voltmeter between the ignition coil (switch side) and a good ground.

2. Jiggle the ignition switch (switch ON) and watch the meter. An unstable needle will indicate a defective ignition switch.

3. With the ignition switch ON (but engine still stopped) the voltmeter should read 5.5 to 7 volts for 12 volt systems.

4. Crank the engine. Voltmeter should read at least 9 volts during cranking period.

5. Now remove the jumper wire from the coil. Start the engine. voltmeter should read from 9.0 volts to 11.5 volts (depending upon generator output) while running.

PRIMARY CIRCUIT WITH OHMMETER

To check ignition coil resistance, primary side, switch ohmmeter to low scale. Connect the ohmmeter leads across the primary terminals of the coil and read the low ohms scale.

Coils requiring ballast resistors should read about 1.0 ohm resistance. 12 volt coils, not requiring external ballast resistors, should read about 4.0 ohms resistance.

SECONDARY CIRCUIT WITH OHMMETER

To check ignition coil resistance, secondary side, switch ohmmeter to high scale. Connect one test lead to the distributor cap end of the coil secondary cable. Connect the other test lead to the distributor terminal of the coil. A coil in satisfactory condition should show between 4K and 8K on the scale. Some special coils (Mallory, etc.) may show a resistance as high as 13K. If the reading is much lower than 4K, the coil probably has shorted secondary turns. If the reading is extremely high (40K or more) the secondary winding is either open, there is a bad connection at the coil terminal, or resistance is high in the cable.

If both primary and secondary windings of the coil test good, but the ignition system is still unsatisfactory, check the system further.

REMOVAL & INSTALLATION

1964-74

1. Disconnect the negative battery cable.
2. Remove the ignition switch-to-coil lead from the coil.
3. Unfasten the distributor leads from the coil.

4. Remove the screws which secure the coil to the engine, then lift the coil from the vehicle.

To install:

5. Position the coil assembly to the engine and secure using the retaining screws.
6. Connect the distributor leads to the coil.
7. Connect the ignition switch-to-coil lead.
8. Connect the negative battery cable.

ELECTRONIC IGNITION

High Energy Ignition (HEI) System

▶ **See Figures 31 and 32**

The General Motors/Delco-Remy High Energy Ignition (HEI) system is breakerless, pulse-triggered, transistor-controlled, inductive discharge ignition system. It was available as an option in 1974 and was standard all 1975 and later vehicles. With the exception of the inline 6-cylinder engine used through 1977, the entire HEI system is contained within the distributor cap. Inline 6-cylinder engines through 1977 are the only engines covered here to utilize an external coil. But with the exception of the external coil, the ignition systems are the same.

The distributor, in addition to housing the mechanical and vacuum advance mechanisms, contains the ignition coil (except on some inline six engines), the electronic ignition module, and the magnetic pick-up assembly which contains a permanent magnet, a pole piece with internal teeth, and a pick-up coil (not to be confused with the ignition coil).

For 1981 and later an HEI distributor with Electronic Spark Timing is used (for more information on EST, refer to Section 4). This system uses a one piece distributor cap, similar to 1980. All spark timing changes in the 1981 and later distributors are controlled electronically by the Electronic Control Module (ECM) which monitors information from various engine sensors, computes the desired spark timing and then signals the distributor to change the timing accordingly. No vacuum or mechanical advance systems are used whatsoever.

In the HEI system, as in other electronic ignition systems, the breaker points have been replaced with an electronic switch, a transistor, which is located within the ignition module. This switching transistor performs the same function the points did in a conventional ignition system; it simply turns coil primary current on and off at the correct time. Essentially then, electronic and conventional ignition systems operate on the same principle.

The module which houses the switching transistor is controlled (turned on and off) by a magnetically generated impulse induced in the pick-up coil. When the teeth of the rotating timer align with the teeth of the pole piece, the induced voltage in the pick-up coil signals the electronic module to open the coil primary circuit. The primary current then decreases and a high voltage is induced in the ignition coil secondary windings which is then directed through the rotor and high voltage leads (spark plug wires) to fire the spark plugs.

In essence then, the pick-up coil module system simply replaces the conventional breaker points and condenser. The condenser found within the distributor is for radio suppression purposes only and has nothing to do with the ignition process.

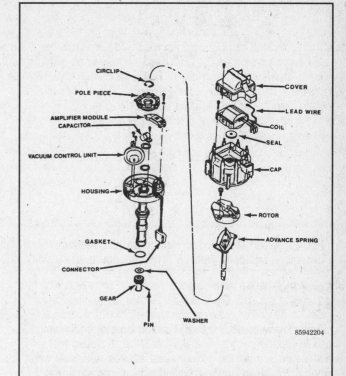

Fig. 31 Exploded view of a common HEI distributor assembly, (1981 and later models will have no vacuum advance unit)

The module automatically controls the dwell period, increasing it with increasing engine speed. Since dwell is automatically controlled, it cannot be adjusted. The module itself is non-adjustable and non-repairable and must be replaced if found defective.

HEI SYSTEM PRECAUTIONS

Before proceeding with troubleshooting or HEI system service, please note the following precautions:

Timing Light Use

Inductive pick-up timing lights are the best kind of use with the HEI system. Timing lights which connect between the spark plug and the spark plug wire occasionally (not always) give false readings.

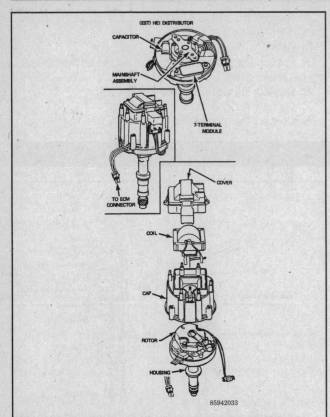

Fig. 32 A partial exploded view of an HEI distributor assembly, equipped with EST (no vacuum advance unit)

Spark Plug Wires

▶ **See Figure 33**

The plug wires used with HEI systems are of a different construction than conventional wires. When replacing them, make sure you get the correct wires, since conventional wires won't carry the voltage. Also, handle them carefully to avoid cracking or splitting them and never pierce them.

Tachometer Use

Not all tachometers will operate or indicate correctly when used on a HEI system. While some tachometers may give a reading, this does not necessarily mean the reading is correct. In addition, some tachometers hook up differently from others. If you can't figure out whether or not your tachometer will work

Fig. 33 HEI distributors are equipped with a spark plug wiring retainer which allows removal of all wires from the distributor at the same time and without the need for labelling

on your car, check with the tachometer manufacturer. Dwell readings, or course, have no significance at all.

HEI System Testers

Instruments designed specifically for testing HEI systems are available from several tool manufacturers. Some of these will even test the module itself. However, the tests given in the following section will require only ohmmeter and a voltmeter.

TROUBLESHOOTING THE HEI SYSTEM

The symptoms of a defective component within the HEI system are exactly the same as those you would encounter in a conventional system. Some of these symptoms are:

- Hard or no Starting
- Rough Idle
- Poor Fuel Economy
- Engine misses under load or while accelerating

If you suspect a problem in your ignition system, there are certain preliminary checks which you should carry out before you begin to check the electronic portions of the system. First, it is extremely important to make sure the vehicle battery is in a good state of charge. A defective or poorly charged battery will cause the various components of the ignition system to read incorrectly when they are being tested. Second, make sure all wiring connections are clean and tight, not only at the battery, but also at the distributor cap, ignition coil, and at the electronic control module.

Since the only change between electronic and conventional ignition systems is in the distributor component area, it is imperative to check the secondary ignition circuit first. If the secondary circuit checks out properly, then the engine condition is probably not the fault of the ignition system. To check the secondary ignition system, perform a simple spark test. Remove one of the plug wires and insert some sort of extension in the plug socket. An old spark plug with the ground electrode removed makes a good extension. Hold the wire so the extension is positioned about ¼ in. away from the block, then crank the engine. If a normal spark occurs, then the problem is most likely not in the ignition system. Check for fuel system problems, or fouled spark plugs.

If, however, there is no spark or a weak spark, then further ignition system testing will have to be performed. Troubleshooting techniques fall into two categories, depending on the nature of the problem. The categories are (1) Engine cranks, but won't start or (2) Engine runs, but runs rough or cuts out. To begin with, let's consider the first case.

Engine Fails to Start

If the engine won't start, perform a spark test as described earlier. This will narrow the problem area down considerably. If no spark occurs, check for the presence of normal battery voltage of the battery (BAT) terminal in the distributor cap. The ignition switch must be in the ON position for this test. Either a voltmeter or a test light may be used for this test. Connect the test light wire to ground and probe end to the BAT terminal at the distributor. If the light comes on, you have voltage on the distributor. If the light fails to come on, this indicates an open circuit in the ignition primary wiring leading to the distributor. In this case, you will have to check wiring continuity back to the ignition switch using a test light. If there is battery voltage at the BAT terminal, but no spark at the plugs, then the problem lies within the distributor assembly. Go on to the distributor components test section.

Engine Runs, But Runs Rough or Cuts Out

1. Make sure the plug wires are in good shape first. There should be no obvious cracks or breaks. You can check the plug wires with an ohmmeter, but do not pierce the wires with a probe. Check the chart for the correct plug wire resistance.

2. If the plug wires are OK, remove the cap assembly and check for moisture, cracks, chips, carbon tracks, or any other high voltage leaks or failures. Replace the cap if any defects are found. Make sure the timer wheel rotates when the engine is cranked. If everything is all right so far, go on to the distributor components test section following.

DISTRIBUTOR COMPONENTS TESTING

▶ See Figures 34, 35 and 36

If the trouble has been narrowed down to the units within the distributor, the following tests can help pinpoint the defective component. An ohmmeter with both high and low ranges should be used. These tests are made with the cap assembly removed (on internal-coil distributor caps) and the battery wire disconnected. If a tachometer is connected to the TACH terminal, disconnect it before making these tests.

1. Connect an ohmmeter between the TACH and BAT terminals in the distributor cap. The primary coil resistance should be less than 1Ω.

2. To check the coil secondary resistance, connect an ohmmeter between the rotor button and BAT terminal. Note the reading. Connect the ohmmeter between the rotor button and the TACH terminal. Note the reading. The resistance in both cases should be between 6,000 and $30,000\Omega$. Be sure to test between the rotor button and both the BAT and TACH terminals.

3. Replace the coil only if the readings in Step 1 and Step 2 are infinite.

➡These resistance checks will not disclose shorted coil windings. This condition can only be detected with scope analysis or a suitably designed coil tester. If these instruments are unavailable, replace the coil with a known good component as a final coil test.

SPARK PLUG WIRE RESISTANCE CHART — HEI IGNITION SYSTEM

Wire Length	Minimum	Maximum
0–15 inches	3000 ohms	10,000 ohms
15–25 inches	4000 ohms	15,000 ohms
25–35 inches	6000 ohms	20,000 ohms
Over 35 inches		25,000 ohms

85942034

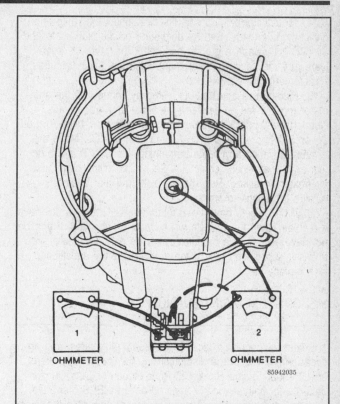

Fig. 35 Testing an internal HEI coil, Test 1: measures the primary coil resistance. Test 2: shows the secondary resistance connection.

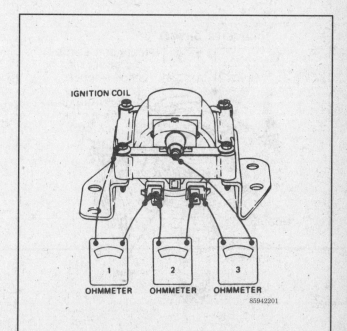

Fig. 34 Testing an external HEI coil, Test 1: uses the high scale setting and the reading should be very high or infinite. Test 2: uses the low setting and the reading should be very low or zero. Test 3: uses the high scale, the reading should NOT be infinite.

4. To test the pick-up coil, first disconnect the white and green module leads. Set the ohmmeter on the high scale and connect it between a ground and either the white or green lead. Any resistance measurement less than infinity requires replacement of the pick-up coil.

5. Pick-up coil continuity is tested by connecting the ohmmeter (on low range) between the white and green leads. Normal resistance is between 650 and 850Ω on 1975-76 models or 500 and 1500Ω on 1977 and later models. Move the vacuum advance arm while performing this test. This will detect any break in coil continuity. Such a condition can cause intermittent misfiring. Replace the pick-up if the reading is outside the specified limits.

6. If no defects have been found at this time, you still have a problem, then the module will have to be checked. If you do not have access to a module tester, the only possible alternative is a substitution test. If the module fails the substitution test, replace it.

HEI SYSTEM MAINTENANCE

Except for periodic checks of the spark plug wires, and an occasional check of the distributor cap for cracks (see Steps 1 and 2 under Engine Runs, But Runs Rough or Cuts Out for details), no maintenance is required on the HEI System. No periodic lubrication is necessary; engine oil lubricates the lower bushing, and an oil-filled reservoir lubricates the upper bushing.

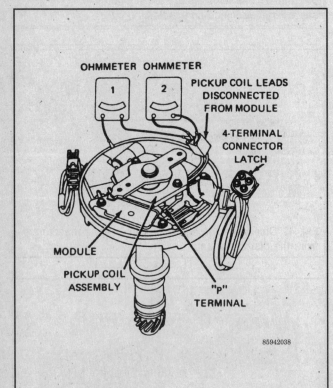

Fig. 36 Ohmmeter 1 shows testing the pickup coil. Ohmmeter 2 shows the testing the pickup coil continuity (1980 shown, most models similar)

COMPONENT REPLACEMENT

Integral Ignition Coil
▶ **See Figures 37, 38, 39, 40, 41, 42, 43, 44, 45 and 46**

1. Disconnect the negative battery cable, then if necessary for access, remove the air cleaner assembly.
2. Remove the ignition wire set retainer along with the spark plug wires from the top of the distributor cap.
3. If necessary, disengage the feed and module wire terminal connectors from the distributor cap.

➡**On some vehicles, interference with the cowl may make access to the cover and coil screws difficult. If necessary, the distributor cap may be removed from the vehicle to continue the service.**

4. As applicable, remove the coil cover-to-distributor cap screws or unsnap the retainers and remove the coil cover.
5. Remove the coil-to-distributor cap retaining screws.
6. Using a pair of needle nose pliers, remove the coil wire spade terminals from the cap. If the cap was removed, you may also use a blunt drift to press the coil wire spade terminals up out of the distributor cap.
7. Lift the coil up out of the distributor cap.
8. Remove and clean the coil spring, rubber seal washer and coil cavity of the distributor cap.

To install:
9. Coat the rubber seal with a dielectric compound furnished in the replacement ignition coil package.
10. Install the rubber arc seal washer and the coil spring, then position the coil into the distributor assembly. Make sure the wire spade terminals are properly positioned in the distributor cap.
11. Install and secure the coil retaining screws.
12. Install the coil cover to the distributor cap and secure using the fasteners.
13. If removed, engage the feed and module wire terminal connectors to the distributor cap.
14. Install the spark plug wires and ignition set retainer assembly to the top of the distributor cap.
15. Connect the negative battery cable.

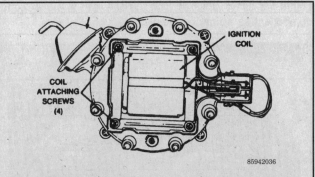

Fig. 37 The integral coil found in most HEI distributor assemblies is retained by 4 coil attaching screws

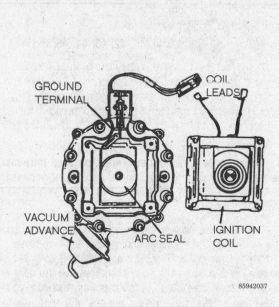

Fig. 38 Check the condition of the rubber arc seal located under the coil

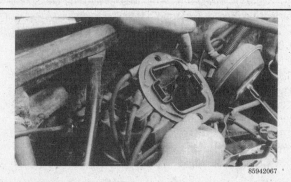

Fig. 39 Remove the ignition wire set retainer and wires from the top of the distributor cap

Fig. 40 Loosen the coil cover retaining screws

Fig. 41 Remove the coil cover for access to the ignition coil assembly

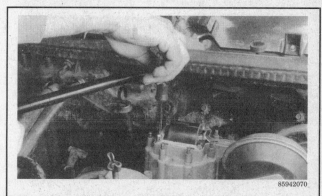

Fig. 42 Remove the coil retaining screws

Fig. 43 Disengage the spade terminal wire connectors from the distributor cap

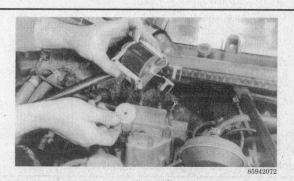

Fig. 44 Lift the coil from the distributor cap, then remove the rubber arc seal found under the coil

Fig. 45 Wipe the top of the distributor cap to remove any dirt, debris or moisture

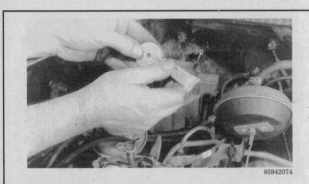

Fig. 46 Coat the rubber arc seal with dielectric compound

Fig. 47 If the wires must be repositioned further away for access, tag and disconnect wires from the harness retainer

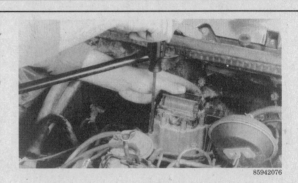

Fig. 48 Depress and turn the cap locktabs in order to release the cap from the distributor housing

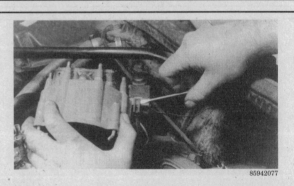

Fig. 49 Use a screwdriver to carefully release the wiring connector tabs, then disengage the tabs from the cap

Distributor Cap

▶ See Figures 47, 48, 49 and 50

1. Disconnect the negative battery cable and if necessary for access, remove the air cleaner assembly.
2. Remove the retainer and spark plug wires from the cap.
3. Remove the feed and module wire terminal connectors from the distributor cap.

➡If wire removal is difficult with the cap installed, release the cap locktabs and reposition the cap for better access to the wire connectors.

4. Depress and release the 4 distributor cap-to-housing locktabs and lift off the cap assembly.
5. If necessary for component replacement, remove the integral coil from the distributor cap.

To install:

6. If removed, install the integral coil to the distributor cap.
7. Install the cap to the distributor assembly and secure using the housing retainers.
8. Engage the feed and module wire terminal connectors to the distributor cap assembly.
9. Install the spark plug wires and retainer to the cap.
10. Connect the negative battery cable.

Rotor

▶ See Figures 51, 52, 53 and 54

1. Disconnect the negative battery cable and if necessary for access, remove the air cleaner assembly.

2. Remove the distributor cap from the housing assembly.

➡Although most rotors can only be installed in 1 direction, it is still wise to note the rotors position before removal.

3. Remove the two rotor attaching screws and note the position of the rotor, then remove the rotor from the distributor.

To install:

4. Install the rotor facing in the direction noted earlier, then secure the rotor using the 2 attaching screws.
5. Install the distributor cap to the housing assembly.
6. Connect the negative battery cable.

Fig. 50 Check the cap for corrosion or damage and clean or replace, as necessary

Fig. 51 Release the locktabs and remove the distributor cap

Fig. 52 Check the rotor for moisture, corrosion or damage

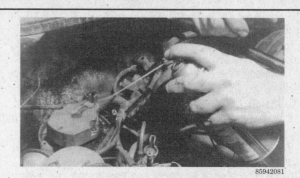

Fig. 53 A moisture displacing lubricant may get a wet engine running again, at least enough to get you home

Fig. 54 Loosen the rotor retaining screws and remove the rotor from the distributor assembly

Pick-Up Coil

▶ **See Figures 55 and 56**

1. Disconnect the negative battery cable.
2. Matchmark and remove the distributor assembly from the vehicle. Be sure to mark both the rotor-to-housing position and housing-to-engine position for assembly purposes. For details on distributor removal, refer to Section 3 of this manual.
3. Remove the rotor from the distributor, then mount the distributor assembly in a suitable soft-jawed vise. Be careful not to damage the distributor housing.
4. Mark the distributor shaft and gear so they may be reassembled in the same position, then drive out the roll pin from the base of the shaft.

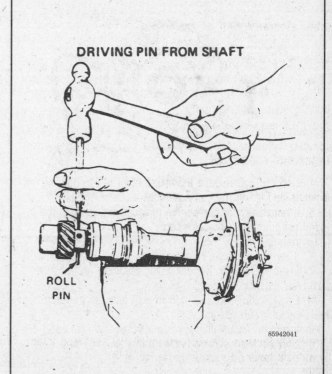

Fig. 55 Drive out the roll pin from the base of the distributor shaft using a punch

5. Remove the gear and pull the shaft assembly from the distributor.

6. Remove the 3 attaching screws, then remove the magnetic shield, as applicable.

7. Remove the retaining ring, pick-up coil, magnet and pole piece.

To install:

8. Install the pole piece, magnet, pick-up coil and retaining ring.

9. As applicable, install the magnetic shield and the 3 attaching screws.

10. Install the shaft assembly and gear to the distributor.

11. Make sure the shaft and gear are aligned as noted during removal, then drive roll pin into position.

12. Install the rotor to the distributor assembly as noted during removed, then remove the assembly from the vise.

13. Install the distributor assembly to the vehicle aligning the marks made during removal. When the distributor is inserted into the block, then rotor must turn and face the original rotor-to-housing alignment mark in order to assure correct engine timing.

14. Connect the negative battery cable.

Vacuum Advance (1975-80)

1. Disconnect the negative battery cable.

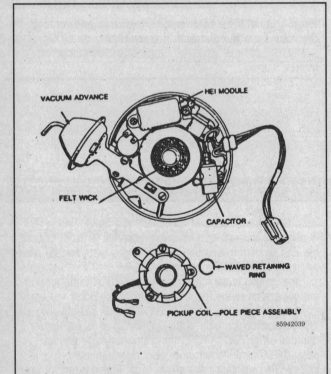

Fig. 56 Pick-up coil removal (note that 1981 and later models have no vacuum advance unit)

2. Remove the distributor cap and rotor as previously described.

3. Disconnect the vacuum hose from the vacuum advance unit.

4. Remove the two vacuum advance retaining screws, pull the advance unit outward, rotate and disengage the operating rod from its tang.

To install:

5. Install the vacuum advance unit to the distributor assembly by engaging the operating rod to the tang, then rotating and pushing the advance unit inward.

6. Secure the advance unit using the retaining screws.

7. Connect the vacuum hose to the unit.

8. Install the rotor and the distributor cap to the assembly.

9. Connect the negative battery cable.

Module

▶ **See Figures 57, 58, 59 and 60**

1. Disconnect the negative battery cable.

2. Remove the distributor cap and rotor as previously described.

3. Disengage the harness connector and pick-up coil spade connectors from the module while noting their positions for installation purposes. Be careful not to damage the wires when removing the connector.

➡**If difficulty is encountered, it may be easier to separate the module from the distributor, then disengage the wiring.**

4. Remove the two screws and module from the distributor housing.

To install:

5. Coat the bottom of the new module with dielectric compound supplied with the new module.

6. Install the ignition module to the distributor housing and secure using the retaining screws.

7. Carefully engage the harness connector and the pick-up coil space connectors to the module.

8. Install the rotor and the distributor cap to the distributor assembly.

9. Connect the negative battery cable.

Fig. 57 Remove the module retainers

Fig. 58 Gently pry the module upward to remove it

Fig. 59 Ignition module replacement, be sure to coat the mating surfaces with silicone lubricant

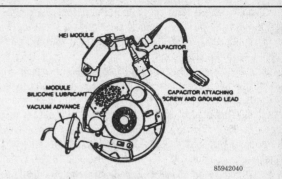

Fig. 60 View of the distributor housing with the ignition module/capacitor assembly removed

HEI SYSTEM TACHOMETER HOOKUP

For all vehicles with an internal coil distributor assembly, there should be a terminal marked TACH on the factory installed distributor cap. Connect one tachometer lead to this terminal and the other lead to a ground. On some tachometers, leads must be connected to the TACH terminal and to the battery positive terminal.

✱✱CAUTION

Never ground the TACH terminal; serious ignition module and coil damage will result. If there is any doubt as to the correct tachometer hookup, check with the tachometer manufacturer.

1975-77 models with an inline 6-cylinder engine utilize an HEI distributor with an external coil. For these particular vehicles, connect one tachometer lead to the TACH terminal on the ignition coil and connect the other one to a suitable ground.

IGNITION TIMING

Ignition timing is the measurement, in degrees of crankshaft rotation, of the point at which the spark plugs fire in each of the cylinders. It is measured in degrees before or after Top Dead Center (TDC) of the compression stroke.

Because it takes a fraction of a second for the spark plug to ignite the mixture in the cylinder, the spark plug must fire a little before the piston reaches TDC. Otherwise, the mixture will not be completely ignited as the piston passes TDC and the full power of the explosion will not be used by the engine.

The timing measurement is given in degrees of crankshaft rotation before the piston reaches TDC (BTDC). If the setting for the ignition timing is 5° BTDC, the spark plug must fire 5° before each piston reaches TDC. This only holds true, however, when the engine is at idle speed.

As the engine speed increases, the pistons go faster. The spark plugs have to ignite the fuel even sooner if it is to be completely ignited when the piston reaches TDC. To do this, most distributors have two means to advance the timing of the spark as the engine speed increases. This is accomplished by centrifugal weights within the distributor, and a vacuum diaphragm mounted on the side of the distributor. Later model vehicles may be equipped with Electronic Spark Timing (EST) in which no vacuum or mechanical advance is used. Instead, the EST system makes all timing changes electronically based on signals from various sensors.

If the ignition is set too far advanced (BTDC), the ignition and expansion of the fuel in the cylinder will occur too soon and tend to force the piston down while it is still traveling up. This causes engine ping. If the ignition spark is set too far retarded, after TDC (ATDC), the piston will have already passed TDC and started on its way down when the fuel is ignited. This will cause the piston to be forced down for only portion of its travel. This will result in poor engine performance and lack of power.

Timing marks consist of a notch on the rim of the crankshaft pulley and a scale of degrees attached to the front of the engine. The notch corresponds to the position of the piston in the number 1 cylinder. A stroboscopic (dynamic) timing light is used, which is hooked into the circuit of the No. 1 cylinder spark plug. Every time the spark plug fires, the timing light flashes. By aiming the timing light at the timing marks while the engine is running, the exact position of the piston within the cylinder can be read, since the stroboscopic flash makes the mark on the pulley appear to be standing still. Proper timing is indicated when the notch is aligned with the correct number on the scale.

There are three basic types of timing lights available. The first is a simple neon bulb with two wire connections (one for the spark plug and one for the plug wire, connecting the light in series). This type of light is quite dim, and must be held closely to the marks to be seen, but it is quite inexpensive. The second type of light operated from the car's battery. Two alligator clips connect to the battery terminals, while a third wire connects to the spark plug with an adapter. This type of light is more expensive, but the xenon bulb provides a nice bright flash which can even be seen in sunlight. The third type replaces the battery source with 110 volt house current, but still attaches to the No. 1 spark plug wire in order to determine when the plug is fired. Some timing lights have other functions built into them, such as dwell meters, tachometers, or remote starting switches. These are convenient, in that they reduce the tangle of wires under the hood, but may duplicate the functions of tools you already have.

➡Never pierce a spark plug wire in order to attach a timing light or perform tests. The pierced insulation will eventually lead to an electrical arc and related ignition troubles.

If your car has electronic ignition, you should use a timing light with an inductive pickup. This pickup simply clamps onto the No. 1 spark plug wire, eliminating the adapter. It is not susceptible to cross-firing or false triggering, which may occur with a conventional light, due to the greater voltages produced by electronic ignition.

Checking & Adjustment

▸ See Figures 61, 62 and 63

The vehicle emission label, which is found underhood, will often contain specifications or procedures for checking and adjusting timing that have been updated during production. The information contained on the label should always be used if it differs from these instructions.

The tachometer hookup for cars 1964-74 is the same as that shown for the dwell meter in the Tune-Up section. On 1975-77 HEI systems, the tachometer connects to the TACH terminal on the distributor for V8s, or on the coil for 6-cylinders, and to a ground. For 1978 and later models, all tachometer connec-

tions are to the TACH terminal. Some tachometers must connect to the TACH terminal and to the positive battery terminal. Some tachometers won't work at all with HEI. Consult the tachometer manufacturer if the instructions supplied with the unit do not give the proper connection.

1. Set the parking brake and block the drive wheels, warm the engine to normal operating temperature. Shut off the engine and connect the timing light to the No. 1 spark plug (left front on V8 and V6 or front on an inline 6-cyl.). Do not, under any circumstances, pierce a wire to hook up a light.

2. Clean off the timing marks, then label the pulley or damper notch and the timing scale with while chalk or paint for better visibility. If the timing notch on the damper or pulley is not visible from the top, the crankshaft should be bumped around using the starter or turned using a wrench on the front pulley bolt, in order to bring the mark to an accessible position.

3. Disconnect and plug the vacuum advance hose (if equipped) at the distributor, to prevent any distributor advance. The vacuum line is the rubber hose connected to the metal cone-shaped canister on the side of the distributor. A short screw, pencil, or a golf tee can be used to plug the hose.

➡1981 models with Electronic Spark Timing have no vacuum advance, therefore you may skip the previous step, but you must disconnect the four terminal EST connector in order to disable the electronic spark advance before proceeding.

4. Start the engine and adjust the idle speed to specification, refer to the Tune-Up Specifications chart. Some cars require that the timing be set with the transmission in Neutral.

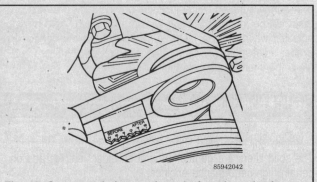

Fig. 62 Common timing mark scale found on the front of the engine

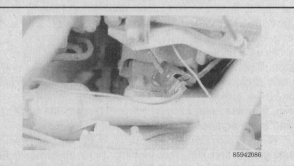

Fig. 61 Connect the timing light to the No. 1 spark plug wire. This type using an inductive clamp is easiest to use

Fig. 63 With the engine running, aim the timing light at the marks to determine ignition timing

You can disconnect the idle solenoid, if any, to get the speed down. Otherwise, adjust the idle speed screw. This is to prevent any centrifugal advance of timing in the distributor.

5. Aim the timing light at the timing marks. Be careful not to touch the fan, which may appear to be standing still. Keep your clothes and hair, and the light's wires clear of the fan, belts and pulleys. If the pulley or damper notch isn't aligned with the proper timing mark (see the Tune-Up Specifications chart), the timing will have to be adjusted.

➡ TDC or Top Dead Center corresponds to 0° mark on the scale. Either B, BTDC, or Before Top Dead Center, may be shown as BEFORE on the scale, while A, ATDC or After Top Dead Center, may be shown as AFTER.

6. Loosen the distributor base clamp locknut. You can buy special wrenches which make this task a lot easier on V8 and V6 engines. Turn the distributor slowly to adjust the timing, holding it by the body and not the cap. Turn the distributor in the direction of rotor rotation (found in the Firing Order illustration in this Section) to retard, and against the direction to advance.

➡ The 231 V6 engine has two timing marks on the crankshaft pulley. One timing mark is 1/8 in. wide and the other, four inches away, is 1/16 in. wide. The smaller mark is used for setting the timing with a hand-held timing light. The larger mark is used with the magnetic probe and is only of use to a dealer or garage that is equipped with such equipment. Make sure you set the timing using the smaller mark.

7. Once the timing is properly set, hold the distributor to keep it from the turning and tighten the locknut. Check the timing again after finishing with the nut in case the distributor moved as you tightened it.

8. If applicable, remove the plug and connect the distributor vacuum hose.

9. If necessary check and/or adjust the idle speed.

10. Shut off the engine and reconnect the EST wire (if equipped), then disconnect the timing light and tachometer.

VALVE LASH

Adjustment

▶ See Figures 64 and 65

Hydraulic valve lifters which are found in most late-model engines rarely require adjustment, and are not adjusted as part of a normal tune-up. All adjustment procedures concerning them will be found in Section 3. Hydraulic valve lifters must be adjusted whenever the rocker arms have been loosened. Proper adjustment will center the pushrods on the lifters and allow the lifters to perform their job of maintaining zero lash.

SOLID LIFTERS (1964-71)

Before adjusting solid lifters, thoroughly warm the engine. The solid lifters are generally found on older vehicles and on certain high-performance engines.

Engine Running

1. Set the parking brake and block the drive wheels, then start and run the engine until it reaches normal operating temperature.

2. Remove the valve covers retainers, then remove the covers and gaskets by tapping the end of the cover rearward to break the seal. Do not attempt to pry the cover off.

➡ Until you are thoroughly familiar with the technique, it may take some time to adjust the valves. It is likely that while you are adjusting the valve, some oil will drip onto the exhaust manifold and smoke causing a highly unpleasant working condition. This may be avoided using an extra set of valve covers which can be purchased from a junk yard for only a few dollars. The tops may be cut off the

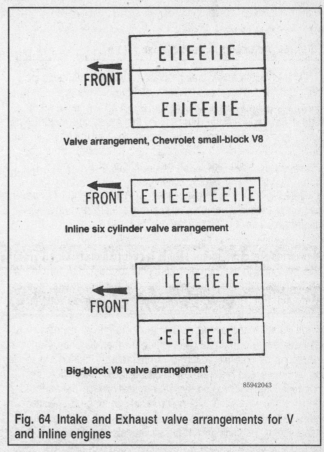

Valve arrangement, Chevrolet small-block V8

Inline six cylinder valve arrangement

Big-block V8 valve arrangement

85942043

Fig. 64 Intake and Exhaust valve arrangements for V and inline engines

extra covers and they may be temporarily installed on the cylinder heads. The walls of the these covers will keep oil from spilling on the manifolds, while the open tops will allow access to the rocker arm nuts for lash adjustment.

Adjusting the solid valve lifters

85942044

Fig. 65 Adjusting the solid valve lifters

3. If possible, avoid being splashed with hot oil using oil deflector clips. Place one at each oil hole in the rocker arm.

4. Measure between the rocker arm and the valve stem with a flat feeler gauge, then adjust the rocker arm stud nut until clearance agrees with the specification in the chart. If you are using the modified valve covers for oil control, it may be necessary to make additional modifications in the covers to allow access with the feeler gauge.

5. After adjusting all the valves, stop the engine. If you are using the modified valve covers, remove them from the cylinder heads.

6. Clean the gasket surfaces, then install the valve covers using new gaskets.

Engine Not Running

These are initial adjustments usually required after assembling an engine or performing a valve job. They should be followed up by an adjustment with the engine running as described above.

1. Set the engine to the No. 1 firing position (No. 1 TDC). This can be accomplished by removing the No. 1 spark plug and feeling for compression and the engine is slowly turned or by removing the valve cover and watching the valves for the No. 1 cylinder as the engine is turned. If the valves move while the timing notch approaches the 0 mark on the timing scale, then the engine crankshaft is 360 degrees away from No. 1 TDC. If the valves do not move while the notch approaches the 0 mark, then the No. 1 cylinder is at TDC.

2. Adjust the clearance between the valve stems and the rocker arms using a feeler gauge. Check the chart for the proper clearance. Adjust the following valves in the No. 1 firing position: Intake No. 2, 7, Exhaust No. 4, 8.

3. Turn the crankshaft ½ revolution clockwise. Adjust the following valves: Intake no. 1,8, Exhaust No. 3, 6.

4. Turn the crankshaft ½ revolution clockwise to the top of the No. 1 piston's exhaust stroke (this is TDC for No. 6 cylinder on V8 engines). Adjust the following valves in this position: Intake No. 3, 4, Exhaust No. 5, 7.

5. Turn the crankshaft ½ revolution clockwise. Adjust the following valves: Intake No. 5, 6, Exhaust No. 1, 2.

6. Run the engine until the normal operating temperature is reached. Reset all clearances, using the procedures listed above under Engine Running.

HYDRAULIC LIFTERS — 1972 AND LATER

All models, with the exception of those few already discussed, use a hydraulic tappet system with adjustable rocker mounting nuts to obtain zero lash. No periodic adjustment is necessary.

IDLE SPEED AND MIXTURE ADJUSTMENTS

Carburetor

Idle mixture and speed adjustments are critical aspects of exhaust emission control. It is important that all tune-up instructions be carefully followed to ensure satisfactory engine performance and minimum exhaust pollution. The different combinations of emission system applications on the various engines have resulted in a great variety of tune-up specifications. See the Tune-Up Specifications chart at the beginning of this section. Beginning in 1968, all models should have a decal conspicuously placed in the engine compartment that gives tune-up specifications. Because this label will often contain changes to specification made during production, it's information should always supersede that on the specification chart.

When adjusting a carburetor with two idle mixture screws, adjust them alternately and evenly, unless otherwise stated.

ADJUSTING THE IDLE SPEED AND MIXTURE

▶ **See Figures 66, 67, 68, 69 and 70**

In the following adjustment procedures the term lean roll means turning the mixture adjusting screws in (clockwise) from optimum setting to obtain an obvious drop in engine speed (usually 20 rpm). See Section 5 for additional adjustments and specifications for Carter and Rochester carburetors.

1964-66

Turn the idle screw(s) slightly in to seat, and then back out 1½ turns (3 when equipped with A.I.R.). Do not turn the idle mixture screws tightly against their seats or you could damage the screws. With the engine idling at operating temperature (air cleaner installed, preheater valve and choke valve wide open), adjust the idle speed to specification (automatic transmission in Drive; manual in Neutral).

Adjust the mixture screw to obtain the highest steady idle speed, then adjust the idle speed screw to the specified rpm. Adjust the mixture screw in to obtain a 20 rpm drop, then back the screw out 1/4 turn. Repeat this operation on the second mixture, if so equipped. Readjust the idle speed screw as necessary until the specified rpm is reached.

1967 Without Air

Adjust with the air cleaner removed.
1. Remove the air cleaner.
2. Connect a tachometer and vacuum gauge to the engine, set the parking brake, and place the transmission in Neutral.
3. Turn in the idle mixture screws until they gently seat, then back out 1½ turns.
4. Start the engine and allow it to come to the normal operating temperature. Make sure the choke is fully open, then adjust the idle speed screw to obtain the specified idle speed (automatic in Drive, manual in Neutral).
5. Adjust the idle mixture screw(s) to obtain the highest steady vacuum at the specified idle speed, except for the Rochester BV. For this carburetor, adjust the idle mixture screw out 1/4 turn from lean drop-off (the point where a 20-30 rpm drop is achieved by leaning the mixture).

➡ **On carburetors having a hot idle compensator valve (A/C models), hold the brass valve down with a pencil while making the mixture adjustment.**

6. Repeat Steps four and five as necessary.
7. Turn off the engine, remove the gauges, and install the air cleaner.

1967 With Air

Adjust with the air cleaner removed.

➡ **During this adjustment, air conditioning should be turned off on 327 and 350 cu. in. engines.**

1. Remove the air cleaner.
2. Connect a tachometer and a vacuum gauge to the engine, set the parking brake, and place the transmission in Neutral.
3. Turn in the idle mixture screw(s) until they gently seat, then back them out three turns.
4. Start the engine and allow it to reach normal operating temperature. Make sure the choke is fully open, then adjust the idle speed screw(s) to obtain the specified idle speed (automatic in Drive, manual in Neutral).
5. Turn the idle mixture screw(s) clockwise (in) to the point where a 20-30 rpm drop in the speed is achieved; this is the lean drop off point. Back out the screws 1/4 turn from this point.
6. Repeat Steps four and five if necessary.
7. Turn off the engine, remove the gauges, and install the air cleaner.

1968-69

Adjust with the air cleaner installed.

➡ **Turn off the air conditioner (if applicable) unless you car is a 1968 model with the 6-cylinder engine and automatic transmission. These cars should have the air conditioner turned on when setting the idle.**

1. Turn in the idle mixture screw(s) until they seat gently, then back them out three turns.
2. Start the engine and allow it to reach operating temperature. Make sure the choke is fully open and the preheater valve is open, then adjust the idle speed screw to obtain the specified idle speed (automatic in Drive, manual in Neutral).
3. Adjust the idle mixture screw(s) to obtain the highest steady idle speed, then readjust the idle speed screw to obtain the specified speed. On cars with an idle stop solenoid adjust as follows:
   a. Adjust the idle speed to 500 RPM (6 cylinder) or 600 rpm (1968 V8) by turning the hex on the solenoid plunger. Refer to the tune-up decal in the engine compartment for 1969 idle speeds.
   b. Disconnect the wire at the solenoid. This allows the throttle lever to seat against the idle screw.
   c. Adjust the idle screw to obtain 400 rpm (1968), then reconnect the wire. On 1969 models, adjust the idle as specified on the tune-up decal in the engine compartment.
4. Adjust one mixture screw to obtain a 20 rpm drop in idle speed, and back out the screw 1/4 turn from this point.
5. Repeat Steps three and four for the second mixture screw (if so equipped).
6. Readjust the idle speed to obtain the specified idle speed.

1970 Initial Adjustments

Adjust with the air cleaner installed.
1. Disconnect the fuel tank line from the vapor canister (EEC).
2. Connect a tachometer to the engine, start the engine and allow it to reach operating temperature. Make sure the choke and preheater valves are fully open.
3. Turn off the air conditioner and set the parking brake. Disconnect and plug the distributor vacuum line.
4. Make the following adjustments:

6-CYLINDER 250 ENGINE

1. Turn in the mixture screw until it gently seats, then back out the screw four turns.
2. Adjust the solenoid screw to obtain 830 rpm for manual transmissions (in Neutral) or 630 rpm for automatic transmission (in Drive).
3. Adjust the mixture screw to obtain 750 rpm for manual transmissions (in Neutral) or 600 rpm for automatic transmissions (in Drive).
4. Disconnect the solenoid wire and set the idle speed to 400 rpm, then reconnect it.
5. Reconnect the distributor vacuum line.

V8-307 & 400 ENGINES

1. Turn in the mixture screws until they seat gently, then back them out four turns.

2. Adjust the carburetor idle speed screw to obtain 800 rpm for manual transmissions (in Neutral), or adjust the solenoid screw to obtain 630 rpm for automatic transmissions (in Drive).

3. Adjust both mixture screws equally inward to obtain 700 rpm for manual transmissions, 600 rpm for automatic transmissions (in Drive).

4. On cars with automatic transmissions, disconnect the solenoid wire, set the carburetor idle screw to obtain 450 rpm and reconnect the solenoid.

5. Reconnect the distributor vacuum line.

V8-350 (250 HP) ENGINE

1. Turn in the mixture screws until they gently seat, then back them out four turns.

2. Adjust the solenoid screw to obtain 830 rpm for manual transmissions (in Neutral), or 630 rpm for automatic transmissions (in Drive).

3. Adjust both mixture screw equally inward to obtain 750 rpm for manual transmissions or 600 rpm for automatics (in Drive).

4. Disconnect the solenoid wire, set the carburetor idle screw to obtain 450 rpm, and reconnect the solenoid.

5. Reconnect the distributor vacuum line.

V8-350 (300 HP) & 402 (330 HP) ENGINES

1. Turn in both mixture screws until they gently seat, then back them out four turns.

2. Adjust the carburetor idle screw to obtain 775 rpm for manual transmission, 630 rpm for automatics (in Drive).

3. Adjust the mixture screw equally to obtain 700 rpm for manual transmission, 600 rpm for automatics (in Drive).

4. Reconnect the distributor vacuum line.

V8-402 (350 HP) & 454 ENGINES

1. Turn in both mixture screws until they gently seat, then back them out four turns.

2. Adjust the carburetor idle screw to obtain 700 rpm for manual transmission or 630 rpm for automatics (in Drive).

3. For cars with automatic transmission: adjust the mixture screws equally to obtain 600 rpm with the transmission in Drive.

4. For cars with manual transmissions: Turn in one mixture screw until the speed drops to 400 rpm, then adjust the carburetor idle screw to obtain 700 rpm. Turn in the other mixture screw until the speed drops 400 rpm, then regain 700 rpm by adjusting the carburetor idle screw.

5. Reconnect the distributor vacuum line.

1971-72 Initial Adjustments

Adjust with air cleaner installed. The following initial idle adjustments are part of the normal engine tune-up. There should be a tune-up decal placed conspicuously in the engine compartment outlining the specific procedure and settings for each engine application. Follow all of the instructions when adjusting the idle. These tuning procedures are necessary to obtain the delicate balance of variables for the maintenance of both reliable engine performance and efficient exhaust emission control.

➡**All engines have limiter caps on the mixture adjusting screws. The idle mixture is preset and the limiter caps installed at the factory in order to meet emission control**

standards. Do not remove these limiter caps unless all other possible causes of poor idle condition have been thoroughly checked out. The solenoid used on 1971 carburetors is different from the one used on earlier models. The Combination Emission Control System (C.E.C.) solenoid valve regulates distributor vacuum as a function of transmission gear position. The C.E.C solenoid is adjusted only after: 1) replacement of the solenoid, 2) major carburetor overhaul, or 3) after the throttle body is removed or replaced.

All initial adjustments described below are made:
1. With the engine warmed up and running.
2. With the choke fully open.
3. With the fuel tank line disconnected from the Evaporative Emission canister on all models.
4. With the vacuum hose disconnected at the distributor and plugged.

Be sure to reconnect the distributor vacuum hose and to connect the fuel tank-to-evaporative emission canister line or install the gas cap when idle adjustments are complete.

6-CYLINDER 250 ENGINE

1. Adjust the carburetor idle speed screw to obtain 550 rpm (700 rpm of 1972) for manual transmissions (in Neutral) or 550 rpm (600 rpm for 1972) for automatics (in Drive). Do not adjust the solenoid screw. Using the solenoid screw to set idle or incorrectly adjusting it may result in a decrease in engine braking.

2. Reconnect the vapor line and distributor vacuum advance line.

V8-307 & 350 (2-BBL) ENGINES

1. On 1971 models, adjust the carburetor idle speed screw to obtain 600 rpm for manual transmission (in Neutral) with the air conditioning turned off, or 550 rpm for automatic transmissions (in Drive) with the air conditioning turned on. Do not adjust the solenoid screw. On 1972 models, turn the air conditioning off and adjust the idle stop solenoid screw to obtain 900 rpm for manual transmissions (in Neutral) or 600 rpm for automatics (in Drive). Place the transmission in Park or Neutral and adjust the fast idle cam screw to get 1,850 rpm on 307 engines and 2,200 rpm on 350 engines.

2. Reconnect the vapor line and distributor vacuum advance line.

V8-350 (4-BBL) ENGINE

1. On 1971 models, adjust the carburetor idle speed screw to obtain 600 rpm for manual transmissions (in Neutral) with the air conditioning turned off, or 550 rpm for automatics (in Drive) with the air conditioning turned on. Do not adjust the solenoid screw. On 1972 models, turn the air conditioning off and adjust the idle stop solenoid screw to get 800 rpm for manual transmissions (in Neutral) or 600 rpm for automatic transmissions (in Drive).

2. For both 1971 and 1972 models, place the fast idle cam follower on the second step of the fast idle cam, turn the air conditioning off and adjust the fast idle to 1,350 rpm for manual transmissions (in Neutral) or 1,500 rpm for automatics (in Park).

3. Reconnect the vapor line and the distributor vacuum advance line on all models.

V8-402 & 454 ENGINES

1. On 1971 models, turn off the air condltioner and adjust the carburetor idle speed screw to obtain 600 rpm with manual transmissions in Neutral and automatics in Drive. Do not adjust the solenoid screw. On 1972 cars, turn off the air conditioning and adjust the idle stop solenoid screw to 800 rpm (in Neutral) for manual transmissions and 600 rpm (in Drive) for automatics.

2. On both 1971 and 1972 cars, place the fast idle cam follower on the second stop of the fast idle cam, turn off the air conditioner and adjust the fast idle to 1,350 rpm for manual transmissions (in Neutral) or 1,500 rpm for automatics (in Park).

3. Reconnect the vapor line and the distributor vacuum line on 1971 and 1972 cars.

1973

INITIAL ADJUSTMENTS

All models are equipped with idle limiter caps and idle solenoids. Disconnect the fuel tank line from the evaporative canister. The engine must be running at operating temperature, choke off, parking brake on, and rear wheels blocked. Disconnect the distributor vacuum hose and plug it. After adjustment, reconnect the vacuum and evaporative hoses.

6-CYLINDER 250 ENGINE

Adjust the idle stop solenoid for 700 rpm on manual transmission models or 600 rpm on automatics (in Drive). On manual models, make no attempt to adjust the CEC solenoid (the larger of the two carburetor solenoids) or a decrease in engine braking could result.

V8-307, 350 & 400 (2-BBL) ENGINES

1. With the air conditioning Off, adjust the idle stop solenoid screw for a speed of 900 rpm on manual models; 600 rpm for automatics in Drive.

2. Disconnect the idle stop solenoid electrical connector and adjust the idle speed screw (screw resting on lower stop of the cam) for 450 rpm on all 307 cu. in. engines, 400 rpm on 350 and 400 engines with automatic transmissions, or 500 rpm or 350 and 400 cu. in engine with manual transmissions.

V8-350 & 400 (4-BBL) ENGINES

1. Adjust the idle stop solenoid screw to 900 rpm (manual), 600 rpm (automatic in Drive).

2. Connect the distributor vacuum hose and position the fast idle cam follower on the top step of the fast idle cam (turn air conditioning off) and adjust the fast idle to 1,300 rpm on manual transmission 350 engines; 1,600 rpm for all automatics in Park.

V8-454 ENGINE

1. With the air conditioning off, adjust the idle stop solenoid screw to 900 rpm for the manual transmission; 700 rpm with the automatic transmission in Drive.

2. Connect the distributor vacuum hose and place fast idle cam follower on the top step of the fast idle cam. Adjust the fast idle to 1,300 rpm for manual transmission; and 1,600 rpm for automatic transmissions (in Park).

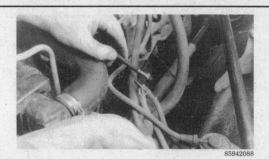

Fig. 66 Disconnect EVAP canister vapor line from carburetor to prevent canister purge from enrichening mixture during adjustment

1974

INITIAL ADJUSTMENTS

All models are equipped with idle limiter caps and idle solenoids. Disconnect the fuel tank line from the evaporative canister. The engine must be running at operating temperature, choke off, parking brake on, and rear wheels blocked. Disconnect the distributor vacuum hose and plug it. After adjustment, reconnect the vacuum and evaporative hoses.

6-CYLINDER 250 ENGINE

Using the hex nut on the end of the solenoid body, turn the entire solenoid to get 850 rpm for the manual transmission, 600 rpm for automatic transmissions in Drive.

V8-350 & 400 (2-BBL) ENGINES

1. Turn the air conditioning off. Adjust the idle stop solenoid screw for 900 rpm on manual; 600 rpm on automatic (in Drive).

2. De-energize the solenoid and adjust the carburetor idle cam screw (on low step of cam) for 400 rpm on automatic models (in Drive); 500 rpm on 350 engines with manual transmission.

V8-350 & 400 (4-BBL) ENGINES

1. Turn the air conditioning off. Adjust the idle stop solenoid screw for 900 rpm on manual transmission models; 600 rpm on automatic (in Drive).

2. Connect the distributor vacuum hose. Position the fast idle cam follower on the top step of the fast idle cam and

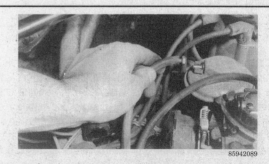

Fig. 67 If equipped with an EGR valve, most adjustments require that the line be disconnected and plugged as well

adjust the fast idle speed to 1,300 rpm on manual; 1,600 on automatic (in Park).

V8-454 ENGINE

1. With the air conditioning off, adjust the idle stop solenoid screw for 800 rpm with the manual transmission; 600 with the automatic transmission in Drive.

2. Reconnect the distributor vacuum advance hose and place the fast idle cam follower on the top step of the fast idle cam. With the air conditioning off, adjust the fast idle to 1,600 rpm for manual transmissions; 1,500 rpm for all automatics in Park.

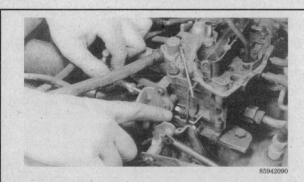

Fig. 68 On most carburetors, adjust the slow idle speed using throttle stop screw

Fig. 69 On carburetors so equipped, adjust the idle-up solenoid using a wrench

Fig. 70 On most carburetors, adjust the fast idle speed using the choke adjustment screw

1975-76

▶ See Figure 71

6-CYLINDER 250 (1-BBL) ENGINE

1. Idle speed is adjusted with the engine at normal operating temperature, air cleaner on, choke open, and air conditioning off (air models). Hook up a tachometer to the engine.

2. Block the rear wheels and apply the parking brake.

3. Disconnect the fuel tank hose from the evaporative canister.

4. Disconnect and plug the distributor vacuum advance hose.

5. Start the engine and check the ignition timing. Adjust if necessary.

Reconnect the vacuum hose. To adjust the idle speed, turn the solenoid in or out to obtain the higher of the two specifications listed on the decal. With the automatic transmission in Drive or the manual transmission in Neutral, disconnect the solenoid electrical connector and turn the 1/8 in. Allen screw in the end of the solenoid body to the lower idle speed.

6. Place the shift lever in Drive on cars with automatic transmissions and have an assistant apply the brakes. On cars with manual transmissions, put it into Neutral.

7. Cut the tab off the mixture limiter cap, but don't remove the cap. Turn the screw counterclockwise until the highest idle speed is reached.

8. Set the idle speed to the higher of the two listed idle speed by turning the solenoid in or out.

9. Check the tachometer and turn the mixture screw clockwise until the idle speed is at the lower of the two listed idle speeds.

10. Shut off the engine, remove the tachometer, and reconnect the carbon canister hose.

V8-350 (2-BBL) ENGINE

1. Idle speed is adjusted with the engine at normal operating temperature, air cleaner on, choke open, and air conditioning off. Hook up a tachometer to the engine.

2. Block the rear wheels and apply the parking brake.

3. Disconnect the fuel tank hose from the evaporative canister.

4. Disconnect and plug the distributor vacuum advance hose.

5. Start the engine and check the ignition timing. Adjust if necessary, then reconnect the vacuum hose.

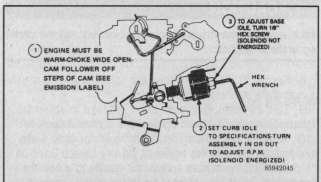

Fig. 71 Idle speed adjustment on a common carburetor for the 1976-78 6-cylinder engines

6. Adjust the idle speed screw to the specified rpm. If the figures given in the Tune-Up Specifications chart differ from those on the tune-up decal, those on the decal take precedence. Automatic transmissions should be in Drive, manual transmissions should be in Neutral.

❄❄CAUTION

Make doubly sure that the rear wheels are blocked and that the parking brake is applied.

7. Adjust the idle speed to the higher of the two figures on the tune-up decal. Back out the two mixture screws equally until the highest idle is reached. Reset the speed if necessary to the higher one on the tune-up decal. Next, turn the screws in equally until the lower of the two figures on the decal is obtained.

8. Shut off the engine, reconnect hose to evaporative canister, and remove blocks from wheels.

V8-350, 400 & 454 ENGINES

1975 4-barrel carburetors are equipped with idle stop solenoids. There are two idle speeds, one with the solenoid energized and second with the solenoid de-energized. Both are set using the solenoid. The slower speed (solenoid de-energized) is necessary to prevent dieseling by allowing the throttle plate to close further than at a normal idle speed.

1. Idle speed is set with the engine at normal operating temperature, air cleaner on, choke open, and air conditioning off. Hook up a tachometer to the engine.

2. Block the rear wheels and apply the parking brake.

3. Disconnect the fuel tank hose from the evaporative canister.

4. Disconnect and plug the distributor vacuum advance hose.

5. Start the engine and check the ignition timing. Adjust if necessary, then reconnect the vacuum hose.

➡For 1976, the idle solenoid has been dropped. To adjust the idle, follow Steps 1-5, skip Steps 6, 7, and 8, then follow Steps 9 and 10, using the idle speed screw.

6. Disengage the electrical connector at the idle solenoid.

7. Set the transmission in Drive, then adjust the low idle speed screw for the lower of the two figures given for idle speed.

❄❄CAUTION

Make sure that the drive wheels are blocked and the parking brake is applied.

8. Reconnect the idle solenoid and open the throttle slightly to extend the solenoid plunger.

9. Turn the solenoid plunger screw in or out to obtain the higher of the two idle speed figures (this is normal curb-idle)

10. To adjust the mixture, break off the limiter caps. Make sure that the idle is at the higher of the two speeds listed on the decal. Turn the mixture screws out equally to obtain the highest idle. Reset the idle speed with the plunger screw if necessary. Turn the mixture screw in until the lower of the two figures on the decal is obtained.

11. Shut off the engine, remove blocks from drive wheels, and reconnect hose to evaporative canister.

1977

▶ See Figures 72 and 73

1. First satisfy all the following requirements:
a. Set parking brake and block drive wheels.
b. Bring the engine to operating temperature.
c. Remove the air cleaner for access, but make sure all hoses stay connected.
d. Consult the Emission Control Information label under the hood, and disconnect and plug hoses as required by the instructions there.
e. Connect an accurate tach to the engine.

2. Set ignition timing as described above.

3. Remove the cap(s) from the idle mixture screw(s). Remove caps carefully, to prevent bending these screws.

4. Turn in the screw(s) till they seat very lightly, then back screw(s) out just far enough to permit the engine to run.

5. Put automatic transmission in Drive.

6. Back out screw(s) $\frac{1}{8}$ turn at a time, going alternately from screw to screw after each $\frac{1}{8}$ turn where there are two screws, until the highest possible idle speed is achieved. Then, set the idle speed as follows: 250 CID engine with manual transmission - 950; with automatic - 575; with automatic in California - 640; with automatic used in higher altitude area - 650; 305 V8 with manual transmission - 650; with automatic - 550; standard 350 V8 with automatic - 550; 350 V8 used at high altitudes - 650.

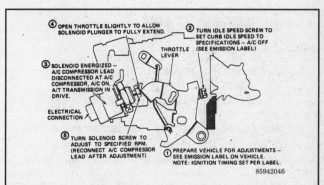

Fig. 72 Idle speed adjustment on a 4BBL, V8 engine with solenoid — 1977

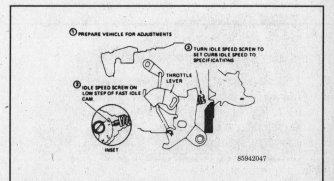

Fig. 73 Idle speed adjustment on a 4BBL, V8 engine without solenoid — 1977

7. After setting the idle speed, repeat the mixture adjustment to ensure that mixture is at the point where highest idle speed is obtained. Then, if idle speed has increased, repeat idle speed adjustment of Step 6.

8. Now, turn screw(s) in, going evenly in 1/8 turn increments where there are two, until the following idle speed are obtained: 250 CID engine with manual transmission - 750; with automatic - 550; with automatic in California - 600; with automatic used in high altitude areas - 600; 305 V8 with manual transmission - 600; with automatic - 500; standard 350 V8, manual transmission - 700; standard 350 V8 with automatic - 500; 350 V8 used at high altitudes - 600.

9. Reset idle speed to the value shown on the engine compartment sticker, if that differs from the final setting in the step above.

10. Check and adjust fast idle as described on the engine compartment sticker. See Section 5.

11. Reconnect any vacuum hoses that were disconnect for the procedure, and install the air cleaner.

12. If idle speed has changed, reset according to the engine compartment sticker. Disconnect tach.

1978-80
▶ **See Figures 74, 75, 76, 77, 78 and 79**

These models have sealed idle mixture screws; in most cases these are concealed under staked-in plugs. Idle mixture is adjustable only during carburetor overhaul, and requires the addition of propane as an artificial mixture enrichener.

See the emission control label in the engine compartment for procedures and specifications not supplied here. Prepare the car for adjustment (engine warm, choke open, fast idle screw off the fast idle cam) as per the label instructions.

1-BBL

1. Run the engine to normal operating temperature.
2. Make sure that the choke is fully opened.
3. Turn the A/C off and disconnect the vacuum line at the vapor canister. Plug the line.
4. Set the parking brake, block the drive wheels and place the transmission in Drive (AT) or Neutral (MT). Connect a tachometer to the engine according to the manufacturer's instructions.
5. Turn the solenoid assembly to achieve the solenoid-on speed.
6. Disconnect the solenoid wire and turn the 1/8 in. hex screw in the solenoid end, to achieve the solenoid-off speed.
7. Remove the tachometer, connect the canister vacuum line and shut off the engine.

2-BBL AND 4-BBL (EXCEPT V8-350 ENGINE)

1. Run the engine to normal operating temperature.
2. Make sure that the choke is fully opened, turn the A/C off, set the parking brake, block the drive wheels and connect a tachometer to the engine according to the manufacturer's instructions.
3. Disconnect and plug the vacuum hoses at the EGR valve and the vapor canister.
4. If equipped with an automatic transmission, place the transmission in Park. If equipped with a manual transmission, place transmission in Neutral.

5. Disconnect and plug the vacuum advance hose at the distributor. Check and adjust the timing.
6. Connect the distributor vacuum line.
7. Manual transmission cars without A/C and without solenoid: place the idle speed screw on the low step of the fast idle cam and turn the screw to achieve the specified idle speed.
8. If equipped with A/C: set the idle speed screw to the specified rpm. Disconnect the compressor clutch wire and turn the A/C on. Open the throttle momentarily to extend the solenoid plunger. Turn the solenoid screw to obtain the specified rpm. Finally, adjust the fast idle speed using the choke screw on the opposite side of the carburetor assembly.
9. Automatic transmission cars without A/C: manual transmission cars without A/C, solenoid-equipped carburetor: momentarily open the throttle to extend the solenoid plunger. Turn the solenoid screw to obtain the specified rpm. Disconnect the solenoid wire and turn the idle speed screw to obtain the slow engine idle speed.

V8-350 ENGINE

1. Run the engine to normal operating temperature.
2. Set the parking brake and block the drive wheels.
3. Connect a tachometer to the engine according to the manufacturer's instructions.
4. Disconnect and plug the purge hose at the vapor canister, then disconnect and plug the EGR vacuum hose at the EGR valve.
5. Turn the A/C off.
6. Place the transmission in Park (Automatic) or Neutral (Manual).
7. Disconnect and plug the vacuum advance line at the distributor. Check and adjust the timing.
8. Connect the vacuum advance line. Place the automatic transmission in Drive.
9. Manual transmission cars without A/C: adjust the idle stop screw to obtain the specified rpm. If equipped with A/C: with the A/C Off, adjust the idle stop screw to obtain the specified rpm. Disconnect the compressor clutch wire and turn the A/C On. Open the throttle slightly to allow the solenoid plunger to extend. Turn the solenoid screw to obtain the solenoid rpm listed on the underhood emission sticker.
10. Connect all hoses and remove the tachometer.

1981-82
▶ **See Figure 80**

Most of the E2ME (two barrel) and E4ME (four barrel) carburetors used on these models are equipped with an Idle Speed Control (ISC) assembly, monitored by the ECM, which controls which controls engine idle speed. The curb idle is programmed into the ECM and is not adjustable. Some models with A/C may be equipped with an Idle Speed Solenoid (ISS), if so, refer to the 1978-80 procedure.

1983-88
▶ **See Figures 80 and 81**

The E2ME (two barrel) and the E4ME (four barrel) carburetors used on these models all are equipped with an Idle Speed Control (ISC) assembly, monitored by the ECM, which controls engine idle speed. The curb idle is programmed into the ECM and is not adjustable.

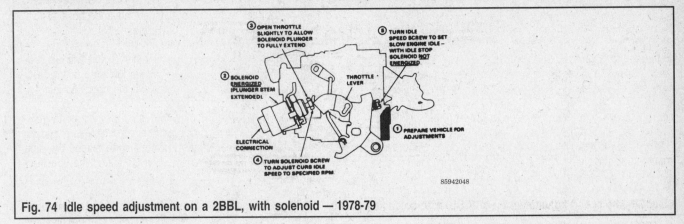

Fig. 74 Idle speed adjustment on a 2BBL, with solenoid — 1978-79

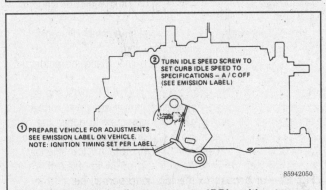

Fig. 75 Idle speed adjustment on a 2BBL, without solenoid — 1978-79

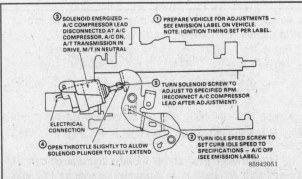

Fig. 76 Idle speed adjustment on a 4BBL, without solenoid — 1979 and later vehicles

Fig. 77 Idle speed adjustment on a 4BBL, with solenoid — 1979 and later vehicles

On the E4MC models, an Idle Load Compensator (ILC) mounted on the float bowl is used to control curb idle speeds. No attempt should be made to adjust this since it is controlled by the ECM.

On vehicles that do not include an ISC or ILC but are equipped with air conditioning, an Idle Speed Solenoid (ISS) is used to maintain curb idle speed any time the air conditioner compressor clutch is engaged. If so refer to the 1978-80 procedures.

Throttle Body Injection (TBI)

MINIMUM IDLE SPEED ADJUSTMENT

▶ See Figure 82

Beginning in 1985, some engines were available with a throttle body fuel injection system. All throttle body injected vehicles are controlled by a computer which regulates idle speeds and supplies the correct amount of fuel during all engine operating conditions. No periodic adjustments are necessary. However, if throttle body is replaced and a proper idle speed cannot be obtained, there is an adjustment which may be made. An idle stop screw is set at the factory and then covered to discourage tampering. If all other components of the fuel system are working properly and there is still a problem with the idle speed, the screw may be adjusted.

➡ Incorrectly adjusting the minimum idle speed stop screw will result in the IAC valve pintle to constantly bottom on its seat leading to an early valve failure.

1. Set the parking brake and block the drive wheels.
2. Start and run the engine until it reaches normal operating temperature. Make sure all accessories are turned OFF.
3. Stop the engine, then disconnect and plug any vacuum lines, as required.
4. Using an awl, pierce the idle stop screw cap and carefully pry the cap from the throttle body. The cap and screw can be found on the opposite side of the throttle body from the Idle Air Control (IAC) valve and Throttle Position (TP) sensor.
5. Connect a tachometer to the engine.
6. Ground the diagnostic terminal of the Assembly Line Data Link (ALDL) connector by using a jumper wire to connect the terminal to the Electronic Control Module (ECM) system

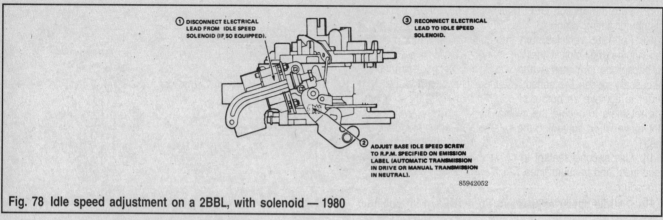

Fig. 78 Idle speed adjustment on a 2BBL, with solenoid — 1980

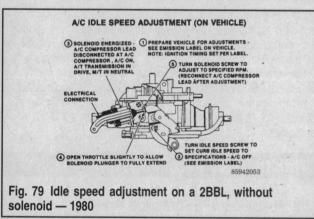

Fig. 79 Idle speed adjustment on a 2BBL, without solenoid — 1980

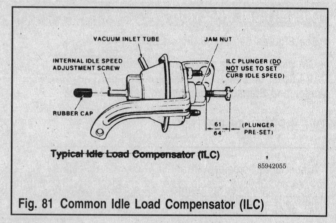

Fig. 81 Common Idle Load Compensator (ILC)

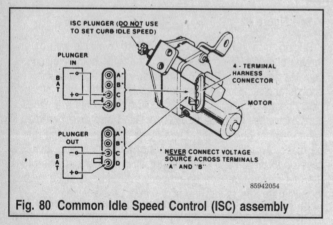

Fig. 80 Common Idle Speed Control (ISC) assembly

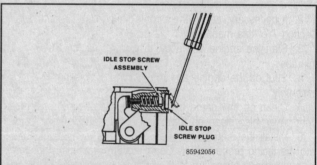

Fig. 82 For access to the idle stop screw, pierce the cap with an awl and carefully pry the cap from the side of the throttle body

ground terminal. The diagnostic and ground terminals are the 2 top right terminals on the ALDL connector which is found under the dash, near the steering column.

7. Turn the ignition ON, but DO NOT start the engine. Wait at least 45 seconds for the IAC valve pintle to extend and seat in the throttle body.

8. With the ignition ON and the ALDL test terminal still grounded, unplug the IAC valve connector. This will keep the pintle extended throughout the procedure and prevent the ECM from adjusting idle speed using the valve.

9. Remove the ground from the ALDL terminal, then disengage the distributor set timing connector in order to prevent the possibility of engine speed changing during the procedure due to timing changes.

10. Place the transmission in Neutral, then start the engine and allow it to idle.

➡If equipped, double check to make sure that the cruise control cables do not hold the throttle open.

11. Wait until the idle stabilizes, then check and adjust the idle speed as necessary:

   a. For 1985 vehicles, set the idle screw to obtain 500-600 rpm.

   b. For 1986 vehicles, have an assistant place the transmission in Drive and apply the brake pedal, then set the idle speed to 400-450 rpm.

   c. For 1987-88 vehicles, set the idle screw to obtain 400-450 rpm.

12. Turn the ignition **OFF**, then reconnect the IAC valve and distributor timing wiring.

13. For 1985 vehicles, turn the ignition **ON**, but do not start the engine, then adjust the TP sensor using a digital voltmeter to backprobe terminals A and B of the TP sensor connector. If necessary loosen the sensor retainers and pivot the switch in order to achieve an output of 0.525-0.075 volts, then tighten the retainers to secure the switch. Make sure the switch does not move when tightening the retainers or adjustment will be lost.

14. Use silicone sealant to cover the idle stop screw, then reconnect and vacuum lines which were plugged for the procedure.

15. Start the engine and check for proper idle operation.

Diesel Fuel Injection

▶ See Figures 83, 84, 85, 86 and 87

➡GM diesel engines are equipped with Roosa-Master, CAV-Lucas, or Stanadyne injection pumps. The Roosa-Master and Stanadyne pumps are nearly identical.

IDLE SPEED ADJUSTMENT

A special tachometer with an RPM counter suitable for the 263 V6 and 350 V8 diesels is necessary for this adjustment; a standard tach suitable for gasoline engines will not work.

1. Place the transmission in Park, block the rear wheels and firmly set the parking brake.

2. If necessary, adjust the throttle linkage as described in Section 7 of this manual.

3. Start the engine and allow it to warm up for 10-15 minutes.

4. Shut off the engine and remove the air cleaner assembly.

5. Clean off any grime from the timing probe holder on the front cover; also clean off the crankshaft balancer rim.

6. Install the magnetic probed end of the tachometer fully into the timing probe holder. Complete the remaining tachometer connections according to the tach manufacturer's instructions.

7. On V6 diesels equipped with air conditioning, disconnect the A/C compressor clutch lead at the compressor.

8. Make sure all electrical accessories are OFF, then disengage the 2 lead connector from the generator.

➡**At no time should either the steering wheel or brake pedal be touched.**

9. Start the engine and place the transmission in Drive (after first making sure the parking brake is firmly applied).

10. Check the slow idle speed reading against the one printed on the underhood emissions sticker. Reset if necessary.

11. Unplug the connector from the fast idle cold advance (engine temperature) switch, and install a jumper wire between the connector terminals.

➡**DO NOT allow the jumper to ground.**

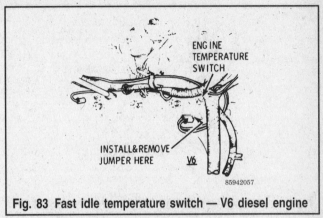

Fig. 83 Fast idle temperature switch — V6 diesel engine

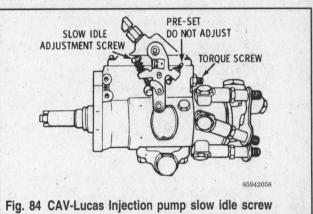

Fig. 84 CAV-Lucas Injection pump slow idle screw

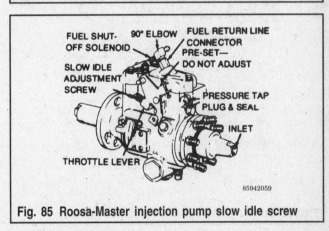

Fig. 85 Roosa-Master injection pump slow idle screw

12. Check the fast idle speed and reset if necessary according to the specification printed on the underhood emissions sticker.

13. Remove the jumper wire and reconnect the temperature switch.

14. Recheck the slow idle speed and reset if necessary.

15. Shut off the engine.

16. Reconnect the wiring leads at the generator and A/C compressor, as applicable.

17. Disconnect and remove the tachometer.

18. If equipped with cruise control, adjust the servo throttle rod to minimum slack, then put the clip in the first free hole closest to the bellcrank or throttle lever.

19. Install the air cleaner assembly.

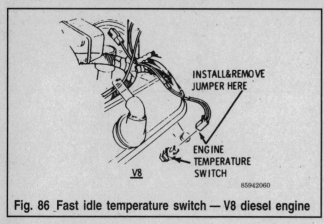

Fig. 86 Fast idle temperature switch — V8 diesel engine

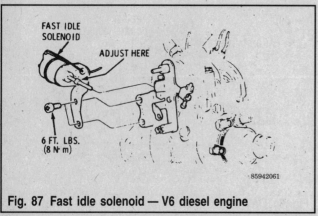

Fig. 87 Fast idle solenoid — V6 diesel engine

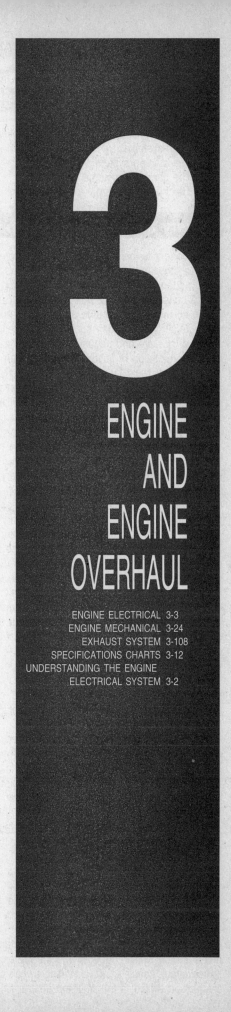

3

ENGINE
AND
ENGINE
OVERHAUL

UNDERSTANDING THE ENGINE ELECTRICAL SYSTEM

The engine electrical system can be broken down into three distinct sub-systems:

1. The starting system
2. The charging system
3. The ignition system.

Battery and Starting System

The battery is the first link in the chain of mechanisms which work together to provide cranking of the automobile engine. In most modern cars, the battery is a lead-acid electrochemical device consisting of six 2 volt (2V) subsections connected in series so the unit is capable of producing approximately 12V of electrical current. Each subsection, or cell, consists of a series of positive and negative plates held a short distance apart in a solution of sulfuric acid and water. The two types of plates are of dissimilar metals. This causes a chemical reaction to be set up, and it is this reaction which produces current flow from the battery when its positive and negative terminals are connected to an electrical appliance such as a lamp or motor. The continued transfer of electrons would eventually convert the sulfuric acid in the electrolyte to water, and make the two plates identical in chemical composition. As electrical energy is removed from the battery, its voltage output tends to drop. Thus, measuring battery voltage and battery electrolyte composition are two ways of checking the ability of the unit to supply power. During the starting of the engine, electrical energy is removed from the battery. However, if the charging circuit is in good condition and the operating conditions are normal, the power removed from the battery will be replaced by the generator (or alternator) which will force electrons back through the battery, reversing the normal flow, and restoring the battery to its original chemical state.

The battery and starting motor are linked by very heavy electrical cables designed to minimize resistance to the flow of current. Generally, the major power supply cable that leaves the battery goes directly to the starter, while other electrical system needs are supplied by a smaller cable. During the starter operation, power flows from the battery to the starter and is grounded through the car's frame and the battery's negative ground strap.

The starting motor is a specially designed, direct current electric motor capable of producing a very great amount of power for its size. One thing that allows the motor to produce a great deal of power is its tremendous rotating speed. It drives the engine through a tiny pinion gear (attached to the starter's armature), which drives the very large flywheel ring gear at a greatly reduced speed. Another factor allowing it to produce so much power is that only intermittent operation is required of it. Thus, little allowance for air circulation is required, and the windings can be built into a very small space.

The starter solenoid is a magnetic device which employs the small current supplied by the starting switch circuit of the ignition switch. This magnetic action moves a plunger which mechanically engages the starter and electrically closes the heavy switch which connects it to the battery. The starting switch circuit consists of the starting switch contained within the ignition switch, a transmission neutral safety switch or clutch pedal switch, and the wiring necessary to connect these with the starter solenoid or relay.

A pinion, which is a small gear, is mounted to a one-way drive clutch. This clutch is splined to the starter armature shaft. When the ignition switch is moved to the start position, the solenoid plunger slides the pinion toward the flywheel ring gear via a collar and spring. If the teeth on the pinion and flywheel match properly, the pinion will engage the flywheel immediately. If the gear teeth butt one another, the spring will be compressed and will force the gears to mesh as soon as the starter turns far enough to allow them to do so. As the solenoid plunger reaches the end of its travel, it closes the contacts that connect the battery and starter and then the engine is cranked.

As soon as the engine starts, the flywheel ring gear begins turning fast enough to drive the pinion at an extremely high rate of speed. At this point, the one-way clutch begins allowing the pinion to spin faster that the starter shaft so that the starter will not operate at excessive speed. When the ignition switch is released from the starter position, the solenoid is de-energized, and a spring contained within the solenoid assembly pulls the gear out of mesh and interrupts the current flow to the starter.

Some starters employ a separate relay, mounted away from the starter, to switch the motor and solenoid current on and off. The relay thus replaces the solenoid electrical switch, but does not eliminate the need for a solenoid mounted on the starter used to mechanically engage the starter drive gears. The relay is used to reduce the amount of current the starting switch must carry.

The Charging System

The automobile charging system provides electrical power for operation of the vehicle's ignition system, starting system and all the electrical accessories. The battery serves as an electrical surge or storage tank, storing (in chemical form) the energy originally produced by the belt driven generator/alternator. The system also provides a means of regulating generator/alternator output to protect the battery from being overcharged and to avoid excessive voltage to the accessories.

The storage battery is a chemical device incorporating parallel lead plates in a tank containing a sulfuric acid-water solution. Adjacent plates are slightly dissimilar, and the chemical reaction of the two dissimilar plates produces electrical energy when the battery is connected to a load such as the starter motor. The chemical reaction is reversible, so that when the generator/alternator is producing a voltage greater then that produced by the battery, electricity is forced into the battery, and the battery is returned to its fully charged state.

The vehicle's alternator or generator is driven mechanically, through a V-belt, by the engine crankshaft. It consists of two coils of fine wire, one stationary (the stator), and one movable (the rotor). The rotor may also be known as the armature and consists of fine wire wrapped around an iron core which is mounted on a shaft. The electricity which flows through the two coils of wire (provided initially by the battery in some cases) creates an intense magnetic field around both rotor and stator, and the interaction between the two fields creates voltage, allowing the generator/alternator to power the accessories and charge the battery.

All vehicles covered in this manual will be equipped with either a generator or an alternator. The earlier of the 2 (generator) is the direct current (DC) type. The DC generator voltage is produced in the armature and carried off the spinning armature by stationary brushes contacting the commutator. The commutator is a series of smooth metal contact plates on the end of the armature. The commutator plates, which are separated from one another by a very short gap, are connected to the armature circuits so that current will flow in one direction only in wires carrying the generator output. The generator stator consists of two stationary coils of wire which draw some of the output current of the generator to form a powerful magnetic field and create the interaction of fields which generates the voltage. The generator field is wired in series with the regulator.

Newer automobiles use alternating current generators or alternators because they are more efficient, can be rotated at higher speeds, and have fewer brush problems, In an alternator, the field rotates while all the current produced passes only through the stator windings. The brushes bear against continuous slip rings rather than a commutator. This causes the current produced to periodically reverse the direction of its flow. Diodes (electrical one-way switches) block the flow of current from traveling in the wrong direction. A series of diodes is wired together to permit the alternating flow of the stator to be converted to a pulsating, but unidirectional, flow of current from traveling in the wrong direction. The alternator's field is wired in series with the voltage regulator.

The regulator consist of several circuits. Each circuit has a core, or magnetic coil of wire, which operates a switch. Each switch is connected to ground through one or more resistors. The coil of wire responds directly to system voltage. When the voltage reaches the required level, the magnetic field created by the winding of wire closes the switch and inserts a resistance into the generator field circuit, thus reducing the output. The contacts of the switch cycle open and close many times each second to precisely control voltage.

While alternators are self-limiting as far as maximum current is concerned, DC generators employ a current regulating circuit which responds directly to the total amount of current flowing through the generator circuit rather than to the output voltage. The current regulator is similar to the voltage regulator except all system current must flow through the energizing coil on its way to the various accessories.

Safety Precautions

Observing these precautions will help avoid damage to the vehicle's electrical system and ensure safe handling of the system components:

• Be absolutely sure of the polarity of a booster battery before making connections. Connect the cables positive to positive, and negative to a good ground. Connect positive cables first and then make the last connection to ground on the body of the booster vehicle so that arcing cannot ignite hydrogen gas that may have accumulated near the battery. Even momentary connection of a booster battery with the polarity reversed will damage alternator diodes.

• Disconnect both vehicle battery cables before attempting to charge a battery.

• Never ground the alternator or generator output or battery terminal. Be cautious when using metal tools around a battery to avoid creating a short circuit between the terminals.

• Never ground the field circuit between the generator and regulator.

• Never run an alternator or generator without load unless the field circuit is disconnected.

• Never attempt to polarize an alternator.

• Keep the regulator cover in place when taking voltage and current limiter readings.

• Use insulated tools when adjusting the regulator.

• Whenever DC generator-to-regulator wires have been disconnected, the generator must be repolarized. To do this with an externally grounded, light duty generator, momentarily place a jumper wires between the battery terminal and the generator terminal of the regulator. With an internally grounded heavy duty unit, disconnect the wire to the regulator field terminal and touch the regulator battery terminal with it.

ENGINE ELECTRICAL

Distributor

➡For ignition system service not found below, please refer to Section 2 of this manual.

REMOVAL & INSTALLATION

▶ See Figures 1 and 2

Point-Type Ignition, 1964-74

1. Disconnect the negative battery cable.
2. Remove the distributor cap and position it out of the way.
3. Disconnect the primary coil wire and the vacuum advance hose.

4. Scribe a mark on the distributor body and the engine block showing their relationship. Mark the distributor housing to show the direction in which the rotor is pointing. Note the positioning of the vacuum advance unit.

5. Remove the hold-down bolt and clamp and remove the distributor.

6. To install the distributor with the engine undisturbed:

   a. Reinsert the distributor into its opening, aligning the previously made marks on the housing and the engine block.

   b. The rotor may have to be turned either way a slight amount to align the rotor-to-housing marks.

   c. Install the retaining clamp and bolt. Install the distributor cap, primary wire or electrical connector, and the vacuum hose.

   d. Start the engine and check the ignition timing.

7. To install the distributor with the engine disturbed:

a. Turn the engine to bring the No. 1 piston to the top of its compression stroke. This may be determined by inserting a rag into the No. 1 spark plug hole and slowly turning the engine over. When the timing mark on the crankshaft pulley aligns with the 0 on the timing scale and the rag is blown out by compression, the No. 1 piston is at top dead center (TDC).

➡ On Mark IV (big block) V8 engines there is a punch mark on the distributor drive gear which indicates the rotor position. Thus, the distributor may be installed with the cap in place. Align the punch mark 2 degrees clockwise from the No. 1 cap terminal, then rotate the distributor body 1/8 turn counterclockwise and push the distributor down into the block.

b. Install the distributor to the engine block so that the vacuum advance unit points in the correct direction.

c. Turn the rotor so that it will point to the No. 1 terminal in the cap.

d. Install the distributor into the engine block. It may be necessary to turn the rotor a little in either direction in order to engage the gears.

e. Connect the negative battery cable, then tap the starter a few times to ensure that the oil pump shaft is mated to the distributor shaft.

f. Bring the engine to No. 1 TDC again and check to see that the rotor is indeed pointing toward the No. 1 terminal of the cap.

g. After correct positioning is assured, turn the distributor housing so that the points are just opening. Tighten the retaining clamp.

h. Install the cap and primary wire. Check the ignition timing. Install the vacuum hose.

HEI Distributor, 1975 and later

1. Disconnect the negative cable from the battery.

2. Tag and disengage the feed and module terminal connectors from the distributor cap.

3. Disconnect the hose from the distributor vacuum advance unit (1975-80 only).

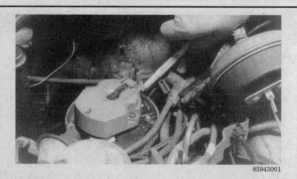

Fig. 1 Scribe matchmarks for the distributor housing and rotor alignment

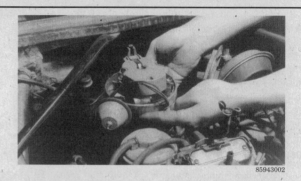

Fig. 2 Lift upward until the shaft clears the bore in the intake manifold, then tilt and remove the distributor

4. Depress and release the 4 distributor cap-to-housing retainers and lift off the cap assembly.

5. Scribe a mark on the distributor body and the engine block showing their relationship. Mark the distributor housing to show the direction in which the rotor is pointing or otherwise matchmark the rotor with the housing.

6. Loosen and remove the distributor hold-down bolt and clamp, then carefully lift the distributor out of the engine. Note the position of the rotor alignment mark on the housing and make a second mark on the housing to align with the rotor. You may wish to reinstall the distributor cap in order to protect the internal components from damage.

UNDISTURBED ENGINE

1. With a new O-ring on the distributor housing and the rotor aligned with the second mark on the housing, install the distributor, taking care to align the distributor body mark with the mark scribed on the engine. When fully installed, the rotor should turn and align with the first distributor housing mark and therefore point in the same direction as before removal. It may be necessary to lift the distributor and turn the rotor slightly to properly align the gears and the oil pump driveshaft.

2. With the respective marks aligned, install the clamp and bolt finger-tight.

3. Install and secure the distributor cap.

4. Engage the feed and module connectors to the distributor cap.

5. Connect a timing light to the engine and either plug the vacuum hose or disconnect the distributor set timing connector, as applicable.

6. Connect the negative cable to the battery.

7. Start the engine and set the timing, then secure the distributor clamp bolt.

8. Recheck the timing to assure it was not changed while tightening the clamp bolt, then shut the engine **OFF**. Disconnect the timing light and either unplug and connect the hose to the vacuum advance or reconnect the distributor timing connector.

DISTURBED ENGINE

1. Remove the No. 1 spark plug.

2. Place a finger over the No. 1 spark plug hole and rotate the engine by hand until the compression can be felt.

➡**An alternate method of finding No. 1 TDC when the valve cover for that cylinder bank is removed involves watching to see if the valves open as the timing mark approaches 0. If any valves open, then the engine is 360 degrees out of No. 1 TDC and should be turned one full revolution. If the valves remain closed, it signifies that the cylinder was on its compression stroke and is at TDC when the mark reaches 0 on the timing plate.**

3. Align the timing mark on the crankshaft pulley with the **0** mark on the timing plate.

4. Align the distributor rotor near the No. 1 spark plug tower.

5. Install the distributor, the hold down clamp, the bolt and the cap. It may be necessary to turn the rotor a little in either direction in order to engage the gears.

➡**With the distributor installed, make sure that the rotor is aligned with the No. 1 spark plug tower of the cap.**

6. Start and run the engine, then check and adjust the ignition timing.

Alternator

▸ **See Figures 3, 4 and 5**

Though the earliest vehicles covered by this manual may be equipped with a generator, most are equipped with an alternator of either external regulator (through early 1970's) or internal regulator (mid 1970's and later) type. Of the internal regulator alternators, there are 2 types used on these vehicles; the SI Delcotron series with 2 terminal integral regulator and the CS Delcotron series with the 4 terminal integral regulator. Once again, most vehicles will be equipped with one type, the SI series alternator, though a few late 1980's vehicles may be equipped with the CS series.

The alternating current generator (alternator) supplies a continuous output of electrical energy at all engine speeds. The alternator generates electrical energy and recharges the battery by supplying it with electrical current. This unit consists of four main assemblies: two end frame assemblies, a rotor assembly, and a stator assembly. The rotor assembly is supported in the drive end frame by a ball bearing and at the other end by a roller bearing. These bearings are lubricated during assembly and require no maintenance. There are six diodes in the end frame assembly. These diodes are electrical check valves that also change the alternating current developed within the stator windings to a direct (DC) current at the output (BAT) terminal. Three of these diodes are negative and are mounted flush with the end frame while the other three are positive and are mounted into a strip called a heat sink. The positive diodes are easily identified as the ones within small cavities or depressions.

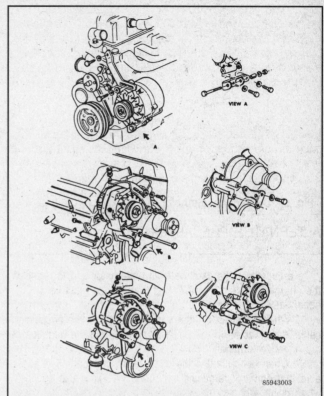

85943003

Fig. 3 Examples of common alternator mounting- inline 6-cylinder (top), V6 and small block V8 (center) and big-block V8 (bottom)

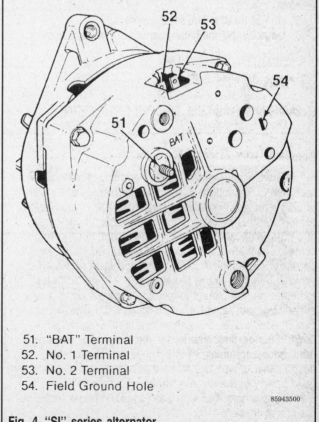

51. "BAT" Terminal
52. No. 1 Terminal
53. No. 2 Terminal
54. Field Ground Hole

85943500

Fig. 4 "SI" series alternator

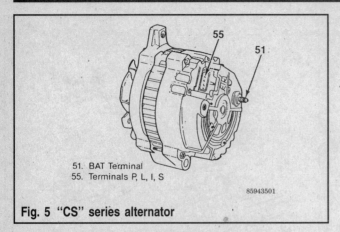

51. BAT Terminal
55. Terminals P, L, I, S

85943501

Fig. 5 "CS" series alternator

ALTERNATOR PRECAUTIONS

To prevent serious damage to the alternator and the rest of the charging system, the following precautions must be observed.

1. When installing a battery, make sure that the positive cable is connected to the positive terminal and the negative to the negative terminal

2. When jump-starting the car with another battery, make sure that only like terminals are connected. This also applies when using a battery charger.

3. Never operate the alternator with the battery disconnected or otherwise on an uncontrolled open circuit. Double check to see that all connections are tight.

4. Do not short across or ground any alternator or regulator terminals.

5. Do not try to polarize the alternator.

6. Do not apply full battery voltage to the field (brown) connector.

7. Always disconnect the battery ground cable before disconnecting the alternator lead.

CHARGING SYSTEM TROUBLESHOOTING

Alternator With External Regulator

There are many ways in which the charging system can malfunction. Though the source of a problem is often difficult to diagnose, requiring special equipment and a good deal of experience, it is not always the case. If the charging system fails completely and causes the dash board warning light to come on or the battery to become dead, troubleshooting may be easier. To troubleshoot a complete system failure on these vehicles only two pieces of equipment are needed: a test light, to determine that current is reaching a certain point; and a current indicator (ammeter), to determine the direction of the current flow and its measurement in amps. This test works under three assumptions:

• The battery is known to be good and fully charged. (If in doubt, either charge and test the battery or substitute a known good battery of the same rating from another vehicles)

• The alternator belt is in good condition and adjusted to the proper tension.

• All connections in the system are clean and tight.

➡In order for the current indicator to give a valid reading, the car must be equipped with battery cables which are of the same gauge size and quality as original equipment battery cables.

1. Turn off all electrical components on the car. Make sure the doors of the car are closed. If the car is equipped with a clock, disconnect the clock by removing the lead wire from the rear of the clock. Disconnect the positive battery cable from the battery and connect the ground wire on a test light to the disconnected positive battery cable. Touch the probe end of the test light to the positive battery post. The test light should not illuminate. If the test light does come on, there is a short or open circuit on the car.

2. Disengage the voltage regulator wiring harness connector at the voltage regulator. Turn the ignition key **ON**. Connect the wire on a test light to a good ground (engine bolt), then touch the probe end of a test light to the ignition wire connector into the voltage regulator wiring connector. This wire corresponds to the **I** terminal on the regulator. If the test light goes ON, the charging system warning light circuit is complete. If the test light does not illuminate and the warning light on the instrument panel is ON either the resistor wire, which is parallel with the warning light, or the wiring to the voltage regulator, is defective. If the test light does not come illuminate and the warning light is not ON, either the bulb is defective or the power supply wire from the battery through the ignition switch to the bulb has an open circuit. Connect the wiring harness to the regulator.

3. Examine the fusible link wire in the wiring harness from the starter relay to the alternator. If the insulation on the wire is cracked or split, the fuse link may be melted. Connect a test light to the fuse link by attaching the ground wire on the test light to an engine bolt and touching the probe end of the light to the bottom of the fuse link wire where it splices into the alternator output wire. If the bulb in the test light does not light, the fuse link is melted.

4. Start the engine and place a current indicator on the positive battery cable. Turn off all electrical accessories and make sure the doors are closed. If the charging system is working properly, the gauge will show a draw of less than 5 amps. If the system is not working properly, the gauge will show a draw of more than 5 amps. A charge moves the needle toward the battery, a draw moves the needle away from the battery. Turn the engine off.

5. Disconnect the wiring harness from the voltage regulator at the regulator connector. Connect a male spade terminal (solderless connector) to each end of a jumper wire. Insert one end of the wire into the wiring harness connector which corresponds to the **A** terminal on the regulator. Insert the other end of the wire into the wiring harness connector which corresponds to the **F** terminal on the regulator. Position the connector with the jumper wire installed so that it cannot contact any metal surface under the hood. Position a current indicator gauge on the positive battery cable. Have an assistant start the engine. Observe the reading on the current indicator. Have your assistant slowly raise the speed of the engine to about 2,000 rpm or until the current indicator needle stops moving, whichever comes first. Do not run the engine for more than a short period of time in this condition. If the wiring harness connector or jumper wire becomes excessively hot during this test, turn off the engine and check for a grounded wire in the

regulator wiring harness. If the current indicator shows a charge of about three amps less than the output of the alternator, the alternator is working properly. If the previous tests showed a draw, the voltage regulator is defective. If the gauge does not show the proper charging rate, the alternator is defective.

Delcotron "SI" Series Alternator With Internal Regulator
▶ See Figure 6

➡Delcotron "SI" alternators can be identified by having a two terminal integral voltage regulator connector. Delcotron "CS" alternators are identified by having a four terminal integral voltage regulator connector on the alternator.

PRELIMINARY CHARGING SYSTEM TESTS

1. If you suspect a defect in your internal regulator charging system, first perform these general checks before going on to more specific tests.
2. Check the condition of the alternator belt and tighten it if necessary.
3. Clean the battery cable connections at the battery. Make sure the connections between the battery wires and the battery clamps are good.
4. Test the battery cables as outlined in Section 1 of this manual.
5. Check the charging system wiring for any obvious breaks or shorts.
6. Check the battery to make sure it is fully charged and in good condition.
7. If all the previous checks were ok, proceed to the applicable test.

CHARGING SYSTEM STATIC TEST

1. Disconnect the two terminal connector at the alternator.
2. With the ignition **ON**, connect a voltmeter between the alternator's harness connector terminal 1 (brown wire) and ground.
   • If 10 volts or greater is measured go to the next step.
   • If no voltage is measured, repair the short to ground in the wiring between the generator light in the instrument panel and the alternator connector.
3. With the ignition **ON**, connect a voltmeter between the alternator's harness connector terminal 2 (red wire) and ground.
   • If 10 volts or greater is measured, go to the next step.
   • If no voltage is measured, repair the open or short to ground in the wire between the alternator and the fusible link at the starter solenoid.
4. Measure voltage at the alternator between the "BAT" ring terminal and ground.
   • If 10 volts or greater is measured, perform the alternator output test.
   • If no voltage is measured, repair the open in the wiring.

ALTERNATOR OUTPUT TEST

This test can only be performed on Delcotron "SI" type alternators which have the alternator field ground tab test hole.

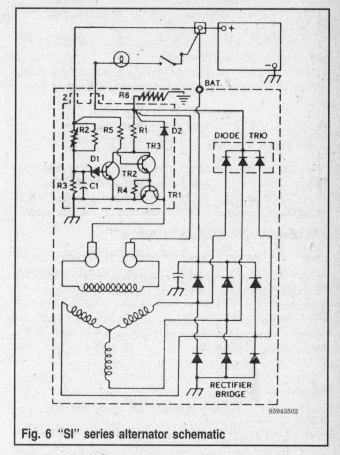

Fig. 6 "SI" series alternator schematic

This test cannot be performed on the Delcotron "CS" type alternators. An ammeter is required to perform this test.

➡Delcotron "SI" alternators can be identified by having a two terminal integral voltage regulator connector. Delcotron "CS" alternators are identified by having a four terminal integral voltage regulator connector on the alternator.

1. Disconnect the negative battery cable.
2. Disconnect the battery terminal on the alternator.
3. Connect the ammeter's negative lead to the battery wire disconnected in the previous step.
4. Reconnect the negative battery cable and turn on all lights and accessories. Leave the lights and accessories on for a minute or two to draw down the battery a little before going on to the next step.
5. Start the engine and run it until you obtain a maximum current reading on the ammeter. Make sure all accessories are ON (blower motor, wipers, air conditioning, high beam headlights, etc.). Record the reading and compare to the alternator's rated output, which is stamped onto the frame of the alternator. If the reading is:
   • Within 10 percent of the rated output, the alternator is good.
   • Not within 10 percent of the rated output go to the next step.
6. With the engine running at moderate speed and all accessories ON, ground the alternator field. This can be done by inserting a insulated screwdriver in the alternator field test hole and allowing the screwdriver shaft to touch the alternator case. Again record the reading and compare to the alternator's rated

output, which is stamped onto the frame of the alternator. If the reading is:

• Within 10 percent of the rated output, the alternator's regulator is most likely defective.

• Not within 10 percent of the rated output, the problem is with either the alternator's field winding, diode trio, rectifier bridge or stator.

Delcotron "CS" Altnerator With Internal Regulator

▶ See Figure 7

➡Delcotron "SI" alternators can be identified by having a two terminal integral voltage regulator connector. Delcotron "CS" alternators are identified by having a four terminal integral voltage regulator connector on the alternator.

PRELIMINARY CHARGING SYSTEM TESTS

1. If you suspect a defect in your internal regulator charging system, first perform these general checks before going on to more specific tests.

2. Check the condition of the alternator belt and tighten it if necessary.

3. Clean the battery cable connections at the battery. Make sure the connections between the battery wires and the battery clamps are good.

4. Test the battery cables as outlined in Section 1 of this manual.

5. Check the charging system wiring for any obvious breaks or shorts.

6. Check the battery to make sure it is fully charged and in good condition.

7. If all the previous checks were ok, proceed to the applicable test.

STATIC TEST

1. Disconnect the four terminal connector at the alternator.

2. With the ignition **ON**, connect a voltmeter between the alternator's harness connector terminal "L" (brown wire) and ground.

• If 10 volts or greater is measured go to the next step.

• If no voltage is measured, repair the short to ground in the wiring between the generator light in the instrument panel and the alternator connector.

3. With the ignition **ON**, connect a voltmeter between the alternator's harness connector terminal "I" (red or pink wire) and ground.

• If 10 volts or greater is measured, go to the next step.

• If no voltage is measured, repair the open or short to ground in the wire between the alternator and the fusible link at the starter solenoid.

4. Measure voltage at the alternator between the "BAT" ring terminal and ground.

• If 10 volts or greater is measured, the problem is in the alternator. Remove the alternator for repair or replacement.

• If no voltage is measured, repair the open in the wiring.

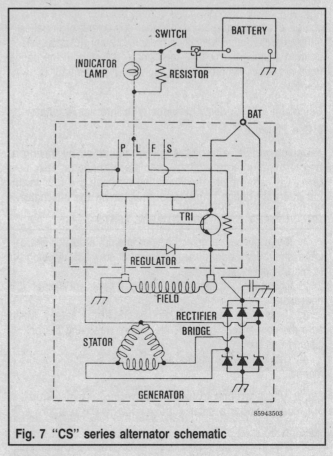

Fig. 7 "CS" series alternator schematic

REMOVAL

▶ See Figures 8, 9, 10, 11, 12 and 13

1. Disconnect the negative battery cable to prevent diode damage and prevent the chance of shorting the battery cables.

2. Tag and disconnect the alternator wiring. Use a small screwdriver to release the locktab on the alternator connector, then use a wrench to loosen the stud nut and disconnect the terminal wiring.

3. Loosen the alternator lower though-bolt, then remove the alternator brace/adjuster bolt.

4. On some vehicles equipped with power steering, it may be necessary to loosen the pump brace and mount nuts, then detach the pump drive belt.

5. Pivot the alternator inward and remove the drive belt from the pulley.

6. Support the alternator and remove the lower mount bolt(s), then remove the unit from the vehicle.

INSTALLATION AND BELT ADJUSTMENT

➡For more details on belt adjustment procedures, please refer to Section 1 of this manual.

1. Position the alternator in the vehicle and install, but do not fully tighten, the lower mount through-bolt(s).

2. Pivot the alternator inward and position the drive belt over the pulley.

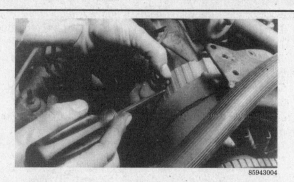

Fig. 8 Use a small screwdriver to release the locktab on the alternator connector

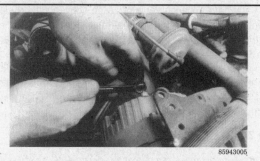

Fig. 9 Use a wrench to loosen the wiring terminal stud nut located under a small rubber boot on the rear of the alternator

Fig. 10 Loosen the lower alternator mounting through-bolt (pivot bolt)

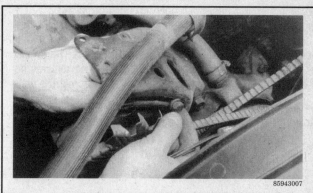

Fig. 11 Remove the alternator bracket/adjuster bolt

Fig. 12 Pivot the alternator inward and remove the drive belt from the pulley

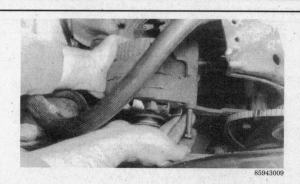

Fig. 13 Support the alternator and remove the through-bolt, then remove the alternator from the vehicle

3. If removed earlier, install the power steering pump drive belt, adjust the tension and tighten the pump fasteners.

➡Determine belt tension at a point halfway between the pulleys by pressing on the belt with moderate thumb pressure while the component is held or pried outward from the engine. The belt should deflect about ½ in. at the halfway point if the distance between the pulleys (measured from the center of each pulley) is 13-16 in. The belt should deflect ¼ in. if the distance is 7-10 in. Once the proper deflection is achieved, the adjuster bolt should be tightened.

4. Pivot the alternator outward in order to properly adjust the belt tension, then tighten the pivot bolt and the lower though-bolt(s).

5. Install the alternator wiring as noted during removal. If equipped, make sure the rubber boot is properly positioned over the stud nut terminal at the rear of the alternator.

6. Connect the negative battery cable.

Regulator

▶ See Figures 14, 15 and 16

The voltage regulator combines with the battery and alternator to comprise the charging system. Just as the name implies, the voltage regulator controls (regulates) the alternator voltage output to a safe level. A properly working regulator prevents excessive voltage from burning out wiring, bulbs, or contact points, and prevents overcharging of the battery. Mechanical adjustments (air gap, point opening) must be followed by electrical adjustments and not vice versa.

Since 1973 all GM cars have been equipped with alternators which have built-in solid state voltage regulators. The regulator is in the end frame (inside) of the alternator and requires no adjustment. The following adjustment apply to pre-1973 units.

→Although standard since 1973, this integral alternator/regulator has been available as an option since 1969.

REMOVAL & INSTALLATION

1. Disconnect the negative battery cable.

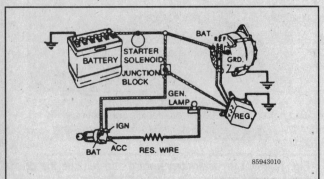

Fig. 14 Non-integral voltage regulator charging system schematic

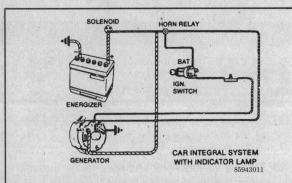

Fig. 15 Integral voltage regulator charging system schematic

2. Disconnect the wiring harness from the regulator.
3. Remove the mounting screws and remove the regulator.
To install:
4. Make sure that the regulator base gasket is in place before installation.
5. Clean the attaching area for proper grounding.
6. Install the regulator. Do not overtighten the mounting screws, as this will cancel the cushioning effect of the rubber grommets.
7. Engage the wiring harness to the regulator
8. Connect the negative battery cable.

ADJUSTMENTS — 1964-72

The standard voltage regulator is the conventional double contact type; however, an optional transistorized regulator was available from 1964-68. Voltage adjustment procedures are the same for both except for the adjustment points. The double contact adjustment screw is under the regulator cover (also on the 1964 transistorized regulator); the 1965-68 transistorized regulator is adjusted externally after removing an Allen screw from the adjustment hole.

Field Relay Adjustments (Mechanical)

As explained earlier, mechanical adjustments must be made first and then followed by electrical adjustments.

Point Opening

Using a feeler gauge, check the point opening. To change the opening, carefully bend the armature stop. The point opening for all regulators should be 0.014 in.

Air Gap

Check the air gap under the armature on which the points are mounted. Check the gap with the points just touching. The gap should be 0.067 in. If the point opening setting is correct, then the relay will operate OK even if the air gap is off. To adjust air gap, bend the flat contact spring. Some units are equipped with an air gap star wheel adjusting nut.

Voltage Adjustment (Electrical)

1. Connect a $\frac{1}{4}\Omega$, 25 watt fixed resistor (a knife blade switch using a $\frac{1}{4}\Omega$ resistor) into the charging circuit (as shown in the regulator voltage setting illustration) at the battery posi-

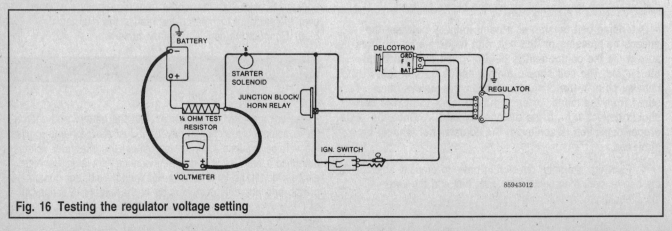

Fig. 16 Testing the regulator voltage setting

Troubleshooting Basic Charging System Problems

Problem	Cause	Solution
Noisy alternator	• Loose mountings • Loose drive pulley • Worn bearings • Brush noise • Internal circuits shorted (High pitched whine)	• Tighten mounting bolts • Tighten pulley • Replace alternator • Replace alternator • Replace alternator
Squeal when starting engine or accelerating	• Glazed or loose belt	• Replace or adjust belt
Indicator light remains on or ammeter indicates discharge (engine running)	• Broken fan belt • Broken or disconnected wires • Internal alternator problems • Defective voltage regulator	• Install belt • Repair or connect wiring • Replace alternator • Replace voltage regulator
Car light bulbs continually burn out— battery needs water continually	• Alternator/regulator overcharging	• Replace voltage regulator/alternator
Car lights flare on acceleration	• Battery low • Internal alternator/regulator problems	• Charge or replace battery • Replace alternator/regulator
Low voltage output (alternator light flickers continually or ammeter needle wanders)	• Loose or worn belt • Dirty or corroded connections • Internal alternator/regulator problems	• Replace or adjust belt • Clean or replace connections • Replace alternator or regulator

85943013

Fig. 17 Basic charging system diagnosis

tive terminal. One end of the resistor connects to the battery positive terminal while the other connects to the voltmeter.

2. Operate the engine at 1,500 rpm or more for at least 15 minutes. Disconnect and reconnect the regulator connector and read the voltage on the voltmeter. If the regulator is functioning properly, the reading should be 13.5-15.2V. If the reading is not within this range, keep the engine running at 1,500 rpm and perform the following:

a. Disengage the terminal connector (four terminal connector) and remove the regulator cover. Re-engage the connector and adjust the voltage to 14.2-14.6V by turning the adjusting screw at the base of the regulator behind the armatures.

❋❋WARNING

When removing the regulator cover ALWAYS disengage the connector first to prevent regulator damage by short circuits.

b. Disengage the connector, install the cover, and then re-engage the connector.

c. Increase the regulator temperature by running the engine at 1,500 rpm for 10 more minutes.

d. Disengage and re-engage the connector, then read the voltmeter. A reading of 13.5-15.2V indicates a good regulator.

ALTERNATOR AND REGULATOR SPECIFICATIONS

Year	Alternator Part No. or Manufacturer	Alternator Field Current @ 12 V	Output (amps)	Field Relay Air Gap (in.)	Field Relay Point Gap (in.)	Field Relay Volts to Close	Regulator Air Gap (in.)	Regulator Point Gap (in.)	Volts @ 75°
1964	1100668	1.9–2.3	42	0.15	0.30	2.3–3.7	0.067	0.014	13.5–14.4
	1100669	1.9–2.3	40	0.15	0.30	2.3–3.7	0.067	0.014	13.5–14.4
	1100670	1.9–2.3	37	0.15	0.30	2.3–3.7	0.067	0.014	13.5–14.4
	1117765	3.7–4.4	62	0.15	0.30	2.3–3.7	0.067	0.014	①
1965–67	1100693	2.2–2.6	37	0.15	0.30	2.3–2.7	0.067	0.014	13.5–14.4
	1100695	2.2–2.6	32	0.15	0.30	2.3–2.7	0.067	0.014	13.5–14.4
	1100794	2.2–2.6	37	0.15	0.30	2.3–2.7	0.067	0.014	13.5–14.4
1968	1100813	2.2–2.6	37	0.15	0.30	2.3–2.7	0.067	0.014	13.5–14.4
	1100693	2.2–2.6	37	0.15	0.30	2.3–2.7	0.067	0.014	13.5–14.4
1969	1100834	2.2–2.6	37	0.15	0.30	2.3–2.7	0.067	0.014	13.5–14.4
	1100836	2.2–2.6	37	0.15	0.30	2.3–2.7	0.067	0.014	13.5–14.4
1970	1100834	2.2–2.6	37	0.15	0.30	2.3–2.7	0.067	0.014	13.5–14.4
	1100837	2.2–2.6	37	0.15	0.30	2.3–2.7	0.067	0.014	13.5–14.4
1971	1100838	2.2–2.6	37	0.15	0.30	2.3–2.7	0.067	0.014	13.5–14.4
	1100839	2.2–2.6	37	0.15	0.30	2.3–2.7	0.067	0.014	13.5–14.4
1972	1100566	2.2–2.6	35	0.15	0.30	1.5–3.2	0.067	0.014	13.8–14.8
	1100917	2.8–3.2	59	0.30	0.30	1.5–3.2	0.067	0.014	13.8–14.8
	1100843	2.8–3.2	58	Integrated with Alternator					13.8–14.8
1973	1100497	2.8–3.2	36	Integrated with Alternator					13.8–14.8
	1100934	2.8–3.2	37	Integrated with Alternator					13.8–14.8
1974	1100934	4–4.5	37	Integrated with Alternator					13.8–14.8
	1102347	4–4.5	61	Integrated with Alternator					13.8–14.8
	1100497	4–4.5	37	Integrated with Alternator					13.8–14.8
	1100573	4–4.5	42	Integrated with Alternator					13.8–14.8
	1100597	4–4.5	61	Integrated with Alternator					13.8–14.8
	1100560	4–4.5	55	Integrated with Alternator					13.8–14.8
	1100575	4–4.5	55	Integrated with Alternator					13.8–14.8
1975	1100497	4–4.5	37	Integrated with Alternator					13.8–14.8
	1102397	4–4.5	37	Integrated with Alternator					13.8–14.8
	1102483	4–4.5	37	Integrated with Alternator					13.8–14.8
	1100560	4–4.5	55	Integrated with Alternator					13.8–14.8
	1100575	4–4.5	55	Integrated with Alternator					13.8–14.8
	1100597	4–4.5	61	Integrated with Alternator					13.8–14.8
	1102347	4–4.5	61	Integrated with Alternator					13.8–14.8
1976–79	1102491	4–4.5	37	Integrated with Alternator					13.8–14.8
	1102480	4–4.5	61	Integrated with Alternator					13.8–14.8
	1102486	4–4.5	61	Integrated with Alternator					13.8–14.8
	1102394	4–4.5	37	Integrated with Alternator					13.8–14.8

85943014

Battery

For additional information on battery maintenance and service, refer to Section 1 of this manual.

REMOVAL & INSTALLATION

1. Disconnect the negative (ground) cable from the battery terminal, then disconnect the positive cable. Special pullers are available to remove post cable clamps, if they seem stuck.

➡To avoid sparks, always disconnect the ground cable first, and connect it last.

2. Remove the battery hold-down clamp.
3. Remove the battery, being careful not to spill the acid.

➡Spilled acid can be neutralized with a baking soda/water solution. If you somehow get acid into your eyes, flush it out with lots of water and get to a doctor.

To install:
4. Clean the battery posts thoroughly before installing a new or used battery.
5. Clean the cable clamps, using a wire brush, both inside and out.
6. Install the battery and hold-down clamp or strap. Connect the positive, and then the negative cable (see Note above). Do not hammer post cables onto the terminal posts. The complete terminals should be coated lightly (externally) with petroleum jelly or grease to help prevent corrosion. There are also felt washers impregnated with an anti-corrosion substance which are slipped over the battery posts before installing the cables; these are available in most auto parts stores.

❄❄WARNING

Make absolutely sure that the battery is connected properly (positive to positive, negative to negative) before you turn the ignition key. Reversed polarity can burn out your alternator and regulator in a matter of seconds.

Starter

REMOVAL & INSTALLATION

▶ **See Figures 18, 19, 20, 21 and 22**

Starter removal on some models may necessitate the removal of the front support which runs from the corner of the frame to the front crossmember. If so, loosen the mounting bolt which attaches the support the frame first, then remove the crossmember bolt and swing the support out of the way.

➡The starters on some engines require the addition of shims to provide proper clearance between the starter pinion gear and the flywheel. These shims are available in 0.015 in. sizes from Chevrolet dealers. Flat washers can be used if shims are unavailable.

1. Disconnect the negative battery cable.
2. Raise and support the vehicle safely using jackstands.

➡If access to the wiring is difficult, the starter may be partially lowered before disconnecting it, but be careful not to stretch or damage the wiring.

3. Disconnect all wiring from the starter solenoid. Replace each nut as the connector is removed, as thread sizes differ from connector to connector. Note or tag the wiring positions for installation purposes.
4. If equipped, remove the front bracket from the starter. On engines with a solenoid heat shield, remove the front bracket upper bolt and detach the bracket from the starter.
5. Remove the starter mounting bolts. If a starter shim tab can be seen protruding out from between the mating surfaces of the starter and the block, remove the outer bolt first, then loosen the inner bolt. With the outer bolt removed and the inner loosened, most shims may be grasped and pulled from the top of the starter at this point. Once the bolts are removed, lower the starter front end first, and remove the unit from the car.

➡If no shim tab could be seen, yet shims or flat washers fall from the starter as it is withdrawn, stop and attempt to determine their locations. If possible, gather the shims for reuse during assembly. Shims without tabs must be positioned on the starter prior to installation, but the bolts may be held through the starter assembly in order to hold the shims in position.

To install:
6. If flat washers or shims without tabs were found on removal, position them on top of the starter using the mounting bolts to hold them in position.
7. Position the starter to the engine block and loosely install the mounting bolts. If tabbed shims were withdrawn during removal, position them before the outer mounting bolt is threaded.
8. Once the starter and shims are properly positioned, tighten the two mounting bolts to 25-35 ft. lbs. (34-47 Nm).
9. If equipped, install the front bracket and/or heat shield to the starter assembly.
10. Attach the starter wiring to the solenoid, as noted during removal.
11. Remove the jackstands and carefully lower the vehicle.
12. Connect the negative battery cable.

SHIMMING THE STARTER

▶ **See Figures 23, 24 and 25**

Starter noise during cranking and after the engine fires is often a result of too much or tool little distance between the starter pinion gear and the flywheel. A high pitched whine during cranking (before the engine fires) can be caused by the pinion and flywheel being too far apart. Likewise, a whine after the engine starts (as the key is released) is often a result of the pinion-flywheel relationship being too close. In both cases flywheel damage can occur. Shims are available in 0.015 in. sizes to properly adjust the starter on its mount. In order to check and adjust the shims, you will also need a flywheel

ALTERNATOR AND REGULATOR SPECIFICATIONS

Year	Alternator Part No. or Manufacturer	Alternator Field Current @ 12 V	Output (amps)	Regulator Field Relay Air Gap (in.)	Point Gap (in.)	Volts to Close	Regulator Air Gap (in.)	Regulator Point Gap (in.)	Volts @ 75°
1980–81	1103161	4–4.5	37	Integrated with Alternator					13.8–14.8
	1103118	4–4.5	37	Integrated with Alternator					13.8–14.8
	1103043	4–4.5	42	Integrated with Alternator					13.8–14.8
	1103162	4–4.5	37	Integrated with Alternator					13.8–14.8
	1103092	4–4.5	55	Integrated with Alternator					13.8–14.8
	1103088	4–4.5	55	Integrated with Alternator					13.8–14.8
	1103100	4–4.5	55	Integrated with Alternator					13.8–14.8
	1103085	4–4.5	55	Integrated with Alternator					13.8–14.8
	1103044	4–4.5	63	Integrated with Alternator					13.8–14.8
	1103091	4–4.5	63	Integrated with Alternator					13.8–14.8
	1103169	4–4.5	63	Integrated with Alternator					13.8–14.8
	1103102	4–4.5	63	Integrated with Alternator					13.8–14.8
	1103122	4–4.5	63	Integrated with Alternator					13.8–14.8
	1101044	4–4.5	70	Integrated with Alternator					13.8–14.8
	1101071	4–4.5	70	Integrated with Alternator					13.8–14.8
1982–84	1103161	4–4.5	37	Integrated with Alternator					13.8–14.8
	1103118	4–4.5	37	Integrated with Alternator					13.8–14.8
	1103043	4–4.5	42	Integrated with Alternator					13.8–14.8
	1103162	4–4.5	37	Integrated with Alternator					13.8–14.8
	1103092	4–4.5	55	Integrated with Alternator					13.8–14.8
	1103088	4–4.5	55	Integrated with Alternator					13.8–14.8
	1103100	4–4.5	55	Integrated with Alternator					13.8–14.8
	1103085	4–4.5	55	Integrated with Alternator					13.8–14.8
	1103044	4–4.5	63	Integrated with Alternator					13.8–14.8
	1103091	4–4.5	63	Integrated with Alternator					13.8–14.8
	1103169	4–4.5	63	Integrated with Alternator					13.8–14.8
	1101044	4–4.5	70	Integrated with Alternator					13.8–14.8
	1101066	4–4.5	70	Integrated with Alternator					13.8–14.8
	1101071	4–4.5	70	Integrated with Alternator					13.8–14.8
	1100226	4–4.5	37	Integrated with Alternator					13.8–14.8
	1100246	4–4.5	63	Integrated with Alternator					13.8–14.8
	1100270	4–4.5	78	Integrated with Alternator					13.8–14.8
	1100239	4–4.5	55	Integrated with Alternator					13.8–14.8
	1100247	4–4.5	63	Integrated with Alternator					13.8–14.8
	1100200	4–4.5	78	Integrated with Alternator					13.8–14.8
	1100230	4–4.5	42	Integrated with Alternator					13.8–14.8
	1100260	4–4.5	78	Integrated with Alternator					13.8–14.8
	1100263	4–4.5	78	Integrated with Alternator					13.8–14.8
	1105022	4–4.5	78	Integrated with Alternator					13.8–14.8
	1100237	4–4.5	55	Integrated with Alternator					13.8–14.8
	1100228	4–4.5	37	Integrated with Alternator					13.8–14.8
	1100300	4–4.5	63	Integrated with Alternator					13.8–14.8
	1105041	4–4.5	78	Integrated with Alternator					13.8–14.8

85943015

ALTERNATOR AND REGULATOR SPECIFICATIONS

| | Alternator | | | Regulator | | | | | |
| | | | | Field Relay | | | Regulator | | |
Year	Part No. or Manufacturer	Field Current @ 12 V	Output (amps)	Air Gap (in.)	Point Gap (in.)	Volts to Close	Air Gap (in.)	Point Gap (in.)	Volts @ 75°
1985	1100246	4–4.5	66	Integrated with Alternator					13.8–14.8
	1100237	4–4.5	56	Integrated with Alternator					13.8–14.8
	1105652	4–4.5	78	Integrated with Alternator					13.8–14.8
	1105521	4–4.5	78	Integrated with Alternator					13.8–14.8
	1105523	4–4.5	56	Integrated with Alternator					13.8–14.8
	1105652	4–4.5	78	Integrated with Alternator					13.8–14.8
	1105523	4–4.5	56	Integrated with Alternator					13.8–14.8
1986–88	1100200	—	78	Integrated with Alternator					13.8–14.8
	1100239	—	56	Integrated with Alternator					13.5–16.0
	1105197	—	70	Integrated with Alternator					13.5–16.0
	1105651	—	94	Integrated with Alternator					13.5–16.0
	1105673	—	56	Integrated with Alternator					13.5–16.0
	1105652	—	78	Integrated with Alternator					13.5–16.0
	1105676	—	56	Integrated with Alternator					13.5–16.0
	1105674	—	66	Integrated with Alternator					13.5–16.0

① 13.0–13.6 @ 80°

85943016

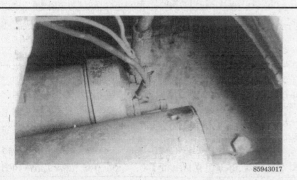

Fig. 18 The starter wiring is connected to the solenoid which is attached to the top of the assembly

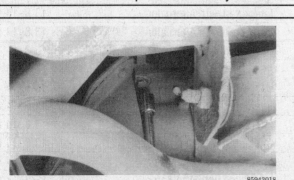

Fig. 19 Remove the outer mounting bolt from the starter assembly

Fig. 20 With the outer mounting bolt removed and inner bolt loosened, a tabbed shim may be withdrawn from between the starter and engine block

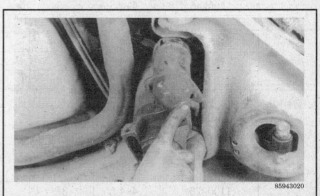

Fig. 21 Tilt and lower the starter motor from the vehicle

85943021

Fig. 22 This photograph shows the orientation between the top of the starter assembly and the mounting shim

turning tool, available at most auto parts stores or from any auto tool store or salesperson.

If your car's starter emits the above noises, follow the shimming procedure below:

1. Disconnect the negative battery cable.
2. Raise and support the vehicle safely using jackstands.
3. Remove the flywheel inspection cover on the bottom of the bellhousing.
4. Using the flywheel turning tool, turn the flywheel and examine the flywheel teeth. If damage is evident, the flywheel should be replaced.
5. Insert a screwdriver into the small hole in the bottom of the starter, then move the starter pinion and clutch assembly so the pinion and flywheel teeth mesh. If necessary, rotate the flywheel so that a pinion tooth is directly in the center of the two flywheel teeth and on the centerline of the two gears, as shown in the accompanying illustration.
6. Check the pinion-to-flywheel clearance by using a 0.020 in. wire gauge (a spark plug wire gauge may work here, or you can make your own). Make sure you center the pinion tooth between the flywheel teeth and the gauge - NOT in the corners, as you may get a false reading. If the clearance is under this minimum, shim the starter away from the flywheel by adding shim(s) one at a time to the starter mount. Check clearance after adding each shim.
7. If the clearance is a good deal over 0.020 in. (in the vicinity of a 0.050 in. plug), shim the starter towards the flywheel. Broken or severely mangled flywheel teeth are also a good indicator that the clearance here is too great. Shimming the starter towards the flywheel is done by adding shims to the outboard starter mounting pad only. Check the clearance after each shim is added. A shim of 0.015 in. at this location will decrease the clearance about 0.010 in.

STARTER OVERHAUL

♦ See Figures 26, 27, 28, 29, 30 and 31

Drive Replacement

1. Disconnect the field coil straps from the solenoid.

2. Remove the through-bolts, and separate the commutator end frame, field frame assembly, drive housing, and armature assembly from each other.

➡**On diesel starter, remove the insulator from the end frame. The armature on the diesel starter remains in the drive end frame. On diesel starters, remove the shift lever pivot bolt. ON the diesel 25 MT starter only, remove the center bearing screws and remove the drive gear housing from the armature shaft. The shift lever and plunger assembly will now fall away from the starter clutch.**

3. Slide the two piece thrust collar off the end of the armature shaft.
4. Slide a suitably sized metal cylinder, such as a standard ½ in. pipe coupling, or an old pinion, onto the shaft so that the end of the coupling or pinion butts up against the edge of the pinion retainer.
5. Support the lower end of the armature securely on a soft surface, such as a wooden block, and tap the end of the coupling or pinion, driving the retainer towards the armature end of the snapring.
6. Remove the snapring from the groove in the armature shaft with a pair of pliers. Then, slide the retainer and starter drive from the shaft.

To assemble:

7. Lubricate the drive end of the armature shaft with silicone lubricant and then slide the starter drive onto the shaft with the pinion facing outward. Slide the retainer onto the shaft with the cupped surface facing outward.
8. Again support the armature on a soft surface, with the pinion at the upper end. Center the snapring on the top of the shaft (use a new snapring if the original was damaged during removal). Gently place a block of wood flat on top of the snapring so as not to move it from a centered position. Tap the wooden block with a hammer in order to force the snapring around the shaft. Then, slide the ring down into the snapring groove.
9. Lay the armature down flat on the surface you're working on. Slide the retainer close up on to the shaft and position it and the thrust collar next to the snapring. Using two pairs of pliers on opposite sides of the shaft, squeeze the thrust collar and the retainer together until the snapring is forced into the retainer.
10. Lube the drive housing bushing with a silicone lubricant. Then, install the armature and the clutch assembly into the drive housing, engaging the solenoid shift lever yoke with the clutch, and positioning the front of the armature shaft into the bushing.

➡**On non-diesel starters the shift lever may be installed in the drive gear housing first. On the 25 MT diesel starter only, install the center bearing screws and the shift lever pivot bolt, and tighten securely.**

11. Apply a sealing compound approved for this application onto the drive housing; then position the field frame around the armatures shaft and against the drive housing. Work slowly and carefully to prevent damaging the starter brushes.
12. Lubricate the bushing in the commutator end frame with a silicone lubricant, place the leather brake washer onto the armature shaft, and then slide the commutator end frame over the shaft and into position against the field frame. Line up the bolt holes, then install and tighten the through-bolts.

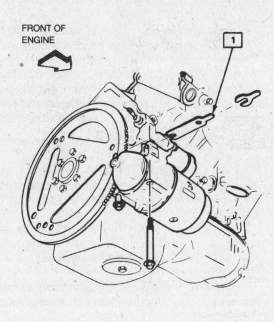

FRONT OF ENGINE

1

1. Use shims as required
2. Shield

Starter noise diagnostic procedure
1. Starter noise during cranking: remove 1–.015″ double shim or add single .015″ shim to *outer* bolt only.
2. High pitched whine after engine fires: add .015″ double shims until noise disappears.
See text for complete procedure.

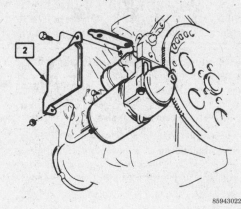

2

85943022

Fig. 23 Starter motor mounting-V6 at left, diesel at right (most engines similar)

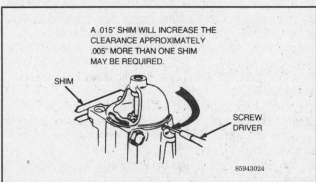

A .015″ SHIM WILL INCREASE THE CLEARANCE APPROXIMATELY .005″ MORE THAN ONE SHIM MAY BE REQUIRED.

SHIM

SCREW DRIVER

85943024

Fig. 24 Meshing the starter and flywheel teeth in order to check and adjust clearance

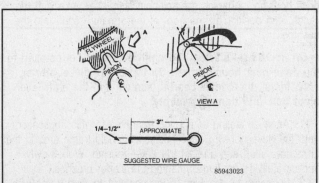

FLYWHEEL

PINION

PINION

VIEW A

1/4–1/2″

3″ APPROXIMATE

SUGGESTED WIRE GAUGE

85943023

Fig. 25 Fabricating and using a flywheel-to-pinion gauge

13. Reconnect the field coil straps to the MOTOR terminal of the solenoid.

➤**If replacement of the starter drive fails to cure improper engagement of starter pinion to flywheel, there are probably defective parts in the solenoid and/or shift lever. The best procedure would probably be to take the assembly to a shop where a pinion clearance check can be made by energizing the solenoid on a test bench. If the pinion clearance is incorrect, disassemble the solenoid and shift lever, inspect, and replace worn parts.**

Brush Replacement

1. Disassemble the starter by following Steps 1 and 2 of the Drive Replacement procedure above.

2. Replace the brushes one at a time to avoid having to mark the wiring. For each brush; remove the brush holding screw; remove the old brush and position the new brush in the same direction (large end toward center of of field frame), position wire connector on top of brush, line up holes, and reinstall screw. Make sure the screw is snug enough to ensure good contact.

3. Reassemble starter according to the applicable steps above.

Solenoid Replacement

1. Remove the screw and washer from the motor connector strap terminal.

2. Remove the two solenoid retaining screws.

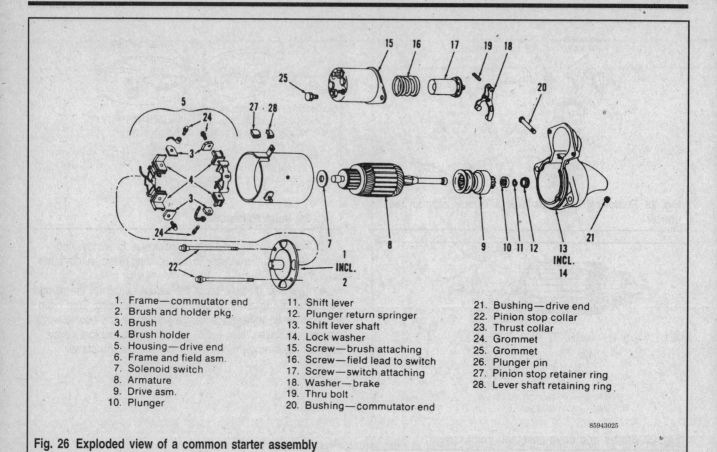

Fig. 26 Exploded view of a common starter assembly

1. Frame—commutator end
2. Brush and holder pkg.
3. Brush
4. Brush holder
5. Housing—drive end
6. Frame and field asm.
7. Solenoid switch
8. Armature
9. Drive asm.
10. Plunger
11. Shift lever
12. Plunger return springer
13. Shift lever shaft
14. Lock washer
15. Screw—brush attaching
16. Screw—field lead to switch
17. Screw—switch attaching
18. Washer—brake
19. Thru bolt
20. Bushing—commutator end
21. Bushing—drive end
22. Pinion stop collar
23. Thrust collar
24. Grommet
25. Grommet
26. Plunger pin
27. Pinion stop retainer ring
28. Lever shaft retaining ring

85943025

Fig. 27 Exploded view of the 15MT/GR starter used on diesel engines

85943026

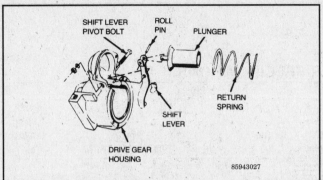

Fig. 28 Removing the shaft lever and plunger from the starter

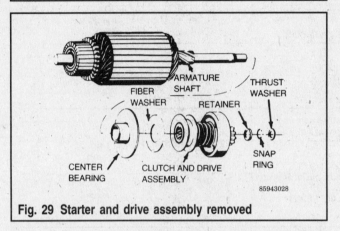

Fig. 29 Starter and drive assembly removed

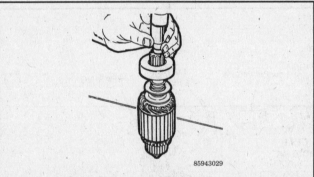

Fig. 30 Use a piece of pipe to drive the retainer toward the armature end of the snapring

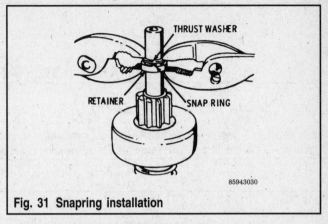

Fig. 31 Snapring installation

3. Twist the solenoid housing clockwise to remove the flange key from the keyway in the housing. Then remove the housing.

4. To install the unit, place the return spring on the plunger and place the solenoid body on the drive housing. Turn counterclockwise to engage the flange key. Place the two retaining screws in position, then install the screw and washer which secures the strap terminal. Install the unit on the starter.

BATTERY AND STARTER SPECIFICATIONS

Year	Engine No. Cyl. Displacement (cu. in.)	Battery			Starter							Brush Spring Tension (oz.)
		Ampere Hour Capacity	Volts	Terminal Grounded	Lock test		Torque (ft. lbs.)	No-Load Test				
					Amps	Volts		Amps	Volts	RPM		
1964–65	All	44	12	Neg	Not Recommended			49–76	10.6	7,800		35
1966–67	6, 8-283	44	12	Neg	Not Recommended			49–76	10.6	7,800		35
	8-327, 396	14	12	Neg	Not Recommended			65–100	10.6	4,200		35
1968–69	6, 8-307	45	12	Neg	Not Recommended			—	10.6	—		35
	8-302, 327, 350, 396	61	12	Neg	Not Recommended			—	9	—		35
1970–71	6, 8-307	45	12	Neg	Not Recommended			50–80	9	5,500–10,500		35
	8-350	61	12	Neg	Not Recommended			55–80	9	3,500–6,000		35
	8-402 (396)	61	12	Neg	Not Recommended			65–95	9	7,500–10,500		35
	8-454	62	12	Neg	Not Recommended			65–95	9	7,500–10,500		35
1972	6-250	45	12	Neg	Not Recommended			50–80	9	5,500–10,500		35
	8-307, 350, 402	61	12	Neg	Not Recommended			50–80①	9	5,500–10,500		35
	8-454	76	12	Neg	Not Recommended			65–95	9	7,500–10,500		35
1973	6-250	45	12	Neg	Not Recommended			50–80	9	5,500–10,500		35
	8-307	61	12	Neg	Not Recommended			50–80	9	5,500–10,500		35
	8-350, 454	76	12	Neg	Not Recommended			65–95	9	5,500–10,500		35
1974	6-250	2300②	12	Neg	Not Recommended			50–80	9	5,500–10,500		35
	8-350, 400	2900②	12	Neg	Not Recommended			65–95	9	7,500–10,500		35
	8-454	3750②	12	Neg	Not Recommended			65–95	9	7,500–10,500		35
1975–76	6-250	2500②	12	Neg	Not Recommended			50–80	9	5,500–10,500		35
	8-350, 400	3200②	12	Neg	Not Recommended			65–95	9	7,500–10,500		35
	8-454	4000②	12	Neg	Not Recommended			65–95	9	7,500–10,500		35

85943032

Troubleshooting Basic Starting System Problems

Problem	Cause	Solution
Starter motor rotates engine slowly	• Battery charge low or battery defective	• Charge or replace battery
	• Defective circuit between battery and starter motor	• Clean and tighten, or replace cables
	• Low load current	• Bench-test starter motor. Inspect for worn brushes and weak brush springs.
	• High load current	• Bench-test starter motor. Check engine for friction, drag or coolant in cylinders. Check ring gear-to-pinion gear clearance.
Starter motor will not rotate engine	• Battery charge low or battery defective	• Charge or replace battery
	• Faulty solenoid	• Check solenoid ground. Repair or replace as necessary.
	• Damage drive pinion gear or ring gear	• Replace damaged gear(s)
	• Starter motor engagement weak	• Bench-test starter motor
	• Starter motor rotates slowly with high load current	• Inspect drive yoke pull-down and point gap, check for worn end bushings, check ring gear clearance
	• Engine seized	• Repair engine
Starter motor drive will not engage (solenoid known to be good)	• Defective contact point assembly	• Repair or replace contact point assembly
	• Inadequate contact point assembly ground	• Repair connection at ground screw
	• Defective hold-in coil	• Replace field winding assembly
Starter motor drive will not disengage	• Starter motor loose on flywheel housing	• Tighten mounting bolts
	• Worn drive end busing	• Replace bushing
	• Damaged ring gear teeth	• Replace ring gear or driveplate
	• Drive yoke return spring broken or missing	• Replace spring
Starter motor drive disengages prematurely	• Weak drive assembly thrust spring	• Replace drive mechanism
	• Hold-in coil defective	• Replace field winding assembly
Low load current	• Worn brushes	• Replace brushes
	• Weak brush springs	• Replace springs

85943031

Fig. 32 Starting system diagnosis

Sending Units and Sensors

REMOVAL & INSTALLATION

Coolant Temperature

On most vehicles covered in this manual the coolant temperature sensor is located in the left cylinder head between spark plugs. The coolant sensor may also be found on the opposite cylinder head or even in the intake manifold. For most fuel injected vehicles the coolant sensor is threaded into the front of the intake manifold.

1. Disconnect the negative battery cable.

2. Drain the engine cooling system to a level below the sensor.

3. Disengage the sensor connector.

4. Using a special sensor tool or a 12-point socket, loosen the sensor, then carefully unthread and remove it from the engine.

To install:

5. Thread the sensor into the engine by hand, then tighten using the socket or tool. If a replacement sensor came with instructions use a torque wrench to assure proper tightening.

6. Engage the sensor wiring harness.

7. Connect the negative battery cable.

8. Properly refill the engine cooling system, then run the engine and check for leaks.

BATTERY AND STARTER SPECIFICATIONS

Year	Engine No. Cyl. Displacement (cu. in.)	Battery			Starter							Brush Spring Tension (oz.)
		Ampere Hour Capacity	Volts	Terminal Grounded	Lock test		Torque (ft. lbs.)	No-Load Test				
					Amps	Volts		Amps	Volts	RPM		
1977–78	6-250	275③	12	Neg	Not Recommended			50–80	9	5,500–10,500		35
	8-305	350③	12	Neg	Not Recommended			50–80	9	7,500–10,500		35
	8-350	350③	12	Neg	Not Recommended			65–95	9	7,500–10,500		35
1979	6-250	275③	12	Neg	Not Recommended			60–88	10.6	6,500–10,100		35
	6-231	350③	12	Neg	Not Recommended			50–80	10.6	7,500–11,400		35
	6-200	350③	12	Neg	Not Recommended			50–80	10.6	7,500–11,400		35
	8-305	350③	12	Neg	Not Recommended			50–80	10.6	7,500–11,400		35
	8-350	350③	12	Neg	Not Recommended			65–95	10.6	7,500–10,500		35
1980–81	6-229	350③	12	Neg	Not Recommended			50–80	10.6	7,500–11,400		35
	6-231	350③	12	Neg	Not Recommended			50–80	10.6	7,500–11,400		35
	8-267	250③	12	Neg	Not Recommended			50–80	10.6	7,500–11,400		35
	8-305	350③	12	Neg	Not Recommended			50–80	10.6	7,500–11,400		35
1982–84	6-229	350③	12	Neg	Not Recommended			50–80	10.6	7,500–11,400		35
	6-231	350③	12	Neg	Not Recommended			50–80	10.6	7,500–11,400		35
	6-263	465③④	12	Neg	Not Recommended			160–220	10.6	4,000–5,500		35
	8-267	350③	12	Neg	Not Recommended			45–70	10.6	7,500–11,400		35
	8-305	350③	12	Neg	Not Recommended			44–70	10.6	7,500–11,400		35
	8-350	465③④	12	Neg	Not Recommended			160–220	10.6	4,000–5,500		35
1985	6-262	630③	12	Neg	Not Recommended			50–75	10	6,000–11,900		35
	8-305	500③	12	Neg	Not Recommended			50–75	10	6,000–11,900		35
1986–88	6-262	630③	12	Neg	Not Recommended			70–120	10	5,500–10,700		—
	8-305	525③	12	Neg	Not Recommended			70–120	10	5,500–10,700		—

① 350 & 402 use 454 starter
② Cranking power in watts @ 0°F
③ Cranking power in amps @ 0°F
④ 115 minute reserve capacity, 2 batteries used

Oil Pressure

The oil pressure switch is usually threaded into the rear of the intake manifold, just in front of the distributor. If the switch is not there, possible alternate locations include the block, above the starter or the oil filter adapter.

1. Disconnect the negative battery cable.
2. Disengage the sensor electrical connector.
3. Using a special sensor tool or a 12-point socket, loosen the sensor, then carefully unthread and remove it from the engine.

To install:

4. Thread the sensor into the engine by hand, then tighten using the socket or tool. If a replacement sensor came with instructions use a torque wrench to assure proper tightening.
5. Engage the sensor wiring harness.
6. Connect the negative battery cable, then check for proper sensor operation.

Oxygen Sensor

▶ **See Figure 33**

Beginning in the early 1980s most GM vehicles were equipped with an oxygen sensor for feedback carburetor control. Fuel injected engines, introduced in the later years of this manual also required an oxygen sensor for computer air/fuel mixture management. On vehicles so equipped, the oxygen sensor is usually mounted in an exhaust manifold. On some engines, the sensor is mounted at the end of the crossover pipe.

The oxygen sensor must be replaced every 30,000 miles (48,000 km.). The sensor may be difficult to remove when the engine temperature is below 120°F (48°C). Excessive removal force may damage the threads in the exhaust manifold or pipe so follow the removal procedure carefully.

1. Disconnect the negative battery cable.
2. Locate the oxygen sensor. On the V8 engines, it is normally on the front of the left side exhaust manifold, just above the point where it connects to the exhaust pipe. On the V6 engines, it is on the inside of the exhaust pipe where it bends toward the back of the car.

➡**On the V6 engine you may find it necessary to raise the front of the car and remove the oxygen sensor from underneath.**

3. Trace the wires leading from the oxygen sensor back to the first connector and then disengage the sensor harness connector (the connector on the V6 engine is attached to a bracket mounted on the right, rear of the engine block, while the connector in the V8 engine is attached to a bracket mounted on the top of the left side exhaust manifold).

➡**The sensor may be extremely difficult to remove when engine temperature is below 120°F (48°C). Be careful as excessive force could damage threads in the exhaust manifold or pipe.**

4. Using a special sensor tool or a socket, loosen the sensor, then carefully unthread and remove it from the engine. If sensor removal is difficult, spray a small amount of commercial heat riser solvent onto the sensor threads and allow it to soak in for at least five minutes, then attempt to loosen and remove the sensor again.

✳✳CAUTION

Avoid using cleaning solvents of any type on the oxygen sensor. Keep the louvered end free of grease, dirt or other contaminants. Do not drop or roughly handle the sensor. If any of these cautions are ignored, the sensor could be damaged resulting in poor engine performance and excessive exhaust emissions.

To install:

5. New oxygen sensors will be packaged with an anti-seize lubricant already applied to the threads. If a sensor is removed from the exhaust and is to be reinstalled for any reason, the sensor threads must be coated with a fresh anti-seize compound. Use G.M. anti-seize compound No. 5613695 or the equivalent. This is not a conventional anti-seize paste. The use of a regular compound may electrically insulate the sensor, rendering it inoperative. You must coat the threads with an electrically conductive anti-seize compound.
6. Carefully thread the sensor into the exhaust bore, then tighten to 30 ft. lbs. (41 Nm) using a torque wrench.
7. Engage the sensor harness.
8. Connect the negative battery cable, then start and run the engine to check for proper operation.

Knock Sensor

▶ **See Figures 34, 35 and 36**

1. Disconnect the negative battery cable.
2. Disengage the wiring harness connector from the knock sensor
3. Loosen and remove the sensor from the engine.

To install:

4. Apply thread sealer (such as soft sealing tape) to the sensor threads.
5. Install the sensor to the engine and tighten.
6. Engage the sensor wiring harness.
7. Connect the negative battery cable and check for proper engine operation.

ENGINE MECHANICAL

Design

All Chevrolet engines, whether inline sixes (L6), V6 or V8, are water cooled, overhead valve powerplants. Most engines use cast iron blocks and heads, with the exception of some high performance 454s, which use aluminum heads.

The crankshaft in the 230 and 250 cu. inch inline 6-cylinder engines is supported in seven main bearings, with the thrust being taken by the No. 7 bearing. The camshaft is low in the block and is gear driven. Relatively long pushrods actuate the valve through ball jointed rocker arms.

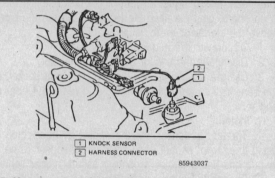

| 1 | KNOCK SENSOR |
| 2 | HARNESS CONNECTOR |

85943037

Fig. 35 Knock sensor installation — late-model carbureted engines

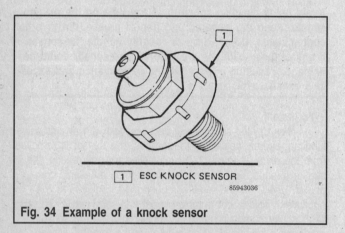

| 1 | ESC KNOCK SENSOR |

85943036

Fig. 34 Example of a knock sensor

The small block family of V8 engines, which has included the 267, 283, 305, 307, 327, 350 and 400 cu. in. blocks, have all evolved from the design of the 1955 265 cu. in. V8. It was this engine that introduced the ball joint type rocker arm design which is now used by many car makers. The Chevrolet built 229 and 262 V6s are also similar.

This line of engines features a great deal of interchangeability, and later parts may be utilized on earlier engines for increased reliability and/or performance. For example, in 1968 the 283 was dropped and replace by the 307, which is in effect a 327 crankshaft in a 283 block. And the 267, 305, and 350 V8s all share the same stroke, making crankshaft and bore dimensions, the main difference between the engines.

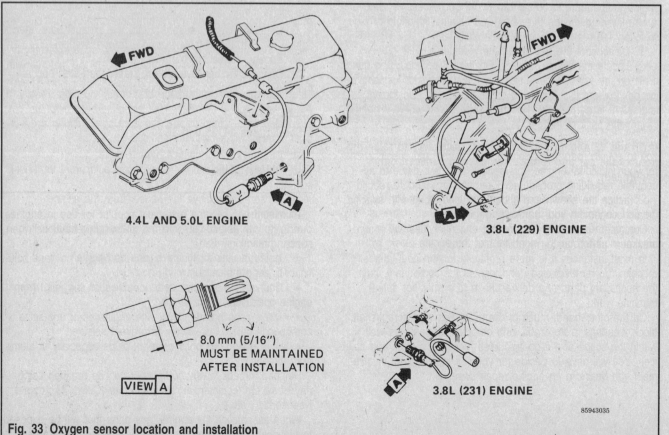

4.4L AND 5.0L ENGINE

3.8L (229) ENGINE

8.0 mm (5/16")
MUST BE MAINTAINED
AFTER INSTALLATION

VIEW A

3.8L (231) ENGINE

85943035

Fig. 33 Oxygen sensor location and installation

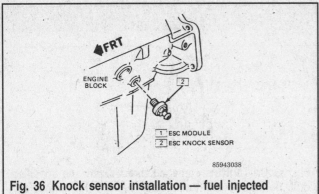

Fig. 36 Knock sensor installation — fuel injected engines

The 396, 402 and 454 engines are known as the big blocks, or less frequently, the Mark IV engines. They are available in the high performance SS versions of the Chevelle, and feature many tuning modifications such as high lift camshafts, solid lifters (in some cases), high compression ratios and large carburetors. These big blocks engines are similar to their small block little brothers in basic design.

The 350 V8 diesel is derived from the 350 gasoline engines, except that the cylinder block, crankshaft, main bearings, connecting rods and wrist pins are heavier duty in the diesel (due to the much higher compression ratio). The 263 V6 diesel is nearly a 6-cylinder copy of the 350 V8, sharing the same bore and stroke and many engine components. Both V6 and V8 diesel cylinder heads, intake manifold, ignition and fuel systems are also different from their gasoline engine counterparts. Aircraft-type hydraulic roller valve lifters are used in the diesels.

The Buick built 231 V6 is the only engine used in the midsized Chevrolets which is substantially different. This engine follows Buick V8 practice in that its valve gear incorporates rocker shafts instead of the ball joint style rockers on the other engines.

Engine Overhaul Tips

Most engine overhaul procedures are fairly standard. In addition to specific parts replacement procedures and specifications for your individual engine, this section also is a guide to acceptable rebuilding procedures. Examples of standard rebuilding practice are shown and should be used along with specific details concerning your particular engine.

Competent and accurate machine shop services will ensure maximum performance, reliability and engine life.

In most instances it is more profitable for the do-it-yourself mechanic to remove, clean and inspect the component, buy the necessary parts and deliver these to a shop for actual machine work.

On the other hand, much of the rebuilding work (crankshaft, block, bearings, piston rods, and other components) is well within the scope of the do-it-yourself mechanic's tools and abilities. You will have to decide for yourself the depth of involvement you desire in an engine repair or rebuild.

TOOLS

The tools required for an engine overhaul or parts replacement will depend on the depth of your involvement. With a few exceptions, they will be the tools found in a mechanic's tool kit (see Section 1 of this manual). More in-depth work will require some or all of the following:
- a dial indicator (reading in thousandths) mounted on a universal base
- micrometers and telescope gauges
- jaw and screw-type pullers
- scraper
- valve spring compressor
- ring groove cleaner
- piston ring expander and compressor
- ridge reamer
- cylinder hone or glaze breaker
- Plastigage®
- engine stand

The use of most of these tools is illustrated in this chapter. Many can be rented for a one-time use from a local parts jobber or tool supply house specializing in automotive work.

Occasionally, the use of special tools is called for. See the information on Special Tools and Safety Notice in the front of this book before substituting another tool.

INSPECTION TECHNIQUES

Procedures and specifications are given in this chapter for inspecting, cleaning and assessing the wear limits of most major components. Other procedures such as Magnaflux® and Zyglo® can be used to locate material flaws and stress cracks. Magnaflux® is a magnetic process applicable only to ferrous materials. The Zyglo® process coats the material with a fluorescent dye penetrant and can be used on any material. Checking for suspected surface cracks can be more readily made using spot check dye. The dye is sprayed onto the suspected area, wiped off and the area sprayed with a developer. Cracks will show up brightly.

OVERHAUL TIPS

Aluminum has become extremely popular for use in engines, due to its low weight. Observe the following precautions when handling aluminum parts:
- Never hot tank aluminum parts (the caustic hot tank solution will eat the aluminum.
- Remove all aluminum parts (identification tag, etc.) from engine parts prior to the tanking.
- Always coat threads lightly with engine oil or anti-seize compounds before installation, to prevent seizure.
- Never overtorque bolts or spark plugs especially in aluminum threads.

Stripped threads in any component can be repaired using any of several commercial repair kits (Heli-Coil®, Microdot®, Keenserts®, etc.).

When assembling the engine, any parts that will be exposed to frictional contact, the parts must be prelubed to provide lubrication at initial start-up. Any product specifically formulated for this purpose can be used, but engine oil is not recommended as a prelube in most cases.

When semi-permanent (locked, but removable) installation of bolts or nuts is desired, threads should be cleaned and coated with Loctite® or other similar, commercial non-hardening sealant.

REPAIRING DAMAGED THREADS

▶ **See Figures 37, 38, 39, 40, 41 and 42**

Several methods of repairing damaged threads are available. Heli-Coil® (shown here), Keenserts® and Microdot® are among the most widely used. All involve basically the same principle — drilling out stripped threads, tapping the hole and installing a prewound insert — making welding, plugging and oversize fasteners unnecessary.

Two types of thread repair inserts are usually supplied: a standard type for most Inch Coarse, Inch Fine, Metric Course and Metric Fine thread sizes and a spark lug type to fit most spark plug port sizes. Consult the individual manufacturer's catalog to determine exact applications. Typical thread repair kits will contain a selection of prewound threaded inserts, a tap (corresponding to the outside diameter threads of the insert) and an installation tool. Spark plug inserts usually differ because they require a tap equipped with pilot threads and a combined reamer/tap section. Most manufacturers also supply blister-packed thread repair inserts separately in addition to a

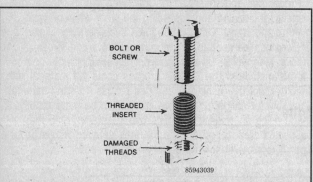

Fig. 37 Damaged bolt hole threads can be replaced with thread repair inserts

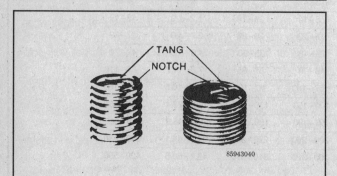

Fig. 38 Standard thread repair insert (left), and spark plug thread insert

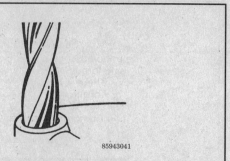

Fig. 39 Drill out the damaged threads with the specified drill. Be sure to drill completely through the hole or to the bottom of a blind hole

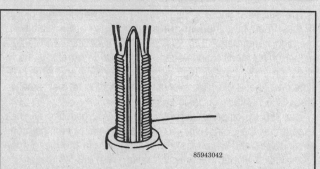

Fig. 40 Using the kit, tap the hole in order to receive the thread insert. Keep the tap well oiled and back it out frequently to avoid clogging the threads.

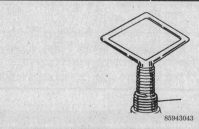

Fig. 41 Screw the threaded insert onto the installer tool until the tang engages the slot. Thread the insert into the hole until it is $\frac{1}{4}$ or $\frac{1}{2}$ turn below the top surface, then remove the tool and break off the tang using a punch.

master kit containing a variety of taps and inserts plus installation tools.

Before effecting a repair to a threaded hole, remove any snapped, broken or damaged bolts or studs. Penetrating oil can be used to free frozen threads. The offending item can be removed with locking pliers or with a screw or stud extractor. After the hole is clear, the thread can be repaired, as shown in the series of accompanying illustrations and in the kit manufacturer's instructions.

Checking Engine Compression

A noticeable lack of engine power, excessive oil consumption and/or poor fuel mileage measured over an extended period are all indicators of internal engine wear. Worn piston

Standard Torque Specifications and Fastener Markings

In the absence of specific torques, the following chart can be used as a guide to the maximum safe torque of a particular size/grade of fastener.

- There is no torque difference for fine or coarse threads.
- Torque values are based on clean, dry threads. Reduce the value by 10% if threads are oiled prior to assembly.
- The torque required for aluminum components or fasteners is considerably less.

U.S. Bolts

SAE Grade Number	1 or 2			5			6 or 7		
Number of lines always 2 less than the grade number.	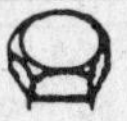			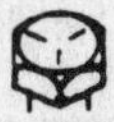			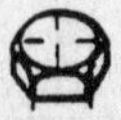		
	Maximum Torque			Maximum Torque			Maximum Torque		
Bolt Size (Inches)—(Thread)	Ft./Lbs.	Kgm	Nm	Ft./Lbs.	Kgm	Nm	Ft./Lbs.	Kgm	Nm
¼—20	5	0.7	6.8	8	1.1	10.8	10	1.4	13.5
—28	6	0.8	8.1	10	1.4	13.6			
5/16—18	11	1.5	14.9	17	2.3	23.0	19	2.6	25.8
—24	13	1.8	17.6	19	2.6	25.7			
⅜—16	18	2.5	24.4	31	4.3	42.0	34	4.7	46.0
—24	20	2.75	27.1	35	4.8	47.5			
7/16—14	28	3.8	37.0	49	6.8	66.4	55	7.6	74.5
—20	30	4.2	40.7	55	7.6	74.5			
½—13	39	5.4	52.8	75	10.4	101.7	85	11.75	115.2
—20	41	5.7	55.6	85	11.7	115.2			
9/16—12	51	7.0	69.2	110	15.2	149.1	120	16.6	162.7
—18	55	7.6	74.5	120	16.6	162.7			
⅝—11	83	11.5	112.5	150	20.7	203.3	167	23.0	226.5
—18	95	13.1	128.8	170	23.5	230.5			
¾—10	105	14.5	142.3	270	37.3	366.0	280	38.7	379.6
—16	115	15.9	155.9	295	40.8	400.0			
⅞—9	160	22.1	216.9	395	54.6	535.5	440	60.9	596.5
—14	175	24.2	237.2	435	60.1	589.7			
1—8	236	32.5	318.6	590	81.6	799.9	660	91.3	894.8
—14	250	34.6	338.9	660	91.3	849.8			

Metric Bolts

Relative Strength Marking	4.6, 4.8			8.8		
Bolt Markings	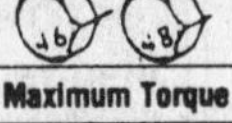			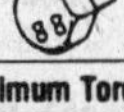		
	Maximum Torque			Maximum Torque		
Bolt Size Thread Size x Pitch (mm)	Ft./Lbs.	Kgm	Nm	Ft./Lbs.	Kgm	Nm
6 x 1.0	2–3	.2–.4	3–4	3–6	.4–.8	5–8
8 x 1.25	6–8	.8–1	8–12	9–14	1.2–1.9	13–19
10 x 1.25	12–17	1.5–2.3	16–23	20–29	2.7–4.0	27–39
12 x 1.25	21–32	2.9–4.4	29–43	35–53	4.8–7.3	47–72
14 x 1.5	35–52	4.8–7.1	48–70	57–85	7.8–11.7	77–110
16 x 1.5	51–77	7.0–10.6	67–100	90–120	12.4–16.5	130–160
18 x 1.5	74–110	10.2–15.1	100–150	130–170	17.9–23.4	180–230
20 x 1.5	110–140	15.1–19.3	150–190	190–240	26.2–46.9	160–320
22 x 1.5	150–190	22.0–26.2	200–260	250–320	34.5–44.1	340–430
24 x 1.5	190–240	26.2–46.9	260–320	310–410	42.7–56.5	420–550

85943044

Fig. 42 Using proper specifications will prevent the need for most thread repairs. If a specification is not given, this chart of standards may be used to help determine the proper torque.

rings, scored or worn cylinder bores, blown head gaskets, sticking or burnt valves and worn valve seats are all possible culprits here. A check of each cylinder's compression will help you locate the problems.

As mentioned under Tools and Equipment in Section 1 of this manual, a screw-in type compression gauge is more accurate that the type you simply hold against the spark plug hole. Although it takes slightly longer to use, it's worth it to obtain a more accurate reading. Follow the procedures below.

GASOLINE ENGINES

▶ See Figure 43

1. Warm up the engine to normal operating temperature.
2. Remove all the spark plugs.
3. Disconnect the high tension lead from the ignition coil.
4. Fully open the throttle either by operating the carburetor throttle linkage by hand or by having an assistant floor the accelerator pedal.
5. Screw the compression gauge into the No. 1 spark plug hole until the fitting is snug.

❋❋WARNING

Be careful not to crossthread the plug hole. On aluminum cylinder heads use extra care, as the threads in these heads are easily ruined.

6. Ask an assistant to depress the accelerator pedal fully on both carbureted and fuel injected vehicles. Then, while you read the compression gauge, ask the assistant to crank the engine two or three times in short bursts using the ignition switch.
7. Read the compression gauge at the end of each series of cranks, and record the highest of these readings. Repeat this procedure for each of the engine's cylinders. Compare the highest reading of each cylinder to the readings on the other cylinders. Readings should be similar for all of the cylinders.

➡A cylinder's compression pressure is usually acceptable if it is not less than 80% of the highest reading. For example, if the highest reading is 150 psi, the lowest should be no lower than 120 psi. No cylinder should be less than 100 psi.

8. If a cylinder is unusually low, pour a tablespoon of clean engine oil into the cylinder through the spark plug hole and repeat the compression test. If the compression comes up

after adding the oil, it appears that the cylinder's piston rings or bore are damaged or worn. If the pressure remains low, the valves may not be seating properly (a valve job is needed), or the head gasket may be blown near that cylinder. If compression in any two adjacent cylinders is low, and if the addition of oil doesn't help the compression, there is leakage past the head gasket. Oil and coolant water in the combustion chamber can result from this problem. There may be evidence of water droplets on the engine dipstick when a head gasket has blown.

DIESEL ENGINES

Checking cylinder compression on diesel engines is basically the same procedure as on gasoline engines except for the following:

1. A special compression gauge adaptor suitable for diesel engines (because these engines have much greater compression pressures) must be used.
2. Remove the injector tubes and remove the injectors from each cylinder.

❋❋WARNING

Don't forget to remove the washer underneath each injector. Otherwise, it may get lost when the engine is cranked.

3. When fitting the compression gauge adaptor to the cylinder head, make sure the bleeder on the gauge (if equipped) is closed.
4. When reinstalling the injector assemblies, install new washers underneath each injector.

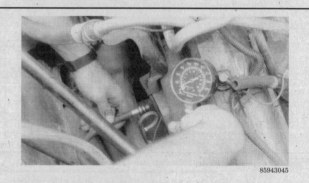

85943045

Fig. 43 Using a screw-in type compression gauge will yield more accurate results

GENERAL ENGINE SPECIFICATIONS

Year	Engine No. Cyl. Displacement (cu. in.)	Type Carburetor	Horsepower @ rpm ■	Torque @ rpm (ft. lbs.) ■	Bore and Stroke (in.)	Compression Ratio	Oil Pressure @ 2000 rpm (psi)
1964	6-194	1-bbl	120 @ 4400	177 @ 2400	3.563 × 3.250	8.5:1	35
	6-230	1-bbl	155 @ 4400	215 @ 2000	3.875 × 3.250	8.5:1	35
	8-283	2-bbl	195 @ 4800	285 @ 2800	3.875 × 3.000	9.25:1	35
	8-283	4-bbl	220 @ 4800	295 @ 3200	3.875 × 3.000	9.25:1	35
	8-327	4-bbl	250 @ 4400	350 @ 2800	4.000 × 3.250	10.5:1	35
	8-327	4-bbl	300 @ 5000	360 @ 3200	4.000 × 3.250	10.5:1	35
1965	6-194	1-bbl	120 @ 4400	177 @ 2400	3.563 × 3.250	8.5:1	35
	6-230	1-bbl	140 @ 4400	220 @ 1600	3.875 × 3.250	8.5:1	35
	8-283	2-bbl	195 @ 4800	285 @ 2400	3.875 × 3.000	9.25:1	35
	8-283	4-bbl	220 @ 4800	295 @ 3200	3.875 × 3.000	9.25:1	35
	8-327	4-bbl	250 @ 4400	350 @ 2800	4.001 × 3.250	10.5:1	35
	8-327	4-bbl	300 @ 5000	360 @ 3200	4.001 × 3.250	10.5:1	35
	8-327	4-bbl	350 @ 5800	360 @ 3600	4.001 × 3.250	11.0:1	35
1966	6-194	1-bbl	120 @ 4400	177 @ 2400	3.563 × 3.250	8.5:1	38 ①
	6-230	1-bbl	140 @ 4400	220 @ 1600	3.875 × 3.250	8.5:1	38 ①
	8-283	2-bbl	195 @ 4800	285 @ 2800	3.875 × 3.000	9.25:1	38 ①
	8-283	4-bbl	220 @ 4800	295 @ 3200	3.875 × 3.000	9.25:1	38 ①
	8-327	4-bbl	275 @ 4800	335 @ 2800	4.001 × 3.250	10.5:1	38 ①
	8-327	4-bbl	350 @ 5800	360 @ 3600	4.001 × 3.250	11.0:1	38 ①
	8-396	4-bbl	325 @ 4800	410 @ 3200	4.094 × 3.760	10.25:1	62
	8-396	4-bbl	360 @ 5200	420 @ 3600	4.096 × 3.760	10.25:1	62
	8-396	4-bbl	375 @ 5600	415 @ 3600	4.094 × 3.760	11.0:1	62
1967	6-230	1-bbl	140 @ 4400	220 @ 1600	3.875 × 3.250	8.5:1	38
	6-250	1-bbl	155 @ 4200	235 @ 1600	3.875 × 3.530	8.5:1	38 ①
	8-283	2-bbl	195 @ 4600	285 @ 2400	3.875 × 3.000	9.25:1	38 ①
	8-327	2-bbl	210 @ 4600	320 @ 2400	4.001 × 3.250	8.75:1	38 ①
	8-327	4-bbl	275 @ 4800	355 @ 3200	4.001 × 3.250	10.0:1	38 ①
	8-396	4-bbl	325 @ 4800	410 @ 3200	4.094 × 3.760	10.25:1	57
	8-396	4-bbl	350 @ 5200	415 @ 3400	4.094 × 3.760	10.25:1	57
1968	6-230	1-bbl	145 @ 4400	220 @ 1600	3.875 × 3.250	8.5:1	58
	6-250	1-bbl	155 @ 4200	235 @ 1600	3.875 × 3.530	8.5:1	58
	8-307	2-bbl	200 @ 4600	300 @ 2400	3.875 × 3.250	9.0:1	58
	8-327	2-bbl	210 @ 4600	320 @ 2400	4.001 × 3.250	8.75:1	58
	8-327	4-bbl	275 @ 4800	355 @ 3200	4.001 × 3.250	10.0:1	58
	8-396	4-bbl	325 @ 4800	410 @ 3200	4.094 × 3.760	10.25:1	62
	8-396	4-bbl	350 @ 5200	415 @ 3400	4.094 × 3.750	10.25:1	62
	8-396	4-bbl	375 @ 5600	415 @ 3600	4.094 × 3.760	11.0:1	62
1969	6-230	1-bbl	140 @ 4400	220 @ 1600	3.875 × 3.250	8.5:1	58
	6-250	1-bbl	155 @ 4200	235 @ 1600	3.875 × 3.530	8.5:1	58
	8-307	2-bbl	200 @ 4600	300 @ 2400	3.875 × 3.250	9.0:1	58
	8-350	2-bbl	250 @ 4800	345 @ 2800	4.000 × 3.480	9.0:1	62
	8-350	4-bbl	300 @ 4800	380 @ 3200	4.000 × 3.480	10.25:1	62

85943047

GENERAL ENGINE SPECIFICATIONS

Year	Engine No. Cyl. Displacement (cu. in.)	Type Carburetor	Horsepower @ rpm ▪	Torque @ rpm (ft. lbs.) ▪	Bore and Stroke (in.)	Compression Ratio	Oil Pressure @ 2000 rpm (psi)
	8-396	4-bbl	325 @ 4800	410 @ 3200	4.094 × 3.760	10.25:1	62
	8-396	4-bbl	350 @ 5200	415 @ 3400	4.094 × 3.760	10.25:1	62
	8-396	4-bbl	375 @ 5600	415 @ 3600	4.094 × 3.760	11.0:1	62
1970	6-230	1-bbl	140 @ 4400	220 @ 1600	3.875 × 3.250	8.5:1	40
	6-250	1-bbl	155 @ 4200	235 @ 1600	3.875 × 3.530	8.5:1	40
	8-307	2-bbl	200 @ 4600	300 @ 2400	3.875 × 3.250	9.0:1	40
	8-350	2-bbl	250 @ 4800	345 @ 2800	4.000 × 3.480	9.0:1	40
	8-350	4-bbl	300 @ 4800	380 @ 3200	4.000 × 3.480	10.25:1	40
	8-400	2-bbl	265 @ 4400	400 @ 2400	4.125 × 3.760	9.0:1	40
	8-402	4-bbl	330 @ 4800	410 @ 3200	4.126 × 3.760	10.25:1	40
	8-402	4-bbl	350 @ 5200	415 @ 3400	4.126 × 3.760	10.25:1	40
	8-454	4-bbl	360 @ 4400	500 @ 3200	4.251 × 4.000	10.25:1	40
1971	6-250	1-bbl	145 @ 4200	230 @ 1600	3.875 × 3.530	8.5:1	40
	8-307	2-bbl	200 @ 4600	300 @ 2400	3.875 × 3.250	8.5:1	40
	8-350	2-bbl	245 @ 4800	350 @ 2800	4.000 × 3.480	8.5:1	40
	8-350	4-bbl	270 @ 4800	360 @ 3200	4.000 × 3.480	8.5:1	40
	8-350	4-bbl	330 @ 5000	275 @ 5600	4.000 × 3.480	9.0:1	40
	8-402	4-bbl	300 @ 4800	400 @ 3200	4.126 × 3.760	8.5:1	40
	8-454	4-bbl	365 @ 4800	465 @ 3200	4.251 × 4.000	8.5:1	40
	8-454	4-bbl	425 @ 5600	475 @ 4000	4.251 × 4.000	9.0:1	40
1972	6-250	1-bbl	110 @ 3800	185 @ 1600	3.875 × 3.530	8.5:1	40
	8-307	2-bbl	130 @ 4000	230 @ 2400	3.875 × 3.250	8.5:1	40
	8-350	2-bbl	165 @ 4000	280 @ 2400	4.000 × 3.480	8.5:1	40
	8-350	4-bbl	200 @ 4400	300 @ 2800	4.000 × 3.480	8.5:1	40
	8-350	4-bbl	225 @ 5600	280 @ 4000	4.000 × 3.480	9.0:1	40
	8-402	4-bbl	240 @ 4400	345 @ 3200	4.126 × 3.760	8.5:1	40
	8-454	4-bbl	270 @ 4000	390 @ 3200	4.251 × 4.000	8.5:1	40
1973	6-250	1-bbl	100 @ 3800	175 @ 1600	3.875 × 3.530	8.25:1	40
	8-307	2-bbl	115 @ 4000	205 @ 2000	3.875 × 3.250	8.5:1	40
	8-350	2-bbl	145 @ 4000	255 @ 2400	4.000 × 3.480	8.5:1	40
	8-350	4-bbl	175 @ 4400	270 @ 2400	4.000 × 3.480	8.5:1	40
	8-350	4-bbl	245 @ 5200	280 @ 4000	4.000 × 3.480	9.0:1	40
	8-454	4-bbl	245 @ 4000	375 @ 2800	4.251 × 4.000	8.5:1	40
1974	6-250	1-bbl	100 @ 3600	175 @ 1800	3.875 × 3.530	8.25:1	40
	8-350 ②	2-bbl	145 @ 3600	250 @ 2200	4.000 × 3.480	8.5:1	40
	8-350 ③	4-bbl	160 @ 3800	245 @ 2400	4.000 × 3.480	8.5:1	40
	8-350	4-bbl	185 @ 4000	270 @ 2600	4.000 × 3.480	8.5:1	40
	8-400 ②	2-bbl	150 @ 3200	295 @ 2600	4.126 × 3.750	8.5:1	40
	8-400 ③	4-bbl	180 @ 3800	290 @ 2400	4.126 × 3.750	8.5:1	40
	8-454	4-bbl	235 @ 4000	360 @ 2800	4.251 × 4.000	8.25:1	40
1975	6-250	1-bbl	105 @ 3800	185 @ 1200	3.875 × 3.530	8.25:1	40
	8-350 ②	2-bbl	145 @ 3800	250 @ 2200	4.000 × 3.480	8.5:1	40
	8-350 ③	4-bbl	155 @ 3800	250 @ 2400	4.000 × 3.480	8.5:1	40

85943048

GENERAL ENGINE SPECIFICATIONS

Year	Engine No. Cyl. Displacement (cu. in.)	Type Carburetor	Horsepower @ rpm ■	Torque @ rpm (ft. lbs.) ■	Bore and Stroke (in.)	Compression Ratio	Oil Pressure @ 2000 rpm (psi)
1975	8-400	4-bbl	175 @ 3600	305 @ 2000	4.126 × 4.000	8.5:1	40
	8-454 ②	4-bbl	215 @ 4000	350 @ 2400	4.251 × 4.000	8.15:1	40
1976–77	6-250	1-bbl	105 @ 3800	185 @ 1200	3.875 × 3.530	8.25:1	40
	8-305	2-bbl	140 @ 3800	245 @ 2000	3.736 × 3.480	8.5:1	40
	8-350	2-bbl	145 @ 3800	250 @ 2200	4.000 × 3.480	8.5:1	40
	8-350	4-bbl	165 @ 3800	260 @ 2400	4.000 × 3.480	8.5:1	40
	8-400	4-bbl	175 @ 3600	305 @ 2000	4.126 × 4.000	8.5:1	40
1978–79	6-200	2-bbl	95 @ 3800	160 @ 2000	3.500 × 3.480	8.2:1	40
	6-231	2-bbl	105 @ 3400	185 @ 2000	3.800 × 3.400	8.0:1	37
	6-250	1-bbl	110 @ 3800	190 @ 1600	3.875 × 3.530	8.1:1	40
	8-305	4-bbl	155 @ 3800	260 @ 2800	3.736 × 3.480	8.4:1	45
	8-305	2-bbl	145 @ 3800	245 @ 2400	3.736 × 3.480	8.5:1	40
	8-267	2-bbl	125 @ 3800	215 @ 2400	3.500 × 3.480	8.2:1	45
	8-350	4-bbl	170 @ 3800	270 @ 2400	4.000 × 3.480	8.5:1	40
1980	6-229	2-bbl	115 @ 4000	175 @ 2000	3.736 × 3.480	8.6:1	45
	6-231	2-bbl	110 @ 3800	190 @ 1600	3.800 × 3.400	8.0:1	45
	6-231	Turbo	170 @ 4000	265 @ 2400	3.800 × 3.400	8.0:1	37
	8-267	2-bbl	120 @ 3600	215 @ 2000	3.500 × 3.480	8.3:1	45
	8-305	4-bbl	155 @ 4000	240 @ 1600	3.736 × 3.480	8.6:1	45
	8-305 (Calif.)	4-bbl	155 @ 4000	230 @ 2400	3.736 × 3.480	8.6:1	45
1981	6-229	2-bbl	110 @ 4200	170 @ 2000	3.736 × 3.480	8.6:1	45
	6-231	2-bbl	110 @ 3800	190 @ 1600	3.800 × 3.400	8.0:1	45
	6-231	Turbo	170 @ 4000	275 @ 2400	3.800 × 3.400	8.0:1	37
	8-267	2-bbl	115 @ 4000	200 @ 2400	3.500 × 3.480	8.3:1	45
	8-305	4-bbl	150 @ 3800	240 @ 2400	3.736 × 3.480	8.6:1	45
1982–84	6-229	2-bbl	110 @ 4200	170 @ 2000	3.736 × 3.480	8.6:1	45
	6-231	2-bbl	110 @ 3800	190 @ 1600	3.800 × 3.400	8.0:1	45
	6-263	Diesel	85 @ 3600	165 @ 1600	4.057 × 3.385	22.5:1	45 ①
	8-267	2-bbl	115 @ 4000	205 @ 2400	3.50 × 3.48	8.3:1	45
	8-305	4-bbl	145 @ 4000	240 @ 1600	3.736 × 3.480	8.6:1	45
	8-350	Diesel	105 @ 3200	200 @ 1600	4.057 × 3.385	22.5:1	45 ①
1985–86	6-262	TBI	130 @ 3600	218 @ 2000	4.000 × 3.480	9.3:1	45
	8-305	4-bbl	134 @ 4800	319 @ 3200	3.736 × 3.480	9.5:1	45
	8-305	4-bbl	150 @ 3800	240 @ 2400	3.736 × 3.480	8.6:1	45
1987–88	6-262	TBI	145 @ 4200	225 @ 2000	4.000 × 3.480	9.3:1	50–65
	8-305	4-bbl	150 @ 4000	240 @ 2000	3.736 × 3.480	8.6:1	50–65
	8-305	4-bbl	180 @ 4800	225 @ 3200	3.736 × 3.480	9.5:1	50–65

TBI—Throttle Body Injection

■ Starting 1972, horsepower and torque are SAE net figures. They are measured at the rear of the transmission with all accessories installed and operating. Since the figures vary when a given engine is installed in different models, some are representative rather than exact.

① Oil pressure at 1500 rpm
② Not available—Calif.
③ Calif. only

85943049

VALVE SPECIFICATIONS

Year	Engine No. Cyl. Displacement (cu. in.)	Seat Angle (deg.)	Fact Angle (deg.)	Spring Test Pressure (lbs. @ in.)	Spring Installed Height (in.)	Stem to Guide Clearance (in.) Intake	Exhaust	Stem diameter (in.) Intake	Exhaust
1964-65	6-194	46	45	170 @ 1.33	$1^2/_3$	0.0010–0.0027	0.0015–0.0033	0.3404–0.3417	0.3410–0.3417
	6-230	46	45	175 @ 1.26	$1^2/_3$	0.0010–0.0027	0.0015–0.0033	0.3404–0.3417	0.3410–0.3417
	8-283	46	45	175 @ 1.26	$1^2/_3$	0.0010–0.0027	0.0015–0.0033	0.3404–0.3417	0.3410–0.3417
	8-327	46	45	175 @ 1.26	$1^2/_3$	0.0010–0.0027	0.0010–0.0027	0.3404–0.3417	0.3410–0.3417
1966	6-194	46	45	60 @ 1.33	$1^{21}/_{32}$	0.0010–0.0037	0.0010–0.0047	0.3414	0.3414
	6-230	46	45	60 @ 1.66	$1^{21}/_{32}$	0.0010–0.0037	0.0010–0.0047	0.3414	0.3414
	8-283	46	45	82 @ 1.66	$1^{21}/_{32}$	0.0010–0.0037	0.0010–0.0047	0.3414	0.3414
	8-327	46	45	82 @ 1.66	$1^{21}/_{32}$	0.0010–0.0037	0.0010–0.0047	0.3414	0.3414
	8-396 [1]	46	45	90 @ 1.88	$1^7/_8$	0.0010–0.0037	0.0010–0.0047	0.3414	0.3414
	8-396 [2]	46	45	100 @ 1.88	$1^7/_8$	0.0010–0.0037	0.0010–0.0047	0.3414	0.3414
1967	6-230	46 [3]	45	60 @ 1.66	$1^{21}/_{32}$	0.0010–0.0037	0.0015–0.0052	0.3414	0.3414
	6-250	46 [3]	45	60 @ 1.66	$1^{21}/_{32}$	0.0010–0.0047	0.0015–0.0052	0.3414	0.3414
	8-283	46 [3]	45	80 @ 1.70	$1^5/_{32}$	0.0010–0.0037	0.0010–0.0047	0.3414	0.3414
	8-327	46 [3]	45	80 @ 1.70	$1^5/_{32}$	0.0010–0.0037	0.0010–0.0047	0.3414	0.3414
	8-396 [1]	46 [3]	45	90 @ 1.88	$1^7/_8$	0.0010–0.0035	0.0012–0.0047	0.3417	0.3417
	8-396 [2]	46	45	100 @ 1.88	$1^7/_8$	0.0010–0.0035	0.0012–0.0047	0.3417	0.3417
1968	6-230	46 [3]	45	59 @ 1.66	$1^{21}/_{32}$	0.0010–0.0037	0.0015–0.0052	0.3414	0.3414
	6-250	46 [3]	45	59 @ 1.66	$1^{21}/_{32}$	0.0010–0.0037	0.0015–0.0052	0.3414	0.3414
	8-307	46 [3]	45	80 @ 1.70	$1^5/_{32}$	0.0010–0.0037	0.0010–0.0047	0.3414	0.3414
	8-327	46 [3]	45	80 @ 1.70	$1^5/_{32}$	0.0010–0.0037	0.0010–0.0047	0.3414	0.3414
	8-350	46 [3]	45	80 @ 1.70	$1^5/_{32}$	0.0010–0.0037	0.0010–0.0047	0.3414	0.3414
	8-396	46 [3]	45	90 @ 1.88	$1^7/_8$	0.0010–0.0035	0.0012–0.0047	0.3719	0.3717
1969	6-230	46 [3]	45	59 @ 1.66	$1^{21}/_{32}$	0.0010–0.0037	0.0015–0.0052	0.3414	0.3414
	6-250	46 [3]	45	59 @ 1.66	$1^{21}/_{32}$	0.0010–0.0037	0.0015–0.0052	0.3414	0.3414
	8-307	46 [3]	45	80 @ 1.70	$1^{23}/_{32}$	0.0010–0.0037	0.0012–0.0049	0.3414	0.3414
	8-350	46 [3]	45	80 @ 1.70	$1^5/_{32}$	0.0010–0.0037	0.0010–0.0047	0.3414	0.3414
	8-396 [1]	46 [3]	45	90 @ 1.88	$1^7/_8$	0.0010–0.0035	0.0012–0.0047	0.3719	0.3719
	8-396 [4]	46 [3]	45	100 @ 1.88	$1^7/_8$	0.0010–0.0035	0.0012–0.0047	0.3719	0.3719
1970	6-230	46 [3]	45	59 @ 1.66	$1^{21}/_{32}$	0.0010–0.0037	0.0015–0.0052	0.3414	0.3414
	6-250	46 [3]	45	59 @ 1.66	$1^{21}/_{32}$	0.0010–0.0037	0.0015–0.0052	0.3414	0.3414
	8-307	46 [3]	45	80 @ 1.70	$1^{23}/_{32}$	0.0010–0.0037	0.0012–0.0049	0.3414	0.3414
	8-350	46 [3]	45	80 @ 1.70	$1^{23}/_{32}$	0.0010–0.0037	0.0012–0.0049	0.3414	0.3414
	8-400	46 [3]	45	80 @ 1.70	$1^7/_8$	0.0010–0.0037	0.0012–0.0047	0.3414	0.3414
	8-402	46 [3]	45	75 @ 1.88 [5]	$1^7/_8$	0.0010–0.0037	0.0012–0.0047	0.3719	0.3717
	8-454	46 [4]	45	75 @ 1.88 [5]	$1^7/_8$	0.0010–0.0037	0.0012–0.0047	0.3717	0.3719
1971	6-250	46	45	60 @ 1.66	$1^{21}/_{32}$	0.0010–0.0037	0.0015–0.0052	0.3414	0.3414
	8-307	46	45	80 @ 1.70	$1^{23}/_{32}$	0.0010–0.0037	0.0012–0.0049	0.3414	0.3414
	8-350	46	45	80 @ 1.70	$1^{23}/_{32}$	0.0010–0.0037	0.0012–0.0049	0.3414	0.3414
	8-402	46	45	75 @ 1.88 [5]	$1^7/_8$	0.0010–0.0037	0.0012–0.0047	0.3719	0.3717
	8-454	46	45	75 @ 1.88 [5]	$1^7/_8$	0.0010–0.0037	0.0012–0.0047	0.3719	0.3717

85943051

VALVE SPECIFICATIONS

Year	Engine No. Cyl. Displacement (cu. in.)	Seat Angle (deg.)	Fact Angle (deg.)	Spring Test Pressure (lbs. @ in.)	Spring Installed Height (in.)	Stem to Guide Clearance (in.)		Stem diameter (in.)	
						Intake	Exhaust	Intake	Exhaust
1972	6-250	46	45	60 @ 1.66	$1\frac{21}{32}$	0.0010–0.0037	0.0015–0.0052	0.3414	0.3414
	8-307	46	45	80 @ 1.70	$1\frac{23}{32}$	0.0010–0.0037	0.0012–0.0049	0.3414	0.3414
	8-350	46	45	80 @ 1.70	$1\frac{23}{32}$	0.0010–0.0037	0.0012–0.0049	0.3414	0.3414
	8-402	46	45	75 @ 1.88 [5]	$1\frac{7}{8}$	0.0010–0.0037	0.0012–0.0047	0.3719	0.3717
	8-454	46	45	75 @ 1.88 [5]	$1\frac{7}{8}$	0.0010–0.0037	0.0012–0.0047	0.3719	0.3717
1973	6-250	46	45	60 @ 1.66	$1\frac{21}{32}$	0.0010–0.0027	0.0015–0.0032	0.3414	0.3414
	8-307	46	45	80 @ 1.61	$1\frac{5}{8}$	0.0010–0.0037	0.0012–0.0047	0.3414	0.3414
	8-350	46	45	80 @ 1.70	$1\frac{23}{32}$	0.0012–0.0027	0.0012–0.0029	0.3414	0.3414
	8-454	46	45	80 @ 1.88	$1\frac{7}{8}$	0.0010–0.0027	0.0012–0.0027	0.3719	0.3717
1974	6-250	46	45	60 @ 1.66	$1\frac{21}{32}$	0.0010–0.0027	0.0012–0.0027	0.3414	0.3414
	8-350	46	45	80 @ 1.70	$1\frac{23}{32}$	0.0010–0.0027	0.0010–0.0027	0.3414	0.3414
	8-400	46	45	80 @ 1.70	$1\frac{23}{32}$	0.0010–0.0027	0.0010–0.0027	0.3414	0.3414
	8-454	46	45	80 @ 1.88	$1\frac{7}{8}$	0.0010–0.0027	0.0010–0.0027	0.3719	0.3719
1975–77	6-250	46	45	60 @ 1.66	$1\frac{21}{32}$	0.0010–0.0027	0.0010–0.0027 [6]	0.3414	0.3414
	8-305	46	45	80 @ 1.70	$1\frac{23}{32}$	0.0010–0.0027	0.0010–0.0027	0.3414	0.3414
	8-350	46	45	80 @ 1.70 [7]	$1\frac{23}{32}$	0.0010–0.0027	0.0010–0.0027	0.3414	0.3414
	8-400	46	45	80 @ 1.70 [7]	$1\frac{23}{32}$	0.0010–0.0027	0.0010–0.0027	0.3414	0.3414
	8-454	46	45	90 @ 1.88	$1\frac{7}{8}$	0.0010–0.0027	0.0010–0.0027	0.3719	0.3719
1978–79	6-200	46	45	200 @ 1.25	$1\frac{23}{32}$ [8]	0.0012–0.0027	0.0010–0.0027	0.3414	0.3414
	6-231	45	45	168 @ 1.33	$1\frac{47}{64}$	0.0015–0.0032	0.0015–0.0032	0.3407	0.3409
	6-250	46	45	175 @ 1.26	$1\frac{21}{32}$	0.0010–0.0027	0.0015–0.0032	0.3414	0.3414
	8-267	46	45	200 @ 1.25	$1\frac{23}{32}$	0.0010–0.0027	0.0010–0.0027	0.3414	0.3414
	8-305	46	45	200 @ 1.25	$1\frac{23}{32}$ [8]	0.0010–0.0027	0.0010–0.0027	0.3414	0.3414
	8-350	46	45	200 @ 1.25	$1\frac{23}{32}$ [8]	0.0010–0.0027	0.0010–0.0027	0.3414	0.3414
1980–81	6-229	46	45	200 @ 1.25	$1\frac{23}{32}$	0.0010–0.0027	0.0010–0.0027	0.3414	0.3414
	6-231	45	45	168 @ 1.33	$1\frac{47}{64}$	0.0015–0.0032	0.0015–0.0032	0.3407	0.3409
	8-267	46	45	200 @ 1.25	$1\frac{23}{32}$	0.0010–0.0027	0.0010–0.0027	0.3414	0.3414
	8-305	46	45	200 @ 1.25	$1\frac{23}{32}$	0.0010–0.0027	0.0010–0.0027	0.3414	0.3414
1982–84	6-229	46	45	200 @ 1.25	$1\frac{23}{32}$	0.0010–0.0027	0.0010–0.0027	0.3414	0.3414
	6-231	45	45	168 @ 1.33	$1\frac{47}{64}$	0.0015–0.0032	0.0015–0.0032	0.3407	0.3409
	6-263	46	45	189 @ 1.30	$1\frac{43}{64}$	0.0010–0.0027	0.0015–0.0032	0.3429	0.3423
	8-267	46	45	200 @ 1.25	$1\frac{23}{32}$	0.0010–0.0027	0.0010–0.0027	0.3414	0.3414
	8-305	46	45	200 @ 1.25	$1\frac{23}{32}$	0.0010–0.0027	0.0010–0.0027	0.3414	0.3414
	8-350	46	45	189 @ 1.30	$1\frac{43}{64}$	0.0010–0.0027	0.0015–0.0032	0.3429	0.3423
1985–88	6-262	46	45	200 @ 1.25	$1\frac{23}{32}$	0.0010–0.0027	0.0010–0.0027	0.3414	0.3414
	8-305	46	45	200 @ 1.25	$1\frac{23}{32}$	0.0010–0.0027	0.0010–0.0027	0.3414	0.3414

[1] 327 hp
[2] 360 hp and 375 hp
[3] 45° on aluminum heads
[4] 350 hp
[5] Inner spring—30 @ 1.78
[6] 1976 and later: 0.0015–0.0032
[7] 80 @ 1.61 for exhaust
[8] Exhaust valve—$1\frac{19}{32}$

85943052

CRANKSHAFT AND CONNECTING ROD SPECIFICATIONS

(All measurements are given in inches)

Year	Engine No. Cyl. Displacement (cu. in.)	Crankshaft			Thrust on No.	Connecting Rod		
		Main Brg. Journal Dia.	Main Brg. Oil Clearance	Shaft End-play		Journal Diameter	Oil Clearance	Side Clearance
1964	6-194	2.2983–2.2993	0.0008–0.004	0.002–0.006	7	1.999–2.000	0.0007–0.0028	0.008–0.014
	6-230	2.2983–2.2993	0.0008–0.004	0.002–0.006	7	1.999–2.000	0.0007–0.0028	0.008–0.014
	8-283	2.2978–2.2988	0.0008–0.004	0.002–0.006	5	1.999–2.000	0.0007–0.0028	0.008–0.014
1965	6-194	2.2983–2.2993	0.0003–0.0029	0.002–0.006	7	1.999–2.000	0.0007–0.0027	0.009–0.013
	6-230	2.2983–2.2993	0.0003–0.0029	0.002–0.006	7	1.999–2.000	0.0007–0.0027	0.009–0.013
	8-283	2.2978–2.2988	0.0003–0.0029*	0.002–0.006	5	1.999–2.000	0.0007–0.0027	0.009–0.013
	8-327	2.2978–2.2988	0.0008–0.0034*	0.002–0.006	5	1.999–2.000	0.0007–0.0028	0.009–0.013
1966	6-194	2.2983–2.2993	0.0003–0.0029	0.002–0.006	7	1.999–2.000	0.0007–0.0027	0.009–0.013
	6-230	2.2983–2.2993	0.0003–0.0029	0.002–0.006	7	1.999–2.000	0.0007–0.0027	0.009–0.013
	8-283	②	0.0003–0.0029①	0.003–0.011	5	1.999–2.000	0.0007–0.0027	0.009–0.013
	8-327	②	0.0003–0.0034①	0.003–0.011	5	1.999–2.000	0.0007–0.0028	0.009–0.013
	8-396	③	④	0.006–0.010	5	2.199–2.200	0.0007–0.0028	0.015–0.021
1967	6-230	2.2983–2.2993	0.0003–0.0029	0.002–0.006	7	1.999–2.000	0.0007–0.0027	0.009–0.013
	6-250	2.2983–2.2993	0.0003–0.0029	0.002–0.006	7	1.999–2.000	0.0007–0.0027	0.009–0.013
	8-283	⑤	⑦	0.003–0.011	5	1.999–2.000	0.0007–0.0027	0.009–0.013
	8-327	⑤	⑦	0.003–0.011	5	1.999–2.000	0.0007–0.0028	0.009–0.013
	8-396	③	④	0.006–0.010	5	2.199–2.200	0.0007–0.0028	0.015–0.021
1968	6-230	2.2983–2.2993	0.0003–0.0029	0.002–0.006	7	1.999–2.000	0.0007–0.0027	0.009–0.013
	6-250	2.2983–2.2993	0.0003–0.0029	0.002–0.006	7	1.999–2.000	0.0007–0.0027	0.009–0.013
	8-307	2.4484–2.4493⑥	0.0008–0.002⑧	0.003–0.011	5	2.099–2.100	0.0007–0.0028	0.009–0.013
	8-327	2.4484–2.4493⑥	0.0008–0.002⑧	0.003–0.011	5	2.099–2.100	0.0007–0.0027	0.009–0.013
	8-350	2.4484–2.4493⑥	0.0008–0.002⑧	0.003–0.011	5	2.099–2.100	0.0007–0.0028	0.009–0.013
	8-396	⑨	⑪	0.006–0.010	5	2.199–2.200	0.0009–0.0025	0.015–0.021
	8-396 (375 HP)	⑩	0.0013–0.0025⑫	0.006–0.010	5	2.1985–2.1995	0.0014–0.0030	0.019–0.025
1969	6-230	2.2983–2.2993	0.0003–0.0029	0.002–0.006	7	1.999–2.000	0.0007–0.0027	0.009–0.013
	6-250	2.2983–2.2993	0.0003–0.0029	0.002–0.006	7	1.999–2.000	0.0007–0.0027	0.009–0.013
	8-307	2.4479–2.4488	0.0008–0.002⑧	0.003–0.011	5	2.099–2.100	0.0007–0.0027	0.009–0.013
	8-350	2.4479–2.4488	0.0008–0.002⑧	0.003–0.011	5	2.099–2.100	0.0007–0.0028	0.009–0.013
	8-396	⑨	⑪	0.006–0.010	5	2.199–2.200	0.0009–0.0025	0.015–0.021
	8-396 (375 HP)	⑩	0.0013–0.0025⑫	0.006–0.010	5	2.1985–2.1995	0.0014–0.0030	0.019–0.025
1970	6-230	2.2983–2.2993	0.0003–0.0029	0.002–0.006	7	1.999–2.000	0.0007–0.0027	0.009–0.013
	6-250	2.2983–2.2993	0.0003–0.0029	0.002–0.006	7	1.999–2.000	0.0007–0.0027	0.009–0.013
	8-307	2.4484–2.4493⑥	0.0003–0.0015⑬	0.002–0.006	5	2.099–2.100	0.0007–0.0028	0.008–0.014
	8-350	2.4484–2.4493⑥	0.0003–0.0015⑬	0.002–0.006	5	2.099–2.100	0.0007–0.0028	0.008–0.014
	8-400 (Monte Carlo)	2.6584–2.6493⑱	0.0008–0.0020㉑	0.002–0.006	5	2.099–2.100	0.0009–0.0025	0.008–0.014
	8-402	2.7487–2.7496⑮	0.0007–0.0019⑯	0.006–0.010	5	2.199–2.200	0.0009–0.0025	0.013–0.023
	8-454	2.7485–2.7494⑩	0.0013–0.0025⑰	0.006–0.010	5	2.199–2.200	0.0009–0.0025	0.015–0.021

85943054

CRANKSHAFT AND CONNECTING ROD SPECIFICATIONS

(All measurements are given in inches)

| Year | Engine No. Cyl. Displacement (cu. in.) | Crankshaft | | | Thrust on No. | Connecting Rod | | |
		Main Brg. Journal Dia.	Main Brg. Oil Clearance	Shaft End-play		Journal Diameter	Oil Clearance	Side Clearance
1971	6-250	2.2983–2.2993	0.0003–0.0029	0.002–0.006	7	1.999–2.000	0.0007–0.0027	0.009–0.014
	8-307	2.4484–2.4493 [20]	0.0008–0.0020 [21]	0.002–0.006	5	2.099–2.100	0.0013–0.0035	0.008–0.014
	8-350	2.4484–2.4493 [20]	0.0008–0.0020 [21]	0.002–0.006	5	2.099–2.100	0.0013–0.0035	0.008–0.014
	8-402	2.7487–2.7496 [15]	0.0007–0.0019 [16]	0.006–0.010	5	2.199–2.200	0.0009–0.0025	0.013–0.023
	8-454 (365 HP)	2.7485–2.7494 [10]	0.0013–0.0025 [17]	0.006–0.010	5	2.199–2.200	0.0009–0.0025	0.015–0.021
	8-454 (425 HP)	2.7481–2.7490 [6]	0.0013–0.0025 [19]	0.006–0.010	5	2.1985–2.1995	0.0009–0.0025	0.019–0.025
1972	6-250	2.2983–2.2993	0.0003–0.0029	0.002–0.006	7	1.999–2.000	0.0007–0.0027	0.009–0.014
	8-307	2.4484–2.4493 [20]	0.0008–0.0020 [21]	0.002–0.006	5	2.099–2.100	0.0013–0.0035	0.008–0.014
	8-350	2.4484–2.4493 [20]	0.0008–0.0020 [21]	0.002–0.006	5	2.099–2.100	0.0013–0.0035	0.008–0.014
	8-402	2.7487–2.7496 [15]	0.0007–0.0019 [16]	0.006–0.010	5	2.199–2.200	0.0009–0.0025	0.013–0.023
	8-454	2.7485–2.7494 [10]	0.0013–0.0025 [17]	0.006–0.010	5	2.199–2.200	0.0009–0.0025	0.015–0.021
1973	6-250	2.3004	0.0003–0.0029	0.002–0.006	7	1.999–2.000	0.0007–0.0027	0.009–0.014
	8-307, 350	2.4502 [22]	0.0008–0.0020 [21]	0.002–0.006	5	2.009–2.100	0.0013–0.0035	0.008–0.014
	8-454	2.7492 [23]	0.0007–0.0019 [24]	0.006–0.010	5	2.199–2.200	0.0009–0.0025	0.015–0.023
1974–77	6-250	2.2988	0.0003–0.0029	0.002–0.006	7	1.9928–2.000	0.0007–0.0027	0.007–0.016
	8-305	2.4489 [26]	[25]	0.002–0.006	5	2.099–2.100	0.0013–0.0035	0.008–0.014
	8-350	2.4489 [26]	[25]	0.002–0.006	5	2.099–2.100	0.0035–0.0035	0.008–0.014
	8-400	2.6489 [27]	0.0008–0.0002 [28]	0.002–0.006	5	2.099–2.100	0.0035–0.0035	0.008–0.014
	8-454	2.7490	0.0013–0.0025 [29]	0.006–0.010	5	2.199–2.200	0.0009–0.0025	0.015–0.021
1978–79	6-200	2.4489	0.0011–0.0023 [30]	0.002–0.006	5	2.0988–2.0998	0.0013–0.0035	0.008–0.014
	6-231	2.4995	0.0004–0.0015	0.004–0.008	2	2.2487–2.2495	0.0005–0.0026	0.006–0.027
	6-250	2.2988	0.0010–0.0024	0.002–0.006	7	1.9980–2.0000	0.0010–0.0026	0.006–0.017
	8-267	2.4489 [31]	0.0020–0.0035 [21]	0.002–0.007	5	2.0978–2.0988	0.0013–0.0035	0.006–0.016
	8-305	2.4489 [31]	0.0011–0.0023 [30]	0.002–0.006	5	2.0988–2.0998	0.0013–0.0035	0.008–0.014
	8-350	2.4489 [31]	0.0011–0.0023 [30]	0.002–0.006	5	2.0988–2.0998	0.0013–0.0035	0.008–0.014
1980–81	6-229	[32]	[33]	0.002–0.006	4	2.0986–2.0998	0.0013–0.0035	0.006–0.014
	6-231	2.4995	0.0004–0.0015	0.004–0.008	2	2.2495–2.2487	0.0005–0.0026	0.006–0.027
	8-267	[32]	[33]	0.002–0.006	5	2.0986–2.0998	0.0013–0.0035	0.006–0.014
	8-305	[32]	[33]	0.002–0.006	5	2.0986–2.0998	0.0013–0.0035	0.006–0.014
1982–84	6-229	[32]	[33]	0.002–0.006	4	2.0986–2.0998	0.0013–0.0035	0.006–0.014
	6-231	2.4995	0.0004–0.0015	0.004–0.008	2	2.2495–2.2487	0.0005–0.0026	0.006–0.027
	6-263	2.9998	[34]	0.0035–0.0135	3	2.3742–2.375	0.0003–0.0025	.0082–.0214
	8-267	[32]	[33]	0.002–0.006	5	2.0986–2.0998	0.0013–0.0035	0.006–0.014
	8-305	[32]	[33]	0.002–0.006	5	2.0986–2.0998	0.0013–0.0035	0.006–0.014
	8-350	2.9998	[35]	0.0035–0.0135	3	2.1238–2.1248	0.0005–0.0026	0.006–0.020

85943055

CRANKSHAFT AND CONNECTING ROD SPECIFICATIONS

(All measurements are given in inches)

Year	Engine No. Cyl. Displacement (cu. in.)	Crankshaft			Thrust on No.	Connecting Rod		
		Main Brg. Journal Dia.	Main Brg. Oil Clearance	Shaft End-play		Journal Diameter	Oil Clearance	Side Clearance
1985-88	6-262	2.4484-2.4493 ㊱	0.0008-0.0020 ⑭	0.002-0.006	4	2.0986-2.0998	0.0013-0.0035	0.006-0.014
	8-305	㉜	㉝	0.002-0.006	5	2.0986-2.0998	0.0013-0.0035	0.006-0.014

*No. 5: 0.0010-0.0036
① No. 5: 0.0010-0.0036
② No. 1: 2.2987-2.29977
  Nos. 2-4: 2.2983-2.2993
  No. 5: 2.2978-2.2988
③ Nos. 1-2: 2.7487-2.7497
  Nos. 3-4: 2.7482-2.7492
  No. 5: 2.7478-2.7488
④ Nos. 1-2: 0.0004-0.002
  Nos. 3-4: 0.0009-0.0025
  No. 5: 0.0013-0.0029
⑤ No. 1: 2.2984-2.2993
  Nos. 2-4: 2.2988-2.2993
  No. 5: 2.2978-2.2988
⑥ No. 5: 2.4478-2.4488
⑦ No. 1: 0.0008-0.002
  Nos. 2-4: 0.0018-0.002
  No. 5: 0.0010-0.0036
⑧ No. 5: 0.0018-0.0034
⑨ Nos. 1-2: 2.7484-2.7493
  Nos. 3-4: 2.7481-2.7490
  No. 5: 2.7478-2.7488
⑩ No. 1: 2.7484-2.7493
  Nos. 2-4: 2.7481-2.7490
  No. 5: 2.7478-2.7488

⑪ Nos. 1-2: 0.0010-0.0022
  Nos. 3-4: 0.0013-0.0025
  No. 5: 0.0015-0.0031
⑫ No. 5: 0.0015-0.0031
⑬ Nos. 2-4: 0.0006-0.0018
  No. 5: 0.0008-0.0023
⑭ Intermediate: 0.0011-0.0023
  Rear: 0.0017-0.0032
⑮ Nos. 3-4: 2.7481-2.7490
  No. 5: 2.7473-2.7483
⑯ Nos. 2-4: 0.0013-0.0025
  No. 5: 0.0019-0.0025
⑰ No. 5: 0.0024-0.0040
⑱ No. 5: 2.6479-2.6488
⑲ No. 5: 0.0024-0.0045
⑳ Nos. 2-4: 2.4481-2.4490
  No. 5: 2.4479-2.4488
㉑ Nos. 2-4: 0.0011-0.0023
  No. 5: 0.0017-0.0033
㉒ No. 5: 2.4508
㉓ No. 5: 2.7504
  No. 5: 2.7499
㉔ Nos. 2-4: 0.0013-0.0028
  No. 5: 0.0019-0.0035

㉕ w/Auto trans./No. 1: 0.0019-0.0031
  Nos. 2-4: 0.0013-0.0025
  No. 5: 0.0023-0.0033
㉖ Nos. 2-4: 2.4486
  No. 5: 2.4485
㉗ Np. 5: 2.6485
㉘ Nos. 2-4: 0.001-0.0023
  No. 5: 0.0017-0.0033
㉙ No. 5: 0.0024-0.0070
㉚ No. 1: 0.0008-0.0020
㉛ Nos. 2-4: 2.4486
  No. 5: 2.4485
㉜ No. 1: 2.4484-2.4493
  Nos. 2,3,4: 2.4481-2.4490
  No. 5: 2.4479-2.4488
㉝ No. 1: .0008-.0020
  Nos. 2-4: .0011-.0023
  No. 5: .0017-.0032
㉞ Nos. 1,2,3: .0005-.0021
  No. 4: .0020-.0034
㉟ Nos. 1,2,3: .0005-.0021
  No. 4: .0015-.0031
㊱ Intermediate: 2.4481-2.4490
  Rear: 2.4479-2.4488

85943056

PISTON AND RING SPECIFICATIONS

(All measurements are given in inches. To convert inches to metric units, refer to the Metric Information section.)

Year	Engine Type Displacement (cu. in.)	Piston-to-Bore Clearance	Ring Gap			Ring Side Clearance		
			Top Compression	Bottom Compression	Oil Control	Top Compression	Bottom Compression	Oil Control
1964	All Engines	—	0.010–0.020	0.010–0.020	0.015–0.055	0.0012–0.0027	0.0012–0.0032	0.0000–0.0050
1965	6-194, 6-230	—	0.010–0.020	0.010–0.020	0.015–0.055	0.0012–0.0027	0.0012–0.0032	0.0000–0.0050
	8-283, 8-327	—	0.013–0.023	0.013–0.028	0.015–0.055	0.0012–0.0027	0.0012–0.0032	0.0012–0.0050
1966	6-194	—	0.010–0.020	0.010–0.020	0.015–0.055	0.0012–0.0027	0.0012–0.0032	0.0000–0.0050
1966–69	6-230	0.0005–0.0011	0.010–0.020	0.010–0.020	0.015–0.055	0.0012–0.0027	0.0012–0.0032	0.0000–0.0050
1966–67	8-283	0.0024–0.0030	0.010–0.020	0.010–0.020	0.015–0.055	0.0012–0.0027	0.0012–0.0032	0.0000–0.0050
1966–68	8-327	0.0005–0.0011	0.013–0.023	0.013–0.025	0.015–0.055	0.0012–0.0027	0.0012–0.0032	0.0000–0.0050
1966–67	8-396	0.0007–0.0013	0.010–0.020	0.010–0.020	0.010–0.030	0.0012–0.0032	0.0012–0.0032	0.0012–0.0060
1967	6-250	0.0005–0.0011	0.010–0.020	0.010–0.020	0.015–0.055	0.0020–0.0035	0.0020–0.0040	0.0012–0.0050
1968–79	6-250	0.0005–0.0015	0.010–0.020	0.010–0.020	0.015–0.055	0.0012–0.0027	0.0012–0.0032	0.0000–0.0050
1968–73	8-307	0.0005–0.0011	0.010–0.020	0.010–0.020	0.015–0.055	0.0012–0.0032	0.0012–0.0027	0.0000–0.0050
1968–70	8-396	0.0010–0.0018 ①	0.010–0.020	0.010–0.020	0.010–0.030	0.0017–0.0032	0.0017–0.0032	0.0005–0.0065
1969	8-350	0.0005–0.0011	0.013–0.025	0.013–0.025	0.0015–0.0055	0.0012–0.0032	0.0012–0.0027	0.0000–0.0050
1970–79	8-350	0.0007–0.0013	0.010–0.020 ②	0.013–0.025 ②	0.015–0.055	0.0012–0.0032 ④	0.0012–0.0027 ⑤	0.0000–0.0050 ③ ⑧
1970–76	8-400	0.0034	0.010–0.020	0.010–0.020	0.015–0.055	0.0012–0.0027 ⑥	0.0012–0.0032 ⑥	0.0000–0.0050
1970–76	8-454	0.0049 ⑦	0.010–0.020	0.010–0.020	0.015–0.055	0.0017–0.0032	0.0017–0.0032	0.0005–0.0065
1971–72	8-402	0.0018–0.0026	0.010–0.020	0.010–0.020	0.015–0.055	0.0017–0.0032	0.0017–0.0032	0.0005–0.0065
1976–77	8-305	0.0007–0.0017	0.010–0.020	0.010–0.020	0.015–0.055	0.0012–0.0032	0.0012–0.0027	0.0000–0.0050
1978–79	6-200	0.0007–0.0017	0.010–0.020	0.010–0.025	0.010–0.030	0.0012–0.0032	0.0012–0.0032	0.002–0.007
1978–84	6-231	0.0008–0.0020	0.010–0.020	0.010–0.020	0.015–0.035	0.003–0.005	0.003–0.005	0.0035 max.
1978–88	8-305	0.0007–0.0017	0.010–0.020	0.010–0.025	0.015–0.055	0.0012–0.0032	0.0012–0.0032	0.002–0.007
1980–84	6-229	0.0007–0.0017	0.010–0.020	0.010–0.025	0.015–0.055	0.0012–0.0032	0.0012–0.0032	0.002–0.007

85943058

PISTON AND RING SPECIFICATIONS

(All measurements are given in inches. To convert inches to metric units, refer to the Metric Information section.)

Year	Engine Type Displacement (cu. in.)	Piston-to-Bore Clearance	Ring Gap			Ring Side Clearance		
			Top Compression	Bottom Compression	Oil Control	Top Compression	Bottom Compression	Oil Control
1979–84	8-267	0.0007–0.0017	0.010–0.020	0.010–0.025	0.015–0.055	0.0012–0.0032	0.0012–0.0032	0.002–0.007
1980–84	8-350 ⑨	0.005–0.006	0.015–0.025	0.015–0.025	0.015–0.055	0.005–0.007	0.0018–0.0038	0.001–0.005
1982–84	6-263 ⑨	0.0035–0.0045	0.015–0.025	0.015–0.025	0.015–0.055	0.005–0.007	0.003–0.005	0.001–0.005
1985–88	6-262	0.0007–0.0017	0.010–0.020	0.010–0.025	0.015–0.055	0.0012–0.0032	0.0012–0.0032	0.001–0.007

① 0.0036–0.0044; 11:1 compression
② 325, 350 hp: Top 0.010–0.020
　　　　　　　2nd 0.013–0.023
③ 1978–82: 0.002–0.007
④ 0.0012–0.0027 on 1975 2-bbl
⑤ 165, 245, 250 hp: 0.0012–0.0032
⑥ 300 hp: Top 0.0017–0.0032
　　　　　　2nd 0.0017–0.0032
⑦ 425 hp—1971: 0.0065
　　　1973–75: 0.0035
⑧ 1978–80: 0.015–0.050
⑨ Diesel

85943059

TORQUE SPECIFICATIONS

Year	Model	Cylinder Head Bolts (ft. lbs.)	Rod Bearing Bolts (ft. lbs.)	Main Bearing Bolts (ft. lbs.)	Crankshaft Pulley Bolt (ft. lbs.)	Flywheel to Crankshaft Bolts (ft. lbs.)	Manifold (ft. lbs.) Intake	Manifold (ft. lbs.) Exhaust
1964-65	All 6 cyl.	90-95	35-40	60-70	Press Fit	50-65	25-65	⑰
1964-65	All 8 cyl.	60-70	30-35	60-80	Press Fit	55-65	25-35	25-35
1966-75	All 6 cyl.	95	36	65	—	60	30⑧	27⑦
1966-67	8-283, 327	60-70	35	80	60⑥	60	30	20
1968-77	8-305, 307, 327, 350	60-70	45	72②⑨	60⑥	60	30	⑤
1966-77	8-396, 402	80①	50	105③	85⑥	65	30	30
	8-427, 454	80①	50④	105③	85	65	30	30
1978-84	6-200, 229 8-267, 305, 350	65	45	70	60	60	30	20⑩
1978-84	6-231	80	40	100	175	60	45	25
1982-84	6-263⑭	⑪	42	107	⑫	48	41⑬	29
1982-84	8-350⑭	130⑬	42	120	⑮	60	40	25
1985-88	6-262	60-75	45	70-85	65-75	70	25-45	20
	8-305	60-75	45	70-85	65-75	60	25-45	20⑯

① Aluminum Heads—Short bolts: 65,
   Long bolts: 75
② Engines with 4-bolt mains—Outer bolts: 65
③ 1966-68 2-bolt mains: 95
   1966-67 4-bolt mains: 115
④ 7/16 Rod bolts: 70
⑤ Center bolts: 25-30, end bolts: 15-20
⑥ Where applicable
⑦ Exhaust-to-intake
⑧ Manifold-to-head
⑨ 70 starting 1976
⑩ Inside bolts on 350: 30 ft. lbs.
⑪ All bolts except Nos. 5, 6, 11, 12, 13, 14:
   142 ft. lbs.
   Nos. 5, 6, 11, 12, 13, 14: 59 ft. lbs.
⑫ Pulley-to-balancer bolts: 30 ft. lbs.
   Balancer-to-crankshaft bolt, 160: 350 ft. lbs.
⑬ Dip bolts in engine oil before torquing
⑭ Diesel engine
⑮ Pulley-to-balancer bolts: 27 ft. lbs.
   Balancer-to-crankshaft bolt, 271: 420 ft. lbs.
⑯ Inside bolts: 25 ft. lbs.
⑰ Inner 7 bolts: 30-35 ft. lbs.
   Intermediate 2 bolts: 25-30 ft. lbs.
   Outer 4 bolts: 10-23 ft. lbs.

85943060

Engine

REMOVAL & INSTALLATION

▶ See Figures 44, 45 and 46

❈❈CAUTION

Please refer to Section 1 before discharging the compressor or disconnecting air conditioning lines. Damage to the air conditioning system or personal injury could result.

Consult your local laws concerning refrigerant discharge and recycling. In many areas it may be illegal for anyone but a certified technician to service the A/C system. Always use an approved recovery station when discharging the air conditioning.

Inline 6-Cylinder Gasoline Engine

1. Scribe alignment marks around the hood hinges and remove the hood.
2. Disconnect the negative battery cable and remove the air cleaner.

3. Drain the cooling system and the crankcase.

✳✳CAUTION

When draining the coolant, keep in mind that cats and dogs are attracted by the ethylene glycol antifreeze, and are quite likely to drink any that is left in an uncovered container or in puddles on the ground. This will prove fatal in sufficient quantity. Always drain the coolant into a sealable container. Coolant should be reused unless it is contaminated or several years old.

4. Disconnect the radiator and the heater hoses, then remove the radiator and the fan shroud.

➡**If equipped with an automatic transmission, disconnect and plug the oil cooler lines at the radiator.**

5. Disconnect and label the wires at the ignition coil, the starter, the alternator, the temperature switch and the oil pressure switch.

6. Disconnect accelerator control cable at the inlet manifold, the fuel inlet line from the fuel pump, the hoses from the vapor canister and (if equipped) the power brake vacuum line from the intake manifold.

7. If equipped with power steering, remove the power steering pump and move it aside.

8. Raise and support the vehicle on jackstands.

9. Disconnect the exhaust pipe from the exhaust manifold and (if equipped) the converter bracket from the rear transmission mount.

10. Remove the starter and the flywheel splash shield or the converter housing cover.

11. If equipped with an automatic transmission, remove the converter-to-flexplate bolts.

12. Attach a vertical hoist to the engine and support the transmission with a floor jack, then raise the engine slightly.

13. Remove the engine mount through bolts and the bell housing-to-engine bolts.

14. Carefully remove the engine from the vehicle. Pause several times while lifting the engine to make sure no components, wires or hoses are caught.

To install:

15. Attach the engine hoist and lower the engine into position.

16. Support the transmission with a floor jack and install the engine mount through bolts and the bell housing-to-engine.

17. If equipped with an automatic transmission, install the converter-to-flexplate bolts.

18. Install the starter and the flywheel splash shield or the converter housing cover.

19. Connect the exhaust pipe to the exhaust manifold and (if equipped) the converter bracket to the rear transmission.

20. Lower the vehicle.

21. If equipped with power steering, install the power steering pump.

22. Connect accelerator control cable at the inlet manifold, the fuel inlet line to the fuel pump, the hoses to the vapor canister and (if equipped) the power brake vacuum line to the intake manifold.

23. Connect the labeled wires at the ignition coil, the starter, the alternator, the temperature switch and the oil pressure switch.

➡**If equipped with an automatic transmission, connect the oil cooler lines at the radiator.**

24. Install the radiator and fan shroud, then connect the heater and radiator hoses.

25. Fill the cooling system and the crankcase.

26. Connect the negative battery cable and install the air cleaner.

27. Install the hood.

✳✳WARNING

Please refer to Section 1 before servicing the compressor or damage to the air conditioning system or personal injury could result.

V6 Gasoline Engine

1. Scribe alignment marks at the hood hinges and remove the hood.

2. Disconnect the negative battery cable.

3. Disconnect the exhaust pipe from the exhaust manifold.

4. Remove the bell housing cover and drain the transmission oil cooler lines at the oil pan.

5. Remove the left engine mount through-bolt and loosen the right engine mount through-bolt.

6. If equipped with an automatic transmission, remove the torque converter cover, the converter-to-flex plate bolts and the engine-to-transmission bolts.

➡**Before removing the torque converter bolts, scribe a mark to ensure the proper relationship between the torque converter and flex plate during installation.**

7. Disconnect the CCC wiring harness from the transmission and the knock sensor wiring from the engine.

8. Disconnect the fuel hoses from the frame and the lower fan shroud.

9. Lower the vehicle and remove the windshield washer bottle.

10. Disengage and label the CCC wiring harness, other necessary wiring connectors and the vacuum hoses from the engine.

11. Remove the air cleaner, the upper fan shroud, the accelerator and the T.V. cables.

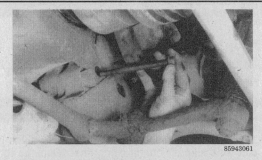

85943061

Fig. 44 Most V-type engines are attached to the frame with motor mounts utilizing through-bolts — once removed, the block is free to be lifted from the frame.

Fig. 45 Typical engine mounts

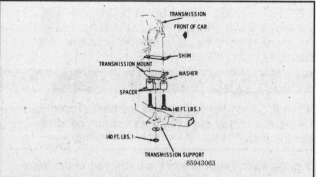

Fig. 46 Some rear engine (transmission) mounts are shimmed

12. Drain the cooling system, then remove the heater and the radiator hoses.

✳✳CAUTION

When draining the coolant, keep in mind that cats and dogs are attracted by the ethylene glycol antifreeze, and are quite likely to drink any that is left in an uncovered container or in puddles on the ground. This will prove fatal in sufficient quantity. Always drain the coolant into a sealable container. Coolant should be reused unless it is contaminated or several years old.

13. If equipped with air conditioning and power steering, remove the compressor and the power steering pump from the engine, then position them aside.

14. Disconnect the transmission oil cooler lines and the overflow tube from the radiator, then remove the radiator.

15. Remove the air conditioning hose and the adjusting bracket from the alternator.

16. Disconnect the battery cables from the frame and the heater hose from the bracket.

17. Secure a vertical lifting device to the engine and remove the remaining motor mount through-bolt, then remove the engine from the vehicle. Pause several times while lifting the engine to make sure no components, wires or hoses are caught.

✳✳CAUTION

When removing the engine from the transmission, be careful that the torque converter does not pull out of the transmission.

To install:

18. Secure a vertical lifting device to the engine and install the engine in the vehicle. Loosely install the right motor mount through-bolt.

19. Connect the battery cables to the frame and the heater hose to the bracket.

20. Secure the air conditioning hose and the adjusting bracket to the alternator.

21. Connect the transmission oil cooler lines and the overflow tube to the radiator, then secure the radiator.

22. As applicable, reposition and secure the compressor and/or the power steering pump.

23. Install the heater and the radiator hoses.

24. Install the air cleaner, the upper fan shroud, the accelerator and the T.V. cables.

25. Engage the CCC wiring harness, other necessary wiring connectors and the vacuum hoses to the engine as tagged or noted during removal.

26. Lower the vehicle and install the windshield washer bottle.

27. Connect the fuel hoses to the frame and the lower fan shroud.

28. Connect the CCC wiring harness to the transmission and the knock sensor.

29. If equipped with an automatic transmission, install the torque converter cover, the converter-to-flex plate bolts and the engine-to-transmission bolts.

30. Install the left engine mount through-bolt and tighten the right engine mount through-bolt.

31. Install the bell housing cover and connect the transmission oil cooler lines at the oil pan.

32. Connect the exhaust pipe to the exhaust manifold.

33. Connect the negative battery cable.

34. Refill the radiator with the proper coolant mixture.

35. Install the hood.

V8 Gasoline Engines

1. Scribe alignment marks on hood and remove hood from hinges.

2. Disconnect the negative battery cable.

3. Drain cooling system, then remove the heater hoses and the radiator hoses from the engine.

✳✳CAUTION

When draining the coolant, keep in mind that cats and dogs are attracted by the ethylene glycol antifreeze, and are quite likely to drink any that is left in an uncovered container or in puddles on the ground. This will prove fatal in sufficient quantity. Always drain the coolant into a sealable container. Coolant should be reused unless it is contaminated or several years old.

4. Remove the upper fan shroud and the fan assembly.

5. If equipped with air conditioning and power steering, remove the compressor and the power steering pump from the engine, then position them aside.

6. Disconnect the accelerator and the T.V. cables.

7. Remove the transmission oil cooler lines (if equipped) from the radiator and remove the radiator.

8. Disconnect and label the vacuum hoses and the CCC wiring harness connector(s) from the engine.

9. If equipped, remove the AIR pipe from the converter.

10. Remove the windshield washer bottle.

11. Disconnect and mark the wiring harness and related engine wiring.

12. Remove the distributor cap and the cruise control cable (if equipped).

13. Disconnect the positive battery cable from the battery and, if equipped, the frame straps. Disconnect the negative battery cable from the air conditioning hose/alternator bracket.

14. Raise and support the vehicle on jackstands.

15. Remove the crossover pipe and the catalytic converter as an assembly.

16. If equipped with an automatic transmission, remove the torque converter cover and the torque converter bolts.

➡**Before removing the torque converter bolts, scribe a mark to ensure the relationship between the torque converter and the flex plate.**

17. Remove the engine-to-mount bolts.

18. Disconnect the fuel line from the fuel pump.

19. If equipped with an automatic transmission, disconnect the torque converter clutch wiring from the transmission. Disconnect the transmission oil cooler lines from the clip at the engine oil pan.

20. Remove the engine-to-transmission bolts.

21. Lower the vehicle and support the transmission.

22. Secure a vertical lifting device to the engine and remove the engine from the vehicle. Pause several times while lifting the engine to make sure no components, wires or hoses are caught.

✳✳CAUTION

When removing the engine from the transmission, be careful that the torque converter does not pull out of the transmission.

To install:

23. Secure a vertical lifting device to the engine and install the engine to the vehicle.

24. Support the transmission.

25. Install the engine-to-transmission bolts.

26. If equipped with an automatic transmission, connect the torque converter clutch wiring to the transmission. Connect the transmission oil cooler lines to the clip at the engine oil pan.

27. Connect the fuel line to the fuel pump.

28. Install the engine-to-mount bolts.

29. If equipped with an automatic transmission, install the torque converter bolts and the torque converter cover.

30. Install the crossover pipe and the catalytic converter as an assembly.

31. Lower the vehicle.

32. Connect the positive battery cable to the battery and, if applicable, to the frame straps. Connect the negative battery cable to the air conditioning hose/alternator bracket.

33. Install the distributor cap and, if equipped, the cruise control cable.

34. Engage the wiring harness and related engine wiring connectors.

35. Install the windshield washer bottle.

36. If equipped, install the AIR pipe to the converter.

37. Connect the vacuum hoses and the CCC wiring harness connector(s) to the engine.

38. Install the transmission oil cooler lines (if equipped) to the radiator and install the radiator.

39. Connect the accelerator and the T.V. cables.

40. As applicable, reposition and secure the compressor and/or the power steering pump.

41. Install the upper fan shroud and the fan assembly.

42. Install the heater hoses and the radiator hoses to the engine, then fill the cooling system.

43. Connect the negative battery cable.

44. Install the hood.

Diesel Engines

1. Drain the cooling system.

❋❋CAUTION

When draining the coolant, keep in mind that cats and dogs are attracted by the ethylene glycol antifreeze, and are quite likely to drink any that is left in an uncovered container or in puddles on the ground. This will prove fatal in sufficient quantity. Always drain the coolant into a sealable container. Coolant should be reused unless it is contaminated or several years old.

2. Remove the air cleaner assembly.

3. Mark the hood-to-hinge position and remove the hood from the vehicle.

4. Disconnect the ground cables from the batteries.

5. Disconnect the ground wires at the fender panels and the ground strap at the cowl.

6. Disconnect the radiator hoses, cooler lines, heater hoses, vacuum hoses, power steering pump hoses, air conditioning compressor (hoses attached), fuel inlet hose and all attached wiring.

7. Remove the bellcrank clip.

8. Disconnect the throttle and transmission cables.

9. Remove the upper radiator support and the radiator.

10. Raise and support the vehicle safely using jackstands.

11. Disconnect the exhaust pipes at the manifold.

12. Remove the torque converter cover and the three bolts holding the converter to the flywheel.

13. Remove the engine mount bolts or nuts.

14. Remove the three right side transmission-to-engine bolts. Remove the starter.

15. Lower the car and attach a hoist to the engine.

16. Slightly raise the transmission with a jack.

17. Remove the three left side transmission-to-engine bolts and lift out the engine. Pause several times while lifting the engine to make sure no components, wires or hoses are caught.

To install

18. With a hoist, lower the engine into position and support the transmission with a jack.

19. Install the three left side transmission-to-engine bolts.

20. Install the three right side transmission-to-engine bolts. Install the starter.

21. Install the engine mount bolts or nuts.

22. Install the torque converter cover and the three bolts holding the converter to the flywheel. Torque to 40 ft. lbs. (350 V8) and 35 ft. lbs. (263 V6).

23. Connect the exhaust pipes at the manifold.

24. Lower the car.

25. Install the upper radiator support and the radiator.

26. Connect the throttle and transmission cables.

27. Install the bellcrank clip.

28. Connect the radiator hoses, cooler lines, heater hoses, vacuum hoses, power steering pump hoses, air conditioning compressor (hoses attached), fuel inlet hose and all attached wiring.

29. Connect the ground wires at the fender panels and the ground strap at the cowl.

30. Connect the ground cables to the batteries.

31. Install the hood.

32. Install the air cleaner.

33. Fill the cooling system.

Rocker Arm (Valve) Cover

◗ **See Figures 47, 48, 49 and 50**

REMOVAL & INSTALLATION

Inline 6-Cylinder Gasoline Engine

1. Disconnect the negative battery cable.

2. At the rocker arm cover, disconnect the ventilation hoses, then remove the air cleaner assembly.

3. Disconnect the wires, the fuel and the vacuum tubes from the rocker arm cover clips.

4. If equipped, disconnect the air injection hose from the check valve of the AIR pipe.

5. Remove the cover-to-cylinder head screws and the cover by rotating it from under the air pipe (if equipped).

➡**DO NOT pry on the cover to remove it. If it sticks, use your hand palm or a rubber mallet to bump it rearwards, from the front.**

6. Using a putty knife, clean the gasket mounting surfaces.

To install:

7. Position a new gasket and/or RTV sealant, then install the cover.

➡When installing the cover, use a new gasket (1964-76) or an ⅛ in. bead of RTV sealant (1977-79).

8. Secure the cover using the retaining screws.

9. If equipped, connect the air injection hose to the AIR pipe check valve.

10. Connect the wires, fuel and vacuum tubes to the rocker arm cover clips, as necessary.

11. Install the air cleaner assembly and connect the ventilation hoses.

12. Connect the negative battery cable, then start the engine and check for leaks.

V6 Gasoline Engine

RIGHT SIDE

1. Disconnect the negative battery cable, then remove the air cleaner assembly.

2. Disconnect the dipstick tube bracket from the alternator bracket. Then remove the dipstick tube head.

3. At the engine, disconnect the heater hoses from the evaporator case and bracket.

4. At the intake manifold, disconnect the heater hose and the wiring harness bracket.

5. Remove the rocker arm cover bolts and disconnect the breather pipe.

6. Disconnect the fuel lines, the clips and the spark plug wires (at the distributor).

Fig. 47 On vehicles equipped with A/C, the rocker cover must be removed by lifting the end, and pulling the cover out from under the compressor hoses and bracket

Fig. 48 On the right side of the engine, carefully pull the rocker cover out from underneath the heater hoses

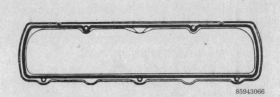

Fig. 49 If needed, a bead of RTV sealant should be run around the inner perimeter of the valve cover-to-cylinder head mating surface

Fig. 50 Be sure to clean the mating surface of the cylinder head, as well as the surface on the valve cover

7. Remove the rocker arm cover from the engine.

8. Using a putty knife, clean the gasket mounting surfaces.

To install:

9. Position a new gasket or sealant on the valve cover mating surface.

10. Install the rocker arm cover to the engine.

11. Connect the fuel lines, clips and spark plug wires, as necessary.

12. Install the rocker arm cover bolts and tighten, taking care not to overtighten and distort the cover.

13. Connect the breather pipe.

14. Connect the heater hose and the wiring harness bracket at the intake manifold.

15. Connect the heater hoses to the evaporator case and bracket.

16. Install the dipstick tube head and connect the tube bracket to the alternator bracket.

17. Install the air cleaner assembly and connect the negative battery cable.

18. Start the engine and check for leaks.

LEFT SIDE

1. Disconnect the negative battery cable.

2. At the rocker arm cover, disconnect the PCV valve.

3. If equipped with air conditioning, remove the compressor and the brace.

➡When removing the air conditioning compressor, DO NOT disconnect the hoses. Simply disconnect the bracket from the engine and reposition the assembly out of the way.

4. Remove the rocker arm cover bolts, then remove the cover from the engine.

5. Using a putty knife, clean the gasket mounting surfaces.

To install:

6. Position a new gasket or sealant on the valve cover mating surface.

7. Install the rocker arm cover to the engine, then secure using the cover bolts. Be careful not to overtighten the bolts and distort the cover.

8. If equipped with A/C, reposition the compressor and bracket assembly, then secure them to the engine.

9. Connect the PCV valve.

10. Connect the negative battery cable.

11. Start the engine and check for leaks.

V8 Gasoline Engines

RIGHT SIDE

1. Disconnect the negative battery cable, then remove the air cleaner assembly.

2. On the 1985-88 models, disconnect the CCC harness from the intake manifold and the oxygen sensor.

3. If equipped, disconnect the AIR hose at the exhaust manifold.

4. As necessary, disconnect the wires from the alternator, the choke and the spark plugs, then the harness from the rocker cover (lay it aside).

5. If necessary, remove the EGR valve.

6. Remove the rocker arm cover bolts, then remove the rocker cover from the engine.

7. Using a putty knife or gasket scraper, clean the gasket mounting surfaces.

To install:

8. Position a new gasket or sealant on the valve cover mating surface.

9. Install the rocker arm cover to the engine, then secure using the cover bolts. Be careful not to overtighten the bolts and distort the cover.

10. If removed, install the EGR valve.

11. Position the wiring harness, then engage the connectors to the alternator, choke and/or spark plugs, as applicable.

12. If equipped, connect the AIR hose at the exhaust manifold.

13. For 1985-88 models, connect the CCC harness to the intake manifold and to the oxygen sensor.

14. Install the air cleaner assembly, then connect the negative battery cable.

15. Start the engine and check for leaks.

LEFT SIDE

1. Disconnect the negative battery cable, then remove the air cleaner assembly.

2. Disconnect the power brake vacuum pipe from the carburetor and the booster, then reposition the pipe as necessary for clearance, but be careful not to damage the pipe. If equipped with cruise control, it may be necessary to loosen the actuator bracket lower bolt and remove the upper bolt in order to pivot the bracket, thereby repositioning the booster pipe.

3. If applicable, disconnect the AIR hose from the exhaust manifold.

4. At the rocker arm cover, either remove the PCV valve from the cover or disconnect the hose from the valve.

5. If applicable, disconnect the wire from the oxygen sensor.

➡Some late model vehicles are equipped with engine compartment stress bars which may interfere with rocker arm cover removal. If necessary, loosen the rear bolt and remove the front bolt, then pivot the bar out of the way.

6. Remove the rocker arm cover bolts, then remove the rocker cover from the engine.

7. Using a putty knife, clean the gasket mounting surfaces.

To install:

8. To install, use a new gasket or sealant and reverse the removal procedures. Start the engine and check for leaks.

9. Position a new gasket or sealant on the valve cover mating surface.

10. Install the rocker arm cover to the engine, then secure using the cover bolts. Be careful not to overtighten the bolts and distort the cover.

11. If removed, reposition and secure the engine compartment stress bar.

12. If applicable, connect the oxygen sensor wiring.

13. Either install the PCV valve to the rocker cover or connect the hose to the valve.

14. If applicable, connect the AIR hose to the exhaust manifold.

15. Reposition, then connect the power brake vacuum pipe to the carburetor and the booster. If applicable, pivot the cruise control actuator bracket and tighten the retaining bolts.

16. Install the air cleaner assembly and connect the negative battery cable.

17. Start and run the engine, then check for leaks.

V6 and V8 Diesel Engines

1. Refer to the Injection Lines, Removal and Installation procedures, in the Diesel Fuel System of Section 5 and remove the fuel injection lines.

2. Remove the rocker arm cover-to-cylinder head screws and any accessory mounting brackets (if necessary).

3. Using the valve cover removal tool No. J-34144 or BT-8315, place it midway between the ends of the valve cover (on the upper side), then tighten the screw to lift the rocker arm cover.

4. Using a rubber mallet and a shop cloth (placed on the rocker arm cover above the removal tool to absorb the blow), strike the cover to completely remove break the gasket seal and remove it from the engine.

5. Using a putty knife, clean the gasket mounting surfaces.

To install:

6. Using RTV sealant, apply a ¼ in. bead to the rocker arm cover.

➡When installing the rocker arm cover, the sealant must be wet to the touch.

7. Install the rocker arm cover to the engine, then secure using the retaining bolts and, if applicable, the mounting brackets. Be careful not to overtorque the bolts and distort the cover.

8. Install the fuel injection lines. Refer to Section 5 of this manual for details.

Rocker Arms

REMOVAL & INSTALLATION

▶ See Figures 51, 52, 53, 54 and 55

All Gasoline Engines, Except 231 V6

To access the rocker arms, first remove the rocker arm covers. With the covers removed, loosen and remove the adjusting nuts and the rocker arm pivots. The rocker arms are then free to be removed from the cylinder head studs. Be sure to adjust the valve lash after replacing the rocker arms. Coat the replacement rocker arm and ball with SAE 90 gear oil before installation. Make sure the valves are closed on the cylinder you are working on before installation.

➡When replacing an exhaust rocker, move an old intake rocker to the exhaust rocker arm stud and install the new rocker arm on the intake stud. This will prevent burning of the new rocker arm on the exhaust position.

Rocker arms studs that have damaged threads or are loose in the cylinder heads may be replaced by reaming the bore and installing oversize studs. Oversizes available are 0.003 in. and 0.013 in. The bore may also be tapped and screw-in studs installed. Several aftermarket companies produce complete rocker arm stud kits with installation tools. Mark IV and late high performance small block engines use screw-in studs and pushrod guide plates.

231 V6 Engines

▶ See Figures 56, 57, 58, 59 and 60

1. Disconnect the negative battery cable.
2. Remove the rocker arm covers.
3. Remove the rocker arm shaft assembly bolts.
4. Remove the rocker arm shaft assembly.

➡It may be easier to remove the nylon arm retainers with the rocker arm shafts still installed to the cylinder head

5. To remove the rocker arms from the shaft, the nylon arm retainers must be removed. They can be removed with a pair of water pump pliers, or they can be broken by hitting them below the head with a chisel.
6. Remove the rocker arms from the shaft. Make sure you keep them in order. Also note that the external rib on each

Fig. 51 The rocker covers must be removed in order to access the rocker arms

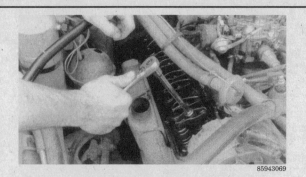

Fig. 52 Use a ratchet to loosen the rocker arm adjusting nuts

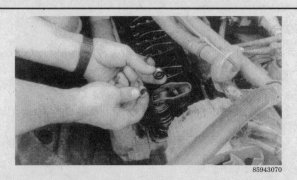

Fig. 53 Remove the rocker arm nut and pivot, then the rocker arm will be free for removal

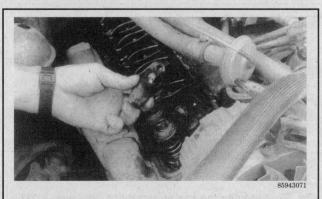

Fig. 54 Lift the rocker arm from the stud

arm points away from the rocker arm shaft bolt located between each pair of rocker arms.

To install:

7. If you are installing new rocker arms, note that the replacement rocker arms are marked **R** and **L** for right and left side installation. Do not interchange them.
8. Install the rocker arms on the shaft, as noted, and lubricate them with oil.
9. Center each arm on the $1/4$ in. hole in the shaft. Install new nylon rocker arm retainers in the holes using a $1/2$ in. drift.
10. Install the shaft to the cylinder head while locating the push rods in the rocker arms, then insert the shaft bolts. Tighten the bolts a little at a time until they are tight.
11. Install the rocker covers using new gaskets.
12. Connect the negative battery cable.

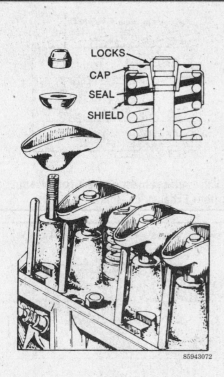

Fig. 55 Rocker arm components for the inline 6-cylinder engine (most V8's similar)

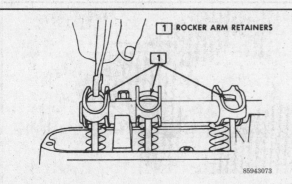

Fig. 56 Removing the rocker arm nylon retainers — 231 V6 rocker shafts

Fig. 57 Loosen the rocker shaft retaining bolts using a ratchet

Fig. 58 Remove the shaft retaining bolts in order to free the shaft assembly

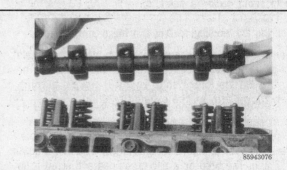

Fig. 59 With the bolts removed, the shaft and rocker arm assembly is free to be removed from the cylinder head

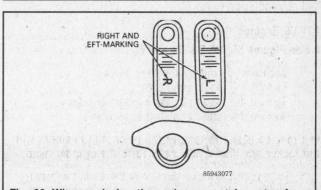

Fig. 60 When replacing the rocker arms take note of the markings for proper installation — 231 V6 engine

V6 and V8 Diesel Engines

➡When the diesel engine rocker arms are removed or loosened, the lifters must be bled down to prevent oil pressure buildup inside each lifter, which could cause it to raise up higher than normal and bring the valves within striking distance of the pistons.

1. Remove the valve cover.
2. Remove the rocker arm pivot bolts, the bridged pivot and rocker arms.
3. Remove each rocker set as a unit.
4. To install, lubricate the pivot wear points and position each set of rocker arms in its proper location. Do not tighten the pivot bolts for fear of bending the pushrods when the engine is turned. Bleed-down the valve lifters.

Diesel Engine Bleed-Down

1. Before installing any removed rocker arms, rotate the crankshaft so that No. 1 cylinder is 32°BTDC. This is 50mm (2 in.) counterclockwise from the 0 degree pointer on the timing indicator on the front of the engine. If only the right valve cover was removed, remove the glow plug from No. 1 cylinder to determine if the piston is in the correct position. If the left valve cover wash removed, rotate the crankshaft until the No. 5 cylinder intake valve pushrod ball is 7.0mm (0.28 in.) above the No. 5 cylinder exhaust valve pushrod ball.

✳✳WARNING

Use only hand wrenches to torque the rocker arm pivot bolts to avoid pushrod damage.

2. If the No. 5 cylinder pivot and rocker arms were removed, install them. Torque the bolts alternately between the intake and exhaust valves until the intake valve begins to open, then stop.

3. Install the remaining rocker arms except No. 3 exhaust valve for (V6) or No. 3 and No. 8 intake valves for (V8), if these rockers were removed.

4. If removed, install the No. 3 valve pivots, but do not torque them beyond the point that the valve would be fully open. This is indicated by a strong resistance while still turning the pivot retaining bolts. Going beyond this will bend the pushrod. Torque the bolts slowly, allowing the lifter to bleed-down.

5. Finish torquing the No. 5 cylinder rocker arm pivot bolt slowly. Do not go beyond the point that the valve would be fully open. this is indicated by a strong resistance while still turning the pivot retaining bolts. Going beyond this will bend the pushrod.

6. DO NOT turn the engine crankshaft for at least 45 minutes, allowing the lifters to bleed-down. This is important.

7. Finish reassembling the engine as the lifters are being bled.

Valve Lash Adjustment

▶ **See Figures 61, 62 and 63**

Although some of the earlier vehicles covered by this book are equipped with solid lifters that are adjusted as a part of routine engine tune-ups, most engines described in this book use hydraulic lifters, which require no periodic adjustment. However, on all vehicles, in the event of cylinder head removal or any operation requiring the rocker arms to be disturbed, adjustment of the arms will be necessary to assure proper valve operation.

SOLID LIFTERS (1964-71)

For vehicle's equipped with solid lifters, refer to the valve lash adjustment procedures in Section 2 of this manual.

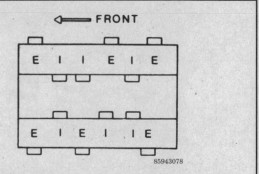

Fig. 61 Valve arrangement of the Chevrolet-built V6 engines (E — Exhaust, I — Intake)

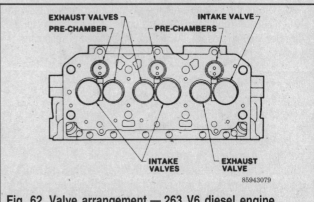

Fig. 62 Valve arrangement — 263 V6 diesel engine

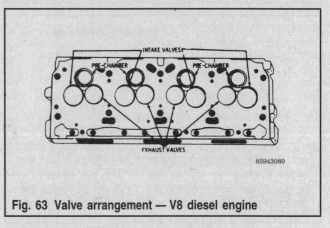

Fig. 63 Valve arrangement — V8 diesel engine

HYDRAULIC LIFTERS (1972 AND LATER)

▶ **See Figure 64**

➡**The valve lash adjustment procedure is for hydraulic lifters which are filled with oil either from previous use (old lifters on which the oil has not drained) or from priming before installation (new lifters or old lifters on which oil had drained while removed from the engine).**

1. Remove the rocker covers and gaskets.
2. Adjust the valves on inline 6-cylinder engines as follows:
   a. Mark the distributor housing with a piece of chalk at the No. 1 and 6 plug wire positions. Remove the distributor cap with the plug wires attached.

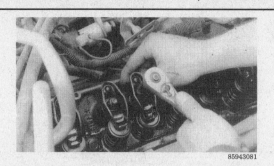

85943081

Fig. 64 Adjust the valve lash on hydraulic lifter engines by tightening the rocker arm nut while turning the pushrod by hand to determine lash

  b. Crank the engine until the distributor rotor points to the No. 1 cylinder and the No. 1 piston is at TDC (both No. 1 cylinder valves closed). At this point, adjust the following valves:
- No. 1 - Exhaust and Intake
- No. 2 - Intake
- No. 3 - Exhaust
- No. 4 - Intake
- No. 5 - Exhaust

  c. Back out the adjusting nut until lash is felt at the pushrod, then turn the adjusting nut in until all lash is removed. This can be determined by checking pushrod endplay while turning the adjusting nut. When all play has been removed, turn the adjusting nut in 1 full turn.

  d. Crank the engine until the distributor rotor points to the No. 6 cylinder and the No. 6 piston is at TDC (both No. 6 cylinder valves closed). The following valves can be adjusted:
- No. 2 - Exhaust
- No. 3 - Intake
- No. 4 - Exhaust
- No. 5 - Intake
- No. 6 - Intake and Exhaust

  3. Adjust the valves on V6 and V8 engines as follows:

  a. Crank the engine until the mark on the damper aligns with the TDC or 0 degree mark on the timing tab and the engine is in the No. 1 firing position. This can be determined by placing the fingers on the No. 1 cylinder valves as the marks align. If the valves do not move, it is in the No. 1 firing position. If the valves move, it is in the No. 6 firing position (No. 4 on V6) and the crankcase should be rotated one more revolution to the No. 1 firing position.

  b. With the engine in the No. 1 firing position, the following valves can be adjusted:
- V8 - Exhaust: 1, 3, 4, 8
- V8 - Intake: 1, 2, 5, 7
- V6 - Exhaust: 1, 5, 6
- V6 - Intake: 1, 2, 3

  c. Back out the adjusting nut until lash is felt at the pushrod, then turn the adjusting nut in until all lash is removed. This can be determined by checking pushrod endplay while turning the adjusting nut. When all play has been removed, turn the adjusting nut in:
- 1/2-1 1/4 additional turn (flat lifter)
- 3/4-1 1/4 additional turn (roller lifter V8)
- 3/4 additional turn (roller lifter V6)

  d. Crank the engine 1 full revolution until the marks are again in alignment. This is the No. 6 firing position (No. 4 on V6). The following valves can now be adjusted:
- V8 - Exhaust: 2, 5, 6, 7
- V8 - Intake: 3, 4, 6, 8
- V6 - Exhaust: 2, 3, 4
- V6 - Intake: 4, 5, 6

  4. Reinstall the rocker arm covers using new gaskets or sealer.

  5. Install the distributor cap and wire assembly.

  6. Adjust the carburetor idle speed.

Thermostat

▶ **See Figures 65, 66, 67 and 68**

REMOVAL & INSTALLATION

  1. Drain the radiator until the level is below the thermostat level (below the level of the intake manifold).

❊❊CAUTION

When draining the coolant, keep in mind that cats and dogs are attracted by the ethylene glycol antifreeze, and are quite likely to drink any that is left in an uncovered container or in puddles on the ground. This will prove fatal in sufficient quantity. Always drain the coolant into a sealable container. Coolant should be reused unless it is contaminated or several years old.

  2. Some late model vehicles will contain 1 or more Thermal Vacuum Switches (TVS) threaded into the top of the thermostat housing. If so equipped, tag and disconnect the vacuum lines from the valves.

  3. Loosen the retaining bolts, then remove the water outlet elbow (thermostat housing) assembly from the engine.

  4. Grasp the top of the thermostat and withdraw it from the bore. If necessary, use a pair of pliers to grip the top of the thermostat and pull it from the opening. Note the direction of the thermostat which was facing the engine for installation purposes.

  To install:

  5. Clean the gasket mating surfaces on the water outlet elbow and the intake manifold.

  6. Install the thermostat assembly into the bore in the direction noted during removal.

  7. Install the water outlet elbow (thermostat housing) to the intake manifold. Use a new gasket when installing the elbow to the manifold. On later models the thermostat housing may have been sealed with RTV sealant. If so, place a 1/8 in. bead of RTV sealer all around the thermostat housing sealing surface on the intake manifold and install the housing while it is still wet.

  ➡**If the thermostat is equipped with a pin hole, be sure to install pin side facing upwards.**

  8. Secure the thermostat housing using the retaining bolts.

  9. If applicable, connect the vacuum lines to the TVS(s) as noted during removal.

10. Refill the engine cooling system, then start the engine and check for leaks.

Intake Manifold

REMOVAL & INSTALLATION

◗ See Figures 69, 70 and 71

Inline 6-Cylinder With Combination Manifold

Most the inline 6-cylinder engines covered in this manual are equipped with a combination intake/exhaust manifold. Once

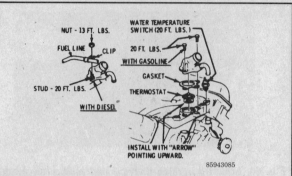

Fig. 68 Diesel (left) and gasoline engine thermostat mounting locations

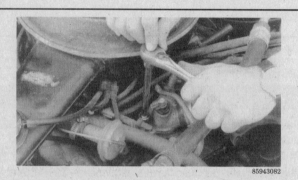

Fig. 65 Loosen the water outlet elbow (thermostat housing) retaining bolts

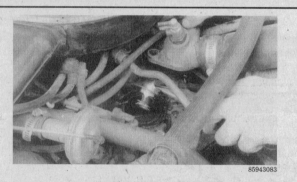

Fig. 66 If necessary, use a pair of pliers to grasp and pull the thermostat from the bore

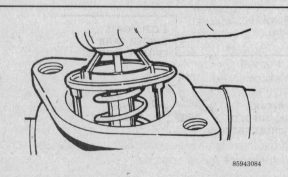

Fig. 67 Removing the thermostat from a water outlet elbow

this combination manifold is removed from the vehicle, the fasteners may be removed and the 2 pieces separated. Certain late-model versions of the inline 250 engine are equipped with an integral intake in which the intake was actually part of the cylinder head. For these engines, which were used in the mid to late 1970's refer to the cylinder head procedure for removal of the integral intake and cylinder head. If your vehicle is equipped with a 250 engine, determine if it has an integral or combination intake by looking for intake manifold mounting bolts and/or a gasket seam between the cylinder head and the intake. If either are found, you have a combination manifold.

1. Disconnect the negative battery cable, then remove the air cleaner assembly.

2. Disconnect the throttle rods at the bellcrank and remove the throttle return spring.

3. Disconnect the fuel and vacuum lines from the carburetor.

4. Disconnect the crankcase ventilation hose from the valve cover and the evaporation control hose from the carbon canister.

5. Disconnect the exhaust pipe from the manifold and throw away the packing.

6. Remove the manifold assembly and scrape off the gaskets.

7. Check the condition of the manifold. If a manifold is cracked or distorted 0.030 in. or more, it should be replaced to prevent exhaust leakage. To detect distortion, lay a straight-edge along the length of the exhaust port faces. If, at any point, a gap of 0.030 in. or more exists between the straight-edge and the manifold, distortion of that amount is present.

8. If necessary for replacement or service separate the manifold by removing one bolt and two nuts.

To install:

9. If separated, assemble the manifold and tighten the retainers.

10. Install the intake manifold using a new gasket, then carefully tighten the retainers.

11. Connect the exhaust pipe to the manifold.

12. Connect the evaporation control hose to the carbon canister and the crankcase ventilation hose to the valve cover.

13. Connect the fuel and vacuum lines to the carburetor.

14. Connect the throttle rods to the bellcrank and remove the throttle return spring.

15. Install the air cleaner assembly, then connect the negative battery cable.

16. Start and run the engine, then check for leaks.

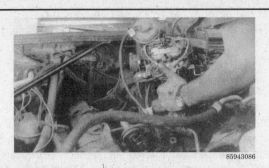

Fig. 69 With the retainers, lines and wiring removed, the intake manifold may be lifted from the engine with most of it's mounted components attached

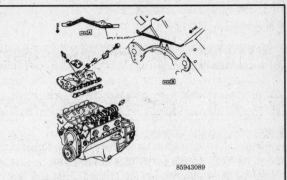

Fig. 72 V6 intake manifold and seal location (most V8 gasoline engines similar)

Fig. 70 Remove the old manifold gaskets and clean the mating surfaces thoroughly before installation

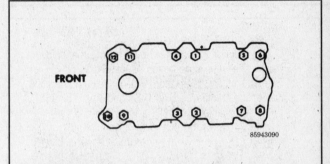

Fig. 73 Intake manifold torque sequence — 229 V6 and small block V8 engines

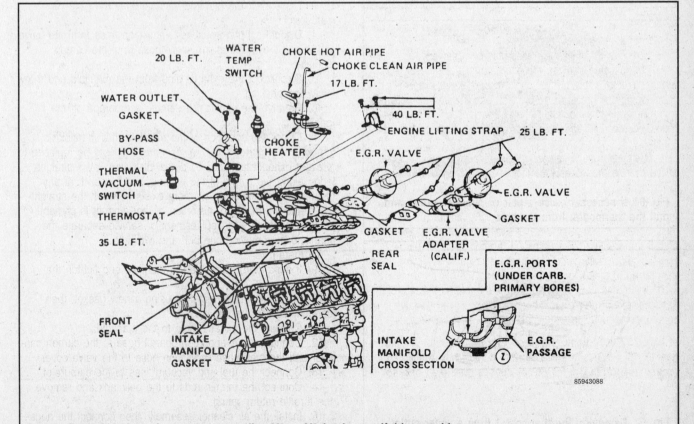

Fig. 71 Exploded view of a common gasoline V6 or V8 intake manifold assembly

Gasoline V6 and V8 (Except 231 V6)

▶ See Figures 72, 73, 74 and 75

1. Disconnect the negative battery cable, then remove the air cleaner assembly.
2. Drain the radiator to a level below the intake manifold.

✳✳CAUTION

When draining the coolant, keep in mind that cats and dogs are attracted by the ethylene glycol antifreeze, and are quite likely to drink any that is left in an uncovered container or in puddles on the ground. This will prove fatal in sufficient quantity. Always drain the coolant into a sealable container. Coolant should be reused unless it is contaminated or several years old.

3. Disconnect:
   a. Battery cables at the battery.
   b. Upper radiator and heater hoses at the manifold.
   c. Crankcase ventilation hoses as required.
   d. Fuel line at the carburetor (V8) or the fuel line clips and lines at the throttle body (if equipped with TBI V6).
   e. Accelerator linkage and TV cables (if equipped).
   f. Vacuum hose at the distributor (if equipped).
   g. Power brake hose at the carburetor base or manifold, if applicable.
   h. Ignition coil, the spark plug wires and temperature sending switch wires.
   i. Water pump bypass at the water pump (Mark IV only).
   j. If equipped with CCC (V8), disconnect the electrical harness and lay it aside.
4. Remove the distributor cap and scribe the rotor position relative to the distributor body.
5. Remove the distributor assembly from the engine.
6. If applicable, remove the alternator upper bracket. As required, remove the oil filler bracket, air cleaner bracket, air conditioning compressor and bracket, and accelerator bellcrank.
7. Remove the manifold-to-head attaching bolts, then remove the manifold and carburetor or throttle body as an assembly.
8. Using a putty knife clean the gasket and seal surfaces of the cylinder heads and manifold.

To install:

9. If the manifold is to be replaced, transfer the carburetor (and mounting studs), water outlet and thermostat (use a new gasket) heater hose adapter, EGR valve (use new gasket) and, if applicable, TVS switch and the choke coil. 1975-79 engines use a new carburetor heat choke tube which must be transferred to a new manifold.
10. Install the new manifold end seals, folding the tabs if applicable, and the manifold/head gaskets, using a sealing compound around the water passages.

➡1974-75 V8 engines require a new intake manifold side gasket on 4-bbl engines. The new gasket has restricted crossover ports. The 350 2-bbl uses a restricted crossover

gasket on the right hand side and an open gasket on the left. The 350 4-bbl uses restricted crossover gaskets on both sides. The correct gaskets are essential.

11. Install the intake manifold assembly, taking care not to dislocate the end seals. It is helpful to use a pilot in the distributor opening. Tighten the manifold bolts to 30-35 ft. lbs. (41-47 Nm) in the proper torque sequence.
12. If applicable, install the alternator upper bracket. As required, install the oil filler bracket, air cleaner bracket, air conditioning compressor and bracket, and accelerator bellcrank.
13. Align the matchmarks made earlier and install the distributor to the engine making sure the rotor is facing the last of the matchmarks when the distributor housing is fully installed.
14. Connect all hoses, cables and wires which were disconnected for intake manifold removal.
15. Connect the negative battery cable, then properly refill the engine cooling system.
16. Start and run the engine, then check for leaks.
17. Check and adjust the timing, as necessary.

231 V6

▶ See Figure 76

➡A special wrench adapter, available from several tool manufacturers, is necessary to remove the left front intake manifold bolt.

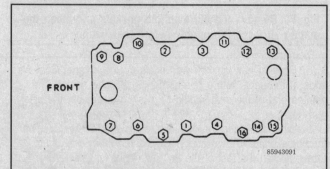

Fig. 74 Intake manifold torque sequence — big-block V8 engine

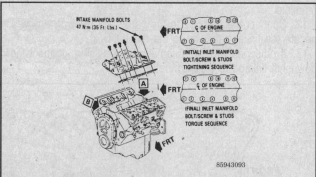

Fig. 75 Intake manifold torque sequence — 262 V6 engine

1. Disconnect the negative battery cable, then drain the engine cooling system.

✳✳CAUTION

When draining the coolant, keep in mind that cats and dogs are attracted by the ethylene glycol antifreeze, and are quite likely to drink any that is left in an uncovered container or in puddles on the ground. This will prove fatal in sufficient quantity. Always drain the coolant into a sealable container. Coolant should be reused unless it is contaminated or several years old.

2. Remove the upper radiator hose and the coolant bypass hose from the manifold.

3. Remove the air cleaner assembly. Disconnect the throttle linkage from the carburetor. If necessary, remove the linkage bracket from the manifold. If the car is equipped with an automatic transmission, remove the downshift linkage.

4. Disconnect the fuel line from the carburetor. If equipped with power brakes, disconnect the power brake line from the manifold. Disconnect the choke pipe and all vacuum lines. Disconnect the anti-dieseling solenoid wire.

5. Remove the manifold bolts. It will be necessary to remove the distributor cap and rotor to gain access to the front left manifold bolt. This is a special fastener, known as a Torx® bolt. Remove the plug wires from the plugs.

6. Remove the manifold.

7. Thoroughly clean the gasket mating surfaces on the engine and the intake manifold.

To install:

8. Position new gaskets and seals on the engine. Coat the ends of the seals with a non-hardening silicone sealer. The pointed end of the seal should be a snug fit against the block and head.

9. When installing the manifold, start with the center bolts (numbers one and two) and slowly tighten them until snug. Continue with the rest of the bolts in sequence, tightening them in several stages to the correct torque.

10. Connect the anti-dieseling solenoid wire, the choke pipe and all vacuum lines.

11. If equipped with power brakes, connect the line to the manifold.

12. Connect the fuel line to the carburetor, then if removed, secure the linkage bracket to the manifold.

13. If equipped with an automatic transmission, connect the downshift linkage to the carburetor.

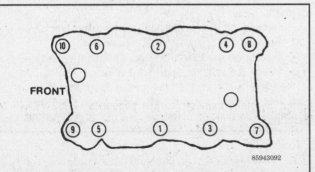

Fig. 76 Intake manifold torque sequence — 231 V6 engine

14. Connect the throttle linkage to the carburetor.

15. Install the air cleaner assembly, then connect the upper radiator hose and coolant bypass hose to the intake.

16. Connect the negative battery cable, then properly refill the engine cooling system.

17. Start and run the engine, then check for leaks.

V6 and V8 Diesel
▶ See Figures 77, 78 and 79

1. Disconnect the negative battery cable, then remove the air cleaner assembly.

2. Drain the radiator and loosen the upper bypass hose clamp. Remove the thermostat housing bolts, the housing and the thermostat from the intake manifold.

✳✳CAUTION

When draining the coolant, keep in mind that cats and dogs are attracted by the ethylene glycol antifreeze, and are quite likely to drink any that is left in an uncovered container or in puddles on the ground. This will prove fatal in sufficient quantity. Always drain the coolant into a sealable container. Coolant should be reused unless it is contaminated or several years old.

3. Remove the breather pipes from the rocker covers and the air crossover. Remove the air crossover.

4. Disconnect the throttle rod and the return spring. If equipped with cruise control, remove the servo.

5. Remove the hairpin clip at the bellcrank and disconnect the cables. Remove the throttle cable from the bracket on the manifold; position the cable away from the engine. Disconnect and label any wiring as necessary.

6. If necessary, remove the alternator bracket. If equipped with air conditioning, remove the compressor mounting bolts and move the compressor aside, without disconnecting any of the hoses. Remove the compressor mounting bracket from the intake manifold.

7. Disconnect the fuel line from the pump and the fuel filter. Remove the fuel filter and bracket.

8. Remove the fuel injection pump and lines. Refer to Section 5, Fuel System, for details and procedures.

9. Disconnect and remove the vacuum pump or oil pump drive assembly from the rear of the engine.

10. Remove the intake manifold drain tube.

11. Remove the intake manifold bolts and the manifold. Remove the adapter seal and the injection pump adapter.

12. Clean the mating surfaces of the cylinder heads and the intake manifold using a putting knife.

To install:

13. For the V8 engine, coat both sides of the gasket surface that seal the intake manifold to the cylinder heads with G.M. sealer # 1050026 or the equivalent.

14. For the V6 engine, DO NOT coat the gasket or sealing surfaces with any sealer. Use an RTV sealer only on the end seals.

15. Position the intake manifold gaskets on the cylinder heads. Install the end seals, making sure that the ends are positioned under the cylinder heads.

16. Carefully lower the intake manifold into place on the engine.

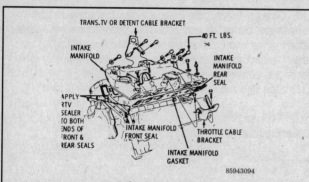

Fig. 77 Exploded view of a diesel intake manifold and gaskets

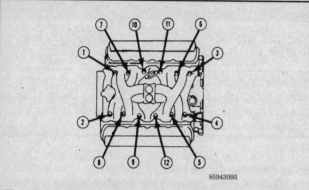

Fig. 78 V8 diesel intake manifold bolt torque sequence

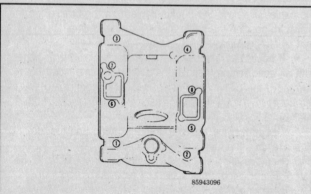

Fig. 79 V6 diesel intake manifold bolt torque sequence

17. Clean the intake manifold bolts thoroughly, then dip them in clean engine oil. Install the bolts and tighten to 15 ft. lbs. (20 Nm) in the sequence shown. In a second pass of the sequence, tighten all the bolts to 30 ft. lbs. (41 Nm). Finally, in a third pass of the sequence, tighten the bolts to 40 ft. lbs. (54 Nm).

18. Install the intake manifold drain tube and clamp.

19. Install injection pump adapter. Refer to Section 5 of this manual for details. If a new adapter is not being used, be sure to skip the steps for preparing a new adapter, as noted.

20. Install and connect the vacuum pump or oil pump drive assembly from the rear of the engine.

21. Install the fuel injection pump and lines.

22. Install the fuel filter and bracket, then connect the fuel line to the pump and filter.

23. If equipped with A/C, install the compressor bracket to the intake manifold, then reposition and secure the compressor assembly.

24. If removed, install the alternator bracket.

25. Connect the wiring as tagged during removal.

26. Connect the throttle cable and secure it in the bracket. Connect the cables and install the hairpin clip at the bellcrank.

27. If equipped with cruise control, install the servo.

28. Connect the throttle rod and return spring.

29. Install the air crossover, then connect the breather pipes to the rocker covers and the crossover.

30. Install the thermostat housing and tighten the retaining bolts, then connect and tighten the upper bypass hose clamp.

31. Connect the negative battery cable and properly refill the engine cooling system.

32. Start and run the engine, then check for leaks.

Exhaust Manifold

REMOVAL & INSTALLATION

▶ See Figures 81, 82, 83, 84 and 85

Inline Six With Combination Manifold

Most the inline 6-cylinder engines covered in this manual are equipped with a combination intake/exhaust manifold. Once this combination manifold is removed from the vehicle, the fasteners may be removed and the 2 pieces separated. Certain late-model versions of the inline 250 engine are equipped with an integral intake in which the intake was actually part of the cylinder head. For these engines, which were used in the mid to late 1970's refer to the cylinder head procedure for removal of the integral intake and cylinder head. If your vehicle is equipped with a 250 engine, determine if it has an integral or combination intake by looking for intake manifold mounting bolts and/or a gasket seam between the cylinder head and the intake. If either are found, you have a combination manifold.

For removal and installation procedures regarding the combination intake/exhaust manifold, refer to the intake manifold procedure found earlier in this section.

Inline Six With Integral Intake Manifold/Cylinder Head, Except 1979

▶ See Figure 80

1. Disconnect the negative battery cable, then remove the air cleaner assembly.

2. Remove the power steering and air pump brackets.

3. Remove the EFE valve bracket.

4. Disconnect the throttle linkage and return spring.

5. Unbolt the exhaust pipe from the flange. The fasteners on the exhaust system are often rusted into place, in order to save your knuckles, spray the fasteners with a penetrating lubricant a few minutes before you attempt to remove them.

6. Unbolt and remove the manifold.

To install:

7. Position the manifold and gaskets (if used) to the engine, then loosely install the fasteners. Tighten the fasteners to specification using the required sequence (the four end bolts are tightened last).

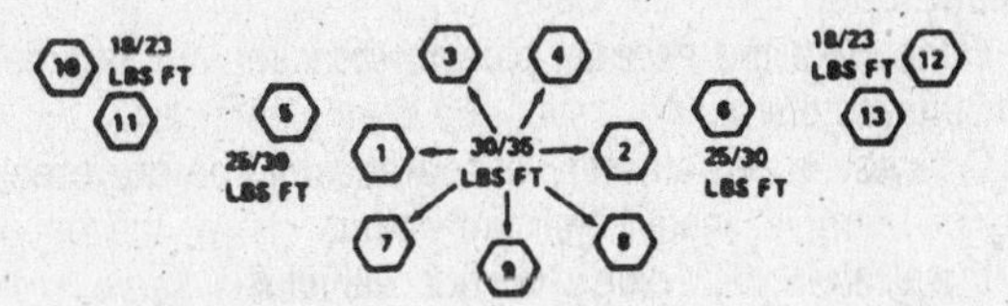

Fig. 80 Exhaust manifold torque sequence — inline 6-cylinder engines equipped with an integral intake/cylinder head

8. Connect the exhaust pipe to the flange and tighten the retainers.

9. Connect the throttle linkage and return spring.

10. Install the EFE valve bracket.

11. Install the power steering pump and air pump brackets.

12. Install the air cleaner assembly and connect the negative battery cable.

13. Start and run the engine, then check for leaks.

Inline Six With Integral Intake Manifold/Cylinder Head, 1979

▶ See Figure 80

1. Disconnect negative battery cable, then remove the air cleaner assembly.

2. Remove the power steering and/or AIR pumps and brackets, where they are present. (You need not disconnect power steering hoses - just support the pump out of the way).

➡The fasteners on the exhaust system are often rusted into place, in order to save your knuckles, spray the fasteners with a penetrating lubricant a few minutes before you attempt to remove them.

3. Working from below, with the vehicle safely supported by jackstands, disconnect the exhaust pipe at the manifold and at the catalytic converter bracket near the transmission mount. If the car uses an exhaust manifold mounted converter, disconnect the pipe at the bottom of the converter and remove the converter.

4. Working from above, remove the rear heat shield and accelerator cable bracket.

5. Remove the exhaust manifold bolts, and pull the manifold off the engine.

6. If the manifold is to be replaced, transfer the EFE valve, actuator, and rod assembly to the new part. Otherwise, inspect the manifold as described below.

7. Clean and then inspect the manifold carefully for cracks, and for free operation of the EFE valve. Repair or replace parts, and free up the EFE valve with solvent, as necessary.

To install:

8. Make sure the gasket surface is clean and free of deep scratches. Position a new gasket on the manifold, and then put the manifold in position on the block, and install the bolts hand tight.

9. Torque all bolts in the proper order and to the specified torque.

10. Install the rear heat shield and the accelerator cable bracket.

11. Working from underneath, connect the exhaust pipe at the manifold flange and connect the converter bracket at the transmission mount. If the car has an exhaust manifold converter, first install the converter to the manifold loosely; then attach the exhaust pipe to the converter and align the exhaust system; finally, torque the converter mounting bolts to 15 ft. lbs. (20 Nm), in an X pattern, and torquing in several stages.

12. Working from above, install the power steering and A.I.R. pumps as necessary.

13. Install the air cleaner assembly and connect the negative battery cable.

1964-84 V6 and V8

▶ See Figures 86 and 87

1. Disconnect the negative battery cable and, if necessary, remove the air cleaner assembly.

2. If equipped with AIR (Air Injection Reaction), remove the air injector manifold assembly. The ¼ in. pipe threads in the manifold are straight threads. Do not use a ¼ in. tapered pipe tap to clean the threads.

3. If applicable, remove the air cleaner preheater shroud.

4. Remove the spark plug wire heat shields. On Mark IV, remove spark plugs.

5. On the left exhaust manifold, disconnect and remove the alternator.

➡The fasteners on the exhaust system are often rusted into place, in order to save your knuckles, spray the fasteners with a penetrating lubricant a few minutes before you attempt to remove them.

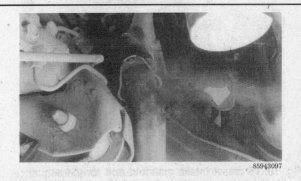

Fig. 81 Before attempting to loosen exhaust system fasteners, spray them with a penetrating lubricant

Fig. 82 Loosen the exhaust pipe-to-manifold flange bolts using a deep socket

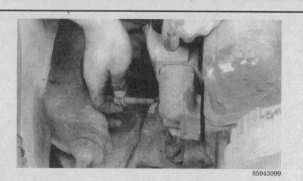

Fig. 83 Support the exhaust manifold and remove the retaining bolts

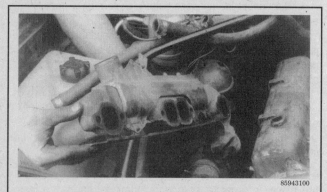

Fig. 84 Lift the manifold from the vehicle

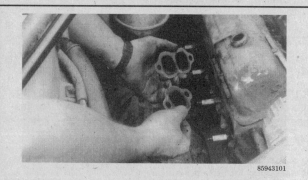

Fig. 85 Make sure the old manifold gaskets are removed from the mating surface and discarded

6. Disconnect the exhaust pipe from the manifold and hang it from the frame out of the way.

7. Bend the locktabs and remove the end bolts, then the center bolts. With the retainers removed, carefully pull the manifold from the cylinder head and remove it from the vehicle.

➡A ⁹/₁₆ in. thin wall 6-point socket, sharpened at the leading edge and tapped onto the head of the bolt, will simplify bending the locktabs. When installing a new manifold on the right side on 1978-84 V8s you must transfer the heat stove from the old manifold to the new one.

To install:
8. Thoroughly clean the gasket mating surfaces.

9. Install the exhaust manifold to the engine using new gaskets. Torque all bolts to specification working from the inner bolts towards to the outer bolts.

10. Reconnect the exhaust pipe to the manifold flange, then tighten the fasteners.

11. If removed, install and connect the alternator assembly.

12. For Mark IV, install the spark plugs.

13. Install the spark plug wire head shields.

14. If applicable, install the air cleaner preheater shroud.

15. If equipped, install the air injector manifold assembly.

16. If removed, install the air cleaner assembly.

17. Connect the negative battery cable.

18. Start and run the engine, then check for leaks.

V6 Engines, 1985 and Later

▶ See Figures 86 and 87

RIGHT SIDE

1. Disconnect the negative battery cable.

2. Remove the air cleaner assembly.

3. Raise and support the vehicle safely using jackstands. If possible, raise the vehicle to a height where access is available both underhood and undervehicle. This will keep you from having to keep raising and lowering it during the procedure.

➡The fasteners on the exhaust system are often rusted into place, in order to save your knuckles, spray the fasteners with a penetrating lubricant a few minutes before you attempt to remove them.

4. Remove the exhaust pipe bolts, then lower the vehicle, as necessary for underhood access.

5. If equipped with air management valve, disconnect the bracket.

6. If equipped with AIR, disconnect the hoses, then disconnect the pipes to the converter, the cylinder head and the exhaust manifold.

7. Tag and disconnect the spark plug wires.

8. Support the manifold and remove the bolts, then remove the manifold from the vehicle.

To install:
9. Before installing, use a putty knife and clean the gasket mounting surfaces.

10. Install the exhaust manifold to the vehicle using new gaskets, then torque the retaining bolts to the proper specification working from the inner bolts towards the outer bolts.

11. Connect the spark plug wires as noted.

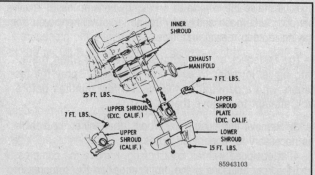

Fig. 86 Exploded view of a common exhaust manifold and hot air shroud assembly

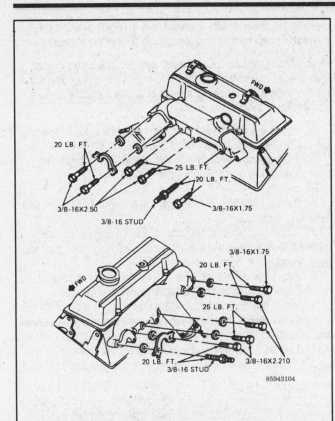

Fig. 87 Exhaust manifold installation — 1980 V6 and V8 engines (most V-engines similar)

12. If equipped with AIR, connect the hoses, then connect the pipes to the converter, cylinder head and the exhaust manifold.

13. If equipped with an air management valve, connect the bracket.

14. Connect the pipe to the exhaust manifold and tighten the retainers, then remove the jackstands and carefully lower the vehicle.

15. Install the air cleaner assembly and connect the negative battery cable.

16. Start and run the engine, then check for leaks.

LEFT SIDE

1. Disconnect the negative battery cable, and if necessary, remove the air cleaner assembly.

2. Raise and support the vehicle safely using jackstands. If possible, raise the vehicle to a height where access is available both underhood and undervehicle. This will keep you from having to keep raising and lowering it during the procedure.

➡ **The fasteners on the exhaust system are often rusted into place, in order to save your knuckles, spray the fasteners with a penetrating lubricant a few minutes before you attempt to remove them.**

3. Remove the exhaust pipe bolts, then lower the vehicle, as necessary for underhood access.

4. If equipped with air conditioning, remove the compressor and the rear adjusting brace, then reposition the compressor aside with the lines still connected.

5. If equipped with power steering, remove the power steering pump and the rear lower power steering adjusting brace, then position the pump aside with the lines still connected.

6. Tag and disconnect the spark plug wires from the spark plugs.

7. Support the manifold and remove the retaining bolts, then remove the manifold from the vehicle.

To install:

8. Before installing, use a putty knife and clean the gasket mounting surfaces.

9. Install the exhaust manifold to the vehicle using new gaskets, then torque the retaining bolts to the proper specification working from the inner bolts towards the outer bolts.

10. Connect the spark plug wires as noted.

11. If equipped with power steering, reposition and secure the pump along with the rear lower adjusting brace.

12. If equipped with A/C, reposition and secure the compressor along with the rear adjusting brace.

13. Connect the exhaust pipe to the manifold and tighten the retainers, then remove the jackstands and carefully lower the vehicle.

14. If removed, install the air cleaner assembly.

15. Connect the negative battery cable.

16. Start and run the engine, then check for leaks.

V8 Engines, 1985 and Later
▶ **See Figures 86 and 87**

RIGHT SIDE

1. Disconnect the negative battery cable and remove the air cleaner assembly.

2. Raise and support the vehicle safely using jackstands. If possible, raise the vehicle to a height where access is available both underhood and undervehicle. This will keep you from having to keep raising and lowering it during the procedure.

➡ **The fasteners on the exhaust system are often rusted into place, in order to save your knuckles, spray the fasteners with a penetrating lubricant a few minutes before you attempt to remove them.**

3. Remove the exhaust pipe bolts, then lower the vehicle, as necessary for underhood access.

4. Tag and disconnect the spark plug wires from the spark plugs, the vacuum hoses from the carbon canister and, if equipped, the AIR hose(s).

5. If equipped, loosen the alternator belt, then remove the lower alternator bracket and the AIR valve. Disconnect the converter's AIR pipe from the back of the manifold.

6. Support the manifold and remove the retaining bolts, then remove the manifold from the vehicle.

To install:

7. Before installing, use a putty knife and clean the gasket mounting surfaces.

8. Install the exhaust manifold to the vehicle using new gaskets, then torque the retaining bolts to the proper specification working from the inner bolts towards the outer bolts.

9. If equipped, connect the AIR pipe to the back of the manifold, then install the AIR valve and the lower alternator bracket. Adjust the drive belt tension.

10. Connect the spark plug wires as noted.

11. Connect the exhaust pipe to the manifold and tighten the retainers, then remove the jackstands and carefully lower the vehicle.

12. Install the air cleaner assembly and connect the negative battery cable.

13. Start and run the engine, then check for leaks.

LEFT SIDE

1. Disconnect the negative battery cable and, if necessary, remove the air cleaner assembly.

2. Raise and support the vehicle safely using jackstands. If possible, raise the vehicle to a height where access is available both underhood and undervehicle. This will keep you from having to keep raising and lowering it during the procedure.

➡The fasteners on the exhaust system are often rusted into place, in order to save your knuckles, spray the fasteners with a penetrating lubricant a few minutes before you attempt to remove them.

3. Remove the exhaust pipe bolts, then lower the vehicle, as necessary for underhood access.

4. Tag and disconnect the spark plug wires from the plugs.

5. If equipped, disconnect the AIR hose.

6. If equipped with air conditioning, loosen the bracket at the front of the head, then remove the rear bracket and the compressor. Position the compressor aside with the lines intact.

7. If equipped with power steering, remove the power steering pump and the lower adjusting bracket. Position the pump aside with the lines intact.

8. Support the manifold and remove the retaining bolts, then remove the wire loom holder and the valve cover and remove the manifold from the vehicle.

To install:

9. Before installing, use a putty knife and clean the gasket mounting surfaces.

10. Install the exhaust manifold and the wire loom holder to the vehicle using new gaskets, then torque the retaining bolts to the proper specification working from the inner bolts towards the outer bolts.

11. If equipped, reposition and secure the power steering pump, along with the lower adjusting bracket.

12. If equipped, reposition and secure the A/C compressor, along with the front and rear brackets.

13. If equipped, connect the AIR hose.

14. Connect the spark plug wires as noted during removal.

15. Connect the exhaust pipe to the manifold and tighten the retainers, then remove the jackstands and carefully lower the vehicle.

16. If removed, install the air cleaner assembly.

17. Connect the negative battery cable.

18. Start and run the engine, then check for leaks.

Diesel Engines

LEFT SIDE

1. Disconnect the negative battery cable and remove the air cleaner assembly.

2. Remove the alternator lower bracket.

3. Raise and support the vehicle safely using jackstands. If possible, raise the vehicle to a height where access is available both underhood and undervehicle. This will keep you from having to keep raising and lowering it during the procedure.

➡The fasteners on the exhaust system are often rusted into place, in order to save your knuckles, spray the fasteners with a penetrating lubricant a few minutes before you attempt to remove them.

4. Remove the exhaust crossover pipe, then lower the vehicle, as necessary for underhood access.

5. Support the manifold and remove the retaining bolts, then remove the manifold from the vehicle.

To install:

6. Before installing, use a putty knife and clean the gasket mounting surfaces.

7. Install the exhaust manifold to the engine using new gaskets, then tighten the retaining bolts working from the inner bolts towards the outer bolts.

8. Install the crossover pipe and tighten the retainers, then remove the jackstands and carefully lower the vehicle.

9. Install the alternator lower bracket.

10. Install the air cleaner assembly and connect the negative battery cable.

11. Start and run the engine, then check for leaks.

RIGHT SIDE

1. Disconnect the negative battery cable.

2. Raise and support the safely using jackstands.

3. Remove the crossover pipe.

4. Disconnect the exhaust pipe.

5. Remove the right front wheel.

6. Support the manifold and remove the retaining bolts, then lower and remove the manifold from under the vehicle.

To install:

7. Before installing, use a putty knife and clean the gasket mounting surfaces.

8. Install the exhaust manifold to the engine using new gaskets, then tighten the retaining bolts working from the inner bolts towards the outer bolts.

9. Install the right front wheel.

10. Connect the exhaust pipe and install the crossover pipe.

11. Remove the jackstands and carefully lower the vehicle.

12. Connect the negative battery cable.

Turbocharger and Actuator - 231 V6

◗ See Figures 88, 89, 90 and 91

REMOVAL & INSTALLATION

1. Disconnect the negative battery cable.

2. Disconnect the exhaust inlet and outlet pipes at the turbocharger.

3. Disconnect the oil feed pipe from the center housing rotating assembly.

4. Remove the nut attaching the air intake elbow to the carburetor and remove the elbow; still attached to the flex tube, from the carburetor.

5. Disconnect the accelerator, cruise and detent linkage at the carb. Remove the linkage bracket from the plenum.

6. Remove the two bolts attaching the plenum to the side bracket.

7. Disconnect the fuel line and all the vacuum hoses.

8. Drain the cooling system.

✻✻CAUTION

When draining the coolant, keep in mind that cats and dogs are attracted by the ethylene glycol antifreeze, and are quite likely to drink any that is left in an uncovered container or in puddles on the ground. This will prove fatal in sufficient quantity. Always drain the coolant into a sealable container. Coolant should be reused unless it is contaminated or several years old.

9. Disconnect the coolant hoses from the front and rear of the plenum.

10. Disconnect the plenum front bracket by removing one bolt attaching the bracket to the intake manifold. Leave the bracket attached to the manifold.

11. Remove the two bolts attaching the turbine housing to the bracket on the intake manifold.

12. Unscrew the two mounting bolts and then remove the EGR valve manifold.

13. Loosen the clamp attaching the hose from the air bypass to the pipe to the check valve.

14. Unscrew the three compressor housing-to-intake manifold mounting bolts.

15. Remove the turbocharger, actuator (still attached to the carburetor) and plenum assembly from the engine.

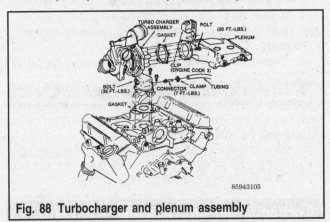
Fig. 88 Turbocharger and plenum assembly

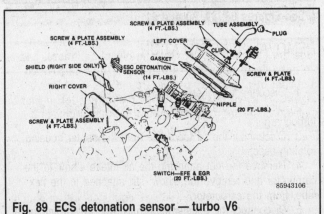
Fig. 89 ECS detonation sensor — turbo V6

16. Unscrew the six bolts and separate the turbocharger assembly from the carburetor.

17. Remove the oil drain from the center housing rotating assembly.

To install:

18. Install the oil drain to the center housing rotating assembly.

➡**Throughout the installation procedure, use new gaskets wherever necessary.**

19. Connect the turbocharger assembly to the carburetor and secure using the six bolts.

20. Install the turbocharger, actuator and plenum assembly to the engine.

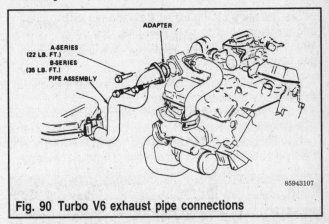
Fig. 90 Turbo V6 exhaust pipe connections

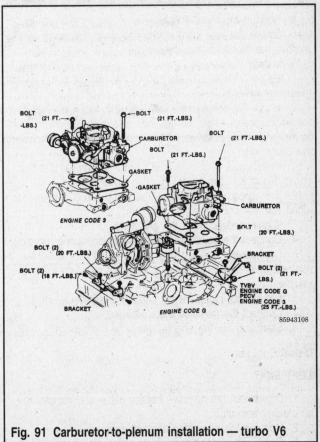
Fig. 91 Carburetor-to-plenum installation — turbo V6

21. Install and tighten the three compressor housing-to-intake manifold mounting bolts.

22. Make sure the hose from the air by-pass to the pipe to the check valve is in position and tighten the retaining clamp.

23. Install the EGR valve and tighten the two mounting bolts.

24. Secure the turbine housing to the bracket on the intake manifold using the retaining bolts.

25. Reposition the plenum front bracket and tighten the retaining bolts.

26. Connect the coolant hoses to the front and rear of the plenum.

27. Connect the fuel line and the vacuum hoses.

28. Secure the plenum to the side bracket using the two bolts.

29. Install the linkage bracket to the plenum, then connect the accelerator, cruise and detent linkage at the carb.

30. Install the elbow, still attached to the flex tube, to the carburetor and secure using the nut.

31. Connect the oil feed pipe to the center housing rotating assembly.

32. Connect the exhaust inlet and outlet pipes to the turbocharger.

33. Connect the negative battery cable and properly refill the engine cooling system.

Air Conditioning Compressor

✳✳CAUTION

Please refer to Section 1 before discharging the compressor or disconnecting air conditioning lines. Damage to the air conditioning system or personal injury could result. Consult your local laws concerning refrigerant discharge and recycling. In many areas it may be illegal for anyone but a certified technician to service the A/C system. Always use an approved recovery station when discharging the air conditioning.

REMOVAL

▶ **See Figure 92**

1. Disconnect the negative battery cable.
2. Disconnect the compressor clutch coil wire.
3. Remove the engine fan and fan shroud.
4. Remove the drive belt from the compressor.
5. Remove the compressor bracket.
6. Refer to Section 1 of this manual and discharge the air conditioning system into a suitable recovery station.
7. Remove the screw attaching the muffler to the compressor support.
8. Remove the hose and muffler assembly from the compressor.
9. Remove the vacuum pump hose from the metal vacuum line.
10. Remove the four nuts and one bolt and spacer from the compressor support.
11. Remove the compressor support by pulling forward.
12. Pull the compressor forward to remove.

Fig. 92 Most compressor brackets/housings have openings which will accept ratchet drives to assist when loosening/tightening the drive belt

INSTALLATION

1. Position the compressor to the engine.
2. Install the compressor support by pulling forward.
3. Install the four nuts and one bolt and spacer from the compressor support.
4. Install the vacuum pump hose to the metal vacuum line.
5. Install the hose and muffler assembly to the compressor.
6. Install the screw attaching the muffler to the compressor support.
7. Install the compressor bracket.
8. Install the drive belt to the compressor and adjust the belt tension.
9. Install the engine fan and fan shroud.
10. Connect the compressor clutch coil wire.
11. Refer to Section 1 of this manual for system evacuation and charging procedures.
12. Connect the negative battery cable.

Radiator

REMOVAL & INSTALLATION

▶ **See Figures 93, 94, 95 and 96**

1. Disconnect the negative battery cable and drain the engine cooling system.

✳✳CAUTION

When draining the coolant, keep in mind that cats and dogs are attracted by the ethylene glycol antifreeze, and are quite likely to drink any that is left in an uncovered container or in puddles on the ground. This will prove fatal in sufficient quantity. Always drain the coolant into a sealable container. Coolant should be reused unless it is contaminated or several years old.

2. As necessary, remove the fan, the upper fan shroud and/or the upper support.

➡**If the fan is removed on vehicle equipped with a clutch type fan, be sure to keep it in an upright position to prevent the fluid from leaking.**

3. Disconnect upper and lower hoses.

4. If equipped with an automatic transmission, disconnect and plug the oil cooler lines. The lines should be plugged to prevent system contamination or excessive fluid loss.

5. Lift radiator straight up and out of the vehicle.

To install:

6. Carefully lower the radiator into the vehicle, making sure the lower cradles are properly located.

7. If equipped with an automatic transmission, remove the plugs and reconnect the cooler lines.

8. Connect the upper and lower hoses.

9. If removed, install the cooling fan, upper fan shroud and/or upper support.

10. Connect the negative battery cable and properly refill the engine cooling system.

11. Start and run the engine, then check for leaks.

12. If equipped, check and add automatic transmission fluid, as necessary.

Condenser

REMOVAL & INSTALLATION

✳✳CAUTION

Please refer to Section 1 before discharging the compressor or disconnecting air conditioning lines. Damage to the air conditioning system or personal injury could result.

Fig. 93 The upper shroud must be removed for access. If equipped with a 1 piece shroud, it may be disconnected from the radiator and pushed backwards, over the cooling fan.

Fig. 94 If equipped, disconnect the automatic transmission lines from the radiator

Fig. 95 The transmission lines should be plugged to prevent system contamination or excessive fluid loss

Fig. 96 With the shroud out of the way and all hoses or lines disconnected, the radiator may be lifted from the engine compartment

Consult your local laws concerning refrigerant discharge and recycling. In many areas it may be illegal for anyone but a certified technician to service the A/C system. Always use an approved recovery station when discharging the air conditioning.

1. Disconnect the negative battery cable.

2. Discharge the air conditioning system into a suitable recovery station.

3. Remove the upper radiator shroud.

4. Disconnect the air conditioning lines at the condenser. Plug all openings to prevent system contamination

5. Push the radiator forward and pull the condenser out from the top.

To install:

6. Carefully lower the condenser into position in the vehicle.

7. Unplug and connect the A/C lines to the condenser.

8. Install the upper radiator shroud.

9. Refer to Section 1 of this manual for system evacuation and charging procedures.

10. Connect the negative battery cable.

Water Pump

The water pump is a die cast, centrifugal-type with sealed bearings. Since it is pressed together, it must be serviced as a unit.

REMOVAL & INSTALLATION

◆ See Figures 97, 98, 99, 100 and 101

All Engines Except Diesel

1. Disconnect the negative battery cable and drain the cooling system.

❋❋CAUTION

When draining the coolant, keep in mind that cats and dogs are attracted by the ethylene glycol antifreeze, and are quite likely to drink any that is left in an uncovered container or in puddles on the ground. This will prove fatal in sufficient quantity. Always drain the coolant into a sealable container. Coolant should be reused unless it is contaminated or several years old.

2. If necessary for access, remove the fan shroud and/or the upper radiator support.
3. Loosen and remove the necessary drive belts.
4. Remove the fan and water pump pulley.
5. Remove the alternator and, if equipped, the power steering pump brackets as necessary and reposition the components for access to the water pump.
6. Remove the heater hose and the lower radiator hose from the pump.
7. Support the water pump and remove the retaining bolts, then remove the pump from the block. Because the water pump is held by bolts of various lengths, the bolt positions should be noted during removal.

To install:

8. Be sure to remove all traces of gasket or sealer material from the gasket mating surfaces.
9. Position the pump to the block using new gaskets. The gaskets may be held in place using small amount of RTV sealer or bolts may be held through the pump mounting holes in order to correctly position the gaskets.

➡Use an anti-seize compound on the water pump bolt threads.

10. Install all of the water pump bolts and torque to 30 ft. lbs. (41 Nm).
11. Connect the heater hose and the lower radiator hose to the pump.
12. As applicable, reposition and secure the alternator and/or power steering pump.
13. Install the water pump pulley and the cooling fan.
14. Install and adjust the drive belts.
15. If removed, install the fan shroud and/or the upper radiator support.
16. Connect the negative battery cable, then properly refill the engine cooling system.
17. Start and run the engine, then check for leaks.

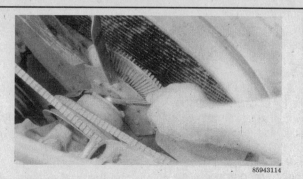

Fig. 97 Loosen the retainers holding the fan assembly to the water pump pulley

Fig. 98 Once the retainers are removed, carefully lift the fan out of the vehicle

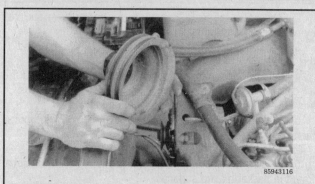

Fig. 99 With the fan removed, the pulley should be free to be pulled from the water pump hub

Diesel

1. Disconnect the negative battery cable and drain the engine cooling system.

❋❋CAUTION

When draining the coolant, keep in mind that cats and dogs are attracted by the ethylene glycol antifreeze, and are quite likely to drink any that is left in an uncovered container or in puddles on the ground. This will prove fatal in sufficient quantity. Always drain the coolant into a sealable container. Coolant should be reused unless it is contaminated or several years old.

Fig. 100 Pull the water pump from the front of the block. Make sure all remains of the gaskets and/or sealer are removed from the mating surfaces.

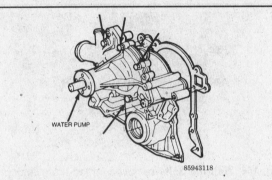

WATER PUMP

Fig. 101 Example of a V8 water pump showing pump, gasket and mounting bolts

2. Disconnect the lower radiator hose, heater hose and the by-pass hose from the water pump.

3. Remove the cooling fan assembly, the drive belts and the water pump pulley.

4. Remove the alternator, the power steering pump and the air conditioning compressor (if equipped) brackets, then position the components aside with their lines intact.

5. Support the water pump and remove the mounting bolts, then remove the pump from the block.

To install:

6. Be sure to remove all traces of gasket or sealer material from the gasket mating surfaces.

7. Position the pump to the block using new gaskets. The gaskets may be held in place using small amount of RTV sealer or bolts may be held through the pump mounting holes in order to correctly position the gaskets.

➡**Apply sealer to the lower water pump bolts.**

8. Install and tighten the water pump bolts to 22 ft. lbs. (30 Nm).

9. Reposition and secure the A/C compressor, power steering pump and/or alternator and bracket(s).

10. Install the water pump pulley, the cooling fan assembly and the drive belt.

11. Adjust the drive belt tension.

12. Connect the lower radiator hose, heater hose and the by-pass hose to the water pump.

13. Connect the negative battery cable and properly refill the engine cooling system.

14. Start and run the engine, then check for leaks.

Cylinder Head

REMOVAL & INSTALLATION

▶ **See Figures 103, 104, 105 and 106**

➡**The engine should be allowed to cool overnight before the cylinder head is removed in order to prevent warpage.**

Inline 6-Cylinder

▶ **See Figure 102**

1. Disconnect the negative battery cable.

2. Drain engine cooling system, then remove air cleaner assembly and disconnect the PCV hose.

✳✳CAUTION

When draining the coolant, keep in mind that cats and dogs are attracted by the ethylene glycol antifreeze, and are quite likely to drink any that is left in an uncovered container or in puddles on the ground. This will prove fatal in sufficient quantity. Always drain the coolant into a sealable container. Coolant should be reused unless it is contaminated or several years old.

3. Disconnect accelerator pedal rod at the bellcrank on the manifold, the fuel and the vacuum lines at the carburetor.

➡**On some late model inline 6-cylinder engines, only the exhaust manifold may be removed as the intake is an integral part of the cylinder head.**

4. Disconnect the exhaust pipe at the manifold flange, then remove the manifold bolts and clamps. Either remove the manifolds and carburetor as an assembly or remove the exhaust manifold, as applicable.

5. Remove the fuel and the vacuum line retaining clip from the water outlet. Disconnect the wiring harness from the temperature sending unit and the coil, leaving the harness clear of the clips on the rocker arm cover.

6. Disconnect the radiator hose at the water outlet housing and the negative battery cable from the cylinder head.

7. Tag and disconnect the wires, then remove the spark plugs.

8. Remove the rocker arm cover, then back off the rocker arm nuts. Pivot the rocker arms to clear the push rods and remove the push rods.

9. Remove the cylinder head bolts, the cylinder head and the gasket.

10. Using a putty knife, clean the gasket mounting surfaces.

To install:

11. Position a new cylinder head gasket on the block, then carefully lower the cylinder head assembly into position.

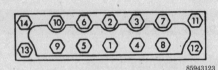

Fig. 102 Cylinder head torque sequence — inline 6-cylinder engines

12. Lubricate the cylinder head bolts using clean engine oil, then install and finger-tighten them. Torque the bolts using the proper torque sequence.

➡️On vehicles equipped with solid lifters, once the valves have been set up properly and given a static adjustment, temporarily place the rocker arm cover on the engine to prevent the entrance of dirt or debris. After the valves have been adjusted with the engine running (dynamic adjustment), the cover will be fastened in place.

13. Install the push rods, then pivot the rocker arms into position and install the retaining nuts. Adjust the valves and, unless the engine is equipped with solid lifters, install the rocker arm covers.

14. Install the spark plugs, then connect the wires as noted during removal.

15. Connect the radiator hose at the water outlet housing and the negative battery cable to the cylinder head.

16. Connect the wiring harness to the temperature sending unit and the coil, making sure the harness is properly positioned in the clips of the rocker arm cover (unless equipped with solid lifters).

17. Connect the fuel and the vacuum line retaining clip to the water outlet.

18. Install the exhaust manifold or the intake/exhaust manifold assembly, as applicable.

19. Connect the accelerator pedal rod at the bellcrank on the manifold, then connect the fuel and the vacuum lines at the carburetor.

20. Install the air cleaner assembly and connect the PCV hose.

21. Connect the negative battery cable and properly refill the engine cooling system

22. Run the engine and check for leaks.

23. If equipped with solid lifters, adjust the valves with the engine running, then shut the engine **OFF** and install the rocker arm cover.

V6 and V8 Gasoline Engines, Except 231 V-6
◆ See Figures 107, 108, 109, 110 and 111

1. Disconnect the negative battery cable.
2. Remove the intake manifold from the cylinder heads. Refer to the Intake Manifold Removal and Installation procedures earlier in this section for details.
3. If necessary, remove the alternator's lower mounting bolt and reposition the unit aside.

Fig. 103 Evenly loosen the cylinder head retaining bolts using a large breaker bar and socket

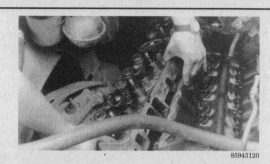

Fig. 104 With the bolts removed, grasp the cylinder head and lift it from the engine. Be careful as the head (unless aluminum) is quite heavy.

Fig. 105 Remove the old head gasket from the engine block

4. Remove the exhaust manifold(s) and the rocker arm cover(s), then remove the rocker arm and pushrod assemblies.

➡️If rocker arms and pushrods are to be reused, be sure to sort or label all parts to assure installation in their original locations.

5. If necessary, remove the diverter valve.
6. Gradually loosen and remove the cylinder head bolts, then remove the cylinder head(s) from the engine block. If necessary, a prybar may be used to gently loosen the gasket seal, but be VERY careful not to damage the sealing surfaces or the engine or cylinder head. Always protect surfaces being pried using wood or cloth.
7. Using a putty knife, clean the gasket mounting surfaces.

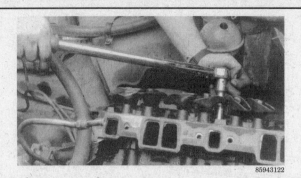

Fig. 106 Once the head is installed, use a torque wrench to tighten the bolts in the proper sequence

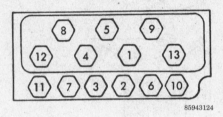

Fig. 107 Cylinder head torque sequence — 229 and 262 V6 engines

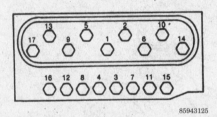

Fig. 108 Cylinder head torque sequence — small block V8 engines

To install:

8. Position a new cylinder head gasket on the block, then carefully lower the cylinder head assembly into position.

9. Install and finger-tighten the cylinder head retaining bolts, then tighten them to specification using the proper torque sequence.

10. If removed, install the diverter valve.

➡ On vehicles equipped with solid lifters, once the valves have been set up properly and given a static adjustment, temporarily place the rocker arm cover on the engine to prevent the entrance of dirt or debris. After the valves have been adjusted with the engine running (dynamic adjustment), the cover will be fastened in place.

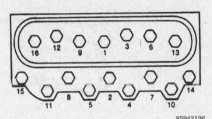

Fig. 109 Cylinder head torque sequence — big block V8 engines

11. Install the pushrod and rocker arm assemblies, then adjust the valves. Engines equipped with solid lifters will require a dynamic adjustment once the engine is running.

12. Unless the engine is equipped with solid lifters, install the rocker arm cover(s).

13. Install the exhaust manifold(s) using new gaskets.

14. Install the intake manifold assembly.

15. If not done already, reposition and secure the alternator, then adjust the drive belt.

16. Connect the negative battery cable, then properly refill the engine cooling system.

17. Run the engine and check for leaks.

18. If equipped with solid lifters, adjust the valves with the engine running, then shut the engine **OFF** and install the rocker arm cover.

231 V6

▶ **See Figure 112**

➡ On vehicles equipped with AIR, disconnect the rubber hose at the injection tubing check valve. This way the tubing will not have to be removed from the exhaust manifold.

1. Disconnect the negative battery cable.

2. Remove the intake manifold from the engine. Refer to the Intake Manifold Removal and Installation procedures earlier in this section for details.

   a. Loosen and remove all drive belts.

   b. Tag and disconnect the wires leading from the rear of the alternator.

   c. Remove the air conditioning compressor (if so equipped) and position it out of the way with all the hoses still connected.

   d. Remove the alternator and its mounting bracket.

3. When removing the left cylinder head:

   a. Remove the oil gauge rod.

   b. Remove the power steering pump (if so equipped) and its bracket and then position it out of the way with the hoses still attached.

4. Tag and disconnect the spark plug wires and then remove the spark plug wires clips from the cylinder head cover studs.

5. Remove the exhaust manifold mounting bolts from the head which is being removed, and then pull the manifold away from the head.

6. Use an air hose if available, or a bunch of clean rags and clean the dirt off the head and surrounding areas thor-

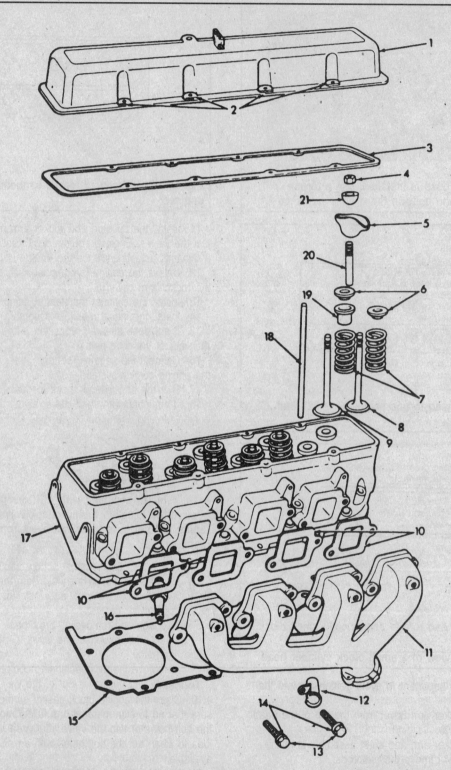

1. Valve cover
2. Screw reinforcements
3. Gasket
4. Adjusting nut
5. Rocker arm
6. Valve spring retainer
7. Valve spring
8. Exhaust valve
9. Intake valve
10. Gasket
11. Exhaust manifold
12. Spark plug shield
13. Bolt
14. Washer
15. Head gasket
16. Spark plug
17. Cylinder head
18. Pushrod
19. Spring shield
20. Rocker arm stud
21. Rocker arm ball

85943127

Fig. 110 Exploded view of a big block cylinder head

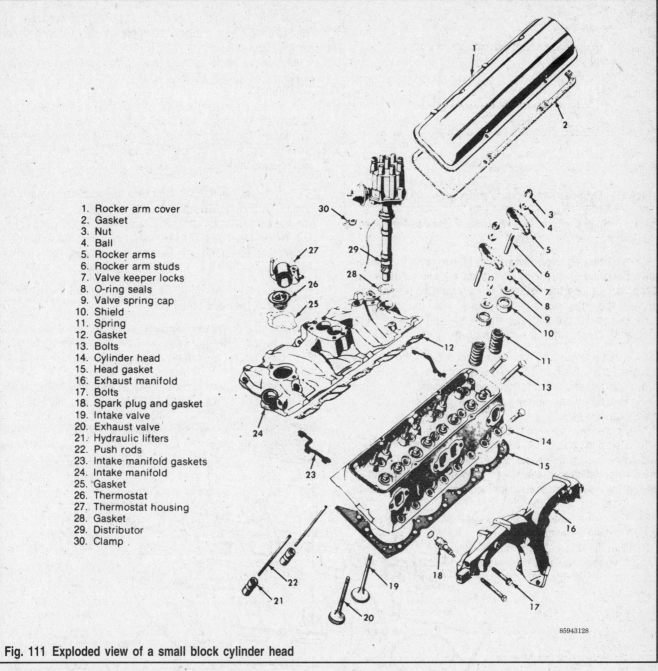

1. Rocker arm cover
2. Gasket
3. Nut
4. Ball
5. Rocker arms
6. Rocker arm studs
7. Valve keeper locks
8. O-ring seals
9. Valve spring cap
10. Shield
11. Spring
12. Gasket
13. Bolts
14. Cylinder head
15. Head gasket
16. Exhaust manifold
17. Bolts
18. Spark plug and gasket
19. Intake valve
20. Exhaust valve
21. Hydraulic lifters
22. Push rods
23. Intake manifold gaskets
24. Intake manifold
25. Gasket
26. Thermostat
27. Thermostat housing
28. Gasket
29. Distributor
30. Clamp

Fig. 111 Exploded view of a small block cylinder head

oughly. It is extremely important to avoid getting dirt into the hydraulic valve lifters.

7. Remove the rocker arm cover from the top of the head that you wish to remove.

8. Remove the rocker arm and shaft assembly from the cylinder head and then remove the pushrods.

➡**If the valve lifters are to serviced, remove them at this time. Otherwise, protect the lifters and the camshaft from dust and dirt by covering the entire area with a clean cloth. Whenever the lifters or the pushrods are removed from the head it is always a good idea to place them in a wooden block with numbered holes to keep them identified as to their position in the engine.**

9. Loosen and remove all the cylinder head bolts, then then lift the head off the engine block.

To install:

10. Clean the engine block gasket surface thoroughly. Make sure that no foreign material has fallen into the cylinder bores, the bolt holes or into the valve lifter area. It is always a good idea to clean out the bolt holes with an air hose if one is available.

11. Install a new head gasket with the bead facing down toward the cylinder block. The dowels in the block will hold the gasket in place.

12. Clean the gasket surface of the cylinder head and carefully set it into place on the dowels in the cylinder block.

13. Use a heavy body thread sealer on all of the head bolts since the bolt holes go all the way through into the coolant.

14. Install the head bolts. Tighten the bolts a little at a time about three times around in the sequence shown in the illus-

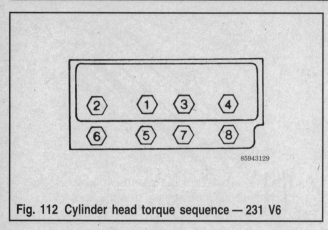

Fig. 112 Cylinder head torque sequence — 231 V6

tration. Tighten the bolts to a final torque equal to that given in the Torque Specifications chart.

➡**On vehicles equipped with solid lifters, once the valves have been set up properly and given a static adjustment, temporarily place the rocker arm cover on the engine to prevent the entrance of dirt or debris. After the valves have been adjusted with the engine running (dynamic adjustment), the cover will be fastened in place.**

15. Install the pushrod and rocker arm assemblies, then adjust the valves. Engines equipped with solid lifters will require a dynamic adjustment once the engine is running.

16. Unless the engine is equipped with solid lifters, install the rocker arm cover(s).

17. Reposition and secure the exhaust manifold.

18. Route the spark plug wires through the retaining clips and connect them to the plugs, as noted during removal.

19. If the left cylinder head was removed, reposition and secure the power steering pump, then install the oil gauge rod.

20. Install the intake manifold assembly.

21. Connect the negative battery cable and properly refill the engine cooling system.

22. Run the engine and check for leaks.

23. If equipped with solid lifters, adjust the valves with the engine running, then shut the engine **OFF** and install the rocker arm cover.

Diesel Engines

▶ **See Figures 113 and 114**

1. Disconnect the negative battery cable.

2. Remove the intake manifold. Refer to the procedure earlier in this section for details.

3. Remove the rocker arm cover(s), after removing any accessory brackets which interfere with cover removal.

4. Tag and disconnect the glow plug wiring.

5. If the right cylinder head is being removed, disconnect the ground strap from the head.

6. Remove the rocker arm bolts, the bridged pivots, the rocker arms, and the pushrods, keeping all the parts in order so that they can be returned to their original locations. It is a good practice to number or mark the parts to avoid interchanging them.

7. Remove the fuel return lines from the nozzles.

8. Remove the exhaust manifold(s). Refer to the procedure earlier in this section for details.

9. Remove the engine block drain plug on the side of the engine from which the cylinder head is being removed. On V6s, remove the pipe thread plugs covering the upper cylinder head bolts.

10. Remove the head bolts, then remove the cylinder head assembly.

To install:

11. Clean the mating surfaces thoroughly. Install new head gaskets on the engine block. DO NOT coat the gaskets with any sealer. The gaskets have a special coating that eliminates the need for sealer. The use of sealer will interfere with this coating and cause leaks. Install the cylinder head onto the block.

12. Clean the head bolts (and pipe thread plugs - V6s) thoroughly. On the V8, dip the bolts in clean engine oil and install into the cylinder block until the heads of the bolts lightly contact the cylinder head. On V6s, coat the plug threads, bolt threads and the area under the bolt threads with sealer/lubricant part No. 1052080 or equivalent.

➡**The correct sealer must be used or coolant leaks and bolt torque loss will result.**

13. On the V8, tighten the bolts, in the sequence illustrated, to 100 ft. lbs. (136 Nm). When all bolts have been tightened to this figure, begin the tightening sequence again, and torque all bolts to 130 ft. lbs. (176 Nm).

14. On V6s, tighten all head bolts in sequence to the following torques: all except bolts 5, 6, 11, 12, 13 and 14: 100 ft. lbs. (136 Nm); bolts 5, 6, 11, 12, 13, and 14: 41 ft. lbs. (56 Nm). Finally, tighten all bolts except 5, 6, 11, 12, 13 and 14 to 142 ft. lbs. (192 Nm), and bolts 5, 6, 11, 12, 13, and 14 to 59

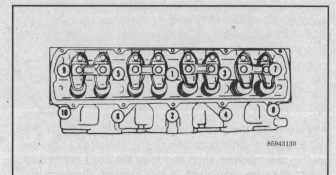

Fig. 113 Cylinder head torque sequence — 350 V8 diesel engine

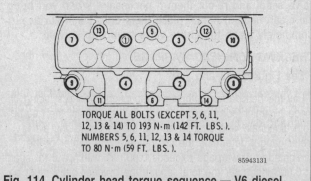

TORQUE ALL BOLTS (EXCEPT 5, 6, 11, 12, 13 & 14) TO 193 N·m (142 FT. LBS.). NUMBERS 5, 6, 11, 12, 13 & 14 TORQUE TO 80 N·m (59 FT. LBS.).

Fig. 114 Cylinder head torque sequence — V6 diesel engine

ft. lbs. (80 Nm) in the proper sequence. Install the pipe thread plugs.

15. Install the engine block drain plug(s), the exhaust manifold(s), the fuel return lines, the glow plug wiring, and the ground strap for the right cylinder head.

16. Install the valve train assembly. Refer to diesel engine, rocker arm replacement, earlier in this section, for valve lifter bleeding procedures.

17. Install the intake manifold.

18. Install the rocker cover(s). The valve covers are sealed with RTV (room temperature vulcanizing) silicone sealer instead of a gasket. Use GM No. 1052434 or its equivalent. Install the cover to the head within 10 minutes (while the sealer is still wet).

19. Connect the negative battery cable and properly refill the engine cooling system.

CLEANING & INSPECTION

→Any diesel cylinder head work should be handled by a reputable machine shop familiar with diesel engines. Disassembly, valve lapping, and assembly can be completed by following the gasoline engine procedures.

Gasoline Engines

REMOVING GASKET MATERIAL AND CARBON DEPOSITS

▶ See Figures 115, 116 and 117

Once the complete valve train has been removed from the cylinder head(s), the head itself can be inspected, cleaned and machined (if necessary). Set the head(s) on a clean work space, so the combustion chambers are facing up. Begin cleaning the gasket surface, chambers and ports with a hardwood chisel or other non-metallic tool (to avoid nicking or gouging the chamber, ports, and especially the valve seats). Chip away the gasket material and the major carbon deposits, then remove the remainder with a wire brush fitted to an electric drill.

→Be sure that the carbon is actually removed, rather than just burnished. After decarbonizing is completed, take the head(s) to a machine shop and have the head hot tanked (unless they are aluminum). In this process, the head is lowered into a hot chemical bath that very effectively cleans all grease, corrosion, and scale from all internal and external head surfaces. Also have the machinist check the valve seats and re-cut them if necessary. When you bring the clean head(s) home, place them on a clean surface. Completely clean the entire valve train with solvent.

CHECKING FOR HEAD WARPAGE

▶ See Figures 118 and 119

Lay the head down with the combustion chamfers facing up. Place a straightedge across the gasket surface of the head, both diagonally and straight across the center. Using a flat feeler gauge, determine the clearance at the center of the straightedge. If warpage exceeds 0.003 in. within a 6 in. span, or 0.006 inch over the total length, the cylinder head must be

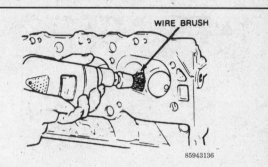

Fig. 117 The electric drill and wire brush may also be used to remove carbon deposits from the tops of the combustion chambers

resurfaced (which is akin to planing a piece of wood). Resurfacing can be performed at most machine shops.

→When resurfacing the cylinder head(s) of V6 or V8 engines, the intake manifold mounting position is altered, and must be corrected by machining a proportionate amount from the intake manifold flange.

LAPPING THE VALVES

▶ See Figures 120 and 121

When valve faces and seats have been refaced and recut, or if they are determined to be in good condition, the valves must be lapped in to ensure efficient sealing when the valve closes against the seal.

1. Invert the cylinder head so that the combustion chambers are facing up.

Fig. 115 Use a gasket scraper to remove the bulk of the old head gasket from the mating surface

Fig. 116 An electric drill equipped with a wire wheel will expedite complete gasket removal

Fig. 118 Check the cylinder head for warpage along the center using a straightedge and a feeler gauge

Fig. 119 Be sure to check for warpage across the cylinder head at both diagonals

2. Lightly lubricate the valve stems with clean oil, and coat the valve seats with valve grinding compound. Install the valves in the head as numbered.

3. Attach the suction cup of a valve lapping tool to a valve head. You'll probably have to moisten the cup to securely attach the tool to the valve.

4. Rotate the tool between the palms, changing position and lifting the tool often to prevent grooving. Lap the valve until a smooth, polished seat is evident (you may have to add a bit more compound after some lapping is done).

5. Remove the valve and tool, and remove ALL traces of grinding compound with solvent-soaked rag, or rinse the head with solvent.

➡**Valve lapping can also be done by fastening a suction cup to a piece of drill rod in a hand eggbeater type drill. Proceed as above, using the drill as a lapping tool. Due to the higher speeds involved when using the hand drill, care must be exercised to avoid grooving the seat. Lift the tool and change direction of rotation often.**

RESURFACING

➡**This procedure should only be performed by a qualified machine shop.**

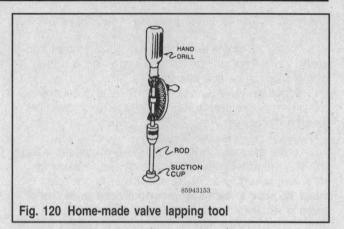

Fig. 120 Home-made valve lapping tool

Fig. 121 Lapping the valves by hand

Valves

REMOVAL & INSTALLATION

▶ **See Figures 122, 123, 124, 125, 126 and 127**

New valve seals must be installed when the valve train is put back together. Certain seals slip over the valve stem and guide boss, while others require that the boss be machined. In some applications Teflon guide seals are available. Check with a machinist and/or automotive parts store for a suggestion on the proper seals to use.

1. Remove the head(s), and place on a clean surface.

2. Using a suitable spring compressor (either a leverage or jawed type that is designed for pushrod overhead valve engines), compress the valve spring and remove the valve spring cap key. Carefully release the spring compressor and remove the valve spring and cap (and valve rotator on some engines).

➡**Use care in removing the keys; they are easily lost.**

3. Remove the valve seals from the intake valve guides. Throw these old seals away, as you'll be installing new seals during reassembly.

4. Slide the valves out of the head from the combustion chamber side.

5. Make a holder for the valves out of a piece of wood with drilled holes or cardboard. Make sure you number each hole in the holder to keep the valves in proper order. Slide the

Fig. 122 Use a valve spring compressor tool to relieve spring tension from the valve caps

Fig. 123 A small magnet will help in removal of the valve keys

Fig. 124 Be careful not to lose the valve keys

Fig. 125 Once the spring has been removed, the O-ring may be removed from the valve stem

Fig. 126 Invert the cylinder head and withdraw the valve from the cylinder head bore

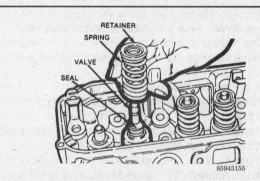
Fig. 127 Exploded view of the valve spring, retainer (cap) and seal assembly

valve out of the head from the combustion chamber side; they MUST be installed in their original locations.

To install:

➡Remember that when installing valve seals, a small amount of oil is able to pass the seal to lubricate the valve guides; otherwise, excessive wear will result.

To install the valve and rocker assembly:

6. Lubricate the valve stems with clean engine oil.
7. Install the valves in the cylinder head, one at a time, as numbered.

8. Lubricate and position the seals and valve springs, again a valve at a time.
9. Install the spring caps, and compress the springs.
10. With the valve key groove exposed above the compressed valve spring, wipe some wheel bearing grease around the groove. This will retain the keys as you release the spring compressor.
11. Using needle nose pliers (or your fingers), place the keys in the key grooves. The grease should hold the keys in place. Slowly release the spring compressor; the valve cap or rotator will raise up as the compressor is released, retaining the key.
12. Install the cylinder head(s).

INSPECTION

▶ **See Figures 128, 129, 130, 131, 132, 133 and 134**

Inspect the valve faces and seats (in the head) for pits, burned spots and other evidence of poor seating. If a valve face is in such bad shape that the head of the valve must be ground in order to true up the face, discard the valve because the sharp edge will run too hot. The correct angle for valve faces is 45 degrees. We recommend the refacing be done at a reputable machine shop.

Check the valve stem for scoring and burned spots. If not noticeably scored or damaged, clean the valve stem with solvent to remove all gum and varnish. Clean the valve guides using solvent and an expanding wire type valve guide cleaner. If you have access to a dial indicator for measuring valve stem-to-guide clearance, mount it so that the stem of the indicator is at 90 degrees to the valve stem, and is as close to the valve guide as possible. Move the valve off its seat, and measure the valve guide-to-stem clearance by rocking the stem back and forth to actuate the dial indicator. Measure the valve stems using a micrometer, and compare to specifications to determine whether stem or guide wear is responsible for the excess clearance. If a dial indicator and micrometer are not available to you, take your cylinder head and valves to a reputable machine shop of inspection.

Make sure the valve stem is not bent. The valve may be rolled on a flat surface such as a mirror or glass. An even better indication of valve stem bending can be determined by carefully chocking the stem into an electric drill. Use the drill the spin the stem while you watch the valve head. A bent stem will be obvious by the wobbling of the head. Be very careful if this method is used. If the valve stem is not properly chocked in position it could come flying out of the drill and cause injury.

Some of the engines covered in this guide are equipped with valve rotators, which double as valve spring caps. In normal operation the rotators put a certain degree of wear on the tip of the valve stem; this ear appears as concentric rings on the stem tip. However, if the rotator is not working properly, the wear may appear as straight notches or **X** patterns across the valve stem tip. Whenever the valves are removed from the cylinder head, the tips should be inspected for improper pattern, which could indicate valve rotator problems. Valve stem tips will have to be ground flat if rotator patterns are severe.

Fig. 128 A dial gauge may be used to check valve stem-to-guide clearance

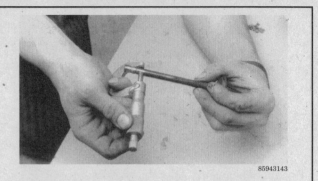
Fig. 129 Use a micrometer to measure the valve stem diameter

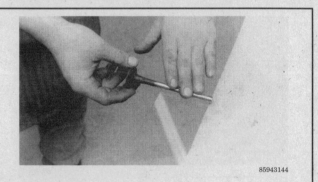
Fig. 130 Valve stems may be rolled on a flat surface to check for bends

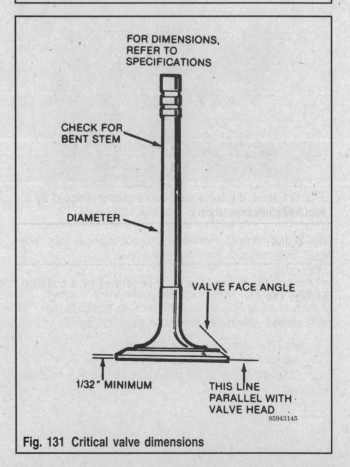
FOR DIMENSIONS, REFER TO SPECIFICATIONS

CHECK FOR BENT STEM

DIAMETER

1/32" MINIMUM

VALVE FACE ANGLE

THIS LINE PARALLEL WITH VALVE HEAD

Fig. 131 Critical valve dimensions

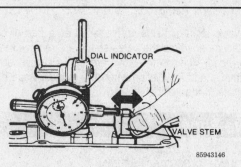

Fig. 132 When using a dial gauge to check stem-to-guide clearance, rock the stem back and forth a check the gauge readings

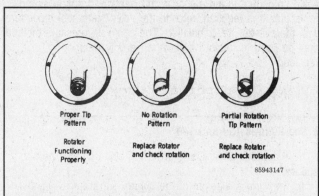

Fig. 133 Valve stem wear patterns

Fig. 134 Have the valve seat concentricity checked by a reputable machine shop

REFACING

➡ This procedure should only be performed by a qualified machine shop.

Valve Stem Seals

REPLACEMENT

Cylinder Head Installed
◗ See Figures 135, 136, 137 and 138

The valve stem seals on the most engines covered by this manual may be replaced with the cylinder head either on or off the engine. The removal procedure with the cylinder head installed utilizes compressed air in the cylinder to hold the valve in place and keep it from dropping into the cylinder once the valve key, cap and spring are removed.

➡ If air pressure is lost while the valve keepers are removed, the valve will drop into the cylinder. If this happens, the cylinder head must be removed in order to recover the valve.

1. Disconnect the negative battery cable.
2. Remove the rocker arm cover.
3. Remove the rocker arm and pushrod assemblies from the cylinders on which the valves are being serviced.

➡ The cylinder must be on it's compression stroke in order to follow this procedure. On the compression stroke, the cylinder's valves will be closed allowing the air pressure to hold the valve in position. The engine must therefore be turned slightly for each cylinder's valve seals.

4. Remove the spark plug from the cylinder which is on it's compression stroke and install a spark plug air fitting adapter with an in-line gauge set between the adapter and air compressor. Apply compressed air to hold the valve in place.
5. Compress the valve spring using a suitable compressor tool and remove the valve key. Carefully release the spring tension, then remove the valve cap and spring.

➡ If the air pressure has forced the piston to the bottom of the cylinder, any removal of air pressure will allow the valves to fall into the cylinder. A rubber band, tape or string wrapped around the end of the valve stem will prevent this.

6. Remove the old seal using a suitable removal tool.
To install:
7. Install the new seal using the valve stem seal tool.

Fig. 135 Remove the rocker cover from the head on which the valve stem seals are being replaced

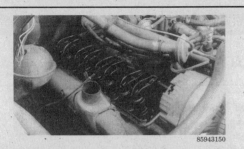

Fig. 136 With the cover removed, the valve stems seals may be accessed, but if the mechanisms were just removed at this point the valves would fall into the cylinders

Fig. 137 With an adapter fitting threaded into the spark plug bore air pressure from a compressor may be used to hold the cylinder's valves in position

Fig. 138 With the valve spring out of the way, the valve stem seals may now be replaced

8. Install the valve spring and cap, then compress the spring and install the valve key.

9. When the valve springs are properly installed, release the air pressure from the cylinder using the gauge set, then remove the spark plug adapter.

10. Install the spark plug and turn the engine sufficiently to work on the next cylinder. Repeat the above steps until all seals are replaced.

11. Install the rocker arm and pushrod assemblies, then install the rocker cover and connect the negative battery cable.

Cylinder Heads Removed

The valve stem oil seals are replaced as a part of normal valve service any time the valve stems are removed from the cylinder head. Refer to the valve procedure in this section for seal removal and installation when the cylinder head has been removed from the vehicle.

Valve Springs

REMOVAL & INSTALLATION

The valve springs are removed and installed as part of the valve procedure found earlier in this section. If only a spring replacement is required, refer to the valve stem seal procedure with the cylinder head installed. The same air pressure method may be used to retain the valve while only a spring is replaced.

HEIGHT AND PRESSURE CHECK

▶ **See Figures 139 and 140**

1. Place the valve spring on a flat, clean surface next to a square.

2. Measure the height of the spring, and rotate it against the edge of the square to measure distortion (out-of-roundness). If spring height varies between springs by more than $1/16$ in. or if the distortion exceeds $1/16$ in., replace the spring.

A valve spring tester is needed to test spring test pressure, so the valve springs must usually be taken to a professional machine shop for this test. Spring pressure at the installed and compressed heights is checked, and a tolerance of plus or minus 5 lbs. (plus or minus 1 lb. on the 231 V6) is permissible on the springs covered in this guide.

VALVE ADJUSTMENT

In the event of cylinder head removal or any operation that requires disturbing or removing the rocker arms, the rocker arms must be adjusted. See the Valve Lash procedure found earlier in this section.

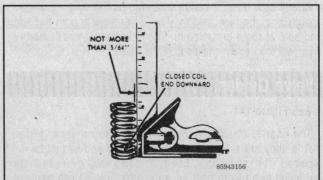

Fig. 139 Check the valve spring for proper length and squareness

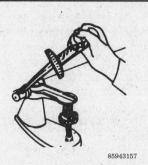

Fig. 140 If a spring pressure testing tool is not available, have the spring checked professionally

Valve Seats

REMOVAL & INSTALLATION

Due to the high degree of precision and special equipment required, valve seat replacement should be left to an automotive machine shop. Seat replacement procedures vary depending on whether the engine is equipped with cast iron or aluminum heads. Iron heads use a valve seat which is originally an integral part of the head. To replace these, a bore must be cut in the head which will accept an insert. The bore must be drilled to exacting specifications for the insert to work.

Aluminum cylinder heads are already equipped with a valve seat insert. There are various methods to replace these inserts, and although most are similar, the specifications are unique to each cylinder head application. The following procedure can be construed as what is generally acceptable for aluminum cylinder heads; the actual method employed should be the decision of the machinist.

The replaceable inserts can be removed by cutting them out to within a few thousandths of their outside diameter and then collapsing the remainder. Another method sometimes used to remove aluminum head seat inserts is to heat the head to a high temperature and drive the seat out.

Upon installation, the new seat may be installed with the aluminum cylinder head heated to a high temperature, then the seat, which is at room temperature or slightly chilled, is pressed into the head. The aluminum head is then allowed to cool and as it does, it contracts and grips the seat. In certain applications, the new seat may be driven in with both the head and seat at room temperature. The calculated press-fit interference will then retain the seat in the head.

Valve Guides

▶ See Figure 141

The engines covered in this guide use integral valve guides; that is, they are a part of the cylinder head and cannot be replaced. The guides can, however, be reamed oversize if they are found to be worn past an acceptable limit. Occasionally, a valve guide bore will be oversize as manufactured. These are marked on the inboard side of the cylinder heads on the machined surface just above the intake manifold.

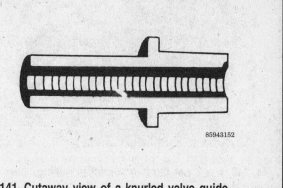

Fig. 141 Cutaway view of a knurled valve guide

If the guides must be reamed (this service is available at most machine shops) then valves with oversize stems must be fitted. Valves are usually available in 0.001 in., 0.003 in. and 0.005 in. stem oversizes. Valve guides which are not excessively worn or distorted may, in some cases, be knurled rather than reamed. Knurling is a process which the metal on the valve guide bore is displaced and raised, thereby reducing clearance. Knurling also provides excellent oil control. The option of knurling rather than reaming valve guides should be discussed with a reputable machinist or engine specialist.

Valve Lifters

REMOVAL & INSTALLATION

▶ See Figures 142, 143, 144, 145 and 146

➡Valve lifters and pushrods should be kept in order so they can be reinstalled in their original position. Some engines will have both standard size and 0.010 in. oversize valve lifters as original equipment. The oversize lifters are etched with an O on their sides; the cylinder block will also be marked with an O if the oversize lifter is used.

1. Remove the intake manifold and gasket.
2. Remove the rocker arm covers.
3. On 1988 models (roller lifters), remove the valve lifter retainer and restrictor.
4. Remove the rocker arm assemblies and pushrods.

Fig. 142 Withdraw the pushrod from the head so the valve lifter may be removed

Fig. 143 A magnet is often helpful in pulling lifters from their bores

5. If the lifters are coated with varnish, apply carburetor cleaning solvent to the lifter body. The solvent should dissolve the varnish in about 10 minutes.

6. Remove the lifters. On diesels, remove the lifter retainer guide bolts, and remove the guides. A magnet or a special tool designed for removing lifters is available, and is helpful for this procedure.

7. New lifters must be primed before installation, as dry lifters will seize when the engine is started. On the diesel lifters, submerge the lifters in clean diesel fuel or kerosene and work the lifter plunger up and down to prime. On gasoline engine lifters, submerge the lifters in SAE 10 oil, which is very thin. Carefully insert the end of a 1/8 in. (3mm) drift or an old pushrod into the lifter and push down on the plunger. Hold the plunger down while the lifter is still submerged; do not pump the plunger. Release the plunger and the lifter is now primed.

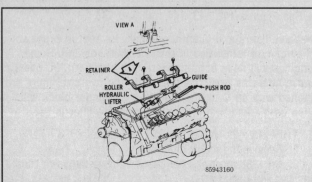

Fig. 144 Exploded view of the diesel pushrod, valve lifter guide, retainer and lifter installation

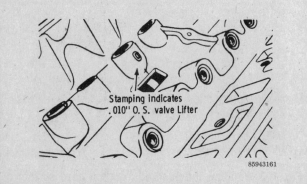

Fig. 145 Oversize valve lifter bore marking

8. Coat the bottoms of the gasoline engine lifters, and the rollers of the diesel engine lifters with Molykote® or an equivalent molybdenum-disulfide lubricant before installation. Install the lifters and pushrods into the engine in their original order. On diesels, install the lifter retainer guide.

9. Install the intake manifold gaskets and manifold.

10. Position the rocker arms, pivots and bolts on the cylinder head.

11. On 1988 models (roller lifters) install the valve lifter retainer and restrictor.

12. On the 231 V6, position and install the rockers and rocker shafts.

13. Refer to the Rocker Arm Removal and Installation procedure earlier in this section for lifter bleed-down. New lifters must be bled-down on diesel engines; valve-to-piston contact could occur if this procedure is neglected.

➡An additive containing EP lube, such as EOS, should always be added to crankcase oil for break-in when new lifters or a new camshaft is installed. This additive is generally available in automotive parts stores.

14. Once all valves are properly adjusted, install the rocker arm covers.

Oil Pan

REMOVAL & INSTALLATION

◗ **See Figures 147 and 148**

Inline 6-Cylinder

➡Pan removal for all engines may be easier if the engine is turned to No. 1 cylinder firing position. This positions the crankshaft in the path of least resistance for pan removal.

1. Disconnect the battery ground cable.

2. Remove the upper radiator mounting bolts or side mount bolt.

3. Position a drain pan to catch any escaping fluid, then remove the upper and lower hoses for the water pump.

4. Install a piece of heavy cardboard between the fan and the radiator in order to protect the components.

5. Disconnect the fuel suction line from the fuel pump.

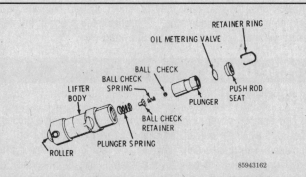

Fig. 146 Exploded view of a roller type hydraulic valve lifter

6. Raise and support the vehicle safely using jackstands, then drain the oil.

7. Remove the starter assembly.

8. Remove the flywheel lower pan or converter lower pan and splash shield.

9. Rotate the crankshaft until the timing mark on the damper is at the six o'clock position.

10. Remove the brake line retaining bolts from the crossmember and move the brake line out of the way.

11. Remove the through-bolts from the front motor mounts.

12. Remove the oil pan bolts.

13. Slowly raise the engine until the motor mounts can be removed from the frame brackets.

14. Remove the mounts and continue to raise the engine until it has been raised three inches. Make sure that none of the engine mounted components are damaged by contact with the vehicle's body or frame.

15. Remove the oil pan by pulling it down from the engine and then twisting it into the opening left by the removal of the left engine mount.

16. When the pan is clear of the engine, tilt the front up and remove it by pulling it down and to the rear.

To install:

17. Thoroughly clean the gasket mating surfaces.

18. Install the oil pan to the engine block by reversing the tilting necessary to remove it. Be sure to use a new gasket during installation.

19. Install the oil pan retaining bolts, then torque the side bolts to 6-8 ft.lbs. (8-11 Nm) and the end bolts to 9-12 ft. lbs. (12-16 Nm).

20. Install the motor mounts, then carefully lower the engine into position and install the mount through-bolts.

21. Reposition the brake line and install the brake line retaining bolts to the crossmember.

22. Install the flywheel lower pan or converter lower pan and splash shield.

23. Install the starter assembly.

24. Make sure the oil pan drain plug is installed, then remove the jackstands and carefully lower the vehicle.

25. Fill the engine crankcase with the proper amount of clean engine oil. This should be done right away to eliminate the danger of forgetting it later and attempting to start a dry engine.

26. Connect the fuel suction line to the fuel pump.

27. Remove the cardboard from between the fan and the radiator.

28. Connect the upper and lower hoses to the water pump.

29. Install the upper radiator mounting bolts or side mount bolt.

30. Connect the negative battery cable.

31. Check the engine oil level and add, as necessary.

32. Run the engine and check for leaks, then check and top off the coolant, as necessary.

V8 Engines

1964-68

1. Remove the engine from the chassis.
2. Remove the bellhousing or converter underpan.
3. Remove the starter assembly.
4. Remove the oil pan retaining bolts, then remove the pan from the engine block.

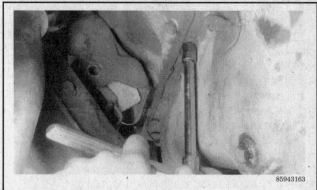

Fig. 147 Loosen and remove the oil pan retaining bolts

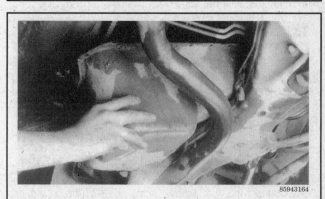

Fig. 148 Tilt and lower the oil pan from the engine

To install:

5. Using a new gasket and/or sealer, as applicable, install the oil pan to the engine block and secure using the retaining bolts.

6. Install the starter assembly.

7. Install the bellhousing or converter underpan.

8. Install the engine to the chassis.

1969 WITH 8-396 ,1969 WITH MANUAL TRANSMISSION OR 1970-72 WITH 8-396 AND 8-402

1. Disconnect the negative battery cable.

2. Remove the air cleaner, dipstick, distributor cap, radiator shroud and upper mounting panel.

3. On big block models, place a piece of heavy cardboard between the radiator and the fan in order to protect the components.

4. Disconnect the engine ground straps. Remove the fuel pump on 307 and 350 engines.

5. Disconnect the accelerator control cable.

6. Drain the engine oil. Remove the filter on 307 and 350 engines.

7. Remove the driveshaft and plug the rear of transmission.

8. Remove the starter assembly.

9. Disconnect the transmission linkage at the transmission or remove the floorshift lever.

10. Disengage the speedometer cable and the back-up switch connector.

11. On manual transmission vehicles, disconnect the clutch cross-shaft at the frame. On automatic transmission vehicles, disconnect the cooler lines, detent cable, rod or switch wire, and the modulator pipe.

12. Remove the crossmember bolts. Jack up the engine and move the crossmember rearward.

13. Disconnect the dual exhaust pipes or remove the crossover.

14. Remove the flywheel housing cover.

15. Remove the transmission assembly.

16. Remove the flywheel housing and throwout bearing (manual transmission only).

17. Remove the front engine mount through-bolts.

18. Raise the rear of the engine approximately 4 in. and support the engine using a hoist.

19. Raise the front of the engine approximately 4 in. and insert 2 in. blocks under the front engine mounts.

20. Rotate the crankshaft until the timing mark on the torsional damper is at the six o'clock position.

21. Unbolt and remove the oil pan.

To install:

22. Thoroughly clean the gasket mating surfaces.

23. Using a new gasket and/or sealer, as applicable, install the oil pan to the engine block and secure using the retaining bolts.

24. Remove the blocks and lower the engine into position, then install the engine mount through-bolts.

25. Install the flywheel housing and throwout bearing (manual transmission only).

26. Install the transmission assembly.

27. Install the flywheel housing cover.

28. Connect the dual exhaust pipes or install the crossover.

29. Reposition and secure the crossmember using the retaining bolts. If necessary, jack up the engine slightly for the necessary clearance.

30. On manual transmission vehicles, connect the clutch cross-shaft at the frame.

31. On automatic transmission vehicles, connect the cooler lines, detent cable, rod or switch wire, and the modulator pipe.

32. Engage the speedometer cable and the back-up switch connector.

33. Connect the transmission linkage at the transmission or install the floorshift lever.

34. Install the starter assembly.

35. Install the driveshaft and plug the rear of transmission.

36. For 307 and 350 engines, install a new oil filter.

37. Refill the engine crankcase with oil.

38. Connect the accelerator control cable.

39. Connect the engine ground straps.

40. For 307 and 350 engines, install the fuel pump assembly.

41. If applicable, remove the cardboard from between the radiator and the fan.

42. Install the air cleaner, dipstick, distributor cap, radiator shroud and upper mounting panel.

43. Connect the negative battery cable.

44. Run the engine and check for leaks.

1969-78

1. Disconnect the negative battery cable.

2. As a precaution, remove the distributor cap to keep it from breaking from contact with the firewall when the engine is raised.

3. Remove the fan shroud retaining bolts.

4. On earlier models, it may be necessary to remove the radiator upper mounting panel.

5. Raise and support the vehicle safely using jackstands, then drain the engine oil.

6. Disconnect the exhaust pipes or crossover pipes.

7. On automatic transmission equipped vehicles, remove the converter housing underpan and splash shield.

8. Rotate the crankshaft until the timing mark on the torsional dampener is at the six o'clock position.

9. The starter can be swung out of the way by disconnecting the brace at the starter, removing the inboard starter bolt and loosening the outboard starter bolts. On 1970 small block V8 engines, remove the fuel pump.

10. Remove the front engine mount through-bolts.

11. Raise the engine and insert blocks, at least 3 inches thick, under the engine mounts.

12. Remove the oil pan bolts and remove the oil pan.

To install:

13. Thoroughly clean the gasket and seal surfaces .

➡ **If the crankshaft was rotated while the pan was off, place the timing mark at the six o'clock position.**

14. Install the oil pan to the engine using new gaskets and seals.

15. Remove the blocks and carefully lower the engine, then install the front engine mount through-bolts.

16. Swing the starter back into position and secure.

17. On 1970 small block V8 engines, install the fuel pump.

18. On automatic transmission equipped vehicles, install the converter housing underpan and splash shield.

19. Connect the exhaust pipes or crossover pipes.

20. Make sure the oil pan drain plug is installed, then remove the jackstands and carefully lower the vehicle.

21. Refill the engine crankcase with clean oil right away. This will prevent an accidental attempt to start a dry engine.

22. If removed, install the radiator upper mounting panel.

23. Install the fan shroud retaining bolts.

24. Install the distributor cap.

25. Connect the negative battery cable.

26. Run the engine and check for leaks.

1979-88

1. Disconnect the negative battery cable.

2. Remove the air cleaner assembly, the upper radiator mounting panel and the fan shroud.

3. Raise and support the vehicle safely using jackstands. Drain the oil from the engine.

4. Remove the distributor cap and the fan assembly.

5. If equipped, disconnect the AIR hose from the converter pipe and the AIR pipe from the exhaust manifold.

6. Remove the exhaust crossover pipe from the manifold and the catalytic converter.

➡ **On some models, it may be necessary to remove the starter.**

7. If equipped with an automatic transmission, remove torque converter housing cover plate and disconnect the transmission oil cooler lines at the oil pan.

8. If equipped with a manual transmission, remove the starter and the flywheel housing cover plate.

9. Rotate crankshaft until timing mark on torsional damper is at 6 o'clock position, this positions the crankshaft throw in the horizontal place.

10. Remove front engine mount through bolts.

11. Carefully raise the engine and insert blocks under engine mounts.

➡ **The block thickness should be 3 in.**

12. Remove the oil pan bolts and lower the pan from the engine block.

To install:

13. Using a putty knife, clean the gasket mounting surfaces.

14. Install the oil pan using a new gasket and sealant, then torque the oil pan bolts to 7 ft. lbs. (9 Nm).

15. Remove the blocks and carefully lower the engine, then install the engine mount bolts and tighten to 50 ft. lbs. (68 Nm).

16. If equipped with a manual transmission, install the starter and the flywheel housing cover plate.

17. If equipped with an automatic transmission, install the torque converter housing cover plate and connect the transmission oil cooler lines at the oil pan.

18. Install the exhaust crossover pipe to the manifold and the catalytic converter.

19. If removed, install the starter assembly.

20. If equipped, connect the AIR hose to the converter pipe and the AIR pipe to the exhaust manifold.

21. Install the distributor cap and the fan assembly.

22. Make sure the drain plug is installed in the oil pan, then remove the jackstands and carefully lower the vehicle.

23. Refill the engine crankcase with clean oil right away. This will prevent an accidental attempt to start a dry engine.

24. Install the air cleaner assembly, the upper radiator mounting panel and the fan shroud.

25. Connect the negative battery cable.

26. Run the engine and check for leaks.

V6 Engines

1. Disconnect the negative battery cable.

2. Remove the upper half of the radiator fan shroud.

3. Raise the front of the vehicle and support safely using jackstands, then drain the engine oil.

4. Unscrew the exhaust pipe cross-over tube mounting nuts at the manifold. Lower the crossover tube.

5. On models which are equipped with an automatic transmission, remove the torque converter cover, and the oil cooler lines at the oil pan.

6. Remove the upper bolt on the starter brace and then remove the inboard starter bolt ad swing the starter assembly aside.

7. If equipped with Air Injection Reaction (AIR) system, disconnect the AIR hose from the converter pipe and the AIR pipe from the exhaust manifold.

8. Loosen and remove the left hand motor mount through-bolt and then loosen the through-bolt on the right hand mount.

9. Raise the engine and then reinstall the through-bolt in the left hand motor mount. Do not tighten the bolt.

10. Unscrew the attaching bolts and remove the oil pan from under the engine.

To install:

11. Thoroughly clean the gasket and seal surfaces.

12. Install the oil pan to the engine using new gaskets and seals.

13. Remove the left motor mount through bolt, carefully lower the engine into position.

14. Install and tighten the motor mount through-bolts.

15. If equipped with Air Injection Reaction (AIR) system, connect the AIR hose to the converter pipe and the AIR pipe to the exhaust manifold.

16. Swing the starter assembly into position and secure.

17. On models which are equipped with an automatic transmission, install the torque converter cover, and connect the oil cooler lines to the oil pan.

18. Reposition the crossover tube, then secure using the mounting nuts.

19. Make sure the oil pan drain plug is installed, then remove the jackstands and carefully lower the vehicle.

20. Refill the engine crankcase with clean oil. This should be done right away in order to prevent an accidental attempt to start a dry engine.

21. Install the upper half of the radiator fan shroud.

22. Connect the negative battery cable, then run the engine and check for leaks.

Diesel Engines

▶ **See Figure 149**

1. Disconnect the batteries and remove the dipstick.

2. Remove the vacuum pump and drive (with air conditioning) or the oil pump drive (without air conditioning).

3. Remove the upper radiator support and fan shroud.

4. Raise and support the vehicle safely using jackstands, then drain the engine oil from the crankcase.

5. Remove the flywheel cover.

6. Disconnect the exhaust and crossover pipes.

7. Remove the oil cooler lines at the filter base.

8. Remove the starter assembly. Support the engine with a jack.

9. Remove the engine mounts from the block.

10. Raise the front of the engine and remove the oil pan.

To install:

11. Thoroughly clean the gasket and seal surfaces.

12. Install the oil pan to the engine using new gaskets and seals.

13. Lower the front of the engine and secure the engine mounts to the block.

14. Remove the engine support jack, then install the starter assembly.

15. Install the oil cooler lines at the filter base.

16. Connect the exhaust and crossover pipes.

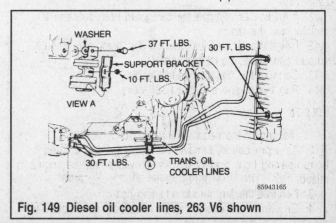

Fig. 149 Diesel oil cooler lines, 263 V6 shown

85943165

17. Install the flywheel cover.

18. Make sure the oil drain plug is installed, then remove the jackstands and carefully lower the vehicle.

19. Immediately refill the engine crankcase with clean oil. This will prevent an accidental attempt to start a dry engine.

20. Install the upper radiator support and fan shroud.

21. Install the vacuum pump and drive (with air conditioning) or the oil pump drive (without air conditioning).

22. Install the dipstick and connect the batteries.

23. Run the engine and check for leaks.

Oil Pump

REMOVAL & INSTALLATION

▶ **See Figure 150**

In Line 6-Cylinder

1. Remove the oil pan as described earlier in this section.

2. Remove the two flange mounting bolts along with the pick-up bolt, then remove the pump and screen together.

To install:

3. Align the oil pump driveshafts to match with the distributor tang and position the flange over the distributor lower bushing.

4. Support the pump in this position, then install and tighten the pump mounting bolts.

5. Install the oil pan to the engine block.

Gasoline and Diesel V6 and V8 (Except 231 V6)

1. Remove the oil pan as described earlier in this section.

2. Remove the pump-to-rear main bearing cap bolts and remove the pump and extension shaft.

To install:

3. Align the slot on the top end of the extension shaft with the drive tang on the lower end of the distributor driveshaft (or until the shaft mates into the oil pump drive gear on diesels) and install the rear main bearing cap bolts.

4. Position the pump screen so that the bottom edge is parallel to the oil pan rails.

5. Install the oil pan to the engine block.

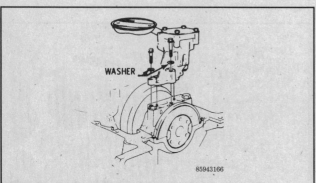

WASHER

85943166

Fig. 150 Typical oil pump installation — V6 diesel engine shown

231 V6

The oil pump is located in the timing chain cover and is connected by a drilled passage to the oil screen housing and pipe assembly in the oil pan. All oil is discharged from the pump to the oil pump cover assembly, on which the oil filter is mounted.

1. For access to the oil pump cover and gears, first remove the oil filter.

2. Remove the screws which attach the oil pump cover assembly to the timing chain cover.

3. Remove the cover assembly and slide out the oil pump gears. Clean the gears and inspect them for any obvious defects such as chipping or scoring.

4. Remove the oil pressure relief valve cap, spring and valve. Clean them and inspect them for wear or scoring. Check the relief valve spring to see that it is not worn on its side or collapsed. Replace the spring if it seems questionable.

5. Check the relief valve for a correct fit in its bore. It should be an easy slip fit and no more. If any perceptible shake can be felt, the valve and/or cover should be replaced.

To install:

6. Lubricate the pressure relief valve and spring and place them in the cover. Install the cap and the gasket. Torque the cap to 35 ft. lbs. (47 Nm).

7. Pack the oil pump gear cavity full of petroleum jelly. Do not use gear lube. Reinstall the oil pump gears so that the petroleum jelly is forced into every cavity of the gear pocket, and between the gear teeth. There must be no air spaces. This step is very important. Unless the pump is packed, it may not begin to pump oil as soon as the engine is started.

8. Install the cover assembly using a new gasket and sealer. Tighten the screws to 10 ft. lbs. (14 Nm).

9. Install the oil filter.

INSPECTION & OVERHAUL

▶ **See Figures 151, 152 and 153**

231 V6 Engine

The oil pump is located in the timing chain cover and is connected by a drilled passage to the oil screen housing and pipe assembly in the oil pan. All oil is discharged from the pump to the oil pump cover assembly, on which the oil filter is mounted.

1. For access to the oil pump cover and gears, first remove the oil filter.

2. Remove the screws which attach the oil pump cover assembly to the timing chain cover.

3. Remove the cover assembly and slide out the oil pump gears. Clean the gears and inspect them for any obvious defects such as chipping or scoring.

4. Remove the oil pressure relief valve cap, spring and valve. Clean them and inspect them for wear or scoring. Check the relief valve spring to see that it is not worn on its side or collapsed. Replace the spring if it seems questionable.

5. Check the relief valve for a correct fit in its bore. It should be an easy slip fit and no more. If any perceptible shake can be felt the valve and/or the cover should be replaced.

6. Install the oil pump gears (if removed) and the shaft in the oil pump body section of the timing chain cover to check the gear end clearance and gear side clearance. Check gear end clearance by placing a straight edge over the gears and measure the clearance between the straight edge and the gasket surface. Clearance should be between 0.002-0.006 in. Check gear side clearance by inserting the feeler gauge between the gear teeth and the side wall of the pump body. Clearance should be between 0.002-0.005 in.

7. Check the pump cover flatness by placing a straight edge across the cover face, with the feeler gauge between the straight edge and the cover. If clearance is 0.001 in. or more, replace the cover.

8. To install, lubricate the pressure relief valve and spring and place them in the cover. Install the cap and the gasket. Torque the cap to 35 ft. lbs. (47 Nm).

9. Pack the oil pump gear cavity full of petroleum jelly. Do not use gear lube. Reinstall the oil pump gears so that the petroleum jelly is forced into every cavity of the gear pocket, and between the gear teeth. There must be no air spaces. This step is very important.

❊❊WARNING

Unless the pump is primed this way, it may not produce any oil pressure when the engine is started.

10. Install the cover assembly using a new gasket and sealer. Tighten the screws to 10 ft. lbs. (14 Nm).
11. Install the oil filter.

Gasoline and Diesel V6 and V8 (Except 231 V6)

1. Remove the oil pump drive shaft extension.
2. Remove the cotter pin, spring and the pressure regulator valve.

➡**Place your thumb over the regulator bore before removing the cotter pin, as the spring is under pressure.**

3. Remove the oil pump cover attaching screws and remove the oil pump cover and gasket. Clean the pump in solvent or kerosene, and wash out the pick-up screen.
4. Remove the drive gear and idler gear from the pump body.
5. Check the gears for scoring and other damage. Install the gears if in good condition, or replace them if damaged. Check gear end clearance by placing a straight edge over the gears and measure the clearance between the straight edge

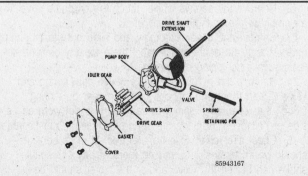

Fig. 151 Exploded view of a common oil pump assembly

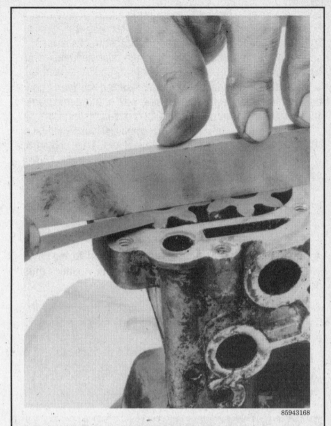

Fig. 152 Checking oil pump gear end clearance

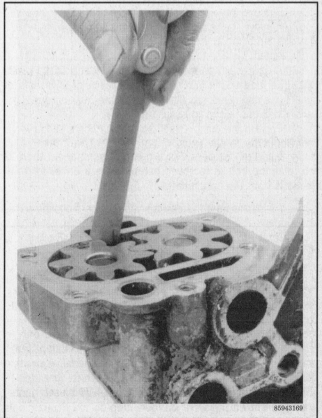

Fig. 153 Checking oil pump gear side clearance

and the gasket surface with a feeler gauge. End clearance for both diesels is 0.0005-0.0075 in. and other V8s is 0.002-0.0065 in. If end clearance is excessive, check for scores in the cover that would bring the total clearance over specification.

6. Check gear side clearance by inserting the feeler gauge between the gear teeth and the side wall of the pump body. Clearance should be between 0.002-0.005 in.

7. Pack the inside of the pump completely with petroleum jelly. DO NOT use engine oil The pump MUST be primed this way or it may not produce any oil pressure when the engine is started.

8. Install the cover screws and tighten alternately and evenly to 8 ft. lbs. (11 Nm).

9. Position the pressure regulator valve into the pump cover, closed end first, then install the spring and retaining pin.

➡**When assembling the driveshaft extension to the drive shaft, the end of the extension nearest the washers must be inserted into the drive shaft.**

10. Insert the driveshaft extension through the opening in the main bearing cap and block until the shaft mates into the distributor drive gear.

11. Install the pump onto the rear main bearing cap and install the attaching bolts. Torque the bolts to 35 ft. lbs. (47 Nm).

12. Install the oil pan to the engine block.

Crankshaft Damper

REMOVAL & INSTALLATION

▶ **See Figures 154, 155, 156 and 157**

1. Disconnect the negative battery cable.
2. Loosen and remove the drive belts from the crankshaft damper.
3. If necessary for access, remove the fan and pulley assembly from the water pump.

➡**Some early model vehicles are equipped with press fit pulleys and/or dampers. For a press fit component there is no retaining bolt to removed before using a puller to remove it from the crankshaft.**

4. If separate from the damper, remove the mounting bolts, then remove the crankshaft pulley from the damper.

5. Spray the damper bolt with penetrating oil and allow it to soak in for at least a few minutes. Loosen and remove the crankshaft damper bolt.

➡**If damper bolt removal is difficult, various methods may be used to hold the crankshaft while loosening or tightening the bolt. One method involves installing a flywheel holding fixture. Another method which can be used on manual transmission vehicles is to have an assistant put the vehicle in gear and depress the brake pedal. A holding tool may be available for some dampers which threads into the pulley bolt holes. But most of all, allow the penetrating oil to do the work on loosening an old damper bolt and reapply oil, as necessary.**

6. Remove the damper from the end of the crankshaft using a suitable threaded damper puller, NOT a jawed-type puller which would most likely destroy the damper.

✳✳WARNING

The use of any other type of puller, such as a universal claw type which pulls on the outside of the hub, can destroy the balancer. The outside ring of the balancer is bonded in rubber to the hub. Pulling on the outside will break the bond.

To install:

7. If removal of the damper was difficult, check the damper inner diameter and the crankshaft outer diameter for corrosion. A small amount of corrosion may be removed using steel wool, then the surface may be lubricated slightly with clean engine oil.

8. Coat the front cover seal contact edge of the damper lightly with clean engine oil, then install the damper on the end of the crankshaft. Do not hammer the damper into position, instead use a damper installation tool to slowly draw the hub into position. If the damper can be positioned far enough over the end of the crankshaft, the damper bolt may be used to draw it into position, but be careful that enough of the threads are in contact to prevent stripping the bolt or crankshaft.

9. Once the damper is fully seated, install and tighten the retaining bolt to specification.

10. If separate, install and secure the damper pulley.

11. If removed, install the fan and pulley to the water pump.

12. Install the drive belts to the crankshaft pulley, then adjust their tension.

13. Connect the negative battery cable.

Timing Gear Cover

REMOVAL & INSTALLATION

▶ **See Figures 158, 159, 160, 161, 162, 163 and 164**

Inline 6-Cylinder

1. Disconnect the negative battery cable.
2. For 1964-72 models, raise and support the vehicle safely using jackstands, then drain the engine oil and remove the oil pan.

85943170

Fig. 154 Remove the pulley from the crankshaft damper

Fig. 155 Use a threaded damper puller to draw the hub from the end of the crankshaft. If equipped, use the end cap attachment to keep the puller center bolt from damaging the crankshaft threads

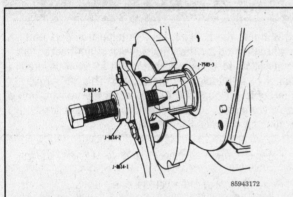

Fig. 156 Cutaway view of a GM damper puller assembly

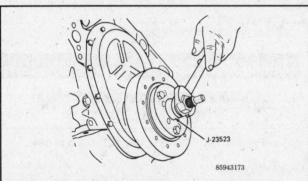

Fig. 157 Use a damper installer to push the hub into position on the crankshaft

3. Drain the engine cooling system, then remove the radiator from the vehicle.

✳✳CAUTION

When draining the coolant, keep in mind that cats and dogs are attracted by the ethylene glycol antifreeze, and are quite likely to drink any that is left in an uncovered container or in puddles on the ground. This will prove fatal in sufficient quantity. Always drain the coolant into a sealable container. Coolant should be reused unless it is contaminated or several years old.

4. Remove the fan, pulley, and belt. Remove any power steering and/or AIR pump drive belts. Remove any braces for

the above pumps which will interfere with cover removal and position the pumps out of the way.

5. Remove the crankshaft pulley and damper. Use the puller tool No. J-16516 to remove the damper. Do NOT attempt to pry or hammer the damper off, or it will be damaged.

6. Remove the retaining bolts, then for 1964-72 models, remove the front cover.

7. On 1973-79 models, pull the cover forward slightly and cut the oil pan front seal off flush with the block. Remove the cover. On installation, be sure to cut the tabs off a new oil pan front seal and install it on the cover.

To install:

8. Thoroughly clean the gasket mating surfaces, then check and if necessary, replace the front cover oil seal.

9. Install the front cover to the engine using a new gasket. Coat the gasket with sealer and use a 1/8 in. bead of silicone sealer at the oil pan-to-cylinder block joint. Install the damper before tightening the cover bolts down, so that the cover seal will align. The damper must be drawn into place as hammering it into position will likely destroy it.

➡When installing the timing cover, place the centering tool J-23042 inside the oil seal, slide the timing cover into position, install 2 screws and remove the tool.

10. Install any braces for the power steering and/or AIR pumps which were removed for access.

11. Install the engine cooling fan and pulley, then install the drive belts and adjust their tension.

12. Install the radiator to the vehicle.

13. If removed, install the oil pan, then remove the jackstands and carefully lower the vehicle.

14. Check and add clean engine oil, as necessary.

15. Connect the negative battery cable, then properly fill the engine cooling system.

V6 and V8 Except 231

1964-74 (EXCEPT 231)

1. Disconnect the negative battery cable.

2. Raise and support the vehicle safely using jackstands, then drain the engine oil.

3. Except for 1974 and later small block engines, remove the oil pan.

4. Drain the engine cooling system and remove the radiator assembly from the vehicle.

✳✳CAUTION

When draining the coolant, keep in mind that cats and dogs are attracted by the ethylene glycol antifreeze, and are quite likely to drink any that is left in an uncovered container or in puddles on the ground. This will prove fatal in sufficient quantity. Always drain the coolant into a sealable container. Coolant should be reused unless it is contaminated or several years old.

5. Remove the fan, pulley, and belt. Remove any power steering and/or AIR pump drive belts. Remove any braces for these pumps which will interfere with cover removal and position the pumps out of the way.

6. Remove the water pump assembly.

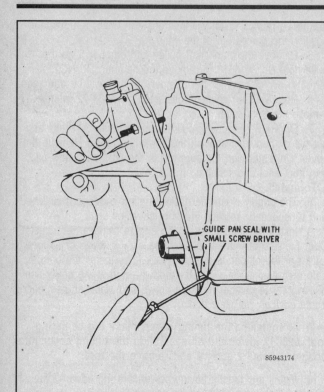

Fig. 158 On most applications the front cover must be carefully guided into place in order to assure a proper seal between the cover and the oil pan

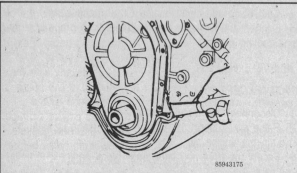

Fig. 159 On some applications, the oil pan seal should be cut flush with the front of the engine block

7. Remove the crankshaft pulley and damper. Use a puller on the damper. Do not attempt to pry or hammer the damper off.

8. Remove the retaining bolts, the carefully remove the timing cover from the front of the engine block.

To install:

9. Thoroughly clean the gasket mating surfaces, then check and if necessary, replace the front cover oil seal.

10. Install the front cover to the engine using a new gasket. Apply a 1/8 in. bead of silicone rubber sealer to the oil pan and cylinder block joint faces. Lightly coat the bottom of the seal with engine oil.

11. Install the crankshaft damper and pulley to the engine.

12. Install the water pump assembly.

13. Install any braces for the power steering and/or AIR pumps which were removed for access.

14. Install the engine cooling fan and pulley, then install the drive belts and adjust their tension.

15. Install the radiator assembly to the vehicle.

16. If removed, install the oil pan assembly, then remove the jackstands and carefully lower the vehicle.

17. Check and add clean engine oil, as necessary.

18. Connect the negative battery cable, then properly fill the engine cooling system.

1975-88 (EXCEPT 231)

1. Disconnect the negative battery cable and drain the cooling system.

✻✻CAUTION

When draining the coolant, keep in mind that cats and dogs are attracted by the ethylene glycol antifreeze, and are quite likely to drink any that is left in an uncovered container or in puddles on the ground. This will prove fatal in sufficient quantity. Always drain the coolant into a sealable container. Coolant should be reused unless it is contaminated or several years old.

2. Remove the fan assembly, the drive belts and the fan pulley.

3. Raise and support the vehicle safely using jackstands.

4. Remove the alternator and the brackets. If equipped with power steering, remove the lower pump bracket and swing aside.

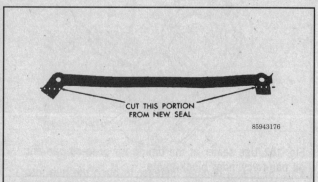

Fig. 160 When the timing gear cover is replaced on most engine, the oil pan front seal must be modified

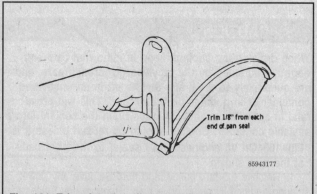

Fig. 161 Trimming the oil pan seal using a razor blade

5. Disconnect the heater and the lower radiator hoses from the water pump.

6. Remove the water pump bolts, then remove the pump from the engine.

7. Remove the crankshaft pulley and the damper pulley bolt.

8. Using tool J-23523, remove the damper pulley.

9. Remove the timing cover bolts and carefully remove the timing cover from the front of the engine block.

To install:

10. Thoroughly clean the gasket mating surfaces, then check and if necessary, replace the front cover oil seal.

11. Install the front cover to the engine using a new gasket, then tighten the timing cover retaining bolts to 8 ft. lbs. (11 Nm).

12. Install the crankshaft damper and pulley to the engine.

13. Install the water pump assembly to the engine, then connect the hoses.

14. Install the alternator and brackets to the engine. If equipped with power steering reposition and secure the pump using the lower bracket.

15. Remove the jackstands and carefully lower the vehicle.

16. Install the water pump pulley and fan, then install the drive belts and adjust their tension.

17. Check and add clean engine oil, as necessary.

18. Connect the negative battery cable, then properly refill the engine cooling system.

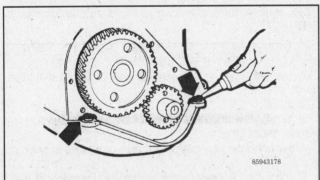

Fig. 162 Use sealer at the timing cover-to-oil pan and oil pan-to-cylinder block joints

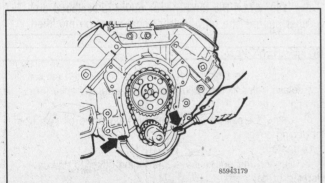

Fig. 163 On V8 engines, apply sealer to the front pads at the area shown

231 V6

1. Disconnect the negative battery cable.

2. Drain the cooling system and disconnect the radiator hoses, then remove the radiator.

> **✳✳CAUTION**
>
> **When draining the coolant, keep in mind that cats and dogs are attracted by the ethylene glycol antifreeze, and are quite likely to drink any that is left in an uncovered container or in puddles on the ground. This will prove fatal in sufficient quantity. Always drain the coolant into a sealable container. Coolant should be reused unless it is contaminated or several years old.**

3. Loosen and remove all the drive belts, then remove the fan and fan pulley. Remove the bypass hose.

4. Remove the crankshaft pulley, the fuel pump and the distributor. Scribe matchmarks for the distributor housing and rotor before removal.

5. Remove the alternator and its bracket.

6. Remove the harmonic balancer using a suitable damper puller. DO NOT use a jawed-type puller.

7. Remove the two bolts which attach the oil pan to the front cover. Remove the bolts which attach the cover to the block, then carefully remove the cover from the front of the engine.

To install:

8. Thoroughly clean the mating surfaces of any remaining gasket or sealer.

9. Before installing the timing cover, it is first necessary to remove the oil pump cover and pack the space around the oil pump gears completely full of petroleum jelly. Do not use gear lube. There must be no air space left inside the pump. Reinstall the pump cover using a new gasket. This step is very important since the oil pump may lose its prime any time the pump, pump cover or timing cover is disturbed. If the pump is not packed, it may not begin to pump oil as soon as the engine is started which could result in serious engine damage.

10. Install the front cover, using a sealer and new gaskets. Make sure the dowel pins engage the dowel pin holes before starting the bolts. Apply sealer to the bolt threads.

11. Install the harmonic balancer, bolt and washer. It will be necessary to lock the flywheel in some way to torque the balancer bolt to specifications. Most mechanics remove the flywheel cover and lock the flywheel with suitable locking device.

12. Install the alternator and bracket assembly.

13. Install the distributor, aligning the matchmarks made earlier for the housing and for the rotor.

14. Install the fuel pump, then install the crankshaft pulley.

15. Connect the bypass hose.

16. Install the water pump fan and pulley, then install the drive belts and adjust their tension.

17. Install the radiator assembly and connect the hoses.

18. Check and add clean engine oil, as necessary.

19. Connect the negative battery cable, then properly refill the engine cooling system.

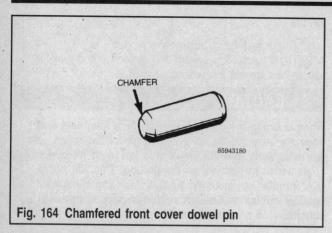

CHAMFER

85943180

Fig. 164 Chamfered front cover dowel pin

V6 and V8 Diesel Engines

1. Drain the cooling system and disconnect the radiator hoses.

❋❋CAUTION

When draining the coolant, keep in mind that cats and dogs are attracted by the ethylene glycol antifreeze, and are quite likely to drink any that is left in an uncovered container or in puddles on the ground. This will prove fatal in sufficient quantity. Always drain the coolant into a sealable container. Coolant should be reused unless it is contaminated or several years old.

2. Remove all belts, then remove the water pump fan and pulley.

3. Remove the crankshaft pulley and balancer, using a balancer puller.

❋❋WARNING

The use of any other type of puller, such as a universal claw type which pulls on the outside of the hub, can destroy the balancer. The outside ring of the balancer is bonded in rubber to the hub. Pulling on the outside will break the bond. The timing mark is on the outside ring. If it is suspected that the bond is broken, check that the center of the keyway is 16 degrees from the center of the timing slot. In addition, there are chiseled aligning marks between the weight and the hub.

4. Unbolt and remove the cover, timing indicator, water pump and both dowel pins. It may be necessary to grind a flat on the cover for gripping purposes.

To install:

5. Grind a chamfer on one end of each dowel pin.

6. Cut the excess material from the front end of the oil pan gasket on each side of the block.

7. Clean the block, oil pan and front cover mating surfaces with solvent.

8. Trim about 1/8 in. off each end of a new front pan seal.

9. Install a new front cover gasket on the block and a new seal in the front cover.

10. Apply an R.T.V. sealer to the gasket around the coolant holes.

11. Apply an R.T.V. sealer to the block at the junction of the pan and front cover.

12. Place the cover on the block and press down to compress the seal. Rotate the cover left and right and guide the pan seal into the cavity using a small screwdriver. Oil the bolt threads and install two bolts to hold the cover in place. Install both dowel pins (chamfered end first), then install the remaining front cover bolts.

➡ **The front cover-to-block bolts on the V6 diesel must be coated with an adhesive, GM part # 1052624 or equivalent to avoid coolant leaks and loss of bolt torque.**

13. Apply a lubricant, compatible with rubber, on the balancer seal surface.

14. Install the balancer and pulley. Torque the damper bolt to 271-420 ft. lbs. (367-569 Nm) for the V8 engine or to 160-350 ft. lbs. (217-474 Nm) on V6 engines.

15. Install the water pump fan and pulley.

16. Install the drive belts and adjust their tension.

17. Connect the radiator hoses.

18. Properly refill the engine cooling system.

Timing Cover Oil Seal

REMOVAL & INSTALLATION

◆ **See Figures 165, 166, 167 and 168**

Inline 6-Cylinder

1. Remove the timing cover from the engine. For details, refer to the timing cover procedure earlier in this section.

2. Using a small pry bar, carefully remove the oil seal from the timing cover.

To install:

3. Support the underside of the timing cover to prevent warping or damage.

4. Lubricate the new seal with a light coat of clean engine oil.

5. Place the new seal's open end toward the inside of the cover, then drive the seal into position using the oil seal installation tool J-23042 or an equivalent sized driver.

6. Install the timing cover to the front of the engine.

V6 and V8

COVER REMOVED

1. Remove the timing cover from the front of the engine. For details, refer to the timing cover procedures earlier in this section.

2. Using a small pry bar, carefully remove the oil seal from the timing cover.

To install:

3. Support the underside of the timing cover to prevent warping or damage.

4. Lubricate the new seal with a light coat of clean engine oil.

5. Place the new seal's open end toward the inside of the cover, then drive the seal into position using the oil seal installation tool J-23042 or an equivalent sized driver.

6. Install the timing cover to the front of the engine.

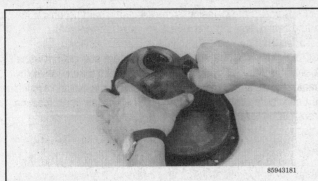

Fig. 165 Carefully pry the old seal from the front of the timing cover

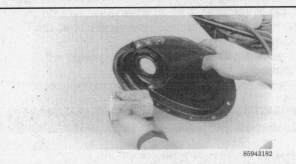

Fig. 166 Support the rear of the timing cover (in this case with a small block of wood) in order to prevent cover damage

Fig. 167 Drive the seal into the cover using a suitable driver. If using a socket or pipe, be sure that the end touching the seal is smooth and will not tear or damage the seal.

COVER INSTALLED

1. Remove the crankshaft damper from the engine. For details, refer to the crankshaft damper procedure earlier in this section.

2. Using a small pry bar, carefully remove the oil seal from the timing cover. Take extra care to prevent scoring and damaging the end of the crankshaft.

To install:

3. Lubricate the new seal with a light coat of clean engine oil.

4. Place the new seal (open end toward the engine) on the timing cover and carefully drive it into the cover using tool J-23042.

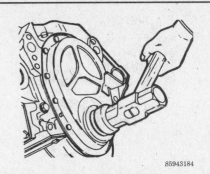

Fig. 168 Oil seal installation with the front cover installed

5. Install the crankshaft damper to the engine.

Timing Gear

REMOVAL & INSTALLATION

▶ See Figure 169

Inline 6-Cylinder

➡The timing gear is pressed onto the camshaft. An arbor must be used to remove or install the timing gear.

1. Remove the camshaft from the engine. For details, refer to the camshaft removal procedure found later in this section.

2. Using an arbor press, a press plate and gear removal tool J-971 (or equivalent), press the timing gear from the camshaft.

➡When pressing the timing gear from the camshaft, be certain that the position of the press plate does not contact the woodruff key.

To install:

3. Position the press plate to support the camshaft at the back of the front journal. Place the gear spacer ring and the thrust plate over the end of the camshaft, then install the woodruff key. Press the timing gear onto the camshaft, until it bottoms against the gear spacer ring.

➡The end clearance of the thrust plate should be 0.0015-0.005 in. If less than 0.0015 in., replace the thrust plate.

4. Align the timing marks and install the camshaft.

Timing Chain

REMOVAL & INSTALLATION

▶ See Figures 170, 171, 172, 173, 174, 175 and 176

231 V6

1. Remove the timing chain cover. For details, refer to the procedure earlier in this section.

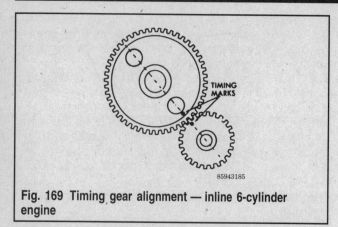

Fig. 169 Timing gear alignment — inline 6-cylinder engine

2. Before removing anything else, make sure the timing marks on the crankshaft and camshaft sprockets are aligned. This will greatly ease reinstallation of parts.

➡It is not necessary to remove the timing chain tensioners unless they are worn or damaged.

3. Remove the front crankshaft oil slinger.

4. Remove the bolt and the special washer that hold the camshaft distributor drive gear and fuel pump eccentric at the forward end of the camshaft.

5. Using a pair of prybars, alternately pry the camshaft sprocket, then the crankshaft sprocket forward until the camshaft sprocket is free. Be careful not to damage the sprockets or the ends of the shafts.

6. Remove the camshaft sprocket along with the chain, then finish pulling the crankshaft sprocket off the shaft.

To install:

7. If the engine has been disturbed, turn the the crankshaft so that the number one piston is at top dead center. With the crankshaft turned to No. 1 TDC, temporarily install the sprocket key and the camshaft sprocket on the camshaft, then turn the camshaft so that the index mark of the sprocket is pointing downward. Remove the key and the sprocket from the camshaft.

8. Make sure the sprocket keys are properly installed. Arrange the sprockets in the timing chain so the marks are aligned at the point closest together. Slide the sprocket and chain assembly on both the crankshaft and camshaft at the same time, making sure the marks remain aligned. An assistant may be helpful as it will be necessary to hold the chain tensioners out of the way while installing the timing chain and sprocket assembly.

9. Install the front oil slinger on the crankshaft with the concave side toward the front of the engine.

10. Install the fuel pump eccentric with the oil groove forward.

11. Install the distributor drive gear on the camshaft.

12. Install the front cover.

V6 and V8 Gasoline Engines (Except 231 V6)

1. Remove the timing chain cover. For details, refer to the procedure earlier in this section.

2. Turn the crankshaft until the mark on the camshaft sprocket aligns with the mark on the crankshaft sprocket.

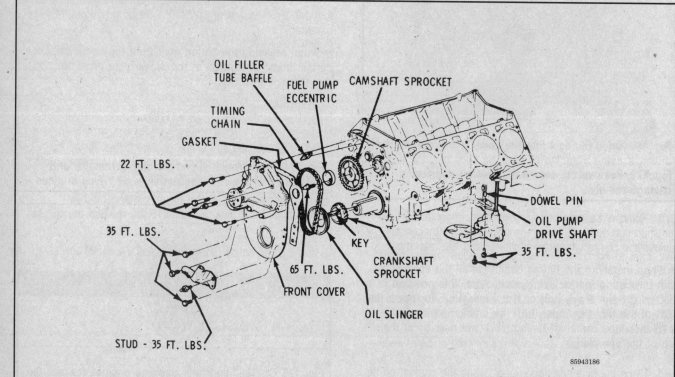

Fig. 170 Exploded view of a common timing cover, gear and chain assembly

Fig. 171 Remove the timing cover from the engine for access to the timing chain and gears

Fig. 172 Before removal, make sure the timing marks are aligned at their closest point of rotation

Fig. 173 Remove the camshaft sprocket and timing chain assembly

3. Remove the camshaft sprocket bolts, then remove the camshaft sprocket and timing chain assembly. If necessary, remove the crankshaft sprocket with or after the assembly.

➡When installing the timing chain, install the sprockets with the timing marks facing each other; this position is TDC of the No. 6 cyl. (V8) or No. 4 cyl. (V6). To locate the TDC of the No. 1 cylinder, turn the crankshaft one full revolution, the camshaft timing mark will now be at the top of the sprocket.

To install:
4. If removed, install the crankshaft sprocket. Make sure the timing mark is at the top of the sprocket so the pistons are properly positioned to set engine timing.
5. Insert the camshaft timing sprocket into the timing chain so the mark on the sprocket is facing downward.
6. Install the bottom of the chain under the crankshaft sprocket as you install the camshaft sprocket to the end of the shaft. Make sure the sprockets are properly installed and seated, then make sure the timing marks are properly aligned.
7. Install and tighten the camshaft sprocket retaining bolts to 13-23 ft. lbs. (18-31 Nm).
8. Install the timing chain cover.

350 V8 Diesel

1. Remove the timing chain cover. For details, refer to the procedure earlier in this section.
2. Align the timing marks for ease of installation.
3. Remove the oil slinger and camshaft bolts, then remove the camshaft and crankshaft sprockets along with the timing chain as an assembly.
4. If replacement is necessary, remove the fuel pump eccentric from the crankshaft.
To install:
5. If removed, install the key in the crankshaft and/or the fuel pump eccentric.
6. Position the sprockets in the timing chain with the timing marks aligned. Install the camshaft and crankshaft sprockets along with the timing chain as an assembly.

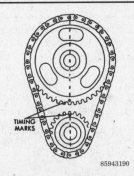

Fig. 174 Timing mark alignment during removal and installation of the chain assembly — all V-type engines

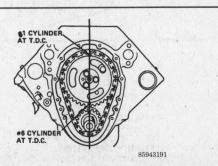

Fig. 175 On 1980 and later gasoline engines (except the 231 V6) and all V8 diesel engines, camshaft timing mark alignment results in these engine timing positions

7. Make sure the timing marks are still in alignment, then install and tighten the camshaft sprocket bolt to 65 ft. lbs. (88 Nm).

➡When the two timing marks are in alignment at the point they are closest together, the number six cylinder is at TDC. To obtain TDC for number one cylinder, slowly rotate the crankshaft one revolution. This will bring the camshaft sprocket mark to the top and the number one piston will then be in firing position.

8. Install the oil slinger.
9. Install the timing chain front cover.

➡Any time the timing chain and gears are replaced, it will be necessary to retime the injection system. Refer to diesel engine injection timing in Section 5 of this manual.

263 V6 Diesel

1. Remove the timing chain cover. For details, refer to the procedure earlier in this section.
2. Remove the rocker arm covers and loosen all of the rocker arm pivot bolts evenly so that lash exists between the rocker arms and the valves (the pushrods and rocker arms are loose). It is not necessary to remove the rockers completely.
3. Align the timing marks for ease of installation.
4. Remove the crankshaft oil slinger.

5. Remove the camshaft-to-camshaft sprocket bolt and washer, then remove the timing chain, camshaft and crankshaft sprockets as an assembly.

➡If the crank sprocket is a tight fit on the end of the crankshaft, you may have to use a sprocket puller to remove it.

To install:

6. If the camshaft sprocket key should come out with the camshaft sprocket, perform the following by referring to the exploded drawing of the V6 diesel front cover and timing assembly.
   a. Remove the front camshaft bearing retainer.
   b. Install the key with the injection pump drive gear.
   c. Install the bearing retainer and bolts loose on the block.
   d. Install the camshaft sprocket.
   e. Rotate the camshaft at least 4 turns to center the retainer.
   f. Remove the camshaft sprocket.
   g. Torque the bearing retainer-to-block bolts evenly to 48 ft. lbs. (65 Nm).
   h. Rotate the camshaft to make sure it's free. If it is not, repeat steps a-h.
7. If removed, install the key in the crankshaft.
8. Position the camshaft and crankshaft sprockets into the timing chain with the timing marks aligned. Install the camshaft and crankshaft sprockets along with the timing chain as an assembly
9. Make sure the timing marks are still aligned, then install and tighten the camshaft sprocket bolt to 70 ft. lbs. (95 Nm).

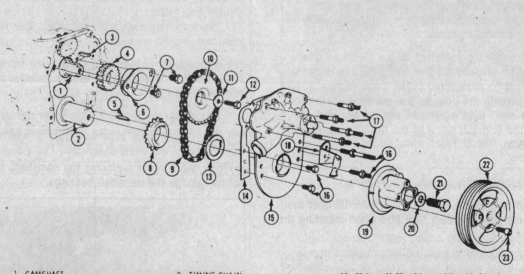

1. CAMSHAFT
2. CRANKSHAFT
3. CAMSHAFT SPROCKET KEY
4. INJECTION PUMP DRIVE GEAR
5. CRANKSHAFT SPROCKET KEY
6. FRONT CAMSHAFT BEARING RETAINER
7. 65 N·m (48 FT. LBS.)
8. CRANKSHAFT SPROCKET
9. TIMING CHAIN
10. CAMSHAFT SPROCKET
11. WASHER
12. 95 N·m (70 FT. LBS.)
13. SLINGER
14. GASKET
15. FRONT COVER
16. 57 N·m (42 FT. LBS.) - APPLY ADHESIVE
17. 28 N·m (21 FT. LBS.) - APPLY ADHESIVE
18. PROBE HOLDER (RPM COUNTER)
19. CRANKSHAFT BALANCER
20. WASHER
21. 217-475 N·m (160 - 350 FT. LBS.)
22. PULLEY ASSEMBLY
23. 40 N·m (30 FT. LBS.)

85943192

Fig. 176 Exploded view of the timing cover and chain assembly (along with bolt torques) — 263 V6 diesel engine

10. Install the oil slinger.

11. Install the engine timing chain front cover.

12. Bleed-down the valve lifters as described under rocker arm service earlier in this section.

13. Install the valve covers and check and reset the injection pump timing.

Camshaft

REMOVAL & INSTALLATION

▶ See Figure 177

Inline 6-Cylinder

Due to the length of the inline 6-cylinder camshaft, a large amount of working room will be required in front of the engine to remove the camshaft. There are two ways to go about this task: either remove the engine from the car, or remove the radiator, grille and all supports which are mounted directly in front of the engine. If the second alternative is chosen, you must also disconnect the motor mounts and raise the front of the engine.

1. Either remove the engine from the vehicle, or remove the radiator, grille and supports.

2. Remove the timing cover assembly from the vehicle.

3. Remove the valve cover and gasket, loosen all the valve rocker arm nuts and pivot the arms clear of the pushrods.

4. Remove the distributor and the fuel pump.

5. Remove the coil, the side cover and its gasket. Remove the pushrods and valve lifters.

6. Remove the two camshaft thrust plate retaining screws by working through the holes in the camshaft gear.

7. Remove the camshaft and gear assembly by pulling it out through the front of the block.

➡If replacing either the camshaft or the camshaft gear, the gear must be pressed off the camshaft. The replacement parts must be assembled in the same manner (under pressure). In placing the gear on the camshaft, press the gear onto the shaft until it bottoms against the gear spacer ring. The end clearance of the thrust plate should be 0.001-0.005 in.

To install:

8. Install the camshaft assembly in the engine.

➡Pre-lube the cam lobes with E.O.S. or SAE 90 gear lubricant. Do not dislodge the cam bearings when inserting the camshaft.

9. Turn the crankshaft and the camshaft to align the timing marks together. Push the camshaft into this aligned position. Install the camshaft thrust plate-to-block screws and torque them to 6-7½ ft. lbs. (8-10 Nm).

10. Runout on either the crankshaft or the camshaft gear should not exceed 0.003 in.

11. Backlash between the two gears should be between 0.004-0.006 in.

12. Install the timing gear cover and its gasket.

13. Install the oil pan and gaskets.

14. Install the harmonic balancer.

15. Line up the keyway in the balancer with the key on the crankshaft and the drive balancer onto the shaft until it bottoms against the crankshaft gear.

16. Install the valve lifters and pushrods. Install the side cover with new gasket. Attach the coil wires; install the fuel pump.

17. Install the distributor and set the timing as described under distributor installation at the beginning of this section.

18. Pivot the rocker arms over the pushrods and then adjust the valves.

19. Add oil to the engine. Install and adjust the fan belt.

20. Install the radiator or shroud.

21. Install the grille assembly and connect the negative battery cable.

22. Fill the cooling system, start the engine and check for leaks.

23. Check and adjust the timing.

Gasoline V6 and V8 (except 231 V6)

1. Remove the timing chain and camshaft sprocket from the engine. For details, refer to the timing chain procedure found earlier in this section.

➡If the camshaft sprocket is tight on the camshaft, use a plastic hammer to carefully bump it loose.

2. On the V8, remove the oil cooler lines and the hoses from the radiator, then remove the radiator from the vehicle.

3. Remove the intake manifold and the rocker arm covers.

4. If equipped on the V8, remove the AIR pump bracket.

5. On the V8, disconnect the fuel lines at the fuel pump, then remove the fuel pump assembly.

6. If equipped with air conditioning on the V8, remove the compressor and the condenser, then reposition them aside with the lines intact.

7. Remove the rocker arm assemblies, then remove the push rods and the valve lifters.

➡If components of the valve train are to be reused, be sure to sort or label them to assure installation in their original locations.

8. Install two ⁵⁄₁₆-18 x 4 in. bolts in the camshaft and carefully pull it from the front of the engine while rotating it back and forth.

➡When removing or replacing the camshaft, be careful not to damage the camshaft bearings.

85943193

Fig. 177 When removing the camshaft, be careful to pull straight back so as not to damage the camshaft journals or bearings

To install:

9. Coat the camshaft journals and lobes with clean engine oil or with an approved pre-lube.

10. Carefully guide the camshaft into the engine block and through the bearings.

11. Install the valve lifters, pushrods and rocker arm assemblies, then adjust the valves.

12. If applicable, reposition and secure the A/C compressor and condenser.

13. If equipped, install the V8 engine's air pump bracket.

14. Install the intake manifold and the rocker arm covers. If the engine is equipped with solid lifters, do not bolt the covers in place at this time.

15. On the V8, install the radiator assembly to the vehicle, then install the hoses and oil cooler lines.

16. Install the timing chain and camshaft sprocket to the engine.

17. If the engine is equipped with solid lifters, make a final valve clearance adjustment with the engine running, then secure the rocker covers to the cylinder heads.

231 V6

1. Disconnect the negative battery cable, then drain the engine cooling system.

2. Disconnect the hoses and remove the radiator.

✳✳CAUTION

When draining the coolant, keep in mind that cats and dogs are attracted by the ethylene glycol antifreeze, and are quite likely to drink any that is left in an uncovered container or in puddles on the ground. This will prove fatal in sufficient quantity. Always drain the coolant into a sealable container. Coolant should be reused unless it is contaminated or several years old.

3. Remove the water pump and all the drive belts. Remove the alternator assembly.

4. Remove the crankshaft pulley and the vibration damper.

5. Remove the intake manifold. Mark the location of the distributor and remove the distributor.

6. Remove the fuel pump. Remove the timing chain cover and the oil pump.

7. Remove the timing chain and the camshaft sprocket, along with the distributor drive gear and the fuel pump eccentric.

8. Remove the rocker arm covers and the rocker arm assemblies. Mark the pushrods and remove them. Remove the lifters. mark them so they can be returned to their original position.

9. Carefully remove the camshaft from the engine. Make sure you don't damage the bearings.

To install:

10. Coat the camshaft journals and lobes with clean engine oil or with an approved pre-lube.

11. Carefully insert the camshaft to the engine, taking care not to damage the bearings.

12. Install the lifters and pushrods. If these components are being reused, they must be installed in their original locations.

13. Install the rocker arm assemblies and adjust the valves.

14. Install the timing chain and camshaft sprocket, along with the distributor drive gear and the fuel pump eccentric.

15. Install the fuel pump assembly.

16. Remember to pack the oil pump with petroleum jelly, then install the timing chain cover and oil pump.

17. Install the intake manifold and install the distributor (while aligning the matchmarks made earlier).

18. Install the crankshaft pulley and the vibration damper.

19. Install the alternator assembly, water pump and all the drive belts.

20. Install the radiator and hoses, then connect the negative battery cable and properly refill the engine cooling system.

V6 and V8 Diesel Engines

▶ See Figure 178

➡**If equipped with air conditioning, the system must be discharged and recovered by an air conditioning specialist before the camshaft is removed. The condenser must also be removed from the car. Removal of the camshaft also requires removal of the injection pump drive and driven gears, removal of the intake manifold, disassembly of the valve lifters, and re-timing of the injection pump.**

1. Disconnect the negative battery cables, then drain the coolant and remove the radiator.

✳✳CAUTION

When draining the coolant, keep in mind that cats and dogs are attracted by the ethylene glycol antifreeze, and are quite likely to drink any that is left in an uncovered container or in puddles on the ground. This will prove fatal in sufficient quantity. Always drain the coolant into a sealable container. Coolant should be reused unless it is contaminated or several years old.

2. Remove the intake manifold along with the gasket, front and rear intake manifold seals. For details, refer to the intake manifold removal and installation procedures earlier in this section.

3. Remove the crankshaft damper pulley and damper. Do NOT use a jawed type puller or the balancer will likely be destroyed.

4. Remove the rocker covers, then remove the rocker arms, pushrods and valve lifters. Be sure to keep the parts in order to that they may be returned to their original position.

5. Remove the camshaft sprocket retaining bolt, and remove the timing chain and sprockets.

6. Position the camshaft dowel pin at the 3 o'clock position on the V8.

7. On V8s, push the camshaft rearward and hold it there, but be careful not to dislodge the oil gallery plug at the rear of the engine. Remove the fuel injection pump drive gear by sliding it from the camshaft while rocking the pump driven gear.

8. To remove the fuel injection pump driven gear, remove the pump adapter, the snapring, and remove the selective washer. Remove the driven gear and spring.

9. Remove the camshaft by sliding it out the front of the engine. On the V6, install a longer bolt into the front hole on the camshaft, to act as a handle. Be extremely careful not to allow the cam lobes or journals to contact any of the bearings this could result in bearing damage or dislodgment. Do not

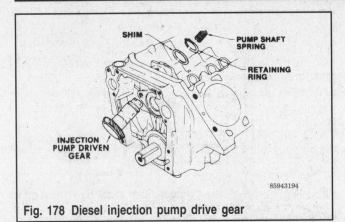

Fig. 178 Diesel injection pump drive gear

force the camshaft to move at any time during removal, or bearing damage will result.

To install:

10. If either the injection pump drive or driven gears are to be replaced, replace both gears.

11. Coat the camshaft and the cam bearings with a heavy-weight engine oil, GM lubricant #1052365 or the equivalent.

12. Carefully slide the camshaft into position in the engine.

13. Fit the crankshaft and camshaft sprockets, aligning the timing marks as shown in the timing chain removal and installation procedures, above. Remove the sprockets without disturbing the timing.

14. Install the injection pump driven gear, spring, shim, and snapring. Check the gear end-play. If the end-play is not within 0.002-0.006 in. on V8s through 1979 and 0.002-0.015 in. on 1980-84 engines, replace the shim to obtain the specified clearance. Shims are available in 0.003 in. increments, from 0.008-0.0115 in.

15. Position the camshaft dowel pin at the 3 o'clock position. Align the zero marks on the pump drive gear and pump driven gear. Hold the camshaft in the rearward position and slide the pump drive gear onto the camshaft. Install the camshaft bearing retainer.

16. Install the timing chain and sprockets, making sure the timing marks are aligned.

17. Install the lifters, pushrods, and rocker arms. Refer to the rocker arm procedures earlier in this section for lifter bleed-down procedures. Failure to bleed-down the lifters could bend valves when the engine is turned over.

18. Install the injection pump adapter and injection pump. Refer to the appropriate procedures under the Fuel System section of this manual.

19. If not done already, install the rocker arm covers.

20. Install the crankshaft damper and pulley.

21. Install the intake manifold using new gaskets and seals.

22. Install the radiator assembly and connect the hoses.

23. Connect the negative battery cables, then properly refill the engine cooling.

24. Run the engine and check for leaks.

CAMSHAFT INSPECTION

Completely clean the camshaft with solvent, paying special attention to cleaning the oil holes. Visually inspect the cam lobes and bearing journals for excessive wear. If the lobe is

questionable, have the cam checked at a reputable machine shop; if a journal or lobe is worn, the camshaft must be reground or replaced. Also have the camshaft checked for straightness on a dial indicator.

➡️**If a cam journal is worn, there is a good chance that the bushings are worn.**

Camshaft Bearings

REMOVAL & INSTALLATION

▶ **See Figures 179, 180 and 181**

If excessive camshaft wear is found, or if the engine is being completely rebuilt, the camshaft bearings should be replaced.

➡️**The front and rear bearings should be removed last, and installed first. Those bearings act as guides for the other bearings and pilot.**

1. Drive the camshaft rear plug from the block.

2. Assemble the removal puller with is shoulder on the bearing to be removed. Gradually tighten the puller nut until the bearing is removed.

3. Remove the remaining bearings, leaving the front and rear for last. To remove these, reverse the position of the puller, so as to pull the bearings towards the center of the block. Leave the tool in this position, pilot the new front and rear bearings on the installer, and pull them into position.

4. Return the puller to its original position and pull the remaining bearings into position.

➡️**Ensure that the oil holes align when install the bearings. This is very important! You can make a simple tool out of the piece of $\frac{5}{32}$ in. brass rod to check alignment.**

5. Replace the camshaft rear plug, and stake it into position.

Pistons and Connecting Rods

REMOVAL

▶ **See Figures 182, 183, 184, 185, 186, 187, 188, 189, 190 and 191**

Before removing the pistons, the top of the cylinder bore must be examined for a ridge. A ridge at the top of the bore is the result of normal cylinder wear, caused by the piston rings only traveling so far up the bore in the course of the piston stroke. The ridge can be felt by hand; it must be removed before the pistons are removed.

A ridge reamer is necessary for this operation. Place the piston at the bottom of its stroke, and cover it with a rag. Cut the ridge away with the ridge reamer, using extreme care to avoid cutting too deeply. Remove the rag, and remove the cuttings that remain on the piston with a magnet and a rag soaked in clean oil. Make sure the piston top and cylinder bore are absolutely clean before moving the piston. For more

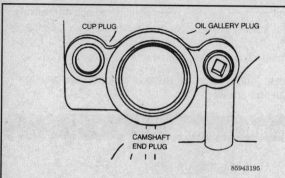

Fig. 179 Camshaft and oil gallery plugs at the rear of the engine block

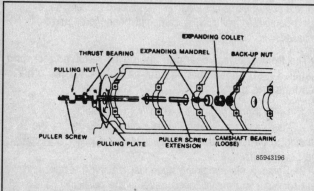

Fig. 180 Remove the camshaft bearings using a puller

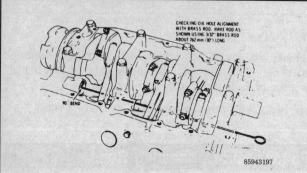

Fig. 181 Camshaft bearing alignment may be checked using this homemade tool

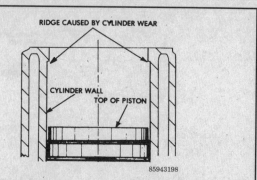

Fig. 182 If present, the cylinder ridge must be removed before the pistons are removed from the block

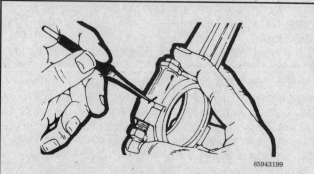

Fig. 183 Match connecting rods to their caps using a scribe mark

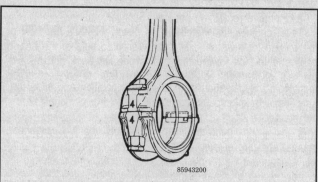

Fig. 184 Match the connecting rods to their cylinders using a number stamp

details, refer to the ridge removal and honing procedures later in this section.

1. Remove intake manifold and cylinder head or heads.
2. Remove oil pan.
3. If necessary, remove the oil pump assembly.
4. Matchmark the connecting rod cap to the connecting rod with a scribe; each cap must be reinstalled on its proper rod in the proper direction. Remove the connecting rod bearing cap and the rod bearing. Number the top of each piston with silver paint or a felt-tip pen for later assembly.
5. Cut lengths of ⅜ in. diameter host to use as rod bolt guides. Install the hose over the threads of the rod bolts, to prevent the bolt threads from damaging the crankshaft journals and cylinder walls when the piston is removed.

6. Squirt some clean engine oil onto the cylinder wall from above, until the wall is coated. Carefully push the piston and rod assembly up and out of the cylinder by tapping on the bottom of the connecting rod with a wooden hammer handle.
7. Place the rod bearing and cap back on the connecting rod, and install the nut temporarily. Using a number stamp or punch, stamp the cylinder number on the side of the connecting rod and cap; this will help keep the proper piston and rod assembly on the proper cylinder.

➡ On V6 engines, starting at the front the cylinders are numbered 2-4-6 on the right bank and 1-3-5 on the left. On all V8s, starting at the front of the left bank the cylinders are numbered 1-3-5-7 and from the front of the right bank cylinders are 2-4-6-8.

Fig. 185 Cut lengths of rubber hose for connecting rod bolt guides

Fig. 186 Carefully tap the piston and rod assembly out using a wooden hammer handle

8. Remove remaining pistons in similar manner.

On all engines, the notch on the piston will face the front of the engine for assembly. The chamfered corners of the bearing caps should face toward the front of the left bank and toward the rear of the right bank, and the boss on the connecting rod should face toward the front of the engine for the right bank and to the rear of the engine on the left.

On various engines, the piston compression rings are marks with a dimple, a letter **T**, a letter **O**, **GM** or the word **TOP** to identify the side of the ring which must face toward the top of the piston.

CLEANING AND INSPECTION

▶ **See Figures 192, 193, 194, 192 and 197**

A piston ring expander is necessary for removing piston rings without damaging them; any other method (screwdriver blades, pliers, etc.) usually results in the ring being bent, scratched or distorted, or the piston itself being damaged. When the rings are removed, clean the piston grooves using an appropriate ring groove cleaning tool, using care not to cut

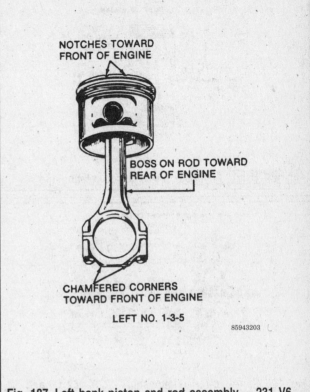

Fig. 187 Left bank piston and rod assembly — 231 V6 engine

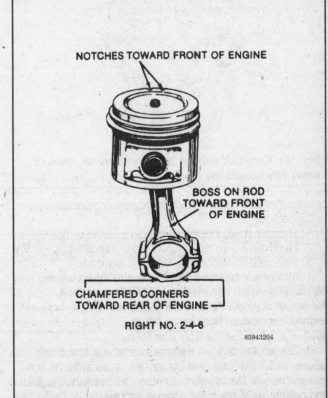

Fig. 188 Right bank piston and rod assembly — 231 V6 engine

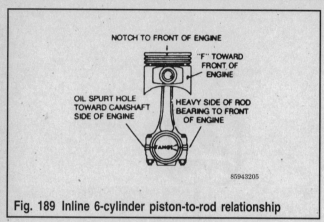

Fig. 189 Inline 6-cylinder piston-to-rod relationship

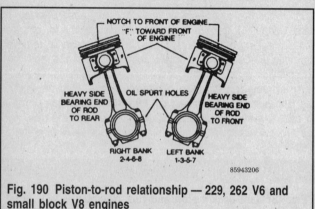

Fig. 190 Piston-to-rod relationship — 229, 262 V6 and small block V8 engines

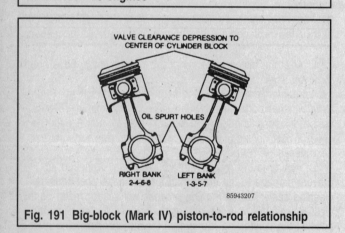

Fig. 191 Big-block (Mark IV) piston-to-rod relationship

too deeply. Thoroughly clean all carbon and varnish from the piston with solvent.

✳✳WARNING

Do not use a wire brush or caustic solvent (acids, etc.) on piston. Inspect the pistons for scuffing, scoring, cranks, pitting, or excessive ring groove wear. If these are evident, the piston must be replaced.

The piston should also be checked in relation to the cylinder diameter. Using a telescoping gauge and micrometer, or a dial gauge, measure the cylinder bore diameter perpendicular (90 degrees) to the piston pin, 2½ in. below the cylinder block deck (surface where the block mates with the heads). Then,

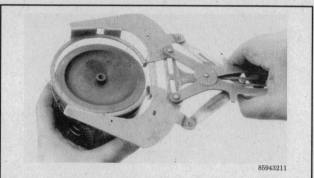

Fig. 192 Use a ring expander tool to remove the piston rings

Fig. 193 Clean the piston grooves using a ring groove cleaner

with the micrometer, measure the piston perpendicular to its wrist pin on the skirt. The difference between the two measurements is the piston clearance.

If the clearance is within specifications or slightly below (after the cylinders have been bored or honed), finish honing is all that is necessary. If the clearance is excessive, try to obtain a slightly larger piston to bring clearance to within specifications. If this is not possible obtain the first oversize piston and hone (or if necessary, bore) the cylinder to size. Generally, if the cylinder bore is tapered 0.005 in. or more, and/or is out-of-round 0.003 in. or more, it is advisable to rebore for the smallest possible oversize piston and rings. After measuring, mark pistons with a felt-tip pen for both reference and assembly.

➡Cylinder block boring should be performed by a reputable machine shop with the proper equipment. In some cases, cleanup honing can be done with the cylinder block in the car, but most excessive honing and all cylinder boring must be done with the block stripped and removed from the car.

RIDGE REMOVAL & HONING

▶ See Figures 198, 199 and 200

1. Before the piston is removed from the cylinder, check for a ridge at the top of the cylinder bore. This ridge occurs because the piston ring does not travel all the way to the top of the bore, thereby leaving an unworn portion of the bore.

Fig. 194 An telescoping gauge may be used to measure the cylinder bore diameter

Fig. 195 Measure the piston's outer diameter using a micrometer

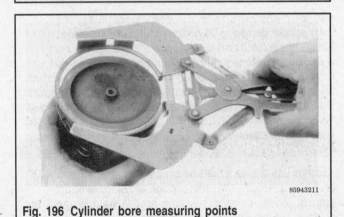

Fig. 196 Cylinder bore measuring points

2. Clean away any carbon buildup at the top of the cylinder with sand paper, in order to see the extent of the ridge more clearly. If the ridge is slight, it will be safe to remove the pistons without damaging the rings or piston ring lands. If the ridge is severe, and easily catches your fingernail, it will have to be removed using a ridge reamer.

➡A severe ridge is an indication of excessive bore wear. Before removing the piston, check the cylinder bore diameter with a bore gauge, as explained in the cleaning and inspection procedure. Compare your measurement with engine specification. If the bore is excessively worn, the cylinder will have to bored oversize and the piston and rings replaced.

Fig. 197 The cylinder bore may also be measured using a dial gauge

3. Install the ridge removal tool in the top of the cylinder bore. Carefully follow the manufacturers instructions for operation. Only remove the amount of material necessary to remove the ridge. Place the piston at the bottom of its stroke, and cover it with a rag. Cut the ridge away with the ridge reamer, using extreme care to avoid cutting too deeply. Remove the rag, and remove the cuttings that remain on the piston with a magnet and a rag soaked in clean oil. Make sure the piston top and cylinder bore are absolutely clean before moving the piston.

✳✳WARNING

Be very careful if you are unfamiliar with operating a ridge reamer. It is very easy to remove more cylinder bore material than you want, possibly requiring a cylinder overbore and piston replacement that may not have been necessary.

4. After the piston and connecting rod assembly have been removed, check the clearances as explained earlier in this section under the cleaning and inspection procedure, to determine whether boring and honing or just light honing are required. If boring is necessary, consult an automotive machine shop. If light honing is all that is necessary, proceed with the next step.

5. Honing is best done with the crankshaft removed, to prevent damage to the crankshaft and to make post-honing cleaning easier, as the honing process will scatter metal particles. However, if you do not want to remove the crankshaft, position the connecting rod journal for the cylinder being honed as far away from the bottom of the cylinder bore as possible, and wrap a shop cloth around the journal.

6. Honing can be done either with a flexible glaze breaker type hone or with a rigid hone that has honing stones and guide shoes. The flexible hone removes the least amount of metal, and is especially recommended if your piston-to-cylinder bore clearance is on the loose side. The flexible hone is useful to provide a finish on which the new piston rings will seat. A rigid hone will remove more material than the flexible hone and requires more operator skill.

7. Regardless of which type of hone you use, carefully follow the manufacturers instructions for operation.

8. The hone should be moved up and down the bore at sufficient speed to obtain a uniform finish. A rigid hone will provide a definite cross-hatch finish; operate the rigid hone at a speed to obtain a 45-65 degree included angle in the cross-

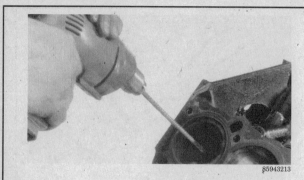

Fig. 198 Removing cylinder glazing using a flexible hone

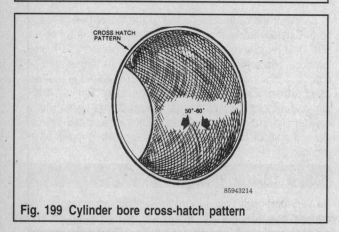

Fig. 199 Cylinder bore cross-hatch pattern

Fig. 200 A properly cross-hatched cylinder bore

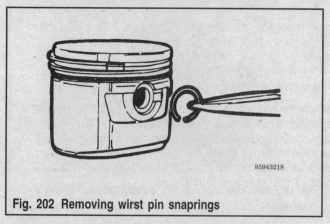

Fig. 202 Removing wirst pin snaprings

hatch. The finish marks should be clean but not sharp, free from embedded particles and torn or folded metal.

9. Periodically during the honing procedure, thoroughly clean the cylinder bore and check the piston-to-bore clearance with the piston for that cylinder.

10. After honing is completed, thoroughly wash the cylinder bores and the rest of the engine with hot water and detergent. Scrub the bores well with a stiff bristle brush and rinse thoroughly with hot water. Thorough cleaning is essential, for if any abrasive material is left in the cylinder bore, it will rapidly wear the new rings and the cylinder bore. If any abrasive material is left in the rest of the engine, it will be picked up by the oil and carried throughout the engine, damaging bearings and other parts.

11. After the bores are cleaned, wipe them down with a clean cloth coated with light engine oil, to keep them from rusting.

PISTON RING AND WRIST PIN

▶ See Figures 201, 202, 203, 204, 205, 206 and 207

Removal

Some of the engines covered in this guide utilize pistons with pressed-in wrist pins; these must be removed by a special press designed for this purpose. Other pistons have their wrist pins secured by snaprings, which are easily removed with snapring pliers. Determine which piston type your engine is equipped with and separate the piston from the connecting rod using the appropriate method.

A piston ring expander is necessary for removing piston rings without damaging them; any other method (screwdriver blades, pliers, etc.) usually results in the rings being bent, scratched or distorted, or the piston itself being damaged. When the rings are removed, clean the ring grooves using an appropriate ring groove cleaning tool, using care not to cut too deeply. Thoroughly clean all carbon and varnish from the piston with solvent.

✲✲WARNING

Do not use a wire brush or caustic solvent (Acids, etc.) on pistons. Inspect the pistons for scuffing, scoring, cracks, pitting, or excessive ring groove wear. If these are evident, the piston must be replaced.

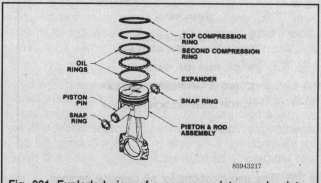

Fig. 201 Exploded view of a common piston and wrist pin assembly

The piston should also be checked in relation to the cylinder diameter. Using a telescoping gauge and micrometer, or a dial gauge, measure the cylinder bore diameter perpendicular (90 degrees) to the piston pin, 2½ in. below the cylinder block deck (surface where the block mates with the heads). Then, with the micrometer, measure the piston perpendicular to its wrist pin on the skirt. The difference between the two measurements is the piston clearance.

If the clearance is within specifications or slightly below (after the cylinders have been bored or honed), finish honing is all that is necessary. If the clearance is excessive, try to obtain a slightly larger piston to bring clearance to within specifications. If this is not possible obtain the first oversize piston and hone (or if necessary, bore) the cylinder to size. Generally, if the cylinder bore is tapered 0.005 in. or more, and/or is out-of-round 0.003 in. or more, it is advisable to rebore for the smallest possible oversize piston and rings. After measuring, mark pistons with a felt-tip pen for both reference and assembly.

After measuring, mark pistons with a felt-tip pen for reference and for assembly.

➡ Cylinder honing and/or boring should be performed by a reputable, professional mechanic with the proper equipment. In some cases, clean-up honing can be done with the cylinder block in the car, but most excessive honing and all cylinder boring must be done with the block stripped and removed from the car.

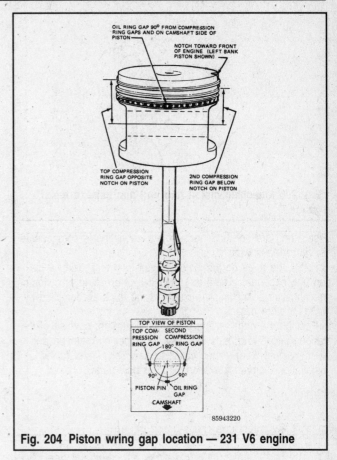

Fig. 204 Piston wring gap location — 231 V6 engine

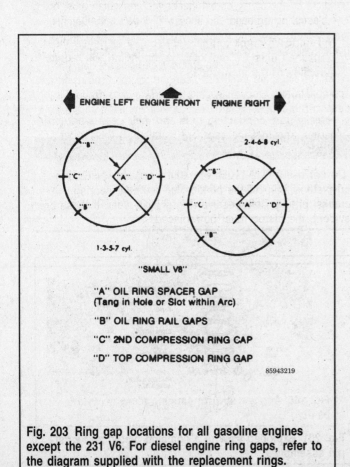

Fig. 203 Ring gap locations for all gasoline engines except the 231 V6. For diesel engine ring gaps, refer to the diagram supplied with the replacement rings.

Piston Ring End Gap

Piston ring end gap should be checked while the rings are removed from the pistons. Incorrect end gap indicates the wrong size rings are being used; ring breakage could occur and engine damage could result.

Squirt clean engine oil into the cylinder, then carefully compress and insert the piston rings to be used in a cylinder, one at a time, into that cylinder. Position the rings approximately 1 in. below the deck of the block (on diesels, measure ring gap clearance with the ring positioned at the bottom of ring travel in the bore). The ring can be carefully positioned using the top of the piston, this will assure that the ring is properly squared to the cylinder walls. Measure the ring end gap with a feeler gauge, and compare to the piston and ring chart earlier in this chapter. Carefully pull the ring out of the cylinder and, if a larger clearance is necessary, file the ends squarely with a fine file to obtain the proper clearance.

Piston Ring Side Clearance Check & Installation

Check the pistons to see that the ring grooves and oil return holes have been properly cleaned. Slide a piston ring into its groove, and check the side clearance with a feeler gauge. On gasoline engines, make sure you insert the gauge between the ring and its lower land (lower edge of the groove), because any wear that occurs forms a step at the inner portion of the lower land. On diesels, insert the gauge between the ring and the upper land. If the piston grooves have worn to the extent that relatively high steps exist on the lower land, the piston should be replaced, because these will interfere with the operation of the new rings and ring clearance will be excessive.

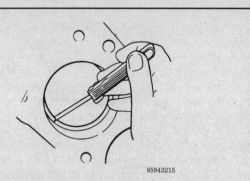

Fig. 205 Checking piston ring end gap using a feeler gauge

Piston ring are not furnished in oversize widths to compensate for ring groove wear.

Install the rings on the piston, lowest ring first, using a piston ring expander. There is a high risk of breaking or distorting the rings, or scratching the piston, if the rings are installed by hand or other means.

Position the rings on the piston as illustrated; spacing of the various piston ring gaps is crucial to proper oil retention and even cylinder wear. When installing new rings, refer to the installation diagram furnished with the new parts.

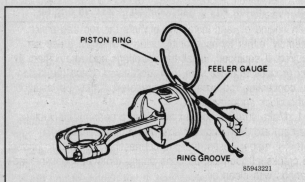

Fig. 206 Checking ring side clearance on a piston from a gasoline engine

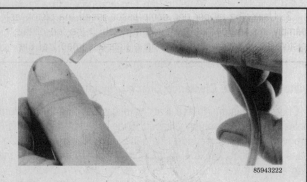

Fig. 207 Most rings are marked to show which side should face upward

ROD BEARING REPLACEMENT

▶ **See Figures 208, 209, 210, 211 and 212**

Connecting rod bearings for the engines covered in this guide consist of two halves or shells which are interchangeable in the rod and cap. When the shells are placed in position, the ends extend slightly beyond the rod and cap surfaces so that when the rod bolts are torqued the shells will be clamped tightly in place to insure positive seating and to prevent turning. A tang holds the shells in place.

➡The ends of the bearing shells must never be filed flush with the mating surface of the rod and cap.

If a rod bearing becomes noisy or is worn so that its clearance on the crank journal is sloppy, a new bearing of the correct undersize must be selected and installed since there is no provision for adjustment.

✳✳WARNING

Under no circumstances should the rod end or cap be filed to adjust the bearing clearance, nor should shims of any kink be used.

Inspect the rod bearings while the rod assemblies are out of the engine. If the shells are scored or show flaking, they should be replaced. If they are in good shape check for proper clearance on the crank journal (see below). Any scoring or ridges on the crank journal means the crankshaft must be replaced, or reground and fitted with undersized bearings.

➡If turbo V6 crank journals are scored or ridged the crankshaft must be replaced, as regrinding will reduce the durability of the crankshaft.

Checking Bearing Clearance and Replacing Bearings

➡Make sure connecting rods and their caps are kept together, and that the caps are installed in the proper direction.

Replacement bearings are available in standard size, and in undersizes for reground crankshaft. Connecting rod-to-crankshaft bearing clearance is checked using Plastigage® or an

Fig. 208 Apply a strip of gauging material to the bearing

Fig. 209 Install the bearing cap and tighten to specification

Fig. 210 Remove the bearing cap and compare the gauging material to the scale provided with the package

Fig. 211 Always oil the bearings prior to installation

equivalent gauging material at either the top or bottom of each crank journal. The Plastigage® has a range of 0.001-0.003 in.

1. Remove the rod cap with the bearing shell. completely clean the bearing shell and the crank journal, and blow any oil from the oil hole in the crankshaft; Plastigage® is soluble in oil.

2. Place a piece of Plastigage® lengthwise along the bottom center of the lower bearing shell, then install the cap with shell and torque the bolt or nuts to specification. DO NOT turn the crankshaft with Plastigage® in the bearing.

3. Remove the bearing cap with the shell. the flattened Plastigage® will be found sticking to either the bearing shell or crank journal. Do not remove it yet.

4. Use the scale printed on the Plastigage® envelope to measure the flattened material to its widest point. The number within the scale which most closely corresponds to the width of the Plastigage® indicates bearing clearance in thousandths of an inch.

5. Check the specifications chart earlier this section for the desired clearance. It is advisable to install a new bearing if clearance exceeds 0.003 in.; however, if the bearing is in good condition and is not being checked because of bearing noise, bearing replacement is not necessary.

6. If you are installing new bearings, try a standard size, then each undersize in order until one is found that is within the specified limits when checked for clearance with Plastigage®. Each undersize shell has its size stamped on it.

7. When the proper size shell is found, clean off the Plastigage® and oil the bearing thoroughly, then reinstall the cap with its shell and torque the rod fasteners to specification.

➡ **With the proper bearing selected and the nuts torqued, it should be possible to move the connecting rod back and forth freely on the crank journal as allowed by the specified connecting rod end clearance. If the rod cannot be moved, either the rod bearing is too far undersize or the rod is misaligned.**

ASSEMBLY AND INSTALLATION

◆ **See Figures 213, 214 and 215**

Install the connecting rod to the piston, making sure the piston installation notches and any marks on the rod are in proper relation to one another. Lubricate the wrist pin with clean engine oil, and install the pin into the rod and piston assembly, either by hand or by using a wrist pin press as required. If equipped, install the snaprings and rotate them in their grooves to make sure they are seated. Once the piston and connecting rod assembly is prepared, it may be installed to the block and crankshaft.

1. Make sure connecting rod big-end bearings (including end cap) are of the correct size and properly installed.

2. Fit rubber hoses over the connecting rod bolts to protect the crankshaft journals, as done during removal. Coat the rod bearings with clean oil.

➡ **It is a good idea to lightly coat the walls of the cylinder bore with clean engine oil during assembly.**

3. Using the proper ring compressor, insert the piston assembly into the cylinder so that the notch in the top of the piston faces the front of the engine (this assumes that the

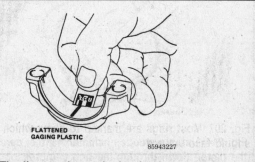

FLATTENED GAGING PLASTIC

Fig. 212 The line on the scale that is closest to the thickness of the gauging material represents the bearing clearance

dimple(s) or other markings on the connecting rods are in correct relation to the piston notch(s). The marks made during disassembly should serve as a guide here.

4. From beneath the engine, coat each crank journal with clean oil. Pull the connecting rod, with the bearing shell in place, into position against the crank journal.

5. Remove the rubber hoses. Install the bearing cap and cap nuts, then torque to specification.

➡️**When more than one rod and piston assembly is being installed, the connecting rod cap attaching nuts should only be tightened enough to keep each rod in position until all have been installed. This will ease the installation of the remaining piston assemblies.**

6. Check the clearance between the sides of the connecting rods and the crankshaft using a feeler gauge. Spread the rods slightly with a small prybar and insert the gauge. If clearance is below the minimum tolerance, the rod may be machined to provide adequate clearance. If clearance is excessive, substitute an unworn rod, and recheck. If clearance is still outside specifications, the crankshaft must be welded and reground, or replaced.

7. Replace the oil pump if removed and the oil pan.

8. Install the cylinder head(s) and intake manifold.

Freeze Plugs

On most cast iron blocks, round metal plugs are used to seal coolant jackets. These plugs allow for a certain amount of

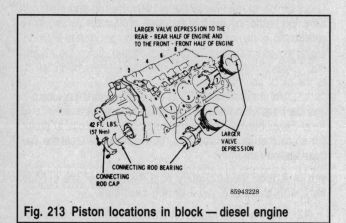

Fig. 213 Piston locations in block — diesel engine

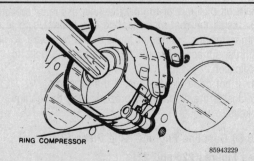

Fig. 214 Using a wooden hammer handle, carefully tap the piston down through the ring compressor and into the cylinder bore

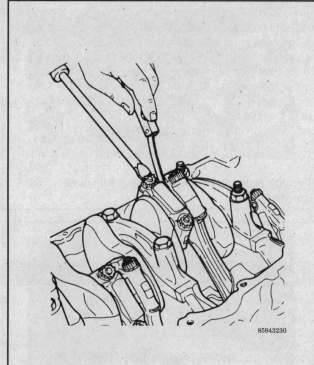

Fig. 215 Check the connecting rod side clearance using a feeler gauge. A small prybar should be used to carefully spread the connecting rods.

water and block expansion should water (without anti-freeze) ever be left in the coolant system. Although the cooling system should NEVER be filled with plain water only, an emergency and unavailability of coolant could force the situation to occur.

In the event that water only is placed in the cooling system and the engine is subject to sub-freezing temperatures, it is likely that the water will freeze and expand. It is also quite possible that the block will expand and crack. If you are lucky though, the expansion may only cause freeze plugs to become dislodged.

During engine block overhaul, it is often standard procedure to remove and replace all of the freeze plugs.

REMOVAL & INSTALLATION

1. If necessary, remove the engine from the vehicle or remove the interfering components, in order to access the freeze plug(s).

❊❊CAUTION

Always wear proper eye protection when using a chisel, especially when attempting to dislodge a freeze plug.

2. Using a hammer and a suitable chisel, cock the plug in the bore.

3. Using the chisel or a small prybar, drive/pry the freeze plug from the bore. Be careful not to score the block or the new freeze plug may not fit well.

To install:

➡Some auto part stores may offer easy to install freeze plugs consisting of a grommet with metal plates and an adjustment bolt. These plugs are positioned, then the bolt is tightened to expand the grommet sealing the block bore. Although these might be handy to get the vehicle home quickly, they should not be installed as a permanent fix.

4. Freeze plugs are interference fitted to the block. Make sure you have the proper plug size and an equalled sized driver. The proper sized driver will ease the installation process by preventing the plug from cocking in the bore as it is driven into position.

5. Position the plug to the bore and drive into position.

6. Install the interfering components or the engine, as applicable.

Rear Main Oil Seal

REMOVAL & INSTALLATION

All Gasoline Engines Through 1985 (Except 231)
▶ **See Figures 216, 217, 218 and 219**

1. Remove the oil pan from the engine. For details, refer to the oil pan procedures earlier in this section.

2. Remove the oil pump and the rear main bearing cap.

3. Using a small pry bar, carefully pry the oil seal from the rear main bearing cap.

4. Using a small hammer and a brass pin punch, drive the top half of the oil seal from the rear main bearing. Drive it out far enough, so it may be removed with a pair of pliers.

5. Using a non-abrasive cleaner, clean the rear main bearing cap and the crankshaft.

To install:

6. Fabricate an oil seal installation tool from 0.004 in. shim stock, shape the end to $1/2$ in. long by $1/64$ in. wide.

7. Coat the new oil seal with engine oil; DO NOT coat the ends of the seal.

8. Position the fabricated tool between the crankshaft and the seal seat in the cylinder case.

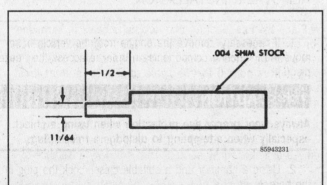

Fig. 216 Dimensions for making an oil seal installation tool

(image labels: .004 SHIM STOCK, 1/2, 11/64, 85943231)

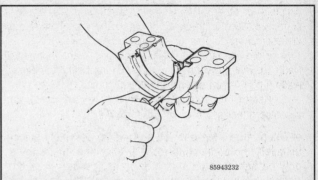

Fig. 217 Removing the lower rear main seal from the bearing cap

(image label: 85943232)

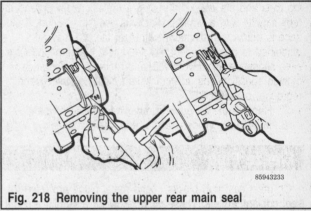

Fig. 218 Removing the upper rear main seal

(image label: 85943233)

9. Position the new half seal between the crankshaft and the top of the tool, so that the seal bead contacts the tip of the tool.

➡**Make sure that the seal lip is positioned toward the front of the engine.**

10. Using the fabricated tool as a shoe horn, to protect the seal's bead from the sharp edge of the seal seat surface in the cylinder case, roll the seal around the crankshaft. When the seal's ends are flush with the engine block, remove the installation tool.

11. Using the same manner of installation, install the lower half of the seal onto the lower half of the rear main bearing cap.

12. Apply sealant to the cap-to-case mating surfaces and install the lower rear main bearing half to the engine; keep the sealant off of the seal's mating line.

13. Install the rear main bearing cap bolts. Using a lead hammer, tap the crankshaft forward and rearward, to line up the thrust surfaces. Torque the main bearing bolts to specification.

14. If not done already, install the oil pump

15. Install the oil pan and properly refill the engine crankcase.

1986-88 Gasoline Engines (One Piece Seal)
▶ **See Figures 220 and 221**

1. Remove the transmission assembly from the vehicle. Refer to Section 7 of this manual for removal procedures.

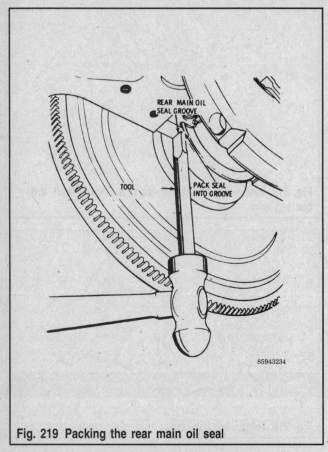

Fig. 219 Packing the rear main oil seal

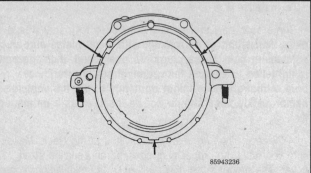

Fig. 220 Carefully pry the seal from the retainer at these locations

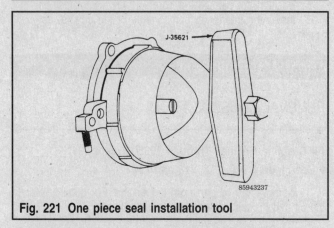

Fig. 221 One piece seal installation tool

2. Using the notches provided in the rear seal retainer, carefully pry out the seal using a small tool.

➡Extreme care should be taken when removing the seal so as not to nick and damage the crankshaft sealing surface.

To install:
3. Before installation lubricate the new seal with clean engine oil.
4. Install the seal on J-3561 or an equivalent seal installation tool. Thread the tool into the rear of the crankshaft and tighten the screws snugly, this is to insure that the seal will be installed squarely over the crankshaft. With the tool properly positioned, tighten the tool wing nut until it bottoms.
5. Remove the tool from the crankshaft.
6. Install the transmission assembly to the vehicle.

ONE PIECE SEAL RETAINER AND GASKET

1. Remove the transmission assembly from the vehicle. Refer to Section 7 of this manual for removal procedures.
2. Remove the oil pan bolts, then lower the oil pan from the engine.
3. Remove the retainer and seal assembly.
4. Remove the gasket and seal from the retainer assembly.

➡Whenever the retainer is removed a new retainer gasket and rear main seal must be installed.

To install:
5. Thoroughly clean the gasket mating surfaces.

6. Position a new gasket, then install and secure the seal retainer.
7. Install the oil pan and tighten the retainers.
8. Install a new one piece seal to the retainer using a suitable installation tool.
9. Install the transmission assembly to the vehicle.

231 V6

◗ See Figures 222 and 223

On this engine, the upper half of the rear main bearing oil seal may be repaired, but not replaced, with the crankshaft installed in the block. To completely replace the seal, the crankshaft must be removed. The lower part of the seal may be replaced in the conventional manner when the bearing cap is removed.

➡Place the new bearing cap neoprene seals in kerosene for two minutes before installing them. The neoprene seals will swell up once exposed to the oil and heat when in the engine. It is normal for the seals to leak for a short time, until they become properly seated. The neoprene seals must NOT be cut to fit.

1. Remove the oil pan and the rear main bearing cap.
2. Using a blunt-edged tool, drive the upper seal into its groove until it is tightly packed. This is usually a distance of $1/4$-$3/4$ in.
3. Cut pieces of a new seal $1/16$ in. longer than required to fill the grooves and install them, packing them into place.
4. Carefully trim any protruding edges of the fabric seal. Do NOT cut the neoprene seals on the bearing cap.

5. Remove the old seal from the bearing cap, and install a new seal.

➡️To help eliminate oil leakage at the joint where the cap meets the crankcase, apply RTV type sealer to the rear main bearing cap split line. When applying sealer, use only a thin coat as an over abundance will not allow the cap to seat properly.

6. Reinstall the cap and the oil pan.

Diesel

▶ **See Figures 216 and 224**

The crankshaft need not be removed to replace the rear main bearing upper oil seal. The lower seal is installed in the bearing cap.

1. Drain the crankcase oil and remove the oil pan, then remove the rear main bearing cap.

2. Using a special main seal tool or a tool that can be made from a dowel (see illustration), drive the upper seal into its groove on each side until it is tightly packed. This is usually ¼-¾ in.

3. Measure the amount the seal was driven up on one side; add ¹⁄₁₆ in and cut this length from the old seal that was removed from the main bearing cap. Use a single-edge razor blade. Measure the amount the seal was driven up on the other side; add ¹⁄₁₆ in. and cut another length from the old seal. Use the main bearing cap as a holding fixture when cutting the seal as illustrated. Carefully trim the protruding seal.

4. Work these two pieces of seal up into the cylinder block on each side with two nail sets or small screwdrivers. Using

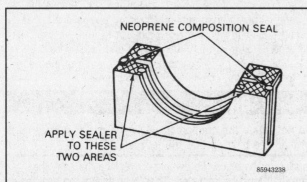

Fig. 222 DO NOT over-apply sealant to the lower main bearing cap — 231 V6

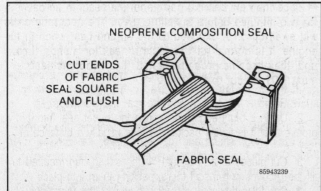

Fig. 223 The new lower seal may be rolled into position

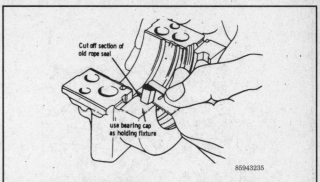

Fig. 224 Use the bearing cap as a holding fixture when cutting off lengths of the old seal

the packing tool again, pack these pieces into the block, then trim them flush with a razor blade or hobby knife. Do not scratch the bearing surfaces with the razor.

5. Install a new seal in the rear main bearing cap. Run a ¹⁄₁₆ in. bead of sealer onto the outer mating surface of the bearing cap. Install the cap to the block and torque to specification.

6. Install the oil pan and properly refill the crankcase with clean engine oil.

Crankshaft and Main Bearings

CRANKSHAFT REMOVAL

▶ **See Figures 225 and 226**

1. Drain the crankcase oil and remove the engine from the car. Mount the engine on a work stand in a suitable working area. Invert the engine, so the oil pan is facing up.

2. Remove the engine front (timing) cover.

3. Remove the timing chain and gears.

4. Remove the oil pan.

5. Remove the oil pump assembly.

6. Stamp the cylinder number on the machined surfaces of the bolt bosses of the connecting rods and caps for identification when reinstalling. If the pistons are to be removed eventually from the connecting rod, mark the cylinder number on the pistons with silver paint or felt-tip pen for proper cylinder identification and cap-to-rod location.

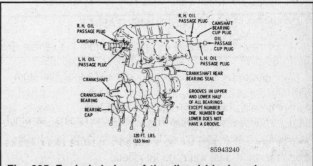

Fig. 225 Exploded view of the diesel block and crankshaft assembly. Gasoline engines similar, though bearing configuration will vary upon application.

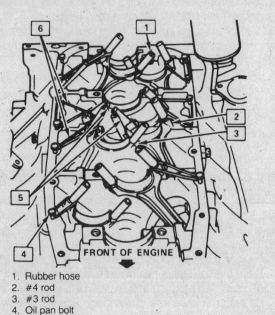

1. Rubber hose
2. #4 rod
3. #3 rod
4. Oil pan bolt
5. Note overlap of adjacent rods
6. Rubber bands

85943241

Fig. 226 Crankshaft removal showing hose lengths and rubber bands installed on rod bolts for crankshaft protection

7. Remove the connecting rod caps. Install lengths of rubber hose on each of the connecting rod bolts, to protect the crank journals when the crank is removed.

8. Mark the main bearing caps with a number punch or punch so that they can be reinstalled in their original positions.

9. Remove all main bearing caps.

10. Note the position of the keyway in the crankshaft so it can be installed in the same position.

11. Install rubber bands between a bolt on each connecting rod and oil pan bolts that have been reinstalled in the block (see illustration). This will keep the rods from banging on the block when the crank is removed.

12. Carefully lift the crankshaft out of the block. The rods will pivot to the center of the engine when the crank is removed.

MAIN BEARING INSPECTION AND REPLACEMENT

Like connecting rod big-end bearings, the crankshaft main bearings are shell-type inserts that do not utilize shims and cannot be adjusted. The bearings are available in various standard and undersizes; if main bearing clearance is found to be too sloppy, a new bearing (both upper and lower halves) is required.

➡**Factory-undersized crankshafts are marked, sometimes with a "9" and/or a large spot of light green paint; the bearing caps also will have the paint on each side of the undersized journal.**

Generally, the lower half of the bearing shell (except No. 1 bearing) shows greater wear and fatigue. If the lower half only shows the effects of normal wear (no heavy scoring or discoloration), it can usually be assumed that the upper half is also in good shape; conversely, if the lower half is heavily worn or damaged, both halves should be replaced. Never replace one bearing half without replacing the other.

CHECKING CLEARANCE

▶ **See Figures 227, 228 and 229**

Main bearing clearance can be checked both with the crankshaft in the car and with the engine out of the car. If the engine block is still in the car, the crankshaft should be supported both front and rear (by the damper and flywheel to remove clearance from the upper bearing. Total clearance can then be measured between the lower bearing and journal. If the block has been removed from the car, and is inverted, the crank will rest on the upper bearings and the total clearance can be measured between the lower bearing and journal. Clearance is checked in the same manner as the connecting rod bearings, using Plastigage® or an equivalent gauging material.

➡**Crankshaft bearing caps and bearing shells should NEVER be filed flush with the cap-to-block mating surface to adjust for wear in the old bearings. Always install new bearings.**

1. If the crankshaft has been removed, install it (block removed from car). If the block is still in the car, remove the oil pan and oil pump, then support the shaft against the upper bearings. Starting with the rear bearing cap, remove the cap and wipe all oil from the crank journal and bearing cap.

2. Place a strip of Plastigage® the full width of the bearing, (parallel to the crankshaft), on the journal.

✳✳WARNING

Do not rotate the crankshaft while the gauging material is between the bearing and the journal.

3. Install the bearing cap and evenly torque the cap bolts to specification.

4. Remove the bearing cap. The flattened Plastigage® will be sticking to either the bearing shell or the crank journal.

5. Use the graduated scale on the Plastigage® envelope to measure the material at its widest point.

➡**If the flattened Plastigage® tapers towards the middle or ends. there is a difference in clearance indicating the bearing or journal has a taper, low spot or other irregularity. If this is indicated, measure the crank journal with a micrometer.**

6. If bearing clearance is within specifications, the bearing insert is in good shape and may be reused. Replace the insert if the clearance is not within specifications. Always replace both upper and lower inserts as a unit.

7. Standard, 0.001 in. or 0.002 in. undersize bearings should produce the proper clearance. If these sizes still produce too sloppy a fit, the crankshaft must be reground for use

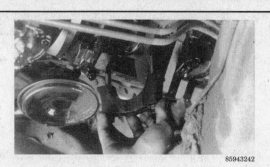

Fig. 227 Bearing clearance may be checked with the engine still installed in the vehicle, simply remove the oil pan for access to the bearing caps

Fig. 228 Apply a strip of gauging material to the bearing, then install and torque the cap

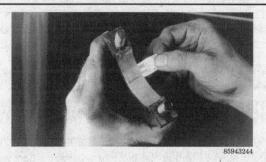

Fig. 229 Like with the connecting rod bearings, remove the cap and compare the gauging material to the provided scale in order to determine clearance

with the next undersize bearing. Recheck all clearances after installing new bearings.

8. Replace the rest of the bearings in the same manner. After all bearings have been checked, rotate the crankshaft to make sure there is no excessive drag. When checking the No. 1 main bearing, loosen the accessory drive belts (engine in car) to prevent a tapered reading with Plastigage®.

MAIN BEARING REPLACEMENT

Engine Out of Car

1. Remove and inspect the crankshaft.

2. Remove the main bearings from the bearing saddles in the cylinder block and main bearing caps.

3. Coat the bearing surfaces of the new, correct size main bearings with clean engine oil and install them in the bearing saddles in the block and in the main bearing caps.

4. Install the crankshaft. Refer to the crankshaft installation procedure, later in this section.

Engine in Car

▶ See Figures 230 and 231

1. With the oil pan, oil pump and spark plugs removed, remove the cap from the main bearing needing replacement, then remove the bearing from the cap.

2. Make a bearing roll-out pin, using a bent cotter pin as shown in the illustration. Install the end of the pin on the oil hole in the crankshaft journal.

3. Rotate the crankshaft clockwise as viewed from the front of the engine. This will roll the upper bearing out of the block.

4. Lube the new upper bearing with clean engine oil and insert the plain (un-notched) end between the crankshaft and the indented or notched side of the block. Roll the bearing into place, making sure that the oil holes are aligned. Remove the roll pin from the oil hole.

5. Lube the new lower bearing and install it to the bearing cap. Install the main bearing cap, making sure it is positioned in proper direction with the matchmarks in alignment.

6. Torque the main bearing cap bolts to specification.

➡See Crankshaft Installation for thrust bearing alignment.

CRANKSHAFT END-PLAY AND INSTALLATION

▶ See Figure 232

When main bearing clearance has been checked, bearings examined and/or replaced, the crankshaft can be installed. Thoroughly clean the upper and lower bearing surfaces, and lube them with clean engine oil. Install the crankshaft and main bearing caps.

Dip all main bearing cap bolts in clean oil, and torque all main bearings caps, excluding the thrust bearing cap, to specifications (see the crankshaft and connecting rod chart earlier in this section to determine which bearing is the thrust bearing). Tighten the thrust bearing bolts finger-tight. To align the thrust bearing, pry the crankshaft to the extent of it axial travel several times, holding the last movement toward the front of the

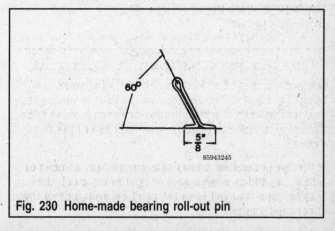

Fig. 230 Home-made bearing roll-out pin

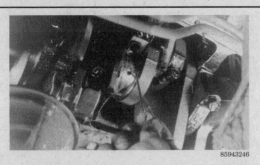

Fig. 231 Position the roll-out pin in the crankshaft oil hole in order to push out the upper bearing when the crankshaft is rotated

engine. Add thrust washers if required for proper alignment. Torque the thrust bearing cap to specifications.

To check crankshaft end-play, pry the crankshaft to the extreme rear of its axial travel, then to the extreme front of its travel. Using a feeler gauge, measure the end-play at the front of the rear main bearing. End-play may also be measured at the thrust bearing. Install a new rear main bearing oil seal in the cylinder block and main bearing cap. Continue to reassemble the engine.

EXHAUST SYSTEM

▶ **See Figures 234 and 235**

➡**Safety glasses should be worn at all times when working on or near the exhaust system. Older exhaust systems will almost always be covered with loose rust particles which will shower you when disturbed. These particles are more than a nuisance and could injure your eye.**

Whenever working on the exhaust system always keep the following in mind:

1. Check the complete exhaust system for open seams, holes loose connections, or other deterioration which could permit exhaust fumes to seep into the passenger compartment.

2. The exhaust system is supported by free-hanging rubber mountings which permits some movement of the exhaust system, but does not permit transfer of noise and vibration into the passenger compartment. Do not replace the rubber mounts with solid ones.

3. Before removing any component of the exhaust system, ALWAYS squirt a liquid rust dissolving agent onto the fasteners for ease of removal. A lot of knuckle skin will be saved by following this rule.

4. Annoying rattles and noise vibrations in the exhaust system are usually caused by misalignment of the parts. When aligning the system, leave all bolts and nuts loose until all parts are properly aligned, then tighten, working from front to rear.

5. When replacing a muffler and/or resonator, the tailpipe(s) should be checked. Often, the same wear or damage which caused a vehicle's muffler or resonator to fail will have taken the same toll on the tailpipe.

6. When installing exhaust system parts, make sure there is enough clearance between the hot exhaust parts and pipes and hoses that would be adversely affected by excessive heat.

Flywheel and Ring Gear

REMOVAL & INSTALLATION

▶ **See Figure 233**

The ring gear is an integral part of the flywheel and is not replaceable.

1. Remove the transmission assembly from the vehicle.
2. Remove the six bolts attaching the flywheel to the crankshaft flange, then remove the flywheel.

To install:

3. Inspect the flywheel for cracks, and inspect the ring gear for burrs or worn teeth. Replace the flywheel if any damage is apparent. Remove burrs with a mill file.

4. Install the flywheel. The flywheel will only attach to the crankshaft in one position, as the bolt holes are unevenly spaced. Install the bolts and torque to specification using a criss-cross pattern.

5. Install the transmission assembly to the vehicle.

Also make sure there is adequate clearance from the floor pan to avoid possible overheating of the floor.

7. Exhaust pipe sealers should be used at all slip joint connections except at the catalytic convertor. Do not use any sealers at the convertor as the sealer will not withstand convertor temperatures.

Tailpipe

REMOVAL & INSTALLATION

➡**Safety glasses should be worn at all times when working on or near the exhaust system. Older exhaust systems will almost always be covered with loose rust particles which will shower you when disturbed. These particles are more than a nuisance and could injure your eye.**

1. Raise and support the vehicle safely using jackstands.
2. Spray all fasteners which are to be disconnected using a penetrating oil.
3. Loosen and remove the hanger clamps from the tailpipe.
4. Remove the tailpipe-to-muffler clamp.
5. Disengage the tailpipe from the muffler and remove the tailpipe.
6. Inspect the tailpipe hangers; replace, if necessary.

To install:

7. Add sealer to the connecting surfaces.
8. Engage the tailpipe to the muffler, then loosely install the retaining clamp.
9. Install the hanger clamps to the tailpipe.
10. Check the clearance and tighten the attachments.
11. Remove the jackstands and carefully lower the vehicle.

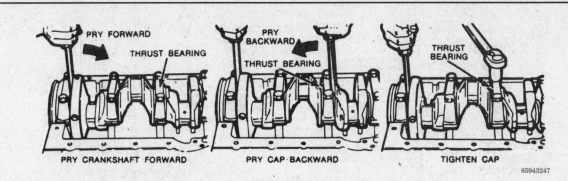

Fig. 232 Aligning the crankshaft thrust bearing

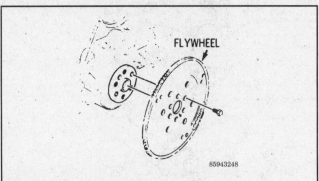

Fig. 233 Flywheel installation — follow the torque specifications closely

12. Run the engine and check for leaks, but be careful NOT to touch the hot exhaust pipes.

Crossover Pipe

➡Safety glasses should be worn at all times when working on or near the exhaust system. Older exhaust systems will almost always be covered with loose rust particles which will shower you when disturbed. These particles are more than a nuisance and could injure your eye.

V6 or V8 engines which are not equipped with dual exhausts utilize a crossover pipe so both manifolds can utilize the single exhaust system.

REMOVAL & INSTALLATION

1. Raise and support the front of the vehicle safely on jackstands.
2. Spray all fasteners which are to be disconnected using a penetrating oil.
3. Remove the exhaust pipe-to-exhaust manifolds nuts.

➡The left side has an extension and packing; the right side has a heat riser valve assembly.

4. If equipped, loosen the catalytic converter-to-transmission bracket.

5. Remove the crossover-to-catalytic converter or intermediate pipe clamp and the pipe from the converter.

➡Check and lubricate the heat riser valve to make sure that it is operating properly.

To install:
6. Add sealer to the connecting surfaces.
7. Connect the crossover to the catalytic converter or the intermediate pipe, then loosely install the clamp.
8. Connect the crossover to the exhaust manifold, then check the clearance and tighten the retaining nuts. Work backwards on the system to tighten the remaining fasteners.
9. Remove the jackstands and carefully lower the vehicle.
10. Run the engine and check for leaks, but be careful NOT to touch the hot exhaust pipes. Be especially careful near the catalytic converter, if equipped.

Front Pipe

➡Safety glasses should be worn at all times when working on or near the exhaust system. Older exhaust systems will almost always be covered with loose rust particles which will shower you when disturbed. These particles are more than a nuisance and could injure your eye.

REMOVAL & INSTALLATION

1. Raise and support the front of the vehicle safely using jackstands.
2. Spray all fasteners which are to be disconnected using a penetrating oil.
3. Remove the exhaust pipe-to-manifold nuts.
4. Support the catalytic converter or muffler and disconnect the front pipe. Remove the pipe.

To install:
5. Add sealer to the connecting surfaces, except where a gasket is used.
6. Loosely install the front pipe to the exhaust manifold, using a new gasket.
7. Connect the rear of the front pipe to the converter or muffler, as applicable.
8. Check the clearance, then tighten the fasteners.
9. Remove the jackstands and carefully lower the vehicle.

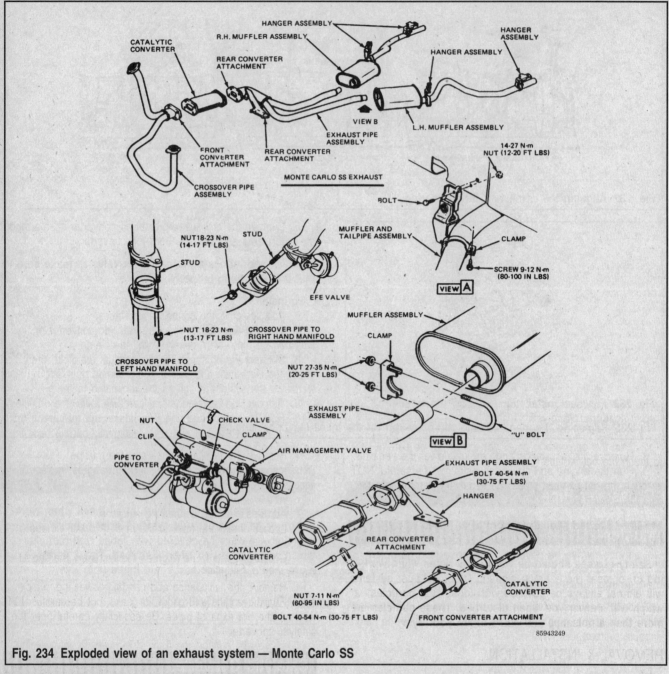

Fig. 234 Exploded view of an exhaust system — Monte Carlo SS

10. Run the engine and check for leaks, but be careful NOT to touch the hot exhaust pipes. Be especially careful near the catalytic converter, if equipped.

Intermediate Pipe

The intermediate pipe is the section between the catalytic converter and the muffler.

➡ **Safety glasses should be worn at all times when working on or near the exhaust system. Older exhaust systems will almost always be covered with loose rust particles which will shower you when disturbed. These particles are more than a nuisance and could injure your eye.**

REMOVAL & INSTALLATION

1. Raise and support the front of the vehicle safely using jackstands.
2. Spray all fasteners which are to be disconnected using a penetrating oil.
3. Disconnect the intermediate pipe from the catalytic converter.
4. At the muffler, remove the clamp and the intermediate pipe.

To install:
5. During installation, use a new clamp and nuts/bolts.
6. Connect the intermediate pipe to the muffler, then to the converter.
7. Check the clearance, then tighten the fasteners.

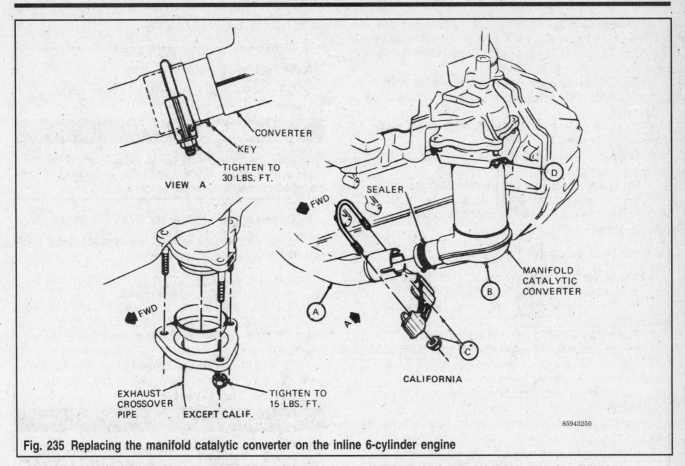

Fig. 235 Replacing the manifold catalytic converter on the inline 6-cylinder engine

8. Remove the jackstands and carefully lower the vehicle.

9. Run the engine and check for leaks, but be careful NOT to touch the hot exhaust pipes. Be especially careful near the catalytic converter.

Muffler

➡️ **Safety glasses should be worn at all times when working on or near the exhaust system. Older exhaust systems will almost always be covered with loose rust particles which will shower you when disturbed. These particles are more than a nuisance and could injure your eye.**

REMOVAL & INSTALLATION

1. Raise and support the vehicle safely using jackstands.

2. Spray all fasteners which are to be disconnected using a penetrating oil.

3. On the single pipe system, cut the exhaust pipe (wearing safety glasses) near the front of the muffler. ON the dual pipe system, remove the U-bolt clamp at the front of the muffler and disengage the muffler from the exhaust pipe.

➡️ **Before cutting the exhaust pipe, measure the service muffler exhaust pipe extension and make certain to allow 1½ in. for the exhaust pipe-to-muffler extension engagement.**

4. At the rear of the muffler, remove the U-bolt clamp and disengage the muffler from the tailpipe.

5. Remove the tailpipe clamps and the tailpipe.

6. Inspect the muffler and the tailpipe hangers; replace if necessary.

To install:

7. Add sealer to the connecting surfaces.

8. Loosely install the front of the muffler to the exhaust pipe and to the tailpipe.

9. Check alignment, then tighten the fasteners starting at the front of the muffler.

10. Remove the jackstands and carefully lower the vehicle.

11. Run the engine and check for leaks, but be careful NOT to touch the hot exhaust pipes. Be especially careful near the catalytic converter.

Catalytic Converter

➡️ **Safety glasses should be worn at all times when working on or near the exhaust system. Older exhaust systems will almost always be covered with loose rust particles which will shower you when disturbed. These particles are more than a nuisance and could injure your eye.**

REMOVAL & INSTALLATION

◗ See Figure 236

Except California Inline 6-Cylinder

1. Raise and support the front of the vehicle safely using jackstands.

2. Remove the clamp at the front of the converter, then unfasten or cut the pipe at the front of the converter, as applicable. Remember to wear safety glasses when cutting the pipes.

3. Remove the converter-to-intermediate pipe nuts/bolts.

4. Disconnect the converter-to-crossover pipe or front pipe.

To install:

5. Install the converter to the front/crossover pipe and to the intermediate pipe.

6. Check all clearances, then tighten the fasteners starting at the front of the converter, moving backwards.

7. Remove the jackstands and carefully lower the vehicle.

8. Run the engine and check for leaks, but be careful NOT to touch the hot exhaust pipes. Be especially careful near the catalytic converter.

California Inline 6-Cylinder

This model has a catalytic converter mounted to the exhaust manifold in addition to the one under the floor.

1. Raise and support the front of the vehicle safely using jackstands.

2. Remove the manifold converter-to-front pipe.

3. Remove the manifold converter-to-exhaust manifold nuts.

4. Remove the underfloor converter from the hanger and lower the front pipe with the manifold converter.

5. Remove the manifold converter from the front pipe.

To install:

6. Loosely assemble the exhaust system using new clamps, nuts and bolts.

7. Check alignment, then tighten the fasteners.

8. Remove the jackstands and carefully lower the vehicle.

9. Run the engine and check for leaks, but be careful NOT to touch the hot exhaust pipes. Be especially careful near the catalytic converter.

Catalyst (Gasoline)

On some older vehicles, the catalyst can be replaced while the converter is on the vehicle.

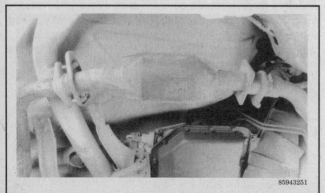

Fig. 236 Late model catalytic converter mounting

85943251

REMOVAL & INSTALLATION

Through 1981

1. Raise and support the front of the vehicle safely using jackstands.

✱✱WARNING

The catalytic converter can be the hottest part of the exhaust system. Make sure the system is thoroughly cooled before attempting to remove the catalyst.

2. Connect an Aspirator tool No. J-25077 to the tailpipe.

➡**If the vehicle has dual exhaust systems, attach the aspirator to one pipe and plug the other.**

3. Connect a 60 psi air hose to the aspirator, to hold the beads in place when the plug is removed.

4. To remove the converter fill plug, perform the following:

   a. Threaded Plug - Using a ¾ in. Allen wrench or tool No. J-25077-3, remove the plug from the bottom of the converter.

   b. Pressed Plug - Place a cold chisel between the plug and the converter shell. Deform the plug until it can be removed with a pair of pliers.

✱✱WARNING

When using the chisel, be careful not to damage the converter shell. DO NOT pry on the plug, for it may damage the converter's sealing opening.

5. Connect the Vibrator tool J-25077-6 to the converter so that the canister aligns with the converter opening.

6. Disconnect the air hose from the aspirator and allow the beads to drop into the collecting canister.

7. Connect a 60 psi air hose to the vibrator and allow the excess beads to be removed from the converter, then disconnect the air hose. Remove the canister from the vibrator and discard the used catalyst.

8. Fill the container with an approved replacement catalyst.

9. Install the fill tube extension to the vibrator fixture.

10. Connect the air hoses to the aspirator and the vibrator, then attach the canister.

11. After the catalyst stops flowing, disconnect the air hose from the vibrator. Remove the vibrator from the converter and check to see if the catalyst if lush with the fill plug hole (add catalyst if necessary).

12. To install the converter plug, perform the following:

   a. Threaded Plug - Apply an anti-seize compound to the threaded fill plug; install it and torque to 60 ft. lbs. (81 Nm)

   b. Press Plug - Use a service plug. Install the bolt into the bridge, then the bridge into the converter's hole, by moving the bridge back-and-forth to dislodge the catalyst beads until the bridge is positioned. Remove the bolt from the bridge then position the washer and the fill plug (dished side out) over the bolt. Install the assembly to the bridge 4-5 turns and release the full plug (the aspirator will pull the plug into position). Torque the bolt to 28 ft. lbs. (38 Nm).

13. Disconnect the air hose from the aspirator.

14. Start the vehicle and check for leaks.

TORQUE SPECIFICATIONS

Component	U.S.	Metric
Camshaft bearing retainer bolts 263 V6 diesel engine (front):	48 ft. lbs.	65 Nm
Camshaft thrust plate-to-block screws inline 6-cylinder gasoline engine:	6.0–7.5 ft. lbs.	8–10 Nm
Camshaft sprocket retaining bolts Gasoline V6 and V8 engines, except 231 V6: 350 V8 diesel engine: 263 V6 diesel engine:	13–23 ft. lbs. 65 ft. lbs. 70 ft. lbs.	18–31 Nm 88 Nm 95 Nm
Catalytic converter Threaded filler plug (Apply an anti-seize compound): Push plug bridge bolt:	60 ft. lbs. 28 ft. lbs.	81 Nm 38 Nm
Connecting Rod Bearing Inline 6-cylinder gasoline engine 1964–65: 1966–75: V6 and V8 gasoline engines 1964–65: 1966–67 Small block: Big block Except 427 & 454 with 7/16 bolts: 427 & 454 with 7/16 rod bolts: 1968–77 Small block: Big block Except 427 & 454 with 7/16 bolts: 427 & 454 with 7/16 rod bolts: 1978–88 All except 231 V6: 231 V6 engine: Diesel engines:	 35–40 ft. lbs. 36 ft. lbs. 30–35 ft. lbs. 35 ft. lbs. 50 ft. lbs. 70 ft. lbs. 45 ft. lbs. 50 ft. lbs. 70 ft. lbs. 45 ft. lbs. 40 ft. lbs. 42 ft. lbs.	 47–54 Nm 49 Nm 41–47 47 Nm 68 Nm 95 Nm 61 Nm 68 Nm 95 Nm 61 Nm 54 Nm 57 Nm
Crankshaft Damper/Balancer bolt Inline 6-cylinder gasoline engines Early models: Late models: V6 and V8 gasoline engines 1964–65: 1966–77 * Small block: * Big block: 1978–84 All except 231 V6: 231 V6 engine: 1985–88: Diesel engines V6: V8:	 Press Fit 60 ft. lbs. Press Fit 60 ft. lbs. 85 ft. lbs. 60 ft. lbs. 175 ft. lbs. 65–75 ft. lbs. 160–350 ft. lbs. 271–420 ft. lbs.	 Press Fit 81 Nm Press Fit 81 Nm 115 Nm 81 Nm 237 Nm 88–102 Nm 217–474 Nm 367–569 Nm

85943C03

TORQUE SPECIFICATIONS

Component	U.S.	Metric
Cylinder head bolts (in the proper sequence)		
Inline 6-cylinder gasoline engines		
1964–65:	90–95 ft. lbs.	122–129 Nm
1966–75:	95 ft. lbs.	129 Nm
V6 and V8 gasoline engines		
Small block		
Except 231 V6:	60–70 ft. lbs.	81–95 Nm
231 V6 engine:	80 ft. lbs.	108 Nm
Big block		
Iron heads:	80 ft. lbs.	108 Nm
Aluminum heads		
Short bolts:	65 ft. lbs.	88 Nm
Long bolts:	75 ft. lbs.	102 Nm
Diesel engines		
V6 bolt numbers		
5, 6, 11, 12, 13, and 14:	59 ft. lbs.	80 Nm
except 5, 6, 11, 12, 13 and 14:	142 ft. lbs.	192 Nm
V8 (dipped in clean engine oil):	130 ft. lbs.	176 Nm
Engine front cover/timing chain cover		
Gasoline engines		
Except 231 V6 engine:	8 ft. lbs.	11 Nm
231 V6 engine:	10 ft. lbs.	14 Nm
Diesel engine		
V6		
Upper mounting studs:	21 ft. lbs.	28 Nm
Lower studs and bolts:	41 ft. lbs.	56 Nm
V8		
Upper fasteners (through water pump):	22 ft. lbs.	30 Nm
Lower fasteners (through cover/probe):	35 ft. lbs.	47 Nm
Exhaust Manifold		
Inline 6-cylinder gasoline engines		
1964–65 (in sequence)		
Inner 7 bolts:	30–35 ft. lbs.	41–47 Nm
Intermediate 2 bolts:	25–30 ft. lbs.	34–41 Nm
Outer 4 bolts:	10–23 ft. lbs.	14–31 Nm
1966–75		
Exhaust-to-intake:	27 ft. lbs.	37 Nm
V6 and V8 gasoline engines		
1964–65:	25–35 ft. lbs.	34–47 Nm
1966–67		
Small block:	20 ft. lbs.	27 Nm
Big block:	30 ft. lbs.	41 Nm
1968–77		
Small block		
Center bolts:	25–30 ft. lbs.	34–41 Nm
End bolts:	15–20 ft. lbs.	20–27 Nm
Big block:	30 ft. lbs.	41 Nm
1978–84		
All except 231 V6		
Except center on 350 engine:	20 ft. lbs.	27 Nm
Center bolts on 350 engine:	30 ft. lbs.	41 Nm
231 V6 engine:	25 ft. lbs.	34 Nm
1985–88		
All except center on 305 engine:	20 ft. lbs.	27 Nm
Center bolts on 305 engine:	25 ft. lbs.	34 Nm
Diesel engines		
V6:	29 ft. lbs.	39 Nm
V8:	25 ft. lbs.	34 Nm

85943C04

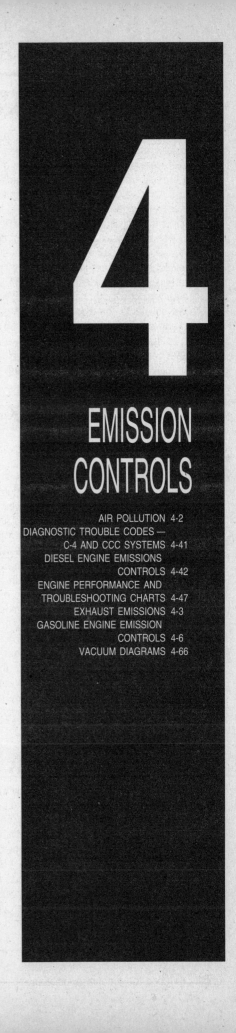

4

EMISSION
CONTROLS

AIR POLLUTION

The earth's atmosphere, at or near sea level, consists approximately of 78% nitrogen, 21% oxygen and 1% other gases. If it were possible to remain in this state, 100% clean air would result. However, many varied causes allow other gases and particulates to mix with the clean air, causing the air to become unclean or polluted.

Certain of these pollutants are visible while others are invisible, with each having the capability of causing distress to the eyes, ears, throat, skin and respiratory system. Should these pollutants become concentrated in a specific area and under certain conditions, death could result due to the displacement or chemical change of the oxygen content in the air. These pollutants can also cause great damage to the environment and to the many man made objects that are exposed to the elements.

To better understand the causes of air pollution, the pollutants can be categorized into 3 separate types, natural, industrial and automotive.

Natural Pollutants

Natural pollution has been present on earth since before man appeared and continues to be a factor when discussing air pollution, although it causes only a small percentage of the overall pollution problem existing in our country today. It is the direct result of decaying organic matter, wind born smoke and particulates from such natural events as plain and forest fires (ignited by heat or lightning), volcanic ash, sand and dust which can spread over a large area of the countryside.

Such a phenomenon of natural pollution has been recently seen in the form of volcanic eruptions, with the resulting plume of smoke, steam and volcanic ash blotting out the sun's rays as it spreads and rises higher into the atmosphere. As it travels into the atmosphere the upper air currents catch and carry the smoke and ash, while condensing the steam back into water vapor. As the water vapor, smoke and ash traveled on their journey, the smoke dissipates into the atmosphere while the ash and moisture settle back to earth in a trail hundred of miles long. In some cases, lives are lost and millions of dollars of property damage result. Ironically, man can only stand by and watch it happen.

Industrial Pollution

Industrial pollution is caused primarily by industrial processes, the burning of coal, oil and natural gas, which in turn produce smoke and fumes. Because the burning fuels contain large amounts of sulfur, the principal ingredients of smoke and fumes are sulfur dioxide and particulate matter. This type of pollutant occurs most severely during still, damp and cool weather, such as at night. Even in its less severe form, this pollutant is not confined to just cities. Because of air movements, the pollutants move for miles over the surrounding countryside, leaving in its path a barren and unhealthy environment for all living things.

Working with Federal, State and Local mandated regulations and by carefully monitoring the emissions, big business has greatly reduced the amount of pollutant emitted from its industrial sources, striving to obtain an acceptable level. Because of the mandated industrial emission clean up, many land areas and streams in and around the cities that were formerly barren of vegetation and life, have now begun to move back in the direction of nature's intended balance.

Automotive Pollutants

The third major source of air pollution is automotive emissions. The emissions from the internal combustion engine were not an appreciable problem years ago because of the small number of registered vehicles and the nation's small highway system. However, during the early 1950's, the trend of the American people was to move from the cities to the surrounding suburbs. This caused an immediate problem in transportation because the majority of suburbs were not afforded mass transit conveniences. This lack of transportation created an attractive market for the automobile manufacturers, which resulted in a dramatic increase in the number of vehicles produced and sold, along with a marked increase in highway construction between cities and the suburbs. Multi-vehicle families emerged with a growing emphasis placed on an individual vehicle per family member. As the increase in vehicle ownership and usage occurred, so did pollutant levels in and around the cities, as suburbanites drove daily to their businesses and employment, returning at the end of the day to their homes in the suburbs.

It was noted that a fog and smoke type haze was being formed and at times, remained in suspension over the cities, taking time to dissipate. At first this "smog", derived from the words "smoke" and "fog", was thought to result from industrial pollution but it was determined that automobile emissions shared the blame. It was discovered that when normal automobile emissions were exposed to sunlight for a period of time, complex chemical reactions would take place.

It is now known that smog is a photo chemical layer which develops when certain oxides of nitrogen (NOx) and unburned hydrocarbons (HC) from automobile emissions are exposed to sunlight. Pollution was more severe when smog would become stagnant over an area in which a warm layer of air settled over the top of the cooler air mass, trapping and holding the cooler mass at ground level. The trapped cooler air would keep the emissions from being dispersed and diluted through normal air flows. This type of air stagnation was given the name "Temperature Inversion".

Temperature Inversion

In normal weather situations, the surface air is warmed by heat radiating from the earth's surface and the sun's rays and will rise upward, into the atmosphere. Upon rising it will cool through a convection type heat exchange with the cooler upper air. As warm air rises, the surface pollutants are carried upward and dissipated into the atmosphere.

When a temperature Inversion occurs, we find the higher air is no longer cooler but warmer than the surface air, causing the cooler surface air to become trapped. This warm air blanket can extend from above ground level to a few hundred or even a few thousand feet into the air. As the surface air is trapped, so are the pollutants, causing a severe smog condition. Should this stagnant air mass extend to a few thousand feet high, enough air movement with the inversion takes place to allow the smog layer to rise above ground level but the pollutants still cannot dissipate. This inversion can remain for days over an area, with the smog level only rising or lowering from ground level to a few hundred feet high. Meanwhile, the pollutant levels increase, causing eye irritation, respiratory problems, reduced visibility, plant damage and in some cases, disease.

This inversion phenomenon was first noted in the Los Angeles, California area. The city lies terrain resembling a basin and with certain weather conditions, a cold air mass is held in the basin while a warmer air mass covers it like a lid.

Because this type of condition was first documented as prevalent in the Los Angeles area, this type of trapped pollution was named Los Angeles Smog, although it occurs in other areas where a large concentration of automobiles are used and the air remains stagnant for any length of time.

Internal Combustion Engine Pollutants

Consider the internal combustion engine as a machine in which raw materials must be placed so a finished product comes out. As in any machine operation, a certain amount of wasted material is formed. When we relate this to the internal combustion engine, we find that through the input of air and fuel, we obtain power during the combustion process to drive the vehicle. The by-product or waste of this power is, in part, heat and exhaust gases with which we must dispose.

EXHAUST EMISSIONS

Composition Of The Exhaust Gases

The exhaust gases emitted into the atmosphere are a combination of burned and unburned fuel. To understand the exhaust emission and its composition, we must review some basic chemistry.

When the air/fuel mixture is introduced into the engine, we are mixing air, composed of nitrogen (78%), oxygen (21%) and other gases (1%) with the fuel, which is 100% hydrocarbons (HC), in a semi-controlled ratio. As the combustion process is accomplished, power is produced to move the vehicle while the heat of combustion is transferred to the cooling system. The exhaust gases are then composed of nitrogen, a diatomic gas (N_2), the same as was introduced in the engine, carbon dioxide (CO_2), the same gas that is used in beverage carbonation and water vapor (H_2O). The nitrogen (N_2), for the most part passes through the engine unchanged, while the oxygen (O_2) reacts (burns) with the hydrocarbons (HC) and produces the carbon dioxide (CO_2) and the water vapors (H_2O). If this chemical process would be the only process to take place, the exhaust emissions would be harmless. However, during the combustion process, other compounds are formed which are considered dangerous. These pollutants are carbon monoxide (CO), hydrocarbons (HC), oxides of nitrogen (NOx) oxides of sulfur (SOx) and engine particulates.

Heat Transfer

The heat from the combustion process can rise to over 4000°F (2204°C). The dissipation of this heat is controlled by a ram air effect, the use of cooling fans to cause air flow and having a liquid coolant solution surrounding the combustion area to transfer the heat of combustion through the cylinder walls and into the coolant. The coolant is then directed to a thin-finned, multi-tubed radiator, from which the excess heat is transferred to the atmosphere by 1 of the 3 heat transfer methods, conduction, convection or radiation.

The cooling of the combustion area is an important part in the control of exhaust emissions. To understand the behavior of the combustion and transfer of its heat, consider the air/fuel charge. It is ignited and the flame front burns progressively across the combustion chamber until the burning charge reaches the cylinder walls. Some of the fuel in contact with the walls is not hot enough to burn, thereby snuffing out or quenching the combustion process. This leaves unburned fuel in the combustion chamber. This unburned fuel is then forced out of the cylinder and into the exhaust system, along with the exhaust gases.

Many attempts have been made to minimize the amount of unburned fuel in the combustion chambers due to the snuffing out or quenching, by increasing the coolant temperature and lessening the contact area of the coolant around the combustion area. Design limitations within the combustion chambers prevent the complete burning of the air/fuel charge, so a certain amount of the unburned fuel is still expelled into the exhaust system, regardless of modifications to the engine.

HYDROCARBONS

Hydrocarbons (HC) are essentially fuel which was not burned during the combustion process or which has escaped into the atmosphere through fuel evaporation. The main sources of incomplete combustion are rich air/fuel mixtures, low engine temperatures and improper spark timing. The main sources of hydrocarbon emission through fuel evaporation on most cars used to be the vehicle's fuel tank and carburetor bowl.

To reduce combustion hydrocarbon emission, engine modifications were made to minimize dead space and surface area in the combustion chamber. In addition the air/fuel mixture was made more lean through the improved control which feedback carburetion and fuel injection offers and by the addition of external controls to aid in further combustion of the hydrocarbons outside the engine. Two such methods were the addition of an air injection system, to inject fresh air into the exhaust manifolds and the installation of a catalytic converter, a unit that is able to burn traces of hydrocarbons without affecting the internal combustion process or fuel economy. The vehicles covered in this manual may utilize either, both or none of these methods, depending on the year and model.

To control hydrocarbon emissions through fuel evaporation, modifications were made to the fuel tank to allow storage of the fuel vapors during periods of engine shut-down.

Modifications were also made to the air intake system so that at specific times during engine operation, these vapors may be purged and burned by blending them with the air/fuel mixture.

CARBON MONOXIDE

Carbon monoxide is formed when not enough oxygen is present during the combustion process to convert carbon (C) to carbon dioxide (CO_2). An increase in the carbon monoxide (CO) emission is normally accompanied by an increase in the hydrocarbon (HC) emission because of the lack of oxygen to completely burn all of the fuel mixture.

Carbon monoxide (CO) also increases the rate at which the photo chemical smog is formed by speeding up the conversion of nitric oxide (NO) to nitrogen dioxide (NO_2). To accomplish this, carbon monoxide (CO) combines with oxygen (O_2) and nitric oxide (NO) to produce carbon dioxide (CO_2) and nitrogen dioxide (NO_2). ($CO + O_2 + NO = CO_2 + NO_2$).

The dangers of carbon monoxide, which is an odorless and colorless toxic gas are many. When carbon monoxide is inhaled into the lungs and passed into the blood stream, oxygen is replaced by the carbon monoxide in the red blood cells, causing a reduction in the amount of oxygen being supplied to the many parts of the body. This lack of oxygen causes headaches, lack of coordination, reduced mental alertness and should the carbon monoxide concentration be high enough, death could result.

NITROGEN

Normally, nitrogen is an inert gas. When heated to approximately 2500°F (1371°C) through the combustion process, this gas becomes active and causes an increase in the nitric oxide (NO_x) emission.

Oxides of nitrogen (NO_x) are composed of approximately 97-98% nitric oxide (NO). Nitric oxide is a colorless gas but when it is passed into the atmosphere, it combines with oxygen and forms nitrogen dioxide (NO_2). The nitrogen dioxide then combines with chemically active hydrocarbons (HC) and when in the presence of sunlight, causes the formation of photo chemical smog.

OZONE

To further complicate matters, some of the nitrogen dioxide (NO_2) is broken apart by the sunlight to form nitric oxide and oxygen. ($NO_2 + sunlight = NO + O$). This single atom of oxygen then combines with diatomic (meaning 2 atoms) oxygen (O_2) to form ozone (O_3). Ozone is 1 of the smells associated with smog. It has a pungent and offensive odor, irritates the eyes and lung tissues, affects the growth of plant life and causes rapid deterioration of rubber products. Ozone can be formed by sunlight as well as electrical discharge into the air.

The most common discharge area on the automobile engine is the secondary ignition electrical system, especially when inferior quality spark plug cables are used. As the surge of high voltage is routed through the secondary cable, the circuit

builds up an electrical field around the wire, acting upon the oxygen in the surrounding air to form the ozone. The faint glow along the cable with the engine running that may be visible on a dark night, is called the "corona discharge." It is the result of the electrical field passing from a high along the cable, to a low in the surrounding air, which forms the ozone gas. The combination of corona and ozone has been a major cause of cable deterioration. Recently, different and better quality insulating materials have lengthened the life of the electrical cables.

Although ozone at ground level can be harmful, ozone is beneficial to the earth's inhabitants. By having a concentrated ozone layer called the "ozonosphere", between 10 and 20 miles (16-32km) up in the atmosphere much of the ultra violet radiation from the sun's rays are absorbed and screened. If this ozone layer were not present, much of the earth's surface would be burned, dried and unfit for human life.

There is much discussion concerning the ozone layer and its density. A feeling exists that this protective layer of ozone is slowly diminishing and corrective action must be directed to this problem. Much experimentation is presently being conducted to determine if a problem exists and if so, the short and long term effects of the problem and how it can be remedied.

OXIDES OF SULFUR

Oxides of sulfur (SO_x) were initially ignored in the exhaust system emissions, since the sulfur content of gasoline as a fuel is less than 1/10 of 1%. Because of this small amount, it was felt that it contributed very little to the overall pollution problem. However, because of the difficulty in solving the sulfur emissions in industrial pollutions and the introduction of catalytic converter to the automobile exhaust systems, a change was mandated. The automobile exhaust system, when equipped with a catalytic converter, changes the sulfur dioxide (SO_2) into the sulfur trioxide (SO_3).

When this combines with water vapors (H_2O), a sulfuric acid mist (H_2SO_4) is formed and is a very difficult pollutant to handle since it is extremely corrosive. This sulfuric acid mist that is formed, is the same mist that rises from the vents of an automobile battery when an active chemical reaction takes place within the battery cells.

When a large concentration of vehicles equipped with catalytic converters are operating in an area, this acid mist will rise and be distributed over a large ground area causing land, plant, crop, paints and building damage.

PARTICULATE MATTER

A certain amount of particulate matter is present in the burning of any fuel, with carbon constituting the largest percentage of the particulates. In gasoline, the remaining particulates are the burned remains of the various other compounds used in its manufacture. When a gasoline engine is in good internal condition, the particulate emissions are low but as the engine wears internally, the particulate emissions increase. By visually inspecting the tail pipe emissions, a determination can be made as to where an engine defect may exist. An engine with light gray smoke emitting from the tail pipe normally indicates an increase in the oil consumption through burning due to internal engine wear. Black smoke would indicate a defective fuel delivery system, causing the engine to operate in a rich mode. Regardless of the color of the smoke, the internal part of the engine or the fuel delivery system should be repaired to a "like new" condition to prevent excess particulate emissions.

Diesel and turbine engines emit a darkened plume of smoke from the exhaust system because of the type of fuel used. Emission control regulations are mandated for this type of emission and more stringent measures are being used to prevent excess emission of the particulate matter. Electronic components are being introduced to control the injection of the fuel at precisely the proper time of piston travel, to achieve the optimum in fuel ignition and fuel usage. Other particulate after-burning components are being tested to achieve a cleaner emission.

Good grades of engine lubricating oils should be used, which meet the manufacturers specification. "Cut-rate" oils can contribute to the particulate emission problem because of their low "flash" or ignition temperature point. Such oils burn prematurely during the combustion process causing emissions of particulate matter.

The cooling system is an important factor in the reduction of particulate matter. With the cooling system operating at a temperature specified by the manufacturer, the optimum of combustion will occur. The cooling system must be maintained in the same manner as the engine oiling system, as each system is required to perform properly in order for the engine to operate efficiently for a long time.

Other Automobile Emission Sources

Before emission controls were mandated on the internal combustion engines, other sources of engine pollutants were discovered, along with the exhaust emission. It was determined the engine combustion exhaust produced 60% of the total emission pollutants, fuel evaporation from the fuel tank and carburetor vents produced 20%, with the another 20% being produced through the crankcase as a by-product of the combustion process.

CRANKCASE EMISSIONS

Crankcase emissions are made up of water, acids, unburned fuel, oil fumes and particulates. The emissions are classified as hydrocarbons (HC) and are formed by the small amount of unburned, compressed air/fuel mixture entering the crankcase from the combustion area during the compression and power strokes, between the cylinder walls and piston rings. The head of the compression and combustion help to form the remaining crankcase emissions.

Since the first engines, crankcase emissions were allowed into the atmosphere through a road draft tube, mounted on the lower side of the engine block. Fresh air came in through an open oil filler cap or breather. The air passed through the crankcase mixing with blow-by gases. The motion of the vehicle and the air blowing past the open end of the road draft tube caused a low pressure area at the end of the tube.

Crankcase emissions were simply drawn out of the road draft tube into the air.

To control the crankcase emission, the road draft tube was deleted. A hose and/or tubing was routed from the crankcase to the intake manifold so the blow-by emission could be burned with the air/fuel mixture. However, it was found that intake manifold vacuum, used to draw the crankcase emissions into the manifold, would vary in strength at the wrong time and not allow the proper emission flow. A regulating type valve was needed to control the flow of air through the crankcase.

Testing, showed the removal of the blow-by gases from the crankcase as quickly as possible, was most important to the longevity of the engine. Should large accumulations of blow-by gases remain and condense, dilution of the engine oil would occur to form water, soots, resins, acids and lead salts, resulting in the formation of sludge and varnishes. This condensation of the blow-by gases occur more frequently on vehicles used in numerous starting and stopping conditions, excessive idling and when the engine is not allowed to attain normal operating temperature through short runs.

FUEL EVAPORATIVE EMISSIONS

Gasoline fuel is a major source of pollution, before and after it is burned in the automobile engine. From the time the fuel is refined, stored, pumped and transported, again stored until it is pumped into the fuel tank of the vehicle, the gasoline gives off unburned hydrocarbons (HC) into the atmosphere. Through redesigning of the storage areas and venting systems, the pollution factor was diminished, but not eliminated, from the refinery standpoint. However, the automobile still remained the primary source of vaporized, unburned hydrocarbon (HC) emissions.

Fuel pumped from an underground storage tank is cool but when exposed to a warmer ambient temperature, will expand. Before controls were mandated, an owner would fill the fuel tank with fuel from an underground storage tank and park the vehicle for some time in warm area, such as a parking lot. As the fuel would warm, it would expand and should no provisions or area be provided for the expansion, the fuel would spill out the filler neck and onto the ground, causing hydrocarbon (HC) pollution and creating a severe fire hazard. To correct this condition, the vehicle manufacturers added overflow plumbing and/or gasoline tanks with built in expansion areas or domes.

However, this did not control the fuel vapor emission from the fuel tank. It was determined that most of the fuel evaporation occurred when the vehicle was stationary and the engine not operating. Most vehicles carry 5-25 gallons (19-95 liters) of gasoline. Should a large concentration of vehicles be parked in one area, such as a large parking lot, excessive fuel vapor emissions would take place, increasing as the temperature increases.

To prevent the vapor emission from escaping into the atmosphere, the fuel system is designed to trap the fuel vapors while the vehicle is stationary, by sealing the fuel system from the atmosphere. A storage system is used to collect and hold the fuel vapors from the carburetor and the fuel tank when the engine is not operating. When the engine is started, the storage system is then purged of the fuel vapors, which are drawn into the engine and burned with the air/fuel mixture.

GASOLINE ENGINE EMISSION CONTROLS

▶ **See Figure 1**

There are three sources of automotive pollutants: Crankcase fumes, exhaust gases and gasoline evaporation. The pollutants formed from these substances all into three categories: unburned hydrocarbons (HC), carbon monoxide (CO) and oxides of nitrogen (NOx). The equipment that is used to limit these pollutants is commonly called emission control equipment.

Positive Crankcase Ventilation

OPERATION

▶ **See Figures 2, 3 and 4**

Until 1967, most mid-size Chevrolets were available with two types of crankcase ventilation systems: The closed type found on all California cars and some non-California cars, or the open type. The open ventilation system (non-California cars) receives outside air through a vented oil filler cap was usually equipped with a PCV valve that is threaded into the base of the carburetor. The vented oil cap permits outside air to enter the crankcase, but also allows crankcase vapors to escape from the valve cover into the atmosphere.

The 1967 California law and later Federal law requires that this filler cap be non-vented to prevent the emission of vapors into the air. To supply this closed system with fresh air, a breather hose runs from the carburetor air cleaner to an inlet hole in the valve cover. The carburetor end of the hose fits into a cup-shaped flame arrestor and breather filter in the air cleaner cover. In the event of a carburetor backfire, this arrestor prevents the spread of fire to the valve cover where it could create an explosion.

Included in the closed system is a PCV (positive crankcase ventilation) valve that fits into an outlet hole in the top of the valve cover. A hose connects this valve to a vacuum outlet at the intake manifold. Contained within the PCV housing is a unidirectional valve (pointed at one end, flat at the other) positioned within a coiled spring. During idle or low speed operation, when manifold vacuum is highest, the valve spring tension is overcome by the high vacuum pull and, as a result, the valve is pulled up to very nearly seal off the manifold end of

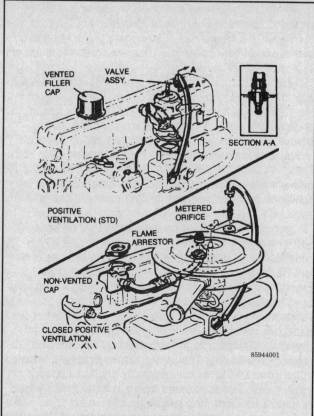

Fig. 2 Open (top) and closed PCV systems

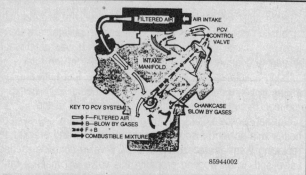

Fig. 3 PCV system schematic for a common V8 engine (most closed systems similar)

the valve housing. This restricts the flow of crankcase vapors to the intake manifold at a time when crankcase pressures are lowest and least disruptive to engine performance. At times of acceleration or constant speed, intake manifold vacuum is reduced to a point where it can no longer pull against the valve spring and so, spring force pulls the valve away from the housing outlet allowing crankcase vapors to escape through the hose to the intake manifold. Once inside the manifold, the gases enter the combustion chambers to be reburned. At times of engine backfire (at the carburetor) or when the engine is turned off, manifold vacuum ceases permitting the spring to pull the valve against the inlet (crankcase end) end of the

Fig. 1 The vehicle emission control information label includes vacuum diagrams and engine control system adjustment information

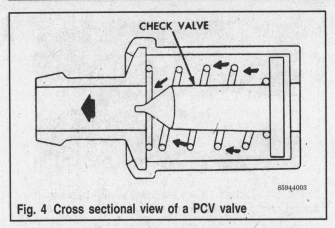

Fig. 4 Cross sectional view of a PCV valve

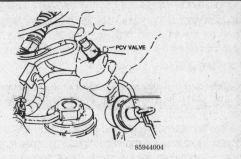

Fig. 5 The valve and hose may be checked by removing the valve from the grommet and feeling for vacuum while the engine is running

valve housing. This seals off the inlet, thereby stopping the entrance of crankcase gases into the valve and preventing the possibility of a backfire spreading through the hose and valve to ignite these gases. The carburetor used with is system is set to provide a richer gas mixture to compensate for the additional air and gases going to the intake manifold. A valve that is clogged and stuck closed will not allow this extra air to reach the manifold. Consequently, the engine will run roughly and plugs will foul due to the creation, of an overly rich air/fuel mixture.

It can be said that the PCV system performs three functions. It reduces air pollution by reburning the crankcase gases rather than releasing them to the atmosphere, it increases engine life and it increase fuel economy. By recirculating crankcase gases, oil contamination that is harmful to engine parts is kept to a minimum. Recirculated gases returned to the intake manifold are combustible and, when combined with the air/fuel mixture from the carburetor, becomes fuel for operation, slightly increasing fuel economy. In 1968, all cars were required to use the closed system and vented filler caps became a thing of the past.

SERVICE

▶ See Figure 5

Normal service entails cleaning the passages of the system hoses with solvent, inspecting them for cracks and breaks, and replacing them as necessary. The PCV valve contains a check valve and, when working properly, this valve will make a rattling sound when the outside case is tapped. If it fails to rattle, then it is probably stuck in a closed position and needs to be replaced.

The PCV system is designed to prevent the emission of gases from the crankcase into the atmosphere. It does this by connecting a crankcase outlet (valve cover, oil filler tube, back of engine) to the intake manifold with a hose. The crankcase gases travel through the hose to the intake manifold where they are returned to the combustion chamber and burned. If maintained properly, this system reduces condensation in the crankcase and the resultant formation of harmful acids and oil dilution. A clogged PCV valve will often cause a slow or rough idle due to a richer fuel mixture. A car equipped with a PCV system has air going through a hose to the intake manifold from an outlet at the valve cover, oil filler tube, or rear of the engine. To compensate for this extra air going to the manifold,

carburetor specifications require a richer mixture (more gas) at the carburetor. If the PCV valve or hose is clogged, the additional air doesn't go to the intake manifold and the fuel mixture is too rich. A rough, slow idle results. The valve should be checked before making any carburetor adjustments. Disconnect the valve from the engine or merely clamp the hose shut. If the engine speed decreases less than 50 rpm, the valve is clogged and should be replaced. If the engine speed decreases much more than 50 rpm, then the valve is good. The PCV valve is an inexpensive item and is easily replaced during routine maintenance. If the new valve doesn't noticeably improve engine idle, the problem might be a restriction in the PCV hose. For more information regarding testing and service intervals, please refer to Section 1 of this manual.

REMOVAL & INSTALLATION

▶ See Figure 6

The valve is inserted into a rubber grommet in the valve cover at the large end (on 1964-66 V8 engines, the valve is located in, or near the carburetor base). At the narrow end, it is inserted into a hose and clamped. To remove it, gently pull it out of the valve cover, then open the clamp with a pair of pliers. Hold the clamp open while sliding it an inch or two down the hose (away from the valve), and then remove the valve.

If the end of the hose is hard or cracked where it holds the valve, it may be feasible to cut the end off if there is plenty of extra hose. Otherwise, replace the hose. Replace the grommet in the valve cover if it is cracked or hard. Replace the clamp if

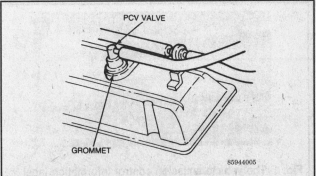

Fig. 6 On most gasoline engines, the PCV valve is located in the rocker arm (valve) cover

it is broken or weak. In replacing the valve, make sure it is fully inserted in the hose, that the clamp is moved over the ridge on the valve so that the valve will not slip out of the hose, and that the valve is fully inserted into the grommet in the valve cover.

PCV Breather

Most breathers are located inside the air cleaner assembly, though they may be mounted directly to a valve cover. Although a breather may in some cases be removed and cleaned, it is an inexpensive part and it is wise to replace it if dirty. Breathers which are mounted directly to the valve cover may be simply grasped and pulled from the cover grommet. For breathers which are mounted inside the air cleaner follow the procedure listed below.

REMOVAL & INSTALLATION

▶ See Figures 7 and 8

1. Loosen the wing nut and remove the top of the air cleaner assembly.
2. Slide the rubber coupling that joins the tube coming from the valve cover to the breather off the breather nipple.
3. Slide the spring clamp off the breather nipple which is protruding from the air cleaner housing, then withdraw the breather from inside the air cleaner assembly.
4. Inspect the rubber grommet in the valve cover and the rubber coupling for brittleness or cracking. Replace parts as necessary.
   To install:
5. Insert the new PCV breather through the hole in the air cleaner with the open portion of the breather upward. Make sure that the square portion of breather behind the nipple fits into the (square) hole in the air cleaner.
6. Install a new spring clamp onto the nipple. Make sure the clamp goes under the ridge on the breather nipple all the way around.
7. Reconnect the rubber coupling.
8. Install the air cleaner cover and tighten the wing nut.

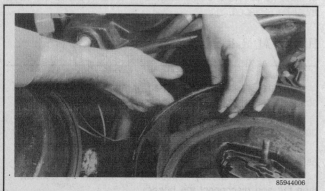

Fig. 7 Disconnect the hose from the breather nipple

Fig. 8 This picture shows the relationship between the spring clamp and the breather

Evaporative Emission Control

OPERATION

▶ See Figures 9 and 10

This system which was introduced to California cars in 1970, and other cars in 1971, reduces the amount of escaping gasoline vapors. Float bowl emissions are controlled by internal carburetor modifications and, in some later vehicles, by a vapor line to the canister. Redesigned bowl vents, reduced bowl capacity, heat shields, and improved intake manifold-to-carburetor insulation reduce vapor loss into the atmosphere. The venting of fuel tank vapors into the air has been stopped by means of the carbon canister storage method. This method transfers fuel vapors to an activated carbon storage device which absorbs and stores the vapor that is emitted from the engine's induction system while the engine is not running. When the engine is running, the stored vapor is purged from the carbon storage device by the intake air flow and then consumed in the normal combustion process. As the manifold vacuum reaches a certain point, it opens a purge control valve mounted atop or near the charcoal storage canister. This allows air to be drawn into the canister, thus forcing the existing fuel vapors back into the engine to be burned normally.

The purge function on many earlier model vehicles was controlled by a Thermal Vacuum Switch (TVS) located inline between the canister and the carburetor/intake manifold. The thermal vacuum switch was threaded into a coolant passage or the thermostat housing and would be activated by engine cool-

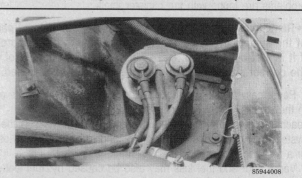

Fig. 9 The evaporative emission canister is usually mounted in the side of the engine compartment

85944009

Fig. 10 Certain engine adjustments, such a carburetor idle speed, often require disconnecting and plugging the canister purge line

ant temperature. Later vehicles switched from thermal to electronic control. The purge control on the 231 and 262 (1985-88) V6 engines is electronically controlled by an inline purge solenoid which is itself activated by the Electronic Control Module (ECM). When the system is in the Open Loop mode, the solenoid valve is energized, blocking all vacuum to the purge valve. When the system is in the Closed Loop mode, the solenoid is de-energized, thus allowing existing vacuum to operate the purge valve. This releases the trapped fuel vapor and it is forced into the induction system.

On late model vehicles that are equipped with a float bowl vent to the canister, a vacuum valve is used to prevent vapor purge from the float bowl when the engine is running. Whenever the engine is off, the valve allows vapors to travel from the float bowl to the canister.

Most carbon canisters used are of the "Open" design, meaning that air is drawn in through the bottom (filter) of the canister. Some 231 V6 canisters are of the "Closed" design which means that the incoming air is drawn directly from the air cleaner.

SERVICE

▶ **See Figures 11, 12 and 13**

Besides a periodic visual inspection of the system's components, the only periodic service necessary (on early model vehicles so equipped) is canister filter replacement. Later vehicles are equipped with a sealed canister that is not equipped with a replaceable cartridge. On these vehicles, the entire canister assembly must be replaced if any damage occurs or any problems are found with the canister itself.

➡**Remember that the fuel tank filler cap is an integral part of the system in that it is designed to seal in fuel vapors. If it is lost or damaged, make sure the replacement is of the correct size and fit so a proper seal can be obtained.**

Periodically check for cracks or leaks in the vacuum lines or in the canister itself. The lines and fittings can usually be reached without removing the canister. Cracks or leaks in the system may cause poor idle, stalling, poor driveability, fuel loss or a fuel vapor odor.

Vapor odor and fuel loss may also be caused by; fuel leaking from the lines, tank or injectors, loose, disconnected or kinked lines or an improperly seated air cleaner and gasket.

If the system passes the visual inspection and a problem is still suspected, check the basic operation of the components:

1. The line from the fuel tank to the canister must be clear and unobstructed. When the engine is **OFF**, air should pass from the fuel tank towards the canister freely in order to allow vapors to collect in the canister. Make sure the line is free of kinks or obstructions. While the engine is not running, air should NOT be allowed out of the canister.

2. If equipped with a float bowl vent, the vacuum valve should only allow air to be blown from the carburetor float bowl towards the canister when no vacuum is applied (engine is not running). To test this valve, attempt to blow air through the valve towards the canister with the engine **OFF**, there should be little or no restriction. Use a hand vacuum pump to apply approximately 15 in. Hg (51 kPa) to the valve, now air should no longer flow towards the canister.

3. Thermal valves are usually designed to open, allowing vacuum or air pressure towards the canister or control valve only when the engine is warm. Attach a length of hose to the engine side fitting and try blowing towards the canister. Air should be felt at the canister side fitting, only when the engine is at normal operating temperature.

➡**When testing valves by blowing air through them, be careful that you are blowing in the proper direction of flow. Many valves are designed to only allow air to flow in one direction and a proper working valve may seem defective if it is tested with air flow only in the wrong direction.**

4. Solenoid valves, used on some late model engines, should close when energized and open when de-energized. Try blowing air through the valve fittings when the engine is **OFF**, it should flow with little or no resistance. When the engine is running the solenoid should energize during engine warm-up and de-energize only once it has reached normal operating temperature.

5. Most vacuum and control valves, with the exception of the float bowl valve, are designed to open when vacuum is applied. In either case, all are designed to allow air to pass through only during one condition (vacuum on or off depending on design). To test vacuum valves, try to blow air through the valve with and without vacuum applied. If air can pass through during only 1 of these conditions the valve is likely operating properly. On the other hand if air can always or never flow, the valve is defective. Use a hand vacuum pump to apply approximately 15 in. Hg (51 kPa) to the valve. The valve should open or close (as applicable) and hold the vacuum for at least 20 seconds, or the diaphragm is leaking and the valve must be replaced.

REMOVAL & INSTALLATION

1. If the hoses can be reached at this time, tag and disconnect them from the canister assembly.

2. Loosen the screw(s) fastening the canister retaining bracket to the vehicle.

3. Rotate the bracket and carefully remove the canister assembly.

4. If not done already, reposition the canister for access, then tag and disconnect the hoses.

5. Remove the canister assembly from the vehicle.

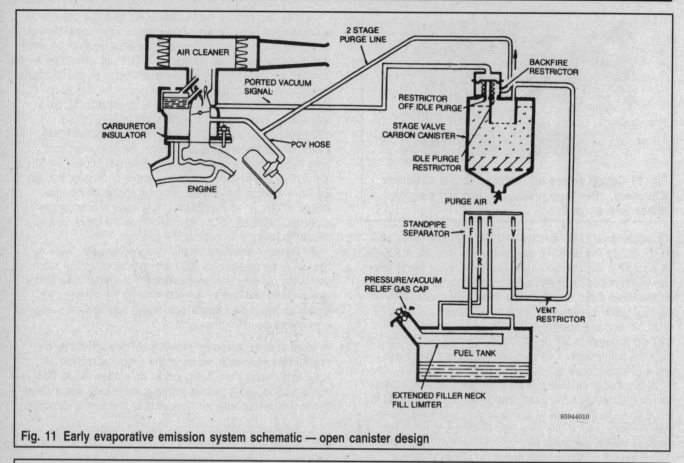

Fig. 11 Early evaporative emission system schematic — open canister design

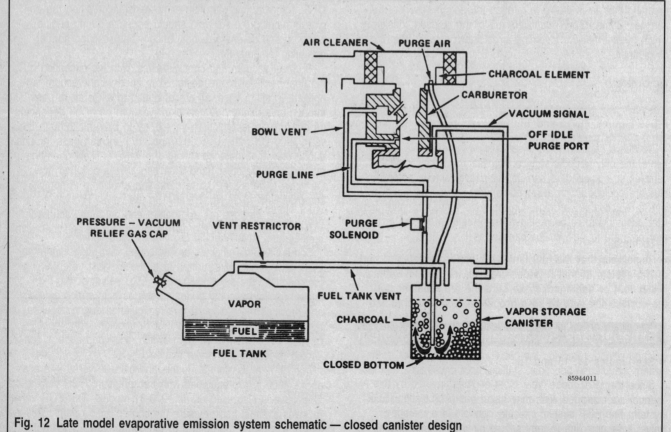

Fig. 12 Late model evaporative emission system schematic — closed canister design

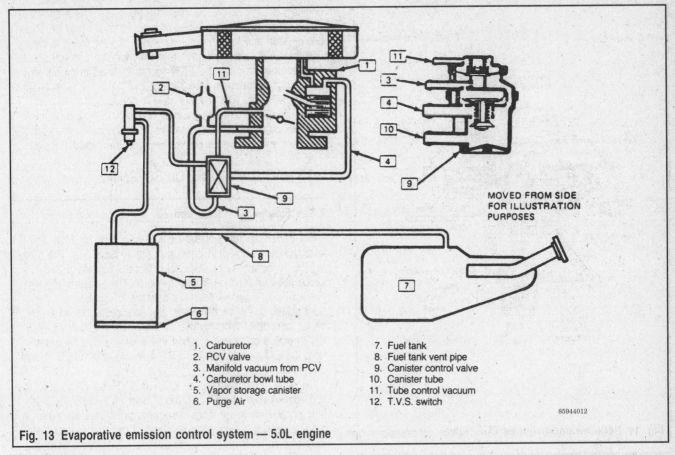

1. Carburetor
2. PCV valve
3. Manifold vacuum from PCV
4. Carburetor bowl tube
5. Vapor storage canister
6. Purge Air
7. Fuel tank
8. Fuel tank vent pipe
9. Canister control valve
10. Canister tube
11. Tube control vacuum
12. T.V.S. switch

MOVED FROM SIDE
FOR ILLUSTRATION
PURPOSES

85944012

Fig. 13 Evaporative emission control system — 5.0L engine

To install:

6. Position the canister in the vehicle.

7. If the hoses cannot be accessed once the canister is secured, connect them now as noted during removal.

8. Install the canister to the retaining bracket and secure using the retaining screw(s).

9. If not done earlier, connect the lines to the canister assembly as noted during removal.

FILTER REPLACEMENT

1. Remove the vapor canister from the vehicle.

2. Grasp the filter in the bottom of the canister with your fingers, then squeeze and pull it out from under the lip surface or from under the retainer bar.

To install:

3. Install a new filter to the bottom of the canister by squeezing and carefully inserting the filter into the canister. Make sure the edges are tucked under the canister lip.

4. Install the canister assembly to the vehicle.

Exhaust Gas Recirculation (EGR) System

▶ See Figures 14, 15 and 16

Since the 1970 model year most engines covered by this manual are equipped with an exhaust gas recirculation (EGR) system. The EGR system typically consists of a metering valve, a vacuum line to the carburetor, and cast-in exhaust gas passages in the intake manifold. The EGR valve is con-

trolled by carburetor vacuum, and accordingly opens and closes to admit exhaust gases into the fuel/air mixture. The exhaust gases lower the combustion temperature, thereby reducing the amount of nitrogen oxides (NOx) produced. The valve is closed at idle and open between the two extreme throttle positions.

In most installations, vacuum to the EGR valve is controlled by a thermal vacuum switch (TVS). The switch, which is installed into the engine block or thermostat housing, shuts off vacuum to the EGR valve until the engine is properly warmed. This prevents the stalling and lumpy idle which would result if EGR occurred when the engine was cold.

As the car accelerates, the carburetor throttle plate uncovers the vacuum port for the EGR valve. At 3-5 in. Hg, the EGR valve opens and some of the exhaust gases are allowed to flow into the air/fuel mixture in order to lower the combustion temperature. At full throttle the valve closes again.

Some California engines are equipped with dual diaphragm EGR valve. This valve further limits the exhaust gas opening (compared to the single diaphragm EGR valve) during high intake manifold vacuum periods, such as high speed cruising, and provides more exhaust gas recirculation during acceleration when manifold vacuum is low. In addition to the hose running to the thermal vacuum switch, a second hose is connected directly to the intake manifold.

For 1977, all California models and cars delivered in areas above 4000 ft. are equipped with backpressure EGR valves. This valve is also used on all 1978-81 models. The EGR valve receives exhaust backpressure through its hollow shaft. This exerts a force on the bottom of the control valve diaphragm, opposed by a light spring. Under low exhaust pressure (low

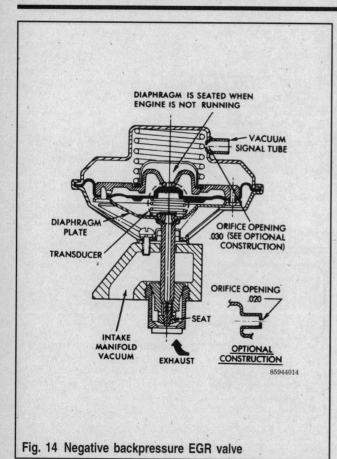

Fig. 14 Negative backpressure EGR valve

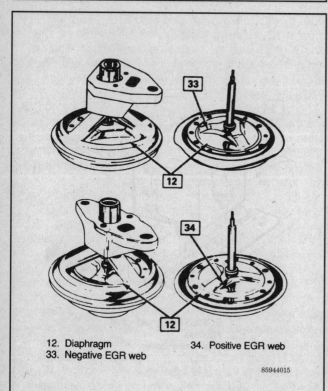

12. Diaphragm
33. Negative EGR web
34. Positive EGR web

Fig. 15 Both negative and positive backpressure EGR valves may be found on Chevrolet mid-size vehicles

engine load and partial throttle), the EGR signal is reduced by an air bleed. Under conditions of high exhaust pressure (high engine load and large throttle opening), the air bleed is closed and the EGR valve responds to an unmodified vacuum signal. At wide open throttle, the EGR flow is reduced in proportion to the amount of vacuum signal available.

The 1979 and later models have a ported signal vacuum EGR valve. The valve opening is controlled by the amount of vacuum obtained from a ported vacuum source on the carburetor and the amount of backpressure in the exhaust system.

EGR VACUUM CONTROL SOLENOID

▶ See Figures 17, 18, 19 and 20

For better control over the EGR system flow on 1981 and later models, a solenoid is used in the vacuum line. The solenoid is controlled by the Electronic Control Module (ECM), which uses information from the coolant temperature, throttle position, and manifold pressure sensors to regulate the vacuum solenoid. On most models, the solenoid is turned on or off for periods of time in order to cut or allow vacuum to the EGR valve. For example, when the engine is cold, a signal from the ECM energizes the EGR solenoid, thus blocking vacuum to the EGR valve.

On some later models, the ECM uses "Pulse Width Modulation" during cold engine operation (meaning it turns the solenoid on and off many times a second) to achieve an even more exact control over the amounts of exhaust gas that are recirculated. After engine warm up, the ECM allows vacuum and backpressure to take over control as in the earlier solenoid controlled models.

For all solenoid controlled systems, the solenoid is also energized during cranking and wide-open throttle. When the engine warms up, the EGR solenoid is turned off by the ECM, and the EGR valve operates according to normal ported vacuum and exhaust backpressure signals.

FAULTY EGR VALVE SYMPTOMS

▶ See Figure 21

An EGR valve that stays open when it should be closed causes weak combustion, resulting in a rough running engine and/or frequent stalling. Too much EGR flow at idle, cruise, or when cold can cause any of the following:
- Engine stopping after a cold start
- Engine stopping at idle after deceleration
- Surging during cruising
- Rough idle

An EGR valve which is stuck closed and allows little or no EGR flow causes extreme combustion temperatures (too hot) during acceleration. Spark knock (detonation or pinging), engine overheating and excess engine emissions can all be a result, as well as engine damage.

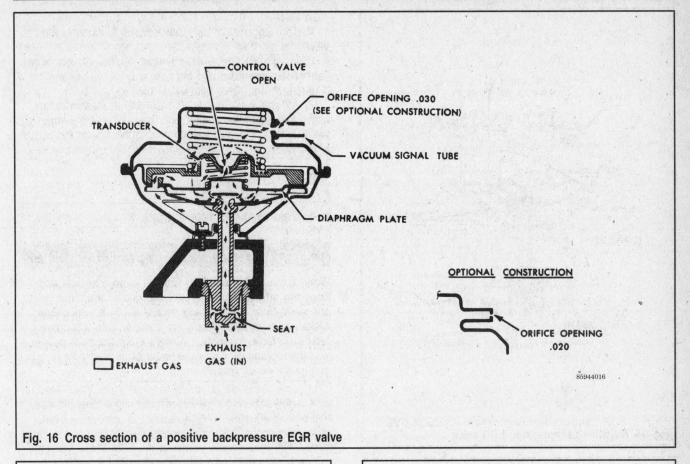

Fig. 16 Cross section of a positive backpressure EGR valve

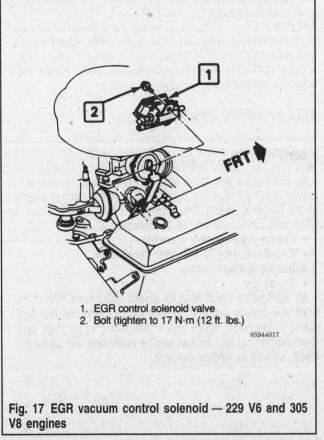

1. EGR control solenoid valve
2. Bolt (tighten to 17 N·m (12 ft. lbs.)

Fig. 17 EGR vacuum control solenoid — 229 V6 and 305 V8 engines

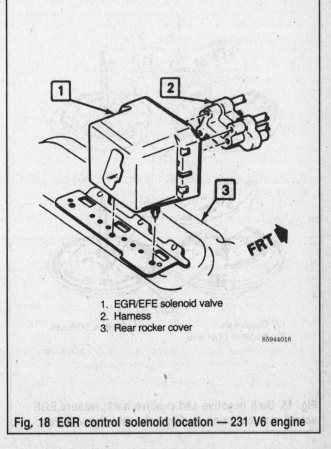

1. EGR/EFE solenoid valve
2. Harness
3. Rear rocker cover

Fig. 18 EGR control solenoid location — 231 V6 engine

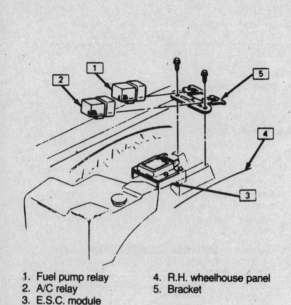

1. Fuel pump relay
2. A/C relay
3. E.S.C. module
4. R.H. wheelhouse panel
5. Bracket

85944019

Fig. 19 EGR control solenoid location — 1985 262 V6 engine

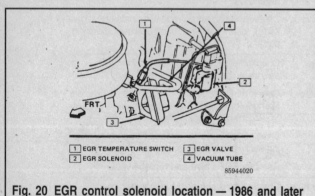

FRT.

| 1 | EGR TEMPERATURE SWITCH | 3 | EGR VALVE |
| 2 | EGR SOLENOID | 4 | VACUUM TUBE |

85944020

Fig. 20 EGR control solenoid location — 1986 and later 262 V6 engine

REMOVAL & INSTALLATION

EGR Valve

▶ See Figures 22 and 23

1. Detach the vacuum line(s) from the EGR valve. If there is more than one line, be sure to label them to assure proper installation.

2. Unfasten the two bolts or bolt and clamp which attach the valve to the manifold, then remove the valve.

3. Make sure the old valve gasket is removed from the manifold.

To install:

4. Thoroughly clean the gasket mating surfaces of the valve and manifold.

5. Install the valve to the manifold. Always use a new gasket between the valve and the manifold.

6. Install and tighten the valve retainers.

7. Attach the vacuum line(s). On dual diaphragm valves, attach the carburetor vacuum line to the tube at the top of the valve, and the manifold vacuum line to the tube at the center of the valve.

TVS Switch

▶ See Figures 24 and 25

1. Drain the engine cooling system to a level below the TVS switch.

✳✳CAUTION

When draining the coolant, keep in mind that cats and dogs are attracted by the ethylene glycol antifreeze, and are quite likely to drink any that is left in an uncovered container or in puddles on the ground. This will prove fatal in sufficient quantity. Always drain the coolant into a sealable container. Coolant should be reused unless it is contaminated or several years old.

2. Disconnect the vacuum lines from the switch noting their locations for assembly purposes.

3. Carefully unthread the switch from the bore.

To install:

4. Apply sealer to the threaded portion of the switch.

5. Install the switch to the bore and tighten it to 15 ft. lbs. (20 Nm).

6. If possible, rotate the head of the switch to a position that will permit easy hookup of vacuum hoses.

7. Connect the vacuum hoses to the proper connectors as noted during removal.

EGR VALVE CLEANING

✳✳WARNING

Do not wash the valve assembly in solvents or degreasers. Permanent damage to the valve diaphragm may result.

Valves That Protrude from Mounting Face

▶ See Figure 26

1. Remove the EGR valve from the intake manifold.

2. Holding the valve assembly in hand, use a small plastic hammer to tap the valve lightly and remove exhaust deposits from the valve seat. Shake out any loose particles. DO NOT put the valve in a vise.

3. Carefully remove any exhaust deposits from the mounting surface of the valve with a wire wheel or putty knife. Be careful not to score or damage the mounting surface.

4. Depress the valve diaphragm and inspect the valve seating areas through the valve outlet for cleanliness. If the valve

EGR System Diagnosis

Condition	Possible Cause	Correction
Engine idles abnormally rough and/or stalls.	EGR valve vacuum hoses mis-routed.	Check EGR valve vacuum hose routing. Correct as required.
	Leaking EGR valve.	Check EGR valve for correct operation.
	EGR valve gasket failed or loose EGR attaching bolts.	Check EGR attaching bolts for tightness. Tighten as required. If not loose, remove EGR valve and inspect gasket. Replace as required.
	EGR control solenoid.	Check vacuum into control solenoid from carburetor EGR port with engine at normal operating temperature and at curb idle speed. Then check the vacuum out of the EGR control solenoid to EGR valve. If the two vacuum readings are not equal within ± 1/2 in. Hg. (1.7 kPa), then problem could be within EGR solenoid or ECM unit.
	Improper vacuum to EGR valve at idle.	Check vacuum from carburetor EGR port with engine at stabilized operating temperature and at curb idle speed. Vacuum should not exceed 1.0 in. Hg. If vacuum exceeds this, check carburetor idle.
Engine runs rough on light throttle acceleration and has poor part load performance.	EGR valve vacuum hose misrouted.	Check EGR valve vacuum hose routing. Correct as required.
	Check for loose valve.	Torque valve.
	Failed EGR control solenoid.	Same as listing in "Engine Idles Rough" condition.
	Sticky or binding EGR valve.	Clean EGR passage of all deposits.
		Remove EGR valve and inspect. Replace as required.
	Wrong or no EGR gasket(s) and/or Spacer.	Check and correct as required. Install new gasket(s), install spacer (if used), torque attaching parts.
Engine stalls on decelerations.	Control valve blocked or air flow restricted.	Check internal control valve function per service procedure.
	Restriction in EGR vacuum line or control solenoid signal tube.	Check EGR vacuum lines for kinks, bends, etc. Remove or replace hoses as required. Check EGR control solenoid function.
		Check EGR valve for excessive deposits causing sticky or binding operation. Replace valve.
	Sticking or binding EGR valve.	Remove EGR valve and replace valve.
Part throttle engine detonation.	Control solenoid blocked or air flow restricted.	Check control solenoid function per check chart.
	Insufficient exhaust gas recirculation flow during part throttle accelerations.	Check EGR valve hose routing. Check EGR valve operation. Repair or replace as required. Check EGR control solenoid as listed in "Engine Idles Rough" section. Check EGR passages and valve for excessive deposit. Clean as required.

(NOTICE: Non-Functioning EGR valve could contribute to part throttle detonation.)

		Check EGR per service procedure.

(NOTICE: Detonation can be caused by several other engine variables. Perform ignition and carburetor related diagnosis.)

Engine starts but immediately stalls when cold.	EGR valve hoses misrouted.	Check EGR valve hose routings.
	EGR control solenoid system malfunctioning when engine is cold.	Perform check to determine if the EGR solenoid is operational. Replace as required.

(NOTICE: Stalls after start can also be caused by carburetor problems.)

85944021

Fig. 21 Possible causes of EGR system faults

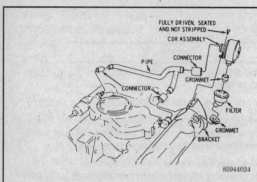

Fig. 22 Pull the EGR valve and gasket from the top of the intake manifold

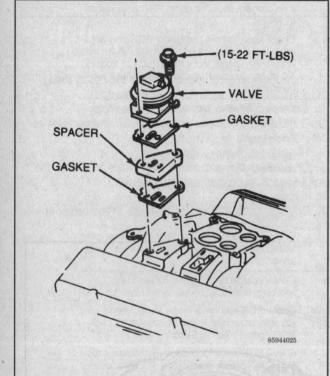

Fig. 23 Exploded view of a common EGR valve mounting — note that the spacer is not used in all applications

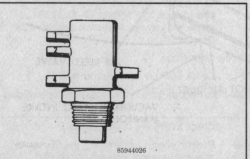

Fig. 24 Example of a Thermostatic Vacuum Switch (TVS) — Nipple 1 is to the distributor; 2 is to the TCS solenoid and 4 is to the intake manifold

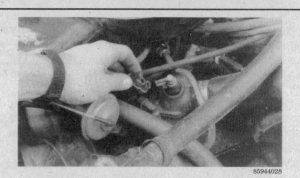

Fig. 25 Some thermostatic switch vacuum lines are harness attached to ease service

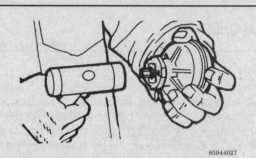

Fig. 26 On EGR assemblies whose valves are protruding from the mounting face, tap the valve lightly with a small plastic hammer to loosen exhaust deposits

and/or seat are not completely clean, attempt to remove the remaining deposits using the plastic hammer.

5. Look for exhaust deposits in the valve outlet, and remove any deposits with an old screwdriver or small prytool.

6. Clean the mounting surfaces of the intake manifold and valve assembly, then install the valve to the intake.

Shielded Valves or Valves That Do Not Protrude

1. Remove the valve from the intake manifold.

2. Clean the base of the valve with a wire brush or wheel to remove exhaust deposits from the mounting surface.

3. Clean the valve seat and valve in an abrasive-type spark plug cleaning machine or sand-blaster. Most machine shops provide this service. Make sure the valve portion is cleaned (blasted) for about 30 seconds, and that the valve is also cleaned with the diaphragm spring fully compressed (valve unseated). The cleaning should be repeated until all deposits are removed.

4. The valve must be blown out with compressed air thoroughly to ensure all abrasive material is removed from the valve.

5. Clean the mounting surface of the intake manifold and valve assembly, then install the valve.

Thermostatic Air Cleaner

▶ See Figures 27 and 28

All late model engines utilize the THERMAC system (in 1978 it was called TAC, but was the same). This system is designed to warm the air entering the carburetor when underhood temperatures are low, and to maintain a controlled air temperature into the carburetor at all times. By allowing preheated air to enter the carburetor, the amount of time the choke is on can be reduced, resulting in quicker warm-up time, better fuel economy and lower emissions.

The Thermac system is composed of the air cleaner body, an air filter, sensor unit, vacuum diaphragm, damper door, and associated hoses and connections. Heat radiating from the exhaust manifold is trapped by a heat stove and is ducted to the air cleaner in order to supply heated air to the carburetor. A movable door in the air cleaner case snorkel allows air to be drawn in from the heat stove (cold operation) or from underhood air (warm operation). The door position is controlled by the vacuum motor, which receives intake manifold vacuum as modulated by the temperature sensor.

SYSTEM CHECKS

1. Check the vacuum hoses for leaks, kinks, breaks, or improper connections and correct any defects.
2. With the engine off, check the position of the damper door within the snorkel. A mirror can be used to make this job easier. The damper door should be open to admit outside air.
3. Using a hand vacuum pump, apply at least 7 in. Hg of vacuum to the damper diaphragm unit. The door should close. If it doesn't, check the diaphragm linkage for binding and correct hookup. With vacuum still applied and the door closed, clamp the tube to trap the vacuum. If the door doesn't remain closed, there is a leak in the diaphragm assembly.

4. If a vacuum pump is not available or the cleaner passed the other tests and a problem is still suspected, leave the end of the air cleaner snorkel disconnected from the air intake duct-work, then perform a cold start of the engine. The door in the snorkel should close allowing heater air from the exhaust manifold and heat stove to enter the air cleaner.
5. Allow the engine to come to normal operating temperature, then check and make sure the door has opened. If the door does not operate properly, make sure the vacuum lines and temperature sensor are in good condition. If the door opened with the hand-held vacuum pump, but not when the engine warmed, the temperature sensor or the lines are likely at fault.

REMOVAL & INSTALLATION

▶ **See Figure 29**

Vacuum Motor

1. Loosen the wing nut and disconnect the hoses, then remove the air cleaner assembly from the vehicle.
2. Disconnect the vacuum hose from the motor.
3. Drill out the spot welds with a ⅛ in. bit, then enlarge as necessary to remove the retaining strap.
4. Remove the retaining strap.
5. Lift up the motor and cock it to one side to unhook the motor linkage at the control damper assembly.
   To install:
6. Drill a ⁷/₆₄ in. hole in the snorkel tube at the center of the vacuum motor retaining strap.

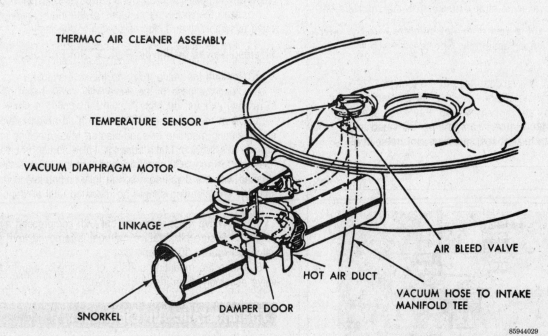

THERMAC AIR CLEANER ASSEMBLY

TEMPERATURE SENSOR

VACUUM DIAPHRAGM MOTOR

LINKAGE

SNORKEL

DAMPER DOOR

HOT AIR DUCT

AIR BLEED VALVE

VACUUM HOSE TO INTAKE MANIFOLD TEE

85944029

Fig. 27 Example of a THERMAC air cleaner assembly

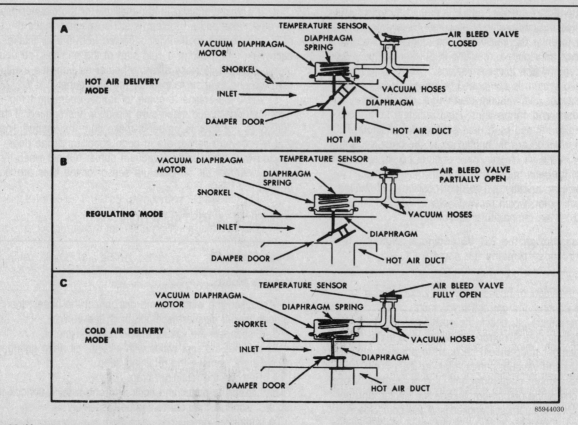

Fig. 28 Vacuum motor operation schematic

7. Insert and engage the vacuum motor linkage into the control damper assembly.

8. Use the motor retaining strap and a sheet metal screw to secure the retaining strap and motor to the snorkel tube.

➡**Make sure the screw does not interfere with the operation of the damper assembly. Shorten the screw if necessary.**

9. Connect the vacuum hose to the motor.

10. Install the air cleaner assembly to the vehicle making sure the hoses are properly seated. Pay close attention to the brittle heat stove to make sure it is not damaged and it is fully seated on both the exhaust manifold and the snorkel.

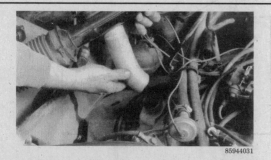

Fig. 29 When removing and installing the air cleaner housing, pay close attention to the fragile heat stove to make sure it is not damaged

Temperature Sensor

1. Loosen the wing nut and disconnect the hoses, then remove the air cleaner assembly from the vehicle.

2. Disconnect the air cleaner hoses from the temperature sensor.

3. Pry up the tabs on the sensor retaining clip, then remove the clip and sensor from the air cleaner.

To install:

4. Install the sensor to the vehicle using a new retaining clip, then secure the tabs to hold the sensor in place.

5. Connect the air cleaner hoses to the temperature sensor.

6. Install the air cleaner assembly to the vehicle making sure the hoses are properly seated. Pay close attention to the brittle heat stove to make sure it is not damaged and it is fully seated on both the exhaust manifold and the snorkel.

Air Injection Reactor (AIR) System

▶ **See Figures 30, 31 and 32**

The AIR system was first introduced on California cars in 1966 and was later used on most vehicles covered in this manual through 1980. A form of the system may be found on all 231 V6 engines as late as 1984. In the early 1980's most other engines for the Chevrolet mid-sized vehicles changed to another, very similar, system known as Air Management and is covered later in this section.

The AIR system injects compressed air into the exhaust system near the exhaust valves. The fresh air allows exhaust gases, which normally remain unburned as they are expelled from the system, to continue burning and thereby lower emissions. To do this it employs an air injection pump and and a system of hoses, valves, tubes, etc., necessary to carry the compressed air from the pump to the exhaust manifolds. Carburetors and distributors for AIR engines have specific modifications to adapt them to the air injection system; those components should not be interchanged with those intended for use on engines that do not have the system.

A diverter valve is used to prevent backfiring. The valve senses sudden increases in manifold vacuum and ceases the injection of air during fuel-rich periods. During coasting, this valve diverts the entire air flow through the pump muffler and during high engine speeds, expels it through a relief valve. Check valves in the system prevent exhaust gases from entering the pump.

➡The AIR system on the 231 V6 engine is slightly different, but its purpose remains the same.

SERVICE

The AIR system's effectiveness depends on correct engine idle speed, ignition timing, and dwell. These settings should be strictly adhered to and checked frequently. Refer to the engine tune-up procedures in Section 2 of this manual for more information on engine settings. In addition to engine control adjustments, all hoses and fittings should be inspected for condition and connection tightness. Check the drive belt for wear and tension every 12 months or 12,000 miles.

REMOVAL & INSTALLATION

Air Pump

✶✶WARNING

Do not pry on the pump housing or clamp the pump in a vise; the housing is soft and may become distorted.

1. Disconnect the air hose(s) at the pump.
2. If necessary, hold the pump pulley form turning and loosen the pulley bolts.
3. Loosen the pump mounting bolt and adjustment bracket bolt. Remove the drive belt.
4. Remove the mounting bolts, and then remove the pump.
To install:
5. Position the pump in the vehicle and loosely install the mounting bolts
6. If loosened or removed, install and tighten the pulley bolts.
7. Position the drive belt over the pulley, then adjust the belt tension and tighten the pump bolts.
8. Connect the air hose(s) to the pump.

Diverter (Anti-afterburn) Valve

1. Detach the vacuum sensing line from the valve.
2. Disconnect the remaining hose(s) from the valve.
3. Unfasten the diverter valve from the elbow or the pump body and remove the valve from the vehicle.

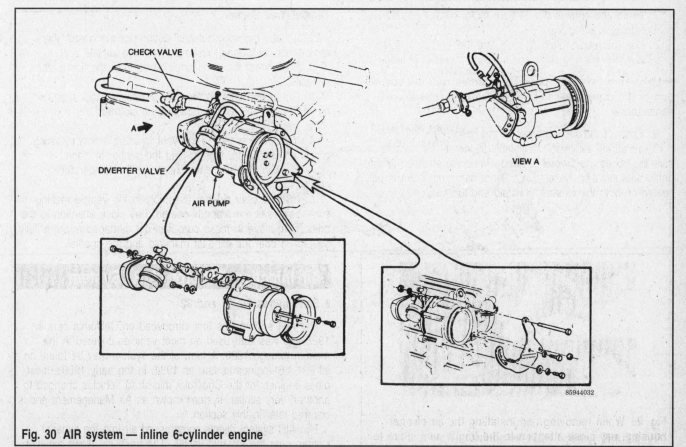

Fig. 30 AIR system — inline 6-cylinder engine

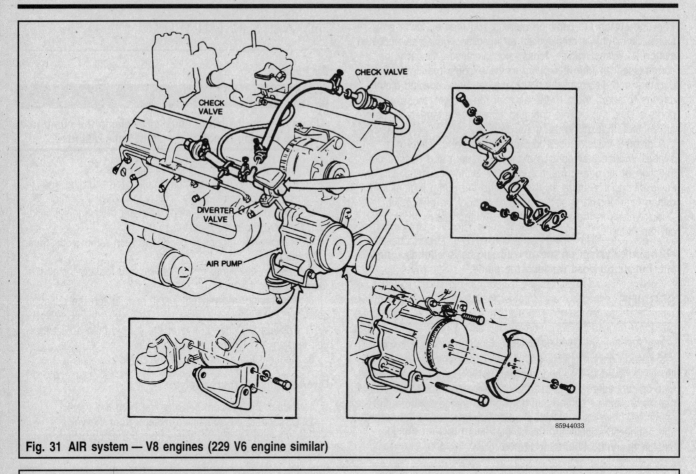

Fig. 31 AIR system — V8 engines (229 V6 engine similar)

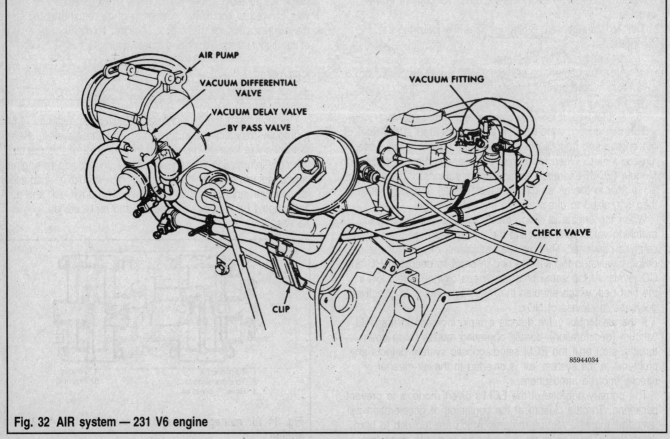

Fig. 32 AIR system — 231 V6 engine

To install:

4. Install the diverter valve to the elbow or the pump body using a new gasket.

5. Tighten the valve securing bolts to 85 in. lbs. (10 Nm).

6. Connect the vacuum sensing line and hoses(s) to the valve.

Air Management System

▶ **See Figures 33, 34 and 35**

With the exception of the 231 V6 engine (which does not use a dual-bed converter and is equipped with the standard AIR system through 1984) the air management system was used on most vehicles 1981 and later. The air management system is used to provide additional oxygen to continue the combustion process after the exhaust gases leave the combustion chamber; much the same as the AIR system described earlier in this chapter. Air is injected into either the exhaust port(s), the exhaust manifold(s) or the catalytic converter by an engine driven air pump. The system is in operation at all times and will bypass air only momentarily during deceleration and at high speeds. The bypass function is performed by the air management valve, while the check valve protects the air pump by preventing any backflow of exhaust gases.

The AIR system helps to reduce HC and CO content in the exhaust gases by injecting air into the exhaust ports during cold engine operation. This air injection also helps the catalytic converter to reach the proper temperature quicker during warm-up. When the engine is warm (closed loop), the AIR system injects air into the beds of the three-way converter, so equipped, in order to lower the HC and CO content in the exhaust.

The Air Management System utilizes the following components:

1. An engine driven air pump
2. Air management valves (Air Control and Air Switching)
3. Airflow and control hoses
4. Check valves
5. A dual-bed, three-way catalytic converter.

The belt driven, vane-type air pump is located at the front of the engine and supplies clean air to the system for purposes already stated. When the engine is cold, the Electronic Control Module (ECM) energizes an air control solenoid. This allows air to flow to the air switching valve. The air switching valve is then energized to direct air into the exhaust port.

When the engine is warm, the ECM de-energizes the air switching valve, thus directing the air between the beds of the catalytic converter. This provides additional oxygen for the oxidizing catalyst in the second bed in order to decrease HC and CO levels. At the same time this keeps oxygen levels low in the first bed, which enables the reducing catalyst to effectively decrease the levels of NOx.

If the air control valve detects a rapid increase in manifold vacuum (deceleration), certain operating modes (wide open throttle, etc.) or if the ECM self-diagnostic system detects any problems in the system, air is diverted to the air cleaner or directly into the atmosphere.

The primary purpose of the ECM's divert mode is to prevent backfiring. Throttle closure at the beginning of deceleration will temporarily create air/fuel mixtures which are too rich to burn completely. These mixtures will become burnable when they

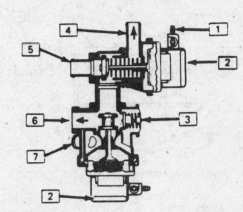

1. Vacuum signal
2. Solenoid
3. Relief valve
4. Converter air
5. Port air
6. Air from pump
7. Divert air

Fig. 33 Electric Divert/Electric air Switching (EDES) valve

reach the exhaust if they are combined with injection air. If this was allowed to occur, the next firing of the engine would ignite the mixture causing an exhaust backfire. Momentary diverting of the injection air from the exhaust prevents this.

SERVICE

The air managements system's effectiveness depends upon a properly maintained and tuned engine control system. Refer to the engine tune-up procedures in Section 2 of this manual for more information on engine settings. In addition to engine control adjustments, all hoses and fittings should be inspected for condition and connection tightness. The drive belt and air filter should be checked periodically and replaced, as necessary.

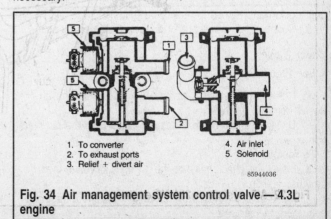

1. To converter
2. To exhaust ports
3. Relief + divert air
4. Air inlet
5. Solenoid

Fig. 34 Air management system control valve — 4.3L engine

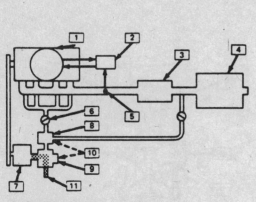

1. Closed loop fuel control
2. ECM
3. Reducing catalyst
4. Oxidizing catalyst
5. O_2 sensor
6. Check valve
7. Air pump
8. Air switching valve
9. Air divert valve
10. Electrical signals from ECM
11. By-pass air to air cleaner

85944037

Fig. 35 Air management system operation

REMOVAL & INSTALLATION

Air Pump

1. Disconnect the valves and/or adapter at the air pump.
2. Loosen the air pump adjustment bolt(s) and remove the drive belt.
3. Unscrew the three mounting bolts and then remove the pump pulley.
4. Unscrew the pump mounting bolts and then remove the pump.
To install:
5. Position the pump in the vehicle, then install the mounting bolts.
6. Install the pump pulley and tighten the mounting bolts.
7. Position the drive belt over the pulley, then adjust the belt tension and tighten the adjusting bolt(s).
8. Connect the valves and/or adapter to the air pump.

Check Valve
▶ See Figure 36

1. Release the retaining clamp, then disconnect the air hoses from the valve.
2. Unscrew and remove the check valve from the air injection pipe.
To install:
3. Install the check valve to the air injection pipe, then carefully tighten.
4. Make sure the hoses are properly positioned, then connect them to the valve.

5. Position and secure the retaining clamp to the hoses.

Air Management Valve
▶ See Figure 37

1. Disconnect the negative battery cable.
2. Remove the air cleaner assembly.
3. Tag and disconnect the vacuum hose(s) from the valve.
4. Tag and disconnect the air outlet hoses from the valve.
5. Bend back the lock tabs and then remove the bolts holding the elbow to the valve.
6. Tag and disengage any electrical connections at the valve, then remove the valve from the elbow.
To install:
7. Position the valve in the vehicle and install it to the elbow, then engage the electrical connections, as noted during removal.
8. Tighten the retaining bolts, then bend the lock tabs into position.
9. Connect the air outlet hoses to the valve, as noted during removal.
10. Connect the vacuum hose(s) to the valve, as noted during removal.
11. Install the air cleaner assembly.
12. Connect the negative battery cable.

Pump Filter Removal
▶ See Figure 38

1. Remove the drive belt and pump pulley.
2. Using needle nose pliers, carefully pull the fan from the pump.

➡Use care to prevent any dirt or fragments from entering the air intake hole. DO NOT insert a screwdriver between the pump and the filter, and do not attempt to remove the metal hub. It is seldom possible to remove the filter without destroying it.

3. To install a new filter, draw it on with the pulley and pulley bolts. DO NOT hammer or press the filter on the pump.
4. Draw the filter down evenly by torquing the bolts alternately and evenly. Make sure the outer edge of the filter slips into the housing. A slight amount of interference with the housing bore is normal.

➡The new filter may squeal initially until the sealing lip on the pump outer diameter has worn in.

Anti-Dieseling Solenoid

▶ See Figure 39

Beginning in 1968 some models may be equipped with an idle speed (idle stop) solenoid on the carburetor. All 1972-75 models are equipped with these idle solenoids. Due to the leaner carburetor settings required for emission control, the engine may have a tendency to diesel or run-on after the ignition is turned off. The carburetor solenoid, energized when the ignition is on, maintains the normal idle speed. When the ignition is turned off, the solenoid is de-energized and permits the throttle valves to fully close, thus preventing run-on. For adjustment of carburetors with idle solenoids see the section on carburetor adjustments in Section 2 of this manual.

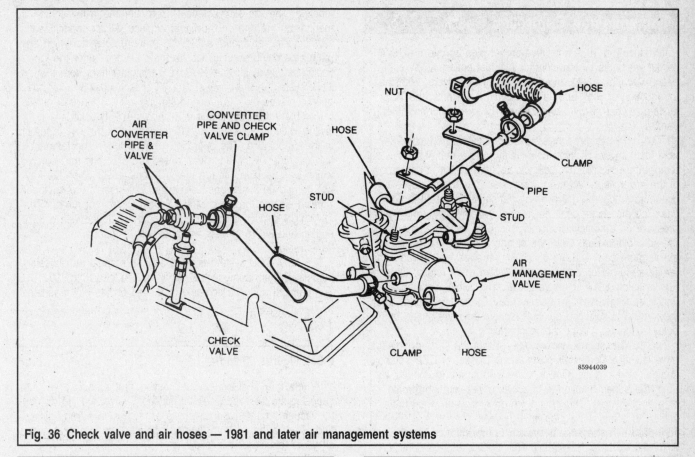

Fig. 36 Check valve and air hoses — 1981 and later air management systems

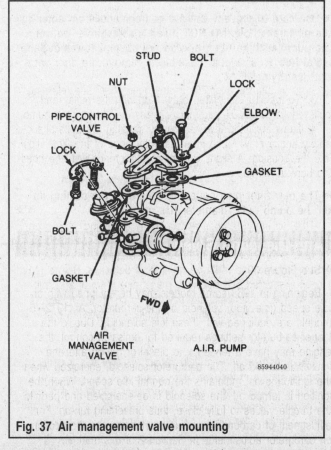

Fig. 37 Air management valve mounting

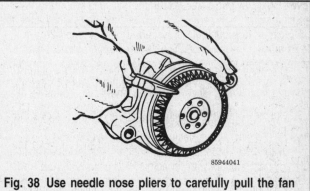

Fig. 38 Use needle nose pliers to carefully pull the fan from the pump

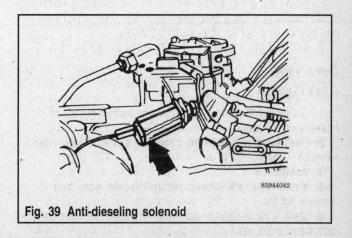

Fig. 39 Anti-dieseling solenoid

Transmission Controlled Spark

Introduced in 1970 and used on vehicles up into the 1974 model year, this system controls exhaust emissions by eliminating vacuum advance in the lower forward gears. With the introduction of High Energy Ignition (HEI) systems, the TCS system fell out of favor and was not used in 1975 and later cars.

The 1970 system consists of a transmission switch, solenoid vacuum switch, time delay relay, and a thermostatic water temperature switch. The solenoid vacuum switch is energized in the lower gears via the transmission switch and closes off distributor vacuum. The two-way transmission switch is activated by the shifter shaft on manual transmissions, and by oil pressure on automatic transmissions. The switch de-energizes the solenoid in High gear, the plunger extends and uncovers the vacuum port, and the distributor receives full vacuum. The temperature switch overrides the system when engine temperature is below 63°F or above 232°F. This allows vacuum advance in all gears. A time delay relay opens 15 seconds after the ignition is switched on. Full vacuum advance during this delay eliminates the possibility of stalling.

The 1971 system is similar, except that the vacuum solenoid (now called a Combination Emissions Control or CEC solenoid) serves two functions. One function is to control distributor vacuum; the added function is to act as a deceleration throttle stop in High gear. This cuts down on emissions when the vehicle is coming to a stop in High gear. The CEC solenoid is controlled by a temperature switch, a transmission switch, and a 20 second time delay relay. This system also contains a reversing delay, which energizes the solenoid when the transmission switch, temperature switch or time delay completes the CEC circuit to ground. This system is directly opposite the 1970 system in operation. The 1970 vacuum solenoid was normally open to allow vacuum advance and when energized, closed to block vacuum. The 1971 system is normally closed blocking vacuum advance and when energized, opens to allow vacuum advance. The temperature switch completes the CEC circuit to ground when engine temperature is below 82°F. The time delay relay allows vacuum advance (and raised idle speed) for 200 seconds after the ignition key is turned to the ON position. Models with an automatic transmission and air conditioning also have a solid state timing device which engages the air conditioning compressor for three seconds after the ignition key is turned to the OFF position to prevent the engine from running on.

The 1972 6-cylinder system is similar to that used on 1971, except that an idle stop (anti-dieseling) solenoid has been added to the system. In the energized position, the solenoid maintains engine speed at a predetermined fast idle. When the solenoid is de-energized by turning off the ignition, the solenoid allows the throttle plates to close beyond the normal idle position; thus cutting off their air supply and preventing engine run-on. The 6-cylinder is the only 1972 engine with a C.E.C. valve, which serves the same deceleration function as in 1971. The 1972 time delay relay delays full vacuum 20 seconds after the transmission is shifted into High gear. V8 engines use a vacuum advance solenoid similar to that used in 1970. This relay is normally closed to block vacuum and opens when energized to allow vacuum advance. The solenoid controls distributor vacuum advance and performs no throttle positioning function. The idle stop solenoid used operates in the same manner as the one on 6-cylinder engines. All air conditioned cars have an additional anti-diesel (run-on) solenoid which engages the compressor clutch for three seconds after the ignition is switched off. The 1973 TCS system differs from the 1972 system in three ways. The 23 second upshift delay has been replaced by a 20 second starting relay. This relay closes to complete the TCS circuit and open the TCS solenoid, allowing vacuum advance, for 20 seconds after the key is turned to the on position. The operating temperature of the temperature override switch has been raised to 93°F, and the switch which was used to engage the A/C compressor when the key was turned OFF has been eliminated. All models are equipped with an electric throttle control solenoid to prevent run-on. The 1973 TCS system is used on all models equipped with a 307 engine and all V8 models equipped with a manual transmission.

The 1974 TCS system is used only on manual transmission models. System components remain unchanged from 1973. The vacuum advance solenoid is located on the coil bracket.

TESTING

▶ **See Figures 40 and 41**

If there is a TCS system malfunction, first connect a vacuum gauge in the hose between the solenoid valve and the distributor vacuum unit. Drive the vehicle or raise it on a frame lift and observe the vacuum gauge. If full vacuum is available in all gears, check for the following:
- Blown fuse.
- Disconnected wire at the solenoid-operated vacuum valve.
- Disconnected wire at the transmission switch.
- Temperature override switch energized due to low engine temperature.
- Solenoid failure.

If no vacuum is available in any gear, check the following:
- Solenoid valve vacuum lines switched.
- Clogged solenoid vacuum valve.
- Distributor or manifold vacuum lines leaking or disconnected.
- Transmission switch or wire grounded.

The individual components may be tested as follows:

Idle Stop Solenoid

This unit may be checked simply by observing it while an assistant switches the ignition on and off. The solenoid's piston should extend further with the current switched on. The unit is not repairable and must be replaced if defective. Before replacing a suspected bad solenoid, make sure it is not the fault of the wiring. A voltmeter may be used to check for voltage at the solenoid connector when the ignition is switched on.

Solenoid Vacuum Valve

Check that proper manifold vacuum is available. Connect the vacuum gauge in the line between the solenoid valve and the distributor. Check the system descriptions above to determine if the valve should be energized or de-energized to allow vacuum. Simulate the proper control conditions by applying or denying 12 volts to the solenoid. If vacuum is still not available, the valve is defective, either mechanically or electrically.

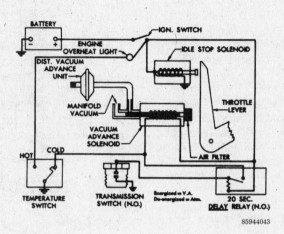

Fig. 40 Small Block V8 TCS system in the engine OFF mode (Big block V8 and inline systems similar)

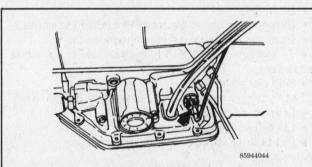

Fig. 41 TCS switch location — turbo hydro-matic 350 shown (most transmissions similar, though side may vary)

The unit is not repairable. If the valve is satisfactory, check the relay next.

➡A valve of this type may also be checked by attempting to blow are through its passages while the solenoid is energized and while it is de-energized. Air should be allowed to blow through under only 1 of these conditions. If air passes is allowed through or blocked under both conditions, the solenoid valve is faulty.

Relay

1. With the engine at normal operating temperature and the ignition on, ground the solenoid vacuum valve terminal with the black lead. The solenoid should energize (vacuum/no vacuum depending upon application) if the relay is satisfactory.

2. With the solenoid energized (allowing or denying vacuum, as applicable) as in Step 1, connect a jumper from the relay terminal with the green/white stripe lead to ground. The solenoid should de-energize if the relay is satisfactory.

3. If the relay worked properly in Steps 1 and 2, check the temperature switch. The relay unit is not repairable.

Temperature Switch

The vacuum valve solenoid should be either de-energized or energized (depending upon application) in order to allow vacuum for distributor advance when the engine is cold. The easiest way to check switch conditions is through continuity tests with the engine cold and the engine warmed. The switch should open or close (again, depending upon application) once a certain temperature is reached. First check switch continuity with the engine cold (coolant temperature below 63°F for 1970 engines, 82°F for 1971 engines or 93°F for 1973-74 engines). Then start and run the engine until normal operating temperature is reached. At a coolant temperature above these listed values, recheck for switch continuity. The switch should have opened or closed once these temperatures were surpassed. If the switch was satisfactory, check the transmission switch.

Transmission Switch

With the engine at normal operating temperature and the transmission in one of the no-vacuum gears (check the system description for year applications), the vacuum valve solenoid should be energized (no vacuum). If not, remove the ground switch electrical lead. If the solenoid energizes, replace the switch.

Early Fuel Evaporation (EFE) System

▶ See Figures 42, 43, 44 and 45

Most 1975 and later models (except TBI) are equipped with this system to reduce engine warm-up time, improve driveability, and reduce emissions. On start-up, a vacuum motor acts to close a heat valve in the exhaust manifold which causes exhaust gases to enter the intake manifold heat riser passages and enter the thermostatic air cleaner. Incoming fuel mixture is then heated and more complete fuel evaporation is provided during warm-up.

The system consists of a Thermal Vacuum Switch (TVS), along with an exhaust heat valve and actuator. The Thermal Vacuum Switch is located on the coolant outlet housing on V8s, and on the block on inline 6-cylinder engines. When the engine is cold, the TVS conducts manifold vacuum to the actuator to close the valve. When engine coolant, or oil on the 6-cylinder engine, warms up, vacuum is interrupted and the actuator should open the valve.

➡ On 231 V6 (1981 and later) engines and 262 V6 (1985 and later) engines, the EFE system is controlled by the ECM.

As of 1981, some 231 V6 turbo engines utilize a heater grid system instead of the vacuum servo system. Although the purpose of heater grid system remains the same (to reduce engine warm-up time, improve driveability and to reduce emissions) the operation is entirely different. The new system is electric and uses a ceramic heater grid located underneath the primary bore of the carburetor as part of the carburetor insulator/gasket. When the engine coolant is below the specified calibration level, electrical current is supplied to the heater through an ECM controlled relay.

CHECKING THE EFE SYSTEM

Vacuum Servo Systems

1. With the engine overnight cold, have someone start the engine while you observe the vacuum servo exhaust heat valve (on some V8s, the EFE valve actuator arm is covered by a two-piece metal cover, which must be removed for service). The valve should snap to the closed position.

2. Watch the valve as the engine warms up. By the time coolant starts circulating through the radiator on most V-type engines or the oil is hot on inline engines, the valve should snap open.

3. If the valve does not close, immediately disconnect the hose at the actuator, and check for vacuum by placing your finger over the end of the hose, or with a vacuum gauge. If there is vacuum, immediately disconnect the hose leading to the TVS from the manifold at the TVS. If there is vacuum here, but not at the actuator, replace the TVS. If vacuum does not exist at the hose going to the TVS, check that the vacuum hose is free of cracks or breaks and tightly connected at the manifold, and that the manifold port is clear.

4. If the valve does not open when the engine coolant or oil warms up, disconnect the hose at the actuator, and check for vacuum by placing your finger over the end of the hose or

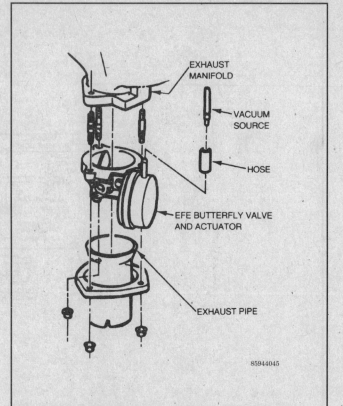

Fig. 42 The vacuum-servo type EFE system is most prevalent on these vehicles

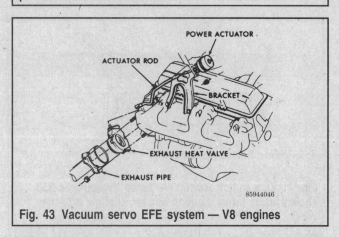

Fig. 43 Vacuum servo EFE system — V8 engines

using a vacuum gauge. If there is vacuum, replace the TVS. If there is no vacuum, replace the actuator.

Heater Grid Systems

▶ See Figure 46

1. With the engine overnight cold, disengage the connector from the heater grid. Connect a test light or voltmeter between the harness connector terminals. Turn the ignition ON and energize the relay and check to see if power is available to the heater grid. The relay may be energized in 2 ways. The diagnostic test terminal of the underdash ECM connector may be grounded setting the ECM into diagnostic mode, at the end of which the ECM will energize the relay. Also, the relay connector terminal C (ECM ground wire) may be grounded to close the relay and provide power to the grid.

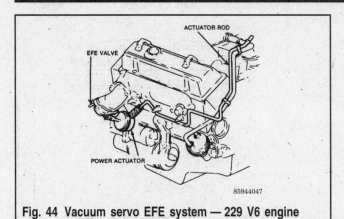

Fig. 44 Vacuum servo EFE system — 229 V6 engine

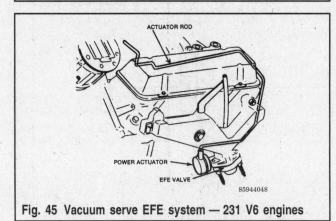

Fig. 45 Vacuum serve EFE system — 231 V6 engines

2. If no power is available, check the wiring supplying power to the relay. Make sure the fusible link and the ignition fuse are both good.

3. If power was present, check the heater grid using an ohmmeter. Take a resistance reading across the grid connector terminals. If the reading is under 3 ohms, the heater is good. If resistance is over 3 ohms, replace the heater.

REMOVAL & INSTALLATION

Thermo Vacuum Switch (TVS)

The TVS is located on the engine coolant outlet housing for V8 engines or on the block for inline 6-cylinder engines. In order to replace the switch on V8 engines, the coolant must be drained to a level is below the outlet housing. No oil need be drained on 6-cylinder engines. Upon installation, be sure to apply sealer to sensor threads on V8 engines. Use no sealer on 6-cylinder engines. Note that the valve must be installed until just snug (approximately 120 in. lbs.) and then turned by hand just far enough to line up the fittings for hose connection.

Heater Grid
▶ See Figure 47

1. Disconnect the negative battery cable.
2. Remove the air cleaner assembly.
3. Tag and disconnect all electrical, vacuum and fuel connections from the carburetor.
4. Disconnect the EFE heater electrical connection.

5. Remove the carburetor assembly from the intake manifold. For details, refer to the procedure in Section 5 of this manual.
6. Lift the EFE heater from the intake manifold.
To install:
7. Install the EFE heater to the intake manifold.
8. Install the carburetor assembly.
9. Engage the EGE heater electrical connection.
10. Engage all electrical, vacuum and fuel connections to the carburetor as noted during removal.
11. Install the air cleaner assembly, then connect the negative battery cable.
12. Start the engine and check for any leaks.

Controlled Combustion System

▶ See Figure 48

The CCS system relies upon leaner air/fuel mixtures and altered ignition timing to improve combustion efficiency. A special air cleaner with a thermostatically controlled opening is used on most CCS equipped models to ensure that air entering the carburetor is kept at 100°F. This allows leaner carburetor settings and improves engine warm-up. A 15°F higher temperature thermostat is employed on CCS cars to further improve emission control.

SERVICE

Since the only extra component added with a CCS system is the thermostatically controlled air cleaner, there is no additional maintenance required; however, tune-up adjustments such as idle speed, ignition timing, and dwell become much more critical. Care must be taken to ensure that these settings are correct, both for trouble-free operation and a low emission level.

Computer Controlled Catalytic Converter (C-4) System

The C-4 System, installed on certain 1979 and all 1980 cars sold in California, is an electronically controlled exhaust emission system. The purpose of the system is to maintain the ideal air/fuel ratio at which the catalytic converter is most effective. As the system is designed around feedback control of the air/fuel mixture, it was a predecessor of engine control systems that were soon to follow.

Major components of the system include an Electronic Control Module (ECM), an oxygen sensor, an electronically controlled carburetor, and a three-way oxidation reduction catalytic converter. The system also includes a maintenance reminder flag connected to the odometer which becomes visible in the instrument cluster at regular intervals, signaling the need for oxygen sensor replacement.

The oxygen sensor, installed in the exhaust manifold, generates a voltage which varies with exhaust gas oxygen content. Lean mixtures (more oxygen) reduce voltage; rich mixtures (less oxygen) increase voltage. The voltage output is monitored by the ECM which uses the information in engine control calculations.

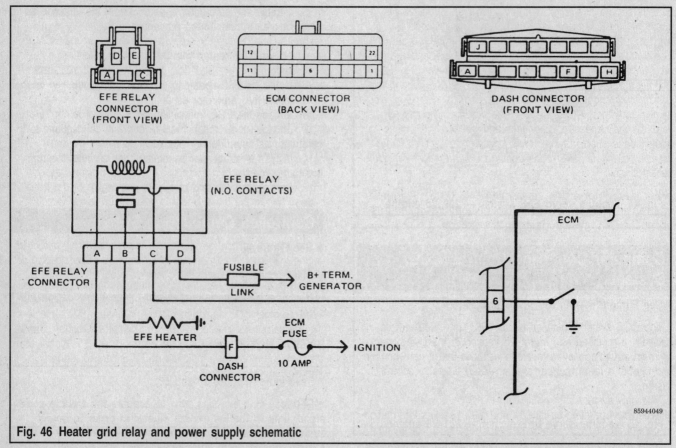

Fig. 46 Heater grid relay and power supply schematic

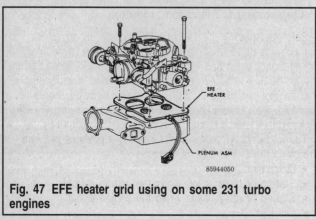

Fig. 47 EFE heater grid using on some 231 turbo engines

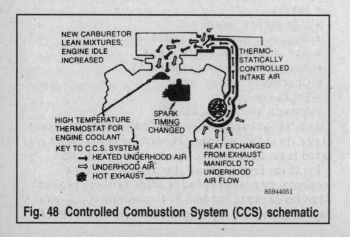

Fig. 48 Controlled Combustion System (CCS) schematic

An engine temperature sensor installed in the engine coolant outlet monitors engine coolant temperatures. Vacuum control switches and throttle position sensors also monitor engine conditions and supply signals to the ECM.

The Electronic Control Module receives input signals from all sensors. It processes these signals and generates a control signal sent to the carburetor. The control signal cycles between on (lean command) and off (rich command). The amount of on and off time is a function of the input voltage sent to the ECM by the oxygen sensor.

Rochester Dualjet (2-barrel) E2ME and E4ME (4-barrel) carburetors are used with the C-4 system. Basically, an electrically operated mixture control solenoid is installed in the carburetor float bowl. The solenoid controls the air/fuel mixture which is metered to the idle and main metering systems. Air metering to the idle system is controlled by an idle air bleed valve. It follows the movement of the mixture solenoid to control the amount of air bled into the idle system, enriching or leaning out the mixture as appropriate. Air/fuel mixture enrichment occurs when the fuel valve is open and the air bleed valve is closed. All cycling of this system, which occurs ten times per second, is controlled by the ECM. A throttle position switch informs the ECM of the open or closed throttle operation. A number of different switches are used, varying with application. When the ECM receives a signal from the throttle switch, indicating a change of position, it immediately searches its memory for the set of operating conditions that result in an ideal air/fuel ratio, and shifts to that set of conditions. The memory is continually updated during normal operation.

A Check-Engine light is included in the C-4 System installation. When a fault develops, the light comes on, and a trouble code is set into the ECM memory. However, if the fault is intermittent, the light will go out, but the trouble code will remain in the ECM memory as long as the engine is running. The trouble codes are used as a diagnostic aid, and are pre-programmed.

Unless the required tools are available, troubleshooting the C-4 System should be confined to mechanical checks of electrical connectors, vacuum hoses and the like. Should you access to the necessary diagnostic equipment, a diagnostic trouble code chart may be found later in this section. Otherwise, all diagnosis and repair should be performed by a qualified mechanic.

➡For more information concerning C-4 System diagnosis and repair, refer to the Basic Troublshooting procedures under the CCC system, later in this section.

Computer Command Control (CCC) System

▶ See Figures 49, 50, 51, 52, 53 and 54

The CCC system, installed on all 1981 and later cars, is basically a modified and improved version of the C-4 system. Its main advantage over its predecessor is that it can monitor and control a large number of interrelated emission control systems.

This new system can monitor up to 15 various engine/vehicle operating conditions and then use this information to control as many as 9 engine related systems. The system is thereby making constant adjustments to maintain optimum vehicle performance under all normal driving conditions while at the same time allowing the catalytic converter to effectively control the emissions of NOx, HC and CO.

In addition, the Electronic Control Module (ECM) contains a built in diagnostic system that recognizes and identifies possible operational problems and alerts the driver through a Check Engine (or Service Engine Soon) light in the instrument panel. The light will remain ON until the problem is corrected. The ECM also has built in back-up systems that, in most cases of operational problems, will allow for the continued operation of the vehicle in a near normal manner until the repairs can be made.

The CCC system has some components in common with the C-4 system, although they are not interchangeable. These components include the Electronic Control Module (ECM), which, as previously stated, controls many more functions than does it predecessor, an oxygen sensor, an electronically controlled variable mixture carburetor, a three-way catalytic converter, throttle position and coolant sensors, a Barometric Pressure (BARO) sensor, a Manifold Absolute Pressure (MAP) sensor and a Check Engine light in the instrument panel.

Components unique to the CCC system include the Air Injection Reaction (AIR) management system, a charcoal canister purge solenoid, EGR valve controls, a vehicle speed sensor (in the instrument panel), a transmission converter clutch solenoid (only on models with automatic transmission), idle speed control and Electronic Spark timing (EST).

The ECM, in addition to monitoring sensors and sending out control signals to the carburetor, also controls the following components or sub-systems: charcoal canister purge control, the AIR system, idle speed, automatic transmission converter

lock-up, distributor ignition timing, the EGR valve, and the air conditioner converter clutch.

The EGR valve control solenoid is activated by the ECM in a fashion similar to that of the charcoal canister purge solenoid. When the engine is warm, the ECM de-energizes the solenoid and the vacuum signal is allowed to reach and open the EGR valve.

The Transmission Converter Clutch (TCC) lock is controlled by the ECM through an electrical solenoid in the automatic transmission. When the vehicle speed sensor in the dash signals the ECM that the car has attained the predetermined speed, the ECM energizes the solenoid which allows the torque converter to mechanically couple the engine to the transmission. When the brake pedal is pushed, or during deceleration or passing, etc., the ECM returns the transmission to fluid drive.

The idle speed control adjusts the idle speed to all particular engine load conditions and will lower the idle under no-load or low-load conditions in order to conserve fuel.

➡Not all engines use all systems. Control application may differ.

BASIC TROUBLESHOOTING

▶ See Figures 55, 56, 57 and 58

➡The following explains how to activate the trouble code signal light in the instrument cluster in order to begin system troubleshooting. Because of the complexity of the system, this is not a complete C-4 or CCC system troubleshooting and isolation procedure.

Before suspecting the C-4 or CCC system, or any of its components as faulty, check the ignition system (distributor, timing, spark plugs and wires). Check the engine compression, the air cleaner and any of the emission control components that are not controlled by the ECM. Also check the intake manifold, the vacuum hoses and hose connectors for any leaks. Check the carburetor mounting bolts for tightness.

The following symptoms could indicate a possible problem area with the C-4 or CCC systems:
• Detonation
• Stalling or rough idling when the engine is cold
• Stalling or rough idling when the engine is hot
• Missing
• Hesitation
• Surging
• Poor gasoline mileage
• Sluggish or spongy performance
• Hard starting when engine is cold
• Hard starting when the engine is hot
• Objectionable exhaust odors
• Engine cuts out
• Improper idle speed (CCC only)

As a bulb and system check, the Check Engine (or Service Engine Soon) light will come ON when the ignition switch is turned to the ON position but the engine is not started.

The Check Engine light will also produce the trouble code/codes by a series of flashes which translate as follows: When the diagnostic test lead (C-4) or terminal (CCC) under the instrument panel is grounded with the ignition in the ON

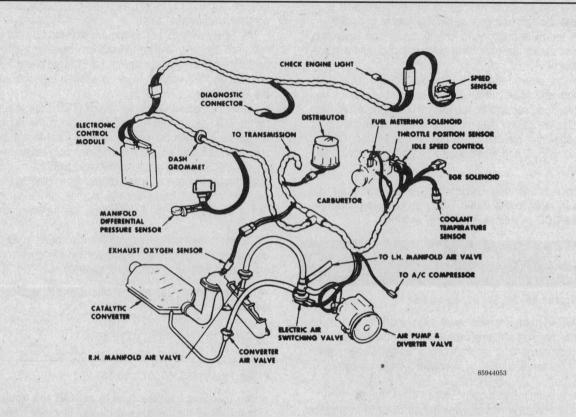

CHECK ENGINE LIGHT

DIAGNOSTIC
CONNECTOR

SPEED
SENSOR

ELECTRONIC
CONTROL
MODULE

DISTRIBUTOR

FUEL METERING SOLENOID

THROTTLE POSITION SENSOR

TO TRANSMISSION

IDLE SPEED CONTROL

DASH
GROMMET

EGR SOLENOID

CARBURETOR

COOLANT
TEMPERATURE
SENSOR

MANIFOLD
DIFFERENTIAL
PRESSURE SENSOR

TO L.H. MANIFOLD AIR VALVE

EXHAUST OXYGEN SENSOR

TO A/C COMPRESSOR

CATALYTIC
CONVERTER

ELECTRIC AIR
SWITCHING VALVE

AIR PUMP &
DIVERTER VALVE

R.H. MANIFOLD AIR VALVE

CONVERTER
AIR VALVE

85944053

Fig. 49 Computer Command Control (CCC) system components and wiring

position and the engine not running. The Check Engine light will flash once, pause, and then flash twice in rapid succession. This is a Code 12, which indicates that the diagnostic system is working. After a long pause, the Code 12 will repeat itself until the engine is started or the ignition switch is turned OFF. For fuel injected engines, the ECM will continue in diagnostic mode and flash any stored trouble codes while the engine is NOT running. Should the engine be started with the test terminal grounded, fuel injected vehicles will enter the field service mode.

➡Trouble code diagnosis on 4.3L TBI vehicles is almost identical to the carbureted CCC vehicles. The major difference is that to begin code flashing on fuel injected vehicles, the diagnostic connector terminals should be grounded while the engine is NOT running. Once the engine is running, the indicator light will flash for 30 seconds to 2 minutes indicating open loop operation. After the system enters closed loop operation, the light will indicate engine rich or lean operation. When the Service Engine Soon light is out, a lean signal is being indicated. When the light is on the ECM is receiving a rich oxygen sensor signal.

Whenever the engine is started, the Check Engine light will remain ON for a few seconds as a bulb and system check, then the lifht will turn off. If the Check Engine light remains ON, the self-diagnostic system has detected a problem. If the test lead (C-4) or test terminal (CCC) is then grounded (with the engine running except for 4.3L TBI engines), the trouble code will flash (3) three times. If more than one problem is found, each trouble code will flash (3) three times and then

change to the next one. Trouble codes will flash in numerical order (lowest code number to highest). The trouble code series will repeat themselves for as long as the test leads or terminal remains grounded.

➡For more information regarding the ECM and fuel injection system, refer to Section 5 of this manual.

A trouble code indicates a problem with a given circuit. For example, trouble code 14 indicates a problem in the cooling sensor circuit. This includes the coolant sensor, its electrical harness and the Electronic Control Module (ECM). The entire circuit must then be checked, starting with the harness and the sensor. The ECM should always be the last component that is suspected because it is usually the most expensive and most difficult to test (if testing is even possible).

Since the self-diagnostic system cannot diagnose every possible fault in the system, the absence of a trouble code does not necessarily mean that the system is trouble free. To determine whether or not a problem with the system exists that does not activate a trouble code, a system performance check must be made. This job should be left to a qualified service technician.

In case of an intermittent fault in the system, the Check Engine light will go out when the fault goes away, but the trouble code will remain in the memory of the ECM. Therefore, if a trouble code can be obtained even though the Check Engine light is not on, it must still be evaluated. It must be determined if the fault is intermittent or if the engine must be operating under certain conditions (acceleration, deceleration, etc.) before the Check Engine light will come on. In some cases, certain trouble codes will not be recorded in the ECM

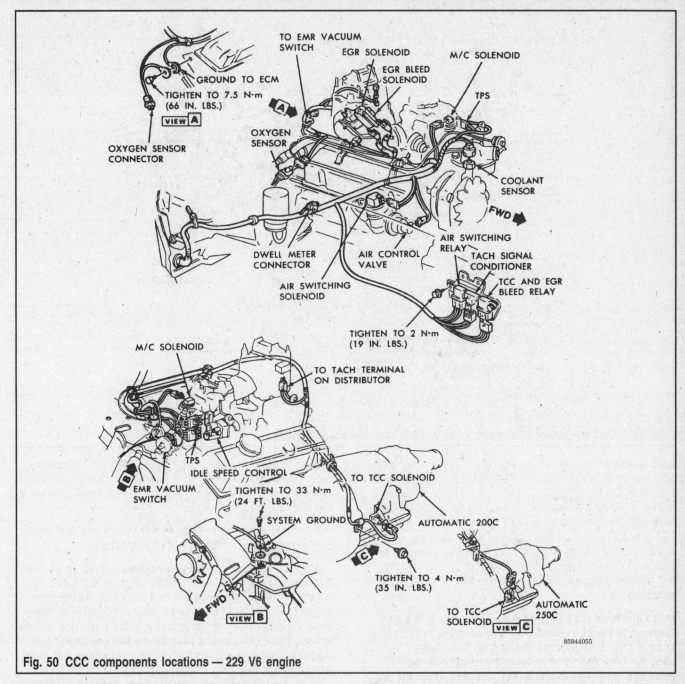

TO EMR VACUUM SWITCH

GROUND TO ECM

TIGHTEN TO 7.5 N·m (66 IN. LBS.)

VIEW A

OXYGEN SENSOR CONNECTOR

OXYGEN SENSOR

EGR SOLENOID

EGR BLEED SOLENOID

M/C SOLENOID

TPS

COOLANT SENSOR

FWD

DWELL METER CONNECTOR

AIR CONTROL VALVE

AIR SWITCHING SOLENOID

AIR SWITCHING RELAY

TACH SIGNAL CONDITIONER

TCC AND EGR BLEED RELAY

TIGHTEN TO 2 N·m (19 IN. LBS.)

M/C SOLENOID

TO TACH TERMINAL ON DISTRIBUTOR

TPS

EMR VACUUM SWITCH

IDLE SPEED CONTROL

TIGHTEN TO 33 N·m (24 FT. LBS.)

SYSTEM GROUND

TO TCC SOLENOID

AUTOMATIC 200C

FWD

VIEW B

TIGHTEN TO 4 N·m (35 IN. LBS.)

TO TCC SOLENOID

AUTOMATIC 250C

VIEW C

85944055

Fig. 50 CCC components locations — 229 V6 engine

until the engine has been operated at part throttle for at least 5 to 8 minutes.

Intermittent fault codes are often due to loose or damaged wiring and connectors. If an intermittent code is present, check the wiring for breaks or damage. Locate the wiring connectors and make sure they are not corroded and that they are properly engaged. Sometimes simply by grasping and wiggling a poor connection (while the engine is running) will set an intermittent code.

On the C-4 system, the ECM erases all trouble codes every time that the ignition is turned off. In the case of intermittent faults, a long term memory is desirable. This can be produced by temporarily connecting the orange connector/lead from terminal S of the ECM directly to the battery (or to a the CCC system, a trouble code will be stored until the terminal "R" at

the ECM has been disconnected from the battery for at least 10 seconds.

Activating Trouble Code Read Out

On the C-4 system, activate the trouble code read out by grounding the trouble code test lead. Use the illustrations to help you locate the test lead under the instrument panel (usually a white and black wire and/or a green connector).

On the CCC system, locate the multi-terminal test connector under the left side of the instrument panel. Use a jumper wire and ground the test terminal (2nd terminal from the top right of the connector). This can be easily accomplished by jumpering the test terminal to the connector ground terminal (top right terminal). Remember that on carbureted vehicles the read out can only be activated while the engine is running, while on fuel

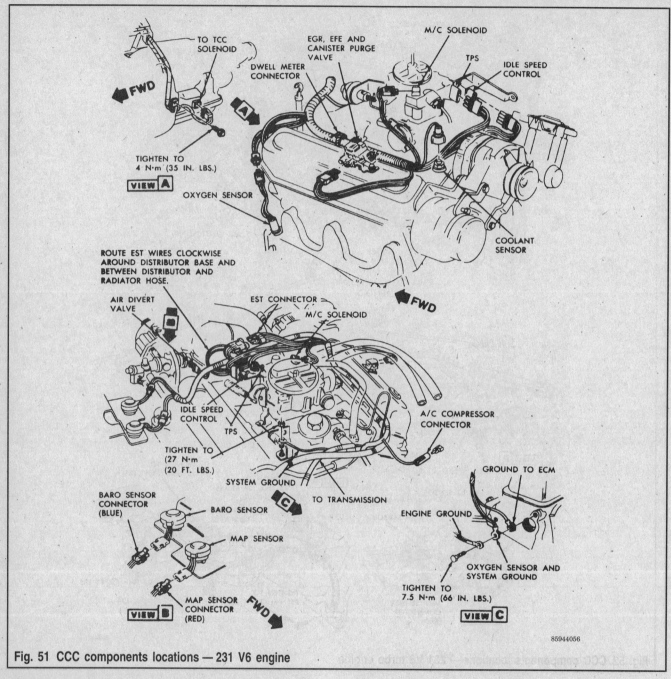

Fig. 51 CCC components locations — 231 V6 engine

injected vehicles, the read out can only be activated when the engine is stopped.

➡Ground the test lead/terminal according to the instructions given previously in the Basic Troubleshooting section.

Mixture Control Solenoid (M/C)

On all computer controlled (feedback) vehicles, the fuel flow through the carburetor idle main metering circuits is controlled by a mixture control (M/C) solenoid located in the carburetor. The M/C solenoid changes the air/fuel mixture to the engine by controlling the fuel flow through the carburetor. The ECM controls the solenoid by providing a ground. When the solenoid is energized, the fuel flow through the carburetor is reduced,

providing a leaner mixture. When the ECM removes the ground, the solenoid is de-energized, increasing the fuel flow and providing a richer mixture. The M/C solenoid is energized and de-energized at a rate of 10 times per second.

The mixture control solenoid is mounted under the carburetor air horn assembly. Adjustment or replacement requires a partial rebuild of the carburetor unit. In the event of air horn removal, most of the carburetor internal and external adjustments must be checked and adjusted.

Throttle Position Sensor (TPS)

▶ See Figure 59

On feedback vehicles, the throttle position sensor is mounted in the carburetor body and is used to supply throttle position

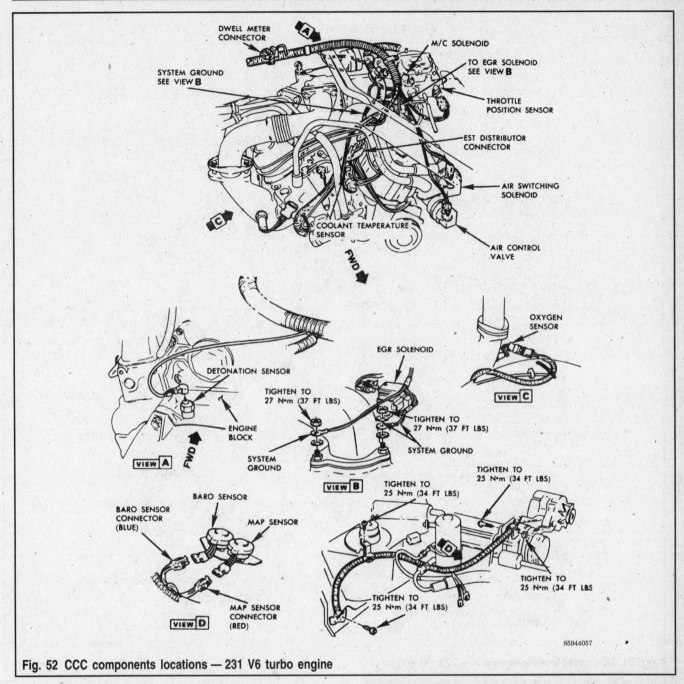

DWELL METER
CONNECTOR

SYSTEM GROUND
SEE VIEW **B**

M/C SOLENOID

TO EGR SOLENOID
SEE VIEW **B**

THROTTLE
POSITION SENSOR

EST DISTRIBUTOR
CONNECTOR

AIR SWITCHING
SOLENOID

COOLANT TEMPERATURE
SENSOR

AIR CONTROL
VALVE

FWD

DETONATION SENSOR

EGR SOLENOID

OXYGEN
SENSOR

TIGHTEN TO
27 N•m (37 FT LBS)

TIGHTEN TO
27 N•m (37 FT LBS)

VIEW **C**

ENGINE
BLOCK

SYSTEM GROUND

VIEW **A**   FWD

SYSTEM
GROUND

VIEW **B**

TIGHTEN TO
25 N•m (34 FT LBS)

TIGHTEN TO
25 N•m (34 FT LBS)

BARO SENSOR

BARO SENSOR
CONNECTOR
(BLUE)

MAP SENSOR

TIGHTEN TO
25 N•m (34 FT LBS)

TIGHTEN TO
25 N•m (34 FT LBS

MAP SENSOR
CONNECTOR
(RED)

TIGHTEN TO
25 N•m (34 FT LBS)

VIEW **D**

85944057

Fig. 52 CCC components locations — 231 V6 turbo engine

information to the ECM. The ECM memory stores an average of operation conditions with the ideal air/fuel ratios for each of those conditions. When the ECM receives a signal that indicates throttle position change, it immediately shifts to the last remembered set of operating conditions that resulted in an ideal air/fuel ratio control. The memory is continually being updated during normal operations.

Idle Speed Control (ISC)

229, 231 V6 (Except Turbo)

◗ **See Figure 60**

The Idle Speed Control (ISC) does just what its name implies - it controls the idle. The ISC is used to maintain low engine speeds while at the same time preventing stalling due to engine load changes. The system consists of a motor assembly mounted on the carburetor which moves the throttle lever so as to open or close the throttle blades.

The whole operation is controlled by the ECM. The ECM monitors engine load to determine the proper idle speed. To

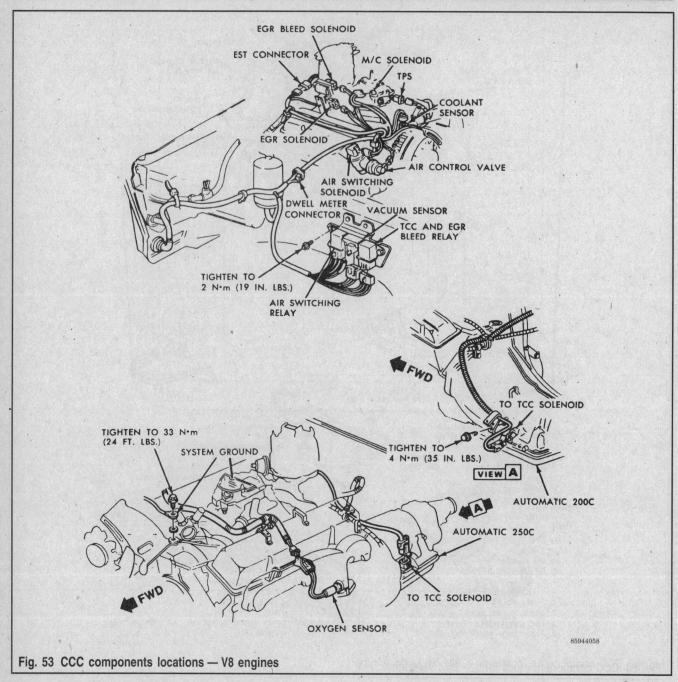

Fig. 53 CCC components locations — V8 engines

prevent stalling, it monitors the air conditioning compressor switch, the transmission, the park/neutral switch and the ISC throttle switch. The ECM processes all this information and then uses it to control the ISC motor which in turn will vary the idle speed as necessary.

Electronic Spark Timing (EST)

▶ See Figures 61 and 62

All 1980 models with the 231 V6 engine and all 1981 and later models, except those with the 229 V6 engine, are equipped with EST. The EST distributor, as described in Sections 2 and 3 of this manual, contains no vacuum or centrifugal advance mechanism, but is instead equipped with a seven terminal HEI module. It has four wires going to a four

terminal connector in addition to the connectors normally found on the HEI distributors. A reference pulse, indicating engine rpm is sent to the ECM; terminal R on the 7-terminal HEI provides this pulse on all models (except the 229 V6 engine). The ECM determines the proper spark advance for the engine operating conditions and then sends an EST pulse back to the distributor.

➡ **The distributor for the 1985 and later 262 V6 engine is equipped with a modified module which has eight terminals.**

Under most normal operating conditions, the ECM will control spark advance. However, under certain operating conditions such as cranking or when setting base timing, the distributor is capable of operating without ECM control. This condition is called BYPASS and is determined by the BYPASS

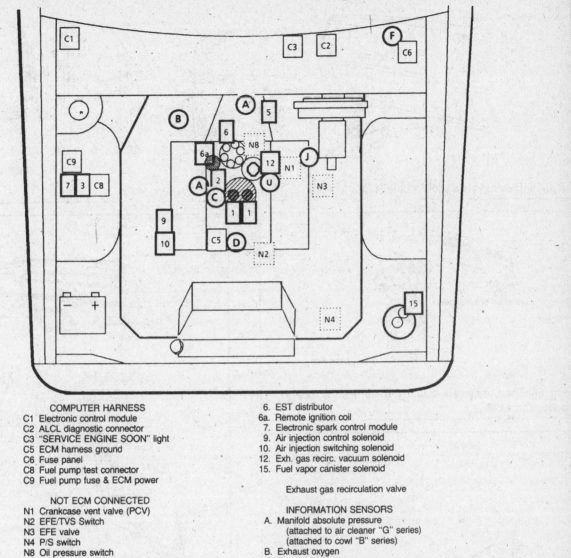

COMPUTER HARNESS
C1 Electronic control module
C2 ALCL diagnostic connector
C3 "SERVICE ENGINE SOON" light
C5 ECM harness ground
C6 Fuse panel
C8 Fuel pump test connector
C9 Fuel pump fuse & ECM power

NOT ECM CONNECTED
N1 Crankcase vent valve (PCV)
N2 EFE/TVS Switch
N3 EFE valve
N4 P/S switch
N8 Oil pressure switch

CONTROLLED DEVICES
1. Fuel injectors
2. Idle air control motor
3. Fuel pump relay
5. Trans. conv. clutch connector

6. EST distributor
6a. Remote ignition coil
7. Electronic spark control module
9. Air injection control solenoid
10. Air injection switching solenoid
12. Exh. gas recirc. vacuum solenoid
15. Fuel vapor canister solenoid

Exhaust gas recirculation valve

INFORMATION SENSORS
A. Manifold absolute pressure
    (attached to air cleaner "G" series)
    (attached to cowl "B" series)
B. Exhaust oxygen
C. Throttle position
D. Coolant temperature
F. Vehicle speed
J. ESC knock
U. EGR temp. diagnostic switch
    on base of valve

85944059

Fig. 54 CCC components locations — 262 V6 engine

lead which runs from the ECM to the distributor. When the BYPASS lead is at the proper voltage, the ECM will control the spark. If the lead is grounded or open circuited, the HEI module itself will control the spark. Disconnecting the 4-terminal EST connector will also cause the engine to operate in the BYPASS mode.

Electronic Spark Control (ESC)

▶ **See Figures 63 and 64**

The Electronic Spark Control (ESC) system can be found on most 231 V6 TURBO engine 1981 and later. The system was also used on all engine in 1984 and later vehicle. The ESC system is a closed loop system that controls engine detonation by adjusting the spark timing. There are two basic components in this system, the controller and the sensor.

The controller processes the sensor signal and re-modifies the EST signal to the distributor in order to adjust the spark timing. The process is continuous so that the presence of detonation is monitored and controlled. The controller is not capable of memory storage.

The sensor is a magneto restrictive device, mounted in the engine block that detects the presence, or absence, and intensity of detonation according to the vibration characteristics of the engine. The output is an electrical signal which is sent to the controller.

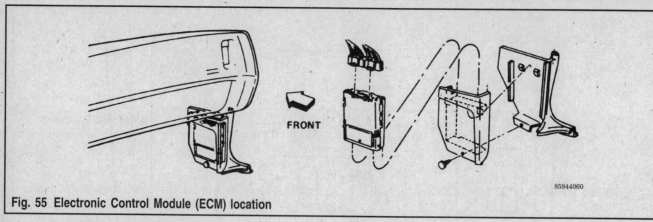

Fig. 55 Electronic Control Module (ECM) location

85944060

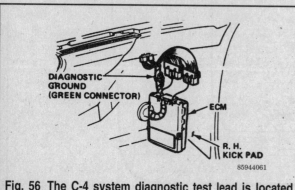

Fig. 56 The C-4 system diagnostic test lead is located above the ECM

85944061

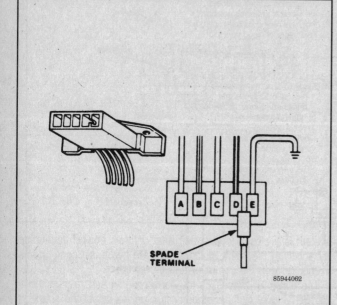

Fig. 57 Early CCC system diagnostic test terminal (pre 1982), located under the left side of the instrument panel

85944062

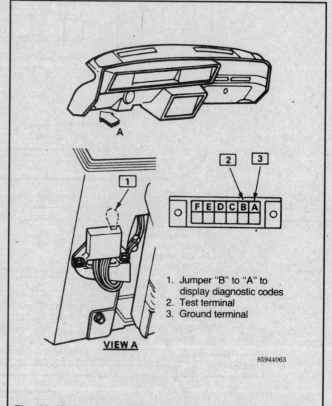

1. Jumper "B" to "A" to display diagnostic codes
2. Test terminal
3. Ground terminal

VIEW A

85944063

Fig. 58 Under dash terminal location — 1982 and later CCC systems

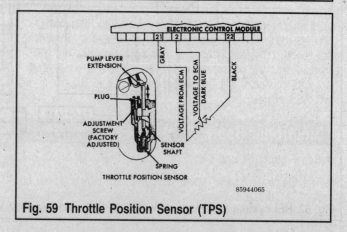

Fig. 59 Throttle Position Sensor (TPS)

85944065

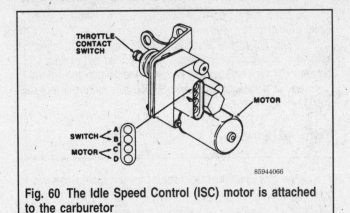

Fig. 60 The Idle Speed Control (ISC) motor is attached to the carburetor

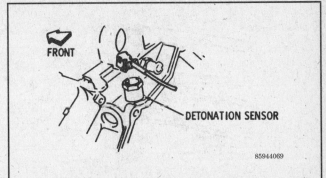

Fig. 63 The detonation sensor is mounted on the intake manifold — 231 V6 turbo engine

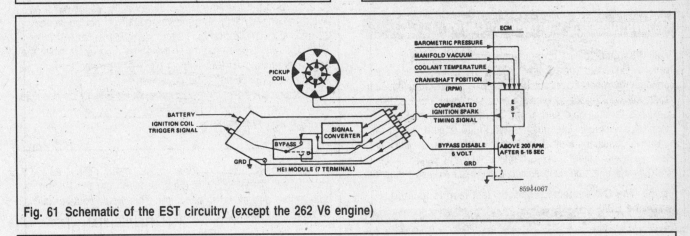

Fig. 61 Schematic of the EST circuitry (except the 262 V6 engine)

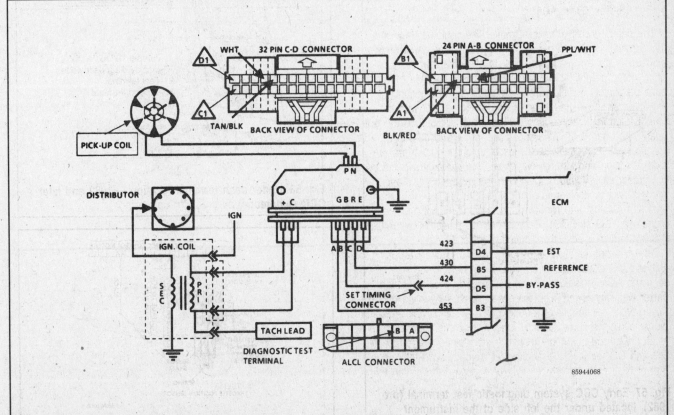

Fig. 62 HEI system schematic with EST — 1985 and later 262 V6 engine

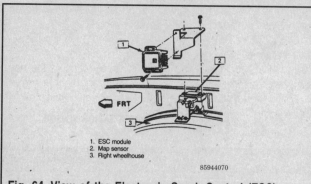

1. ESC module
2. Map sensor
3. Right wheelhouse

85944070

Fig. 64 View of the Electronic Spark Control (ESC) module

Transmission Converter Clutch (TCC)

All 1981 models with an automatic transmission use a Transmission Converter Clutch (TCC). The ECM controls the converter by means of a solenoid mounted in the transmission. When the vehicle speed reaches a certain level, the ECM energizes the solenoid and allows the torque converter to mechanically couple the transmission to the engine. When the operating conditions indicate that the transmission should operate as a normal fluid coupled transmission, the ECM will de-energize the solenoid. Depressing the brake will also return the transmission to normal automatic operation.

Catalytic Converter

▶ **See Figures 65 and 66**

The catalytic converter is a muffler-like container built into the exhaust system to aid in the reduction of exhaust emissions. The catalyst element consists of individual pellets or a honeycomb monolithic substrate coated with a noble metal such as platinum, palladium, rhodium or a combination of them. When the exhaust gases come into contact with the catalyst, a chemical reaction occurs which will reduce the pollutants into harmless substances like water and carbon dioxide.

There are essentially two types of catalytic converters: an oxidizing type and a three-way type. The oxidizing type is used on almost all 1975-80 models with the exception of those 1980 models built for California. It requires the addition of oxygen to spur the catalyst into reducing the engine's HC and CO emissions into H_2O and CO_2. Because of this need for oxygen, the AIR system is used with all these models.

The oxidizing catalytic converter, while effectively reducing HC and CO emissions, does little, if anything in the way of reducing NOx emissions. Thus, the three-way catalytic converter was developed. The three-way converter, unlike the oxidizing type, is capable of reducing HC, CO and NOx emissions; all at the same time. In theory, it seems impossible to reduce all three pollutants in one system since the reduction of HC and CO requires the addition of oxygen, while the reduction of NOx calls for the removal of oxygen. In actuality, the three-way system can reduce all three pollutants, but only if the amount of oxygen in the exhaust system is precisely controlled. Due to this precise control of exhaust oxygen content which is necessary for this system to operate properly, it can

only be used in cars equipped with an oxygen sensor (feedback) air/fuel control system.

There are no service procedures required for the catalytic converter, although the converter body should be inspected occasionally for damage. Some early models with the V6 engine require a catalyst charge at 30,000 mile intervals (consult your Owner's Manual).

PRECAUTIONS

1. Use only unleaded fuel. Use of leaded fuel in catalytic converter equipped vehicles will quickly clog and destroy a converter.
2. Due to the extreme temperatures a converter will reach. Avoid prolonged idling; the engine should run no longer than 20 min. at curb idle and no longer than 10 min. at fast idle.
3. Do not disconnect any of the spark plug leads while the engine is running. The raw fuel which will be expelled from that cylinder will damage the converter.
4. Make engine compression checks as quickly as possible.

CATALYST TESTING

Testing the catalytic converter in the field is difficult as it necessitates sampling the exhaust gasses from the system both before and after the converter. This would require drilling an additional hole in the exhaust system of most vehicles

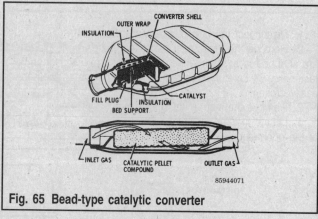

85944071

Fig. 65 Bead-type catalytic converter

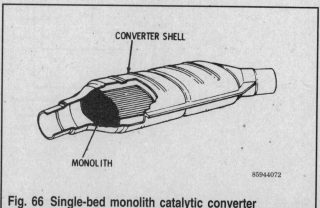

85944072

Fig. 66 Single-bed monolith catalytic converter

covered in this manual and is not desirable under most circumstances.

The 2 reasons catalytic converters normally fail is from clogging (coating of the noble metals) or damage. Clogging could occur from use of leaded gasoline or from the use of silicone sealer which is not approved for use on engines with oxygen sensors. Damage could occur from a physical blow (contact with a curb or pothole) that collapses the converter structure or from overheating.

The chemical reactions which occur inside a catalytic converter generate a great deal of heat. Many converter problems can be traced to fuel or ignition system problems which cause unusually high emissions. As a result of the increased intensity of the chemical reactions, the converter literally burns itself up.

As long as you avoid severe overheating, physical damage and the use of leaded fuels or unapproved sealer it is reasonably safe to assume that the converter is working properly.

Maintenance Reminder System

An emissions indicator flag may appear in the odometer window of the speedometer on some vehicles. The flag could say SENSOR, EMISSIONS or CATALYST depending on the part or assembly that is scheduled for regular emissions maintenance replacement. The word SENSOR indicates a need for oxygen sensor replacement and the words EMISSIONS or CATALYST indicate the need for catalytic converter catalyst replacement.

RESET PROCEDURE

1. Disconnect the negative battery cable.
2. Remove the instrument panel trim plate. Some plates are snapped in position while others use visible or hidden fasteners. Be careful when removing trim pieces as they are easily broken.
3. Remove the instrument cluster lens.
4. Locate the flag indicator reset notches at the drivers side of the odometer.
5. Use a pointed tool to apply light downward pressure on the notches, until the indicator is reset.
6. When the indicator is reset an alignment mark will appear in the left center of the odometer window.
7. Once the indicator is reset, temporarily connect the negative battery cable and check to make sure the light is extinguished. Then disconnect the battery cable again for safety.
8. Install the instrument cluster lens and the trim plate.
9. Connect the negative battery cable.

Oxygen Sensor

▶ See Figures 67 and 68

An oxygen sensor protrudes into the exhaust stream and monitors the oxygen content of the exhaust gases. The difference between the oxygen content of the exhaust gases and that of outside air generates a voltage signal to the ECM. The ECM monitors this voltage and, depending upon the value of the signal received, issues a command to adjust for a rich or a lean condition.

No attempt should ever be made to measure the voltage output of the sensor. The current drain of any conventional voltmeter would be such that it would permanently damage the sensor. Use these tools ONLY on the ECM side of the wiring harness connector AFTER disconnecting it from the sensor.

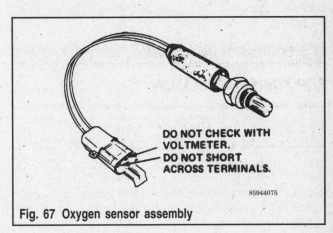

DO NOT CHECK WITH VOLTMETER.
DO NOT SHORT ACROSS TERMINALS.

85944075

Fig. 67 Oxygen sensor assembly

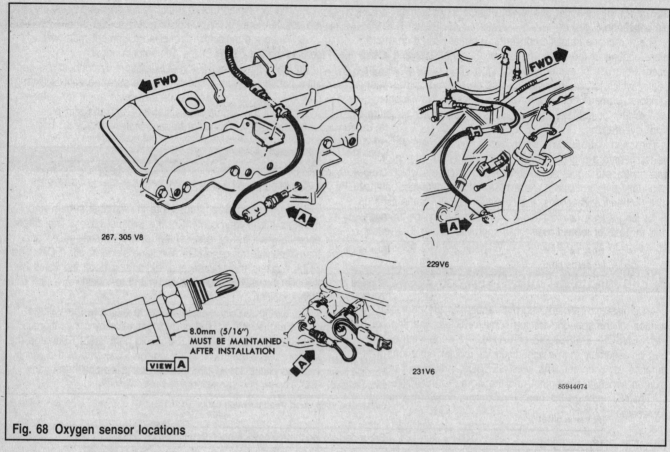

267, 305 V8

229V6

8.0mm (5/16")
MUST BE MAINTAINED
AFTER INSTALLATION

VIEW A

231V6

85944074

Fig. 68 Oxygen sensor locations

REMOVAL & INSTALLATION

For oxygen sensor removal and installation procedures, refer to Section 3 of this manual. The sensor is a delicate compo- nent which must be handled properly. Be sure to follow all instructions closely when removing the sensor.

DIAGNOSTIC TROUBLE CODES — C-4 AND CCC SYSTEMS

Trouble Code Identification Chart

NOTE: Always ground the test lead/terminal AFTER the engine is running

Trouble Code	Applicable System	Possible Problem Area
12	C-4, CCC	No reference pulses to the ECM. This is not stored in the memory and will only flash when the fault is present (not to be confused with the Code 12 discussed earlier).
13	C-4, CCC	Oxygen sensor circuit. The engine must run for at least 5 min. (18 min. on the C-4 equipped 231 V6) at part throttle before this code will show.
13 & 14 (at same time)	C-4	See code 43.
13 & 14 (at same time)	C-4	See code 43.
14	C-4, CCC	Shorted coolant sensor circuit. The engine must run 2–5 min. before this code will show.
15	C-4, CCC	Open coolant sensor circuit. The engine must run for at least 5 min. (18 min. on the C-4 equipped 231 V6) before this code will show.
21	C-4	Shorted wide open throttle switch and/or open closed-throttle switch circuit (when used).
	C-4, CCC	Throttle position sensor circuit. The engine must run for at least 10 sec. (25 sec.—CCC) below 800 rpm before this code will show.
21 & 22 (at same time)	C-4	Grounded wide open throttle switch circuit (231 V6).
22	C-4	Grounded closed throttle or wide open throttle switch circuit (231 V6).
23	C-4, CCC	Open or grounded carburetor mixture control (M/C) solenoid circuit.
24	CCC	Vehicle speed sensor circuit. The engine must run for at least 5 min, at normal speed before this code will show.
32	C-4, CCC	Barometric pressure sensor (BARO) circuit output is low.
32 & 55 (at same time)	C-4	Grounded +8V terminal or V(REF) terminal for BARO sensor, or a faulty ECM.
34	C-4	Manifold absolute pressure sensor (MAP) output is high. The engine must run for at least 10 sec. below 800 rpm before this code will show.
	CCC	Manifold absolute pressure sensor (MAP) circuit or vacuum sensor circuit. The engine must run for at least 5 min. below 800 rpm before this code will show.
35	CCC	Idle speed control circuit shorted. The engine must run for at least 2 sec. above ½ throttle before this code will show.
42	CCC	Electronic spark timing (EST) bypass circuit grounded.

85944064

Trouble Code Identification Chart (cont.)

NOTE: Always ground the test lead/terminal AFTER the engine is running

Trouble Code	Applicable System	Possible Problem Area
43	C-4	Throttle position sensor adjustment. The engine must run for at least 10 sec. before this code will show.
44	C-4, CCC	Lean oxygen sensor indication. The engine must run for at least 5 min. in closed loop (oxygen sensor adjusting carburetor mixture) at part throttle under load (drive car) before this code will show.
44 & 45 (at same time)	C-4, CCC	Faulty oxygen sensor circuit.
45	C-4, CCC	Rich oxygen sensor indication. The engine must run for at least 5 min. before this code will show (see 44 for conditions).
51	C-4, CCC	Faulty calibration unit (PROM) or improper PROM installation in the ECM. It will take at least 30 sec. before this code will show.
52 & 53	C-4	"Check Engine" light off: intermittent ECM problem. "Check Engine" light on: faulty ECM—replace.
52	C-4, CCC	Faulty ECM.
53	CCC	Faulty ECM.
54	C-4, CCC	Faulty mixture control solenoid circuit and/or faulty ECM.
55	C-4	Faulty throttle position sensor or ECM (all but 231 V6). Faulty oxygen sensor, open MAP sensor or faulty ECM (231 V6 only).
	CCC	Grounded +8V supply (terminal 19 on ECM connector), grounded 5V reference (terminal 21 on ECM connector), faulty oxygen sensor circuit or faulty ECM.

NOTE: *Not all codes will apply to every model.*

85944a64

DIESEL ENGINE EMISSIONS CONTROLS

Crankcase Ventilation

▶ See Figures 69, 70 and 71

A Crankcase Depression Regulator Valve (CDRV) is used to regulate (meter) the flow of crankcase gases back into the engine for burning. The CDRV is designed to limit vacuum in the crankcase as the gases are drawn from the valve covers through the CDRV and into the intake manifold (air crossover).

Fresh air enters the engine through the combination filter, check valve and oil fill cap. The fresh air mixes with blow-by gases and enters both valve covers. The gases then pass through a filter installed on the valve covers and are drawn into connecting tubing.

Intake manifold vacuum acts against a spring loaded diaphragm to control the flow of crankcase gases. Higher intake vacuum levels pull the diaphragm closer to the top of the outlet tube. This reduces the amount of gases being drawn from the crankcase and decreases the vacuum level in the crankcase. As the intake vacuum decreases, the spring pushes the diaphragm away from the top of the outlet tube allowing more gases to flow into the intake manifold.

For more information regarding CDRV maintenance and service, refer to Section 1 of this manual.

➡ Do not allow any solvent to come in contact with the diaphragm of the Crankcase Depression Regulator Valve because the diaphragm will fail.

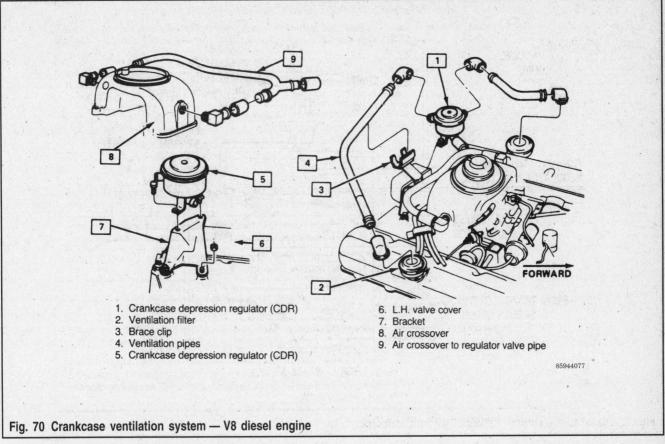

1. Crankcase depression regulator (CDR)
2. Ventilation filter
3. Brace clip
4. Ventilation pipes
5. Crankcase depression regulator (CDR)
6. L.H. valve cover
7. Bracket
8. Air crossover
9. Air crossover to regulator valve pipe

85944077

Fig. 70 Crankcase ventilation system — V8 diesel engine

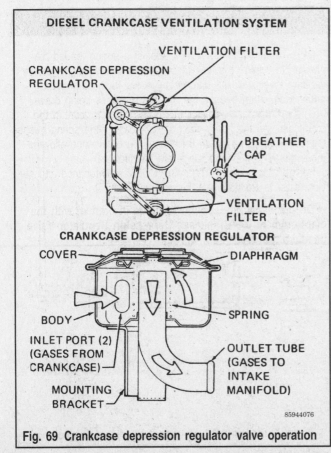

Fig. 69 Crankcase depression regulator valve operation

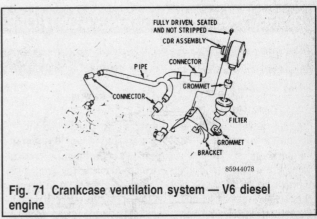

Fig. 71 Crankcase ventilation system — V6 diesel engine

Exhaust Gas Recirculation (EGR)

▶ **See Figures 72, 73 and 74**

To lower the formation of nitrogen oxides (NOx) in the exhaust, it is necessary to reduce combustion temperatures. This is accomplished with diesel engines in the same method as with gasoline engines, by introducing small amount of exhaust gases into the cylinders using an EGR valve.

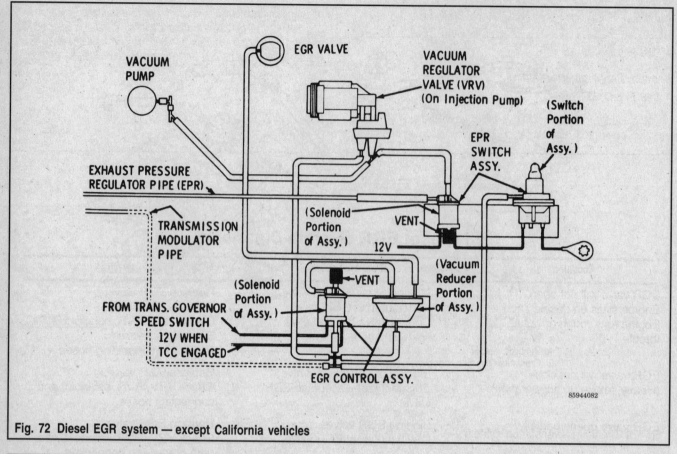

Fig. 72 Diesel EGR system — except California vehicles

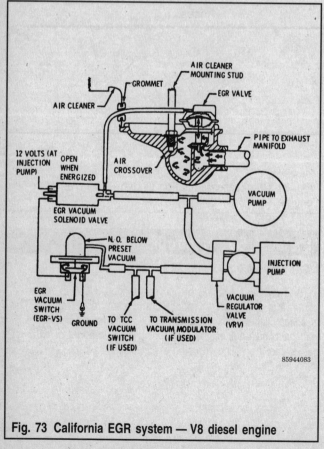

Fig. 73 California EGR system — V8 diesel engine

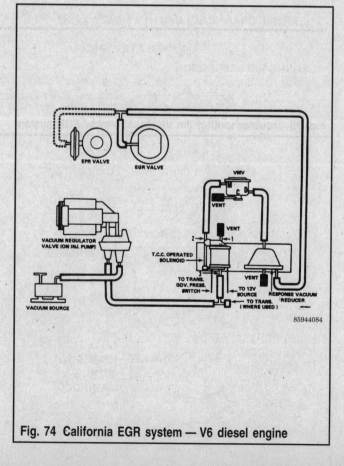

Fig. 74 California EGR system — V6 diesel engine

FUNCTIONAL TESTS OF COMPONENTS

▶ **See Figures 75 and 76**

Vacuum Regulator Valve (VRV)

▶ **See Figure 77**

The Vacuum Regulator Valve is attached to the side of the injection pump and regulates vacuum in proportion to throttle angel. Vacuum from the vacuum pump is supplied to port A and vacuum at port B is reduced as the throttle is opened. At closed throttle, the vacuum is 15 in. Hg; at half throttle, 6 in. Hg; at wide open throttle there is no vacuum.

V8 Diesel EGR System Diagnosis

Condition	Possible Causes	Correction
EGR valve will not open. Engine stalls on deceleration Engine runs rough on light throttle	Binding or stuck EGR valve. No vacuum to EGR valve. Control valve blocked or air flow restricted.	Replace EGR valve. Replace EGR valve. Check VRV, RVR, solenoid, T.C.C. Operation, Vacuum Pump and connecting hoses.
EGR valve will not close. (Heavy smoke on acceleration).	Binding or stuck EGR valve. Constant high vacuum to EGR valve.	Replace EGR valve. Check VRV, RVR, solenoid, and connecting hoses.
EGR valve opens partially.	Binding EGR valve. Low vacuum at EGR valve.	Replace EGR valve. Check VRV, RVR, solenoid, vacuum pump, and connecting hoses.

85944080

Fig. 75 Troubleshooting the V8 diesel engine EGR system

V6 Diesel EGR System Diagnosis

Condition	Possible Cause	Correction
EGR valve will not open.	Binding or stuck EGR valve. No vacuum to EGR valve.	Replace EGR valve. Check VRV, RVR, solenoid TCC Operation (See Section 7A), Vacuum Pump, VMV, and connecting hoses.
EGR valve will not close, or EPR valve will not open. (Heavy smoke on acceleration).	Binding or stuck EGR or EPR valve.	Replace EGR or EPR valve
	Constant high vacuum to EGR and EPR valve.	Check VRV, RVR, solenoid VMV and connecting hoses.
EGR valve opens partially.	Binding EGR valve. Low vacuum at EGR valve.	Replace EGR valve. Check VRV, RVR, solenoid, vacuum pump, VMV and connecting hoses.
Loss of power and heavy smoke on acceleration, EGR valve functions normally.	Binding or stuck EPR valve, constant high vacuum to EPR valve.	Replace EPR valve. Check vacuum hose routing.

85944081

Fig. 76 Troubleshooting the V6 diesel engine EGR system

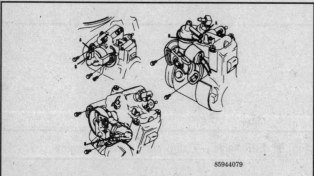

Fig. 77 The vacuum regulator valve is mounted to diesel injection pumps

85944079

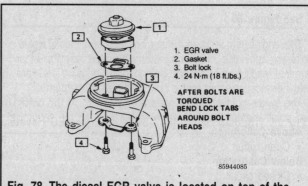

1. EGR valve
2. Gasket
3. Bolt lock
4. 24 N·m (18 ft.lbs.)

AFTER BOLTS ARE TORQUED BEND LOCK TABS AROUND BOLT HEADS

85944085

Fig. 78 The diesel EGR valve is located on top of the intake manifold

Exhaust Gas Recirculation (EGR) Valve
▶ See Figure 78

Apply vacuum to vacuum port. The valve should be fully open at 10.6 in. Hg and closed below 6 in. Hg.

Response Vacuum Reducer (RVR)
▶ See Figure 79

The Response Vacuum Reducer (sometimes known as the vacuum reducer valve) may be tested using a hand vacuum pump. Connect a vacuum gauge to the port marked To EGR valve or T.C.C solenoid. Connect a hand operated vacuum pump to the RVR port. Draw a 15 in. Hg (50.66 kPa) vacuum on the pump and the reading on the vacuum gauge should be lower than the vacuum pump reading as follows:
1981-83
- 0.75 in. Hg (2.53 kPa) Except High Altitude
- 2.50 in. Hg (8.44 kPa) High Altitude
1984
- 2.00 in. Hg (6.75 kPa)

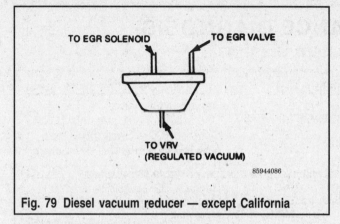

Fig. 79 Diesel vacuum reducer — except California

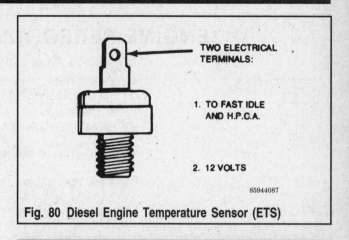

Fig. 80 Diesel Engine Temperature Sensor (ETS)

Torque Converter Clutch Operated Solenoid

When the torque converter clutch is engaged, an electrical signal energizes the solenoid allowing ports 1 and 2 to be interconnected. When the solenoid is not energized, port 1 is closed and ports 2 and 3 are interconnected.

Solenoid Energized
- Ports 1 and 3 are connected.

Solenoid De-energized
- Ports 2 and 3 are connected.

Engine Temperature Sensor (ETS)

OPERATION

▶ See Figure 80

The engine temperature sensor has two terminals. Twelve volts are applied to one terminal and the wire from the other terminal leads to the fast idle solenoid and housing pressure cold advance solenoid that is part of the injection pump.

The switch contacts are closed below 125°F. At the calibration point, the contacts are open which turns off the solenoids.

Above Calibration
- Open circuit

Below Calibration
- Closed circuit.

EPR Valve (California V6)

▶ See Figure 81

This valve is found between the right hand exhaust manifold and the exhaust pipe on California V6 diesel cars. The EPR valve is used in the exhaust flow to increase back pressure in the exhaust system, thus increasing exhaust flow through the EGR system. The valve operates from the same vacuum source as the EGR valve. It should be fully closed at idle, and will open as the throttle is opened.

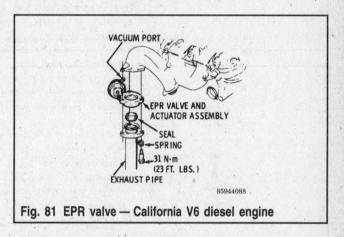

Fig. 81 EPR valve — California V6 diesel engine

TESTING THE EPR VALVE

To test the EPR valve, apply vacuum to the vacuum port on the valve. The valve should be fully closed at 12 in. Hg of vacuum, and open below 6 in. Hg. of vacuum.

ENGINE PERFORMANCE AND TROUBLESHOOTING CHARTS

Below are a listing of basic engine performance and driveability troubleshooting charts for both gasoline and diesel engines. The charts give possible explanations for various engine performance and mechanical symptoms. They should be used along with the information in Sections 1, 2, 3 & 5 to help diagnose suspected engine problems.

ENGINE PERFORMANCE DIAGNOSIS

A. Dieseling

1. Make visual checks of the following for sticking.
   a. Carburetor, choke, and throttle linkage
   b. Fast idle cam
   See cleaning, inspection, and adjustment of carburetor

2. See ISC diagnosis if applicable.

3. Check and reset ignition timing and idle speed settings. Refer to emission label.

4. Remove carbon with top engine cleaner. Follow instructions on can.
   If condition still exists, suggest that owner try different gasoline.

B. Detonation

1. Check for obvious overheating problems.
   a. Low coolant
   b. Loose fan belt
   c. Restricted air flow, etc.

2. For "non-EST" check ignition timing per emission control information label.

3. For "EST or ESC" see diagnosis Section

4. Perform EGR functional check

5. Remove carbon with top engine cleaner. Follow instructions on can.
   If condition still exists, suggest that owner try different gasoline.

C. Stalls or Rough Idle - Cold

1. With engine running, remove air cleaner cover and filter. Damper door in air cleaner snorkel should be closed when engine is cold. It may be necessary to place cold wet rag over sensor to close it if engine is too warm. If damper door does not close, apply vacuum directly to vacuum motor. If door closes, replace sensor. If door stays open, replace vacuum motor.

2. Visually check the following:
   a. Hot air tube to air cleaner connection and condition of hot air stove.
   b. Vacuum hoses for splits, kinks and proper connections. See Hose Routing Schematic on Vehicle Emission Control Information Label.
   c. Air leaks at carburetor mounting and intake manifold.
   d. Ignition wires for cracking, hardness and proper connections.
   Repair or replace as necessary.

85944301

Fig. 82 Engine performance diagnosis

3. Check the following for sticking:
   a. Carburetor, choke, and throttle linkage.
   b. Fast idle cam.
   c. Carburetor flooding.
    See cleaning, inspection and adjustment of carburetor

4. With engine running, visually check vacuum break linkage for movement while removing and reinstalling vacuum hose. If the linkage does not move and vacuum is at hose, replace vacuum break assembly.

5. With engine off, check all choke adjustments.

6. Check engine timing and idle speed. See Emission Control Information Label.

7. Remove vacuum hose from E.G.R. valve and connect an extra hose from any manifold vacuum source to valve. If rpm doesn't drop, valve is leaking.
See E.G.R. Section for further functional tests, cleaning, and/or replacement.

8. Check E.F.E. valve.
Disconnect E.F.E. hose from tube and connect an extra vacuum hose from any manifold vacuum source to E.F.E. tube.
Observe actuator linkage for movement. If no movement, repair as necessary.

9. See Computer Command Control diagnosis

D. Stalls or Rough Idle - Hot	1. With engine running, remove air cleaner cover and filter. Damper door in air cleaner snorkel should be open. If closed and engine is hot, check temperature operation of sensor unit.
	
	2. Visually check the following:
	  a. Vacuum hoses for splits, kinks and proper connections. See hose routing Schematic, Vehicle Emission Control Information Label.
	  b. Air leaks at carburetor mounting and intake manifold.
	  c. Ignition wires for cracking, hardness and proper connections. Repair or replace as necessary.
	  d. Check idle solenoid - Replace as necessary
	
	3. Check engine timing and idle speed. See emission control information label.
	
	4. Check P.C.V. valve for proper operation by placing finger over inlet hole in valve end several times. Valve should snap back. If not, replace valve.
	
	5. Remove vacuum hose from E.G.R. valve and connect an extra hose from any manifold source to valve. If rpm doesn't drop, valve is leaking. See E.G.R. Section for further functional tests, cleaning and/or replacement.
	
	6. Remove carbon with top engine cleaner. Follow instructions on can. If idle is still rough, run a cylinder compression check.
	
	7. See Computer Command Control Diagnosis

E. Miss	1. Visually check the following:
	  a. Vacuum hoses for splits, kinks and proper connections. See hose routing Schematic, Vehicle Emission Control Information Label.
	  b. Air leaks at carburetor mounting and intake manifold.
	  c. Ignition wires for cracking, hardness and proper connections. Repair or

85944302

Fig. 83 Engine performance diagnosis

replace as necessary.

2. Disconnect air cleaner and E.G.R. vacuum hoses and cap both vacuum sources.

3. Remove one spark plug wire at a time with insulated pliers. If there is an rpm drop on all cylinders, go to rough idle (hot) diagnosis charts.

4. If there is no rpm drop on one or more cylinders
                                        remove spark plug(s)
and check for:
   a. Cracks
   b. Wear
   c. Improper gap
   d. Burned Electrodes
   e. Heavy Deposits
Repair or replace as necessary.

5. Check spark plug wires by connecting ohmmeter to ends of each wire in question. If meter reads over 50,000 ohms, replace wire(s).

6. Visually check distributor cap and rotor for moisture, dust, cracks, burns, etc. Clean and/or repair as necessary.

7. Perform compression check on questionable cylinder(s). If compression is low, repair as necessary.

8. Remove rocker covers. Check for bent push rods, worn rocker arms, broken valve springs, worn cam shaft lobes. Repair as necessary.
9. See Computer Command Control Diagnosis

F. Hesitates

1. Visually check the following:
   a. Vacuum hoses for splits, kinks and proper connections. See hose routing

   b. Air leaks at carburetor mounting and intake manifold.
   c. Check ignition wires for cracking, hardness and proper connections.
      Repair and replace as necessary.

2. Note: Cold Engine Only
Check the following for sticking or faulty operation:
   a. Carburetor, choke, and throttle linkage.
   b. Fast idle cam.
      See cleaning, inspection and adjustment of carburetor

3. Check carburetor accelerator pump operation. With air cleaner removed and engine off, hold choke valve open and look for gas squirt in carburetor bore while moving throttle.

4. If weak or no pump squirt, remove carburetor air horn and repair pump system as necessary.
                    Check float level adjustment before replacing air horn
and pump rod adjustment after assembly.

5. Disconnect and plug vacuum advance hose,(Non-EST) on EST equipped engines disconnect EST connector, connect tachometer and timing light. Check ignition timing and idle speed against specs on emission label.

6. With engine running, remove air cleaner cover and filter. Damper door in

85944303

Fig. 84 Engine performance diagnosis

air cleaner snorkel should be closed when engine is cold. It may be necessary
to place cold wet rag over sensor to close if engine is too warm.
If damper door does not close, apply vacuum directly to vacuum motor. If
door closes, replace sensor. If door stays open, replace vacuum motor.

7. Check TPS adjustment if applicable
8. See Computer Command Control Diagnosis

G. Surges	1. With engine running, remove air cleaner cover and filter. Damper door in air cleaner snorkel should be closed when engine is cold. It may be necessary to place cold wet rag over sensor to close if engine is too warm.

2. Visually check the following:
   a. Vacuum hoses for splits, kinks and proper connections. See hose routing
  Schematic, Vehicle Emission Control Information Label.
   b. Air leaks at carburetor mounting and intake manifold.
   c. Ignition wires for cracking, hardness and proper connections. Repair or
  replace as necessary.

3. "Non EST" check ignition timing per emission control information label.
To check mechanical advance, observe timing marks. It should advance
as throttle is opened and return to mark as throttle is closed.
Check EST operation if applicable.

4. "Non EST" with engine off, remove vacuum hose from distributor vacuum advance
Connect vacuum pump and apply 15" vacuum. Vacuum should hold steady for 15
seconds. If vacuum drops, replace vacuum advance unit.

5. Check carburetor fuel inlet filter. Replace if dirty or plugged.

6. Test fuel pump by connecting hose from carburetor fuel feed line to a suitable
container. Start engine and let idle for 15 seconds.
   a. Mechanical pump should supply 1/2 pint or more. If not, go to step 7.
  If OK, go to step 9.

7. To check mechanical fuel pump connect a vacuum gage. Crank or run
engine until maximum vacuum is reached. If less than 12 inches, replace
pump. If vacuum reading is 12 inches or more, go to step 8.

8. Check fuel lines and hoses for splits, leaks or kinks by disconnecting each
section of line and connect vacuum gage. Crank or run engine until vacuum
gage peaks. Vacuum should be at least 12 inches. If less, repair or replace
defective line or hose.

9. If fuel lines and pump check OK, remove tank unit, replace strainer and
clean fuel tank, if necessary.

10. Remove spark plugs, Check for cracks, wear, improper gap, burned electrodes,
heavy deposits. Repair or replace as necessary.

11. See Computer Command Control diagnosis

85944304

Fig. 85 Engine performance diagnosis

H. Sluggish or Spongy

1. Remove air cleaner and check air filter for dirt or being plugged. Replace as necessary.

2. With engine running, damper door in air cleaner snorkel should be closed when engine is cold. It may be necessary to place cold wet rag over sensor to close if engine is too warm.
If damper door does not close, apply vacuum directly to vacuum motor. If door closes, replace sensor. If door stays open, replace vacuum motor.

**3. Check ignition timing per emission label.
Without EST check mechanical advance as throttle is
opened and closed.
Check EST if applicable**

4. Remove air cleaner and check for full throttle valve opening in carburetor by depressing accelerator pedal to floor; also check for full choke valve opening and free operating air valve (if equipped). Repair as necessary. See carburetor cleaning and inspection

5. Remove vacuum hose from E.G.R. valve and connect an extra hose from any manifold vacuum source to valve. If rpm doesn't drop, valve is leaking. See E.G.R. Section for further functional tests, cleaning, and/or replacement.

6. "Non EST" with engine off, remove vacuum hose from distributor vacuum advance vacuum pump and apply 15" vacuum. Vacuum should hold steady for 15 seconds. If vacuum drops, replace vacuum advance unit.

7. Remove spark plugs. Check for cracks, wear, improper gap, burned electrodes, heavy deposits. Repair or replace as necessary.

8. "Non-Computer Command Control" remove carburetor air horn and check the following:
   a. Power piston for freeness
   b. Dirt in carburetor
   c. Float adjustment
   d. Metering rods
   e. Power valve(s)
Refer to carburetor cleaning and inspection
9. See Computer Command Control Diagnosis

I. Poor Gasoline Mileage

1. With engine running, remove air cleaner cover and filter. Check filter for dirt or being plugged. Replace as necessary. Damper door in air cleaner snorkel should be closed when engine is cold. It may be necessary to place cold wet rag over sensor to close it if engine is too warm.
If damper door does not close, apply vacuum directly to vacuum motor. If door closes, replace sensor. If door stays open, replace vacuum motor.

2. Visually check the following:
   a. Vacuum hoses for splits, kinks and proper connections. See hose routing Schematic, Vehicle Emission Control Information Label.
   b. Air leaks at carburetor mounting and intake manifold.
   c. Ignition wires for cracking, hardness and proper connections. Repair or replace as necessary.

3. Check ignition timing per emission control information label.
"Non EST" To check mechanical advance, observe timing mark. It should advance throttle is opened and return to mark as throttle is closed.

Fig. 86 Engine performance diagnosis

Check EST if applicable

4. Check carburetor choke linkage and settings. Clean and repair as necessary.
See carburetor choke adjustments, cleaning and inspection

5. "NON EST" with engine off, remove vacuum hose from distributor vacuum advance
vacuum pump and apply 15" vacuum. Vacuum should hold steady for 15 seconds.
If vacuum drops, replace vacuum advance unit.

6. Remove spark plugs, check for cracks, wear, improper gap, burned electrodes,
heavy deposits. Repair or replace as necessary.
See Computer Command Control diagnosis

7. "Non Computer Command Control" if in previous checks, adjustments
have not been made that could improve
mileage, remove carburetor air horn and check the following:
  a. Power piston for freeness
  b. Dirt in jets and metering passages
  c. Metering rods
  d. Power valve(s)
  e. Float adjustment
See carburetor cleaning, inspection, and adjustments

8. Computer Command Control

9. Suggest owner fill tank and recheck mileage.

J. Cuts Out

1. Check ignition wires, boots, cap and coil for:
  a. Damage
  b. Deterioration
  c. Loose connections
  d. Carbon tracking
Clean, tighten and/or replace defective parts as necessary.

2. Check ignition system
Check distributor for:
  a. Worn shaft
  b. Bare or shorted wires
Repair or replace defective parts as necessary.

3. Remove spark plugs. Check for cracks, wear, improper gap, burned electrodes,
heavy deposits. Repair or replace as necessary.

4. Check carburetor fuel inlet filter. Replace if dirty or plugged.

5. Test fuel pump by connecting hose from carburetor fuel feed line to a
suitable container. Start engine and let idle for 15 seconds.
  a. Fuel pump should supply 1/2 pint or more. If not, go to step 7.

6. To check mechanical fuel pump, disconnect inlet hose at pump and connect
a vacuum gage. Crank or run engine until maximum vacuum is reached. If
less than 12 inches, replace pump. If vacuum reading is 12 inches or more,
go to step 8.

85944306

Fig. 87 Engine performance diagnosis

7. Check fuel lines and hoses for splits, leaks or kinks by disconnecting each section of line and connecting a vacuum gage. Crank or run engine until vacuum gage peaks. Vacuum should be at least 12 inches. If less, repair or replace defective line or hose as necessary.

8. If fuel pump and fuel lines check OK, remove tank unit, replace strainer and clean fuel tank, if necessary.

9. See Computer Command Control system diagnosis

10. "Non Computer Command Control"
if carburetor is suspected, remove the air horn and check the following:
    a. Power Piston(s) or main fuel piston for freeness.
    b. Dirt in jets and metering passages.
    c. Metering rods.
    d. Power valve(s) or main fuel valve(s).
    e. Float adjustment.
See Carburetor Cleaning Inspection and Adjustment

K. Hard Starting - Cold (Engine Cranks OK)

1. Visually check the following:
    a. Vacuum hoses for splits, kinks and proper connections. See hose routing charts
    b. Air leaks at carburetor mounting and intake manifold.
    c. Ignition wires for cracking, hardness, proper connections, and carbon tracking. Repair or replace as necessary.
    d. Check choke and vacuum break operation and adjustment.

2. Check ignition timing per emission control information label.
"Non EST" if timing is too early - speed up engine to see if timing mark moves
If not, check for stuck mechanical advanace.   Repair
as necessary and recheck timing.
Check EST if applicable

3. Check the following:
    a. Choke, throttle linkage and fast idle cam for sticking.
    b. Carburetor flooding.
Clean and repair as necessary. If repairs are necessary, see carburetor, cleaning and inspection.

4. Check ignition system
Check distributor for:
    a. Worn shaft
    b. Bare and shorted wires
    c. Repair or replace as necessary.

5. Remove spark plugs. Check for cracks, wear, improper gap, burned electrodes, heavy deposits. Repair or replace as necessary.

6. Test fuel pump by connecting hose from carburetor fuel feed line to a suitable container.
Start engine and let idle for 15 seconds. Pump should supply 1/2 pint or more.
If more than 1/2 pint, check filter in carburetor. Replace if necessary.
If less than 1/2 pint, for mechanical pump go to step 7.

7. Disconnect inlet hose at pump and connect a vacuum gage. Crank or run engine

85944307

Fig. 88 Engine performance diagnosis

until maximum vacuum is reached. If less than 12 inches, replace pump. If more than 12 inches, go to step 8.

8. Check fuel lines and hoses for splits, leaks or kinks by disconnecting each section of line and connect vacuum gage. Crank or run engine until vacuum gage peaks. Vacuum should be at least 12 inches. If less, repair or replace defective line or hose.

9. If fuel lines and pump check OK, remove tank unit, replace strainer and clean fuel tank, if necessary.

L. Hard Starting - Hot
(Engine cranks OK)

1. Visually check the following:
   a. Vacuum hoses for splits, kinks and proper connections. See hose routing Schematic, Vehicle Emission Control Information Label.
   b. Air leaks at carburetor mounting and intake manifold.
   c. Ignition wires for cracking, hardness, proper connections, and carbon tracking. Repair or replace as necessary.
2. Check ignition timing per emission control information label.
   "Non EST" If timing is too early - speed up engine to see if timing mark moves If not, check for stuck mechanical advance.   Repair as necessary and recheck timing.
Check EST if applicable

3. Check the following:
   a. Choke, throttle linkage and fast idle cam for sticking.
   b. Carburetor flooding.
   Clean and repair as necessary. If repairs are necessary, see carburetor, cleaning and inspection

4. Check ignition system
Check distributor for:
   a. Worn shaft
   b. Bare and shorted wires
   c. Faulty pick up coil, module, ignition coil, and shorted condenser. Repair or replace as necessary.

5. Remove spark plugs. Check for cracks, wear, improper gap, burned electrodes, heavy deposits. Repair or replace as necessary.

6. Also check steps 6, 7, 8, 9 - Hard Starting - Cold.

ENGINE MECHANICAL DIAGNOSIS

The following diagnostic information covers common problems and possible causes. When the proper diagnosis is made, the problem should be corrected by adjustment, repair or part replacement as required. Refer to the appropriate section of the manual for these procedures.

CONDITION	POSSIBLE CAUSE	CORRECTION
Excessive Oil Loss	a. External oil leaks.	1. Tighten bolts and/or replace gaskets and seals as necessary.
	b. Improper reading of dipstick.	1. Check oil with car on a level surface and allow adequate drain down time.

85944308

Fig. 89 Engine performance and mechanical diagnosis

	c. Improper oil viscosity.	1. Use recommended S.A.E. viscosity for prevailing temperatures.
	d. Continuous high speed driving and/or severe usage such as trailer hauling.	1. Continuous high speed operation and/or severe usage will normally cause decreased oil mileage.
	e. P.C.V. system malfunctioning.	1. Service as necessary.
	f. Valve guides and/or valve stem seals worn, or seals omitted.	1. Ream guides and install oversize service valves and/or new valve stem seals.
	g. Piston rings not seated, broken or worn.	1. Allow adequate time for rings to seat. 2. Replace broken or worn rings as necessary.
	h. Piston improperly installed or misfitted.	1. Replace piston or repair as necessary.
Low Oil Pressure	a. Slow idle speed	1. Set idle speed to spec.
	b. Incorrect or malfunctioning oil pressure switch.	1. Replace with proper switch.
	c. Incorrect or malfunctioning oil pressure gage.	1. Replace with proper gage.
	d. Improper oil viscosity or diluted oil.	1. Install oil of proper viscosity for expected temperature. 2. Install new oil if diluted with moisture or unburned fuel mixtures.
	e. Oil pump worn or dirty.	1. Clean pump and replace worn parts as necessary.
	f. Plugged oil filter.	1. Replace filter and oil.
	g. Oil pickup screen loose or plugged.	1. Clean or replace screen as necessary.
	h. Hole in oil pickup tube.	1. Replace tube.
	i. Excessive bearing clearance.	1. Replace as necessary.
	j. Cracked, porous or plugged oil galleys.	1. Repair or replace block.
	k. Galley plugs missing or misinstalled.	1. Install plugs or repair as necessary

85944309

Fig. 90 Engine mechanical diagnosis

	l. Poor seal at timing cover gasket (231 engine only).	1. Replace gasket.
Valve Train Noise	a. Low oil pressure.	1. Repair as necessary. (See diagnosis for low oil pressure.)
	b. Loose rocker arm attachments.	1. Inspect and repair as necessary.
	c. Worn rocker arm and/or pushrod.	1. Replace as necessary.
	d. Broken valve spring.	1. Replace spring.
	e. Sticking valves.	1. Free valves.
	f. Lifters worn, dirty or defective.	1. Clean, inspect, test and replace as necessary.
	g. Camshaft worn or poor machining.	1. Replace camshaft.
	h. Worn valve guides.	1. Repair as necessary.

ENGINE KNOCK DIAGNOSIS

CONDITION	POSSIBLE CAUSE	CORRECTION
a. Engine knocks cold and continues for two to three minutes. Knock increases with torque.	1. EFE equipped engines may have valve knock. 2. Flywheel contacting splash shield. 3. Loose or broken balancer or drive pulleys. 4. Excessive piston to bore clearance.[1]	1. Replace EFE valve. 2. Reposition splash shield. 3. Tighten or replace as necessary. 4. Replace piston.
b. Engine has heavy knock hot with torque applied.	1. Broken balancer or pulley hub. 2. Loose torque converter bolts. 3. Accessory belts too tight or nicked. 4. Exhaust system grounded. 5. Flywheel cracked. 6. Excessive main bearing clearance. 7. Excessive rod bearing clearance.	1. Replace parts as necessary. 2. Tighten bolts. 3. Replace and/or tension to specs as necessary. 4. Reposition as necessary. 5. Replace flywheel. 6. Replace as necessary. 7. Replace as necessary.

85944310

Fig. 91 Engine mechanical and knock diagnosis

c. Engine has light knock hot in light load conditions.	1. Detonation or spark knock. 2. Loose torque converter bolts. 3. Exhaust leak at manifold. 4. Excessive rod bearing clearance.	1. EST or ESC Check engine timing and fuel quality. 2. Tighten bolts. 3. Tighten bolts and/or replace gasket. 4. Replace bearings as necessary.
d. Engine knocks on initial start up but only lasts a few seconds.	1. Fuel pump. 2. Improper oil viscosity. 3. Hydraulic lifter bleed down. 4. Excessive crankshaft end clearance.	1. Replace pump. 2. Install proper oil viscosity for expected temperatures. 3. Clean, test and replace as necessary. 4. Replace crankshaft thrust bearing.
e. Engine knocks at idle hot.	1. Loose or worn drive belts. 2. Compressor or generator bearing. 3. Fuel pump. 4. Valve train. 5. Improper oil viscosity. 6. Excessive piston pin clearance. 7. Connecting rod alignment. 8. Insufficient piston to bore clearance.	1. Tension and/or replace as necessary. 2. Replace as necessary. 3. Replace pump. 4. Replace parts as necessary. 5. Install proper viscosity oil for expected temperature. 6. Ream and install oversize pins. 7. Check and replace rods as necessary. 8. Hone and fit new piston.

   Cold engine piston knock usually disappears when the cylinder is grounded out. Cold engine piston knock which disappears in 1.5 minutes should be considered acceptable.

   [2]When the engine is stopped, some valves will be open. Spring pressure against lifters will tend to bleed lifter down. Attempts to repair should be made only if the problem is consistent and appears each time engine is started.

85944311

Fig. 92 Engine knock diagnosis

DIESEL ENGINE DIAGNOSIS

Diesel Engine Mechanical Diagnosis such as noisy lifters, rod bearings, main bearings, valves, rings and pistons is the same as for a gasoline engine. This diagnosis covers only those conditions that are different for the diesel engine.

CONDITION	POSSIBLE CAUSE	CORRECTION
Engine Will Not Crank	1. Loose or Corroded Battery Cables	Check connections at batteries, engine block and starter solenoid.
	2. Discharged Batteries	Check generator output and generator belt adjustment.
	3. Starter Inoperative	Check voltage to starter and starter solenoid. If OK, remove starter for repair.
Engine Cranks Slowly – Will Not Start (Minimum Engine Cranking Speed – 100 RPM COLD, 240 RPM HOT)	1. Battery Cable Connections Loose or Corroded	Check connections at batteries, engine block and starter.
	2. Batteries Undercharged	Check charging system.
	3. Wrong Engine Oil	Drain and refill with oil of recommended viscosity.
Engine Cranks Normally – Will Not Start	1. Incorrect Starting Procedure	Use recommended starting procedure.
	2. Glow Plugs Inoperative	
	3. Glow Plug Control System Inoperative	
	4. No Fuel Into Cylinders	Remove any one glow plug. Depress the throttle part way and crank the engine for 5 seconds. If no fuel vapors come out of the glow plug hole, go to step 5. If fuel vapors are noticed remove the remainder of the glow plugs and see if fuel vapors come out of each hole when the engine is cranked. If fuel comes out of one glow plug hole only replace the injection nozzle in that cylinder. Crank the engine and check to see that fuel vapors are coming out of all glow plug holes. If fuel is coming from each cylinder, go to step 11.
	5. Plugged Fuel Return System	Disconnect fuel return line at injection pump and route hose to a metal container. Connect a hose to the injection pump connection, route it to the metal container. Crank the engine. If it starts and runs, correct restriction in fuel return lines. If it does not start, remove the ball check connector from the top of the injection pump and make sure that it is not plugged.
	6. No Fuel To Injection Pump	Loosen the line coming out of the filter. Crank the engine, the fuel should spray out of the fitting, use care to direct fuel away from sources of ignition. If fuel sprays from the fitting go to step 10.
	7. Restricted Fuel Filter	Loosen the line going to the filter, if fuel sprays from the fitting, the filter is plugged and should be replaced. Use care to direct the fuel away from sources of ignition.

Fig. 93 Diesel engine performance diagnosis

	8. Fuel Pump Inoperative	Remove inlet hose to fuel pump. Connect a hose to the pump from a separate container that contains fuel. Loosen the line going to the filter. If fuel does not spray from the fitting, replace the pump. Use care to direct the fuel away from source of ignition.
	9. Restricted Fuel Tank Filter	Remove fuel tank and check filter. (Filter for diesel fuel is blue).
	10. No Voltage To Fuel Solenoid	Connect a volt meter to the wire at the injection pump solenoid and ground. The voltage should be a minimum of 9 volts.
Engine Cranks Normally – Will Not Start (Contd)	11. Incorrect or Contaminated Fuel	Flush fuel system and install correct fuel.
	12. Pump Timing Incorrect	Make certain that pump timing mark is aligned with mark on adapter or use timing meter J-33075.
	13. Low Compression	Check compression to determine cause.
	14. Injection Pump Malfunction	Remove injection pump for repair.
Engine Starts But Will Not Continue To Run At Idle	1. Slow Idle Incorrectly Adjusted	Adjust idle screw to specification.
	2. Fast Idle Solenoid Inoperative	With engine cold, start engine; solenoid should move to hold injection pump lever in "fast idle position".
	3. Restricted Fuel Return System	Disconnect fuel return line at injection pump and route hose to a metal container. Connect a hose to the injection pump connection; route it to the metal container. Crank the engine and allow it to idle. If engine idles normally, correct restriction in fuel return line. If engine does not idle normally, remove the return line check valve fitting from the top of the pump and make sure it is not plugged.
	4. Glow Plugs Turn Off Too Soon	
	5. Pump Timing Incorrect	Make certain that timing mark on injection pump is aligned with mark on adapter or use timing meter J-33075
	6. Limited Fuel To Injection Pump	Test the engine fuel pump, check for plugged filters; check fuel lines. Replace or repair as necessary.
	7. Incorrect or Contaminated Fuel	Flush fuel system and install correct fuel.
	8. Low Compression	Check compression to determine cause.
	9. Fuel Solenoid Closes In Run Position	Ignition switch out of adjustment.
	10. Injection Pump Malfunction	Remove injection pump for repair.
Excessive Surge at Light Throttle, Under Load.	1. Torque Converter Clutch Engages too Soon.	
	2. Timing Retarded	Reset Timing. Make certain that timing mark on injection pump is aligned with mark on adapter or use timing meter J-33075

85944313

Fig. 94 Diesel engine performance diagnosis

Note: If Engine has a Rough Idle, use Rough Idle Diagnosis and Correct Prior to Re-evaluation for this Condition.	3. Clogged Fuel Filter	Check Fuel Pump Pressure on Inlet and Outlet Sides of Filter
	4. Injection Pump Housing Pressure too High	Correct Pressure
	5. Injection Line Volume too Low	Replace Affected Line(s).
Engine Starts and Idles Rough WITH Excessive Noise and/or Smoke But Clears Up After Warmup	1. Injection Pump Timing Incorrect	Be sure timing mark on injection pump is aligned with mark on adapter or use tool J-33075.
	2. Insufficient Engine Break-in Time	Break-in engine 2000 or more miles.
	3. Air in System	Install a section of clear plastic tubing on the fuel return fitting from the engine. Evidence of bubbles in fuel when cranking or running indicates the presence of an air leak in the suction fuel line. Locate and correct.
	4. Nozzle(S) Malfunction	Remove and clean or replace.
	5. Housing Pressure Cold Advance In-Op	Check Operation
Engine Misfires Above Idle But Idles Correctly	1. Plugged Fuel Filters	Replace filters.
	2. Incorrect Injection Pump Timing	Be sure timing mark on injection pump is aligned with mark on adapter or use tool J-33075.
	3. Incorrect or Contaminated Fuel	Flush fuel system and install correct fuel.
Engine Will Not Return To Idle	1. External Linkage Binding Or Misadjusted	Free up linkage. Adjust or replace as required.
	2. Fast Idle Malfunction	Check fast idle adjustment.
	3. Internal Injection Pump Malfunction	Remove injection pump for repair.
Fuel Leaks On Ground – No Engine Malfunction	1. Loose or Broken Fuel Line or Connection	Examine complete fuel system, including tank, and injection lines. Determine source and cause of leak and repair.
	2. Injection Pump Internal Seal Leak	Remove injection pump for repair.
Noticeable Loss Of Power	1. Restricted Air Intake	Check air cleaner element.
	2. Timing not to Specification	Reset Timing. Align marks on adapter or use tool J-33075.
	3. EGR Malfunction	
	4. Restricted or Damaged Exhaust System	Check system and replace as necessary.
	5. Plugged Fuel Filter	Replace filter.

Fig. 95 Diesel engine performance diagnosis

	6. Plugged Fuel Tank Vacuum Vent In Fuel Cap	Remove fuel cap. If loud "hissing" noise is heard, vacuum vent in fuel cap is plugged. Replace cap. (Slight hissing sound is normal).
	7. Restricted Fuel Supply From Fuel Tank To Injection Pump	Examine fuel supply system to determine cause of restriction. Repair as required.
	8. Restricted Fuel Tank Filter	Remove fuel tank and check filter. (Filter for diesel fuel is blue).
	9. Pinched or Otherwise Restricted Return System	Examine system for restriction and correct as required.
	10. Incorrect or Contaminated Fuel	Flush fuel system and install correct fuel.
	11. External Compression Leaks	Check for compression leaks at all nozzles and glow plugs, using "Leak-Tec" or equivalent. If leak is found, tighten nozzle or glow plug.
	12. Plugged Nozzle(s)	Remove nozzles. Have them checked for plugging and repair or replace.
	13. Low Compression	Check compression to determine cause.
Noise – "Rap" From One or More Cylinders (Sounds Like Rod Bearing Knock)	1. Nozzle(s) Sticking Open or with very low Nozzle Opening Pressure	Remove nozzle for test and replace as necessary.
	2. Mechanical Problem	
	3. Piston Hitting Head	**Refer to Mechanical Diagnosis. Replace Parts.**
Excessive Black Smoke and/or Objectionable Overall Combustion Noise	1. Timing Not Set To Specification	Make certain that timing mark on injection pump is aligned with mark on adapter or use tool J-33075.
	2. EGR Malfunction	Refer to Emission Diagnosis.
	3. Injection Pump Housing Pressure Out Of Specifications	**Check housing pressure**
	4. Injection Pump Internal Problem	Remove injection pump for repair.
Engine Noise – Internal Or External	1. Engine Fuel Pump, Generator, Water Pump, Valve Train, Vacuum Pump, Bearings, Etc.	Repair or replace as necessary. If noise is internal, see Diagnosis For Noise – Rap From One or More Cylinders and Engine Starts and Idles Rough With Excessive Noise and/or Smoke.
Engine Overheats	1. Coolant System Leak, Oil Cooler System Leak or Coolant Recovery System Not Operating	Check for leaks and correct as required. Check coolant recovery jar, hose and radiator cap.
	2. Belt Slipping or Damaged	Replace or adjust as required.
	3. Thermostat Stuck Closed	Check and replace if required.
	4. Head Gasket Leaking	Check and repair as required.

85944315

Fig. 96 Diesel engine performance diagnosis

Oil Warning Lamp
"ON" at Idle

1. Oil Cooler or Oil or
Cooler Line Restricted

Remove restriction in cooler or cooler line.

2. Oil Pump Pressure Low

Engine Will Not Shut
Off With Key

NOTE With engine at
idle, pinch the fuel
return line at the
flexible hose to
shut off engine.

1. Injection Pump Fuel
Solenoid Does Not
Return Fuel Valve To
"OFF" Position

VACUUM PUMP DIAGNOSIS

Excessive noise or clattering
noise.

1. Loose screws between pump
assy. and drive assy.

1. A – Tighten screws to spec.
   B– Replace pump assy.

2. Loose tube on pump assy.

2. Replace pump assy.

Hooting noise.

Valves not functioning properly.

Replace pump assy.

Pump assy. loose on drive assy.

Stripped threads.

Replace pump assy.

Oil around end plug.

Loose plug.

1. Seat Plug.
2. Replace drive assy.

Oil leaking out crimp.

Bad crimp.

Replace pump assy.

Install hose and vacuum gage
to pump, engine running, gage
should have reading of 20
inches vacuum minimum. With
engine off, vacuum level loss
should not drop from 20
inches to 19 inches in less than
1-1/2 seconds.

1. Defective valves.

Replace pump assy.

2. Defective diaphragm.

3. Worn push rod seal.

4. Loose tube.

85944316

Fig. 97 Diesel engine performance diagnosis

DIESEL ENGINE IDLE ROUGHNESS DIAGNOSIS PROCEDURE

CONDITION

IDLE ROUGHNESS

Idle roughness is defined as an uneven shaking of the engine in comparison to others with the same number of cylinders and in the same body style.

A rough idle condition may be caused by a difference in the output between cylinders on diesel engines. By selection of parts it is possible to alter the output between cylinders, and smooth out the idle quality.

CORRECTION

Follow the diesel engine idle roughness diagnosis procedure. Make all necessary adjustments and corrections. The idle roughness procedure must be followed step by step prior to performing the glow plug resistance check. The glow plug resistance check will only be successful after the idle roughness procedure is performed and corrections made.

CONDITION

COAST DOWN ROUGHNESS

A condition may exist where a roughness is observed on coast down at 50 mph or less with a closed throttle.

CORRECTION

Confirm that this condition is engine roughness rather than a tire waddle or a bent wheel by coasting down through the roughness period in neutral with the engine at 1500 to 2000 RPM. If roughness still exists, during the coast down, the condition is not caused by engine roughness. If the roughness condition is gone, follow the idle roughness diagnosis procedure. If not corrected prior to the glow plug resistance procedure, correct the roughness using the glow plug resistance procedures.

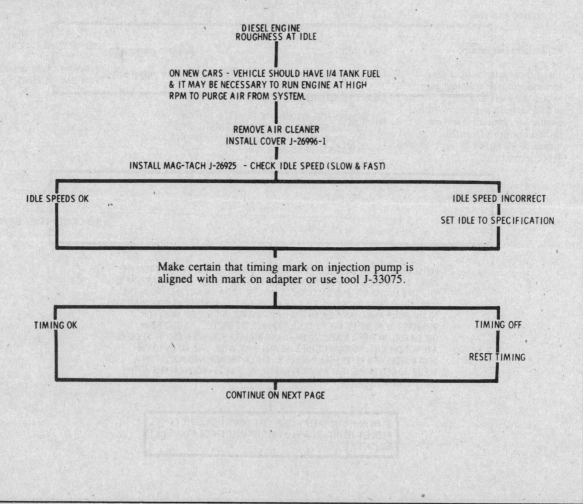

Fig. 98 Diesel engine idle diagnosis

DIESEL ENGINE IDLE ROUGHNESS DIAGNOSIS PROCEDURE (CONT'D)

EXAMINE NOZZLES FOR LEAKS AT NOZZLE BODY
OR AT FUEL LINE CONNECTION. (ENGINE RUNNING)

NO LEAKS

LEAKS

CORRECT

CHECK FOR LEAK AT INJECTION PUMP TO HIGH PRESSURE LINES

NO LEAKS

LEAKS

CORRECT

CHECK FOR FUEL PRESSURE BY CRACKING LINE AT
FITTING BETWEEN FUEL FILTER AND INJECTION PUMP

PRESSURE EVIDENT

NO PRESSURE EVIDENT

DETERMINE CAUSE OF LACK
OF/OR LOW PRESSURE

REMOVE FUEL RETURN LINE FROM TOP OF PUMP.
INSTALL SHORT PIECES OF CLEAR PLASTIC TUBE
BETWEEN RETURN LINE AND CHECK FOR PRESENCE
OF BUBBLES OR FOAM IN TUBE.

NO BUBBLES OR FOAM

BUBBLES EVIDENT

FIND CAUSE IN FUEL SUPPLY

LOOSEN THE LINE AT THE NOZZLES TO BLEED A SMALL AMOUNT OF FUEL FROM THE
LINE. IF SOLID FUEL APPEARS, GO ON TO THE NEXT NOZZLE. IF FOAM APPEARS
SHUT THE ENGINE OFF AND DISCONNECT THE LINE FROM THE NOZZLE. MOVE THE
LINE SO THE INLET TO THE NOZZLE CAN BE OBSERVED. REMOVE THE PINK WIRE
TO THE PUMP AND CRANK THE ENGINE AND OBSERVE THE NOZZLE INLET FOR
BUBBLES. IF BUBBLES ARE EVIDENT, REPLACE THE NOZZLE. SQUIRT SOME
OIL OR FUEL IN THE NEW NOZZLE INLET AND RECHECK FOR BUBBLES. IF BUBBLES
ARE NOT EVIDENT, RECONNECT THE LINE AND PINK WIRE, AND GO ON TO THE
NEXT NOZZLE AND REPEAT THE PROCESS. CHECK THE REMOVED NOZZLE ON A
TESTER TO DETERMINE IF IT IS INOPERATIVE OR IF IT IS INCOMPATIBLE WITH
THE CYLINDER HEAD.

IF AN OBJECTIONABLE ROUGH IDLE CONDITION STILL EXISTS,
PROCEED USING GLOW PLUG RESISTANCE CHECK TO CORRECT
ROUGH IDLE.

85944318

Fig. 99 Diesel engine idle diagnosis

VACUUM DIAGRAMS

Below is a listing of vacuum diagrams for most of the engine and emissions package combinations covered by this manual. Because vacuum circuits will vary based on various engine and vehicle options, always refer first to the vehicle emission control information label, if present. Should the label be missing, or should vehicle be equipped with a different engine from the car's original equipment, refer to the diagrams below for the same or similar configuration.

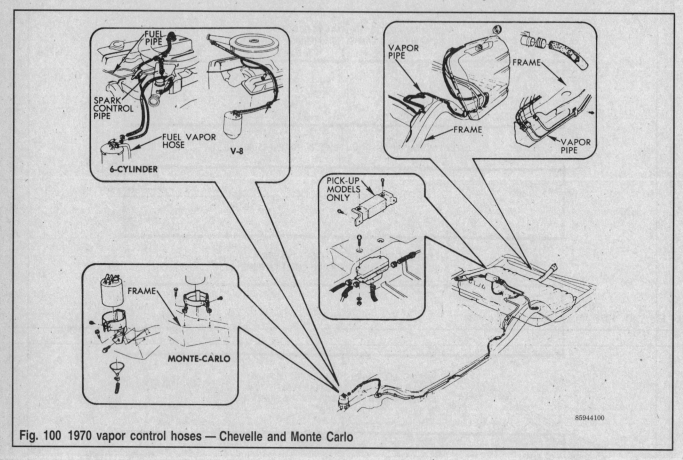

Fig. 100 1970 vapor control hoses — Chevelle and Monte Carlo

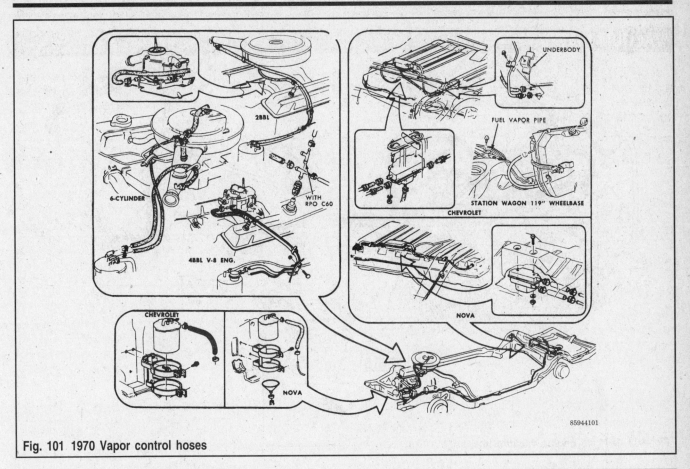

Fig. 101 1970 Vapor control hoses

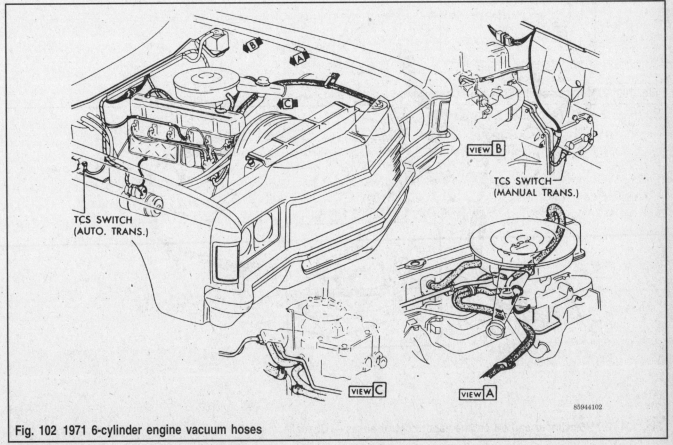

Fig. 102 1971 6-cylinder engine vacuum hoses

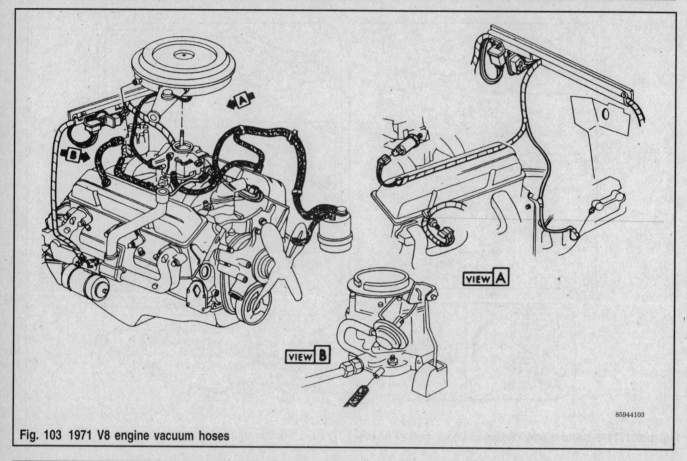

Fig. 103 1971 V8 engine vacuum hoses

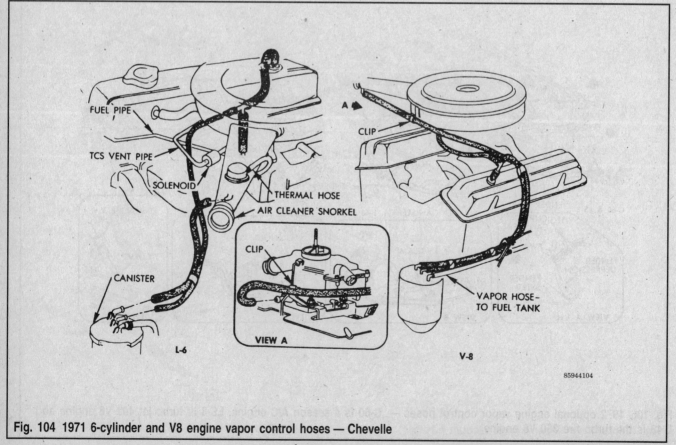

Fig. 104 1971 6-cylinder and V8 engine vapor control hoses — Chevelle

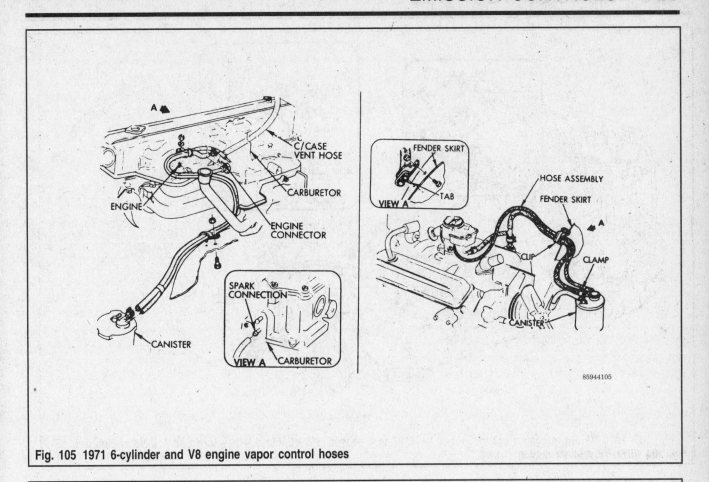

Fig. 105 1971 6-cylinder and V8 engine vapor control hoses

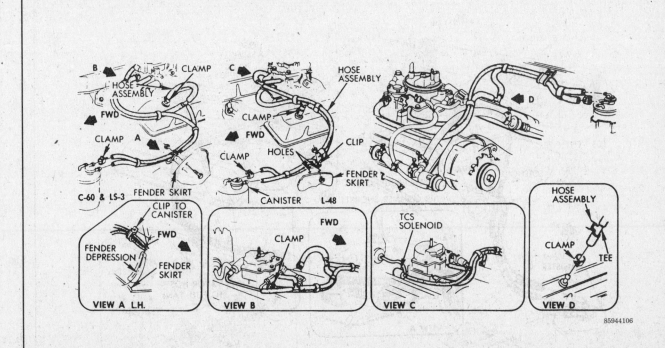

Fig. 106 1972 optional engine vapor control hoses — C-60 is 4 season A/C engine, LS-3 is turbo jet 402 V8 engine and L-48 is the turbo fire 350 V8 engine

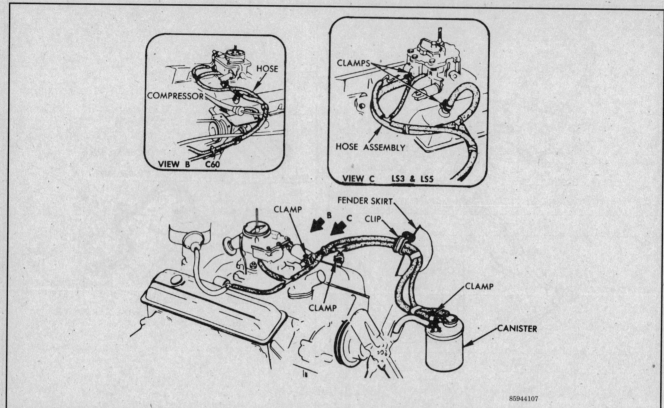

Fig. 107 1972 V8 engine vapor control hoses — C-60 is 4 season A/C engine, LS-3 is turbo jet 402 V8 engine and LS-5 is the turbo jet 454 V8 engine

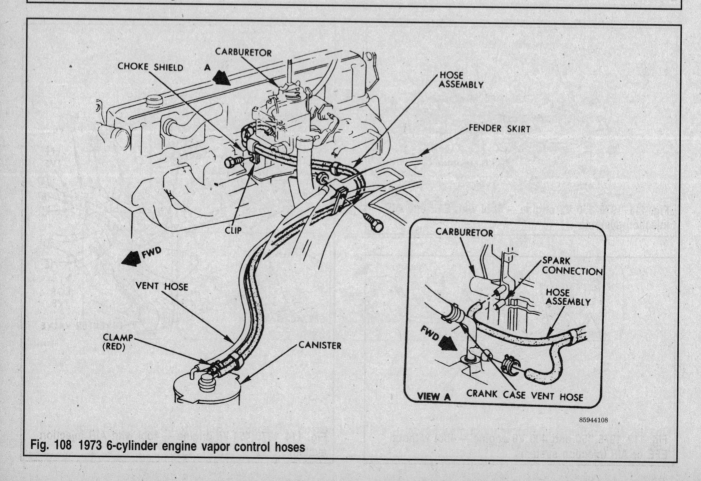

Fig. 108 1973 6-cylinder engine vapor control hoses

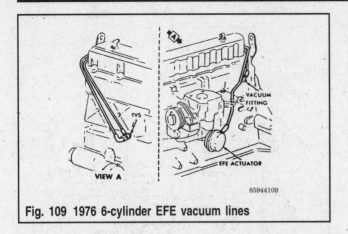

Fig. 109 1976 6-cylinder EFE vacuum lines

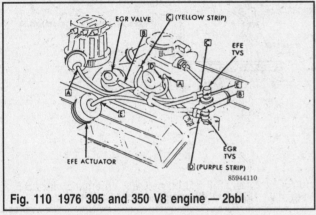

Fig. 110 1976 305 and 350 V8 engine — 2bbl

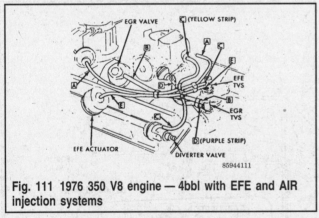

Fig. 111 1976 350 V8 engine — 4bbl with EFE and AIR injection systems

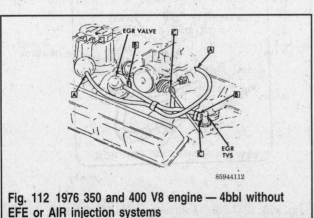

Fig. 112 1976 350 and 400 V8 engine — 4bbl without EFE or AIR injection systems

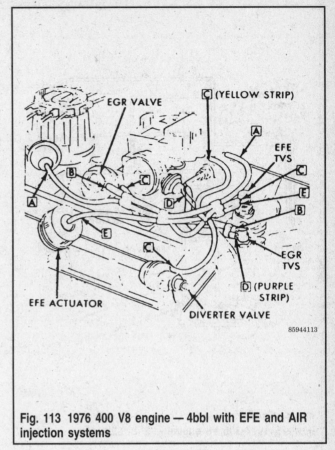

Fig. 113 1976 400 V8 engine — 4bbl with EFE and AIR injection systems

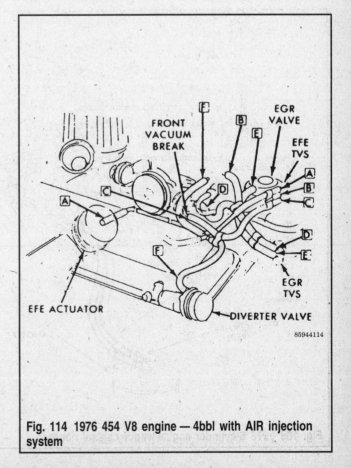

Fig. 114 1976 454 V8 engine — 4bbl with AIR injection system

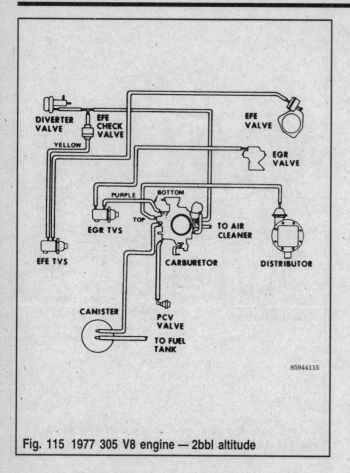

Fig. 115 1977 305 V8 engine — 2bbl altitude

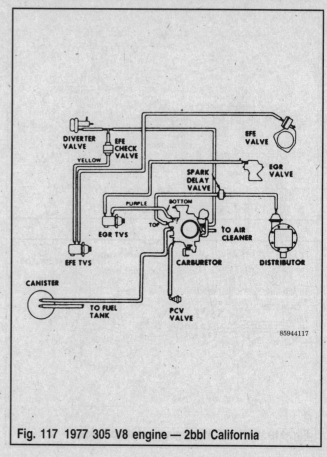

Fig. 117 1977 305 V8 engine — 2bbl California

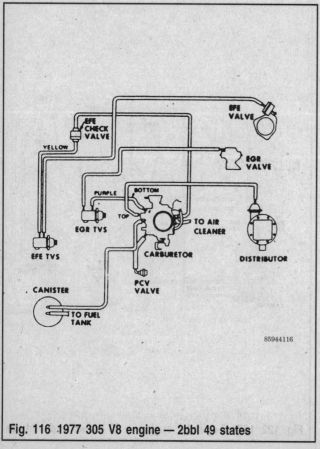

Fig. 116 1977 305 V8 engine — 2bbl 49 states

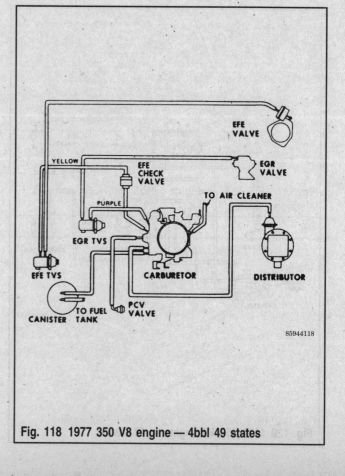

Fig. 118 1977 350 V8 engine — 4bbl 49 states

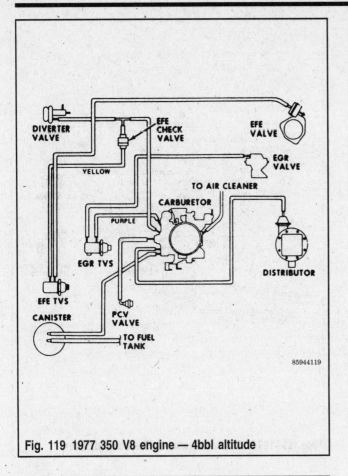

Fig. 119 1977 350 V8 engine — 4bbl altitude

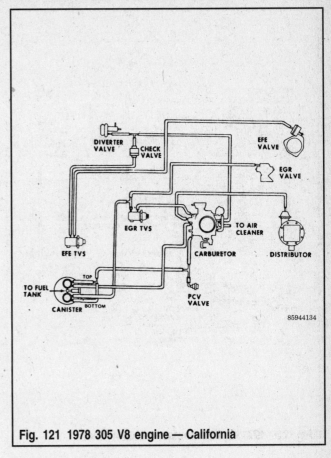

Fig. 121 1978 305 V8 engine — California

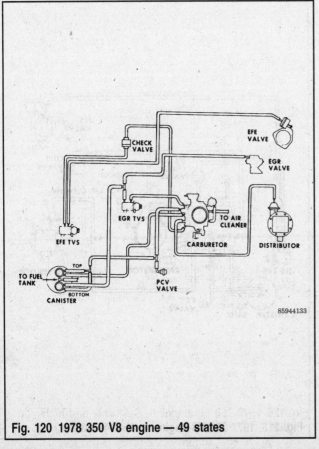

Fig. 120 1978 350 V8 engine — 49 states

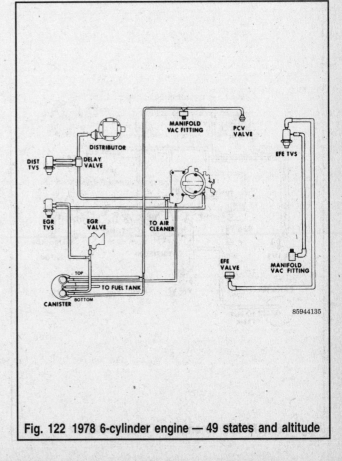

Fig. 122 1978 6-cylinder engine — 49 states and altitude

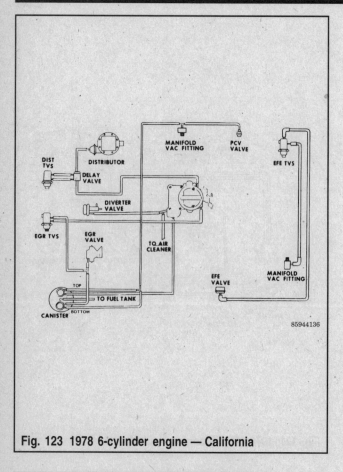

Fig. 123 1978 6-cylinder engine — California

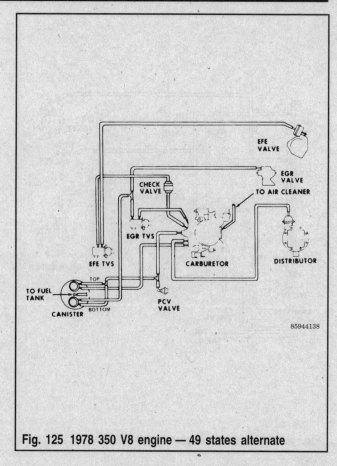

Fig. 125 1978 350 V8 engine — 49 states alternate

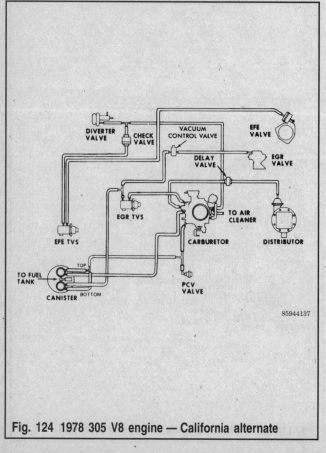

Fig. 124 1978 305 V8 engine — California alternate

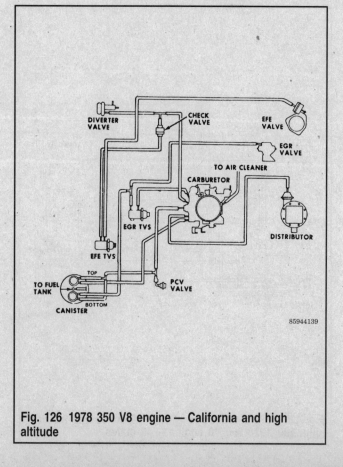

Fig. 126 1978 350 V8 engine — California and high altitude

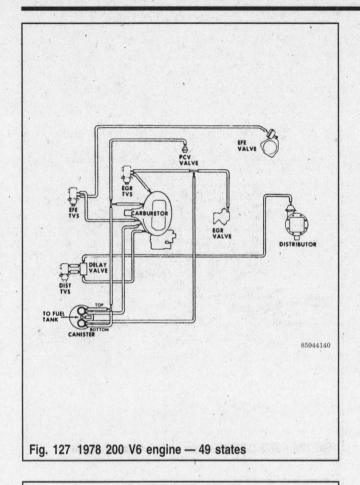

Fig. 127 1978 200 V6 engine — 49 states

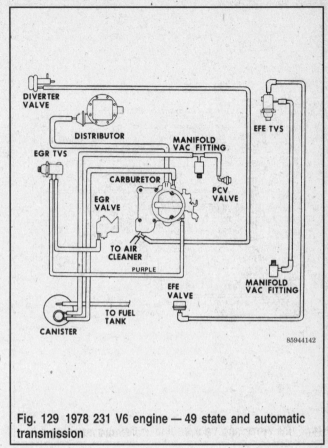

Fig. 129 1978 231 V6 engine — 49 state and automatic transmission

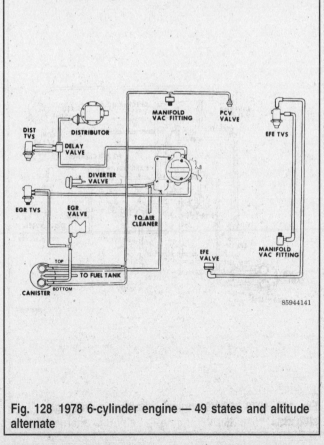

Fig. 128 1978 6-cylinder engine — 49 states and altitude alternate

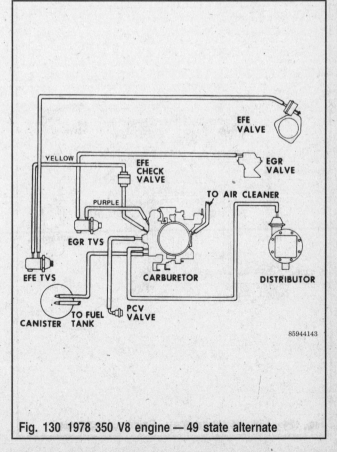

Fig. 130 1978 350 V8 engine — 49 state alternate

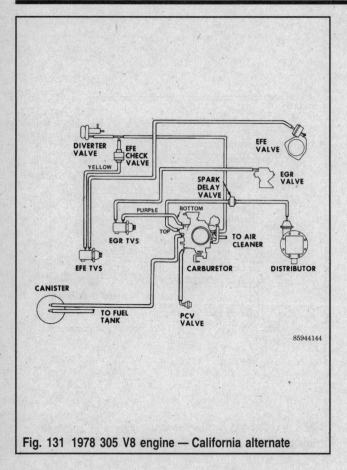

Fig. 131 1978 305 V8 engine — California alternate

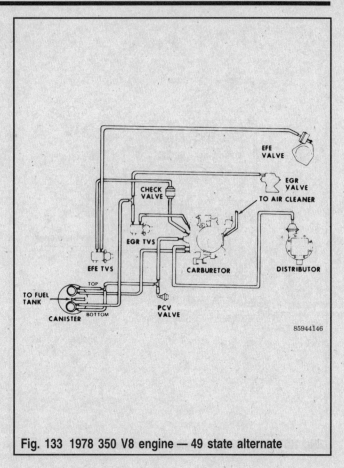

Fig. 133 1978 350 V8 engine — 49 state alternate

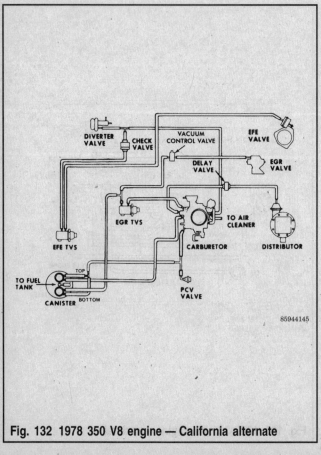

Fig. 132 1978 350 V8 engine — California alternate

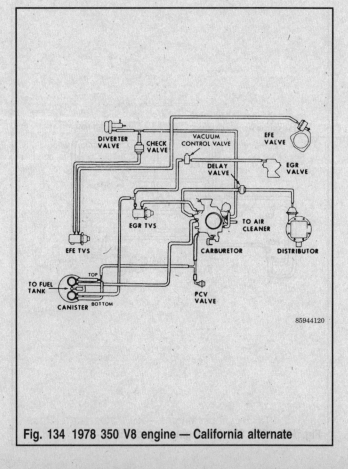

Fig. 134 1978 350 V8 engine — California alternate

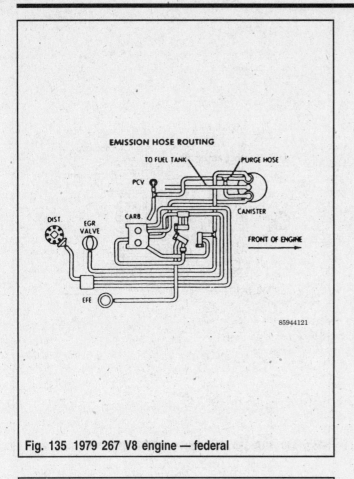

Fig. 135 1979 267 V8 engine — federal

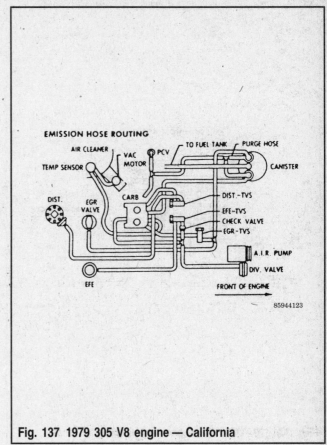

Fig. 137 1979 305 V8 engine — California

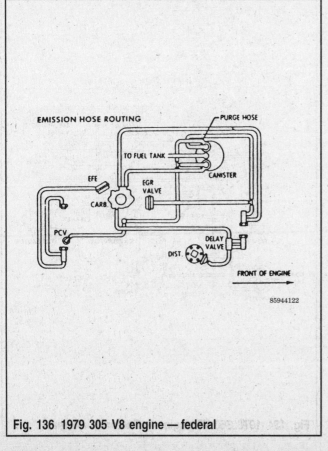

Fig. 136 1979 305 V8 engine — federal

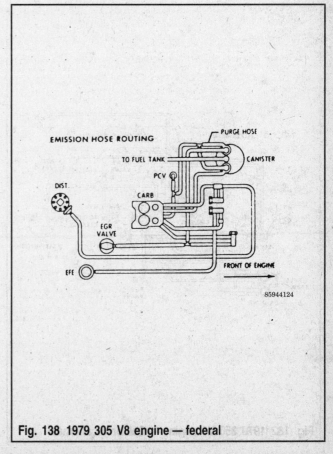

Fig. 138 1979 305 V8 engine — federal

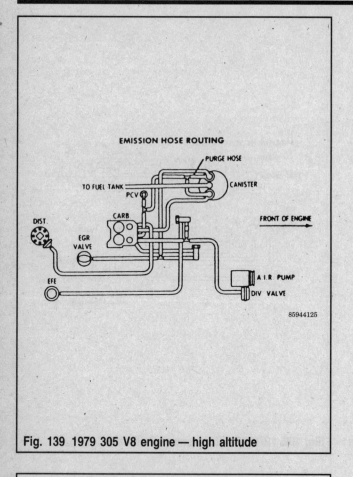

Fig. 139 1979 305 V8 engine — high altitude

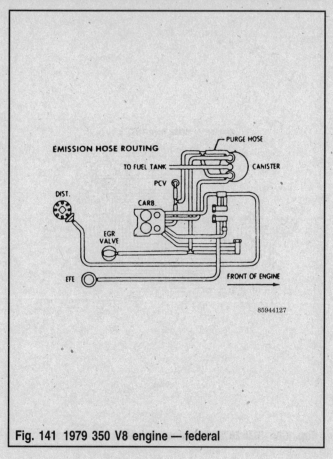

Fig. 141 1979 350 V8 engine — federal

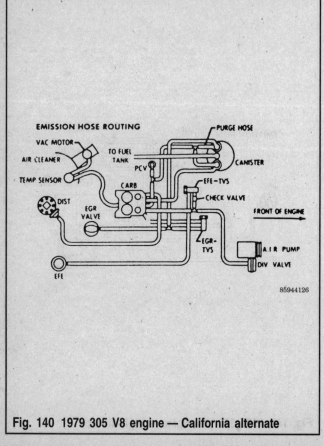

Fig. 140 1979 305 V8 engine — California alternate

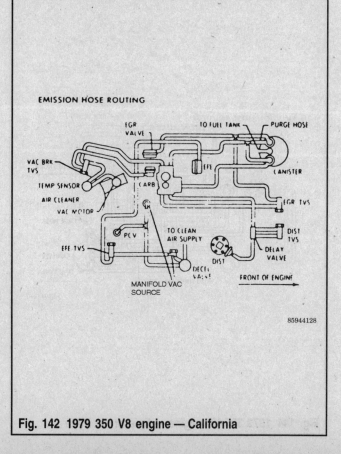

Fig. 142 1979 350 V8 engine — California

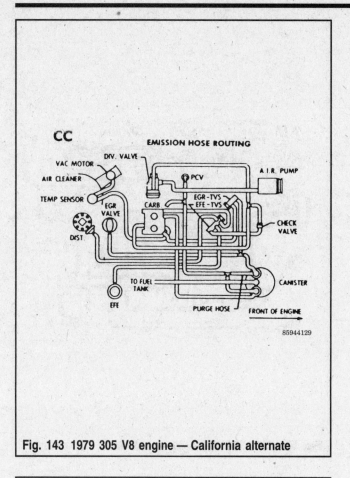

Fig. 143 1979 305 V8 engine — California alternate

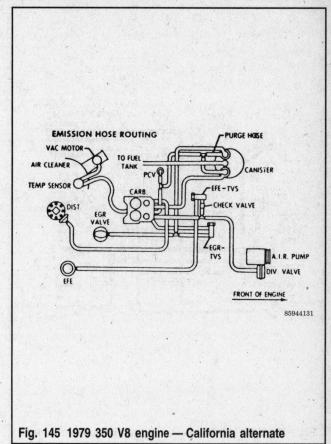

Fig. 145 1979 350 V8 engine — California alternate

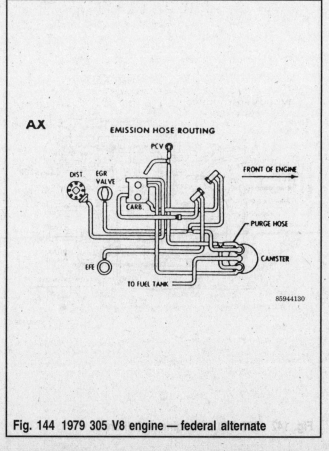

Fig. 144 1979 305 V8 engine — federal alternate

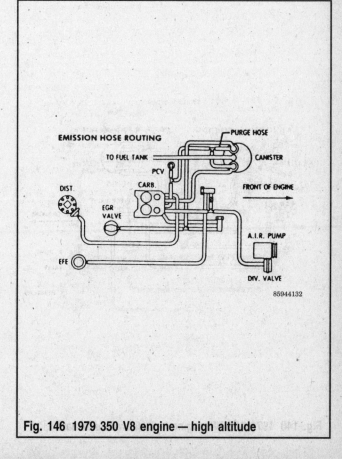

Fig. 146 1979 350 V8 engine — high altitude

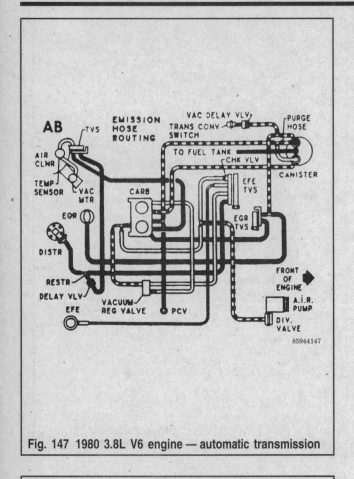

Fig. 147 1980 3.8L V6 engine — automatic transmission

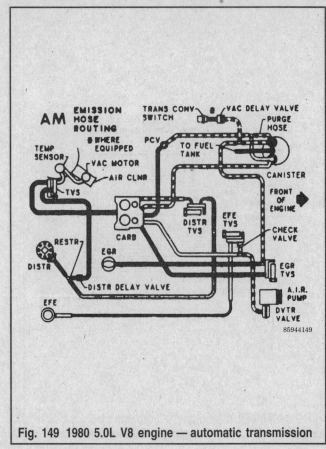

Fig. 149 1980 5.0L V8 engine — automatic transmission

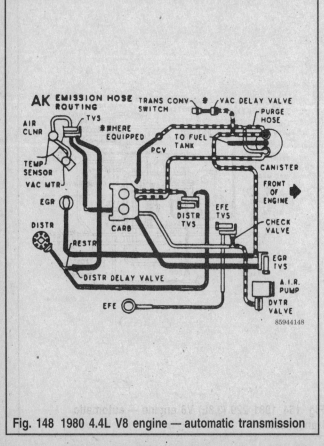

Fig. 148 1980 4.4L V8 engine — automatic transmission

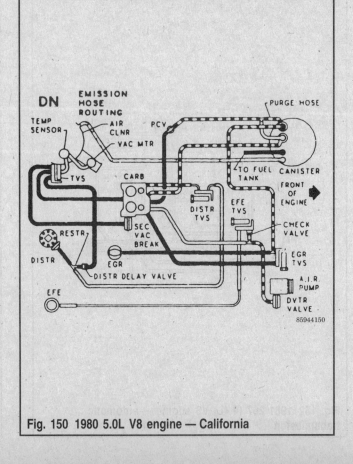

Fig. 150 1980 5.0L V8 engine — California

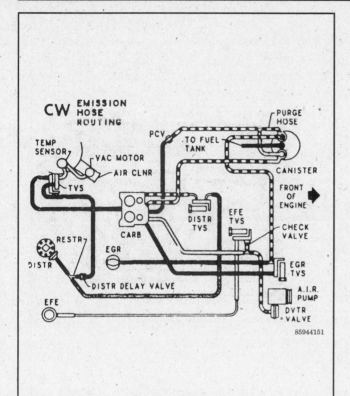

Fig. 151 1980 5.7L V8 engine — automatic transmission federal

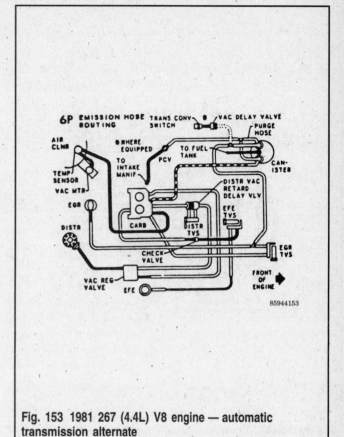

Fig. 153 1981 267 (4.4L) V8 engine — automatic transmission alternate

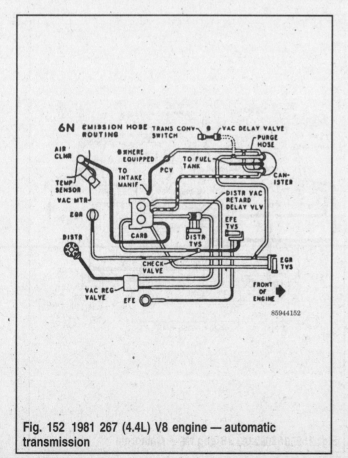

Fig. 152 1981 267 (4.4L) V8 engine — automatic transmission

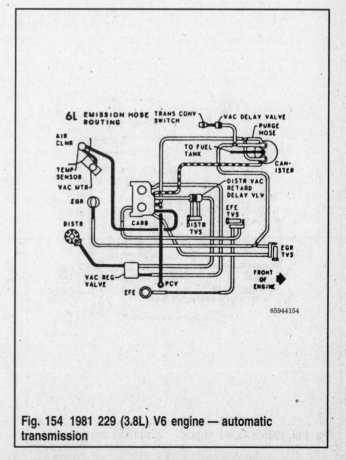

Fig. 154 1981 229 (3.8L) V6 engine — automatic transmission

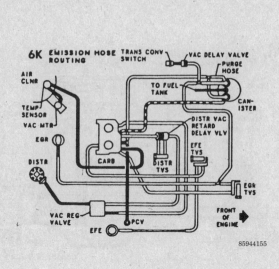

Fig. 155 1981 229 (3.8L) V6 engine — automatic transmission alternate

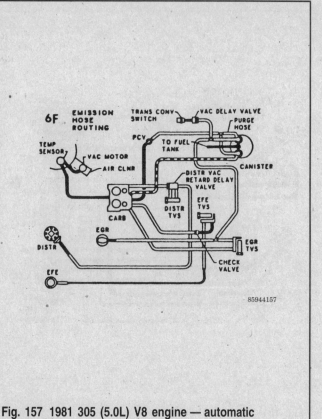

Fig. 157 1981 305 (5.0L) V8 engine — automatic transmission

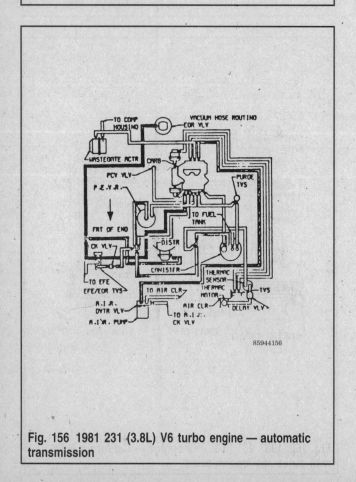

Fig. 156 1981 231 (3.8L) V6 turbo engine — automatic transmission

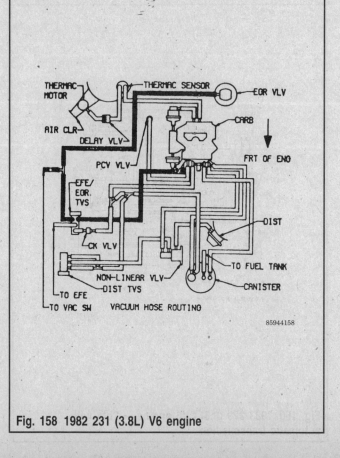

Fig. 158 1982 231 (3.8L) V6 engine

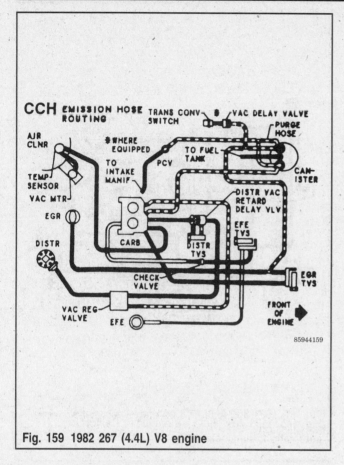

Fig. 159 1982 267 (4.4L) V8 engine

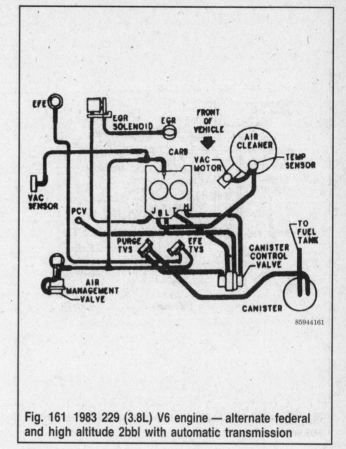

Fig. 161 1983 229 (3.8L) V6 engine — alternate federal and high altitude 2bbl with automatic transmission

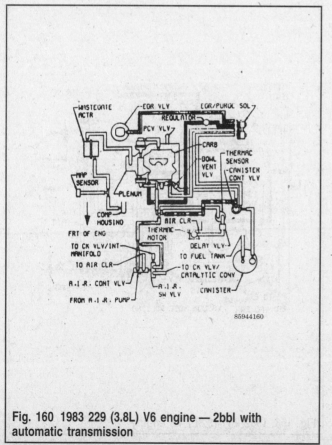

Fig. 160 1983 229 (3.8L) V6 engine — 2bbl with automatic transmission

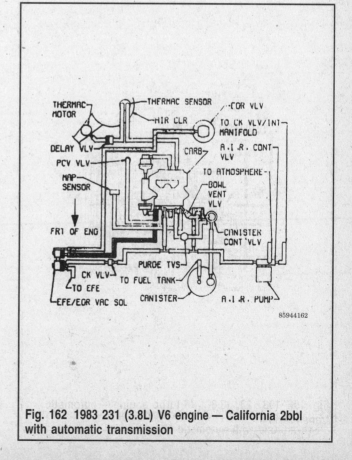

Fig. 162 1983 231 (3.8L) V6 engine — California 2bbl with automatic transmission

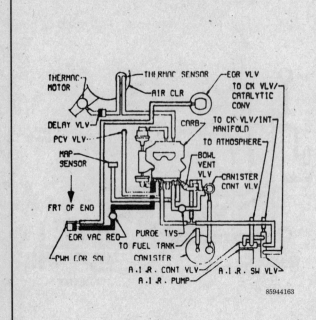

Fig. 163 1983 231 (3.8L) V6 engine — federal 2bbl with automatic transmission

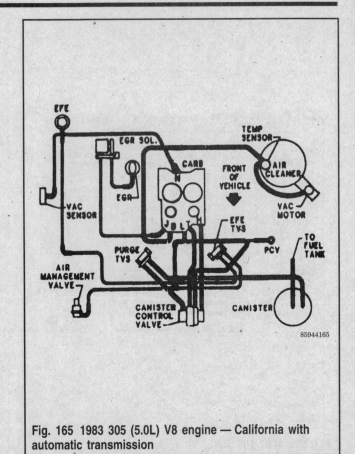

Fig. 165 1983 305 (5.0L) V8 engine — California with automatic transmission

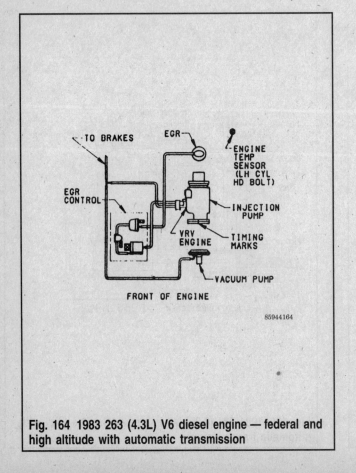

Fig. 164 1983 263 (4.3L) V6 diesel engine — federal and high altitude with automatic transmission

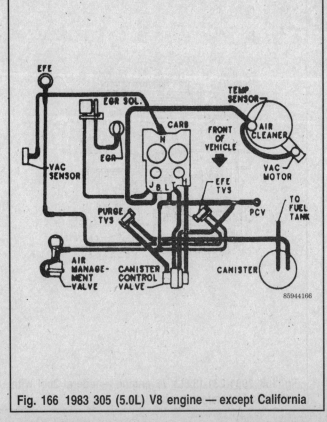

Fig. 166 1983 305 (5.0L) V8 engine — except California

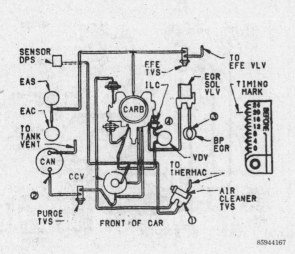

Fig. 167 1983 305 (5.0L) V8 engine — automatic transmission

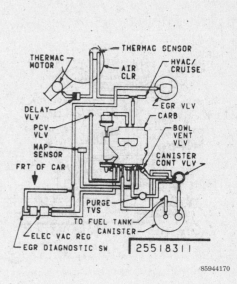

Fig. 169 1984 231 (3.8L) V6 engine — California 2bbl with automatic transmission

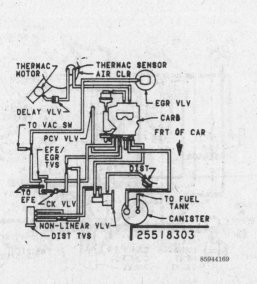

Fig. 168 1984 231 (3.8L) V6 engine — federal 2bbl with automatic transmission alternate

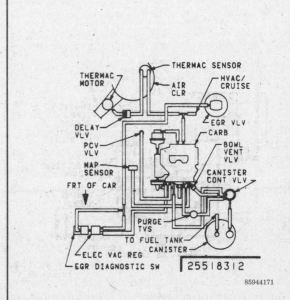

Fig. 170 1984 231 (3.8L) V6 engine — Canada 2bbl with automatic transmission

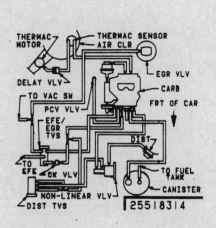

Fig. 171 1984 231 (3.8L) V6 engine — export 2bbl with automatic transmission

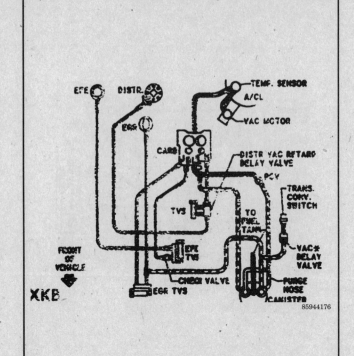

Fig. 173 1984 305 (5.0L) V8 engine — Canada 4bbl with automatic transmission

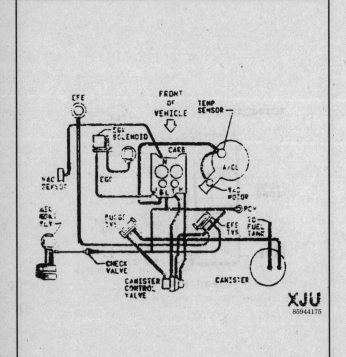

Fig. 172 1984 305 (5.0L) V8 engine — California 4bbl with automatic transmission

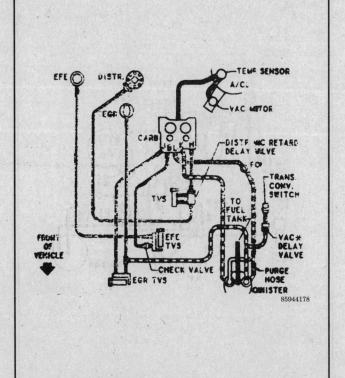

Fig. 174 1984 305 (5.0L) V8 engine — export 4bbl with automatic transmission

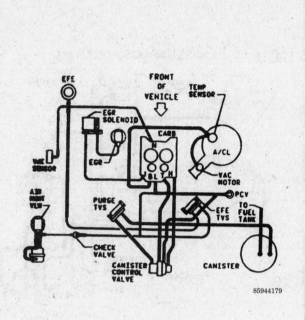

Fig. 175 1984 305 (5.0L) V8 engine — federal 4bbl with automatic transmission alternate

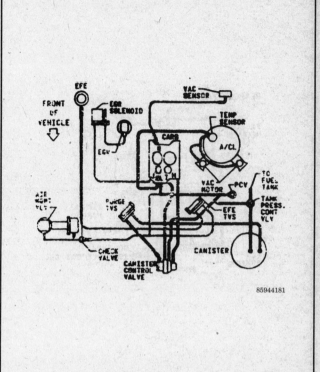

Fig. 177 1984 305 (5.0L) V8 engine — California 4bbl with manual or automatic transmission

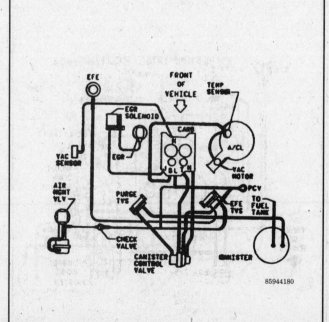

Fig. 176 1984 305 (5.0L) V8 engine — federal 4bbl with automatic transmission alternate

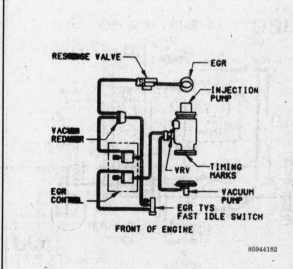

Fig. 178 1984 350 (5.7L) V8 diesel engine — federal low altitude with automatic transmission

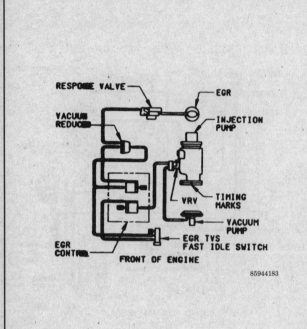

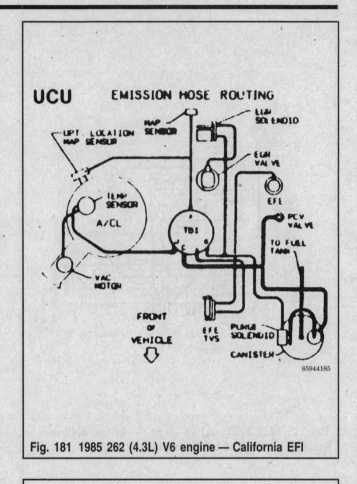

Fig. 179 1984 350 (5.7L) V8 diesel engine — federal high altitude with automatic transmission

Fig. 181 1985 262 (4.3L) V6 engine — California EFI

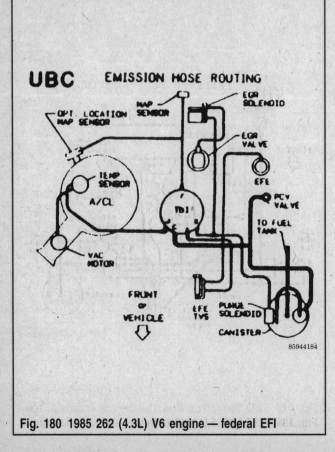

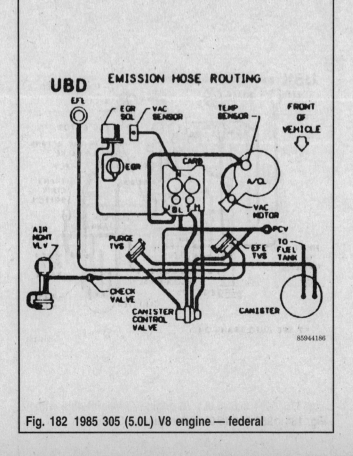

Fig. 180 1985 262 (4.3L) V6 engine — federal EFI

Fig. 182 1985 305 (5.0L) V8 engine — federal

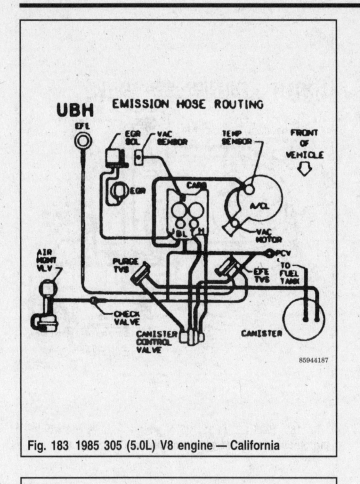

Fig. 183 1985 305 (5.0L) V8 engine — California

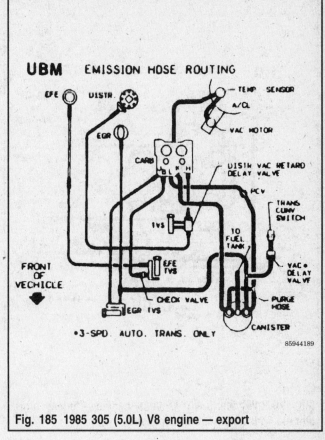

Fig. 185 1985 305 (5.0L) V8 engine — export

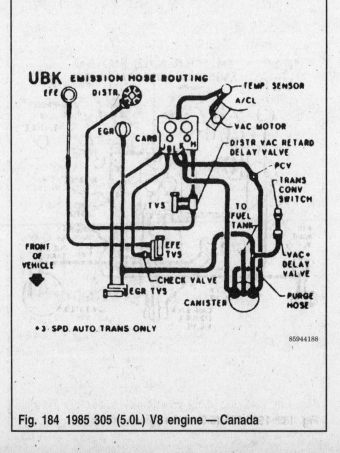

Fig. 184 1985 305 (5.0L) V8 engine — Canada

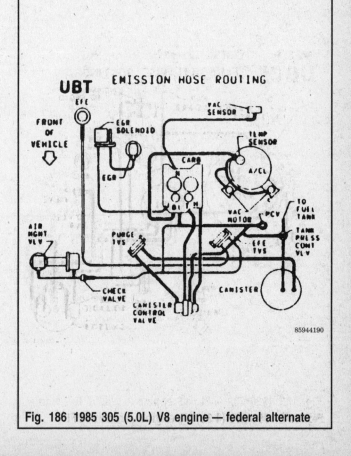

Fig. 186 1985 305 (5.0L) V8 engine — federal alternate

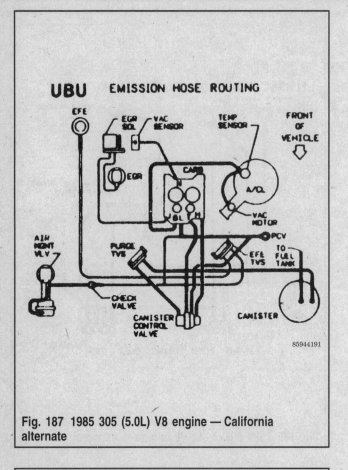

Fig. 187 1985 305 (5.0L) V8 engine — California alternate

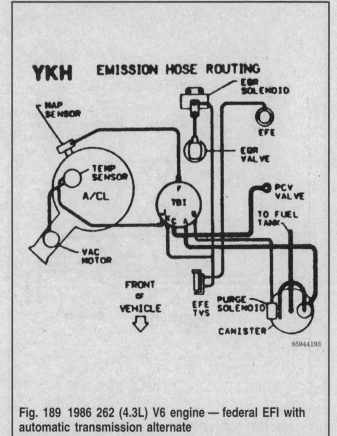

Fig. 189 1986 262 (4.3L) V6 engine — federal EFI with automatic transmission alternate

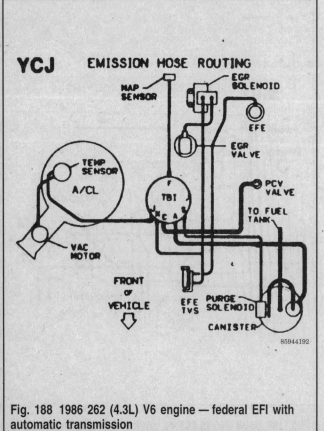

Fig. 188 1986 262 (4.3L) V6 engine — federal EFI with automatic transmission

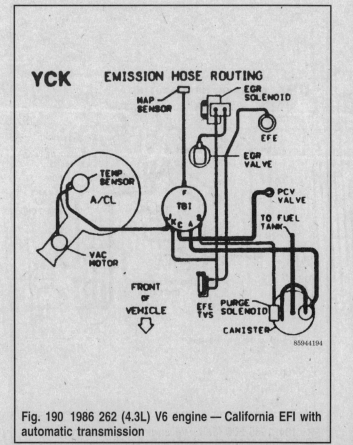

Fig. 190 1986 262 (4.3L) V6 engine — California EFI with automatic transmission

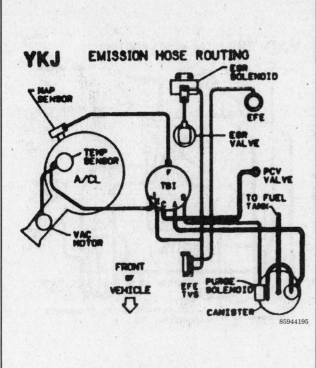

Fig. 191 1986 262 (4.3L) V6 engine — California EFI with automatic transmission alternate

Fig. 193 1986 305 (5.0L) V8 engine — federal with automatic transmission alternate

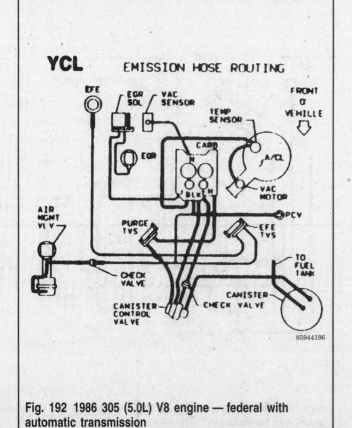

Fig. 192 1986 305 (5.0L) V8 engine — federal with automatic transmission

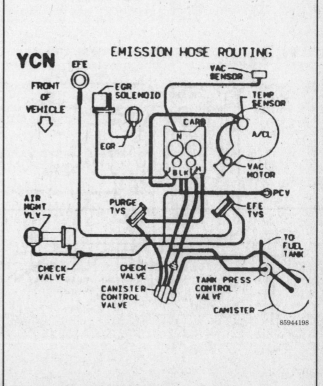

Fig. 194 1986 305 (5.0L) V8 engine — federal with automatic transmission alternate

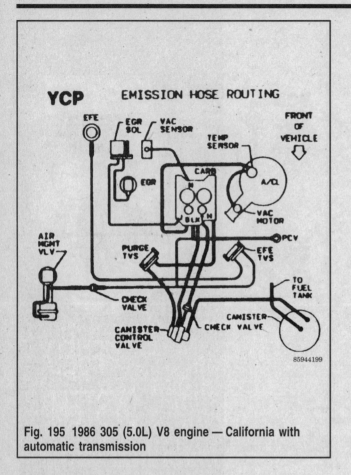

Fig. 195 1986 305 (5.0L) V8 engine — California with automatic transmission

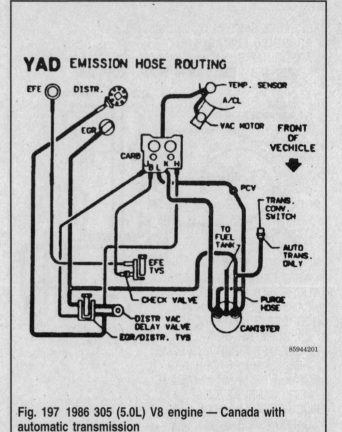

Fig. 197 1986 305 (5.0L) V8 engine — Canada with automatic transmission

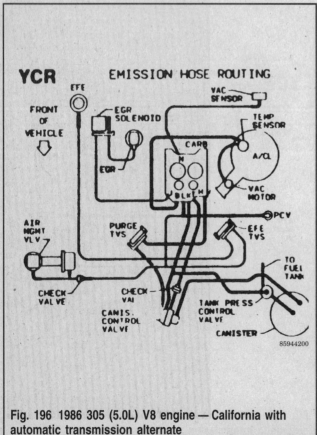

Fig. 196 1986 305 (5.0L) V8 engine — California with automatic transmission alternate

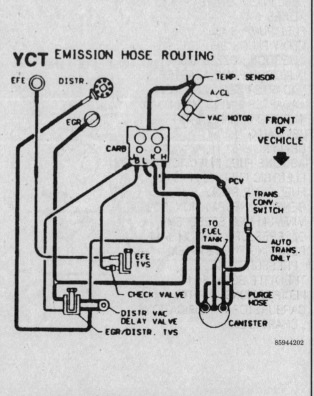

Fig. 198 1986 305 (5.0L) V8 engine — Canada with automatic transmission alternate

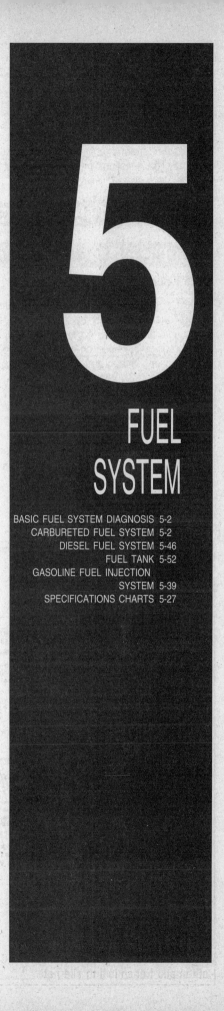

5

FUEL
SYSTEM

BASIC FUEL SYSTEM DIAGNOSIS

When there is a problem starting or driving a vehicle, two of the most important checks involve the ignition and the fuel systems. The questions most mechanics attempt to answer first, "is there spark?" and "is there fuel?" will often lead to solving most basic problems. For ignition system diagnosis and testing, please refer to Section 2 of this manual. If the ignition system checks out (there is spark), then you must determine if fuel system is operating properly (is there fuel?).

CARBURETED FUEL SYSTEM

Fuel Pump

▶ See Figures 1, 2, 3 and 4

The fuel pump is the single action AC diaphragm type. Two types of fuel pumps may be found on these vehicles; serviceable and non-serviceable. The serviceable type was original equipment used on all 1964 and 1965 engines, 1966 in-line engines without the AIR emission control system, and 1966 282 and 327 V8s. All other engines were equipped with the non-serviceable type.

The pump is actuated by an eccentric located on the engine camshaft. On inline engines and on the 231 V6 engine, the eccentric actuates the pump rocker arm directly. On V8 and the 200 V6 engines, a pushrod between the camshaft eccentric and the fuel pump actuates the pump rocker arm.

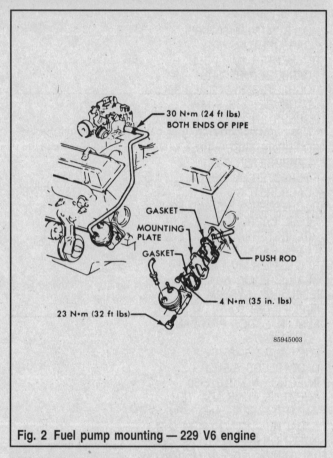

Fig. 2 Fuel pump mounting — 229 V6 engine

TESTING THE FUEL PUMP

The fuel pump should always be tested on the vehicle. The larger line between the pump and tank is the suction side of the system and the smaller line, between the pump and carburetor is the pressure side. A leak in the pressure side would be apparent because of dripping fuel. A leak in the suction side is often only noticed from the reduced volume of fuel delivered to the pressure side. However, fuel may leak out on the suction side when the engine is off.

1. Tighten any loose line connections and look for any kinks or restrictions. Inspect rubber hoses for cracks or leaks and replace if necessary. Inspect the fuel filter for clogging and clean or replace it as necessary.

2. Disconnect the fuel line at the carburetor. Disconnect the distributor-to-coil primary wire or, on HEI systems, the distributor connector. Place a container at the end of the fuel line and crank the engine a few revolutions. If little or no gasoline flows from the line, either the fuel pump is inoperative or the line is

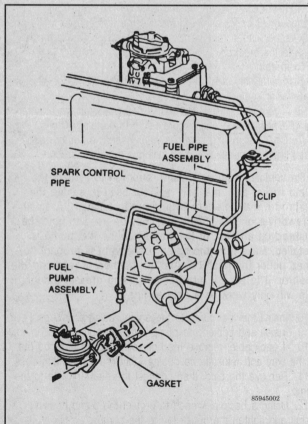

Fig. 1 Fuel pump mounting — inline 6-cylinder engine

plugged. Blow through the lines with compressed air and try the test again. Reconnect the line.

3. Attach a pressure gauge to the pressure side of the fuel line using a Tee fitting.

4. Run the engine and note the reading on the gauge. Stop the engine and compare the reading with the specifications listed in the Tune-Up Specifications chart located in Section 2 of this manual. If the pump is operating properly, the pressure will be as specified and will be constant at idle speed. If pressure varies sporadically or is too high/low, the pump should be replaced.

5. Remove the pressure gauge, then reconnect and secure all fuel lines.

REMOVAL & INSTALLATION

▶ **See Figures 5, 6, 7, 8, 9, 10 and 11**

➡**When you disconnecting or connecting the fuel pump outlet fitting, always use 2 wrenches to avoid damaging the pump.**

1. Disconnect the fuel intake and outlet lines at the pump. Be sure to plug the pump intake line in order to prevent system contamination or excessive fuel loss.

2. On small block V6 and V8 engines, remove the upper bolt from the right front mounting boss. Insert a longer bolt (⅜-16 x 2″) in this hole to hold the fuel pump pushrod up and out of the way.

3. Remove the two pump mounting bolts and lockwashers; then remove the pump and its gasket from the engine.

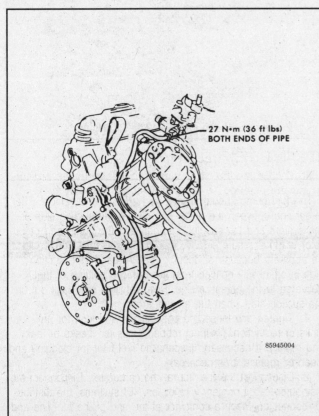

Fig. 3 Fuel pump mounting — 231 V6 engine

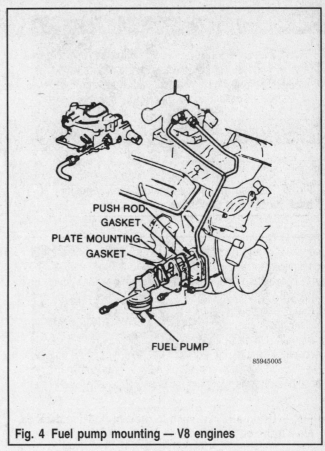

Fig. 4 Fuel pump mounting — V8 engines

4. If the rocker arm pushrod is to be removed from equipped V6 or V8 engines, remove the two adapter bolts and lockwashers, then remove the adapter and its gasket for access to the pushrod.

To install:

5. Thoroughly clean the gasket mating surfaces of all old material or sealer.

6. If removed, install the pushrod, then install the adapter using a new gasket and secure using the retaining bolts.

7. Coat the mating surfaces with a suitable sealer, then install the fuel pump assembly using a new gasket.

➡**On vehicles equipped with a pushrod to actuate the fuel pump rocker arm, if a bolt was not used to secure the pushrod it may interfere with pump installation. A small screwdriver or thin plastic tool may be used to hold the pushrod up and out of the way while the fuel pump is installed. Make sure the pump rocker arm is properly located under the pushrod. Another method of retaining the pushrod it to pack it into position using grease, though this will only work on a cold engine**

8. Install the fuel pump to the engine using a new gasket

9. Install and tighten the pump retaining bolts.

10. If applicable, remove the bolt retaining the pushrod out of the way and reinstall the original bolt to the mounting boss.

11. Remove the plug, then connect the fuel tank line to the pump.

12. Using a backup wrench to protect the pump housing, install and tighten the outlet line to the pump.

13. Start and run the engine, then check for leaks.

Fig. 5 Release the clamp tension, then reposition it back on the fuel tank hose

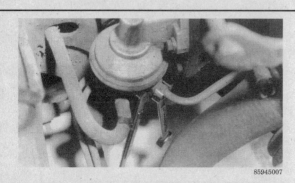

Fig. 6 Using a backwrench to prevent housing damage, loosen the outlet pipe fitting

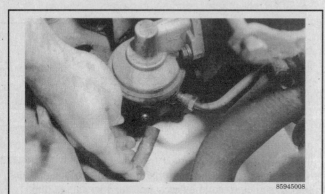

Fig. 7 Disconnect the fuel tank line from the pump

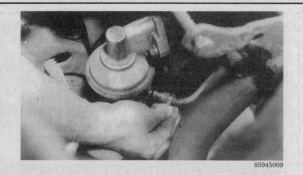

Fig. 8 With the fitting loosened, carefully unthread the outlet pipe from the pump housing

Fig. 9 Loosen and remove the pump retaining bolts

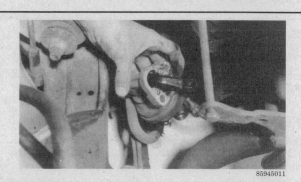

Fig. 10 Remove the pump from the engine mounting surface

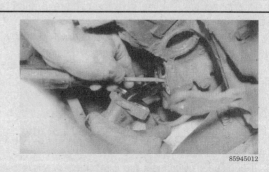

Fig. 11 On models so equipped, it will be necessary to hold the pushrod so the pump rocker arm may be positioned beneath it during installation

Carburetors

Since their introduction in 1964, mid-size Chevrolets have been factory equipped with at least nineteen different carburetors:

- Carter AFB 4 bbl — 1964-65
- Carter WCFB 4-bbl — 1964-65
- Carter YF 1-bbl — 1966-67
- Carter AVS 4-bbl — 1966
- Holley 4150 4-bbl — 1965-70
- Holley 4160 4-bbl — 1966-71
- Rochester BV 1-bbl — 1964-67
- Rochester MV 1-bbl — 1968-71
- Rochester ME 1-bbl — 1977-79
- Rochester 2GV 2-bbl — 1968-74

- Rochester 2GC 2-bbl — 1975-79
- Rochester M2ME 2-bbl — 1980
- Rochester E2ME 2-bbl — 1980 and later
- Rochester 4GC 4-bbl — 1964-66
- Rochester 4MV 4-bbl — 1967-74
- Rochester M4MC 4-bbl — 1975-77
- Rochester 4MC 4-bbl — 1977-79
- Rochester M4ME 4-bbl — 1980
- Rochester E4ME 4-bbl — 1980 and later

MODEL IDENTIFICATION

▶ **See Figure 12**

General Motors Rochester carburetors are identified by their model code. The first number indicates the number of barrels, while one of the last letters indicates the type of choke used. Possible codes include V for the manifold mounted choke coil, C for the choke coil mounted in the carburetor body, and E for electric choke, also mounted on the carburetor. Model codes ending in A indicate an altitude compensating carburetor.

REMOVAL & INSTALLATION

▶ **See Figures 13, 14, 15, 16, 17, 18 and 19**

All Carburetors

1. Disconnect the negative battery cable, then remove the air cleaner assembly and its gasket.
2. Disconnect the fuel line from the carburetor, then tag and disconnect the vacuum lines.
3. Disconnect the choke coil rod, heated air line tube, or electrical connector.
4. Disconnect the throttle linkage, and if equipped, the cruise control linkage.
5. On automatic transmission vehicles, disconnect the throttle valve linkage if equipped.
6. Disconnect the throttle return spring(s).
7. If CEC equipped, remove the CEC valve vacuum hose and electrical connector.
8. If equipped, disconnect the EGR line.
9. If equipped, remove the idle stop solenoid.

10. Remove the carburetor attaching nuts and/or bolts, then remove the carburetor and gasket or insulator.

➡**Immediately cover the opening in the intake manifold to prevent dirt, debris or even loose bolts from falling into the engine, necessitating manifold removal.**

To install:
11. If desired, fill the float bowl with gasoline before installing the carburetor. This will help ease starting the engine later.
12. Remove the cover from the intake manifold, then install the carburetor using a new gasket or insulator and tighten the retaining bolts.
13. If equipped, install the idle stop solenoid.
14. If equipped, connect the EGR line.
15. If CEC equipped, install the CEC valve vacuum hose and electrical connector.
16. Connect the throttle return spring(s).
17. On automatic transmission vehicles, connect the throttle valve linkage, if equipped.
18. Connect the throttle linkage, and if equipped, the cruise control linkage.
19. Connect the choke coil rod, heated air line tube, or electrical connector.
20. Connect the vacuum lines as noted during removal, then connect the fuel line to the carburetor.
21. Install the air cleaner assembly and gasket, then connect the negative battery cable.
22. Start and run the engine, then check for leaks.
23. Check and adjust the carburetor, as necessary.

OVERHAUL

All Types
▶ **See Figures 20 and 21**

Efficient carburetion depends greatly on careful cleaning and inspection during overhaul, since dirt, gum, water, or varnish in or on the carburetor parts are often responsible for poor performance. Always overhaul your carburetor in a clean, dustfree area. Carefully disassemble the carburetor, referring often to the exploded views and directions packaged with the rebuilding kit. Keep similar and look-alike parts segregated during disassembly and cleaning to avoid accidental interchange during assembly. Make a note of all jet sizes.

When the carburetor is disassembled, wash all parts (except diaphragms, electric choke units, pump plunger, and any other

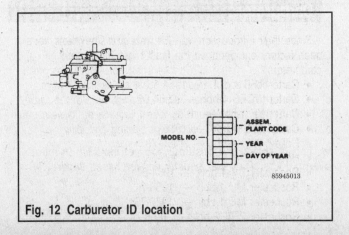

Fig. 12 Carburetor ID location

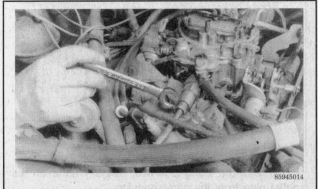

Fig. 13 Disconnect the fuel line from the carburetor

Fig. 14 Tag all hoses and vacuum lines which must be disconnected to assure ease of assembly

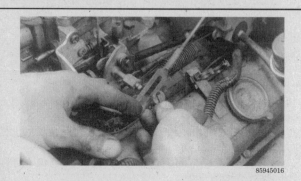

Fig. 15 Disconnect the throttle, cruise control and automatic transmission linkage, as applicable

Fig. 16 Disconnect the throttle return springs

Fig. 17 Use a ratchet and long extension to loosen the flange lower mounting bolts

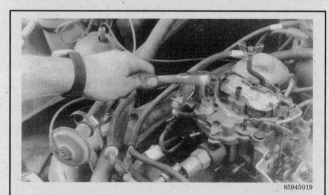

Fig. 18 Loosen the upper carburetor mounting bolts

Fig. 19 Lift the carburetor and gasket or insulator from the intake manifold

plastic, leather, fiber, or rubber parts) in clean carburetor solvent. Do not leave parts in the solvent any longer than is necessary to sufficiently loosen the deposits. Excessive cleaning may remove the special finish from the float bowl and choke valve bodies, leaving these parts unfit for service. Rinse all parts in clean solvent and blow them dry with compressed air or allow them to air dry. Wipe clean all cork, plastic, leather, and fiber parts with clean, lint-free cloth.

Blow out all passages and jets with compressed air and be sure that there are no restrictions or blockages. Never use wire or similar tools to clean jets, fuel passages, or air bleeds. Clean all jets and valves separately to avoid accidental interchange.

Check all parts for wear or damage and, if found, replace the defective parts. Especially check the following:

1. Check the float needle and seat for wear. If wear is found, replace the complete assembly.

2. Check the float hinge pin for wear and the float(s) for dents or distortion. Replace the float if fuel has leaked into it.

3. Check the throttle and choke shaft bores for wear or an out-of-round condition. Damage or wear to the throttle arm, shaft, or shaft bore will often require replacement of the throttle body. These parts require a close tolerance of fit; wear may allow air leakage, which could affect starting and idling.

➡ Throttle shafts and bushings are not included in most overhaul kits. They can usually be purchased separately.

4. Inspect the idle mixture adjusting needles for burrs or grooves. Any such condition requires replacement of the needle, since you will not be able to obtain a satisfactory idle.

5. Test the accelerator pump check valves. They should pass air one way but not the other. Test for proper seating by blowing and sucking on the valve. Replace the valve check ball and spring as necessary. If the valve is satisfactory wash the valve parts again to remove breath moisture.

6. Check the bowl cover for warped surfaces with a straightedge.

7. Closely inspect the accelerator pump plunger for wear and damage, replacing as necessary.

8. During assembly, pay close attention to torque specifications or sequences, when provided. If no sequence is provided, it is usually a good idea to start and the center of the component and gradually work outwards.

9. After the carburetor is assembled, check the choke valve for freedom of operation.

Carburetor overhaul kits are recommended for each overhaul. These kits contain all gaskets and new parts to replace those which deteriorate most rapidly. Failure to replace all parts supplied with the kit (especially gaskets) can result in poor performance later.

Some carburetor manufacturers supply overhaul kits of three basic types: minor repair; major repair; and gasket kits. Basically, they contain the following:

Minor Repair Kits:
- All gaskets
- Float needle valve
- All diagrams
- Spring for the pump diaphragm

Major Repair Kits:
- All jets and gaskets
- All diaphragms
- Float needle valve
- Pump ball valve
- Float
- Complete intermediate rod
- Intermediate pump lever
- Some cover hold-down screws and washers

Gasket Kits:
- All gaskets

After cleaning and checking all components, reassemble the carburetor, using new parts and referring to the exploded view.

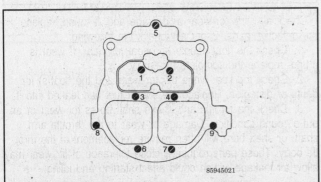

Fig. 20 Example of air horn fastener tightening sequence — M4MC shown

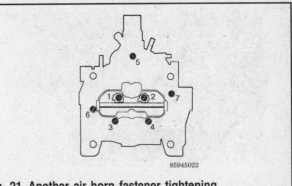

Fig. 21 Another air horn fastener tightening sequence — M2MC carburetor

When reassembling, make sure that all screws and jets are tight in their seats, but do not overtighten as the tips will be distorted. Tighten all screws gradually, in rotation. Do not tighten needle valves into their seats; uneven jetting will result. Always use new gaskets. Be sure to adjust the float level when reassembling.

PRELIMINARY CHECKS (ALL CARBURETORS)

▶ **See Figures 22 and 23**

The following should be observed before attempting any adjustments.

1. Thoroughly warm the engine. If the engine is cold, be sure that it reaches operating temperature.

2. Check the torque of all carburetor mounting nuts and assembly screws. Also check the intake manifold-to-cylinder head bolts. If air is leaking at any of these points, any attempts at adjustment will inevitably lead to frustration.

3. Check the manifold heat control valve (if used) to be sure that it is free.

4. Check and adjust the choke as necessary.

5. Adjust the idle speed and mixture. If the mixture screws are capped, don't adjust them unless all other causes of rough idle have been eliminated. If any other adjustments are performed that might possibly change the idle speed or mixture, adjust the idle and mixture again when you are finished with the other engine adjustments.

Before you make any carburetor adjustments make sure that the engine is in tune. Many problems which are thought to be carburetor related can be traced to an engine which is simply out-of-tune. Any trouble in these areas will have symptoms like those of carburetor problems.

Carter AFB 4-BBL Carburetor

AUTOMATIC CHOKE ADJUSTMENT

The automatic choke is correctly adjusted when the scribe mark on the coil housing is aligned with the center notch in the choke housing for automatic transmission cars and one notch toward lean for manual transmission cars.

Fig. 22 Check the carburetor when the engine is fully closed, the choke should be closed

Fig. 23 Check the carburetor again when the engine has been fully warmed, the carburetor choke should open

FLOAT ADJUSTMENT

Remove the metering rods and the bowl cover. Align the float by sighting down its side to determine if it is parallel with the outer edge of the air horn. Carefully bend the float, as necessary, to adjust. Float level is adjusted with the air horn inverted and the air horn gasket in place. Clearance between each float (at the outer end) and the air horn gasket should be 5/16 in. Carefully bend to adjust.

FLOAT DROP ADJUSTMENT

Float drop is adjusted by holding the air horn in an upright position and bending the float arm until the vertical distance from the air horn gasket to the outer end of each float measures 3/4 in.

INTERMEDIATE CHOKE ROD ADJUSTMENT

Remove the choke coil housing assembly, gasket, and baffle plate. Position a 0.026 in. (0.6604mm) wire gauge between the bottom of the slot in the piston and the top of the float in the choke piston housing. Close the choke piston against the gauge and secure it with a rubber band. Bend the intermediate choke rod so that the distance between the top edge of the choke valve and the air horn divider measures 0.070 in. (1.778mm).

ACCELERATOR PUMP ADJUSTMENT

The first step in adjusting the accelerator pump is to push aside the fast idle cam and firmly seat the throttle valves. Bend the pump rod at the lower angle to obtain a ½ in. clearance between the air horn and the top of the plunger shaft.

UNLOADED, CLOSING SHOE, AND SECONDARY THROTTLE ADJUSTMENT

To adjust the unloader, hold the throttle wide open and bend the unloaded tang to obtain a 3/16 in. clearance between the upper edge of the choke valve and the inner wall of the air horn.

The clearance between the positive closing shoes on the primary and secondary throttle valves is checked with the valves closed. Bend the secondary closing shoe as required to obtain a clearance of 0.020 (0.508mm).

The secondary throttle opening is governed by the pick-up lever on the primary throttle shaft. It has two points of contact with the loose lever on the primary shaft. If the contact points do not simultaneously engage, bend the pick-up lever to obtain proper engagement. The primary and secondary throttle valve opening must be synchronized.

Carter AVS 4-BBL Carburetor

AIR VALVE ADJUSTMENT

1. Turn the air valve bearing retainer until the air valve freely falls open.
2. Wind the air valve bearing counterclockwise until the air valve just starts to close.
3. Continue to wind the bearing an additional 2⅛ turns, and then tighten the retainer.

ACCELERATOR PUMP ADJUSTMENT

1. With the fast idle cam out of the way, back the idle speed screw out until the throttle valves seat in their bores.
2. Hold the throttle valves closed and measure the distance from the air horn to the bottom of the pump S-link.
3. If this distance is not 11/16 in., bend the pump rod to obtain a proper measurement.

IDLE VENT ADJUSTMENT

Holding the choke valve open and the throttle valve closed, the clearance at the idle vent valve should be 0.030 in. (0.762mm). Bend the vent valve lever, as necessary, to adjust.

FAST IDLE CHOKE ROD ADJUSTMENT

Bend the fast idle rod at a lower angle until the fast idle cam index mark lines up with the fast idle adjustment screw. Perform this adjustment while holding the choke valve closed.

FLOAT LEVEL AND DROP ADJUSTMENT

These adjustments are made in the same manner as on the Carter AFB. Refer to the procedures earlier in this section.

CHOKE UNLOADER ADJUSTMENT

1. Hold the throttle wide open and the choke valve toward the closed position with a rubber band.
2. Bend the unloader tang on the throttle shaft lever to obtain a clearance of 0.170 in. (4.318mm) between the upper edge of the choke valve and the dividing wall of the air horn.

CHOKE VACUUM BREAK ADJUSTMENT

1. Hold the vacuum break in against its stop and the choke valve toward the closed position with a rubber band.
2. Bend the vacuum break link at an offset to obtain 0.120 in. (3.048mm) clearance between the upper edge of the choke valve and the air horn.

CLOSING SHOE ADJUSTMENT

1. Hold the primary and secondary throttle valves closed.
2. Bend the secondary closing shoe to obtain 0.020 (0.508mm) clearance between the positive closing shoes on the primary and secondary throttle levers.

SECONDARY THROTTLE OPENING

1. Check to see that the pickup lever contacts the loose lever on the primary shaft at both points simultaneously. Bend the pickup lever to obtain proper contact, if necessary.
2. If the primary and secondary throttle valve do not come to the wide open position simultaneously, bend the connecting link until they do.

SECONDARY LOCKOUT ADJUSTMENT

1. When the choke valve is closed, the lockout tang on the secondary throttle lever should engage the lockout dog. When the valve is open, the lockout dog should swing free of the tang.
2. Bend the lockout tang on the secondary throttle lever, if an adjustment is necessary.

Carter YF 1-BBL Carburetor

AUTOMATIC CHOKE ADJUSTMENT

1. Disconnect the choke rod from the choke lever.
2. Hold the choke valve closed and pull the rod up against the stop in the thermostat housing.
3. The top of the rod should be about one rod diameter above the top of the hole in the choke lever. If not, adjust the length of the rod by bending it at the elbow.
4. Connect the choke rod at the lever.

HAND CHOKE ADJUSTMENT

1. Push in the hand choke knob until the knob is within 1/8 in. of the dash.
2. Loosen the cable clamp at the carburetor and adjust the cable until the choke is wide open.
3. Tighten the cable clamp and check the operation of the choke.

IDLE VENT ADJUSTMENT

1. With the choke open, back out the idle speed screw until it is free to close the throttle valve.
2. Insert a feeler gauge between the air horn and the vent valve. Adjust to get 0.065 in. (1.651mm) clearance.

FAST IDLE AND CHOKE VALVE ADJUSTMENT

1. Hold the choke valve closed.
2. Close the throttle and mark the position of the throttle lever tang on the fast idle cam.
3. The mark on the fast idle cam should align with the upper edge of the tang on the throttle lever. If not, bend the choke rod as necessary to obtain proper alignment.

CHOKE UNLOADER ADJUSTMENT

1. Open the throttle to the wide open position.
2. Using a rubber band, hold the choke valve closed.
3. Bend the unloader tang on the throttle lever to get the proper clearance of 0.250 in. (6.35mm) between the lower edge of the choke valve and the air horn wall.

VACUUM BREAK ADJUSTMENT

1. Hold the vacuum break arm against its stop and hold the choke closed with a rubber band.
2. Bend the vacuum break link to establish a clearance of 0.220 in. (5.588mm) for automatic transmissions or 0.240 in. (6.096mm) for standard transmissions between the lower edge of the choke valve and the air horn wall.

FLOAT LEVEL ADJUSTMENT

1. Turn the bowl cover upside down and measure the float level by measuring the distance between the float (free end) and cover. This distance should be $\frac{7}{32}$ in.; if not, bend the lip of the float, not the float arm.
2. Hold the cover in the proper position (not upside down) and measure the float drop from the cover to the float bottom at the end opposite the hinge. This distance should be $1\frac{9}{16}$ in.
3. Make any necessary adjustments with the stop tab on the float arm.

ACCELERATOR PUMP ADJUSTMENT

1. Seat the throttle valve by backing off the idle speed screw.
2. Hold the throttle valve closed.
3. Fully depress the diaphragm shaft and check the contact between the lower retainer and the lifter link.
4. This retainer (upper pump spring) should just contact the pump lifter link. Do not compress the spring.
5. Bend the pump connector link at its U-bend to make corrections.

METERING ROD ADJUSTMENT

1. Insert the metering rod through the metering jet and close the throttle valve. Press down on the upper pump spring until the pump bottoms.
2. The metering rod arm must rest on the pump lifter link; the rod eye should just slide over the arm pin.
3. To adjust, carefully bend the metering rod arm, as necessary.

Rochester BV 1-BBL Carburetor

AUTOMATIC CHOKE ADJUSTMENT

1. Disconnect the choke rod from the choke lever at the carburetor.
2. While holding the choke valve shut, pull the choke rod up against the stop in the thermostat housing.
3. Adjust the length of the choke rod so that the bottom edge of the choke rod is even with the top edge of the hole in the choke lever.
4. Check the linkage for freedom of operation.

IDLE VENT ADJUSTMENT

▶ **See Figure 24**

1. Position the carburetor lever on the low step of the fast idle cam.
2. The distance between the choke valve and the body casting should be 0.050 in. (1.27mm).

3. If an adjustment is necessary, turn the valve using a screwdriver.

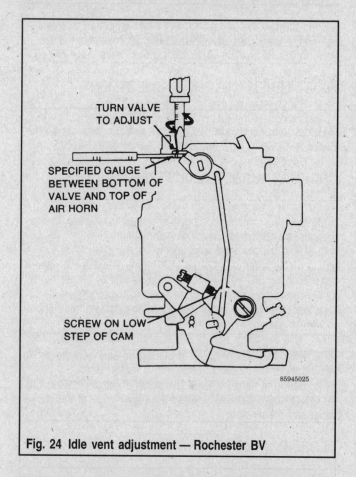

Fig. 24 Idle vent adjustment — Rochester BV

TURN VALVE TO ADJUST

SPECIFIED GAUGE BETWEEN BOTTOM OF VALVE AND TOP OF AIR HORN

SCREW ON LOW STEP OF CAM

85945025

FAST IDLE AND CHOKE VALVE ADJUSTMENT

1. Position the end of the idle adjusting screw on the next to highest step of the fast idle cam.
2. A 0.050 in. (1.27mm) feeler gauge should slide easily between the lower edge of the choke valve and the carburetor bore.
3. If necessary, bend the choke rod until the correct clearance is obtained.

UNLOADER ADJUSTMENT

1. Open the throttle to the wide open position.
2. A 0.230/0.270 in. (5.842/6.858mm) gauge should slide freely between the lower edge of the choke valve and the bore of the carburetor.
3. If necessary, carefully bend the throttle tang to obtain the proper clearance.

VACUUM BREAK ADJUSTMENT

1. Hold the diaphragm lever against the diaphragm body.
2. The clearance between the lower edge of the choke valve and the air horn wall should be 0.136-0.154 in.

(3.454-3.912mm) on Powerglide cars and 0.154-0.173 in. (3.912-4.394mm) on manual cars.

3. Bend the diaphragm link, if adjustment is necessary.

FLOAT LEVEL ADJUSTMENT

▶ See Figure 25

1. Remove the air cleaner assembly.
2. Disconnect the fuel line, fast idle rod, cam-to-choke kick lever, vacuum hose at the diaphragm, and the choke rod at the choke lever.
3. Remove the bowl cover screws and careful lift the cover off the carburetor. Use extra caution not to drop and loose the screws in the engine.
4. Install a new gasket on the cover before making any adjustments.
5. Invert the cover assembly and measure the float level with a float gauge.

➡Rebuilding kits include a float level gauge.

6. Check float centering while holding the cover sideways. Use the same gauge as in Step Five. The floats should not touch the gauge.
7. Hold the cover upright and measure the float drop. If the drop is more or less than 1¾ in., bend the stop tang until the drop is correct.
8. Install the cover and carefully tighten the retaining screws, then reconnect the lines and linkage

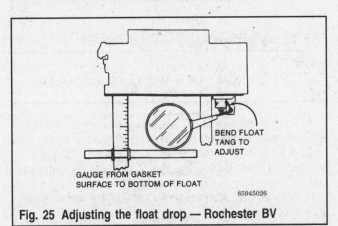

BEND FLOAT TANG TO ADJUST

GAUGE FROM GASKET SURFACE TO BOTTOM OF FLOAT

85945026

Fig. 25 Adjusting the float drop — Rochester BV

Rochester MV 1-BBL Carburetor

▶ See Figure 26

The model MV carburetor is a single bore, downdraft carburetor with an aluminum throttle body, automatic choke, internally balanced venting, and a hot idle compensating system for cars equipped with automatic transmissions. Newer models are also equipped with Combination Emission Control valves (C.E.C.) and an Exhaust Gas Recirculation (EGR) system. An electrically operated idle stop solenoid replaces the idle stop screw of older models.

The MV carburetor is used on six cylinder cars from 1968 and service procedures apply to all MV carburetors.

FAST IDLE ADJUSTMENT

➡The fast idle adjustment must be made with the transmission in Neutral.

1. Position the fast idle lever on the high step of the fast idle cam.
2. Be sure that the choke is properly adjusted and in the wide open position with the engine warm.
3. Bend the fast idle lever until the specified speed is obtained.

CHOKE ROD (FAST IDLE CAM) ADJUSTMENT

▶ See Figure 27

➡Adjust the fast idle before making choke rod adjustments.

1. Place the fast idle cam follower on the second step of the fast idle cam and hold it firmly against the rise to the high step.
2. Rotate the choke valve in the direction of the closed choke by applying force to the choke coil lever.
3. Bend the choke rod, at the partial elbow that exists partway up the rod from the thermostatic coil, in order to give the specified opening between the lower edge (upper edge-1976), of the choke valve and the inside air horn wall.

➡Measurement must be made at the center of the choke valve.

CHOKE VACUUM BREAK ADJUSTMENT

▶ See Figure 28

The adjustment of the vacuum break diaphragm unit ensures correct choke valve opening after engine starting.

1. Remove the air cleaner assembly for access. On vehicles with the THERMAC air cleaner, plug the sensor's vacuum take off port.
2. Using an external vacuum source, apply vacuum to the vacuum break diaphragm until the plunger is fully seated.
3. When the plunger is seated, push the choke valve toward the closed position.

CHOKE UNLOADER ADJUSTMENT

1. While holding the choke valve closed, apply pressure to the choke operating lever.
2. Turn the throttle lever to the wide open position.
3. Measure the distance between the lower edge of the choke plate and the air horn wall.
4. If an adjustment is necessary, carefully bend the unloader tang on the throttle lever.

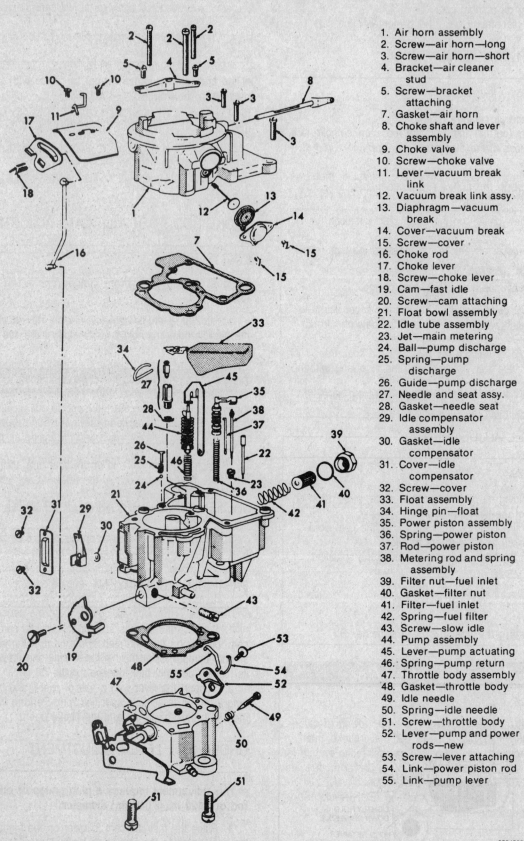

1. Air horn assembly
2. Screw—air horn—long
3. Screw—air horn—short
4. Bracket—air cleaner stud
5. Screw—bracket attaching
7. Gasket—air horn
8. Choke shaft and lever assembly
9. Choke valve
10. Screw—choke valve
11. Lever—vacuum break link
12. Vacuum break link assy.
13. Diaphragm—vacuum break
14. Cover—vacuum break
15. Screw—cover
16. Choke rod
17. Choke lever
18. Screw—choke lever
19. Cam—fast idle
20. Screw—cam attaching
21. Float bowl assembly
22. Idle tube assembly
23. Jet—main metering
24. Ball—pump discharge
25. Spring—pump discharge
26. Guide—pump discharge
27. Needle and seat assy.
28. Gasket—needle seat
29. Idle compensator assembly
30. Gasket—idle compensator
31. Cover—idle compensator
32. Screw—cover
33. Float assembly
34. Hinge pin—float
35. Power piston assembly
36. Spring—power piston
37. Rod—power piston
38. Metering rod and spring assembly
39. Filter nut—fuel inlet
40. Gasket—filter nut
41. Filter—fuel inlet
42. Spring—fuel filter
43. Screw—slow idle
44. Pump assembly
45. Lever—pump actuating
46. Spring—pump return
47. Throttle body assembly
48. Gasket—throttle body
49. Idle needle
50. Spring—idle needle
51. Screw—throttle body
52. Lever—pump and power rods—new
53. Screw—lever attaching
54. Link—power piston rod
55. Link—pump lever

85945027

Fig. 26 Exploded view of the Rochester MV carburetor

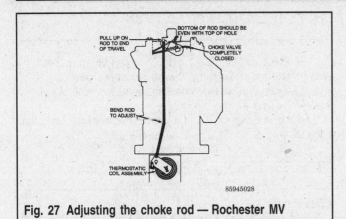

Fig. 27 Adjusting the choke rod — Rochester MV

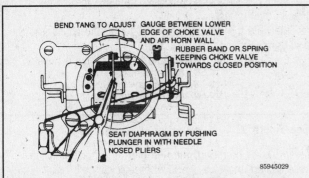

Fig. 28 Choke vacuum break adjustment — Rochester MV

FLOAT LEVEL ADJUSTMENT

▶ **See Figure 29**

1. While holding the float retainer in place, push down on the outer end of the float arm.

2. Measure the distance from the top of the float bowl casting (no gasket) and the toe of the float.

3. Bend the float as necessary to obtain the specified measurement.

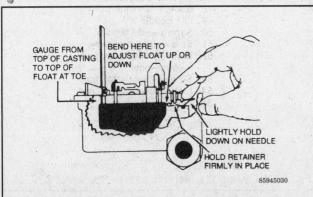

Fig. 29 Adjusting the float level on a Rochester MV

METERING ROD ADJUSTMENT

1. Back out the idle adjusting screw or idle stop solenoid to close the throttle valve.

2. Apply pressure to the power piston hanger and hold the piston against its stop.

3. While holding the power piston down, turn the metering rod holder over the float surface of the bowl casting until the metering rod lightly touches the inside edge of the bowl.

4. Measure the space between the bowl and the bottom of the metering rod holder. This dimension should be 0.070-0.078 in. (1.778-1.981mm).

5. Bend the metering rod holder if an adjustment is necessary.

CHOKE ROD ADJUSTMENT

1. Disconnect the choke rod from the upper choke lever and hold the choke valve closed.

2. Push the choke rod down to the bottom of its travel.

3. The top of the rod should be even with the bottom of the hole in the choke lever, carefully bend the rod if adjustment is necessary.

Rochester 1ME 1-BBL Carburetors

FLOAT LEVEL ADJUSTMENT

1. Push down on the end of the float arm and against the top of the float needle to hold the retaining pin firmly in place.

2. While holding the position of the retaining pin, gauge from the top of the casting to the top of the index point at the toe of the float.

3. If float level needs to be changed do it by bending the float arm just on the float side of the float needle.

FAST IDLE ADJUSTMENT

1. If the carburetor has a stepped fast idle cam, put the cam follower on the high step of the cam. If the cam has a smooth contour, open the throttle slightly and rotate the cam to its highest position, then release throttle.

2. Support the lever with a pair of pliers, and bend the tang in or out to achieve specified rpm. Perform the adjustment with the engine hot and the choke open.

CHOKE COIL LEVER ADJUSTMENT

➡ **This adjustment requires a plug gauge or other metal rod of 0.120 in. (3.048mm) diameter.**

1. Place the fast idle cam follower on the highest step of the cam or rotate the cam to its highest possible position. Close the choke all the way and hold.

2. Insert the plug gauge through the small hole in the out end of the choke lever. Bend the link at the lowest point of the

curved portion until the gauge will enter the hole in the carburetor casting.

CHOKE ADJUSTMENT

1. Place the fast idle cam follower on the high step of the cam or rotate the cam until it is at the highest position.
2. Slightly loosen the three screws which retain the choke cover just enough to turn the cover. Don't loosen them more than necessary, or the lever may slip out of the tang inside.
3. Turn the cover until the mark on the cover lines up with the appropriate mark on the choke housing. See specifications.

METERING ROD ADJUSTMENT

1. Hold the throttle wide open. Push downward on the metering rod until it can be slid out of the slot in the holder. Slide the rod out of the holder and remove it from the main metering jet.
2. Back out the solenoid hex screw until the throttle can be closed all the way.
3. Remove the float bowl gasket.
4. Holding power piston down and throttle closed, swing the metering rod holder over the flat surface of the bowl casting next to the throttle bore. Measure the distance from the float surface to the outer end of the rod holder with the specified gauge (see specifications), or a metal rod of equivalent diameter.
5. Bend the horizontal portion of the rod holder where is joins the vertical portion until the gauge just passes between the holder and surface of the bowl casting with power piston bottomed.

Rochester 2GC, 2GV 2-BBL Carburetors

These procedures are for both the 1¼ and 1½ models; where there are differences these are noted. The 1½ model has larger throttle bores and an additional fuel feed circuit to make it suitable for use on the 350 V8 engines.

FAST IDLE ADJUSTMENT

On 2GC and 2GV models the fast idle is set automatically when the curb idle and mixture is set.

FAST IDLE CAM ADJUSTMENT

▶ See Figure 30

1. Turn the idle screw onto the second step of the fast idle cam, abutting against the top step.
2. Hold the choke valve toward the closed position and check the clearance between the upper edge of the choke valve and the air horn wall.
3. If this measurement varies from specifications, bend the tang on the choke lever.

CHOKE UNLOADER ADJUSTMENT

1. Hold the throttle valves wide open and use a rubber band to hold the choke valve toward the closed position.
2. Measure the distance between the upper edge of the choke valve and the air horn wall.
3. If this measurement is not within specifications, bend the unloader tang on the throttle lever to correct it.

ACCELERATOR PUMP ROD ADJUSTMENT

▶ See Figure 31

1. Back out the idle stop screw and close the throttle valves in their bores.
2. Measure the distance from the top of the air horn to the top of the pump rod.
3. Bend the pump rod at angle to correct this dimension.

FLOAT LEVEL ADJUSTMENT

▶ See Figure 32

Invert the air horn and, with the gasket in place and the needle seated, measure the level as follows:
- On nitrophyl floats, measure the air horn gasket to the lip on the toe of the float.
- On brass floats, measure the air horn gasket to the lower edge of the float seam.

Bend the float tang to adjust the level.

FLOAT DROP ADJUSTMENT

▶ See Figure 33

Holding the air horn right side up, measure float drop as follows:
- On nitrophyl floats, measure from the air horn gasket to the lip at the toe of the float.
- On brass floats, measure from the air horn gasket to the bottom of the float.

Bend the float tang to adjust either type of float.

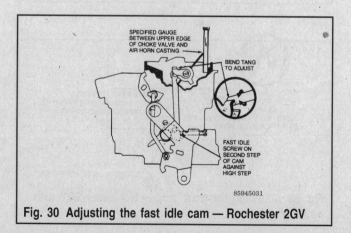

Fig. 30 Adjusting the fast idle cam — Rochester 2GV

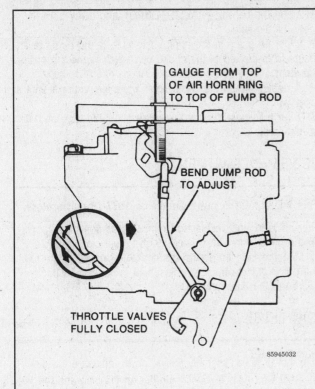

Fig. 31 Adjusting the accelerator pump rod — Rochester 2GV

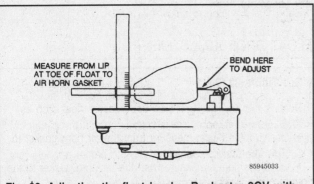

Fig. 32 Adjusting the float level — Rochester 2GV with a nitrophyl float

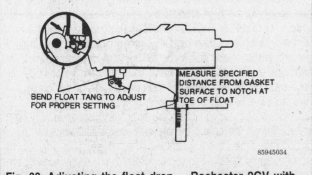

Fig. 33 Adjusting the float drop — Rochester 2GV with a nitrophyl float

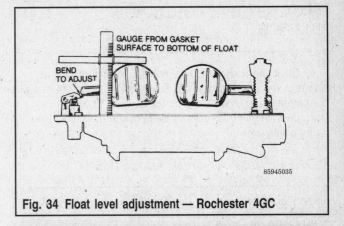

Fig. 34 Float level adjustment — Rochester 4GC

Rochester 4GC 4-BBL Carburetor

AUTOMATIC CHOKE ROD

Set the cover index mark to the one notch lean mark on the housing.

INTERMEDIATE CHOKE ROD

The intermediate choke rod is adjusted with the choke cover and baffle removed.
1. Hold the choke valve closed, exert a light pressure on the choke piston to take up any lash, and then note if the choke piston is at the end of its sleeve.
2. If necessary, bend the intermediate choke rod for correct piston positioning.
3. Install the choke baffle and cover.

CHOKE ROD ADJUSTMENT

1. Turn the idle speed screw in until it just touches the second step of the fast idle cam.
2. Ensure that the choke trip lever is touching the choke counterweight lever.
3. While holding the idle speed screw on the second cam step and against the shoulder of the high step, there should be 0.043 in. (1.092mm) clearance between the choke valve edge and the air horn dividing wall.
4. Bend the choke rod at a lower angle, if necessary.

CHOKE UNLOADER ADJUSTMENT

1. Hold the throttle valve wide open, while the choke trip lever touches the choke counterweight.
2. Clearance between the top of the choke valve and the dividing wall of the air horn should now be 0.235 in. (5.969mm). Bend the fast idle cam tang, if necessary.

SECONDARY THROTTLE LOCKOUT ADJUSTMENT

1. Close the choke valve so that the secondary lockout tang is in the fast idle cam slot. Clearance between the fast idle cam and the tang should be 0.015 in. (0.381mm).

2. Bend the tang horizontally as necessary to obtain the correct clearance.

FLOAT LEVEL AND DROP ADJUSTMENT

▶ **See Figure 34**

1. Remove the bowl cover.

2. Install a new gasket on the bowl cover surface.

3. Invert the cover and install the float lever gauges supplied with the carburetor rebuilding kit over the primary and secondary floats. The floats should just touch the gauges. The height from the bottom of the float to the bowl cover gasket is $1\frac{33}{64}$ in. for the primaries and $1\frac{37}{64}$ in. for the secondaries. Bend the float arms as necessary to obtain the correct level.

4. Center the floats in the level gauge, bending them to the left or right as necessary.

5. While holding the bowl cover in an upright position, measure the distance from the bowl cover gasket to the bottom of the float. This distance, float drop, should be $2\frac{1}{4}$ in. Bend the float tang on the end of the hinge arm to correct the drop.

6. Install the bowl cover.

Rochester 4 MC, 4MV, M4MC 4-BBL Carburetors

The Rochester Quadrajet carburetor is a two stage, 4-barrel downdraft carburetor. The designation MC or MV refers to the type of choke system the carburetor is designed for. The MV model is equipped with a manifold thermostatic choke coil. The MC model has a choke housing and coil mounted on the side of the float bowl.

The primary side of the carburetor is equipped with $1\frac{3}{8}$ in. diameter bores and a triple venturi with plain tube nozzles. During off idle and part throttle operation, the fuel is metered through tapered metering rods operating in specially designed jets positioned by a manifold vacuum responsive piston.

The secondary side of the carburetor contains two $2\frac{1}{4}$ in. bores. An air valve is used on the secondary side for metering control and supplements the primary bores.

The secondary air valve operates tapered metering rods which regulate the fuel in constant proportion to the air being supplied.

ACCELERATOR PUMP

1. Close the primary throttle valves by backing out the slow idle screw and making sure that the fast idle cam follower is off the steps of the fast idle cam.

2. Bend the secondary throttle closing tang away from the primary throttle lever.

3. With the pump in the appropriate hole in the pump lever, measure from the top of the choke valve wall to the top of the pump stem.

4. To adjust, bend the pump lever while supporting it with a screwdriver.

5. After adjusting, reset the secondary throttle tang and the slow idle screw.

IDLE VENT ADJUSTMENT

➡ **This adjustment is not required on 1977-79 carburetors.**

After adjusting the accelerator pump rod as specified above, open the primary throttle valve enough to just close the idle vent. Measure from the top of the choke valve wall to the top of the pump plunger stem. If adjustment is necessary, bend the wire tang on the pump lever.

FLOAT LEVEL

With the air horn assembly upside down, measure the distance from the air horn gasket surface (gasket removed) to the top of the float at the toe. Measure at a point $\frac{3}{16}$ in. back from the top of the float on 1977-79 carburetors.

➡ **Make sure the retaining pin is firmly held in place and that the tang of the float is firmly against the needle and seat assembly.**

FAST IDLE

1. Position the fast idle lever on the high step of the fast idle cam. Disconnect and plug the vacuum hose at the EGR valve.

2. Be sure that the choke is wide open and the engine is warm.

3. Turn the fast idle screw to gain the proper fast idle rpm.

CHOKE ROD ADJUSTMENT

Position the cam follower on the second step of the fast idle cam, touching the high step. Close the choke valve directly on models up to 1976. On 1977 models, remove the choke thermostatic cover, and then hold the choke closed by pushing upward on the choke coil lever. Gauge the clearance between the lower edge of the choke valve and the carburetor body on models to 1975, and between the upper edge of the choke valve and the carburetor body on 1976 and 1977 models. Bend the choke rod to obtain the specified clearance. On 1977 models, install the choke thermostatic cover and adjust it to specification when the adjustment is complete. This adjustment requires highly specialized tools on 1978 and later models, and so is not included here.

AIR VALVE DASHPOT ADJUSTMENT

▶ See Figure 35

Set the vacuum break diaphragm. On 1977-79 models, this requires plugging the bleed purge hole on the back of the diaphragm with tape, and the use of an external vacuum source. Hold the air valve tightly closed on all models. Gauge the clearance between the dashpot rod and the end of the slot in the air valve lever. Bend the rod to adjust. Remove the tape from the bleed purge hole.

CHOKE COIL ROD

1967-76

1. Close the choke valve by rotating the choke coil lever counterclockwise.
2. Disconnect the thermostatic coil rod from the upper lever.
3. Push down on the rod until it contacts the bracket of the coil.
4. The rod must fit in the notch of the upper lever.
5. If it does not, it must be carefully bent at the curved portion just below the upper lever.

CHOKE COIL LEVER AND CHOKE THERMOSTATIC COIL

1977-79

1. Remove the three mounting screws and retainers, then pull the thermostatic coil cover assembly off the choke housing and set it aside.
2. Place the fast idle cam follower on the high step of the cam and then push up on the thermostatic coil tang in the choke housing until the choke is closed.
3. Insert a 0.120 in. (3.048mm) plug gauge or rod of that diameter into the hole in the housing located just below the lever. With the choke closed, the lever should just touch the gauge.
4. If necessary, adjust the choke rod by changing the angle of the bend it makes just below the choke itself.
5. Then, install the coil cover back on the choke housing, making sure that the thermostatic coil engages the tang. Install

the three retainers and screws, but do not tighten. With the fast idle cam follower still on the high step of the cam, rotate the cover assembly counterclockwise until the choke closes. Set all models 2 notches lean except 1977 models with manual transmission; set these three notches lean. Hold the position of the housing while tightening screws evenly.

VACUUM BREAK

1967-76

1. Fully seat the vacuum break diaphragm using an outside vacuum source.
2. Open the throttle valve enough to allow the fast idle cam follower to clear the fast idle cam.
3. The end of the vacuum break rod should be at the outer end of the slot in the vacuum break diaphragm plunger.
4. The specified clearance should register from the lower end of the choke valve to the inside air horn wall.
5. If the clearance is not correct, bend the vacuum break link.

1977

➡**Adjustment procedures for 1978 and later models require the use of an expensive and sophisticated special tool, so procedures are not included here.**

1. Remove the choke thermostatic cover. Place the fast idle cam follower on the high step of the cam.
2. Where there is a purge bleed hole on the back of the choke vacuum break, put tape over the hole. Then, set the diaphragm using an outside vacuum source.
3. Push the inside choke coil lever counterclockwise until the tang on the vacuum break lever touches the tang on the vacuum break plunger stem.
4. Place a gauge of the proper diameter between the upper edge of the choke butterfly and the inside wall of the air horn:
   - California Engines: 0.165 in. (4.191mm)
   - All Other Engines: 0.160 in. (4.064mm)
5. If the dimension is incorrect, adjust the screw on the vacuum break plunger stem until all play is taken up and choke butterfly just touches the gauge when it's held vertically.
6. Reconnect the vacuum line to vacuum break port of carburetor, remove tape from purge hole (if applied), then reinstall and adjust choke thermostat (see above).

CHOKE UNLOADER ADJUSTMENT

➡**Performing this adjustment on 1978 and later models requires the use of sophisticated special tools, so the procedure is not included here.**

On 1977 models, make sure the choke thermostatic spring is properly adjusted (see above). Close the choke valve and secure it with a rubber band hooked to the vacuum break lever. Open the primary throttles all the way. Then measure the distance between the air horn and edge of the choke butterfly. On models up to and including 1976, use the bottom side of the butterfly for this measurement; on 1977 models, use the top side. Bend the fast idle lever tang to achieve the proper opening of the choke.

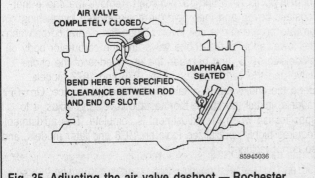

AIR VALVE
COMPLETELY CLOSED

DIAPHRAGM
SEATED

BEND HERE FOR SPECIFIED
CLEARANCE BETWEEN ROD
AND END OF SLOT

85945036

Fig. 35 Adjusting the air valve dashpot — Rochester 4MV

SECONDARY LOCKOUT

1967-76

Completely open the choke valve and rotate the vacuum break lever clockwise. Bend the lever if the measurement between the lever and the secondary throttle exceeds specifications. Close the choke and gauge the distance between the lever and the secondary throttle shaft pin. Bend the lever to adjust.

1977-79

▶ See Figure 36

With the throttle valves and choke valve closed use a gauge pin to check clearance between the lockout lever and the choke arm. Clearance should be no more than 0.015 in. (0.381mm). If clearance is more than specification, carefully bend the lockout lever to achieve proper clearance.

Hold the choke valve wide open by pushing down on the tail of the fast idle cam, then check lockout lever for opening clearance using the gauge pin. If necessary, file the end of the pin if additional clearance is necessary.

AIR VALVE SPRING ADJUSTMENT

➡**Loosening and tightening the locking screw to adjust the air valve spring requires a hex wrench on 1977 and later models carburetors.**

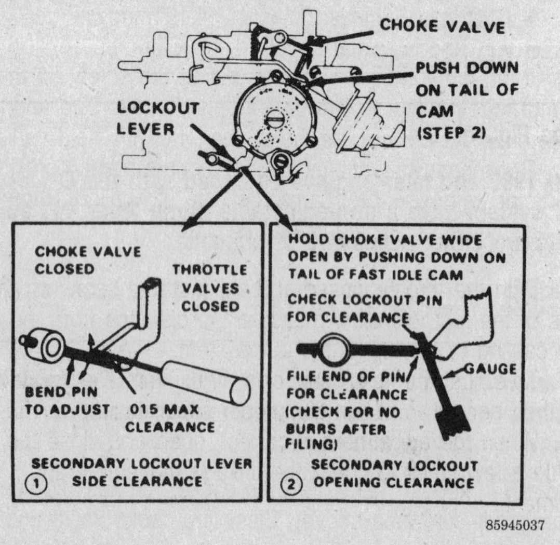

Fig. 36 Adjusting the secondary lockout — 1977-79

Remove all spring tension by loosening the locking screw and backing out the adjusting screw. Close the air valve and turn the adjusting screw in until the torsion spring touches the pin on the shaft, then turn it the additional number of turns specified. Secure the locking screw.

SECONDARY CLOSING ADJUSTMENT

This adjustment assures proper closing of the secondary throttle plates.

1. Set the idle as per instructions in the appropriate section. Make sure that the fast idle cam follower is not resting on the fast idle cam.
2. There should be 0.020 in. (0.508mm) clearance between the secondary throttle actuating rod and the front of the slot on the secondary throttle lever when the throttle lever closing tang is resting against the actuating lever.
3. Bend the tang on the primary throttle actuating rod to adjust.

SECONDARY OPENING ADJUSTMENT

1. Open the primary throttle valves until the actuating link contacts the upper tang on the secondary lever.
2. With 2-point linkage, the bottom of the link should be in the center of the secondary lever slot.
3. With three point linkage, there should be 0.070 in. (1.778mm) clearance between the link and the middle tang.
4. Bend the upper tang on the secondary lever to adjust as necessary.

Holley 4150, 4160 4-BBL Carburetors

These carburetors are basically similar in design. The 4160 is an end-inlet carburetor, while the 4150 carburetor has been both an end-inlet and center inlet design.

CHOKE ADJUSTMENT

The 1965 model 4150 uses a bimetallic choke mounted on the carburetor. It is correctly set when the cover scribe mark aligns with the specified notch mark. The later model 4150 and 4160 employ a remotely located choke. To adjust, disconnect the choke rod at the choke lever and secure the choke lever shut. Bend the rod so that when the rod is depressed to the contact stop, the top is even with the bottom of the hole in the choke lever.

FLOAT LEVEL ADJUSTMENT

Position the car on a flat, level surface and start the engine. Remove the sight plugs and check to see that the fuel level reaches the bottom threads of the sight plug port. A plus or minus tolerance of $1/32$ in. is acceptable. To change the level, loosen the fuel inlet needle locking screw and adjust the nut. Turning it clockwise lowers the fuel level and counterclockwise raises it. Turn the nut $1/6$ of a turn for each $1/16$ in. desired change. Open the primary throttle slightly to assure a stabilized adjusting condition on the secondaries. There is no required float drop adjustment.

FAST IDLE ADJUSTMENT

1965 4150

Bring the engine to normal operating temperature with the air cleaner off. Open the throttle. Place the fast idle cam on its high step and close the throttle. Adjust the fast idle screw to reach the specified idle speed.

1966 and Later 4150 and 4160

Open the throttle and place the choke plate fast idle lever against the top step of the fast idle cam. Bend the fast idle lever to obtain the specified throttle plate opening.

CHOKE UNLOADER ADJUSTMENT

Adjustment should be make with the engine not running. Fully open and secure the throttle plate. Force the choke valve toward a closed position, so that contact is made with the unloader tang. Bend the choke rod to gain the specified clearance between the main body and the lower edge of the choke valve.

ACCELERATOR PUMP ADJUSTMENT

With the engine off, block the throttle open and push the pump lever down, Clearance between the pump lever arm and the spring adjusting nut should be 0.015 (0.381mm) minimum. Turn the screw or nut to adjust this clearance.

SECONDARY THROTTLE VALVE ADJUSTMENT

Close the throttle plates, and then turn the adjustment screw until it contacts the throttle lever. Advance the screw ½ turn more.

AIR VENT VALVE ADJUSTMENT

Close the throttle valves and open the choke valve so that the throttle arm is free of the idle screw. Bend the air vent valve rod to obtain the specified clearance between the choke valve and seat. Advance the idle speed screw until it touches the throttle lever, and then advance it 1½ turns.

VACUUM BREAK ADJUSTMENT

Secure the choke valve closed and the vacuum break against the stop. Bend the vacuum break link to gain the specified clearance between the main body and the lower edge of the choke valve.

Rochester M2ME and E2ME 2-BBL Carburetors

FLOAT ADJUSTMENT

▶ See Figure 37

1. Remove the air horn from the throttle body.
2. Using your fingers, hold the retainer in place and then push the float down into light contact with the needle.
3. Measure the distance from the toe of the float (furthest from the hinge) to the top of the carburetor (gasket removed).
4. To adjust, remove the float and gently bend the are to specifications. After adjustment, check the float alignment in the chamber. On engines equipped with the C-4 or the CCC system, where the float level varies more than $1/16$" from specifications, adjust the float as follows:

Float too High:

Hold the retainer firmly in place and then push down the center of the float pontoon until the correct setting is obtained.

Float too Low:

1. Lift out the meter rods and remove the solenoid connector screw.
2. Turn the lean mixture solenoid screw clockwise until the screw is bottomed lightly in the float bowl. Count and record the number of turns before the screw is bottomed.
3. Turn the screw counterclockwise and remove it. Lift the solenoid and the connector from the float bowl.
4. Remove the float and bend the arm up to adjust it. Put the float back in and check its alignment.
5. Upon installation make sure that the solenoid lean mixture screw is backed out of the float bowl EXACTLY the same number of turns as were recorded in Step 2.

PUMP ADJUSTMENT

▶ See Figure 38

➡ All 1980 and later engines equipped with the C-4 or the CCC system have a non-adjustable pump lever. No adjustments are either necessary or possible.

1. With the throttle closed and the fast idle screw off the steps of the fast idle cam, measure the distance from the air horn casting to the top of the pump stem.
2. To adjust the lever, support it firmly with a screwdriver and then bend it to obtain the proper specifications.
3. When the adjustment is correct, open and close the throttle a few times to check the linkage movement and alignment.

CHOKE COIL LEVER ADJUSTMENT

▶ See Figure 39

➡ To complete this procedure you will need a start cover retainer kit; available at most auto parts suppliers.

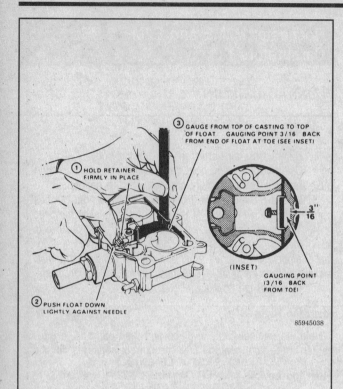

Fig. 37 Adjusting the float — Rochester M2ME and E2ME

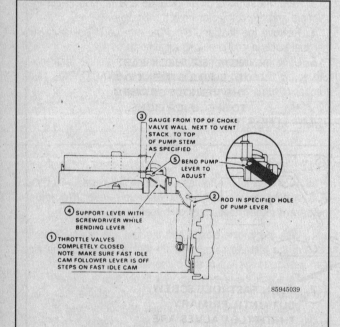

Fig. 38 Pump adjustment — Rochester M2ME and E2ME except for C-4 or CCC systems

1. Drill out and remove the rivets. Retain the choke housing cover and then remove the thermostatic cover and coil assembly from the choke housing.

2. Place the fast idle cam follower on the high step of the fast idle cam.

3. Close the choke valve by pushing up on the thermostatic coil tang (counterclockwise).

4. Insert a drill or gauge of the specified size into the hole in the choke housing. The lower edge of the choke lever should be just touching the side of the gauge.

5. If the choke lever is not touching the side of the gauge, bend the choke rod until you see that it does.

FAST IDLE ADJUSTMENT

▶ See Figure 40

1. Set the ignition timing and curb idle speed. Disconnect and plug any hoses as directed on the emission control label.

2. Place the fast idle screw on the highest step of the fast idle cam.

3. Start the engine and adjust the engine speed to specifications with the fast idle screw.

FAST IDLE CAM (CHOKE ROD) ADJUSTMENT

▶ See Figure 41

➡A special angle gauge should be used. If it is not available, an inch measurement may be substituted.

1. Adjust the choke coil lever and the fast idle as previously detailed.

2. Rotate the degree scale until it is zeroed.

3. Close the choke valve completely and place the magnet on top of it.

4. Center the bubble.

5. Rotate the scale so that the specified degree is opposite the pointer.

6. Place the fast idle screw on the second step of the cam, against the rise of the high step.

7. Close the choke by pushing up on the choke coil lever or the vacuum break lever tang. You may hold it in position with a rubber band.

8. To adjust, bend the tang on the fast idle cam until the bubble is centered.

FRONT VACUUM BREAK ADJUSTMENT

▶ See Figure 42

1. Follow Steps 1-5 of the Fast Idle Cam Adjustment procedure.

2. Set the choke vacuum diaphragm using an outside vacuum source.

3. Close the choke valve by pushing up on the choke coil lever or the vacuum break lever. You may hold it in position with a rubber band.

4. To adjust, turn the screw in or out until the bubble in the gauge is centered.

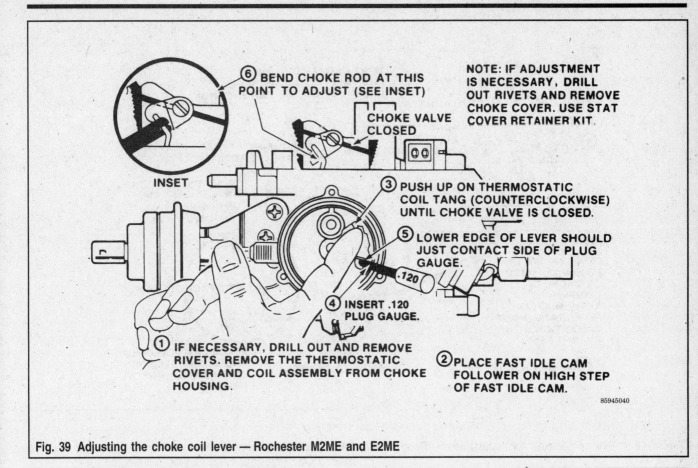

6 BEND CHOKE ROD AT THIS POINT TO ADJUST (SEE INSET)

INSET

CHOKE VALVE CLOSED

NOTE: IF ADJUSTMENT IS NECESSARY, DRILL OUT RIVETS AND REMOVE CHOKE COVER. USE STAT COVER RETAINER KIT.

3 PUSH UP ON THERMOSTATIC COIL TANG (COUNTERCLOCKWISE) UNTIL CHOKE VALVE IS CLOSED.

5 LOWER EDGE OF LEVER SHOULD JUST CONTACT SIDE OF PLUG GAUGE.

.120

4 INSERT .120 PLUG GAUGE.

1 IF NECESSARY, DRILL OUT AND REMOVE RIVETS. REMOVE THE THERMOSTATIC COVER AND COIL ASSEMBLY FROM CHOKE HOUSING.

2 PLACE FAST IDLE CAM FOLLOWER ON HIGH STEP OF FAST IDLE CAM.

85945040

Fig. 39 Adjusting the choke coil lever — Rochester M2ME and E2ME

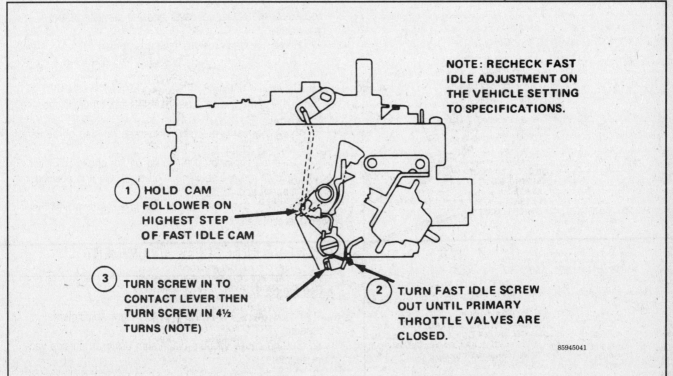

NOTE: RECHECK FAST IDLE ADJUSTMENT ON THE VEHICLE SETTING TO SPECIFICATIONS.

1 HOLD CAM FOLLOWER ON HIGHEST STEP OF FAST IDLE CAM

3 TURN SCREW IN TO CONTACT LEVER THEN TURN SCREW IN 4½ TURNS (NOTE)

2 TURN FAST IDLE SCREW OUT UNTIL PRIMARY THROTTLE VALVES ARE CLOSED.

85945041

Fig. 40 Preliminary setting of the fast idle with the carburetor assembly removed from the engine — Rochester M2ME and E2ME

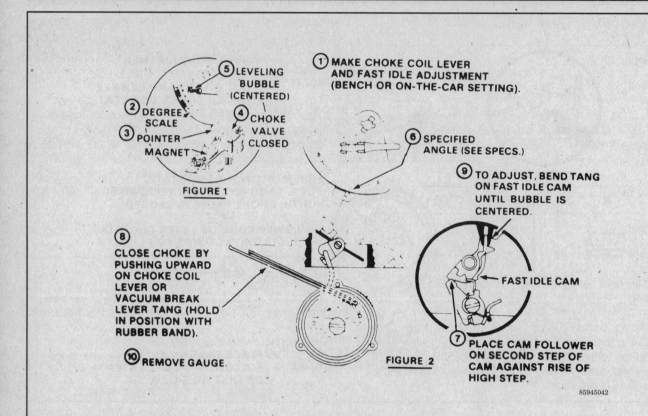

Fig. 41 Fast idle cam (choke rod) adjustment — Rochester M2ME and E2ME

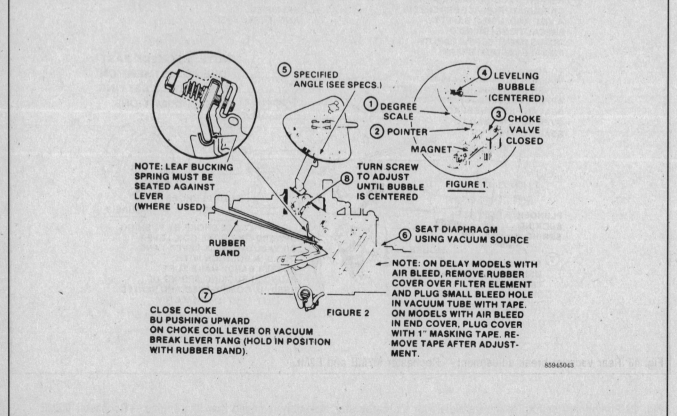

Fig. 42 Front vacuum break adjustment — Rochester M2ME and E2ME

REAR VACUUM BREAK ADJUSTMENT

▶ **See Figure 43**

1. Follow Steps 1-3 of the Front Vacuum Break Adjustment procedure.
2. To adjust, use a ⅛ in. Allen wrench to turn the screw in the rear cover until the bubble is centered. After adjusting, apply silicone sealant RTV over the screw head to seal the setting.

UNLOADER ADJUSTMENT

▶ **See Figure 44**

1. Follow Steps 1-5 of the Fast Idle Cam Adjustment procedure.
2. If they have been previously removed, install the choke thermostatic cover and the coil assembly into the choke housing.
3. Close the choke valve by pushing up on the tang on the vacuum break lever (you may hold it with a rubber band).
4. Hold the primary throttle valves wide open.
5. To adjust, bend the tang on the fast idle lever until the bubble on the gauge is centered.

Rochester M4ME and E4ME 4-BBL Carburetors

▶ **See Figures 45 and 46**

➡Float, pump, choke coil lever, fast idle, fast idle cam (choke rod), front and rear vacuum break and unloader adjustments on these two carburetors are identical to those detailed in the preceding M2ME and E2ME section. Please refer to them. There are, however, a number of procedures that apply only to the 4-bbl carburetors and to specific years. Please refer to the appropriate procedure or illustration.

AIR VALVE ROD ADJUSTMENT

▶ **See Figures 47, 48 and 49**

1. Using an outside vacuum source, seat the choke vacuum diaphragm. Put a piece of tape over the purge bleed hole if so equipped.
2. Close the air valve completely.
3. Insert the gauge between the rod and the end of the slot in the lever.
4. Bend the rod to adjust the clearance.

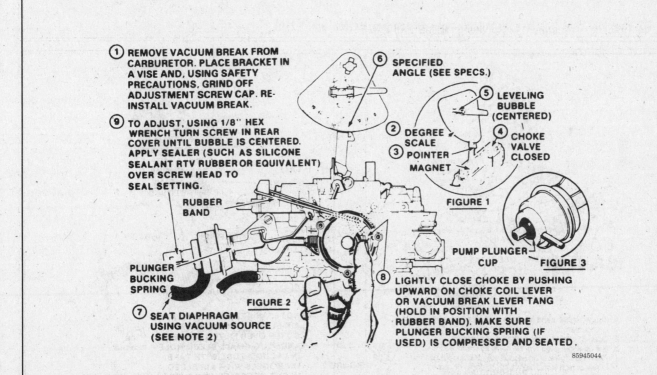

Fig. 43 Rear vacuum break adjustment — Rochester M2ME and E2ME

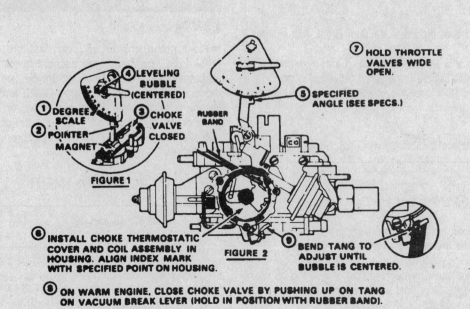

⑦ HOLD THROTTLE VALVES WIDE OPEN.

⑤ SPECIFIED ANGLE (SEE SPECS.)

④ LEVELING BUBBLE (CENTERED)

① DEGREE SCALE

② POINTER MAGNET

③ CHOKE VALVE CLOSED

RUBBER BAND

FIGURE 1

FIGURE 2

⑥ INSTALL CHOKE THERMOSTATIC COVER AND COIL ASSEMBLY IN HOUSING. ALIGN INDEX MARK WITH SPECIFIED POINT ON HOUSING.

⑨ BEND TANG TO ADJUST UNTIL BUBBLE IS CENTERED.

⑧ ON WARM ENGINE, CLOSE CHOKE VALVE BY PUSHING UP ON TANG ON VACUUM BREAK LEVER (HOLD IN POSITION WITH RUBBER BAND).

85945045

Fig. 44 Unloader adjustment — Rochester M2ME and E2ME

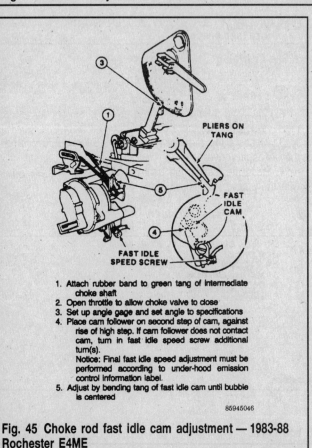

PLIERS ON TANG

FAST IDLE CAM

FAST IDLE SPEED SCREW

1. Attach rubber band to green tang of intermediate choke shaft
2. Open throttle to allow choke valve to close
3. Set up angle gage and set angle to specifications
4. Place cam follower on second step of cam, against rise of high step. If cam follower does not contact cam, turn in fast idle speed screw additional turn(s).
   Notice: Final fast idle speed adjustment must be performed according to under-hood emission control information label.
5. Adjust by bending tang of fast idle cam until bubble is centered

85945046

Fig. 45 Choke rod fast idle cam adjustment — 1983-88 Rochester E4ME

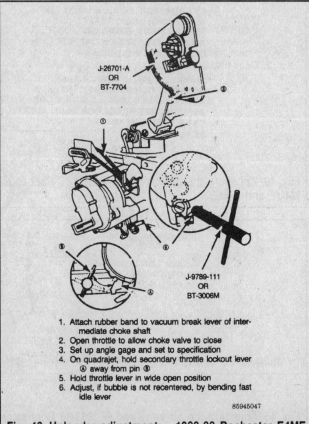

J-26701-A OR BT-7704

J-9789-111 OR BT-3006M

1. Attach rubber band to vacuum break lever of intermediate choke shaft
2. Open throttle to allow choke valve to close
3. Set up angle gage and set to specification
4. On quadrajet, hold secondary throttle lockout lever Ⓐ away from pin Ⓑ
5. Hold throttle lever in wide open position
6. Adjust, if bubble is not recentered, by bending fast idle lever

85945047

Fig. 46 Unloader adjustment — 1983-88 Rochester E4ME

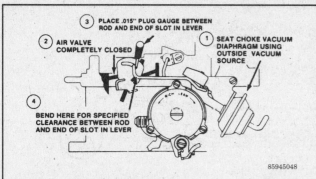

Fig. 47 Adjusting the air valve rod — Rochester M4ME and E4ME (through 1982)

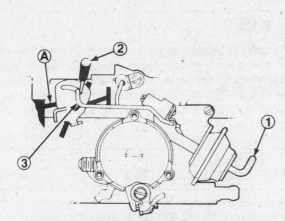

1. Plug vacuum break bleed holes, if applicable. Air valves Ⓐ closed. Apply 15" Hg (51 k Pa) vacuum to seat vacuum break plunger.
2. Gage the clearance between air valve link and end of slot in lever.
3. Adjust, if necessary, by bending link.

85945050

Fig. 49 Adjusting the air valve rod — 1986-88 Rochester M4ME and E4ME

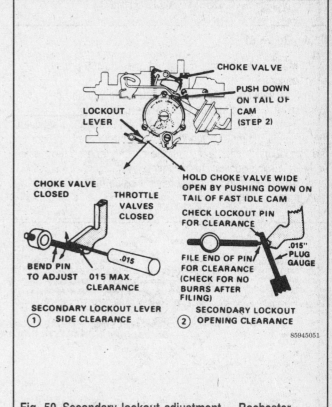

Fig. 50 Secondary lockout adjustment — Rochester M4ME and E4ME

SECONDARY LOCKOUT ADJUSTMENT

▶ **See Figure 50**

1. Pull the choke wide open by pushing out on the choke lever.
2. Open the throttle until the end of the secondary actuating lever is opposite the toe of the lockout lever.
3. Measure the clearance between the lockout lever and the secondary lever.
4. Bend the lockout pin until the clearance is in accordance with the proper specifications.

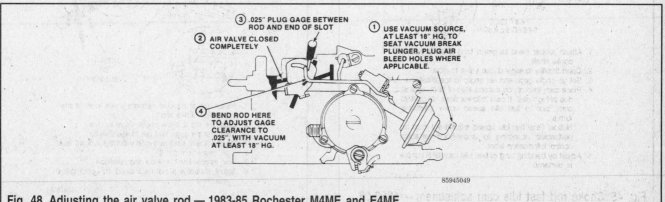

Fig. 48 Adjusting the air valve rod — 1983-85 Rochester M4ME and E4ME

SECONDARY CLOSING ADJUSTMENT

▶ **See Figure 51**

1. Make sure that the idle speed is set to the proper specifications.

2. The choke valve should be wide open with the cam follower off of the steps of the fast idle cam.

3. There should be 0.020 in. (0.508mm) clearance between the secondary throttle actuating rod and the front of the slot on the secondary throttle lever with the closing tang on the throttle lever resting against the actuating lever.

4. To adjust, bend the secondary closing tang on the primary throttle actuating rod.

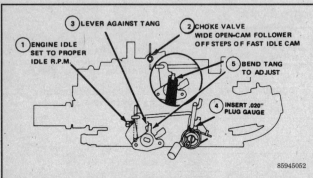

Fig. 51 Secondary closing adjustment — Rochester M4ME and E4ME

SECONDARY OPENING ADJUSTMENT

▶ **See Figure 52**

1. Open the primary throttle valves until the actuating link contacts the upper tang on the secondary lever.

2. With the two point linkage, the bottom of the link should be in the center of the secondary lever slot.

3. With the three point linkage, there should be 0.070 in. (1.778mm) clearance between the link and the middle tang.

4. To adjust, bend the upper tang on the secondary lever.

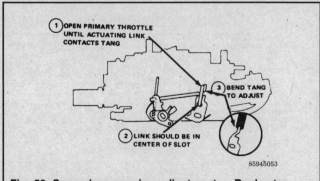

Fig. 52 Secondary opening adjustment — Rochester M4ME and E4ME

AIR VALVE SPRING ADJUSTMENT

▶ **See Figure 53**

To adjust the air valve spring windup, loosen the Allen lockscrew, then turn the adjusting screw counterclockwise so as to remove all spring tension. With the air valve closed, turn the adjusting screw clockwise the specified number of turns after the torsion spring contacts the pin on the shaft. Hold the adjusting screw in this position and tighten the lockscrew.

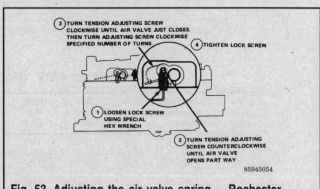

Fig. 53 Adjusting the air valve spring — Rochester M4ME and E4ME

Carter Specifications

Year	Model or Type ①	Float Level (in.)		Float Drop (in.)		Pump Travel Setting (in.)	Choke Setting		Secondary Locknut Adj.
		Prim	Sec	Prim	Sec		Unloader (in.)	Housing	
1964–65	AFB-All	$7/32$	$7/32$	$3/4$	$3/4$	$1/2$	$1/4$	1-Lean	0.020
	WCFB-All	$7/32$	$1/4$	$3/4$	$3/4$	$1/2$	$3/16$	Index	—
1966	6-Cyl-YF-4079S, 4080S	$1/2$	—	$1^{3}/16$	—	—	0.260	—	—
	V8-AVS-4027S, 4028S	$1^{15}/32$	—	2	—	$1^{1}/32$	0.170	—	—
1967	6 Cyl-YF	$7/32$	—	$1^{3}/16$	—	—	0.250	—	—

① Model number located on the tag or casting

85945055

Rochester BV Specifications

Year	Carburetor Identification ①	Float Level (in.)	Float Drop (in.)	Pump Rod (in.)	Idle Vent (in.)	Vacuum Break (in.)	Automatic Choke	Choke Rod (in.)	Choke Unloader (in.)	Fast Idle Speed
1964–66	All	$1^{9}/32$	$1^{3}/4$	—	0.050	—	—	—	0.350	—
1967	7025000	$1^{9}/32$	$1^{3}/4$	—	0.050	0.140	—	0.090	0.350	—
	7022503	$1^{9}/32$	$1^{3}/4$	—	0.050	0.160	—	0.100	0.350	—
	7026028	$1^{9}/32$	$1^{3}/4$	—	0.050	0.140	—	0.090	0.350	—
	7026027	$1^{9}/32$	$1^{3}/4$	—	0.050	0.160	—	0.100	0.350	—
	7027110	$3/4$	$1^{3}/4$	—	1	0.110	—	0.060	0.215	—
	7027101	$3/4$	$1^{3}/4$	—	1	0.120	—	0.060	0.215	—

① The carburetor identification tag is located at the rear of the carburetor on one of the air horn screws

85945056

Rochester 4MV, 4MC, M4MC Specifications

Year	Carburetor Identification ①	Float Level (in.)	Air Valve Spring	Pump Rod (in.)	Idle Vent (in.)	Vacuum Break (in.)	Secondary Opening (in.)	Choke Rod (in.)	Choke Unloader (rpm)	Fast Idle Speed
1967	7027202	$9/32$	$7/8$ turn	$13/32$	$3/8$	0.160	0.015	0.100	0.260	—
	7027203	$9/32$	$7/8$ turn	$13/32$	$3/8$	0.200	0.015	0.100	0.300	—
	7027200	$9/32$	$7/8$ turn	$13/32$	$3/8$	0.160	0.015	0.100	0.300	—
	7027201	$9/32$	$7/8$ turn	$13/32$	$3/8$	0.240	0.015	0.100	0.300	—
	7027202	$9/32$	$7/8$ turn	$13/32$	$3/8$	0.160	0.015	0.100	0.260	—
	7027203	$9/32$	$7/8$ turn	$13/32$	$3/8$	0.200	0.015	0.100	0.300	—

85945063

Rochester 4MV, 4MC, M4MC Specifications (cont.)

Year	Carburetor Identification ①	Float Level (in.)	Air Valve Spring	Pump Rod (in.)	Idle Vent (in.)	Vacuum Break (in.)	Secondary Opening (in.)	Choke Rod (in.)	Choke Unloader (rpm)	Fast Idle Speed
1968	7028212	9/32	3/8 turn	9/32	3/8	0.160	0.010	0.100	0.260	—
	7028213	9/32	3/8 turn	9/32	3/8	0.245	0.010	0.100	0.300	—
	7028229	9/32	7/8 turn	9/32	3/8	0.245	0.010	0.100	0.300	—
	7028208	9/32	3/8 turn	9/32	3/8	0.160	0.010	0.100	0.260	—
	7028207	9/32	3/8 turn	9/32	3/8	0.245	0.010	0.100	0.300	—
	7028219	9/32	7/8 turn	9/32	3/8	0.245	0.010	0.100	0.300	—
	7028218	3/16	7/8 turn	9/32	3/8	0.160	0.010	0.100	0.300	—
	7028217	3/16	7/8 turn	9/32	3/8	0.245	0.010	0.100	0.300	—
	7028210	3/16	7/8 turn	9/32	3/8	0.160	0.010	0.100	0.300	—
	7028211	3/16	7/8 turn	9/32	3/8	0.245	0.010	0.100	0.300	—
	7028216	3/16	7/8 turn	9/32	3/8	0.160	0.010	0.100	0.300	—
	7028209	3/16	7/8 turn	9/32	3/8	0.245	0.010	0.100	0.300	—
1969	7029203	7/32	7/16 turn	5/16	3/8	0.245	0.015	0.100	0.450	—
	7029202	7/32	7/16 turn	5/16	3/8	0.180	0.015	0.100	0.450	—
	7029207	3/16	13/16 turn	5/16	3/8	0.245	0.015	0.100	0.450	—
	7029215	1/4	13/16 turn	5/16	3/8	0.245	0.015	0.100	0.450	—
	7029204	1/4	13/16 turn	5/16	3/8	0.180	0.015	0.100	0.450	—
1970	7040202	1/4	7/16 turn	5/16	—	0.245	—	0.100	0.450	—
	7040203	1/4	7/16 turn	5/16	—	0.275	—	0.100	0.450	—
	7040207	1/4	13/16 turn	5/16	—	0.275	—	0.100	0.450	—
	7040200	1/4	13/16 turn	5/16	—	0.245	—	0.100	0.450	—
	7040201	1/4	13/16 turn	5/16	—	0.275	—	0.100	0.450	—
	7040204	1/4	13/16 turn	5/16	—	0.245	—	0.100	0.450	—
	7040205	1/4	13/16 turn	5/16	—	0.275	—	0.100	0.450	—
1971	7041200	1/4	7/16 turn	—	—	0.260	—	0.100	—	—
	7041202	1/4	7/16 turn	—	—	0.260	—	0.100	—	—
	7041204	1/4	7/16 turn	—	—	0.260	—	0.100	—	—
	7041212	1/4	7/16 turn	—	—	0.260	—	0.100	—	—
	7041201	1/4	7/16 turn	—	—	0.275	—	0.100	—	—
	7041203	1/4	7/16 turn	—	—	0.275	—	0.100	—	—
	7041205	1/4	7/16 turn	—	—	0.275	—	0.100	—	—
	7041213	1/4	7/16 turn	—	—	0.275	—	0.100	—	—
1972	7042202	1/4	1/2 turn	3/8	—	0.215	—	0.100	0.450	—
	7042203	1/4	1/2 turn	3/8	—	0.215	—	0.100	0.450	—
	7042902	1/4	1/2 turn	3/8	—	0.215	—	0.100	0.450	—
	7042903	1/4	1/2 turn	3/8	—	0.215	—	0.100	0.450	—
1973	7043212	7/32	1 turn	13/32	—	0.250	—	0.430	0.450	—
	7043213	7/32	1 turn	13/32	—	0.250	—	0.430	0.450	—
1974	7044202	1/4	7/8 turn	13/32 ②	—	0.230	—	0.430	0.450	1600 ③ – 1300 ④

85945064

Rochester 4MV, 4MC, M4MC Specifications (cont.)

Year	Carburetor Identification ①	Float Level (in.)	Air Valve Spring	Pump Rod (in.)	Idle Vent (in.)	Vacuum Break (in.)	Secondary Opening (in.)	Choke Rod (in.)	Choke Unloader (rpm)	Fast Idle Speed
1974	7044203	1/4	7/8 turn	13/32 ②	—	0.230	—	0.430	0.450	1600 ③– 1300 ④
	7044208	1/4	1 turn	13/32 ②	—	0.230	—	0.430	0.450	1600 ③– 1300 ④
	7044209	1/4	1 turn	13/32 ②	—	0.230	—	0.430	0.450	1600 ③– 1300 ④
	7044502	1/4	7/8 turn	13/32 ②	—	0.230	—	0.430	0.450	1600 ③– 1300 ④
	7044503	1/4	7/8 turn	13/32 ②	—	0.230	—	0.430	0.450	1600 ③– 1300 ④
1975	7045202	15/32	7/8 turn	0.275 ⑤	—	0.180 ⑥	—	0.300	0.325	—
	7045203	15/32	7/8 turn	0.275 ⑤	—	0.180 ⑥	—	0.300	0.325	—
	7045208	15/32	7/8 turn	0.275 ⑤	—	0.180 ⑥	—	0.300	0.325	—
	7045209	15/32	7/8 turn	0.275 ⑤	—	0.180 ⑥	—	0.300	0.325	—
1976	17056202	13/32	7/8 turn	9/32	—	0.185	—	0.325	0.325	—
	17056203	13/32	7/8 turn	9/32	—	0.170	—	0.325	0.325	—
	17056528	13/32	7/8 turn	9/32	—	0.185	—	0.325	0.325	—
1977	17057203	15/32	7/8	9/32 ⑤	—	0.160	—	0.325	0.280	1300
	17057202	15/32	—	9/32 ⑤	—	0.160	—	0.325	—	1600 ⑤
	17057502	15/32	7/8	9/32 ⑤	—	0.165	—	0.325	0.280	1600 ⑤
1978	17058203	15/32	7/8	9/32	—	0.179	—	0.314	0.277	⑦
	17058202	15/32	7/8	9/32	—	0.179	—	0.314	0.277	⑦
	17058502	15/32	7/8	9/32	—	0.187	—	0.314	0.277	⑦
1979	17059203	15/32	7/8	1/4	—	0.157	—	0.243	0.243	⑦
	17059207	15/32	7/8	1/4	—	0.157	—	0.243	0.243	⑦
	17059216	15/32	7/8	1/4	—	0.157	—	0.243	0.243	⑦
	17059217	15/32	7/8	1/4	—	0.157	—	0.243	0.243	⑦
	17059218	15/32	7/8	1/4	—	0.164	—	0.243	0.243	⑦
	17059222	15/32	7/8	1/4	—	0.164	—	0.243	0.243	⑦
	17059502	15/32	7/8	1/4	—	0.164	—	0.243	0.243	⑦
	17059504	15/32	7/8	1/4	—	0.164	—	0.243	0.243	⑦
	17059582	15/32	7/8	11/32	—	0.203	—	0.243	0.314	⑦
	17059584	15/32	7/8	11/32	—	0.203	—	0.243	0.314	⑦
	17059210	15/32	1	9/32	—	0.157	—	0.243	0.243	⑦
	17059211	15/32	1	9/32	—	0.157	—	0.243	0.243	⑦
	17029228	15/32	1	9/32	—	0.157	—	0.243	0.243	⑦

① The carburetor identification tag is located at the rear of the carburetor on one of the air horn screws
② Without vacuum advance
③ With automatic transmission; vacuum advance connected and EGR disconnected after the throttle positioned on the high step of cam
④ With manual transmission; without vacuum advance and the throttle positioned on the high step of cam
⑤ Inner pump rod location
⑥ Front vacuum break given; rear—0.170 in.
⑦ See engine compartment sticker

Rochester MV Specifications

Year	Carburetor Identification ①	Float Level (in.)	Metering Rod (in.)	Pump Rod	Idle Vent (in.)	Vacuum Break (in.)	Auxiliary Vacuum Break (in.)	Fast Idle Off Car (in.)	Choke Rod (in.)	Choke Unloader (in.)	Fast Idle Speed (rpm)
1968	7028014	9/32	0.120	—	0.050	0.245	—	1½	0.150	0.350	2400 ②
	7028015	9/32	0.130	—	0.050	0.275	—	1½	0.150	0.350	2400 ②
	7028017	9/32	0.130	—	0.050	0.275	—	1½	0.150	0.350	2400 ②
1969	7029014	¼	0.070	—	0.050	0.245	—	0.100	0.170	0.350	2400 ②
	7029015	¼	0.090	—	0.050	0.275	—	0.100	0.200	0.350	2400 ②
	7029017	¼	0.090	—	0.050	0.275	—	0.100	0.200	0.350	2400 ②
1970	7040014	¼	0.070	—	—	0.200	—	0.110	0.170	0.350	2400 ②
	7040017	¼	0.090	—	—	0.160	—	0.100	0.190	0.350	2400 ②
1971	7041014	¼	0.080	—	—	0.200	—	0.100	0.160	0.350	—
	7041017	¼	0.080	—	—	0.230	—	0.100	0.180	0.350	—
	7041023	1/16	—	—	—	0.200	—	0.110	0.120	0.350	—
1972	7042014	¼	0.080	—	—	0.190	—	—	0.125	0.500	2400 ②
	7042017	¼	0.078	—	—	0.225	—	—	0.150	0.500	2400 ②
	7042984	¼	0.078	—	—	0.190	—	—	0.125	0.500	2400 ②
	7042987	¼	0.076	—	—	0.225	—	—	0.150	0.500	2400 ②
1973	7043014	¼	0.080	—	—	0.300	—	—	0.245	0.500	1800 ②
	7043017	¼	0.080	—	—	0.350	—	—	0.275	0.500	1800 ②
1974	7044014	3/10	0.079	—	—	0.275	—	—	0.230	0.500	1800 ② ③
	7044017	3/10	0.072	—	—	0.350	—	—	0.275	0.500	1800 ② ③
	7044314	3/10	0.073	—	—	0.300	—	—	0.245	0.500	1800 ② ③
1975	7045013	11/32	0.080	—	—	0.200	0.215	—	0.160	0.215	1800 ④
	7045012	11/32	0.080	—	—	0.350	0.312	—	0.275	0.275	1800 ④
	7045314	11/32	0.080	—	—	0.275	0.312	—	0.230	0.275	1800 ④
1976	17056012	11/32	0.084	—	—	0.140	0.265	—	0.100	0.260	⑤
	17056013	11/32	0.082	—	—	0.140	0.325	—	0.140	0.260	⑤
	17056014	—	—	—	—	—	—	—	—	—	—

① The carburetor identification tag is located at the rear of the carburetor on one of the air horn screws
② High step of cam
③ Without vacuum advance
④ 1700 rpm with automatic transmission in Neutral
⑤ 2100 rpm—49 states with transmission in Neutral; 2200 rpm—49 states with non-integral head; 1700 rpm—California

85945057

Rochester 2GC, 2GV Specifications

Year	Carburetor Identifi-cation [1]	Float Level (in.)	Float Drop (in.)	Pump Rod (in.)	Idle Vent (in.)	Vacuum Break (in.)	Auto-matic [2] Choke	Choke Rod (in.)	Choke Unloader (in.)	Fast Idle Speed
1967	7027101	3/4	1 3/4	1 1/8	1.000	0.120	—	0.060	0.215	—
	7027103	3/4	1 3/4	1 1/8	1.000	0.120	—	0.060	0.215	—
	7027110	3/4	1 3/4	1 1/8	1.000	0.110	—	0.060	0.215	—
	7027112	3/4	1 3/4	1 1/8	1.000	0.110	—	0.060	0.215	—
	7037103	3/4	1 3/4	1 1/8	1.000	0.130	—	0.060	0.215	—
	7037110	3/4	1 3/4	1 1/8	1.000	0.110	—	0.060	0.215	—
	7037112	3/4	1 3/4	1 1/8	1.000	0.110	—	0.060	0.215	—
1968	7028110	3/4	1 3/4	1 1/8	1.000	0.100	—	0.060	0.200	—
	7028101	3/4	1 3/4	1 1/8	1.000	0.100	—	0.060	0.200	—
	7028112	3/4	1 3/4	1 1/8	1.000	0.100	—	0.060	0.200	—
	7028103	3/4	1 3/4	1 1/8	1.000	0.100	—	0.060	0.200	—
1969	7029101	27/32	1 3/4	1 1/8	0.020	0.100	—	0.060	0.215	—
	7029103	27/32	1 3/4	1 1/8	0.020	0.100	—	0.060	0.215	—
	7029110	27/32	1 3/4	1 1/8	0.020	0.100	—	0.060	0.215	—
	7029112	27/32	1 3/4	1 1/8	0.020	0.100	—	0.060	0.215	—
	7029102	3/4	1 3/4	1 13/32	0.020	0.215	—	0.085	0.275	—
	7029104	3/4	1 3/4	1 13/32	0.020	0.215	—	0.085	0.275	—
	7029127	3/4	1 3/4	1 13/32	0.020	0.215	—	0.085	0.275	—
	7029129	3/4	1 3/4	1 13/32	0.020	0.215	—	0.085	0.275	—
	7029117	3/4	1 3/4	1 13/32	0.020	0.215	—	0.085	0.275	—
	7029118	3/4	1 3/4	1 13/32	0.020	0.215	—	0.085	0.275	—
	7029119	5/8	1 3/4	1 13/32	0.020	0.215	—	0.085	0.275	—
	7029120	5/8	1 3/4	1 13/32	0.020	0.215	—	0.085	0.275	—
1970	7040110	27/32	1 3/4	1 1/8	0.020	0.100	—	0.060	0.215	—
	7040112	27/32	1 3/4	1 1/8	0.020	0.100	—	0.060	0.215	—
	7040101	27/32	1 3/4	1 1/8	0.020	0.125	—	0.060	0.160	—
	7040103	27/32	1 3/4	1 1/8	0.020	0.125	—	0.060	0.225	—
	7040114	23/32	1 3/8	1 17/32	0.020	0.200	—	0.085	0.325	—
	7040116	23/32	1 3/8	1 17/32	0.020	0.200	—	0.085	0.325	—
	7040113	23/32	1 3/8	1 17/32	0.020	0.215	—	0.085	0.275	—
	7040115	23/32	1 3/8	1 17/32	0.020	0.215	—	0.085	0.275	—
	7040118	23/32	1 3/8	1 17/32	0.020	0.215	—	0.085	0.325	—
	7040120	23/32	1 3/8	1 17/32	0.020	0.215	—	0.085	0.325	—
	7040117	23/32	1 3/8	1 17/32	0.020	0.215	—	0.085	0.325	—
	7040119	23/32	1 3/8	1 17/32	0.020	0.215	—	0.085	0.325	—
1971	7041024	1/16	—	—	—	0.140	—	0.080	0.350	—
	7041101	13/16	1 3/4	1 3/64	—	0.110	—	0.075	0.215	—
	7041110	13/16	1 3/4	1 3/64	—	0.080	—	0.040	0.215	—
	7041102	25/32	1 3/8	1 5/32	—	0.170	—	0.100	0.325	—
	7041114	25/32	1 3/8	1 5/32	—	0.170	—	0.100	0.325	—

Rochester 2GC, 2GV Specifications (cont.)

Year	Carburetor Identification ①	Float Level (in.)	Float Drop (in.)	Pump Rod (in.)	Idle Vent (in.)	Vacuum Break (in.)	Automatic ② Choke	Choke Rod (in.)	Choke Unloader (in.)	Fast Idle Speed
1971	7041113	23/32	1 3/8	1 5/32	—	0.180	—	0.100	0.325	—
	7041127	23/32	1 3/8	1 5/32	—	0.180	—	0.100	0.325	—
	7041118	23/32	1 3/8	1 5/32	—	0.170	—	0.100	0.325	—
	7041181	5/8	1 3/4	1 3/8	—	0.120	—	0.080	0.180	—
	7041182	5/8	1 3/4	1 3/8	—	0.120	—	0.080	0.180	—
1972	7042111	23/32	1 9/32	1 1/2	—	0.180	—	0.100	0.325	—
	7042831	23/32	1 9/32	1 1/2	—	0.180	—	0.100	0.325	—
	7042112	23/32	1 9/32	1 1/2	—	0.170	—	0.100	0.325	—
	7042832	23/32	1 9/32	1 1/2	—	0.170	—	0.100	0.325	—
	7042100	25/32	1 31/32	1 5/16	—	0.080	—	0.040	0.215	—
	7042820	25/32	1 31/32	1 5/16	—	0.080	—	0.040	0.215	—
	7042101	25/32	1 31/32	1 5/16	—	0.110	—	0.075	0.215	—
	7042821	25/32	1 31/32	1 5/16	—	0.110	—	0.075	0.215	—
1973	7043100	21/32	1 9/32	1 5/16	—	0.080	—	0.150	0.215	—
	7043101	21/32	1 9/32	1 5/16	—	0.080	—	0.150	0.215	—
	7043120	21/32	1 9/32	1 5/16	—	0.080	—	0.150	0.215	—
	7043105	21/32	1 9/32	1 5/16	—	0.080	—	0.150	0.215	—
	7043112	19/32	1 9/32	1 7/16	—	0.130	—	0.245	0.325	—
	7043111	19/32	1 9/32	1 7/16	—	0.140	—	0.200	0.250	—
1974	7043100	21/32	1 9/32	1 5/16	—	0.080	—	0.150	0.215	—
	7043101	21/32	1 9/32	1 5/16	—	0.080	—	0.150	0.215	—
	7043120	21/32	1 9/32	1 5/16	—	0.080	—	0.150	0.215	—
	7043105	21/32	1 9/32	1 5/16	—	0.080	—	0.150	0.215	—
	7043112	19/32	1 9/32	1 7/16	—	0.130	—	0.245	0.325	—
	7043111	19/32	1 9/32	1 7/16	—	0.140	—	0.200	0.250	—
1975	7045111	21/32	31/32	1 5/8	—	0.130	—	—	0.350	—
	7045112	21/32	31/32	1 5/8	—	0.130	—	—	0.350	—
1976	17056111	9/16	1 9/32	1 21/32	—	0.140	—	—	0.325	—
	17056112	9/16	1 9/32	1 21/32	—	0.140	—	—	0.325	—
	17056412	9/16	1 9/32	1 11/16	—	0.140	—	—	0.325	—
1977	17057111	19/32	1 9/32	1 21/32	—	0.130 ③	Index	—	0.325	—
	17057108	19/32	1 9/32	1 21/32	—	0.130 ③	Index	—	0.325	—
	17057412	21/32	1 9/32	1 21/32	—	0.140 ③	1/2 CCW	—	0.325	—
1978	17058102	15/32	1 9/32	1 17/32	0	0.130 ④	Index	—	0.325	—
	17058103	15/32	1 9/32	1 17/32	0	0.130 ④	Index	—	0.325	—
	17058104	15/32	1 9/32	1 21/32	0	0.130 ③	Index	—	0.325	—
	17058105	15/32	1 9/32	1 21/32	0	0.130 ③	Index	—	0.325	—
	17058107	15/32	1 9/32	1 17/32	0	0.130 ③	Index	—	0.325	—
	17058109	15/32	1 9/32	1 17/32	0	0.130 ③	Index	—	0.325	—
	17058404	1/2	1 9/32	1 21/32	0	0.140 ③	1/2 CCW	—	0.325	—

Rochester 2GC, 2GV Specifications (cont.)

Year	Carburetor Identification [1]	Float Level (in.)	Float Drop (in.)	Pump Rod (in.)	Idle Vent (in.)	Vacuum Break (in.)	Automatic [2] Choke	Choke Rod (in.)	Choke Unloader (in.)	Fast Idle Speed
1978	17058405	½	1⁹/₃₂	1²¹/₃₂	0	0.140 [3]	½ CCW	—	0.325	—
1979	17059135	—	—	Information not available					
	17059134	—	—	Information not available					
	17059434	—	—	Information not available					

[1] The carburetor identification tag is located at the rear of the carburetor on one of the air horn screws
[2] Index or notches clockwise (CW) or counterclockwise (CCW)
[3] .160 after 22,500 miles or first tune-up
[4] .150 after 22,500 miles or first tune-up

85945061

Rochester ME Specifications

Year	Carburetor Identification	Float Level (in.)	Metering Rod (in.)	Pump Rod	Idle Vent (in.)	Vacuum Break (in.)	Auxiliary Vacuum Break (in.)	Fast Idle Off Car (in.)	Choke [1] Rod (in.)	Choke Unloader (in.)	Fast Idle Speed (rpm) [2]
1977	17057013	³/₈	.070	—	—	.125	—	—	1 CCW	.375	2000
	17057014	³/₈	.070	—	—	.120	—	—	2 CCW	.325	2000
	17057310	³/₈	.070	—	—	—	—	—	Index	—	1800
1978	17058013	³/₈	.080	—	—	.200	—	—	Index	.200	2000
	17058014	⁵/₁₆	.160	—	—	.200	—	—	Index	.200	2100
	17058314	³/₈	.160	—	—	.243	—	—	Index	.245	2000
1979	17059013	—	—	Information not available							
	17059014	—	—	Information not available							
	17059314	—	—	Information not available							

[1] Choke adjustment—Index, CCW—counterclockwise in notches, or CW—clockwise in notches
[2] Transmission in Neutral

85945058

Rochester 4GC Specifications

Year	Model or Type	Float Level (in.)		Float Drop (in.)		Pump Travel Setting (in.)	Choke Setting	
		Prim	Sec	Prim	Sec		Unloader (in.)	Housing
1964	All	1³³/₆₄	1³³/₆₄	2¼	2¼	1¹/₁₆	0.235	Index
1965	All	1³³/₆₄	1³⁷/₆₄	2¼	2¼	1¹/₁₆	0.250	Index
1966	All	1¹⁷/₃₂	1¹⁹/₃₈ ¼	2¼	2¼	1¹/₁₆	0.250	Index

85945062

Rochester M2ME, E2ME Specifications

Year	Carburetor Identification ①	Float Level (in.)	Choke Rod (deg./in.)	Choke Unloader (deg./in.)	Vacuum Break Lean or Front (deg./in.)	Vacuum Break Rich or Rear (deg./in.)	Pump Rod (in.)	Choke Coil Lever (in.)	Automatic Choke (notches)
1980	17080108	3/8	38/0.243	38/0.243	25/0.142	—	5/16 ②	0.120	Fixed
	17080110	3/8	38/0.243	38/0.243	25/0.142	—	5/16 ②	0.120	Fixed
	17080130	5/16	38/0.243	38/0.243	25/0.142	—	5/16 ②	0.120	Fixed
	17080131	5/16	38/0.243	38/0.243	25/0.142	—	5/16 ②	0.120	Fixed
	17080132	5/16	38/0.243	38/0.243	25/0.142	—	5/16 ②	0.120	Fixed
	17080133	5/16	38/0.243	38/0.243	25/0.142	—	5/16 ②	0.120	Fixed
	17080138	3/8	38/0.243	38/0.243	25/0.142	—	5/16 ②	0.120	Fixed
	17080140	3/8	38/0.243	38/0.243	25/0.142	—	5/16 ②	0.120	Fixed
	17080493	5/16	38/0.139	38/0.243	25/0.117	−/0.179	Fixed	0.120	Fixed
	17080495	5/16	38/0.139	38/0.243	25/0.117	−/0.179	Fixed	0.120	Fixed
	17080496	5/16	38/0.139	38/0.243	25/0.117	−/0.203	Fixed	0.120	Fixed
	17080498	5/16	38/0.139	38/0.243	25/0.117	−/0.203	Fixed	0.120	Fixed
1981	17080185	9/32	24.5/0.139	38/0.243	19/0.103	14/0.071	1/4 ②	0.120	Fixed
	17080187	9/32	24.5/0.139	38/0.243	19/0.103	14/0.071	1/4 ②	0.120	Fixed
	17080191	9/32	24.5/0.139	38/0.243	18/0.096	18/0.096	1/4 ②	0.120	Fixed
	17080491	5/16	24.5/0.139	38/0.243	21/0.117	35/0.220	Fixed	0.120	Fixed
	17080496	5/16	24.5/0.139	38/0.243	21/0.117	33/0.203	Fixed	0.120	Fixed
	17080498	5/16	24.5/0.139	38/0.243	21/0.117	33/0.203	Fixed	0.120	Fixed
	17081130	3/8	20/0.110	38/0.243	25/0.142	—	Fixed	0.120	Fixed
	17081131	3/8	20/0.110	38/0.243	25/0.142	—	Fixed	0.120	Fixed
	17081132	3/8	20/0.110	38/0.243	25/0.142	—	Fixed	0.120	Fixed
	17081133	3/8	20/0.110	38/0.243	25/0.142	—	Fixed	0.120	Fixed
	17081138	3/8	20/0.110	40/0.260	25/0.142	—	Fixed	0.120	Fixed
	17081140	3/8	20/0.110	40/0.260	25/0.142	—	Fixed	0.120	Fixed
	17081191	5/16	24.5/0.139	38/0.243	28/0.139	24/0.136	Fixed	0.120	Fixed
	17081192	5/16	24.5/0.139	38/0.243	28/0.139	24/0.136	Fixed	0.120	Fixed
	17081194	5/16	24.5/0.139	38/0.243	21/0.117	24/0.136	Fixed	0.120	Fixed
	17081196	5/16	24.5/0.139	38/0.243	28/0.139	24/0.136	Fixed	0.120	Fixed
	17081197	5/16	18/0.096	38/0.243	28/0.139	24/0.136	Fixed	0.120	Fixed
	17081198	3/8	24.5/0.139	38/0.243	28/0.139	24/0.136	Fixed	0.120	Fixed
	17081199	3/8	18/0.096	38/0.243	28/0.139	24/0.136	Fixed	0.120	Fixed
1982	17082130	3/8	20/−	38/0.243	27	—	Fixed	0.120	Fixed
	17082132	3/8	20/−	38/0.243	27	—	Fixed	0.120	Fixed
	17082138	3/8	20/−	38/0.243	27	—	Fixed	0.120	Fixed
	12082140	3/8	20/−	38/0.243	27	—	Fixed	0.120	Fixed
	17082497	5/16	24.5/0.139	32/−	28	24	Fixed	0.120	Fixed
1983	17082130	3/8	20/−	38/−	27	—	Fixed	0.120	Fixed
	17082132	3/8	20/−	38/−	27	—	Fixed	0.120	Fixed
	17083130	3/8	20/−	38/−	27	—	Fixed	0.120	Fixed

Rochester M2ME, E2ME Specifications (cont.)

Year	Carburetor Identification ①	Float Level (in.)	Choke Rod (deg./in.)	Choke Unloader (deg./in.)	Vacuum Break Lean or Front (deg./in.)	Vacuum Break Rich or Rear (deg./in.)	Pump Rod (in.)	Choke Coil Lever (in.)	Automatic Choke (notches)
1983	17083132	3/8	20/–	38/–	27	—	Fixed	0.120	Fixed
	17083190	5/16	18/–	32/–	28	24	Fixed	0.120	Fixed
	17083192	5/16	18/–	32/–	28	24	Fixed	0.120	Fixed
	17083193	5/16	17/–	27/–	23	28	Fixed	0.120	Fixed
1984	17082130	3/8	20/–	38/–	27	—	Fixed	0.120	Fixed
	17082132	12/32	20/–	38/–	27	—	Fixed	0.120	Fixed
	17084191	10/32	18/–	32/–	28	24	Fixed	0.120	Fixed

① The carburetor identification number is stamped on the float bowl, next to the fuel inlet nut.
② Inner hole.

85945068

Holley 4150, 4160 Specifications

Year	Model or Type	Float Level (in.) Prim	Sec	Float Drop (in.) Prim	Sec	Pump Travel Setting (in.)	Choke Setting Unloader (in.)	Housing	Secondary Locknut Adj.
1965	327 (4150)	①	①	—	0.015		0.375	—	—
1966	327-350 hp (4150)	①	①	0.065	0.015		0.260	—	—
	327 (4160)	①	①	0.065	0.015		0.260	—	—
	396 (4160)	①	①	0.065	0.015		0.260	—	—
1967–68	327-325 hp-4 bbl (4150)	A①	A①	0.065	0.015		0.265	—	—
1967	327, 396, 427-4 bbl (4160)	A①	A①	0.065	0.015		0.265	—	—
1968–69	V8-396 (4150)	B①	B①	0.065	0.015		0.350	—	—
1970	454 (4150)	0.350	—	—	0.015		0.350	—	—
1971	454 (4160)	②	①	—	0.015		0.350	—	—

A—Primary 0.170, Secondary 0.300
B—Primary 0.350, Secondary 0.500
① Float adjustment: Fuel level should be plus or minus 1/32 in. with threads at bottom of sight holes. To adjust turn adjusting nut on top of bowl clockwise, to lower, counterclockwise to raise.
② Float centered in bowl

85945066

Rochester M4ME, E4ME Specifications

Year	Carburetor Identification ①	Float Level (in.)	Air Valve Spring (turn)	Pump Rod (in.)	Primary Vacuum Break (deg./in.)	Secondary Vacuum Break (deg./in.)	Secondary Opening (in.)	Choke Rod (deg./in.)	Choke Unloader (deg./in.)	Fast Idle Speed ② (rpm)
1980	17080828	7/16	7/8	1/4 ③	27/0.157	—	⑤	20/0.110	38/0.243	⑥
	17080204	7/16	7/8	1/4 ③	27/0.157	—	⑤	20/0.110	38/0.243	⑥
	17080207	7/16	7/8	1/4 ③	27/0.157	—	⑤	20/0.110	38/0.243	⑥
	17080228	7/16	7/8	9/32 ③	30/0.179	—	⑤	20/0.110	38/0.243	⑥
	17080243	3/16	9/16	9/32 ③	16/0.016	−/0.083	⑤	14.5/0.074	30/0.179	⑥
	17080274	15/32	5/8	5/16 ④	20/0.110	−/0.164	⑤	16/0.083	33/0.203	⑥
	17080282	7/16	7/8	11/32 ④	25/0.142	—	⑤	20/0.110	38/0.243	⑥
	17080284	7/16	7/8	11/32 ④	25/0.142	—	⑤	20/0.110	38/0.243	⑥
	17080502	1/2	7/8	Fixed	−/0.136	−/0.179	⑤	20/0.110	38/0.243	⑥
	17080504	1/2	7/8	Fixed	−/0.136	−/0.179	⑤	20/0.110	38/0.243	⑥
	17080542	3/8	9/16	Fixed	−/0.103	−/0.066	⑤	14.5/0.074	38/0.243	⑥
	17080543	3/8	9/16	Fixed	−/0.103	−/0.129	⑤	14.5/0.074	38/0.243	⑥
1981	17081202	11/32	7/8	Fixed	26/0.149	—	⑤	20/0.110	38/0.243	⑦
	17081203	11/32	7/8	Fixed	26/0.149	—	⑤	20/0.110	38/0.243	⑦
	17081204	11/32	7/8	Fixed	26/0.149	—	⑤	20/0.110	38/0.243	⑦
	17081207	11/32	7/8	Fixed	26/0.149	—	⑤	20/0.110	38/0.243	⑦
	17081216	11/32	7/8	Fixed	26/0.149	—	⑤	20/0.110	38/0.243	⑦
	17081217	11/32	7/8	Fixed	26/0.149	—	⑤	20/0.110	38/0.243	⑦
	17081218	11/32	7/8	Fixed	26/0.149	—	⑤	20/0.110	38/0.243	⑦
	17081242	5/16	7/8	Fixed	17/0.090	−/0.077	⑤	24.5/0.139	38/0.243	⑦
	17081243	1/4	7/8	Fixed	19/0.103	−/0.090	⑤	24.5/0.139	38/0.243	⑦
1982	17082202	11/32	7/8	Fixed	27	—	⑤	20/−	38/−	⑦
	17082204	11/32	7/8	Fixed	27	—	⑤	20/−	38/−	⑦

85945069

Rochester M4ME, E4ME Specifications (cont.)

Year	Carburetor Identification ①	Float Level (in.)	Air Valve Spring (turn)	Pump Rod (in.)	Primary Vacuum Break (deg./in.)	Secondary Vacuum Break (deg./in.)	Secondary Opening (in.)	Choke Rod (deg./in.)	Choke Unloader (deg./in.)	Fast Idle Speed ② (rpm)
1983	17083202	11/32	7/8	Fixed	—	27/—	⑤	20/—	38/—	⑦
	17083203	11/32	7/8	Fixed	—	27/—	⑤	38/—	38/—	⑦
	17083204	11/32	7/8	Fixed	—	27/—	⑤	20/—	38/—	⑦
	17083207	11/32	7/8	Fixed	—	27/—	⑤	38/—	38/—	⑦
	17083216	11/32	7/8	Fixed	—	27/—	⑤	20/—	38/—	⑦
	17083218	11/32	7/8	Fixed	—	27/—	⑤	20/—	38/—	⑦
	17083236	11/32	7/8	Fixed	—	27/—	⑤	20/—	38/—	⑦
	17083506	7/16	7/8	Fixed	27/—	36/—	⑤	20/—	36/—	⑦
	17083508	7/16	7/8	Fixed	27/—	36/—	⑤	20/—	36/—	⑦
	17083524	7/16	7/8	Fixed	25/—	36/—	⑤	20/—	36/—	⑦
	17083526	7/16	7/8	Fixed	25/—	36/—	⑤	20/—	36/—	⑦
1984	17084201	11/32	7/8	Fixed	27/—	—	⑤	20/—	38/—	—
	17084205	11/32	7/8	Fixed	27/—	—	⑤	38/—	38/—	—
	17084208	11/32	7/8	Fixed	27/—	—	⑤	20/—	38/—	—
	17084209	11/32	7/8	Fixed	27/—	—	⑤	38/—	38/—	—
	17084210	11/32	7/8	Fixed	27/—	—	⑤	20/—	38/—	—
	17084507	7/16	1	Fixed	27/—	36/—	⑤	20/—	36/—	—
	17084509	7/16	1	Fixed	27/—	36/—	⑤	20/—	36/—	—
	17084525	7/16	1	Fixed	25/—	36/—	⑤	20/—	36/—	—
	17084527	7/16	1	Fixed	25/—	36/—	⑤	20/—	36/—	—
1985	17085202	11/32	7/8	Fixed	27/—	—	⑤	20/—	38/—	—
	17085203	11/32	7/8	Fixed	27/—	—	⑤	20/—	38/—	—
	17085204	11/32	7/8	Fixed	27/—	—	⑤	20/—	38/—	—
	17085207	11/32	7/8	Fixed	27/—	—	⑤	38/—	38/—	—
	17085218	11/32	7/8	Fixed	27/—	—	⑤	20/—	38/—	—
	17085502	7/16	7/8	Fixed	26/—	36/—	⑤	20/—	39/—	—
	17085503	7/16	7/8	Fixed	26/—	36/—	⑤	20/—	39/—	—
	17085506	7/16	1	Fixed	27/—	36/—	⑤	20/—	36/—	—
	17085508	7/16	1	Fixed	27/—	36/—	⑤	20/—	36/—	—
	17085524	7/16	1	Fixed	25/—	36/—	⑤	20/—	36/—	—
	17085526	7/16	1	Fixed	25/—	36/—	⑤	20/—	36/—	—
1986	17085502	7/16	7/8	Fixed	26/—	36/—	⑤	20/—	39/—	—
	17085503	7/16	7/8	Fixed	26/—	36/—	⑤	20/—	39/—	—
	17085506	7/16	1	Fixed	27/—	36/—	⑤	20/—	36/—	—
	17085508	7/16	1	Fixed	27/—	36/—	⑤	20/—	36/—	—
	17085524	7/16	1	Fixed	25/—	36/—	⑤	20/—	36/—	—
	17085526	7/16	1	Fixed	25/—	36/—	⑤	20/—	36/—	—
	17086003	11/32	7/8	Fixed	27/—	—	⑤	20/—	38/—	—
	17086004	11/32	7/8	Fixed	27/—	—	⑤	20/—	38/—	—

85945070

Rochester M4ME, E4ME Specifications (cont.)

Year	Carburetor Identification ①	Float Level (in.)	Air Valve Spring (turn)	Pump Rod (in.)	Primary Vacuum Break (deg./in.)	Secondary Vacuum Break (deg./in.)	Secondary Opening (in.)	Choke Rod (deg./in.)	Choke Unloader (deg./in.)	Fast Idle Speed ② (rpm)
	17086005	11/32	7/8	Fixed	27/–	—	⑤	38/–	38/–	—
	17086006	11/32	7/8	Fixed	27/–	—	⑤	20/–	38/–	—
	17086040	11/32	7/8	Fixed	27/–	—	⑤	38/–	38/–	—
1987	17087129	11/32	7/8	Fixed	27/–	—	⑤	20/–	38/–	—
	17087130	11/32	7/8	Fixed	27/–	—	⑤	20/–	38/–	—
	17087132	11/32	7/8	Fixed	27/–	—	⑤	20/–	38/–	—
1988	17087306	11/32	7/8	Fixed	27/–	—	—	20/–	32/–	—
	17087129	11/32	7/8	Fixed	27/–	—	—	20/–	32/–	—
	17087132	11/32	7/8	Fixed	27/–	—	—	20/–	32/–	—

① The carburetor identification number is stamped on the float bowl, near the secondary throttle lever.
② With manual transmission; w/o vacuum advance and the throttle positioned on the high step of the cam
③ Inner hole
④ Outer hole
⑤ No measurement necessary on two point linkage; see text
⑥ 4 turns after contacting lever for preliminary setting
⑦ 4½ turns after contacting lever for preliminary setting

85945071

Troubleshooting Basic Fuel System Problems

Problem	Cause	Solution
Engine cranks, but won't start (or is hard to start) when cold	• Empty fuel tank • Incorrect starting procedure • Defective fuel pump • No fuel in carburetor • Clogged fuel filter • Engine flooded • Defective choke	• Check for fuel in tank • Follow correct procedure • Check pump output • Check for fuel in the carburetor • Replace fuel filter • Wait 15 minutes; try again • Check choke plate
Engine cranks, but is hard to start (or does not start) when hot— (presence of fuel is assumed)	• Defective choke	• Check choke plate
Rough idle or engine runs rough	• Dirt or moisture in fuel • Clogged air filter • Faulty fuel pump	• Replace fuel filter • Replace air filter • Check fuel pump output
Engine stalls or hesitates on acceleration	• Dirt or moisture in the fuel • Dirty carburetor • Defective fuel pump • Incorrect float level, defective accelerator pump	• Replace fuel filter • Clean the carburetor • Check fuel pump output • Check carburetor
Poor gas mileage	• Clogged air filter • Dirty carburetor • Defective choke, faulty carburetor adjustment	• Replace air filter • Clean carburetor • Check carburetor
Engine is flooded (won't start accompanied by smell of raw fuel)	• Improperly adjusted choke or carburetor	• Wait 15 minutes and try again, without pumping gas pedal • If it won't start, check carburetor

85945001

GASOLINE FUEL INJECTION SYSTEM

✳✳CAUTION

The 262 V6 engine with the 220 TBI has a bleed in the pressure regulator to relieve pressure any time the engine is turned off, however a small amount of fuel may be released when a fuel line is disconnected. As a precaution, cover the fuel line with a cloth and dispose of properly.

General Information

▶ See Figure 54

The 262 (4.3L) V6 engine is equipped with a Throttle Body Injection (TBI) system. Instead of a carburetor, the system uses an intake manifold mounted throttle body assembly which is equipped with 2 electric fuel injectors. All fuel injection and ignition functions are controlled by the Electronic Control Module (ECM, sometimes referred to as the Engine Control Module). It accepts inputs from various sensors and switches, calculates the optimum air/fuel mixture and operates the various output devices to provide peak performance within specific emissions limits. The ECM will attempt to maintain the air/fuel mixture of 14.7:1 in order to optimize catalytic converter operation. If a system failure occurs that is not serious enough to stop the engine, the ECM will illuminate the SERVICE ENGINE SOON light and will continue to operate the engine, although it may need to operate in a backup or fail-safe mode.

Fuel is supplied to the injectors through an electric fuel pump assembly which is mounted in the vehicle's fuel tank. The ECM provides a signal to operate the fuel pump though the fuel pump relay and oil pressure switch.

Other system components include a pressure regulator, an Idle Air Control (IAC) valve, a Throttle Position Sensor (TPS), Manifold Air Temperature (MAT) sensor, Coolant Temperature Sensor (CTS), a Manifold Absolute Pressure (MAP) sensor and an oxygen sensor. The fuel injectors are solenoid valves that the ECM pulses on and off many times per second to promote proper fuel atomization. The pulse width determines how long an injector is ON each cycle and this regulates the amount of fuel supplied to the engine.

The system pressure regulator is part of the throttle body fuel meter cover which is designed to keep fuel pressure constant at the injector regardless of engine rpm. This is accomplished by controlling the flow in the return line (a calibrated bypass).

The idle air control valve is a stepper motor that controls the amount of air allowed to bypass the throttle plate. With this valve the ECM can closely control idle speed even when the engine is cold or when there is a high engine load at idle.

OPERATING MODES

Starting Mode

When the ignition switch is first turned **ON**, the fuel pump relay is energized by the ECM for 2 seconds in order to build system pressure. In the start mode, the ECM checks the CTS,

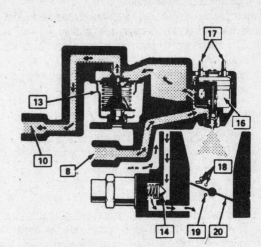

8. Fuel supply
10. Fuel return
13. Pressure regulator (part of fuel meter cover)
14. Idle air control (IAC) valve (shown open)
16. Fuel injector
17. Fuel injector terminals
18. Ported vacuum sources*
19. Manifold vacuum source*
20. Throttle valve

*May Be Different on some Models.

85945072

Fig. 54 A cross-sectional view of TBI operation

TPS and crank signal to determine the best air/fuel ratio for starting. Ratios could range from 1.5:1 at -33°F (-36°C), to 14.7:1 at 201°F (94°C).

Clear Flood Mode

If the engine becomes flooded, it can be cleared by opening the accelerator to the full throttle position. When the throttle is open all the way and engine rpm is less than 600, the ECM will pulse the fuel injector at a air/fuel ratio of 20:1 while the engine is turning over in order to clear the engine of excess fuel. If throttle position is reduced below 80 percent, the ECM will return to the start mode.

Open Loop Mode

When the engine first starts and engine speed rises above 400 rpm, the ECM operates in the Open Loop mode until specific parameters are met. In Open Loop mode, the fuel requirements are calculated based on information from the MAP sensor and the CTS. The oxygen sensor signal is ignored during initial engine operation because it needs time to warm up.

Closed Loop Mode

▶ See Figure 55

When the correct parameters are met, the ECM will use O_2 sensor output and adjust the air/fuel mixture in order to maintain a narrow band of exhaust gas oxygen concentration.

When the ECM is correcting and adjusting fuel mixture based on the oxygen sensor signal along with the other sensors, this is known as feedback air/fuel ratio control. The ECM will shift into this Closed Loop mode when:

• Oxygen sensor output voltage is varied, indicating that the sensor has warmed up to operating temperature
• The CTS shows an engine coolant temperature above a specified level.
• The engine has been operating for a programmed amount of time.

Acceleration Mode

If the throttle position and manifold pressure is quickly increased, the ECM will provide extra fuel for smooth acceleration.

Deceleration Mode

As the throttle closes and the manifold pressure changes, fuel flow is reduced by the ECM. If both conditions remain for a specific number of engine revolutions indicating a very fast deceleration, the ECM decides fuel flow is not needed and stops the flow by temporarily shutting off the injectors.

Battery Low Mode

If the ECM detects a low battery, it will increase injector pulse width to compensate for the low voltage and provide proper fuel delivery. It will also increase idle speed and ignition dwell time to increase alternator output and allow for proper engine operation.

Field Service Mode

When terminals the diagnostic terminal of the test connector is grounded with the engine running, the ECM will enter the Field Service Mode. If the engine is running in Open Loop Mode, the SERVICE ENGINE SOON light will flash quickly, about 2½ times per second. When the engine is in Closed Loop Mode, the light will flash only about once per second. If the light stays OFF most of the time in Close Loop, the engine is running lean. If the light is ON most of the time, the engine is running rich.

While the engine continues to operate in Field Service Mode certain conditions will apply:
• The distributor operate with a fixed spark advance.
• New trouble codes cannot be stored in ECM memory.
• The closed loop timer is bypassed.

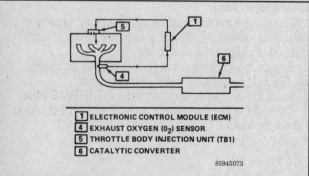

1 ELECTRONIC CONTROL MODULE (ECM)
4 EXHAUST OXYGEN (0₂) SENSOR
5 THROTTLE BODY INJECTION UNIT (TB1)
6 CATALYTIC CONVERTER

85945073

Fig. 55 ECM fuel control schematic for common closed loop engine operation

➡️**For more information concerning the ECM and Computer Command Control (CCC) system, refer to Section 4 of this manual.**

Relieving Fuel System Pressure

The 220 TBI has a bleed in the pressure regulator to relieve system pressure any time the engine is turned **OFF**, however a small amount of fuel may be released when a fuel line is disconnected. As a precaution, cover the fuel line with a cloth and dispose of properly. Also, the fuel tank filler cap should be removed, then reinstalled in order to release tank pressure before disconnecting any fittings.

Electric Fuel Pump

TESTING

1. Properly relieve the fuel system pressure.
2. Remove the air cleaner assembly and plug the THERMAC vacuum port on the TBI unit.
3. Raise and support the rear of the vehicle safely using jackstands.
4. Remove the flexible fuel line between the fuel tank and the fuel filter (located near the tank).
5. Install a fuel pressure gauge, such as J-29658 or equivalent, inline between the fuel tank and fuel filter. If necessary use an adapter or Tee fitting in order to connect the gauge and complete the fuel circuit.

➡️**A Tee fitting may be fabricated for this purpose. Depending on the fuel gauge being used, short lengths of steel tubing, appropriately sized flare nuts and a flare nut adapter may be used.**

6. Make sure the vehicle is secure, then start the engine.
7. Check to be sure the lines are intact and there are no leaks, then observe the fuel pressure, it should be 9-13 psi (62-90 kPa).
8. Once the test is completed, depressurize the fuel system and remove the gauge.
9. Secure the fuel lines and check for leaks.
10. Remove the plug from the THERMAC vacuum port, then install the air cleaner assembly.
11. Remove the jackstands and carefully lower the rear of the vehicle.

REMOVAL & INSTALLATION

▶ **See Figures 56 and 57**

1. Properly relieve the fuel system pressure.
2. Disconnect the negative battery cable.
3. Raise the rear of the vehicle and support safely using jackstands.
4. Drain the fuel tank, then remove it from the vehicle.
5. Using a hammer and a drift punch, carefully drive the lockring (located on top of the fuel tank) for the fuel level sending unit/pump assembly counterclockwise. Lift the assem-

bly from the tank and remove the pump from the fuel lever sending device.

6. Pull the pump up into the attaching hose while pulling it outward away from the bottom support. Be careful not to damage the rubber insulator and strainer during removal. After the pump assembly is clear of the bottom support, pull it out of the rubber connector.

To install:

7. Install the fuel pump attaching hose for any signs of deterioration and replace, as necessary. Also, check the rubber sound insulator at bottom of pump.

8. Push the fuel pump assembly into the attaching hose.

9. Install the fuel level sending unit/pump assembly into the tank using a new O-ring.

➡**Special care should be taken when installing the pump assembly to the tank not to fold or twist the fuel strainer or flow will be restricted.**

10. Install the lockring and secure the sending unit/pump assembly by turning the lockring clockwise.

11. Install the fuel tank to the vehicle.

12. Remove the jackstands and carefully lower the vehicle.

13. Connect the negative battery cable, then start the engine and check for leaks.

Throttle Body

REMOVAL & INSTALLATION

▶ **See Figures 58 and 59**

1. Properly relieve fuel system pressure, then disconnect the negative battery cable.

2. Disconnect the THERMAC hose from the engine fitting and remove the air cleaner assembly.

3. Tag and disengage the electrical connectors from the idle air control valve, throttle position sensor and the fuel injectors.

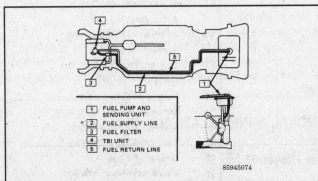

Fig. 56 Fuel supply system — Throttle Body Injection (TBI) system

1. FUEL PUMP AND SENDING UNIT
2. FUEL SUPPLY LINE
3. FUEL FILTER
4. TBI UNIT
5. FUEL RETURN LINE

85945074

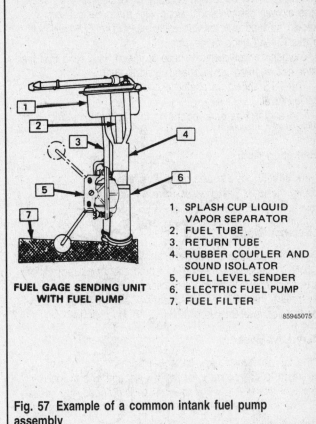

1. SPLASH CUP LIQUID VAPOR SEPARATOR
2. FUEL TUBE
3. RETURN TUBE
4. RUBBER COUPLER AND SOUND ISOLATOR
5. FUEL LEVEL SENDER
6. ELECTRIC FUEL PUMP
7. FUEL FILTER

FUEL GAGE SENDING UNIT WITH FUEL PUMP

85945075

Fig. 57 Example of a common intank fuel pump assembly

4. Disconnect the throttle linkage, return spring(s) and cruise control (if equipped).

5. Tag and disconnect the throttle body vacuum hoses, the fuel supply and fuel return lines.

6. Loosen and remove the fasteners securing the throttle body to the intake manifold, then remove it and the gasket.

7. If the throttle body is to remain off the engine for any length of time, cover the opening in the intake manifold to keep debris out of the engine.

To install:

8. Thoroughly clean the gasket mating surfaces of any remaining gasket material.

9. Install the throttle body to the intake manifold using a new gasket, then install the retainers and tighten to 11 ft. lbs. (15 Nm).

10. Connect the fuel supply and return lines to the throttle body using new O-rings.

11. Connect the throttle body vacuum hoses as noted during removal, then connect the throttle linkage and return spring(s). If equipped, connect the cruise control.

12. Engage the electrical connectors to the idle air control valve, TPS and injectors, as noted during removal.

13. Install the air cleaner and connect the THERMAC hose.

14. Connect the negative battery cable, then start the engine and check for leaks.

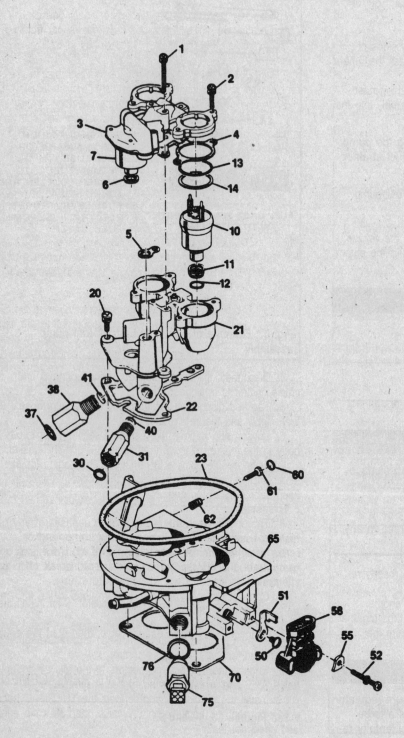

1	Screw Assembly - Fuel Meter Cover Attaching - Long
2	Screw Assembly - Fuel Meter Cover Attaching - Short
3	Fuel Meter Cover Assembly
4	Gasket - Fuel Meter Cover
5	Gasket - Fuel Meter Outlet
6	Seal - Pressure Regulator
7	Pressure Regulator
10	Injector - Fuel
11	Filter - Fuel Injector Inlet
12	O-ring - Fuel Injector - Lower
13	O-ring - Fuel Injector - Upper
14	Washer - Fuel Injector
20	Screw Assembly - Fuel Meter Body - Throttle Body Attaching
21	Fuel Meter Body Assembly
22	Gasket - Throttle Body to Fuel Meter Body
23	Gasket - Air Filter
30	O-ring - Fuel Return Line
31	Nut - Fuel Outlet
37	O-ring - Fuel Inlet Line
38	Nut - Fuel Inlet
40	Gasket - Fuel Outlet Nut
41	Gasket - Fuel Inlet Nut
50	Screw - TPS Lever Attaching
51	Lever - TPS
52	Screw Assembly - TPS Attaching
55	Retainer - TPS Attaching Screw
58	Sensor - Throttle Position (TPS)
60	Plug - Idle Stop Screw
61	Screw Assembly - Idle Stop
62	Spring - Idle Stop Screw
65	Throttle Body Assembly
70	Gasket - Flange
75	Valve Assembly - Idle Air Control (IAC)
76	Gasket - Idle Air Control Valve Assembly

85945076

Fig. 58 Exploded view of the model 220 TBI assembly

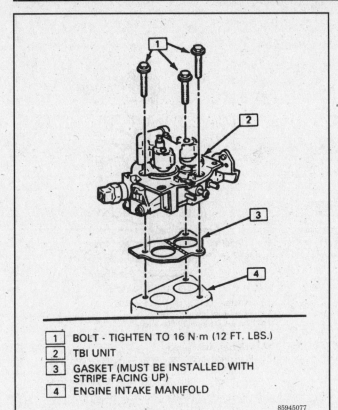

1. BOLT - TIGHTEN TO 16 N·m (12 FT. LBS.)
2. TBI UNIT
3. GASKET (MUST BE INSTALLED WITH STRIPE FACING UP)
4. ENGINE INTAKE MANIFOLD

85945077

Fig. 59 Removing the TBI unit from the intake manifold

INJECTOR REPLACEMENT

▶ See Figures 60, 61 and 62

✳✳WARNING

When removing the injectors, be careful not to damage the electrical connector pins (on top of the injector), the injector fuel filter and the nozzle. The fuel injector is serviced as a complete assembly ONLY. The injector is an electrical component and should not be immersed in any kind of cleaner.

1. Disconnect the negative battery cable and properly relieve the fuel system pressure.
2. Remove the air cleaner assembly from the engine.
3. At the injector connector, squeeze the two tabs together and pull straight up to disengage the connector from the injector.

✳✳CAUTION

Do not remove the screws retaining the pressure regulator to the fuel meter cover. The regulator includes a large spring under heavy compression which, if accidentally released, could cause personal injury.

4. Loosen the screws, then remove the screws and lockwashers securing the fuel meter cover. Remove the cover from the fuel meter body, but leave the cover gasket in place.

5. Using a small pry bar and a round fulcrum, or tool No. J-26868, carefully pry or lift the injector until it is free of the fuel meter body.
6. Remove the small O-ring from the nozzle end of the injector. Carefully rotate the injector's fuel filter back and forth to remove it from the base of the injector.
7. Remove and discard the fuel meter cover gasket.
8. Remove the large O-ring and back-up washer from the top of the counterbore of the fuel meter body injector cavity.
To install:
9. With the larger end of the filter facing the injector (so that the filter covers the raised rib of the injector base) install the filter by twisting it into position on the injector.
10. Lubricate the new O-rings with clean automatic transmission fluid, then install the small O-ring on the nozzle end of the injector. Be sure the O-ring is pressed up against the injector fuel filter.
11. Install the steel backup washer in the top counterbore of the fuel meter body's injector cavity, then install the new large O-ring directly over the backup washer. Make sure the O-ring is properly seated in the cavity and is flush with the top of the fuel meter body casting surface.

➡**If the backup washer and large O-ring are not properly installed BEFORE the fuel injector, a fuel leak will likely result.**

12. Install the fuel injector into the cavity by aligning the raised lug on the injector base with the cast notch in the fuel meter body cavity. Once the injector is aligned, carefully push down on the injector by hand until it is fully seated in the cavity. When properly aligned and installed, the injector terminals will be approximately parallel to the throttle shaft.
13. Install a new dust seal into the recess on the fuel meter body and a new fuel outlet gasket on the fuel meter cover.
14. Position a new cover-to-body gasket, then install the fuel meter cover to the body making sure all new gaskets are properly in position.
15. Coat the threads of the cover retaining screws with a threadlocking compound such as Loctite® 262, or equivalent. Install the screws and lockwashers, then carefully tighten to 28 inch lbs. (3 Nm).

➡**Do not use a stronger threadlocking compound or screw removal may be excessively difficult. If the improper compound is used, the screw heads could break off when attempting to loosen them at some future time.**

16. Engage the injector electrical connector, then install the air cleaner assembly.
17. Connect the negative battery cable, then start the engine and check for leaks.

IDLE AIR CONTROL (IAC) VALVE REPLACEMENT

▶ See Figures 63, 64 and 65

1. Disconnect the negative battery cable.
2. Remove the air cleaner assembly from the engine.
3. Disengage the electrical connector from the idle air control valve.

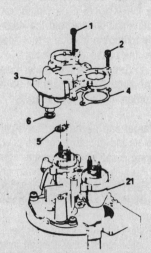

1. Screw assembly–fuel meter cover attaching–long
2. Screw assembly–fuel meter cover attaching–short
3. Fuel meter cover assembly
4. Gasket–fuel meter cover
5. Gasket–fuel meter outlet
6. Seal–pressure regulator
21. Fuel meter body assembly

85945078

Fig. 60 Exploded view of the fuel meter cover

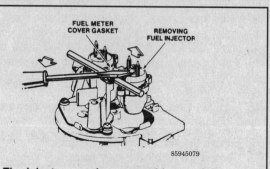

Fig. 61 The injector may be removed by carefully prying upward using a small prytool and a round fulcrum

4. Using a 1¼ (32mm) wrench or tool J-33031, loosen and remove the idle air control valve from the throttle body assembly.
   To install:

❋❋WARNING

Before installing a new idle air control valve, measure the distance that the valve extends (from the motor housing to the end of the cone); the distance should be no greater than 1⅛ in. (28mm). If it is extended too far, damage will occur to the valve when it is installed.

5. Measure the valve pintle extension. If it is excessive, identify the valve as a type-I or type-II. The type I valve has a collar at the electric terminal end while the type-II does not.

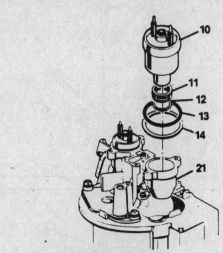

10. Injector–fuel
11. Filter–fuel injector inlet
12. "O" ring–fuel injector–lower
13. "O" ring–fuel injector–upper
14. Washer–fuel injector
21. Fuel meter body assembly

85945080

Fig. 62 Exploded view of the fuel injector and O-ring seal installation

To retract the valve pintle on a type-I valve, use firm thumb pressure and, if necessary, rock the pintle with a slight side-to-side motion. For type-II valves, compress the retaining spring by hand and turn the valve inward using a clockwise motion. Once the pintle is retracted for type-II valves, make sure the straight portion of the spring is again aligned with the flat on the valve.

6. Install the valve to the throttle body using a new gasket, then carefully tighten the valve to 13 ft. lbs. (18 Nm).
7. Engage the valve electrical connector, then install the air cleaner assembly.
8. Connect the negative battery cable, then start and run the engine until it reaches normal operating temperature.
9. Shut the engine **OFF** and the ECM will reset the IAC valve pintle.

THROTTLE POSITION SENSOR (TPS) SERVICE

The throttle position sensor used on the fuel injected engine is non-adjustable. If sensor problems are suspected, test sensor output using a scan tool or voltmeter. The sensor must be replaced if defective.

Testing

1. If available, connect a scan tool to the ECM test connector. If a scan tool is not available, use a voltmeter to back-probe the TPS connector terminals A (black wire on end of connector) and B (dark blue wire at center of connector). By backprobing the connector a voltage reading can be taken without disconnecting the circuit and without piercing the wires.

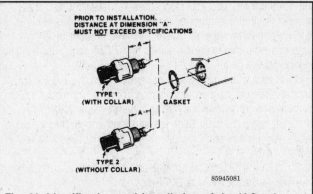

Fig. 63 Identification and installation of the IAC valve

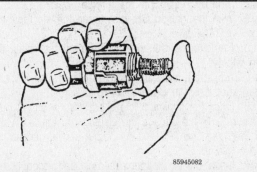

Fig. 64 Retracting the IAC valve pintle on type-I valves (with collar at terminal end)

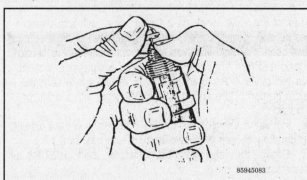

Fig. 65 Retracting the IAC valve pintle on type-II valves (without collar)

2. Turn the ignition **ON**, but do not start the engine. Check the voltmeter or scan tool for TPS output. Voltage should be 1.25 volts or less with the throttle closed. Voltage may go as high as 4.5 volts at wide open throttle.

3. If voltage with the throttle closed is greater than 1.25 volts, replace the switch.

Replacement

➡The throttle position sensor is an electrical component. Do NOT soak it or clean it with solvent or the sensor could be damaged.

1. Disconnect the negative battery cable, then remove the air cleaner assembly for access.

2. Disengage the TPS electrical connector.

3. Loosen the TPS attaching screws, then remove the sensor from the throttle body.

To install:

4. Install the TPS to the throttle body assembly while aligning the TPS lever with the drive lever on the throttle body.

5. Install the retaining screws and tighten to 18 inch lbs. (2.0 Nm).

6. Engage the sensor connector, then install the air cleaner assembly.

7. Connect the negative battery cable.

Fuel Pump Relay

REPLACEMENT

▶ See Figure 66

The fuel pump relay is located in the engine compartment. Other than checking for loose electrical connections, the only service necessary is to replace the relay if found defective.

Oil Pressure Switch

REPLACEMENT

▶ See Figure 67

The oil pressure switch is mounted to the top rear of the engine.

1. Disconnect the negative battery cable.

2. Remove the electrical connector from the switch.

3. Remove the oil pressure switch.

To install:

4. Install the switch to the engine.

5. Engage the switch electrical connector.

6. Connect the negative battery cable.

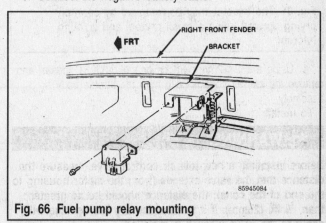

Fig. 66 Fuel pump relay mounting

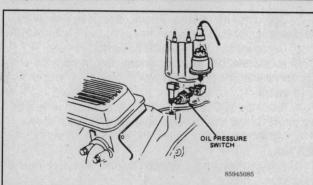

Fig. 67 The oil pressure switch is mounted to the top rear of the engine, near the distributor

Minimum Idle Speed

On fuel injected engines, idle speed is controlled by the ECM using the IAC valve. No periodic adjustments are necessary. However, if a throttle body has been replaced and no other causes can be found for an incorrect idle speed, then base or minimum idle speed may be adjusted. ONLY use this adjustment as a last resort. If this adjustment is improperly altered, the ECM will be unable to properly control engine idle.

ADJUSTMENT

Only if parts of the throttle body have been replaced should this procedure be performed; the engine should be at operating temperature. The idle stop screw is set at the factory to allow a minimum amount of air when the IAC valve pintle is fully extended into the throttle body. This amount of air will determine the minimum idle speed the ECM can order by fully extending the pintle.

1. Remove the air cleaner assembly from the engine for access. Be sure to plug any vacuum ports which were disconnected in order to remove the air cleaner assembly.
2. Remove the plug over the idle stop screw plug by piercing it with an awl and carefully prying the plug free of the throttle body.
3. With the IAC valve connected, ground the diagnostic test terminal of the underdash ECM diagnostic connector.
4. Turn the ignition **ON**, but DO NOT start the engine and wait for 30 seconds. This allows time for the ECM to fully extend the IAC valve into the throttle body.
5. With the ignition **ON**, disengage the electrical connector from the IAC valve.
6. Remove the ground from the diagnostic lead, then start the engine.
7. Adjust the idle stop screw to obtain 400-450 rpm with the transmission in Drive.
8. Once the minimum idle speed has been set, turn the ignition OFF and engage the electrical to the IAC valve.
9. Check the TPS voltage output and, if necessary, replace the sensor.
10. Install the air cleaner assembly and reconnect any vacuum hoses.
11. Start the engine and inspect for proper idle operation.

DIESEL FUEL SYSTEM

Fuel Pump

REMOVAL & INSTALLATION

V8 Models

The fuel supply pump on the V8 engine is serviced in the same manner as the fuel pump on the carbureted gasoline engine. For details, refer to the mechanical fuel pump procedure found earlier in this section.

V6 Models

▶ **See Figures 68 and 69**

➡The fuel pump used on the V6 diesel engine is located at the front of the engine, next to the fuel heater.

1. Disconnect the negative battery cable, then remove the air cleaner assembly.
2. Tag and unplug all electrical connectors from the pump.
3. Place a rag under the pump inlet and outlet fittings, then carefully unscrew the fittings from the pump. Cap all fittings to prevent system contamination

4. Remove the pump mounting bracket nut, then remove the pump from the engine.
To install:
5. Install the pump and mounting bracket to the engine, then tighten the bracket nut to 18 ft. lbs. (24 Nm).
6. Thread the inlet and outlet fittings to the pump by hand, then tighten them to 19 ft. lbs. (26 Nm)

➡**In some cases you may have to adjust pump position slightly to align pump fittings with the fuel lines.**

7. Engage all electrical connectors to the pump as noted during removal.
8. Install the air cleaner assembly and connect the negative battery cable.
9. After installing the fuel pump, position a catch basin and disconnect the fuel line at the filter. Turn the ignition switch **ON** in order to prime and bleed the lines. If after torquing the fuel line, the pump runs with a click-like sound, or the fuel bubbles, check for leaks in the fuel lines. The system is properly primed and bled when the pump quiets down. Be sure the fitting is properly tightened.

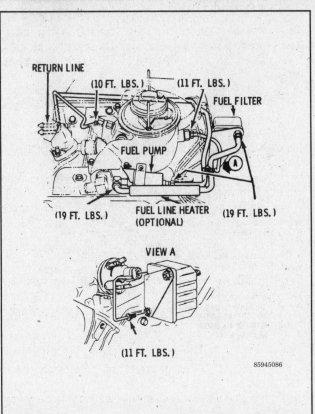

Fig. 68 Fuel pump (shown above) and filter locations —
V6 diesel engine

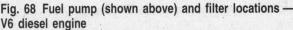
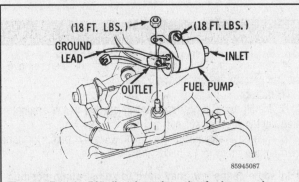

Fig. 69 For the V6 diesel engine, the fuel pump is
mounted on the intake manifold

Fuel Filter

REMOVAL & INSTALLATION

The fuel filter is a square assembly located at the back of
the engine above the intake manifold. Disconnect the fuel lines
in order to remove the filter. When installing, carefully thread
and tighten the lines to the new filter. Start the engine and
check for leaks.

Water in Fuel

Water is the worst enemy of the diesel fuel injection system.
Both the injection pump, which is designed and constructed to

extremely close tolerances, and the injectors can be easily
damaged if enough water is forced through them along with
the fuel. Engine performance will also be drastically affected,
and engine damage can occur.

Diesel fuel is much more susceptible than gasoline to water
contamination. Most diesel engine cars are equipped with an
indicator lamp system that turns on an instrument panel lamp
if water (1 to 2½ gallons) is detected in the fuel tank. The
lamp will come on for 2 to 5 seconds each time the ignition is
turned ON, assuring the driver the lamp is working. If there is
water in the fuel, the light will come back on after a 15 to 20
second off delay, and then remain ON throughout engine
operation.

Purging the Fuel Tank

Cars on which the Water in Fuel light has illuminated may
have the water removed from the tank with a siphon pump.
The pump hose should be hooked up to the ¼ in. fuel return
hose (the smaller of the two hoses) above the rear axle or
under the hood near the fuel pump. Siphoning should continue
until all water is removed from the tank. Use a clear plastic
hose or observe the filter bowl on the siphon pump (if
equipped) to determine when clear fuel begins to flow. Be sure
to remove the cap on the fuel tank while purging. Replace the
cap when finished. Discard the fuel filter and replace with a
new filter.

Fuel Injection Pump and Lines

REMOVAL & INSTALLATION

▶ See Figures 70, 71 and 72

➡The V6 and V8 diesel injection system may use either a
CAV injection pump, or a Roosa-Master/Stanadyne pump.

1. Disconnect the negative battery cable, then remove the
air cleaner assembly.
2. Remove the filters and pipes from the valve covers and
air crossover.
3. Remove the air crossover, then cap the intake manifold
with screen covers (tool J-26996-1).
4. Disconnect the throttle rod and return spring.
5. Remove the bellcrank.
6. Remove the throttle and transmission cables from the
intake manifold brackets.
7. Disconnect the fuel lines from the filter, then remove the
filter from the vehicle.
8. Disconnect the fuel inlet line from the pump.
9. Remove the rear A/C compressor brace and the fuel
line.
10. Disconnect the fuel return line from the injection pump.
11. Remove the clamps and pull the fuel return line from
each injection nozzle.
12. Using two wrenches to prevent damage to the fittings,
disconnect the high pressure line from the nozzles.
13. Remove the three injection pump retaining nuts with tool
J-26987 or its equivalent.
14. Remove the pump. then cap all lines and nozzles in
order to prevent system contamination.

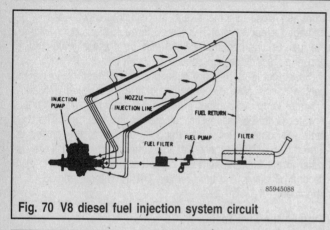

Fig. 70 V8 diesel fuel injection system circuit

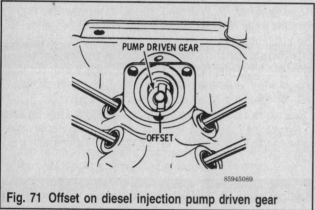

Fig. 71 Offset on diesel injection pump driven gear

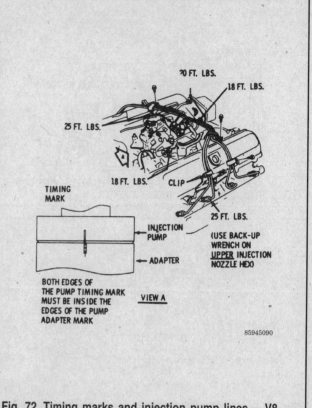

Fig. 72 Timing marks and injection pump lines — V8 diesel engine

To install:

15. Remove the protective caps.

16. Line up the offset tang on the pump driveshaft with the pump driven gear and install the pump.

17. Install, but do not tighten the pump retaining nuts.

18. Connect the high pressure lines to the nozzles.

19. Using two wrenches, torque the high pressure line nuts to 25 ft. lbs. (34 Nm).

20. Connect the fuel return lines to the nozzles and pump.

21. Align the timing mark on the injection pump with the line on the timing mark adaptor and torque the mounting nuts to 35 ft. lbs. (47 Nm).

➡**A ¾ in. open end wrench on the boss at the front of the injection pump will aid in rotating the pump to align the marks.**

22. Adjust the throttle rod:

a. Remove the clip from the cruise control rod and the rod from the bellcrank.

b. Loosen the locknut on the throttle rod a few turns, then shorten the rod several turns.

c. Rotate the bellcrank to the full throttle stop, then lengthen the throttle rod until the injection pump lever contacts the injection pump full throttle stop, then release the bellcrank.

d. Tighten the throttle rod locknut.

23. Install the fuel inlet line between the transfer pump and the filter.

24. Install the rear A/C compressor brace.

25. Install the bellcrank and clip.

26. Connect the throttle rod and return spring.

27. To adjust the transmission cable:

a. Push the snap-lock to the disengaged position.

b. Rotate the injection pump lever to the full throttle stop and hold it there.

c. Push the snap-lock until it is flush.

d. Release the injection pump lever.

28. Connect the negative battery cable, then start the engine and check for fuel leaks.

29. Shut the engine **OFF**, then remove the screened covers and install the air crossover.

30. Install the tubes in the air flow control valve in the air crossover and install the ventilation filter in the valve covers.

31. Install the air cleaner assembly.

32. Start the engine and allow it to run for two minutes. Stop the engine, let it stand for two minutes, then restart. This permits the air to bleed off within the pump.

SLOW IDLE SPEED ADJUSTMENT

▶ **See Figures 73 and 74**

1. Run the engine to normal operating temperature.

2. Insert the probe of a magnetic pickup tachometer into the timing indicator hole.

3. Set the parking brake and block the drive wheels.

4. Place the transmission in Drive and turn the A/C off.

5. Turn the slow idle screw on the injection pump to obtain the idle specification on the emission control label.

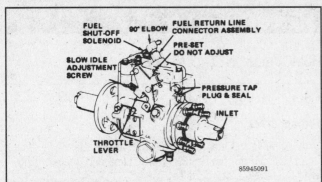

Fig. 73 Diesel injection pump slow idle screw — Roosa Master/Stanodyne

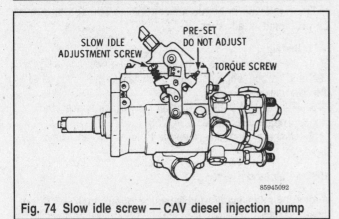

Fig. 74 Slow idle screw — CAV diesel injection pump

FAST IDLE SOLENOID ADJUSTMENT

▶ See Figure 75

Through 1979

1. Set the parking brake and block the drive wheels.
2. Run the engine to normal operating temperature.
3. Place the transmission in Drive.
4. If equipped with A/C disconnect the compressor clutch wire and turn the A/C on. Then disconnect the solenoid wire and connect jumper wires to the solenoid terminals. Ground one of the wires and connect the other to a 12 volt power source in order to activate the solenoid.
5. Adjust the fast idle solenoid plunger to obtain 650 rpm.

Fig. 75 The fast idle solenoid is mounted on the side of the injection pump

1980 and Later

1. With the ignition OFF, disconnect the single green wire from the fast idle relay located on the front of the firewall.
2. Set the parking brake and block the drive wheels.
3. Start the engine and adjust the solenoid (energized) to the specifications on the underhood emission control label.
4. Turn the ignition switch OFF and reconnect the green wire.

CRUISE CONTROL SERVO RELAY ROD ADJUSTMENT

1. Turn the engine Off.
2. Adjust the rod to minimum slack then put the clip in the first free hole closest to the bellcrank, but within the servo bail.

Injection Timing

CHECKING

➡A special diesel timing meter is needed in order to check injection timing. There are a few variations of this meter, but the type desirable here uses a signal through a glow plug probe to determine combustion timing. The meter picks up the engine speed in rpm and the crankshaft position from the crankshaft balancer. This tool is available at automotive supply houses and from tool jobbers; it is the counterpart to a gasoline engine timing light, coupled with a tachometer. An intake manifold cover is also needed. The marks on the pump and adapter flange will normally be aligned within 0.030 in. on the V8 and 0.050 in. on the V6.

1. Place the transmission shift lever in PARK, apply the parking brake and block the rear wheels.
2. Start the engine and let it run at idle until fully warm. Shut the engine OFF.

➡If the engine is not allowed to completely warm up, the probe may soot up, causing incorrect timing readings.

3. Remove the air cleaner assembly and carefully install cover J-26996-1, or equivalent. This cover over the intake is important. Disconnect the EGR valve hose.
4. Clean away ALL dirt from the engine probe holder (rpm counter) and the crankshaft balancer rim.
5. Clean the lens on both end of the glow plug probe and clean the lens in the photoelectric pick-up. Use a tooth pick to scrape the carbon from the combustion chamber side of the glow plug probe, then look through the probe to make sure it's clean. Cleanliness is crucial for accurate readings.
6. Install the probe into the crankshaft rpm counter (probe holder) on the engine front cover.
7. Remove the glow plug from No. 3 cylinder on the V8 engine and from No. 1 on the V6 engine. Install the glow plug probe in the glow plug opening and torque to 8 ft. lbs. (11 Nm).
8. Set the timing meter offset selector to **B** (99.5) on the V8 engine, and to **A** (20) on the V6 engine.

9. Connect the battery leads, red to positive, black to negative.

10. Disengage the two-lead connector from the alternator.

11. Start the engine. Adjust the engine rpm to the speed specified on the emissions control decal.

12. Observe the timing reading, then observe it again in 2 minutes. When the readings stabilize over the 2 minutes intervals, compare that final stabilized reading to the one specified on the emissions control decal. The timing reading will be at ATDC (After Top Dead Center) reading when set to specifications.

13. Disconnect the timing meter and install the removed glow plug, torquing it to 12 ft. lbs. (16 Nm) on the V8 engine and 15 ft. lbs. (20 Nm) on the V6 engine.

14. Engage the generator two-lead connection.

15. Install the air cleaner assembly and connect the EGR valve hose.

ADJUSTMENT

1. Shut the engine **OFF**.

2. Note the relative position of the marks on the pump flange and either the pump intermediate adapter (V6 engine) or pump adapter (V8 engine).

3. Loosen the nuts or bolts holding the pump to a point where the pump can just be rotated. Use a ¾ in. open-end wrench on the boss at the front of the injection pump on the V8 engine and a 1 in. open-end wrench on the V6 engine. You may need a wrench with a slight offset to clear the fuel return line on the V6 engine.

4. Rotate the pump to the left to advance the timing and to the right to retard the timing. On the V8 engine the width of the mark on the adaptor is equal to about 1° of timing. On the V6 engine the width of the mark on the intermediate adaptor is about ⅔ degrees. Move the pump the amount that is needed and tighten the pump retaining nuts to 18 ft. lbs. (24 Nm) on the V8 engine and 35 ft. lbs. (47 Nm) on the V6 engine.

5. Start the engine and recheck the timing as described earlier. Reset the timing if necessary.

6. Adjust the injection pump rod on the V8 engine. On both engines, reset the fast and curb idle speeds.

➡**Wild needle fluctuations on the timing meter indicate a cylinder not firing properly. Correction of this condition must be made prior to adjusting the timing.**

7. If after resetting the timing, the marks are far apart and the engine still runs poorly, the dynamic timing could still be off. It is possible that a malfunctioning cylinder will cause incorrect timing. If this occurs, it is essential that timing be checked in cylinders 2 or 3 on the V8 engine and 1 or 4 on the V6 engine. If different timing exists between cylinders, try both positions to determine which timing works best.

Injection Nozzle

REMOVAL & INSTALLATION

◆ **See Figures 76, 77 and 78**

Through 1979

1. Remove the fuel return line from the nozzle.

2. Remove the nozzle hold-down clamp and spacer using tool No. J-26952, or equivalent.

3. Remove the nozzle form the engine, then cap the high pressure line and nozzle tip.

➡**The nozzle tip is highly susceptible to damage and must be protected at all times.**

To install:

4. If an old nozzle is to be reinstalled, a new compression seal and carbon stop seal must be installed after removal of the used seals.

5. Remove the caps and install the nozzle, spacer and clamp. Torque to 25 ft. lbs. (34 Nm).

6. Connect return line, then start the engine and check for leaks.

1982-84 Models

After the fuel lines are removed, the injection nozzles on these engines are simply unbolted from the cylinder head in similar fashion to a spark plug. Be careful not to damage the nozzle end and make sure you remove the copper nozzle

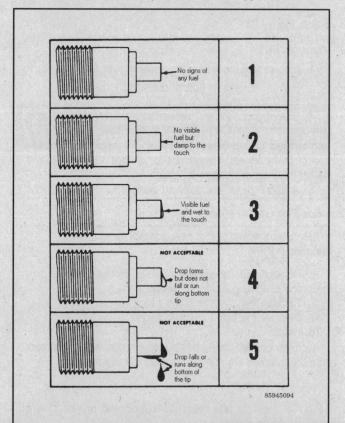

85945094

Fig. 76 Checking injection nozzle seat tightness

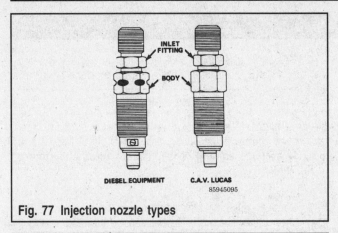

Fig. 77 Injection nozzle types

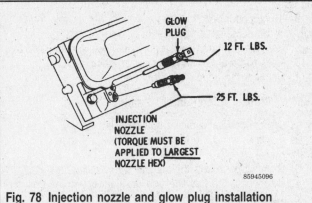

Fig. 78 Injection nozzle and glow plug installation

gasket from the cylinder head if it does not come off with the injection nozzle. Clean the carbon off the tip of the nozzle with a soft brass wire brush and install the nozzles, with gaskets.

➡1981 and later models use two types of injectors, CAV Lucas or Diesel Equipment. When installing the inlet fittings, torque the Diesel Equipment injector fitting to 45 ft. lbs. (61 Nm) and the CAV Lucas to 25 ft. lbs. (34 Nm).

Injection Pump Adapter, Adapter Seal, and New Adapter Timing Mark

REMOVAL & INSTALLATION

▸ **See Figures 79, 80 and 81**

➡**Skip steps 4 and 9 if a new adapter is not being installed.**

1. Remove injection pump and lines. For details, refer to the procedure found earlier in this section.
2. Remove the injection pump adapter.
3. Remove the seal from the adapter.
To install:
4. If the old adapter is being installed, file the timing mark from the adapter. Do not file the mark off the pump.

5. Position the engine at TDC of No. 1 cylinder. Align the mark on the balancer with the zero mark on the indicator. The index is offset to the right when No. 1 is at TDC.
6. Apply a chassis lube to the seal areas. Install, but do not tighten the injection pump.
7. Install the new seal on the adapter using tool J-28425, or its equivalent.
8. Torque the adapter bolts to 25 ft. lbs. (34 Nm).
9. If the old adapter is being used, install timing tool J-26896, or equivalent, into the injection pump adapter. Torque the tool, toward No. 1 cylinder to 50 ft. lbs. (68 Nm). Mark the injection pump adapter, then remove the tool.
10. Install the injection pump and lines to the engine.

Glow Plugs

There are two types of glow plugs used on General Motors Corp. diesels; the fast glow type and the slow glow type. The fast flow type use pulsing current applied to 6 volt glow plugs while the slow glow type use continuous current applied to 12 volt glow plugs.

An easy way to tell the plugs apart is that the fast glow (6 volt) plugs have an $5/16$ in. wide electrical connector plug while the slow glow (12 volt) connector plug is $1/4$ in. wide. Do not attempt to interchange any parts of these two glow plug systems.

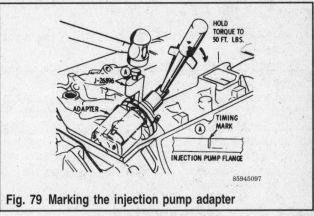

Fig. 79 Marking the injection pump adapter

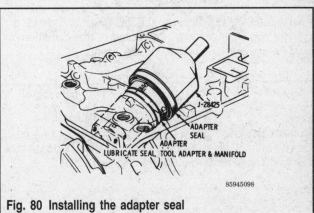

Fig. 80 Installing the adapter seal

FUEL TANK

DRAINING

1. Remove the fuel tank filler cap.
2. Connect a siphon pump to the ¼ in. fuel feed hose (the smaller of the two hoses when applicable) above the rear axle, or under the hood near the fuel pump on the passenger's side of the engine, near the front.
3. Operate the siphon pump until all fuel is removed from the fuel tank. Be sure to reinstall the fuel return hose and the fuel cap.

REMOVAL & INSTALLATION

▶ **See Figures 82 and 83**

1964 Sedan, 1964 Station Wagon and El Camino

1. Disconnect the negative battery cable.
2. Properly pump the fuel from the tank, as there is no drain plug.
3. Raise and support the vehicle safely using jackstands.
4. Disconnect the fuel line and the gauge sending unit wire from the tank.
5. If equipped, disconnect the vent hose from the tank.

6. Remove the retaining bolts from the tank straps, lower the support straps and then carefully lower the tank from the vehicle.

➡ **Be sure to store the fuel tank in a cool dry area out of direct sunlight. Keep any source of flame away from the tank, even though it has been drained of most fuel, there is likely an large amount of flammable vapors still stored in the tank.**

To install:

7. Carefully raise the tank into position (an assistant is helpful here), then secure using the support straps and retaining bolts.
8. If equipped, connect the vent hose to the tank, then connect the sending unit connector and fuel line.
9. Remove the jackstands and carefully lower the vehicle.
10. Refill the fuel tank and check for leaks.
11. Connect the negative battery cable.

1965-67 Station Wagon and El Camino

1. Disconnect the negative battery cable.
2. Properly pump the fuel from the tank, as there is no drain plug.
3. Raise and support the vehicle safely using jackstands.
4. Disconnect the fuel line and the gauge sending unit wire from the tank.
5. If equipped, disconnect the vent hose from the tank.
6. Remove the tank support straps.

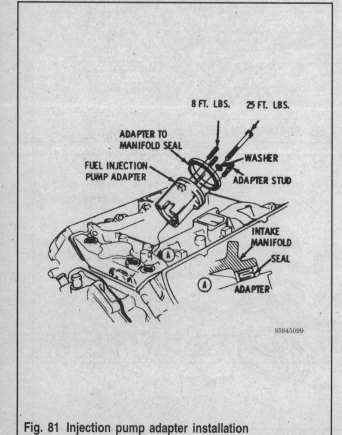

Fig. 81 Injection pump adapter installation

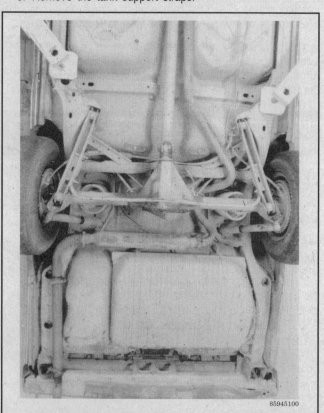

Fig. 82 The fuel tank is secured under the rear of the vehicle by retaining straps

7. Remove the frame attaching screws from the front support.

8. Slide the tank forward and then carefully lower it from the car.

➡️Be sure to store the fuel tank in a cool dry area out of direct sunlight. Keep any source of flame away from the tank, even though it has been drained of most fuel, there is likely an large amount of flammable vapors still stored in the tank.

To install:

9. Carefully raise the fuel tank and slide it into position.
10. Install the frame attaching screws to the front support.
11. Install and secure the tank support straps.
12. If equipped, connect the vent hose to the tank, then connect the sending unit connector and fuel line.
13. Remove the jackstands and carefully lower the vehicle.
14. Refill the fuel tank and check for leaks.
15. Connect the negative battery cable.

1968-77 Sedan and El Camino

1. Disconnect the negative battery cable.
2. Properly pump the fuel from the tank, as there is no drain plug.
3. Disconnect the fuel gauge sending unit wire from the rear wiring harness connector. On sedans, push the grommet out and work the gauge wire through the trunk floor hole.
4. Raise and support the vehicle safely using jackstands.
5. Remove the fuel gauge wire screw from the underbody.
6. Disconnect the fuel line at the sending unit pickup line.

7. Remove the vent hose (hoses for evaporative control on 1970 and later models).
8. Remove the tank filler neck bolt on the El Camino.
9. Remove the strap retaining bolts, lower the support straps, and carefully lower the tank from the car.

➡️Be sure to store the fuel tank in a cool dry area out of direct sunlight. Keep any source of flame away from the tank, even though it has been drained of most fuel, there is likely an large amount of flammable vapors still stored in the tank.

To install:

10. Carefully raise the tank into position (an assistant is helpful here), then position and secure the tank support straps.
11. For the El Camino, install the filler neck bolt.
12. For 1970 and later models so equipped, install the vent hose.
13. Connect the fuel line at the sending unit pickup line.
14. Install the fuel gauge wire screw to the under body.
15. Remove the jackstands and carefully lower the vehicle.
16. Connect the fuel gauge sending unit wire to the rear harness connector. On sedans, be sure to push the gauge through the trunk floor hole and properly seat the grommet.
17. Refill the fuel tank and check for leaks.
18. Connect the negative battery cable.

1968-77 Station Wagon

1. Disconnect the negative battery cable.
2. Properly pump the fuel from the tank, as there is no drain plug.

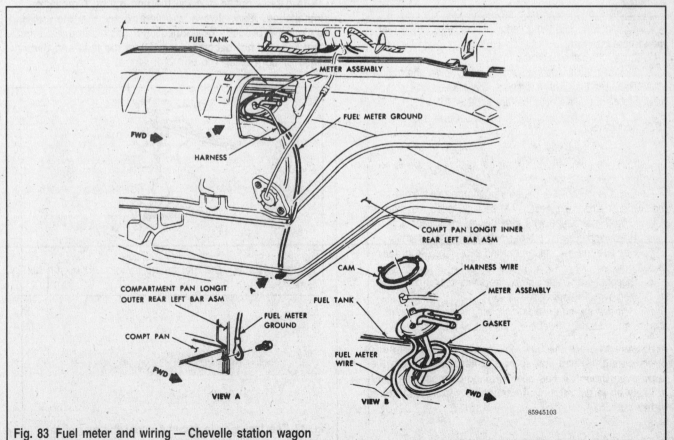

Fig. 83 Fuel meter and wiring — Chevelle station wagon

3. Raise and support the vehicle safely using jackstands. Position the jackstands under the frame, leaving the rear axle free.

4. Lower the rear axle into the full rebound position, and remove the left rear wheel assembly.

5. Disconnect the fuel gauge sending unit wire at the rear wiring harness.

6. Remove the fuel tank front shield.

7. Remove the fuel gauge ground wire from the rear quarter panel.

8. Remove the fuel line and wires from the gauge sending unit.

9. On 1974 and later models, remove the left rear shock absorber and lift the right rear wheel slightly to allow movement of the left wheel down and out of the way.

10. Remove the strap retaining bolts and carefully lower the tank from the vehicle.

➡Be sure to store the fuel tank in a cool dry area out of direct sunlight. Keep any source of flame away from the tank, even though it has been drained of most fuel, there is likely an large amount of flammable vapors still stored in the tank.

To install:

11. Carefully raise the tank into position (an assistant is helpful here), then position and secure the tank support straps.

12. For 1974 and later models, reposition the axle, as necessary, and reconnect the shock absorber.

13. Install the fuel line and wires to the gauge sending unit.

14. Install the fuel gauge ground wire to the rear quarter panel.

15. Install the fuel tank front shield.

16. Connect the fuel gauge sending unit wire to the rear wiring harness.

17. Install the left wheel assembly.

18. Remove the jackstands and carefully lower the vehicle.

19. Refill the fuel tank and check for leaks.

20. Connect the negative battery cable.

1978 and Later

1. Disconnect the negative battery cable.

2. Properly pump the fuel from the tank, as there is no drain plug.

3. Disconnect the fuel gauge sending unit wire from the rear wiring harness connector. On sedans, push the grommet out and work the gauge wire through the trunk floor hole.

4. Raise and support the car safely using jackstands.

5. Remove the fuel gauge ground wire screw from the underbody.

6. Disconnect the fuel line at the sending unit pickup line.

7. Remove the vent hose.

8. Remove the strap retaining bolts, lower the support straps, and carefully lower the tank out of the car.

➡Be sure to store the fuel tank in a cool dry area out of direct sunlight. Keep any source of flame away from the tank, even though it has been drained of most fuel, there is likely an large amount of flammable vapors still stored in the tank.

To install:

9. Carefully raise the tank into position (an assistant is helpful here), then position and secure the tank support straps.

10. Install the vent hose.

11. Connect the fuel line(s) to the sending unit or sending unit/pump assembly (fuel injected vehicles).

12. Install the fuel gauge wire screw to the under body.

13. Remove the jackstands and carefully lower the vehicle.

14. Connect the fuel gauge sending unit wire to the rear harness connector. On sedans, be sure to push the gauge through the trunk floor hole and properly seat the grommet.

15. Refill the fuel tank and check for leaks.

16. Connect the negative battery cable.

SENDING UNIT REPLACEMENT

▶ **See Figure 84**

➡**For details on sending unit/fuel pump assembly removal and installation on fuel injected vehicles, refer to the procedure earlier in this section.**

The sending unit (or sending unit/fuel pump assembly on fuel injected vehicles) is located in the fuel tank assembly. The tank must be removed from the vehicle in order to access the unit which is mounted through the top of the tank. For most vehicles covered in this manual a lockring is used to hold the unit in position. The lockring may be loosened using a hammer and drift punch to carefully drive it counterclockwise, then the unit may be withdrawn from the vehicle.

➡**Be careful not to damage the unit during removal or installation. Also, always take care to see that the arm and pickup are properly positioned upon installation. Be sure that they do not become hung up on the tank and damaged or bent when the unit is inserted.**

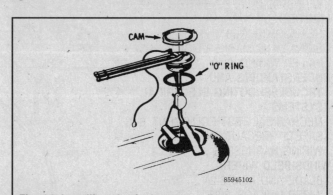

Fig. 84 Installing the fuel gauge unit to a common fuel tank

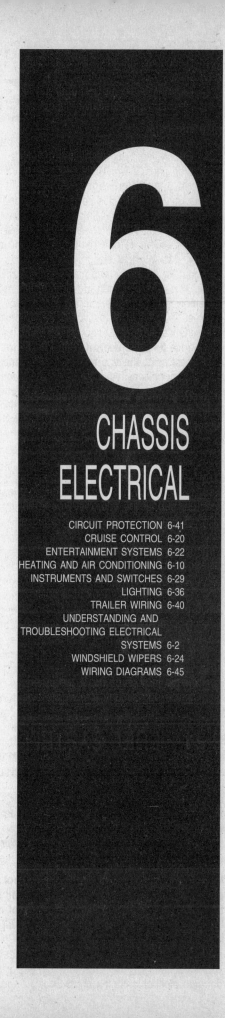

6

CHASSIS
ELECTRICAL

UNDERSTANDING AND TROUBLESHOOTING ELECTRICAL SYSTEMS

At the rate which both import and domestic manufacturers are incorporating electronic control systems into their production lines, it won't be long before every new vehicle is equipped with one or more on-board computer, like the unit installed on later vehicles covered in this manual. These electronic components (with no moving parts) should theoretically last the life of the vehicle, provided nothing external happens to damage the circuits or memory chips.

While it is true that electronic components should never wear out, in the real world malfunctions can, and often do, occur. It is also true that any computer-based system is extremely sensitive to electrical voltages and cannot tolerate careless or haphazard testing or service procedures. An inexperienced individual can easily cause major damage looking for a minor problem by using the wrong kind of test equipment or connecting test leads or connectors under improper conditions. Always pay close attention to the circumstances when a test should be performed. NEVER disconnect an ECM connector with the ignition switch ON. When selecting test equipment, make sure the manufacturer's instructions state that the tester is compatible with whatever type of electronic control system is being serviced. Read all instructions carefully and double check all test points before installing probes or making any test connections.

The following section outlines basic diagnosis techniques for dealing with computerized automotive control systems. Along with a general explanation of the various types of test equipment available to aid in servicing modern electronic automotive systems, basic repair techniques for wiring harnesses and connectors is given. Read the basic information before attempting any repairs or testing on any computerized system, to provide the background of information necessary to avoid the most common and obvious mistakes that can cost both time and money. Although the replacement and testing procedures are simple in themselves, the systems are not, and unless one has a thorough understanding of all components and their function within a particular computerized control system, the logical test sequence these systems demand cannot be followed. Minor malfunctions can make a big difference, so it is important to know how each component affects the operation of the overall electronic system in order to find the ultimate cause of a problem without replacing good components unnecessarily. It is not enough to use the correct test equipment; the test equipment must be used correctly.

Safety Precautions

✳✳CAUTION

Whenever working on or around any computer based microprocessor control system, always observe these general precautions to prevent the possibility of personal injury or damage to electronic components.

• Never install or remove battery cables with the ignition switch ON or the engine running. Jumper cables should be connected with the key OFF to avoid power surges that can damage electronic control units. Engines equipped with

computer controlled systems should avoid both giving and getting jump starts due to the possibility of serious damage to components from arcing in the engine compartment when connections are made with the ignition ON.

• Always remove the battery cables before charging the battery. Never use a high output charger on an installed battery or attempt to use any type of "hot shot" (24 volt) starting aid.

• Exercise care when inserting test probes into connectors to insure good connections without damaging the connector or spreading the pins. Always probe connectors from the rear (wire) side, NOT the pin side, in order to avoid accidental shorting of terminals during test procedures.

• Never remove or attach wiring harness connectors with the ignition switch ON, especially to an electronic control unit.

• Do not drop any components during service procedures and never apply 12 volts directly to any component (like a solenoid or relay) unless instructed specifically to do so. Some component electrical windings are designed to safely handle only 4 or 5 volts and can be destroyed in seconds if 12 volts are applied directly to the connector.

• Remove the electronic control unit if the vehicle is to be placed in an environment where temperatures exceed approximately 176°F (80°C), such as a paint spray booth or when arc or gas welding near the control unit location in the car.

ORGANIZED TROUBLESHOOTING

When diagnosing a specific problem, organized troubleshooting is a must. The complexity of a modern automobile demands that you approach any problem in a logical, organized manner. There are certain troubleshooting techniques that are standard:

1. Establish when the problem occurs. Does the problem appear only under certain conditions? Were there any noises, odors, or other unusual symptoms?

2. Isolate the problem area. To do this, make some simple tests and observations; then eliminate the systems that are working properly. Check for obvious problems such as broken wires, dirty connections or split or disconnected vacuum hoses. ALWAYS check the obvious before assuming something complicated is the cause.

3. Test for problems systematically to determine the cause once the problem area is isolated. Are all the components functioning properly? Is there power going to electrical switches and motors? Is there vacuum at vacuum switches and/or actuators? Is there a mechanical problem such as bent linkage or loose mounting screws? Performing careful, systematic checks will often turn up most causes on the first inspection without wasting time checking components that have little or no relationship to the problem.

4. Test all repairs after the work is done to make sure that the problem is fixed. Some causes can be traced to more than one component, so a careful verification of repair work is important to pick up additional malfunctions that may cause a problem to reappear or a different problem to arise. A blown fuse, for example, is a simple problem that may require more

than another fuse to repair. If you don't look for a problem that caused a fuse to blow, for example, a shorted wire may go undetected.

Experience has shown that most problems tend to be the result of a fairly simple and obvious cause, such as loose or corroded connectors or air leaks in the intake system; making a careful inspection of components during testing is essential to quick and accurate troubleshooting. Special, hand held computerized testers designed specifically for diagnosing the system are available from a variety of aftermarket sources, as well as from the vehicle manufacturer, but care should be taken that any test equipment being used is designed to diagnose that particular computer controlled system accurately without damaging the Electronic control Module (ECM) or components being tested.

➡Pinpointing the exact cause of trouble in an electrical system can sometimes only be accomplished by the use of special test equipment. The following describes commonly used test equipment and explains how to put it to best use in diagnosis. In addition to the information covered below, the manufacturer's instructions booklet provided with the tester should be read and clearly understood before attempting any test procedures.

TEST EQUIPMENT

Jumper Wires

Jumper wires are simple, yet extremely valuable, pieces of test equipment. Jumper wires are merely wires that are used to bypass sections of a circuit. The simplest type of jumper wire is merely a length of multi-strand wire with an alligator clip at each end. Jumper wires are usually fabricated from lengths of standard automotive wire and whatever type of connector (alligator clip, spade connector or pin connector) that is required for the particular vehicle being tested. The well equipped tool box will have several different styles of jumper wires in several different lengths. Some jumper wires are made with three or more terminals coming from a common splice for special purpose testing. In cramped, hard-to-reach areas it is advisable to have insulated boots over the jumper wire terminals in order to prevent accidental grounding, sparks, and possible fire, especially when testing fuel system components.

Jumper wires are used primarily to locate open electrical circuits, on either the ground (-) side of the circuit or on the hot (+) side. If an electrical component fails to operate, connect the jumper wire between the component and a good ground. If the component operates only with the jumper installed, the ground circuit is open. If the ground circuit is good, but the component does not operate, the circuit between the power feed and component is open. You can sometimes connect the jumper wire directly from the battery to the hot terminal of the component, but first make sure the component uses 12 volts in operation. Some electrical components, such as fuel injectors, are designed to operate on about 4 volts and running 12 volts directly to the injector terminals can burn out the wiring. By inserting an in-line fuseholder between a set of test leads, a fused jumper wire can be used for bypassing open circuits. Use a 5 amp fuse to provide protection against voltage spikes. When in doubt, use a voltmeter to check the

voltage input to the component and measure how much voltage is being applied normally. By moving the jumper wire successively back from the lamp toward the power source, you can isolate the area of the circuit where the open is located. When the component stops functioning, or the power is cut off, the open is in the segment of wire between the jumper and the point previously tested.

❋❋CAUTION

Never use jumpers made from wire that is of lighter gauge than used in the circuit under test. If the jumper wire is of too small gauge, it may overheat and possibly melt. Never use jumpers to bypass high resistance loads (such as motors) in a circuit. Bypassing resistances, in effect, creates a short circuit which may, in turn, cause damage and fire. Never use a jumper for anything other than temporary bypassing of components in a circuit.

12 Volt Test Light

The 12 volt test light is used to check circuits and components while electrical current is flowing through them. It is used for voltage and ground tests. Twelve volt test lights come in different styles but all have three main parts; a ground clip, a probe, and a light. The most commonly used 12 volt test lights have pick-type probes. To use a 12 volt test light, connect the ground clip to a good ground and probe wherever necessary with the pick. The pick should be sharp so that it can penetrate wire insulation to make contact with the wire, without making a large hole in the insulation. The wrap-around light is handy in hard to reach areas or where it is difficult to support a wire to push a probe pick into it. To use the wrap around light, hook the wire to probed with the hook and pull the trigger. A small pick will be forced through the wire insulation into the wire core.

❋❋CAUTION

Do not use a test light to probe electronic ignition spark plug or coil wires. Never use a pick-type test light to probe wiring on computer controlled systems unless specifically instructed to do so. Any wire insulation that is pierced by the test light probe should be taped and sealed with silicone after testing.

Like the jumper wire, the 12 volt test light is used to isolate opens in circuits. But, whereas the jumper wire is used to bypass the open to operate the load, the 12 volt test light is used to locate the presence of voltage in a circuit. If the test light glows, you know that there is power up to that point; if the 12 volt test light does not glow when its probe is inserted into the wire or connector, you know that there is an open circuit (no power). Move the test light in successive steps back toward the power source until the light in the handle does glow. When it does glow, the open is between the probe and point previously probed.

➡The test light does not detect that 12 volts (or any particular amount of voltage) is present; it only detects that some voltage is present. It is advisable before using the test light to touch its terminals across the battery posts to make sure the light is operating properly.

Self-Powered Test Light

The self-powered test light usually contains a 1.5 volt penlight battery. One type of self-powered test light is similar in design to the 12 volt test light. This type has both the battery and the light in the handle and pick-type probe tip. The second type has the light toward the open tip, so that the light illuminates the contact point. The self-powered test light is dual purpose piece of test equipment. It can be used to test for either open or short circuits when power is isolated from the circuit (continuity test). A powered test light should NOT be used on any computer controlled system or component unless specifically instructed to do so. Many engine sensors can be destroyed by even this small amount of voltage applied directly to the terminals.

Open Circuit Testing

To use the self-powered test light to check for open circuits, first isolate the circuit from the vehicle's 12 volt power source by disconnecting the battery or wiring harness connector. Connect the test light ground clip to a good ground and probe sections of the circuit sequentially with the test light. (start from either end of the circuit). If the light is out, the open is between the probe and the circuit ground. If the light is on, the open is between the probe and end of the circuit toward the power source.

Short Circuit Testing

By isolating the circuit both from power and from ground, and using a self-powered test light, you can check for shorts to ground in the circuit. Isolate the circuit from power and ground. Connect the test light ground clip to a good ground and probe any easy-to-reach test point in the circuit. If the light comes on, there is a short somewhere in the circuit. To isolate the short, probe a test point at either end of the isolated circuit (the light should be on). Leave the test light probe connected and open connectors, switches, remove parts, etc., sequentially, until the light goes out. When the light goes out, the short is between the last circuit component opened and the previous circuit opened.

➡The 1.5 volt battery in the test light does not provide much current. A weak battery may not provide enough power to illuminate the test light even when a complete circuit is made (especially if there are high resistances in the circuit). Always make sure that the test battery is strong. To check the battery, briefly touch the ground clip to the probe; if the light glows brightly the battery is strong enough for testing. Never use a self-powered test light to perform checks for opens or shorts when power is applied to the electrical system under test. The 12 volt vehicle power will quickly burn out the 1.5 volt light bulb in the test light.

Voltmeter

A voltmeter is used to measure voltage at any point in a circuit, or to measure the voltage drop across any part of a circuit. It can also be used to check continuity in a wire or circuit by indicating current flow from one end to the other. Voltmeters usually have various scales on the meter dial and a selector switch to allow the selection of different voltages. The voltmeter has a positive and a negative lead. To avoid damage to the meter, always connect the negative lead to the negative (-) side of circuit (to ground or nearest the ground side of the circuit) and connect the positive lead to the positive (+) side of the circuit (to the power source or the nearest power source). Note that the negative voltmeter lead will always be black and that the positive voltmeter will always be some color other than black (usually red). Depending on how the voltmeter is connected into the circuit, it has several uses.

A voltmeter can be connected either in parallel or in series with a circuit and it has a very high resistance to current flow. When connected in parallel, only a small amount of current will flow through the voltmeter current path; the rest will flow through the normal circuit current path and the circuit will work normally. When the voltmeter is connected in series with a circuit, only a small amount of current can flow through the circuit. The circuit will not work properly, but the voltmeter reading will show if the circuit is complete or not.

✳✳CAUTION

Do not use a multimeter to probe electronic ignition spark plug or coil wires. Small pin holes in secondary ignition wires will allow high voltage to arc from the wire to a metal part, external to the secondary ignition circuit. This arcing may cause misfiring, leading to a driveability complaint.

Available Voltage Measurement

Set the voltmeter selector switch to the 20V position and connect the meter negative lead to the negative post of the battery. Connect the positive meter lead to the positive post of the battery and turn the ignition switch **ON** to provide a load. Read the voltage on the meter or digital display. A well charged battery should register over 12 volts. If the meter reads below 11.5 volts, the battery power may be insufficient to operate the electrical system properly. This test determines voltage available from the battery and should be the first step in any electrical trouble diagnosis procedure. Many electrical problems, especially on computer controlled systems, can be caused by a low state of charge in the battery. Excessive corrosion at the battery cable terminals can cause a poor contact that will prevent proper charging and full battery current flow.

Normal battery voltage is 12 volts when fully charged. When the battery is supplying current to one or more circuits it is said to be "under load". When everything is off the electrical system is under a "no-load" condition. A fully charged battery may show about 12.5 volts at no load; will drop to 12 volts under medium load; and will drop even lower under heavy load. If the battery is partially discharged the voltage decrease under heavy load may be excessive, even though the battery shows 12 volts or more at no load. When allowed to discharge further, the battery's available voltage under load will decrease more severely. For this reason, it is important that the battery be fully charged during all testing procedures to avoid errors in diagnosis and incorrect test results.

Voltage Drop

When current flows through a resistance, the voltage beyond the resistance is reduced (the larger the current, the greater the reduction in voltage). When no current is flowing, there is no voltage drop because there is no current flow. All points in the circuit which are connected to the power source are at the same voltage as the power source. The total voltage drop always equals the total source voltage. In a long circuit with many connectors, a series of small, unwanted voltage drops due to corrosion at the connectors can add up to a total loss of voltage which impairs the operation of the normal loads in the circuit.

INDIRECT COMPUTATION OF VOLTAGE DROPS

1. Set the voltmeter selector switch to the 20 volt position.
2. Connect the meter negative lead to a good ground.
3. Probe all resistances in the circuit with the positive meter lead.
4. Operate the circuit in all modes and observe the voltage readings.

DIRECT MEASUREMENT OF VOLTAGE DROPS

1. Set the voltmeter switch to the 20 volt position.
2. Connect the voltmeter negative lead to the ground side of the resistance load to be measured.
3. Connect the positive lead to the positive side of the resistance or load to be measured.
4. Read the voltage drop directly on the 20 volt scale.

Too high a voltage indicates too high a resistance. If, for example, a blower motor runs too slowly, you can determine if there is too high a resistance in the resistor pack. By taking voltage drop readings in all parts of the circuit, you can isolate the problem. Too low a voltage drop indicates too low a resistance. If, for example, a blower motor runs too fast in the MED and/or LOW position, the problem can be isolated in the resistor pack by taking voltage drop readings in all parts of the circuit to locate a possibly shorted resistor. The maximum allowable voltage drop under load is critical, especially if there is more than one high resistance problem in a circuit because all voltage drops are cumulative. A small drop is normal due to the resistance of the conductors.

HIGH RESISTANCE TESTING

1. Set the voltmeter selector switch to the 4 volt position.
2. Connect the voltmeter positive lead to the positive post of the battery.
3. Turn on the headlights and heater blower to provide a load.
4. Probe various points in the circuit with the negative voltmeter lead.
5. Read the voltage drop on the 4 volt scale. Some average maximum allowable voltage drops are:
   FUSE PANEL — 7 volts
   IGNITION SWITCH — 5 volts
   HEADLIGHT SWITCH — 7 volts
   IGNITION COIL (+) — 5 volts
   ANY OTHER LOAD — 1.3 volts

➡Voltage drops are all measured while a load is operating; without current flow, there will be no voltage drop.

Ohmmeter

The ohmmeter is designed to read resistance (ohms) in a circuit or component. Although there are several different styles of ohmmeters, all will usually have a selector switch which permits the measurement of different ranges of resistance (usually the selector switch allows the multiplication of the meter reading by 10, 100, 1000, and 10,000). A calibration knob allows the meter to be set at zero for accurate measurement. Since all ohmmeters are powered by an internal battery (usually 9 volts), the ohmmeter can be used as a self-powered test light. When the ohmmeter is connected, current from the ohmmeter flows through the circuit or component being tested. Since the ohmmeter's internal resistance and voltage are known values, the amount of current flow through the meter depends on the resistance of the circuit or component being tested.

The ohmmeter can be used to perform continuity test for opens or shorts (either by observation of the meter needle or as a self-powered test light), and to read actual resistance in a circuit. It should be noted that the ohmmeter is used to check the resistance of a component or wire while there is no voltage applied to the circuit. Current flow from an outside voltage source (such as the vehicle battery) can damage the ohmmeter, so the circuit or component should be isolated from the vehicle electrical system before any testing is done. Since the ohmmeter uses its own voltage source, either lead can be connected to any test point.

➡When checking diodes or other solid state components, the ohmmeter leads can only be connected one way in order to measure current flow in a single direction. Make sure the positive (+) and negative (-) terminal connections are as described in the test procedures to verify the one-way diode operation.

In using the meter for making continuity checks, do not be concerned with the actual resistance readings. Zero resistance, or any resistance readings, indicate continuity in the circuit. Infinite resistance indicates an open in the circuit. A high resistance reading where there should be none indicates a problem in the circuit. Checks for short circuits are made in the same manner as checks for open circuits except that the circuit must be isolated from both power and normal ground. Infinite resistance indicates no continuity to ground, while zero resistance indicates a dead short to ground.

RESISTANCE MEASUREMENT

The batteries in an ohmmeter will weaken with age and temperature, so the ohmmeter must be calibrated or "zeroed" before taking measurements. Many modern digital meters are self-zeroing and will require no adjustment. If your meter must be zeroed, be sure to check this each time it is used. To zero the meter, place the selector switch in its lowest range and touch the two ohmmeter leads together. Turn the calibration knob until the meter needle is exactly on zero.

➡All analog (needle) type ohmmeters must be zeroed before use, but some digital ohmmeter models are automatically calibrated when the switch is turned on. Self-calibrating digital ohmmeters do not have an adjusting knob, but its a good idea to check for a zero readout before use by touching the leads together. All computer controlled systems require the use of a digital ohmmeter with at least 10 megohms impedance for testing. Before any test procedures are attempted, make sure the ohmmeter used is compatible with the electrical system or damage to the on-board computer could result.

To measure resistance, first isolate the circuit from the vehicle power source by disconnecting the battery cables or the harness connector. Make sure the ignition key is **OFF** when disconnecting any components or the battery. Where necessary, also isolate at least one side of the circuit to be checked to avoid reading parallel resistances. Parallel circuit resistances will always give a lower reading than the actual resistance of either of the branches. When measuring the resistance of parallel circuits, the total resistance will always be lower than the smallest resistance in the circuit. Connect the meter leads to both sides of the circuit (wire or component) and read the actual measured ohms on the meter scale. Make sure the selector switch is set to the proper ohm scale for the circuit being tested to avoid misreading the ohmmeter test value.

✳✳CAUTION

Never use an ohmmeter with power applied to the circuit. Like the self-powered test light, the ohmmeter is designed to operate on its own power supply. The normal 12 volt automotive electrical system current could damage the meter.

Ammeters

An ammeter measures the amount of current flowing through a circuit in units called amperes or amps. Amperes are units of electron flow which indicate the speed at which electrons are flowing through the circuit. Since Ohms Law dictates that current flow in a circuit is equal to the circuit voltage divided by the total circuit resistance, increasing voltage also increases the current level (amps). Likewise, any decrease in resistance will increase the amount of amps in a circuit. At normal operating voltage, most circuits have a characteristic amount of amperes, called "current draw" which can be measured using an ammeter. By referring to a specified current draw rating, measuring the amperes, and comparing the two values, one can determine what is happening within the circuit to aid in diagnosis. An open circuit, for example, will not allow any current to flow so the ammeter reading will be zero. More current flows through a heavily loaded circuit or when the charging system is operating.

An ammeter is always connected in series with the circuit being tested. All of the current that normally flows through the circuit must also flow through the ammeter; if there is any other path for the current to follow, the ammeter reading will not be accurate. The ammeter itself has very little resistance to current flow and therefore will not affect the circuit, but it will measure current draw only when the circuit is closed and electricity is flowing. Excessive current draw can blow fuses and drain the battery, while a reduced current draw can cause motors to run slowly, lights to dim and other components to not operate properly. The ammeter can help diagnose these conditions by locating the cause of the high or low reading.

Multimeters

Different combinations of test meters can be built into a single unit designed for specific tests. Some of the more common combination test devices are known as Volt/Amp testers, Tach/Dwell meters, or Digital Multimeters. The Volt/Amp tester is used for charging system, starting system or battery tests and consists of a voltmeter, an ammeter and a variable resistance carbon pile. The voltmeter will usually have at least two ranges for use with 6, 12 and 24 volt systems. The ammeter also has more than one range for testing various levels of battery loads and starter current draw and the carbon pile can be adjusted to offer different amounts of resistance. The Volt/Amp tester has heavy leads to carry large amounts of current and many later models have an inductive ammeter pickup that clamps around the wire to simplify test connections. On some models, the ammeter also has a zero-center scale to allow testing of charging and starting systems without switching leads or polarity. A digital multimeter is a voltmeter, ammeter and ohmmeter combined in an instrument which gives a digital readout. These are often used when testing solid state circuits because of their high input impedance (usually 10 megohms or more).

The tach/dwell meter combines a tachometer and a dwell (cam angle) meter and is a specialized kind of voltmeter. The tachometer scale is marked to show engine speed in rpm and the dwell scale is marked to show degrees of distributor shaft rotation. In most electronic ignition systems, dwell is determined by the control unit, but the dwell meter can also be used to check the duty cycle (operation) of some electronic engine control systems. Some tach/dwell meters are powered by an internal battery, while others take their power from the car battery in use. The battery powered testers usually require calibration much like an ohmmeter before testing.

Special Test Equipment

A variety of diagnostic tools are available to help troubleshoot and repair computerized engine control systems. The most sophisticated of these devices are the console type engine analyzers that usually occupy a garage service bay, but there are several types of aftermarket electronic testers available that will allow quick circuit tests of the engine control system by plugging directly into a special connector located in the engine compartment or under the dashboard. Several tool and equipment manufacturers offer simple, hand held testers that measure various circuit voltage levels on command to check all system components for proper operation. Although these testers usually cost about $300-$500, consider that the average computer control unit (or ECM) can cost just as much and the money saved by not replacing perfectly good sensors or components in an attempt to correct a problem could justify the purchase price of a special diagnostic tester the first time it's used.

These computerized testers can allow quick and easy test measurements while the engine is operating or while the car is being driven. In addition, the on-board computer memory can be read to access any stored trouble codes; in effect allowing the computer to tell you where it hurts and aid trouble diagnosis by pinpointing exactly which circuit or component is malfunctioning. In the same manner, repairs can be tested to make sure the problem has been corrected. The biggest advantage these special testers have is their relatively easy hookups that minimize or eliminate the chances of making the wrong connections and getting false voltage readings or damaging the computer accidentally.

➡️It should be remembered that these testers check voltage levels in circuits; they don't detect mechanical problems or failed components if the circuit voltage falls within the preprogrammed limits stored in the tester PROM unit. Also, most of the hand held testers are designed to work only on one or two systems made by a specific manufacturer.

A variety of aftermarket testers are available to help diagnose different computerized control systems. Owatonna Tool Company (OTC), for example, markets a device called the OTC Monitor which plugs directly into the Assembly Line Diagnostic Link (ALDL). The OTC tester makes diagnosis a simple matter of pressing the correct buttons and, by changing the internal PROM or inserting a different diagnosis cartridge, it will work on any model from full size to subcompact, over a wide range of years. An adapter is supplied with the tester to allow connection to all types of ALDL links, regardless of the number of pin terminals used. By inserting an updated PROM into the OTC tester, it can be easily updated to diagnose any new modifications of computerized control systems.

Wiring Harnesses

The average automobile contains about 1/2 mile of wiring, with hundreds of individual connections. To protect the many wires from damage and to keep them from becoming a confusing tangle, they are organized into bundles, enclosed in plastic or taped together and called wire harnesses. Different wiring harnesses serve different parts of the vehicle. Individual wires are color coded to help trace them through a harness where sections are hidden from view.

A loose or corroded connection or a replacement wire that is too small for the circuit will add extra resistance and an additional voltage drop to the circuit. A ten percent voltage drop can result in slow or erratic motor operation, for example, even though the circuit is complete. Automotive wiring or circuit conductors can be in any one of three forms:

1. Single strand wire
2. Multi-strand wire
3. Printed circuitry

Single strand wire has a solid metal core and is usually used inside such components as alternators, motors, relays and other devices. Multi-strand wire has a core made of many small strands of wire twisted together into a single conductor. Most of the wiring in an automotive electrical system is made up of multi-strand wire, either as a single conductor or grouped together in a harness. All wiring is color coded on the insulator, either as a solid color or as a colored wire with an identification stripe. A printed circuit is a thin film of copper or other conductor that is printed on an insulator backing. Occasionally, a printed circuit is sandwiched between two sheets of plastic for more protection and flexibility. A complete printed circuit, consisting of conductors, insulating material and connectors for lamps or other components is called a printed circuit board. Printed circuitry is used in place of individual wires or harnesses in places where space is limited, such as behind instrument panels.

WIRE GAUGE

Since computer controlled automotive electrical systems are very sensitive to changes in resistance, the selection of properly sized wires is critical when systems are repaired. The wire gauge number is an expression of the cross section area of the conductor. The most common system for expressing wire size is the American Wire Gauge (AWG) system.

Wire cross section area is measured in circular mils. A mil is $1/_{1000}$ in. (0.001 in.); a circular mil is the area of a circle one mil in diameter. For example, a conductor 1/4 in. diameter is 0.250 in. or 250 mils. The circular mil cross section area of the wire is 250 squared (250^2) or 62,500 circular mils. Imported car models usually use metric wire gauge designations, which is simply the cross section area of the conductor in square millimeters (mm^2).

Gauge numbers are assigned to conductors of various cross section areas. As gauge number increases, area decreases and the conductor becomes smaller. A 5 gauge conductor is smaller than a 1 gauge conductor and a 10 gauge is smaller than a 5 gauge. As the cross section area of a conductor decreases, resistance increases and so does the gauge number. A conductor with a higher gauge number will carry less current than a conductor with a lower gauge number.

➡️ Gauge wire size refers to the size of the conductor, not the size of the complete wire. It is possible to have two wires of the same gauge with different diameters because one may have thicker insulation than the other.

12 volt automotive electrical systems generally use 10, 12, 14, 16 and 18 gauge wire. Main power distribution circuits and larger accessories usually use 10 and 12 gauge wire. Battery cables are usually 4 or 6 gauge, although 1 and 2 gauge wires are occasionally used. Wire length must also be considered when making repairs to a circuit. As conductor length increases, so does resistance. An 18 gauge wire, for example, can carry a 10 amp load for 10 feet without excessive voltage drop; however if a 15 foot wire is required for the same 10 amp load, it must be a 16 gauge wire.

WIRING DIAGRAMS

An electrical schematic shows the electrical current paths when a circuit is operating properly. It is essential to understand how a circuit works before trying to figure out why it doesn't. Schematics break the entire electrical system down into individual circuits and show only one particular circuit. In a schematic, no attempt is made to represent wiring and components as they physically appear on the vehicle; switches and other components are shown as simply as possible. Face views of harness connectors show the cavity or terminal locations in all multi-pin connectors to help locate test points.

If you need to backprobe a connector while it is on the component, the order of the terminals must be mentally reversed. The wire color code can help in this situation, as well as a keyway, lock tab or other reference mark.

WIRING REPAIR

Soldering is a quick, efficient method of joining metals permanently. Everyone who has the occasion to make wiring repairs should know how to solder. Electrical connections that are soldered are far less likely to come apart and will conduct electricity much better than connections that are only "pig-tailed" together. The most popular (and preferred) method of soldering is with an electrical soldering gun. Soldering irons are available in many sizes and wattage ratings. Irons with higher wattage ratings deliver higher temperatures and recover lost heat faster. A small soldering iron rated for no more than 50 watts is recommended, especially on electrical systems where excess heat can damage the components being soldered.

There are three ingredients necessary for successful soldering; proper flux, good solder and sufficient heat. A soldering flux is necessary to clean the metal of tarnish, prepare it for soldering and to enable the solder to spread into tiny crevices. When soldering, always use a resin flux or resin core solder which is non-corrosive and will not attract moisture once the job is finished. Other types of flux (acid core) will leave a residue that will attract moisture and cause the wires to corrode. Tin is a unique metal with a low melting point. In a molten state, it dissolves and alloys easily with many metals. Solder is made by mixing tin with lead. The most common proportions are 40/60, 50/50 and 60/40, with the percentage of tin listed first. Low priced solders usually contain less tin, making them very difficult for a beginner to use because more heat is required to melt the solder. A common solder is 40/60 which is well suited for all-around general use, but 60/40 melts easier, has more tin for a better joint and is preferred for electrical work.

Soldering Techniques

Successful soldering requires that the metals to be joined are heated to a temperature that will melt the solder — usually 360-460°F (182-238°C). Contrary to popular belief, the purpose of the soldering iron is not to melt the solder itself, but to heat the parts being soldered to a temperature high enough to melt the solder when it is touched to the work. Melting flux-cored solder on the soldering iron will usually destroy the effectiveness of the flux.

➡**Soldering tips are made of copper for good heat conductivity, but must be "tinned" regularly for quick transference of heat to the project and to prevent the solder from sticking to the iron. To "tin" the iron, simply heat it and touch the flux-cored solder to the tip; the solder will flow over the hot tip. Wipe the excess off with a clean rag, but be careful as the iron will be hot.**

After some use, the tip may become pitted. If so, simply dress the tip smooth with a smooth file and "tin" the tip again. An old saying holds that "metals well cleaned are half soldered." Flux-cored solder will remove oxides but rust, bits of insulation and oil or grease must be removed with a wire brush or emery cloth. For maximum strength in soldered parts, the joint must start off clean and tight. Weak joints will result in gaps too wide for the solder to bridge.

If a separate soldering flux is used, it should be brushed or swabbed on only those areas that are to be soldered. Most solders contain a core of flux and separate fluxing is unnecessary. Hold the work to be soldered firmly. It is best to solder on a wooden board, because a metal vise will only rob the piece to be soldered of heat and make it difficult to melt the solder. Hold the soldering tip with the broadest face against the work to be soldered. Apply solder under the tip close to the work, using enough solder to give a heavy film between the iron and the piece being soldered, while moving slowly and making sure the solder melts properly. Keep the work level or the solder will run to the lowest part and favor the thicker parts, because these require more heat to melt the solder. If the soldering tip overheats (the solder coating on the face of the tip burns up), it should be retinned. Once the soldering is completed, let the soldered joint stand until cool. Tape and seal all soldered wire splices after the repair has cooled.

Wire Harness and Connectors

The on-board computer (ECM) wire harness electrically connects the control unit to the various solenoids, switches and sensors used by the control system. Most connectors in the engine compartment or otherwise exposed to the elements are protected against moisture and dirt which could create oxidation and deposits on the terminals. This protection is important because of the very low voltage and current levels used by the computer and sensors. All connectors have a lock which secures the male and female terminals together, with a secondary lock holding the seal and terminal into the connector. Both terminal locks must be released when disconnecting ECM connectors.

These special connectors are weather-proof and all repairs require the use of a special terminal and the tool required to service it. This tool is used to remove the pin and sleeve terminals. If removal is attempted with an ordinary pick, there is a good chance that the terminal will be bent or deformed. Unlike standard blade type terminals, these terminals cannot be straightened once they are bent. Make certain that the connectors are properly seated and all of the sealing rings in place when connecting leads. On some models, a hinge-type flap provides a backup or secondary locking feature for the terminals. Most secondary locks are used to improve the connector reliability by retaining the terminals if the small terminal lock tangs are not positioned properly.

Molded-on connectors require complete replacement of the connection. This means splicing a new connector assembly into the harness. All splices in on-board computer systems should be soldered to insure proper contact. Use care when probing the connections or replacing terminals in them as it is possible to short between opposite terminals. If this happens to the wrong terminal pair, it is possible to damage certain components. Always use jumper wires between connectors for circuit checking and never probe through weatherproof seals.

Open circuits are often difficult to locate by sight because corrosion or terminal misalignment are hidden by the connectors. Merely wiggling a connector on a sensor or in the wiring harness may correct the open circuit condition. This should always be considered when an open circuit or a failed sensor is indicated. Intermittent problems may also be caused by oxidized or loose connections. When using a circuit tester for diagnosis, always probe connections from the wire side. Be careful not to damage sealed connectors with test probes.

All wiring harnesses should be replaced with identical parts, using the same gauge wire and connectors. When signal wires are spliced into a harness, use wire with high temperature insulation only. With the low voltage and current levels found in the system, it is important that the best possible connection at all wire splices be made by soldering the splices together. It is seldom necessary to replace a complete harness. If replacement is necessary, pay close attention to insure proper harness routing. Secure the harness with suitable plastic wire clamps to prevent vibrations from causing the harness to wear in spots or contact any hot components.

➡**Weatherproof connectors cannot be replaced with standard connectors. Instructions are provided with replacement connector and terminal packages. Some wire harnesses have mounting indicators (usually pieces of colored tape) to mark where the harness is to be secured.**

In making wiring repairs, it's important that you always replace damaged wires with wires that are the same gauge as the wire being replaced. The heavier the wire, the smaller the gauge number. Wires are color-coded to aid in identification and whenever possible the same color coded wire should be used for replacement. A wire stripping and crimping tool is necessary to install solderless terminal connectors. Test all crimps by pulling on the wires; it should not be possible to pull the wires out of a good crimp.

Wires which are open, exposed or otherwise damaged are repaired by simple splicing. Where possible, if the wiring harness is accessible and the damaged place in the wire can be located, it is best to open the harness and check for all possible damage. In an inaccessible harness, the wire must be bypassed with a new insert, usually taped to the outside of the old harness.

When replacing fusible links, be sure to use fusible link wire, NOT ordinary automotive wire. Make sure the fusible segment is of the same gauge and construction as the one being replaced and double the stripped end when crimping the terminal connector for a good contact. The melted (open) fusible link segment of the wiring harness should be cut off as close to the harness as possible, then a new segment spliced in as described. In the case of a damaged fusible link that feeds two harness wires, the harness connections should be replaced with two fusible link wires so that each circuit will have its own separate protection.

➡**Most of the problems caused in the wiring harness are due to bad ground connections. Always check all vehicle ground connections for corrosion or looseness before performing any power feed checks to eliminate the chance of a bad ground affecting the circuit.**

Repairing Hard Shell Connectors

Unlike molded connectors, the terminal contacts in hard shell connectors can be replaced. Weatherproof hard-shell connectors with the leads molded into the shell have non-replaceable terminal ends. Replacement usually involves the use of a special terminal removal tool to depress the locking tangs (barbs) on the connector terminal and allow the connector to be removed from the rear of the shell. The connector shell should be replaced if it shows any evidence of burning, melting, cracks, or breaks. Replace individual terminals that are burnt, corroded, distorted or loose.

➡**The insulation crimp must be tight to prevent the insulation from sliding back on the wire when the wire is pulled. The insulation must be visibly compressed under the crimp tabs, and the ends of the crimp should be turned in for a firm grip on the insulation.**

The wire crimp must be made with all wire strands inside the crimp. The terminal must be fully compressed on the wire strands with the ends of the crimp tabs turned in to make a firm grip on the wire. Check all connections with an ohmmeter to insure a good contact. There should be no measurable resistance between the wire and the terminal when connected.

Mechanical Test Equipment

VACUUM GAUGE

Most gauges are graduated in inches of mercury (in. Hg), although a device called a manometer reads vacuum in inches of water (in. H_2O). The normal vacuum reading usually varies between 18 and 22 in. Hg at sea level. To test engine vacuum, the gauge must be connected to a source of manifold vacuum. Many engines have a plug in the intake manifold which can be removed and replaced with an adapter fitting. Connect the vacuum gauge to the fitting with a suitable rubber hose or, if no manifold plug is available, connect the vacuum gauge to any device using manifold vacuum, such as EGR valves, etc. The vacuum gauge can be used to determine if enough vacuum is reaching a component to allow its actuation.

HAND VACUUM PUMP

Small, hand-held vacuum pumps come in a variety of designs. Most have a built-in vacuum gauge and allow the component to be tested without removing it from the vehicle. Operate the pump lever or plunger to apply the correct amount of vacuum required for the test specified in the diagnosis routines. The level of vacuum in inches of Mercury (in. Hg) is indicated on the pump gauge. For some testing, an additional vacuum gauge may be necessary.

Intake manifold vacuum is used to operate various systems and devices on late model vehicles. To correctly diagnose and solve problems in vacuum control systems, a vacuum source is necessary for testing. In some cases, vacuum can be taken from the intake manifold when the engine is running, but vacuum is normally provided by a hand vacuum pump. These hand vacuum pumps have a built-in vacuum gauge that allow testing while the device is still attached to the component. For some tests, an additional vacuum gauge may be necessary.

HEATING AND AIR CONDITIONING

Blower Motor

REMOVAL & INSTALLATION

▶ **See Figures 1, 2, 3, 4, 5 and 6**

1964-67

1. Disconnect the negative battery cable.
2. Unclip the hoses from the fender skirt.
3. Disengage the electrical feed from the motor.
4. Turn the front wheels to the extreme right.
5. Remove the right front fender skirt bolts and allow the skirt to drop, resting it on top of the tire. It may be wedged away from the fender lower flange with a block of wood to provide better access to the bolts.
6. Remove the screws attaching the blower motor mounting plate to the air inlet housing.
7. Remove the screws attaching the blower motor to the mounting plate.
8. Remove the clip attaching the cage to the shaft and remove the blower motor.

To install:
9. Position the blower motor in the vehicle, then install the attaching clip to the cage and shaft
10. Install and tighten the screws attaching the motor to the mounting plate, then install and tighten the screws attaching the mounting plate to the inlet housing.
11. Remove the wooden block, then reposition the fender skirt and secure using the retaining bolts.
12. Engage the motor electrical feed, then clip the hoses back into position in the fender skirt.
13. Connect the negative battery cable and check for proper motor operation.

1968-72

1. Disconnect the negative battery cable.
2. Disconnect the hoses and wiring from the fender skirt.
3. Remove all fender skirt attaching bolts except those attaching the skirt to the radiator support.
4. Pull out, then down, on the skirt. Place a block between the skirt and the fender.
5. Remove the blower-to-case attaching screw, then carefully remove the blower assembly.
6. If necessary, remove the blower wheel retaining nut, then separate the motor and the wheel.

To install:
7. If removed, engage the motor and the wheel, then secure using the retaining nut.
8. Install the motor assembly and install the attaching screw. The open end of the blower should be away from the motor.
9. Remove the block, then reposition and secure the fender skirt.
10. Connect the hoses and wiring to the fender skirt.
11. Connect the negative battery cable, then check for proper motor operation.

1973 and Later

1. Disconnect the negative battery cable.
2. Disconnect the motor lead wire.

➡**If equipped with A/C, disconnect the cooling tube.**

3. If equipped, remove the ground wire from the blower motor housing.
4. Remove the blower-to-case screws, then carefully withdraw the blower.
5. If necessary, remove the retaining nut to separate the motor and wheel.

To install:
6. If removed, install the wheel to the motor and secure using the retaining nut.
7. Insert the blower motor into the module and secure using the case screws. If applicable, be sure to position the ground wire under the appropriate case screw before tightening.
8. If equipped with A/C, connect the cooling tube.
9. Connect the motor lead wire.
10. Connect the negative battery cable, then check for proper motor operation.

Heater Core

REMOVAL & INSTALLATION

▶ **See Figures 7 and 8**

1964-67 Except Air Conditioned Cars

1. Disconnect the negative battery cable, then drain the radiator.

✳✳CAUTION

When draining the coolant, keep in mind that cats and dogs are attracted by the ethylene glycol antifreeze, and are quite likely to drink any that is left in an uncovered container or in puddles on the ground. This will prove fatal in sufficient quantity. Always drain the coolant into a sealable container. Coolant should be reused unless it is contaminated or several years old.

2. Remove the heater hoses from the core. The top hose connects to the water pump and the lower hose goes to the thermostat housing.
3. Remove the cables and all electrical connections from the heater and defroster assembly.
4. Remove the nuts from the core case studs located on the firewall.
5. From inside the car, remove the case-to-firewall mounting screws and also the heater and defroster assembly.
6. Remove the retaining springs and core.

To install:
7. Install the core and retaining spring, making sure the core-to-case sealer is in good shape.

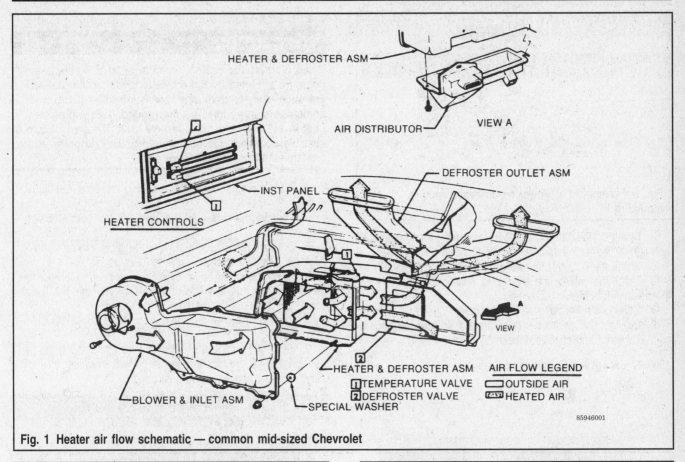

Fig. 1 Heater air flow schematic — common mid-sized Chevrolet

Fig. 2 Disconnect the blower motor wiring harness

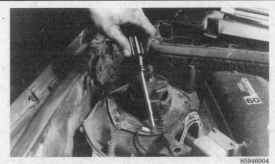

Fig. 4 Disconnect any ground wires from the motor housing, if present

Fig. 3 If equipped, disconnect any hoses from the blower motor housing

Fig. 5 Lift the blower motor assembly from the housing

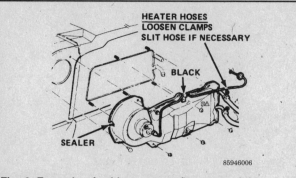

Fig. 6 Example of a blower motor/heater module mounting

8. Install the heater and defroster assembly, then install and tighten the case-to-firewall mounting screws.

9. Install the nuts to the core case studs on the firewall.

10. Install the cables and engage all electrical connectors to the heater and defroster assembly.

11. Engage the heater hoses to the core.

12. Connect the negative battery cable, then refill the engine cooling system and check for leaks.

1968-77 Except Air Conditioned Cars

1. Disconnect the negative battery cable.

2. Drain the radiator.

✳✳CAUTION

When draining the coolant, keep in mind that cats and dogs are attracted by the ethylene glycol antifreeze, and are quite likely to drink any that is left in an uncovered container or in puddles on the ground. This will prove fatal in sufficient quantity. Always drain the coolant into a sealable container. Coolant should be reused unless it is contaminated or several years old.

3. Disconnect the heater hoses. Plug the core inlet and outlet.

4. Remove the nuts from the air distributor duct studs on the firewall.

5. On post-1969 models remove the glove box and radio, then the defroster duct-to-distributor duct screw.

6. Pull the defroster duct out of the way, and then pull the distributor duct from the firewall mounting. Remove the resistor wires. Lay the duct on the floor.

7. Remove the core assembly from the distributor duct.

To install:

8. Install the core assembly to the distributor duct, the reposition and secure the duct to the firewall mounting. If necessary, use new sealer on the duct flange.

9. On post-1969 models, install the defroster duct-to-distributor duct screw, then install the glove box and radio.

10. Install the nuts to the air distributor duct studs on the firewall.

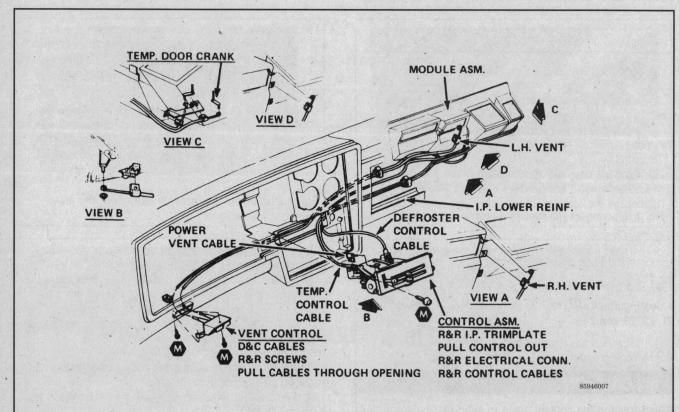

Fig. 7 Example of a heater control cable assembly — 1978 shown

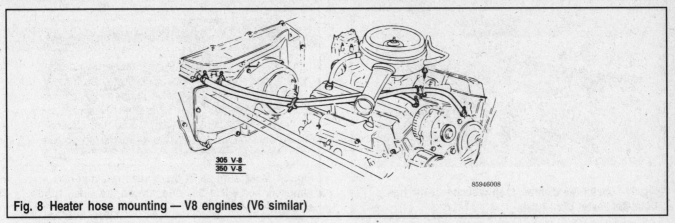

Fig. 8 Heater hose mounting — V8 engines (V6 similar)

11. Remove the plugs, then connect the heater hoses to the core tubes.

12. Connect the negative battery cable, then properly refill the engine cooling system and check for leaks.

1978 and Later Without A/C

1. Disconnect the negative battery cable and drain the cooling system.

✳✳CAUTION

When draining the coolant, keep in mind that cats and dogs are attracted by the ethylene glycol antifreeze, and are quite likely to drink any that is left in an uncovered container or in puddles on the ground. This will prove fatal in sufficient quantity. Always drain the coolant into a sealable container. Coolant should be reused unless it is contaminated or several years old.

2. Disconnect and plug the heater hoses from the core tubes.

3. Disengage the electrical connectors from the module case.

4. Unbolt and remove the module's front cover and lift out the core.

To install:

5. Install the core and apply sealant to the module cover, then install the cover and secure.

6. Engage the electrical connectors to the module case.

7. Remove the plugs, then connect the heater hoses to the core tubes.

8. Connect the negative battery cable, then refill the engine cooling system and check for leaks.

1967 and Later With A/C

▶ See Figures 9, 10, 11, 12, 13, 14, 15, 16, 17, 18, 19, 20, 21, 22, 23 and 24

1. Disconnect the negative battery cable, then drain the engine cooling system to a level below heater core.

✳✳CAUTION

When draining the coolant, keep in mind that cats and dogs are attracted by the ethylene glycol antifreeze, and are quite likely to drink any that is left in an uncovered

container or in puddles on the ground. This will prove fatal in sufficient quantity. Always drain the coolant into a sealable container. Coolant should be reused unless it is contaminated or several years old.

2. Disconnect and plug the heater hoses at the core tubes. Plugging the hoses will help prevent excessive coolant leakage.

3. Remove the module's rubber seal and screen. If necessary, disconnect the washer nozzle from the cowl.

4. If necessary, remove the right windshield wiper arm.

5. As applicable, remove or disengage, the diagnostic connector, high blower relay, thermostatic switch, ground strap and/or electrical connectors from the heater core module cover.

6. Loosen the retainers and remove the module's top cover. The cover is sealed to the module and this seal must be broken before the cover can be removed. Be absolutely sure that all cover fasteners are removed before attempting to break the seal or cover damage will result. Take your time and be careful not to force and crack or otherwise damage the cover.

➡On many late model vehicles, cover interference with the vehicle's bulkhead will may removal difficult. On these vehicles it will be necessary to loosen the windshield's chromed lower trim plate for the necessary clearance.

7. With the top cover removed, loosen or unclip the core retainer, then carefully lift the core from the vehicle.

To install:

8. Thoroughly clean the mating surfaces of the cover and the module of all old sealer.

9. Install the heater core to the module and secure the retaining bracket.

10. Apply a coating of sealant to the cover, then install the cover and tighten the fasteners. If the windshield trim plate was loosened for clearance, reposition and secure it.

11. Engage the electrical connectors and components to the module cover, as applicable.

12. If removed, install the right wiper arm.

13. Install the module screen and rubber seal. If removed, install the washer nozzle to the cowl.

14. Remove the plugs and reconnect the heater hoses to the core tubes.

15. Connect the negative battery cable, then properly refill the engine cooling system and check for leaks.

Fig. 9 Loosen the clamps, then disconnect the hoses from the heater core tubes

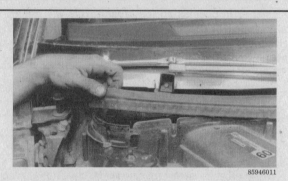
Fig. 10 Remove the rubber seal from the module top cover

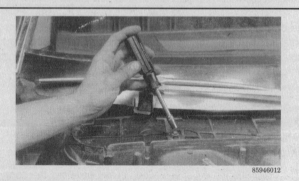
Fig. 11 Loosen and remove the module cowl screen retainers

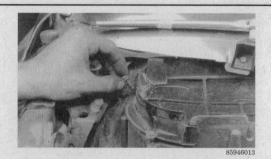
Fig. 12 Make sure all of the screen retainers are removed, some like this one, are on the side of the screen

Fig. 13 If necessary, remove the retainer and reposition the washer nozzle

Fig. 14 Some retaining bolts may be partially hidden, check under the wiper arm

Control Head

REMOVAL & INSTALLATION

▶ **See Figures 25 and 26**

1. Disconnect the negative battery cable.
2. As equipped, remove the radio knobs and/or the clock set knob.
3. Remove the instrument bezel retaining screws.
4. Pull the bezel out to disconnect the rear defogger switch, remote mirror and/or cigarette lighter, as equipped.

5. If necessary, remove the instrument panel retaining screws.
6. Remove the control head-to-dash screws and pull the head out for access.
7. Disengage the electrical connectors and/or control cable(s) (as equipped), then remove the control head from the vehicle.

To install:
8. Hold the control head just in front of the instrument panel, then engage the connectors and/or control cable(s).
9. Install the control head to the dash, then secure using the retaining screws.
10. If removed, install the instrument panel retaining screws.
11. Hold the bezel in front of the dash and engage any necessary wiring.

Fig. 15 With all of the fasteners removed, carefully lift the screen from the top of the module

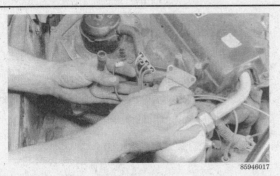

Fig. 16 Disengage all electrical wiring and components from the top of the module

Fig. 17 Loosen and remove the module top cover retaining bolts

Fig. 18 As with the cowl screen, the top cover bolts may be difficult to find

Fig. 19 If the windshield's chrome trimplate interferes with cover removal, it will have to be loosened or removed for additional clearance

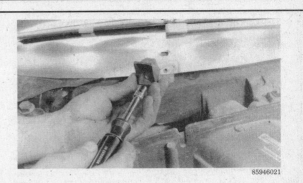

Fig. 20 Remove the bolt and bracket from the passenger side of the trim plate

12. Install the bezel to the dash and secure using the retaining screws.
13. Install the clock set knob and/or radio knobs, as applicable.
14. Connect the negative battery cable.

Compressor

For compressor removal and installation procedures, please refer to Section 3 of this manual. Also, be sure to fully read the Air Conditioning service procedures/precautions in Section 1 of this manual before proceeding.

Condenser

For condenser removal and installation procedures, please refer to Section 3 of this manual. Also, be sure to fully read the Air Conditioning service procedures/precautions in Section 1 of this manual before proceeding.

Fig. 21 With the bolt and bracket removed, the trim plate support may be removed for clearance

Fig. 22 Once all of the bolts are removed, break the seal by lifting the top cover from the module

Fig. 23 Remove the core retaining bracket; in this case by loosening the retaining bolt

Fig. 24 Lift the heater core from the module, but remember it still may contain a fair amount of coolant

Fig. 25 Remove the instrument bezel retaining screws

Fig. 26 Carefully pull the bezel forward for access to any electrical connector mounted behind it

Evaporator Core

REMOVAL & INSTALLATION

✳✳CAUTION

Please refer to Section 1 before discharging the compressor or disconnecting air conditioning lines. Damage to the air conditioning system or personal injury could result. Consult your local laws concerning refrigerant discharge and recycling. In many areas it may be illegal for anyone but a certified technician to service the A/C system. Always use an approved recovery station when discharging the air conditioning.

1964-70

1. Properly discharge and recover the refrigerant in the A/C system using a suitable recovery station.
2. Remove the right fender skirt and hood hinge.
3. Disconnect the high pressure line at the condenser and the suction throttling valve to the compressor line at the suction throttling valve. Cover all lines immediately to prevent system contamination and subsequent damage.
4. Take out the three screws attaching the duct assembly to the evaporator housing and the blower assembly.

5. Take out the nine bolts holding the evaporator assembly to the cowl and lift out the assembly.

6. The core can be removed by removing the screws attaching the core to the case and lifting the core from the case.

7. After installing the evaporator core and tightening the refrigerant lines, evacuate, leak test and charge the system.

1971-73

➡Core removal and installation may be made without removing the entire evaporator assembly.

1. Properly discharge and recover the refrigerant in the A/C system using a suitable recovery station.

2. Disconnect the negative battery cable, then remove the carburetor air cleaner assembly.

3. Remove the expansion valve bulb from the core outlet line and the core outlet line at the POA valve. Disconnect the core outlet line at the expansion valve.

4. Remove the clamp screw and move the expansion valve and line out of the way.

5. Disconnect all wires and hoses attached the the evaporator assembly.

6. Remove the nuts and screws from the evaporator cover, and carefully pull the cover upward and outward.

7. Remove the core retaining screws and remove the core.

To install:

8. Install the core and tighten the retaining screws.

9. Install the cover, then secure using the nuts and screws.

10. Connect all wires and hoses to the evaporator assembly.

11. Reposition the expansion valve and line, then tighten the clamp screw.

12. Connect the core outlet line to the expansion valve, then install the expansion valve bulb to the core outlet line and the the core outlet line to the POA valve.

13. Install the carburetor air cleaner assembly, then connect the negative battery cable.

14. After checking that all the refrigerant lines are properly tightened, evacuate, leak test and charge the system.

1974-77

➡Core removal and installation may be made without removing the entire evaporator assembly.

1. Properly discharge and recover the refrigerant in the A/C system using a suitable recovery station.

2. Disconnect the negative battery cable.

3. Remove the carburetor air cleaner assembly, AIR pipe at the manifold, PCV, carburetor heat stove and engine thermal switch, where necessary.

4. Disconnect the oil bleed and the core inlet and outlet lines at the VIR or accumulator assembly.

5. Remove the bracket screw and move the VIR or accumulator assembly out of the way.

6. Disconnect the vacuum lines and remove the vacuum tank and bracket.

7. Disconnect all wires and hoses attached to the evaporator case.

8. Remove the nuts securing the evaporator cover to the dash panel and the screws attaching the cover to the evaporator.

9. Remove the cover upward and outward.

10. Remove the core.

To install:

11. Install the core, then install the core cover and secure using the retaining nuts.

12. Connect the wires and hoses to the evaporator case, then install the vacuum tank and bracket. Connect the vacuum lines.

13. Reposition the VIR or accumulator assembly and install the bracket screw.

14. Connect the oil bleed and the core inlet/outlet lines at the VIR or accumulator assembly.

15. Where removed, install the carburetor heat stove, PCV, AIR pipe to the manifold and the air cleaner assembly.

16. Connect the negative battery cable.

17. After checking that all the refrigerant lines are properly tightened, evacuate, leak test and charge the system.

1978-88

1. Properly discharge and recover the refrigerant in the A/C system using a suitable recovery station.

2. Disconnect the negative battery cable.

3. Remove the module's rubber seal and screen. If necessary, disconnect the washer nozzle from the cowl.

4. If necessary, remove the right windshield wiper arm.

5. As applicable, remove or disengage, the diagnostic connector, high blower relay, thermostatic switch, ground strap and/or electrical connectors from the heater core module cover.

6. Loosen the retainers and remove the module's top cover. The cover is sealed to the module and this seal must be broken before the cover can be removed. Be absolutely sure that all cover fasteners are removed before attempting to break the seal or cover damage will result. Take your time and be careful not to force and crack or otherwise damage the cover.

➡On many late model vehicles, cover interference with the vehicle's bulkhead will may removal difficult. On these vehicles it will be necessary to loosen the windshield's chromed lower trim plate for the necessary clearance.

7. Remove the accumulator bracket screws.

8. Disconnect and tape the refrigerant lines at the accumulator and liquid line.

9. Remove the evaporator core.

To install:

10. Thoroughly clean the mating surfaces of the cover and the module of all old sealer.

11. Install the evaporator core, then remove the tap and connect the refrigerant lines at the accumulator and liquid line.

➡When connecting the refrigerant lines, use new O-rings dipped in clean refrigerant oil.

12. Install the accumulator bracket screws.

13. Apply a coating of sealant to the cover, then install the cover and tighten the fasteners. If the windshield trim plate was loosened for clearance, reposition and secure it.

14. Engage the electrical connectors and components to the module cover, as applicable.

15. If removed, install the right wiper arm.

16. Install the module screen and rubber seal. If removed, install the washer nozzle to the cowl.

17. Connect the negative battery cable.

18. After checking that all the refrigerant lines are properly tightened, evacuate, leak test and charge the system.

Expansion Valve

An expansion valve is used on most early air conditioning systems which were installed on Chevrolet mid-sized vehicles by the factory or dealer. The expansion valve is used to regulate the flow of refrigerant to the evaporator, so is found inline between the condenser and the evaporator. It is designed to ensure that the evaporator remains as full of liquid refrigerant, as possible without allowing any liquid to pass into the compressor suction line. An expansion valve was used on these vehicles until the mid-1970's when an expansion tube (orifice) took the valve's place.

REMOVAL & INSTALLATION

❊❊CAUTION

Please refer to Section 1 before discharging the compressor or disconnecting air conditioning lines. Damage to the air conditioning system or personal injury could result. Consult your local laws concerning refrigerant discharge and recycling. In many areas it may be illegal for anyone but a certified technician to service the A/C system. Always use an approved recovery station when discharging the air conditioning.

1. Properly discharge and recover the refrigerant in the A/C system using a suitable recovery station.
2. Disconnect the negative battery cable.
3. Remove the expansion valve power element bulb from the lower pressure line.
4. Remove the equalizing line from the POA valve.
5. Remove the low and high pressure lines from the valve in that order.

➡Immediately cover all open lines to prevent system contamination and damage.

6. Remove the screw and bracket attaching the expansion valve to the case, then remove the valve from the vehicle.
To install:
7. Attach the expansion valve to the case.
8. Connect the low and high pressure lines to the valve.
9. Connect the equalizing line to the POA valve.
10. Install the power element bulb on the lower pressure line. Carefully replace the insulation.
11. Connect the negative battery cable.
12. After checking that all the refrigerant lines are properly tightened, evacuate, leak test and charge the system.

Expansion Tube (Orifice)

On later models (mid-1970's and later) covered by this manual, the expansion valve has been replaced by an expansion tube (orifice). The orifice performs the same function of metering the liquid refrigerant that the expansion valve was designed for. The orifice is usually found in the evaporator inlet, but is relocated on some models to the connection at the condenser.

REMOVAL & INSTALLATION

❊❊CAUTION

Please refer to Section 1 before discharging the compressor or disconnecting air conditioning lines. Damage to the air conditioning system or personal injury could result. Consult your local laws concerning refrigerant discharge and recycling. In many areas it may be illegal for anyone but a certified technician to service the A/C system. Always use an approved recovery station when discharging the air conditioning.

1. Properly discharge and recover the refrigerant in the A/C system using a suitable recovery station.
2. Disconnect the negative battery cable.

➡On some models, the orifice tube has been relocated from the inlet of the evaporator to the connection at the condenser. The relocated orifice tube can usually be seen by looking through the driver's side grille opening.

3. Loosen the nut holding the liquid line to the evaporator inlet pipe. Remove the tube using needle nose pliers
4. If the tube is broken or difficult to remove:
   a. Using a heat gun, apply heat approximately 1/4 in. from the inlet pipe dimples.

➡If a pressure switch is located near the orifice, remove it before applying heat so as to prevent damaging the circuit.

   b. Using a twisting motion, loosen the orifice tube and remove it from the holder.
   c. Make sure the inside of the evaporator pipe or condenser is clean and free of debris.
   To install:
5. Lubricate the new orifice tube and O-ring using clean refrigeration oil.
6. Install the orifice tube. If installing the tube to an evaporator inlet pipe, be sure to position it with the shorter screen end inserted first.
7. Install the liquid line to the evaporator inlet pipe.
8. Connect the negative battery cable.
9. After checking that all the refrigerant lines are properly tightened, evacuate, leak test and charge the system.

Receiver-Dehydrator

REMOVAL & INSTALLATION

An receiver-dehydrator is used on most early air conditioning systems which were installed on Chevrolet mid-sized vehicles by the factory or dealer. The receiver-dehydrator is a metal cylinder normally found at the outlet of the condenser. It serves as a storage space for liquid refrigerant (thus ensuring a steady flow to the evaporator) and as a moisture eliminator for the system. These units have a great thirst for moisture and should ALWAYS be sealed to the atmosphere. Removal or installation should take place as quickly as possible in order to minimize exposure of the unit to the atmosphere. An expansion valve was used on these vehicles until the mid-1970's when an Accumulator/Drier took the receiver's place.

✳✳CAUTION

Please refer to Section 1 before discharging the compressor or disconnecting air conditioning lines. Damage to the air conditioning system or personal injury could result. Consult your local laws concerning refrigerant discharge and recycling. In many areas it may be illegal for anyone but a certified technician to service the A/C system. Always use an approved recovery station when discharging the air conditioning.

1. Properly discharge and recover the refrigerant in the A/C system using a suitable recovery station.
2. Disconnect the negative battery cable. On some early models, such as the 1968 Chevelle, it may be necessary to completely remove the battery for access.
3. Disconnect the inlet and outlet lines from the unit. Immediately cover all openings to prevent system contamination.
4. Remove the bracket attaching screws, then remove the receiver-dehydrator assembly from the vehicle.
   To install:
5. Add 1 oz. of fresh refrigerant oil to the new receiver-dehydrator unit, then position the unit in the vehicle.
6. Install the bracket retaining screws to secure the unit in position.
7. Lubricate new O-rings with fresh refrigerant oil, then remove the plugs and quickly connect both the inlet and outlet lines.
8. Connect the negative battery cable.
9. After checking that all the refrigerant lines are properly tightened, evacuate, leak test and charge the system.

Accumulator/Drier

On later models (mid-1970's and later) covered by this manual, the receiver-dehydrator has been replaced by an accumulator/drier. The accumulator performs much in the same way as did the receiver unit on earlier vehicles. The accumulator serves as a storage unit for refrigerant, receiving vapors and liquid from the evaporator and is also used to purge the system of moisture like the receiver. The difference comes in the accumulator's location. It is normally found right after the evaporator in the refrigerant system, instead of before the evaporator (as with receiver-dehydrators). Like with the receiver units, the accumulator/driers have a great thirst for moisture and should ALWAYS be sealed to the atmosphere. Removal or installation should take place as quickly as possible in order to minimize exposure of the unit to the atmosphere.

REMOVAL & INSTALLATION

✳✳CAUTION

Please refer to Section 1 before discharging the compressor or disconnecting air conditioning lines. Damage to the air conditioning system or personal injury could result.

Consult your local laws concerning refrigerant discharge and recycling. In many areas it may be illegal for anyone but a certified technician to service the A/C system. Always use an approved recovery station when discharging the air conditioning.

1. Properly discharge and recover the refrigerant in the A/C system using a suitable recovery station.
2. Disconnect the negative battery cable.
3. Disconnect the accumulator inlet and outlet lines, then immediately cap all openings to prevent system contamination.
4. If equipped, disengage the pressure cycling switch connection, then remove the switch.
5. Remove the accumulator bracket bolts, then remove the accumulator assembly.
   To install:
6. Add the appropriate amount of refrigerant oil to the new accumulator assembly.
7. Position the accumulator in the vehicle and secure using the bracket bolts.
8. If equipped, install the pressure cycling switch and engage the connector.
9. Lubricate the new O-rings with fresh refrigerant oil, then uncap the openings and install the lines.
10. Connect the negative battery cable.
11. After checking that all the refrigerant lines are properly tightened, evacuate, leak test and charge the system.

Refrigerant Lines

REMOVAL & INSTALLATION

1. Properly discharge and recover the refrigerant in the A/C system using a suitable recovery station.
2. Disconnect the negative battery cable.

➡**For some vehicles it may be necessary to remove the radiator grille for access to the lines.**

3. Remove the banjo bolt or loosen the fitting, depending on the application, then disconnect the line at either end. Immediately plug all openings in the system to prevent system contamination and damage.
4. Remove any clips attaching the pipe to the vehicle, then remove the pipe assembly.
   To install:
5. Position the pipe in the vehicle, then remove the plug from 1 end and secure the fitting right away to minimize atmospheric exposure. Remove the plug from the other end and secure that fitting. Make sure the fittings or banjo bolts are properly tightened.
6. Install any clips attaching the pipe.
7. If removed install the radiator grille.
8. Connect the negative battery cable.
9. After checking that all the refrigerant lines are properly tightened, evacuate, leak test and charge the system.

CRUISE CONTROL

Cruise Control Actuator Switch

▶ See Figure 27

REMOVAL & INSTALLATION

The cruise control actuator switch on most Chevrolet mid-sized vehicles with factory or dealer installed systems is located on the steering column. Please refer to Section 8 of this manual for removal and installation procedures.

Brake/Clutch Release Switch

▶ See Figure 28

All factory or dealer installed cruise control systems for these vehicles are equipped with either a brake or clutch release switch. The purpose of the switch is to deactivate the system when the driver begins to depress the pedal. Most of these switches found on earlier models are vacuum break switches which will therefore have a vacuum line attached to the rear of the switch. On later vehicles, many of the switches are electric and may even be combined with other switches (such as the brake light switch).

The switches are mounted using one of two possible methods. Some earlier switches are mounted using a locknut. Later switches are normally mounted using an interference clip which holds ribs on the switches neck.

REMOVAL & INSTALLATION

1. If equipped with an electric switch, disconnect the negative battery cable.
2. Disengage the vacuum line or the electrical connector(s) from the switch.
3. For locknut mounted switches, loosen and remove the locknut, then withdraw the switch from the pedal bracket.
4. For interference fit switches, grasp the switch and withdraw it from the clip. If necessary the clip can be removed from the pedal bracket as well. Some clips are designed with lock tangs and may be pivoted in order to pull them from the bracket. Other clips are also an interference fit and must be squeezed and withdrawn.

To install:

5. Install the switch and locknut or clip, as applicable to the pedal bracket.
6. Adjust the switch plunger height to assure proper operation.
7. Engage the vacuum line or electrical connector(s) to the switch.
8. If removed, connect the negative battery cable.
9. Verify proper switch operation.

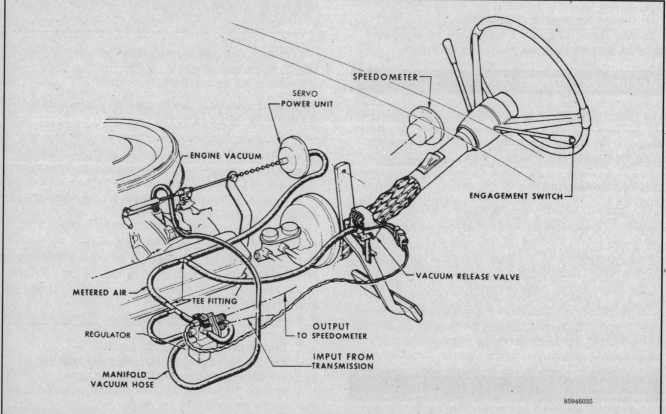

SPEEDOMETER

SERVO POWER UNIT

ENGINE VACUUM

ENGAGEMENT SWITCH

VACUUM RELEASE VALVE

METERED AIR

TEE FITTING

REGULATOR

OUTPUT TO SPEEDOMETER

IMPUT FROM TRANSMISSION

MANIFOLD VACUUM HOSE

85946035

Fig. 27 Example of a common cruise control system — mid-sized Chevrolet

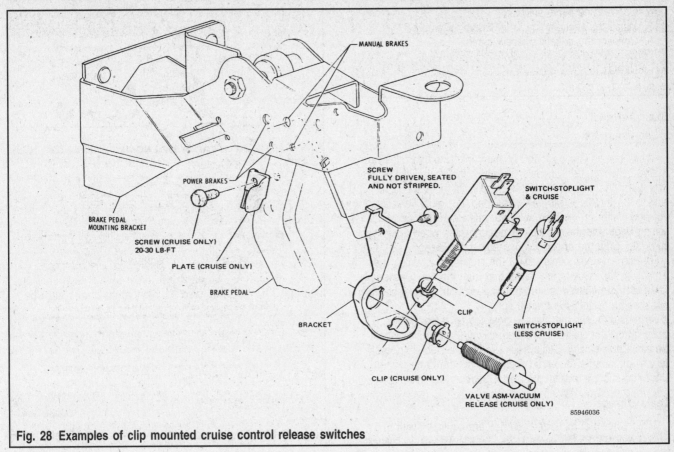

MANUAL BRAKES

SCREW
FULLY DRIVEN, SEATED
AND NOT STRIPPED.

SWITCH-STOPLIGHT
& CRUISE

POWER BRAKES

BRAKE PEDAL
MOUNTING BRACKET

SCREW (CRUISE ONLY)
20-30 LB-FT

PLATE (CRUISE ONLY)

BRAKE PEDAL

BRACKET

CLIP

SWITCH-STOPLIGHT
(LESS CRUISE)

CLIP (CRUISE ONLY)

VALVE ASM-VACUUM
RELEASE (CRUISE ONLY)

85946036

Fig. 28 Examples of clip mounted cruise control release switches

ADJUSTMENT

Locknut Mounted Switches

Locknut mounted switches are adjusted by correctly position-ing the switch in the pedal bracket, then holding the switch in position while tightening the locknut. To position the switch, insert it into the pedal bracket so the plunger is fully de-pressed when the pedal is released, but is at full travel (all of the way out) once the pedal is depressed $\frac{1}{4}$ in. (6.35mm) for electric switches or $\frac{5}{16}$ in. (7.94mm) for vacuum switches.

Clip Mounted Switches

Clip mounted switches are automatically adjusted during in-stallation. The clip holds the switch in position by the raised ribs located on the switche's neck. In order to adjust the switch, first fully seat it into the clip and against the pedal bracket. Grasp the pedal and pull it fully back against the stop. While pulling the pedal backwards, a clicking sound should be heard and the switch is pushed backwards in the clip unit it is in the proper position. Make sure the switch plunger is seated when the pedal is released and that the plunger fully extends as the pedal is depressed. Check the switch operation and adjust again, if necessary.

Vacuum Servo

Most factory or dealer installed cruise control systems for these vehicles utilize a vacuum servo to rotate the throttle plate and hold engine speed. The servo is connected to the throttle plate by linkage, either a chain, rod or cable.

TESTING

Because the vacuum servo is designed to modulate the throttle based on a vacuum signal, the diaphragm must be intact and able to hold vacuum in order to operation properly.

1. Disconnect the vacuum hose from the servo assembly.
2. Use a hand-held vacuum pump to apply 14 inches of vacuum to the servo. Watch the pump gauge for 1 minute and make sure that no more than 5 inches of vacuum leaks down.
3. If no vacuum pump is available, push the diaphragm in by hand, then hold your finger tightly over the vacuum nipple and release the diaphragm. If the diaphragm is intake, it should hold in the pushed in position.
4. Repair or replace any diaphragm which is defective or cannot hold vacuum

REMOVAL & INSTALLATION

1. Disconnect the negative battery cable.
2. Remove the vacuum line from the servo assembly.
3. Disconnect the servo linkage.
4. Remove the servo and bracket assembly retaining bolts, then remove the servo from the vehicle.
   To install:
5. Install the servo and bracket assembly, then secure us-ing the retaining bolts.

6. Connect the servo linkage.

7. Install the vacuum line to the servo assembly.

8. Connect the negative battery cable.

ADJUSTMENT

Chain Linkage

▶ See Figure 29

Chain linkage can be found on most mid-sized vehicles up to and including 1983 models. To adjust the chain linkage, first fully warm the engine, then check and adjust idle speed to assure the throttle is properly positioned. For most vehicles equipped with an idle stop solenoid, make sure the air conditioning is off and the solenoid is disconnected when adjusting curb idle. Shut the engine off and adjust the linkage.

For some older models, adjust the chain by loosening the jamnut on the back of the servo, then turn the servo assembly to adjust. The chain should be positioned with minimal slack, but should not hold the throttle open.

On most models, the chain is adjusted by removing the chain from the connector and the making it as tight as possible while still leaving a little slack. Again, the slack is necessary to make sure the chain does not hold the throttle open. Once the chain is adjusted, install it back to the connector.

Cable Linkage

Some Chevrolet mid-sized vehicles are equipped with a cable linkage from the servo to the throttle. The cable linkage is usually adjusted either by jamnuts or by a servo blade which contains various adjustment holes. In either case, once the engine is fully warmed, position the cable so it is tight, with little slack, but NOT holding the throttle open. For vehicles equipped with the servo blade, if the desired hole seems to open the throttle, take the next hole on the blade in order to leave the required slack.

Rod Linkage

1. Start and warm the engine to normal operating temperature.

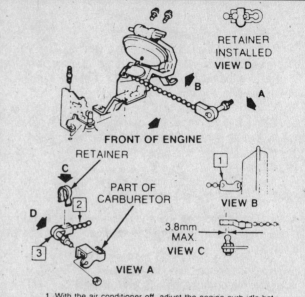

1. With the air conditioner off, adjust the engine curb idle hot speed to 500 rpm with the idle solenoid disconnected. Turn the engine off.

2. Check the bead chain slack by unsnapping the swivel from the ball stud and holding the chain taut at the ball stud. The center of the swivel should extend ⅛ inch beyond the center of the ball stud.

3. Adjust the bead chain slack, as required, by removing the retainer from the swivel and chain assembly.

4. Position the chain into the swivel cavities which permit the chain to have slight slack. Position the retainer over the swivel and the chain assembly.

85946037

Fig. 29 Chain linkage adjustment — late model vehicles

2. Make sure the idle speed is properly adjusted, then shut the engine **OFF**.

3. For diesel engines, adjust the length of the rod to achieve minimum slack with the injection pump on the slow idle screw.

4. For gasoline engines, be sure the idle speed motor is retracted and the throttle is fully closed. Install the rod on the throttle stud at the large end of the slot, then adjust the length so the stud is at the end of the slot and the rod is aligned with the hole in the servo. Install the retainer, insert the rod end of through the holes and snap the retainer into place.

ENTERTAINMENT SYSTEMS

Radio

REMOVAL & INSTALLATION

▶ See Figures 30, 31, 32, 33, 34, 35 and 36

1964-72

1. Disconnect the negative battery cable.

2. Remove the ash tray and ash tray housing, as necessary.

3. Remove the knobs, controls, washers, trim plate, and nuts from radio.

4. Remove the hoses from the center air conditioning duct, as necessary.

5. Disconnect all wiring leads.

6. Remove the screw from the radio rear mounting bracket and lower the radio.

To install:

7. Raise the radio up into position in the vehicle, then install the screw to the rear mounting bracket.

8. Engage all wiring leads.

9. If removed, connect the hoses to the center A/C duct.

10. Install the nuts, trim plate, washers controls and knobs to the radio assembly.

11. If removed, install the ash tray and housing.

12. Connect the negative battery cable and enjoy the tunes.

1973-77

1. Disconnect the negative battery cable.

2. If equipped, remove the left air conditioner lap cooler duct.

3. Pull off the knobs and bezels.

4. Remove the control shaft nuts and washers. You will probably need a deep-well socket or a pair of pliers.

5. Remove the support bracket stud nut. Disconnect the antenna, speaker, and power wires.

6. Move the radio back until the shafts clear the instrument panel, then lower it from behind the panel. On later models, the radio can be removed through the instrument panel opening.

To install:

7. Install the radio to the instrument panel, then connect the antenna, speaker and power wires.

➡**Make sure to hook up the speaker leads before turning the radio on; operating without a speaker will damage the transistors.**

8. Install the support bracket stud nut.

9. Install the control shaft nuts and washers.

10. Install the bezels and control knobs.

11. If equipped, install the left air conditioner lap cooler duct.

12. Connect the negative battery cable and enjoy the tunes.

1978-84

1. Disconnect the negative battery cable.

2. Remove the radio control knobs by pulling them from the shafts.

3. Remove the trim plate screws, then carefully pull the trim plate forward from the instrument panel. If equipped, either disengage the electrical wiring from the cigarette lighter attached to the trim plate or allow the trim plate to hand by the wires out of the way.

4. If applicable, at the right side of the radio bracket, remove the stud nut.

5. Remove the instrument panel bracket screws, then carefully pull the radio and bracket assembly forward for access to the electrical connectors.

6. Disengage the connectors and the antenna wiring from the rear of the radio.

To install:

✳✳WARNING

Before applying power to the radio, ALWAYS attach the speaker wiring harness.

7. Hold the radio and bracket assembly in front of the instrument panel, then connect the wiring and antenna to the rear of the assembly.

8. Insert the radio and bracket assembly to the instrument panel, then secure using the retaining screws.

9. If applicable, install the stud nut to the right side of the radio bracket.

10. If removed, engage the wiring to the cigarette lighter attached to the trim plate.

11. Install the trim plate and secure using the retaining screws.

12. Push the radio control knobs onto the shafts.

13. Connect the negative battery cable and enjoy the tunes.

1985 and Later

1. Disconnect the negative battery cable.

2. To access the temperature control cable, remove the glove box, then disconnect the temperature cable from the temperature door.

3. Remove the radio, heater and A/C control panel-to-dash fasteners.

4. Pull the panel from the dash, then disengage the A/C control vacuum and electrical connectors.

5. Remove the radio and the A/C control knobs, then the trimplate.

6. Remove the radio from the bracket.

To install:

7. Install the radio to the bracket.

Fig. 30 Loosen and remove the trim plate retaining screws

Fig. 31 Carefully pull the trim plate forward from the instrument panel

Fig. 32 If applicable, disengage the wiring from the trim plate so it can be removed from the vehicle

Fig. 33 Loosen and remove the radio bracket retainers

Fig. 34 Pull the radio and bracket assembly from the instrument panel

Fig. 35 Disengage the wiring from the back of the radio assembly

Fig. 36 Unplug the antenna connector from the rear of the radio

8. Install the trimplate, then install the radio and the A/C control knobs.

9. Engage the A/C control vacuum and electrical connectors, then install the panel to the dash.

10. Install and tighten the radio, heater and A/C control panel-to-dash fasteners.

11. Connect and adjust the temperature door cable, then install the glove box.

12. Connect the negative battery cable.

WINDSHIELD WIPERS

Blade and Arm

REMOVAL & INSTALLATION

▶ See Figures 37 and 38

If the wiper assembly has a press type release tab at the center, simply depress the tab and remove the blade. If the blade has no release tab, use a screwdriver to depress the spring at the center. This will release the assembly. To install the assembly, position the blade over the pin at the tip of the arm and press until the spring retainer engages the groove in the pin.

To remove the element, either depress the release button or squeeze the spring type retainer clip at the out end together, and slide the blade element out. Just slide the new element in until it latches.

➡**Removal of the stock wiper arms requires the use of a special tool, G.M. J8966 or its equivalent. Versions of this tool are generally available in auto parts stores.**

1. Insert the tool under the wiper arm and lever the arm off the shaft.

➡**Raising the hood on most later models will facilitate easier wiper arm removal.**

2. Disconnect the washer hose from the arm (if so equipped). Remove the arm.

3. To install the arm, position it over the shaft and carefully snap into position. The proper park position for the arms is with the blades approximately 2 in. (50mm) above the lower molding of the windshield. Be sure that the motor is in the park position before installing the arms.

Wiper Motor

REMOVAL & INSTALLATION

▶ **See Figures 39, 40, 41, 42, 43, 44, 45, 46 and 47**

1964-67

1. Make certain that the wiper motor is in the park position, then disconnect the negative battery cable.
2. Disengage the washer hoses and electrical connectors.
3. Remove the three motor bolts. Pull the wiper motor assembly from the cowl opening and loosen the nuts retaining the drive rod ball stud to the crank arm.

To install:
4. Check the sealing gaskets at the motor, then make sure the motor is in the park position.
5. Hold the motor assembly just in front of the cowl opening and connect the drive rod ball stud to the crank arm, then install and tighten the nuts.
6. Install the motor assembly and secure using the motor bolts.
7. Engage the washer hoses and electrical connectors to the motor assembly.
8. Connect the negative battery cable.

1968-70

1. Make sure that the wiper motor is in the park position, then disconnect the negative battery cable.

2. Disengage the washer hoses and electrical connectors.
3. Remove the plenum chamber grille or access cover. Remove the nut retaining the crank arm to the motor assembly.
4. Remove the retaining screws or nuts and remove the motor. Do not allow the motor to hang by the drive link.

To install:
5. Check the sealing gaskets at the motor, then make sure the motor is in the park position.
6. Install the motor assembly and secure using the retaining screws or nuts.
7. Connect the crank arm, then install and tighten the retaining nut.
8. Install the plenum chamber grille or access cover.
9. Engage the washer hoses and electrical connectors to the motor assembly.
10. Connect the negative battery cable.

1971 and Later

Your car may be equipped with either a round motor or a rectangular motor assembly.
1. Make sure that the wiper motor is in the park position, then disconnect the negative battery cable.
2. If equipped, remove the screen or grille that covers the cowl area.
3. Disengage the wiring from the motor.
4. Reach through the cowl opening and loosen, but do not remove, the nuts which attach the transmission drive link to the motor crank arm. Then, disconnect the drive link from the crank arm.

➡**Some wiper motors will utilize lower retaining screws which are difficult or impossible to access without using an extension. Make sure all bolts are removed before attempting to remove the motor.**

5. Remove the three motor attaching bolts then remove the motor, guiding the crank arm through the hole.

To install:
6. Make sure the motor is in the park position.
7. Install the motor to the cowl while guiding the crank arm through the hole, then install and tighten the motor attaching bolts.
8. With the crank arm attached to the drive link, tighten the retaining nuts.
9. Engage the motor wiring.
10. If equipped, install the screen or grille to the cowl area.
11. Connect the negative battery cable.

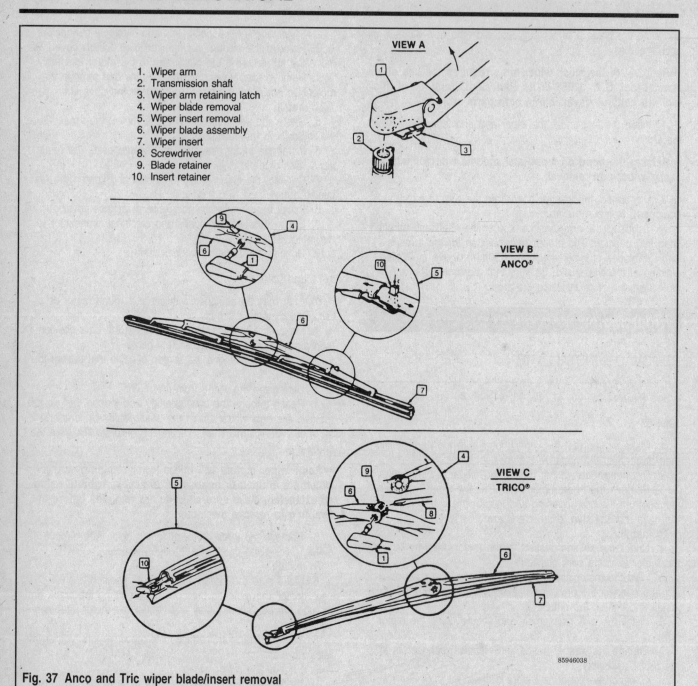

1. Wiper arm
2. Transmission shaft
3. Wiper arm retaining latch
4. Wiper blade removal
5. Wiper insert removal
6. Wiper blade assembly
7. Wiper insert
8. Screwdriver
9. Blade retainer
10. Insert retainer

VIEW A

VIEW B
ANCO®

VIEW C
TRICO®

85946038

Fig. 37 Anco and Tric wiper blade/insert removal

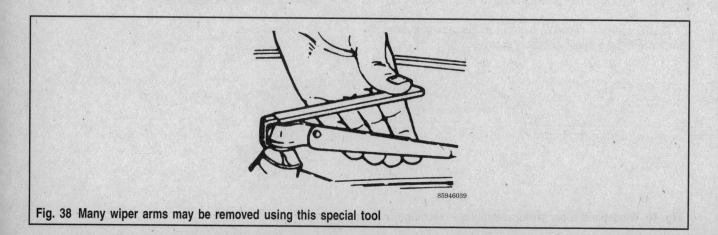

85946039

Fig. 38 Many wiper arms may be removed using this special tool

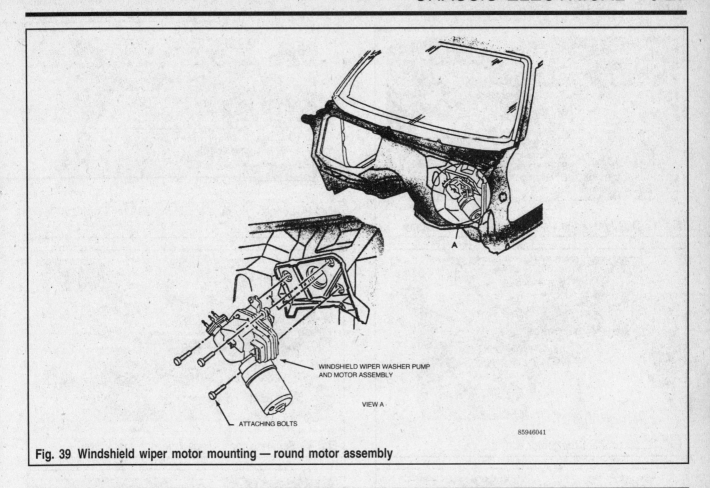

WINDSHIELD WIPER WASHER PUMP
AND MOTOR ASSEMBLY

VIEW A

ATTACHING BOLTS

85946041

Fig. 39 Windshield wiper motor mounting — round motor assembly

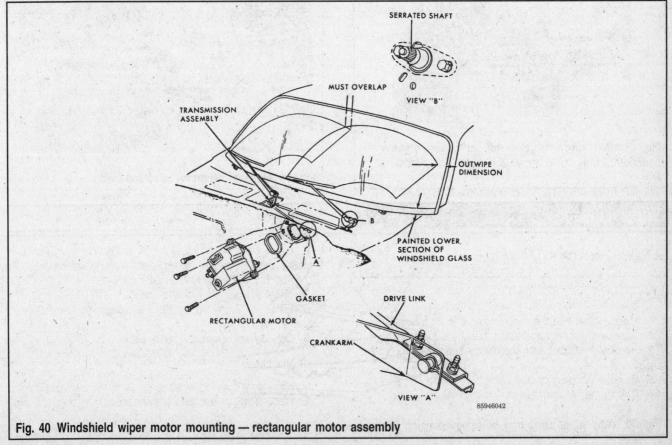

SERRATED SHAFT

MUST OVERLAP

VIEW "B"

TRANSMISSION
ASSEMBLY

OUTWIPE
DIMENSION

B

PAINTED LOWER
SECTION OF
WINDSHIELD GLASS

A

GASKET

DRIVE LINK

RECTANGULAR MOTOR

CRANKARM

VIEW "A"

85946042

Fig. 40 Windshield wiper motor mounting — rectangular motor assembly

Fig. 41 Disconnect the washer hoses from the pump

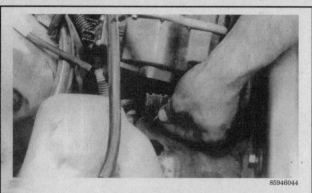

Fig. 42 Disconnect the motor wiring

Fig. 43 Make sure you get all the motor wires, some connectors may be lower on the motor and harder to find

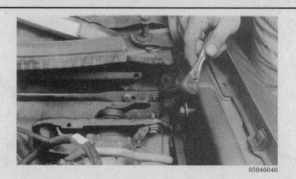

Fig. 44 Loosen the nuts retaining the crank arm to the linkage

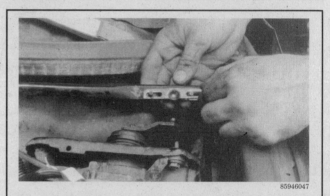

Fig. 45 Separate the linkage from the crank arm

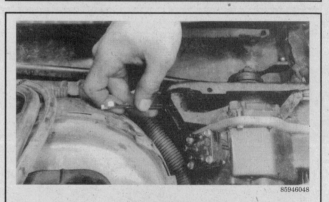

Fig. 46 Remove the motor retaining bolts

Wiper Linkage

REMOVAL & INSTALLATION

1964-67

1. Make certain that the wiper motor is in park position, then disconnect the negative battery cable.
2. Remove the wiper arm and blade assemblies from the transmission shaft.
3. Remove the plenum chamber grille.
4. Detach the linkage from the wiper crank arm.

5. Remove the transmission retaining screws, lower the assembly into the plenum chamber, and remove the unit.
   To install:
6. Install the unit and raise the assembly into the plenum chamber, then install the transmission retaining screws.
7. Attach the linkage to the wiper crank arm.
8. Install the plenum chamber grille.
9. Install the wiper arm and blade assemblies to the transmission shaft.
10. Connect the negative battery cable.

1968 and Later

1. Make sure that the wiper motor is in the park position.
2. Disconnect the negative battery cable.

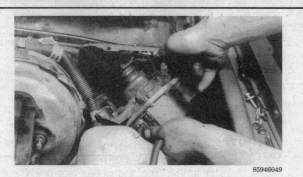

Fig. 47 Remove the motor by carefully guiding the crank arm through the opening

3. Remove the wiper arm and blade assemblies from the transmission. On the articulated left arm assemblies, remove the carburetor type clip retaining the pinned arm to the blade arm.

4. If equipped, remove the plenum chamber air intake grille or screen.

INSTRUMENTS AND SWITCHES

Instrument Cluster

REMOVAL & INSTALLATION

1964-65

▶ See Figure 48

1. Disconnect the negative battery cable.
2. Remove the upper most jacket clamp bolt and carefully bend the clamp away from the steering column.
3. Disconnect the speedometer cable. Disconnect the oil pressure line at the gauge on the SS model.
4. Remove the screws that attach the console to the instrument panel and lean the console forward onto the mast jacket. Remove the radio knobs before removing the console from the panel.
5. Disengage all cluster lamps, harness connectors, and the two harness retaining clips from the rear of the cluster.
6. Lift the console forward and upward to remove.
7. Unscrew and remove the cluster from the console.
To install:
8. Screw the cluster to the console.
9. Hold the console assembly just in front of the dash, then engage all cluster lamps, harness connectors and harness retaining clips at the rear of the cluster.
10. Position the console assembly and install the retaining screws, then install the radio knobs.
11. For SS vehicles, connect the oil pressure line to the gauge.
12. Connect the speedometer cable.
13. Bend the clamp back into position, then install the upper most jacket clamp bolt.
14. Connect the negative battery cable.

5. Loosen the nuts retaining the crank arm drive rod ball stud to the linkage, then detach the linkage.
6. Remove the transmission retaining screws. Lower the transmission and drive rod assemblies into the plenum chamber.
7. Remove the transmission and linkage from the plenum chamber through the cowl opening.
To install:
8. Install the transmission and linkage to the plenum chamber through the cowl opening.
9. Raise the transmission and drive rod assemblies into position, then install the retaining screws.
10. Make sure the linkage and crank arm are both in the park position, then attach the linkage to the crank arm and tighten the retaining nuts.
11. If equipped, install the plenum chamber air intake grille or screen.
12. Install the wiper arm and blade assemblies to the transmission.
13. Connect the negative battery cable.

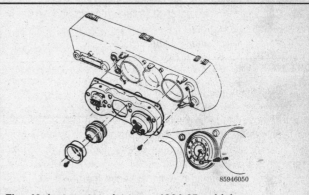

Fig. 48 Instrument cluster — 1964-65 vehicles

1966-67

▶ See Figure 49

1. Disconnect the negative battery cable.
2. Remove the steering coupling bolt and disconnect the steering shaft from the coupling.
3. Loosen the mast jacket lower clamp.
4. On air conditioned cars, remove the air conditioning center distribution duct.
5. Remove the radio rear support bracket screw.
6. Remove the mast jacket trim cover and the support clamp.
7. Loosen the set screw and remove the transmission dial indicator (if so equipped).
8. Disconnect the speedometer shaft at the speedometer head.
9. Remove the instrument panel attaching screws.
10. From under the console, remove the four lower retaining screws from the cluster housing.
11. With the mast jacket padded, pull the instrument panel from the console and lay forward on mast jacket.

12. Disconnect the wiring harness, cluster lamps and wiring terminals from the rear of the cluster assembly.

13. Remove the four screws holding the upper section of the cluster housing to the panel and remove the cluster from the instrument panel.

To install:

14. Install the cluster to the instrument panel, then install the four screws holding the upper section of the cluster housing to the panel.

15. Connect the wiring harness, cluster lamps and wiring terminals to the rear of the cluster assembly.

16. Remove the instrument panel from the padded mast jacket and position it to the console.

17. Under the console, install the four lower retaining screws to the cluster housing.

18. Install the instrument panel attaching screws.

19. Connect the speedometer shaft to the speedometer head.

20. If equipped, install the transmission dial indicator and tighten the set screw.

21. Install the mast jacket trim cover and the support clamp.

22. Install the radio rear support bracket screw.

23. On air conditioned cars, install the air conditioning center distribution duct.

24. Tighten the mast jacket lower clamp.

25. Connect the steering shaft to the coupling, then install the steering coupling bolt.

26. Connect the negative battery cable.

1968-69

1. Disconnect the negative battery cable.
2. Remove the ash tray and retainer.
3. Remove the radio knobs, nuts, electrical connectors, and the radio rear support. Remove the radio.
4. Remove the heater control screws, then push the control head out of the instrument panel.
5. Lower the steering column. Remove the automatic transmission indicator cable from the steering column. Protect the steering column with a cloth.
6. Remove the instrument panel retaining screws at the top, bottom, and sides of the panel. Remove all attachments to the underside of the panel.
7. Lift the panel up and back slightly. Reach behind the cluster to remove the speedometer cable, support the panel on the protected steering column.

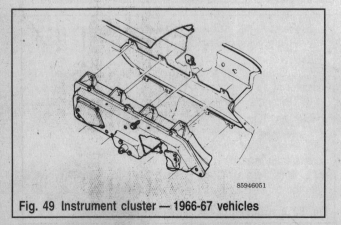

Fig. 49 Instrument cluster — 1966-67 vehicles

8. Remove the clips at the top of the cluster rear cover and remove all connectors at the rear of the cluster.

9. If equipped, remove the oil pressure fitting from the rear of the oil pressure gauge.

10. Remove the screws that secure the twin window clusters to the back of the instrument panel and remove the cluster.

To install:

11. Install the cluster, then install the screws that secure the twin window clusters to the back of the instrument panel.

12. If equipped, install the oil pressure fitting to the rear of the oil pressure gauge.

13. Install the clips to the top of the cluster rear cover and engage all connectors at the rear of the cluster.

14. Position the panel, then reach behind the cluster and connect the speedometer cable.

15. Install all attachments to the underside of the panel, then install the instrument panel retaining screws at the top, bottom, and sides of the panel.

16. Install the automatic transmission indicator cable to the steering column, the carefully raise the column into position.

17. Push the control head into the instrument panel, then install the heater control screws

18. Install the rear radio support, then install the radio knobs, nuts, electrical connectors.

19. Install the ash tray and retainer.

20. Connect the negative battery cable.

1970-72
▶ See Figure 50

1. Disconnect the negative battery cable.
2. Carefully lower and support the steering column.
3. Disconnect the parking brake hand release.
4. Disconnect the speedometer cable.
5. Remove the instrument panel pad.
6. Disconnect the radio speaker bracket from the instrument panel. Disconnect the speaker wire from the radio.
7. Disconnect the air conditioning center outlet and the control head.
8. Remove the radio knobs, washers, bezels, and wiring.
9. Unbolt the radio braces. Roll the radio out from under the instrument panel.
10. Remove the six instrument panel bolts and roll out the instrument panel with the help of an assistant.

To install:

11. With the help of an assistant, carefully roll in the instrument panel, then install the six instrument panel bolts.

12. Roll the radio into position, then bolt the radio braces.

13. Install the radio knobs, washers, bezels, and wiring.

14. Connect the air conditioning center outlet and the control head.

15. Connect the speaker wire to the radio, then connect the radio speaker bracket to the instrument panel.

16. Install the instrument panel pad.

17. Connect the speedometer cable.

18. Connect the parking brake hand release.

19. Carefully raise and secure the steering column.

20. Connect the negative battery cable.

1973-77
▶ See Figure 51

1. Disconnect the negative battery cable.

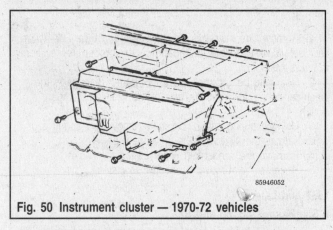

Fig. 50 Instrument cluster — 1970-72 vehicles

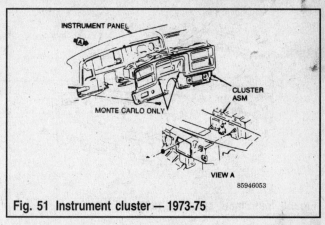

Fig. 51 Instrument cluster — 1973-75

2. Remove the radio knobs and the clock set stem is so equipped.

3. Remove the instrument bezel retaining screws.

4. Pull the bezel out to disconnect the tailgate release or rear defogger switch if so equipped.

5. Remove the instrument bezel.

6. Remove the retaining screws and remove the speedometer head.

7. Remove the retaining screws and remove the fuel gauge and tachometer if so equipped.

8. Remove the clock if so equipped.

9. Disconnect the transmission shift indicator cable from the steering column.

10. Disconnect the wiring and speedometer cable.

11. Remove the instrument cluster case.

To install:

12. Install the instrument cluster case.

13. Connect the wiring and speedometer cable.

14. Connect the transmission shift indicator cable to the steering column.

15. If equipped, install the clock.

16. Install the fuel gauge and, if equipped, the tachometer. Tighten the retaining screws.

17. Install the speedometer head and tighten the retaining screws.

18. If equipped, connect the tailgate release or rear defogger switch.

19. Install the instrument bezel, then tighten the retaining screws.

20. If equipped, install the radio knobs and the clock set stem.

21. Connect the negative battery cable.

1978 And Later

▶ See Figures 52, 53 and 54

MALIBU (STANDARD CLUSTER)

1. Disconnect the negative battery cable.

2. If equipped, remove clock set stem knob.

3. Remove instrument bezel retaining screws.

4. Pull bezel from panel slightly and disconnect rear defogger switch, if equipped.

5. Remove bezel.

6. Remove two screws at transmission selector indicator and lower indicator assembly to disconnect cable.

7. Remove three screws at windshield wiper/light switch mounting plate and pull assembly rearward for access to lower left cluster attaching bolt and nut.

8. Remove nuts attaching cluster to instrument panel.

9. Pull cluster rearward and disconnect the speedometer cable and all wiring and cables.

10. Remove cluster from vehicle.

To install:

11. Position the cluster in the vehicle.

12. Connect the speedometer cable and all wiring and cables.

13. Install the nuts attaching cluster to instrument panel, then install the lower left cluster attaching bolt and nut.

14. Secure the windshield wiper/light switch mounting plate using the mounting screws.

15. Connect the cable, then install the two screws at transmission selector indicator and lower indicator assembly.

16. If equipped, connect rear defogger switch.

17. Install the bezel, then secure using the instrument bezel retaining screws.

18. If equipped, install the clock set stem knob.

19. Connect the negative battery cable.

MALIBU (OPTIONAL CLUSTER) AND MONTE CARLO

1. Disconnect the negative battery cable. Remove the clock set stem knob.

2. Remove the instrument bezel retaining screws.

3. Slightly pull the bezel rearward. Disconnect the rear defogger switch. Remove the remote control mirror control knob, if equipped.

4. Remove the dash panel bezel. Remove the speedometer assembly retaining screws. Pull the assembly from the cluster,

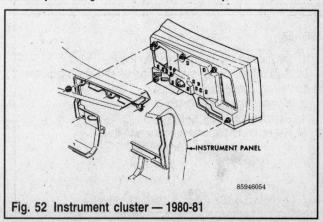

Fig. 52 Instrument cluster — 1980-81

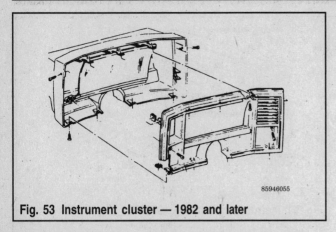

Fig. 53 Instrument cluster — 1982 and later

disengage the speedometer cable from the assembly and remove the speedometer from the vehicle.

5. Remove the fuel gauge or the tachometer retaining screws, disengage the electrical connectors and remove the components.

6. Remove the clock or voltmeter retaining screws, disconnect the electrical connectors and remove the components.

7. Disconnect the transmission shift indicator cable from the steering column.

8. Disengage all wiring connectors and remove the cluster case.

To install:

9. Position the cluster and connect all wiring.

10. Connect the transmission shift indicator cable to the steering column.

11. Install the clock or voltmeter, engage the connectors and install the retaining screws.

12. Install the fuel gauge or the tachometer, engage the connectors and install the retaining screws.

13. Connect the speedometer cable to the speedometer assembly, then install the assembly to the cluster and tighten the retaining screws.

14. Connect the rear defogger switch, then if equipped, install the remote control mirror control knob.

15. Install the instrument bezel retaining screws.

16. Install the clock set stem knob, then connect the negative battery cable.

Windshield Wiper Switch

REMOVAL & INSTALLATION

1964-67

1. Disconnect the negative battery cable.

2. Reach behind the instrument panel and disengage the switch wiring connector.

3. Remove the retaining clip or bezel.

4. Remove the wiper switch switch.

5. Reverse the removal procedure to install.

1968-81

1. Remove the instrument cluster lens and trim. For necessary details, refer to the instrument cluster procedures earlier in this section.

2. Reaching behind the instrument panel, disengage the electrical connector from the rear of the windshield wiper switch.

3. Using a prying action, carefully remove the spring clip which retains the switch to the instrument panel.

4. Remove the windshield wiper switch.

5. Reverse the removal procedure to install.

1982 and Later

▶ **See Figures 55, 56 and 57**

All 1982 and later models utilize a multi-function lever on the steering column. The switch which is actuated by the lever is mounted deep in the steering column assembly.

1. Disconnect the negative battery cable.

2. Remove the steering wheel from the column.

3. Remove the turn signal assembly from the steering column. Refer to Section 8 of this manual for details. It may be possible to leave the signal wiring in position and allow the switch to hang from the wires. If not, attach a piece of mechanic's wire or twine to the connector before pulling the wiring through the column. Leave the string or wire in the column so the connector may be pulled back into position during installation.

4. It may be necessary to loosen the 2 column mounting nuts and remove the four bracket-to-mast jacket screws, then separate the bracket from the mast jacket in order to allow the connector clip on the ignition switch to be pulled out of the column assembly.

5. Disengage the washer/wiper switch lower connector.

6. Remove the screws attaching the column housing to the mast jacket. Be sure to note the position of the dimmer switch actuator rod for reassembly in the same position. Remove the column housing and switch as an assembly.

➡ **The tilt and travel column have a removable plastic cover on the column housing. This provides access to the wiper switch without removing the entire column housing.**

7. Turn the pivot assembly upside down and use a drift to remove the pivot pin from the washer/wiper switch, then remove the switch assembly.

To install:

8. Place the switch into position in the housing, then install the pivot pin.

9. Position the housing onto the mast jacket and attach by installing the retaining screws. Install the dimmer switch actuator rod in the same position as noted earlier. Check switch operation.

10. Connect the lower end of the switch assembly.

11. If removed, install the bracket-to-mast jacket screws and the 2 column mounting nuts.

12. Install the turn signal assembly. For details, refer to Section 8 of this manual.

13. Install the steering wheel to the column assembly.

14. Connect the negative battery cable.

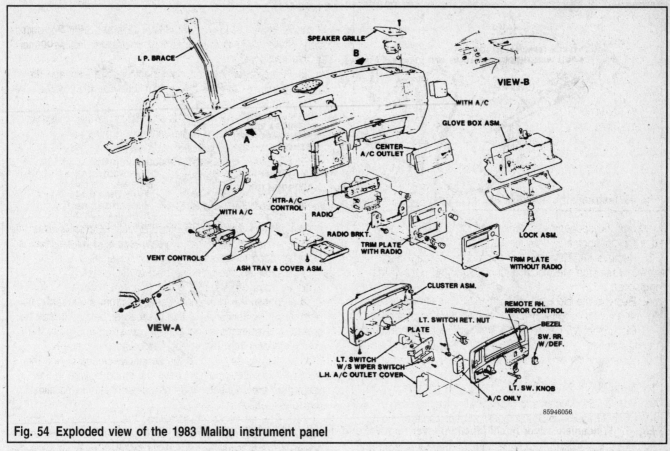

Fig. 54 Exploded view of the 1983 Malibu instrument panel

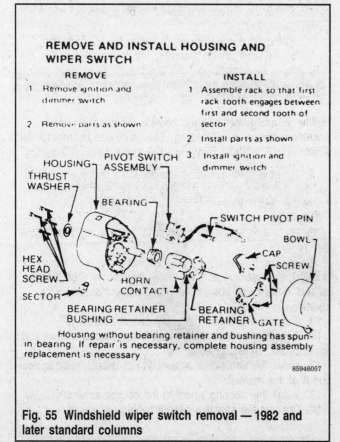

REMOVE AND INSTALL HOUSING AND WIPER SWITCH

REMOVE

1 Remove ignition and dimmer switch

2 Remove parts as shown

INSTALL

1 Assemble rack so that first rack tooth engages between first and second tooth of sector

2 Install parts as shown

3 Install ignition and dimmer switch

Housing without bearing retainer and bushing has spun-in bearing. If repair is necessary, complete housing assembly replacement is necessary.

Fig. 55 Windshield wiper switch removal — 1982 and later standard columns

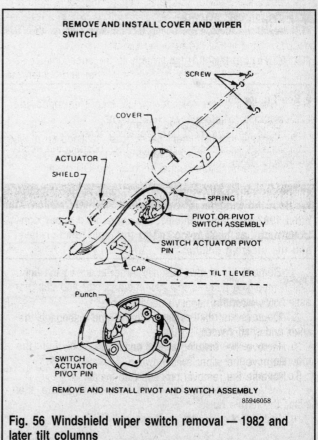

REMOVE AND INSTALL COVER AND WIPER SWITCH

REMOVE AND INSTALL PIVOT AND SWITCH ASSEMBLY

Fig. 56 Windshield wiper switch removal — 1982 and later tilt columns

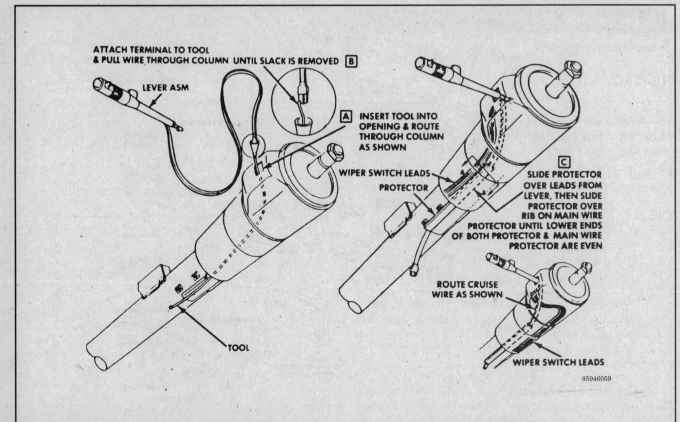

Fig. 57 Windshield wiper (multi-function) lever removal and installation — 1982 and later vehicles

Headlight Switch

REMOVAL & INSTALLATION

▶ **See Figure 58**

1. Disconnect the negative battery cable.
2. Remove the instrument panel bezel, retained on most model years with six screws (varies among models and years).
3. Pull the headlight control knob on the ON position.

➡**The mounting plate on most 1981 and earlier vehicles is for both the windshield wiper switch and light switch. On most 1982 and later vehicles, the windshield wiper control/switch has been relocated to the multi-function lever and the steering column.**

4. Remove the screws (usually three) attaching the light switch mounting plate to the instrument cluster and pull the assembly rearward.
5. Depress the shaft retainer on the switch, then pull the knob and shaft assembly out.
6. Remove the ferrule nut and switch assembly from the mounting plate.
To install:
7. Install the switch assembly to the mounting plate, then install the ferrule nut.
8. Install the knob and shaft assembly.

9. Install the screws attaching the wiper switch/light switch mounting plate to the instrument cluster.
10. Install the instrument panel bezel and retaining screws.
11. Connect the negative battery cable.

Clock

REMOVAL & INSTALLATION

1. Disconnect the negative battery cable.
2. Remove the instrument panel cluster bezel.
3. Remove the clock retaining screws and remove the clock.

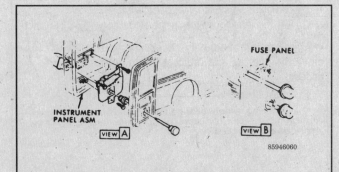

Fig. 58 Example of a common headlight switch mounting

Speedometer Cable

▶ **See Figures 59 and 60**

REPLACEMENT

➡️**Although not necessary in all cases, removing the instrument cluster will give better access to the speedometer cable.**

1. Reach behind the instrument cluster and push the speedometer cable casing toward the speedometer while depressing the retaining spring on the back of the instrument cluster case. Once the retaining spring has released, hold it in while pulling outward on the casing to disconnect the casing from the speedometer.

2. Remove the cable casing sealing plug from the dash panel. Then, pull the casing down from behind the dash and remove the cable from the casing.

3. If the cable is broken and cannot be entirely removed from the top, support the car securely, and then unscrew the cable casing connector at the transmission. Pull the bottom part of the cable out, and then screw the connector back onto the transmission.

4. Lubricate the new cable with a speedometer cable grease. Insert it into the casing until it bottoms. Push inward while rotating it until the square portion at the bottom engages with the coupling in the transmission, permitting the cable to move in another inch or so. Then, reconnect the cable casing to the speedometer and install the sealing plug into the dash panel.

Ignition Switch/Lock Cylinder

REMOVAL & INSTALLATION

Chevrolet mid-sized vehicles from 1964-68 are equipped with a dash mounted ignition switch. The below procedure may be used for these vehicles. All models made in 1969 and later are equipped with ignition switches which are mounted in the steering column. For procedures on vehicles equipped with steering column mounted switches, please refer to Section 8 of this manual.

1. Disconnect the negative battery cable.
2. Put the ignition switch in the Accessory (ACC) position.

➡️**Although not absolutely necessary, you may wish to remove the ashtray and radio at this point for ease of access.**

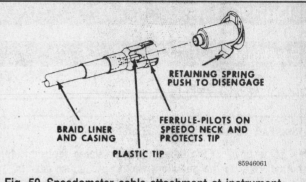

Fig. 59 Speedometer cable attachment at instrument cluster/speedometer housing

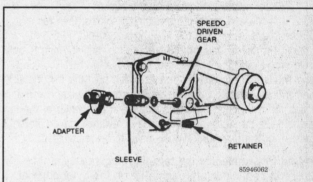

Fig. 60 Example of a speedometer cable-to-drive attachment

3. Insert a wire into the small hole in the face of the lock cylinder. Push in on the wire to depress the plunger. Continue turning the key until the cylinder can be removed from the switch.

4. Remove the switch bezel nut, and then pull the switch out from under the dash.

5. Go in from the front of the switch with a screwdriver and unsnap the theft resistant locking tangs on the connector and then unplug the connector.

To install:

6. Engage the electrical connector to the switch, then position the switch under the dash and install the switch bezel nut.

7. Install the lock cylinder to the switch. It most applications, the key should be installed and turned to the ACC, START or RUN positions in order to install the cylinder. If in doubt, check the switch or cylinder manufacturer's instructions, as applicable.

8. Once the cylinder is installed, turn the key back to the LOCK position.

9. Connect the negative battery cable, then verify proper switch and cylinder operation.

LIGHTING

Headlights

REMOVAL & INSTALLATION

▶ **See Figures 61, 62, 63, 64, 65 and 66**

➡**If some or all of the headlight bulbs being replaced still operate, refer to the headlight aiming procedure later in this section to ease checking or adjustment of the headlights after installation.**

1. Disconnect the negative battery cable.
2. Loosen and remove the retaining screws, then remove the headlight bezel from the front of the vehicle.
3. On most models, the headlight bulb retaining ring is only held on by retaining screws. If so, remove the bulb retaining ring screws. These are the screws which hold the thin metal ring which holds the bulb against the adjusting plate. Do not touch the two headlight aiming screws, at the center of the top and side of the retaining ring (these screws will have different heads), or the headlight aim will have to be re-adjusted.

➡**One way to identify the retaining ring screws is that they will be threaded through a lip on the outer edge of the retaining ring before threading through the adjusting plate. One the other hand, the adjustment screws are threaded through the adjustment plate and a spring loaded holder underneath it.**

4. Some later model vehicles will use a spring on the retaining ring. If so equipped, disengage the spring from the retaining ring, using a cotter pin removal tool, then remove the retaining ring screws.
5. Pull the bulb and ring forward and then separate them. Unplug the electrical connector from the rear of the bulb and remove the bulb from the vehicle.

To install:
6. Plug the new bulb into the electrical connector.
7. Position the retaining ring over the bulb, then install the assembly to the adjusting plate. Secure using the retaining screws and, if applicable, the spring.
8. Install and secure the headlight bezel.
9. Connect the negative battery cable.

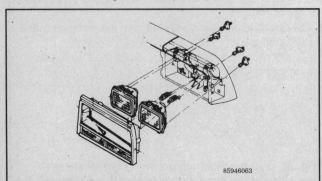

Fig. 61 Exploded view of a common dual headlight mounting assembly — 1983 Malibu shown

Fig. 62 Loosen and remove the headlight bezel retaining screws

Fig. 63 Make sure all of the screws are removed, then pull the bezel from the front of the vehicle

Fig. 64 Loosen and remove the retaining ring screws

HEADLIGHT AIMING

▶ **See Figures 67 and 68**

The headlights must be properly aimed to provide the best, safest road illumination. The lights should be checked for proper aim, and adjusted if necessary, after installing a new sealed beam unit if the front end sheet metal has been replaced. Certain state and local authorities have requirements for headlight aiming; these should be checked before adjustment is made.

Fig. 65 Pull the retaining ring and bulb forward to separate them

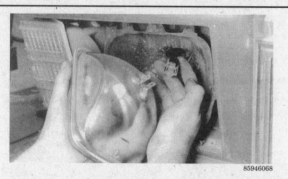

Fig. 66 Unplug the electrical connector from the rear of the headlight

Headlight adjustment may be temporarily made using a wall, as described below, or on the rear of another vehicle. When adjusted, the lights should not glare in oncoming cars windshields, nor should they illuminate the passenger compartment of cars driving in front of you. These adjustments are rough and should always be fine-tuned by a repair shop which is equipped with a headlight aiming tools. Improper adjustments may be both dangerous and illegal.

For most Chevrolet vehicles, horizontal and vertical aiming of each sealed beam unit is provided by two adjusting screws, which move the retaining ring and adjusting plate against the body of the coil spring. There is no adjustment for focus; this is done during headlight manufacturing.

Before removing the headlight bulb or disturbing the headlamp in any way, note the current settings in order to make adjusting the headlights upon reassembly easier. If the high or low beam setting of the old lamp still works, this can be done using the wall of a garage or a building as follows:

1. Park the car on a level surface, with the fuel tank no more than ½ full and with the vehicle empty of all extra cargo (unless normally carried). The vehicle should be facing a wall which is no less the 6 feet high and 12 feet wide. The front of the vehicle should be about 25 feet from the wall.

➡The car's fuel tank should be about half full when adjusting the headlights. Tires should be properly inflated, and if a heavy load is normally carried in the trunk or in the cargo area of station wagons, it should remain there.

2. If this is be performed outdoors, it is advisable to wait until dusk in order to properly see the headlight beams on the wall. If done in a garage, darken the area around the wall as much as possible by closing shades or hanging cloth over the windows.

3. Turn the headlights **ON** and mark the wall at the center of each light's low beam, then switch on the brights and mark the center of each light's high beam. A short length of masking tape which is visible from the front of the car may be used. Although marking all 4 positions is advisable, marking 1 position from each light should be sufficient.

4. If neither beam on 1 side of the vehicle is working, park another like-sized car in the exact spot where the Chevy was and mark the beams using the same side light on that car. Then switch the cars so the Chevy is back in the original spot. The Chevy must be parked no closer to or farther away from the wall than the second vehicle.

5. Perform the necessary repairs, but make sure the car in not moved or is returned to the exact spot from which the lights were marked. Turn the headlights **ON** and adjust the beams to match the marks on the wall.

6. Have the headlight adjustment checked as soon as possible by a reputable repair shop.

Signal and Marker Lights

➡Since the light housing capsules (on the late model vehicles) are constructed by sonic welding, the ONLY service which can be performed are the replacement of the bulbs or the light housing.

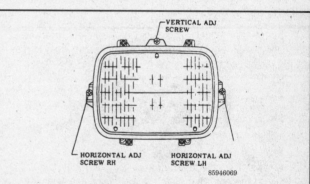

Fig. 67 Headlight adjustment screw locations for most Chevy vehicles

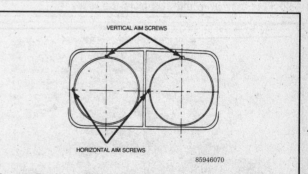

Fig. 68 Dual headlight adjustment screw locations — one side shown here (other side should be a mirror image

REMOVAL & INSTALLATION

Front Turn Signal and Parking Lights
▶ See Figures 69, 70, 71 and 72

1964-79 VEHICLES

1. Disconnect the negative battery cable.
2. Reach up under the fender and twist and withdraw the electrical socket from the rear of the housing. If the bulb can be accessed from here, turn and withdraw the bulb from the socket.
3. If the bulb could not be accessed from under the fender, remove the housing-to-front fender extension screws and the remove the housing for access. Twist and remove the bulb.

To install:

4. Install the new bulb to the electrical socket.
5. If removed, install the housing to the fender.
6. Install the socket and bulb assembly to the housing and lock into place by twisting.
7. Connect the negative battery cable.

1980 AND LATER VEHICLES

1. Disconnect the negative battery cable.
2. Remove the headlight bezel mounting screws and the bezel for access.
3. If necessary for access, remove the parking light housing.

Fig. 69 Most turn signal and parking lamp electrical sockets may be withdrawn from the rear

Fig. 70 Once the socket is withdrawn from the housing, the harness may be pulled outward for better access

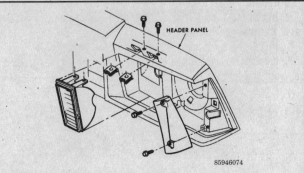

Fig. 71 Exploded view of parking and marker light housings — 1964-79 vehicles

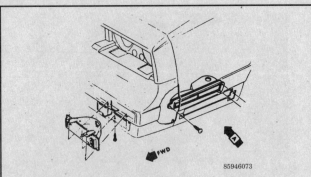

Fig. 72 Exploded view of parking and marker light housings — 1980 and later vehicles

4. Disconnect the twist lock socket from the lens housing, then remove the bulb from the socket.

➡ To remove the bulb, turn the twist lock socket at the rear of the housing) counterclockwise ¼ turn, then remove the socket with the bulb; replace the bulb if defective.

To install:

5. Install the bulb to the electric socket, then install the socket to the housing.
6. If removed for access, position and secure the parking light housing.
7. Install the headlight bezel and mounting screws.
8. Connect the negative battery cable.

Side Marker Lights
▶ See Figures 71, 72, 73 and 74

1964-79 VEHICLES

➡ Before beginning this procedure, check to make sure the marker light electrical socket is not accessible from under the hood or under the vehicle. If the socket is accessible, no bezels or housings will have to be removed.

1. Disconnect the negative battery cable.
2. If necessary for access, remove the headlight bezel mounting screws and the bezel.
3. Disconnect the twist lock socket from the lens housing.
4. Remove the marker light housing, then remove bulb.

➡ To remove the bulb, turn the twist lock socket (at the rear of the housing) counterclockwise ¼ turn, then remove the socket with the bulb; replace the bulb if defective.

To install:

5. Install the bulb to the socket, then if removed for access, install the marker light housing.

6. Install the twist lock socket to the lens housing.

7. If removed, install the headlight bezel and secure using the mounting screws.

8. Connect the negative battery cable.

1981 AND LATER VEHICLES

1. Disconnect the negative battery cable.

2. Remove the marker light housing screws, then remove the housing.

Fig. 73 As with the turn signals, many of the marker light sockets on these vehicles may be accessed from behind without removing and bezels or housings

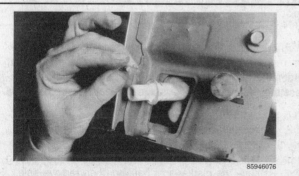

Fig. 74 Position the harness and socket so the bulb is accessible, then remove the bulb for replacement

3. Disconnect the twist lock socket from the lens housing, then remove the bulb from the socket.

→To remove the bulb, turn the twist lock socket (at the rear of the housing) counterclockwise ¼ turn, then remove the socket with the bulb; replace the bulb if defective.

To install:

4. Install the bulb to the socket, then install the socket to the housing.

5. Install the marker light housing and secure using the retaining screws.

6. Connect the negative battery cable.

Rear Turn Signal, Brake and Parking Lights
▶ See Figures 75, 76, 77, 78 and 79

1. Disconnect the negative battery cable.

2. Remove the tail light panel screws and the panel.

→If necessary, once the panel is removed, the lens or lends bezel retaining screws may be accessed in order to replace a cracked or damaged lens.

3. Disconnect the twist lock socket from the lens housing.

→To remove the bulb, turn the twist lock socket (at the rear of the housing) counterclockwise ¼ turn, then remove the socket with the bulb; replace the bulb if defective.

4. Remove the bulb from the twist socket.

To install:

5. Install the bulb to the socket.

6. Install the twist socket to the rear of the lens housing.

7. Install the tail light panel and secure using the retaining screws.

8. Connect the negative battery cable.

License Plate Light
▶ See Figures 80 and 81

Although, some earlier vehicles may not have a housing covering the license plate bulb, most of the vehicles covered by this manual utilize a bulb which is covered by a housing. The housing is mounted adjacent to the license plate using 1 or more retaining screws. If necessary for access to the bulb, loosen the retaining screw(s) and remove the housing, then twist and withdraw the socket. Remove the bulb from the socket and replace using a new part.

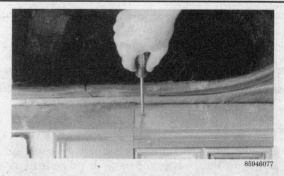

Fig. 75 Loosen and remove the tail light panel retaining screws

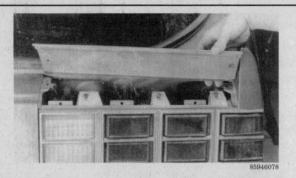

Fig. 76 Remove the tail light panel for access to the bulbs

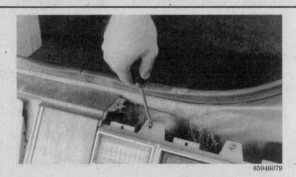

Fig. 77 With the panel removed, a damaged lens may be replaced by removing the lens or bezel retainers

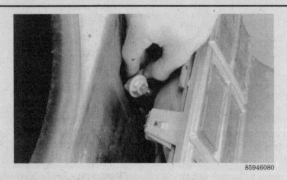

Fig. 78 Twist and remove the rear parking, marker or turn signals light sockets, as necessary

Fig. 79 With the sockets removed from the housing, the bulbs may be replaced

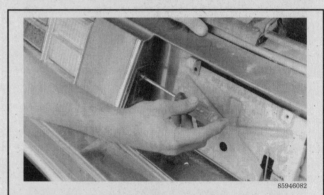

Fig. 80 Loosen the housing retaining screw

Fig. 81 Pull the housing outward, then twist and remove the license plate socket (with bulb) from the rear of the housing

Dome Light

Most dome lamps are covered by a lens cap which is snapped into position. The lens cap may be removed by grasping, gently squeezing and pulling downward. For some earlier models, there may be a fastener holding the cap in place. If so, remove the fastener before attempting to free the lens cap. Once the cap is removed, the bulb may be withdrawn and replaced.

TRAILER WIRING

➡For more information on towing a trailer please refer to Section 1 of this manual.

Wiring the car for towing is fairly easy. There are a number of good wiring kits available and these should be used, rather than trying to design your own. All trailers will need brake lights and turn signals as well as tail lights and side marker lights. Most states require extra marker lights for overly wide trailers. Also, most states have recently required back-up lights for trailers, and most trailer manufacturers have been building trailers with back-up lights for several years. Additionally, some Class I, most Class II and just about all Class III trailers will have electric brakes. Add to this number an accessories wire, to operate trailer internal equipment or to charge the trailer's battery, and you can have as many as seven wires in the harness.

Determine the equipment on your trailer and buy the wiring kit necessary. The kit will contain all the wires needed, plus a plug adapter set which should include the female plug, mounted on the bumper or hitch, and the male plug, wired into, or plugged into the trailer harness. When installing the kit, follow the manufacturer's instructions closely. The color coding of the wires is normally standard throughout the industry.

One point to note, some domestic vehicles, and most imported vehicles, have separate turn signals. On many older domestic vehicles, the brake lights and rear turn signals operate with the same bulb. For vehicles with separate turn signals, you can purchase an isolation unit so that the brake lights won't blink whenever the turn signals are operated, or, you can go to your local electronics supply house and buy four diodes to wire in series with the brake and turn signal bulbs. Diodes will isolate the brake and turn signals. The choice is yours. The isolation units are simple and quick to install, but far more expensive than the diodes. The diodes, however, require more work to install properly, since they require the cutting of each bulb's wire and soldering in place of the diodes.

One final point, the best kits are those with a spring loaded cover on the vehicle mounted socket. This cover prevents dirt and moisture from corroding the terminals. Never let the vehicle socket hang loosely. Always mount it securely to the bumper or hitch.

CIRCUIT PROTECTION

Fusible Links

A fusible link is a protective device used in an electrical circuit and acts very much like a standard fuse. The major difference lies in that fusible links are larger and capable of conducting higher amperages than most fuses. When the current increases beyond the rated amperage for a given link, the fusible metal of the wire link will melt, thus breaking the electrical circuit and preventing further damage to any other components or wiring. Whenever a fusible link is melted because of a short circuit, correct the cause before installing a new one. Most models have four fusible links.

REPLACING FUSIBLE LINKS

▶ See Figures 82 and 83

1. Disconnect the negative battery cable, followed by the positive cables. If the link is connected to the junction block or starter solenoid, disconnect it there as well.
2. Cut the wiring harness right behind the link connector(s) and remove.
3. Strip the insulation off the harness wire back ½ in (12.7mm).
4. Position the clip around the new link and wiring harness or new connector and crimp it securely. Then, solder the connection, using rosin core solder and sufficient heat to guarantee a good connection. Repeat for the remaining connection.
5. Tape all exposed wiring with electrical tape. Where necessary, connect the link to the junction block or started solenoid. Reconnect the positive, followed by the negative battery cables.

Circuit Breakers

One device used to protect electrical components from burning out due to excessive current is a circuit breaker. Circuit breakers open and close the flow path for the electricity rapidly in order to protect the circuit if current is excessive. A circuit breaker is used on components which are more likely to draw excessive current such as the breaker found in the light switch

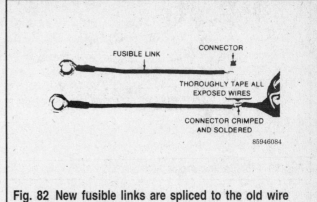

Fig. 82 New fusible links are spliced to the old wire

that protects the headlight circuit. A separate 30 amp breaker mounted on the firewall protects the power window, seat, and power top circuits, as applicable.

Fuse Block

▶ See Figures 84, 85, 86, 87 and 88

The fuse block on most models is located under the instrument panel next to the steering wheel. Other models have the fuse block located on the right side of the dash and access is gained through the glove box.

Each fuse block uses miniature fuses (inline or plug-in blade terminal type) which are designed for increased circuit protection and greater reliability. Later model vehicles are equipped with a compact plug-in or blade terminal design which allows fingertip removal and replacement.

Although most fuses are interchangeable in size, the amperage values are not. Should you install a fuse with too high a value, damaging current could be allowed to destroy the component you were attempting to protect by using a fuse. Inline fuses have a small number molded into 1 or both ends, while plug-in type fuses have a bold number molded on them and are color coded for easy identification. Be sure to only replace a fuse with the proper amperage rated substitute.

A blown fuse can easily be checked by visual inspection or by continuity checking.

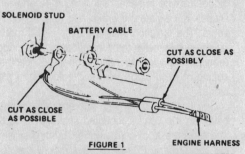

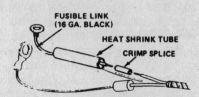

FIGURE 1
REMOVE BATTERY CABLE & FUSIBLE LINK FROM STARTER SOLENOID AND CUT OFF DEFECTIVE WIRE AS SHOWN TWO PLACES.

FIGURE 2
STRIP INSULATION FROM WIRE ENDS. PLACE HEAT SHRINK TUBE OVER REPLACEMENT LINK. INSERT WIRE ENDS INTO CRIMP SPLICE AS SHOWN. NOTE: PUSH WIRES IN FAR ENOUGH TO ENGAGE WIRE ENDS.

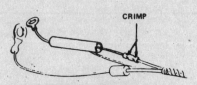

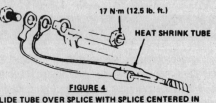

FIGURE 3
CRIMP SPLICE WITH CRIMPING TOOL TWO PLACES TO BIND BOTH WIRES.

FIGURE 4
SLIDE TUBE OVER SPLICE WITH SPLICE CENTERED IN TUBE. APPLY LOW TEMPERATURE HEAT TO SHRINK TUBE AROUND WIRES & SPLICE. REASSEMBLE LINKS & BATTERY CABLE.

Fig: 83 Fusible link repair

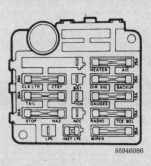

Fig. 84 Early model fuse box designed to accommodate inline fuses — amperage figures may vary

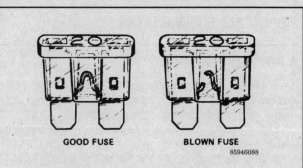

GOOD FUSE   BLOWN FUSE

Fig. 86 Blown fuses can be easily detected through a visual inspection

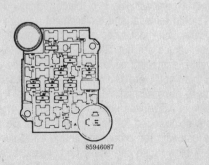

Fig. 85 Plug-in blade type or compact fuse box

Fuse Color-Coding

Fuse (Amps)	Color Stripe
3	Violet
5	Tan
7.5	Brown
10	Red
20	Clear
25	White

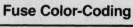

Fig. 87 Plug-in blade type fuses are color coded for easy identification

Fig. 88 The fuse box on most vehicles can be found under the left side of the instrument panel, near the steering column and foot pedals

Buzzers, Relays, and Flashers

▶ See Figure 89

For most vehicles, buzzers and flashers are located in the fuse box, while relays are found throughout the vehicle in various systems. Some newer vehicles are equipped with a convenience center which centrally locates buzzers, flashers and relays. If equipped, the convenience center is a swing down unit located under the instrument panel. Most buzzers, relays and flashers are serviced by plug-in replacements.

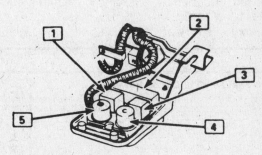

1. Horn relay
2. Seat belt–ignition key–headlight buzzer
3. Choke relay (vacant w/EFI)
4. Hazard flasher
5. Signal flasher

85946091

Fig. 89 View of a common convenience center and components

Troubleshooting Basic Turn Signal and Flasher Problems

Most problems in the turn signals or flasher system can be reduced to defective flashers or bulbs, which are easily replaced. Occasionally, problems in the turn signals are traced to the switch in the steering column, which will require professional service.

F = Front   R = Rear   ● = Lights off   ○ = Lights on

Problem		Solution
Turn signals light, but do not flash		• Replace the flasher
No turn signals light on either side		• Check the fuse. Replace if defective. • Check the flasher by substitution • Check for open circuit, short circuit or poor ground
Both turn signals on one side don't work		• Check for bad bulbs • Check for bad ground in both housings
One turn signal light on one side doesn't work		• Check and/or replace bulb • Check for corrosion in socket. Clean contacts. • Check for poor ground at socket
Turn signal flashes too fast or too slow		• Check any bulb on the side flashing too fast. A heavy-duty bulb is probably installed in place of a regular bulb. • Check the bulb flashing too slow. A standard bulb was probably installed in place of a heavy-duty bulb. • Check for loose connections or corrosion at the bulb socket
Indicator lights don't work in either direction		• Check if the turn signals are working • Check the dash indicator lights • Check the flasher by substitution

85946092

WIRING DIAGRAMS

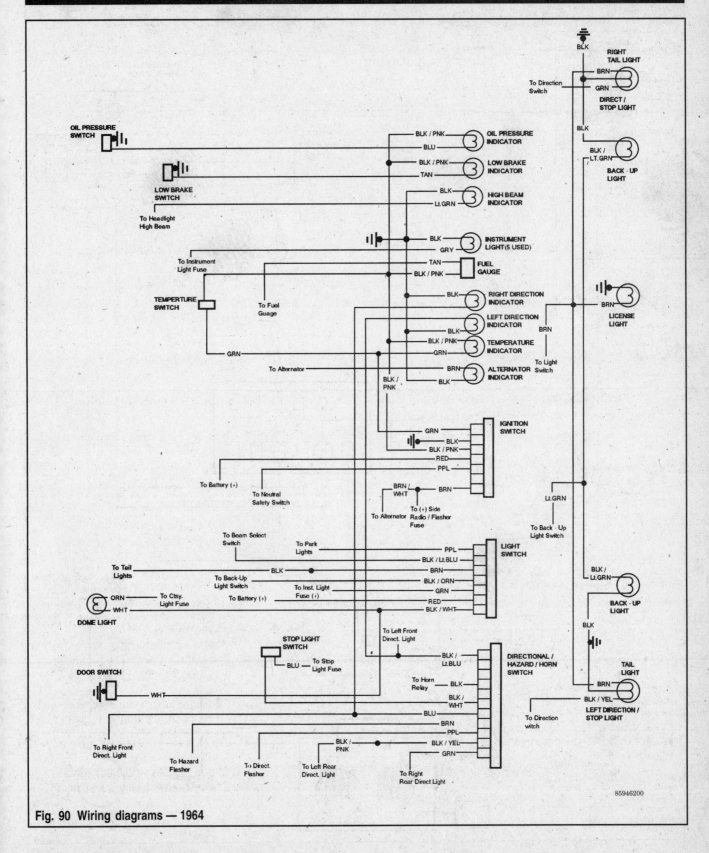

Fig. 90 Wiring diagrams — 1964

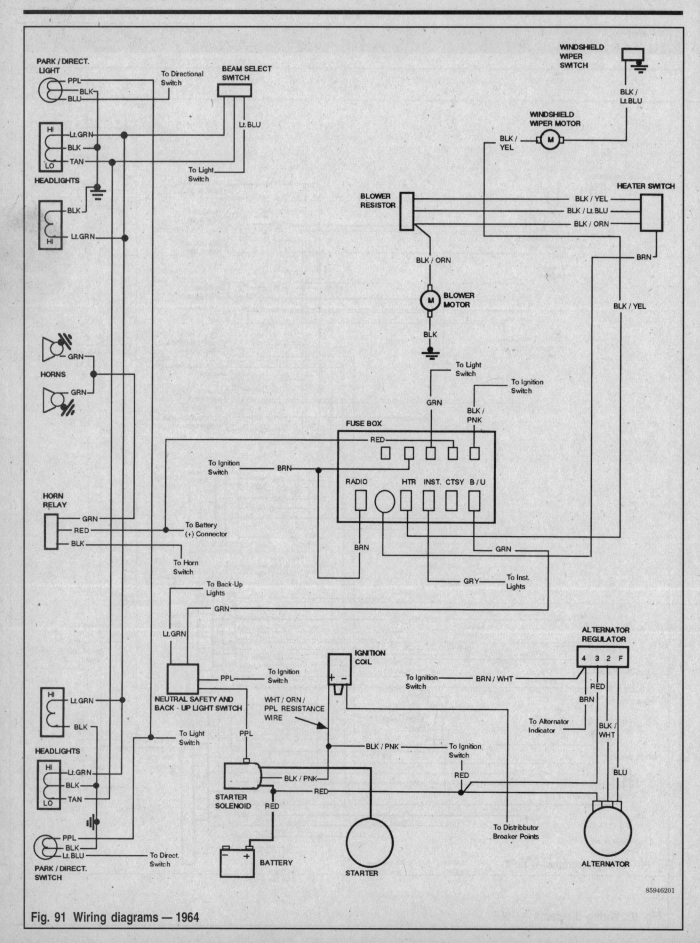

Fig. 91 Wiring diagrams — 1964

85946201

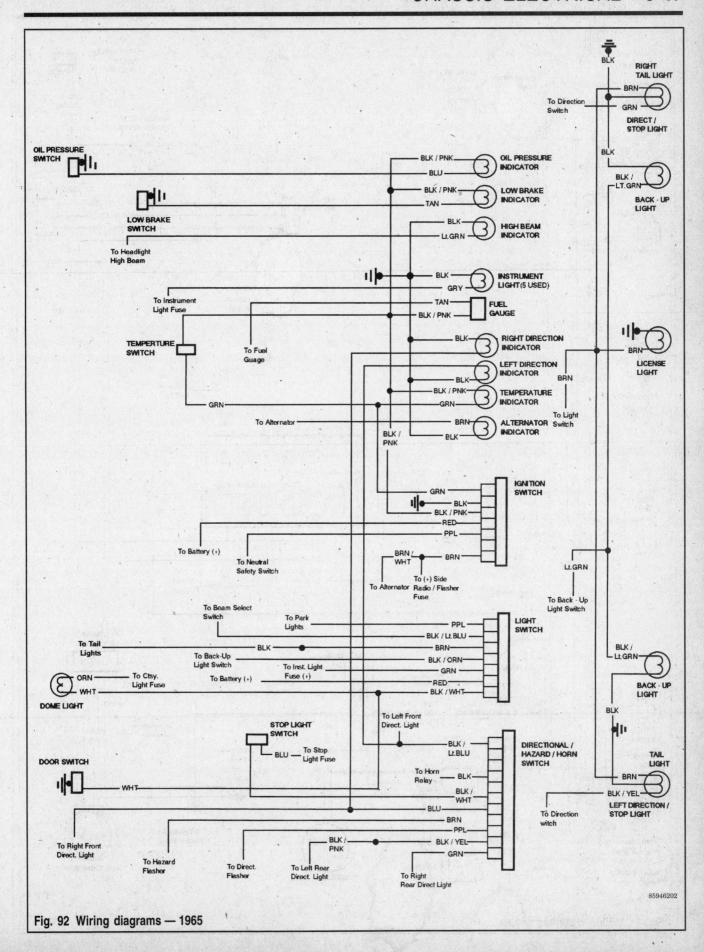

Fig. 92 Wiring diagrams — 1965

85946202

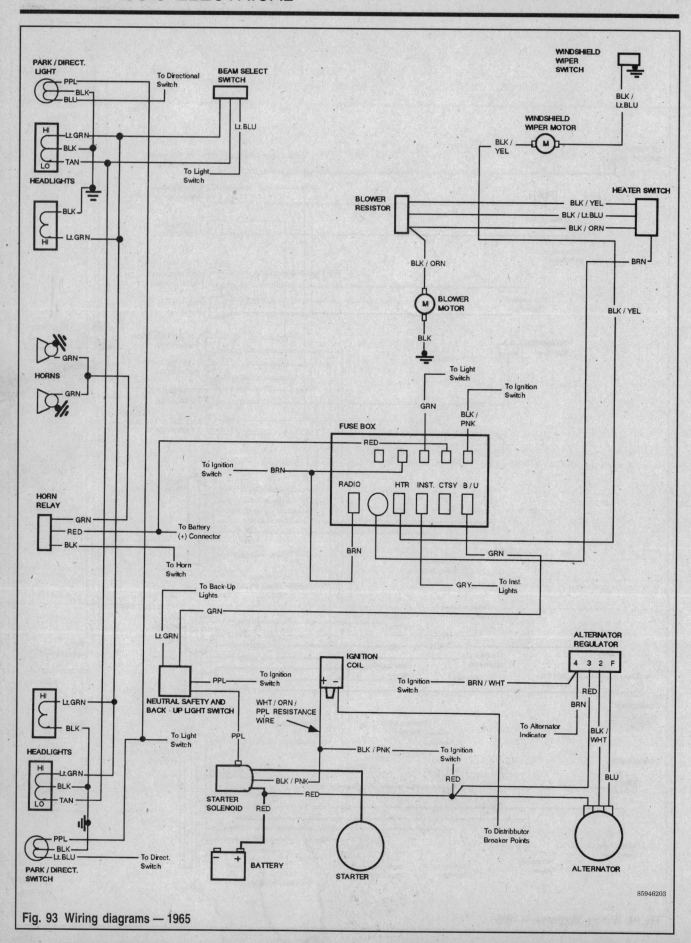

Fig. 93 Wiring diagrams — 1965

85946203

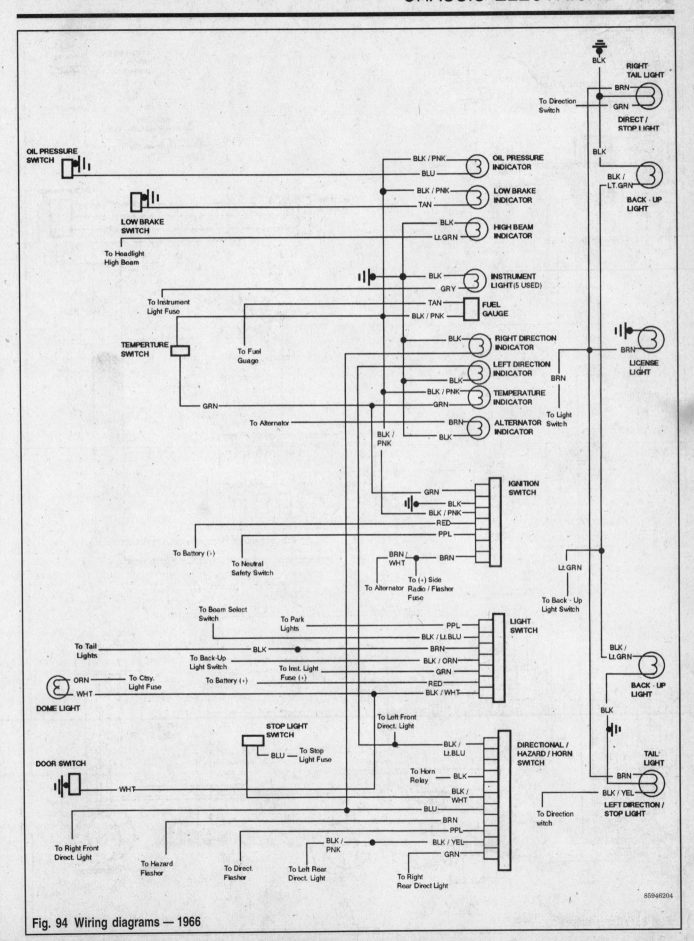

Fig. 94 Wiring diagrams — 1966

85946204

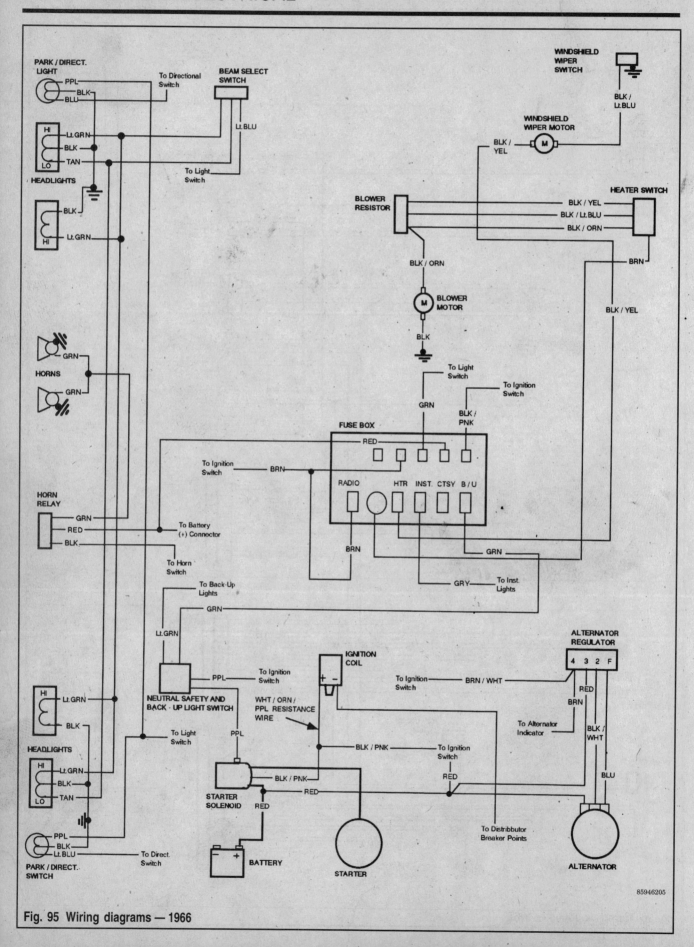

Fig. 95 Wiring diagrams — 1966

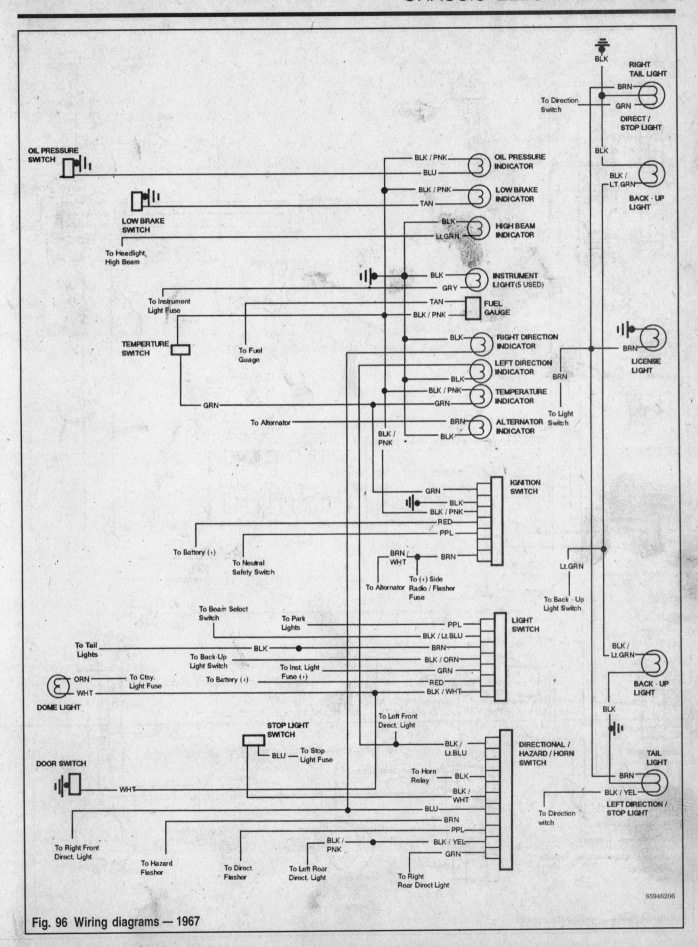

Fig. 96 Wiring diagrams — 1967

85946206

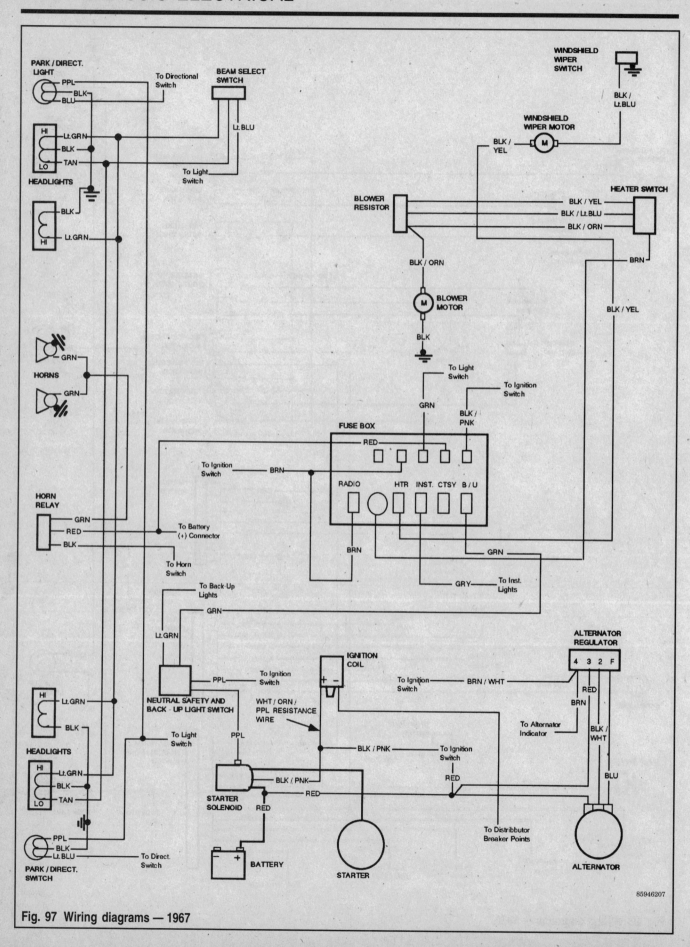

Fig. 97 Wiring diagrams — 1967

85946207

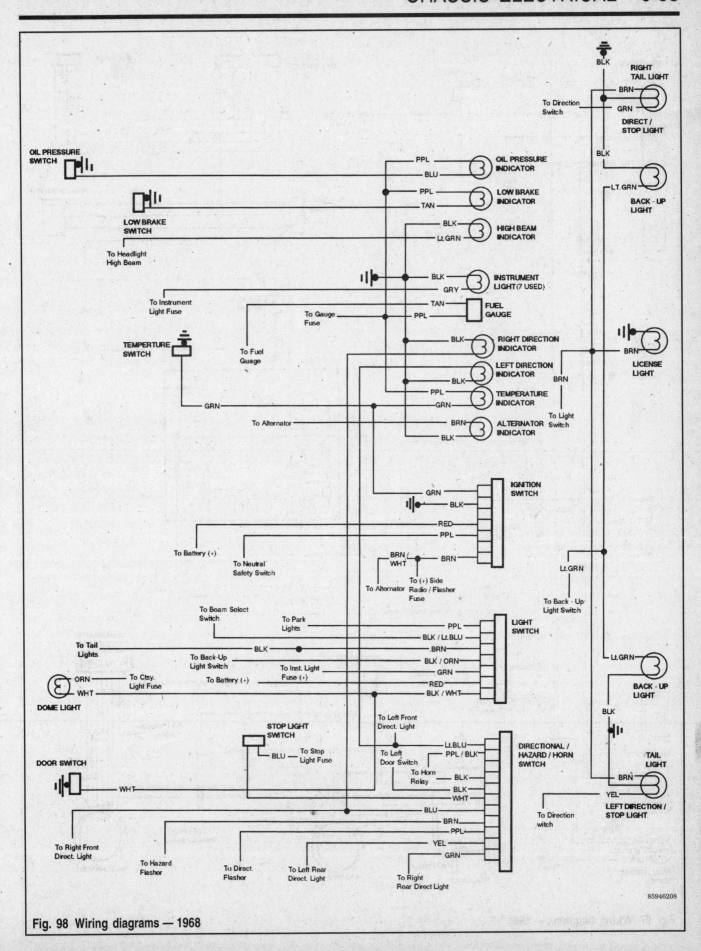

Fig. 98 Wiring diagrams — 1968

85946208

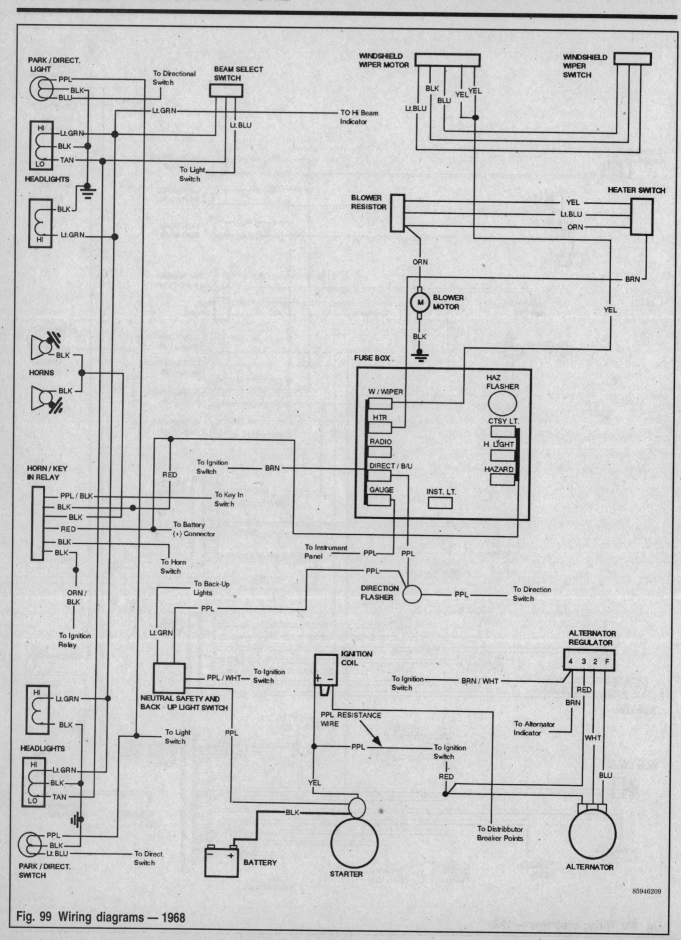

Fig. 99 Wiring diagrams — 1968

85946209

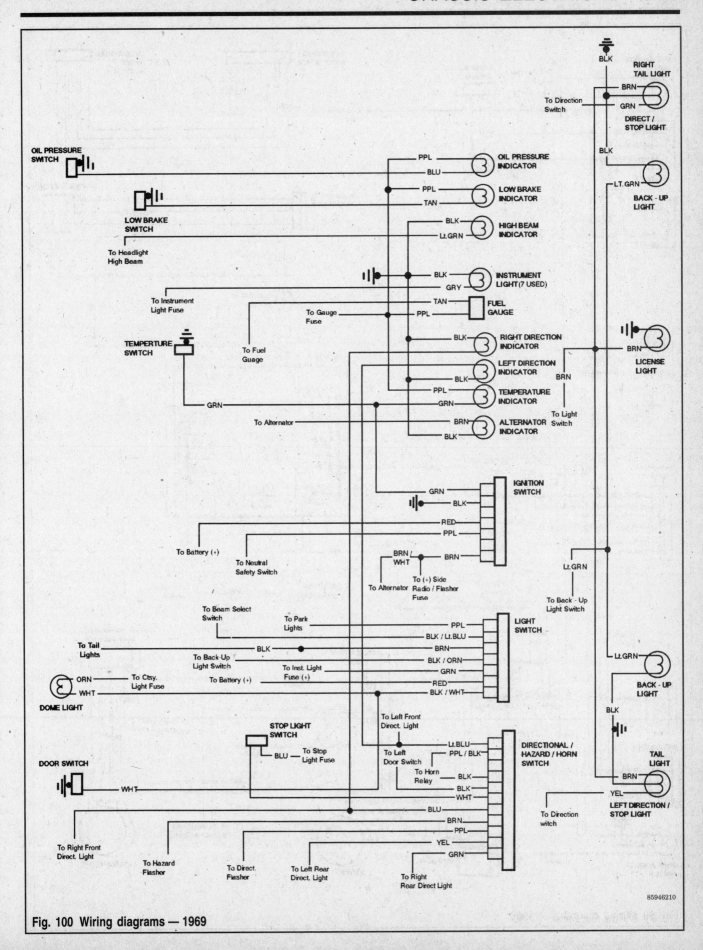

Fig. 100 Wiring diagrams — 1969

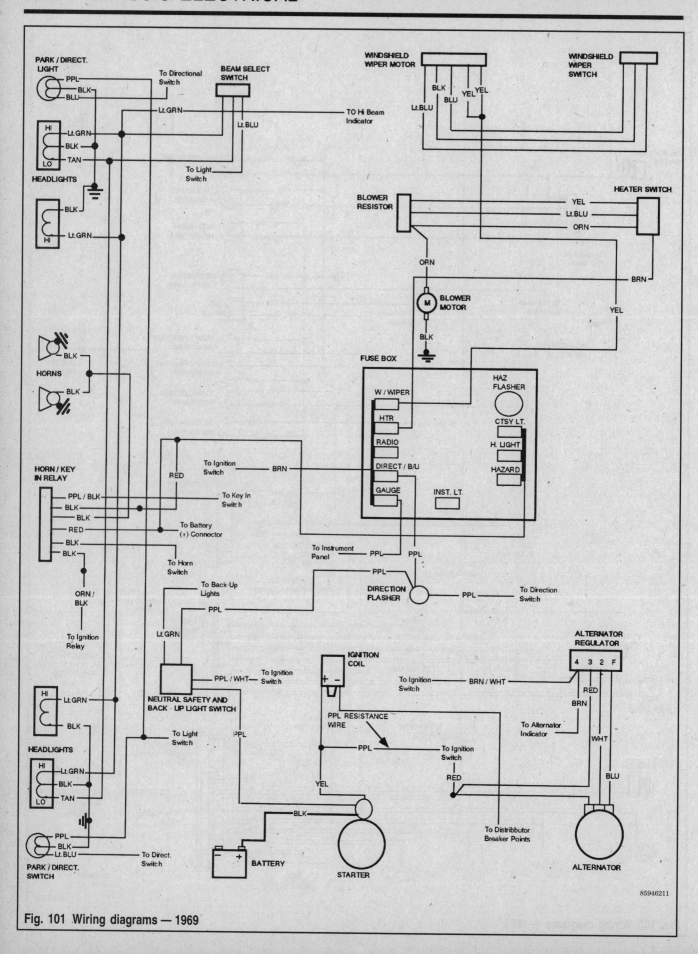

Fig. 101 Wiring diagrams — 1969

85946211

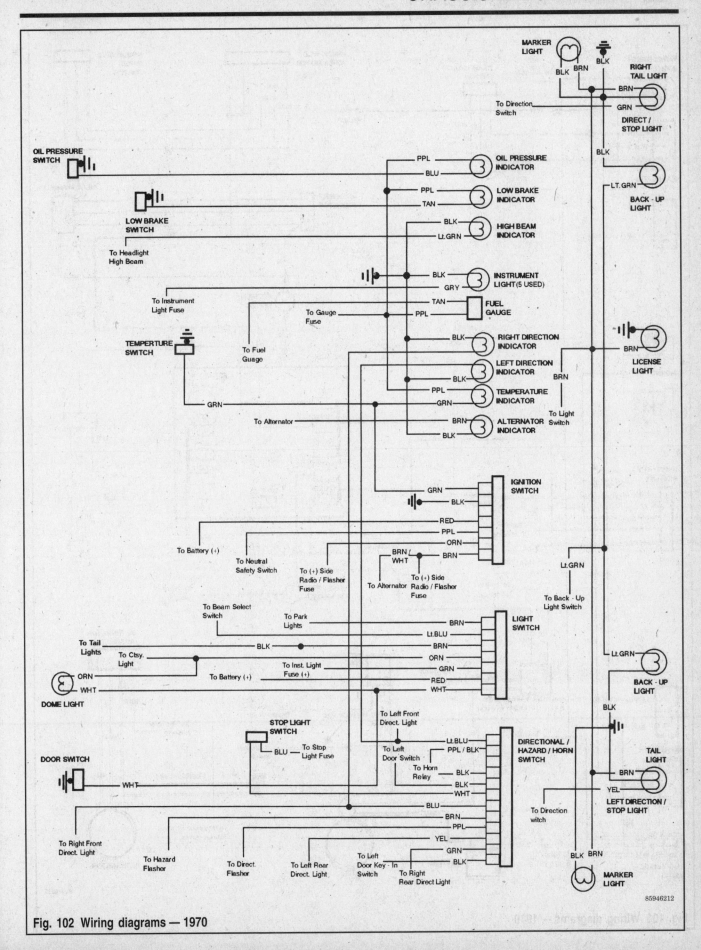

Fig. 102 Wiring diagrams — 1970

85946212

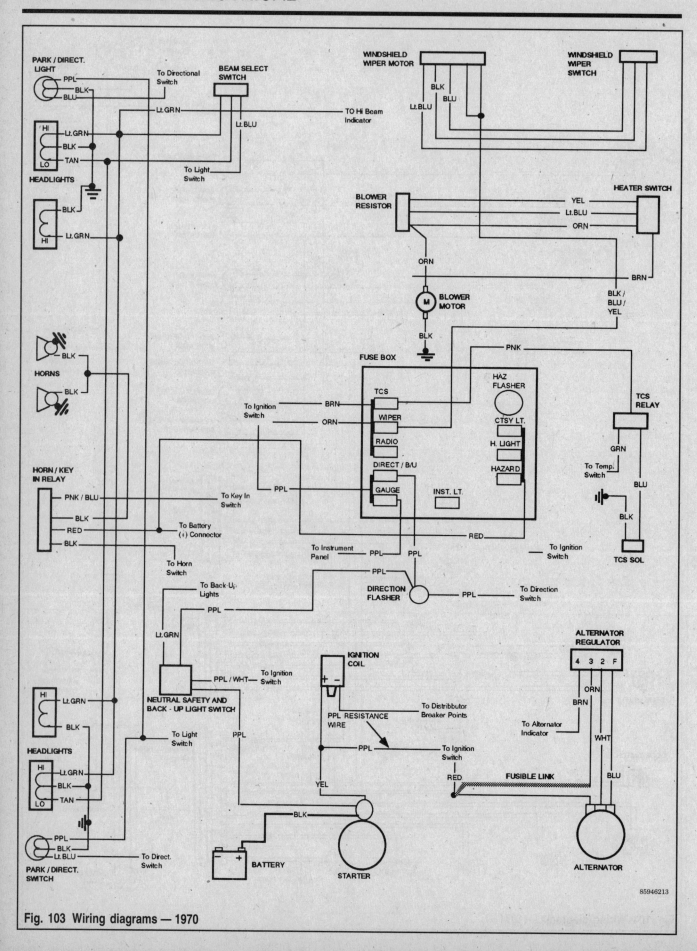

Fig. 103 Wiring diagrams — 1970

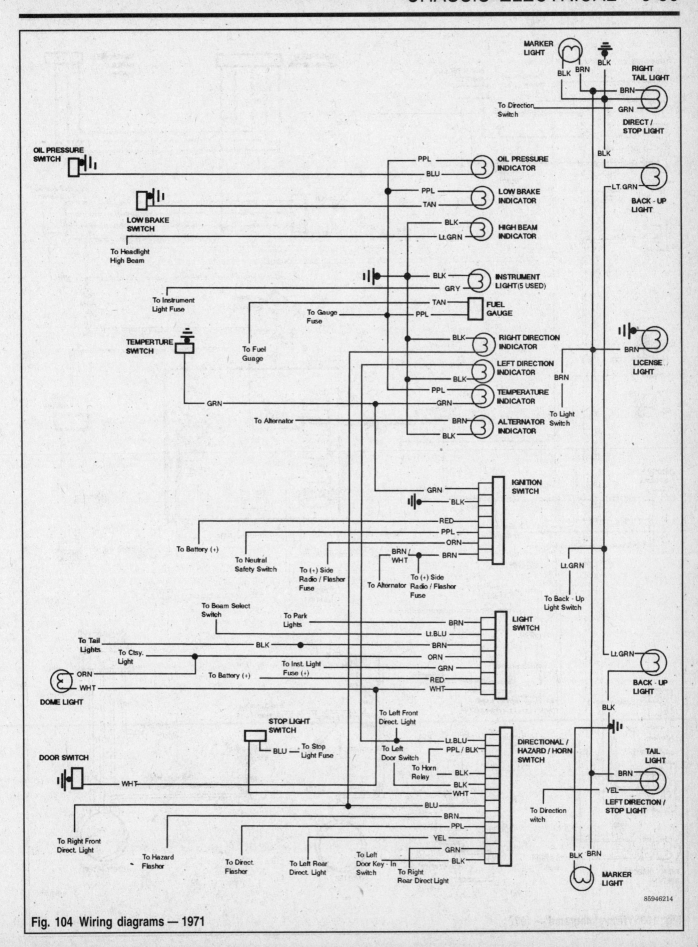

Fig. 104 Wiring diagrams — 1971

85946214

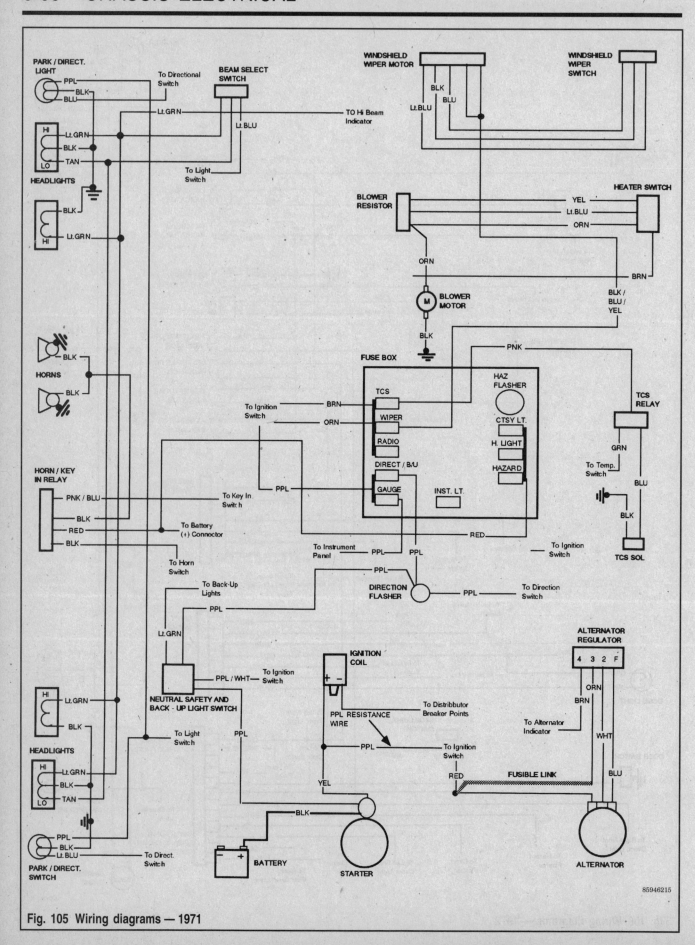

Fig. 105 Wiring diagrams — 1971

85946215

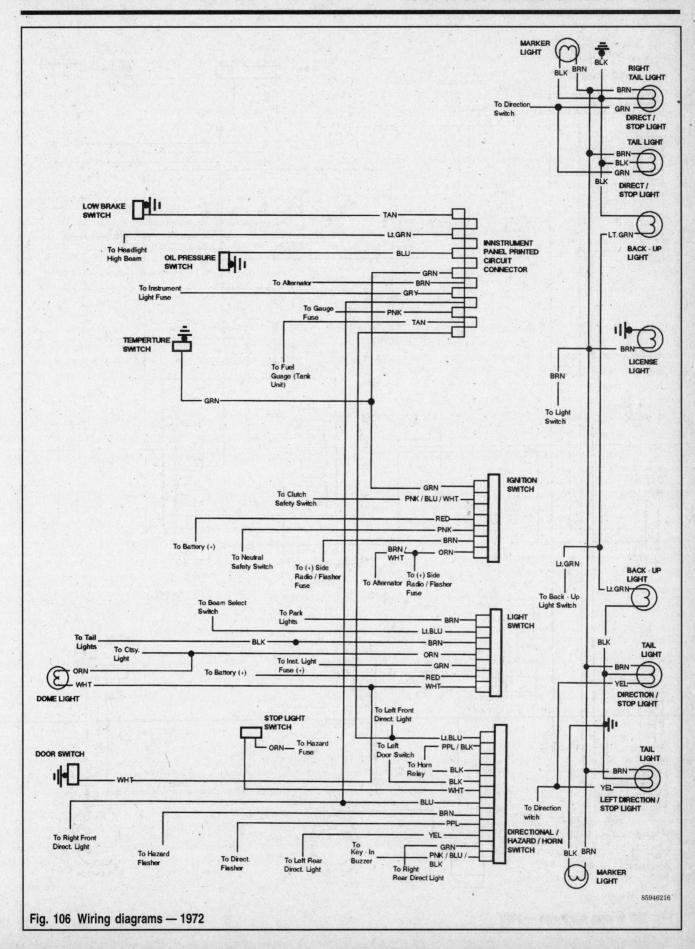

Fig. 106 Wiring diagrams — 1972

85946216

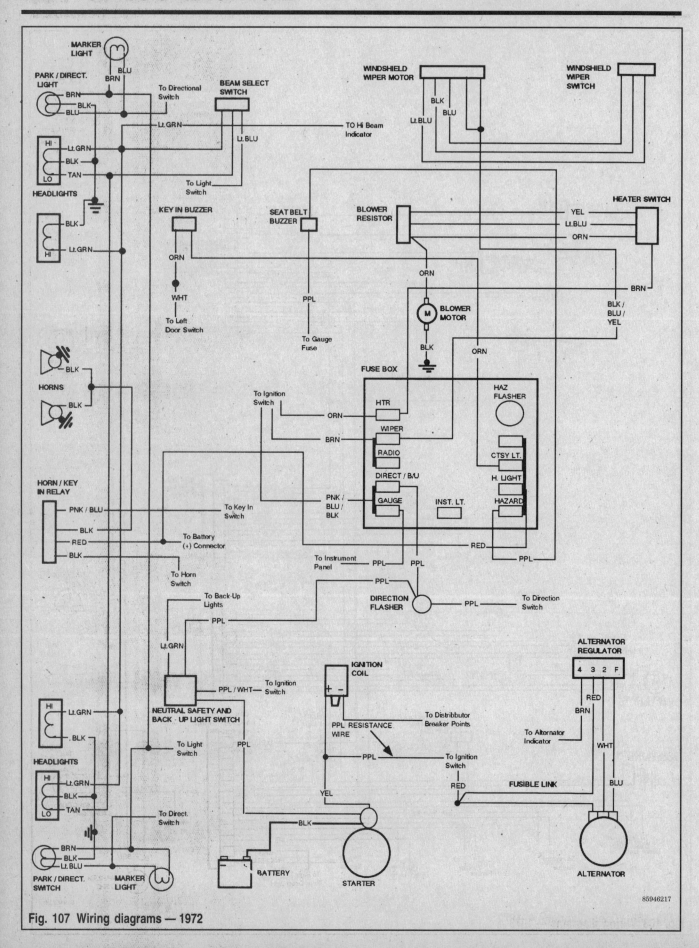

Fig. 107 Wiring diagrams — 1972

85946217

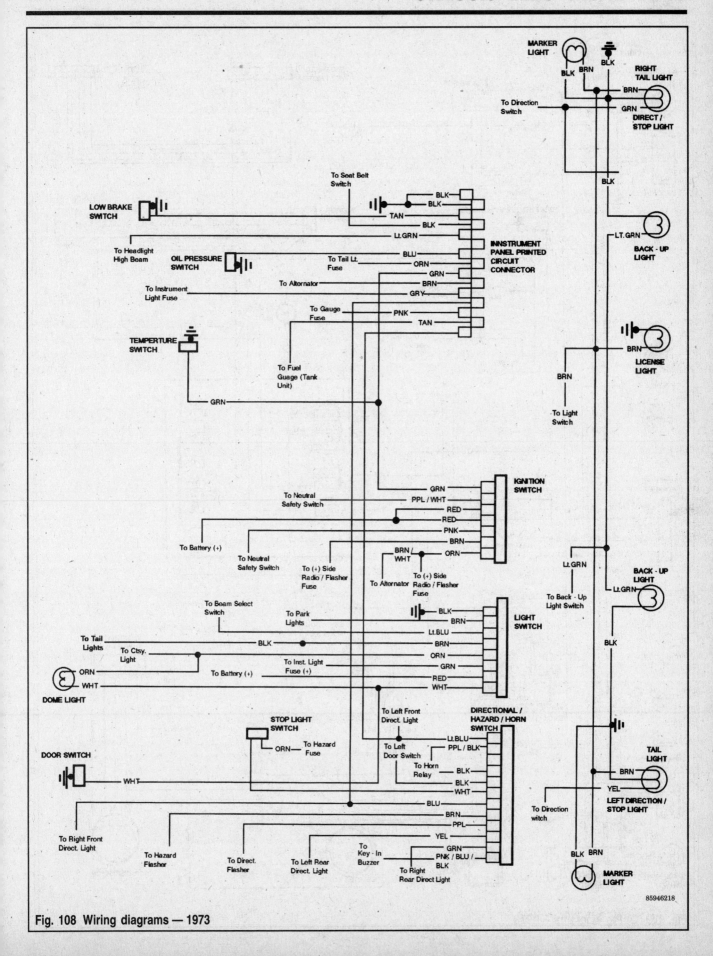

Fig. 108 Wiring diagrams — 1973

85946218

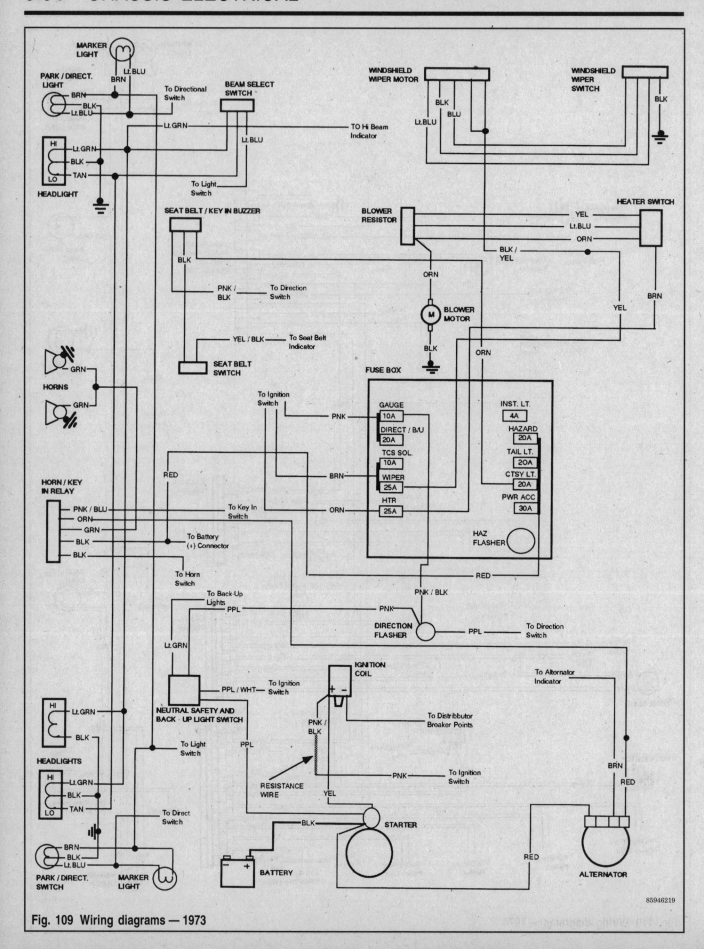

Fig. 109 Wiring diagrams — 1973

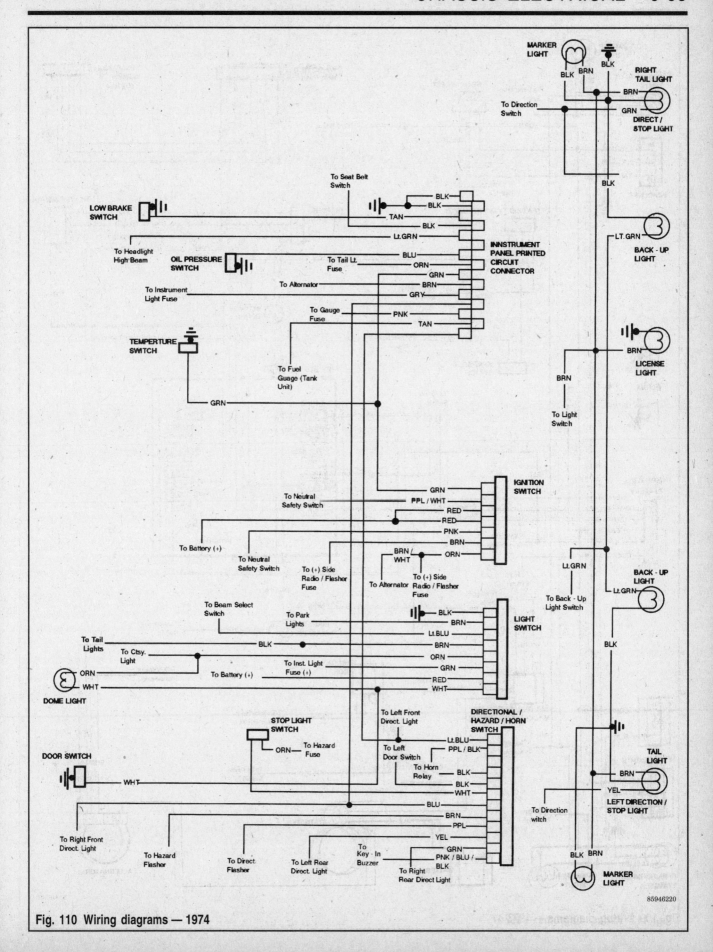

Fig. 110 Wiring diagrams — 1974

85946220

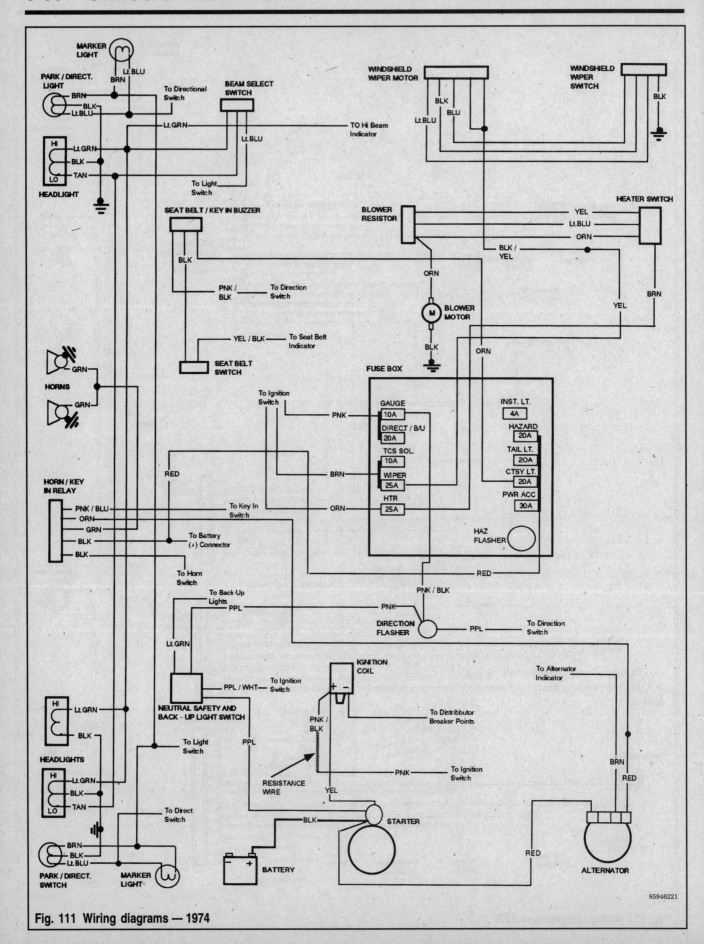

Fig. 111 Wiring diagrams — 1974

85946221

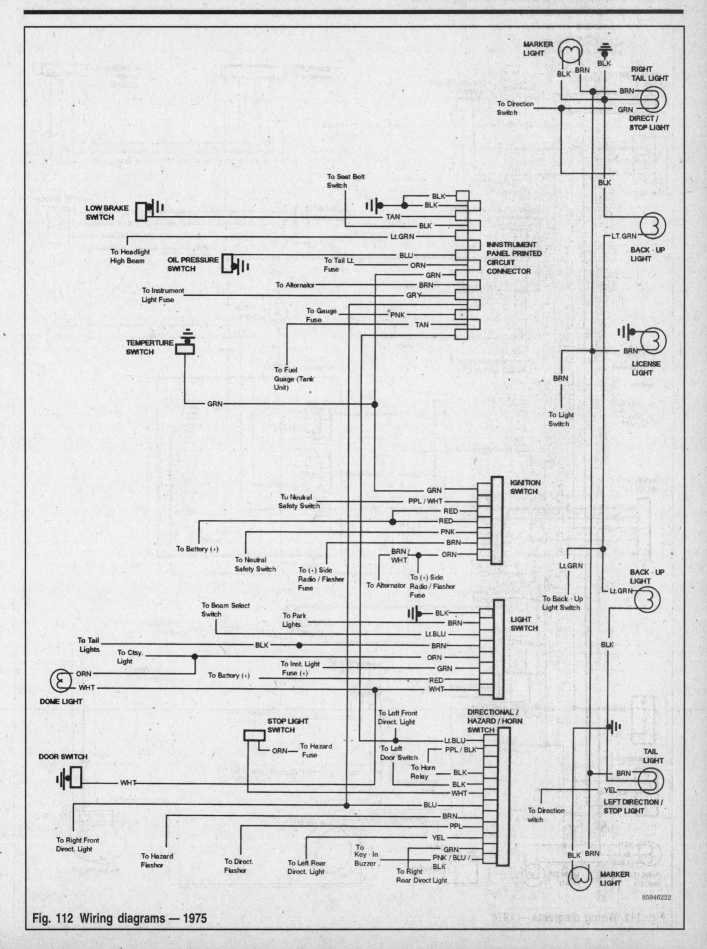

Fig. 112 Wiring diagrams — 1975

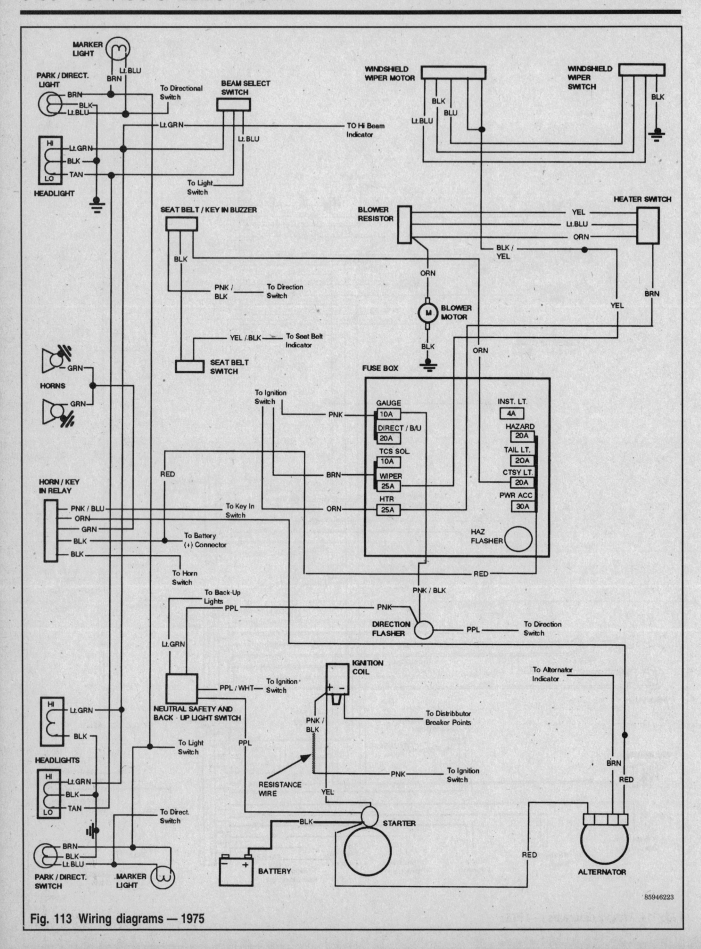

Fig. 113 Wiring diagrams — 1975

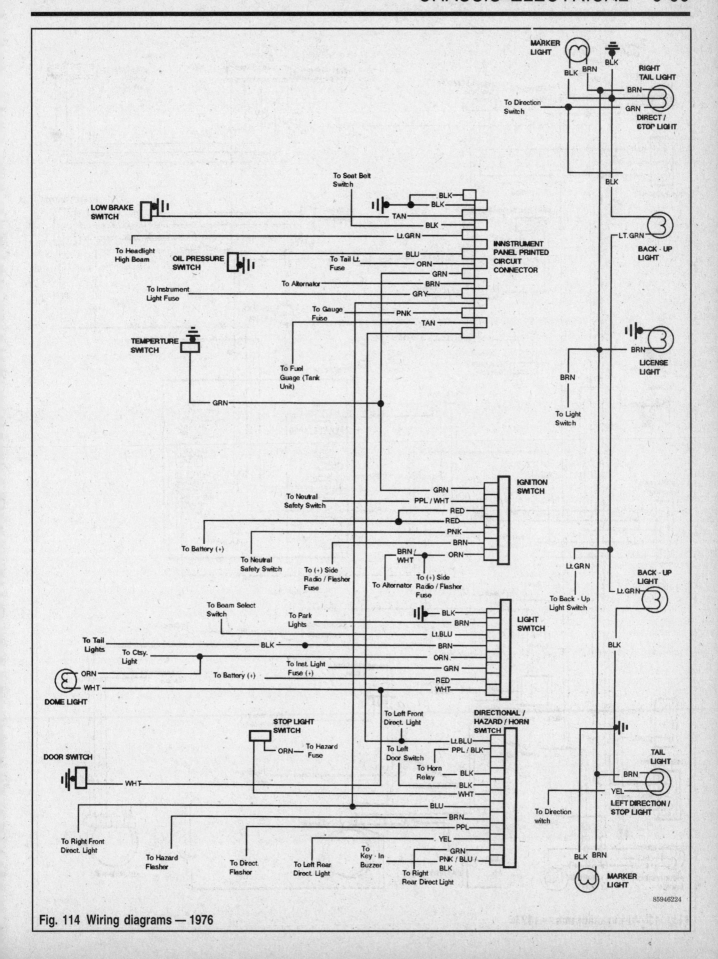

Fig. 114 Wiring diagrams — 1976

85946224

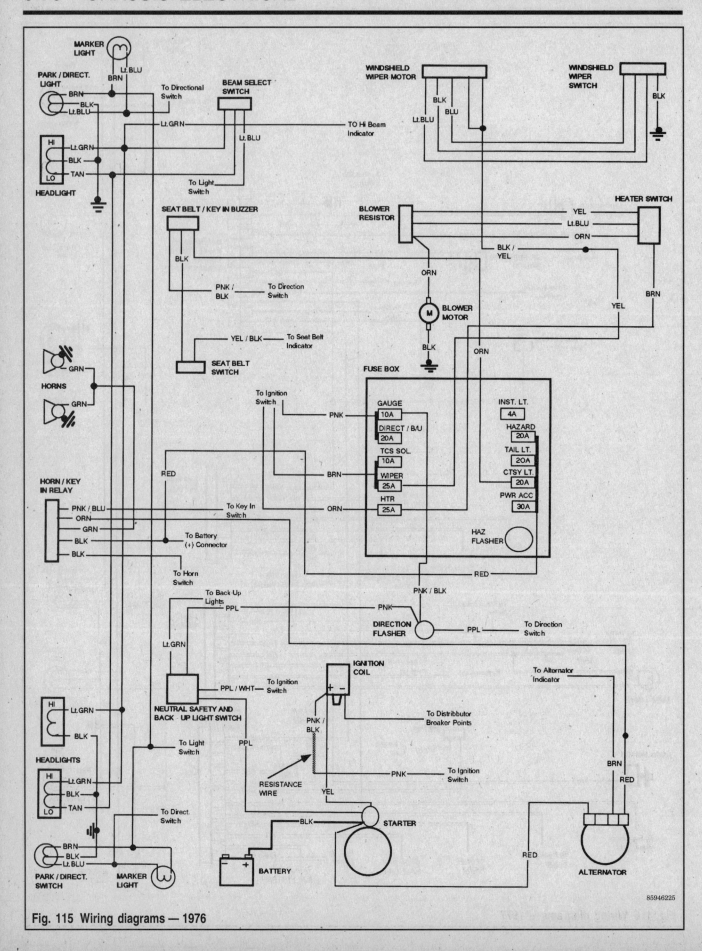

Fig. 115 Wiring diagrams — 1976

85946225

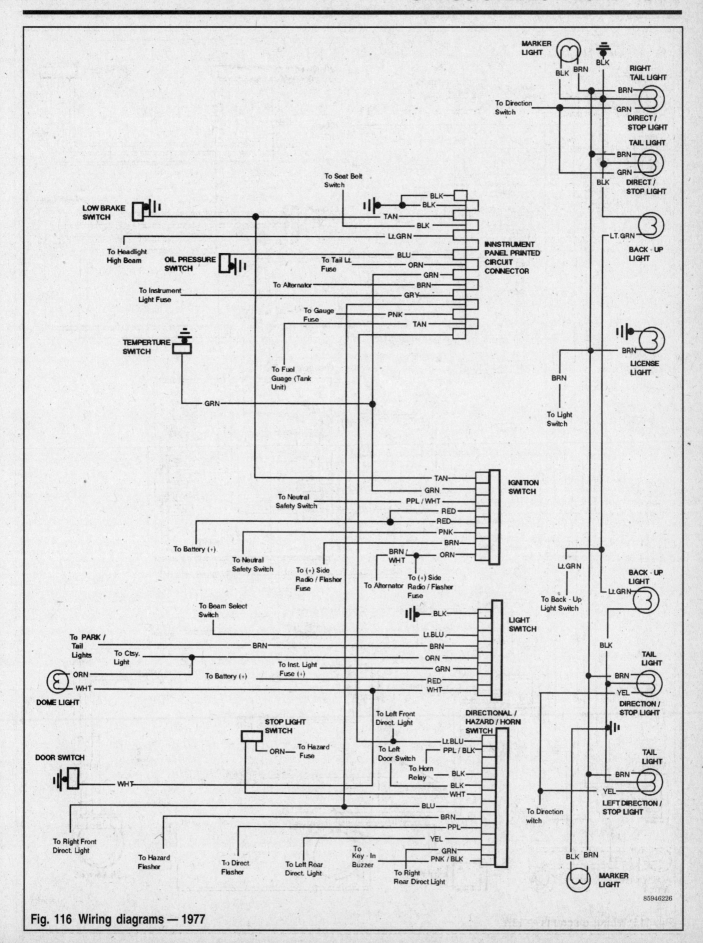

Fig. 116 Wiring diagrams — 1977

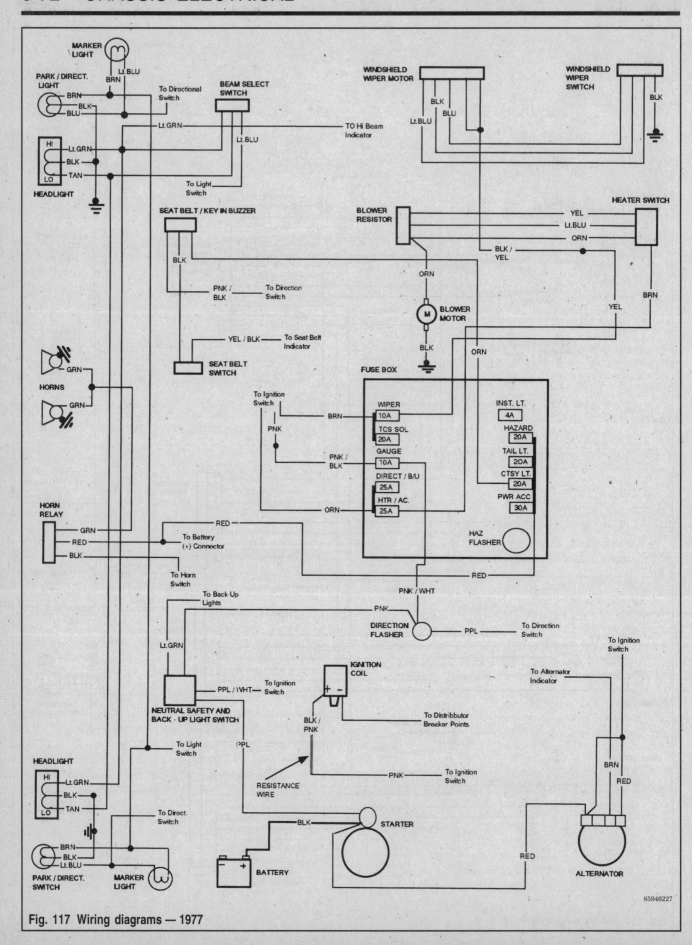

Fig. 117 Wiring diagrams — 1977

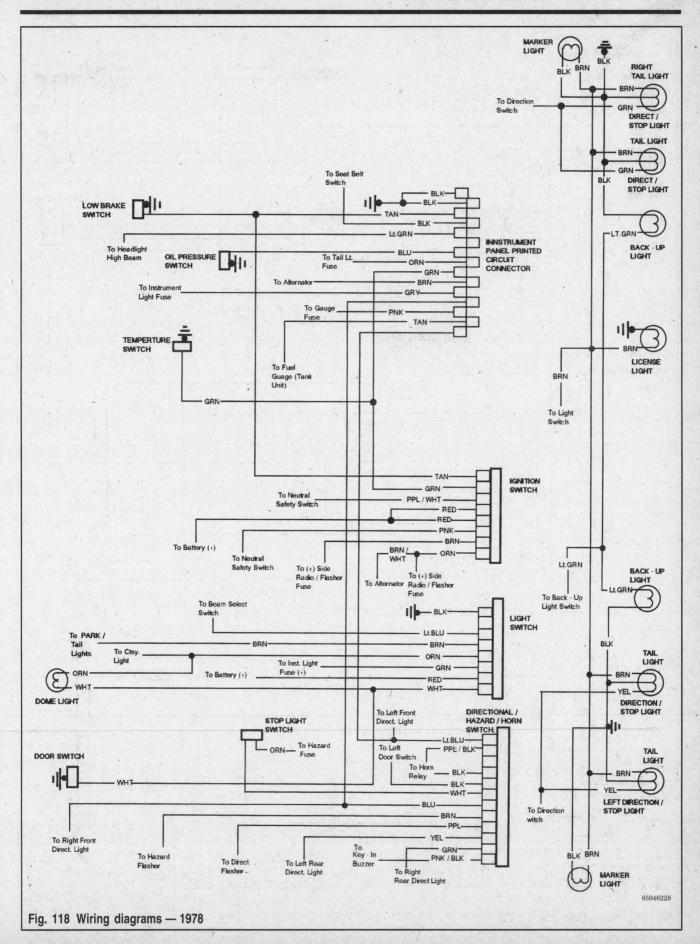

Fig. 118 Wiring diagrams — 1978

85946228

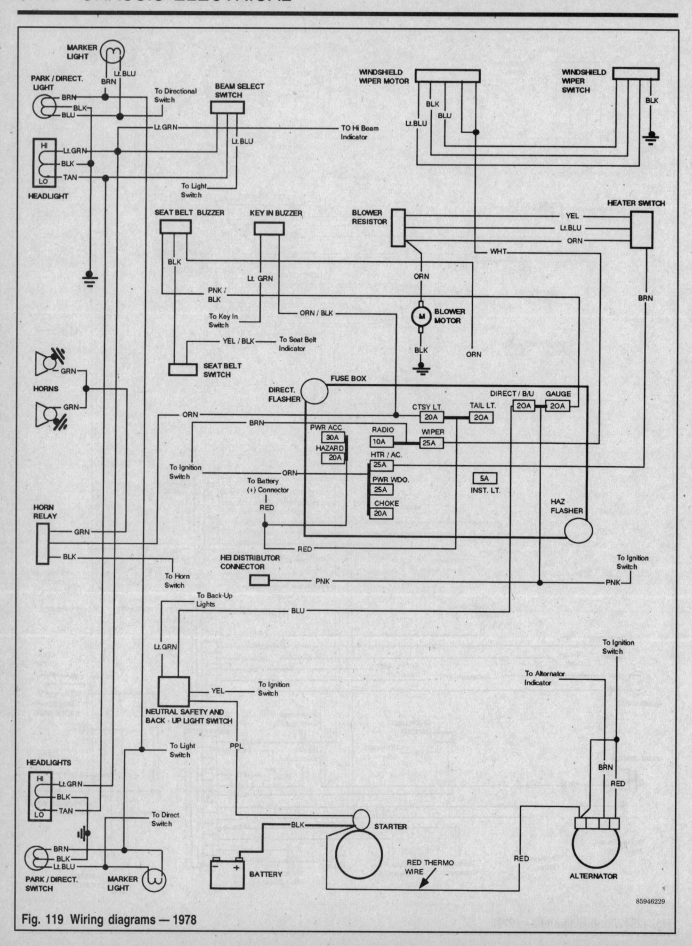

Fig. 119 Wiring diagrams — 1978

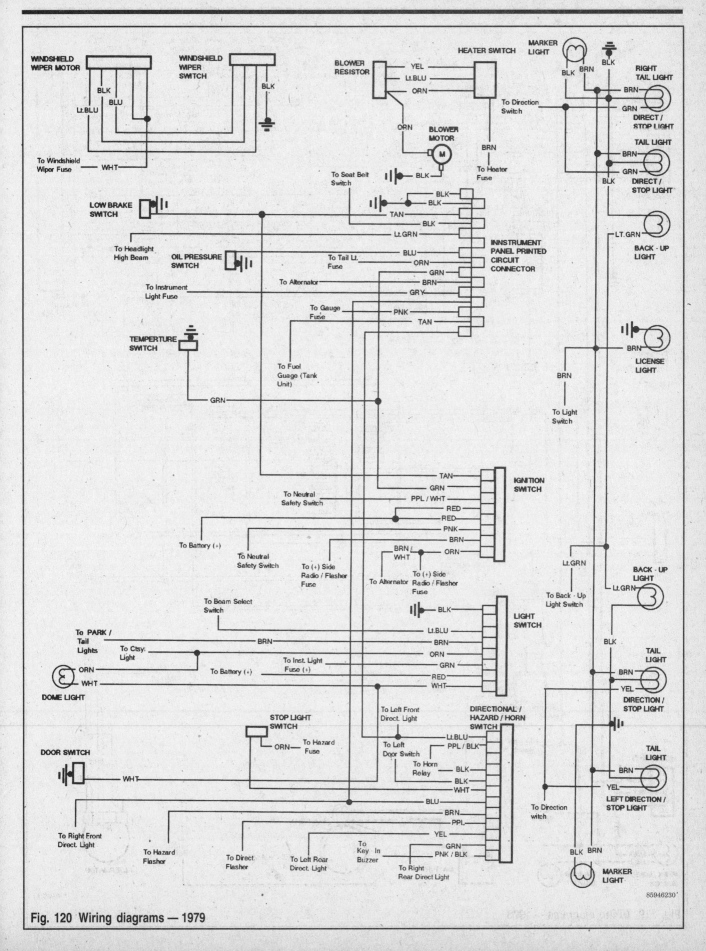

Fig. 120 Wiring diagrams — 1979

85946230

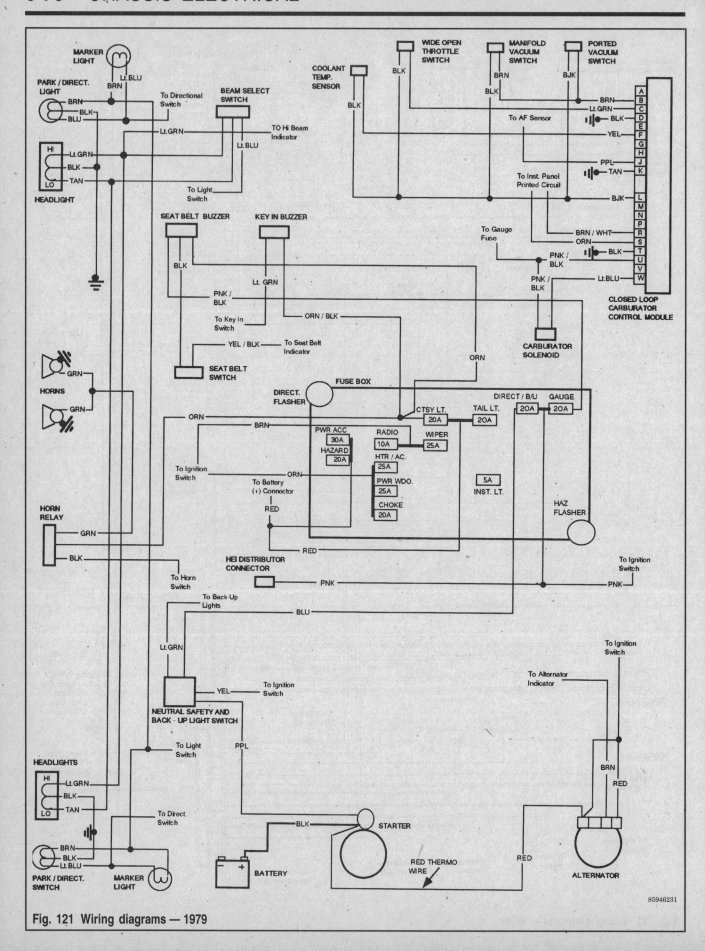

Fig. 121 Wiring diagrams — 1979

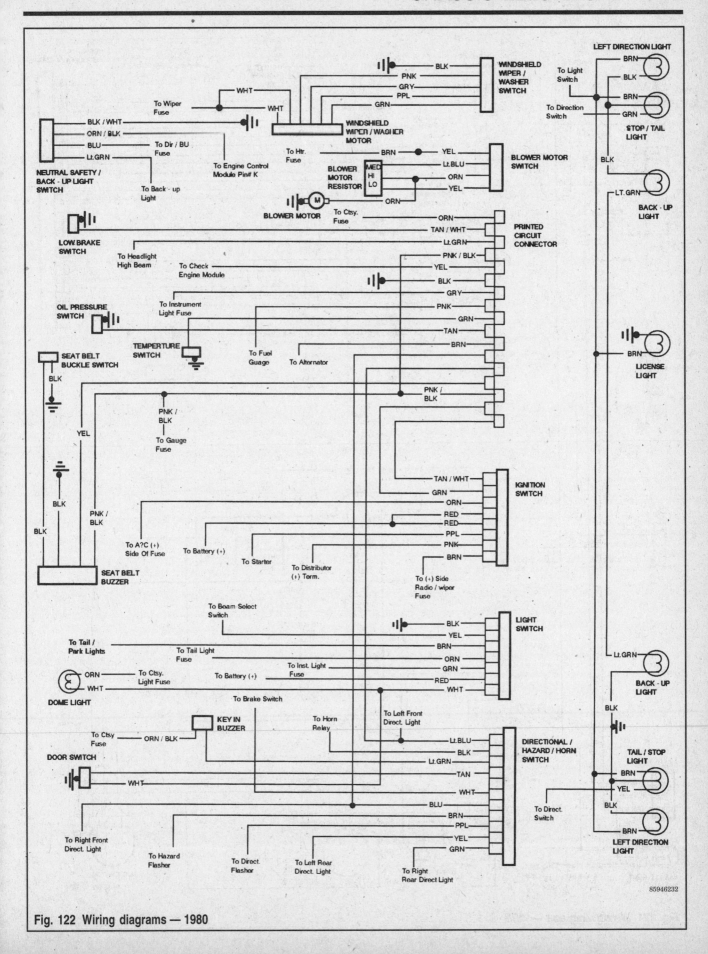

Fig. 122 Wiring diagrams — 1980

85946232

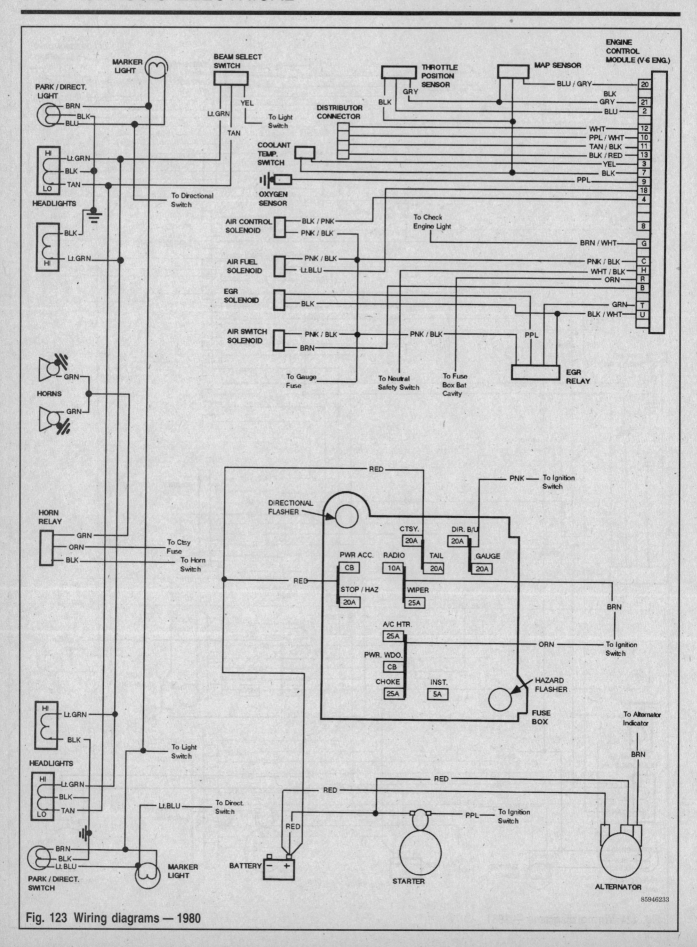

Fig. 123 Wiring diagrams — 1980

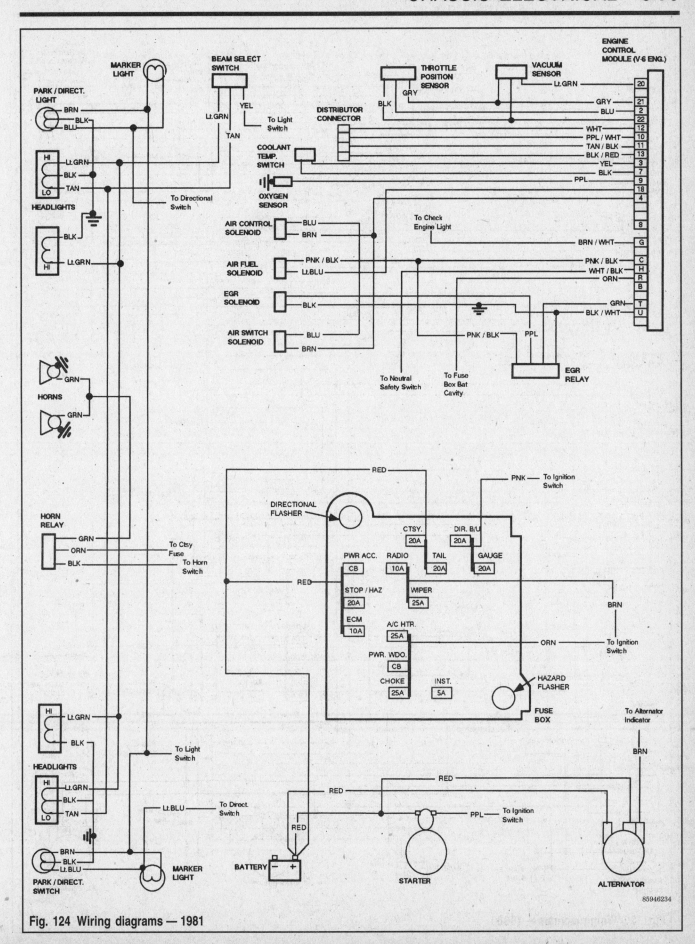

Fig. 124 Wiring diagrams — 1981

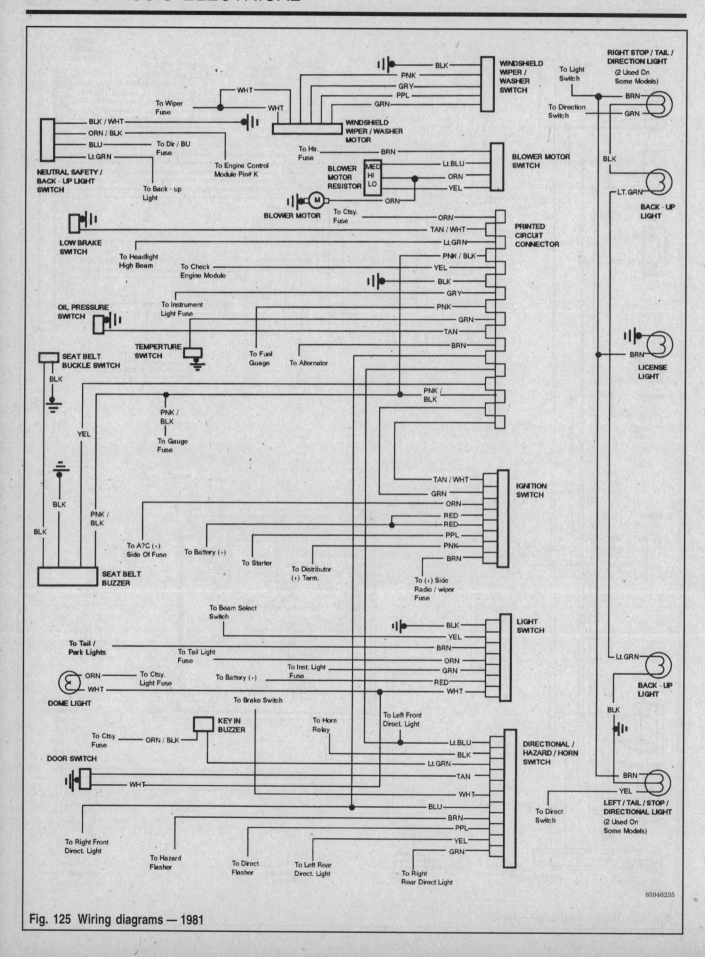

Fig. 125 Wiring diagrams — 1981

85946235

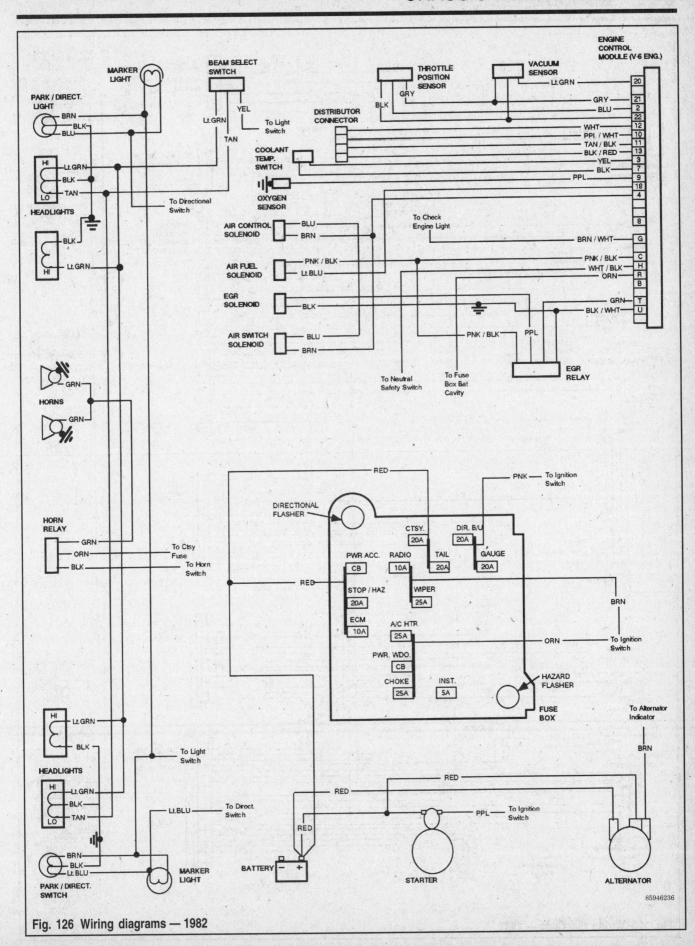

Fig. 126 Wiring diagrams — 1982

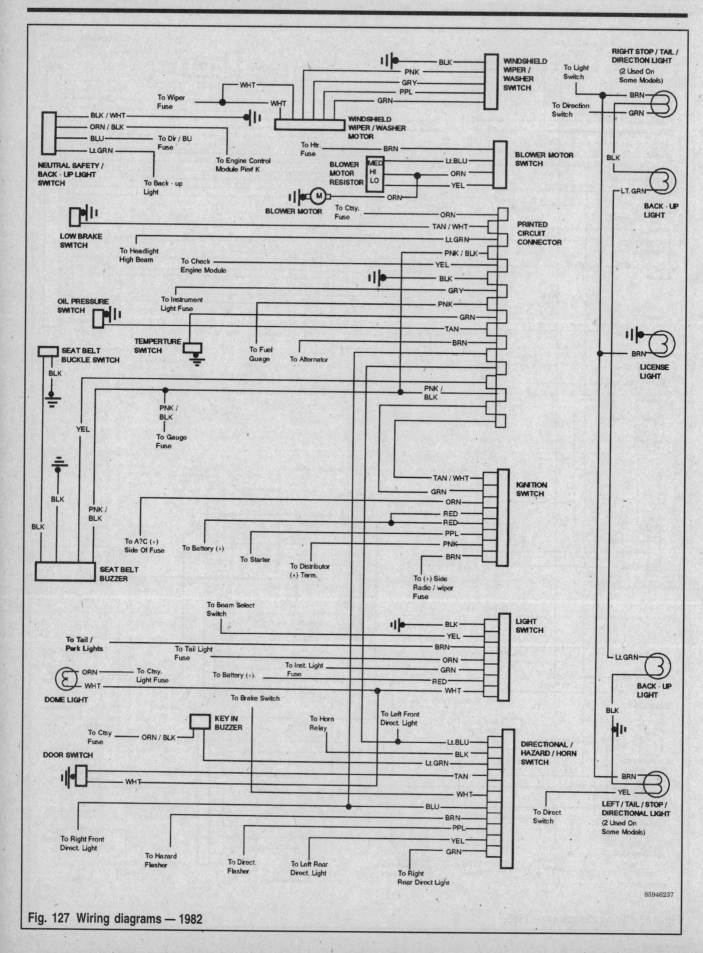

Fig. 127 Wiring diagrams — 1982

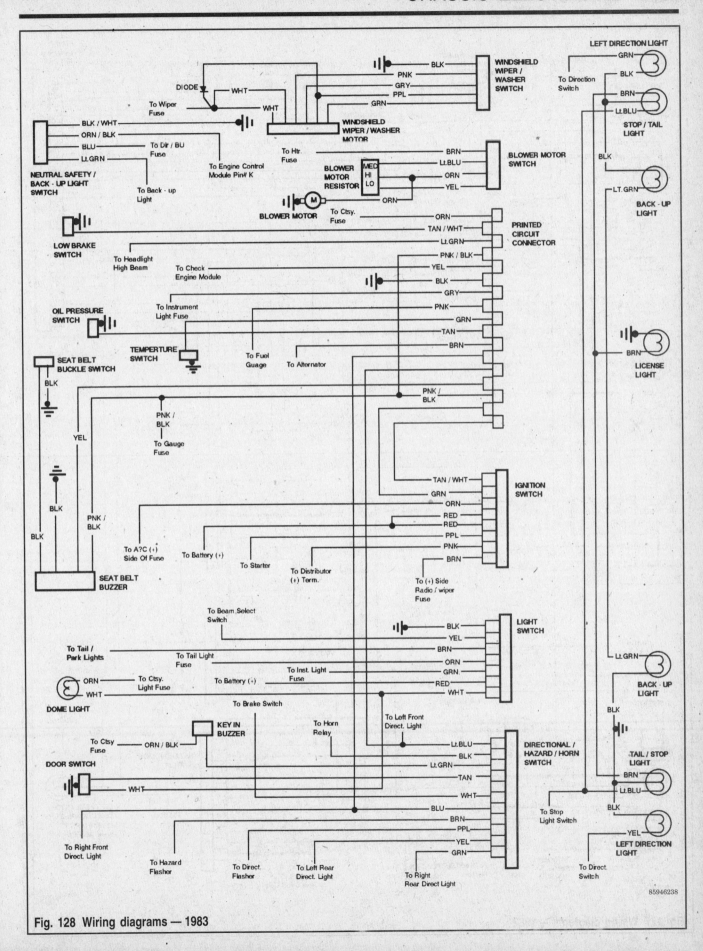

Fig. 128 Wiring diagrams — 1983

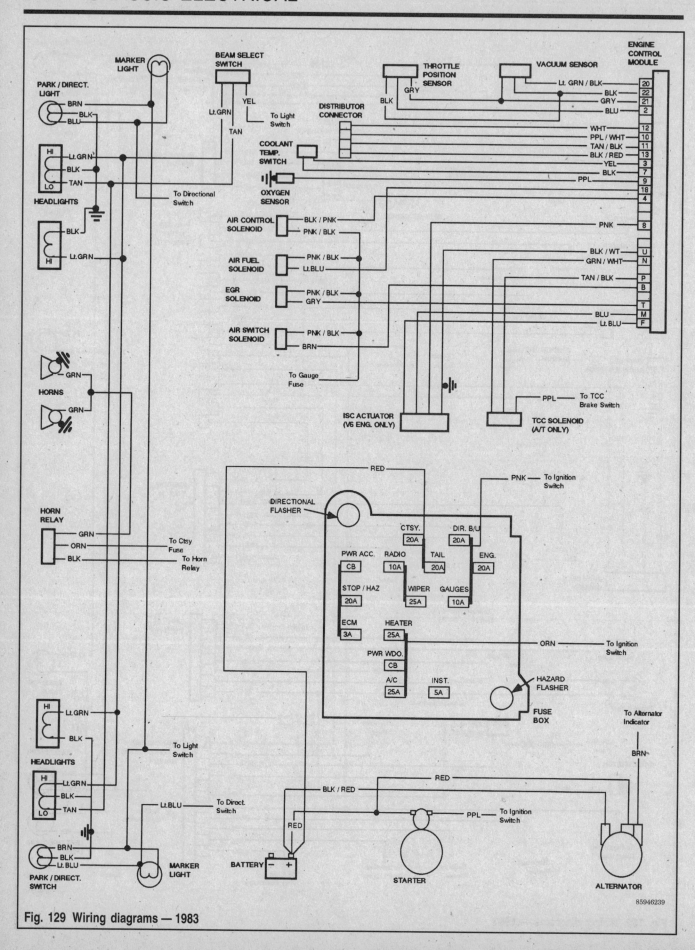

Fig. 129 Wiring diagrams — 1983

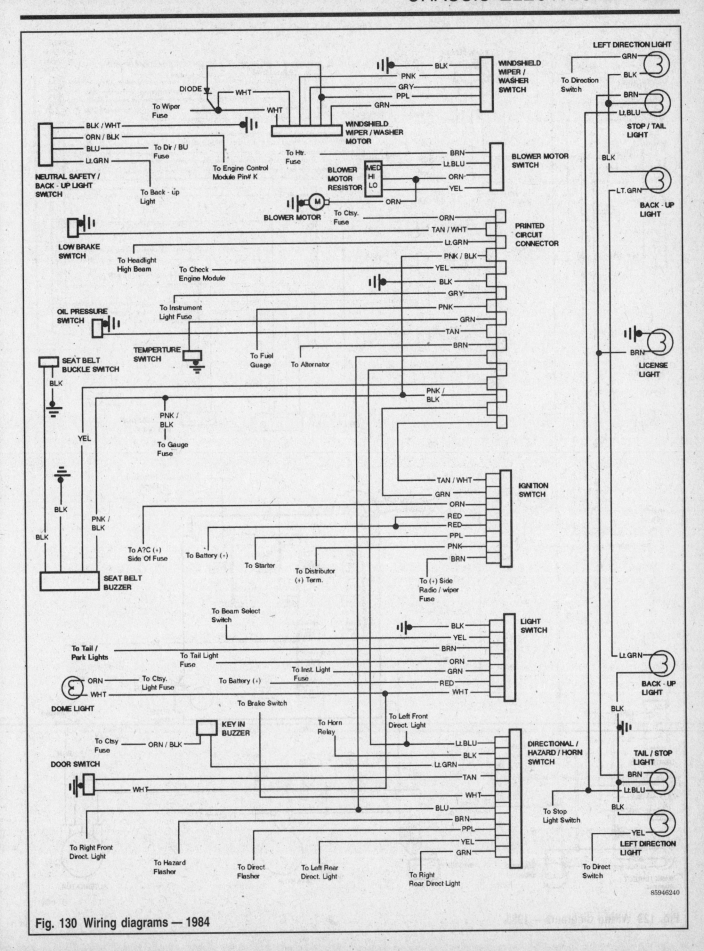

Fig. 130 Wiring diagrams — 1984

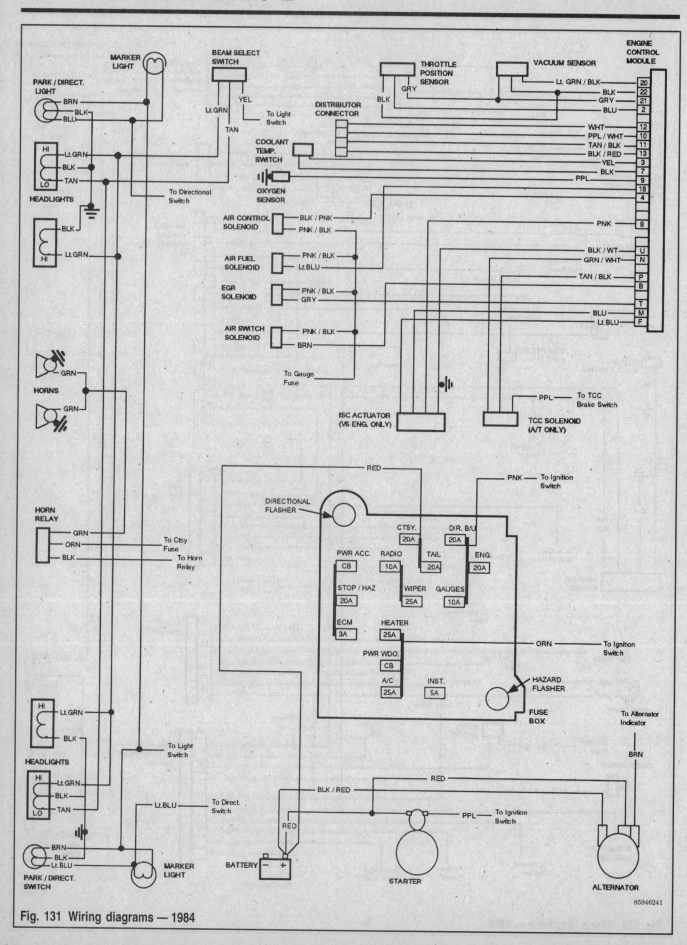

Fig. 131 Wiring diagrams — 1984

85946241

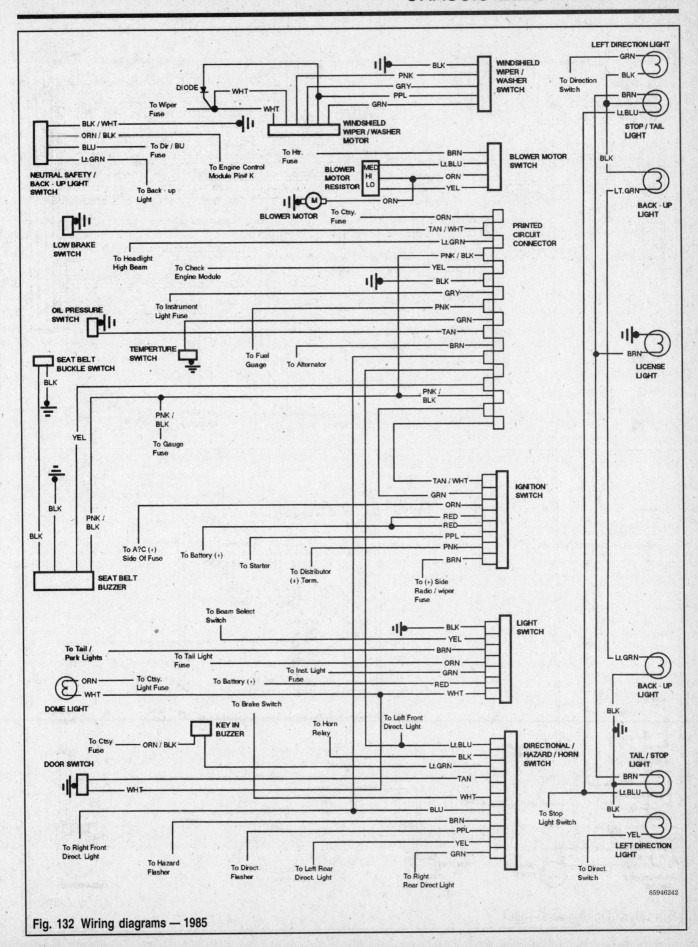

Fig. 132 Wiring diagrams — 1985

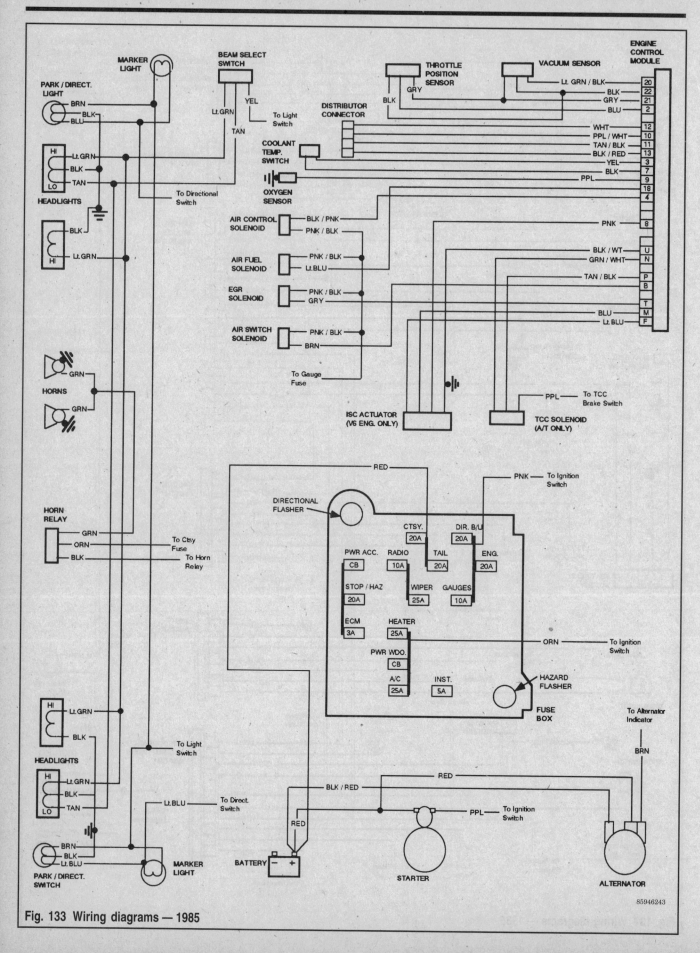

Fig. 133 Wiring diagrams — 1985

85946243

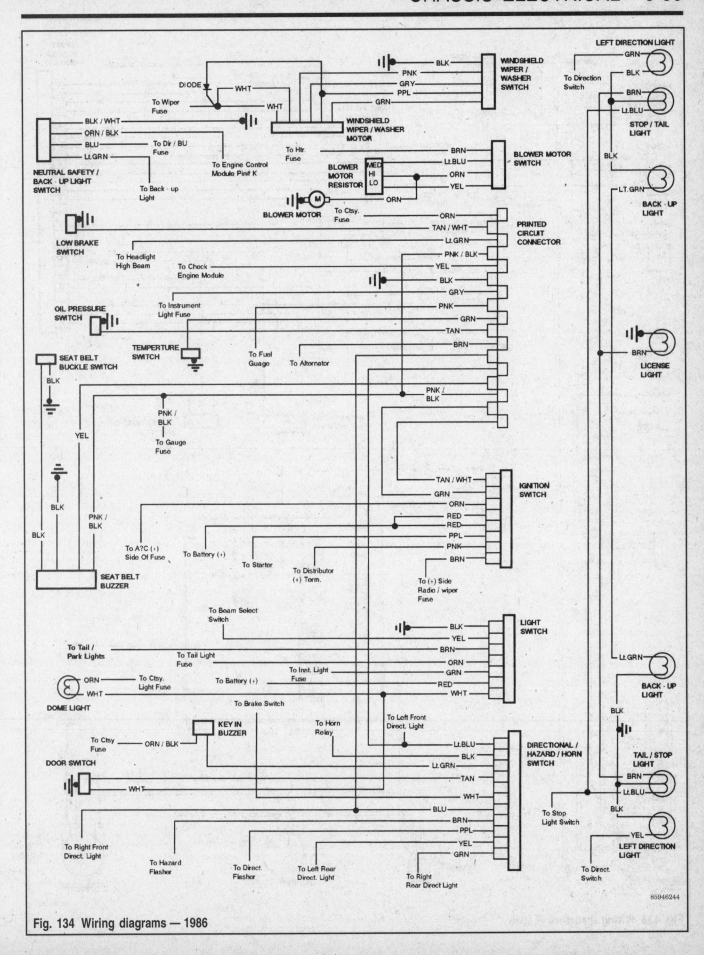

Fig. 134 Wiring diagrams — 1986

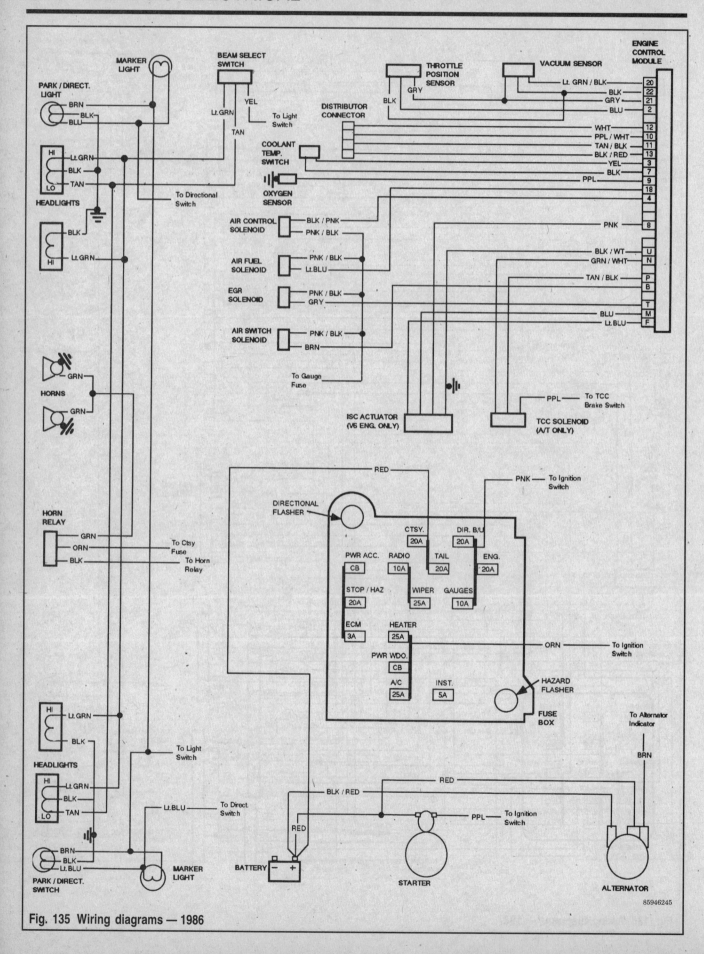

Fig. 135 Wiring diagrams — 1986

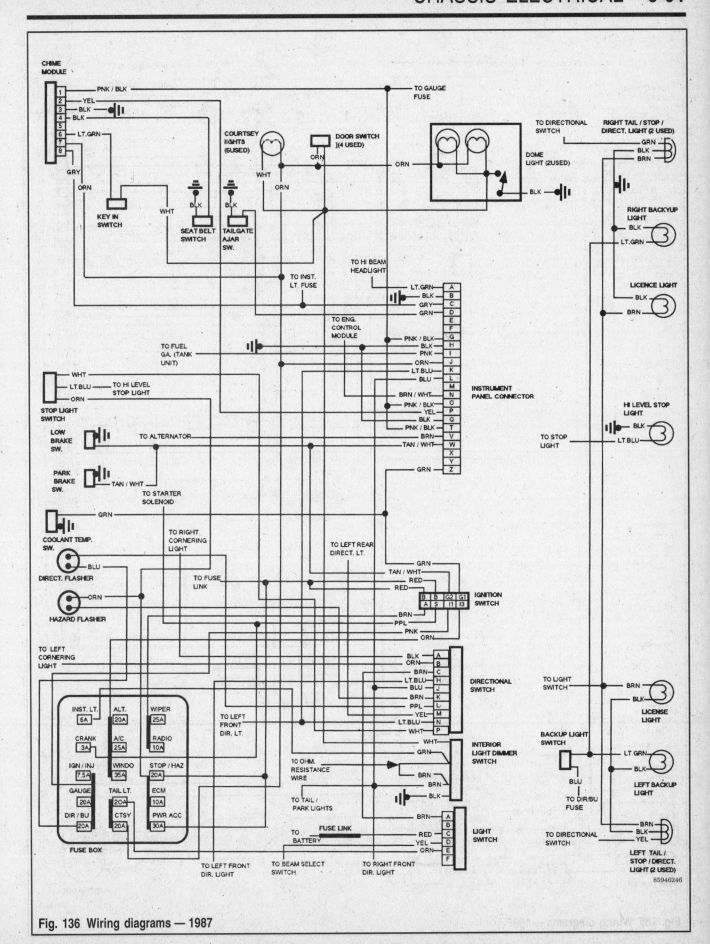

Fig. 136 Wiring diagrams — 1987

85946246

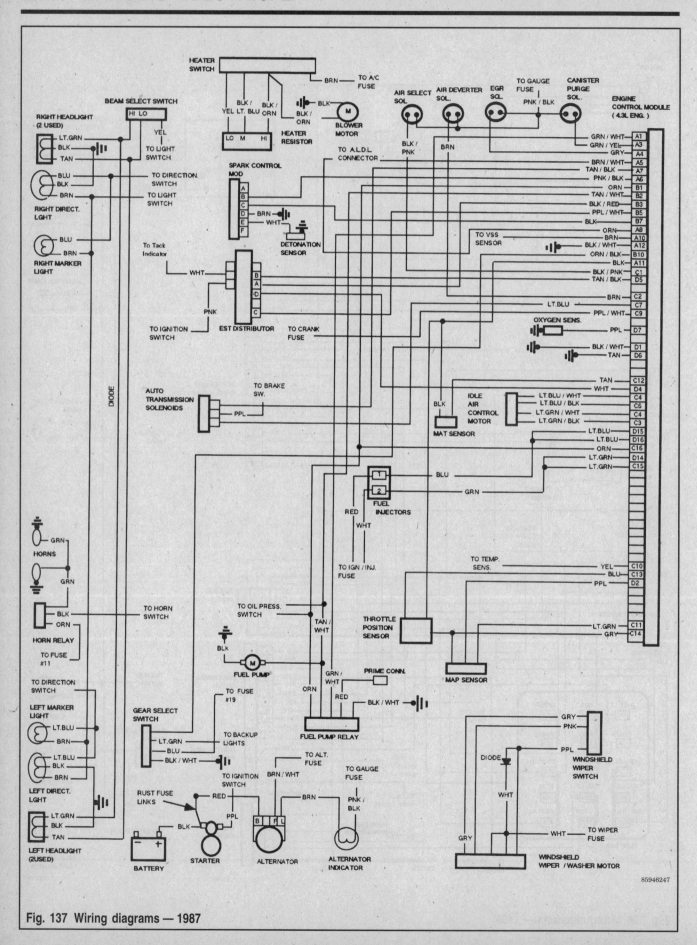

Fig. 137 Wiring diagrams — 1987

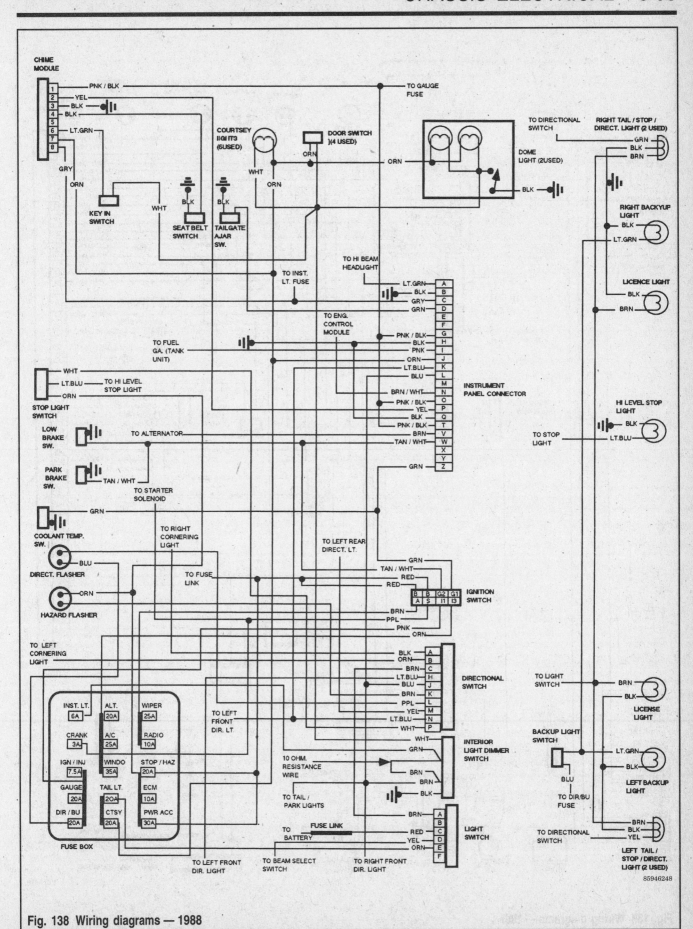

Fig. 138 Wiring diagrams — 1988

85946248

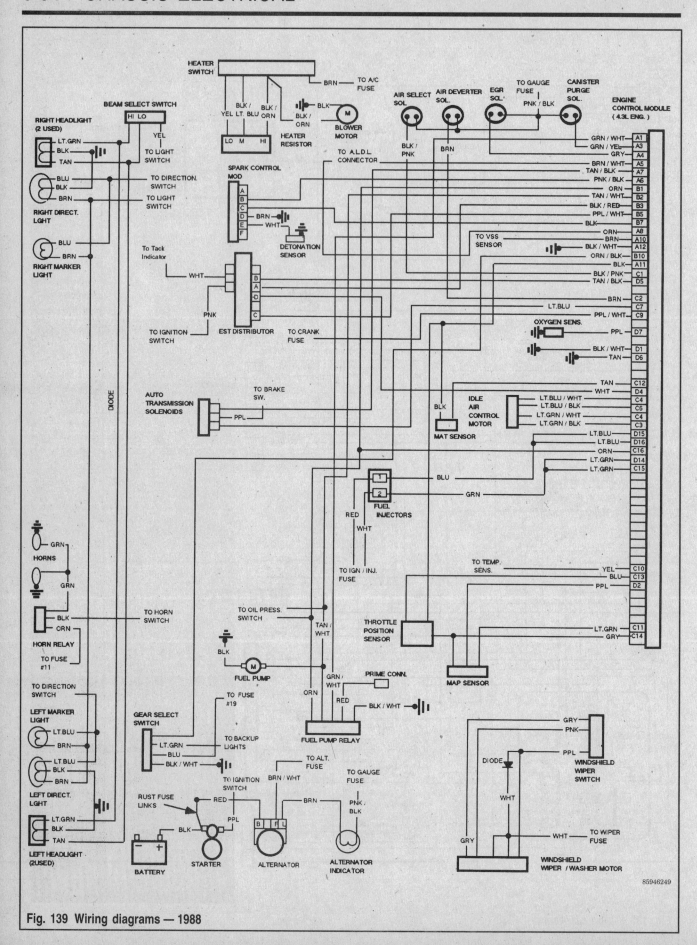

Fig. 139 Wiring diagrams — 1988

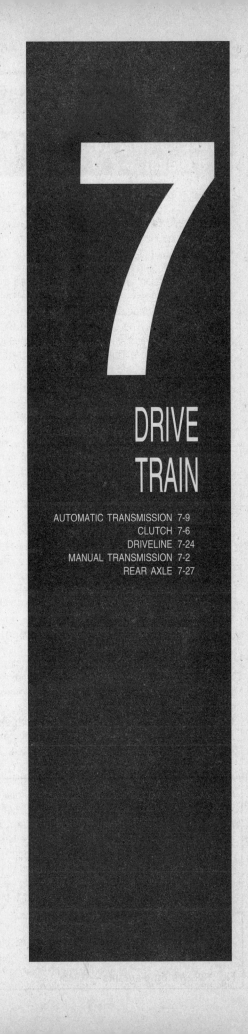

7

DRIVE TRAIN

MANUAL TRANSMISSION

Understanding the Manual Transmission and Clutch

Because of the way an internal combustion gasoline engine breathes, it can produce torque, or twisting force, only within a narrow speed range. Most modern overhead valve engines must turn at about 2,500 rpm to produce their peak torque. By 4,500 rpm they are producing so little torque that continued increases in engine speed produce no power increases.

The transmission and clutch are employed to vary the relationship between engine speed and the speed of the wheels so that adequate engine power can be produced under all circumstances. The clutch allows engine torque to be applied to the transmission input shaft gradually, due to mechanical slippage. The car can, consequently, be started smoothly from a full stop.

The transmission is used to change the ratio between the rotating speeds of the engine and the wheels by the use of gears. 3-speed or 4-speed transmissions are used on these vehicles. The lower gears allow full engine power to be applied to the rear wheels during acceleration at low speeds.

The clutch driven plate is a thin disc, the center of which is splined to the transmission input shaft. Both sides of the disc are covered with a layer of material which is similar to brake lining and which is capable of allowing slippage without roughness or excessive noise.

The clutch cover in bolted to the engine flywheel and incorporates a diaphragm spring which provides the pressure to engage the clutch. The cover also houses the pressure plate. The driven disc is sandwiched between the pressure plate and the smooth surface of the flywheel when the clutch pedal is released, thus forcing it to turn at the same speed as the engine crankshaft.

The transmission housing contains a mainshaft which passes all the way through the transmission, from the clutch to the driveshaft. This shaft is separated at one point, so that front and rear portions can turn at different speeds. Power is transmitted by a countershaft in the lower gears and in reverse. The gears of the countershaft mesh with gears on the mainshaft, allowing power to be carried from one to the other and then back again to the rear half of the mainshaft. All the countershaft gears are integral with that shaft, while several of the mainshaft gears can either rotate independently of the shaft or be locked to it. Shifting from one gear to the next causes one of the gears to be freed from rotating with the shaft, and locks another to it. Gears are locked and unlocked by internal dog clutches which slide between the center of the gear and the shaft. The forward gears usually employ synchronizers: friction members which smoothly bring gear and shaft to the same speed before the toothed dog clutches are engaged.The clutch is operating properly if:

1. It will stall the engine when released with the vehicle held stationary.
2. The shift lever can be moved freely between 1st and reverse gears when the vehicle is stationary and the clutch disengaged (the pedal held downward).

A clutch pedal free-play adjustment is incorporated in the linkage. If there is about 1-2″ of motion before the pedal begins to release the clutch, it is adjusted properly. Inadequate free-play wears all parts of the clutch releasing mechanisms and may cause slippage. Excessive free-play may cause inadequate release and hard shifting of gears.

Identification

Please refer to Section 1 of this manual for a list of the basic manual transmissions and various locations of their serial numbers. By finding the serial number on your transmission and comparing its location with the information there, you should be readily able to determine the type of gearbox used.

Linkage Adjustment

▸ See Figure 1

COLUMN SHIFT

1964-66

1. Position both transmission levers in NEUTRAL.
2. Position the column selector in NEUTRAL. Align the 1st/reverse and 2nd/3rd shifter tube levers on the steering jacket.
3. Install the control rods on the steering jacket levers and secure them with lock clips.
4. Install a swivel on the 1st/reverse shifter control rod and adjust until the swivel can freely enter the transmission shift lever hole (rear). Install a retaining clip on the swivel and insert the swivel in the lever hole and secure with a nut.
5. Install the 2nd/3rd lower rod to the frame mounted idler lever and in the 2nd/3rd transmission lever and secure with retaining clips.
6. Install the upper 2nd/3rd shifter control rod, in the same manner as the 1st/reverse shifter control rod (Step 4), to the frame idler and the jacket shifter lever.

➡Ensure that the shifter tube levers stay in alignment.

7. Check the adjustment by moving the shift lever through all the gear positions.

1967-68

1. Located on the left side of the transmission case are tow levers. Manipulate these levers until the transmission is in NEUTRAL. Verify that the transmission is in NEUTRAL by depressing the clutch pedal, starting the engine, and slowly releasing the pedal. If the car fails to move and the engine is still running with the pedal fully released, the transmission is in NEUTRAL. If the car moves, the transmission is in gear and the levers should be repositioned until NEUTRAL is found.
2. Once the transmission has been verified to be in NEUTRAL, loosen the swivel nuts on both shift rods.
3. Move the shift lever (on the column) to the NEUTRAL position. Raise the hood and locate the shifter tube levers on the steering column. Align the 1st and reverse lever with the 2nd and 3rd lever. Using an alignment pin (a large L-shaped

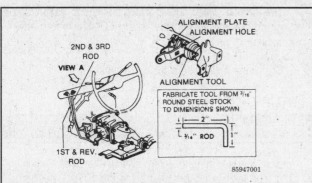

Fig. 1 Column shift linkage adjustment — 1967-69 vehicles

Allen wrench should suffice), hold these levers in alignment (most cars have alignment holes provided in the levers and an alignment plate) until the linkage is connected.

4. Make the final adjustments to align the shift rods and levers at the transmission into the NEUTRAL position. Road test the car and check the shifting operation. If the adjustment is correct, the alignment pin should pass freely through all alignment holes. If not, readjustment is necessary.

1969

1. Turn the ignition switch to the **OFF** position.
2. Loosen the swivel nuts on both shift rods.
3. Place the column mounted shift lever in REVERSE. There are two levers located on the side of the transmission case. The lever to the front of the transmission controls 2nd and 3rd gears while the other lever controls 1st and reverse. Place this 1st and reverse lever into REVERSE. Push up on the 1st/reverse shift rod until the column lever is in the reverse detent position. Tighten the swivel nut.
4. Place the column lever and the transmission levers (located on the side of the case) in NEUTRAL (in order to verify the neutral position, refer to Step No. 1 from the 1967-68 procedure). The shift tube levers are located on the steering column mast jacket. Make sure the column lever is in NEUTRAL and hold it in this position by inserting a pin through the alignment holes in the shift tube levers (a ³/₁₆ in. Allen wrench is perfect for this).
5. Hold the 2nd/3rd shift rod steady (to prevent a change in adjustment) and tighten the swivel locknut.
6. Remove the alignment pin from the shift tube levers and shift the column shift lever to the reverse position. Turn the ignition key to **LOCK** and check the ignition interlock control. If it binds, leave the control in **LOCK** and readjust the 1st/reverse rod at the swivel.
7. Move the column lever through the gear positions and return it to NEUTRAL. The alignment pin should pass freely through the alignment holes of the shift tube levers. If it doesn't loosen the swivel nuts and readjust.

1970-72

1. Place the shift lever (on the column) in REVERSE and the ignition switch in **OFF**.
2. Raise the car and support it safely using jackstands.
3. Loosen the locknuts on the shift rod swivels. Pull down slight on the 1st/reverse control rod on the lower steering col-

umn to remove any slack. Tighten the locknut at the transmission lever.
4. Unlock the ignition switch and shift the column lever into NEUTRAL. Position the shift tube levers (located on the lower steering column) in NEUTRAL by aligning the lever alignment holes. Hold them in this position by inserting a ³/₁₆ in. Allen wrench through the alignment holes.
5. Hold the 2nd/3rd shift rod steady and tighten the rod locknut.
6. Remove the alignment tool from the shift tube levers and check the shifting operation.
7. Place the column lever in REVERSE and check the movement of the ignition key. In reverse and only in reverse, the key must turn freely in and out of **LOCK**.

Floor Shift

▶ See Figures 2, 3 and 4

3-SPEED 1968-72

1. Loosen the locknuts on both shift rod swivels. The shift rods should pass freely through the swivels.
2. Move the floor shift to NEUTRAL and install the locating gauge into the shifter bracket assembly.

➡ **The locating gauge is a piece of ⅛ in. thick flat stock ⁴/₆₄ in. wide and 3 in. long.**

3. Position the levers on the transmission in NEUTRAL. Turn the 1st/reverse shift rod nut down against the swivel, and then tighten the locknut against the swivel.
4. For 1969 vehicles, skip this step. For 1968 vehicles, this is the final step. Turn the 2nd/3rd shift rod nut down against the swivel, and then tighten the locknut against the swivel.

➡ **On 1969 and later cars, skip Step 4 and perform Steps 5-8. Step 4 is the final step for 1968 cars.**

5. Remove the locating gauge, and shift into REVERSE. Turn the ignition switch to the **LOCK** position.
6. Loosen the swivel locknut on the reverse control rod. Pull down slightly on the control rod to take up any slack in the column mechanism, and then tighten the clevis jam nut.
7. The ignition switch should move easily in and out of lock. If there is any binding present, keep the switch in **LOCK** and readjust the reverse control rod.
8. Check the shift pattern for correct operation.

4-SPEED 1964-68

1. Remove the control rods from the transmission levers, and position the levers in NEUTRAL.
2. Move the floor shift lever into NEUTRAL and insert a locating gauge into the bracket assembly (use a ⁵/₁₆ in. rod on 1964 cars. For 1965-74 4-speeds use the same gauge as the 3-speed floor shift).
3. Adjust the length of the control rods and then secure the swivels with the jam nuts and install the clevis pins.
4. Remove the locating gauge and check the shift pattern.

➡ **1965 and later Muncie transmission levers have two control rod holes. Attaching the control rods in the lower holes will result in reduced shift lever travel and allow faster shifting, with increased shifting effort as a minor drawback.**

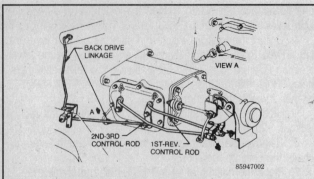

Fig. 2 3-speed floor linkage adjustment — the backdrive shown is on 196-72 models

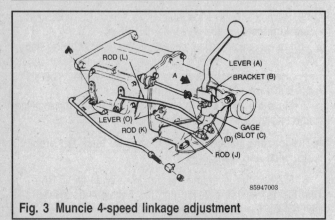

Fig. 3 Muncie 4-speed linkage adjustment

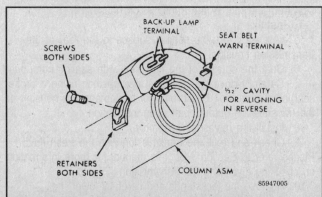

Fig. 4 Saginaw 4-speed linkage adjustment

4-SPEED 1969-81

1. Turn the ignition switch to the **OFF** position, except on 1970 models which should be turned to **LOCK**.

2. Loosen the swivel lock nuts on the shift rods and reverse control rod. Position the transmission side cover levers to their NEUTRAL detent position.

3. Place the floor shift in NEUTRAL and insert a locating gauge (same gauge as 3-speed floor shift) into the lever bracket assembly.

4. Adjust all control rods swivels for easy entry into their respective levers.

5. Tighten the shift rod locknuts and remove the gauge.

6. Shift the lever into REVERSE and pull down slightly on the reverse rod to remove the slack. Tighten the locknut.

7. The ignition switch should move easily into **LOCK** and it must not be possible to turn the key to **LOCK** when in any other position other than REVERSE. Readjust the reverse rod, if necessary.

8. Check the shift pattern for correctness.

CLUTCH SWITCH ADJUSTMENT & REPLACEMENT

A clutch operated neutral safety switch was used beginning in 1970. The ignition switch must be in the START position and the clutch must be fully depressed before the car will start. The switch mounts to the clutch pedal arm. To remove this switch, loosen the fastener(s) or the retaining clip, then pull it from the pedal arm. This switch cannot be adjusted.

Back-up Light Switch

REMOVAL & INSTALLATION

Column Shift
▶ See Figure 5

➡ The back-up light switch is mounted on the mast jacket of the column assembly.

1. Disconnect the negative battery cable.
2. Disengage the wiring connectors at the switch terminals.
3. Remove the screws attaching the switch to the mast jacket, then remove the switch assembly.

To install:
4. Position the column shift tube in the REVERSE detent using the 1st/Reverse lower shift lever.
5. Position the switch on the column with the drive tang in the slot in the shift tube and the right side of the tang contacting the right surface of the shift tube slot.
6. Holding the switch in position, install the two attaching screws.

➡ Moving the gear selector lever out of REVERSE will break the shear pin.

7. Plug the wiring connector on the switch.
8. Connect the negative battery cable, then verify proper switch operation.

Fig. 5 Column mounted back-up light switch

Floor Shift

➡ **The back-up light switch is mounted on the transmission.**

1. Disconnect the negative battery cable, then raise the vehicle and support it safely using jackstands.
2. Disengage the switch wiring from the harness wiring at the in-line connector.
3. Remove the bolt retaining the wiring attaching clip to the transmission.
4. Remove the wire clip retaining the reverse lever rod to the switch.
5. Remove the screws retaining the switch and shield assembly to the transmission, then remove the switch.

➡ **Do not remove the transmission-to-bracket retaining bolts.**

To install:
6. Install the switch and shield assembly to the transmission and secure using the retaining bolts.
7. Engage the reverse lever rod to the switch and secure using the wire clip.
8. Install the bolt retaining the wiring clip to the transmission.
9. Engage the switch wiring to the in-line harness connector.
10. Remove the jackstands and carefully lower the vehicle, then connect the negative battery cable and verify proper switch operation.

Extension Housing Seal

REMOVAL & INSTALLATION

1. Raise and support the vehicle safely using jackstands.
2. Drain the manual transmission oil. If the rear of the vehicle is held significantly higher than the front of the vehicle, it may not be necessary to completely drain the transmission oil.
3. Matchmark and remove the driveshaft. Most vehicles covered in this manual should be equipped with a slip yoke and the front of the driveshaft. In order to remove the shaft, disconnect it from the rear axle, then carefully withdraw the splined yoke from the rear of the transmission.
4. Carefully distort the seal using a punch, then pry the seal from the rear of the transmission housing.

To install:
5. Clean and dry the sealing surface in the rear of the transmission housing.
6. Coat the outside of the new seal with sealing compound.
7. Carefully drive the new seal into position using a proper seal installation tool. Be careful not to damage the housing or the transmission output shaft upon installation.
8. Install the driveshaft assembly.
9. Check and refill the transmission with the fresh fluid. Please refer to Section 1 of this manual for more information on checking and filling the transmission.
10. Remove the jackstands and carefully lower the transmission.

Transmission

REMOVAL & INSTALLATION

▶ **See Figure 6**

1967-69 Vehicles

1. Disconnect the negative battery cable.
2. Raise and support the car safely using jackstands.
3. Matchmark and remove the driveshaft assembly. On floor shift models, remove the trim plate and shifter boot.
4. On 1968-69 models, it may be necessary to disconnect the exhaust pipe at the manifold.
5. Disconnect the speedometer cable and, on floor shift models, disconnect the back-up light switch.
6. Remove the crossmember-to-frame bolts. On the floor shift models, remove the bolts holding the control lever support to the crossmember.
7. Remove the transmission mount bolts.
8. Using a suitable jack and a block of wood (to be placed between the jack and the engine for protection), raise the engine slightly and remove or relocate the crossmember.
9. Remove the shaft levers from the transmission side cover.
10. On floor shift models, remove the stabilizer rod (if so equipped) situated between the shift lever assembly and the transmission.
11. Remove the transmission-to-bellhousing bolts. Remove the top bolts first and insert guide pins into the holes, then remove the bottom bolts.
12. Carefully withdraw the transmission assembly by moving it back, then lower it from the vehicle.

To install:
13. Lift the transmission into position and carefully insert the mainshaft into the bellhousing.
14. Install the transmission-to-bellhousing bolts and lockwashers, then torque them to 50 ft. lbs. (68 Nm).
15. Install the transmission shift levers to the side cover. On floor shift models, install the stabilizer rod (if so equipped).
16. Raise the engine slightly, position the crossmember and install the retaining bolts.
17. Install the transmission mount bolts. On floor shift models, install the bolts holding the shift lever support to the crossmember.

➡ **Lubricate the tailshaft bushing before the driveshafts are installed.**

18. Align the marks made earlier and install the driveshaft assembly. If removed, install the exhaust pipe to the manifold.
19. Connect the speedometer cable and, on floor shift cars, connect the backup light.
20. Check the transmission fluid level and add, as necessary.
21. Remove the jackstands and carefully lower the vehicle.
22. Connect the negative battery cable.

1970 and Later Vehicles

1. Disconnect the negative battery cable.

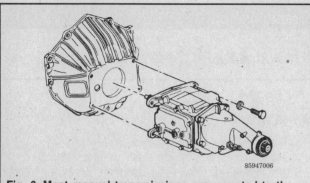

85947006

Fig. 6 Most manual transmissions are mounted to the bellhousing using 4 bolts

2. On floor shift models, remove the shift knob and console trim plate.

3. Raise and support the front of the vehicle safely using jackstands.

4. Disconnect the speedometer cable and the TCS switch wiring.

5. Matchmark and remove the driveshaft assembly.

6. Remove the bolts securing the transmission mounts to the crossmember and also the bolts securing the crossmember to the frame. Remove the crossmember from the vehicle.

7. Remove the shift levers from the side of the transmission.

8. Disconnect the back drive rod from the bellcrank.

9. Remove the bolts from the shift control assembly and carefully lower the assembly until the shift lever clears the rubber shift boot. Remove the assembly from the car.

10. Remove the transmission-to-bellhousing bolts and carefully lower the transmission from the car.

To install:

11. Lift the transmission into position and carefully insert the mainshaft into the bellhousing.

12. Install and torque the transmission-to-clutch housing bolts and lockwashers.

13. Install the shift lever.

14. Install the shift levers to the transmission side cover.

15. Connect the back drive rod to the bellcrank.

16. Raise the engine high enough to position the crossmember. Install and tighten the crossmember-to-frame bolts and transmission mount to crossmember bolts.

17. Align the marks made earlier and install the driveshaft assembly.

18. Connect the speedometer cable and TCS wiring.

19. Fill the transmission with the specified lubricant. If applicable, install the console trim plate and shift knob. Adjust the linkage.

CLUTCH

Understanding the Clutch

▶ See Figure 7

The purpose of the clutch is to smoothly connect and disconnect engine power from the transmission. A car at rest requires a lot of engine torque to get all that weight moving. An internal combustion engine does not develop a high starting torque (unlike steam engines), so it must be allowed to operate without any load until it builds up enough torque to move the car. Torque increases with engine rpm. The clutch allows the engine to build up torque by physically disconnecting the engine from the transmission, relieving the engine of any load or resistance. The transfer of engine power to the transmission (the load) must be smooth and gradual; if it weren't, drive line components would wear out or break quickly. This gradual power transfer is made possible by gradually releasing the clutch pedal. The clutch disc and pressure plate are the connecting link between the engine and transmission. When the clutch pedal is released, the disc and plate contact each other (clutch engagement), physically joining the engine and transmission. When the pedal is pushed in, the disc and plate separate (the clutch is disengaged), disconnecting the engine from the transmission.

The clutch assembly consists of the flywheel, clutch disc, clutch pressure plate, throwout bearing and fork, the actuating linkage and the clutch pedal. The flywheel and clutch pressure plate (driving members) are connected to the engine crankshaft and rotate with it. The clutch disc is located between the flywheel and pressure plate, and is splined to the transmission shaft. A driving member is one that is attached to the engine and transfers engine power to a driven member (clutch disc) on the transmission shaft. A driving member (pressure plate)

rotates (drives) a driven member (clutch disc) on contact and, in so doing, turns the transmission shaft. There is a circular diaphragm spring within the pressure plate cover (transmission side). In a relaxed state (when the clutch pedal is fully released), this spring is convex; that it, it is dished outward toward the transmission. Pushing in the clutch pedal actuates an attached linkage rod. Connected to the other end of this rod is the throwout bearing fork. When the clutch pedal is depressed, the clutch linkage pushes the fork and bearing forward to contact the diaphragm spring of the pressure plate. The outer edges of the spring are secured to the pressure plate and are pivoted on rings so that when the center of the spring is compressed by the throwout bearing, the outer edges bow outward and, by so doing, pull the pressure plate in the same direction - away from the clutch disc. This action separates the disc from the plate, disengaging the clutch and allowing the transmission to be shifted into another gear. A coil type clutch return spring attached to the clutch pedal arm permits full release of the pedal. Releasing the pedal allows this coil spring to pull the throwout bearing away from the diaphragm spring resulting in a reversal of spring position. As bearing pressure is gradually released from the spring center, the outer edges of the spring bow outward, pushing the pressure plate into closer contact with the clutch disc. As the disc and plate move closer together, friction between the two increases and slippage is reduced until, when full diaphragm spring pressure is applied (by fully releasing the pedal), The speed of the disc and plate are the same. This stops all slipping, creating a direct connection between the plate and disc which results in the transfer of power from the engine to the transmission. The clutch disc is now rotating with the pressure plate at engine speed and, because it is splined to the transmission shaft, the shaft now turns at the same engine

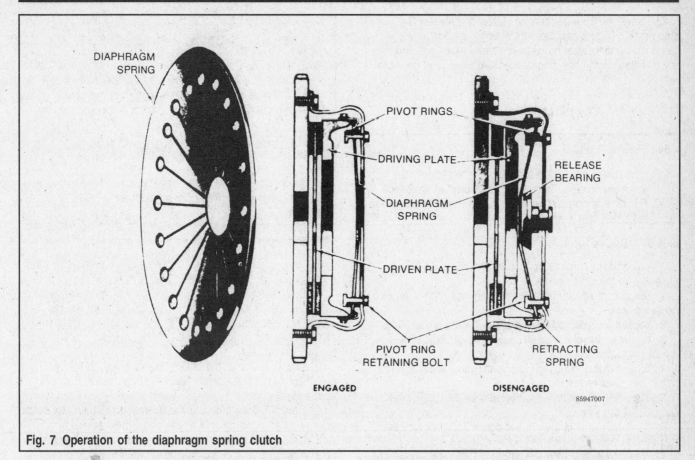

DIAPHRAGM SPRING

PIVOT RINGS

DRIVING PLATE

RELEASE BEARING

DIAPHRAGM SPRING

DRIVEN PLATE

PIVOT RING RETAINING BOLT

RETRACTING SPRING

ENGAGED

DISENGAGED

85947007

Fig. 7 Operation of the diaphragm spring clutch

speed. Understanding clutch operation can be rather difficult at first; if you're still confused after reading this, consider the following analogy. The action of the diaphragm spring can be compared to that of an oil can bottom. The bottom of an oil can is shaped very much like the clutch diaphragm spring and pushing in on the can bottom and then releasing it produces a similar effect. As mentioned earlier, the clutch pedal return spring permits full release of the pedal and reduces linkage slack due to wear. As the linkage wears, clutch free-pedal travel will increase, while free-travel will decrease as the clutch wears. Free-travel is actually throwout bearing lash.

The diaphragm spring type clutches used are available in two different designs: flat diaphragm springs or bent spring. The bent fingers are bent back to create a centrifugal boost ensuring quick re-engagement at higher engine speeds. This design enables pressure plate load to increase as the clutch disc wears and makes low pedal effort possible even with a heavy-duty clutch. The throwout bearing used with the bent finger design is 1¼ in. long and is shorter than the bearing used with the flat finger design. These bearings are not interchangeable. If the longer bearing is used with the bent finger clutch, free-pedal travel will not exist. This results in clutch slippage and rapid wear.

The transmission varies the gear ratio between the engine and rear wheels. It can be shifted to change engine speed as driving conditions and loads change. The transmission allows disengaging and reversing power from the engine to the wheels.

CLUTCH CROSS-SHAFT LUBRICATION

Once every 36,000 miles or sooner if necessary, remove the plug, install a fitting and lubricate with water resistant EP (Extreme Pressure) chassis lubricant.

LINKAGE INSPECTION

A clutch may have all the symptoms of going bad when the real trouble lies in the linkage. To avoid the unnecessary replacement of a clutch, make the following linkage checks when a problem is suspected:

1. Start the engine and depress the clutch pedal until it is about ½ in. from the floor mat, then move the shift lever between 1st and reverse (1st and 2nd on a 4-speed) several times. If this can be done smoothly without any grinding, the clutch is releasing fully. If the shifting is not smooth, the clutch is not releasing fully and adjustment is necessary.

2. Check the condition of the clutch pedal bushings for signs of sticking or excessive wear.

3. Check the throwout bearing fork for proper installation on the ball stud. The fork could possibly be pulled off the ball if not properly lubricated.

4. Check the cross-shaft levers for distortion or damage.

5. Check the car for loose or damaged motor mounts. Bad motor mounts can cause the engine to shift under acceleration and bind the clutch linkage at the cross-shaft. There must be some clearance between the cross-shaft and the motor mount.

6. Check the throwout bearing clearance between the clutch spring fingers and the front bearing retainer on the transmission. If there is no clearance, the fork may be improperly installed on the ball stud or the clutch disc may be worn out.

FREE-PLAY ADJUSTMENT

▶ **See Figures 8 and 9**

This adjustment must be made under the vehicle on the clutch operating linkage. Free-play is measured at the clutch pedal. For access on most vehicles, the car must be raise and supported safely using jackstands.

1964-67 Vehicles

This adjustment is made from under the car. Free-play is measured at the clutch pedal.

1. Disconnect the spring between the cross-shaft lever and the clutch fork.
2. Loosen the pushrod locknut approximately three turns.
3. If no free travel is present, adjust the pushrod until it is free of the clutch fork.
4. While holding the clutch fork to the rear, adjust the rod until it just touches the fork seat.
5. Turn the locknut until $\frac{3}{16}$ in. clearance exists between the nut and the sleeve.
6. Turn the rod until the nut just contacts the sleeve, then hold the rod with a wrench and tighten the nut.
7. Free pedal clearance should be $\frac{3}{4}$-$1\frac{1}{8}$ in. (1964-65 vehicles) or 1-$1\frac{1}{2}$ in. (1966-67 vehicles).

1968-70 Vehicles

1. Disconnect the return spring at the clutch operating fork.
2. Use the linkage to push the clutch pedal up against its rubber bumper stop.
3. Loosen the operating rod locknut and lengthen the adjustment rod until it pushes the fork back enough that the release bearing can just be left to contact the pressure plate fingers.
4. Shorten the rod three turns and tighten the locknut.
5. Replace the spring and check the free-play at the pedal pad. It should be about 1 in. or more.

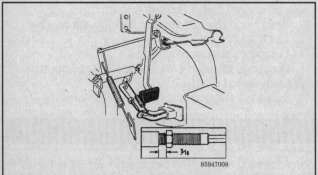

Fig. 8 Clutch pedal free-play adjustment — 1964-67 vehicles

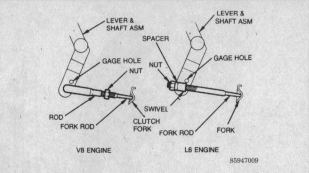

Fig. 9 Clutch pedal free-play adjustment — 1968-72 vehicles

1971 and Later Vehicles

You can use this procedure on any earlier models that have a gauge hole in the clutch pivot shaft arm.

1. Disconnect the return spring at the clutch operating fork.
2. Use the linkage to push the clutch pedal up against its rubber bumper stop. On the 1973 Chevelle, more clearance can be obtained by loosening the rubber bumper bracket and moving the bracket.
3. Push the end of the clutch operating fork to the rear until the release bearing can just be felt to contact the pressure plate fingers.
4. Detach the front end of the operating rod from the clutch pivot shaft arm and place it in the gauge hole on the arm.
5. Loosen the locknut and lengthen the rod just enough to take all the play out of the linkage. Tighten the locknut.
6. Replace the operating rod in its original location.
7. Replace the return spring and check the free-play at the pedal pad. It should be about 1 in. or more.

Driven Disc and Pressure Plate

REMOVAL

▶ **See Figures 10 and 11**

❋❋CAUTION

The clutch driven disc contains asbestos, which has been determined to be a cancer causing agent. NEVER clean the clutch surfaces with compressed air! Avoid inhaling any dust from the clutch surface! When cleaning the clutch surfaces use a commercially available brake cleaning fluid.

1. Support the engine and remove the transmission. For details, refer to the procedures earlier in this section.
2. Disconnect the clutch fork push rod and spring.
3. Remove the flywheel housing.
4. Slide the clutch fork from the ball stud and remove the fork from the dust boot. The ball stud is threaded into the clutch housing and may be replaced if necessary.
5. Install an alignment tool to support the clutch assembly during removal. mark the flywheel and clutch cover for reinstallation, if they do not already have **X** marks.

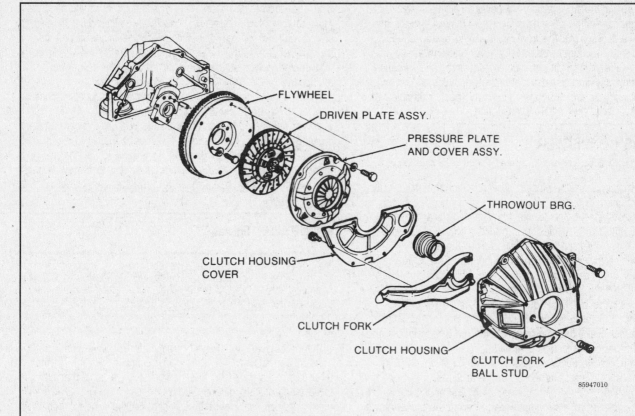

Fig. 10 Exploded view of the clutch and flywheel assembly

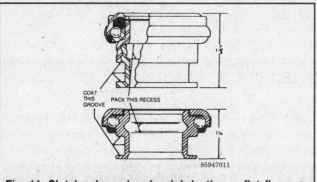

Fig. 11 Clutch release bearing lubrication — flat finger type (top) and bent finger type

6. Loosen the clutch-to-flywheel attaching bolts evenly, one turn at a time, until spring pressure is released. Carefully remove the bolts and clutch assembly. Note the direction which the disc damper springs are facing during removal.

To install:

7. Clean the pressure plate and flywheel face using a commercially available brake cleaner. Inspect the surfaces for cracks or damage.

8. Support the clutch disc and pressure plate with an alignment tool. The driven disc is installed with the damper springs on the transmission side. On some 1964-67 6-cylinder engines, the clutch disc is installed in the reverse manner with the damper springs to the flywheel side.

9. Turn the clutch assembly until the mark on the cover lines up with the mark on the flywheel, then install the bolts. Tighten down evenly and gradually to avoid distortion.

10. Remove the clutch alignment tool.

11. Lubricate the ball socket and fork fingers at the release bearing end with high melting point grease. Lubricate the recess on the inside of the throwout bearing and throwout fork groove with a light coat of graphite grease.

12. Install the clutch fork and dust boot into the housing.

13. Install the flywheel housing.

14. Install the transmission assembly.

15. Connect the fork push rod and spring. Lubricate the spring and pushrod ends.

16. Adjust the shift linkage and clutch pedal free-play.

AUTOMATIC TRANSMISSION

Understanding Automatic Transmissions

The automatic transmission allows engine torque and power to be transmitted to the rear wheels within a narrow range of engine operating speeds. The transmission will allow the engine to turn fast enough to produce plenty of power and torque at very low speeds, while keeping it at a sensible rpm at high vehicle speeds. The transmission performs this job entirely without driver assistance. The transmission uses a light fluid as the medium for the transmission of power. This fluid also works in the operation of various hydraulic control circuits and as a lubricant. Because the transmission fluid performs all three of these functions, trouble within the unit can easily travel from one part to another. For this reason, and because of the complexity and unusual operating principles of the transmission, a very sound understanding of the basic principles of operation is necessary for troubleshooting.

TORQUE CONVERTER

The torque converter replaces the conventional clutch. It has three functions:

1. It allows the engine to idle with the vehicle at a standstill, even with the transmission in gear by effectively disconnecting the engine from the transmission at these times.

2. It allows the transmission to shift from range to range smoothly, without requiring that the driver close the throttle during the shift.

3. It multiplies engine torque to an increasing extent as vehicle speed drops and throttle opening is increased. This has the effect of making the transmission more responsive and reduces the amount of shifting required.

The torque converter is a metal case which is shaped like a sphere that has been flattened on opposite sides. It is bolted to the rear end of the engine's crankshaft. Generally, the entire metal case rotates at engine speed and serves as the engine's flywheel.

The case contains three sets of blades. One set is attached directly to the case. This set forms the torus or pump. Another set is directly connected to the output shaft, and forms the turbine. The third set is mounted on a hub which, in turn, is mounted on a stationary shaft through a one-way clutch. This third set is known as the stator.

A pump, which is driven by the converter hub at engine speed, keeps the torque converter full of transmission fluid at all times. Fluid flows continuously through the unit to provide cooling.

Under low speed acceleration, the torque converter functions as follows:

The torus is turning faster than the turbine. It picks up fluid at the center of the converter and, through centrifugal force, slings it outward. Since the outer edge of the converter moves faster than the portions at the center, the fluid picks up speed.

The fluid then enters the outer edge of the turbine blades. It then travels back toward the center of the converter case along the turbine blades. In impinging upon the turbine blades, the fluid loses the energy picked up in the torus.

If the fluid were now to immediately be returned directly into the torus, both halves of the converter would have to turn at approximately the same speed at all times, and torque input and output would both be the same.

In flowing through the torus and turbine, the fluid picks up two types of flow, or flow in two separate directions. It flows through the turbine blades, and it spins with the engine. The stator, whose blades are stationary when the vehicle is being accelerated at low speeds, converts one type of flow into another. Instead of allowing the fluid to flow straight back into the torus, the stator's curved blades turn the fluid almost 90° toward the direction of rotation of the engine. Thus the fluid does not flow as fast toward the torus, but is already spinning

when the torus picks it up. This has the effect of allowing the torus to turn much faster than the turbine. This difference in speed may be compared to the difference in speed between the smaller and larger gears in any gear train. The result is that engine power output is higher, and engine torque is multiplied.

As the speed of the turbine increases, the fluid spins faster and faster in the direction of engine rotation. As a result, the ability of the stator to redirect the fluid flow is reduced. Under cruising conditions, the stator is eventually forced to rotate on its one-way clutch in the direction of engine rotation. Under these conditions, the torque converter begins to behave almost like a solid shaft, with the torus and turbine speeds being almost equal.

PLANETARY GEARBOX

The ability of the torque converter to multiply engine torque is limited. Also, the unit tends to be more efficient when the turbine is rotating at relatively high speeds. Therefore, a planetary gearbox is used to carry the power output of the turbine to the driveshaft.

Planetary gears function very similarly to conventional transmission gears. However, their construction is different in that three elements make up one gear system, and, in that all three elements are different from one another. The three elements are: an outer gear that is shaped like a hoop, with teeth cut into the inner surface; a sun gear, mounted on a shaft and located at the very center of the outer gear; and a set of three planet gears, held by pins in a ring-like planet carrier, meshing with both the sun gear and the outer gear. Either the outer gear or the sun gear may be held stationary, providing more than one possible torque multiplication factor for each set of gears. Also, if all three gears are forced to rotate at the same speed, the gearset forms, in effect, a solid shaft.

Most modern automatics use the planetary gears to provide either a single reduction ratio of about 1.8:1, or two reduction gears: a low of about 2.5:1, and an intermediate of about 1.5:1. Bands and clutches are used to hold various portions of the gearsets to the transmission case or to the shaft on which they are mounted. Shifting is accomplished, then, by changing the portion of each planetary gearset which is held to the transmission case or to the shaft.

SERVOS AND ACCUMULATORS

The servos are hydraulic pistons and cylinders. They resemble the hydraulic actuators used on many familiar machines, such as bulldozers. Hydraulic fluid enters the cylinder, under pressure, and forces the piston to move to engage the band or clutches.

The accumulators are used to cushion the engagement of the servos. The transmission fluid must pass through the accumulator on the way to the servo. The accumulator housing contains a thin piston which is sprung away from the discharge passage of the accumulator. When fluid passes through the accumulator on the way to the servo, it must move the piston against spring pressure, and this action smooths out the action of the servo.

HYDRAULIC CONTROL SYSTEM

The hydraulic pressure used to operate the servos comes from the main transmission oil pump. This fluid is channeled to the various servos through the shift valves. There is generally a manual shift valve which is operated by the transmission selector lever and an automatic shift valve for each automatic upshift the transmission provides: i.e., 2-speed automatics have a low/high shift valve, while 3-speeds have a 1-2 valve, and a 2-3 valve.

There are two pressures which affect the operation of these valves. One is the governor pressure which is affected by vehicle speed. The other is the modulator pressure which is affected by intake manifold vacuum or throttle position. Governor pressure rises with an increase in vehicle speed and modulator pressure rises as the throttle is opened wider. By responding to these two pressures, the shift valves cause the upshift points to be delayed with increased throttle opening to make the best use of the engine's power output.

Most transmissions also make use of an auxiliary circuit for downshifting. This circuit may be actuated by the throttle linkage or the vacuum line which actuates the modulator, or by a cable or solenoid. It applies pressure to a special downshift surface on the shift valve or valves.

The transmission modulator also governs the line pressure, used to actuate the servos. In this way, the clutches and bands will be actuated with a force matching the torque output of the engine.

Identification

▶ **See Figures 12, 13, 14, 15 and 16**

The five types of pan gaskets used on the automatic transmissions are pictured below for ready identification:

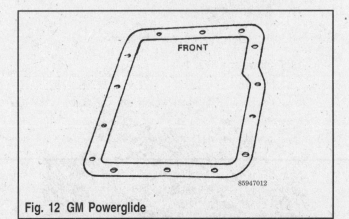

Fig. 12 GM Powerglide

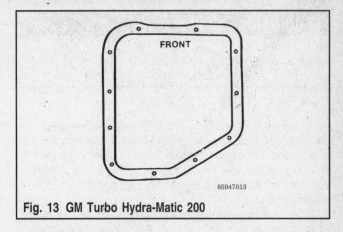

Fig. 13 GM Turbo Hydra-Matic 200

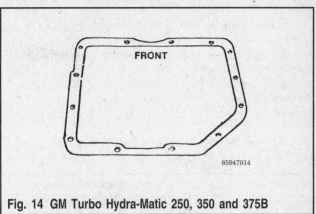

Fig. 14 GM Turbo Hydra-Matic 250, 350 and 375B

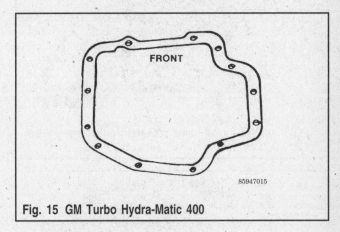

Fig. 15 GM Turbo Hydra-Matic 400

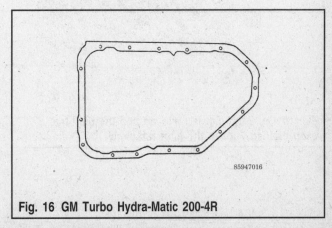

Fig. 16 GM Turbo Hydra-Matic 200-4R

Fluid Pan and Filter

REMOVAL & INSTALLATION

▶ **See Figures 17, 18, 19, 20, 21 and 22**

The fluid should be changed with the transmission warm. A 20 minute drive at highway speeds should accomplish this.

1. Raise and support the vehicle safely using jackstands.

2. If equipped with the Turbo Hydra-Matic 250 or 350, support the transmission and remove the rear support crossmember.

3. Place a large pan under the transmission pan. Remove all the front and side pan bolts. Loosen the rear bolts about four turns.

4. Carefully pry the pan loose and allow most of the fluid to drain.

5. Support the pan and remove the remaining bolts, then carefully lower the pan from the transmission. The pan will still have a fair amount of fluid, so keep it level as is is lowered. Remove the gasket. Clean the pan thoroughly with solvent and air dry it. Be very careful not to get any lint from rags in the pan.

6. Remove the strainer to valve body screws, the strainer, and the gasket. Most 350 transmissions will have a throw-away filter instead of a strainer. On the 400 transmission, remove the filter retaining bolt, filter, and intake pipe O-ring.

7. If there is a strainer, clean it in solvent and allow it to air dry.

To install:

8. Install the new filter or cleaned strainer, as applicable, using a new gasket. Tighten the retaining screws to 12 ft. lbs. (16 Nm). On the 400, install a new intake pipe O-ring and a new filter, tightening the retaining bolt to 10 ft. lbs. (14 Nm).

9. Install the pan using a new gasket. Tighten the bolts evenly to 12 ft. lbs. (16 Nm) for most transmissions or to 8 ft. lbs. (11 Nm) for Powerglide and Torque Drive.

10. Remove the jackstands and carefully lower the vehicle. Immediately add the proper amount of DEXRON®II automatic transmission fluid through the dipstick tube.

➡ **Refer to Section 1 of this manual for more details concerning proper fluid level.**

11. Start the engine in PARK and let it idle. Do not race the engine. Shift into each shift lever position, shift back into PARK, and check the fluid level on the dipstick. The level should be ¼ in. below ADD. Be very careful not to overfill. Recheck the level after the car has been driven long enough to thoroughly warm up the transmission. Add fluid as necessary. The level should then be at (NOT above) FULL.

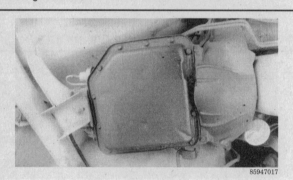

85947017

Fig. 17 Most of the vehicles covered by this manual so not have an automatic transmission fluid drain plug

85947019

Fig. 19 Remove the filter retainers

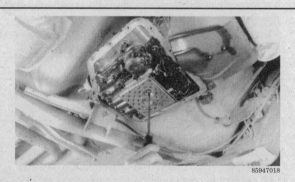

85947018

Fig. 18 Once the pan is removed and the fluid has been drained, loosen the filter retainers

85947020

Fig. 20 With the retainers removed, the filter and gasket may be removed from the transmission

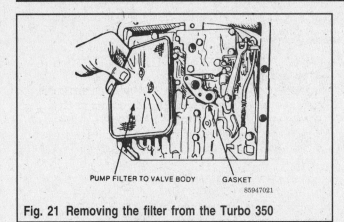

PUMP FILTER TO VALVE BODY   GASKET

85947021

Fig. 21 Removing the filter from the Turbo 350

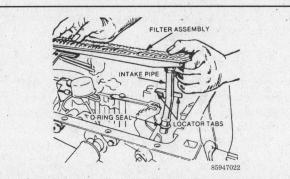

FILTER ASSEMBLY

INTAKE PIPE

O-RING SEAL   LOCATOR TABS

85947022

Fig. 22 Remove the filter, intake pipe and O-ring on the 400 (note that the perspective is from a workstand)

Gasoline Vehicle Transmission Adjustments

BANDS

Powerglide and Torque Drive

LOW BAND

The low band must be adjusted at the first required fluid change or whenever there is slippage.

1. Position the shift lever in NEUTRAL.
2. Remove the protective cap from the adjusting screw on the left side of the transmission.
3. Loosen the locknut ¼ turn and hold it with a wrench during the entire adjusting procedure.
4. Tighten the adjusting nut to 70 inch lbs. (8 Nm), using a ⁷/₃₂ in. Allen wrench drive.
5. Back off the adjusting nut exactly three turns for a band used less than 6,000 miles. Back off exactly four turns for a band used 6,000 miles or more.
6. Torque the locknut to 15 ft. lbs. (20 Nm) and replace the cap.

Turbo Hydra-Matic 250

INTERMEDIATE BAND

The intermediate band must be adjusted with every required fluid change or whenever there is slippage.

1. Position the shift lever in NEUTRAL.
2. Loosen the locknut on the right side of the transmission and tighten the adjusting screw to 30 inch lbs. (3.4 Nm)
3. Back the screw out three turns and then tighten the locknut to 15 ft. lbs. (20 Nm).

Except Powerglide, Torque Drive and Turbo Hydra-Matic 250

There are no band adjustments possible or required for the Turbo Hydra-Matic 200, 200-4R, 350 or 400 transmissions.

TRANSMISSION SHIFT LINKAGE

Powerglide Column Shift

▶ **See Figures 23 and 24**

1. The shift tube and lever assembly must be free in the mast jacket.
2. Lift the selector lever toward the steering wheel and allow the selector lever to be positioned in DRIVE by the transmission detent.
3. Release the selector lever. The lever should be prevented from engaging LOW, unless the lever is lifted.
4. Lift the selector lever toward the steering wheel and allow the lever to be positioned in NEUTRAL by the transmission detent.
5. Release the selector lever. The selector lever should not be kept from engaging REVERSE unless the lever is lifted. If the linkage is adjusted correctly, the selector lever should be prevented from moving beyond both the NEUTRAL detent and the DRIVE detent unless the lever is lifted to pass over the mechanical stop in the steering column.

If adjustment is necessary, perform the following steps:

6. Adjust the linkage by loosening the adjustment clamp at the cross-shaft. Place the transmission lever in DRIVE by rotating the lever counterclockwise to the LOW detent, and then clockwise one detent to DRIVE.
7. Place the selector lever in DRIVE and remove any free-play by holding the cross-shaft up and pulling the shift rod downward.
8. Tighten the clamp and check the adjustment.

On 1969-73 cars, carry out the following additional steps:

9. Place the shift lever in PARK and the ignition switch in **LOCK**. Loosen the reverse rod clamp nut. Remove any lash in the column and tighten the clamp nut.
10. When the selector lever is in PARK, the ignition key should move freely into **LOCK**. The ignition **LOCK** position should be obtainable only when the transmission is in PARK.

Powerglide Floor Shift

1964-67 VEHICLES

▶ **See Figure 25**

1. Loosen the adjustment nuts at the swivel. Place the transmission lever in the DRIVE position by moving it counter-

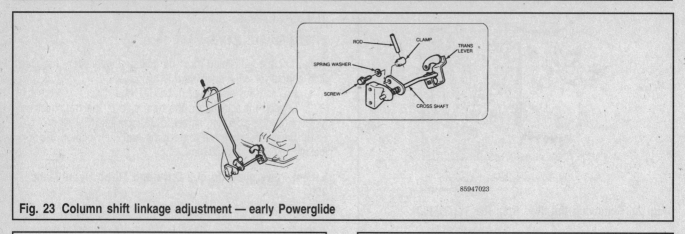

Fig. 23 Column shift linkage adjustment — early Powerglide

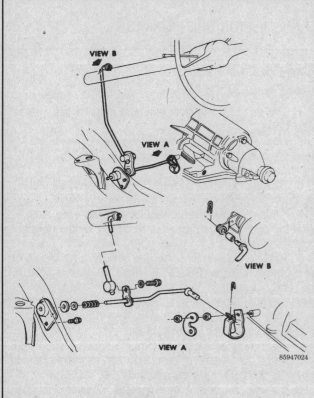

Fig. 24 Column shift linkage adjustment — 1970 and later Powerglide

clockwise to the LOW detent, and then clockwise one detent position to DRIVE.

2. Place the floorshift lever in DRIVE. Hold the floorshift unit lower operating lever for ward against the shift lever detent.

3. Place a $\frac{7}{64}$ in. spacer between the rear nut and the swivel. Tighten the rear nut against the spacer.

4. Remove the spacer and tighten the front nut against the swivel, locking the swivel between the nuts.

1968-73 VEHICLES

▶ See Figures 26 and 27

➡1968 and later cars use a cable-type shift linkage.

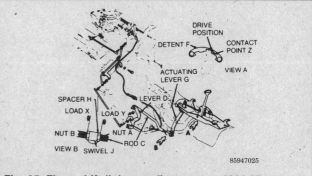

Fig. 25 Floor shift linkage adjustment — 1964-67 Powerglide

1. Place the shift lever in DRIVE.

2. Disconnect the cable from the transmission lever. Place the transmission lever in DRIVE by rotating the lever counterclockwise to the LOW detent, and then clockwise one detent to DRIVE.

3. Measure the distance from the rearward face of the attaching bracket to the center of the cable attaching pin. If this distance is not 5½ in., loosen and move the cable end stud nut to obtain the correct measurement.

➡1969 and later models require an additional backdrive adjustment.

4. Place the shift lever in PARK and the ignition switch in the **LOCK** position.

5. Loosen and adjust the backdrive rod.

6. With the selector lever in PARK, the ignition key should move freely into the **LOCK** position. The ignition **LOCK** position should not be obtainable in any transmission position other than PARK.

Turbo Hydra-Matic Column and Floor Shift Linkage Adjustment

VEHICLES THROUGH 1974

▶ See Figure 28

Linkages used on Turbo Hydra-Matic transmissions are similar to those used on Powerglides. Adjustments are the same, except that the transmission lever is adjusted to DRIVE by moving the lever clockwise to the LOW detent, and then counterclockwise two detent positions to DRIVE.

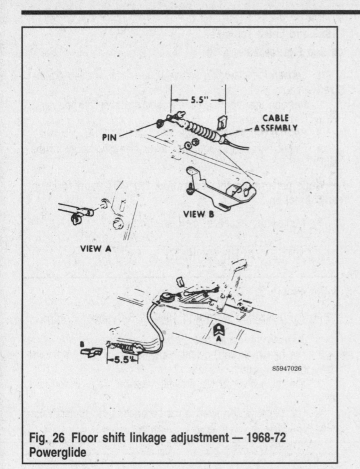

Fig. 26 Floor shift linkage adjustment — 1968-72 Powerglide

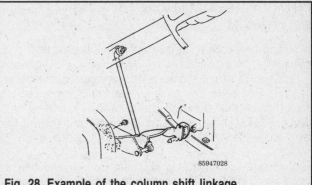

Fig. 28 Example of the column shift linkage components — Turbo Hydra-Matic transmissions

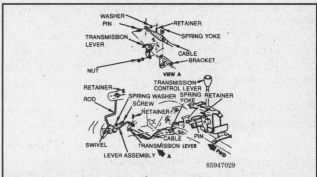

Fig. 29 Floor shift linkage adjustment — 1973 and later Turbo Hydra-Matic

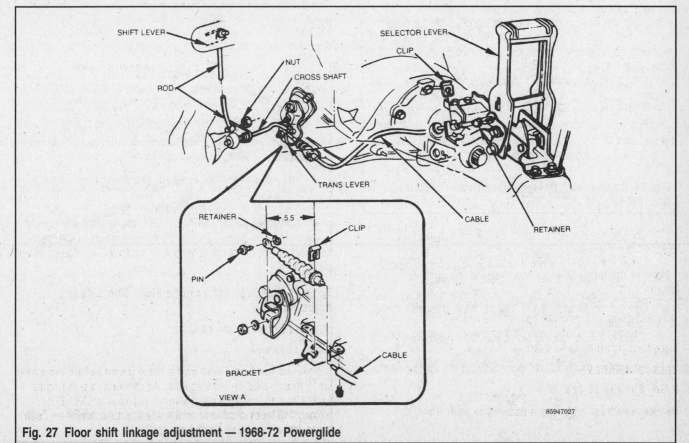

Fig. 27 Floor shift linkage adjustment — 1968-72 Powerglide

Column Shift (Except Turbo Hydra-Matic 200)

▶ See Figure 28

1. Loosen the swivel at the lower end of the rod that comes from the column.

2. On 1973 and later models, set the transmission lever in the NEUTRAL detent by turning the lever counterclockwise to the L1 detent, then clockwise three positions. On models through 1972, set the lever in the DRIVE detent by turning the lever counterclockwise to the L1 detent, then clockwise two positions.

3. Put the column lever in NEUTRAL for 1973 and later models, and in DRIVE for models through 1972. The important thing here is not where the indicator points but that the lever be in the correct position.

4. Tighten the swivel. Readjust the neutral start switch as necessary.

5. Check that the key cannot be removed and that the wheel is not locked with the key in **RUN**. Check that the key can be removed in **LOCK** with the lever in PARK, and that the steering wheel is locked.

Turbo Hydra-Matic 200

▶ See Figure 28

1. Remove the screw and washer from the swivel assembly on the rod which activates the transmission shift lever.

2. Put the transmission shift lever in NEUTRAL by turning it counterclockwise to L1 detent and then clockwise three detent positions. Put the transmission selector lever in NEUTRAL as determined by the mechanical stop in the steering column assembly - do not use the indicator pointer.

3. Turn the swivel until it lines up directly with the hole in the shift lever, and install screw and washer. You should not have to force the transmission lever to move in either direction to install the screw.

4. Adjust the transmission indicator pointer and neutral start switch.

5. Check that the key cannot be removed from the **RUN** position if the transmission selector is in REVERSE and that the key can be removed with the selector in PARK. Make sure the lever will not move from PARK position with key out of ignition.

1975-81 Cars with Cable Linkage

▶ See Figure 29

1. Loosen the swivel at the lower end of the rod that comes from the steering column.

2. Loosen the pin at the transmission end of the cable.

3. Set the floorshift lever in the DRIVE detent.

4. Set the transmission lever in the DRIVE detent by moving it counterclockwise to the L1 detent, then clockwise three detent positions.

5. Tighten the nut on the pin at the transmission end of the cable.

6. Push the floorshift lever in PARK and the ignition switch in **LOCK**.

7. Pull down lightly on the rod from the column and tighten its clamp nut.

1982 and Later Vehicles

▶ See Figures 28 and 30

1. Loosen the clamping screw at the shifting rod-to-equalizer lever.

2. Position the steering column shifting lever into the NEUTRAL position.

3. Set the transmission lever into the NEUTRAL position.

4. Finger tighten the equalizer lever clamping screw to the sifting rod.

➡**While performing this operation, DO NOT exert force in any direction.**

5. Tighten the equalizer clamping screw.

THROTTLE VALVE LINKAGE

▶ See Figure 31

1964-66 Powerglide w/V8 and 1964-73 6-Cylinder Engines

1. Depress the accelerator pedal.

2. The bellcrank on 6-cylinder engines must be at the wide open throttle position.

3. The dash lever at the firewall must be $\frac{1}{64}$-$\frac{1}{16}$ in. off its lever stop.

4. The transmission lever must be against the transmission internal stop.

5. Adjust the linkage to simultaneously obtain the conditions in Steps 1-4.

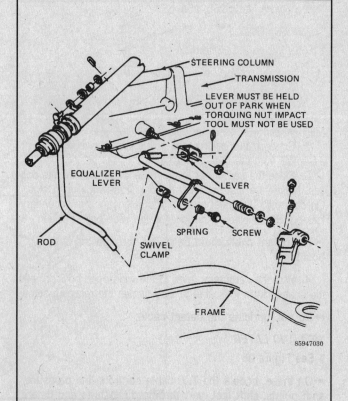

Fig. 30 Steering column shift linkage adjustment — 1982 and later

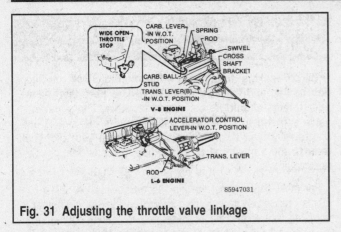

Fig. 31 Adjusting the throttle valve linkage

1967-73 Powerglide w/V8 Engines

1. Remove the air cleaner assembly.
2. Disconnect the accelerator linkage at the carburetor.
3. Disconnect both return springs.
4. Pull the throttle valve upper rod forward until the transmission is through the detent.
5. Open the carburetor to the wide open throttle position. Adjust the swivel on the end of the upper throttle valve rod so that the carburetor reaches wide open throttle position at the same time that the ball stud contact the end of the slot in the upper throttle valve rod. A play of 1/32 in. is allowable.

THROTTLE VALVE DETENT CABLE

Turbo Hydra-Matic 200, 250, 350

THROUGH 1972

▶ See Figures 32, 33 and 34

These transmission utilize a downshift cable instead of a linkage rod between the carburetor and the transmission.
1. Pry up on each side of the detent cable snap-lock with a small pry bar to release the lock. On cars equipped with a retaining screw, loosen the detent cable screw.
2. Squeeze the locking tabs and disconnect the snap-lock assembly from the throttle bracket.
3. Place the carburetor lever in the wide open throttle position. Make sure that the lever is against the wide open stop. On cars with Quadrajet carburetors, disengage the secondary lock-out before placing the lever in the wide open position.

➡The detent cable must be pulled through the detent position.

4. With the carburetor lever in the wide open position, push the snap-lock on the cable or else tighten the retaining screw.

➡Do not lubricate the detent cable.

1973 AND LATER

▶ See Figure 35

➡On these models the T.V. cable controls line pressure, shift points, shift feel, part throttle downshifts and detent downshifts. The T.V. cable operates the throttle valve lever and bracket assembly in the control valve.

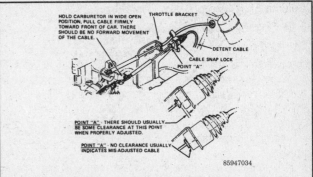

Fig. 32 Downshift cable adjustment — Turbo Hydra-Matic 200

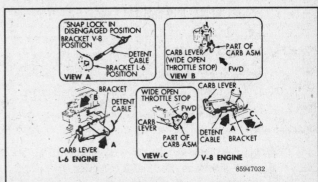

Fig. 33 Detent cable adjustment — Turbo Hydra-Matic 350 (250 model similar)

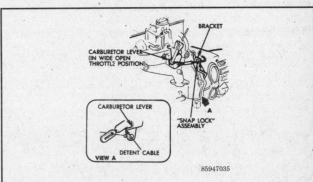

Fig. 34 Detent cable adjustment — Turbo Hydra-Matic 200, 250 and 350

1. Stop the engine.
2. Locate the TV cable adjuster near the carburetor.
3. Depress and hold down the metal tab of the TV cable adjuster.
4. Move the slider until it stops against the fitting.
5. Release the adjuster tab.
6. Turn the carburetor lever to the Full Throttle Stop position and release it.

➡By turning the carburetor lever to the Full Throttle Stop, the TV cable will automatically adjust itself.

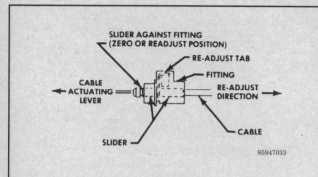

Fig. 35 TV Detent cable adjustment — 1973 and later vehicles

DETENT SWITCH ADJUSTMENT

▶ See Figures 36, 37 and 38

Turbo Hydra-matic 400 transmissions are equipped with an electrical detent, or downshift switch operated by the throttle linkage.

1968 Vehicles

1. Place the carburetor lever in the wide open position.
2. Position the automatic choke so that it is off.
3. Fully depress the switch plunger.
4. Adjust the switch mounting to obtain a distance of 0.05 in. (1.27mm) between the switch plunger and the throttle lever paddle.

1969-78 Vehicles

1. Pull the detent switch driver rearward until the hole in the switch body aligns with the hole in the driver. Insert a #42 wire gauge (approximately 0.094 in. diameter pin) through the aligned holes to hold the driver in position.
2. Loosen the mounting bolt.
3. Press the switch plunger as far forward as possible. This will preset the switch for adjustment, which will occur on the first application of wide open throttle.
4. Tighten the mounting bolt and remove the pin.

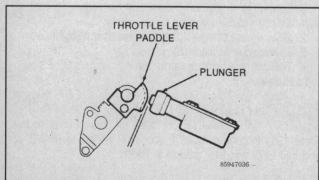

Fig. 36 Adjusting the detent switch — 1968-72 Turbo Hydra-Matic 400

DIESEL VEHICLE TRANSMISSION ADJUSTMENTS

➡ Before making any linkage adjustments, check the injection timing, and adjust if necessary. Also note that these adjustments should be performed together. The vacuum valve adjustment (THM 350s only) requires the use of special tools. If you do not have these tools at your disposal, refer the adjustment to a qualified, professional technician.

For most applications, the automatic transmission adjustments on a given transmission should be the same whether it is mated with a gasoline or diesel engine. Subtle differences may occur if the adjustment is somehow related to the fuel system, such as some detent or throttle valve adjustments. The following procedures are for Chevrolet mid-sized vehicles which are equipped with a diesel engine. For additional adjustments which are not listed here, refer to the gasoline adjustments earlier in this section.

THROTTLE ROD

▶ See Figure 39

1. If equipped with cruise control, remove the clip from the control rod, then remove the rod from the bellcrank.
2. Remove the throttle valve cable (THM 200) or detent cable (THM 350) from the bellcrank.
3. Loosen the locknut on the throttle rod, then shorten the rod several turns.
4. Rotate the bellcrank to the full throttle stop, then lengthen the throttle rod until the injection pump lever contacts the injection pump full throttle stop. Release the bell crank.
5. Tighten the throttle rod locknut.
6. Connect the throttle valve or detent cable and cruise control rod to the bellcrank. Adjust if necessary.

THROTTLE VALVE (TV) OR DETENT CABLE

▶ See Figure 40

Refer to the previous cable adjustment procedures for gasoline engines. Adjust according to the style of cable which is used.

TRANSMISSION VACUUM VALVE

▶ See Figures 41 and 42

1. Remove the air cleaner assembly from the engine.
2. Remove the air intake crossover form the intake manifold. Cover the intake manifold passages to prevent foreign material from entering the engine.
3. Disconnect the throttle rod from the injection pump throttle lever.
4. Loosen the transmission vacuum valve-to-injection pump bolts.
5. Mark and disconnect the vacuum lines from the vacuum valve.

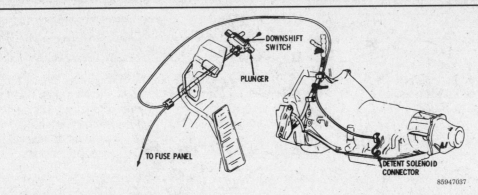

Fig. 37 Detent (downshift) switch wiring

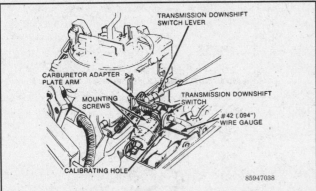

Fig. 38 Adjusting the detent switch — 1969-78 THM 400

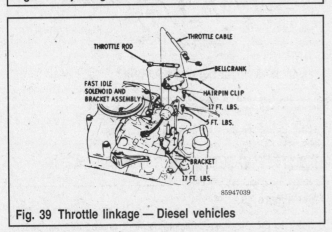

Fig. 39 Throttle linkage — Diesel vehicles

6. Attach a carburetor angle gauge adapter (Kent-Moore tool J-26701-15 or its equivalent) to the injection pump throttle lever. Attach an angle gauge (J-26701 or its equivalent) to the gauge adapter.

7. Turn the throttle lever to the wide open throttle position. Set the angle gauge to zero degrees.

8. Center the bubble in the gauge level.

9. Set the angle gauge to one of the following settings, according to the year and type of engine:

- 1980 — 49-50 degrees
- 1981 California — 49-50 degrees
- 1981 Non-California — 58 degrees
- 1982-83 — 58 degrees

10. Attach a vacuum gauge to port 2 and a hand-held vacuum pump to port 1 of the vacuum valve (as illustrated).

11. Apply 18-22 in. Hg (61-74 kPa) of vacuum to the valve. Slowly rotate the valve until the vacuum reading drops to one of the following values:

- 1980 — 7 in. Hg (24 kPa)
- 1981 California — 7-8 in. Hg (24-27 kPa)
- 1981 Non-California — 8.5-9.0 in. Hg (29-30 kPa)
- 1982-83 — 10.5 in. Hg (35 kPa)

12. Tighten the vacuum valve retaining bolts.

13. Reconnect the original vacuum lines to the vacuum valve.

14. Remove the angle gauge and adapter.

15. Connect the throttle rod to the throttle lever.

16. Install the air intake crossover, using new gaskets.

17. Install the air cleaner assembly.

Neutral Safety/Back-Up Switch

REPLACEMENT

▶ **See Figure 43**

For automatic transmissions both the neutral safety/back-up switches are combined into a single unit. The switch prevents the engine from being started in any transmission position except NEUTRAL or PARK. The switch is located on the upper side of the steering column under the instrument panel on column shift cars and inside the shift console on floor shift models.

Models Through 1981

1. Disconnect the negative battery cable.
2. Remove the console for access on floor shift models.
3. Disengage the electrical connectors.
4. Remove the neutral switch.

To install:

5. Place 1964-70 column shift lever models in DRIVE, and 1971 and later models in NEUTRAL. Locate the lever tang against the transmission selector plate on column shift models. Place 1964 through early 1972 floor shift models in DRIVE, and mid-1972 and later models in PARK.

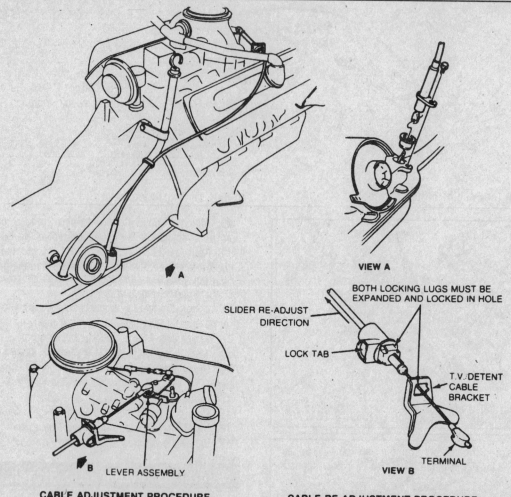

VIEW A

SLIDER RE-ADJUST
DIRECTION

BOTH LOCKING LUGS MUST BE
EXPANDED AND LOCKED IN HOLE

LOCK TAB

T.V. DETENT
CABLE
BRACKET

TERMINAL

VIEW B

B LEVER ASSEMBLY

CABLE ADJUSTMENT PROCEDURE

1. Remove pump rod from lever assembly.

2. After installation to transmission, install cable fitting into cable bracket. **CAUTION** Slider must not be adjusted before or during assembly to bracket.

3. Install cable terminal to lever assembly.

4. Rotate the lever assembly to its full throttle stop position to automatically adjust slider on cable to correct setting.

5. Release lever assembly & reconnect the pump rod to lever assembly

CABLE RE-ADJUSTMENT PROCEDURE

In case re-adjustment is necessary because of inadvertent adjustment before or during assembly, perform the following.

1. Remove pump rod from lever assembly, depress and hold metal lock tab.

2. Move slider through fitting in direction away from lever assembly until slider stops against fitting.

3. Release metal lock tab.

4. Repeat steps 4 & 5 of adjustment procedure.

85947040

Fig. 40 Detent cable adjustment — Diesel engines

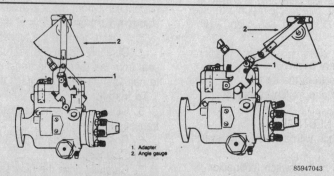

1. Adapter
2. Angle gauge

85947043

Fig. 41 Angle gauge with adaptor for diesel vacuum valve adjustment — NOTE: the gauge is positioned differently depending upon type of throttle lever

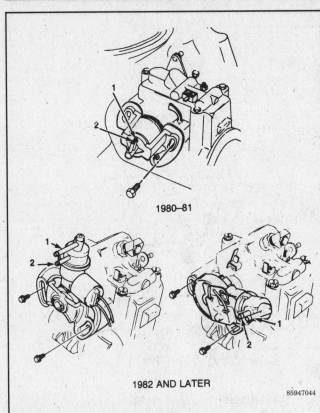

1980–81

1982 AND LATER

85947044

Fig. 42 Vacuum valve adjustment — Diesel equipped vehicles

6. Align the slot in the contact support with the hole in the switch. Insert a ³⁄₃₂ in. pin in place. The switch is now aligned in the DRIVE position.

➡**For 1973-81 applications, replacement neutral safety switches have a shear-pin installed to aid in proper switch alignment so that insertion of a pin is unnecessary. After installation, moving the shift lever from NEUTRAL shears the pin.**

7. Place the contact support drive slot over the drive tang. Install the switch mounting screws.

8. Remove the aligning pin. Engage the electrical wiring and, if applicable, install the console.

9. Connect the negative battery cable.

10. Set the parking brake and hold your foot on the brake pedal. Check to see that the engine will start only in PARK or NEUTRAL.

1982 and Later

1. Disconnect the negative battery cable.

2. Disengage the wiring harness from the switch.

3. Remove the retaining screws and switch assembly.

To install:

4. Position the gear selector in NEUTRAL.

5. Align the actuator on the switch with a hole in the switch tube.

6. Position the rearward portion of the switch (connector side) to fit into the cutout in the lower jacket.

7. Push down on the front of the switch. The two tangs on the housing back will snap into place in rectangular holes in the jacket.

8. Adjust the switch by moving the gear selector to PARK. The main housing and the housing back should ratchet, providing proper switch adjustment.

9. Make sure the switch is properly secured, then engage the wiring harness.

10. Connect the negative battery cable, then verify that the engine will only start in NEUTRAL or PARK. Be sure to firmly apply the brake when checking switch operation.

SWITCH ADJUSTMENT

▶ **See Figure 44**

Models Through 1981

1. Place shift lever in NEUTRAL.

2. If necessary, remove the center console for access to the switch.

3. Move the switch until you can insert a 0.0938 in. (2.381mm) gauge pin through the hole in the switch and through the alignment hole.

4. Loosen the switch securing screws and move the switch, as necessary to insert the pin.

5. Tighten the screws and remove the pin.

6. Step on the brake pedal and check to see that the engine will only start in NEUTRAL or PARK.

7. If removed for access, install the center console assembly.

1982 and Later

1. With the switch installed, move the housing all the way toward LOW.

2. Adjust the switch by moving the gear selector to PARK. The main housing and the housing back should ratchet, providing proper switch adjustment.

Extension Housing Seal

REMOVAL & INSTALLATION

1. Raise and support the vehicle safely using jackstands.

2. Matchmark and remove the driveshaft. Most vehicles covered in this manual should be equipped with a slip yoke and the front of the driveshaft. In order to remove the shaft, disconnect it from the rear axle, then carefully withdraw the splined yoke from the rear of the transmission.

3. If used, remove the tunnel strap.

4. Carefully distort the seal using a punch, then pry the seal from the rear of the transmission housing. Be careful not to damage the sealing surface of the housing.

To install:

5. Clean and dry the sealing surface in the rear of the transmission housing.

6. Coat the outside of the new seal with a non-hardening sealing compound.

7. Carefully drive the new seal into position using a proper seal installation tool. Be careful not to damage the housing or the transmission output shaft upon installation.

8. If used, install the tunnel strap.

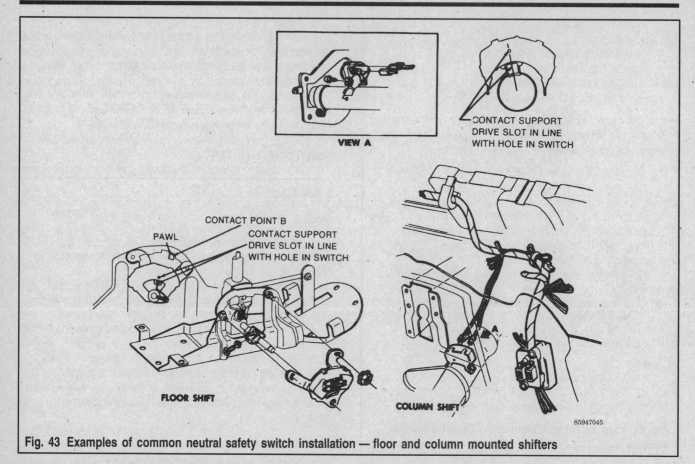

Fig. 43 Examples of common neutral safety switch installation — floor and column mounted shifters

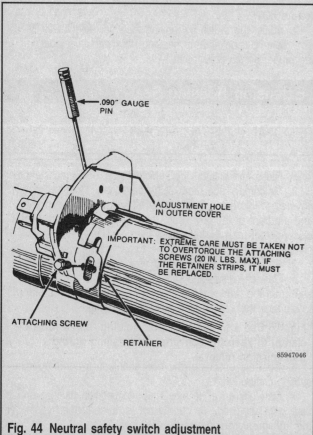

Fig. 44 Neutral safety switch adjustment

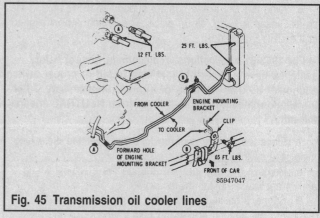

Fig. 45 Transmission oil cooler lines

9. Install the driveshaft assembly.
10. Remove the jackstands and carefully lower the vehicle.
11. Check and, if necessary, add fresh transmission fluid.
Please refer to Section 1 of this manual for details concerning proper methods and type of automatic transmission fluid.

Transmission

REMOVAL & INSTALLATION

▶ **See Figures 45, 46, 47 and 48**

1. Open the hood and place protectors on the fenders, then disconnect the negative battery cable.

2. Remove the air cleaner assembly and cover the air intake for protection.

3. Disconnect the detent cable at its upper end.

4. Remove the transmission oil dipstick, and, if accessible, the bolt holding the dipstick tube.

5. Raise and support the vehicle safely using jackstands.

➡️**If a floor pan reinforcement is used be sure it does not interfere with driveshaft removal. If interference if found, remove the reinforcement.**

6. Disconnect the speedometer cable at the transmission.

7. Disconnect the shift linkage at the transmission.

8. Remove the driveshaft assembly from the transmission.

9. Disconnect all electrical leads at the transmission and any clips that hold these leads to the transmission case.

10. Remove the flywheel cover and matchmark the flywheel and torque converter for later assembly.

11. Remove the torque converter-to-flexplate bolts and/or nuts.

12. On gasoline engine cars, disconnect the catalytic converter support bracket.

13. Remove the transmission support-to-transmission mount bolt and transmission support-to-frame bolts, and any insulators (if used).

14. Position the transmission jack under the transmission and raise it slightly.

15. Slide the transmission support rearward.

16. Loosen the transmission enough to gain access to the oil cooler lines and detent cable attachments.

17. Disconnect the oil cooler lines and detent cable. Plug all openings.

18. Support the engine and remove the engine-to-transmission bolts.

19. Disconnect the transmission assembly, being careful not to damage any cables, lines or linkage.

20. Install a C-clamp or torque converter holding tool onto the transmission housing in order to hold the converter to the housing. Carefully lower the transmission assembly from the vehicle (a hydraulic floor jack is best for this).

To install:

21. With the torque converter held in position, carefully raise the transmission into position. Install the transmission-to-engine bolts and tighten to 35-40 ft. lbs. (47-54 Nm).

22. Connect the detent cable or linkage, then remove the plugs and connect the oil cooler lines.

23. Slide the transmission support into position

24. Install the transmission support-to-transmission mount bolt and transmission support-to-frame bolts along with any insulators (if used).

25. On gasoline engine cars, connect the catalytic converter support bracket.

26. Make sure the weld nuts on the converter are flush with the flexplate and that the converter rotates freely by hand. Align the matchmarks made earlier and hand thread the torque converter-to-flexplate retaining bolts. Once the bolts are threaded, tighten them to 35 ft. lbs. (47 Nm). Re-tighten the first bolt torqued.

27. Install the flywheel cover.

28. Connect all electrical leads at the transmission and any clips that hold these leads to the transmission case.

29. Install the driveshaft assembly to the transmission.

30. Connect the shift linkage to the transmission.

31. Connect the speedometer cable to the transmission.

32. If removed, install the floor pan reinforcement.

33. If access was not possible from above the vehicle, install the transmission dipstick guide tube using a new oil seal.

34. Connect the detent cable at its upper end.

35. Check and adjust the shift and throttle linkage, as necessary. Refer to the adjustment procedures found earlier in this section.

36. Remove the jackstands and carefully lower the vehicle.

37. If not done already, install the transmission dipstick guide tube using a new oil seal.

38. Install the transmission dipstick.

39. Remove the protective cover, then install the air cleaner assembly.

40. If drained, fill the transmission assembly with the proper type and amount of transmission fluid.

41. Connect the negative battery cable, then check and add fluid, as necessary.

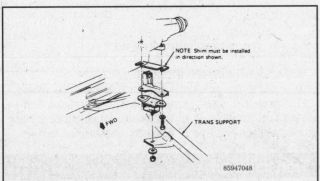

Fig. 46 Note that some transmission mounts are shimmed; DO NOT loose the shim(s) during removal

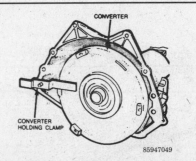

Fig. 47 Use a torque converter holding fixture (or a C-clamp) to keep the converter from falling during transmission removal

DRIVELINE

Driveshaft and U-Joints

▶ See Figure 49

Mid-size Chevrolet driveshafts are of the conventional, open type. Located at either end of the driveshaft is a U-joint or universal joint, which allows the driveshaft to move up and down to match the motion of the rear axle. The front U-joint connects the driveshaft to a slip jointed yoke. This yoke is internally splined, and allows the driveshaft to move in and out on the transmission splines. The rear U-joint is clamped or bolted to a companion flange fastened to the rear axle drive pinion. The rear U-joint is secured in the yoke in one of two ways. Dana and Cleveland design driveshafts (typically found on 1964-81 vehicles) use a conventional type snapring to hold each bearing cup in the yoke. The snapring fits into a groove located in each yoke end, just on top of the bearing cup. A Saginaw design driveshaft (usually found on 1979 and later vehicles) secures the U-joints differently. Nylon material is injected through a small hole in the yoke during manufacture, and flows along a circular groove between the U-joint and the yoke creating a non-metallic snapring. The Nylon joints are sheared during removal and replaced with conventional snapring types, so your vehicle may not contain the Nylon joints if they have been removed previously.

There are toe methods of attaching the rear U-joint to the rear axle. One method employs a pair of straps, while the other method is a set of bolted flanges. Band U-joints, requir-

ing replacement, will produce a clunking sound when the car is put into gear and when the transmission shifts from gear to gear. This is due to worn needle bearings or a scored trunnion end possibly caused by improper lubrication during assembly. U-joints require no periodic maintenance and therefore have no lubrication fittings.

Some driveshafts, generally those in heavy duty applications, use a damper as part of the slip joint. This vibration damper cannot be serviced separately from the slip joint. If either component goes bad, the two must be replaced as a unit.

REMOVAL & INSTALLATION

▶ See Figures 50 and 51

1. Raise the rear of the vehicle and support it safely using jackstands.
2. Matchmark the relationship of the driveshaft to the differential flange to assure that they are reassembled in the same position.
3. Disconnect the rear U-joint by removing the U-bolts or retaining straps.
4. To prevent the loss of the needle bearings, tape the bearing caps in place. If you are replacing the U-joint, this is not necessary.
5. Remove the driveshaft from the transmission by sliding it rearward. There may be some oil leakage from the rear of the transmission. It can be contained by placing a small plastic

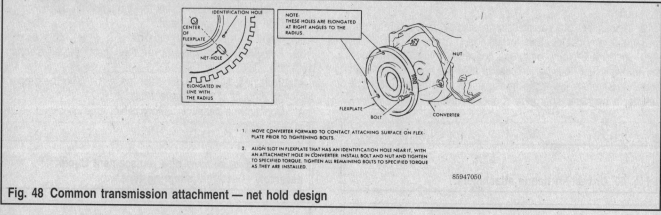

Fig. 48 Common transmission attachment — net hold design

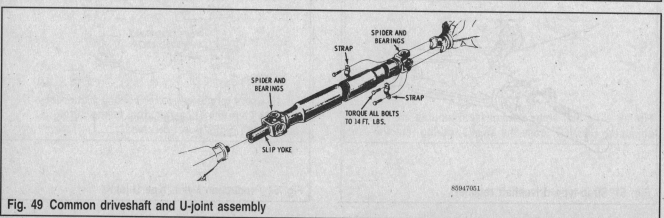

Fig. 49 Common driveshaft and U-joint assembly

bag over the rear of the transmission and holding it in place with a rubber band.

To install:

6. Insert the front yoke into the transmission so that the driveshaft splines mesh with the transmission splines.

7. Using the reference marks made earlier, align the driveshaft with the differential flange and secure it with the U-bolts or retaining straps.

8. Remove the jackstands and carefully lower the vehicle.

U-JOINT OVERHAUL

▶ See Figures 52, 53, 54, 55, 56, 57, 58 and 59

Snapring (Cleveland) Type

1. Matchmark and remove the driveshaft assembly from the vehicle. Refer to the procedure earlier in this section.

✳✳WARNING

NEVER clamp the driveshaft tube in a vise, for this may dent the tube. Support the driveshaft horizontally and clamp on the yokes of the universal joints using a soft-jawed vise or blocks of wood to protect the yokes.

2. Remove the snaprings from the yoke. If the snapring is difficult to remove, tap the end of the bearing cap lightly to relieve pressure from snapring.

3. Support the propeller shaft horizontally in line with the base plate of a bench vise, but never clamp the driveshaft tube.

4. Place the universal joint so the lower ear of the yoke is supported on a 1¼ in. ID pipe or a 1⅛ inch socket, depending on the application. Press the trunnion bearing against the socket/pipe in order to partially press it from the yoke. A cross press such as tool J-9522-3 should be used for this.

5. Grasp the cap and work it out, if necessary use tool J-9522-5 or equivalent spacer to further push the the bearing cap from the trunion, then grasp and work it free.

6. Rotate the shaft and support the other side of the yoke, then press the bearing cap from the yoke and as in previous steps.

7. Remove the trunnion from the driveshaft yoke.

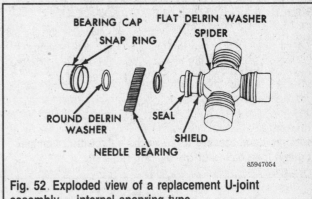
Fig. 52 Exploded view of a replacement U-joint assembly — internal snapring type

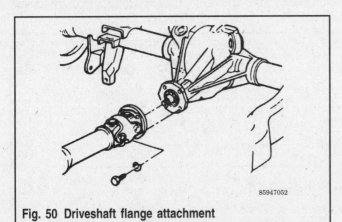
Fig. 50 Driveshaft flange attachment

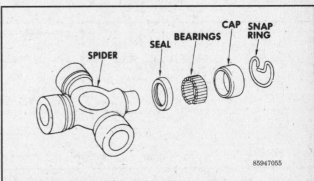
Fig. 53 Exploded view of a replacement U-joint assembly — external snapring type

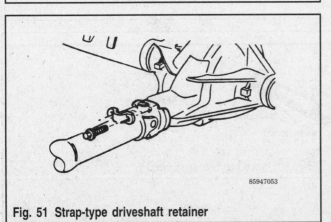
Fig. 51 Strap-type driveshaft retainer

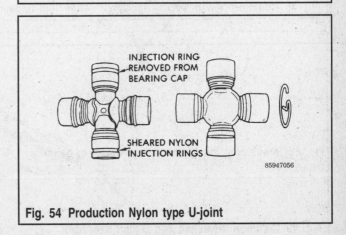
Fig. 54 Production Nylon type U-joint

8. Clean and check the condition of all parts. Use U-joint repair kits to replace all the worn parts or replace the assembly using a new U-joint.

➡**If the used universal joints are going to be reinstalled, repack with new grease.**

To install:

9. Repack the bearings with chassis grease and replace the trunnion dust seals after any operation that requires disassembly of the U-joint. Be sure the lubricant reservoir at the end of the trunnion is full of lubricant. Fill the reservoirs with lubricant from the bottom.

10. Partially insert the cross into the yoke so 1 trunnion seats freely in the bearing cup, then rotate the shaft so this trunion is on the bottom.

11. Install the opposite bearing cap part way. Be sure both trunnions are started straight into the bearing caps.

12. Press against opposite bearing caps, working the cross constantly to be sure the trunions are free in the bearings. If binding occurs, check the needle rollers to be sure 1 or more needles have not become lodged under an end of the trunnion.

13. As soon as 1 bearing retainer groove is exposed, stop pressing and install the bearing retainer snapring.

➡**It may be necessary to strike the yoke with a hammer to align the seating of the bearing retainers.**

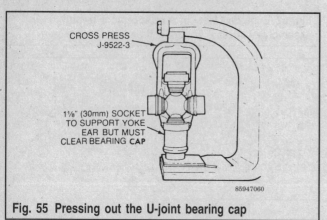

Fig. 55 Pressing out the U-joint bearing cap

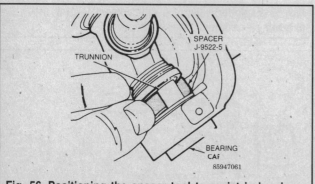

Fig. 56 Positioning the spacer tool to assist in bearing cap removal

14. Continue to press until the opposite bearing retainer can be installed. If difficulty installing the snaprings is encountered, tap the yoke with a hammer to spring the yoke ears slightly.

15. Once the driveshaft and U-joints are properly assembled, align the matchmarks and install the driveshaft to the vehicle.

Nylon Injected (Saginaw) Type

➡**Don't disassemble these joints unless replacing the complete U-joint. These factory installed joints cannot be reused and should instead be replaced by snapring type U-joints.**

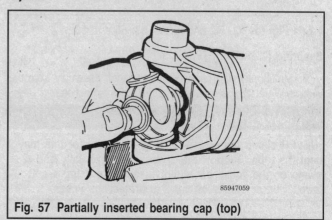

Fig. 57 Partially inserted bearing cap (top)

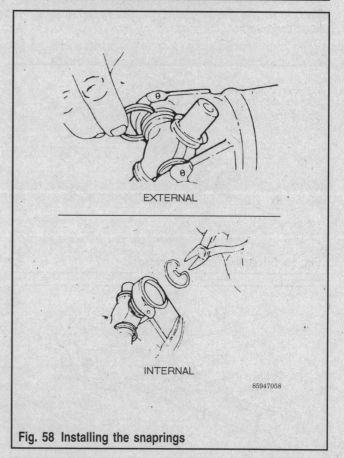

Fig. 58 Installing the snaprings

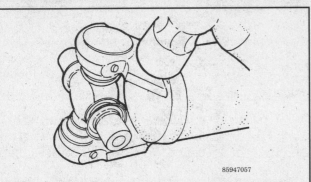

Fig. 59 Tapping the yoke in order to seat the retaining clip

1. Matchmark and remove the driveshaft assembly from the vehicle. Refer to the procedure earlier in this section.

❋❋WARNING

NEVER clamp the driveshaft tube in a vise, for this may dent the tube. Support the driveshaft horizontally and clamp on the yokes of the universal joints using a soft-jawed vise or blocks of wood to protect the yokes.

REAR AXLE

Identification

▶ See Figure 60

The rear axle number is located in the right or left axle tube adjacent to the axle carrier (differential). For more information, please refer to the rear axle identification chart in Section 1 of this manual. Anti-slip differentials are identified by a tab attached to the lower right section of the axle cover.

Determining Axle Ratio

An axle ratio is obtained by dividing the number of teeth on the drive pinion gear into the number of teeth on the ring gear. For instance, on a 4.11 ratio, the driveshaft will turn 4.11 times

2. Support the propeller shaft horizontally in line with the base plate of a bench vise, but never clamp the driveshaft tube.

3. Place the U-joint so the lower ear of the shaft yoke is supported by a 1⅛ inch socket. Press the lower bearing cap out of the yoke ear. This will shear the nylon injected ring retaining the lower bearing cap.

4 If the bearing cup is not completely removed, lift the cross (J-9522-3) and insert J-9522-5 or equivalent spacer, then press the cap completely out.

5. Rotate the driveshaft, shear the opposite plastic retainer, and press the other bearing cup out in the same manner.

6. Remove the cross from the yoke.

➡**Production U-joints cannot be reassembled. There are no bearing retainer grooves in the caps. Discard all parts that were removed and substitute those in the overhaul kit.**

7. If the front U-joint is being removed, separate the bearing caps from the slip yoke in the same manner.

8. Remove the sheared plastic bearing retainer from the yoke. If necessary, drive a small pin or punch through the injection holes to aid in removal.

9. Install the new snapring U-joints. Refer to the snapring type installation procedure found earlier in this section.

for every turn of the rear wheel. The most accurate way to determine the axle ratio is to drain the differential, remove the cover and count the number of teeth on the ring and pinion.

An easier method is to jack and support the car so that both rear wheels are off the ground. make a chalk mark on the rear wheel and the driveshaft. Block the front wheels and put the transmission in NEUTRAL. Turn the rear wheel one complete revolution and count the number of turns made by the driveshaft. The number of driveshaft rotations is the axle ratio. More accuracy can be obtained by going more than one tire revolution and dividing the result by the number of tire rotations.

The axle ratio is also identified by the axle serial number prefix on the axle; the axle ratios are listed in dealer's parts books according to prefix number. Some axles have a tag on the cover.

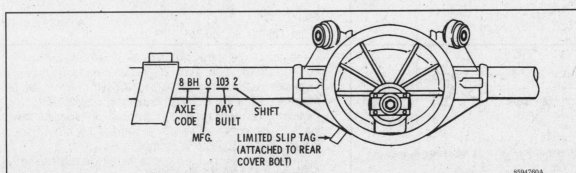

Fig. 60 Rear axle identification — Chevrolet manufacturing codes include C: Chevrolet-Buffalo and G: Chevrolet-Gear and Axle

Axle Shaft and Bearings

♦ See Figures 61, 62, 63 and 64

Two types of axles are used on these models, the C and the non-C type. Axle shafts in the C-type are retained by C-shaped locks, which fit grooves at the inner end of the shaft. Axle shafts in the non C-type are retained by the brake backing plate, which is bolted to the axle housing. Bearings in the C-type axle consist of an outer race, bearing rollers, and a roller cage retained by snaprings. The non C-type axle uses a unit roller bearing (inner race, rollers, and outer race), which is pressed onto the shaft up to a shoulder. When servicing C or non C-type axles, it is imperative to determine the axle type before attempting any service. Before attempting any service to the drive axle or axle shaft, remove the axle carrier cover and visually determine if the axle shaft are retained by C-shaped locks at the inner end, or by the brake backing plate at the outer end.

REMOVAL & INSTALLATION

✳✳CAUTION

Brake shoes contain asbestos, which has been determined to be a cancer causing agent. Never clean the brake surfaces with compressed air! Avoid inhaling any dust from any brake surface! When cleaning brake surfaces, use a commercially available brake cleaning fluid.

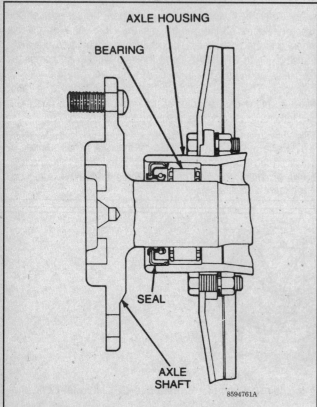

Fig. 61 Cross section of a common axle shaft and bearing assembly

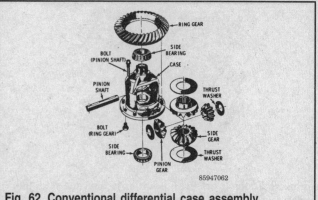

Fig. 62 Conventional differential case assembly

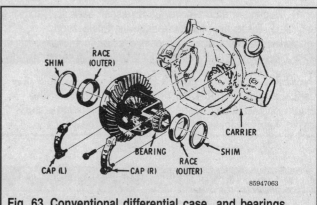

Fig. 63 Conventional differential case and bearings

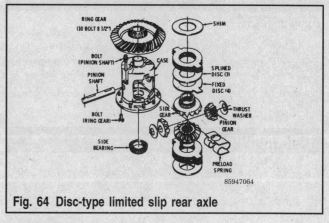

Fig. 64 Disc-type limited slip rear axle

Non C-Type

♦ See Figures 65 and 66

The non C-type is typically found on 1964-79 vehicles with original rear axle assemblies. The design allows for a maximum axle shaft end-play of 0.022 in. (0.559mm), which can be measured with a dial indicator. If end-play is found to be excessive, the bearing should be replaced. Shimming the bearing is not recommended as this ignores end-play of the bearing itself and could result in improper bearing seating.

1. Raise and support the rear of the vehicle safely using jackstands.
2. Remove the wheel and brake drum.

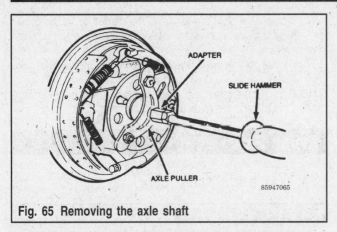

Fig. 65 Removing the axle shaft

3. Remove the nuts holding the retainer plate to the backing plate. Disconnect the brake line, then plug the openings to prevent system contamination or excessive fluid loss.

4. Remove the retainer and install nuts, fingertight, to prevent the brake backing plate from being dislodged.

5. Pull out the axle shaft and bearing assembly, using a slide hammer.

6. Using a chisel, nick the bearing retainer in three or four places. The retainer does not have to be cut, merely collapsed sufficiently, to allow the bearing retainer to be slid from the shaft.

7. Press off and discard the old bearing.

To install:

8. Install the new bearing by pressing it into position.

➡Do not attempt to press the bearing and the retainer on at the same time.

9. Press on the new retainer.

10. Assemble the shaft and bearing in the housing making sure that the bearing is seated properly in the housing.

11. Install the retainer to the backing plate and tighten the nuts.

12. Remove the plugs, then reconnect the brake line.

13. Install the drum, wheel and tire, then properly bleed the hydraulic brake system.

14. Remove the jackstands and carefully lower the vehicle.

1979 and Later C-type

♦ See Figures 67, 68, 69, 70, 71, 72, 73, 74, 75, 76, 77, 78 and 79

1. Raise and support the rear of the vehicle safely using jackstands.

2. Remove the wheel and brake drum.

➡When removing the cover, a small prytool may be used at the base of the cover to gently pry it back from the axle housing, breaking the gasket seal and allowing the lubricant to drain out into the container. Be careful not to use excessive force and damage the cover or housing.

3. Place a large container underneath the rear axle, then clean the area surrounding the rear cover to help prevent dirt from entering the rear axle housing. Unscrew the retaining bolts, drain the gear oil and remove the rear cover.

4. Remove the differential pinion shaft lock-screw and the differential pinion shaft.

5. Push the flanged end of the axle shaft toward the center of the vehicle and remove the C-lock from the retaining groove at the end of the shaft.

6. Remove the axle shaft from the housing, being careful not to damage the oil seal.

7. Remove the oil seal by inserting the bottom end of the axle shaft behind the steel case of the oil seal. Pry the seal loose from the bore.

8. Seat the legs of the bearing puller behind the bearing. Seat a washer against the bearing and hold it in place with a nut. Use a slide hammer to pull the bearing.

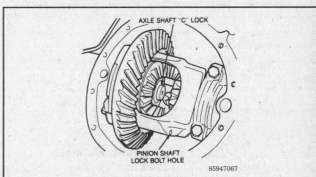

Fig. 67 Rear axle shaft C-lock and pinion shaft lockscrew locations

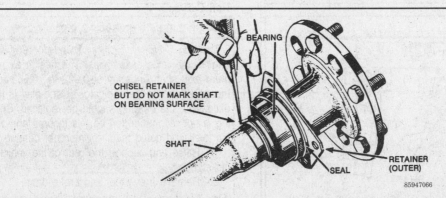

Fig. 66 Cutting the bearing retainer — non C-type axle

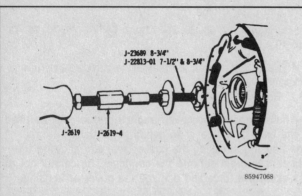

Fig. 68 Removing the axle bearing using a puller

To install:

9. Pack the cavity between the seal lips with wheel bearing lubricant and lubricate a new wheel bearing with same.

10. Use a suitable driver and install the bearing until it bottoms against the tube. Install the oil seal.

11. Slide the axle shaft into place. Be sure that the splines on the shaft do not damage the oil seal. Once the shaft is fully inserted, make sure that the splines engage the differential side gear.

12. Install the axle shaft C-lock on the inner end of the shaft and push the shaft outward so that the C-lock seats in the differential side gear counterbore.

13. Position the differential pinion shaft through the case and pinions, aligning the hole in the case with the hole for the lockscrew. Then install and tighten the lockscrew.

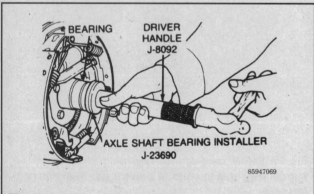

Fig. 69 Installing the axle bearing

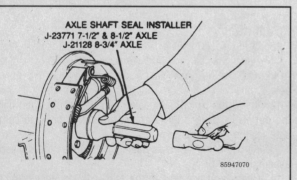

Fig. 70 Using a seal installation tool to drive the new seal into position

14. Use a new gasket and install the carrier cover. Be sure that the gasket surfaces are clean before installing the gasket and cover.

15. Fill the axle with lubricant to the bottom of the filler hole.

16. Install the brake drum and wheels.

17. Remove the jackstands and carefully lower the vehicle.

18. Check for leaks and road test the car.

Pinion Seal

REMOVAL & INSTALLATION

▶ **See Figures 80, 81 and 82**

1. Raise and support the rear of the vehicle safely using jackstands. If the rear of the vehicle is higher than the front, less gear oil will be lost during the procedure.

2. Matchmark the driveshaft and the pinion companion flange so that they can be reassembled in the same position.

3. Disconnect the driveshaft from the pinion companion flange and remove it or support it up in the body tunnel by wiring it to the exhaust pipe.

➡**If the joint bearing caps are not retained by a retainer strap, use a piece of tape to hold the bearing caps on their trunnions.**

4. Matchmark the position of the companion flange, pinion shaft and nut, so that the proper pinion bearing preload can be maintained upon reassembly.

Fig. 71 A spray cleaner will help eliminate some of the mess

Fig. 72 Loosen and remove the lock screw so the pinion shaft may be withdrawn

Fig. 73 If the axle shaft is pushed inward, the C-clock can be accessed

Fig. 74 Remove the C-lock from the shaft groove and the case

Fig. 75 Pull straight back to withdraw the shaft

Fig. 76 A prybar (or the end of the shaft) may be used to dislodge and remove the old bearing seal

Fig. 77 Use a suitably sized driver or the smooth end of a length of pipe to drive the new seal into position

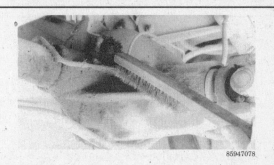

Fig. 78 Before removing the filler plug, clean the surrounding area in order to prevent dirt from entering the case

5. Using Tool J-8614-10 to hold the pinion companion flange, remove the flange retaining nut and washer.

6. With a suitable container in place to hold any fluid that may drain from the rear axle, remove the pinion companion flange with Tool J-8614-10.

7. Remove the seal by driving it out with a blunt chisel.

✳✳WARNING

When driving out the old seal, be extremely careful not to damage the carrier or sealing surfaces.

8. Examine the pinion companion flange for any nicks or damage. If so, replace it.

9. Examine the pinion seal bore in the carrier and remove any burrs.

To install:

10. Using Tool J-23911, or equivalent, install a new seal.

11. Apply Special Seal Lubricant, No. 1050169 or equivalent to the O.D. of the pinion flange and sealing lip of the new seal.

12. Install the pinion companion flange and nut, then tighten the nut 1/16 in. beyond the alignment marks in order to compensate for the new parts.

13. Align the marks made earlier, then install the driveshaft assembly.

14. Check and add fluid to the rear axle, as necessary.

15. Remove the jackstands, then carefully lower the vehicle.

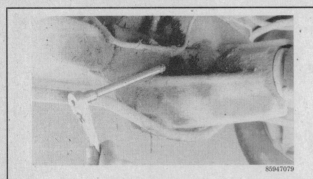

Fig. 79 Use a ratchet and extension to remove the filler plug in order to refill the differential case with gear oil

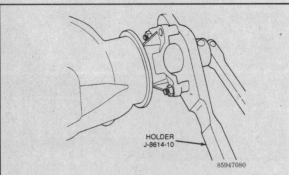

Fig. 80 Use a suitable flange holder to secure the flange while loosening or tightening the retaining nut

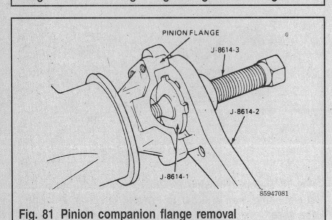

Fig. 81 Pinion companion flange removal

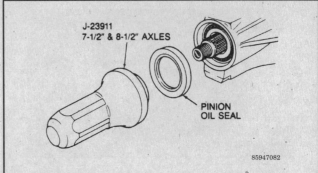

Fig. 82 Install the pinion oil seal with a driver/seal installer tool

Axle Assembly

REMOVAL & INSTALLATION

1. Raise and support the rear of the vehicle safely using jackstands.

�֎CAUTION

Make sure the rear axle assembly is supported safely.

2. Disconnect the shock absorbers from the axle.
3. Matchmark the driveshaft and pinion flange, then disconnect the drive shaft and remove or support out of the way.
4. Remove the brake line junction block bolt at the axle housing. If necessary disconnect the brake lines at the junction block and plug the openings.
5. Disconnect the upper control arms from the axle housing.
6. Lower the rear axle assembly sufficiently and remove the springs.
7. Remove the rear wheels and drums.
8. With the aid of an assistant, carefully continue lowering the rear axle assembly and remove it from the vehicle.
   To install:
9. With the aid of an assistant, carefully raise the axle assembly using a suitable jack or hoist and install the springs.
10. Reconnect the upper and lower control arms.
11. Remove the caps and connect the brake lines and or the junction block.
12. Align and install the driveshaft assembly.
13. Connect the shock absorbers to the axle carrier.
14. Install the brake drums and wheels.
15. If the lines were disconnected, properly bleed the hydraulic brake system.
16. Remove the jackstands and carefully lower the vehicle.

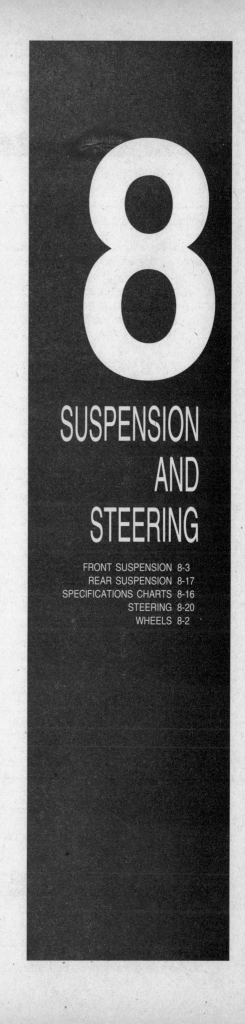

8

SUSPENSION
AND
STEERING

WHEELS

Wheels

REMOVAL & INSTALLATION

▶ **See Figures 1 and 2**

1. Apply the parking brake and block the opposite wheel.
2. If equipped with automatic transmission, place the selector lever in PARK. If equipped with manual transmission, place the gear shifter in reverse.
3. If equipped, remove the wheel cover or hub cap. Carefully pry under the edge of the cap to free it. Do not used excessive force of the thin metal/plastic of the hub cap could be damaged.
4. Break loose the lug nuts using a tire iron. If a nut is stuck, never use heat to loosen it or damage to the wheel and bearings may occur.
5. Raise the vehicle until the tire is clear of the ground. Support the vehicle safely using jackstands.
6. Remove the lug nuts, then remove the tire and wheel assembly.

To install:

7. Make sure the wheel and brake drum or hub mating surfaces and the wheel lug studs are clean and free of all foreign material.
8. Position the wheel on the hub or drum and hand-tighten the lug nuts. Tighten all the lug nuts, in a criss-cross pattern, until they are snug.
9. Remove the supports, if any, and lower the vehicle. Tighten the lug nuts, in a criss-cross pattern. Then recheck the nuts to assure they are properly tightened and that the wheel is fully seated.
10. Install the wheel cover or hub cap to the wheel. A rubber mallet may be used to gently tap the cover into position.

INSPECTION

Check the wheels for any damage. They must be replaced if they are bent, dented, heavily rusted, have elongated bolt holes, or have excessive lateral or radial runout. Wheels with excessive runout may cause a high-speed vehicle vibration.

Replacement wheels must be of the same load capacity, diameter, width, offset and mounting configuration as the original wheels. Using the wrong wheels may affect wheel bearing life, ground and tire clearance, or speedometer and odometer calibrations.

Wheel Lug Studs

REPLACEMENT

1. Raise and support the vehicle safely using jackstands.

Fig. 1 Remove the hub cap or wheel cover by gently prying around the edges

Fig. 2 With the vehicle safely supported, remove the tire and wheel assembly

2. For front suspension stud replacements, remove the wheel hub and bearings. For details, refer to the wheel bearings procedure later in this section or the brake disc procedure in Section 9 of this manual.
3. For rear suspension stud replacements, remove the axle shaft from rear axle assembly.

➡**On some applications it may be possible to replace a rear axle hub stud without removing the axle shaft. In order to accomplish this, carefully knock or press out the damaged stud. Insert the new stud into the hub, then use the flat side of a lug nut and some washers (to protect the outside of the hub) to draw the stud into position in the hub.**

4. Support the disc or shaft hub in a hydraulic press, then press out the damaged stud. If a press is not available, a hammer and suitable driver may be sufficient, but extreme care should be taken not to damage the hub.

To install:

5. Insert the new serrated stud into the disc or shaft hub, then use the press to push the stud into position. If a press is not available, use a washer and the lug nut (installed with the flat side toward the washer) to draw the stud into position by tightening them down on the hub.
6. Install the brake disc and wheel bearings or the rear axle shaft, as applicable.
7. Remove the supports and carefully lower the vehicle.

FRONT SUSPENSION

▶ **See Figures 3 and 4**

The front suspension is designed to allow each wheel to compensate for changes in the read surface level without appreciably affecting the opposite wheel. Each wheel is independently connected to the frame by upper and lower control arms, ball joints and a steering knuckle. The control arms are specifically designed and positioned to allow the steering knuckles to move in a prescribed three dimensional arc. The front wheels are both held in proper relationship to each other and turned by two tie rods which are connected to steering arms on the knuckles and to an intermediate rod.

Coil chassis springs are mounted between the spring housings on the frame or front end sheet metal and the lower control arms. Ride control is provided by double, direct acting, shock absorbers mounted inside the coil springs and attached to the lower control arms by bolts and nuts. The upper portion of each shock absorber extends through the upper control arm's frame bracket and is secured with two grommets, two grommet retainers, and a nut.

Side roll of the front suspension is controlled by a spring steel stabilizer shaft. It is mounted in rubber bushings which are held to the frame side rails by brackets. The ends of the stabilizer are connected to the lower control arms by link bolts isolated by rubber grommets.

85948004

Fig. 3 From underneath, many of the front suspension components are visible — the triangular shaped lower control arms, underside of the shocks and lower ball joints, the tie rods and the intermediate rod

The upper control arm is attached to a cross shaft through isolating rubber bushing. The cross shaft, in turn, is bolted to frame brackets.

A ball joint assembly is riveted to the outer end of the upper arm. It is pre-loaded by a rubber spring to insure proper seating of the ball in the socket. The upper ball joint is attached to the steering knuckle by a torque prevailing nut.

The inner ends of the lower control arms have pressed-in bushings. Bolts, passing through the bushings, attach the arm to the frame. The lower ball joint assembly is a press fit in the arm and attaches to the steering knuckle with a torque prevailing nut.

Rubber grease seals are provided at ball socket assemblies to keep dirt and moisture from entering the joint and damaging the bearing surfaces.

Shock Absorbers

TESTING

Visually inspect the shock absorber. If there is evidence of leakage and the shock absorber is covered with oil, the shock is defective and should be replaced.

If there is no sign of excessive leakage (a small amount of weeping is normal) bounce the car at one corner by pressing down on the fender or bumper and releasing. When you have the car bouncing as much as you can, release the fender or bumper. The car should stop bouncing after the first rebound. If the bouncing continues past the center point of the bounce more than once, the shock absorbers are worn and should be replaced.

REMOVAL & INSTALLATION

▶ **See Figures 5, 6 and 7**

1. Raise and support the front of the vehicle safely using jackstands.
2. Use an open end wrench to hold the upper stem of the shock absorber from turning. Remove the upper stem retaining nut, retainer and grommet.
3. Remove the two bolts retaining the lower shock absorber pivot to the lower control arm, then pull the shock out through the bottom of the control arm.

To install:

4. With the lower retainer and the rubber grommet in place over the upper stem, install the shock (fully extended) back through the lower control arm.
5. Install the upper grommet, retainer and nut onto the upper stem.
6. Hold the upper stem from turning with an open end wrench and tighten the retaining nut.
7. Install the retainers on the lower end of the shock.

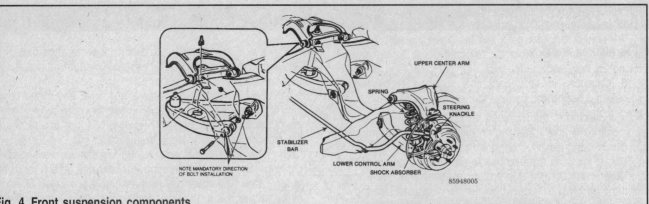

Fig. 4 Front suspension components

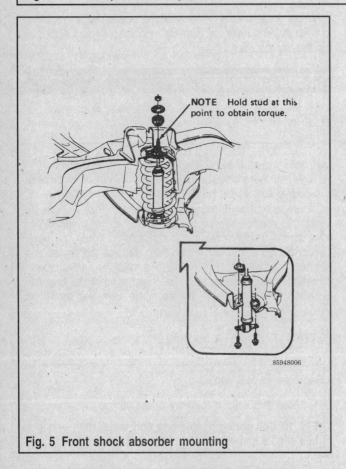

NOTE Hold stud at this point to obtain torque.

Fig. 5 Front shock absorber mounting

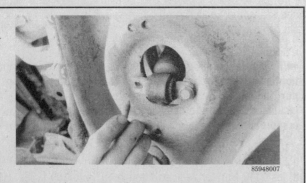

Fig. 6 The lower end of the front shock is usually mounted to the lower control arm using 2 bolts

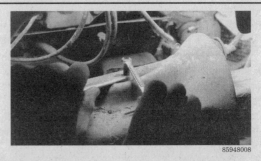

Fig. 7 In order to prevent damage to the shock absorber, hold the stud from turning while tightening the upper retaining nut

Coil Springs

✴✴CAUTION

The coil springs are under a considerable amount of tension. Be extremely careful when removing or installing them; if released suddenly, they can exert enough force to cause serious injury.

REMOVAL & INSTALLATION

▶ See Figures 8, 9 and 10

➡A coil spring compressor should be used for safety during removal and installation. This tool can usually be rented at tool rental shops.

1. Raise and support the front of the vehicle using jackstands at the frame so the control arms hang free.
2. Disconnect the lower shock absorber mounting bolts and push the shock upward into the spring. If necessary for ease of tool installation, remove the upper mounting nut, then remove the shock from the vehicle.
3. Disconnect the stabilizer bar.
4. Support the inner end of the control arm using tool No. J-23028 and a floor jack.
5. Raise the jack enough to take the tension off the lower control arm pivot bolts.
6. Install a spring compressor tool for safety. If a tool is unavailable, loosely install a chain around the spring and

through the lower control arm to keep the spring from suddenly releasing and flying out from the mount under pressure.

7. Remove the rear pivot bolt first, then the front pivot bolt from the control arm. Note the direction which the bolts are facing for installation purposes.

8. Cautiously lower the jack until all spring tension is released. If a spring compressor tool is used, the tool will keep the spring under compression.

9. Note the position in which the spring is installed in relation to the drain holes in the control arm, then remove the spring from the vehicle.

10. If the spring is to be replaced and it is retained by a spring compressor tool, follow the tool manufacturer's instructions to slowly release the spring tension. With the tension eased, remove the spring from the tool.

To install:

11. If a spring compression tool is being used, install the new spring to the tool and carefully compress it for installation.

12. Position the spring to the lower control arm as noted during removal. Make sure that at least part of 1 drain hole is uncovered once the spring is positioned. If no compressor tool is being used, chain the spring to the control arm for safety.

13. Carefully raise the control arm using the jack and fixture until the spring is compressed (no tool being used) and the control arm us properly positioned.

14. Install the pivot bolts in the direction noted during removal, but do not fully tighten at this time.

15. Remove the chain or compressor tool, then lower and remove the jack.

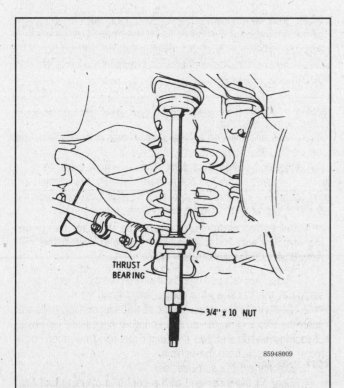

Fig. 8 When removing a coil spring using a compressor tool, always make sure the tool lock is in position and secured

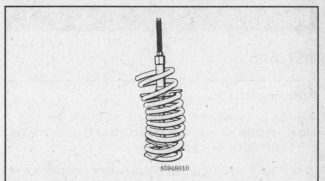

Fig. 9 Spring compressed in a tool and ready for installation

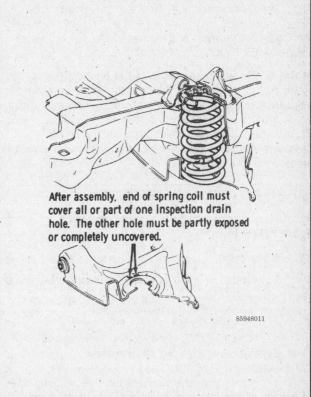

After assembly, end of spring coil must cover all or part of one inspection drain hole. The other hole must be partly exposed or completely uncovered.

Fig. 10 Coil spring positioning and installation — mid to late 1980's shown

16. Connect the stabilizer bar. If removed, install the upper shock absorber mounting nut, then secure the bottom of the shock absorber to the control arm.

17. Remove the jackstands and carefully lower the vehicle.

➡**If there is insufficient clearance in order to access and tighten the lower control arm pivot bolts, raise and support the car on ramps. If ramps are not available, use jackstands under the control arms so the suspension is compressed.**

18. With the vehicle's weight supported by the suspension, tighten the control arm pivot fasteners. Tighten the bolts to 85 ft. lbs. (115 Nm) for vehicles through 1973, to 100 ft. lbs. (136 Nm) for 1974-77 vehicles or to 65 ft. lbs. (88 Nm) for 1978 and later vehicles.

Ball Joints

INSPECTION

▶ See Figures 11 and 12

➡Before performing this inspection, make sure that the wheel bearings are adjusted correctly and that the control arm bushings are in good condition.

1. Raise the car by placing the jack under the lower control arm at the spring seat.
2. Continue raising the car until there is a 1-2 in. clearance under the wheel, then position a jackstand to support the lower control arm as close to the wheel as possible.
3. Insert a bar under the wheel and pry upward. If the wheel raises more than $\frac{1}{8}$ in. the ball joints are worn. Determine whether the upper or lower ball joint is worn by visual inspection while prying on the wheel.

➡Due to the distribution of forces in the suspension, the lower ball joint is usually the defective joint. Because of this, 1974 and later models are equipped with wear indicators on the lower ball joint. As long as the indicator (a $\frac{1}{2}$ in. diameter nipple into which the grease fitting is threaded) extends below the ball stud seat, replacement is unnecessary.

UPPER BALL JOINT REPLACEMENT

▶ See Figure 13

1964-70 Vehicles

1. Support the car using jackstands under the outer end of the lower control arms.
2. Remove the tire and wheel assembly.
3. Remove the cotter pin and nut from the stud.
4. Remove the stud from the steering knuckle.
5. Cut off the ball joint rivets with a chisel.
To install:
6. It may be necessary to enlarge the stud attaching holes in the control arm to accept the larger $\frac{5}{16}$ in. bolts. Inspect and clean the tapered hole in the steering knuckle. If the hole is damaged or deformed, the knuckle must be replaced.

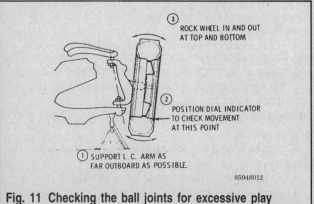

ROCK WHEEL IN AND OUT AT TOP AND BOTTOM

POSITION DIAL INDICATOR TO CHECK MOVEMENT AT THIS POINT

SUPPORT L.C. ARM AS FAR OUTBOARD AS POSSIBLE.

85948012

Fig. 11 Checking the ball joints for excessive play

7. Install the new joint and connect the stud to the steering knuckle. When installing the stud nut, never back off on the nut to align the cotter pin holes; always tighten the nut to the next hole.
8. Replacement ball joints may not include the lube fitting. If not, install a self-threading fitting into the tapped hole.
9. Install the tire and wheel assembly.
10. Remove the jackstands and lower the vehicle.

1971 and Later
▶ See Figures 14, 15 and 16

1. Raise the vehicle and support it securely using jackstands under the lower control arms.
2. Remove the tire and wheel assembly.
3. Remove the upper ball stud cotter pin and loosen the ball stud nut just one turn.
4. Locate the tool No. J-23742 between the upper and lower ball joints, then press the upper joint free in the steering knuckle. Remove the tool.
5. Remove the ball joint stud nut, and separate the joint from the steering knuckle. Lift the upper arm up and place a block of wood between the frame and the arm to support it.
6. With the control arm in the raised position, drill a hole $\frac{1}{4}$ in. deep into each rivet. Use a $\frac{1}{8}$ in. drill bit.
7. Next, use a $\frac{1}{2}$ in. drill bit on each rivet to drill off the heads.
8. Drive out the rivet using a small punch, then remove the ball joint.
To install:
9. Install the new ball joint using the fasteners supplied with the kit. Bolts should come in from the bottom with the nuts going threaded from the top of the control arm. Torque the fasteners to the specification provided with the kit's instructions. If no specification was provided, tighten the bolts to 10-13 ft. lbs. (14-18 Nm).
10. Turn the ball stud cotter pin hole to the fore and aft position. Remove the block of wood from between the upper control arm and frame.
11. Clean and inspect the steering knuckle hole. Replace the steering knuckle if any out of roundness is noted.
12. Insert the ball joint stud into the steering knuckle then install and torque the stud nut to 60 ft. lbs. (81 Nm). Install a new cotter pin. If nut must be turned to align cotter pin holes, tighten it further. Do not back off the specified torque in order to insert the pin.
13. Install a lube fitting and fill the joint with fresh grease.
14. Install the tire and wheel assembly.
15. Remove the jackstands and carefully lower the vehicle.

LOWER BALL JOINT REPLACEMENT

▶ See Figures 17 and 18

1964-1970 Vehicles

1. Raise the front of the vehicle and support it safely using jackstands under the frame. Position a floor jack under the lower control arm spring seat in order to retain spring compression and hold the control arm in position.
2. Remove the tire and wheel assembly. If the vehicle has disc brakes, remove the caliper assembly.

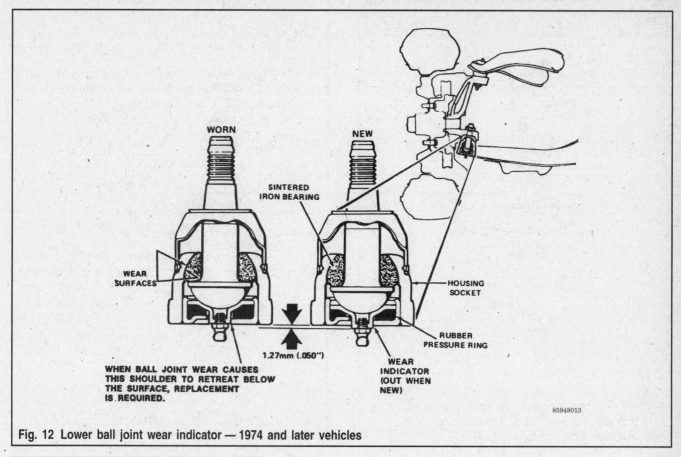

Fig. 12 Lower ball joint wear indicator — 1974 and later vehicles

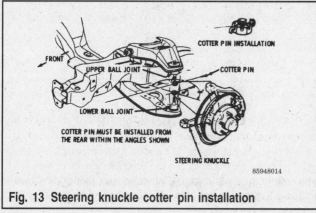

Fig. 13 Steering knuckle cotter pin installation

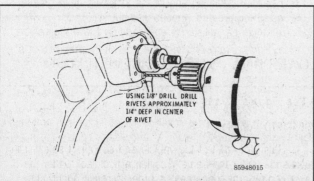

Fig. 14 Start to drill the upper ball joint rivets using a ⅛ in. drill bit — 1971 and later vehicles

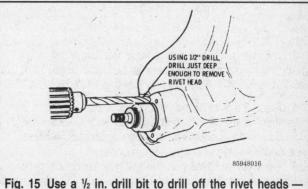

Fig. 15 Use a ½ in. drill bit to drill off the rivet heads — 1971 and later vehicles

3. Remove the lower ball stud cotter pin and nut. Then, using a tool designed for such work, press the ball stud out of the steering knuckle. Wire the steering knuckle out of the way so you'll have more room.

4. Press the joint out of the control arm with a tool designed for that purpose.

To install:

5. Start the replacement joint into the control arm with the air vent in the rubber boot facing inboard.

6. Set the joint in the control arm, pressing it in with a suitable installer tool.

7. Install the stud into the steering knuckle, then install the attaching nut and a new cotter pin.

8. Reinstall the caliper assembly, if applicable.

9. Install the tire and wheel assembly.

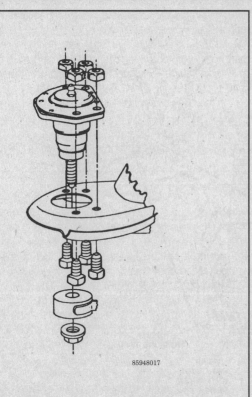

85948017

Fig. 16 When installing the new upper ball joints, make sure that the nuts are threaded from the top of the control arm — 1971 and later vehicles

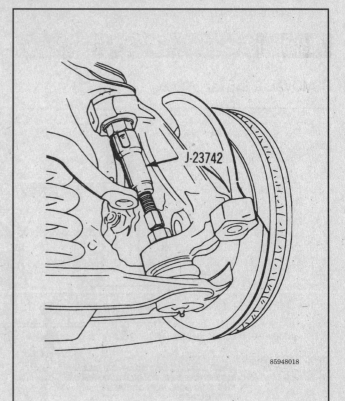

J-23742

85948018

Fig. 17 Use a tool, such as J-23742, to loosen the ball joint from the steering knuckle

10. Remove the supports and carefully lower the vehicle.

1971 and Later

➡On models equipped with a wear indicating ball joint, Chevrolet recommends replacement of both upper and lower ball joints if only the lower ball joint is bad.

1. Raise the front of the vehicle and support it safely using jackstands under the frame. Position a floor jack under the lower control arm spring seat in order to retain spring compression and hold the control arm in position.

2. Remove the lower ball stud cotter pin and loosen the ball stud nut just one turn.

3. Install the tool No. J-23742 between the two ball studs, and press the stud downward in the steering knuckle. Then, remove the stud nut.

4. With your hands on the bottom of the tire, pull the tire outward and, at the same time, upward, in order to free the steering knuckle from the ball stud. Then, remove the tire and wheel assembly.

5. Lift up on the upper control arm and place a block of wood between it and the frame. Be careful not to put any tension on the brake hose while doing this.

6. Press the ball joint out of the lower control arm with a tool made for that purpose. You may have to disconnect the tie rod at the steering knuckle for clearance to do this.

To install:

7. Position the new ball joint onto the control arm with the vent in the rubber boot facing inward. Press the joint fully into the control arm with the tool No. J-9519-10 and J-9519-9, or equivalents.

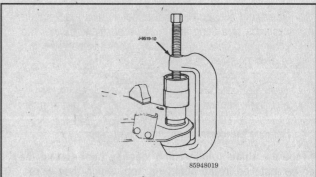

J-9519-10

85948019

Fig. 18 Tools are available to press the ball joint from the lower control arm

8. Turn the ball stud cotter pin hole so it is fore and aft.

9. Remove the block of wood holding the upper control arm out of the way and inspect the tapered hole in the steering knuckle. Remove any dirt from the hole. If the hole is out of round or there is other noticeable damage, replace the entire steering knuckle.

10. Insert the ball joint stud into the steering knuckle, then install the stud nut and torque it to 83 ft. lbs. (112 Nm). Install a new cotter pin, aligning cotter pin holes in the nut and stud only through further tightening. If necessary, tighten the nut additionally in order to insert the cotter pin, but DO NOT loosen the nut from the torque position.

11. Install a lube fitting and lube the joint.

12. Reconnect the tie rod, if disconnected for access.

13. Install the tire and wheel assembly

14. Remove the jackstands, then carefully lower the vehicle.

Stabilizer Bar

REMOVAL & INSTALLATION

1. Raise and support the front of the vehicle safely using jackstands.
2. Disconnect the stabilizer link bolts at the lower control arms.
3. Remove the retainers and the stabilizer-to-frame clamps.
4. Remove the stabilizer bar from the vehicle.

To install:

5. Install the stabilizer bar to the vehicle and loosely secure using the stabilizer-to-frame clamps.
6. Connect the stabilizer link bolts to the lower control arms.
7. Torque the stabilizer-to-lower control arm bolts to 13 ft. lbs (18 Nm) and the stabilizer-to-frame bolts to 24 ft. lbs. (33 Nm).
8. Remove the supports and carefully lower the vehicle.

Upper Control Arm

REMOVAL & INSTALLATION

▶ See Figure 19

1. Raise and support the vehicle safely using jackstands. The jackstands or a floor jack must be positioned under the lower control arm between the spring seat and ball joint in order to allow the vehicle's weight to retain the spring.
2. Remove the tire and wheel assembly.
3. Separate the upper ball joint from the steering knuckle using a suitable separator tool. For details refer to the upper ball joint procedures earlier in this section.
4. Remove the control arm shaft-to-frame nuts.

➡**Tape the shims together and identify them so that they can be installed in the positions from which they were removed.**

5. Remove the bolts which attach the control arm shaft to the frame and remove the control arm. Note the positions of the bolts for installation purposes.

To install:

6. Install the control arm and insert the shaft-to-frame bolts, making sure that they are installed in the same position they were in before removal. Position the shims in their their original positions.
7. Use free running nuts (not locknuts) to pull serrated bolts through the frame. Then install and tighten the locknuts starting with the thinner shim pack first. Tighten the shaft-to-frame nuts to 90 ft. lbs. (122 Nm) for vehicles through 1974, to 75 ft. lbs. (102 Nm) for 1975-77 vehicles or to 40-48 ft. lbs. (54-62 Nm) for 1978 and later models.
8. Install the upper ball joint to the steering knuckle, then install the retaining nut and a new cotter pin. Do not back off the torque specification in order to insert the pin.

9. Install the tire and wheel assembly, then remove the supports and lower the vehicle.
10. If the control arm bushings were replaced or the pivot shaft nuts were loosened, bounce the front end a few times in order to center the bushings. Then, tighten the pivot shaft nuts to 40 ft. lbs. (54 Nm) for vehicles through 1973, to 65 ft. lbs. (88 Nm) for 1974 vehicles, to 75 ft. lbs. (102 Nm) for 1975-80 vehicles or to 85 ft. lbs. (115 Nm) for 1981 and later vehicles.

CONTROL ARM BUSHING REPLACEMENT

▶ See Figure 20

1. Remove the upper control arm from the vehicle.
2. Loosen and remove the nuts from the ends of the pivot shaft.
3. Using a suitable bushing removal tool, press the bushings out of the control arm.

To install:

4. Using a bushing driver, press the new bushings into the control arm and over the ends of the pivot shaft. For late model vehicles the bushings should be installed 0.02-0.50 in. (0.5-13.3mm) from the face of the control arm to the bushing outer sleeve.
5. Loosely install the nuts to the ends of the pivot shaft, then install the upper control arm to the vehicle.
6. Once the control arm is installed and the vehicle is resting on its suspension, bounce the front end a few times in order to center the bushings. Then, tighten the pivot shaft end nuts to 40 ft. lbs. (54 Nm) for vehicles through 1973, to 65 ft. lbs. (88 Nm) for 1974 vehicles, to 75 ft. lbs. (102 Nm) for

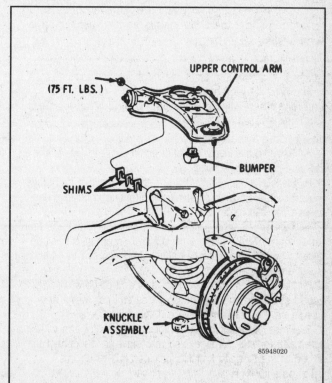

Fig. 19 Example of a common upper control arm installation

1975-80 vehicles or to 85 ft. lbs. (115 Nm) for 1981 and later vehicles.

Lower Control Arm

REMOVAL & INSTALLATION

▶ **See Figure 21**

1. Remove the coil spring from the vehicle. For details, please refer to the coil spring procedure found earlier in this section.
2. Separate the lower ball joint from the steering knuckle using a suitable separator tool. For details refer to the lower ball joint procedures earlier in this section.
3. Note the directions which the control arm pivot bolts are facing for installation purposes. Remove the control arm pivot bolts and the control arm.

To install:

4. Position the control arm to the vehicle and install the pivot bolts in the directions noted during removal. Do not fully tighten the fasteners at this time, the pivot bolts/nuts must be tightened while the vehicle's weight resting on the suspension.
5. Install the lower ball joint to the steering knuckle and secure using the retaining nut. Tighten the nut and insert and new cotter pin. DO NOT back off the torque in order to install the cotter pin.
6. Install the coil spring to the vehicle.

➡**If there is insufficient clearance in order to access and tighten the lower control arm pivot bolts, raise and support the car on ramps. If ramps are not available, use jackstands under the control arms so the suspension is compressed.**

7. With the vehicle's weight supported by the suspension, tighten the control arm pivot fasteners. Tighten the bolts to 85 ft. lbs. (115 Nm) for vehicles through 1973, to 100 ft. lbs. (136 Nm) for 1974-77 vehicles or to 65 ft. lbs. (88 Nm) for 1978 and later vehicles.

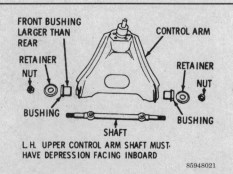

Fig. 20 Exploded view of the control arm and bushing assembly — 1982 and later shown

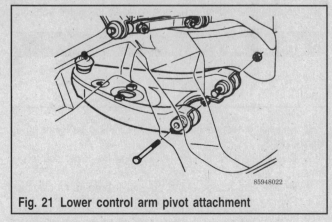

Fig. 21 Lower control arm pivot attachment

CONTROL ARM BUSHING REPLACEMENT

1. Remove the control arm from the vehicle.

➡**Late model vehicles utilize a control arm on which the front bushing is flared during installation. Any flared bushing must be driven down with a blunt chisel prior to removal.**

2. If necessary, use a blunt chisel to drive down the bushing flare until it is even with the rubber.
3. Using a suitable bushing removal tool, drive the bushing from the control arm.

To install:

4. Using a bushing installation driver, press the new bushing into the control arm. If the bushing removed from the arm was flared, you must use a special installation tool which is designed to flare the replacement bushing. For these installations, continue turning the nut on the special installation tool until the new bushing is flared.
5. Install the control arm to the vehicle.

Steering Knuckle

REMOVAL & INSTALLATION

1. Remove some of the fluid from the brake master cylinder using a siphon or a turkey baster. Be VERY careful not to get any of the fluid on the vehicle's paint. Do not allow the fluid to fall below the level of the master cylinder intake or the system may have to bled.
2. Raise and support the front of the vehicle safely using jackstands.
3. Remove the tire and wheel assembly.
4. Remove the caliper from the steering knuckle and support from the suspension using a length of wire. Make sure the weight of the caliper is NEVER supported by the brake line or damage to the hydraulic system could occur.
5. Remove the grease dust cap, the cotter pin, the castle nut and the hub assembly.
6. If applicable, remove the bolts holding the dust shield to the steering knuckle.
7. Using the ball joint removal tool J-6627 or equivalent, disconnect the tie rod from the steering knuckle.

8. Place a floor jack under the lower control arm (near the spring seat) to support the control arm, then use ball joint removal tool J-23742 or equivalent to disconnect the ball joints from the steering knuckle.

9. Remove the steering knuckle from the vehicle.

To install:

10. Position the steering knuckle to the vehicle and insert the control arm ball joints, then loosely install the retaining nuts.

11. Insert the tie rod ball joint to the steering knuckle and loosely install the retaining nut.

12. Torque the upper ball joint-to-steering knuckle nut to 60 ft. lbs. (81 Nm), the lower ball joint-to-steering knuckle nut to 83 ft. lbs. (112 Nm) and the tie rod-to-steering knuckle nut to 35 ft. lbs. (47 Nm).

13. If applicable, install the dust shield the steering knuckle and secure using the retaining bolts.

14. Loosely install the hub and wheel bearings (without the cotter pin or dust cap at this time), then install the caliper followed by the tire and wheel assembly.

15. Properly adjust the bearings, then install a new cotter pin and the dust cap. For details, refer to the procedure later in this section.

16. Remove the supports and carefully lower the vehicle.

17. Refill the master cylinder and check for proper brake operation. Do not attempt to move the vehicle unless a firm pedal is felt.

Wheel Bearings

Properly adjusted bearings have a slightly loose feeling. Wheel bearings must never be preloaded in service. Preloading will damage the bearings and eventually the spindles. If the bearings are too loose, they should be cleaned, inspected and then adjusted.

Hold the tire at the top and bottom and move the wheel in and out of the spindle. If the movement is greater than 0.008 in. (0.203mm) for 1964-73 vehicles or 0.005 in. (0.127mm) for 1974 and later vehicles, the bearings are too loose and must be adjusted.

ADJUSTMENT

▶ **See Figure 22**

1. Raise and support the vehicle safely using a jackstand under the lower control arm.

2. Remove the hub cap from the wheel for access, then remove the dust cap from the hub.

3. Remove the cotter pin and spindle nut.

4. Spin the wheel forward by hand and tighten the nut to 12 ft. lbs. (16 Nm) in order to fully seat the bearings and remove any burrs from the threads.

5. Back off the nut ¼-½ turn until it is just loose, then finger-tighten the nut.

6. Install a new cotter pin. If the pin cannot be installed, loosen the nut until either hole in the spindle lines up with a slot in the nut. This may appear to be too loose, but it is the correct adjustment. The spindle nut should not be even finger-tight.

7. Proper adjustment creates 0.001-0.008 in. (0.025-0.203mm) end-play for vehicles through 1973; 0.001-0.005 in. (0.025-0.127mm) end-play for 1974 and later vehicles.

REMOVAL & INSTALLATION

▶ **See Figures 23, 24, 25, 26, 27, 28, 29, 30, 31, 32, 33, 34, 35 and 36**

Before handling the bearings, there are a few things that you should remember to do and and few things you should not.

Always remember to DO the following:

• Remove all outside dirt from the housing before exposing the bearing.

• Treat a used bearing as gently as you would a new one.

• Work with clean tools in clean surroundings.

• Use clean, dry canvas gloves, or at least clean, dry hands.

• Clean solvents and flushing fluids are a must.

• Use clean paper when laying out the bearings to dry.

• Protect disassembled bearings from rust and dirt. Cover them up.

• Use clean rags to wipe bearings.

• Keep the bearings in oil-proof paper when they are to be stored or are not in use.

• Clean the inside of the housing before replacing the bearing.

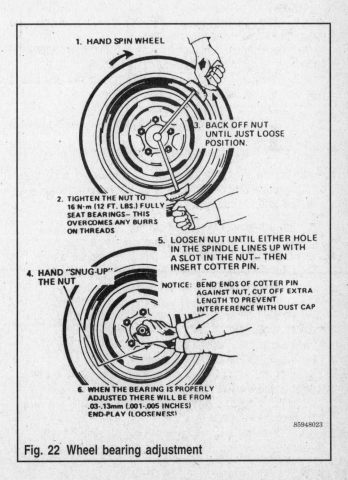

Fig. 22 Wheel bearing adjustment

Do NOT do the following:
- Don't work in dirty surroundings.
- Don't use dirty, chipped or damaged tools.
- Try not to work on wooden work benches or use wooden mallets.
- Don't handle bearings with dirty or moist hands.
- Do not use gasoline for cleaning; use a safe solvent.
- Do not spin-dry bearings with compressed air. They will be damaged.
- Do not spin dirty bearings.
- Avoid using cotton waste or dirty cloths to wipe bearings.
- Try not to scratch or nick bearing surfaces.
- Do not allow the bearing to come in contact with dirt or rust at any time.

1. Raise and support the front of the vehicle safely using jackstands.

2. Remove the tire and wheel assembly.

3. Remove the brake drum or brake caliper, as applicable. On vehicles with disc brakes, remove the caliper mounting bolts and insert a block between the brake pads (if necessary to hold them in position) as the caliper is removed. Remove the caliper and wire it out of the way.

4. Carefully pry out the grease cap, then remove the cotter pin, spindle nut, and washer. Remove the hub, being careful not to drop the wheel bearings.

5. Remove the outer roller bearing assembly from the hub. The inner bearing assembly will remain in the hub and may be removed from the rear of the hub after prying out the inner seal. Discard the seal after removal.

To install:

6. Clean all parts in solvent and allow to air dry, then check for excessive wear or damage.

7. If replacement is necessary, use a hammer and drift to remove the outer or inner bearing races from the hub. When installing new races, make sure they are not cocked and that they are fully seated against the hub shoulder.

8. Using a high melting point bearing lubricant, pack both the inner and outer bearings. Be sure to properly fill the bearings with grease.

9. Lightly grease the spindle and inside of the hub.

➡ Although a seal installation tool is preferable, a section of pipe with a smooth edge or a suitably sized socket may be used to drive the seal into position.

10. Place the inner bearing in the hub, then apply a thin coating of grease to the sealing lip and install a new inner seal, making sure the seal flange faces the bearing cup.

11. Carefully install the wheel hub over the spindle.

12. Using your hands, firmly press the outer bearing into the hub.

13. Loosely install the spindle washer and nut, but do not install the cotter pin or dust cap at this time.

14. If applicable, install the brake caliper.

15. Install the tire and wheel assembly.

16. Properly adjust the wheel bearings, then install a new cotter pin and the dust cap.

17. Install the hub cap, then remove the supports and carefully lower the vehicle.

Fig. 23 Pry the dust cap from the hub taking care not to distort or damage its flange

Fig. 24 Once the bent ends are cut, grasp the cotter pin and pull or pry it free of the spindle

Fig. 25 If difficulty is encountered, gently tap on the pliers with a hammer to help free the cotter pin

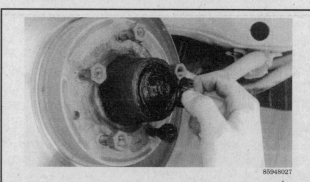
Fig. 26 Loosen and remove the castellated nut from the spindle

Fig. 27 Remove the washer from the spindle

Fig. 28 With the nut and washer out of the way, the outer bearings may be removed from the hub

Fig. 29 Pull the hub and inner bearing assembly from the spindle

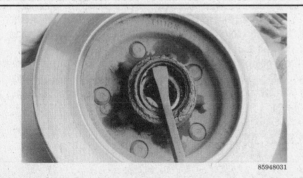

Fig. 30 Use a small prytool to remove the old inner bearing seal

Fig. 31 With the seal removed, the inner bearing may be withdrawn from the hub

Fig. 32 Thoroughly pack the bearing with fresh, high temperature wheel-bearing grease before installation

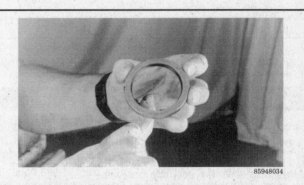

Fig. 33 Apply a thin coat of fresh grease to the new inner bearing seal lip

Fig. 34 Use a suitably sized driver to install the inner bearing seal to the hub

85948036

Fig. 35 With new or freshly packed bearings, tighten the nut to 12 ft. lbs. while gently spinning the wheel, then adjust the bearings

85948037

Fig. 36 After the bearings are adjusted, install the dust cap by gently tapping on the flange — DO NOT damage the cap by hammering on the center

PACKING

Clean the wheel bearings thoroughly with solvent and check their condition before installation.

✳✳WARNING

Do not blow the bearing dry with compressed air as this would allow the bearing to turn without lubrication.

Apply a sizable dab of lubricant to the palm of one hand. Using your other hand, work the bearing into the lubricant so that the grease is pushed through the rollers and out the other side. Keep rotating the bearing while continuing to push the lubricant through it.

Front End Alignment

▶ **See Figures 37 and 38**

CASTER

Caster is a measure of the angle between the steering axis and vertical, as viewed from the side of the vehicle when the wheels are in the straight ahead position. Stated another way, it is the tilting of the front steering axis either forward or backward from the vertical. A backward tilt is said to be positive (+) and a forward tilt is said to be negative (-).

Although is it measured using a special instrument, it can be seen by observing the location of the upper and lower control arm ball joints. A line drawn through the center of these 2 points represents the steering axis. When looking straight downward from the top of the upper control arm you can see if the ball joints are not aligned, indicating that the caster angle is more or less than 0 degrees. If vehicle has positive caster, the lower ball joint would be located ahead of the upper ball joint center line. If the vehicle has negative caster, the lower ball joint would be located behind the upper joint center line.

On most Chevrolet mid-sized vehicles, the caster may be adjusted by changing placement of shims on the 2 upper control arm pivot shaft-to-frame bolts.

CAMBER

Camber is the measure of wheel tilt from the vertical direction, when the wheel is viewed from the rear of the vehicle. Camber is negative when the top of the wheel is inboard and positive when the top is outboard. Always check for bent, damaged or worn suspension components before determining that adjustment is necessary. The amount of tilt is measured in degrees from the vertical and this measurement is called the camber angle.

TOE-IN

Toe is a measurement of how far a wheel is turned in or out from the straight ahead direction. When the front of the wheel is turned in, the toe is positive. When the front of the wheel is turned out, toe is negative. An incorrect toe setting can affect steering feel and cause excessive tire wear.

Stated another way, toe-in is the amount that the fronts of the wheels are closer together than the backs of the same wheels. Some vehicles are set with a slight tow-out (backs of the wheels are closer together than the fronts) in order to prevent excessive toe-in under power.

The actual amount of toe-in is normally only a fraction of a degree. The purpose of toe-in is to ensure parallel rolling of the front wheels. (Excessive toe-in or toe-out will cause tire wear).

CASTER/CAMBER ADJUSTMENT

Caster and camber can be adjusted by moving the position of the upper control arm assembly using shims between the pivot shaft and the frame. Tilting the assembly forward/rearward (by transferring shims from front-to-rear or rear-to-front) adjusts caster. Movement it inboard/outboard (adding or subtracting shims to both ends of the pivot shaft) adjusts camber.

TOE-IN ADJUSTMENT

1. Loosen the clamp bolts at each end of the steering tie rod adjustable sleeves.

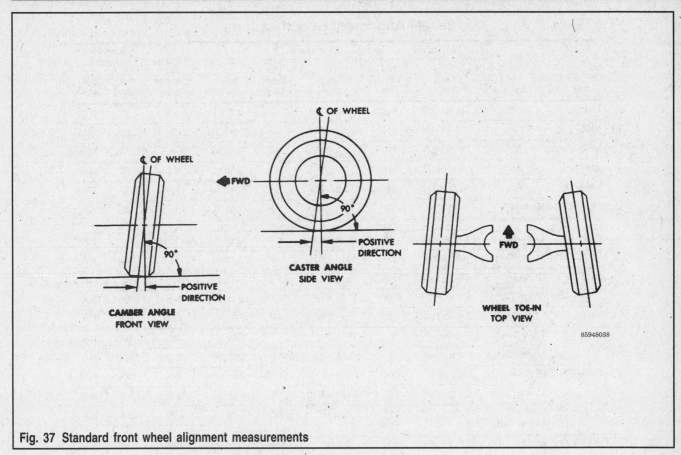

Fig. 37 Standard front wheel alignment measurements

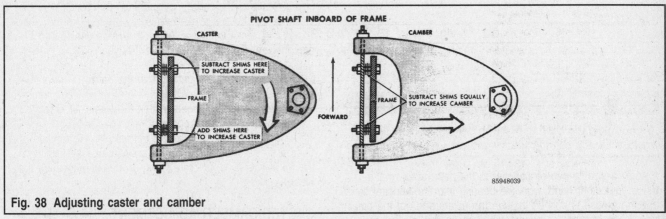

Fig. 38 Adjusting caster and camber

2. With the steering wheel set straight ahead, turn the adjusting sleeves to obtain the proper adjustment.

3. When the adjustment has been completed, check to see that the number the threads showing on each end of the sleeve are equal. Also check that tie rod end housings are at the right angles to the steering arm.

Wheel Alignment Specifications

Year	Model	Caster Range (deg)	Caster Pref Setting (deg)	Camber Range (deg)	Camber Pref Setting (deg)	Toe-in (in.)	Steering Axis Inclination (deg)	Wheel Pivot Ratio Inner Wheel	Wheel Pivot Ratio Outer Wheel
1964	All	¼N to ¾P	¼P	¼ to 1¼P	¾P	0 to ⅛	8¼	20	18¾
1965	All	1½ to ½N	1N	¼N to ¾P	¼P	1/16 to 3/16	8	20	18¾
1966	All	1½ to ½N	1N	0 to 1P	½P	⅛ to ¼	8	20	18¾
1967	All	1½ to ½N ①	1N	0 to 1P	½P	⅛ to ¼	8¼	20	18¾
1968–69	All	1½ to ½N ①	1N	0 to 1P	½P	⅛ to ¼	8¼	20	18½
1970–71	Chevelle, Monte Carlo	1½ to ½N ①	1N	0 to 1P	½P	⅛ to ¼	7¾ to 8¾	20	NA
1972	Chevelle	1½ to ½N	1N	¼ tp 1¼P	¾P	⅛ to ¼	7¾ to 8¾	NA	NA
	Monte Carlo	½N to ½P	0	¼ to 1¼P	¾P	⅛ to ¼	7¾ to 8¾	NA	NA
1973	Chevelle	1¾ to ¾N	1¼N	½ to 1½P	1P ②	⅛ to ¼	9½	NA	NA
	Monte Carlo	4¼ to 5¼P	4¾P	½ to 1½P	1P ②	0 to ⅛	9½	NA	NA
1974	Chevelle ③	1½ to ½N	1N	½ to 1½P	1P	0 to ⅛	10½	NA	NA
	Chevelle ④	½N to ½P	0	½ to 1½P	1P	0 to ⅛	10½	NA	NA
	Monte Carlo	4½ to 5½P	5	½ to 1½P	1P	0 to p1	10½	NA	NA
1975–77	Chevelle	1½ to 2½P	2P ⑤	½ to 1½P ②	1P	0 to ⅛	9¾	NA	NA
	Monte Carlo	4½ to 5½P	5P	¼ to 1½P ②	1P	0 to ⅛	9¾	NA	NA
1978–81	Malibu, Monte Carlo	½ to 1½P	1P	0 to 1P	½P	1/16 to 3/16	7.86	NA	NA
1983–84	Malibu, El Camino Monte Carlo	½ to 1½P ⑥	1P	0 to 1P	½P	1/16 to 3/16	7.86	NA	NA
1985–86	Monte Carlo	½ to 1½P ⑥	1P	0 to 1P	½P	1/16 to 3/16	7.86	NA	NA
1986–87	Monte Carlo El Camino	2.0 to 4.0P	3.0P	0.3N to 0.13P	0.5P	0.05 to 0.1	NA	NA	NA
1988	Monte Carlo	1.8 to 3.8P	2.8P	0.3N to 0.13P	0.5P	0.05 to 0.1	NA	NA	NA

① SS 396 and El Camino—0 to 1P
② Left wheel given; right wheel is ½P ± ½
③ Manual steering
④ Power steering
⑤ Radial tires—1P ± ½ with belted tires
¾ Power steering: 2½P to 3½P, 3P
N Negative   P Positive
NA Not available

85948040

REAR SUSPENSION

▶ **See Figure 39**

The rear axle assembly is attached to the frame through a link-type suspension system. Two rubber bushed lower control arms mounted between the axle assembly and the frame maintain the fore and aft relationship of the axle assembly to the chassis. Two rubber bushed upper control arms, angularly mounted with respect to the centerline of the car, control driving and braking torque and sideways movement of the axle assembly. The rigid axle hold the rear wheels in proper alignment.

The upper control arms are shorter than the lower arms, causing the differential housing to rock or tilt forward on compression. This rocking or titling lowers the rear propeller shaft to make possible the use of a lower tunnel in the rear floor pan area. The rear upper control arms control drive forces, side sway and pinion nose angle. Pinion angle adjustment can greatly affect car smoothness and must be maintained as specified.

The rear chassis springs are located between brackets on the axle tube and spring seats in the frame. The springs are held in the seat pilots by the weight of the vehicle and by the shock absorbers which limit axle movement during rebound.

Ride control is provided by two identical direct double acting shock absorbers angle-mounted between brackets attached to the axle housing and the rear spring seats. Shock absorbers are located behind the axle housing on pre-1968 models. Beginning in 1968, the shock absorbers were staggered to resist axle hop; the right shock in front of the axle and the left behind the axle.

Springs

REMOVAL & INSTALLATION

1964-1972 Vehicles

1. Raise and support the vehicles safely using jackstands under the frame.
2. Position a hydraulic jack under the axle and support it.
3. Disconnect the shock absorber at the bottom on the side where the spring is being replaced.
4. Slowly lower the axle to the bottom of its travel (making sure no brake lines or cables are being stretched), then carefully pry the lower end of the spring over the axle retainer.
5. Remove the spring and its insulator from the vehicle.

➡**On 1964-66 cars, the spring retainer must be removed to remove the spring. It is fastened to the housing with a nut and bolt.**

  To install:
6. Install the spring into the frame seat with its rubber insulation.

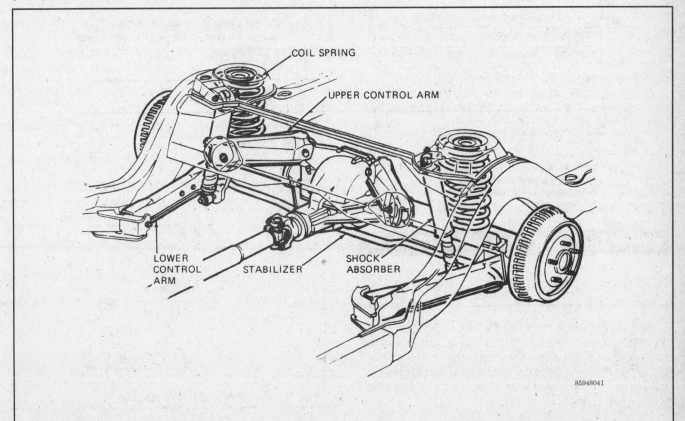

COIL SPRING

UPPER CONTROL ARM

LOWER CONTROL ARM

STABILIZER

SHOCK ABSORBER

85948041

Fig. 39 Rear suspension components

7. Carefully pry the spring into the axle housing retainer. Install the retainer on 1964-66 vehicles and torque the bolt to 45-55 ft. lbs. (61-75 Nm).

8. Slowly raise the axle into position and install the shock absorber. While holding the stud hex, tighten the shock absorber lower nut to 60 ft. lbs. (81 Nm).

9. Remove the jackstands, then carefully lower the vehicle.

1973 and Later Vehicle

1. Raise and support the vehicles safely using jackstands under the frame.

2. Position a hydraulic jack under the axle and support it.

3. Disconnect the shock absorber at the bottom on the side where the spring is being replaced.

4. Remove the brake hose support bolt or junction block retaining bolt, then support the brake hose aside to allow the axle to drop. For most vehicles, this should provide the necessary clearance to lower the rear axle. However, if this is not sufficient, DO NOT allow brake lines to be stretched or bent as they will be damaged. If necessary, disconnect the brake hydraulic line at the junction block located on the axle housing.

5. Disconnect the upper control arm at the axle.

➡Note the direction which the spring ends are pointing for installation purposes.

6. Slowly lower the axle to the bottom of its travel, then carefully pry the lower end of the spring over the axle retainer and remove the spring along with its insulator.

To install:

7. Install the spring in its frame seat along with its rubber insulator.

8. Carefully pry the lower end of the spring over the vertical flange of the axle bracket spring seat.

9. Position the spring so that the coil end is pointing in the direction noted during removal. For most applications, the upper coil points toward the right side of the car.

10. Raise the axle and connect the lower shock absorber mount. While holding the stud hex, tighten the shock absorber lower nut to 60 ft. lbs. (81 Nm).

11. Connect the upper control arm to the axle housing.

12. Secure the brake lines to the axle using the support or junction block bolt, as applicable. If any lines were disconnected, fasten them, then properly bleed the hydraulic brake system.

13. Remove the jackstands, then carefully lower the vehicle.

Shock Absorbers

TESTING

There are 2 possible clues that the shock absorbers are worn and may need replacement. The first is how the vehicle rides and the second is how the shocks appear. The shocks should be checked if the ride of your vehicle has become increasingly bouncy or if oil is visible on the shock, indicating possible fluid leakage.

Visually inspect the shock absorber if trouble or wear is suspected. If the shock absorber is covered with oil and there is evidence of leakage, the shock is defective and should be replaced.

If there is no sign of excessive leakage (a small amount of weeping is normal) but the ride is still suspect, bounce the car at one corner by pressing down on the rear bumper and releasing. When you have the car bouncing as much as you can, release the fender or bumper. The car should stop bouncing after the first rebound. If the bouncing continues past the center point of the bounce more than once, the shock absorbers are worn and should be replaced.

REMOVAL & INSTALLATION

◗ **See Figures 40, 41, 42, 43, 44 and 45**

1. Raise and support the vehicle safely using jackstands under the rear axle.

2. Remove the two upper mounting bolts. On some vehicles, the upper bolts may have a nut positioned above the mount and will require an open-end wrench to keep the nut from turning.

3. If equipped with superlift shock absorbers, disconnect the air line from the shock.

4. While holding the stud hex with a wrench, remove the lower mounting nut. On some vehicles, the tire and wheel assembly may interfere with shock removal. If necessary, remove the tire and wheel assembly from the vehicle.

5. Remove the shock absorber from the car.

To install:

6. Install the upper mounting bolts hand-tight.

7. Install the lower stud into the housing bracket and loosely install the nut.

8. Tighten the two upper bolts to 12 ft. lbs. (16 Nm). Remember to use a backup wrench, if necessary.

9. While holding the stud hex, tighten the lower nut to 60 ft. lbs. (81 Nm).

10. On superlift equipped vehicles, install the air hose and add approximately 10 psi of air.

11. If removed for clearance, install the tire and wheel assembly.

12. Remove the jackstands and carefully lower the vehicle.

STATION WAGON AND PICKUP
85948042

Fig. 40 Rear shock absorber mounting

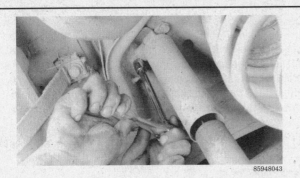

Fig. 41 Loosen and remove the shock absorber upper mounting bolts

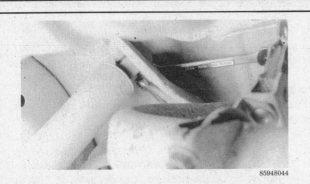

Fig. 42 On some vehicles, a wrench must be used to keep the upper mount nuts from turning

Fig. 43 If the shock absorber is to be reinstalled, DO NOT loosen the lower mounting stud without a backup wrench

Rear Lower Control Arm

REMOVAL & INSTALLATION

➡Remove and install ONLY one lower control arm at a time. If both arms are removed at the same time, the axle could roll or slip sideways, making installation of the arms very difficult.

Fig. 44 The backup wrench should be placed over the rear of the stud

Fig. 45 On most models, there should be sufficient clearance between the stud and the tire/wheel assembly to remove the shock

1. Raise and support the rear of the vehicle using jackstands under the rear axle.
2. If equipped, remove the stabilizer bar.
3. Remove the control arm attaching fasteners, then remove the control arm.

To install:

4. Position the control arm to the vehicle, then install the fasteners, but dot not tighten fully at this time unless the vehicle's weight is being supported by the rear axle. If the weight is on the suspension, tighten the control arm-to-frame nut to 70 ft. lbs. (95 Nm) and the control arm-to-axle bolt to 79 ft. lbs. (107 Nm).

➡The control arm fasteners must be tightened with the vehicle suspension at curb height. If the vehicle is supported by jackstands under the rear axle, this should be sufficient to duplicate that circumstance. If there is sufficient clearance and you so desire, the fasteners may be fully tightened after lowering the vehicle.

5. If equipped with a stabilizer bar, install and tighten the mounting fasteners to 35 ft. lbs. (47 Nm).
6. Remove the jackstands and carefully lower the vehicle. If not done already, tighten the control arm fasteners to specification.

Rear Upper Control Arm

REMOVAL & INSTALLATION

➡Remove and install ONLY one lower control arm at a time. If both arms are removed at the same time, the axle could roll or slip sideways, making installation of the arms very difficult.

1. Raise and support the rear of the vehicle using jackstands under the rear axle.
2. Remove the upper control arm nut at the axle.

➡To remove the mounting bolt from the axle, it may be necessary to rock the axle. On some models, it may also be necessary to remove the lower shock absorber stud to provide clearance for the upper control arm removal.

3. Remove the upper control arm-to-frame nut and bolt, then the remove the control arm from the vehicle.

To install:

4. Position the upper control arm to the vehicle, then install the fasteners, but dot not tighten fully at this time unless the vehicle's weight is being supported by the rear axle. If the weight is on the suspension, tighten the upper control arm-to-axle nut to 70 ft. lbs. (95 Nm), the upper control arm-to-axle

bolt to 79 ft. lbs. (107 Nm) and the upper control arm-to-frame bolt to 70 ft. lbs. (95 Nm).

➡The control arm fasteners must be tightened with the vehicle suspension at curb height. If the vehicle is supported by jackstands under the rear axle, this should be sufficient to duplicate that circumstance. If there is sufficient clearance and you so desire, the fasteners may be fully tightened after lowering the vehicle.

5. Remove the jackstands and carefully lower the vehicle. If not done already, tighten the control arm fasteners to specification.

Stabilizer Bar

REMOVAL & INSTALLATION

1. Raise and support the rear of the vehicle safely using jackstands under the frame or axle.
2. Remove the stabilizer bar-to-lower control arm bolts, then remove the stabilizer bar from the vehicle.

To install:

3. Position the stabilizer bar, then install the mounting fasteners and tighten to 35 ft. lbs. (47 Nm).
4. Remove the jackstands and carefully lower the vehicle.

STEERING

All models have recirculating ball type steering. Forces are transmitted from a worm to a sector gear through ball bearings. Relay type steering linkage is used with a pitman arm connected to one end of the relay rod. The other end of the relay rod is connected to an idle arm which is attached to the frame. The relay rod is connected to the steering arms by two adjustable tie rods. Most models are equipped with a collapsible steering column which is designed to absorb and impact by collapsing, thereby reducing possible chest injuries during accidents. When making any repairs to the steering column or steering wheel, excessive pressure or force capable of collapsing the column must be avoided for this reason. Beginning 1969, the ignition lock, ignition switch, and an anti-theft system were built into each column. The key cannot be removed unless the transmission is in PARK (automatic) or REVERSE (some manuals) with the switch in the LOCK position. Placing the lock in the LOCK position activates a rod within the column which locks the steering wheel and shift lever. On floorshift models, a back drive linkage between the floorshift and the column produces the same effect.

Steering Wheel

✳✳WARNING

Most steering columns are collapsible. When replacing the wheel, do not hammer or exert any force against the column or the column could be irreparably damaged.

REMOVAL & INSTALLATION

Standard Wheel

1964-69 CHEVELLE

▶ See Figure 46

1. Disconnect the negative battery cable.
2. Carefully pry out the center cap and retainer.
3. Remove the receiving cup screws, then remove the cup, belleville spring, bushing, and pivot ring.

➡The 1967-68 simulated wood wheel does not require pulling for removal. The wheel is held to the hub by Phillips screws.

4. Remove the steering wheel nut and washer.
5. Mark the wheel-to-shaft relationship, and then remove the wheel with a puller.

To install:

6. Install the wheel on the shaft, aligning the marks made during removal.
7. Install the nut and washer, then tighten the nut to 35 ft. lbs. (47 Nm).
8. Install the belleville spring (dished side up), pivot ring, bushing, and receiving cup. Secure the receiving cup using the retaining screws.
9. Install the center cap.
10. Connect the negative battery cable.

➡Removal of the 1970 padded steering wheel is similar to the 1964-69 procedure.

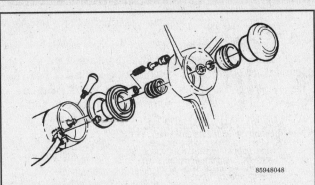

Fig. 46 Exploded view of the steering wheel and horn assembly — 1964-69 vehicles

1969 CHEVELLE DELUXE WHEEL AND STANDARD WHEEL ON ALL MODELS 1970 AND LATER

▶ **See Figures 47, 48, 49, 50, 51, 52, 53, 54, 55, 56, 57 and 58**

1. Disconnect the negative battery cable.
2. Remove the trim retaining screws from behind the wheel.
3. Lift the trim off, then disconnect the horn wire(s).
4. For most 1975 and later models, remove the snapring.
5. Remove the steering wheel retaining nut.

➡**The 1969 simulated wood wheel does not require pulling for removal. The wheel is held to the hub by phillips screws.**

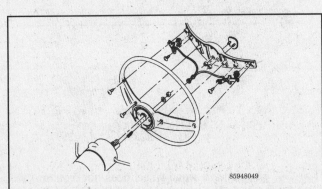

Fig. 47 Steering wheel installation — 1969 deluxe and 1970-72 standard wheel

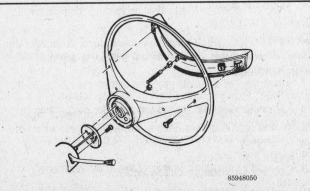

Fig. 48 Steering wheel installation — 1973-74 vehicles

6. Matchmark the wheel-to-shaft relationship, then remove the wheel with a steering wheel puller such, as tool No. J-2927.

To install:

7. Install the wheel on the shaft, aligning the marks made during removal.
8. Install the steering wheel retaining nut, then tighten the nut to 30 ft. lbs. (41 Nm).
9. If equipped, install the snapring.
10. Hold the trim just above position, then connect the horn wire(s)..
11. Install the center trim and secure using the retaining screws.
12. Connect the negative battery cable.

Cushioned Rim Wheel

▶ **See Figure 59**

Some 1971 and later vehicles may be equipped with a cushioned rim wheel.

1. Disconnect the negative battery cable.
2. Remove the horn button cap.
3. Remove the snapring.
4. Loosen and remove the steering wheel nut.
5. Remove the upper horn insulator, receiver, and belleville spring.
6. Matchmark the relationship of the steering wheel to the steering shaft in order to assure proper installation.
7. Install a universal steering wheel puller, turn the puller bolt clockwise to loosen and remove the wheel.

To install:

8. Place the turn signal lever in a Neutral position, then position the wheel to the shaft while aligning the marks made earlier.
9. Position the horn lower insulator, eyelet, and spring in the horn contact tower. Install the belleville spring, receiver, and horn upper insulator.
10. Install the wheel retaining nut and tighten to 30 ft. lbs. (41 Nm), then install the snapring.
11. Install the horn button cap.
12. Connect the negative battery cable.

Turn Signal Switch

REMOVAL & INSTALLATION

1964-66 Chevelle

▶ **See Figure 60**

➡**When servicing any components on the steering column, should any fasteners require replacement, be sure to use only nuts and bolts of the same size and grade as the original fasteners. Using screws that are slightly too long could prevent the column from the collapsing during a collision.**

1. Disconnect the negative battery cable.
2. Matchmark and remove the steering wheel. Refer to the procedure earlier in this section.
3. On column shift cars, remove the shift lever retaining pin and the lever.

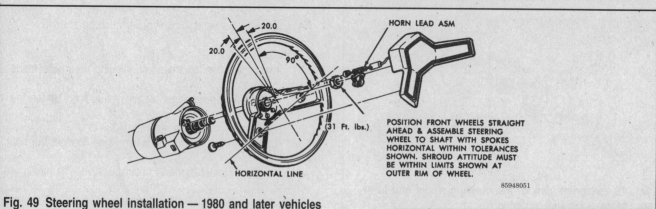

Fig. 49 Steering wheel installation — 1980 and later vehicles

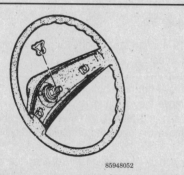

Fig. 50 Most 1975 and later wheels are equipped with a snapring to assure the retaining nut remains in position

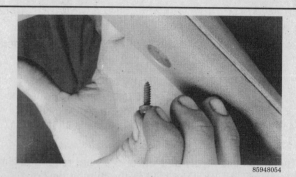

Fig. 52 Once they are loosened, remove the trim pad screws from the back of the steering wheel

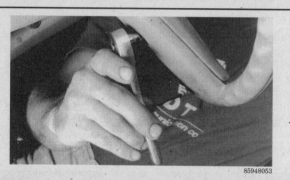

Fig. 51 A ratchet or driver should be used to loosen the trim pad retaining screws

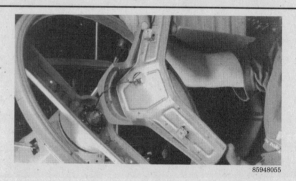

Fig. 53 Pull the trim pad from the steering wheel in order to access the horn wire(s)

4. Disconnect the column wiring harness from the chassis harness.

5. Remove the lower trim plate and the upper mast jacket clamp.

6. On automatic cars, remove the indicator retaining screw and the pointer.

7. Remove the three turn signal-to-housing screws.

8. Remove the turn signal switch, housing, and shift bowl from the steering column. Separate the switch from the wiring harness.

To install:

9. Engage the switch to the wiring harness, then install the turn signal switch, housing, and shift bowl to the steering column.

➡**Two different switch assemblies are used. Although the removal procedures are the same, the parts are not interchangeable.**

10. Install the three turn signal-to-housing screws.

11. On automatic cars, install the indicator pointer and retaining screw.

12. Install the lower trim plate and the upper mast jacket clamp.

13. Connect the column wiring harness to the chassis harness.

Fig. 54 Remove the retaining nut snapring

Fig. 55 Matchmark the relationship between the steering shaft and the wheel in order to assure proper wheel installation

Fig. 56 Loosen and remove the wheel retaining nut

Fig. 57 Use a steering wheel puller to loosen the wheel on the steering shaft

Fig. 58 Once the wheel has been loosened by the puller, the wheel may may be removed from the steering shaft

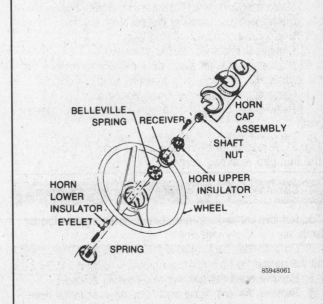

Fig. 59 Exploded view of the cushioned rim wheel found on some 1971 and later vehicles

14. On column shift cars, install the shift lever and retaining pin.
15. Align the marks made earlier and install the steering wheel.
16. Connect the negative battery cable.

1967-68

➡When servicing any components on the steering column, should any fasteners require replacement, be sure to use only nuts and bolts of the same size and grade as the original fasteners. Using screws that are slightly too long could prevent the column from the collapsing during a collision.

1. Disconnect the negative battery cable.

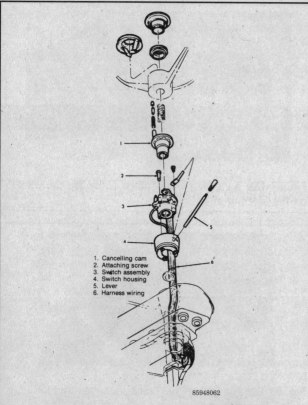

1. Cancelling cam
2. Attaching screw
3. Switch assembly
4. Switch housing
5. Lever
6. Harness wiring

85948062

Fig. 60 Exploded view of the steering column and turn signal installation — 1964-66 vehicles

2. Disconnect the signal switch wiring from the wiring harness under the instrument panel.

3. Matchmark and remove the steering wheel. For details, refer to the procedure earlier in this section.

4. If applicable, remove the shift lever.

5. Remove the four-way flasher lever arm.

6. If equipped with an automatic transmission, remove the dial indicator housing and lamp assembly from the column.

7. Remove the mast jacket lower trim cover.

8. Remove the C-ring and washers from the upper steering shaft.

9. Loosen the signal switch screws, move the switch counterclockwise and remove it from the mast jacket.

10. Remove the upper support bracket assembly.

✳✳WARNING

Support the column; do not allow it to be suspended by the lower reinforcement only.

11. Remove the wiring harness protector and clip, and then reinstall the support bracket and finger-tighten the bolts.

12. Remove the shift lever bowl from the mast jacket and disconnect it from the wiring harness.

13. Remove the three lockplate screws, being careful not to lose the three springs.

14. Disassemble the switch and upper bearing housing from the switch cover.

To install:

15. Insert the upper bearing housing and switch assembly into the switch cover.

16. Align the switch and bearing housing with the mounting holes in the cover and install the three mounting screws.

17. Slide the springs onto the screws and install the lockplate over the springs. Tighten the screws three turns into the lockplate.

18. Position the switch wire through the shift lever bowl and place the upper end assembly on top of the bowl.

19. Place the shift lever down and signal switch assembly on top of the jacket, insert the lockplate tangs into the slots.

20. Push down on the cover assembly and turn clockwise to lock the assembly into position.

21. Tighten the signal mounting screws.

22. Remove the mast jacket support bracket, then install the wiring, wiring cover and clip, and install and tighten the support brackets.

23. Install a C-ring onto the shaft.

24. If equipped, install the dial indicator and lamp assembly on the column.

25. Install the mast jacket lower trim cover if so equipped.

26. Install the four-way flasher knob and the turn signal lever.

27. If applicable, install the shift lever.

28. Align the marks made earlier, then install the steering wheel.

29. Connect the wiring, then connect the negative battery cable.

1969 and Later

▶ **See Figures 61, 62 and 63**

➡**When servicing any components on the steering column, should any fasteners require replacement, be sure to use only nuts and bolts of the same size and grade as the original fasteners. Using screws that are slightly too long could prevent the column from the collapsing during a collision.**

1. Disconnect the negative battery cable.

2. Matchmark and remove the steering wheel. For details, please refer to the procedure earlier in this section.

3. Remove the trim cover from the column.

4. Remove the steering column cover from the shaft by removing the three screws or by prying it out with a screwdriver (1976 and later models).

5. Use a compressing tool, such as No. J-23653, to compress and hold the lockplate. With the plate compressed, pry out and discard the snapring from its shaft groove.

6. Slide the cancelling cam, spring, and washer off the shaft.

7. Remove turn signal lever.

8. Push the four-way flasher knob in and unscrew it.

9. Remove the three switch mounting screws.

10. Pull switch connector out of the bracket and wrap it with tape to prevent it from snagging. Connect a length of twine or mechanic's wire to the connector. When the connector is pulled through the column, leave the twine or wire in the column in order to pull the new switch harness into position during installation.

11. If applicable, place tilt columns in the low and remove the harness cover.

12. Remove the switch and harness assembly from the steering column.

To install:

13. Install the switch and harness assembly to the steering column. Use the length of twine or wire to pull the harness through the column and into position.

14. If applicable, place tilt columns in the low and install the harness cover.

15. Install the switch connector to the bracket.

16. Install and tighten the three switch mounting screws.

17. Push the four-way flasher knob in and secure it.

18. Install the turn signal lever.

➡ **When installing the cancelling cam, spring, and washer, make sure that the switch is in neutral and that the flasher knob is out.**

19. Install the cancelling cam, spring, and washer to the shaft.

20. Use a compressing tool, such as No. J-23653, to compress and hold the lockplate. With the plate compressed, install a new snapring to the shaft groove, then remove the compressing tool.

21. If applicable, install the steering column cover to the shaft and secure using the retaining screws.

22. Install the trim cover to the column.

23. Align the marks made earlier and install the steering wheel.

24. Connect the negative battery cable.

Ignition Switch

REMOVAL & INSTALLATION

The ignition switch on most Chevrolet mid-sized vehicles is located on the steering column. Some earlier models were equipped with a dash-mounted switch. For earlier vehicles, please refer to the procedure in Section 6 of this manual.

The switch is located inside the channel section of the brake pedal support and is completely inaccessible without first lowering the steering column. the switch is actuated by a rod and rack assembly. A gear on the end of the lock cylinder engage the toothed upper end of the rod.

➡ **When servicing any components on the steering column, should any fasteners require replacement, be sure to use only nuts and bolts of the same size and grade as the original fasteners. Using screws that are slightly too long could prevent the column from the collapsing during a collision.**

1. Disconnect the negative battery cable.

2. Carefully support and lower the steering column assembly for access to the switch.

3. Place the ignition switch in the **OFF/UNLOCKED** position and move the actuating rod two detents from the top.

4. Remove the two mounting screws, then remove the ignition switch assembly.

To install:

5. Place the new switch in the **OFF/UNLOCKED** position and make sure the ignition lock cylinder and the actuating rod are both in the **OFF/UNLOCKED** (2nd detent from the top) position.

6. Install the actuating rod into the switch, mount the switch to the column and torque the mounting screws to 3 ft. lbs. (4 Nm).

7. Raise the steering column into position and tighten the column-to-bracket nuts to 25 ft. lbs. (34 Nm).

8. Connect the negative battery cable.

Lock Cylinder

REMOVAL & INSTALLATION

▶ **See Figures 64 and 65**

The ignition switch on most Chevrolet mid-sized vehicles is located on the steering column. Some earlier models were equipped with a dash-mounted switch. For earlier vehicles, please refer to the procedure in Section 6 of this manual.

1. Disconnect the negative battery cable.

2. Matchmark and remove the steering wheel.

3. Remove the turn signal assembly from the steering column. For details, refer to the procedure earlier in this section.

➡ **It is not necessary to pull the turn signal wiring harness out of the column, instead, allow the switch to hang from the wires out of the way.**

4. Place the lock cylinder in **LOCK** for vehicle up to 1970, or **RUN** for 1971 and later vehicles.

5. For most vehicles 1979 and later the switch is retained using a screw. Loosen and remove the retaining screw, taking great care not to drop it into the column (which would require column disassembly), then remove the lock cylinder assembly from the steering column.

6. For most vehicles through 1978 a retaining latch and snapring is used instead of the retaining screw. Insert a sturdy screwdriver or small prytool into the turn signal housing slot. Keeping the tool to the right side of the slot, break the housing flash loose and depress the spring latch at the lower end of the lock cylinder. Remove the lock cylinder.

➡ **Considerable force may be necessary to break this casting flash, but be careful not to damage any other parts. When ordering a new lock cylinder, specify a cylinder assembly. This will save assembling the cylinder washer, sleeve, and adaptor.**

To install:

7. For vehicles through 1978 that are not equipped with a retaining screw, hold the lock cylinder sleeve and rotate the knob clockwise against the stop. Insert the cylinder into the housing, aligning the key and keyway. For 1969-76 vehicles hold a 0.070 in. (1.78mm) drill between the lock bezel and the housing. For all vehicles through 1978, push the cylinder into abutment of cylinder and sector. Rotate the cylinder counterclockwise, maintaining a light pressure until the drive section of the cylinder mates with the sector. Push in until the snapring pops into the grooves. If used, remove the drill. Check the operation of the cylinder.

8. For most vehicles 1979 and later, insert the lock cylinder assembly to the steering column, then install and tighten the retaining screw.

9. Install the turn signal assembly.

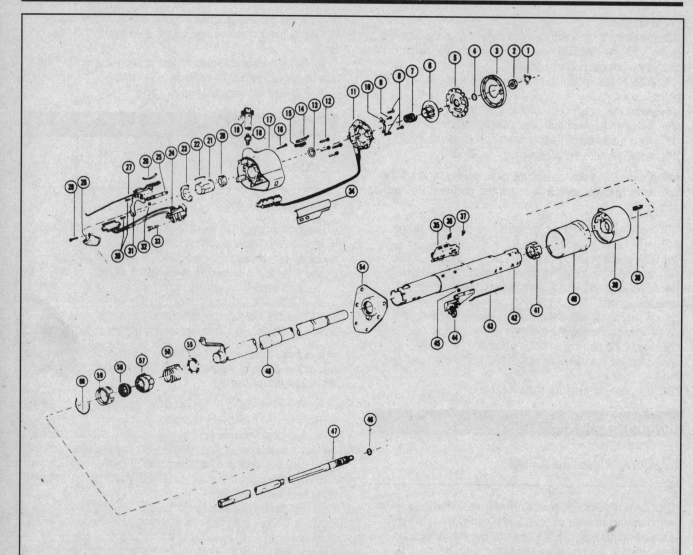

Key No. Part Name	Key No. Part Name	Key No. Part Name
1 - RETAINER	25 - BOLT ASSY, SPRING &	48 - TUBE ASSY, SHIFT
2 - NUT, HEXAGON	26 - SPRING, RACK PRELOAD	49 - NOT USED
3 - COVER, SHAFT LOCK	27 - RACK ASSY, SWITCH ACTUATOR ROD &	50 - NOT USED
4 - RING, RETAINING	28 - COVER, HOUSING	51 - NOT USED
5 - LOCK, STEERING SHAFT	29 - SCREW, BINDING HEAD CROSS RECESS	52 - NOT USED
6 - CAM ASSY, TURN SIGNAL CANCELLING	30 - SCREW, FLAT HEAD CROSS RECESS	53 - NOT USED
7 - SPRING, UPPER BEARING	31 - GATE, SHIFT LEVER	54 - SEAL, DASH
8 - SCREW, BINDING HEAD CROSS RECESS	32 - WASHER, SPRING THRUST	55 - WASHER SPRING THRUST
9 - SCREW, ROUND WASHER HEAD	33 - PIN, SWITCH ACTUATOR PIVOT	56 - SPRING SHIFT TUBE RETURN
10 - ARM ASSY, SWITCH ACTUATOR	34 - PROTECTOR, WIRING	57 - ADAPTER, LOWER BEARING
11 - SWITCH ASSY, TURN SIGNAL	35 - SWITCH ASSY, IGNITION	58 - BEARING ASSEMBLY
12 - SCREW, HEX WASHER HEAD TAPPING	36 - STUD, DIMMER & IGNITION SWITCH MOUNTING	59 - RETAINER BEARING ADAPTER
13 - WASHER, THRUST	37 - SCREW, WASHER HEAD	60 - CLIP, LOWER BEARING ADAPTER
14 - SWITCH ASSY, BUZZER	38 - SPRING, UPPER SHIFT LEVER	
15 - CLIP, BUZZER SWITCH RETAINING	39 - BOWL, GEARSHIFT LEVER	
16 - SCREW, LOCK RETAINING	40 - SHROUD, GEARSHIFT BOWL	
17 - HOUSING, STEERING COLUMN	41 - BEARING, BOWL LOWER	
18 - SECTOR ASSY, SWITCH ACTUATOR	42 - JACKET ASSY, STEERING COLUMN	
19 - LOCK CYLINDER SET, STEERING COLUMN	43 - ROD, DIMMER SWITCH ACTUATOR	
20 - BEARING ASSY	44 - SWITCH ASSY, DIMMER	
21 - BUSHING, BEARING RETAINING	45 - NUT, HEXAGON	
22 - CONTACT, HORN CIRCUIT	46 - RING, RETAINING	
23 - RETAINER, UPPER BEARING	47 - SHAFT ASSY, STEERING	
24 - SWITCH ASSY, PIVOT &		

STANDARD COLUMN

85948065

Fig. 61 Exploded view of a late model standard steering column

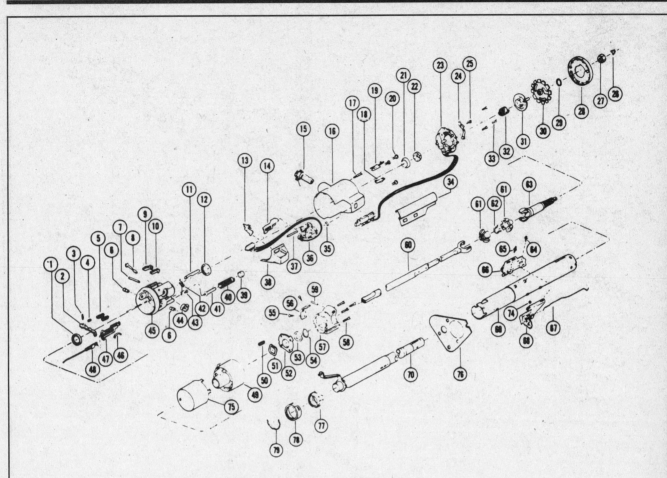

TILT WHEEL STEERING COLUMN

Key No.	Part Name
1	BEARING ASSY
2	LEVER, SHOE RELEASE
3	PIN, RELEASE LEVER
4	SPRING, RELEASE LEVER
5	SPRING, SHOE
6	PIN, PIVOT
7	PIN, DOWEL
8	SHAFT, DRIVE
9	SHOE, STEERING WHEEL LOCK
10	SHOE, STEERING WHEEL LOCK
11	BOLT, LOCK
12	BEARING ASSY
13	SHIELD, TILT LEVER OPENING
14	ACTUATOR, DIMMER SWITCH ROD
15	LOCK CYLINDER SET, STRG COLUMN
16	COVER, LOCK HOUSING
17	SCREW, LOCK RETAINING
18	CLIP, BUZZER SWITCH RETAINING
19	SWITCH ASSY, BUZZER
20	SCREW, PAN HEAD CROSS RECESS
21	RACE, INNER
22	SEAT, UPPER BEARING INNER RACE
23	SWITCH ASSY, TURN SIGNAL
24	ARM ASSY, SIGNAL SWITCH
25	SCREW, ROUND WASHER HEAD
26	RETAINER
27	NUT, HEX JAM
28	COVER, SHAFT LOCK
29	RING, RETAINING

Key No.	Part Name
30	LOCK, SHAFT
31	CAM ASSY, TURN SIGNAL CANCELLING
32	SPRING, UPPER BEARING
33	SCREW, BINDING HEAD CROSS RECESS
34	PROTECTOR, WIRING
35	SPRING, PIN PRELOAD
36	SWITCH ASSY, PIVOT &
37	PIN, SWITCH ACTUATOR PIVOT
38	CAP, COLUMN HOUSING COVER END
39	RETAINER, SPRING
40	SPRING, WHEEL TILT
41	GUIDE, SPRING
42	SPRING, LOCK BOLT
43	SCREW, HEX WASHER HEAD
44	SECTOR, SWITCH ACTUATOR
45	HOUSING, STEERING COLUMN
46	SPRING, RACK PRELOAD
47	RACK, SWITCH ACTUATOR
48	ACTUATOR ASSY, IGNITION SWITCH
49	BOWL, GEARSHIFT LEVER
50	SPRING, SHIFT LEVER
51	WASHER, WAVE
52	PLATE, LOCK
53	WASHER, THRUST
54	RING, SHIFT TUBE RETAINING
55	SCREW, OVAL HEAD CROSS RECESS
56	GATE, SHIFT LEVER
57	SUPPORT, STRG COLUMN HOUSING
58	SCREW, SUPPORT

Key No.	Part Name
59	PIN, DOWEL
60	SHAFT ASSY, LOWER STEERING
61	SPHERE, CENTERING
62	SPRING, JOINT PRELOAD
63	SHAFT ASSY, RACE & UPPER
64	SCREW, WASHER HEAD
65	STUD, DIMMER & IGNITION SWITCH MOUNTING
66	SWITCH ASSY, IGNITION
67	ROD, DIMMER SWITCH
68	SWITCH ASSY, DIMMER
69	JACKET ASSY, STEERING COLUMN
70	TUBE ASSY, SHIFT
71	NOT USED
72	NOT USED
73	NOT USED
74	NUT, HEXAGON
75	SHROUD, GEARSHIFT BOWL
76	SEAL, DASH
77	BUSHING ASSY, STEERING SHAFT
78	RETAINER, BEARING ADAPTER
79	CLIP, LOWER BEARING ADAPTER

85948066

Fig. 62 Exploded view of a late model tilt steering column

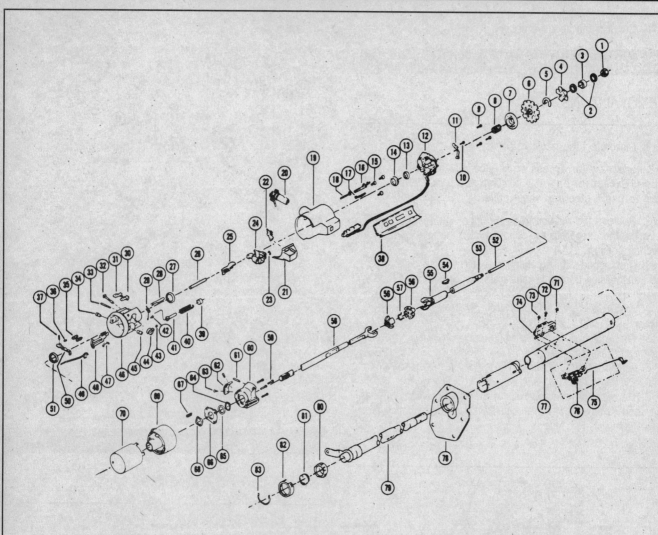

Key No.   Part Name

1 - NUT, HEXAGON JAM
2 - SPACER
3 - BUMPER, RETRACTED STRG SHAFT
4 - RETAINER, CARRIER SNAP RING
5 - RETAINER, SHAFT LOCK
6 - LOCK, STEERING SHAFT
7 - CARRIER ASSY
8 - SPRING, UPPER BEARING
9 - SCREW, BINDING HD CROSS RECESS
10 - SCREW, ROUND CROWN WASHER HEAD
11 - ARM ASSY, SIGNAL SWITCH
12 - SWITCH ASSY, TURN SIGNAL
13 - SEAT, INNER RACE
14 - RACE, INNER
15 - SCREW, OVAL HEAD CROSS RECESS
16 - SWITCH ASSY, BUZZER
17 - CLIP, BUZZER SWITCH RETAINING
18 - SCREW, LOCK RETAINING
19 - COVER, LOCK HOUSING
20 - LOCK CYLINDER SET, STEERING COLUMN
21 - CAP, COLUMN HOUSING COVER END
22 - SHIELD, TILT LEVER OPENING
23 - SPRING, PIN PRELOAD
24 - PIVOT ASSY, SWITCH ACTUATOR &
25 - ACTUATOR, DIMMER SWITCH ROD
26 - PIN, SWITCH ACTUATOR PIVOT
27 - BEARING ASSY
28 - BOLT, LOCK

29 - SPRING, LOCK BOLT
30 - SHOE, STEERING WHEEL LOCK
31 - SHOE, STEERING WHEEL LOCK
32 - SHAFT, DRIVE
33 - PIN, DOWEL
34 - PIN, PIVOT
35 - SPRING, SHOE
36 - SPRING, RELEASE LEVER
37 - PIN, RELEASE LEVER
38 - PROTECTOR, WIRING
39 - RETAINER, SPRING
40 - SPRING, WHEEL TILT
41 - GUIDE, SPRING
42 - SCREW, HEX WASHER HEAD
43 - RING, RETAINING
44 - SECTOR, SWITCH ACTUATOR
45 - PIN, PIVOT
46 - HOUSING, STEERING COLUMN
47 - SPRING, RACK PRELOAD
48 - RACK, SWITCH ACTUATOR
49 - ACTUATOR ASSY, IGNITION SWITCH
50 - LEVER, SHOE RELEASE
51 - BEARING ASSY
52 - ROD, TELESCOPE LOCKING
53 - SHAFT, UPPER STEERING
54 - WEDGE, LOCKING
55 - YOKE ASSY, RACE & STEERING SHAFT
56 - SPHERE, CENTERING

57 - SPRING, JOINT PRELOAD
58 - SHAFT ASSY, LOWER STEERING
59 - SCREW, SUPPORT
60 - SUPPORT, STRG COLUMN HOUSING
61 - PIN, DOWEL
62 - GATE, SHIFT LEVER
63 - SCREW, OVAL HEAD CROSS RECESS
64 - RING, SHIFT TUBE RETAINING
65 - WASHER, THRUST
66 - PLATE, LOCK
67 - SPRING, SHIFT LEVER
68 - WASHER, WAVE
69 - BOWL, GEARSHIFT LEVER
70 - SHROUD, GEARSHIFT BOWL
71 - SCREW, WASHER HEAD
72 - SCREW, FLAT HEAD
73 - SCREW, HEX WASHER HEAD TAPPING
74 - SWITCH ASSY, IGNITION
75 - ROD ASSY, DIMMER SWITCH
76 - SWITCH ASSY, DIMMER
77 - JACKET ASSY, STEERING COLUMN
78 - SEAL, DASH
79 - TUBE ASSY, SHIFT
80 - BEARING ASSY
81 - ADAPTER, LOWER BEARING
82 - RETAINER, BEARING ADAPTER
83 - CLIP, LOWER BEARING ADAPTER

TILT & TELESCOPING STEERING COLUMN

85948067

Fig. 63 Exploded view of a late model tilt and telescoping steering column

10. Align the matchmarks and install the steering wheel.

11. Connect the negative battery cable.

Steering Column

REMOVAL & INSTALLATION

1. Disconnect the negative battery cable.

➡**If necessary for access or service remove the steering wheel. Except for on 1967-69 simulated wood wheels, be sure to use a steering wheel puller.**

2. Remove the nut/bolt from the upper intermediate shaft coupling, then separate the coupling from the lower end of the steering column.

3. If equipped with a column mounted shifter, disconnect the transmission control linkage from the column shift tube levers.

4. If equipped with a floor shifter, disconnect the backdrive linkage.

5. Disengage all of the electrical connectors from the steering column assembly.

6. Remove the floor pan cover-to-floor screws, the floor seal, and the cover.

7. Remove the steering column bracket-to-instrument panel nuts and carefully lower the column. If equipped with an auto-matic transmission, disconnect the shift position indictor pointer.

➡**Once the steering column has been removed from the vehicle, be careful not to drop it (especially on it's end), lean on it or damage it in any way; the column is very susceptible to damage.**

8. Remove the column from the vehicle.

To install:

9. Position the steering column in the vehicle. If equipped with an automatic transmission, connect the shift position indi-cator pointer.

10. Raise the column into position, then install the column bracket-to-instrument panel nuts and tighten to 25 ft. lbs. (34 Nm).

11. Install the floor pan seal and cover, then secure using the retaining screws.

12. Engage all of the electrical connectors to the steering column assembly.

13. If equipped with a floor shifter, connect the backdrive linkage.

14. If equipped with a column mounted shifter, connect the transmission control linkage to the column shift tube levers.

15. Connect the intermediate shaft coupling to the lower end of the steering column, then secure using the nut/bolt.

16. If removed for access or service, align the matchmarks and install the steering wheel.

17. Connect the negative battery cable.

Manual Steering Gear

REMOVAL & INSTALLATION

▶ **See Figure 66**

➡**On 1964-67 models, remove the stabilizer bar-to-frame mounting brackets. Unbolt the left front bumper bracket and brace from the frame after marking their location.**

1. Raise and support the front of the vehicle safely using jackstands.

2. Disconnect the steering shaft coupling.

3. Mark the pitman arm-to-shaft relationship, then remove the pitman arm using a puller.

4. Remove the steering gear-to-frame mounting bolts, then remove the steering gear.

To install:

5. Position the steering gear to the frame, then install and tighten the frame mounting bolts to 70 ft. lbs. (95 Nm).

6. Install the pitman arm while aligning the matchmarks made earlier. Tighten the pitman shaft nut to 180 ft. lbs. (244 Nm).

7. Connect the steering shaft coupling, then tighten the coupling nuts to 20 ft. lbs. (27 Nm).

8. Remove the supports and carefully lower the vehicle.

ADJUSTMENT

1. Disconnect the negative battery cable.

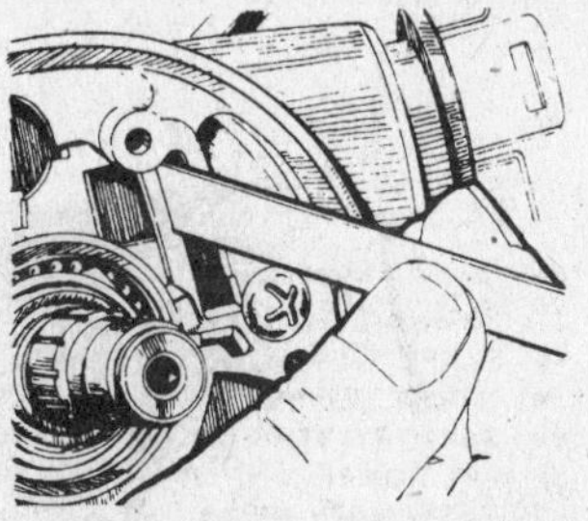

85948068

Fig. 64 For most 1978 and earlier vehicles, depress the lock cylinder spring latch through the slot in the turn signal housing

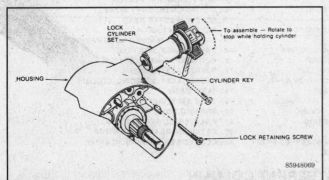

LOCK CYLINDER SET

To assemble — Rotate to stop while holding cylinder

HOUSING

CYLINDER KEY

LOCK RETAINING SCREW

85948069

Fig. 65 Lock cylinder removal — 1979 and later vehicle equipped with a cylinder retaining screw

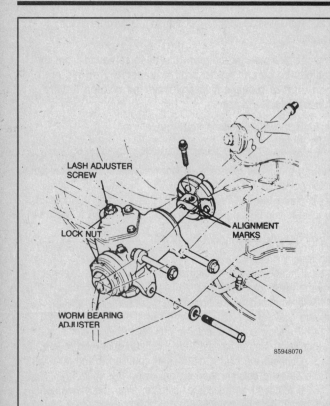

Fig. 66 Example of a common steering gear mounting

2. At the steering wheel, remove the horn ring or button.

➡ **Be sure to mark the relationship of the pitman arm to the steering gear before it is removed.**

3. Remove the pitman arm-to-steering gear nut, then using the puller tool No. J-6632 or equivalent, pull the pitman arm from the steering gear.

4. Turn the steering wheel ½ turn from either stop, then loosen the sector shaft adjusting screw to eliminate the sector load.

✳✳WARNING

Turning the steering wheel too hard against the stops will damage the ball return guides.

5. Place an inch lbs. torque wrench on the steering wheel nut, then turn the wrench 90 degrees and observe the reading (measure preload). If the force is less than 5-8 inch lbs. loosen the steering gear adjuster locknut and turn the worm thrust bearing adjuster to increase the preload.

6. Tighten the adjuster locknut and recheck the preload.

7. Reassemble the pitman arm to the pitman shaft, lining up the marks made during disassembly. Torque the retaining nuts to 180 ft. lbs. (244 Nm).

8. Install the horn cap or ring and connect the battery cable.

Power Steering Gear

REMOVAL & INSTALLATION

▶ **See Figure 67**

Installation and removal of power steering gears is the same as that described for manual steering gears earlier in this section, but with the addition of disconnecting and reconnecting the hydraulic lines. When disconnecting the hoses, use of a line wrench is preferable in order to prevent stripping and damaging the fittings. Remember to cap both hoses and steering gear outlets to prevent foreign material from entering and contaminating the system. Capping the lines will also prevent excessive fluid loss from the pump and reservoir. Upon installation, the power steering fluid level must be topped off and properly bled.

ADJUSTMENT

➡ **The steering gear must be removed from the vehicle in order to adjust the pre-load.**

1. Rotate the stub shaft several times (from stop to stop) to drain the fluid from the steering gear.

2. Mount the steering gear in a vise and remove the adjuster plug locknut.

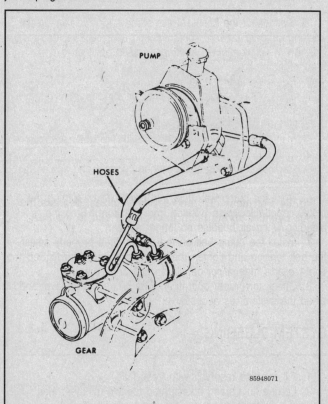

Fig. 67 Example of a common power steering pump and line mounting

3. Using a spanner wrench, turn the adjusting plug clockwise until the plug and the thrust bearing are firmly bottomed (about 20 ft. lbs. (27 Nm).

4. Using the scribe mark on the housing (next to the hole in the adjuster plug), measure counterclockwise (3/16-1/4 in.) and mark the housing.

5. Turn the adjuster plug counterclockwise until the hole in the plug aligned with the second mark.

6. While holding the adjuster plug (to maintain position), tighten the locknut.

7. Using a inch lbs. torque wrench and a 3/4 in. socket, turn the stub shaft to the right stop, then back 1/4 turn. Measure and record the drag, it should be 4-10 inch lbs.

8. Rotate the stub shaft from stop to stop, then back to the center. Using the torque wrench, turn the stub shaft 45 degrees to each side of center and check the reading.

9. Loosen the locknut and turn the pre-load adjusting screw clockwise until the over center (additional torque) reading of 4-8 inch lbs. (new gear, not to exceed 18 inch lbs.) or 4-5 inch lbs. (used gear, not to exceed 14 inch lbs.).

10. While holding the adjuster plug, tighten the locknut.

11. Follow the manual steering gear installation procedure, then be sure to properly fill and bleed the system.

Power Steering Pump

REMOVAL & INSTALLATION

1. Disconnect the hoses at the pump and tape or plug the openings shut to prevent contamination or excessive fluid loss. Position the disconnected lines in a raised position to help prevent leakage.

2. Remove the pump belt.

3. Loosen the retaining bolts and any braces, then remove the pump assembly.

To install:

4. Install the pump on the engine with the retaining bolts hand-tight.

5. Remove the plugs or tape, then connect and tighten the hose fittings.

6. Refill the pump with fluid and pre-bleed by turning the pulley counterclockwise (viewed from the front). Stop the bleeding when air bubbles no longer appear.

7. Install the pump belt on the pulley, then properly adjust the belt tension and tighten the retaining bolts. Refer to Section 1 of this manual for details on belt adjustment.

8. Check for proper operation, then recheck fluid level and bleed the system, as necessary.

SYSTEM BLEEDING

1. Fill the fluid reservoir with fresh fluid.

2. Let the fluid stand undisturbed for two minutes, then crank the engine for about two seconds. Refill reservoir is necessary.

3. Repeat Steps 1 and 2 above until the fluid level remains constant after cranking the engine.

4. Raise the front of the car until the wheels are off the ground, then start and run the engine. Increase the engine speed to about 1,500 rpm.

5. Turn the wheels to the left and right without hitting or only lightly contacting the wheel stops. Check the fluid level and refill, as necessary. If the oil is extremely foamy, allow the car to stand a few minutes with the engine off, then repeat the procedure.

Steering Linkage

REMOVAL & INSTALLATION

▶ **See Figures 68, 69, 70, 71, 72 and 73**

Tie Rod

1. Raise and support the front of the vehicle safely using jackstands.

2. Remove the cotter pins and nuts from the tie rod end studs.

3. Gently tap on the steering arm near the outer tie rod end (use another hammer as backing to prevent damage) or use a ball stud puller tool, such as No. J-6627, and separate the tie rod ball stud.

❋❋WARNING

DO NOT disengage the joint by driving a wedge between the joint and the knuckle, or damage to the seal may result.

4. Remove the inner ball stud in the same manner as the outer.

➡**If a tie rod end is being separated from the adjuster tube, there are various methods which may be used to preserve vehicle toe. The number of turns necessary to unthread the end may be counted. Marks may be made on the end or the adjuster showing how far the end should be threaded. A ruler may be used to measure the installed length of the tie rod end. Using 1 or more of these should help preserve the toe-in adjustment. The use of 2 methods is recommended, because the comparison allows for some correction of an error in measurement.**

5. If either end is being replaced, loosen the clamp bolt and unscrew the end.

To install:

6. Lubricate the tie rod end threads with chassis grease if they were removed. Install each end assembly an equal distance from the sleeve, as noted during removal. Temporarily tighten the sleeve clamps.

7. Install the tie rod assembly to the vehicle by properly positioning the end studs.

8. Install the stud nuts and tighten to 35 ft. lbs. (47 Nm), then install new cotter pins.

➡**Before tightening the sleeve clamps, ensure that the clamps are positioned so that adjusting sleeve sot is covered by the clamp.**

9. Check and adjust the toe-in, as necessary.

10. Remove the jackstands and carefully lower the vehicle.

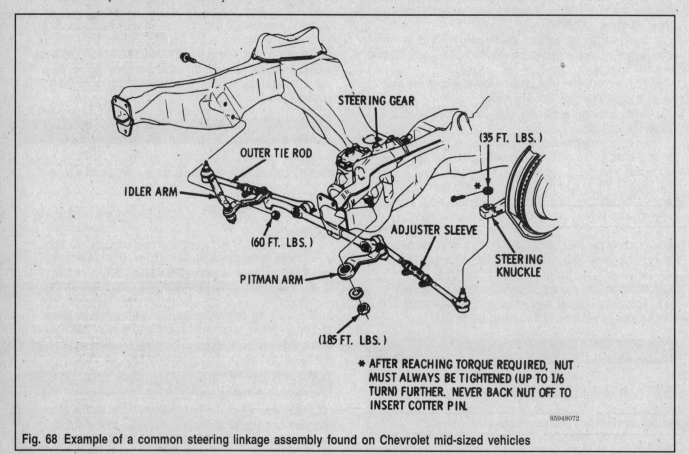

* AFTER REACHING TORQUE REQUIRED, NUT MUST ALWAYS BE TIGHTENED (UP TO 1/6 TURN) FURTHER. NEVER BACK NUT OFF TO INSERT COTTER PIN.

Fig. 68 Example of a common steering linkage assembly found on Chevrolet mid-sized vehicles

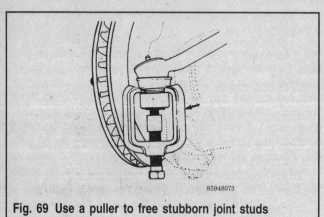

Fig. 69 Use a puller to free stubborn joint studs

Idler Arm

1. Raise and support the front of the vehicle safely using jackstands.
2. Remove the idler arm-to-frame nut, washer, and bolt.
3. Remove the cotter pin and nut from the idler arm-to-relay rod ball end stud.
4. Tap the relay rod with a hammer, using another hammer as backing, or using a steering linkage puller such as No. J-24319-01 to remove the relay rod from the idler arm.

5. Remove the idler arm from the vehicle.

To install:

6. Place the idler arm on the frame and install the retaining bolt, washer and nut, then tighten the fasteners to 35 ft. lbs. (47 Nm).
7. Position the relay rod on the idler arm. Ensure that the seal is on the stud, then install the nut and tighten to 35 ft. lbs. (47 Nm) and install a new cotter pin.
8. Remove the jackstands and carefully lower the vehicle.

Fig. 70 Straighten the ends of the cotter pin so it can be removed

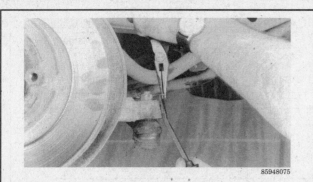

Fig. 71 Use a pair of pliers and a small prytool to pull the cotter pin from the stud

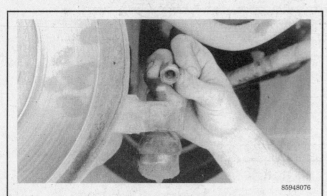

Fig. 72 Remove the steering linkage stud nut

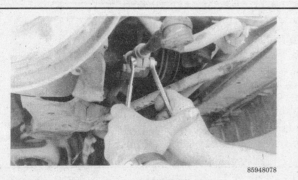

Fig. 73 The adjuster clamp bolt must be loosened in order to adjust toe-in or replace a tie rod end

Relay Rod (Intermediate Rod)

1. Raise and support the front of the vehicle safely using jackstands.
2. Remove the cotter pin and loosen the retaining nuts, then separate the inner tie rod ends from the relay rod.
3. On 1974 models with manual steering, remove the damper from the relay rod.
4. Remove the relay rod stud nut and cotter pin from the pitman arm. Free the relay rod from the pitman arm using the a linkage puller such as No. J-24319-01, moving the steering linkage as necessary. Repeat this operation to remove the relay rod from the idler arm, then remove the relay rod from the vehicle.

To install:

5. Install the relay rod on the idler arm. Tighten the nut to 35 ft. lbs. (47 Nm).
6. Raise the relay and install it on the pitman arm. Tighten the nut to 45 ft. lbs. (61 Nm).
7. Install the damper on 1974 models.
8. Install the tie rod ends to the relay rod.
9. Check and adjust the vehicle toe-in, as necessary.
10. Remove the jackstands and carefully lower the vehicle.

Pitman Arm

1. Raise and support the front of the vehicle safely using jackstands.
2. Remove the pitman arm stud nut and cotter pin.
3. Tap the relay rod off the pitman arm with a hammer, using another hammer as backing, or using a steering linkage puller such as No. J-24319-01 to remove the relay rod from the idler arm.
4. Remove the pitman arm nut and matchmark the arm-to-shaft relationship.
5. Remove the pitman arm using a linkage puller tool such as No. J-6632.

To install:

6. Install the pitman arm on the shaft, aligning the previously made marks.
7. Install the pitman shaft nut and tighten it to 180 ft. lbs. (244 Nm).
8. Install the relay rod on the pitman, then tighten the nut to 45 ft. lbs. (61 Nm) and install a new cotter pin.
9. Check and adjust the alignment, as necessary.
10. Remove the jackstands and carefully lower the vehicle.

TORQUE SPECIFICATIONS

Component	U.S.	Metric
Coil spring rear axle housing retainer bolt 1964–66 vehicles:	45–55 ft. lbs.	61–75 Nm
Idler arm-to-frame retainers:	35 ft. lbs.	47 Nm
Idler arm-to-relay rod nut:	35 ft. lbs.	47 Nm
Lower ball joint stud nut:	83 ft. lbs.	112 Nm
Lower control arm (front suspension) pivot bolts 1964–73:	85 ft. lbs.	115 Nm
pivot bolts 1974–77:	100 ft. lbs.	136 Nm
pivot bolts 1978–88:	65 ft. lbs.	88 Nm
Lower control arm (rear suspension) arm-to-axle bolt:	79 ft. lbs.	107 Nm
arm-to-frame nut:	70 ft. lbs.	95 Nm
Pitman arm-to-pitman shaft nut:	180 ft. lbs.	244 Nm
Pitman arm-to-relay rod nut:	45 ft. lbs.	61 Nm
Shock absorber lower nut:	60 ft. lbs.	81 Nm
Shock absorber upper bolts:	12 ft. lbs.	16 Nm
Stabilizer bar (front suspension) bar-to-frame bolts:	24 ft. lbs.	33 Nm
bar-to-lower control arm bolts:	13 ft. lbs.	18 Nm
Stabilizer bar fasteners (rear suspension):	35 ft. lbs.	47 Nm
Steering column-to-panel bracket nuts:	25 ft. lbs.	34 Nm
Steering gear-to-frame mounting bolts:	70 ft. lbs.	95 Nm
Steering shaft coupling nuts:	20 ft. lbs.	27 Nm
Steering wheel retaining nut 1964–69:	35 ft. lbs.	47 Nm
1969 deluxe or all 1970 and later:	30 ft. lbs.	41 Nm
Tie rod-to-steering knuckle nut:	35 ft. lbs.	47 Nm
Upper ball joint (replacement) retaining bolts:	10–13 ft. lbs.	14–18 Nm
Upper ball joint stud nut:	60 ft. lbs.	81 Nm
Upper control arm (front suspension) pivot shaft end nuts 1964–73:	40 ft. lbs.	54 Nm
1974:	65 ft. lbs.	88 Nm
1975–80:	75 ft. lbs.	102 Nm
1981–88:	85 ft. lbs.	115 Nm
pivot shaft-to-frame nuts 1964–74:	90 ft. lbs.	122 Nm
1975–77:	75 ft. lbs.	102 Nm
1978–88:	40–48 ft. lbs.	54–62 Nm
Upper control arm (rear suspension) arm-to-axle bolt:	79 ft. lbs.	107 Nm
arm-to-axle nut:	70 ft. lbs.	95 Nm
arm-to-frame bolt:	70 ft. lbs.	95 Nm

85948091

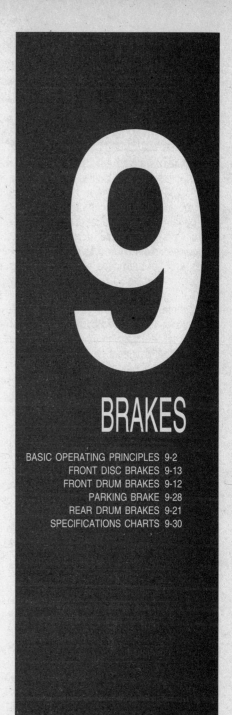

9

BRAKES

BASIC OPERATING PRINCIPLES

Hydraulic Brake Systems

Hydraulic systems are used to actuate the brakes of all automobiles covered by this manual, as well as most vehicles on the roads today. The system transports the power required to force frictional surfaces of the braking system together from the pedal to the individual brake units at each wheel. A hydraulic system is used for two reasons. First, fluid under pressure can be carried to all parts of an automobile by small pipes and flexible hoses without taking up a significant amount of room or posing routing problems. Second, a great mechanical advantage can be given to the brake pedal end of the system, and the foot pressure required to actuate the brakes can be reduced by making the surface area of the master cylinder pistons smaller than that of any of the pistons in the wheel cylinders or calipers.

The master cylinder consists of a fluid reservoir mated to a cylinder and piston assembly. Most of the vehicles covered in this manual utilize a dual circuit cylinder assembly which is designed to separate the front and rear braking systems hydraulically in case a leak should disable one of the circuits. Some of the earlier vehicles covered by this manual may be equipped with a single circuit master cylinder unit.

Steel lines carry the brake fluid to a point on the vehicle's frame near each of the wheels. The fluid is then carried to the calipers or wheel cylinders by flexible tubes in order to allow for suspension and steering movements. In drum brake systems, each wheel cylinder contains two pistons, one at either end, which push outward in opposite directions. In disc brake systems, the cylinder is part of the caliper. One piston in each caliper is used to force the brake pads against the disc.

All pistons employ some type of seal, usually made of rubber, to prevent fluid leakage. A rubber dust boot seals the outer end of the cylinder against dust and dirt. The boot fits around the outer end of the piston on disc brake calipers, and around the brake actuating rod on wheel cylinders.

The hydraulic system operates as follows: When at rest, the entire system, from the piston(s) in the master cylinder to the the pistons in the wheel cylinders and calipers, is full of brake fluid. Upon application of the brake pedal, fluid trapped in front of the master cylinder piston(s) is forced through the lines towards the wheels. Here, it forces the pistons outward toward the shoes (in the case of drum brakes) or inward toward the rotor (in the case of disc brakes). The motion of the pistons is opposed by return springs mounted outside the cylinders in drum brakes, and by spring seals, in disc brakes.

Upon release of the brake pedal, a spring located inside the master cylinder immediately returns the master cylinder pistons to the normal position. Because the springs will return the master cylinder pistons faster than fluid can flow back through the system, fluid from the reservoir is used to prevent a vacuum. Fluid from the reservoir flows to the master cylinder pistons through compensating ports.

Dual circuit master cylinders employ two pistons, located one behind the other, in the same cylinder. The primary piston is actuated directly by mechanical linkage from the brake pedal through the power booster. The secondary piston is actuated

by fluid trapped between the two pistons. If a leak develops in front of the secondary piston, it moves forward until it bottoms against the front of the master cylinder, and the fluid trapped between the pistons will operate the rear brakes. If the rear brakes develop a leak, the primary piston will move forward until direct contact with the secondary piston takes place, and it will force the secondary piston to actuate the front brakes. In either case, the brake pedal moves farther when the brakes are applied, and less braking power is available.

All dual circuit systems use a switch to warn the driver when only half of the brake system is operational. This switch is located in a valve body which is mounted on the firewall or the frame below the master cylinder. A hydraulic piston receives pressure from both circuits, each circuit's pressure being applied to one end of the piston. When the pressures are in balance, the piston remains stationary. When one circuit has a leak, however, the greater pressure in that circuit during application of the brakes will push the piston to one side, closing the switch and activating the brake warning light.

In disc brake systems, this valve body also contains a metering valve and, in some cases, a proportioning valve. The metering valve keeps pressure from traveling to the disc brakes on the front wheels until the brake shoes on the rear wheels have contacted the drums, ensuring that the front brakes will never be used alone. The proportioning valve controls the pressure to the rear brakes to lessen the chance of rear wheel lock-up during very hard braking.

Warning lights may be tested by depressing the brake pedal and holding it while opening one of the wheel cylinder bleeder screws. If this does not cause the light to go on, substitute a new lamp, make continuity checks, and, finally, replace the switch, as necessary to repair the system.

The hydraulic system may be checked for leaks by applying pressure to the pedal gradually and steadily. If the pedal sinks very slowly to the floor, the system has a leak. This is not to be confused with a springy or spongy feel due to the compression of air within the lines. If the system leaks, there will be a gradual change in the position of the pedal with a constant pressure.

Check for leaks along all lines and at wheel cylinders. If no external leaks are apparent, the problem is inside the master cylinder.

Disc Brakes

Instead of the traditional expanding brakes that press outward against a circular drum, disc brake systems utilize a disc (rotor) with brake pads positioned on either side of it. Braking is achieved in a manner similar to the way many bicycle brake work, by squeezing a spinning disc between two pads. The disc (rotor) is a casting with cooling fins between the two braking surfaces. This enables air to circulate between the braking surfaces making them less sensitive to heat buildup and more resistant to fade. Dirt and water do not affect braking action since contaminants are thrown off by the centrifugal action of the rotor or scraped off by the pads. Also, the equal clamping action of the two brake pads tends to ensure uniform, straight line stops. Disc brakes are inherently self-adjusting. There are three general types of disc brake systems:

1. A fixed caliper.
2. A floating caliper.
3. A sliding caliper.

The fixed caliper design uses two pistons mounted on either side of the rotor (in each side of the caliper). The caliper is mounted rigidly and does not move.

The sliding and floating designs are quite similar. In fact, these two types are often lumped together. In both designs, the pad on the inside of the rotor is moved into contact with the rotor by hydraulic force. The caliper, which is not held in a fixed position, moves slightly, bringing the outside pad into contact with the rotor. There are various methods of attaching floating calipers. Some pivot at the bottom or top, and some slide on mounting bolts. In any event, the end result is the same.

All the vehicles covered in this book employ the sliding caliper design.

Drum Brakes

Drum brakes employ two brake shoes mounted on a stationary backing plate. These shoes are positioned inside a circular drum which rotates with the wheel assembly. The shoes are held in place by springs. This allows them to slide toward the drums (when they are applied) while keeping the linings and drums in alignment. The shoes are actuated by a wheel cylinder which is mounted at the top of the backing plate. When the brakes are applied, hydraulic pressure forces the wheel cylinder's actuating links outward. Since these links bear directly against the top of the brake shoes, the tops of the shoes are then forced against the inner side of the drum. This action forces the bottoms of the two shoes to contact the brake drum by rotating the entire assembly slightly (known as servo action). When pressure within the wheel cylinder is relaxed, return springs pull the shoes back away from the drum.

Most modern drum brakes are designed to self-adjust during application when the vehicle is moving in reverse. This motion causes both shoes to rotate very slightly with the drum, rocking an adjusting lever, thereby causing rotation of the adjusting screw.

Power Boosters

Power brakes operate just as non-power brake systems except in the actuation of the master cylinder pistons. A vacuum diaphragm is located on the front of the master cylinder and assists the driver in applying the brakes, reducing both the effort and travel he must use on the brake pedal.

The vacuum diaphragm housing is connected to the intake manifold by a vacuum hose. A check valve is placed at the point where the hose enters the diaphragm housing, so that during periods of low manifold vacuum brake assist vacuum will not be lost.

Depressing the brake pedal closes off the vacuum source and allows atmospheric pressure to enter on one side of the diaphragm. This causes the master cylinder pistons to move and apply the brakes. When the brake pedal is released, vacuum is applied to both sides of the diaphragm and springs

return the diaphragm align with the master cylinder pistons to the released position. If the vacuum fails, the brake pedal rod will butt against the end of the master cylinder actuating rod, and direct mechanical application will occur as the pedal is depressed.

The hydraulic and mechanical problems that apply to conventional brake systems also apply to power brakes, and should be checked for If the tests below do not reveal the problem.

Test for a system vacuum leak as described:

1. Operate the engine at idle without touching the brake pedal for at least one minute.
2. Turn off the engine, and wait one minute.
3. Test for the presence of assist vacuum by depressing the brake pedal and releasing it several times. Light application will produce less and less pedal travel, if vacuum was present. If there is no vacuum, air is leaking into the system somewhere.

Test for system operation as follows:

4. Pump the brake pedal (with engine off) until the supply vacuum is entirely gone.
5. Put a light, steady pressure on the pedal.
6. Start the engine, and operate it at idle. If the system is operating, the brake pedal should fall toward the floor if constant pressure is maintained on the pedal.

Power brake systems may be tested for hydraulic leaks just as ordinary systems are tested.

Adjustments

DRUM BRAKES

▶ See Figure 1

Wheel Installed

1. Raise and support the vehicle safely using jackstands.
2. Remove the rubber plug from the adjusting slot on the backing plate.
3. Insert a brake adjusting spoon into the slot and engage the lowest possible tooth on the starwheel. Move the end of the brake spoon downward to move the starwheel upward and expand the adjusting screw. Repeat this operation until the brakes lock the wheels.
4. Insert a small screwdriver or piece of firm wire (coat hanger wire) into the adjusting slot and push the automatic adjuster lever out and free of the starwheel on the adjusting screw.
5. Holding the adjusting lever out of the way, engage the topmost tooth possible on the starwheel with a brake adjusting spoon. Move the end of the adjusting spoon upward to move the adjusting screw starwheel downward and contact the adjusting screw. Back off the adjusting screw starwheel until the wheel spins freely with a minimum of drag. Keep track of the number of turns the starwheel is backed off.
6. Repeat the operation for the other side. When backing off the brakes on the other side, the adjusting lever must be backed off the same number of turns to prevent side-to-side brake pull.
7. Repeat this operation on the other side of brakes (front or rear).

8. When all 4 brakes are adjusted, make several stops, while backing the car, to equalize all the wheels.

9. Road test the vehicle and check for proper brake operation.

Wheel Removed

Although the previous method (wheel installed) may be used on most vehicles covered by this manual, an alternate method is available for later model vehicles. With the wheel and drum removed, measure the drum inner diameter and the brake shoe outer diameters. The shoes should be adjusted to an outer diameter of 0.050 in. (1.27mm) less than the drum inner diameter. A caliper type brake measuring tool should be used to assure proper and exact measurements. Once the measurements are made and the shoes adjusted, install the drum and the wheel assembly.

BRAKE PEDAL

Travel

The pedal travel is measured as the distance which the pedal moves toward the floor from the fully released position. Inspection should be made with the brake pedal firmly depressed and when the brake system is cold. The brake pedal travel should be 2¼ in. (1964-84), 2¾ in. (1985 and later) or 3⅓ in. (hydro-boost).

➡If equipped with power brakes, be sure to pump the brakes 3 times with the engine OFF, to remove the vacuum reserve before making the travel check.

1. Under the dash, remove the pushrod-to-pedal clevis pin and separate the pushrod from the brake pedal.

2. Loosen the pushrod adjuster lock nut, then adjust the push rod.

3. After the correct travel is established, tighten the locknut, engage the pushrod and secure using the clevis pin.

Brake Light Switch

REMOVAL & INSTALLATION

When the brake pedal is in the fully released position, the stop light switch plunger should be fully depressed against the pedal arm. The switch is adjusted by moving it in or out, as necessary to actuate the plunger and properly operate the brake lights.

1. Disconnect the negative battery cable.
2. Disconnect the brake light switch electrical connector(s).
3. Withdraw the switch from the bracket.

To install:

4. Make sure that the tubular clip is in the brake pedal mounting bracket.

5. Depress the brake pedal and insert the switch into the tubular clip until it seats on the clip.

6. Pull the brake pedal fully rearward, against the pedal stop, until clicking sounds can no longer be heard. The clicks indicate that the switch is adjusting itself in the bracket by moving outward in the tubular retaining clip.

7. Release the brake pedal, then pull the pedal rearward again to assure that the adjustment is complete.

8. Engage the switch electrical connector.

9. Connect the negative battery cable, then verify proper switch operation.

Master Cylinder

REMOVAL & INSTALLATION

▶ **See Figures 2, 3, 4, 5, 6, 7 and 8**

➡Vehicles with disc brakes do not have a check valve in the front outlet port of the master cylinder. If one is installed, the front discs will quickly wear out due to residual hydraulic pressure holding the pads against the rotor.

1. Use a siphon or turkey baster to remove the brake fluid from the master cylinder reservoir.

2. Loosen the fittings and disconnect the hydraulic lines from the master cylinder assembly. Immediately plug or cap all openings to prevent system contamination or excessive fluid loss.

3. Remove the retaining nuts and the lockwashers holding the cylinder to the cowl or the brake booster, as applicable.

➡If equipped with non-power brakes, remove the clevis pin and disconnect the pushrod at the brake pedal.

4. Remove the master cylinder, gasket and, if applicable, the rubber boot.

To install:

5. Position the master cylinder, making sure the gasket and rubber boot, as applicable, are in position.

➡On non-powered brakes, position the master cylinder on the cowl, making sure that the pushrod goes through the rubber boot into the piston.

6. Secure the master cylinder using the retaining nuts, then tighten the nuts to 22 ft. lbs. (30 Nm).

7. If equipped with power brakes, reconnect the pushrod at the brake pedal and secure using the clevis pin.

8. Remove the plugs or caps, then reconnect the hydraulic lines and tighten the fittings to 18 ft. lbs. (24 Nm).

9. Refill the master cylinder with fresh brake fluid, then properly bleed the hydraulic brake system and check the brake

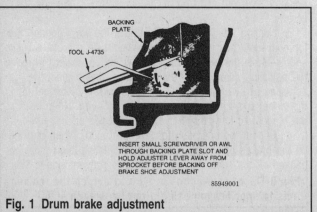

INSERT SMALL SCREWDRIVER OR AWL THROUGH BACKING PLATE SLOT AND HOLD ADJUSTER LEVER AWAY FROM SPROCKET BEFORE BACKING OFF BRAKE SHOE ADJUSTMENT

85949001

Fig. 1 Drum brake adjustment

pedal free-play. Make sure there is a firm brake pedal before attempting to move the vehicle.

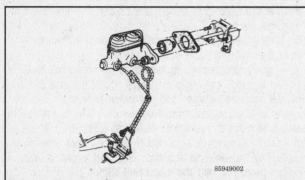

Fig. 2 Common master cylinder mounting — non-power brake vehicles

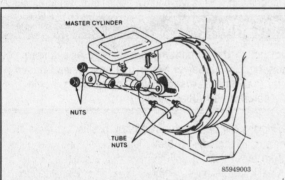

Fig. 3 Common master cylinder mounting — power brake vehicles

Fig. 4 A common turkey baster can be used to remove the brake fluid from the reservoir

Fig. 5 It is best to use a line wrench to loosen the hydraulic line fittings

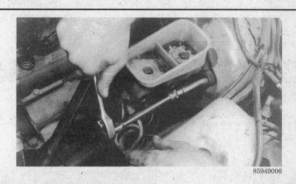

Fig. 6 Loosen and remove the master cylinder retaining nuts

Fig. 7 Remove the master cylinder assembly from the vehicle

Fig. 8 Upon installation, be sure to tighten the retaining nuts to specification using a torque wrench

OVERHAUL

▶ **See Figures 9, 10, 11 and 12**

1964-66 Vehicles

1. Remove the master cylinder assembly from the vehicle, then carefully secure it in a soft-jawed vise.

2. Remove the pushrod assembly and protective boot. This exposes the lock ring which, when removed, allows extraction of the piston stop, secondary cup, and piston.

3. Remove the cylinder end plug and push out the primary cup, spring, valve assembly, and seat.

4. Wash the components with denatured alcohol.

5. Carefully inspect the washed metal parts and the cylinder bore. A corroded cylinder must be replaced. Discoloration or stains can be removed with crocus cloth. When doing this, wrap the cloth around your finger and rotate the cylinder around the cloth.

✳✳WARNING

Do not polish the bore lengthwise, as this can cause a fluid leak.

6. To reassemble, moisten the cylinder bore with brake fluid and replace the valve seat, valve assembly, and spring.

✳✳WARNING

Be sure that the valve and seat are properly installed before proceeding. An incorrectly assembled check valve will distort and fail to provide a check valve seal, which will result in a reduction of brake pedal travel with a corresponding loss in braking.

7. Moisten the primary cup with brake fluid and install it, flat side out, and seated over the spring. The primary cup is distinguished by a brass support ring at its base.

8. Dip the secondary cup in brake fluid and slip it over the end of the piston.

9. Insert the completed assembly, with the bleeder brake end of the piston installed first. Secure the parts with the piston stop and the snapring, and install the end plug.

10. Attach the rubber boot and pushrod, and install the master cylinder.

11. Attach the brake pedal clevis and adjust the pushrod-to-piston clearance. Correct adjustment calls for a barely perceptible free pedal before piston/pushrod contact.

➡**Overhaul of the main cylinder portion of power brake master cylinders is the same as that for manual master cylinders.**

1967 and Later

1. Remove the master cylinder from the car.

2. Remove the mounting gasket and boot, and the main cover. Empty the cylinder of all remaining fluid.

3. Place the cylinder in a vise and remove the pushrod retainer and the secondary piston stop bolt that are found inside the front reservoir.

4. Remove the retaining ring and primary piston assembly.

5. Direct compressed air into the piston stop screw hole to force the secondary piston, spring, and retainer from the cylinder bore. If compressed air isn't available, use a hooked wire to pull out the secondary piston, but be carefully not to score or damage the bore.

6. Check the brass tube fitting inserts and, if damaged, remove them; if not, leave them in place.

7. If insert replacement is necessary, thread a No. 6-32 x $\frac{5}{8}$ in. self-tapping screw into the insert. Hook the end of the screw with a claw hammer and pull out the insert.

8. An alternative (but more troublesome) way to remove the inserts is to drill out the outlet holes with a $\frac{13}{64}$ in. drill and then thread them with a $\frac{1}{4}$-20 tap. Position a thick washer over the hole to serve as a spacer and then thread a $\frac{1}{4}$-20 x $\frac{3}{4}$ in. hex-head bolt into the insert and tighten the bolt until the insert is free.

9. Use only denatured alcohol or brake fluid and compressed air to clean the parts. Slight rust may be removed with crocus cloth.

✳✳WARNING

Do not polish the aluminum bore of type A: cylinders with any type of abrasive. Never use any mineral based solvents (gasoline, kerosene, etc.) for cleaning. It will quickly deteriorate rubber parts.

10. Replace the brass tube inserts by positioning them in their holes and threading a brake line tube nut into the outlet hole. Turn down the nut until the insert is seated.

11. Check the piston assemblies for correct identification and, when satisfied, position the replacement secondary seals in the twin grooves of the secondary piston.

12. The outside seal is correctly placed when its lips face the flat end of the piston.

13. Slip the primary seal and its protector over the end of the secondary piston opposite the secondary seals. The flat side of this seal should face the piston's compensating hole flange.

14. Replace the primary piston assembly with the assembled piece of the overhaul kit.

15. Coat the cylinder bore and the secondary piston's inner and outer seals with brake fluid. Assemble the secondary piston spring to its retainer and place them over the end of the primary seal.

16. Insert the combined spring and piston assembly into the cylinder and, using a pencil or small wooden dowel, seat the spring against the end of the bore.

17. Coat the primary piston seals with brake fluid and push it (pushrod receptacle end out) into the cylinder.

18. Hold the piston in and snap the retaining ring into place.

19. Continue to hold the piston down to make sure that all components are seated and insert the secondary piston stop screw in its hole in the bottom of the front reservoir. Torque the screw to 25-40 inch lbs. (3.0-4.5 Nm).

20. Install the reservoir diaphragm and cover.

21. It will save time later if the master cylinder assembly is bench-bled before installation in the vehicle:

   a. Install plugs in the outlet ports.

   b. Carefully place the unit in a vise with the front end tilted slightly downward. DO NOT OVERTIGHTEN the vise.

   c. Fill both reservoirs with clean fluid.

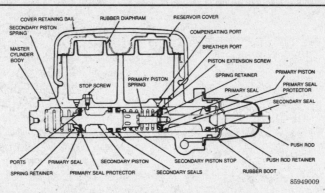

Fig. 9 Cross-sectional view of a common dual circuit master cylinder assembly

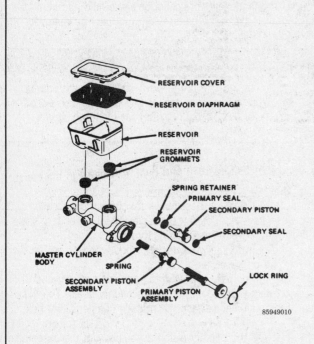

Fig. 10 Exploded view of a late model master cylinder assembly equipped with a removable plastic reservoir

d. Using a smooth, round rod (try the eraser end of a pencil), push in on the primary piston.

e. Release the pressure on the rod and watch for air bubbles in the fluid. Keep repeating this until the bubbles disappear.

f. Loosen the vise and position the cylinder so the front end is tilted slightly upward. Repeat Steps D and E.

g. Place the diaphragm cover on the reservoir.

Combination Valve

REMOVAL & INSTALLATION

▶ See Figure 13

1. Disconnect the negative battery cable.
2. Disengage the electrical lead from the switch.
3. Place rags under the unit to absorb any spilled brake fluid.
4. Clean any dirt from the hydraulic lines and the switch/valve assembly. Disconnect the hydraulic lines from the assembly. If necessary, loosen the line connections at the master cylinder. Tape or plug the open line ends to prevent the entrance of dirt and help impede fluid leakage.
5. Remove the mounting screws, then remove the switch/valve assembly.

To install:

6. Make sure that the new unit is clean and free of dust and lint. If in doubt, wash the new unit in clean brake fluid.
7. Place the new unit in position and secure it to the mounting bracket using the retaining screws.
8. Remove the tape or plugs from the hydraulic lines and connect them to the unit. If loosened for necessary play, tighten the line connections at the master cylinder.
9. Engage the electrical lead.
10. Connect the negative battery cable.
11. Properly refill and bleed the hydraulic brake system. Make sure there is a firm brake pedal before attempting to move the vehicle.

Power Brake Booster

REMOVAL & INSTALLATION

1. Disconnect the vacuum hose from the vacuum check valve.
2. Unbolt the master cylinder and carefully position it aside without disconnecting the hydraulic lines.

➡️If sufficient booster clearance cannot be obtained, it will be necessary to disconnect the hydraulic lines from the master cylinder, then remove the master cylinder assembly from the vehicle.

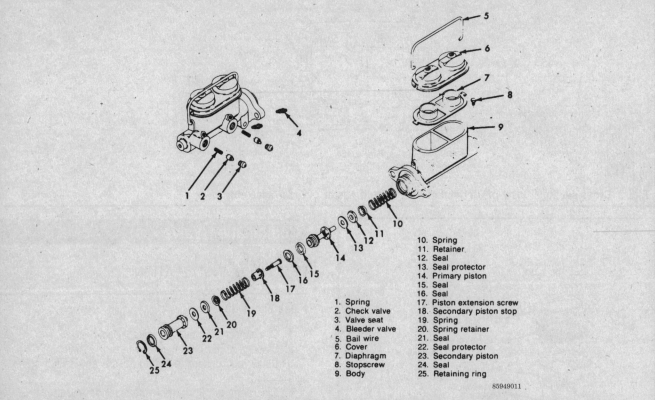

10. Spring
11. Retainer
12. Seal
13. Seal protector
14. Primary piston
15. Seal
16. Seal
17. Piston extension screw
18. Secondary piston stop
19. Spring
20. Spring retainer
21. Seal
22. Seal protector
23. Secondary piston
24. Seal
25. Retaining ring

1. Spring
2. Check valve
3. Valve seat
4. Bleeder valve
5. Bail wire
6. Cover
7. Diaphragm
8. Stopscrew
9. Body

85949011

Fig. 11 Exploded view of a dual circuit master cylinder assembly — note that most 1980 and later vehicles are not equipped with retaining balls on the reservoir cap

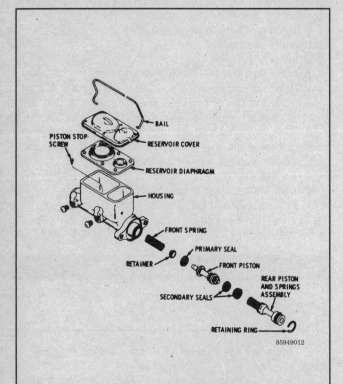

Fig. 12 Moraine cast iron master cylinder with integral reservoir — used on 350 diesel engine vehicles

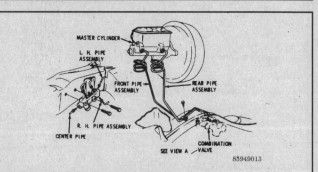

85949013

Fig. 13 The combination valve is usually mounted to the front frame member, below and near the master cylinder assembly

3. Disconnect the pushrod at the brake pedal assembly.

➡Some brake boosters may be held on with sealant, this can be easily removed with tar remover.

4. Remove the booster-to-cowl nuts and lockwashers, then lift the booster from the engine compartment.

To install:

5. Place the booster loosely into position, then connect the pushrod at the brake pedal assembly. If necessary, thread the booster retaining nuts on the ends of the studs in order to hold the booster while connecting the pushrod.

6. Install and tighten the booster-to-cowl retaining nuts to 28 ft. lbs. (38 Nm).

7. Reposition and secure the master cylinder by tightening the nuts to 22 ft. lbs. (30 Nm).

8. If the hydraulic lines were disconnected, install and tighten the fittings, then properly bleed the hydraulic brake system before attempting to move the vehicle.

➡ **Make sure to check the operation of the stop lights. Allow the engine vacuum to build before applying the brakes.**

Hydro-Boost

▶ **See Figure 14**

Hydro-Boost differs from conventional power booster brake systems, in that it operates from power steering pump fluid pressure rather than intake manifold vacuum. The Hydro-Boost unit contains a spool valve with an open center which controls the strength of the pump pressure when braking occurs. A lever assembly controls the valve's position. A boost piston provides the force necessary to operate the conventional master cylinder on the front of the booster.

A reserve of at least two assisted brake applications is supplied by an accumulator which is spring loaded on earlier and pneumatic on later models. The accumulator is an integral part of the Hydro-Boost II unit. The brakes can be applied manually if the reserve system is depleted.

All system checks, tests and troubleshooting procedure are the same for the two systems.

1. Turn the engine off and pump the brake pedal 4 or 5 times to deplete the accumulator.
2. Remove the nuts from the master cylinder, then move the master cylinder away from the booster, with brake lines still attached.
3. Remove the hydraulic lines from the booster. Plug or cap the lines to prevent system contamination or excessive fluid leakage.
4. Remove the retainer and washer at the brake pedal.
5. Remove the nuts retaining the booster to the cowl, then remove the booster assembly from the vehicle.

To install:

6. Position the booster in the vehicle and loosely install the retaining nuts to hold it in place.
7. Remove the caps or plugs and connect the hydraulic lines

8. Reconnect the retainer and washer at the brake pedal, then tighten the booster-to-cowl retaining nuts to 15 ft. lbs. (20 Nm).
9. Reposition and secure the master cylinder by tightening the nuts to 22 ft. lbs. (30 Nm).
10. Bleed the power steering and hydro-booster system. Do not attempt to move the vehicle until and firm brake pedal is obtained.

Brake Hoses and Pipes

HYDRAULIC BRAKE LINE CHECK

The hydraulic brake lines and brake linings are to be inspected at the recommended intervals in the maintenance schedule. Follow the steel tubing (pipe) from the master cylinder to the flexible hose fitting at each wheel. If a section of the tubing is found to be damaged, replace the entire section with tubing of the same type (steel, not copper), size, shape, and length. When installing a new section of brake tubing, flush clean brake fluid or denatured alcohol through the system to remove any dirt or foreign material from the line. Be sure to flare both ends to provide sound, leak-proof connections. When bending the tubing to fit the underbody contours, be careful not to kink or crack the line. Torque all hydraulic connections to 10-15 ft. lbs. (14-20 Nm).

Check the flexible brake hoses that connect the steel tubing to each wheel cylinder. Replace the hose if it shows any signs of softening, cracking, or other damage. When installing a new front brake hose, position the hose to avoid contact with other chassis parts. Place a new copper gasket over the hose fitting and thread the hose assembly into the front wheel cylinder or use the banjo bolt to secure it to the caliper, as applicable. A new rear brake hose must be positioned clear of the exhaust pipe or shock absorber. Thread the hose into the rear brake tube connector. When installing either a new front or rear brake hose, engage the opposite end of the hose to the bracket on the frame. Install the horseshoe type retaining clip and connect the tube to the hose with the tube fitting nut.

Always bleed the system after hose or line replacement. Before bleeding, make sure that the master cylinder is topped up with high temperature, extra heavy duty fluid of at least SAE 70R3 quality.

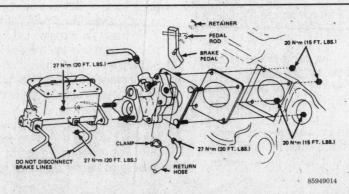

Fig. 14 Exploded view of the Hydro-Boost system mounting and installation

REMOVAL & INSTALLATION

Brake Hose

1. Raise the end of the vehicle which contains the hose to be repaired, then support the vehicle safely using jackstands.

2. If necessary, remove the wheel for easier access to the hose.

3. Note the hose routing to assure correct installation.

4. Disconnect the hose from the wheel cylinder or caliper and plug the opening to avoid system contamination or excessive fluid loss.

5. Disconnect the hose from the brake line and plug the openings to avoid excessive fluid loss or contamination.

To install:

6. Install the brake hose to the brake line, then make sure that the line is routed properly as noted during removal.

7. Tighten all hydraulic connections to 10-15 ft. lbs. (14-20 Nm).

8. Properly bleed the brake system, then check the connections for leaks.

9. Remove the supports and carefully lower the vehicle.

Brake Line

There are 2 options available when replacing a brake line. The first, and probably most preferable, is to replace the entire line using a line of similar length which is already equipped with machined flared ends. Such lines are usually available from auto parts stores and usually require only a minimum of bending in order to properly fit then to the vehicle. The second option is to bend and flare the entire replacement line (or a repair section of line) using the appropriate tools.

Buying a line with machined flares is preferable because of the time and effort saved, not to mention the cost of special tools if they are not readily available. Also, machined flares are of a higher quality than those produced by hand flaring tools or kits.

1. Raise the end of the vehicle which contains the hose to be repaired, then support the vehicle safely using jackstands.

2. Remove the components necessary for access to the brake line which is being replaced.

3. Disconnect the fittings at each end of the line, then plug the openings to prevent system contamination or excessive fluid loss.

4. Trace the line from 1 end to the other and disconnect the line from any retaining clips, then remove the line from the vehicle.

To install:

5. Try to obtain a replacement line that is the same length as the line that was removed. If the line is longer, you will have to cut it and flare the end, or if you have decided to repair a portion of the line, see the procedure on brake line flaring, later in this section.

6. Use a suitable tubing bender to make the necessary bends in the line. Work slowly and carefully; try to make the bends look as close as possible to those on the line being replaced.

➡ **When bending the brake line, be careful not to kink or crack the line. If the brake line becomes kinked or cracked, it must be replaced.**

7. Before installing the brake line, flush it with brake fluid to remove any dirt or foreign material.

8. Install the line into the vehicle. Be sure to attach the line to the retaining clips, as necessary. Make sure the replacement brake line does not contact any components that could rub the line and cause a leak.

9. Connect the brake line fittings, then tighten all hydraulic connections to 10-15 ft. lbs. (14-20 Nm).

10. Properly bleed the brake system and check for leaks.

11. Install any removed components, then remove the supports and carefully lower the vehicle.

BRAKE LINE FLARING

Use only brake line tubing approved for automotive use; never use copper tubing. Whenever possible, try to work with brake lines that are already cut to the length needed. These lines are available at most auto parts stores and have machine made flares, the quality of which is hard to duplicate with most of the available inexpensive flaring kits.

When the brakes are applied, there is a great deal of pressure developed in the hydraulic system. An improperly formed flare can leak with a resultant loss of stopping power. If you have never formed a double-flare, take time to familiarize yourself with the flaring kit; practice forming double-flares on scrap tubing until you are satisfied with the results.

The following procedure applies to a standard GM flaring kit, but should be similar to commercially available brake-line flaring kits. If these instructions differ in any way from those in your kit, follow the instructions in the kit.

1. Determine the length necessary for the replacement or repair and allow an additional $\frac{1}{8}$ in. (3.2mm) for each flare. Select a length of tubing according to the repair/replacement charts in the figure, then cut the brake line to the necessary length using an appropriate saw. Do not use a tubing cutter.

2. Square the end of the tube with a file and chamfer the edges. Remove burrs from the inside and outside diameters of the cut line using a deburring tool.

3. Install the required fittings onto the line.

4. Install the flaring tool, into a vice and install the handle into the operating cam.

5. Loosen the die clamp screw and rotate the locking plate to expose the die carrier opening.

6. Select the required die set and install in the carrier with the full side of either half facing clamp screw and counter bore of both halves facing punch turret.

7. Insert the prepared line through the rear of the die and push forward until the line end is flush with the die face.

8. Make sure the rear of both halves of the die rest against the hexagon die stops, then rotate the locking plate to the fully closed position and clamp the die firmly by tightening the clamp screw.

9. Rotate the punch turret until the appropriate size points towards the open end of the line to be flared.

10. Pull the operating handle against the line resistance in order to create the flare, then return the handle to the original position.

11. Release the clamp screw and rotate the locking plate to the open position.

12. Remove the die set and line, then separate by gently tapping both halves on the bench. Inspect the flare for proper size and shape.

13. If necessary, repeat Steps 2-12 for the other end of the line or for the end of the line which is being repaired.

Bleeding the Brake System

▶ See Figures 15, 16, 17 and 18

The hydraulic brake system must be bled any time one of the lines is disconnected or any time air enters the system. If a point in the system, such as a wheel cylinder or caliper brake line is the only point which was disconnected, the bleeder screws down stream in the hydraulic system are the only ones which must be bleed. If however, the master cylinder fittings are opened, or if the reservoir is allowed to empty, air must be bleed from the entire system. If the brake pedal feels spongy upon application, and goes almost to the floor but regains height when pumped, air has entered the system. It must be bled out. If no fittings were recently opened for service, check for leaks that would have allowed the entry of air and repair before bleeding the system.

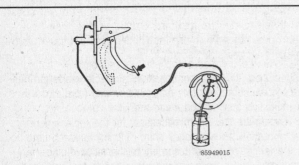

Fig. 15 During bleeding an assitant holds the brake pedal down while you open a bleeder valve (allowing trapped air to escape)

As a general rule, once the master cylinder is bled, the system should be bled starting at the furthest wheel from the master cylinder and working towards the nearest wheel. Therefore, the correct bleeding sequence is: master cylinder, right rear wheel cylinder, left rear, right front and left front. Most master cylinder assemblies on Chevrolet mid-sized vehicles are equipped with bleeder valves, bleed them first then go to the wheel cylinders or calipers. If the master cylinder is not equipped with bleeder valves, it may be bled by loosening and tightening the fittings.

This method of bleeding requires two people, one to depress the brake pedal and the other to open the bleeder screws.

1. Clean the top of the master cylinder, remove the cover and fill the reservoirs with clean fluid. To prevent squirting fluid, and possibly damaging painted surfaces, install the cover during the procedure, but be sure to frequently check and top off the reservoirs with fresh fluid.

➡On cars with front disc brakes, it will be necessary to hold in the metering valve pin during the bleeding procedure. The metering valve is located beneath the master cylinder and the pin is situated under the rubber boot on the end of the valve housing. This may be taped in or held by an assistant.

✳✳CAUTION

Never reuse brake fluid which has been bled from the system.

2. Fill the master cylinder reservoir with fresh brake fluid.
3. If the master cylinder contains any air, start bleeding at the assembly.
4. Install a box-end wrench on the bleeder screw for the master cylinder assembly.
5. Attach a length of small diameter, clear vinyl tubing to the bleeder screw. Submerge the other end of the rubber tubing in a glass jar partially filled with clean brake fluid. Make sure the rubber tube fits on the bleeder screw snugly or you may be squirted with brake fluid when the bleeder screw is opened.

➡While bleeding the system, do not let your friend release the brake pedal if the bleeder screw is still open. Should this occur, air may be drawn back into the system.

6. Have your friend slowly depress the brake pedal and hold. As this is done, open the bleeder screw half a turn and allow the fluid to run through the tube. Close the bleeder screw, then have your friend fully release the pedal.

Fig. 16 Specialized bleeder wrenches are designed to access tight spots such as this wheel cylinder's bleeder screw

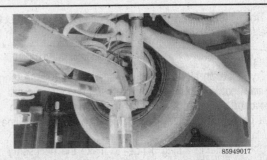

Fig. 17 Be sure one end of the vinyl tubing is submerged in fresh brake fluid to help assure no air is drawn back into the system.

7. Repeat the procedure until no bubbles appear in the jar. Check and refill the master cylinder reservoir.

8. Repeat this procedure on the right rear, left rear, right front, and left front wheels, in that order. Periodically check and refill the master cylinder so it does not run dry. Remember, if the reservoir is allowed to empty of fluid during, air will be drawn into the system and the bleeding procedure must be restarted.

➡Be very careful when bleeding wheel cylinders and brake calipers. The bleeder screws often rust in position and may easily break off if forced. Installing a new bleeder screw will often require removal of the component and may include overhaul or replacement of the wheel cylinder/caliper. To help prevent the possibility of breaking a bleeder screw, spray it with some penetrating oil before attempting to loosen it.

9. If the brake warning light is on, depress the brake pedal firmly. If there is no air in the system, the light will go out.

10. After bleeding, make sure that a firm pedal is achieved before attempting to move the vehicle.

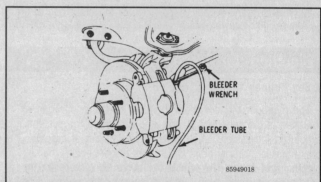

85949018

Fig. 18 Positioning the plastic tubing and wrench on a caliper bleeder nipple

FRONT DRUM BRAKES

❊❊CAUTION

Brake shoes contain asbestos, which has been determined to be a cancer causing agent. Never clean the brake surfaces with compressed air! Avoid inhaling any dust from any brake surface! When cleaning brake surfaces, use a commercially available brake cleaning fluid.

Brake Drums and Shoes

REMOVAL & INSTALLATION

➡For information concerning the wheel bearings, please refer to the wheel bearing procedures in Section 8 of this manual. Disassemble the brakes on only one side of the vehicle at a time so that you may use the assembled side for reference during reassembly. Remember that the opposite side is a mirror image of the side on which you are working.

1. Raise and support the front of the vehicle safely using jackstands.
2. Remove the front wheel and drum as a unit by removing the spindle nut and cotter pin.
3. Free the brake shoe return springs, actuator pull-back spring, hold-down pins and springs, and the actuator assembly.

➡Special tools available from auto supply stores will ease removal of the spring and anchor pin.

4. Disconnect the adjusting mechanism and spring, then remove the primary shoe. The primary shoe has a shorter lining than the secondary and is mounted at the front of the wheel.
5. Remove the secondary shoe.
To install:
6. Clean and inspect all brake parts.
7. Check the wheel cylinders for seal condition and leaking.

8. Repack wheel bearings and replace the seals.

➡Maintenance procedures for the metallic lining option are the same as those for standard linings. Do not substitute these linings in standard drums, unless they have been honed to a 20 micro-inch finish and equipped with special heat resistant springs.

9. Inspect the replacement shoes for nicks or burrs, lubricate the backing plate contact points, brake cable and levers, and adjusting screws and then install the components using the assembled side for reference.
10. Position the secondary shoe. The hold-down spring and pin may be used to retain the shoe in position during the procedure.
11. Position the primary shoe, then connect the adjusting mechanism and spring.

➡Make sure that the right and left hand adjusting screws are not mixed. You can prevent this by working on one side at a time. This will also provide you with a reference for reassembly. The star wheel should be nearest to the secondary shoe when correctly installed.

12. Install the brake shoe return springs, actuator pull-back spring, hold-down pins and springs (if not done earlier), and the actuator assembly.
13. Install the front wheel and drum as a unit, then install the spindle nut and cotter pin. Properly adjust the wheel bearings. For details, refer to Section 8 of this manual.
14. Properly adjust the drum brakes. Refer to the procedure earlier in this section.
15. Remove the jackstands and carefully lower the vehicle.

DRUM INSPECTION

1. Check the drums for any cracks, scores, grooves, or an out-of-round condition. Replace if cracked. Slight scores can be removed with fine emery cloth while extensive scoring requires turning the drum on a lathe.

2. Never have a drum turned more than 0.060 in. (1.524mm).

Wheel Cylinders

REMOVAL & INSTALLATION

1. Raise and support the front of the vehicle safely using jackstands.

2. Remove the wheel and the brake drum for access to the wheel cylinder assembly.

➡**In most cases, the wheel cylinders may be removed from the backing plate without completely removing the brake shoes and related components. Some of the upper springs must be removed in order to allow the shoes to spread and provide the necessary clearance for wheel cylinder removal.**

3. Clean away all dirt, crud and foreign material from around wheel cylinder. It is important that dirt be kept away from the brake line when the cylinder is disconnected.

4. Disconnect the inlet tube line. Plug or cap the line opening to prevent system contamination or excessive fluid loss.

➡**Wheel cylinders are retained to the rear of the brake backing plate by two types of fasteners. One type uses a round retainer with locking clips while the other simply uses two bolts threaded into the wheel cylinder body.**

5. To remove the round retainer type cylinders, insert two awls or pins into the access slots between the wheel cylinder pilot and the retainer locking tabs. Bend both tabs away simultaneously. The wheel cylinder can be removed, as the retainer is released.

6. To remove the bolted wheel cylinders, loosen and remove the bolts from the back side of the backing plate, then remove the wheel cylinder assembly.

To install:

7. For round retainer type wheel cylinders, position the cylinder and hold it in place with a wooden block between the cylinder and the axle flange. Install the new retainer clip, using a 1 1/8 in. 12-point socket and socket extension. The socket is used to assure that the retainer seats evenly.

8. For bolt type wheel cylinders, position the cylinder and secure using the retaining bolts.

9. Remove the cap or plug, then connect and secure the inlet line.

10. Assemble the remaining brake components which were removed, then install the tire and wheel.

11. Bleed the wheel cylinder, then remove the jackstands and carefully lower the vehicle.

OVERHAUL

Wheel cylinder overhaul is virtually the same for front drum brakes as it is for the rear. For information, please refer to the overhaul procedure found later in this section under rear drum brakes. Wheel cylinder overhaul kits may be available, but often at little or no savings over a reconditioned wheel cylinder. It often makes sense with these components to substitute a new or reconditioned part instead of attempting an overhaul.

FRONT DISC BRAKES

✳✳CAUTION

Brake pads contain asbestos, which has been determined to be a cancer causing agent. Never clean the brake surfaces with compressed air! Avoid inhaling any dust from any brake surface! When cleaning brake surfaces, use a commercially available brake cleaning fluid.

Disc Brake Pads

INSPECTION

▶ **See Figures 19, 20 and 21**

Brake pads should be inspected once a year or at 7,500 miles, whichever occurs first. Check both ends of the outboard pad, looking in at each end of the caliper; then check the lining thickness of the inboard pad, looking down through the inspection hole. On riveted pads, the lining should be more than 0.020 in. (0.51mm) above the rivet (so that the lining is thicker than the metal backing) in order to prevent the rivet from scoring the rotor. On all pads, a minimum thickness of 0.063 in. (1.59mm) should be used to determine necessary replacement intervals. Keep in mind that any applicable state inspection standards that are more stringent take precedence. All four front pads must be replaced as a set if one shows excessive wear.

➡**All 1979 and later models have a wear indicator that makes a noise when the linings have worn to a degree where replacement is necessary. The spring clip is an integral part of the inboard pad and lining. When the brake pad reaches a certain degree of wear, the clip will contact the rotor and produce a warning noise.**

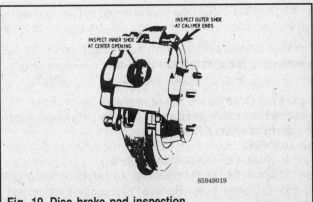

85949019

Fig. 19 Disc brake pad inspection

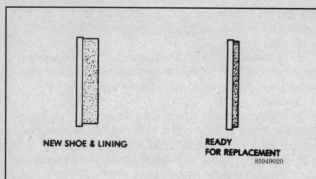

Fig. 20 Relative size differences between a new and worn pad lining

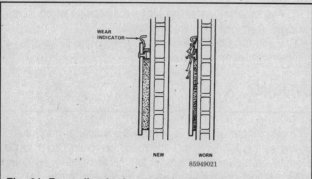

Fig. 21 Front disc brake pads on 1979 and later vehicles have a built-in wear indicator

REMOVAL & INSTALLATION

1966-68 Vehicles

1. Siphon off about ⅔ of the brake fluid from the full master cylinder. A turkey baster may also be used to remove the brake fluid.

✳✳WARNING

The insertion of the thicker replacement pads will push the caliper pistons back into their bores and will cause a full master cylinder to overflow causing paint damage. In addition to siphoning fluid, it would be wise to keep the cylinder cover on during pad replacement.

2. Raise and support the front of the vehicle safely using jackstands.
3. Remove the front wheels.

➡Replacing the pads on just one wheel will result in uneven braking. Always replace the pads on both wheels.

4. Extract and discard the pad retaining pin cotter key.
5. Remove the retaining pin and open the bleed screw on the caliper in order to release some of the fluid, but do not allow all of the fluid to drain from the master cylinder reservoir. This will reduce the pressure and make it easier to push in on the pistons. Compress the piston into the caliper bore and tighten the bleeder screw. Remove the pads, then inspect and compare them with each other. They may be slightly different;

if so, make sure that the replacement pads are installed correctly.
6. After installing the new pads, install the retaining pin and insert a new cotter pin.
7. Refill the master cylinder and bleed the system if necessary.

1969 and Later

▶ See Figures 22, 23, 24, 25, 26, 27, 28, 29 and 30

1. Siphon off about ⅔ of the brake fluid from the full master cylinder. A turkey baster may also be used to remove the brake fluid.

✳✳WARNING

The insertion of the thicker replacement pads will push the caliper pistons back into their bores and will cause a full master cylinder to overflow causing paint damage. In addition to siphoning fluid, keep the cylinder cover on during pad replacement.

2. Raise and support the front of the vehicle safely using jackstands.
3. Remove the front wheels.

➡Replacing the pads on just one wheel will result in uneven braking. Always replace the pads on both wheels.

4. Install a C-clamp on the caliper so that the solid side of the clamp rests against the back of the caliper and the screw end is against the metal part (backing plate) of the outboard pad. Slowly tighten the clamp until the caliper moves enough to bottom the piston in its bore, then remove the clamp.
5. Remove the two Allen-head caliper mounting bolts so that the caliper may be pulled off the disc.
6. Remove the inboard pad and loosen the outboard pad. Place the caliper where it won't strain the brake hose. It would be best to wire it out of the way. NEVER hang the caliper by the hose or the hydraulic system could be damaged.
7. Remove the pad support spring clip from the piston or the rear of the inboard pad.
8. Remove the two bolt ear sleeves and the four rubber bushings from the ears.
   To install:
9. Check the inside of the caliper for leakage and inspect the condition of the piston dust boot.
10. Lubricate the two new sleeves and four bushings with a silicone spray or a suitable grease.
11. Install the bushings in each caliper ear. Install the two sleeves in the two inboard ears.
12. Install the pad support spring clip and pad into the center of the piston.

➡On models with wear sensors, make sure the wear sensor is toward the rear of the caliper.

13. Place the outboard pad in the caliper with its top ears over the caliper ears and the bottom tab engaged in the caliper cutout.
14. After both pads are installed, lift the caliper and place the bottom edge of the outboard pad on the outer edge of the disc to make sure that there is no clearance between the tab on the bottom of the pads and the caliper abutment.

15. Place the caliper over the disc, lining up the hole in the caliper ears with the hole in the mounting bracket. Make sure that the brake hose is not kinked.

16. Start the caliper-to-mounting bracket bolts through the sleeves in the inboard caliper ears and through the mounting bracket making sure the ends of the bolts pass under the retaining ears of the inboard pad.

17. Push the mounting bolts through to engage the holes in the outboard pads and the outboard caliper ears and then threading them into the mounting bracket. Tighten the mounting bolts to 35 ft. lbs. (47 Nm).

18. Pump the brake pedal to seat the linings against the rotors.

19. With a pair of channel lock pliers placed on the notch on the caliper housing, bend the pad upper ears until no clearance exist between the pad and the caliper housing.

20. Install the wheels, lower the car, and refill the master cylinder with fluid. Pump the brake pedal to make sure that it is firm. Do not attempt to move the vehicle until and firm pedal is obtained.

Fig. 24 Wire the caliper to the suspension — an old coat hanger may be easily adapted for this use

Fig. 25 Most replacement pad kits will come with an anti-squeal compound which may be applied to the pad backing plates

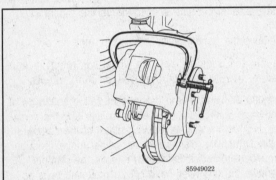

Fig. 22 Use a C-clamp to seat the caliper piston before removing the old pads

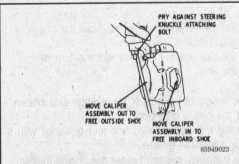

Fig. 23 The caliper may also be compressed using a prybar, but be careful NOT to damage any of the pry surfaces

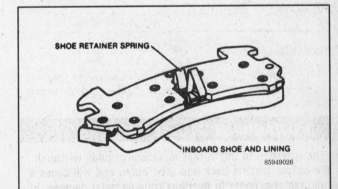

Fig. 26 Proper inboard pad retaining spring installation

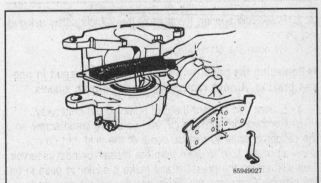

Fig. 27 Installing the pad support spring — 1970 and later vehicles

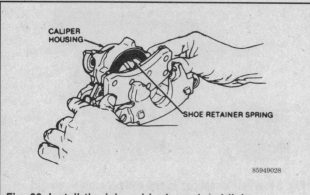

Fig. 28 Install the inboard brake pad and lining

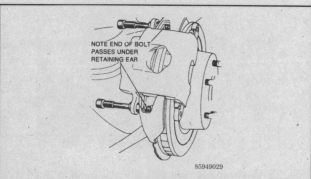

Fig. 29 Caliper bolts must go under the pad retaining ears

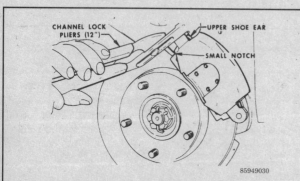

Fig. 30 Use pliers to fit the brake pad to the caliper housing

Caliper

REMOVAL & INSTALLATION

▶ See Figures 31, 32, 33, 34, 35 and 36

1. Raise the front of the vehicle and support safely using jackstands.

2. Remove the tire and wheel assembly from the side on which the caliper is being removed.

3. Disconnect the brake hose from the caliper. Tape or cap the end of the line to prevent system contamination or excessive fluid loss.

4. On 1968 and earlier vehicles, remove the cotter pin from the brake pad and retaining pin, then remove the pin. Then, remove the brake pads and identify them as inboard or outboard if they are being reused.

5. If applicable, remove the U-shaped retainer from the hose fitting and pull the hose from the bracket.

6. Remove the two caliper retaining bolts, then remove the caliper from its mounting bracket. For 1969 and later vehicles, the brake pads will be removed with the caliper, if necessary, separate them from the caliper assembly.

To install:

7. If removed on 1969 and later vehicle, install the brake pads to the caliper.

8. Install the caliper to the mounting bracket and secure using the retaining bolts.

9. Remove the cap or tape, then install the brake hose into the caliper, passing the female end through the support bracket.

10. If applicable, install the hose fitting into the support bracket and install the U-shaped retainer.

11. Turn the steering wheel from side to side to make sure that the hose doesn't interfere with the tire. If it does, turn the hose end one or two points in the bracket until the interference is eliminated.

12. For 1968 and earlier vehicles, install the brake pads, retainer pin and cotter pin.

13. Properly refill and bleed the hydraulic brake system. Be sure to check the brake line for leaks.

14. Install the wheel, then remove the jackstands and lower the vehicle. Do not attempt to move the vehicle until a firm brake pedal has been obtained.

Fig. 31 The tire and wheel assembly must be removed to access the caliper

Fig. 32 Loosen and disconnect the brake line fitting at the caliper

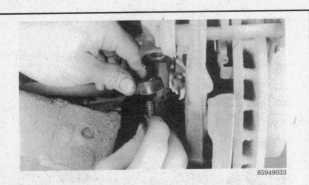

Fig. 33 Most caliper brake lines fittings consist of a banjo bolt, fitting and washer(s)

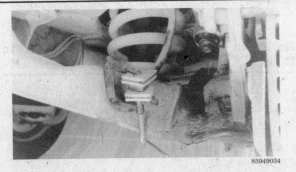

Fig. 34 A banjo fitting may be capped using a C-clamp a 2 smooth, flat pieces of plastic or rubber

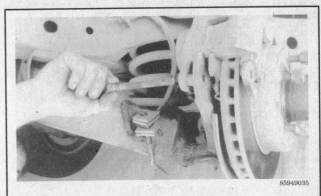

Fig. 35 Remove the caliper mounting bolts

Fig. 36 Remove the caliper from the mounting bracket and brake rotor

OVERHAUL

1966-68

1. Remove the caliper assembly from the vehicle.
2. Separate the caliper halves. Remove the two O-rings from the fluid transfer holes in the caliper.
3. Push the piston all the way down into the caliper. Using the piston as a fulcrum, place a screwdriver under the steel ring in the boot and carefully pry the boot from the caliper half.
4. Remove the pistons and springs, being careful not to damage the seal.
5. Remove the boot and seal from the piston.
6. Clean all metal components with clean brake fluid or denatured alcohol.

**WARNING

Do not use gasoline, kerosene, or any other mineral based solvent for cleaning. These solvents form an oily film on the parts which leads to fluid contamination and the deterioration of rubber parts.

7. Blow out all fluid passages using compressed air.
8. Discard and replace all rubber parts.
9. Inspect all bores for scoring and pitting and replace is necessary. Minor flaws can be removed with very fine crocus cloth but do so with a circular motion.
10. Using a feeler gauge, check the clearance of the piston in its bore. If the bore is not damaged and the clearance

exceeds the maximum limit below, then the piston must be replaced.

- For a 2¹/₁₆ in. diameter, there should be a 0.0045-0.0100 in. clearance.
- For a 1⁷/₈ in. diameter, there should be a 0.0045-0.0100 in. clearance.
- For a 1³/₈: in. diameter, there should be a 0.0035-0.0090 in. clearance.

11. Insert the seal in the piston groove nearest the flat end of the piston. The seal lip must face the large end of the piston. The lips must be in the groove and may not extend beyond.

12. Place the spring in the piston bore.

13. Coat the seal with clean brake fluid.

14. Install the piston assembly into the bore, being careful not to damage the seal lip on the edge of the bore.

15. Install the boot into the piston groove closest to the concave end of the piston.

16. The fold in the boot must face the seal end of the piston.

17. Push the pistons to the bottom of the bore and check for smooth piston movement. The end of the piston must be flush with the end of the bore. If it is not, check the installation of the seal.

18. Seat the piston boot so that its metal ring is even in the counterbore. The ring is even in the counterbore. The ring must be flush or below the machined face of the caliper. If the ring is seated unevenly dirt and moisture could get into the bore.

19. Insert the O-rings around the fluid transfer holes at both ends of the caliper halves.

20. Lubricate the bolts with brake fluid, connect the caliper halves, and tighten the bolts securely.

21. Make sure the pistons are fully retracted, then mount the caliper over the disc. Be careful not to damage the piston boots on the edge of the disc.

22. Install the two mounting bolts and tighten them securely, then finish caliper installation.

1969 and Later

▶ See Figures 37, 38, 39, 40, 41 and 42

1. Clean the outside of the caliper with denatured alcohol.
2. Remove the caliper from the vehicle.
3. If not done already, remove the outboard and inboard shoes from the caliper assembly.
4. Drain any remaining brake fluid from the caliper.

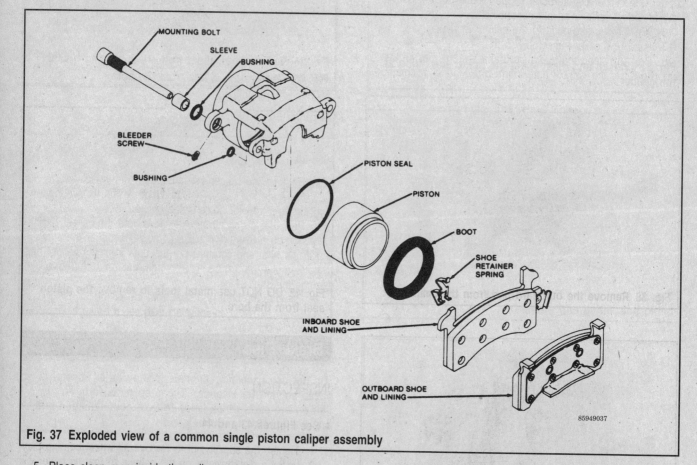

Fig. 37 Exploded view of a common single piston caliper assembly

5. Place clean rags inside the caliper opening to catch the piston when it is released.

6. Apply compressed air to the caliper fluid inlet hole and force the piston out of its bore. Do not blow the piston out; use just enough pressure to inch it out.

7. Use a small screwdriver to carefully pry the boot out of the caliper. Take great care to avoid scratching or otherwise damaging the bore.

8. Remove the piston seal from its groove in the caliper bore. Do not use a metal tool of any type for this operation.

➡**Replace (do not reuse) the boot, piston seal, rubber bushings, and sleeves.**

9. Blow out all passages in the caliper and bleeder valve. Clean the piston and piston bore with fresh brake fluid.

10. Examine the piston for scoring, scratches, or corrosion. If any of these conditions exist, the piston must be replaced because it is plated and cannot be refinished.

11. Examine the bore for the same defects. Light rough spots may be removed by rotating crocus cloth, using finer pressure, in the bore. Do not polish with an in-and-out motion or use any other abrasive.

12. Lubricate the piston bore and the new rubber pars with fresh brake fluid. Position the seal in the piston bore groove.

13. Lubricate the piston with brake fluid and assemble the boot into the piston groove so that the fold faces the open end of the piston.

14. Insert the piston into the bore, taking care not to unseat the seal.

15. Force the piston to the bottom of the bore (this will require a force of approximately 40-100 lbs.). Seat the boot lip around the caliper counterbore. Proper seating of the boot is very important for sealing out contaminants.

16. Install the brake pads to the caliper assembly.

17. Install the caliper assembly to the vehicle.

18. Properly bleed the hydraulic brake system. Do not attempt to move the vehicle until a firm brake pedal is obtained.

Fig. 38 Remove the outboard pad from the caliper

Fig. 39 Remove the inboard pad by releasing the spring clip from the caliper piston

Fig. 40 Use compressed air to free the piston — but KEEP YOUR FINGERS CLEAR when applying the air

Fig. 41 Remove the piston from the bore

Fig. 42 DO NOT use metal tools to remove the piston seal from the bore

Brake Disc

INSPECTION

▶ **See Figures 43 and 44**

1. Tighten the spindle nut to remove all wheel bearing play.

2. Install a dial indicator on the caliper so that its feeler will contact the disc about 1 in. (25.4mm) below its outer edge.

3. Turn the disc and observe the runout reading. If the reading exceeds 0.002 in. (0.051mm) for 1970-83 vehicles or 0.004 in. (0.102mm) for other years, the disc should be replaced.

4. Measure the thickness of the rotor at 5 points around the circumference. The tolerance for difference in thickness is 0.005 in. (0.127mm).

5. Minimum thickness dimensions are cast into the caliper for reference.

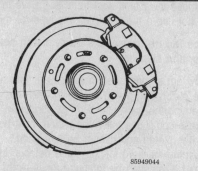

Fig. 44 A discard dimension (in this case 0.965 in.) is stamped onto most brake disc hubs

REMOVAL & INSTALLATION

▶ **See Figure 45**

On some older vehicles covered in this manual, the original brake discs may be separated from the hubs by drilling out the attaching rivets. Before attempting this, check with your local parts supply store to see if replacement hubs or discs are available. In most cases, the entire assembly will have to be replaced.

1. Raise and support the front of the vehicle safely using jackstands.

2. Remove the tire and wheel assembly.

3. Remove the brake caliper from the mounting bracket and wire it out of the way. Be sure not to stretch and damage the brake hose.

4. Carefully pry out the grease cap, then remove the cotter pin, spindle nut and washer. Remove the hub and disc from the spindle being careful not to drop the outer wheel bearings.

To install:

5. Carefully install the wheel hub over the spindle, making sure the outer bearing is in place.

6. Loosely install the spindle washer and nut, but do not install the cotter pin or dust cap at this time.

7. Remove the wire support, then install the brake caliper assembly.

8. Install the tire and wheel assembly.

9. Properly adjust the wheel bearings, then install a new cotter pin and the dust cap. For wheel bearing adjustment procedures, refer to Section 8 of this manual.

10. Install the hub cap, then remove the supports and carefully lower the vehicle.

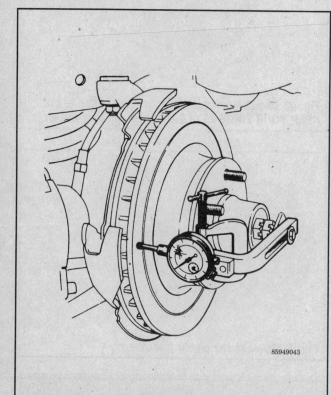

Fig. 43 Use a dial indicator to measure brake disc runout

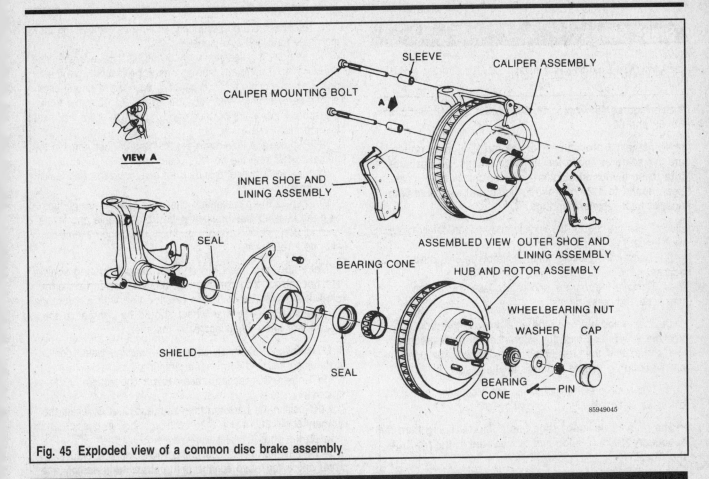

Fig. 45 Exploded view of a common disc brake assembly.

REAR DRUM BRAKES

✳✳CAUTION

Brake shoes contain asbestos, which has been determined to be a cancer causing agent. Never clean the brake surfaces with compressed air! Avoid inhaling any dust from any brake surface! When cleaning brake surfaces, use a commercially available brake cleaning fluid.

Brake Drum

REMOVAL & INSTALLATION

1. Block the front wheels, then release the parking brake.
2. Raise and support the rear of the vehicle safely using jackstands.
3. Remove the tire and wheel assembly.
4. Matchmark the drum to the hub, then pull the brake drum off the hub. It may be necessary to gently tap the rear edge of the drum using a rubber mallet to start it off the studs.

5. If extreme resistance to removal is encountered, it will be necessary to retract the adjusting screw. Knock out the access hole in the brake drum and turn the adjusting to retract the linings from the drum.
6. Install a replacement hole cover before reinstalling drum.
7. After service, install the drums in the same position on the hub as marked during removal.
8. Install the tire and wheel assembly, then remove supports and carefully lower the vehicle.
9. Set the parking brake, then remove the blocks from the front wheels.

DRUM INSPECTION

1. Check the drums for any cracks, scores, grooves, or an out-of-round condition. Replace if cracked. Slight scores can be removed with fine emery cloth while extensive scoring requires turning the drum on a lathe.
2. Never have a drum turned more than 0.060 in. (1.524mm).

Brake Shoes

REMOVAL & INSTALLATION

▶ See Figures 46, 47, 48, 49, 50, 51, 52, 53, 54, 55, 56, 57, 58, 59 and 60

➡ **Maintenance procedures for the metallic lining option are the same as those for standard linings. Do not substitute these linings in standard drums, unless they have been honed to a 20 micro-inch finish and equipped with special heat resistant springs.**

1. Raise the rear of the vehicle and support safely using jackstands.
2. Slacken the parking brake cable by backing off the adjuster.
3. Remove the rear tire and wheel assemblies, then remove the and brake drums.

➡ **Disassemble only one side at a time so that you may use the assembled side for reference during reassembly. Remember that the assembled side opposite the one you are working on will be a mirror image.**

4. Clean the brake components with a commercially available spray cleaner designed for brake systems.

➡ **The primary (leading) shoe has a shorter lining than the secondary (trailing) shoe and is mounted at the front of the wheel.**

5. Free the brake shoe return springs, adjusting screw spring, trailing shoe hold-down pin and spring, the adjusting screw, then finally the actuator assembly, consisting of the actuating link, adjuster levers and lever return spring.

➡ **Special tools available from auto supply stores will ease removal of the spring and anchor pin.**

6. Pull back on the secondary shoe, then remove the parking brake strut and strut spring.
7. Remove the secondary shoe and disengage the parking brake cable. If sufficient tension was not released from the parking brake cable, an assistant will be needed to pull back on the cable spring while you disengage the cable end from the shoe. Three pairs of hands and 2 pairs of pliers will make this job much easier.
8. Remove the hold-down pin and spring, then remove the primary shoe from the backing plate.
9. Check the wheel cylinders for seal condition and leaking.

To install:

10. Inspect the replacement shoes for nicks or burrs, lubricate the backing plate contact points, brake cable and levers, and adjusting screws. Begin assembly using the assembled side as a reference.

➡ **Make sure that the right and left hand adjusting screws are not mixed. You can prevent this by working on one side at a time. This will also provide you with a reference for reassembly. The star wheel should be nearest to the secondary shoe when correctly installed.**

11. Position the primary shoe to the backing plate, then secure using the hold-down pin and spring.
12. Engage the parking brake cable to the bottom of the secondary shoe.
13. Position the parking brake strut and strut spring to the primary shoe, then place the secondary shoe in position and engage the strut.
14. Install the actuator assembly (actuating link, adjuster lever and lever return spring), then secure the assembly and secondary shoe using the hold-down pin and spring assembly.
15. Engage the actuating link, then install and secure the brake shoe return springs, adjuster screw assembly and the adjusting screw spring.
16. Install the brake drums, then install the rear tire and wheel assemblies.
17. Properly adjust the rear drum brakes, followed by the parking brake cable.
18. Remove the supports and carefully lower the vehicle.

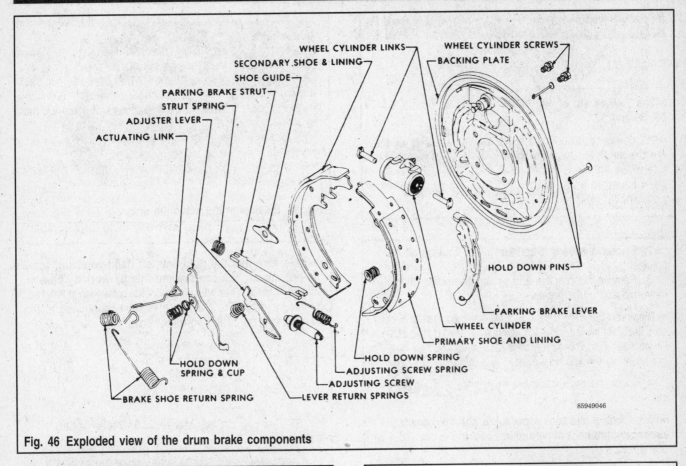

WHEEL CYLINDER LINKS
SECONDARY SHOE & LINING
SHOE GUIDE
PARKING BRAKE STRUT
STRUT SPRING
ADJUSTER LEVER
ACTUATING LINK

WHEEL CYLINDER SCREWS
BACKING PLATE

HOLD DOWN PINS

PARKING BRAKE LEVER
WHEEL CYLINDER
PRIMARY SHOE AND LINING

HOLD DOWN
SPRING & CUP

BRAKE SHOE RETURN SPRING

HOLD DOWN SPRING
ADJUSTING SCREW SPRING
ADJUSTING SCREW
LEVER RETURN SPRINGS

85949046

Fig. 46 Exploded view of the drum brake components

85949047

Fig. 47 Use a commercially available spray cleaner to remove brake dust from the components

85949051

Fig. 49 Pivot and remove the return spring from the primary shoe

85949049

Fig. 48 Remove the return spring from the secondary shoe

85949052

Fig. 50 Remove the adjusting screw spring

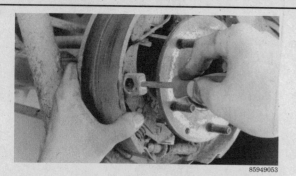

Fig. 51 Removing the hold-down pin and spring is easiest using a brake tool

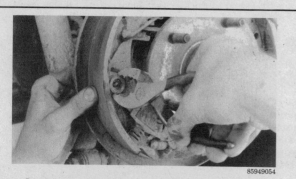

Fig. 52 If no brake tool is available, the hold-down assembly may be removed using pliers

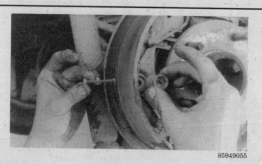

Fig. 53 One the spring and cap are pivoted, the hold-down pin may be withdrawn from behind the backing plate

Fig. 54 Pull outward on the secondary shoe and remove the adjuster screw

Fig. 55 Disengage the actuating link

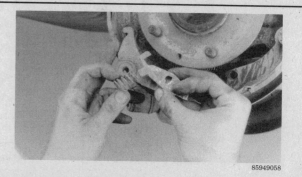

Fig. 56 Remove the adjuster lever and lever return spring

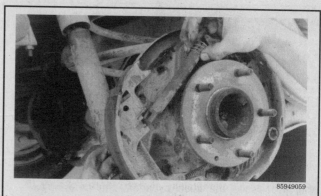

Fig. 57 Remove the parking brake strut

Fig. 58 An assistant is helpful in removing the parking brake cable end from the secondary shoe

Fig. 59 If necessary, the shoe guide may be removed from the backing plate

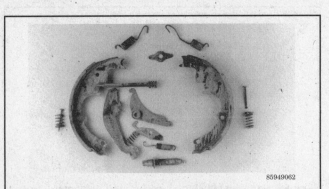

Fig. 60 Exploded view of the brake components once they are removed from the backing plate

Wheel Cylinders

REMOVAL & INSTALLATION

▶ See Figures 61, 62, 63, 64, 65, 66, 67 and 68

1. Raise and support the front of the vehicle safely using jackstands.

2. Remove the wheel and the brake drum for access to the wheel cylinder assembly.

➡In most cases, the wheel cylinders may be removed from the backing plate without completely removing the brake shoes and related components. Some of the upper springs must usually be removed in order to allow the shoes to spread and provide the necessary clearance for wheel cylinder removal.

3. Clean away all dirt, crud and foreign material from around wheel cylinder. It is important that dirt be kept away from the brake line when the cylinder is disconnected.

4. Disconnect the inlet tube line from the back of the wheel cylinder. Immediately plug or cap the line to prevent system contamination or excessive fluid loss.

➡Wheel cylinders are retained to the rear of the brake backing plate by two types of fasteners. One type uses a round retainer with locking clips while the other simply uses two bolts threaded into the wheel cylinder body.

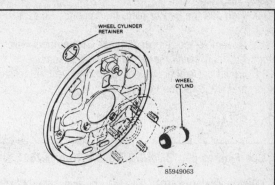

Fig. 61 Exploded view of the round retainer type wheel cylinder

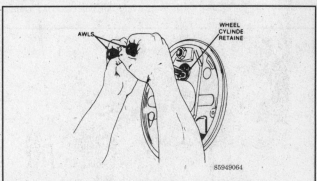

Fig. 62 Two awls may be used to bend the retainer stubs, releasing the wheel cylinder

5. To remove the round retainer type cylinders, insert two awls or pins into the access slots between the wheel cylinder pilot and the retainer locking tabs. Bend both tabs away simultaneously. The wheel cylinder can be removed, as the retainer is released.

6. To remove the bolted wheel cylinders, loosen and remove the bolts from the back side of the backing plate, then remove the wheel cylinder assembly.

To install:

7. For round retainer type wheel cylinders, position the cylinder and hold it in place with a wooden block between the cylinder and the axle flange. Install the new retainer clip, using a 1⅛ in. 12-point socket and socket extension. The socket is used to assure that the retainer seats evenly.

8. For bolt type wheel cylinders, position the cylinder and secure using the retaining bolts.

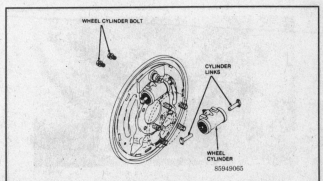

Fig. 63 Exploded view of the bolted wheel cylinder mounting

9. Remove the cap or plug, then connect and secure the inlet line.

10. Assemble the remaining brake components which were removed, then install the tire and wheel assembly.

11. Bleed the wheel cylinder, then remove the jackstands and carefully lower the vehicle.

OVERHAUL

▶ **See Figures 69, 70, 71, 72, 73, 74, 75 and 76**

Wheel cylinder overhaul kits may be available, but often at little or no savings over a reconditioned wheel cylinder. It often

Fig. 64 Use a line wrench to loosen the inlet pipe fitting from the rear of the wheel cylinder

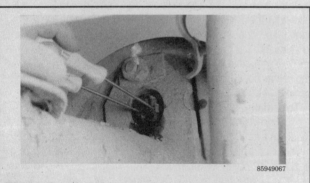

Fig. 65 If equipped, use 2 awls to free the round retainer from the cylinder

Fig. 66 Remove the necessary springs, then carefully spread the brake shoes for access

Fig. 67 A small prytool may be used to assist in freeing the wheel cylinder

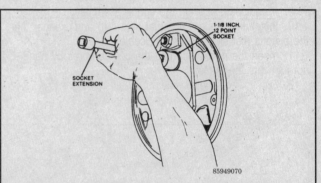

Fig. 68 Upon installation, a socket and extension should be used to seat the round retainer

makes sense with these components to substitute a new or reconditioned part instead of attempting an overhaul.

If no replacement is available, or you would prefer to overhaul your wheel cylinders, the following procedure may be used. When rebuilding and installing wheel cylinders, avoid getting any contaminants into the system. Always install clean, new high-quality brake fluid. If dirty or improper fluid has been used, it will be necessary to drain the entire system, flush the system with proper brake fluid, replace all rubber components, refill, and bleed the system.

➡The wheel cylinder may be equipped with links (often found on the bolted retainer type) or with pistons. The pistons may be identified by the round, flat ends with which they are equipped. Links found on wheel cylinders are often much thinner that the pistons and are equipped with a larger, notched end.

1. Remove the wheel cylinder from the vehicle.

2. For link type cylinders, remove the cylinder links, then remove the rubber boots from the cylinder ends with pliers. Discard the boots. Link type cylinders are equipped with inner pistons and cups.

3. For piston equipped cylinders, first remove and discard the old rubber boots, then withdraw the pistons. Piston cylinders are equipped with seals and a spring assembly all located behind the pistons in the cylinder bore.

4. Remove and discard remaining inner components (pistons, seals, cups and spring(s), as equipped). Compressed air may be useful in removing these components. If no compressed air is available, be VERY careful not to score the wheel cylinder bore when removing parts from it.

5. Wash the cylinder and metal parts in denatured alcohol or clean brake fluid.

✳✳CAUTION

Never use a mineral-based solvent such as gasoline, kerosene, or paint thinner for cleaning purposes. These solvents will swell rubber components and quickly deteriorate them.

6. Allow the parts to air dry or use compressed air. Do not use rags for cleaning since lint will remain in the cylinder bore.

7. Inspect the piston and replace it if it shows scratches.

8. Lubricate the cylinder bore and counterbore with clean brake fluid.

9. If equipped, position the spring assembly.

10. Install the rubber cups (flat side out) and/or inner then the pistons (flat side in), as applicable.

11. Insert the new boots into the counterbores by hand. Do not lubricate the boots.

12. For link equipped cylinders, install the links.

13. Install the wheel cylinder to the vehicle.

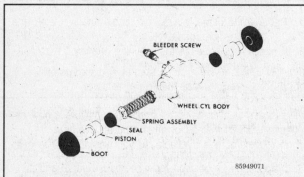

Fig. 69 Exploded view of a piston type wheel cylinder assembly

Fig. 70 If necessary, loosen and remove the bleeder screw from the wheel cylinder

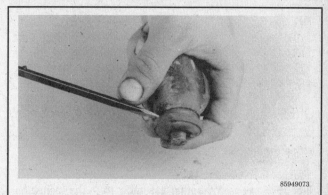

Fig. 71 For piston type cylinders, first pry free old boot

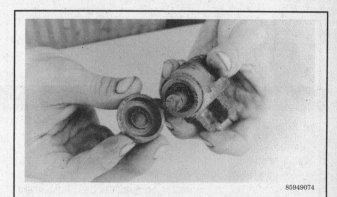

Fig. 72 Once removed, the boot should be discarded

Fig. 73 Remove the piston from the cylinder bore

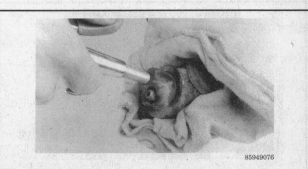

Fig. 74 With the bleeder screw installed, a small amount of compressed air may be used to free the inner components

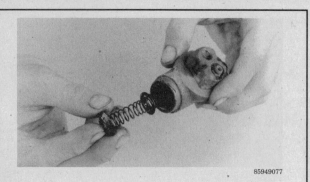

Fig. 75 Remove the spring assembly from the cylinder bore

85949077

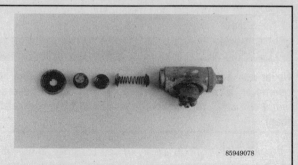

Fig. 76 Exploded view of the spring and end components from a piston cylinder (there is an additional seal, piston and boot on the other end)

85949078

Wheel Bearings

Refer to the Section 7 of this manual for service procedures relating to the rear axle shaft and bearings.

PARKING BRAKE

Most models are equipped with a foot operated ratchet type parking brake, though some may be equipped with a hand operated ratchet type. A cable or cable assembly connects this pedal to an equalizer which controls tension on the 2 rear cables which attach to the secondary brake shoes. Adjustment is made at the equalizer. If equipped, an intermediate cable connects the front cable with the equalizer.

Cables

REMOVAL & INSTALLATION

➡To avoid breaking or damaging the equalizer assembly, ALWAYS clean the exposed threads and lubricate the nuts using a spray penetrant oil before attempting to loosen the adjusting nut(s).

Front Cable
▶ See Figures 77 and 78

1. Raise the rear of the vehicle and support safely using jackstands. Support the vehicle at a height where access to the interior is still convenient, yet the equalizer and cable are still accessible from underneath the car.
2. Slacken the cable by removing the adjusting nut from the equalizer.
3. If equipped, remove the spring retainer clip from the bracket.
4. Remove the cable from the equalizer or from the intermediate cable connector, as applicable.
5. If applicable, remove the lower rear bolt from the wheelhouse panel, then pull the panel outward to gain access to the front cable.
6. If equipped, remove the upper console cover and lower console rear screws, then lift the rear of the lower console for access to the cable retainer at the hand lever.

7. Remove the cable retainer pin, cable retainer, then free the cable from the lever/pedal.
8. If necessary, squeeze the retaining tab using a pair of pliers, then free the cable from the vehicle.
   To install:
9. Place the cable into position and secure to the pedal/lever using the retainer. If equipped, make sure any retaining tabs are engaged.
10. If equipped, reposition the lower console and secure using the retaining screws, then install the upper console cover.
11. If applicable, reposition the wheelhouse panel and secure using the lower rear bolt.
12. Install the cable to the equalizer or from the intermediate cable connector, as applicable.
13. If equipped, install the spring retainer clip to the bracket.
14. Install the adjuster nut to the cable, then properly adjust the parking brake assembly.
15. Remove the jackstands and carefully lower the vehicle.

Intermediate Cable

Some vehicles may be equipped with an intermediate cable which connects the front cable to the equalizer.

1. Raise the rear of the vehicle and support safely using jackstands.
2. Slacken the cable by removing the adjusting nut from the equalizer.
3. Separate the intermediate cable ends from the front cable connector and from the equalizer, then remove the cable from the vehicle.
   To install:
4. Install the cable ends to the front cable connector and to the equalizer.
5. Install the equalizer adjusting nut, then properly adjust the parking brake cable.
6. Remove the supports and carefully lower the vehicle.

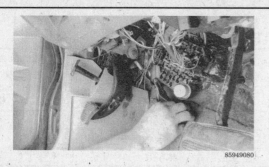

Fig. 77 If equipped, use a pair of pliers to squeeze the retaining tab so the cable may be released from the vehicle

Rear Cable

▶ See Figure 78

1. Raise the rear of the vehicle and support safely using jackstands.
2. Loosen the adjusting nut at the equalizer.
3. Disengage the rear cable at the connector.
4. Remove the wheel assembly and brake drum for access to the cable end.
5. Bend the retainer fingers or squeeze the retaining tab to free the cable from the backing plate.
6. Disengage the cable at the brake shoe operating lever.

To install:

7. Attach the cable to the brake shoe operating lever and make sure the retainer is properly seated on the backing plate.
8. Engage the rear cable at the connector.
9. Install the wheel assembly and brake drum.
10. Adjust the parking brake.
11. Remove the supports and carefully lower the vehicle.

Fig. 78 In some cases, the cable casing may be released from the backing plate by squeezing the retainer tab

ADJUSTMENT

➡To avoid breaking or damaging the equalizer assembly, ALWAYS clean the exposed threads and lubricate the nuts using a spray penetrant oil before attempting to loosen the adjusting nut(s).

▶ See Figures 79 and 80

1. Raise the rear of the vehicle and support safely using jackstands.
2. Apply the parking brake on three notches (ratchet clicks) from the fully released position.
3. Clean and lubricate the threads of the equalizer adjusting rod.

Fig. 79 Adjusting the equalizer may be performed using 2 open end wrenches or 1 wrench and 1 VERY deep socket

4. If equipped with a locknut, loosen the locknut in order to allow the adjusting nut to be turned.
5. Turn the adjuster nut as necessary until the right rear wheel can be just turned backwards using 2 hands, but cannot be turned forward.
6. Release the parking brake and make sure the rear wheels turn freely.
7. If equipped, tighten the locknut.
8. Remove the supports and carefully lower the vehicle.

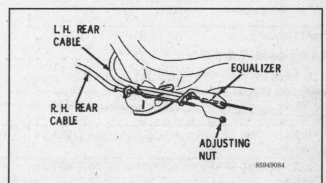

Fig. 80 Parking brake cable adjustment on late model vehicles

BRAKE SPECIFICATIONS

Year	Lug Nut Torque (ft. lbs.)	Master Cylinder Bore	Brake Disc		Brake Drum			Minimum Lining Thickness	
			Minimum Thickness	Maximum Run-Out	Diameter	Max. Machine O/S	Max. Wear Limit	Front	Rear
1964	80	1.0	NA	NA	9.5	9.560	9.590	2/32	2/32
②	80	0.875	NA	NA	9.5	9.560	9.590	2/32	2/32
1965	80	1.0	NA	NA	9.5	9.560	9.590	2/32	2/32
②	80	0.875	NA	NA	9.5	9.560	9.590	2/32	2/32
1966	80	1.125 (disc) 1.0 (drum)	NA	0.004	9.5	9.560	9.590	2/32	2/32
1967	80	1.125 (disc) 1.0 (drum)	NA	0.004	9.5	9.560	9.590	2/32	2/32
1968	80	1.125 (disc) 1.0 (drum)	NA	0.004	9.5	9.560	9.590	2/32	2/32
1969	80	1.0	NA	0.004	9.5	9.560	9.590	2/32	2/32
1970	80	1.125	0.980	0.002	9.5①	9.560	9.590	2/32	2/32
1971	80	1.125	0.980	0.002	9.5①	9.560	9.590	2/32	2/32
1972	80	1.125	0.980	0.002	9.5①	9.560	9.590	2/32	2/32
1973	80	1.125	0.980	0.002	9.5①	9.560	9.590	2/32	2/32
1974	80	1.125	0.980	0.002	9.5①	9.560	9.590	2/32	2/32
1975	80	1.125	0.980	0.002	9.5①	9.560	9.590	2/32	2/32
1976	80	1.125	0.980	0.002	9.5①	9.560	9.590	2/32	2/32
1977	80	1.125	0.980	0.002	9.5①	9.560	9.590	2/32	2/32
1978	80	1.125 (power) 0.9375 (manual)	0.980	0.002	9.5	9.560	9.590	2/32	2/32
1979	80	1.125 (power) 0.9375 (manual)	0.980	0.002	9.5	9.560	9.590	2/32	2/32
1980	80	1.125 (power) 0.9375 (manual)	0.980	0.002	9.5	9.560	9.590	2/32	2/32
1981	80	1.125 (power) 0.9375 (manual)	0.980	0.002	9.5	9.560	9.590	2/32	2/32
1982	80	1.125 (power) 0.9375 (manual)	0.980	0.002	9.5	9.560	9.590	2/32	2/32
1983	80	1.125 (power) 0.9375 (manual)	0.980	0.002	9.5	9.560	9.590	2/32	2/32
1984	80	1.125③	0.980	0.004	9.5 11.0	9.560 11.060	9.590 11.090	2/32	2/32
1985	80	1.125③	0.980	0.004	9.5 11.0	9.560 11.060	9.590 11.090	2/32	2/32
1986	80	1.125③	0.980	0.004	9.5 11.0	9.560 11.060	9.590 11.090	2/32	2/32
1987	80	1.125③	0.980	0.004	9.5 11.0	9.560 11.060	9.590 11.090	2/32	2/32
1988	80	1.125③	0.980	0.004	9.5 11.0	9.560 11.060	9.590 11.090	2/32	2/32

NOTE: Minimum lining thickness is as recommended by the manufacturer. Because of variations in state inspection regulations, the minimum allowable thickness may be different than recommended by the manufacturer.

NA—Not available
① 11.0 inches for 1973–75 station wagons
② Metallic Linings
③ 1985: Hydraboots—1 1/16 in.
    Quicktakeup—15/16 in.
    1986–88: 15/16 (0.937) in.

10

BODY
AND
TRIM

EXTERIOR

Doors

REMOVAL & INSTALLATION

When removing the door, it is easier to remove the hinges because the hinge-to-body retainers are usually more accessible than the hinge-to-door attachment.

1. If equipped with power door accessories, disconnect the negative battery cable.

2. Matchmark the position of the door hinges to the body. This should be done to make the installation easier and assure proper adjustment of the doors during installation.

3. If equipped with power operated components, remove the trim panel and detach the inner panel water deflector sufficiently to disconnect the wiring harness from the components. Separate and remove the rubber conduit and the wiring harness from the door.

4. With the aid of an assistant (to support the door), remove the upper and lower hinge-to-body bolts, then carefully remove the door from the vehicle.

To install:

5. With the help of an assistant to lift and support the door, position the door to the vehicle and loosely install the hinge-to-body bolts.

6. Align the matchmarks made earlier to assure proper door adjustment, then have the assistant hold the door in that position while you tighten the retaining bolts to 15-21 ft. lbs. (20-28 Nm).

7. If equipped, install the rubber conduit and wiring harness to the door, then connect the harness to the power components. Secure the inner panel water deflector, then install the trim panel.

8. Carefully close the door and verify proper adjustment. If necessary, readjust the door for proper operation.

9. If applicable, connect the negative battery cable.

ADJUSTMENT

▶ **See Figures 1 and 2**

The door adjustments are made possible through the use of floating anchor plates in the door and the body hinge pillars.

1. Remove the door lock striker from the body and allow the door to hang freely on it's hinges.

2. Using the Door Hinge tool No. J-28500, or equivalent, loosen the door hinge-to-body pillar bolts.

3. Using the body hinge pillar attachments, adjust the door up/down and fore/aft.

➡ **If a rearward adjustment is made, it may be necessary to replace the jamb switch.**

4. At the door hinge pillar attachments, adjust the door in and out.

5. After adjusting the door, torque the door hinge-to-body pillar to 15-21 ft. lbs. (20-28 Nm).

6. Align and install the door lock striker.

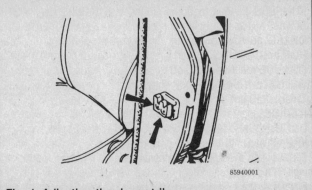

Fig. 1 Adjusting the door striker

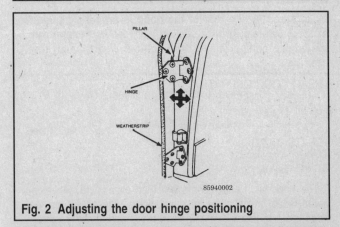

Fig. 2 Adjusting the door hinge positioning

Hood

REMOVAL & INSTALLATION

1. Using a scratch awl or permanent marker, scribe the hinge-to-hood alignment in order to assure proper reinstallation.

2. Using an assistant (to help support the hood), remove the hinge-to-hood bolts. Make sure the hood does not slide down and contact the cowl or windshield as the last bolts are removed.

3. Carefully lift the hood and remove it from the vehicle.

To install:

4. With the aid of the assistant, carefully lift the hood and position it over the hinges, then hold it as you loosely install the retaining bolts in order to keep the hood from sliding into the cowl.

5. Align the hood and hinges using the matchmarks made earlier, then tighten the retaining bolts.

6. Check the hood alignment with the hood latch.

ALIGNMENT

➡ **When aligning the hood and the latch, align the hinge first, then adjust the latch and striker.**

Hinge

▶ **See Figure 3**

The hinge-to-hood mount is slotted to provide forward and rearward adjustment, while the hood hinge-to-body mount is slotted to provide upward and downward movement at the rear of the hood. Additional rearward height adjustment is usually achieved through the use of stop screws. Adjust the hood so that it is flush with the body sheet metal. Once this is accomplished, the latch and striker may be adjusted to provide proper engagement and securing of the hood when closed.

1. Using a scratch awl or permanent marker, scribe the hinge outline onto the hood or body as a reference point.

2. Loosen the appropriate screws and shift the hood or hinge into proper alignment with the vehicle's sheet metal.

❊❊CAUTION

Make sure that the rear of the hood is properly positioned at the cowl seal; proper sealing will restrict fumes (from the engine compartment) from being pulled through the cowl vent.

3. After adjustment, tighten the retainers to secure the hood and hinge adjustment.

4. Check and adjust the latch and striker, as necessary.

Latch and Striker

▶ **See Figures 4, 5 and 6**

The hood latch assembly is mounted on a plate with elongated holes, which allow for adjustments. The striker (on the hood) adjusts laterally to align with the hood latch assembly. Forward height adjustment is achieved through the stop screws. Stop screws may be mounted at the rear of the hood as well.

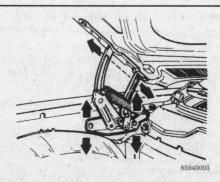

Fig. 3 Hood positioning and rear height adjustments are possible at the hinges

Fig. 4 The base of the hood lock can be repositioned slightly for more positive lock engagement

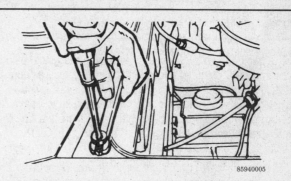

Fig. 5 The hood pin can be adjusted for proper lock engagement

Fig. 6 The hood is adjusted vertically using stop screws at the front, and sometimes at the rear of the hood

Trunk Lid

REMOVAL & INSTALLATION

▶ **See Figure 7**

The trunk lid hinge is usually welded to the body and then bolted to the lid.

1. Open the trunk lid and place protective coverings over the rear fenders (to protect the paint from damage).

2. Mark the location of the hinge-to-trunk lid bolts to ease installation.

3. If equipped, disengage the electrical connections and wiring from the lid.

4. With the help of an assistant (to support the lid), remove the hinge-to-lid bolts, then carefully lift the lid from the vehicle.

To install:

5. With the aid of the assistant, carefully lift the lid and position it on the hinges, then loosely install the retaining bolts to hold it on the hinges.

6. Align the lid and hinges using the matchmarks made earlier, then tighten the retaining bolts.

7. If equipped, engage the electrical connectors and wiring to the lid.

8. Check and adjust the position of the trunk lid to the body, as necessary.

ALIGNMENT

The trunk lid can be aligned by loosening the hinge-to-lid bolts and shifting the lid into position. Only a small amount of adjustment is usually possible with the trunk lid. If greater adjustment is necessary, the bolt holes in the lid will have to be elongated. Before attempting this, verify there are no other repairable causes of misalignment. Trunk lid alignment problems are often the result of other rear body parts being misaligned, possibly from an old accident.

➡**When adjusting the hinge/latch-to-body positions, be sure to use alignment marks as reference points.**

Tailgate

REMOVAL & INSTALLATION

El Camino
▶ **See Figure 8**

1. Open the tailgate and support it in the open position.

2. Remove the support cable bolts and disengage the cable from the tailgate.

3. Using a scratch awl or permanent marker, matchmark the hinge out line onto the panel.

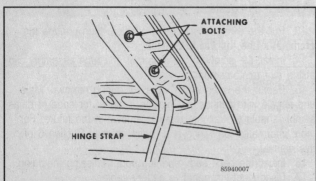

ATTACHING BOLTS

HINGE STRAP

85940007

Fig. 7 The trunk lid is usually attached to the hinges using retaining bolts

4. With the aid of an assistant (to support the tailgate), remove the tailgate hinge-to-body bolts, then carefully remove the the tailgate from the vehicle.

To install:

5. With the aid of the assistant, carefully lift the tailgate and position it to the body, then loosely install the retaining bolts to hold it in position.

6. Align the matchmarks made earlier, then tighten the hinge-to-body bolts to 14-22 ft. lbs. (19-30 Nm).

7. Install the support cable and secure using the retaining bolts.

8. Check and assure proper tailgate operation, if necessary, loosen the bolts and adjust the tailgate for a better fit.

1964-72 Station Wagon

1. Partially open the tailgate to achieve a neutral torque rod position or until tension on the torque rod has been relieved.

2. With the tension relieved remove the torque rod assist link retainer-to-body attaching bolts.

3. Support the tailgate in the full open position and remove the support cable-to-left upper hinge and striker assembly attaching bolt.

4. On styles equipped with electrical options in the tailgate, remove the inner panel water deflector and access hole cover. Disconnect the wiring harness connectors and pull the wiring from the tailgate.

5. With the aid of a helper, remove the left lower hinge-to-body attaching bolts.

6. Using a suitable tool, manually lock the right and left upper locks. Push the arm down and in to lock the left side and rotate the lock forward to second click to lock the right lock.

7. With the aid of a helper support the tailgate, actuate the inside door remote handle (right side) to unlock and free the right lower lock from the striker assembly. Remove the tailgate by lifting upward then rearward.

To install:

8. With the aid of a helper install the tailgate to the vehicle by lowering it into position.

9. Position the tailgate assembly so the hinge bolts may be installed. It may be necessary to temporarily actuate or release the left and right locks, as applicable, to position the tailgate.

10. Install the lower hinge-to-body attaching bolts.

11. On styles equipped with electrical options in the tailgate, install the wiring harness to the tailgate, then engage the connectors. Install the access hole cover and the inner panel water deflector.

12. Support the tailgate in the full open position and install the support cable-to-left upper hinge and striker assembly attaching bolt.

13. With the tension relieved install the torque rod assist link retainer-to-body attaching bolts.

14. Check for proper tailgate operation and adjust the hinges or supports, as necessary.

1973-77 Station Wagon
▶ **See Figures 9 and 10**

1. Disconnect the negative battery cable.

2. Remove the back body opening upper finishing moulding.

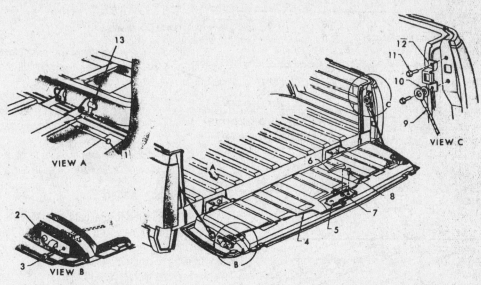

1. Pin
2. Latch assembly
3. Screw (latch assembly)
4. Rod–tailgate remote control to lock
5. Control assembly–tailgate lock remote
6. Handle tailgate lock remote
7. Spindle–remote control
8. Screw–remote control attaching
9. Cable–tailgate support
10. Washer–spacer
11. Screw–striker retainer
12. Striker–tailgate lock
13. Strap–tailgate hinge–gate side

85940008

Fig. 8 Tail gate assembly components — El Camino

3. Peel the tape from the tailgate harness between the bendover tabs and cut the wire(s) that lead into the tailgate.

➡**The number of wires may vary according to power options.**

4. Remove the screw from the grommet and tube assembly clip at the roof reinforcement.

5. Disengage the grommet from the roof reinforcement and pull the harness remaining through the hole and tape to the inner surface of the tailgate.

6. Place a protective covering between the upper edge of the tailgate and the roof panel.

✳✳WARNING

Do not attempt to remove or loosen the counterbalance support assembly (piston support) attaching nuts with the tailgate in any other position except fully open as personal injury may result.

7. With the aid of a helper, remove both gate-side counterbalance support assembly attaching nuts, disengage from the gate and allow the support to rest against the base of the back body opening.

8. Use a 3/16 in. diameter rod, 18 in. long to remove the hinge pins from the hinge. Place the end of the rod against the pointed end of the hinge pin; then, strike the rod firmly to shear the retaining clip tabs and drive the pin through the hinge. Repeat again on the opposite side hinge and remove the tailgate from the body.

To install:

9. Position new retaining rings onto the notches provided in the hinge pins. Position the rings so that the tabs point toward the head of the pin.

10. Place a protective covering between the upper edge of the tailgate and the roof panel.

11. With the aid of a helper, mate the tailgate hinge with the body side hinge and install the hinge pins with the pointed end of the pin facing outboard.

12. With the tailgate held fully open, position the counterbalance support assembly onto the gate side mounting stud and torque a new retaining nut to 14-22 ft. lbs. (19-30 Nm). Repeat for the opposite side.

➡**Replace with new nuts, Part No. 9664875 or equivalent. If not available use old nuts and apply a retaining adhesive such as Loctite®.**

13. Pull the wiring harness into position, then engage the grommet to the roof reinforcement.

14. Install the screw to the grommet and tube assembly clip at the roof reinforcement.

15. Repair the wires which were cut during removal. Male and female wire connectors may be installed for ease of disassembly should the tailgate require removal in the future. For more information on wiring and repair, refer to Section 6 of this manual.

16. Install the back body opening upper finishing moulding.

17. Disconnect the negative battery cable.

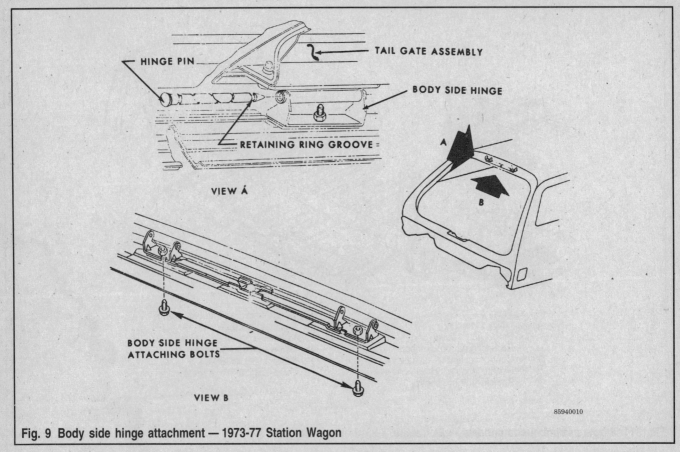

Fig. 9 Body side hinge attachment — 1973-77 Station Wagon

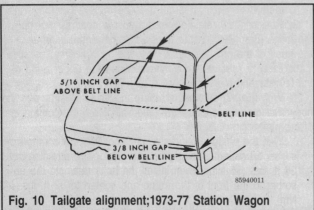

Fig. 10 Tailgate alignment;1973-77 Station Wagon

1978-83

▶ See Figure 11

1. Partially open the tailgate to achieve a neutral torque rod position or until tension on the torque rod has been relieved.

2. Mark the position of the torque rod assist link on the back body pillar and remove the assist link.

3. Use a ³/₁₆ in. diameter rod, 12 in. long to remove the hinge pins from the hinge. Place the end of the rod against the pointed end of the hinge pin; then, strike the rod firmly to

shear the retaining clip tabs and drive the pin through the hinge. Repeat again on the opposite side hinge and remove the tailgate from the body. Note the direction which the pins are facing for installation purposes.

To install:

4. Position new retaining rings onto the notches provided in the pins. Make sure the rings are positioned so the tabs point toward the head of the pin.

5. With the aid of a helper, mate the tailgate hinge with the body hinge and install the pins with the pointed end of the pins facing the directions noted during removal.

6. Align the marks made earlier, then install and secure the torque rod assist link on the back body pillar.

7. Check for proper alignment and tailgate operation.

ALIGNMENT

The tailgate can be aligned slightly by loosening the hinge and/or the latch bolts, then adjusting them. The bottom of the tailgate on 1978-83 models can be adjusted in or out by adding or removing shims between the hinge and body.

➡When adjusting the hinge/latch-to-body positions, be sure to use alignment marks as reference points.

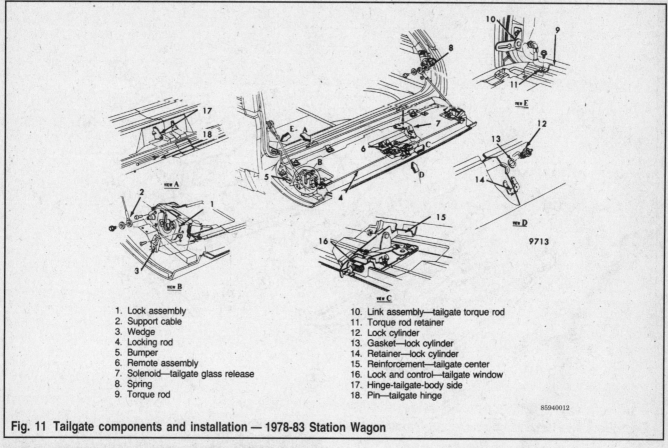

1. Lock assembly
2. Support cable
3. Wedge
4. Locking rod
5. Bumper
6. Remote assembly
7. Solenoid—tailgate glass release
8. Spring
9. Torque rod
10. Link assembly—tailgate torque rod
11. Torque rod retainer
12. Lock cylinder
13. Gasket—lock cylinder
14. Retainer—lock cylinder
15. Reinforcement—tailgate center
16. Lock and control—tailgate window
17. Hinge-tailgate-body side
18. Pin—tailgate hinge

85940012

Fig. 11 Tailgate components and installation — 1978-83 Station Wagon

Bumpers

REMOVAL & INSTALLATION

Front

EXCEPT 1981-88 MONTE CARLO

▶ **See Figures 12, 13 and 14**

1. Raise and support the end of the vehicle safely using jackstands.

2. Support the bumper using a jack, jackstands or a strong friend.

3. On early the models without the energy absorbers, remove the bolts from the frame, then carefully lower the bumper from the vehicle.

4. On later models equipped with energy absorbers, remove the bolts from the reinforcement to the energy absorber (each side), then carefully lower the bumper assembly. If necessary, disassemble the bumper and/or the energy absorber:

   a. Remove the bolts attaching the bumper reinforcement assembly to the bumper face bar and separate the reinforcement from the filler panel.

   b. If equipped with protective strips and bumper guards, remove the bolts and nuts attaching the guards and remove from the bumper. Remove the remaining nuts and squeeze push-in clips with pliers to remove the protective strip from the face bar.

   c. If the energy absorber is to be removed, remove the bolts connecting the front of the energy absorber to the frame. Remove the rear nut from the energy absorber L-bracket where it attaches to the energy absorber and slide forward to remove.

To install:

5. If the energy absorber was removed or the bumper disassembled on later model vehicles, prepare the components for bumper installation:

   a. If the energy absorber was removed, position the absorber L-bracket to the frame and tighten the retaining nut to 26 ft. lbs. (35 Nm). Then install the bolts retaining the absorber to the front of the frame and tighten to 32 ft. lbs. (43 Nm).

   b. If removed, install the protective strip to the face bar using the retaining nuts and push-in clips, then install the guards and secure using the retaining bolts.

   c. Install the bumper reinforcement assembly to the filler panel and secure using the retaining bolts.

6. With the aid of a friend, position the bumper to the vehicle and support in position while the retaining bolts are threaded. Tighten the bolts and remove the support.

7. Remove the jackstands and carefully lower the vehicle.

1981-88 MONTE CARLO

▶ **See Figure 15**

1. Remove the headlamp bezels by removing the bolts from each bezel.

2. Raise and support the end of the vehicle safely using jackstands.

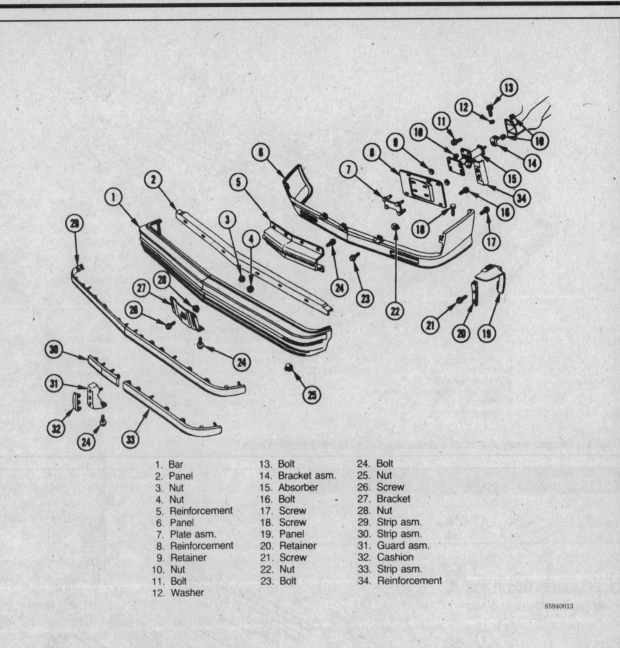

1. Bar	13. Bolt	24. Bolt
2. Panel	14. Bracket asm.	25. Nut
3. Nut	15. Absorber	26. Screw
4. Nut	16. Bolt	27. Bracket
5. Reinforcement	17. Screw	28. Nut
6. Panel	18. Screw	29. Strip asm.
7. Plate asm.	19. Panel	30. Strip asm.
8. Reinforcement	20. Retainer	31. Guard asm.
9. Retainer	21. Screw	32. Cashion
10. Nut	22. Nut	33. Strip asm.
11. Bolt	23. Bolt	34. Reinforcement
12. Washer		

85940013

Fig. 12 Exploded view of a common front bumper assembly — 1978-83 Malibu and El Camino

3. Remove the bolts (usually 10 of them) from the bumper cover to the header and fenders.

4. Disconnect the parking light sockets and remove the screws at either housing, then remove the parking lamp housings.

5. Support the bumper and remove the nuts from the frame bracket, then remove the bumper assembly.

6. Disassemble the bumper, as necessary.

To install:

7. If necessary, assemble the bumper to prepare it for installation.

8. Install and support the bumper assembly, then secure using the retaining nuts at the frame bracket.

9. Install the parking lamp housing, then install the screws and connect the parking light sockets.

10. Secure the bumper cover to the header and fenders using the retaining bolts.

11. Remove the jackstands and carefully lower the vehicle.

12. Install the headlamp bezels and secure using the bolts.

Rear

▶ **See Figures 16 and 17**

Removal and installation of the rear bumper is similar to the front bumper on most vehicles covered by this manual. Please refer to front bumper procedures found earlier in this section.

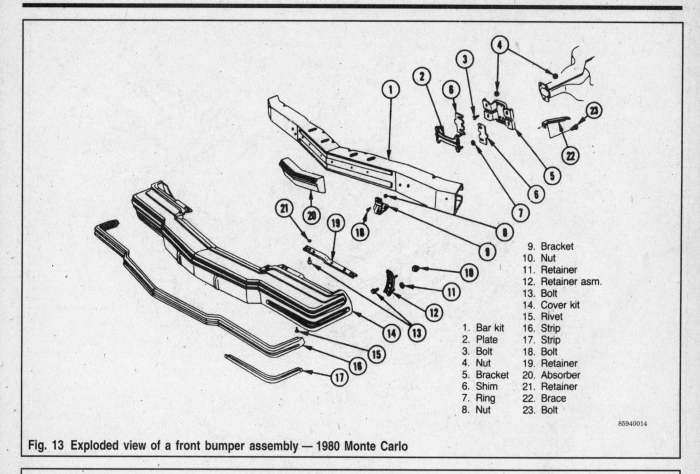

9. Bracket
10. Nut
11. Retainer
12. Retainer asm.
13. Bolt
14. Cover kit
15. Rivet
1. Bar kit   16. Strip
2. Plate   17. Strip
3. Bolt   18. Bolt
4. Nut   19. Retainer
5. Bracket   20. Absorber
6. Shim   21. Retainer
7. Ring   22. Brace
8. Nut   23. Bolt

85940014

Fig. 13 Exploded view of a front bumper assembly — 1980 Monte Carlo

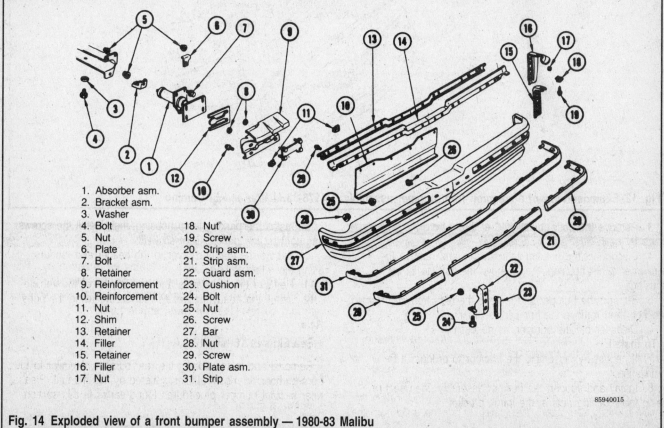

1. Absorber asm.
2. Bracket asm.
3. Washer
4. Bolt   18. Nut
5. Nut   19. Screw
6. Plate   20. Strip asm.
7. Bolt   21. Strip asm.
8. Retainer   22. Guard asm.
9. Reinforcement 23. Cushion
10. Reinforcement 24. Bolt
11. Nut   25. Nut
12. Shim   26. Screw
13. Retainer   27. Bar
14. Filler   28. Nut
15. Retainer   29. Screw
16. Filler   30. Plate asm.
17. Nut   31. Strip

85940015

Fig. 14 Exploded view of a front bumper assembly — 1980-83 Malibu

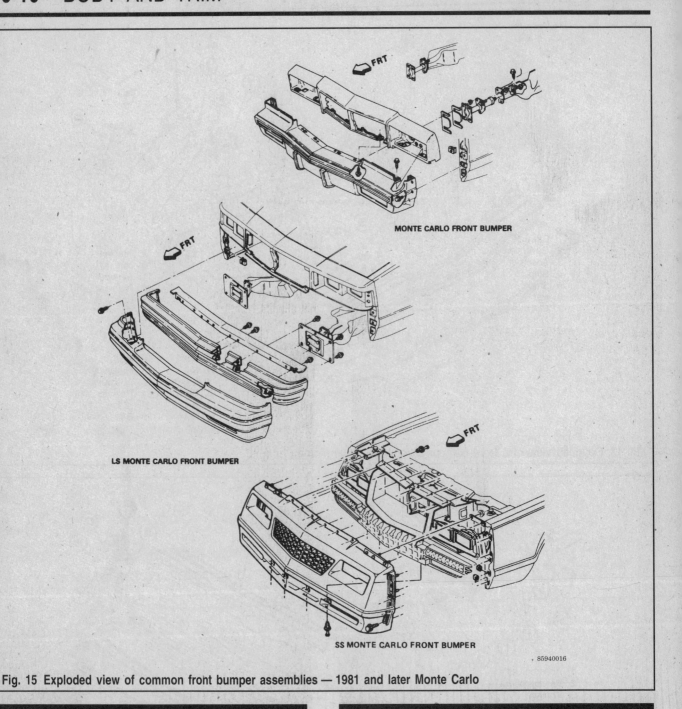

MONTE CARLO FRONT BUMPER

LS MONTE CARLO FRONT BUMPER

SS MONTE CARLO FRONT BUMPER

85940016

Fig. 15 Exploded view of common front bumper assemblies — 1981 and later Monte Carlo

Grille

REMOVAL & INSTALLATION

▶ See Figure 18

The radiator grilles on most models are attached with sheet metal screws to the header panel. The header panel is the painted panel below the hood that surrounds the grille and sometimes the headlights and is attached to the radiator support. To remove the grille, remove the screws which retain the grille to the header panel, then carefully pull the grille from the vehicle.

Outside Mirrors

➡A damaged mirror glass face may be replaced by placing a large piece or multiple strips of tape over the glass then breaking the mirror face. Adhesive back mirror faces should be available for most applications.

REMOVAL & INSTALLATION

▶ See Figures 19, 20, 21 and 22

Standard Mirror

1. Remove the door trim panel. Refer to the procedures later in this section for more information.

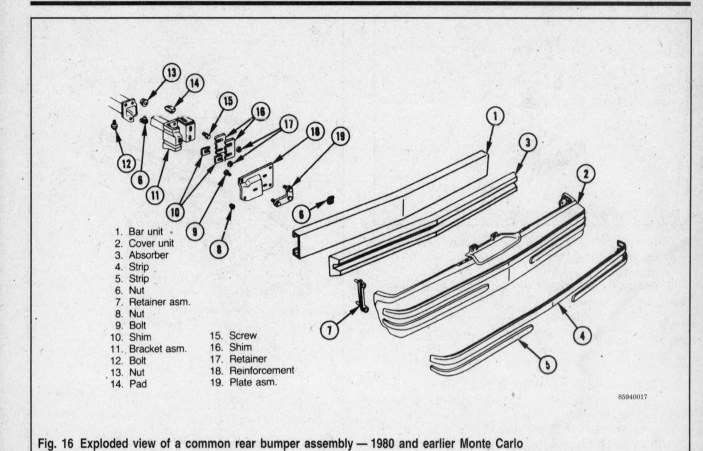

1. Bar unit
2. Cover unit
3. Absorber
4. Strip
5. Strip
6. Nut
7. Retainer asm.
8. Nut
9. Bolt
10. Shim
11. Bracket asm.
12. Bolt
13. Nut
14. Pad
15. Screw
16. Shim
17. Retainer
18. Reinforcement
19. Plate asm.

Fig. 16 Exploded view of a common rear bumper assembly — 1980 and earlier Monte Carlo

1. Reinforcement
2. Nut
3. Bar
4. Nut
5. Bolt
6. Strip asm.
7. Guard asm.
8. Cushion
9. Bolt
10. Strip asm.
11. Strip asm.
12. Plate asm.
13. Bracket
14. Shim
15. Absorber
16. Bracket asm.
17. Washer
18. Bolt
19. Nut
20. Bolt
21. Retainer
22. Bolt
23. Nut
24. Nut

Fig. 17 Exploded view of the rear bumper assembly — 1980 and later Station Wagon and El Camino

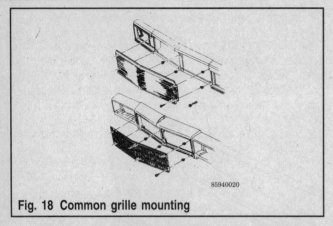

85940020

Fig. 18 Common grille mounting

2. Remove the mirror base-to-door outer panel stud nuts, then remove the mirror from the door.

To install:

3. Position the base gasket, then install the mirror and secure using the retainers.

4. Install the door trim panel.

Manual Remote Mirror

LEFT SIDE

1. Remove the door trim panel and detach the remote control lever. Peel back the insulator and water deflector to gain access to the mirror cable.

2. Detach the cable from any retaining tabs in the door.

3. Remove the attaching nuts, then remove the mirror and cable assembly from the door.

To install:

4. Position the base gasket, then install the mirror and secure using the retainers.

5. Install the cable to any retaining tabs located in the door.

6. Attach the remote control lever, then reposition the insulator and water deflector. Install the door trim panel.

RIGHT SIDE

1. Remove the door trim panel and detach the remote control lever. Peel back the insulator and water deflector to gain access to the mirror cable.

2. On styles with the instrument panel mounted control, remove the set screw from from the control knob.

3. Remove the shroud side finishing panel as follows:

a. Remove the sill plate screws and sill plate.

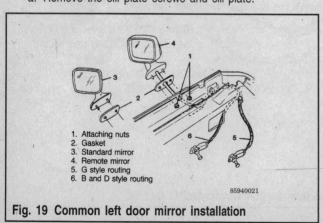

1. Attaching nuts
2. Gasket
3. Standard mirror
4. Remote mirror
5. G style routing
6. B and D style routing

85940021

Fig. 19 Common left door mirror installation

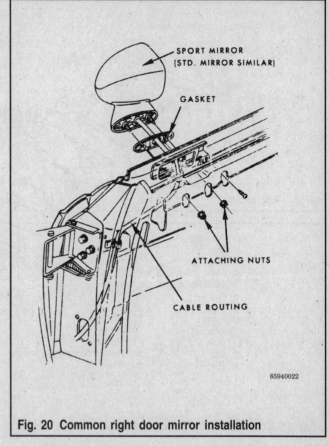

SPORT MIRROR
(STD. MIRROR SIMILAR)

GASKET

ATTACHING NUTS

CABLE ROUTING

85940022

Fig. 20 Common right door mirror installation

b. If equipped, remove the litter container.

c. Remove the screw retaining the hinge pillar pinch-weld upper finishing lace.

d. Grasp the shroud finishing panel at the forward edge toward the dash panel and pull inward to disengage the plastic retaining clip, and slide the panel rearward.

4. Feed the remote cable through the shroud and rubber conduit between the door and pillar, then detach the cable from any retaining tabs in the door.

5. Remove the attaching nuts, then remove the mirror and cable assembly from the door.

To install:

6. Position the base gasket, then install the mirror and secure using the retainers.

7. Feed the remote cable through the shroud and rubber conduit between the door and pillar, making sure it is secured in any door retaining tabs.

8. Install the shroud side finishing panel:

a. Slide the panel into position and engage the plastic retaining clip.

b. Install the screw retaining the hinge pillar pinch-weld upper finishing lace.

c. If equipped, install the litter container.

d. Install the sill plate and secure using the retaining screws.

9. On styles with the instrument panel mounted control, install the set screw to the control knob.

10. Attach the remote control lever, then verify that the mirror is operating properly. Reposition the insulator and water deflector, then install the door trim panel.

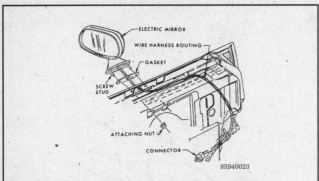

Fig. 21 Common installation of a power operated mirror — left shown

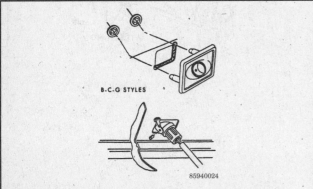

Fig. 22 The remote mirror cable and escutcheon

Power Operated Mirror

RIGHT AND LEFT

1. Remove the door trim panel and disconnect the wire harness at the connector. Peel back the insulator pad and water deflector enough to gain access to the wire harness.

2. Detach the harness from any retaining tabs in the door.

3. Remove the attaching nuts and remove the mirror and harness assembly from the door.

To install:

4. Position the mirror and harness assembly to the door, then secure using the attaching nuts.

5. Install the harness to any retaining tabs present in the door.

6. Engage the wire harness connector, then verify proper mirror operation.

7. Reposition the insulator and water deflector, then install the door trim panel.

Antenna

REMOVAL & INSTALLATION

Manual

1. Unscrew the mast from the top of the fender.

2. Unscrew the nut and the bezel from the top of the fender.

3. On later models it may be necessary to remove a bolt/screw which retains the base of the antenna under the fender. This bolt/screw is accessible under the hood.

4. Disconnect the antenna lead from the antenna. On some later models the antenna lead may even plug into another lead under the hood.

5. Reach under the fender and remove the antenna base.

To install:

6. Install the antenna base by reaching under the fender.

7. Connect the antenna lead.

8. On later models so equipped, install the bolt/screw retaining the base of the antenna under the fender.

9. Install and tighten the nut and bezel to the top of the fender.

➡When installing the antenna to the fender make sure the retaining nut is tight. A loose antenna or one that does not make good contact at the fender can cause radio interference.

10. Thread the mast to the top of the fender.

Power

▶ **See Figures 23 and 24**

1. Lower the antenna by turning the radio and the ignition **OFF**.

➡If the mast has failed in the UP position, and the mast or entire assembly is being replaced, the mast may be cut off to facilitate removal.

2. Disconnect the negative battery cable.

3. Remove the fender skirt attaching screws except those to the battery tray and radiator support.

➡On some models there is an access plate which may reduce the amount of fender skirt bolts that have to be removed.

4. Pull down on the rear edge of the skirt and block with a 2 in. x 4 in. block of wood.

5. Remove the motor bracket attaching screws, then remove the motor.

To install:

➡Be sure the mast is in the fully retracted position before installation. If necessary, the wiring may be temporarily connected in order to retract the mast.

6. Install the motor and secure using the attaching screws.

7. Remove the block of wood and reposition and secure the fender skirt.

8. If equipped, install and secure the access panel.

9. Connect the negative battery cable.

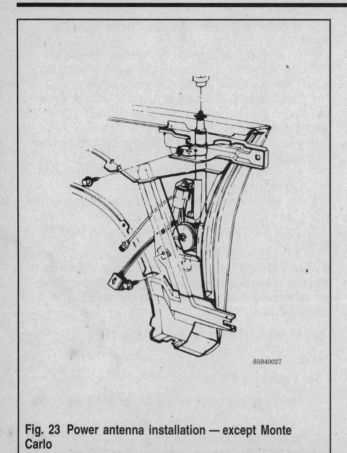

Fig. 23 Power antenna installation — except Monte Carlo

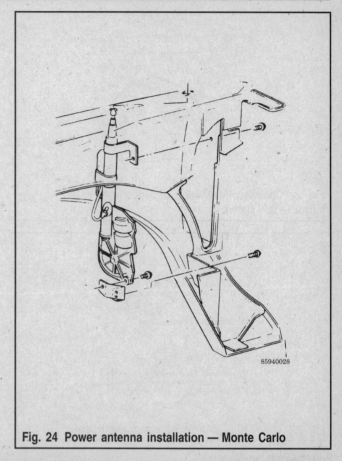

Fig. 24 Power antenna installation — Monte Carlo

INTERIOR

Instrument Panel and Pad

REMOVAL & INSTALLATION

▶ See Figure 25

1. Disconnect the negative battery cable.
2. Open the doors and check for retaining screws on the sides of the instrument panel. If present, remove the screws from the instrument panel sides.
3. If equipped, remove the screws attaching the instrument panel pad to the instrument panel.
4. Remove the defogger grilles and remove the screws located under the grilles and in the front of the panel pad.
5. If equipped, remove the instrument panel pad from the panel.
6. Remove the lower instrument panel trim pieces or sound insulators, as equipped and necessary.

➡When removing any plastic pieces of the dashboard assembly, remember never to force and break the pieces. If a corner or end of a component will not move freely, there is likely a screw or retainer that was missed and must be released before the piece can be removed without damage.

7. Remove the instrument cluster from the panel. For details, please refer to Section 6 of this manual.
8. Remove the steering column retaining nuts and carefully lower the column onto the driver's seat.
9. Remove any upper and lower instrument panel-to-cowl screws.
10. Disconnect and remove all electrical wiring from under the dash panel.
11. Make sure all retainers have been removed, then carefully remove the instrument panel assembly from the vehicle.
To install:
12. Install the instrument panel assembly.
13. Install the electrical wiring to the dash panel.
14. Install any upper and lower instrument panel-to-cowl screws.
15. Carefully raise the column into position and secure using the retaining nuts.
16. Install the instrument cluster assembly.
17. Install the instrument panel sound insulators or lower trim pieces which were removed.
18. If equipped, install the instrument panel pad.
19. Install the defogger grilles.
20. If equipped, install the screws attaching the instrument panel pad to the instrument panel.
21. Install the screws at either side of the instrument panel assembly.
22. Connect the negative battery cable.

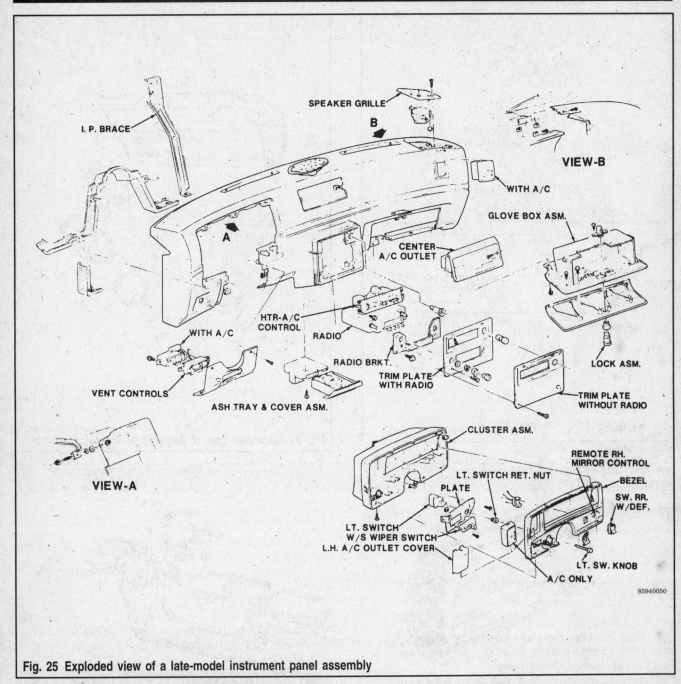

Fig. 25 Exploded view of a late-model instrument panel assembly

Front Door Panels

REMOVAL & INSTALLATION

▶ **See Figures 26, 27, 28, 29, 30 and 31**

1. Remove the door handles and the locking knob from the inside of the doors.

➡**If equipped with screw retained door pull handles, remove the screws through the handle into the door inner panel.**

2. If equipped with remote control mirrors, remove the remote mirror escutcheon, then disengage the end of the mirror control cable from the escutcheon.

3. If equipped with a switch cover plate in the door armrest, remove the cover plate screws, then disconnect the switches and the cigar lighter (if equipped) from the electrical harness.

4. If equipped with an integral armrest, remove the screws inserted through the pull cup into the armrest hanger support. If equipped with an armrest applied after the door trim installation, remove the armrest-to-inner panel screws.

5. If equipped with two-piece trim panels, disengage the retainer clips from the front and the rear of the upper trim panel, using tool No. BT-7323A, then lift the upper door trim

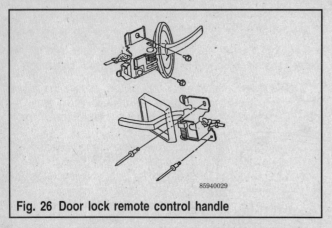

Fig. 26 Door lock remote control handle

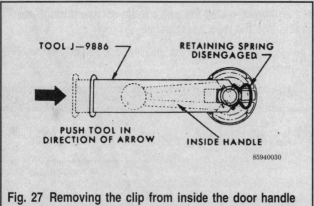

Fig. 27 Removing the clip from inside the door handle

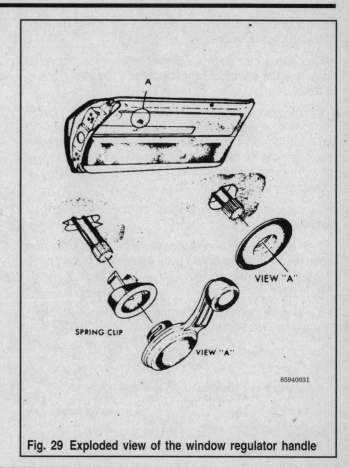

Fig. 29 Exploded view of the window regulator handle

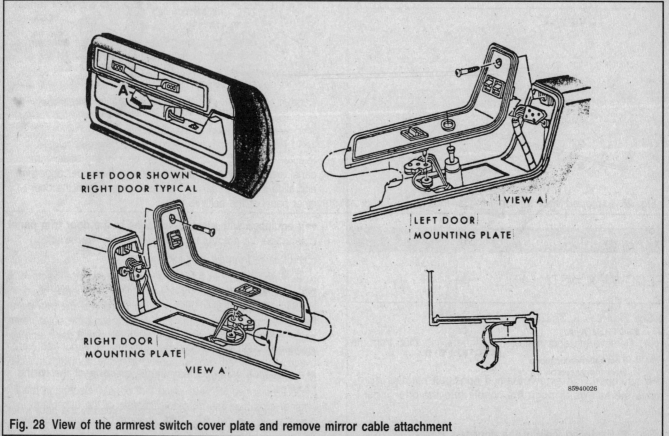

Fig. 28 View of the armrest switch cover plate and remove mirror cable attachment

and slide it slightly rearward to disengage it from the door inner panel at the beltline.

➡**If equipped with electric switches in the door trim panel, disengage the electrical connectors from the switch assembly.**

6. Along the upper edge of the lower trim panel, remove the mounting screws. At the lower edge of the panel, insert tool No. BT-7323A between the inner panel and the trim panel, then disengage the retaining clips from around the outer perimeter. To remove the lower panel, push the panel down and outward to disengage it from the door.

➡**If equipped with courtesy lights, disconnect the wiring harness.**

7. If equipped with an insulator pad glued to the door inner panel, remove the pad (with a putty knife) by separating it from the inner panel.

To install:

➡**If replacing the inner pad to the door inner panel, use 3M General Trim Adhesive No. 8080, glue it to the panel.**

8. If removed, glue a new inner pad to the door inner panel.

➡**If equipped with courtesy lights, connect the wiring harness.**

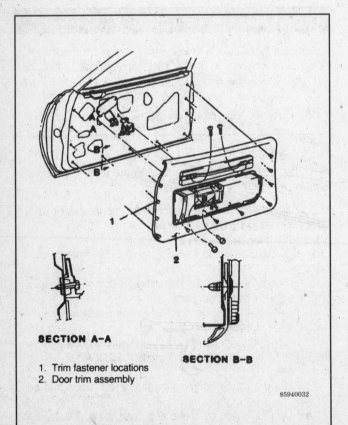

SECTION A–A

SECTION B–B

1. Trim fastener locations
2. Door trim assembly

85940032

Fig. 30 Exploded view of the door trim panel

9. Engage the retaining clips around the edge of the lower trim panel, then install mounting screws.

➡**If equipped with electric switches in the door trim panel, engage the electrical connectors to the switch assembly.**

10. If equipped with two-piece trim panels, engage the retainer clips to the front and the rear of the upper trim panel.

11. If equipped with an integral armrest, install the retaining screws.

12. If equipped with a switch cover plate in the door armrest, engage the switches and cigar lighter (if equipped) harness connectors, then install the cover plate and secure using the plate screws.

13. If equipped with remote control mirrors, engage the control cable, then install the remote mirror escutcheon.

➡**If equipped, install the pull handle screws through the handle into the door inner panel.**

14. Install the door handles and the locking knob to the inside of the doors.

Rear Door Panels

REMOVAL & INSTALLATION

1. Remove the door handles and the locking knob from the inside of the doors.

➡**If equipped with screw retained door pull handles, remove the screws through the handle into the door inner panel.**

2. If equipped with a switch cover plate in the door armrest, remove the cover plate screws, then disconnect the switch from the electrical harness.

3. If equipped with an integral armrest, remove the screws inserted through the pull cup into the armrest hanger support. If equipped with an armrest applied after the door trim installation, remove the armrest-to-inner panel screws.

4. If equipped with two-piece trim panels, disengage the retainer clips from the front and the rear of the upper trim panel, using tool No. BT-7323A, then lift the upper door trim and slide it slightly rearward to disengage it from the door inner panel at the beltline.

➡**If equipped with electric switches in the door trim panel, disengage the electrical connectors from the switch assembly.**

5. Along the upper edge of the lower trim panel, remove the mounting screws. At the lower edge of the panel, insert tool No. BT-7323A between the inner panel and the trim panel, then disengage the retaining clips from around the outer perimeter. To remove the lower panel, push the panel down and outward to disengage it from the door.

➡**If equipped with courtesy lights, disconnect the wiring harness.**

6. If equipped with an insulator pad glued to the door inner panel, remove the pad (with a putty knife) by separating it from the inner panel.

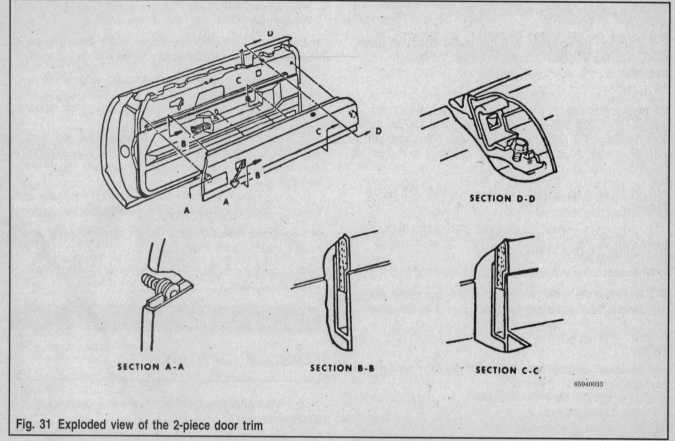

SECTION D-D

SECTION A-A

SECTION B-B

SECTION C-C

85940033

Fig. 31 Exploded view of the 2-piece door trim

To install:

➡If replacing the inner pad to the door inner panel, use 3M General Trim Adhesive No. 8080, glue it to the panel.

7. If removed, glue a new inner pad to the door inner panel.

➡If equipped with courtesy lights, connect the wiring harness.

8. Engage the retaining clips around the edge of the lower trim panel, then install mounting screws.

➡If equipped with electric switches in the door trim panel, engage the electrical connectors to the switch assembly.

9. If equipped with two-piece trim panels, engage the retainer clips to the front and the rear of the upper trim panel.

10. If equipped with an integral armrest, install the retaining screws.

11. If equipped with a switch cover plate in the door armrest, engage the switch harness connector, then install the cover plate and secure using the plate screws.

➡If equipped, install the pull handle screws through the handle into the door inner panel.

12. Install the door handles and the locking knob to the inside of the doors.

Door Locks

The door locks uses a fork bolt lock design which includes a safety interlock feature. The door is securely closed when the door lock fork bolt engages the striker bolt.

REMOVAL & INSTALLATION

▶ **See Figure 32**

➡NEVER attempt to make repairs to the lock assembly; replace it.

1. Remove the door trim, then detach the insulator pad (if equipped) and the inner panel water deflector sufficiently to access the door lock.

2. If working on the front doors, remove the inner panel cam.

3. If working on the rear doors, remove the stationary window and the ventilator assembly.

4. Disengage the inside handle and the power lock connecting rods (if equipped).

5. If equipped with power locks on the front door, remove the electric lock actuator by performing the following procedures;

    a. Using a center punch, drive the center pins out of pop rivets.

    b. Drill the heads off of the pop rivets using a ¼ in. drill bit.

c. Disengage the connecting rod, the electrical connector and the actuator through the access hole.

➡**On some models, it may be necessary to remove the inside handle, the lock and the connecting rod as a unit.**

6. Remove the lock-to-door screws and the lock through the access hole.
   To install:
7. Attach the spring clips to the lock assembly, then install the lock through the access hole and secure using the retaining screws. Tighten the door lock-to-door screws to 80-100 inch lbs. (9-11 Nm).

➡**If working on the front door of the sedan models, engage the lock cylinder-to-lock and the outside handle-to-lock connecting rods.**

8. If equipped with a remote lock button, engage the locking rod from the door lock(s).

➡**When attaching the power door lock actuator to the door, use ¼in. x ½ in. pop rivets or nuts/bolts.**

9. If equipped with power locks on the front door, install the electric lock actuator using pop rivets or retainers.
10. Engage the inside handle and the power lock connecting rods (if equipped).
11. If working on the rear doors, install the stationary window and the ventilator assembly.
12. If working on the front doors, install the inner panel cam.
13. Reposition the inner panel water deflector, then install the insulator pad (if equipped) and the door trim.

Front Door Glass

REMOVAL & INSTALLATION

◗ **See Figure 33**

Coupe

1. Remove the door panel. For more information, refer to the procedure earlier in this section.
2. Remove the armrest, the trim panel(s), the insulator pad (if equipped), and the inner panel water deflector.

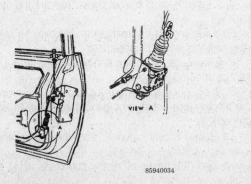

85940034

Fig. 32 View of the power door lock actuator

3. With the glass in the half raised position, mark the location of the mounting screws, then remove the following components:
   a. The front belt stabilizer and trim retainer.
   b. The rear belt stabilizer pin assembly.
   c. The front up-travel stop (on the inner panel).
   d. The rear up-travel stop (on the inner panel).
4. Remove the vertical guide upper and lower screws, then disengage the guide assembly from the roller and lay in the bottom of the door.
5. Position the glass to expose the lower sash channel cam nuts, then remove the nuts through the inner panel access hole.
6. While supporting the glass, separate it from the lower sash channel cam.
7. To remove the glass, perform the following procedures:
   a. Raise the glass slowly and slide it rearward.
   b. Tilt the top of the glass inboard until the front up-stop roller clears the front loading hole at the inner panel bolt reinforcement.
   c. Rotate the glass rearward 45 degrees, then raise it slowly to clear the glass attaching screws through the belt loading holes.
   To install:
8. Carefully lower the glass into position and connect it to the lower sash channel cam.
9. Install the sash channel cam nuts and tighten to 90-125 inch lbs. (10-14 Nm).
10. Engage the guide assembly to the roller, then install the vertical guide upper and lower screws.
11. Install the travel stops on the inner panel, then install the rear belt stabilizer pin and/or the front belt stabilizer and trim retainer.
12. Check and adjust the glass installation, as necessary.
13. Install the inner panel water deflector, insulator pad (if equipped), the trim panel(s) and the armrest.
14. Install the door panel.

Sedan

1. Remove the door panel. For more information, refer to the procedure earlier in this section.
2. To disengage the rear roller, lower the glass to ¾ of the way down, tip the nose of the glass down and slide it backward.
3. To disengage the front roller, raise the nose of the glass 45 degrees and slide it rearward.
4. Lift the outboard of the upper frame to remove the glass. Adjust the regulator position to remove the glass.
5. To install, reverse the removal procedures. Adjust the position of the glass. Torque the fasteners to 90-125 inch lbs. (10-14 Nm)

ADJUSTMENT

Coupe

1. Remove the door panel. For more information, refer to the procedure earlier in this section.
2. To rotate the window, loosen the front and rear up-stops, adjust the inner panel cam and the up-stops, then tighten the screws.

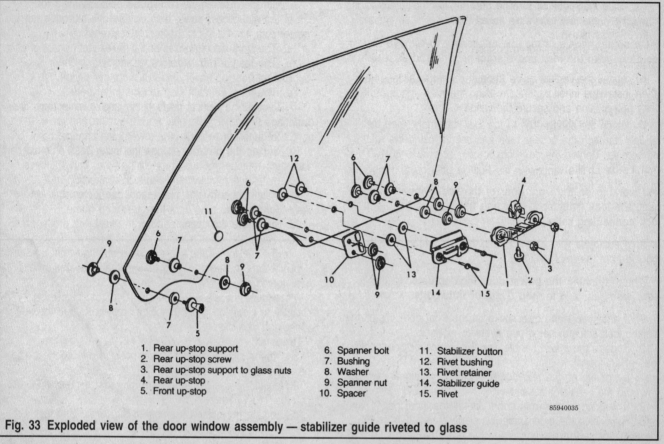

1. Rear up-stop support
2. Rear up-stop screw
3. Rear up-stop support to glass nuts
4. Rear up-stop
5. Front up-stop

6. Spanner bolt
7. Bushing
8. Washer
9. Spanner nut
10. Spacer

11. Stabilizer button
12. Rivet bushing
13. Rivet retainer
14. Stabilizer guide
15. Rivet

85940035

Fig. 33 Exploded view of the door window assembly — stabilizer guide riveted to glass

3. To adjust the window's upper inboard and outboard edge, perform the following procedures:

a. Position the window in the partially down position.

b. Loosen the vertical guide upper support (lower) screws, which are accessible through the inner panel access holes.

c. Loosen the pin assembly screws, the rear up-stop screw and the front belt stabilizer screw.

d. Adjust the vertical guide upper support and pin assembly (in or out as required, then tighten the screws, adjust and tighten the other components.

➡**When adjusting glass, make sure that it remains inboard of the blow-out clip, when cycled.**

4. If the window is too far forward or rearward, position the window partially down, loosen the vertical guide (upper and lower) screws, then adjust as required.

5. If the window is too high or low in it's Up position, adjust the front and rear up-travel stops.

6. If the window is too high or low in the Down position, adjust the down-travel stop.

7. If the window binds during the up and down operation, adjust the front and/or rear belt stabilizer pin assemblies.

Sedan

1. Remove the door panel. For more information, refer to the procedure earlier in this section.

2. If the window is rotated, loosen the inner panel cam adjusting screws, position the glass and tighten the screws.

3. If the window is too high or low in the down position, loosen the down-travel stop screws, position the glass, position the down stop and tighten the screws.

Front Door Regulator

REMOVAL & INSTALLATION

▶ **See Figures 34 and 35**

Coupe

1. Remove the door panel. For more information, refer to the procedure earlier in this section.

2. Prop the window in the half-way position by insert rubber edges between the window and the inner panel (at the belt) at the front and rear of the window.

➡**If rubber stops are not available, remove the windows.**

3. Mark (locate) and remove the inner panel cam and the vertical guide screws. Remove the vertical guide through the large access hole.

4. Using a center punch and a ¼ in. drill bit, drive out the center pins, then drill out the regulator rivets.

5. Remove the lower sash channel cam-to-glass rear nut, then slide the regulator rearward and disengage the rollers from the lower sash channel cam.

6. Remove the regulator through the largest inner panel access hole.

To install:

7. Install the regulator through the largest inner panel access hole.

8. Slide the regulator forward and engage the rollers to the lower sash channel cam, then install the lower sash channel cam-to-glass rear nut.

9. Secure the regulator in position using ¼-20 x ½ in. fasteners

10. Install the vertical guide through the large access hole, then install the inner panel cam using the mark made earlier.

11. Reposition and secure the window.

12. Install the door panel.

Sedan

1. Position the window in the Full-Up position and tape the glass to the frame.

2. Locate and remove the inner panel cam screws and the cam.

3. Remove the remote handle-to-lock connecting rod.

4. Using a center punch and a ¼ in. drill bit, drive out the center pins, then drill out the regulator rivets.

5. Disengage the rollers from the lower sash channel cam.

6. Remove the regulator through the largest inner panel access hole.

To install:

7. Install the regulator through the largest inner panel access hole.

8. Engage the rollers to the lower sash channel cam.

9. Secure the regulator in position using ¼-20 x ½ in. fasteners

10. Install the remote handle-to-lock connecting rod.

11. Install the cam and inner panel cam screws.

12. Remove the tape from the glass and frame.

13. Install the door panel.

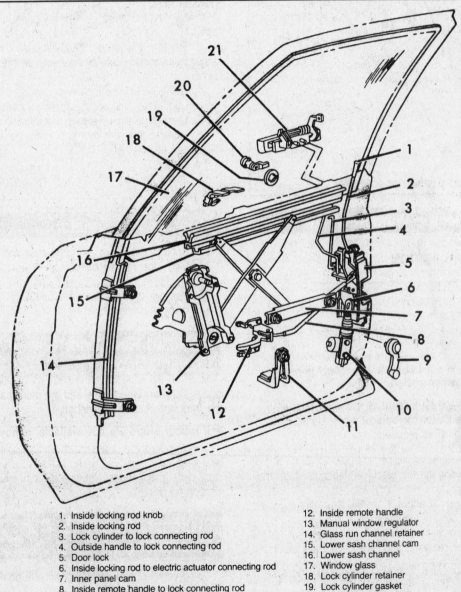

1. Inside locking rod knob
2. Inside locking rod
3. Lock cylinder to lock connecting rod
4. Outside handle to lock connecting rod
5. Door lock
6. Inside locking rod to electric actuator connecting rod
7. Inner panel cam
8. Inside remote handle to lock connecting rod
9. Manual window regulator handle
10. Power door lock actuator
11. Down-travel stop
12. Inside remote handle
13. Manual window regulator
14. Glass run channel retainer
15. Lower sash channel cam
16. Lower sash channel
17. Window glass
18. Lock cylinder retainer
19. Lock cylinder gasket
20. Lock cylinder assembly
21. Outside handle assembly

Fig. 34 Cut-away view of the front door hardware attachments — Sedans

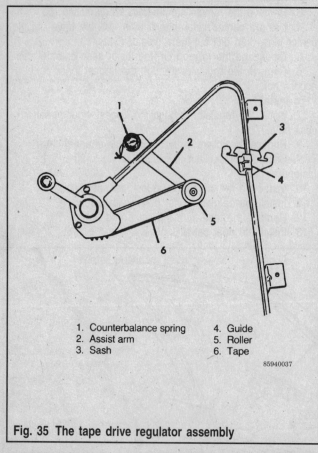

1. Counterbalance spring
2. Assist arm
3. Sash
4. Guide
5. Roller
6. Tape

85940037

Fig. 35 The tape drive regulator assembly

Front Door Electric Window Motor

REMOVAL & INSTALLATION

Coupe

1. Remove the door panel. For more information, refer to the procedure earlier in this section.
2. Prop the window in the half-way position by inserting rubber wedges between the window and the inner panel (at the belt) at the front and rear of the window.

➡**If rubber doors stops are not available, remove the window.**

3. Mark (locate) and remove the inner panel cam and the vertical guide screws. Remove the vertical guide through the large access hole. Disengage the electrical connector from the window regulator motor.
4. Using a center punch and a ¼ in. drill bit, drive out the center pins, then drill out the regulator rivets.
5. Remove the lower sash channel cam-to-glass rear nut, then slide the regulator rearward and disengage the roller from the lower sash channel cam.
6. Remove the regulator and motor through the largest inner panel access hole.

To install:
7. Install the regulator through the largest inner panel access hole.
8. Slide the regulator forward and engage the rollers to the lower sash channel cam, then install the lower sash channel cam-to-glass rear nut.
9. Secure the regulator in position using ¼-20 x ½ in. fasteners
10. Engage the motor electrical connector.
11. Install the vertical guide through the large access hole, then install the inner panel cam using the mark made earlier.
12. Reposition and secure the window.
13. Install the door panel.

Sedan

1. Position the window in the Full-Up position and tape the glass to the frame.
2. Locate and remove the inner panel cam screws and the cam.
3. Remove the remote handle-to-lock connecting rod. Disengage the wiring harness connector at the window regulator motor.
4. Using a center punch and a ¼ in. drill bit, drive out the center pins, then drill out the regulator rivets.
5. Disengage the rollers from the lower sash channel cam.
6. Remove the regulator and motor through the largest inner panel access hole.

To install:
7. Install the regulator through the largest inner panel access hole.
8. Engage the rollers to the lower sash channel cam.
9. Secure the regulator in position using ¼-20 x ½ in. fasteners
10. Engage the motor wiring harness connector.
11. Install the remote handle-to-lock connecting rod.
12. Install the cam and inner panel cam screws.
13. Remove the tape from the glass and frame.
14. Install the door panel.

Standard Rear Door Glass (Sedan/Wagon)

REMOVAL & INSTALLATION

The standard rear glass on most Chevrolet mid-sized sedans and wagons is removed and installed in a similar way to the front door glass. Please refer to the procedures earlier in this section for details.

Stationary Rear Door Glass (Sedan/Wagon)

Some vehicles may be equipped with non-opening (stationary) rear door glass windows.

REMOVAL & INSTALLATION

▶ See Figure 36

➡The rear door window is a frameless solid, safety plate glass window which is retained by two beltline support clips; the window remains in a fixed position.

1. Remove the door panel. For more information, refer to the procedure earlier in this section.
2. Remove the beltline support clips and the trim support retainer.
3. With the use of suction cups, slide the glass down and remove it from the inboard side of the door.

To install:

4. Lubricate the glass channel with silicone spray or liquid soap, then carefully slide the glass into position in the door.
5. Install the trim support retainer and the beltline support clips.
6. Install the door panel.

Rear Door Operating Vent Window Assembly

Some rear doors have a movable vent window which are either manually or electrically operated. The window is held in place by mounting screws in the upper door frame and in the door belt return flange. The manual vent window has a latch handle which locks or opens the window. The electric vent window is operated by an electric motor and a drive cable assembly. It is controlled by a master switch on the left front armrest or by a switch on the rear door trim panel.

REMOVAL & INSTALLATION

▶ See Figures 37 and 38

Manual

1. Remove the rear door glass. For details, refer to the procedures earlier in this section.
2. Remove the frame and the belt mounting screws, then pull the top of vent assembly forward and remove it from inside the door.

To install:

3. Lubricate the glass channel with silicone spray or liquid soap, then install glass.
4. Install the frame and belt mounting screws.
5. Install the rear door glass.

Electric

1. Remove the rear door glass. For details, refer to the procedures earlier in this section.
2. Disconnect the actuator rod-to-actuator lever plastic clip, by rotating the clip inward with a flat-bladed screwdriver.
3. To remove the drive cable plastic retaining clip, depress the tabs and push up.
4. Remove the upper frame screws and the belt screw.
5. Pull the top of vent assembly forward and remove it from inside the door.

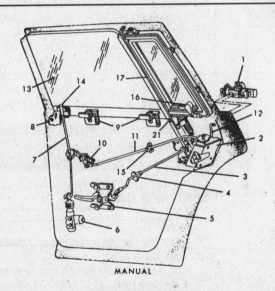
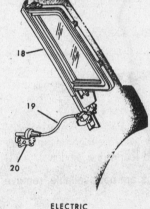

MANUAL

ELECTRIC

1. Outside handle assembly
2. Door lock
3. Inside handle to lock connecting rod
4. Shoe
5. Inside remote handle
6. Power door lock actuator
7. Inside locking rod
8. Trim support retainer
9. Glass support clips
10. Bell crank
11. Bell crank to lock connecting rod
12. Outside handle to lock connecting rod
13. Door glass (stationary)
14. Inside locking rod knob
15. Silencer
16. Manual vent latch assembly
17. Manual vent assembly
18. Electric vent assembly
19. Drive cable
20. Motor assembly—electric vent
21. Belt screw

85940038

Fig. 36 Cut-away view of the rear door hardware — stationary glass door

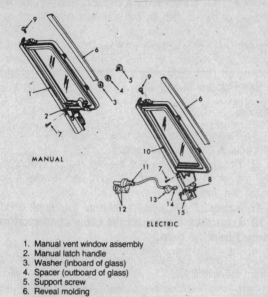

1. Manual vent window assembly
2. Manual latch handle
3. Washer (inboard of glass)
4. Spacer (outboard of glass)
5. Support screw
6. Reveal molding
7. Belt attaching screw
8. Actuator lever
9. Upper frame attaching screw
10. Electric vent window assembly
11. Electric actuator assembly
12. Grommets—motor assembly to rear door inner panel
13. Retaining clip—drive cable to retainer
14. Retaining clip—actuator rod to actuator lever
15. Retainer

85940041

Fig. 37 Exploded view of the rear door vent window hardware

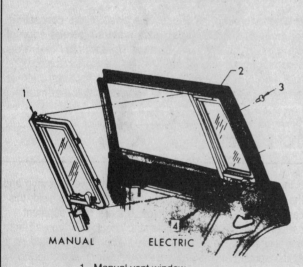

1. Manual vent window
2. Electric vent window
3. Upper frame attaching screw
4. Belt attaching screw

85940040

Fig. 38 Installing the rear door vent window

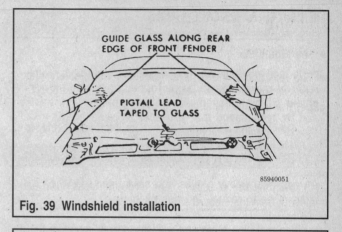

85940051

Fig. 39 Windshield installation

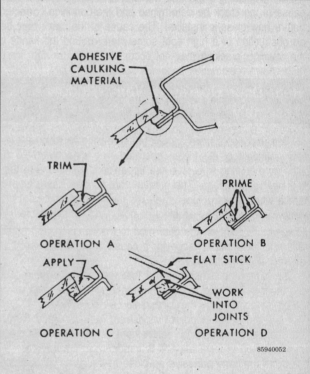

85940052

Fig. 40 Applying sealant to existing windshield to correct water leak

To install:

6. Lubricate the glass channel with silicone spray or liquid soap, then install glass.

7. Install the frame and belt mounting screws.

8. Install the drive cable plastic retaining clip, then connect the actuator rod-to-actuator lever clip.

9. Install the rear door glass.

Front and Rear Glass

▶ See Figures 39, 40 and 41

➡ Bonded windshields require special tools and special removal procedures to be performed to ensure the windshield will be removed without being broken. For this reason we recommend that you refer all removal and installation to a qualified technician.

✳✳CAUTION

Always wear heavy gloves and safety glasses when handling glass to reduce the risk of injury.

When replacing a cracked windshield, it is important that the cause of the crack be determined and the condition corrected, before new glass is installed. The cause of the crack may be an obstruction or a high spot somewhere around the flange of the opening; cracking may not occur until pressure from the high spot or obstruction becomes particularly high due to winds, extremes of temperature or rough terrain.

When a windshield is broken, the glass may have already have fallen or been removed from the weatherstrip. Often, however, it is necessary to remove a cracked or otherwise imperfect windshield that is still intact. In this case, it is a good practice to crisscross the glass with strips of masking tape before removing it; this will help hold the glass together and minimize the risk of injury.

If a crack extends to the edge of the glass, mark the point where the crack meets the weather strip. (Use a piece of chalk to mark the point on the cab, next to the weatherstrip.) Later, examine the window flange for a cause of the crack which started at the point marked.

The higher the temperature of the work area, the more pliable the weather strip will be. The more pliable the weather strip, the more easily the windshield can be removed.

There are two methods of windshield removal, depending on the method of windshield replacement chosen. When using the short method of installation, it is important to cut the glass from the urethane adhesive as close to the glass as possible. This is due to the fact that the urethane adhesive will be used to provide a base for the replacement windshield.

When using the extended method of windshield replacement, all the urethane adhesive must be removed from the pinchweld flange so, the process of cutting the window from the adhesive is less critical.

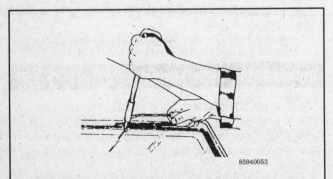
85940053

Fig. 41 Using a hot knife or equivalent to remove the windshield

REMOVAL & INSTALLATION

➡ The following procedure may be used for front and rear glass and requires the use of the Urethane Glass Sealant Remover (hot knife) tool No. J-24709-1 or equivalent, the Glass Sealant Remover Knife tool No. J-24402-A or equivalent.

1. Place a protective covering around the area where the glass will be removed.
2. Remove the windshield wiper arms, the cowl vent grille, the windshield supports, the rear view mirror and the interior garnish moldings.

➡ If equipped with a radio antenna that is embedded in the windshield, disconnect the cable connector from the windshield.

3. Remove the exterior reveal molding and glass supports from the windshield.
4. Using the Urethane Glass Sealant Remover (hot knife) tool No. J-24709-1 or equivalent, and the Glass Sealant Remover Knife tool No. J-24402-A or equivalent, cut the windshield from the urethane adhesive. If the short method of glass replacement is to be used, keep the knife as close to the glass as possible in order to leave a base for the replacement glass.
5. With the help of an assistant, remove the glass.
6. If the original glass is to be reinstalled, place it on a protected bench or a holding or holding fixture. Remove any remaining adhesive with a razor blade or a sharp scraper. Any remaining traces of adhesive material can be removed with denatured alcohol or lacquer thinner.

➡ When cleaning the windshield glass, avoid contacting the edge of the plastic laminate material (on the edge of the glass) with a volatile cleaner. Contact may cause discoloration and deterioration of the plastic laminate. DO NOT use a petroleum based solvent such as gasoline or kerosene; the presence of oil will prevent the adhesion of new material.

INSPECTION

Inspection of the windshield opening, the weather strip and the glass may reveal the cause of a broken windshield; this can help prevent future breakage. If there is no apparent cause of breakage, the weatherstrip should be removed from the flange and the flange inspected. Look for high weld or solder spots, hardened spot welds sealer, or any other obstruction or irregularity in the flange. Check the weatherstrip for irregularities or obstructions in it.

Check the windshield to be installed to make sure that it does not have chipped edges. Chipped edges can be ground off, restoring a smooth edge to the glass and minimizing concentrations of pressure that cause breakage. Remove no more than necessary, in an effort to maintain the original shape of the glass and the proper clearance between it and the flange of the opening.

INSTALLATION

To replace a urethane adhered windshield, a GM Adhesive Service Kit contains some of the materials needed and should be used to ensure the original integrity of the windshield design. Materials in this kit include:

1. One tube of adhesive material.
2. One dispensing nozzle.
3. Steel music wire.
4. Rubber cleaner.
5. Rubber primer.
6. Pinchweld primer.
7. Blackout primer.
8. Filler strip (for use on windshield installations of vehicles equipped with an embedded windshield antenna).
9. Primer applicators.

Other materials required for windshield installation which are not included in the service kit, are:

10. GM rubber lubricant No. 1051717.
11. Alcohol for cleaning the edge of the glass.
12. Adhesive dispensing gun No. J-24811 or equivalent.
13. A commercial type razor knife.
14. Two rubber support spacers.

Short Method

1. Apply masking across the windshield pillar-to-windshield opening, then cut the tape and remove the windshield.
2. Using an alcohol dampened cloth, clean the metal flange surrounding the windshield opening. Allow the alcohol to air dry.
3. Using the pinchweld primer found in the service kit, apply it to the pinchweld area. DO NOT let any of the primer touch the exposed paint or damage to the finish may occur; allow five minutes for the primer to dry.
4. Cut the tip of the adhesive cartridge approximately $3/15$ inch (5mm) from the end of the tip.
5. Apply the adhesive first in and around the spacer blocks. Apply a smooth continuous bead of adhesive into the gap between the glass edge and the sheet metal. If necessary use a flat bladed tool to paddle the material into position. Be sure that the adhesive contacts the entire edge of the glass and extends to fill the gap between the glass and the solidified urethane base.
6. With the aid of a helper, position the windshield on the filler strips against the two support spacers.

➡ **The vehicle should not be driven and should remain at room temperature for six hours to allow the adhesive to cure.**

7. Spray a mist of water onto the urethane. Water will assist in the curing process. Dry the area where the reveal molding will contact the body and glass.
8. Install new reveal moldings. Remove the protective tape covering the butyl adhesive on the underside of the molding. Push the molding caps onto each end of one of the reveal moldings. Press the lip of the molding into the urethane adhesive while holding it against the edge of the windshield. Take care to seat the molding in the corners. The lip must fully contact the adhesive and the gap must be entirely covered by

the crown of the molding. Slide the molding caps onto the adjacent moldings. Use tape to hold the molding in position until the adhesive cures.

9. Install the wiper arms and the interior garnish moldings.

➡ **The vehicle should not be driven and should remain at room temperature for six hours to allow the adhesive to cure.**

Extended Method

1. Using the GM Strip Filler No. 20146247 or equivalent, install the sealing strip onto the pinchweld flange. The joint of the molding should be located at the bottom center of the molding.
2. Apply masking tape across the windshield pillar-to-windshield opening, then cut the tape and remove the windshield.
3. Using an alcohol dampened cloth, clean the metal flange surrounding the windshield opening. Allow the alcohol to air dry.
4. Using the pinchweld primer, found in the service kit, apply it to the pinchweld area. DO NOT let any of the primer touch the exposed paint for damage to the finish may occur; allow five minutes for the primer to dry.
5. With the aid of an assistant, position the windshield on the filler strips against the two support spacers.
6. Cut the tip of the adhesive cartridge approximately $3/8$ in. from the end of the tip.
7. Apply the adhesive first in and around the spacer blocks. Apply a smooth continuous bead of adhesive into the gap between the glass edge and the sheet metal. If necessary, use a flat bladed tool to paddle the material into position. Be sure that the adhesive contacts the entire edge of the glass and extends to fill the gap between the glass and the primed sheet metal.

➡ **The vehicle should not be driven and should remain at room temperature for six hours to allow the adhesive to cure.**

8. Spray a mist of warm or hot water onto the urethane. Water will assist in the curing process. Dry the area where the reveal molding will contact the body and glass.
9. Install the reveal molding onto the windshield and remove the masking tape from the inner surface of the glass.
10. Press the lip of the molding into the urethane adhesive while holding it against the edge of the windshield. Take care to seat the molding in the corners. The lip must fully contact the adhesive and the gap must be entirely covered by the crown of the molding. Use tape to hold the molding in position until the adhesive cures.
11. Install the wiper arms and the interior garnish moldings.

Inside Rear View Mirror

On most vehicles covered by this manual, the rear view mirror is attached to a support which is bonded to the windshield glass. If so mounted, the mirror is usually sliped in place over the mount, then secured using a small hex head set screw.

A few of the older vehicles covered by this manual may have the mirror bolted to the interior roof.

REMOVAL

1. If removing the mirror only, loosen the retaining bolt or set screw, then carefully remove the mirror from the support.

2. If the windshield is being replaced, measure the support location in from points around the windshiled, these measurements will be used during installation to assure proper positioning of the support.

3. If the support has come off the windshield, as is often the case on older vehicles, see if there is a spot of old adhesive remaining. If so, the location should be marked or measured to assure proper installation.

INSTALLATION

▶ **See Figures 42 and 43**

The mirror support is usually installed using a plastic-polyvinyl butyl adhesive. Service replacement windshields often come with the mirror support bonded to the glass assembly. To install a detached mirror support or install a new part, the following items are needed:

• Part No. 1052369, Loctite® Minute-Bond Adhesive 312 two component pack, or equivalent
• Original mirror support (prepared per Steps 4 and 5 of the installation procedure) or replacement rear view mirror support
• Wax marking pencil or crayon
• Rubbing alcohol
• Clean paper towels
• Fine grit emery cloth or sandpaper (No. 320 or No. 360)
• Clean toothpick
• Six-lobed socket bit.

1. Determine the rear view mirror support position on the windshield. Support is to be located at the center of the glass, slightly below the top of the windshield.

2. Mark the location on the outside of the glass with wax pencil or crayon. also make a larger diameter circle around the mirror support circle on the outside of the glass surface.

3. On the inside of the glass surface, clean the large circle with a paper towel and domestic scouring cleanser, glass cleaning solution or polishing compound. Rub until the area is completely clean and dry. When dry, clean the area with an alcohol saturated paper towel to remove any traces of scouring powder of cleaning solution from this area.

4. With a piece of fine grit (No. 320 or No. 360) emery cloth or sandpaper, sand the bonding surface of the new rear view mirror support or factory installed support. If original rear view mirror support is to be reused, all traces of the factory installed adhesive must be removed prior to reinstallation.

5. Wipe the sanded mirror support with a clean paper towel saturated with alcohol and allow it to dry.

6. Follow the directions on the manufacturer's kit to prepare the rear view mirror support prior to installation on the glass.

7. Properly position the support to its premarked location, with rounded end pointed upward, press the support against the glass for 30-60 seconds, exerting steady pressure against the glass. After five minutes, any excess adhesive may be removed with an alcohol moistened paper towel or glass cleaning solution.

8. Install and secure the mirror.

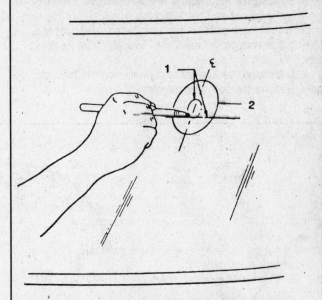

1. LOCATING CIRCLE AND BASE OF SUPPORT LINE ON OUTSIDE GLASS SURFACE
2. CIRCLE ON OUTSIDE GLASS SURFACE INDICATES AREA TO BE CLEANED

85940054

Fig. 42 Locating and marking the bonded rear view mirror support area on the windshield

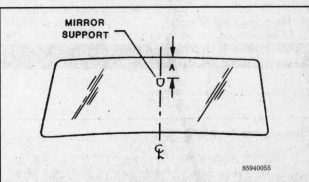

85940055

Fig. 43 Distance "A" should be 4 inches for most late model vehicles covered by this manual

Seats

REMOVAL & INSTALLATION

▶ **See Figure 44**

Front

1. Operate the seat to the full-forward position. If equipped with a six-way power seat and it is still operable, move the seat to the full-forward and up positions. Where necessary to gain access to the adjuster-to-floor pan attaching nuts, remove the adjuster rear foot covers and/or carpet retainers.

2. Remove the track covers where necessary; then remove the adjuster-to-floor pan rear attaching nuts. Operate the seat to the full-rearward position. Remove the adjuster front foot covers; then remove the adjuster-to-floor pan front attaching nuts.

3. Disengage the wire connectors and remove the seat belts. Remove the seat assembly from the car.

To install:

4. Prior to installing the seat assembly, check that both seat adjusters are parallel and in phase with each other.

5. Install the adjuster-to-floor pan attaching nuts by moving the seat forward and rearward, then torque the nuts to 15-21 ft. lbs. (20-28 Nm).

6. Check the operation of the seat assembly to full limits of travel.

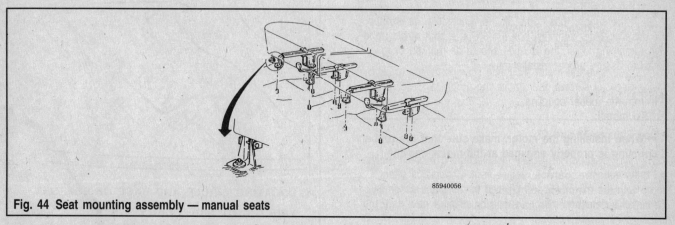

85940056

Fig. 44 Seat mounting assembly — manual seats

REAR

In most cases, the rear seat bottom may be removed by simply pushing rearward at the bottom of the seat, then tilting the assembly up and removing it from the vehicle. On some older vehicles, retaining bolts may be used at the base of the seat bottom. The top (back portion) is usually removed by unthreading the retaining bolts at the bottom of the seatback and lifting up on the assembly.

Seat Belt System

REMOVAL & INSTALLATION

▶ **See Figures 45 and 46**

1. Remove the door pillar trim covers and/or rear seat, as required for access. Remove the cover from the anchor plate.

2. Remove the attaching bolt, anchor plate and washer.

3. Remove the bolt cover from the rear of the retractor assembly.

4. Remove the bolt retaining the retractor to the floor panel, then remove the retractor.

5. Remove the buckle assembly from the floor panel.

6. Remove the cap which conceals the buckle assembly bolt and remove the bolt.

7. Remove the seat belt warning wire from the drivers side buckle and remove the buckle assembly from the vehicle.

8. Installation is the reverse of removal. Tighten all bolts to 31-35 ft. lbs. (43-48 Nm).

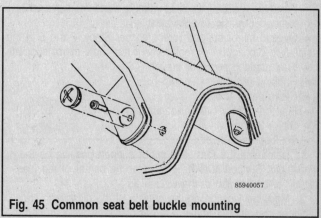

85940057

Fig. 45 Common seat belt buckle mounting

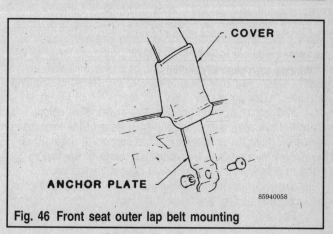

COVER

ANCHOR PLATE

85940058

Fig. 46 Front seat outer lap belt mounting

Power Seat Motor

REMOVAL & INSTALLATION

▶ **See Figure 47**

1. Disengage the electrical harness connector and remove the seat from the vehicle, then place it upside down on a covered workbench to protect the seat.
2. Disconnect the motor feed wires from the motor control relay.
3. Remove the motor mounting screws and the transmission-to-motor screws, then move the motor away to disengage it from the rubber coupling.

To install:

➡ **When installing the motor, make sure that the rubber coupling is properly engaged at the motor and the transmission.**

4. Install the motor, engaging it the the rubber coupling, then install both the the transmission-to-motor and motor mounting screws.
5. Engage the motor feed wires to the motor control relay.
6. Install the seat to the vehicle and engage the harness connector.

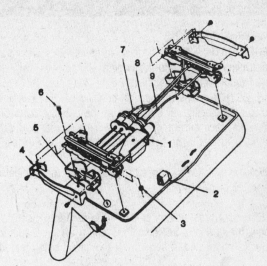

1. Transmission assembly
2. Seat relay
3. Nut
4. Adjuster track lower cover
5. Adjuster track upper cover
6. Adjuster-to-seat frame attaching bolts
7. Horizontal drive cable
8. Rear vertical drive cable
9. Front vertical drive cable

85940042

Fig. 47 Six-way power sear adjuster components

TORQUE SPECIFICATIONS

Component	U.S.	Metric
Bumper energy absorber		
L-bracket-to-frame nuts	26 ft. lbs.	35 Nm
Frame bolts	32 ft. lbs.	43 Nm
Door hinge-to-body bolts	15–21 ft. lbs.	20–28 Nm
Door lock-to-door screws	80–100 in. lbs.	9–11 Nm
Tailgate counterbalance support mounting stud and retaining nut	14–22 ft. lbs.	19–30 Nm
Tailgate hinge-to-body bolts (El Camino)	14–22 ft. lbs.	19–30 Nm
Window sash channel cam nuts	90–125 in. lbs.	10–14 Nm

85940045

GLOSSARY

AIR/FUEL RATIO: The ratio of air to gasoline by weight in the fuel mixture drawn into the engine.

AIR INJECTION: One method of reducing harmful exhaust emissions by injecting air into each of the exhaust ports of an engine. The fresh air entering the hot exhaust manifold causes any remaining fuel to be burned before it can exit the tailpipe.

ALTERNATOR: A device used for converting mechanical energy into electrical energy.

AMMETER: An instrument, calibrated in amperes, used to measure the flow of an electrical current in a circuit. Ammeters are always connected in series with the circuit being tested.

AMPERE: The rate of flow of electrical current present when one volt of electrical pressure is applied against one ohm of electrical resistance.

ANALOG COMPUTER: Any microprocessor that uses similar (analogous) electrical signals to make its calculations.

ARMATURE: A laminated, soft iron core wrapped by a wire that converts electrical energy to mechanical energy as in a motor or relay. When rotated in a magnetic field, it changes mechanical energy into electrical energy as in a generator.

ATMOSPHERIC PRESSURE: The pressure on the Earth's surface caused by the weight of the air in the atmosphere. At sea level, this pressure is 14.7 psi at 32{248}F (101 kPa at 0{248}C).

ATOMIZATION: The breaking down of a liquid into a fine mist that can be suspended in air.

AXIAL PLAY: Movement parallel to a shaft or bearing bore.

BACKFIRE: The sudden combustion of gases in the intake or exhaust system that results in a loud explosion.

BACKLASH: The clearance or play between two parts, such as meshed gears.

BACKPRESSURE: Restrictions in the exhaust system that slow the exit of exhaust gases from the combustion chamber.

BAKELITE: A heat resistant, plastic insulator material commonly used in printed circuit boards and transistorized components.

BALL BEARING: A bearing made up of hardened inner and outer races between which hardened steel balls roll.

BALLAST RESISTOR: A resistor in the primary ignition circuit that lowers voltage after the engine is started to reduce wear on ignition components.

BEARING: A friction reducing, supportive device usually located between a stationary part and a moving part.

BIMETAL TEMPERATURE SENSOR: Any sensor or switch made of two dissimilar types of metal that bend when heated or cooled due to the different expansion rates of the alloys. These types of sensors usually function as an on/off switch.

BLOWBY: Combustion gases, composed of water vapor and unburned fuel, that leak past the piston rings into the crankcase during normal engine operation. These gases are removed by the PCV system to prevent the buildup of harmful acids in the crankcase.

BRAKE PAD: A brake shoe and lining assembly used with disc brakes.

BRAKE SHOE: The backing for the brake lining. The term is, however, usually applied to the assembly of the brake backing and lining.

BUSHING: A liner, usually removable, for a bearing; an anti-friction liner used in place of a bearing.

CALIPER: A hydraulically activated device in a disc brake system, which is mounted straddling the brake rotor (disc). The caliper contains at least one piston and two brake pads. Hydraulic pressure on the piston(s) forces the pads against the rotor.

CAMSHAFT: A shaft in the engine on which are the lobes (cams) which operate the valves. The camshaft is driven by the crankshaft, via a belt, chain or gears, at one half the crankshaft speed.

CAPACITOR: A device which stores an electrical charge.

CARBON MONOXIDE (CO): A colorless, odorless gas given off as a normal byproduct of combustion. It is poisonous and extremely dangerous in confined areas, building up slowly to toxic levels without warning if adequate ventilation is not available.

CARBURETOR: A device, usually mounted on the intake manifold of an engine, which mixes the air and fuel in the proper proportion to allow even combustion.

CATALYTIC CONVERTER: A device installed in the exhaust system, like a muffler, that converts harmful byproducts of combustion into carbon dioxide and water vapor by means of a heat-producing chemical reaction.

CENTRIFUGAL ADVANCE: A mechanical method of advancing the spark timing by using flyweights in the distributor that react to centrifugal force generated by the distributor shaft rotation.

CHECK VALVE: Any one-way valve installed to permit the flow of air, fuel or vacuum in one direction only.

CHOKE: A device, usually a moveable valve, placed in the intake path of a carburetor to restrict the flow of air.

CIRCUIT: Any unbroken path through which an electrical current can flow. Also used to describe fuel flow in some instances.

CIRCUIT BREAKER: A switch which protects an electrical circuit from overload by opening the circuit when the current flow exceeds a predetermined level. Some circuit breakers must be reset manually, while most reset automatically

COIL (IGNITION): A transformer in the ignition circuit which steps up the voltage provided to the spark plugs.

COMBINATION MANIFOLD: An assembly which includes both the intake and exhaust manifolds in one casting.

COMBINATION VALVE: A device used in some fuel systems that routes fuel vapors to a charcoal storage canister instead of venting them into the atmosphere. The valve relieves fuel tank pressure and allows fresh air into the tank as the fuel level drops to prevent a vapor lock situation.

COMPRESSION RATIO: The comparison of the total volume of the cylinder and combustion chamber with the piston at BDC and the piston at TDC.

CONDENSER: 1. An electrical device which acts to store an electrical charge, preventing voltage surges.
2. A radiator-like device in the air conditioning system in which refrigerant gas condenses into a liquid, giving off heat.

CONDUCTOR: Any material through which an electrical current can be transmitted easily.

CONTINUITY: Continuous or complete circuit. Can be checked with an ohmmeter.

COUNTERSHAFT: An intermediate shaft which is rotated by a mainshaft and transmits, in turn, that rotation to a working part.

CRANKCASE: The lower part of an engine in which the crankshaft and related parts operate.

CRANKSHAFT: The main driving shaft of an engine which receives reciprocating motion from the pistons and converts it to rotary motion.

CYLINDER: In an engine, the round hole in the engine block in which the piston(s) ride.

CYLINDER BLOCK: The main structural member of an engine in which is found the cylinders, crankshaft and other principal parts.

CYLINDER HEAD: The detachable portion of the engine, fastened, usually, to the top of the cylinder block, containing all or most of the combustion chambers. On overhead valve engines, it contains the valves and their operating parts. On overhead cam engines, it contains the camshaft as well.

DEAD CENTER: The extreme top or bottom of the piston stroke.

DETONATION: An unwanted explosion of the air/fuel mixture in the combustion chamber caused by excess heat and compression, advanced timing, or an overly lean mixture. Also referred to as "ping".

DIAPHRAGM: A thin, flexible wall separating two cavities, such as in a vacuum advance unit.

DIESELING: A condition in which hot spots in the combustion chamber cause the engine to run on after the key is turned off.

DIFFERENTIAL: A geared assembly which allows the transmission of motion between drive axles, giving one axle the ability to turn faster than the other.

DIODE: An electrical device that will allow current to flow in one direction only.

DISC BRAKE: A hydraulic braking assembly consisting of a brake disc, or rotor, mounted on an axle, and a caliper assembly containing, usually two brake pads which are activated by hydraulic pressure. The pads are forced against the sides of the disc, creating friction which slows the vehicle.

DISTRIBUTOR: A mechanically driven device on an engine which is responsible for electrically firing the spark plug at a predetermined point of the piston stroke.

DOWEL PIN: A pin, inserted in mating holes in two different parts allowing those parts to maintain a fixed relationship.

DRUM BRAKE: A braking system which consists of two brake shoes and one or two wheel cylinders, mounted on a fixed backing plate, and a brake drum, mounted on an axle, which revolves around the assembly.

DWELL: The rate, measured in degrees of shaft rotation, at which an electrical circuit cycles on and off.

ELECTRONIC CONTROL UNIT (ECU): Ignition module, module, amplifier or igniter. See Module for definition.

ELECTRONIC IGNITION: A system in which the timing and firing of the spark plugs is controlled by an electronic control unit, usually called a module. These systems have no points or condenser.

ENDPLAY: The measured amount of axial movement in a shaft.

ENGINE: A device that converts heat into mechanical energy.

EXHAUST MANIFOLD: A set of cast passages or pipes which conduct exhaust gases from the engine.

FEELER GAUGE: A blade, usually metal, of precisely predetermined thickness, used to measure the clearance between two parts.

FIRING ORDER: The order in which combustion occurs in the cylinders of an engine. Also the order in which spark is distributed to the plugs by the distributor.

FLOODING: The presence of too much fuel in the intake manifold and combustion chamber which prevents the air/fuel mixture from firing, thereby causing a no-start situation.

FLYWHEEL: A disc shaped part bolted to the rear end of the crankshaft. Around the outer perimeter is affixed the ring gear. The starter drive engages the ring gear, turning the flywheel, which rotates the crankshaft, imparting the initial starting motion to the engine.

FOOT POUND (ft.lb. or sometimes, ft. lbs.): The amount of energy or work needed to raise an item weighing one pound, a distance of one foot.

FUSE: A protective device in a circuit which prevents circuit overload by breaking the circuit when a specific amperage is present. The device is constructed around a strip or wire of a lower amperage rating than the circuit it is designed to protect. When an amperage higher than that stamped on the fuse is present in the circuit, the strip or wire melts, opening the circuit.

GEAR RATIO: The ratio between the number of teeth on meshing gears.

GENERATOR: A device which converts mechanical energy into electrical energy.

HEAT RANGE: The measure of a spark plug's ability to dissipate heat from its firing end. The higher the heat range, the hotter the plug fires.

HUB: The center part of a wheel or gear.

HYDROCARBON (HC): Any chemical compound made up of hydrogen and carbon. A major pollutant formed by the engine as a byproduct of combustion.

HYDROMETER: An instrument used to measure the specific gravity of a solution.

INCH POUND (in.lb. or sometimes, in. lbs.): One twelfth of a foot pound.

INDUCTION: A means of transferring electrical energy in the form of a magnetic field. Principle used in the ignition coil to increase voltage.

INJECTOR: A device which receives metered fuel under relatively low pressure and is activated to inject the fuel into the engine under relatively high pressure at a predetermined time.

INPUT SHAFT: The shaft to which torque is applied, usually carrying the driving gear or gears.

INTAKE MANIFOLD: A casting of passages or pipes used to conduct air or a fuel/air mixture to the cylinders.

JOURNAL: The bearing surface within which a shaft operates.

KEY: A small block usually fitted in a notch between a shaft and a hub to prevent slippage of the two parts.

MANIFOLD: A casting of passages or set of pipes which connect the cylinders to an inlet or outlet source.

MANIFOLD VACUUM: Low pressure in an engine intake manifold formed just below the throttle plates. Manifold vacuum is highest at idle and drops under acceleration.

MASTER CYLINDER: The primary fluid pressurizing device in a hydraulic system. In automotive use, it is found in brake and hydraulic clutch systems and is pedal activated, either directly or, in a power brake system, through the power booster.

MODULE: Electronic control unit, amplifier or igniter of solid state or integrated design which controls the current flow in the ignition primary circuit based on input from the pick-up coil. When the module opens the primary circuit, the high secondary voltage is induced in the coil.

NEEDLE BEARING: A bearing which consists of a number (usually a large number) of long, thin rollers.

OHM:(Ω) The unit used to measure the resistance of conductor to electrical flow. One ohm is the amount of resistance that limits current flow to one ampere in a circuit with one volt of pressure.

OHMMETER: An instrument used for measuring the resistance, in ohms, in an electrical circuit.

OUTPUT SHAFT: The shaft which transmits torque from a device, such as a transmission.

OVERDRIVE: A gear assembly which produces more shaft revolutions than that transmitted to it.

OVERHEAD CAMSHAFT (OHC): An engine configuration in which the camshaft is mounted on top of the cylinder head and operates the valve either directly or by means of rocker arms.

OVERHEAD VALVE (OHV): An engine configuration in which all of the valves are located in the cylinder head and the camshaft is located in the cylinder block. The camshaft operates the valves via lifters and pushrods.

OXIDES OF NITROGEN (NOx): Chemical compounds of nitrogen produced as a byproduct of combustion. They combine with hydrocarbons to produce smog.

OXYGEN SENSOR: Used with the feedback system to sense the presence of oxygen in the exhaust gas and signal the computer which can reference the voltage signal to an air/fuel ratio.

PINION: The smaller of two meshing gears.

PISTON RING: An open ended ring which fits into a groove on the outer diameter of the piston. Its chief function is to form a seal between the piston and cylinder wall. Most automotive pistons have three rings: two for compression sealing; one for oil sealing.

PRELOAD: A predetermined load placed on a bearing during assembly or by adjustment.

PRIMARY CIRCUIT: Is the low voltage side of the ignition system which consists of the ignition switch, ballast resistor or resistance wire, bypass, coil, electronic control unit and pick-up coil as well as the connecting wires and harnesses.

PRESS FIT: The mating of two parts under pressure, due to the inner diameter of one being smaller than the outer diameter of the other, or vice versa; an interference fit.

RACE: The surface on the inner or outer ring of a bearing on which the balls, needles or rollers move.

REGULATOR: A device which maintains the amperage and/or voltage levels of a circuit at predetermined values.

RELAY: A switch which automatically opens and/or closes a circuit.

RESISTANCE: The opposition to the flow of current through a circuit or electrical device, and is measured in ohms. Resistance is equal to the voltage divided by the amperage.

RESISTOR: A device, usually made of wire, which offers a preset amount of resistance in an electrical circuit.

RING GEAR: The name given to a ring-shaped gear attached to a differential case, or affixed to a flywheel or as part a planetary gear set.

ROLLER BEARING: A bearing made up of hardened inner and outer races between which hardened steel rollers move.

ROTOR: 1. The disc-shaped part of a disc brake assembly, upon which the brake pads bear; also called, brake disc.
  2. The device mounted atop the distributor shaft, which passes current to the distributor cap tower contacts.

SECONDARY CIRCUIT: The high voltage side of the ignition system, usually above 20,000 volts. The secondary includes the ignition coil, coil wire, distributor cap and rotor, spark plug wires and spark plugs.

SENDING UNIT: A mechanical, electrical, hydraulic or electromagnetic device which transmits information to a gauge.

SENSOR: Any device designed to measure engine operating conditions or ambient pressures and temperatures. Usually electronic in nature and designed to send a voltage signal to an on-board computer, some sensors may operate as a simple on/off switch or they may provide a variable voltage signal (like a potentiometer) as conditions or measured parameters change.

SHIM: Spacers of precise, predetermined thickness used between parts to establish a proper working relationship.

SLAVE CYLINDER: In automotive use, a device in the hydraulic clutch system which is activated by hydraulic force, disengaging the clutch.

SOLENOID: A coil used to produce a magnetic field, the effect of which is produce work.

SPARK PLUG: A device screwed into the combustion chamber of a spark ignition engine. The basic construction is a conductive core inside of a ceramic insulator, mounted in an outer conductive base. An electrical charge from the spark plug wire travels along the conductive core and jumps a preset air gap to a grounding point or points at the end of the conductive base. The resultant spark ignites the fuel/air mixture in the combustion chamber.

SPLINES: Ridges machined or cast onto the outer diameter of a shaft or inner diameter of a bore to enable parts to mate without rotation.

TACHOMETER: A device used to measure the rotary speed of an engine, shaft, gear, etc., usually in rotations per minute.

THERMOSTAT: A valve, located in the cooling system of an engine, which is closed when cold and opens gradually in response to engine heating, controlling the temperature of the coolant and rate of coolant flow.

TOP DEAD CENTER (TDC): The point at which the piston reaches the top of its travel on the compression stroke.

TORQUE: The twisting force applied to an object.

TORQUE CONVERTER: A turbine used to transmit power from a driving member to a driven member via hydraulic action, providing changes in drive ratio and torque. In automotive use, it links the driveplate at the rear of the engine to the automatic transmission.

TRANSDUCER: A device used to change a force into an electrical signal.

TRANSISTOR: A semi-conductor component which can be actuated by a small voltage to perform an electrical switching function.

TUNE-UP: A regular maintenance function, usually associated with the replacement and adjustment of parts and components in the electrical and fuel systems of a vehicle for the purpose of attaining optimum performance.

TURBOCHARGER: An exhaust driven pump which compresses intake air and forces it into the combustion chambers at higher than atmospheric pressures. The increased air pressure allows more fuel to be burned and results in increased horsepower being produced.

VACUUM ADVANCE: A device which advances the ignition timing in response to increased engine vacuum.

VACUUM GAUGE: An instrument used to measure the presence of vacuum in a chamber.

VALVE: A device which control the pressure, direction of flow or rate of flow of a liquid or gas.

VALVE CLEARANCE: The measured gap between the end of the valve stem and the rocker arm, cam lobe or follower that activates the valve.

VISCOSITY: The rating of a liquid's internal resistance to flow.

VOLTMETER: An instrument used for measuring electrical force in units called volts. Voltmeters are always connected parallel with the circuit being tested.

WHEEL CYLINDER: Found in the automotive drum brake assembly, it is a device, actuated by hydraulic pressure, which, through internal pistons, pushes the brake shoes outward against the drums.

MASTER

INDEX

10-40 INDEX